# Management

*Ninth Edition*

**Robert Kreitner**

ARIZONA STATE UNIVERSITY

**Houghton Mifflin Company**

BOSTON    NEW YORK

In loving memory of Jean C. Sova

*Editor-in-Chief:* George T. Hoffman
*Technology Manager/Development Editor:* Damaris R. Curran
*Senior Project Editor:* Cathy Labresh Brooks
*Senior Production/Design Coordinator:* Carol Merrigan
*Senior Manufacturing Coordinator:* Marie Barnes
*Marketing Manager:* Steven W. Mikels

*Cover design: Illustration by Andy Powell.*
*Photo credits appear on page G7.*

Printed in the U.S.A.

Library of Congress Catalog Card Number: 00-132081
ISBN: 0-618-27391-3

2 3 4 5 6 7 8 9–VH–07 06 05 04

# Brief Contents

**"** Go confidently in the direction of your dreams.
Live the life you've imagined. **"**

**henry david thoreau**

# Contents

---

### part two

# Planning and Decision Making     175

**part five**

## Organizational Control Processes   561

"...nothing can live well except in a manner suited to the way the Power of the World lives and moves to do its work."

**Black Elk, Oglala Sioux**

# Preface

Today's managers face a complex web of difficult and exciting challenges. A global economy in which world-class quality is the ticket to ride, increased diversity in the work force, the proliferation of technology and e-business, and demands for more ethical conduct promise to keep things interesting. As trustees of society's precious human, material, financial, and informational resources, today's and tomorrow's managers hold the key to a better world. A solid grounding in management is essential to successfully guiding large or small, profit or nonprofit, organizations into the twenty-first century. *Management,* Ninth Edition, represents an important step toward managerial and personal success in an era of rapid change. It is a comprehensive, up-to-date, and highly readable introduction to management theory, research, and practice. This ninth edition is the culmination of my thirty years in management classrooms and management development seminars around the world. Its style and content have been shaped by interaction with literally thousands of students, instructors, reviewers, and managers. All have taught me valuable lessons about organizational life, management, and people in general. Organized along a time-tested functional/process framework, *Management,* Ninth Edition, integrates classical and modern concepts with a rich array of contemporary real-world examples, cases, and Interactive Annotations.

## New Topics and Research Insights

In response to feedback from students, colleagues, and managers who read the previous edition, and reflecting the latest trends in management thinking, more than 56 new topics can be found in this edition.

### Comprehensive New Coverage and New Sections

These major new topics, models, and areas have been added to the Ninth Edition of *Management:*

- The controversial issue of an "Americanized" global culture (Chapter 4)
- Individualistic versus collectivist cultures (Chapter 4)
- How to select project management software (Chapter 6)
- Enterprise resource planning (ERP) pros and cons (Chapter 6)
- Knowledge management; tacit and explicit knowledge (Chapter 8)
- New approach to employee recruitment and selection (Chapter 11)
- Behavioral interviewing (Chapter 11)
- Five communication strategies; model plus complete discussion (Chapter 12)
- Cellphone etiquette; practical tips (Chapter 12)
- Open-book management (Chapter 13)
- How political infighting helped bring down Enron (Chapter 14)
- Building social capital through compassion (Chapter 14)
- Emotional intelligence and leadership (Chapter 15)
- "Tempered radicals" who quietly change the organization's culture (Chapter 16)

# Other New Topics and Significantly Revised Coverage

Comprehensive revision of *Management,* Ninth Edition, is evidenced by these new topics and improvements:

- How goals and productivity improvement helped save Japan's Nissan; globalization and terrorism (post-Sept. 11); how environmentalism pays; e-business definition and overview as a preview of comprehensive coverage in Chapter 7; new small business statistics (Chapter 1)
- Complex adaptive systems (Chapter 2)
- New Hispanic/Latino demographics; the new look of African-American leadership; European ownership of U.S. companies (Chapter 3)
- Assimilating Hispanic workers (Chapter 4)
- Issue of foreign prison-slave labor; Enron's failure as possible indication that classical economic model of business is obsolete; "venture philanthropy;" low public trust in business ethics; "Scared straight" program for college students (Chapter 5)
- First-mover advantage (strategy); expanded coverage of 80/20 principle (priorities); Russian vs. Western views of planning and control; new definition of "project" (Chapter 6)
- E-business strategies for the Internet; "three-tailing" Internet strategy; importance of good sales forecasts (Chapter 7)
- Role of "unintended consequences" in decision making (Chapter 8)
- Organizational decline at Enron; avoiding layoffs with "employee sharing" (Chapter 9)
- Poor current state of organization structure and design; mechanistic structure still relevant for Web hosts (Chapter 10)
- The age of "human capital;" how to interview the blind and visually impaired; current training methods and delivery (Chapter 11)
- Silence as communication; guidelines for touching while communicating (Chapter 12)
- Cost of unscheduled absenteeism relative to the need for flexible work schedules (Chapter 13)
- Corporate boards and groupthink (Chapter 14)
- Empowerment at Germany's Siemans; how empowerment without oversight hurt Enron (Chapter 15)
- Resistance to change because of "competing commitments" (Chapter 16)
- Due diligence as feedforward control; impact of Enron/Andersen scandal on internal auditing; crisis management after Sept. 11; cost of poor crisis management for Ford and Firestone; Deming's PDCA cycle at Intel (Chapter 17)

To make room for these new topics and research insights, outdated material and examples and unnecessary wording were studiously identified and eliminated. The net result is an efficient and very up-to-date introduction to the field of management.

# Complete Harmony with AACSB International's Revised Accreditation Standards

AACSB International (The Association to Advance Collegiate Schools of Business), the leading accrediting organization for business, management, and accounting programs, presently is revising its Standards for Business Accreditation. According to the latest draft, a major "conceptual change" is taking place: "curriculum standards have been replaced with standards requiring 'Assurance of Learning'. This is a shift of perspective from structural input to learning outcome. It asks for evidence, rather than intent." (*Source:* "Second Working Draft: Eligibility Procedures and Standards for Business Accreditation," **www.aacsb.edu**, March 22, 2002, p. 5.) **Learning objectives** at the beginning of each chapter, repeated at appropriate locations in the margin and answered in the chapter summary, make this entire textbook "**outcome-focused.**"

Moreover, topical coverage in *Management*, Ninth Edition, aligns very closely with AACSB International's list of "management-specific knowledge and skills:" creating value by producing goods and services; understanding the economic, political, legal, and global contexts of business; knowledge of individual and group dynamics in organizations; information management; the individual's responsibilities to the organization and society; and "Other management-specific knowledge and abilities as identified by the school." (*Source:* Ibid., p. 25.)

## Major Themes

The study of management takes in a great deal of territory, both conceptually and geographically. Therefore, it is important for those being introduced to the field to have reliable guideposts to help them make sense of it all. Four major themes guiding our progress through the fascinating world of management are change, skill development, diversity, and ethics.

## An Overriding Focus on Change

It may be a cliché to say "the only certainty today is change," but it is nonetheless true. The challenge for today's and especially tomorrow's managers is to be aware of *specific* changes, along with the factors contributing to them and their likely impact on the practice of management. Change has been woven into the fabric of this edition in the following ways:

- Under the heading of "The Changing Workplace," each chapter-opening case introduces students to real-world managers and changes at large and small, domestic and foreign organizations (16 of the 17 opening cases are new to this edition; 7 feature a woman and/or minority).
- Chapter 1 profiles twenty-first-century managers and ten major changes in the practice of management.
- Chapter 1 provides an overview of the Internet and e-business revolution and traces the history of the Internet.
- Chapter 3 is entirely devoted to the changing social, political/legal, economic, and technological environment that management faces. Workplace demographics document the changing face of the work force.
- Chapter 4 discusses the growth of global and transnational corporations and how to adapt to cross-cultural situations.
- Chapter 6 covers project planning/management, underscoring the ad hoc nature of today's workplaces.
- Chapter 7 has a completely updated section titled E-business Strategies for the Internet, including three lessons from the dot-com meltdown.
- Chapter 8, for the first time, introduces knowledge management as a strategic tool for better decision making.

- Chapter 9 discusses learning organizations as well as how to detect and avoid organizational decline.
- Chapter 10 describes the new virtual organizations.
- Chapter 11 introduces the concept of "human capital" and features Pfeffer's seven people-centered practices.
- Chapter 14 covers virtual teams and how to build them.
- Chapter 15 now covers emotional intelligence, a vital trait for adaptable managers and leaders.
- Chapter 16 offers comprehensive treatment of change, resistance to change, and how to bring about unofficial grassroots change.
- Chapter 17 covers the timely topic of crisis management.
- Completely updated (with 27 new URLs) **Internet Exercises** at the end of each chapter help the reader stay in touch with recent changes in the world of management.

## Emphasis on Skill Development

Managers tell us they want job applicants who know more than just management theory. They value people who can communicate well, solve problems, see the big picture, and work cooperatively in teams. Consequently, this edition has a very strong skills orientation.

- **Skills & Tools** sections at the end of each chapter teach students how to manage their career, stay current with management literature, help women break the glass ceiling, have a safe foreign business trip, behave ethically around the world, write a new business plan, reengineer the organization, construct a fishbone diagram (for problem finding), build an organization's learning capability, demonstrate initiative, successfully handle a job interview, develop a more effective speaking style, manage stress, use cooperative conflict to avoid groupthink, empower employees, constructively express anger, and avoid public-relations problems in a crisis.
- **How-to-do-it instructions** are integrated into the text for the following skills and tasks: preparing employees for foreign assignments, examining the ethics of a business decision, using management by objectives (MBO), constructing flow charts and Gantt charts, building a PERT network, performing a break-even analysis, writing planning scenarios, making decisions, avoiding decision-making traps, managing creative people, avoiding layoffs, delegating, cellphone etiquette, interviewing, discouraging sexual harassment, communicating via e-mail, participating in a videoconference, listening, writing effectively, running a meeting, using rewards, making employee participation programs work, curbing organizational politics, preventing groupthink, building trust, modifying behavior, managing change, overcoming resistance to change, managing conflict, negotiating, using Deming's Plan-Do-Check-Act cycle, and improving product and service quality.
- **Video Skill Builders,** following each major part of the text, emphasize the development of essential management skills; and focus on topics such as managing customer service, being an entrepreneur, taking a business international, shaping organizational culture, motivating, leading, and managing quality.

# Emphasis on Diversity

Labor forces and customers around the globe, particularly in the United States, are becoming more diverse in terms of national origin, race, religion, gender, predominant age categories, and personal preferences. Managers are challenged to manage diversity effectively to tap the *full* potential of *every* individual's unique combination of abilities and traits. The following diversity coverage and themes can be found in this edition:

- Six boxed features (5 new) titled **Managing Diversity** throughout the text focus needed attention on the emergence of African-American top executives, accommodating Hispanic patients and employees in a hospital, how Allstate makes diversity pay, interviewing blind and visually impaired people, touching others when communicating, and how to change the organization's culture by being a "tempered radical."
- Women play key managerial roles in the chapter-opening cases for Chapters 1, 3, 6, 8, 14, and 15 and the chapter-closing cases for Chapters 5 and 9.
- A diverse selection of individuals is featured in cases, boxes, examples, and photos.
- Chapter 1 describes the demand for multilingual and multicultural managers.
- Chapter 3 includes a section on managing diversity.
- Chapter 4 discusses managing across cultures and emphasizes the importance of learning foreign languages. Chapter 4 also describes the work goals and leadership styles in different cultures.
- Chapter 5 discusses different value systems.
- Chapter 8 describes different information-processing styles and how to manage creative individuals.
- Chapter 11 discusses moving from tolerance to appreciation when managing diversity. It also covers equal employment opportunity, affirmative action, the Americans with Disabilities Act (ADA), and how to develop policies for sexual harassment and substance abuse.
- Chapter 13 discusses how to motivate a diverse work force and provides coverage of the U.S. Family and Medical Leave Act (FMLA).
- Chapter 14 includes major coverage of teamwork.
- Chapter 15 discusses women and the use of power as well as different leadership styles.
- Chapter 16 discusses *cooperative* conflict and describes different conflict resolution styles.

# Emphasis on Ethics

Simply put, society wants managers to behave better. Ethical concerns are integrated throughout this edition, as well as featured in Chapter 5. Ethical coverage is evidenced by:

- Six (3 new) **Management Ethics** boxes throughout the text
- Discussion of management's ethical reawakening in Chapter 1
- Chapter 5, in Part One, entirely devoted to management's social and ethical responsibilities, providing an ethical context for the entire book
- Ethical aspects of e-business in Chapter 7
- Value judgments in decision making in Chapter 8
- Ethics of downsizing and layoffs in Chapter 9
- Ethical implications of group norms and avoiding groupthink in Chapter 14

- Greenleaf's ethical "servant leader" in Chapter 15
- Covey's ethical win-win negotiating style in Chapter 16
- Timely discussions of Enron's fall and the Ford/Firestone crisis in cases, textual discussions, and examples.

## An Interactive Textbook

Active rather than passive learning is the preferred way to go these days. As well it should be, because active learning is interesting and fun. This textbook employs two interactive-learning strategies: Web-linked Interactive Annotations and Hands-On Exercises.

## Interactive Annotations

This feature, unique to *Management,* Ninth Edition, was introduced two editions ago. The idea was to link the textbook and the Internet to create a dynamic, instructive, and interesting learning tool—in short, to make the textbook come alive. This pedagogical experiment has been a great success. (In fact, students say they read the annotations first when turning to a new page.) Consequently, there are 158 Interactive Annotations in this ninth edition (89 are new and many have been updated) that integrate timely facts, provocative ideas, discussion questions, and back-to-the-opening-case questions into the flow of the book.

Answers and interpretations for the annotations are provided in the *Instructor's Resource Manual* and on the Internet at our Web site (**http://college.hmco.com/ business/instructors/**).

At the instructor's discretion, many of the annotations provide stimulating opportunities for cooperative learning. Valuable new insights are gained and interpersonal skills are developed when students work together in groups and teams.

## Hands-On Exercises

This is a completely new feature for *Management,* Ninth Edition. One Hands-On Exercise follows each chapter. They strive to heighten self-awareness and build essential managerial skills. The exercises can be completed alone or in cooperative-learning teams. Each exercise is followed by a set of questions for personal consideration and/or class discussion. The **17 Hands-On Exercises** include: an entrepreneur's quiz, open-system thinking for dealing with global terrorism, rating the probability of futuristic predictions, a cultural-awareness survey, a personal values survey, how to write good objectives and plans, doing a strategic SWOT analysis, a creativity test, an organizational culture assessment, a field study on organization structure and design, writing behavioral interview questions, communicating in an awkward situation, a quality-of-worklife survey, a management teamwork survey, an emotional intelligence (EQ) test, managing a conflict, and measuring service quality.

## Successful Pedagogical Structure for Students

As with the previous edition, pedagogical features of the text, along with student ancillaries, make *Management,* Ninth Edition, a complete and valuable learning tool—one that will satisfy the needs of both students and professors. This is demonstrated by the following:

- Chapter objectives at the beginning of each chapter focus the reader's attention on key concepts.
- Chapter objectives are repeated at appropriate locations, in the text margin, to pace the reader's progress.
- Key terms are emphasized in bold, where first defined, repeated in marginal notes, and listed at the close of each chapter (with page notations) to reinforce important terminology and concepts.
- A stimulating photo/art program and an inviting, user-friendly layout make the material in this edition visually appealing, accessible, and interesting. Captioned color photographs of managers in action and organizational life enliven the text discussion.
- In-text examples and boxes with three different themes—Global Manager, Management Ethics, Managing Diversity—provide students with extensive, interesting real-world illustrations to demonstrate the application and relevance of topics important to today's managers.
- Clear, comprehensive chapter summaries refresh the reader's memory of important material.
- Cases at the beginning and end of each chapter provide a real-world context for handling management problems. Twenty-five (74 percent) of the cases in this edition are new.
- A Skills & Tools section follows each chapter to give today's and tomorrow's managers practical tools for the twenty-first-century workplace.
- A Hands-On-Exercise following every chapter to provide interactive and experiential learning.
- Internet Exercises at the end of each chapter challenge the reader to learn more about relevant managerial topics and problems.
- Video Skill Builders at the end of each part foster experiential learning by providing how-to-do-it instruction on key managerial skills.
- An end-of-text glossary (with chapter annotations) of all key terms provides a handy reference for the study of management.
- A student Web site (**http://college.hmco.com/business/students**) provides comments on the text annotations, links to the sites discussed in the Internet Exercises and any necessary updates to the exercises, links to the companies highlighted in each chapter's boxes and cases, a description of and additional links to sites of interest, and ACE self-tests.
- A management game called *Manager: A Simulation,* Third Edition, prepared by Jerald R. Smith and Peggy Golden, Florida Atlantic University, offers students the chance to act as managers themselves. The game simulates a business environment in which student management teams produce and market a product. Players make various management decisions and learn from the positive or negative outcomes.
- A *Study Guide* (with answers) helps students to measure their understanding of the terms and concepts in each chapter of the text and to prepare for tests and exams.
- A free CD, *Real Deal Upgrade,* contains a variety of review materials as well as tips on improving study habits.

## Complete Teaching Package

*Management,* Ninth Edition, also includes a comprehensive package of teaching materials:

- An instructor's Web site, accessed via a password, provides teaching tips, links to online publications and professional organizations, electronic lecture notes from the *Instructor's Resource Manual,* and PowerPoint® slides for previewing.

- The *Instructor's Resource Manual,* prepared by Maria Muto, contains the chapter objectives, a lecture outline, case interpretation/solutions, interpretations for the Interactive Annotations, discussion/essay questions, a key issue expansion, a decision case and answers to discussion questions, a cooperative learning tool, and transparency masters for every chapter.
- The completely updated *Test Bank* includes nearly 3,000 true/false, multiple-choice, scenario multiple-choice, and short-answer essay questions with page references and answers. Information about the learning level and the degree of difficulty of each multiple-choice item is also included.
- HMTesting™ is an electronic version of the *Test Bank* that allows instructors to generate and change tests easily on the computer. It is available on the HMClassPrep™ instructor CD-ROM. The program will print an answer key appropriate to each version of the test you have devised, and it lets you customize the printed appearance of the test. A call-in test service is also available. The program also includes the Online Testing System and Gradebook. This feature allows instructors to administer tests via a network system, modem, or personal computer. It also includes a grading function that lets instructors set up a new class, record grades, analyze grades, and produce class and individual statistics.
- An HMClassPrep™ CD-ROM with HMTesting™ for instructors contains over 300 PowerPoint slides and provides an effective presentation tool for lectures. The slides highlight key textual material and provide interesting exercises and discussion questions.
- A Blackboard Course Cartridge and a WebCT Courselet CD-ROM that include chapter review materials, PowerPoint slides, Internet exercises, discussion questions, online quizzes, and hyperlinks allow instructors to customize content for online/distance learning courses.
- 100 color transparencies include figures both from within and outside the text.
- The video package includes ten videos for the Video Skill Builders that follow each part of the text. Bonus videos supplement various chapters and focus on important topics from the text.

## Acknowledgments

Countless people, including colleagues, students, and relatives, have contributed in many ways to the nine editions of this book. For me, this project has been a dream come true; it is amazing where life's journey leads when you have a clear goal, the support of many good people, and a bone-deep belief in the concept of continuous improvement. Whether critical or reinforcing, everyone's suggestions and recommendations have been helpful and greatly appreciated.

While it is impossible to acknowledge every contributor here, some key people need to be identified and sincerely thanked. I particularly appreciate the help and thoughtful comments of my colleague, co-author, and good friend, Professor Angelo Kinicki. I am grateful for the cornerstone reviews of earlier editions by Professors Jack L. Mendleson and Angelo Kinicki. A hearty thank you to Professor Amit Shah, Frostburg State University, for a top-quality job on the *Test Bank.* Sincere thanks also to Maria Muto for her outstanding and creative work on the *Instructor's Resource Manual.*

Warmest thanks are also extended to the following colleagues who have provided valuable input for this and prior editions by serving as content advisers or manuscript reviewers:

Teshome Abebe
*University of Southern Colorado*

Benjamin Abramowitz
*University of Central Florida*

Raymond E. Alie
*Western Michigan University*

Stephen L. Allen
Northwest Missouri State University

Douglas R. Anderson
*Ashland University*

Mark Anderson
*Point Loma Nazarene College*

Eva Beer Aronson
*Interboro Institute*

Debra A. Arvanites
*Villanova University*

Robert Ash
*Rancho Santiago College*

Seymour Barcun
*St. Frances College*

R. B. Barton Jr.
*Murray State University*

Andrew J. Batchelor
*Ohio University—Chillicothe*

Walter H. Beck Sr.
*Kennesaw State University* and
*Reinhardt College*

Roger Best
*Louisiana College*

Gerald D. Biby
*Sioux Falls College*

Glenn M. Blair
*Baldwin-Wallace College*

Bruce Bloom
*DeVry University, Chicago*

Bob Bowles
*Cecils College*

Barbara Boyington
*Brookdale Community College*

Steve Bradley
*Austin Community College*

Molly Burke
*Rosary College*

Marie Burkhead
*University of Southwestern Louisiana*

John Cantrell
*Cleveland State Community College*

Thomas Carey
*Western Michigan University*

Elaine Adams Casmus
*Chowan College*

David Chown
*Minnesota State University—Mankato*

Anthony A. Cioffi
*Lorain County Community College*

Richard Coe
*Richard Stockton College of New Jersey*

George M. Coggins
*High Point College*

Naomi Berger Davidson
*California State University—Northridge*

Pamela Davis
*Eastern Kentucky University*

Richard A. Davis
*Rosary College*

Thomas Daymont
*Temple University—Philadelphia*

Tim Donahue
*Sioux Falls College*

Thomas Duda
*S.U.N.Y. Canton Tech College*

Deborah J. Dwyer
*University of Toledo*

Gary Ernst
*North Central College*

Janice Feldbauer
*Macomb Community College*

Jacque Foust
*University of Wisconsin—River Falls*

Ellen Frank
*Southern Connecticut State University*

Phyllis Goodman
*College of DuPage*

Sue Granger
*Jacksonville State University*

Judith Grenkowicz
*Kirtland Community College*

Ann McClure
*Ft. Hays State University*

John Hall
*University of Florida*

Barbara McIntosh
*University of Vermont*

Susan C. Hanlon
*University of Akron*

Debra Miller
*Ashland Community College*

Nell Hartley
*Robert Morris College*

Peggy M. Miller
*Ohio University—Athens*

Lindle Hatton
*University of Wisconsin—Oshkosh*

John Nagy
*Cleary College*

Rick Hebert
*East Carolina University*

James Nead
*Vincennes University*

Brian R. Hinrichs
*Illinois Wesleyan University*

Joan Nichols
*Emporia State University*

Jerome Hufnagel
*Horry Georgetown Tech*

Alice E. Nuttall
*Kent State University*

Cathy Jensen
*University of Nebraska—Lincoln*

Darlene Orlov
*New York University*

Marvin Karlins
*University of South Florida*

Robert Ottemann
*University of Nebraska—Omaha*

Velta Kelly
*University of Cincinnati*

Clyde A. Painter
*Ohio Northern University*

Sylvia Keyes
*Bridgewater State College*

Herbert S. Parker
*Kean College of New Jersey*

Mary Khalili
*Oklahoma City University*

Gus Petrides
*Borough of Manhattan Community College*

John Lea
*Arizona State University*

J. Stephen Phillips
*Ohio University—Chillicothe*

Charles Lee
*Baldwin-Wallace College*

Allen H. Pike
*Ferrum College*

Roger D. Lee
*Salt Lake Community College*

Khush Pittenger
*Ashland University*

Bob Lower
*Minot State University*

Jyoti N. Prasad
*Eastern Illinois University*

James L. Mann
*Ashland Community College*

Lynn J. Richardson
*Fort Lewis College*

Randall Martin
*Florida International University*

Robert W. Risteen
*Ohio University—Chillicothe*

Irvin Mason
*Herkimer County Community College*

Ralph Roberts
*University of West Florida*

Fredric L. Mayerson
*CUNY—Kingsboro Community College*

Jake Robertson
*Oklahoma State University*

Robert Rowe
*New Mexico State University–Alamogordo*
and *Park College, Holloman Air Force Base*

Daniel James Rowley
*University of Northern Colorado,*
*Monfort College of Business*

Wendell J. Roye
*Franklin Pierce College*

Doug Rymph
*Emporia State University*

Nestor St. Charles
*Dutchess County Community College*

John T. Samaras
*Central State University*

Roger C. Schoenfeldt
*Murray State University*

C. L. Scott III
*Indiana University NW—Gary*

Kathryn Severance
*Viterbo College*

Jane Shuping
*Western Piedmont Community College*

Marc Siegall
*California State University—Chico*

G. David Sivak
*Westmoreland County Community College*

Mick Stahler
*Stautzenberger College*

Jacqueline Stowe
*McMurray University*

Sharon Tarnutzer
*Utah State University*

Margo Underwood
*Brunswick College*

John Valentine
*Kean College of New Jersey*

Joe F. Walenciak
*John Brown University*

Dorothy Wallace
*Chowan College*

Stanley Welaish
*Kean College of New Jersey*

Richard A. Wells
*Aiken Technical College*

Ty Westergaard
*Lincoln University*

Timothy Wiedman
*Ohio University—Lancaster*

Mary Williams
*College of South Nevada*

James Wittman
*Rock Valley College*

My partnership with Houghton Mifflin through the years has been productive and enjoyable. Many Houghton Mifflin Company people have contributed enormously to this project. I would like to offer a hearty thank you to everyone by acknowledging the following key contributors: George Hoffman, Damaris Curran, Cathy Brooks, Steven Mikels, Lisa Boden, Marcy Kagan, Lindsay Frost, Carol Merrigan, Marie Barnes, Bonnie Melton, and Marisa Papile.

    The discussion of mentoring in Chapter 15 is dedicated once again to Professor Fred Luthans, University of Nebraska—Lincoln, for getting me into the textbook business. His love for our field of study and incredible work ethic continue to inspire me. To Margaret—my wife, best friend, and hiking buddy—thanks for being my center of gravity and for keeping the spirit of the dancing bears alive. Our marriage is a cherished treasure. Once again, I must thank our cat, Amaranth, for supervising my every move during the last seventeen years from his cozy napping places in my home office.

    Finally, I would like to thank the thousands of introductory management students I have had the pleasure of working with through the years for teaching me a great deal about tomorrow's managers. Best wishes for a rewarding career in management.

*Bob Kreitner*

**"**If you have built castles in the air,
your work need not be lost;
that is where they should be.
Now put the foundations
under them.**"**

**henry david thoreau**

# part one

# The **Management** Challenge

# chapter one

# Managers and Entrepreneurs

## CHAPTER OBJECTIVES

*When you finish studying this chapter you should be able to*

**1** **Define** the term *management* and **explain** the managerial significance of the terms *effectiveness* and *efficiency*.

**2** **Identify** and **summarize** five major sources of change for today's managers.

**3** **Contrast** the functional and role approaches to explaining what managers do.

**4** **Summarize** the ten facts of managerial life.

**5** **Explain** how managers learn to manage.

**6** **Challenge** two myths about small businesses and **describe** entrepreneurs.

> **"** Some days you wake up, and if you think about all the things that you have to do, it's so overwhelming, you could be paralyzed. . . . You just have to get it done. **"**
>
> Justine Fritz, manager

# Avon's CEO, Andrea Jung, Still Striving for Perfection

ndrea Jung, the Chairman and CEO of Avon, is sitting in her office on the 27th floor of Avon's New York headquarters considering an obvious question: What does it mean to be the first woman to lead the beauty products company in its 115-year history? "I guess it helps," she says wryly. "You know, you go home and you try on a new mascara, and I guess a male CEO can't do that." She's joking, of course, but there's something to what she says. Glamorous, poised, and always impeccably turned out, Jung knows what women want and how to sell it to them. And that's what has made her one of the most successful CEOs—male or female—in recent years.

When Jung, 43, took over Avon in November 1999, the company was in deep trouble. During the greatest economic boom in history, its stock was crumbling. As fewer women wanted to peddle Avon products, its sales sagged. The Avon Lady seemed to have passed out of present time into the sphere of kitsch. "There was that feeling, is the day of the Avon rep over?" recalls board member Ann Moore, an executive vice president at Time Inc. But Jung surprised a lot of people. Over the past 20 months she has overhauled nearly everything about the way Avon does business: how it advertises, manufactures, packages, and even sells its products. Most surprising, she has done it not by abandoning the seemingly outdated Avon Lady, but by reviving her. Under Jung, more Avon Ladies are signing on than ever before. In the U.S., their numbers—after years of decline—will actually grow this year.

"The results under Andrea are strikingly different than they have been under any other CEO," says Heather Hay Murren, an analyst with Merrill Lynch. Indeed, over the past two years sales growth has climbed from 1.5% in 1999 to an expected 6% this year, and revenues should hit $6 billion. Operating profits, which grew at an average of 4% throughout the '90s, are expected to climb this year by 7%. And operating margins are on track to top 14%—their highest level in a decade. . . .

To reward her efforts, Avon's board recently made Jung chairman—a title that had been withheld contingent on how she performed as CEO. "She is really shin-

ing," says Jack Welch, who until his retirement . . . [in 2001] sat with Jung on GE's board. "I think you've got a CEO that is just blossoming on the job."

She blossomed so quickly at the top, perhaps, because she'd spent time getting to know the company and its foibles. Jung came to Avon seven years ago after working for such retailers as Neiman Marcus and Bloomingdale's. At Avon her task was to create a global brand. At the time, each region was in charge of its own campaigns. As a result, the company logo, packaging, and ads in Latin America, for example, looked nothing like those in the U.S. The last memorable slogan was the "Ding-dong, Avon calling" jingle that dates from 1953. Jung created a new "Let's talk" campaign and pushed for the current corporate tag, "The company for women."

She also trusted her own instincts about style and taste. She knew that Avon's largely working- and middle-class customers couldn't afford Lancôme or Estée Lauder, but that couldn't stop them from craving the elegance they associated with those brands. So she redesigned Avon's packaging to make its bottles and jars look as modern and sophisticated as products in upscale department stores.

To get a grip on the desires of her customers, as well as the struggles of the sales force, she signed on as an Avon Lady herself. "I wanted to go through the selling experience," recalls Jung. "I was going door to door in my neighborhood." It was by ringing doorbells on New York's Upper East Side that she really began to understand Avon's larger business. She heard customer gripes over discontinued colors, mishandled orders, confusing promotions. One customer chewed her out for showing up with a catalog that didn't offer her favorite skin cream.

By the time she took over as CEO from Charles Perrin, Jung was familiar with Avon's failings, and she knew she needed to move fast to fix them. Four weeks into her new job, in December 1999, she laid out her turnaround plan at an analysts' conference. She talked about launching an entirely new line of businesses, developing blockbuster products, and selling Avon in retail stores—something it had never done in its long history. At the same time she promised to meet the company's goal of cutting hundreds of millions in costs out of the back end by the end of 2000. It was an ambitious plan, one few believed Jung could pull off. . . .

Jung worked at a breakneck pace to execute her plan. In 2000 she added 46% to Avon's research-and-development budget to get blockbusters to market faster. Normally Avon spends at least three years developing new products, but Janice Teal, head of R&D, recalls Jung saying to her: "You've got two years. I need a breakthrough, and that's the goal." And indeed, by the end of that year, Jung got what she wanted. Last winter, Avon launched Retroactive, an anti-aging skin cream that has been a runaway hit. . . .

To guide Avon through this next phase, Jung's plan is to stick to the plan. "I'm not changing any of our thinking," she insists. "This turnaround is far from complete. I'm probably thinking that we need to be even bolder and faster." . . .

She's striving to cut the time it takes to get a product to market from 88 weeks to less than 50. She's pushing to reduce the number of mishandled orders from 32% to 10%. And over the next two years she expects Avon to cut another $200 million in costs out of its manufacturing and distribution.

She's determined to do all of this. And by way of explaining what drives her determination, she tells a little story. She tells it earnestly, without irony or jest. When she was in fourth grade in Wellesley, Mass., Jung recalls, she desperately wanted a box of 120 colored pencils. Her parents made her a deal. She could get the set if she got straight A's in school—no B's, no A-minuses, just straight A's. By her own admission, Jung was never a natural student, but she badly wanted that pencil set. So while other kids goofed around after school, Jung holed up in her room and studied. She missed out on birthday parties and tennis games, but by the end of the year she delivered to her parents a full set of A's—and in return she got a full set of 120 colored pencils. "I'll never forget that," Jung says. "My parents ingrained in me early on that the perfect score is always something to strive for. I want to win and I want to succeed no matter what." And if the girl would give up a year of fun for a box of pencils, what won't the woman do to make her company succeed?

Andrea Jung is an inspiring example of a modern manager in action. Her overriding goal is to do whatever it takes to achieve her organization's mission in a highly competitive world. Relative to our present challenge to learn more about management, Jung's story underscores four key realities of managing today:

1. The only certainty today is *change.* Challenging *goals* motivate people to strive for improvement and overcome obstacles and resistance to change.
2. *Speed, teamwork,* and *flexibility* are the orders of the day, from both strategic and operational standpoints.
3. Managers at all levels need to stay close to the *customer.* Product/service *quality* is the driving force in the battle to stay competitive.
4. Without *continuous improvement* and *lifelong learning,* there can be no true economic progress for individuals and organizations alike.[1]

Keep these managerial realities in mind as you explore the world of management in this book.

Every one of us—whether as an employee, a customer, a stockholder, or a member of the surrounding community—has a direct stake in the quality of management. As an everyday example, consider the positive connection Hyatt Hotels found among good management, customer satisfaction, and profitability.

*Hyatt Hotels has been surveying all employees at its 106 hotels in North America for 15 years. Although its questionnaire includes some 100 items, the answers to seven key queries—one of which is "Tell us what you think of management"—make up the general morale index, or GMI, that Hyatt's top officers watch most closely. The company has just finished developing a computer program that compares employees' attitudes in each location with what guests say on those how-did-you-like-your-stay postcards in Hyatt's hotel rooms. Guess what: The hotels with the highest GMI scores also rack up the highest ratings from customers—and, not coincidentally, the highest sales and gross operating profits.*[2]

Conversely, bad management is a serious threat to our quality of life. In fact, "studies . . . show the single biggest source of stress is poorly trained and inept supervisors."[3]

Effective management is the key to a better world, but mismanagement squanders our resources and jeopardizes our well-being. Every manager, regardless of level or scope of responsibility, is either part of the solution or part of the problem. Management or mismanagement—the choice is yours. A basic knowledge of management theory, research, and practice will help prepare you for productive and gainful employment in a highly organized world in which virtually everything is managed.

# Management Defined

We now need to define management, in order to highlight the importance, relevance, and necessity of studying it. **Management** is the process of working with and through others to achieve organizational objectives in a changing environment. Central to this process is the effective and efficient use of limited resources.

Five components of this definition require closer examination: (1) working with and through others, (2) achieving organizational objectives, (3) balancing effectiveness and efficiency, (4) making the most of limited resources, and (5) coping with a changing environment (see Figure 1.1).

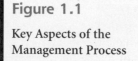

**1** Define the term **management** and explain the managerial significance of the terms *effectiveness* and *efficiency*.

**management**  *the process of working with and through others to achieve organizational objectives in a changing environment*

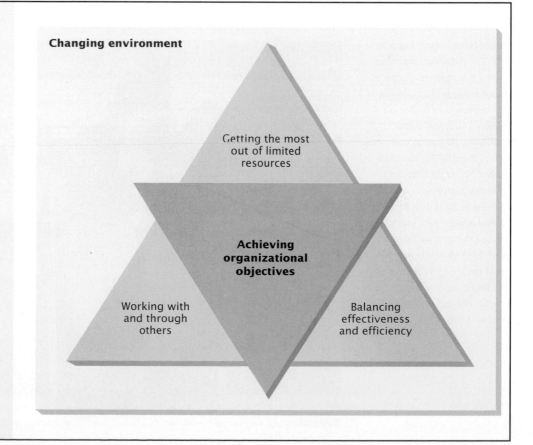

**Figure 1.1**

Key Aspects of the Management Process

**Changing environment**

Getting the most out of limited resources

**Achieving organizational objectives**

Working with and through others

Balancing effectiveness and efficiency

## Working with and Through Others

Management is, above all else, a social process. Many collective purposes bring individuals together—building cars, providing emergency health care, publishing books, and on and on. But in all cases, managers are responsible for getting things done by working with and through others.

Aspiring managers who do not interact well with others hamper their careers. This was the conclusion two experts reached following interviews with 62 executives from the United States, United Kingdom, Belgium, Spain, France, Germany, and Italy. Each of the executives was asked to describe two managers whose careers had been *derailed*. Derailed managers were those who had not lived up to their peers' and superiors' high expectations. The derailed managers reportedly had these shortcomings:

- Problems with interpersonal relationships.
- Failure to meet business objectives.
- Failure to build and lead a team.
- Inability to change and adapt during a transition.[4]

Significantly, the first and third shortcomings involve failure to work effectively with and through others. The derailed managers experienced a number of interpersonal problems; among other things, they were perceived as manipulative, abusive, untrustworthy, demeaning, overly critical, not team players, and poor communicators.[5]

Even managers who make it all the way to the top often have interpersonal problems, according to management consultant Richard Hagberg. His study of 511 chief executive officers led to this conclusion about why managers often fail to inspire loyalty in employees:

*Successful managers put people first. These Agilent employees share a fun moment despite a brutal tech-industry downturn. Although Agilent had to cut salaries and lay off 8,000 employees, the former electronics unit of Hewlett-Packard still ranked No. 31 on Fortune's "100 Best Companies to Work For" list in 2002. Employees ranked Agilent very favorably because the company did everything humanly possible to avoid the layoff. When business gets better, Agilent will reap the benefits of keeping employee trust and hope alive.*

## 1A Getting Along with the Boss

*Quick quiz:* How important is it for you to have a good relationship with your boss at work? (Circle your response on the following scale.)

Not at all important  1  2  3  4  5  Extremely important

*Comparative survey results:* In one survey, 77 percent of the women and 63 percent of the men said "extremely important."

**Source:** Data from "What Makes a Job OK," *USA Today* (May 15, 2000): 1B.

**Question:** *Is "quality of supervision" a major quality of life issue for you? Why or why not?*

For further information about the interactive annotations in this chapter, visit our Web site (http://business.college.hmco.com/students).

*Many are also hobbled by self-importance, which keeps them from hearing feedback about their own strengths and weaknesses. The head of one large company recently told me about an incident that occurred as he and his wife waited in line to get his driver's license renewed. He was frustrated at how long it was taking and grumbled to his wife, "I have a lot to do. Don't they know who I am?" She replied, "Yeah, you're a plumber's son who got lucky." Her remark really got to him. It drove home how far he had gotten caught up in his sense of self-importance.[6]*

## Achieving Organizational Objectives

An objective is a target to be strived for and, one hopes, attained. Like individuals, organizations are usually more successful when their activities are guided by challenging, yet achievable, objectives. From an individual perspective, scheduling a course load becomes more systematic and efficient when a student sets an objective, such as graduating with a specific degree by a given date.

Although personal objectives are typically within the reach of individual effort, organizational objectives or goals always require collective action. A master of powerful organizational objectives is Carlos Ghosn, the Brazilian-born CEO of Nissan. When France's Renault bought a controlling interest in Nissan in 1999 and put Ghosn in charge, the Japanese automaker was a real money loser. Thanks to Ghosn's bold Nissan Revival Plan, based on lots of employee input, Nissan is turning a profit.[7] Now comes the next step:

*Ghosn has laid out what he calls the "180 Plan" for Nissan. It begins April 2003, as his Nissan Revival Plan ends. . . .*

*The "1" in the 180 Plan means Nissan intends to sell 1 million more vehicles a year worldwide than it does now. The "8" refers to the target of 8% profit margin, roughly double what's typical. The "0" means the debt-burdened automaker wants no debt.*

*The goals are to be accomplished before the end of 2005.[8]*

Thus, Ghosn's goal-oriented approach strives to inspire and energize Nissan's employees to achieve greater organizational success.

Organizational objectives also serve later as measuring sticks for performance. Without organizational objectives, the management process, like a trip without a specific destination, would be aimless and wasteful.

## Balancing Effectiveness and Efficiency

**effectiveness**  *a central element in the process of management that entails achieving a stated organizational objective*

**efficiency**  *a central element in the process of management that balances the amount of resources used to achieve an objective against what was actually accomplished*

Distinguishing between effectiveness and efficiency is much more than an exercise in semantics. The relationship between these two terms is important, and it presents managers with a never-ending dilemma. **Effectiveness** entails promptly achieving a stated objective. Swinging a sledgehammer against the wall, for example, would be an effective way to kill a bothersome fly. But given the reality of limited resources, effectiveness alone is not enough. **Efficiency** enters the picture when the resources required to achieve an objective are weighed against what was actually accomplished. The more favorable the ratio of benefits to costs, the greater the efficiency. Although a sledgehammer is an effective tool for killing flies, it is highly inefficient when the wasted effort and smashed walls are taken into consideration. A fly swatter is both an effective and an efficient tool for killing a single housefly.

Managers are responsible for balancing effectiveness and efficiency (see Figure 1.2). Too much emphasis in either direction leads to mismanagement. On the one hand, managers must be effective, although those who waste resources in the process flirt with bankruptcy.

On the other hand, managers need to be efficient by containing costs as much as possible and conserving limited resources. But managers who are too stingy with resources may not get the job done.

At the heart of the quest for *productivity improvement* (a favorable ratio between inputs and output) is the constant struggle to balance effectiveness and efficiency.[9] Returning again to Nissan, recent data show it to be more productive than Germany's Volkswagen. VW annually produces 46 vehicles per worker at its Wolfsburg, Germany, factory "compared with 101 at Nissan Motor Co.'s British factory in Sunderland."[10] At least in terms of labor productivity, Nissan is both more effective and more efficient than VW.

> **1B  Got a Flashlight? I Can't See My Productivity Report!**
>
> *Situation:* When telecommunications equipment maker Lucent Technologies was struggling through bad times in 2001, three out of four of the fluorescent bulbs in some of its office cubicles were darkened in a cost-cutting move.
>
> **Source:** Based on Matthew Boyle, "What We Learned," *Fortune* (December 24, 2001): 179.
>
> **Question:** *Why was this a good (or bad) idea?*

## Making the Most of Limited Resources

We live in a world of scarcity. Those who are concerned with such matters worry not only about running out of nonrenewable energy and material resources but also about the lopsided use of those resources. The United States, for example, with about 5 percent of the world's population, is currently consuming about 25 percent of the world's annual oil production and generating 23 percent of the greenhouse gases linked to global warming.[11]

Although experts and nonexperts alike may quibble over exactly how long it will take to exhaust our nonrenewable resources or come up with exotic new technological alternatives, one bold fact remains. Our planet is becoming increasingly crowded.

Demographers who collect and study population statistics tell us the Earth's human population is growing by 8,741 people every *hour* (as the result of 15,020 births and 6,279 deaths.)[12] The present world population of 6.1 billion people is projected to reach 9 billion within 70 years.[13] Meanwhile, our planet's carrying capacity is open to speculation.

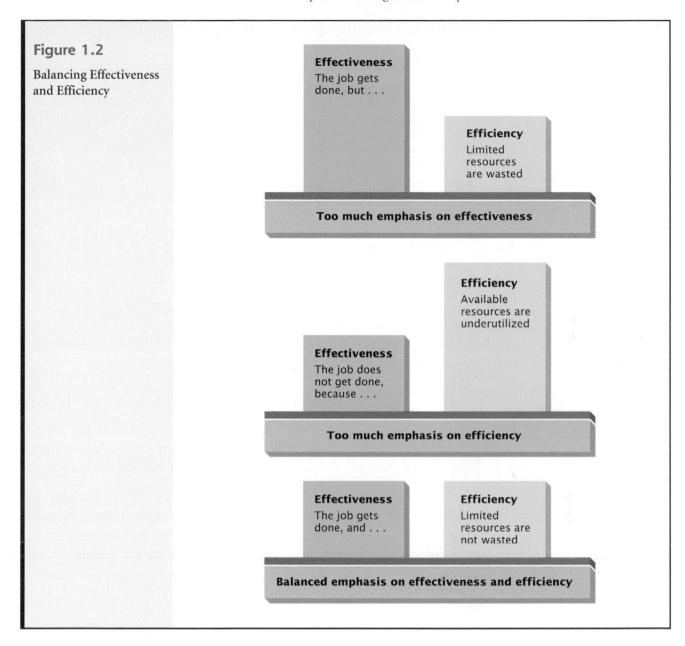

**Figure 1.2**

Balancing Effectiveness
and Efficiency

Approximately 83 percent of the world's population in the year 2020 will live in relatively poor and less-developed countries. Developed and industrialized nations, consequently, will experience increasing pressure to divide the limited resource pie more equitably.[14]

Because of their common focus on resources, economics and management are closely related. Economics is the study of how limited resources are distributed among alternative uses. In productive organizations, managers are the trustees of limited resources, and it is their job to see that the basic factors of production—land, labor, and capital—are used efficiently as well as effectively. Management could be called "applied economics."

## Coping with a Changing Environment

Successful managers are the ones who anticipate and adjust to changing circumstances rather than being passively swept along or caught unprepared. Employers today are hiring managers who can take unfamiliar situations in stride. *Business Week* recently served up this amusing but challenging profile of tomorrow's managers: "The next generation of corporate leaders will need the charm of a debutante, the flexibility of a gymnast, and the quickness of a panther. A few foreign languages and a keen understanding of technology won't hurt either."[15] Also in the mix are a sense of humor, passion, and the ability to make fast decisions.

Chapter 3 provides detailed coverage of important changes and trends in management's social, political-legal, economic, and technological environments. At this point, it is instructive to preview major changes for managers doing business in the twenty-first century[16] (see Table 1.1). This particular collection of changes is the product of five overarching sources of change: globalization, the evolution of product quality, environmentalism, an ethical reawakening, and the Internet revolution. Together, these factors are significantly reshaping the practice of management.

**Globalization.**    Figuratively speaking, the globe is shrinking in almost every conceivable way. Networks of transportation, communication, computers, music, and economics have tied the people of the world together as never before. Companies are having to become global players just to survive, let alone prosper. For example, Thomson Corp., a Canadian media and publishing company, rings up 94 percent of its sales outside the country, and 92 percent of its employees are foreigners.[17] Import and

**2**  Identify and summarize five major sources of change for today's managers.

| **Table 1.1**   The Twenty-First Century Manager: Ten Major Changes | | |
|---|---|---|
| | **Moving away from** | **Moving toward** |
| **Administrative role** | Boss/superior/leader | Team member/facilitator/teacher/ sponsor/advocate/coach |
| **Cultural orientation** | Monocultural/monolingual | Multicultural/multilingual |
| **Quality/ethics/ environmental impacts** | Afterthought (or no thought) | Forethought (unifying themes) |
| **Power bases** | Formal authority; rewards and punishments | Knowledge; relationships; rewards |
| **Primary organizational unit** | Individual | Team |
| **Interpersonal dealings** | Competition; win-lose | Cooperation; win-win |
| **Learning** | Periodic (preparatory; curriculum-driven) | Continuous (lifelong; learner-driven) |
| **Problems** | Threats to be avoided | Opportunities for learning and continuous improvement |
| **Change and conflict** | Resist/react/avoid | Anticipate/seek/channel |
| **Information** | Restrict access/hoard | Increase access/share |

export figures are equally stunning. For instance, the United States currently imports about 60 percent of its oil, with a higher percentage forecasted.[18] On the export side, "Internet infrastructure king Cisco gets 59% of its sales from outside the U.S."[19] In a 1998 American Management Association survey, 1,797 executives from 36 countries were asked to look ten years into the future. "Globalization and foreign markets" was ranked the likely number one issue for managers in ten years.[20] Business and job opportunities show little regard for international borders these days.

On the negative side, some worry about giant global corporations eclipsing the economic and political power of individual nations and their citizens. Indeed, "half of the hundred largest budgets in the world now belong to corporations, not nations."[21]

Today's model manager is one who is comfortable transacting business in multiple languages and cultures. A prime example is Peter Brabeck-Letmathe, the Austrian-born head of Nestlé, the Swiss company with customers in "every country of the world—even in North Korea. . . . Brabeck's wife, an interior designer, is Chilean. He speaks Spanish at home with her and their three grown children. [In addition to his native German language, he is] also fluent in French, Italian, Portuguese, and English."[22]

Unusual? No. There is a rapidly growing army of global managers from all corners of the world, and you can become a member of it through diligent effort and a clear sense of purpose. Chapter 4 is devoted to the topic of international management. The international cases, examples, and The Global Manager features throughout the text are intended to broaden your awareness of international management. (See The Global Manager.)

**The Evolution of Product Quality.**    Managers have been interested in the quality of their products, at least as an afterthought, since the Industrial Revolution. But thanks to U.S. and Japanese quality gurus such as W. Edwards Deming and Kaoru Ishikawa[23] (more about them in Chapter 2), product/service quality has become both a forethought and a driving force in effective organizations of all kinds. Today's hospitals, hotels, universities, and government agencies are as interested in improving product/service quality as are factories, mines, airlines, and railroads.

*You probably don't think about the quality of the products responsible for your Internet connections and telephone calls. That's because an international workforce including Maria Gabriela Gúzman Jiménez, checking the quality of switching gear on an overhead screen in this photo, makes sure key components work properly. Here we also have tangible evidence of the North American Free Trade Association (NAFTA). This factory in Guadalajara, Mexico, is owned by Solectron, a California company, and it assembles and tests products for Canada's Nortel, among others.*

# The Global Manager

## Globalization and Terrorism: Post–September 11, 2001, Perspectives from Around the World

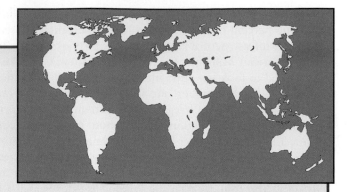

Ricardo Semler, President, Semco SA, a Brazilian manufacturer:

*Will Sept. 11 change the world?* I don't see structural change of any kind. It obviously shakes everyone up on a human level, but not on a structural level. I don't have the impression that we're now dealing with a completely different world, or that we're dealing with different economics or with different political considerations from those we had before.

*Business Week:*

Globalization certainly isn't going to disappear—the world's markets are too vitally integrated to roll back now. But globalization could well become slower and costlier, crimping the high-productivity, low-inflation model of the 1990s. Companies will likely have to pay more to insure and provide security for overseas staff and property. Heightened border inspections could slow movements of cargo, forcing companies to stock more inventory. Tighter immigration policies could curtail the liberal inflows of skilled and blue-collar laborers that allowed companies to expand while keeping wages in check.

Haim Harari, president, Weizmann Institute of Science, an Israeli R&D center:

*Was globalization itself attacked on Sept. 11? Will the World Trade Center attacks slow the progress of the global economy?* Globalization is here to stay. Even terror is globalized. It is operated from several countries, with terrorist acts in other countries, by a multinational consortium, directed against several nations, using international communications and travel. International science and technology, as well as the communications media of the global village, are used quite successfully by terrorists. And illegal immigration, organized crime, and even antiglobalization demonstrations—all of these, too, are globalized. The ultimate example was the Internet message saying, "Join the worldwide fight against globalization."

*Sources:* Excerpted from "Ricardo Semler," *Fortune* (November 26, 2001): 80; Pete Engardio and Rich Miller, "What's at Stake," *Business Week* (October 22, 2001): 35; and "Haim Harari," *Fortune* (November 26, 2001): 98.

In its most basic terms, the emphasis on quality has evolved through four distinct stages since World War II—from "fix it in" to "inspect it in" to "build it in" to "design it in." Progressive managers are moving away from the first two approaches and toward the build-it-in and design-it-in approaches.[24] Here are the key differences:

- *The fix-it approach to quality.* Rework any defective products identified by quality inspectors at the end of the production process.
- *The inspect-it-in approach to quality.* Have quality inspectors sample work in process and prescribe machine adjustments to avoid substandard output.
- *The build-it-in approach to quality.* Make *everyone* who touches the product responsible for spotting and correcting defects. Emphasis is on identifying and eliminating *causes* of quality problems.
- *The design-it-in approach to quality.* Intense customer and employee involvement drives the entire design-production cycle. Emphasis is on *continuous improvement* of personnel, processes, and product.

Notice how each stage of this evolution has broadened the responsibility for quality, turning quality improvement into a true team effort. Also, the focus has shifted from reactively fixing product defects to proactively working to prevent them and to satisfy the customer completely. Today's quality leaders strive to *exceed,* not just meet, the customer's expectations.

A popular label for the build-it-in and design-it-in approaches to quality is *total quality management* (TQM).[25] TQM is discussed in detail in Chapter 17.

**Environmentalism.**    Environmental issues such as deforestation; global warming; depletion of the ozone layer; toxic waste; and pollution of land, air, and water are no longer strictly the domain of campus radicals. Mainstream politicians and managers around the world have picked up the environmental banner. The so-called green movement has spawned successful political parties in Europe and is gaining a foothold in North America and elsewhere. Managers are challenged to develop creative ways to make a profit without unduly harming the environment in the process.[26] Terms such as *industrial ecology* and *eco-efficiency* are heard today under the general umbrella of sustainable development.[27]

Also, cleaning up the environment promises to generate whole new classes of jobs and robust profits in the future. The debate over jobs versus the environment has been rendered obsolete by the need for both a healthy economy *and* a healthy environment.[28] Encouragingly, researchers recently found 80 percent higher stock market valuations for multinational corporations adhering to strict environmental standards, compared with those taking advantage of the lax environmental standards often found in less-developed countries.[29] In short, investors tend to reward "clean" companies and punish "dirty" ones.

**An Ethical Reawakening.**    Managers are under strong pressure from the public, elected officials, and respected managers to behave better. This pressure has resulted from years of headlines about discrimination, illegal campaign contributions, accounting fraud, price fixing, insider trading, the selling of unsafe products, and other unethical practices.

Traditional values such as honesty are being reemphasized in managerial decision making and conduct. This conclusion is supported by the results of a nationwide survey of executives who were asked to rank the desired characteristics of superior leaders. The number one choice was *honest* (87 percent).[30] Ethics and honesty are everyone's concern: *mine, yours,* and *ours.* Every day we have countless opportunities to be honest or dishonest. One survey of more than 4,000 employees uncovered the following ethical problems in the workplace (the percentage of employees observing the problem during the past year appears in parentheses):

- Lying to supervisors (56 percent)
- Lying on reports or falsifying records (41 percent)
- Stealing and theft (35 percent)
- Sexual harassment (35 percent)
- Abusing drugs or alcohol (31 percent)
- Conflict of interest (31 percent)[31]

Because of closer public scrutiny, ethical questions can no longer be shoved aside as irrelevant. The topic of managerial ethics is covered in depth in Chapter 5 and explored in the Management Ethics boxes throughout the text.

**The Internet and E-Business Revolution.**   Like a growing child, the Internet first crawled, then walked, then ran too fast and fell, and now is running more wisely. In concept, the Internet began as a U.S. Department of Defense (DOD) research project during the Cold War era of the 1960s. The plan was to give university scientists a quick and inexpensive way to share their DOD research data. Huge technical problems such as getting incompatible computers to communicate in a fail-safe network were solved in 1969 at UCLA when researchers succeeded in getting two linked computers to exchange data. The Internet was born. Other universities were added to the Internet during the 1970s, and gradually applications such as e-mail emerged. By 1983, technology made it possible to share complex documents and graphics on the Internet, and the World Wide Web came into existence.[32] Time passed and improvements were made. During the early 1990s, individuals and businesses began to log on to the "Web" to communicate via e-mail and to buy and sell things.

Growth of the **Internet**—the worldwide network of personal computers, routers and switches, powerful servers, and organizational computer systems—has been explosive. No one owns the Web, and anyone with a computer modem can be part of it. Within its digital recesses are both trash and treasure. By 2001, there were an estimated 100 million Internet users in the United States alone.[33] Worldwide use is believed to exceed 500 million. The implications of this massive interconnectedness for managers are profound and truly revolutionary. Legal, ethical, security, and privacy issues, however, remain largely unresolved.[34]

**Internet** *global network of servers and personal and organizational computers*

Within the business community, heads are still spinning from the dot-com crash of 2000–2001. Wild hype gave way to doubt as countless dot-com dreams simply vaporized. Internet portal Excite.com, purchased by At Home in 1999 for $6.7 *billion* and sold in 2001 for $10 *million,* is a sobering case in point.[35] Today, the e-business revolution is proceeding in a more measured way and with more realistic expectations.[36] Where their focus before the dot-com crash was primarily on business-to-consumer retailing, Internet strategists are now much more broadly focused. Thus, an **e-business** is one seeking efficiencies via the Internet in all basic business functions—production, marketing, and finance/accounting—and all support activities involving human, material, and financial resources. Craig Barrett, the CEO of Intel, the computer chip giant, recently explained how his firm evolved into what he calls an "Internet company":

**1C  It's a Wired, Wired World**

*Strip away the highfalutin talk, and at bottom, the Internet is a tool that dramatically lowers the cost of communication. That means it can radically alter any industry or activity that depends heavily on the flow of information.*

**Source:** Michael J. Mandel and Robert D. Hof, "Rethinking the Internet," *Business Week* (March 26, 2001): 118.

**Questions:**  *In what ways is the Internet affecting your work and leisure activities these days? What do you see ten years down the road for the Internet?*

**e-business** *a business using the Internet for greater efficiency in every aspect of its operations*

*. . . for Intel, being an Internet company meant turning ourselves into a 100% e-business from front to back—not just in terms of selling and buying, but also in terms of information transfer, education, and customer interaction. We wanted to improve our competitiveness and our productivity, to streamline our internal operations, and to save some money. We also wanted to show that we can use the technology that we sell to the rest of the world.[37]*

Aspects and implications of the Internet and e-business revolution are explored throughout this book, with detailed coverage of Internet strategy in Chapter 7.

Considering the variety of these sources of change in the general environment, managers are challenged to keep abreast of them and adjust and adapt as necessary.

# What Do Managers Do?

Although nearly all aspects of modern life are touched at least indirectly by the work of managers, many people do not really understand what the management process involves. Management is much more, for example, than the familiar activity of telling employees what to do. Management is a complex and dynamic mixture of systematic techniques and common sense. As with any complex process, the key to learning about management lies in dividing it into readily understood subprocesses. Historically, there have been two different approaches to dividing the management process for study and discussion. One approach, dating back to the early part of this century, is to identify managerial functions. A second, more recent approach focuses on managerial roles.

**Managerial functions** are general administrative duties that need to be carried out in virtually all productive organizations. **Managerial roles** are specific categories of managerial behavior. A British management scholar clarified this distinction by pointing out that managerial functions involve "desired outcomes." Those outcomes are achieved through the performance of managerial roles (actual behavior).[38] Stated another way, roles are the *means* and functions are the *ends* of the manager's job. We shall examine both approaches more closely and then have a frank discussion of some managerial facts of life.

**3** Contrast the functional and role approaches to explaining what managers do.

**managerial functions** *general administrative duties that need to be carried out in virtually all productive organizations to achieve desired outcomes*

**managerial roles** *specific categories of managerial behavior*

## Managerial Functions

For nearly a century, the most popular approach to describing what managers do has been the functional view. It has been popular because it characterizes the management process as a sequence of rational and logical steps. Henri Fayol, a French industrialist turned writer, became the father of the functional approach in 1916 when he identified five managerial functions: planning, organizing, command, coordination, and control.[39] Fayol claimed that these five functions were the common denominators of all managerial jobs, whatever the purpose of the organization. Over the years Fayol's original list of managerial functions has been updated and expanded by management scholars. This book, even though it is based on more than just Fayol's approach, is organized around eight different managerial functions: planning, decision making, organizing, staffing, communicating, motivating, leading, and controlling (see Figure 1.3). A brief overview of these eight managerial functions will describe what managers do and will preview what lies ahead in this text.

**Planning.** Commonly referred to as the primary management function, planning is the formulation of future courses of action. Plans and the objectives on which they are based give purpose and direction to the organization, its subunits, and contributing individuals.

**Decision Making.** Managers choose among alternative courses of action when they make decisions. Making intelligent and ethical decisions in today's complex world is a major management challenge.

**Organizing.** Structural considerations such as the chain of command, division of labor, and assignment of responsibility are part of the organizing function. Careful organizing helps ensure the efficient use of human resources.

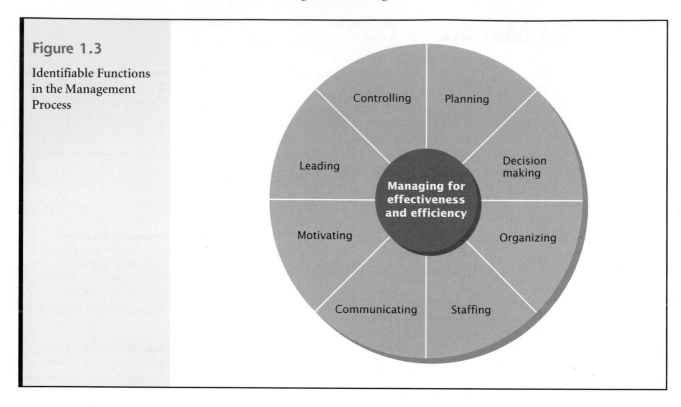

## Figure 1.3

Identifiable Functions in the Management Process

### Back to the Opening Case

What evidence of the eight managerial functions can you detect in the Andrea Jung/Avon case?

**Staffing.**   Organizations are only as good as the people in them. Staffing consists of recruiting, training, and developing people who can contribute to the organized effort.

**Communicating.**   Today's managers are responsible for communicating to their employees the technical knowledge, instructions, rules, and information required to get the job done. Recognizing that communication is a two-way process, managers should be responsive to feedback and upward communications.

**Motivating.**   An important aspect of management today is motivating individuals to pursue collective objectives by satisfying needs and meeting expectations with meaningful work and valued rewards. Flexible work schedules can be motivational for today's busy employees.

**Leading.**   Managers become inspiring leaders by serving as role models and adapting their management style to the demands of the situation. The idea of visionary leadership is popular today.

**Controlling.**   When managers compare desired results with actual results and take the necessary corrective action, they are keeping things on track through the control function. Deviations from past plans should be considered when formulating new plans.

## Managerial Roles

During the 1970s, a researcher named Henry Mintzberg criticized the traditional functional approach as unrealistic. From his firsthand observation of top-level managers and similar studies conducted by others, he concluded that functions "tell us little about what managers actually do. At best they indicate some vague objectives managers have when they work."[40]

Those who agree with Mintzberg believe that the functional approach portrays the management process as far more systematic and rational and less complex than it really is. Even the most casual observation reveals that managers do not plan on Monday, organize on Tuesday, coordinate on Wednesday, and so on, as the functional approach might lead one to believe. Moreover, according to the Mintzberg view, the average manager is not the reflective planner and precise "orchestra leader" that the functional approach suggests. Mintzberg characterizes the typical manager as follows: "The manager is overburdened with obligations; yet he cannot easily delegate his tasks. As a result, he is driven to overwork and is forced to do many tasks superficially. Brevity, fragmentation, and verbal communication characterize his work."[41]

In addition, according to Mintzberg's research, constant interruptions are the order of the day. A more recent study supported Mintzberg's view and provided a somewhat surprising insight into the reality of nonstop interruptions. Stephanie Winston interviewed 48 top U.S. executives, including the late Katharine Graham, former chief executive of *The Washington Post*, and discovered that constant interruptions are not a threat to successful top executives. Indeed, interruptions are what the work of top managers is all about and actually constitute a valuable resource. Winston concluded, "They use a fluid time style to make abundant connections and draw in streams of information. . . . The torrent of questions, comments, updates, requests, and expectations is a rich resource to be mined."[42]

Mintzberg and his followers have suggested that a more fruitful way of studying what managers do is to focus on the key roles they play. Using a method called "structured observation," which entailed recording the activities and correspondence of five top-level executives, Mintzberg isolated ten roles he believes are common to all managers.[43] These roles (see Figure 1.4) have been grouped into three major categories: interpersonal, informational, and decisional roles.

*How about this formula? Take one chemist with a degree from Indiana University, add savvy business experience, and mix with the notion to start a business in 1980 during a severe recession. Doesn't sound so great. But that formula put William Gerard Mays on the road to turning his Indianapolis chemical supply business, Mays Chemical Co., into a $172 million-a-year global winner. His employees admire his ability to mix technical know-how with good business sense and excellent people-management skills.*

## Figure 1.4

Mintzberg's Managerial Roles

| Category | Role | Nature of role |
|---|---|---|
| **Interpersonal roles** | 1. Figurehead | As a symbol of legal authority, performing certain ceremonial duties *(e.g., signing documents and receiving visitors)* |
| | 2. Leader | Motivating subordinates to get the job done properly |
| | 3. Liaison | Serving as a link in a horizontal *(as well as vertical)* chain of communication |
| **Informational roles** | 4. Nerve center | Serving as a focal point for non-routine information; receiving all types of information |
| | 5. Disseminator | Transmitting selected information to subordinates |
| | 6. Spokesperson | Transmitting selected information to outsiders |
| **Decisional roles** | 7. Entrepreneur | Designing and initiating changes within the organization |
| | 8. Disturbance handler | Taking corrective action in nonroutine situations |
| | 9. Resource allocator | Deciding exactly who should get what resources |
| | 10. Negotiator | Participating in negotiating sessions with other parties *(e.g., vendors and unions)* to make sure the organization's interests are adequately represented |

*Source:* Adapted from Henry Mintzberg, "Managerial Work: Analysis from Observation," *Management Science*, 18 (October 1971): B97–B110.

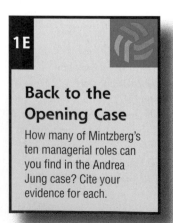

**1E**

## Back to the Opening Case

How many of Mintzberg's ten managerial roles can you find in the Andrea Jung case? Cite your evidence for each.

**Interpersonal Roles.**    Because of their formal authority and superior status, managers engage in a good deal of interpersonal contact with people who report to them. They also interact with other managers. The three interpersonal roles managers play are those of figurehead, leader, and liaison.

**Informational Roles.**    Every manager is a clearinghouse for information relating to the task at hand. Informational roles are important because information is the lifeblood of organizations. Typical roles include acting as nerve center, disseminator, and spokesperson.

**Decisional Roles.**    In their decisional roles, managers balance competing interests and make choices. Through decisional roles, strategies are formulated and put into action. Four decisional roles are those of entrepreneur, disturbance handler, resource allocator, and negotiator.

## Merging Functions and Roles

Both the functional approach and the role approach to explaining management are valuable to the student of management. Managerial functions are a useful categorization of a manager's tasks. It is important for future managers to realize that planning and staffing, for example, require different techniques and perspectives. The role approach is valuable because it injects needed realism, emphasizing that the practice of management is less rational and systematic than the functional approach implies. This text merges the functional and role approaches by explaining how the important roles are played within each functional category.

## Some Managerial Facts of Life (with No Sugar Coating)

Managing is a tough and demanding job today. The hours are long and, at first anyway, the pay may not be generous. Worse yet, managers are visible authority figures who get more than their fair share of criticism and ridicule from politicians and Scott Adams's Dilbert cartoons (see Figure 1.5).[44] Nevertheless, managing can be a very rewarding occupation for those who develop their skills and persist, as evidenced by American Management Association (AMA) research findings:

- Forty-six percent of U.S. managers say they feel more overwhelmed at work today than two years ago, and 22 percent more say they're "somewhat" more overwhelmed.
- Half of U.S. managers say they experience stress every day, but an even greater share—63 percent—say they feel enthusiasm for their jobs.[45]

**A Hectic Pace**  Mintzberg is right. The typical manager's day follows a hectic schedule, with lots of brief and mostly verbal interactions. Interruptions and fragmentation are the norm. Extended quiet periods for contemplation simply don't exist. A landmark observational study by the Center for Creative Leadership gives a realistic picture of managerial life (see Table 1.2). An even quicker pace is in store for future managers.[46]

**4** Summarize the ten facts of managerial life.

**Figure 1.5**   Cartoonist Scott Adams, a former cubicle dweller at a phone company, gets lots of laughs at the pointy-haired boss's expense. Readers tell Adams this is their favorite Dilbert cartoon.

*Source:*  Dilbert reprinted by permission of United Feature Syndicate, Inc.

| **Table 1.2**    Ten Facts of Managerial Life (from direct observation and diaries) |
| --- |

1. **Managers work long hours.** The number of hours worked tends to increase as one climbs the managerial ladder.

2. **Managers are busy.** The typical manager's day is made up of hundreds of brief incidents or episodes. Activity rates tend to decrease as rank increases.

3. **A manager's work is fragmented; episodes are brief.** Given managers' high activity level, they have little time to devote to any single activity. Interruptions and discontinuity are the rule.

4. **The manager's job is varied.** Managers engage in a variety of activities (paperwork, phone calls, scheduled and unscheduled meetings, and inspection tours/visits), interact with a variety of people, and deal with a variety of content areas.

5. **Managers are "homebodies."** Managers spend most of their time pursuing activities within their own organizations. As managerial rank increases, managers spend proportionately more time outside their work areas and organizations.

6. **The manager's work is primarily oral.** Managers at all levels spend the majority of their time communicating verbally (by personal contact or telephone).

7. **Managers use a lot of contacts.** Consistent with their high level of verbal communication, managers continually exchange information with superiors, peers, subordinates, and outsiders on an ongoing basis.

8. **Managers are not reflective planners.** The typical manager is too busy to find uninterrupted blocks of time for reflective planning.

9. **Information is the basic ingredient of the manager's work.** Managers spend most of their time obtaining, interpreting, and giving information.

10. **Managers don't know how they spend their time.** Managers consistently overestimate the time they spend on production, reading and writing, phone calls, thinking, and calculating and consistently underestimate the time spent on meetings and informal discussions.

*Source:* Adapted from Morgan W. McCall, Jr., Ann M. Morrison, and Robert L. Hannan, *Studies of Managerial Work: Results and Methods* (Greensboro, North Carolina: Center for Creative Leadership, 1978), Technical Report No. 9, pp. 6–18. Used by permission of the authors.

**Managers Lose Their Right to Do Many Things.**    Mention the word *manager,* and the average person will probably respond with terms like *power, privilege, authority, good pay,* and so on. Although many managers eventually do enjoy some or all of these good things, they pay a significant price for stepping to the front of the administrative parade.[47] According to one management expert, when you accept a supervisory or managerial position you *lose* your right to do any of the following:

- Lose your temper
- Be one of the gang
- Bring your personal problems to work
- Vent your frustrations and express your opinion at work
- Resist change

- Pass the buck on tough assignments
- Get even with your adversaries
- Play favorites
- Put your self-interests first
- Ask others to do what you wouldn't do
- Expect to be immediately recognized and rewarded for doing a good job[48]

We tell you this not to scare you away from what could be a financially and emotionally rewarding career, but rather to present a realistic picture so you can choose intelligently. Management is not for everyone—it is not for the timid, the egomaniacal, or the lazy. Management requires clear-headed individuals who can envision something better and turn it into reality by working with and through others.

**1F   Managing "Up"**

*Young managers often have as much trouble managing "up"—getting their bosses to respect them—as managing "down."*

**Source:** Dimitry Elias Léger, "Help! I'm the New Boss," *Fortune* (May 29, 2000): 282.

**Question:** *Putting yourself in the place of a manager "fresh out of school," how would you handle this problem?*

# Learning to Manage

Students of management are left with one overriding question: "How do I acquire the ability to manage?" This question has stimulated a good deal of debate among those interested in management education. What is the key, theory or practice? Some contend that future managers need a solid background in management theory acquired through formal education. Others argue that managing, like learning to ride a bicycle, can be learned only by actually doing it.[49] We can leapfrog this debate by looking at how managers learn to manage, understanding how students learn about management, and considering how you can blend the two processes to your best advantage.

**5** Explain how managers learn to manage.

## How Do Managers Learn to Manage?

We have an answer to this simple but intriguing question, thanks to the Honeywell study, which was conducted by a team of management development specialists employed by Honeywell.[50] In a survey, they asked 3,600 Honeywell managers: "How did you learn to manage?" Ten percent of the respondents were then interviewed for additional insights. Successful Honeywell managers reportedly acquired 50 percent of their management knowledge from job assignments (see Figure 1.6). The remaining 50 percent of what they knew about management reportedly came from relationships with bosses, mentors, and coworkers (30 percent) and from formal training and education (20 percent).

Fully half of what the Honeywell managers knew about managing came from the so-called school of hard knocks. To that extent, at least, learning to manage is indeed like learning to ride a bike. You get on, you fall off and skin your knee, you get back on a bit smarter, and so on, until you're able to wobble down the road. But in the minds of aspiring managers, this scenario raises the question of what classes are held in the school of hard knocks. A second study, this one of British managers,

### Figure 1.6

The Honeywell Study:
How Managers Learn to
Manage

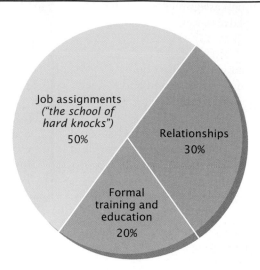

Job assignments
("*the school of
hard knocks*")
50%

Relationships
30%

Formal
training and
education
20%

*Source:* Data from Ron Zemke, "The Honeywell Studies: How Managers Learn to Manage," *Training*, 22 (August 1985): 46–51.

provided an answer. It turns out that the following are considered *hard knocks* by managers:

- Making a big mistake
- Being overstretched by a difficult assignment
- Feeling threatened
- Being stuck in an impasse or dilemma
- Suffering an injustice at work
- Losing out to someone else
- Being personally attacked[51]

These situations are traumatic enough to motivate managers to learn how to avoid repeating the same mistakes.

---

**1G**   **Bouncing Back from a Hard Knock**

Advice from management consultant Andrew Shatté, who teaches managers how to be resilient amid adversity:

*Don't overreact. . . . it's also important to be sure you understand what's really going on. . . . Keep it in perspective. Ask yourself: What's the worst thing that can happen? What's the best outcome that we can hope for? And then keep pressing yourself about the accuracy of those scenarios.*

**Source:** Rekha Balu, "How To Bounce Back from Setbacks." *Fast Company*, no. 45 (April 2001): 155.

---

**Questions:** *What important life lessons have you learned from the school of hard knocks? How will the above advice help you better handle your next major hard knock?*

*The devastating September 11, 2001 terrorist attacks on America produced lots of heroes. But less heralded than the heroics of police and fire fighters were the incredible deeds of surviving employees of affected companies. Consider the situation of then 23-year-old James Colbert. On September 10th, he was a low-paid assistant at Sandler O'Neill & Partners, a small investment banking firm headquartered on the 104th floor of the New York World Trade Center. The next day, 66 of his 171 coworkers were dead, including his boss, and his workplace was in ruins. He immediately took over his former boss's duties and successfully completed a complex $700 million deal. Time is not always a luxury when learning to manage.*

## How Can Future Managers Learn to Manage?

As indicated in Figure 1.7, students can learn to manage by integrating theory and practice and observing role models. Theory can help you systematically analyze, interpret, and internalize the managerial significance of practical experience and observations. Although formal training and education contributed only 20 percent to the Honeywell managers' knowledge, they nonetheless represent a needed conceptual foundation. Returning to our bicycle example, a cross-country trip on a high-tech bike requires more than the mere ability to ride a bike. It requires a sound foundation of knowledge about bicycle maintenance and repair, weather and road conditions, and road safety. So, too, new managers who have a good idea of what lies ahead can go farther and faster with fewer foolish mistakes. The school of hard knocks is inevitable. But you can foresee and avoid at least some of the knocks.[52]

Ideally, an individual acquires theoretical knowledge and practical experience at the same time, perhaps through work-study programs or internships. Usually, though, full-time students get a lot of theory and little practice. This is when simulated and real experience become important. If you are a serious management student, you will put your newly acquired theories into practice wherever and whenever possible (for example, in organized sports; positions of leadership in fraternities, sororities, or clubs; and part-time and summer jobs). What really matters is your personal integration of theory and practice.

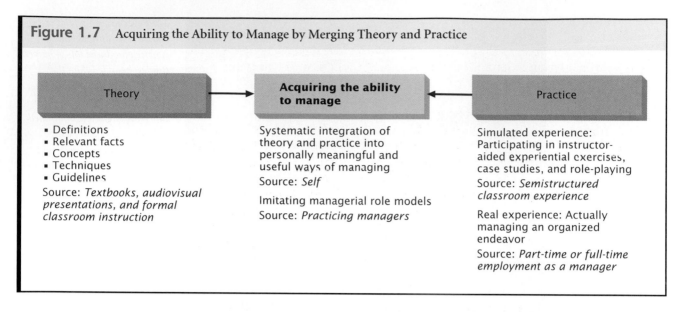

**Figure 1.7**    Acquiring the Ability to Manage by Merging Theory and Practice

| Theory | Acquiring the ability to manage | Practice |
|---|---|---|
| • Definitions<br>• Relevant facts<br>• Concepts<br>• Techniques<br>• Guidelines<br>Source: *Textbooks, audiovisual presentations, and formal classroom instruction* | Systematic integration of theory and practice into personally meaningful and useful ways of managing<br>Source: *Self*<br><br>Imitating managerial role models<br>Source: *Practicing managers* | Simulated experience: Participating in instructor-aided experiential exercises, case studies, and role-playing<br>Source: *Semistructured classroom experience*<br><br>Real experience: Actually managing an organized endeavor<br>Source: *Part-time or full-time employment as a manager* |

# Small-Business Management

Small businesses have been called the "engine" of the U.S. economy. They are often too small to attract much media attention, but collectively they (and their counterparts in other countries) are a *huge* and *vibrant* part of the global economy. As evidence, consider these facts about the 5.6 million small businesses in the United States:

- They represent 99 percent of the nation's employers.[53]
- Each year they account for more than one-quarter of the nation's $1.4 trillion in business capital investment.[54]

Interestingly, about 60 percent of them are "microbusinesses" with fewer than five employees, typically operating out of the owner's home.[55] Free-enterprise capitalism is a rough-and-tumble arena where anyone can play, but only the very best survive. The only guaranteed result for those starting their own business is that they will be tested to their limit.

Few would dispute the facts and claims cited above, but agreement on the definition of a small business is not so easily reached. Some of the many yardsticks used to distinguish small from large businesses include the number of employees, level of annual sales, amount of owner's equity, and total assets. For our present purposes, a **small business** is defined as an independently owned and managed profit-seeking enterprise employing fewer than 100 people. (If the small business is incorporated, the owner/manager owns a significant proportion of the firm's stock.)

The health of every nation's economy depends on how well its small businesses are managed. To get a better grasp of the realm of small-business management, we will clear up two common misconceptions, explore small-business career options, and discuss entrepreneurship.

**small business**

*an independently owned and managed profit-seeking enterprise with fewer than 100 employees*

# Exploding Myths About Small Business

Mistaken notions can become accepted facts if they are repeated often enough. Such is the case with failure rates and job creation for small businesses. Fortunately, recent research sets the record straight.

**The 80-Percent-Failure-Rate Myth.**   An often-repeated statistic says that four out of five small businesses will fail within five years.[56] This 80 percent casualty rate is a frightening prospect for anyone thinking about starting a business. But a study by Bruce A. Kirchhoff of the New Jersey Institute of Technology found the failure rate for small businesses to be *only 18 percent during their first eight years*.[57] Why the huge disparity? It turns out that studies by the U.S. government and others defined business failures much too broadly. Any closing of a business, whether because someone died, sold the business, or retired, was recorded as a business failure. In fact, only 18 percent of the 814,000 small businesses tracked by Kirchhoff for eight years went out of business with unpaid bills. This should be a comfort to would-be entrepreneurs.

**The Low-Wage-Jobs Myth.**   When it came to creating jobs during the 1980s and 1990s, America's big businesses were put to shame by their small and mid-size counterparts. Eighty percent of the new job growth was generated by the smaller

**6**  Challenge two myths about small businesses and describe entrepreneurs.

*Jen-Hsun Huang is a textbook model for entrepreneurs. Born in Taiwan and sent to live with an uncle in the United States when he was nine, he ended up in a Kentucky boarding school full of delinquent kids. Characterized by his friends as intensely competitive, Jen-Hsun worked hard and went on to earn an advanced degree in electrical engineering from Stanford. His impatience to start his own company boiled over at age 30 when he founded Nvidia, now a leading maker of 3D graphics computer chips based in Santa Clara, California. Computer gamers can thank Nvidia for those really cool graphics.*

companies; massive layoffs were the norm at big companies.[58] Critics, meanwhile, claimed that most of the new jobs in the small-business sector went to low-paid clerks and hamburger flippers. Such was not the case, according to a Cambridge, Massachusetts, study by researcher David Birch.

After analyzing new jobs created in the United States between 1987 and 1992, Birch found that businesses with fewer than 100 employees had indeed created most new jobs. Surprisingly, however, only 4 percent of those small firms produced 70 percent of that job growth.[59] Birch calls these rapidly growing small companies "gazelles," as opposed to the "mice" businesses that tend to remain very small. For the period studied, the gazelles added more high-paying jobs than big companies eliminated. Gazelles are not mom-and-pop operations. They tend to be computer software, telecommunications, and specialized engineering or manufacturing firms.[60] So, while small businesses do in fact pay on average less than big companies do, they are not low-wage havens.[61]

Again, as in the case of failure rates, the truth about the prospects of starting or working for a small company is different—and brighter—than traditional fallacies suggest.

## Career Opportunities in Small Business

Among the five small-business career options listed in Table 1.3, only franchises require definition. The other four are self-defining.[62] A franchise is a license to sell another company's products and/or to use another company's name in business. Familiar franchise operations include McDonald's, the National Basketball Association, and Holiday Inn.[63] Notice how each of the career options in Table 1.3 has positive and negative aspects. There is no one best option. Success in the small-business sector depends on the right combination of money, talent, hard work, luck, and opportunity.[64] Fortunately, career opportunities in small business are virtually unlimited.

**Table 1.3**    Career Opportunities in Small Business

| Small-business career options | Capital requirements | Likelihood of steady paycheck | Degree of personal control | Ultimate financial return |
|---|---|---|---|---|
| 1. Become an independent contractor/consultant | Low to moderate | None to low | Very high | Negative to high |
| 2. Take a job with a small business | None | Moderate to high | Low to moderate | Low to moderate |
| 3. Join or buy a small business owned by your family | Low to high | Low to high | Low to high | Moderate to high |
| 4. Purchase a franchise | Moderate to high | None to moderate | Moderate to high | Negative to high |
| 5. Start your own small business | Moderate to high | None to moderate | High to very high | Negative to very high |

## 1H   Got a Good Business Idea? You've Got 45 Seconds

According to new-venture expert Elton B. Sherwin Jr., entrepreneurs who are trying to raise venture capital should be able to answer these "Seven Sacred Questions" in 45 seconds:

1. *What is your product?*

2. *Who is the customer?*

3. *Who will sell it?*

4. *How many people will buy it?*

5. *How much will it cost to design and build?*

6. *What is the sales price?*

7. *When will you break even?*

**Source:** Marc Ballon, "Hot Tips," *Inc.*, 21 (April 1999):104.

**Question:** *Can you pass this 45-second test with your new business idea? Give details.*

## Entrepreneurship

According to experts on the subject, "**entrepreneurship** is the process by which individuals—either on their own or inside organizations—pursue opportunities without regard to the resources they currently control."[65] In effect, entrepreneurs look beyond current resource constraints when they envision new possibilities. Entrepreneurs are preoccupied with "how to," rather than "why not." Entrepreneurs, as we discuss next, are risk takers—and all they want is a chance.

**entrepreneurship**   *process of pursuing opportunities without regard to resources currently under one's control*

## 1I   Do You Have the X Factor?

Norm Brodsky, a successful entrepreneur who founded six businesses, describes what he calls the X Factor:

> *Call it passion, tenacity, stick-to-itiveness, true grit, or just plain stubbornness. Whatever it is and wherever it comes from, it's the most important quality an entrepreneur can have. Ultimately, it determines whether we succeed or fail.*

**Source:** Norm Brodsky, "The X Factor," Inc., 23 (September 2001): 84.

**Questions:** *How do you rate in terms of the X Factor? Do you dream of working for yourself some day? (If so, take the quiz in the Hands-On Exercise at the end of this chapter.) Is the X Factor also good for those willing to work for someone else?*

**A Trait Profile for Entrepreneurs.**    Exactly how do entrepreneurs differ from general managers or administrators? According to the trait profiles in Table 1.4, entrepreneurs tend to be high achievers who focus more on future possibilities, external factors, and technical details. Also, compared with general administrators, entrepreneurs are more comfortable with ambiguity and risk taking. It is important to note that entrepreneurs are not necessarily better or worse than other managers—they are just different.[66]

**Entrepreneurship Has Its Limits.**    Many successful entrepreneurs have tripped over a common stumbling block. Their organizations outgrow the entrepreneur's ability to manage them. In fact, according to "a poll by PriceWaterhouseCoopers, about 40% of CEOs at the fastest-growing companies said that their own ability to manage or reorganize their business could be an impediment to growth."[67] Some refer to this problem as "founder's disease." Moreover, entrepreneurs generally feel stifled by cumbersome and slow-paced bureaucracies. One management consultant praised Microsoft's Bill Gates for knowing his limits in this regard:

> *In January [2000], Gates went from being CEO of the multibillion-dollar business he cofounded to naming himself "chief software architect" and handing over executive responsibility for his company to Steve Ballmer. . . . few people recognized it for what I think it was: a courageous leap into a self-esteem-threatening black hole.*[68]

Entrepreneurs who launch successful and growing companies face a tough dilemma: either grow with the company[69] or have the courage to step aside and turn the reins over to professional managers who possess the administrative traits needed, such as those listed in Table 1.4.

| **Table 1.4**  Contrasting Trait Profiles for Entrepreneurs and Administrators | |
|---|---|
| **Entrepreneurs tend to** | **Administrators tend to** |
| Focus on envisioned futures | Focus on the established present |
| Emphasize external/market dimensions | Emphasize internal/cost dimensions |
| Display a medium-to-high tolerance for ambiguity | Display a low-to-medium tolerance for ambiguity |
| Exhibit moderate-to-high risk-taking behavior | Exhibit low-to-moderate risk-taking behavior |
| Obtain motivation from a need to achieve | Obtain motivation from a need to lead others (i.e., social power) |
| Possess technical knowledge and experience in the innovative area | Possess managerial knowledge and experience |

*Source:* Philip D. Olson, "Choices for Innovation-Minded Corporations," *The Journal of Business Strategy,* 11 (January–February 1990): Exhibit 1, p. 44. Reprinted from *Journal of Business Strategy* (New York: Warren, Gorham & Lamont). © 1990 Warren, Gorham & Lamont Inc. Used with permission.

# Summary

**1.** Formally defined, *management* is the process of working with and through others to achieve organizational objectives in a changing environment. Central to this process is the effective and efficient use of limited resources. An inability to work with people, not a lack of technical skills, is the main reason some managers fail to reach their full potential. A manager is *effective* if he or she reaches a stated objective and *efficient* if limited resources are not wasted in the process. Five overarching sources of change affecting the way management is practiced today are globalization, the evolution of product quality, environmentalism, an ethical reawakening, and e-business on the Internet.

**2.** Two ways to answer the question, "What do managers do?" are the functional approach and role approach. *Managerial functions* relate to the desired outcomes of managerial action, whereas *managerial roles* categorize managers' actual behavior. This text is organized around eight managerial functions: planning, decision making, organizing, staffing, communicating, motivating, leading, and controlling. Having criticized the functional approach for making management appear to be more orderly than it really is, Henry Mintzberg concluded from his observation of managers that management is best explained in terms of roles. Three managerial role categories, according to Mintzberg, are interpersonal, informational, and decisional.

**3.** The ten facts of managerial life, derived from direct observation, characterize managers as hardworking and busy people who engage in many and varied, primarily oral, interactions with others. Interestingly, managers do not have an accurate self-perception of how they spend their time.

**4.** Honeywell researchers found that managers learned 50 percent of what they know about managing from job assignments (or the school of hard knocks). The remaining 50 percent of their management knowledge came from relationships (30 percent) and formal training and education (20 percent). A good foundation in management theory can give management students a running start and help them avoid foolish mistakes.

**5.** *Small businesses* (independently owned and managed profit-seeking companies with fewer than 100 employees) are central to a healthy economy. Contrary to conventional wisdom, 80 percent of new businesses do not fail within five years. In fact, one large study found only an 18 percent failure rate during the first eight years. The belief that small businesses create only low-wage jobs also has been shown to be a myth. Five career opportunities in the small business sector include (1) becoming an independent contractor/consultant; (2) going to work for a small business; (3) joining or buying your family's business; (4) buying a franchise; and (5) starting your own business. Compared with general administrators, entrepreneurs tend to be high achievers who are more future-oriented, externally focused, ready to take risks, and comfortable with ambiguity.

Management (p. 5)

Effectiveness (p. 8)

Efficiency (p. 8)

Internet (p. 14)

E-business (p. 14)

Managerial functions (p. 15)

Managerial roles (p. 15)

Small business (p. 24)

Entrepreneurship (p. 27)

## Terms to Understand

# Skills & Tools

## Career Tips for Today's and Tomorrow's Managers

### How to Find the *Right* Job

1. **Assess yourself.** "Job seekers need to emphasize the things they do best," says Diane Wexler of Career Transition Management in Palo Alto, California. Wexler takes clients through a process of examining goals, interests, skills, and resources. Questions include: What are the 20 things you love to do, both alone and with others? What are the roles you fill, and which aspects would you like to incorporate into a career?

2. **Draft a mission statement.** Just as a company writes and adheres to a mission statement, create one for yourself. Thinking about your mission and putting it on paper will help define your job search.

3. **Brainstorm.** Ask others about what your ideal job would be, and how you should go about landing that position. Nancy Nagel invited eight people with a variety of interests and careers to dinner. "I got these great ideas, ranging from being a talk show host to leading adventure travel," she says. "I ended up tossing most of them out, but the session reminded me that there was a great big world out there."

4. **Network.** Conduct informational interviews. Yes, call those friends-of-friends and ask them for a few minutes of their time. Be prepared with some thoughtful questions.

5. **Research companies.** Job seekers often accept positions without adequately researching their employers, says Valerie Frankel, co-author of the *I Hate My Job Handbook*. "Inevitably, after a year or two, the job becomes intolerable," she says. Before talking to anyone at a company, research its history, values, and priorities.

6. **Be aware of your abilities and the realities of work.** "We have this entitlement problem, that we expect to be completely satisfied with our jobs," says Frankel. "I help people be humble when it comes to their job search," adds Elissa Sheridan of BSR. "You can't walk in with a BA or even an MBA and expect someone to be excited by your background without practical experience."

*Source:* Excerpted from Mary Scott, "Finding the Perfect Job," *Business Ethics*, 10 (March–April 1996): 16. Reprinted with permission from *Business Ethics Magazine*, 52 South 10th Street, #110, Minneapolis, Minn. 55403 (612-962-4700).

### *Secrets to Success* Once You've Found the Right Job

*Investor's Business Daily* has spent years analyzing leaders and successful people in all walks of life. Most have 10 traits that, when combined, can turn dreams into reality.

1. How you think is everything. Always be positive. Think success, not failure. Beware of a negative environment.

2.  Decide upon your true dreams and goals. Write down your specific goals and develop a plan to reach them.

3.  Take action. Goals are nothing without action. Don't be afraid to get started now. Just do it.

4.  Never stop learning. Go back to school or read books. Get training and acquire skills.

5.  Be persistent and work hard. Success is a marathon, not a sprint. Never give up.

6.  Learn to analyze details. Get all the facts, all the input. Learn from your mistakes.

7.  Focus your time and money. Don't let other people or things distract you.

8.  Don't be afraid to innovate; be different. Following the herd is a sure way to mediocrity.

9.  Deal and communicate with people effectively. No person is an island. Learn to understand and motivate others.

10. Be honest and dependable; take responsibility. Otherwise, Numbers 1–9 won't matter.

*Source:* "IBD's 10 Secrets To Success," *Investor's Business Daily* (June 8, 2000): A4. Reprinted by permission.

## Hands-On Exercise

### Do You Have the Right Stuff to Be an Entrepreneur?

Entrepreneurship isn't just about a good business idea. It's a matter of temperament. Some have it, some don't. Do you? Test yourself. And be honest: there are no "right" answers.

**Instructions**

**1.** Where do you think you'll be in 10 years' time?

   a.  I don't think that far ahead; my short-term goals are clear, though.

   b.  I have a career path in mind, and I'm going to stick to it.

   c.  I live and work from day to day.

   d.  I know where I want to be and have ideas on how to get there, but if a better idea comes along, I'll take it.

**2.** How would you describe your attitude toward competition?

   a.  I relish it. Winning isn't everything, it's the only thing.

   b.  I avoid it. Competition brings out the worst in people.

   c.  I compete hard when I have to, but have been known to bluff my rivals.

   d.  I compete hard, but my eye is always on the payoff.

**3.** Your boss says, "That's the way we do things here." How do you react?

  a. I respect established procedures, but I know when to ignore them.

  b. I begin to think I should be working somewhere else.

  c. I accept it and proceed accordingly. After all, I want to keep my job.

  d. I may try to change his mind, but if I don't succeed quickly, I'll go along.

**4.** Which statement comes closest to describing your personal finances?

  a. My checkbook is always balanced, and I pay my bills when they come in.

  b. I have an interest-bearing bank account, and I wait until the end of the statement period to pay my bills. That way the bank doesn't get the interest.

  c. I have multiple credit cards, and every one of them is about maxed out.

  d. I separate my business and personal expenses by using different credit cards.

**5.** What gives you the greatest personal satisfaction at work?

  a. Having an idea and being allowed to run with it.

  b. Receiving praise for a job well done.

  c. Coming out ahead of an office rival.

  d. Knowing my office status is secure.

**6.** How do you handle criticism at work?

  a. It throws me off track and makes my next task more difficult.

  b. Other perspectives are often helpful, so I listen carefully and adjust if the criticism makes sense to me.

  c. While maintaining my dignity, I try to shift at least some of the blame to others.

  d. I don't like it, but what can I do? I absorb the criticism and move on.

**7.** What's best about your current job?

  a. My salary and perks. I do OK compared with people like me.

  b. The fine reputation of my company.

  c. I enjoy a certain amount of freedom to start my own projects.

  d. I get regular promotions, and there's a clear career path to the top.

**8.** Which statement best describes your attitude toward your projects at work?

  a. I like to start projects, but I tend to lose interest and delegate things to other people.

  b. I find myself moving on to new projects before I finish the current one.

  c. I always finish what I start. Personally.

  d. I've been known to put a project on hold if I run into difficulties.

**9.** How much time do you typically invest in your projects at work?

  a. I take pride in being on schedule, so I put in however many hours it takes. Then I take a breather.

   b.  I work hard, but sometimes I'll take a day or two off in midproject.

   c.  I'm pretty much a 9-to-5er.

   d.  My work is my life.

**10.** If you had what you thought was a good idea for a start-up, how would you finance it?

   a.  A loan. That's why banks exist.

   b.  To hold down my exposure, I'd hit up friends and family.

   c.  I'd take out a second mortgage on my house.

   d.  I'd *sell* my house if it came to that.

**Scoring:** Add up your score, using the following key:

| | | | | |
|---|---|---|---|---|
| **1.** | a-2 | b-3 | c-1 | d-4 |
| **2.** | a-3 | b-1 | c-2 | d-4 |
| **3.** | a-3 | b-4 | c-1 | d-2 |
| **4.** | a-1 | b-3 | c-4 | d-2 |
| **5.** | a-4 | b-2 | c-3 | d-1 |
| **6.** | a-1 | b-4 | c-3 | d-2 |
| **7.** | a-2 | b-1 | c-4 | d-3 |
| **8.** | a-2 | b-3 | c-4 | d-1 |
| **9.** | a-4 | b-2 | c-1 | d-3 |
| **10.** | a-1 | b-2 | c-3 | d-4 |

**Results**

**10 TO 19 POINTS:** You are probably a responsible employee, but not a self-starter. You wait to be assigned tasks. Security is important to you. Your tolerance of risk is relatively low. You may derive too much of your sense of self-worth from factors outside yourself, such as the prestige of the company you work for. Stay put.

**20 TO 29 POINTS:** You are capable of initiative, even if it doesn't seem that way. You try to advance your career, but are careful not to offend people along the way. You understand office politics, but are reluctant to make bold moves. If you aren't already in middle management, you may be a good candidate.

**30 TO 35 POINTS:** Lack of ambition is not one of your shortcomings. Neither is a willingness to work hard, and outside normal office hours. You may, however, be somewhat impatient, and reluctant to seek advice from others. These are not good qualities in an entrepreneur. Go for top management instead.

**36 TO 40 POINTS:** You have the makings of an excellent entrepreneur. You have a high tolerance for risk—an essential ingredient. You are passionate about your ideas. Equally important, you are able to balance your own ambition with interest in others' thoughts and regard for their feelings. Go for it.

**For Consideration/ Discussion**

**1.** Well, do you have the right stuff to be an entrepreneur? Is this a valid assessment tool? Why or why not?

**2.** Do you know someone who is a successful entrepreneur? If so, how well does the interpretation for an individual scoring 36 to 40 points characterize that person?

**3.** What would happen if everyone in the business world scored high on this quiz?

**4.** Is it an insult to score low on this quiz? Explain.

*Source:* "The Right Stuff," *Newsweek,* Special Issue, E-Life (2000): 16.

# Internet Exercises

**1. Staying informed about management and managers:** Business managers have their own culture—complete with heroes and villains, legends, myths, literature, and jargon. What better way to begin thinking like a manager than to read what they like to read? *Business Week* magazine offers an excellent collection of online resources at **www.businessweek.com.** A good place to start is by clicking on the tab "Daily Briefing" at the home page. Find a management-related topic or article that interests you and read it. It may be necessary to browse a bit until you find something to your liking. (*Note:* You may want to make a hard copy for later reference and/or discussion in class.)

   *Learning Points:* 1. What linkages did you find between the article you selected and the material in Chapter 1?  2. What useful ideas did you learn about good management and/or mismanagement?  3. What interesting or useful things did you learn about specific managers, companies, industries, or current events?  4. Are you now more (or less) interested in being a manager?

**2. Want to start and run your own business?** When surveyed, nearly two-thirds of Americans say they either own their own business or have dreamed of being their own boss. If you are in that category, here is a must-visit on the Internet. Go to the home page of **www.morebusiness.com**. If your business is already up and running, explore the entire site for useful information and updates. If you are thinking of starting your own business, click on the main menu item "Start Up" and then select the link "Small Business Primer." Work your way through relevant parts of the primer.

   If you are hungry for more information about starting your own business, get down to details with **www.inc.com** (search the "Getting Started" list). This site is run by small-business–oriented *Inc.* magazine. You'll find lots of helpful advice and practical tips.

   *Learning Points:* 1. Does starting your own business entail more than you expected? Explain.  2. Are you more or less inclined to start your own business after this Web exercise? Explain.

**3. Good source for quick management readings and practical tips:** Call up the home page of the Briefings Publishing Group (**www.briefings.com**) and click on the navigation tab "Advice for Managers." Scan the short articles from the most recent issue of *Manager's Edge* and check out archive topics such as "Leadership," "Employee Motivation," and "Teamwork."

*Learning Points:* 1. What was the most useful piece of management information you acquired? 2. How does what you read relate to topics in Chapter 1 of this text? Be specific.

**4. Check it out:** The U.S. Small Business Administration provides a gold mine of free information for small business owners and future entrepreneurs (**www.sba.gov**).

For updates to these exercises, visit our Web site (**http://business.college.hmco.com/ students**).

# Closing Case

## Greg Gianforte: The Bootstrap Entrepreneur

**"B**ootstrap it."

That's how Gianforte launched his first company, software maker Brightwork Development Inc., in 1986. Eight years later he and his partners sold the business to McAfee Associates for more than $10 million—a move that enabled Gianforte to retire to Bozeman, Mont., at age 33. After realizing that he couldn't spend the rest of his life fly-fishing, Gianforte started his second major venture, RightNow Technologies Inc. In almost five years, RightNow has grown from a spare bedroom in Gianforte's home to 230 employees and $30 million in sales. So it's understandable that he might think that he's onto something good here.

And it's also understandable that a whole new generation of entrepreneurs are suddenly hot on bootstrapping, too. There are only two ways to start a business, after all: with capital or without. And in these uncertain times, capital is scarce. But most would-be bootstrappers don't quite get it. They think the process means building

desks out of doors and sawhorses. When Gianforte talks about bootstrapping—which he loves to do—he doesn't mean pinching pennies. Sure, he can trade tightwad stories with any bootstrapper. When RightNow was getting started, for instance, Gianforte couldn't afford to spend thousands of dollars on a phone system. So he got a separate line and an 800 number for each member of his tiny sales force. Employees couldn't transfer calls to one another, but each line cost just $30 a month.

To Gianforte, though, that kind of improvisation isn't really bootstrapping. Not the heart of it, anyway. Bootstrapping is both bigger and simpler than saving a dime whenever you can. If you boiled down his philosophy of bootstrapping, it would run something like this: lack of money, employees, equipment—even lack of product—is actually a huge advantage, because it forces the bootstrapper to concentrate on selling to bring cash into the business. There's an expression that Gianforte likes to quote: "In war you're either making bullets or shooting bullets." In other words, for the bootstrapper, business is all about just two things: making product and selling product. It's not hard to see which one is closer to Gianforte's heart. "Nothing Happens Until Someone Sells Something" reads the sign in his otherwise spartan office.

*Source:* Excerpted from Emily Barker, "Start with . . . Nothing," *Inc.*, February 2002; 66–73. *Inc:* The Magazine for Growing Companies. Copyright 2002 by Bus. Innovator Group Resources/Inc. Reproduced with permission of Bus. Innovator Group Resources/Inc. in the format textbook via the Copyright Clearance Center.

In other words, bootstrapping clears away the clutter and makes you focus single-mindedly on the customer, which is what any smart entrepreneur needs to do anyway. It compels you to be creative, and it's an acid test for figuring out whether you've got a real business or just a plausible-sounding business plan. But bootstrapping is a safety net, too, because if you wind up with no sales, no customers, and no business, well, at least all you've lost is time, not money. "You don't make any fatal mistakes" is how Gianforte puts it.

What sets him apart from most bootstrappers is that he practices bootstrapping by choice. After he sold Brightwork, Gianforte says, he didn't have to work anymore. He moved to Bozeman in 1995 because he'd fallen in love with Montana on a junior-high-school backpacking trip, and because he thought it would be a good place to raise his kids. He settled his family in a rambling, cedar-shingled house just outside Bozeman, on a spread big enough that he gets a couple hundred pounds of buffalo meat every year in exchange for supplying a neighbor's herd with hay from his field. In Montana, Gianforte can camp in the summer, hunt in the fall, and ski in the winter.

But all of that recreation couldn't hold Gianforte's attention. Not that it wasn't fun; it just wasn't enough. Mountain-ringed Bozeman, population 27,500, home of Montana State University, was half college town, half cow town, a place that offered gorgeous scenery, an active outdoor lifestyle, and not much in the way of employment. Gianforte decided that his personal mission was to create 2,000 high-paying high-tech jobs in town. He had the talent for starting companies, he figured, so why not put it to use? First, he launched an incubator and started mentoring local entrepreneurs. He then started a venture of his own, an E-mail stock-quote service. But he got impatient. The companies that he was involved with were just too small. He began looking around for a new business to start.

Given his background and his software-industry connections, Gianforte probably could have raised angel money or venture capital. But the incubator experience had crystalized some ideas about company building that he had been turning over in his head ever since Brightwork. Hoping to spread the word, he created a PowerPoint presentation on bootstrapping and talked his ideas up to a couple of local business groups. "And then I used those lessons to start RightNow," he says.

## Sales Before Product

Admittedly, when Gianforte talks about how he started RightNow, some of what he says sounds like nothing more than good entrepreneurship, period. For example, look at how he figured out what kind of business to start. Gianforte knew that he wanted to launch an Internet-software company—not a hard call, given the business climate and his experience. In the early months of 1997 he surfed the Web, searching for a niche to focus on. No one seemed to be making a product that would help companies respond to E-mail from their customers, he noticed.

So far he was just identifying an opportunity, like any other smart entrepreneur. But here's where it gets interesting. Gianforte started trying to sell that nonexistent product. Armed with a data sheet outlining what such a product might do, Gianforte sat in a spare bedroom and cold-called customer-support managers at hundreds of companies. After talking them through the sheet, he told them that the product would be released in 90 days and asked whether they would use that type of software on their Web sites. If someone said no, he asked why. Sometimes the potential customer needed a feature that Gianforte hadn't thought of. If he thought that he could deliver it in 90 days, he added it to the data sheet.

Some might say that Gianforte was peddling vaporware—the much-criticized practice of hyping the imminent release of new software that is far from ready. Gianforte disagrees. The key is not to promise anything that can't be delivered within the specified time frame. "You never want to lie to your customers," he says. What he did, he says, is "really sales as a method of market research. It allows you to determine very quickly, without much money, if you have a viable business idea."

The same approach will work for bootstrappers outside the software industry, Gianforte insists. Say a would-be entrepreneur wants to open a retail store, he offers. Don't sink capital into leasing space and ordering inventory. Instead, reach out to customers from day one. Advertise the kinds of products that you plan to offer, hand out flyers, put up a sign. Keep it cheap. If you get orders, that's when you rent the storefront.

## Get Something Out the Door

Although rapid prototyping is common in the software industry, Gianforte took it to extremes, says David Bayless, a former venture capitalist in Bozeman who advised Gianforte during RightNow's start-up phase. "Watching the process and seeing it really work was pretty cool," Bayless says. "It struck me as unusual for someone with his technical background. They usually want to polish it and make it perfect before you get it out in front of the customer. He got it in front of people who could actually give him useful feedback."

After a couple of weeks of calling, Gianforte knew exactly what his potential customers wanted. That's when he got around to building the product. He spent two months writing a basic program that allowed a company to judge which information to publish on its Web site, based on E-mail queries that it received. "I don't even want to call it 1.0—it was the .8 release," says Gianforte. "But it was enough that people said they'd start using it."

But he still hadn't closed any sales. At first he gave the software away to anyone who would use it—a move that might seem counterintuitive, given a bootstrapper's appetite for cash. But Gianforte was still working out of his house with no employees and no overhead. It was important to get the product out into customers' hands and hear their reaction, he says. "This is an iterative process," he says. "[The customer] says, 'Uh, that does what your data sheet said, but we really expected *this*.' Well, that's good input. You could say, 'Well, you signed up for that data sheet. You have to take that.' Wrong answer. You go and put those features in."

Gianforte began charging for RightNow software within three months of its release. He set the price point deliberately low—offering customers a two-year license instead of a perpetual one—to jump-start his sales. "He could have tried to sell it for $50,000, and it would have taken six to nine months to get his first sale," says Cindy Taylor, RightNow's former vice-president of field sales. Indeed, most of the other entrants into the Internet customer-relationship-management market have introduced more-expensive software, says senior analyst Charles Rider of Patricia Seybold Group Inc., in Boston. Priced at $5,000, with discounts of up to 50%, RightNow's software attracted a handful of paying customers by September 1997. That year the company's total revenues were a paltry $20,000. But by early 1998 all new customers were paying customers, and Gianforte was selling about $30,000 worth of product a month. "It wasn't until that point that I really concluded that there was a strong business there," he says.

Before that time, Gianforte had invested less than $5,000 of his own money in RightNow, which paid for a computer, a Web site, a phone line, and other office necessities. Now, after selling his share in another small software start-up, Gianforte was ready to put $50,000 of the proceeds into hiring his first employees—and, more important, to devote himself fulltime to the business. . . .

Bootstrapping may be the best way to start a company, but is it the best way to continue to build one? Not always, says Gianforte. "There comes a point in a business where you start to understand the business equation," he explains. "You've got a product you know the

customer is willing to pay for. You have a sales strategy that works. And the business is growing. That's all given. But you believe you could grow the business faster if you had more resources." Then it makes sense to look outside for funding.

But, he cautions, "it's a slippery slope. I think a lot of entrepreneurs think they need money to build the business faster when they actually haven't figured out the business equation yet."

By December 1999, Gianforte was confident enough about his business equation to raise $16 million through a private placement as a first step toward going public. The company filed for an initial public offering in 2000 and got as far as launching its road show, although Gianforte pulled back in the fall of 2000 after the IPO market cooled. . . .

In its bootstrapping past, RightNow was housed first in Gianforte's home, then in a windowless room in the back of a real estate agency, and later in a former elementary school. Now it's based in a cluster of low-slung, spanking-new office buildings on a field near the university. Once Gianforte began to hire more experienced managers, he had to start thinking about the company's image. "When you're trying to recruit a senior product manager from Hewlett-Packard, he doesn't want to work in a garage," he says. Gianforte built the cluster in partnership with a local developer and leased space in it to RightNow. No reason for the company to sink a lot of cash into real estate, he says.

Today the software that RightNow sells offers far more features than the stripped-down version that Gianforte first designed, and a typical two-year license goes for $75,000, not $5,000. In addition, the company has a 12-person marketing department and a slew of glossy brochures that are aimed at developing and promoting RightNow's once-neglected brand. . . .

What of his goal of creating jobs? The average position at RightNow pays just over $50,000 a year. Not bad, considering that the median household income in Bozeman is $30,450. Still, of the 2,000 jobs that Gianforte wants to create, he still has a bit more than 1,600 to go. And a good chunk of RightNow's future growth will likely take place outside Bozeman. So the real test of Gianforte's bootstrapping ethos may be whether he can inspire entrepreneurs around him to create companies and jobs.

"Greg understood that it was important that there would be a business like RightNow Technologies, because people need to see it, touch it, before they can believe it can be done," says Bayless. "There was no company like RightNow here. Greg was out to make the statement 'Look, it can be done here.'"

## For Discussion

**1.** How well does Gianforte fit the entrepreneurial profile in Table 1.4? Explain.

**2.** Do you find this story inspiring? Why or why not?

**3.** What are the risks of selling something to customers *before* you have a product in hand? How can those risks be minimized?

**4.** If you have a good idea for a business, but are short of capital, does the bootstrap concept motivate you to get going?

**5.** Which of Mintzberg's managerial roles, in Figure 1.4, are evident in this case? Explain.

## chapter two

# The Evolution of Management Thought

## CHAPTER OBJECTIVES

*When you finish studying this chapter you should be able to*

**1** **Identify** two key assumptions supporting the universal process approach and briefly **describe** Henri Fayol's contribution.

**2** **Discuss** Frederick W. Taylor's approach to improving the practice of industrial management.

**3** **Identify** at least four key quality improvement ideas from W. Edwards Deming and the other quality advocates.

**4** **Describe** the general aim of the human relations movement and **explain** the circumstances in which it arose.

**5** **Explain** the significance of applying open-system thinking to management.

**6** **Explain** the practical significance of adopting a contingency perspective.

**7** **Identify** and **explain** the nature of at least four of Thomas J. Peters and Robert H. Waterman Jr.'s eight attributes of excellence.

# History Matters at This Wisconsin Boat Builder

**P**roduction manager Rich Auth stood at the boatyard gate and watched his 166 colleagues, some tearful, leave behind the work that had sustained many of their families for generations. On that day, in November 1990, Burger Boat's absentee owner had faxed a message to the staff: the yard would close. Twenty minutes later, at the shift's end, the yard was shut down. Burger's owner had stopped paying employees' health-insurance premiums and had run up $13 million in debt. Still, Auth's coworkers "went out like gentlemen," he says. "There was no foul language, no threats. That's just the way people are here." Or maybe they just knew they'd be back.

Manitowoc's boatyards were famous for building first-class schooners and for constructing submarines and other military vessels. Burger Boat, founded in 1863 and family run until 1986, had constructed boats for three wars when, in the early 1960s, the company repositioned itself as a builder of luxury aluminum motor yachts. The yachts quickly became known for quality craftsmanship.

By 1970, though, all the other shipbuilders in Manitowoc had moved or shut down, and Burger had been sold to its second out-of-towner, an ailing shipbuilding company based in Tacoma, Wash., that used Burger as a cash cow. When the yard closed, says Mayor Kevin Crawford, "everyone felt a ripple go through the community."

Luckily for Burger and Manitowoc, the ripple was felt as far away as Chicago, where David Ross, an entrepreneur who had sold his $55-million commercial-photo-labs company in 1989, heard of Burger's plight. Ross had always admired Burgers—coveted them, even. Now there appeared to be an opportunity to buy the company itself.

As Ross gathered information about Burger, what impressed him even more than the boats were the people who made them. Shortly after the yard closed, 18 Burger employees crawled through a hole in the fence to get the tools and materials they needed to finish a boat they'd been working on. Later a customer with an unfinished boat in the yard—*The Lady Iris*—would help Rich Auth and 70 other employees set up a shell corporation to try to revive the company. There was not only boatbuilding to be done but also a retirement plan to rescue, an employee stock ownership plan to develop, and a blatant violation of state plant-closing laws to redress.

Burger's yard had been filled with men whose fathers and grandfathers had practiced the same craftsmanship before them, who had fashioned gracefully curved bows from sheets of aluminum. The instinct to preserve that tradition was overpowering. "When I met Rich, I determined that this company was zero without the people who made it famous," says Ross. For more than a year, Burger's employees had struggled unsuccessfully to save the company.

Ross, along with his partner, Jim Ruffolo, offered the wary craftspeople a second chance. "They weren't ready to put their trust in just anyone," Ross recalls. "I told them I was going to move here and that I could offer them something they didn't have—a hands-on owner who could speak directly to clients, who could bring strong advertising, marketing, and sales skills."

Ross flew Auth to Chicago to speak with employees of Ross's former company and to examine its financial statements. "We didn't want another silver spoon coming into the yard," says Auth. Ross, he discovered, was genuinely respected by his old employees. By 1992, Burger's former workers decided to throw their lot in with Ross. Most, like Burger designer Don Fogltanz, had landed good jobs elsewhere. But, says Fogltanz, "I wanted to finish off my working years at the company where I had spent my life. I wanted to build boats."

In January 1993, after more than a year of negotiations, a dramatic appearance before a U.S. Bankruptcy Court judge, and more than $250,000 in legal fees, Ross and Ruffolo were permitted to buy Burger. They promised to keep the company in Manitowoc for at least 20 years. "We never would have done the deal if David were staying in Chicago," says Auth. But Ross never had any intention of staying there. What he saw at Burger—a company bonded to its community, and workers impassioned by their craft—had drawn him in.

Today Burger has a three-year backlog of orders, steady revenue growth, and four years of profits on the books. Half of the company's 200 employees are people who returned to Burger when the gates reopened in 1993; Ross keeps them and the company focused around their skills and passions. "In May we launched hull number 491, and it's an 85-foot flush-deck motor-yacht cruiser," says Ross. "In 1901 we launched our first motor yacht, and do you know what it was? It was an 80-foot flush-deck motor-yacht cruiser."

The launch of hull number 491—like most of Burger's launches—was a public event. Twelve hundred admirers crowded the yard to watch the maiden voyage. "It's just a beautiful ceremony," says Auth. "This company was started when Lincoln was president, and today we're building boats on the same shoreline. I know a lot of people here who take great pride in that."

*Source:* Donna Fenn, "Rescuing Tradition," Inc., 23 (August 2001): 48–49. *Inc:* The Magazine for Growing Companies. Copyright 2001 by Bus. Innovator Group Resources/Inc. Reproduced with permission of Bus. Innovator Group Resources/Inc. in the format textbook via Copyright Clearance Center.

**D**avid Ross and his business partner wisely took Burger Boat Company's rich history into full consideration when thinking about rescuing it. In a parallel sense, that is what this chapter is all about. Management historians believe that a better knowledge of the past will lead to a more productive future. They contend that students of management who fail to understand the evolution of management thought are destined to repeat past mistakes.[1] Moreover, historians and managers alike believe that one needs to know where management has been if one is to understand where it is going. For example, while participating in a Harvard Business School roundtable discussion on the value of management history, a top-level executive summarized:

*It is always hard to communicate any sort of abstract idea to someone else, let alone get any acceptance of it. But when there is some agreement on the factual or historical background of that idea, the possibilities for general agreement expand enormously.*[2]

Historians draw a distinction between history and historical perspective. According to one management scholar:

*Historical perspective is the study of a subject in light of its earliest phases and subsequent evolution. Historical perspective differs from history in that the object of historical perspective is to sharpen one's vision of the present, not the past.*[3]

This chapter qualifies as a historical perspective because it is part historical fact and part modern-day interpretation. Various approaches in the evolution of management thought are discussed relative to the lessons each can teach today's managers. The term *evolution* is appropriate here because management theory has developed in bits and pieces through the years. Moreover, pioneering contributors to management theory and practice have come from around the globe (see Figure 2.1). A historical perspective puts these pieces together.

# The Practice and Study of Management

The systemic study of management is relatively new. As an area of academic study, management is essentially a product of the twentieth century. Only three universities—Pennsylvania, Chicago, and California—offered business management courses before 1900.[4]

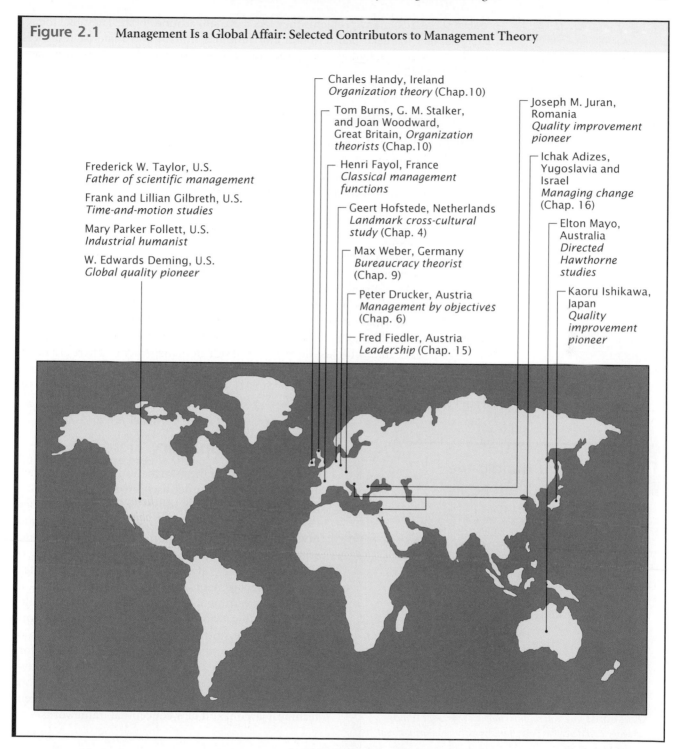

**Figure 2.1    Management Is a Global Affair: Selected Contributors to Management Theory**

Charles Handy, Ireland
*Organization theory* (Chap.10)

Tom Burns, G. M. Stalker,
and Joan Woodward,
Great Britain, *Organization
theorists* (Chap.10)

Henri Fayol, France
*Classical management
functions*

Geert Hofstede, Netherlands
*Landmark cross-cultural
study* (Chap. 4)

Max Weber, Germany
*Bureaucracy theorist*
(Chap. 9)

Peter Drucker, Austria
*Management by objectives*
(Chap. 6)

Fred Fiedler, Austria
*Leadership* (Chap. 15)

Frederick W. Taylor, U.S.
*Father of scientific management*

Frank and Lillian Gilbreth, U.S.
*Time-and-motion studies*

Mary Parker Follett, U.S.
*Industrial humanist*

W. Edwards Deming, U.S.
*Global quality pioneer*

Joseph M. Juran,
Romania
*Quality improvement
pioneer*

Ichak Adizes,
Yugoslavia and
Israel
*Managing change*
(Chap. 16)

Elton Mayo,
Australia
*Directed
Hawthorne
studies*

Kaoru Ishikawa,
Japan
*Quality
improvement
pioneer*

But the actual practice of management has been around for thousands of years. The pyramids of Egypt, for example, stand as tangible evidence of the ancient world's ability to manage. It reportedly took more than 100,000 individuals 20 years to construct the great pyramid of Cheops. This remarkable achievement was the result of systematically managed effort. Although the Egyptians' management techniques were crude by modern standards, many problems they faced are still around today. They, like today's managers, had to make plans, obtain and mobilize human and material resources, coordinate interdependent jobs, keep records, report their progress, and take corrective action as needed.

## Information Overload

Since the building of the pyramids, entire civilizations have come and gone. In one form or another, management was practiced in each. Sadly, during those thousands of years of management experience, one modern element was missing: a systematically recorded body of management knowledge.[5] In early cultures management was something one learned by word of mouth and trial and error—not something one studied in school, read about in textbooks and on the Internet, theorized about, experimented with, or wrote about.

Thanks to modern print and electronic media, the collective genius of thousands of management theorists and practitioners has been compressed into a veritable mountain of textbooks, journals, research monographs, microfilms, movies, audio- and videotapes, and computer files. Never before have present and future managers had so much relevant information at their fingertips, often as close as the nearest Internet-linked computer or library. As an indication of what is available, a 1990 study identified 54 journals dealing with just the behavioral side of management.[6] There are many, many others (see Skills & Tools at the end of this chapter). In fact, so much information on management theory and practice exists today that it is difficult, if not impossible, to keep abreast of all of it.[7]

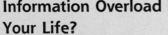

**2A    How Do You Handle the Information Overload in Your Life?**

In a survey, 2,096 employees categorized their work-space habits as follows:

| | |
|---|---|
| Neat freaks | 33% |
| Pilers | 27% |
| Filers | 23% |
| Pack rats | 12% |
| Slobs | 2% |
| Don't know | 3% |

**Source:** Data from Cheryl Comeau-Kirschner, "Neatness Counts for Many Employees," *Management Review*, 88 (April 1999): 7.

**Questions:** *Are you on information overload? Which category best describes your handling of the informational clutter in your life?*

For further information about the interactive annotations in this chapter, visit our Web site (http://business.college.hmco.com/students).

## An Interdisciplinary Field

A principal cause of the information explosion in management theory is its interdisciplinary nature. Scholars from many fields—including psychology, sociology, cultural anthropology, mathematics, philosophy, statistics, political science, economics, logistics, computer science, ergonomics, history, and various fields of engineering—have, at one time or another, been interested in management. In addition, administrators in business, government, religious organizations, health care, and education all have drawn from and contributed to the study of management. Each group of scholars and practitioners has interpreted and reformulated management according to its own perspective. With each new perspective have come new questions and assumptions, new research techniques, different technical jargon, and new conceptual frameworks.[8]

## No Universally Accepted Theory of Management

We can safely state that no single theory of management is universally accepted today.[9] To provide a useful historical perspective that will guide our study of modern management, we shall discuss six different approaches to management: (1) the universal process approach, (2) the operational approach, (3) the behavioral approach, (4) the systems approach, (5) the contingency approach, and (6) the attributes of excellence approach. Understanding these general approaches to the theory and practice of management can help you appreciate how management has evolved, where it is today, and where it appears to be headed.

# The Universal Process Approach

The universal process approach is the oldest and one of the most popular approaches to management thought. It is also known as the universalist or functional approach. According to the **universal process approach,** the administration of all organizations, public or private or large or small, requires the same rational process. The universalist approach is based on two main assumptions. First, although the purpose of organizations may vary (for example, business, government, education, or religion), a core management process remains the same across all organizations. Successful managers, therefore, are interchangeable among organizations of differing purpose. Second, the universal management process can be reduced to a set of separate functions and related principles. Early universal process writers emphasized the specialization of labor (who does what), the chain of command (who reports to whom), and authority (who is ultimately responsible for getting things done).

**universal process approach**
*assumes all organizations require the same rational management process*

## Henri Fayol's Universal Management Process

In 1916, at the age of 75, Henri Fayol published his now classic book *Administration Industrielle et Générale,* though it did not become widely known in Britain and the United States until an English translation became available in 1949.[10] Despite its belated appearance in the English-speaking world and despite its having to compete with enthusiastic scientific management and human relations movements in the United States, Fayol's work has left a permanent mark on twentieth-century management thinking.

Fayol was first an engineer and later a successful administrator in a large French mining and metallurgical concern, which is perhaps why he did not resort to theory in his pioneering management book. Rather, Fayol was a manager who attempted to translate his broad administrative experience into practical guidelines for the successful management of all types of organizations.

As we mentioned in the previous chapter, Fayol believed that the manager's job could be divided into five functions, or areas, of managerial responsibility—planning, organizing, command, coordination, and control—that are essential to managerial success. (Some educators refer to them as the POC[3] functions.) His 14 universal principles of management, as listed in Table 2.1, were intended to show managers how to carry out their functional duties. Fayol's functions and principles have withstood the test of time because of their widespread applicability. In spite of years of reformulation, rewording, expansion, and revision, Fayol's original management functions still can be found in nearly all management texts. In fact, after an extensive review of studies of managerial work, a pair of management scholars concluded:

> *The classical functions still represent the most useful way of conceptualizing the manager's job, especially for management education, and perhaps this is why it is still the most favored*

**1** Identify two key assumptions supporting the universal process approach and briefly describe Henri Fayol's contribution.

| **Table 2.1**   Fayol's 14 Universal Principles of Management |
|---|

1. **Division of work.** Specialization of labor is necessary for organizational success.

2. **Authority.** The right to give orders must accompany responsibility.

3. **Discipline.** Obedience and respect help an organization run smoothly.

4. **Unity of command.** Each employee should receive orders from only one superior.

5. **Unity of direction.** The efforts of everyone in the organization should be coordinated and focused in the same direction.

6. **Subordination of individual interests to the general interest.** Resolving the tug of war between personal and organizational interests in favor of the organization is one of management's greatest difficulties.

7. **Remuneration.** Employees should be paid fairly in accordance with their contribution.

8. **Centralization.** The relationship between centralization and decentralization is a matter of proportion; the optimum balance must be found for each organization.

9. **Scalar chain.** Subordinates should observe the formal chain of command unless expressly authorized by their respective superiors to communicate with each other.

10. **Order.** Both material things and people should be in their proper places.

11. **Equity.** Fairness that results from a combination of kindliness and justice will lead to devoted and loyal service.

12. **Stability and tenure of personnel.** People need time to learn their jobs.

13. **Initiative.** One of the greatest satisfactions is formulating and carrying out a plan.

14. **Esprit de corps.** Harmonious effort among individuals is the key to organizational success.

*Source:*  Adapted from Henri Fayol, *General and Industrial Management*, trans. Constance Storrs (London: Isaac Pitman & Sons, 1949). Copyright 1949 by Lake Publishing Company. Reprinted by permission.

## 2B

### Back to the Opening Case

Which of Fayol's 14 universal principles of management in Table 2.1 are evident in the Burger Boat case? Explain your reasoning for each principle selected.

*description of managerial work in current management textbooks. The classical functions provide clear and discrete methods of classifying the thousands of different activities that managers carry out and the techniques they use in terms of the functions they perform for the achievement of organizational goals.*[11]

## Lessons from the Universal Process Approach

Fayol's main contribution to management thought was to show how the complex management process can be separated into interdependent areas of responsibility, or functions. Fayol's contention that management is a continuous process beginning with planning and ending with controlling also remains popular today. Contemporary adaptations of Fayol's functions offer students of management a useful framework for analyzing the management process. But as we mentioned in Chapter 1, this sort of rigid functional approach has been criticized for creating the impression that the management process is more rational and orderly than it really is. Fayol's functions, therefore, form a skeleton that needs to be fleshed out with concepts, techniques, and situational refinements from more modern approaches. The functional approach is useful because it specifies what managers *should* do, but the other approaches help explain *why* and *how*.

# The Operational Approach

The term **operational approach** is a convenient description of the production-oriented area of management dedicated to improving efficiency, cutting waste, and improving quality. Since the turn of the twentieth century, it has had a number of labels, including scientific management, management science, operations research, production management, and operations management. Underlying this somewhat confusing evolution of terms has been a consistent purpose: to make person-machine systems work as efficiently as possible. Throughout its historical development, the operational approach has been technically and quantitatively oriented.

**operational approach**
*production-oriented field of management dedicated to improving efficiency and cutting waste*

## Frederick W. Taylor's Scientific Management

**2** Discuss Frederick W. Taylor's approach to improving the practice of industrial management.

Born in 1856, the son of a Philadelphia lawyer, Frederick Winslow Taylor was the epitome of the self-made man. Because a temporary problem with his eyes kept him from attending Harvard University, Taylor went to work as a common laborer in a small Philadelphia machine shop. In just four years he picked up the trades of pattern maker and machinist.[12] Later, Taylor went to work at Midvale Steel Works in Philadelphia, where he quickly moved up through the ranks while studying at night for a mechanical engineering degree. As a manager at Midvale, Taylor was appalled at industry's unsystematic practices. He observed little, if any, cooperation between the managers and the laborers. Inefficiency and waste were rampant. Output restriction among groups of workers, which Taylor called "systematic soldiering," was widespread. Ill-equipped and inadequately trained workers were typically left on their own to determine how to do their jobs. Hence, the father of scientific management committed himself to the relentless pursuit of "finding a better way."[13] Taylor sought nothing less than what he termed a "mental revolution" in the practice of industrial management.[14]

**scientific management**
*developing performance standards on the basis of systematic observation and experimentation*

According to an early definition, **scientific management** is "that kind of management which *conducts* a business or affairs by *standards* established by facts or truths gained through *systematic* observation, experiment, or reasoning."[15] The word *experiment* deserves special emphasis because it was Taylor's trademark. While working at Midvale and later at Bethlehem Steel, Taylor started the scientific management movement in industry in four areas: standardization, time and task study, systematic selection and training, and pay incentives.[16]

**Standardization.** By closely studying metal-cutting operations, Taylor collected extensive data on the optimum cutting-tool speeds and the rates at which stock should be fed into the machines for each job. The resulting standards were then posted for quick reference by the machine operators. He also systematically catalogued and stored the expensive cutting tools that usually were carelessly thrown aside when a job was completed. Operators could go to the carefully arranged tool room, check out the right tool for the job at hand, and check it back in when finished. Taylor's approach caused productivity to jump and costs to fall.

*Frederick W. Taylor, 1856–1915*

### Time and Task Study.
According to the traditional rule-of-thumb approach, there was no "science of shoveling." But after thousands of observations and stopwatch recordings, Taylor detected a serious flaw in the way various materials were being shoveled—each laborer brought his own shovel to work. Taylor knew the company was losing, not saving, money when a laborer used the same shovel for both heavy and light materials. A shovel load of iron ore weighed about 30 pounds, according to Taylor's calculations, whereas a shovel load of rice coal weighed only 4 pounds. Systematic experimentation revealed that a shovel load of 21 pounds was optimum (permitted the greatest movement of material in a day). Taylor significantly increased productivity by having workers use specially sized and shaped shovels provided by the company—large shovels for the lighter materials and smaller ones for heavier work.

### Systematic Selection and Training.
Although primitive by modern standards, Taylor's experiments with pig iron handling clearly reveal the intent of this phase of scientific management. The task was to lift a 92-pound block of iron (in the steel trade, a "pig"), carry it up an incline (a distance of about 36 feet), and drop it into an open railroad car. Taylor observed that on the average, a pig iron handler moved about 12½ tons in a ten-hour day of constant effort. After careful study, Taylor found that if he selected the strongest men and instructed them in the proper techniques of lifting and carrying the pigs of iron, he could get each man to load 47 tons in a ten-hour day. Surprisingly, this nearly fourfold increase in output was achieved by having the pig iron handlers spend only 43 percent of their time actually hauling iron. The other 57 percent was spent either walking back empty-handed or sitting down. Taylor reported that the laborers liked the new arrangement because they were less fatigued and took home 60 percent more pay.

Management historians recently have disputed Taylor's pig iron findings, suggesting his conclusions were unfounded and/or exaggerated.[17] As mentioned earlier, our present historical perspective is an evolving blend of fact and interpretation.

## 2C  Piece-Rate Puzzle

Suppose you were a college student about to take a part-time job in the school library. The job involves taking books and bound periodicals from the sorting room and returning them on a hand cart to their proper shelves throughout the library. Library officials have observed that an average of 30 items can be reshelved during one hour of steady effort. You have the option of being paid $9 an hour or 30 cents per item reshelved. The quality of your work will be randomly checked, and 30 cents will be deducted from your pay for each item found to be improperly shelved. How do you want to be paid? Why? Which pay plan is probably better for the library? Why?

### Pay Incentives.
According to Taylor, "What the workmen want from their employers beyond anything else is high wages."[18] This "economic man" assumption led Taylor to believe that piece rates were important to improved productivity. Under traditional piece-rate plans, an individual received a fixed amount of money for each unit of output. Thus, the greater the output, the greater the pay. In his determination to find a better way, Taylor attempted to improve the traditional piece-rate scheme with his differential piece-rate plan.

Figure 2.2 illustrates the added incentive effect of Taylor's differential plan. (The amounts are typical rates of pay in Taylor's time.) Under the traditional plan, a worker would receive a fixed amount (for example, 5 cents) for each unit produced. Seventy-five cents would be received for producing 15 units and $1.00 for 20 units. In contrast, Taylor's plan required that a time study be carried out to determine the company's idea of a fair day's work. Two piece rates were then put into effect. A low rate would be paid if the worker finished the day below the company's standard, and a high rate when the day's output met or exceeded the standard. As the lines in Figure 2.2 indicate, a hard worker who produced 25 units would earn $1.25 under the traditional plan and $1.50 under Taylor's plan.

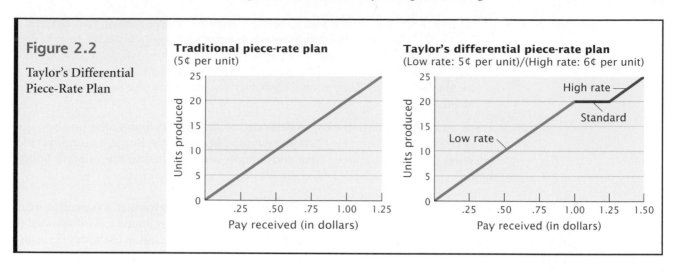

**Figure 2.2**

Taylor's Differential
Piece-Rate Plan

**Traditional piece-rate plan**
(5¢ per unit)

Units produced

Pay received (in dollars)

**Taylor's differential piece-rate plan**
(Low rate: 5¢ per unit)/(High rate: 6¢ per unit)

Units produced

High rate

Standard

Low rate

Pay received (in dollars)

## Taylor's Followers

Among the many who followed in Taylor's footsteps, Frank and Lillian Gilbreth and
Henry L. Gantt stand out.

**Frank and Lillian Gilbreth.**   Inspired by Taylor's time studies and motivated by a
desire to expand human potential, the Gilbreths turned motion study into an exact
science. In so doing, they pioneered the use of motion pictures for studying and
streamlining work motions. They paved the way for modern work simplification by
cataloguing 17 different hand motions, such as "grasp" and "hold." These they called
"therbligs" (actually the name *Gilbreth* spelled backward with the *t* and *h* reversed).
Their success stories include the following:

*Lillian M. Gilbreth, 1878–1972,
at right, and Frank B. Gilbreth,
1868–1924, at left, with 11 of
their dozen children*

*In laying brick, the motions used in laying a single brick were reduced from eighteen to five—with an increase in output, from one hundred and twenty bricks an hour to three hundred and fifty an hour, and with a reduction in the resulting fatigue. In folding cotton cloth, twenty to thirty motions were reduced to ten or twelve, with the result that instead of one hundred and fifty dozen pieces of cloth, four hundred dozen were folded, with no added fatigue.*[19]

Frank and Lillian Gilbreth were so dedicated to the idea of finding the one best way to do every job that 2 of their 12 children wrote *Cheaper by the Dozen,* a humorous recollection of scientific management and motion study applied to the Gilbreth household.[20]

**Henry L. Gantt.**    Gantt, a schoolteacher by training, contributed to scientific management by refining production control and cost control techniques. As illustrated in Chapter 6, variations of Gantt's work-scheduling charts are still in use today.[21] He also humanized Taylor's differential piece-rate system by combining a guaranteed day rate (minimum wage) with an above-standard bonus. Gantt was ahead of his time in emphasizing the importance of the human factor and in urging management to concentrate on service rather than profits.[22]

*Henry L. Gantt, 1861–1919*

**3**  Identify at least four key quality improvement ideas from W. Edwards Deming and the other quality advocates.

## The Quality Advocates

Today's managers readily attach strategic importance to quality improvement. The road to this enlightened view, particularly for U.S. managers, was a long and winding one. It started in factories and eventually made its way through service businesses, nonprofit organizations, and government agencies. An international cast of quality advocates took much of the twentieth century to pave the road to quality. Not until 1980, when NBC ran a television documentary titled *If Japan Can . . . Why Can't We?* did Americans begin to realize fully that *quality* was a key to Japan's growing dominance in world markets. Advice from the following quality advocates finally began to sink in during the 1980s.[23]

**Walter A. Shewhart.**    A statistician for Bell Laboratories, Shewhart introduced the concept of statistical quality control in his 1931 landmark text, *Economic Control of Quality of Manufactured Product.*

**Kaoru Ishikawa.**    The University of Tokyo professor advocated quality before World War II and founded the Union of Japanese Scientists and Engineers (JUSE), which became the driving force behind Japan's quality revolution. Ishikawa proposed a preventive approach to quality. His expanded idea of the customer included both *internal and external customers.* Ishikawa's fishbone diagrams, discussed in Chapter 8, remain a popular problem-solving tool to this day.

**W. Edwards Deming.**    This Walter Shewhart understudy accepted an invitation from JUSE in 1950 to lecture on his principles of statistical quality control. His ideas, detailed later in Chapter 17, went far beyond what his Japanese hosts expected from a man with a mathematics Ph.D. from Yale. Japanese manufacturers warmly embraced Deming and his unconventional ideas about encouraging employee participation and striving for continuous improvement. His 1986 book *Out of the Crisis* is "a guide to the 'transformation of the style of American management,' which became a bible for Deming disciples."[24]

*W. Edwards Deming, 1900–1993*

**Joseph M. Juran.**   Juran's career bore a striking similarity to Deming's. Both were Americans (Juran was a naturalized U.S. citizen born in Romania) schooled in statistics, both strongly influenced Japanese managers via JUSE, and both continued to lecture on quality into their nineties. Thanks to extensive training by the Juran Institute, the concept of internal customers is well established today.[25] Teamwork, partnerships with suppliers, problem solving, and brainstorming are all Juran trademarks. "A specific term associated with Juran is *Pareto analysis*, a technique for separating major problems from minor ones. A Pareto analysis looks for the 20 percent of possible causes that lead to 80 percent of all problems."[26] (The 80/20 rule is discussed in Chapter 6 under the heading of priorities.)

**Armand V. Feigenbaum.**   While working on his doctorate at MIT, Feigenbaum developed the concept of *total quality control*. He expanded on his idea of an organizationwide program of quality improvement in his 1951 book, *Total Quality Control*. He envisioned all functions of the business cycle—from purchasing and engineering, to manufacturing and finance, to marketing and service—as necessarily involved in the quest for quality. The *customer*, according to Feigenbaum, is the one who ultimately determines quality.[27]

| 2D | Juran on Quality |  |
|---|---|---|

Just before his 94th birthday in 1998, Joseph M. Juran made this observation in a *Fortune* magazine interview:

*There's a lot of confusion as to whether quality costs money or whether it saves money. In one sense, quality means the features of some product or service that make people willing to buy it. So it's income-oriented—has an effect on income. Now to produce features, ordinarily you have to invest money. In that sense, higher quality costs more. Quality also means freedom from trouble, freedom from failure. This is cost-oriented. If things fail internally, it costs the company. If they fail externally, it also costs the customer. In these cases, quality costs less.*

**Source:** Thomas A. Stewart, "A Conversation with Joseph Juran," *Fortune* (January 11, 1999): 170.

**Questions:** *What sorts of product and/or service quality problems have you observed lately? How could they have been prevented?*

**Philip B. Crosby.**   The author of the 1979 best-seller *Quality Is Free*, Crosby learned about quality improvement during his up-from-the-trenches career at ITT (a giant global corporation in many lines of business). His work struck a chord with top managers because he documented the huge cost of having to rework or scrap poor-quality products. He promoted the idea of *zero defects*, or doing it right the first time.[28]

## Lessons from the Operational Approach

Scientific management often appears rather unscientific to those who live in a world of genetic engineering, manned space flight, industrial robots, the Internet, and laser technology. *Systematic management* might be a more accurate label. Within the context of haphazard, turn-of-the-twentieth-century industrial practices, however, scientific management was indeed revolutionary. Heading the list of its lasting contributions is a much-needed emphasis on promoting production efficiency and combating waste. Today, dedication to finding a better way is more important than ever in view of uneven productivity growth and diminishing resources.

Nevertheless, Taylor and the early scientific management proponents have been roundly criticized for viewing workers as unidimensional economic beings interested only in more money. These critics fear that scientific management techniques have dehumanized people by making them act like mindless machines. Not all would agree. According to one respected management scholar who feels that Taylor's work is widely misunderstood and unfairly criticized, Taylor actually improved working conditions by reducing fatigue and redesigning machines to fit people. A systematic analysis of Taylor's contributions led this same management scholar to conclude: "Taylor's track record is remarkable. The point is not, as is often claimed, that he was 'right in the context of his time' but is now outdated, but that *most of his insights are still valid today*."[29]

Contributions by the quality advocates are subject to less debate today. The only question is, Why didn't we listen to them earlier? (See Chapter 17.)

An important post–World War II outgrowth of the operational approach is operations management. Operations management, like scientific management, aims at promoting efficiency through systematic observation and experimentation. However, operations management (sometimes called production/operations management) tends to be broader in scope and application than scientific management was. Whereas scientific management was limited largely to hand labor and machine shops, operations management specialists apply their expertise to all types of production and service operations, such as the purchase and storage of materials, energy use, product and service design, work flow, safety, quality control, and data processing. Thus, **operations management** is defined as the process of transforming raw materials, technology, and human talent into useful goods and services.[30] Operations managers could be called the frontline troops in the battle for productivity growth.

**operations management**
*the process of transforming material and human resources into useful goods and services*

# The Behavioral Approach

**4** Describe the general aim of the human relations movement and explain the circumstances in which it arose.

Like the other approaches to management, the behavioral approach has evolved gradually over many years. Advocates of the behavioral approach to management point out that people deserve to be the central focus of organized activity. They believe that successful management depends largely on a manager's ability to understand and work with people who have a variety of backgrounds, needs, perceptions, and aspirations. The progress of this humanistic approach from the human relations movement to modern organizational behavior has greatly influenced management theory and practice.

## The Human Relations Movement

**human relations movement**
*an effort to make managers more sensitive to their employees' needs*

The **human relations movement** was a concerted effort among theorists and practitioners to make managers more sensitive to employee needs. It came into being as a result of special circumstances that occurred during the first half of the twentieth century. As illustrated in Figure 2.3, the human relations movement may be compared to the top of a pyramid. Just as the top of a pyramid must be supported, so too the human relations movement was supported by three very different historic influences: (1) the threat of unionization, (2) the Hawthorne studies, and (3) the philosophy of industrial humanism.

**Threat of Unionization.**    To understand why the human relations movement evolved, one needs first to appreciate its sociopolitical background. From the late 1800s to the 1920s, American industry grew by leaps and bounds as it attempted to satisfy the many demands of a rapidly growing population. Cheap immigrant labor was readily available, and there was a seller's market for finished goods. Then came the Great Depression in the 1930s, and millions stood in bread lines instead of pay lines. Many held business somehow responsible for the depression, and public sympathy swung from management to labor. Congress consequently began to pass prolabor legislation.

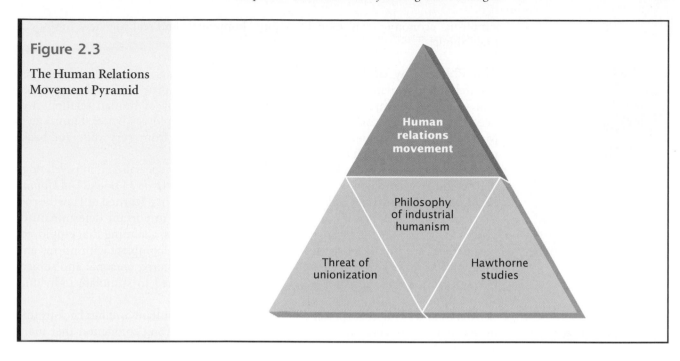

**Figure 2.3**

**The Human Relations Movement Pyramid**

When the Wagner Act of 1935 legalized union-management collective bargaining, management began searching for ways to stem the tide of all-out unionization. Early human relations theory proposed an enticing answer: satisfied employees would be less inclined to join unions. Business managers subsequently began adopting morale-boosting human relations techniques as a union-avoidance tactic.

**The Hawthorne Studies.**    As the sociopolitical climate changed, a second development in industry took place. Behavioral scientists from prestigious universities began to conduct on-the-job behavior studies. Instead of studying tools and techniques in the scientific management tradition, they focused on people. Practical behavioral research such as the famous Hawthorne studies stirred management's interest in the psychological and sociological dynamics of the workplace.

The Hawthorne studies began in 1924 in a Western Electric plant near Chicago as a small-scale scientific management study of the relationship between light intensity and productivity. Curiously, the performance of a select group of employees tended to improve no matter how the physical surroundings were manipulated. Even when the lights were dimmed to moonlight intensity, productivity continued to climb! Scientific management doctrine could not account for what was taking place, and so a team of behavioral science researchers, headed by Elton Mayo, was brought in from Harvard to conduct a more rigorous study.

By 1932, when the Hawthorne studies ended, more than 20,000 employees had participated in one way or another. After extensive interviewing of the subjects, it became clear to researchers that productivity was much less affected by changes in work conditions than by the attitudes of the workers themselves. Specifically, relationships between members of a work group and between workers and their supervisors were found to be more significant. Though the experiments and the theories that evolved from them are criticized today for flawed methodology and statistical inaccuracies, the Hawthorne studies can be credited with turning management theorists away from the simplistic "economic man" model to a more humanistic and realistic view, the "social man" model.[31]

### The Philosophy of Industrial Humanism.

Although unionization prompted a search for new management techniques and the Hawthorne studies demonstrated that people were important to productivity, a philosophy of human relations was needed to provide a convincing rationale for treating employees better. Elton Mayo, Mary Parker Follett, and Douglas McGregor, although from very different backgrounds, offered just such a philosophy.

Born in Australia, Elton Mayo was a Harvard professor specializing in psychology and sociology when he took over the Hawthorne studies. His 1933 book, *The Human Problems of an Industrial Civilization*, inspired by what he had learned at Hawthorne, cautioned managers that emotional factors were a more important determinant of productive efficiency than were physical and logical factors. Claiming that employees create their own unofficial yet powerful workplace culture complete with norms and sanctions, Mayo urged managers to provide work that fostered personal and subjective satisfaction. He called for a new social order designed to stimulate individual cooperation.[32]

Mary Parker Follett's experience as a management consultant and her background in law, political science, and philosophy produced her strong conviction that managers should be aware that each employee is a complex collection of emotions, beliefs, attitudes, and habits. She believed managers had to recognize the individual's motivating desires to get employees to work harder. Accordingly, Follett urged managers to motivate performance rather than simply demand it. Cooperation, a spirit of unity, and self-control were seen as the keys to both productivity and a democratic way of life.[33] Historians credit Follett, who died in 1933, with being decades ahead of her time in terms of behavioral and systems management theory.[34] Her influence as a management consultant in a male-dominated industrial sector was remarkable as well.

A third philosophical rallying point for industrial humanism was provided by an American scholar named Douglas McGregor. In his 1960 classic, *The Human Side of Enterprise,* McGregor outlined a set of highly optimistic assumptions about human nature. McGregor viewed the typical employee as an energetic and creative individual who could achieve great things if given the opportunity. He labeled the set of assumptions for this optimistic perspective **Theory Y.** McGregor's Theory Y assumptions are listed in Table 2.2, along with what he called the traditional Theory X assumptions. These two sets of assumptions about human nature enabled McGregor to contrast the modern or enlightened view he recommended (Theory Y) with the prevailing traditional view (Theory X), which he criticized for being pessimistic, stifling, and outdated. Because of its relative recency (compared with Mayo's and Follett's work), its catchy labels, and its intuitive appeal, McGregor's Theory X/Y philosophy has left an indelible mark on modern management thinking.[35] Some historians have credited McGregor with launching the field of organizational behavior.

*Elton Mayo, 1880–1949*

*Mary Parker Follett, 1868–1933*

**Theory Y**  *McGregor's optimistic assumptions about working people*

*Douglas McGregor, 1906–1964*

**2E  Back to the Opening Case**

Is David Ross a Theory X or Theory Y manager? Explain.

| Table 2.2   McGregor's Theories X and Y | |
|---|---|
| **Theory X: Some traditional assumptions about people** | **Theory Y: Some modern assumptions about people** |
| 1. Most people dislike work, and they will avoid it when they can. | 1. Work is a natural activity, like play or rest. |
| 2. Most people must be coerced and threatened with punishment before they will work. They require close direction. | 2. People are capable of self-direction and self-control if they are committed to objectives. |
| 3. Most people prefer to be directed. They avoid responsibility and have little ambition. They are interested only in security. | 3. People will become committed to organizational objectives if they are rewarded for doing so. |
| | 4. The average person can learn to both accept and seek responsibility. |
| | 5. Many people in the general population have imagination, ingenuity, and creativity. |

## Organizational Behavior

**Organizational behavior** is a modern approach to management that attempts to determine the causes of human work behavior and translate the results into effective management techniques. As such, it has a strong research orientation. Organizational behaviorists have borrowed an assortment of theories and research techniques from all of the behavioral sciences and applied them to people at work in modern organizations. The result is an interdisciplinary field in which psychology predominates. In spite of its relatively new and developing state, organizational behavior has had a significant impact on modern management thought by helping to explain why employees behave as they do. Because human relations has evolved into a practical, how-to-do-it discipline for supervisors, organizational behavior amounts to a scientific extension of human relations. Many organizational behavior findings will be examined in Part Four of this text.

**organizational behavior**
*a modern approach seeking to discover the causes of work behavior and develop better management techniques*

## Lessons from the Behavioral Approach

Above all else, the behavioral approach makes it clear to present and future managers that *people* are the key to productivity. According to advocates of the behavioral approach, technology, work rules, and standards do not guarantee good job performance. Instead, success depends on motivated and skilled individuals who are committed to organizational objectives.[36] Only a manager's sensitivity to individual concerns can foster the cooperation necessary for high productivity.

On the negative side, traditional human relations doctrine has been criticized as vague and simplistic. According to these critics, relatively primitive on-the-job behavioral research does not justify such broad conclusions. For instance, critics do not believe that supportive supervision and good human relations will lead automatically to higher morale and hence to better job performance. Also, recent analyses of the Hawthorne studies, using modern statistical techniques, have generated debate about the validity of the original conclusions.[37]

Fortunately, organizational behavior, as a scientific extension of human relations, promises to fill in some of the gaps left by human relationists while at the same time retaining an emphasis on people. Today, organizational behaviorists are trying to piece together the multiple determinants of effective job performance in various work situations and across cultures.

# The Systems Approach

**system** *a collection of parts that operate interdependently to achieve a common purpose*

A **system** is a collection of parts operating interdependently to achieve a common purpose. Working from this definition, the systems approach represents a marked departure from the past; in fact, it requires a completely different style of thinking.

Universal process, scientific management, and human relations theorists studied management by taking things apart. They assumed that the whole is equal to the sum of its parts and can be explained in terms of its parts. Systems theorists, in contrast, study management by putting things together and assume that the whole is greater than the sum of its parts. The difference is analytic versus synthetic thinking. According to one management systems expert, "Analytic thinking is, so to speak, outside-in thinking; synthetic thinking is inside-out. Neither negates the value of the other, but by synthetic thinking we can gain understanding that we cannot obtain through analysis, particularly of collective phenomena."[38]

Systems theorists recommend synthetic thinking because management is not practiced in a vacuum. Managers affect and are, in turn, affected by many organizational and environmental variables. Systems thinking has presented the field of management with an enormous challenge: to identify all relevant parts of organized activity and to discover how they interact. Two management writers predicted that systems thinking offers "a basis for understanding organizations and their problems which may one day produce a revolution in organizations comparable to the one brought about by Taylor with scientific management."[39]

## Chester I. Barnard's Early Systems Perspective

In one sense, Chester I. Barnard followed in the footsteps of Henri Fayol. Like Fayol, Barnard established a new approach to management on the basis of his experience as a top-level manager. But the approach of the former president of New Jersey Bell Telephone differed from Fayol's. Rather than isolating specific management functions and principles, Barnard devised a more abstract systems approach. In his landmark 1938

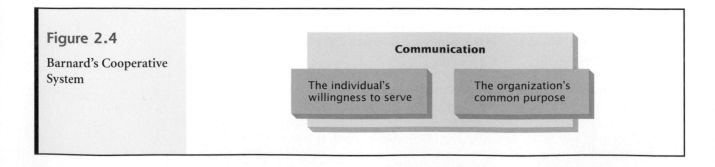

**Figure 2.4**

Barnard's Cooperative System

**Communication**

The individual's willingness to serve

The organization's common purpose

# Management Ethics

## Rebecca Webb Lukens (1794–1854): America's First Female Chief Executive Officer

As America's first female CEO of an industrial company, Rebecca Lukens was a woman more than a century ahead of her time. For her, the critical year was 1825. Lukens, a devout Quaker, was raising three children and was pregnant with another in Coatesville, Pennsylvania, when her husband became mortally ill. On his deathbed, he urged Rebecca to take over his job of operating the Brandywine Iron Works and Nail Factory, founded by her late father.

She agreed and went on to run it for 24 years. Lukens not only rescued the mill from near bankruptcy but also built it into the country's premier manufacturer of boilerplate, high-quality iron essential to the making of steam boilers in what was the dawn of the age of steam....

Lukens was an unusual woman from the start. Her father taught her to ride and often took her to his ironworks. A book lover, she sometimes read secretly in her room until dawn. When she was a teenager, her parents sent her to a boarding school in Wilmington, Delaware, where she developed a love of chemistry. About that time,

she recalled later, "vanity began to whisper to me that I was of some importance, and my beloved tutor often warned me against its siren power." Fortunately, she listened to the whisper and ignored the tutor.

A hands-on executive, Lukens made many purchases and sales. When revenues slumped during the panic of 1837, she laid in a little inventory and then assigned her employees to do maintenance on the factory or gave them work on her farm. She laid off no one. When cash flow ran dry, she paid workers with farm produce. Near the end of her business career, she wrote: "There was difficulty and danger on every side. Now I look back and wonder at my daring."

*Update:* Lukens Inc. merged with Bethlehem Steel Corp. in 1998, thus beginning a new era for America's longest-running steel mill.

*Source:* Excerpted from Peter Nulty, "The National Business Hall of Fame," *Fortune* (April 4, 1994): 126. © 1994 Time, Inc. All rights reserved. Update information from **www.bethsteel.com.**

book, *The Functions of the Executive,* Barnard characterized all organizations as cooperative systems: "A cooperative system is a complex of physical, biological, personal, and social components which are in a specific systematic relationship by reason of the cooperation of two or more persons for at least one definite end."[40]

According to Barnard, willingness to serve, common purpose, and communication are the principal elements in an organization (or cooperative system).[41] He felt that an organization did not exist if these three elements were not present and working interdependently. As illustrated in Figure 2.4, Barnard viewed communication as an energizing force that bridges the natural gap between the individual's willingness to serve and the organization's common purpose.

Barnard's systems perspective has encouraged management and organization theorists to study organizations as complex and dynamic wholes instead of piece by piece. Significantly, he was also a strong advocate of business ethics in his speeches and writings.[42] (See Management Ethics for a profile of another business ethics pioneer.) Barnard opened some important doors in the evolution of management thought.

## General Systems Theory

**General systems theory** is an interdisciplinary area of study based on the assumption that everything is part of a larger, interdependent arrangement. According to Ludwig von Bertalanffy, a biologist and the founder of general systems theory, "In order to

**general systems theory**
*an area of study based on the assumption that everything is part of a larger, interdependent arrangement*

understand an organized whole we must know the parts and the relations between them."[43] This interdisciplinary perspective was eagerly adopted by Barnard's followers because it categorized levels of systems and distinguished between closed and open systems.

**Levels of Systems.**    Envisioning the world as a collection of systems was only the first step for general systems theorists. One of the more important recent steps has been the identification of hierarchies of systems, ranging from very specific systems to general ones. Identifying systems at various levels has helped translate abstract general systems theory into more concrete terms.[44] A hierarchy of systems relevant to management is the seven-level scheme of living systems shown in Figure 2.5. Notice that each system is a subsystem of the one above it.

**Closed Versus Open Systems.**    In addition to identifying hierarchies of systems, general systems theorists have distinguished between closed and open systems. A **closed system** is a self-sufficient entity, whereas an **open system** depends on the surrounding environment for survival. In reality, these two kinds of systems cannot be completely separated from each other. The key to classifying a system as relatively closed or relatively open is to determine the amount of interaction between the system and its environment. A battery-powered digital watch, for example, is a relatively closed system; after the battery is in place, it runs without help from the outside environment. In contrast, a solar-powered clock is a relatively open system; it cannot operate without a continuous supply of outside energy. The human body is a highly open system because life depends on the body's ability to import oxygen and energy and to export waste. In other words, the human body is highly dependent on the environment for survival.

Along the same lines, general systems theorists say that all organizations are open systems because organizational survival depends on interaction with the surrounding environment. Just as no person is an island, no organization or organizational subsystem is an island, according to this approach.

**5** Explain the significance of applying open-system thinking to management.

**closed system**   *a self-sufficient entity*

**open system**   *something that depends on its surrounding environment for survival*

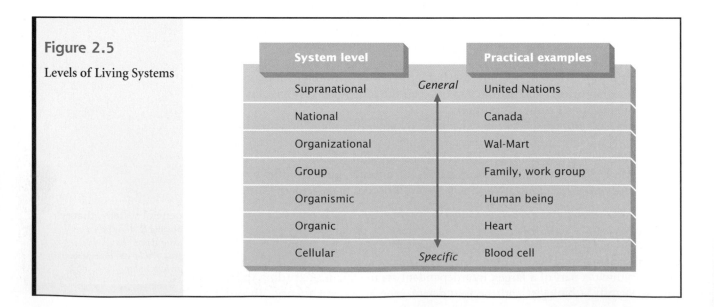

**Figure 2.5**

Levels of Living Systems

| System level | | Practical examples |
|---|---|---|
| Supranational | *General* | United Nations |
| National | | Canada |
| Organizational | | Wal-Mart |
| Group | | Family, work group |
| Organismic | | Human being |
| Organic | | Heart |
| Cellular | *Specific* | Blood cell |

# New Directions in Systems Thinking

Two very different streams of thought are taking systems thinking in interesting new directions today. No one knows for sure where these streams will lead, but they promise to stimulate creative ideas about modern organizations.

**Organizational Learning and Knowledge Management.**  An organizational learning perspective portrays the organization as a living and *thinking* open system. Like the human mind, organizations rely on feedback to adjust to changing environmental conditions. In short, organizations are said to learn from experience, just as humans and higher animals do. Organizations thus engage in complex mental processes such as anticipating, perceiving, envisioning, problem solving, and remembering. According to two organization theorists:

> Some forms of organizational learning occur regularly in many organizations. Human resource development activities, strategic and other planning activities, and the introduction and mastering of new technologies for doing work are three common learning processes. They often do not fulfill their potential for true organizational learning, however.
>
> Organizational learning is more than the sum of the learning of its parts—more than cumulative individual learning. The training and development of individuals with new skills, knowledge bases, theories, and frameworks does not constitute organizational learning unless such individual learning is translated into altered organizational practices, policies, or design features. Individual learning is necessary but not sufficient for organizational learning.[45]

When organizational learning becomes a strategic initiative to identify and fully exploit valuable ideas from both inside and outside the organization, a *knowledge management* program exists.[46] You will find more about knowledge management in Chapter 8 and organizational learning in Chapter 9.

**Chaos Theory and Complex Adaptive Systems.**
Chaos theory has one idea in common with organizational learning: systems are influenced by feedback. Work in the 1960s and 1970s by mathematicians Edward Lorenz and James Yorke formed the basis of modern chaos theory. So-called chaologists are trying to find order among the seemingly random behavior patterns of everything from weather systems to organizations to stock markets.[47] Behind all this is the intriguing notion that every complex system has a life of its own, with its own rule book. The challenge for those in the emerging field known as *complex adaptive systems theory* is to discover "the rules" in seemingly chaotic systems.

As indicated in Table 2.3, complex adaptive systems theory casts management in a very different light than do traditional models. Managers are challenged to be more flexible and adaptive than in the past.[48] They need to acknowledge the limits of traditional command-and-control management because complex systems have *self-organizing* tendencies. (For

---

**2F**  **Managing at the Edge of Chaos**

Richard T. Pascale, author of *Surfing the Edge of Chaos: The Laws of Nature and the New Laws of Business*:

*The important thing to remember is that innovations rarely emerge from systems with high degrees of order and stability. On the other hand, completely chaotic systems are simply too hot to handle. That's why it's important to find the edge of chaos, where a company can experience upheaval but not dissolution. The edge of chaos is not the abyss. It's the sweet spot for productive change.*

**Source:**  As quoted in Alan M. Webber, "How Business Is a Lot Like Life," *Fast Company*, no. 45 (April 2001): 135.

**Questions:**  *Why is this true? How comfortable would you be as an "on the edge" manager? Explain.*

**Table 2.3**   Complex Adaptive Systems Thinking Helps Managers Make Sense Out of Chaos

| Complex adaptive systems theory | Classical management theory |
| --- | --- |
| Change and transformation are inherent qualities of dynamic systems. The goal of management is to increase learning and self-organizing in continuously changing contexts. | Organizations exist in equilibrium, therefore change is a nonnormal process. The goal of management is to increase stability through planning, organizing, and controlling behavior. |
| Organizational behavior is inherently nonlinear, and results may be nonproportional to corresponding actions. New models and methods are needed to understand change. | Organizational behavior is essentially linear and predictable, and results are proportional to causes. Thus linear regression models explain most of the variance of organizational change. |
| Inputs do not cause outputs. The elements of a system are interdependent and mutually causal. | System components are independent, and can be analyzed by separating them from the rest of the system, as well as from their outcomes. |
| An organization is defined, first of all, according to its underlying order and principles. These give rise to surface-level organizing structures, including design, strategy, leadership, controls, and culture. | An organization can be completely defined in terms of its design, strategy, leadership, controls, and culture. |
| Change should be encouraged through embracing tension, increasing information flow, and pushing authority downwards. | Change should be controlled by minimizing uncertainty and tension, limiting information, and centralizing decision making. |
| Long-term organizational success is based on optimizing resource flow and continuous learning. A manager's emphasis is on supporting structures that accomplish these goals. | Organizational success is based on maximizing resource utilization, to maximize profit and increase shareholder wealth. A manager's emphasis is on efficiency and effectiveness, and avoiding both transformation and chaos. |

*Source:* Benyamin Bergmann Lichtenstein, "Self-Organized Transitions: A Pattern amid the Chaos of Transformative Change," *Academy of Management Executive,* 14 (November 2000): Table 1, p. 129. Copyright 2000 by Academy of Management. Reproduced with permission of Academy of Management in the format textbook via Copyright Clearance Center.

example, labor unions have historically thrived in eras when management was oppressive.) The twenty-first-century manager, profiled in the previous chapter (Table 1.1), is up to the challenge. Importantly, chaos theory and complex adaptive systems theory are launching pads for new and better management models, not final answers. Stay tuned.

## Lessons from the Systems Approach

Because of the influence of the systems approach, managers now have a greater appreciation for the importance of seeing the whole picture. Open-system thinking does not permit the manager to become preoccupied with one aspect of organizational management while ignoring other internal and external realities. The manager of a business, for instance, must consider resource availability, technological developments, and market trends when producing and selling a product or service. Another positive aspect of the systems approach is how it tries to integrate various management theories. Although quite different in emphasis, both operations management and organizational behavior have been strongly influenced by systems thinking.

There are critics of the systems approach, of course. Some management scholars see systems thinking as long on intellectual appeal and catchy terminology and short on verifiable facts and practical advice.

# The Contingency Approach

A comparatively new line of thinking among management theorists has been labeled the contingency approach. Contingency management advocates are attempting to take a step away from universally applicable principles of management and toward situational appropriateness. In the words of Fred Luthans, a noted contingency management writer, "The traditional approaches to management were not necessarily wrong, but today they are no longer adequate. The needed breakthrough for management theory and practice can be found in a contingency approach."[49] Formally defined, the **contingency approach** is an effort to determine through research which managerial practices and techniques are appropriate in specific situations. Imagine using Taylor's approach with a college-educated computer engineer! Different situations require different managerial responses, according to the contingency approach.

Generally, the term *contingency* refers to the choice of an alternative course of action. For example, roommates may have a contingency plan to move their party indoors if it rains. Their subsequent actions are said to be contingent (or dependent) on the weather. In a management context, contingency has become synonymous with situational management. As one contingency theorist put it, "The effectiveness of a given management pattern is contingent upon multitudinous factors and their interrelationship in a particular situation."[50] This means the application of various management tools and techniques must be appropriate to the particular situation because each situation presents to the manager its own problems. A contingency approach is applicable in intercultural dealings where customs and habits cannot be taken for granted.

In real-life management, the success of any given technique is dictated by the situation. For example, researchers have found that rigidly structured organizations with many layers of management function best when environmental conditions are relatively stable. Unstable surroundings dictate a more flexible and streamlined organization that can adapt quickly to change. Consequently, traditional principles of management that call for rigidly structured organizations, regardless of the situation, have come into question.

**contingency approach**
*research effort to determine which managerial practices and techniques are appropriate in specific situations*

**6** Explain the practical significance of adopting a contingency perspective.

## Contingency Characteristics

Some management scholars are attracted to contingency thinking because it is a workable compromise between the systems approach and what can be called a purely situational perspective. Figure 2.6 illustrates this relationship. The systems approach is often

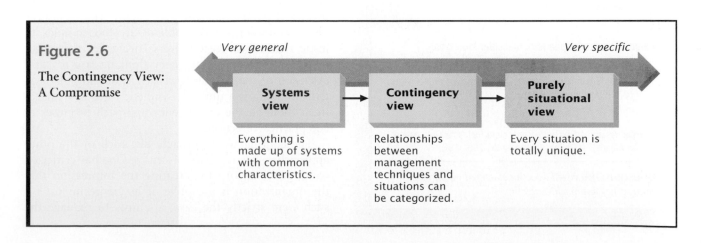

**Figure 2.6**

The Contingency View: A Compromise

Very general ← → Very specific

Systems view → Contingency view → Purely situational view

Everything is made up of systems with common characteristics.

Relationships between management techniques and situations can be categorized.

Every situation is totally unique.

criticized for being too general and abstract, although the purely situational view, which assumes that every real-life situation requires a distinctly different approach, has been called hopelessly specific. Contingency advocates have tried to take advantage of common denominators without getting trapped into simplistic generalization. Three characteristics of the contingency approach are (1) an open-system perspective, (2) a practical research orientation, and (3) a multivariate approach.

**An Open-System Perspective.**    Open-system thinking is fundamental to the contingency view. Contingency theorists are not satisfied with focusing on just the internal workings of organizations. They see the need to understand how organizational subsystems combine to interact with outside social, cultural, political, and economic systems.

**A Practical Research Orientation.**    Practical research is that which ultimately leads to more effective on-the-job management. Contingency researchers attempt to translate their findings into tools and situational refinements for more effective management.

**A Multivariate Approach.**    Traditional closed-system thinking prompted a search for simple one-to-one causal relationships. This approach is called bivariate analysis. For example, the traditional human relations assumption that higher morale leads automatically to higher productivity was the result of bivariate analysis. Only one variable, morale, was seen as the sole direct cause of changes in a second variable, productivity. Subsequent multivariate analysis has shown that many variables, including the employee's personality, the nature of the task, rewards, and job and life satisfaction, collectively account for variations in productivity. **Multivariate analysis** is a research technique used to determine how a combination of variables interact to cause a particular outcome. For example, if an employee has a conscientious personality, the task is highly challenging, and the individual is highly satisfied with his or her life and job, then analysis might show that productivity could be expected to be high. Contingency management theorists strive to carry out practical and relevant multivariate analyses.

**multivariate analysis**
*research technique used to determine how a combination of variables interact to cause a particular outcome*

## Lessons from the Contingency Approach

Although still not fully developed, the contingency approach is a helpful addition to management thought because it emphasizes situational appropriateness. People, organizations, and problems are too complex to justify rigid adherence to universal principles of management. In addition, contingency thinking is a *practical* extension of the systems approach. Assuming that systems thinking is a unifying synthetic force in management thought, the contingency approach promises to add practical direction.

The contingency approach, like each of the other approaches, has its share of critics. One has criticized contingency theory for creating the impression that the organization is a captive of its environment.[51] If such were strictly the case, attempts to manage the

**2G  Words of Wisdom**

Peter F. Drucker, management's elder statesman:

*A decision is a judgment. It is a choice between alternatives. It is rarely a choice between right and wrong. It is at best a choice between "almost right" and "probably wrong."*

**Source:** As quoted in Bruce Rosenstein, "91-Year-Old Legend Shares Advice," *USA Today,* (August 20, 2001): 6B.

**Question:** *How well does this statement mesh with the contingency approach? Explain.*

organization would be in vain. In actual fact, organizations are subject to various combinations of environmental forces and management practices.

Whether the contingency management theorists have bitten off more than they can chew remains to be seen. At present they appear to be headed in a constructive direction. But it is good to keep in mind that the contingency approach is a promising step rather than the end of the evolution of conventional management thought.

# Attributes of Excellence: A Modern Unconventional Approach

In 1982, Thomas J. Peters and Robert H. Waterman Jr., a pair of management consultants, wrote a book that took the management world by storm. It topped the nonfiction best-seller lists for months, was translated into several foreign languages, and later appeared in paperback. Just five years later, an astounding 5 million copies had been sold worldwide.[52] *In Search of Excellence* attempted to explain what makes America's best-run companies successful. Many respected corporate executives hailed Peters and Waterman's book as the remedy for America's productivity problems. Certain management scholars, however, called the book simplistic and accused the authors of pandering to management's desire for a quick fix. Moreover, they called Peters and Waterman's research methods weak. If for no reason other than its widespread acceptance in the management community, *In Search of Excellence* deserves discussion in any historical perspective of management thought.[53]

Peters and Waterman's approach to management was unconventional for three reasons. First, they attacked conventional management theory and practice for being too conservative, rationalistic, analytical, unemotional, inflexible, negative, and preoccupied with bigness. Second, they replaced conventional management terminology (such as planning, management by objectives, and control) with catch phrases gleaned from successful managers (for example, "Do it, fix it, try it" and "management by wandering around"). Third, they made their key points with stories and anecdotes rather than with objective, quantified data and facts. All this added up to a challenge to take a fresh new look at management. In this section we explore that challenge by discussing the eight attributes of excellence uncovered by Peters and Waterman. Subsequent interpretations of their approach are also examined.

*Thomas J. Peters*

*Robert H. Waterman Jr.*

## 2H  Still Searching for Excellence

Bill Zollars, president, Yellow Freight System, with 13,000 trucks across the United States:

> *During his first year at Yellow, Zollars spent most of his time in the field. "It's the only place where you find out what's really going on with customers and operations without any filters," he says. "At headquarters, you don't hear any of the bad stuff."*

**Source:** Chuck Salter, "On the Road Again," *Fast Company*, no. 54 (January 2002): 57.

**Questions:** *Which of Peters and Waterman's attributes of excellence are evident here? Is this a good way to manage? Why?*

# Eight Attributes of Excellence

Peters and Waterman employed a combination of subjective and objective criteria to identify 62 of the best-managed companies in the United States. Among the final subsample of 36 "excellent" companies that boasted 20-year records of innovation and profitability were such familiar names as Boeing, Caterpillar, Delta Air Lines, Eastman Kodak, IBM, Johnson & Johnson, McDonald's, and 3M. Extensive interviews were conducted at half of these firms and less extensive interviewing took place at the rest.[54] After analyzing the results of their interviews, Peters and Waterman isolated the eight attributes of excellence summarized in Table 2.4. Importantly, the authors noted: "Not all eight attributes were present or conspicuous to the same degree in all of the excellent companies we studied. But in every case at least a preponderance of the eight was clearly visible, quite distinctive."[55]

---

**7** Identify and explain the nature of at least four of Thomas J. Peters and Robert H. Waterman Jr.'s eight attributes of excellence.

# A Critical Appraisal of the Excellence Approach

Critics took Peters and Waterman to task for giving managers more questions than answers, ignoring the contingency approach to management, and relying too heavily on unsupported generalizations. They also criticized them for taking an overly narrow viewpoint of organizational success. According to one skeptical management consultant:

> *The authors fail to position management effectiveness among the several nonmanagement variables that are also important to sustained corporate excellence. Technology, finances, government policy, raw materials, and others must be acknowledged, if only to forestall unreasonable expectations of and for management.[56]*

In fact, after reviewing research evidence that 14 of Peters and Waterman's "excellent" companies had fallen on hard times by 1984, *Business Week* observed:

> *One major lesson from all this is that the excellent companies of today will not necessarily be the excellent companies of tomorrow. But the more important lesson is that good management requires much more than following any one set of rules. In Search of Excellence was a response to an era when management put too much emphasis on number-crunching. But companies can also get into trouble by overemphasizing Peters' and Waterman's principles.[57]*

Subsequent research has reinforced the foregoing criticisms of the excellence approach. Unlike Peters and Waterman, Michael Hitt and Duane Ireland conducted a *comparative* analysis of "excellent" companies and industry norms. Companies that satisfied all of Peters and Waterman's excellence criteria turned out to be no more effective than a random sample of *Fortune* 1000 companies.[58] This outcome prompted Hitt and Ireland to offer five tips for avoiding what they termed "the quick-fix mentality"[59] (see Table 2.5).

**Table 2.4**    Peters and Waterman's Eight Attributes of Excellence

| Attributes of excellence | Key indicators |
|---|---|
| 1. A bias for action | Small-scale, easily managed experiments to build knowledge, interest, and commitment.<br><br>Managers stay visible and personally involved in all areas through active, informal communication and spontaneous MBWA ("management by wandering around"). |
| 2. Close to the customer | Customer satisfaction is practically an obsession.<br>Input from customers is sought throughout the design/production/marketing cycle. |
| 3. Autonomy and entrepreneurship | Risk taking is encouraged; failure is tolerated.<br><br>Innovators are encouraged to "champion" their pet projects to see them through to completion.<br><br>Flexible structure permits the formation of "skunk works" (small teams of zealous innovators working on a special project).<br><br>Lots of creative "swings" are encouraged to ensure some "home runs" (successful products). |
| 4. Productivity through people | Individuals are treated with respect and dignity.<br><br>Enthusiasm, trust, and a family feeling are fostered.<br><br>People are encouraged to have fun while getting something meaningful accomplished.<br><br>Work units are kept small and humane. |
| 5. Hands-on, value driven | A clear company philosophy is disseminated and followed.<br><br>Personal values are discussed openly, not buried.<br><br>The organization's belief system is reinforced through frequently shared stories, myths, and legends.<br><br>Leaders are positive role models, not "Do-as-I-say, not-as-I-do" authority figures. |
| 6. Stick to the knitting | Management sticks to the business it knows best.<br><br>Emphasis is on internal growth, not mergers. |
| 7. Simple form, lean staff | Authority is decentralized as much as possible.<br><br>Headquarters staffs are kept small; talent is pushed out to the field. |
| 8. Simultaneous loose-tight properties | Tight overall strategic and financial control is counterbalanced by decentralized authority, autonomy, and opportunities for creativity. |

*Source:* "Eight Attributes of Excellence" from *In Search of Excellence: Lessons from America's Best-Run Companies* by Thomas J. Peters and Robert H. Waterman Jr. Copyright © 1982 by Thomas J. Peters and Robert H. Waterman Jr. Reprinted by permission of HarperCollins Publishers, Inc.

**Table 2.5**   How to Avoid the Quick-Fix Mentality in Management

Our research suggests that practicing managers should embrace appealing ideas when appropriate, but anticipate that solutions typically are far more complex than the type suggested by Peters and Waterman's search for excellence. To avoid the quick-fix mentality, managers should:

1. Remain current with literature in the field, particularly with journals that translate research into practice.

2. Ensure that concepts applied are based on science or, at least, on some form of rigorous documentation, rather than purely on advocacy.

3. Be willing to examine and implement new concepts, but first do so using pilot tests with small units.

4. Be skeptical when simple solutions are offered; analyze them thoroughly.

5. Constantly anticipate the effects of current actions and events on future results.

*Source:* Michael A. Hitt and R. Duane Ireland, "Peters and Waterman Revisited: The Unended Quest for Excellence," *Academy of Management Executive* 2, no. 2 (May 1987): 96. Reprinted by permission.

## Lessons from the Excellence Approach

Certainly more than anything else, Peters and Waterman did a good job of reminding managers to pay closer attention to *basics* such as customers, employees, and new ideas. While reviewing their findings, they noted:

> The project showed, more clearly than could have been hoped for, that the excellent companies were, above all, brilliant on the basics. Tools didn't substitute for thinking. Intellect didn't overpower wisdom. Analysis didn't impede action. Rather, these companies worked hard to keep things simple in a complex world. They persisted. They insisted on top quality. They fawned on their customers. They listened to their employees and treated them like adults. They allowed their innovative product or service "champions" long tethers. They allowed some chaos in return for quick action and regular experimentation.[60]

Although discussion of these basics may strike some as a tedious review of the obvious, it is precisely neglect of the basics that keeps many organizations and individuals from achieving excellence.

Despite Peters and Waterman's subjective research methodology,[61] they deserve credit for reminding managers of the importance of on-the-job experimentation. All the planning in the world cannot teach the practical lessons that one can learn by experimentally rearranging things and observing the results, trying an improved approach, observing, and so on.[62]

A concluding comment is in order to help put the foregoing historical overview into proper perspective. The theoretical tidiness of this chapter, although providing a useful conceptual framework for students of management, generally does not carry over to the

**21  Management Wisdom: Beyond Quick Fixes**

*. . . if you look hard at the history of the* Fortune *500 over the past 40 years, there emerges through all the static a set of golden management rules that have surviving power. They don't have labels—once you stick a name on something, it's fast on its way to becoming a flavor-of-the-month disappointment— but are broad management principles. They are (1) Management is a practice. (2) People are a resource. (3) Marketing and innovation are the key functions of a business. (4) Discover what you do well. (5) Quality pays for itself.*

**Source:** Excerpted from Brian Dumaine, "Distilled Wisdom: Buddy, Can You Paradigm?" Fortune (May 15, 1995): 205.

**Question:** *What lesson does each of these broad management principles teach you?*

practice of management. As the excellence approach makes clear, managers are, first and foremost, pragmatists. They use whatever works. Instead of faithfully adhering to a given school of management thought, successful managers tend to use a "mixed bag" approach. This chapter is a good starting point for you to begin building your own personally relevant and useful approach to management by blending theory, the experience and advice of others, and your own experience.

# Summary

**1.** Management is an interdisciplinary and international field that has evolved in bits and pieces over the years. Six approaches to management theory are (1) the universal process approach, (2) the operational approach, (3) the behavioral approach, (4) the systems approach, (5) the contingency approach, and (6) the attributes of excellence approach. Useful lessons have been learned from each approach.

   Henry Fayol's universal approach assumes that all organizations, regardless of purpose or size, require the same management process. Furthermore, it assumes that this rational process can be reduced to separate functions and principles of management. The universal approach, the oldest of the various approaches, is still popular today.

**2.** Dedicated to promoting production efficiency and reducing waste, the operational approach has evolved from scientific management to operations management. Frederick W. Taylor, the father of scientific management, and his followers revolutionized industrial management through the use of standardization, time-and-motion study, selection and training, and pay incentives.

**3.** The quality advocates taught managers about the strategic importance of high-quality goods and services. Shewhart pioneered the use of *statistics* for quality control. Japan's Ishikawa emphasized *prevention* of defects in quality and drew management's attention to *internal* as well as external *customers*. Deming sparked the Japanese quality revolution with calls for *continuous improvement* of the entire production process. Juran trained many U.S. managers to improve quality through *teamwork*, *partnerships with suppliers*, and *Pareto analysis* (the 80/20 rule). Feigenbaum developed the concept of *total quality control*, thus involving all business functions in the quest for quality. He believed that the *customer* determined quality. Crosby, a champion of *zero defects*, emphasized how costly poor-quality products could be.

**4.** Management has turned to the human factor in the human relations movement and organizational behavior approach. Emerging from such influences as unionization, the Hawthorne studies, and the philosophy of industrial humanism, the human relations movement began as a concerted effort to make employees' needs a high management priority. Today, organizational behavior theory tries to identify the multiple determinants of job performance.

**5.** Advocates of the systems approach recommend that modern organizations be viewed as open systems. Open systems depend on the outside environment for survival, whereas closed systems do not. Chester I. Barnard stirred early interest in systems thinking in 1938 by suggesting that organizations are cooperative systems energized by communication. General systems theory, an interdisciplinary field based on the assumption that everything is systematically related, has identified a hierarchy of systems and has differentiated between closed and open systems. New directions in systems thinking are organizational learning and chaos theory.

**6.** A comparatively new approach to management thought is the contingency approach, which stresses situational appropriateness rather than universal principles. The contingency approach is characterized by an open-system perspective, a practical research orientation, and a multivariate approach to research. Contingency thinking is a practical extension of more abstract systems thinking.

**7.** *In Search of Excellence,* Peters and Waterman's best-selling book, challenged managers to take a fresh, unconventional look at managing. They isolated eight attributes of excellence after studying many of the best-managed and most successful companies in America. Generally, the excellent companies were found to be relatively decentralized and value-driven organizations dedicated to humane treatment of employees, innovation, experimentation, and customer satisfaction. Critics of the excellence approach caution managers to avoid the quick-fix mentality, in which organizational problems and solutions are oversimplified.

## Terms to Understand

Universal process approach (p. 45)

Operational approach (p. 47)

Scientific management (p. 47)

Operations management (p. 52)

Human relations movement (p. 52)

Theory Y (p. 54)

Organizational behavior (p. 55)

System (p. 56)

General systems theory (p. 57)

Closed system (p. 58)

Open system (p. 58)

Contingency approach (p. 61)

Multivariate analysis (p. 62)

# Skills & Tools

## Recommended Periodicals for Staying Current in the Field of Management

### Academic Journals (with a research orientation)

*Academy of Management Journal*
*Academy of Management Review*
*Administrative Science Quarterly*
*Human Relations*
*Journal of Applied Psychology*
*Journal of Management*

*Journal of Organizational Behavior*
*Journal of Vocational Behavior*
*Journal of World Business*
*Nonprofit Management & Leadership*

## Scholarly Journals (with a practical orientation)

*Academy of Management Executive*
*Business Horizons*
*Harvard Business Review*
*Journal of Organizational Excellence* (formerly *National Productivity Review*)
*MIT Sloan Management Review*
*Organizational Dynamics*
*Public Administration Review*

## General Periodicals

*Business 2.0*
*Business Week*
*Canadian Business*
*The Economist*
*Fast Company*
*Forbes*
*Fortune*
*Industry Week*
*International Management* (Europe)
*The Wall Street Journal*
*Wired* (business with an attitude)

## Practitioner Journals (special interest)

*Black Enterprise*
*Business Ethics*
*CIO* (information technology)
*Entrepreneur*
*Executive Female*
*Hispanic Business*
*HR Magazine* (human resource management)
*Inc.* (small business)
*Information Week* (information technology)
*Inside Supply Management* (formerly *Purchasing Today*)
*Macworld* (Apple computer users)
*Money* (personal finance and investing)
*Nonprofit World* (not-for-profit organizations)
*PC World* (personal computing and Internet)
*Technology Review* (new technology)
*Training*
*Web Bound* (Internet)
*Working Mother* (work/family issues)

# Hands-On Exercise

## Managers Need Open-System Thinking to Deal with Global Terrorism

**Instructions**

To borrow a phrase from crisis management specialists, this is an exercise in "thinking about the unthinkable," with an eye toward being better prepared. After you have read the section on the systems approach to management (with special attention to Table 2.3), read the brief piece below about the threat of terrorism. The systems thinking you will need to get your mind around this huge issue will be enhanced by reading the description of organizations as open systems in Chapter 9 and the discussion of crisis management in Chapter 17. *Note:* An excellent background article on complex systems theory is "Simple, Yet Complex" by Megan Santosus in the April 15, 1998, issue of *CIO* magazine (available in full text on the Web at **www.cio.com/archive/**).

**The Problem**

*"The likelihood of cyberterrorism happening has gone from a possibility to almost a certainty."*

*That assessment of the post–Sept. 11 world comes from Fred Rica, threat and vulnerability practice leader at PricewaterhouseCoopers. Rica is weighing the likelihood that the nation's economic arteries—banks, oil companies, communication companies, water systems, you name it—could be brought down by a terrorist hacker. And the reality, he says, is that "everybody is a potential target." . . .*

*The very systems that have increased productivity and driven efficiencies have also made the United States more susceptible to attack. The electrical grid and telecommunications, for example, increasingly are connected to Internet protocol-based networks that have been opened by deregulation and, as a result, are shared by many competitors. On the corporate level, supply chains have expanded the reach of company networks— and multiplied the potential points of attack.*[63]

**For Consideration/ Discussion**

**1.** From a personal standpoint, how could your life be disrupted by terrorism?

**2.** Focusing on a specific organization of your choice, determine its major vulnerabilities to terrorist acts.

**3.** What do today's managers need to do to protect their organizations, employees, and customers from acts of terrorism?

**4.** On a global scale, what needs to be done to make terrorism less likely in the first place?

**5.** Why is systems thinking useful for issues as complex as global terrorism?

# Internet Exercises

1. **Managerial shortcut to the information superhighway:** Busy managers typically cannot afford the luxury of spending hours surfing the Internet for needed information. Fortunately, **www.ceoexpress.com** offers managers a handy one-stop information clearinghouse. Hundreds of "hot links" instantly tap into current information in relevant areas such as news, weather, technology, travel, health, investing, statistics, sports, and shopping. Useful and interesting reference items include everything from a guide to writing and grammar, to a currency-exchange calculator, to an Internet public library, to a worldwide list of public holidays. Take some time to browse the links in this valuable Web site. Be sure to call up material of both managerial and personal interest.

   *Learning Points:* 1. Which links would you recommend to a parent or a friend who is a manager? Why? 2. What useful or interesting things did you learn about management during this Internet session? 3. What personally relevant or useful things did you pick up during this exploratory session?

2. **Check it out:** There's only one thing better than useful information on the Internet, and that's *free* useful information! At the home page of **www.mapnp.org**, select "Free Management Library" from the menu. You will find more than 70 topical areas relevant to modern management. Simply click through to a rich array of resources for topics such as business planning, supervision, crisis management, personal wellness, leadership development, career development, interpersonal skills, and systems thinking.

   For updates to these exercises, visit our Web site (**http://business.college.hmco. com/students**).

# Closing Case

## Russia's New Management Style

**M**oscow—The rise of Russian capitalism is giving birth to a uniquely Russian brand of business management.

Helping with the delivery is a small but growing cadre of Russian management consultants, homegrown counterparts to the horde of organizational experts who advise Corporate America.

But what Russian consultants are preaching isn't exactly what they teach at the Harvard Business School. In a country still reeling from the collapse of socialism, they're blending Western practices—such as Total Quality Management—with Russian techniques, including some inherited from Soviet days.

"We have our own ideas and our own theories, even though no one in the West knows about them," says Anatoli Levenchuk, director of the Institute for Commercial Engineering, a Russian consulting firm.

The idea that the Soviet era might yield useful management insights is startling, to say the least. The conventional view is that under communism, Russian managers were little more than glorified foremen, blindly obeying production plans handed down by the Soviet bureaucracy.

The truth is more complex. Most Soviet factories were inefficient nightmares, producing refrigerators that didn't refrigerate and washing machines that didn't wash. But the fact the system functioned at all is a tribute to the resourcefulness of Russian managers.

"Given the realities of centralized planning, state monopoly and constant shortage, a remarkable number of Soviet enterprises produce usable, sophisticated products," economists Paul Lawrence and Charalambos Vlachoutsicos concluded in a 1990 study.

Communism also didn't prevent Russian managers from developing shrewd bargaining skills. Unworkable central plans forced them to craft elaborate barter deals to obtain crucial components. Just-in-time inventories were routine—out of necessity, not choice. Those survival

skills have grown even sharper in the post-communist era, as managers have wrestled with the economic chaos, crime, and corruption unleashed by the breakup of the Soviet Union.

But harnessing all that ingenuity to the profit motive hasn't been easy. Many Russian managers remain deeply suspicious of the free market. While some have become owners, most still believe their main loyalty should be to their workers and fellow managers, not to company shareholders.

Levenchuk is trying to change that mentality by stressing the cooperative aspects of capitalism. He encourages his clients to view suppliers, customers—even competitors—as potential strategic partners, to use the Western buzzword.

"We're trying to teach people that they can work together as a team," Levenchuk says.

His theory draws heavily on the work of Ronald Coase, a Nobel Prize–winning economist at the University of Chicago who emphasized the need to lower "transactional costs"—the social, legal and personal barriers that impede efficiency.

But Levenchuk also makes wide use of games and role-playing exercises developed in the 1970s by a Soviet sociologist, Georgi Shedrovitski.

"If anything, the need for such techniques was greater under socialism," Levenchuk says, "because the system itself was so inefficient."

Many Western analysts remain pessimistic about the possibility of converting Soviet-era managers into modern business executives. Bringing modern management to Russia, they say, will take time—and the rise of a

*Source:* Bill Montague, "Russia's New Management Style," *USA Today* (August 12, 1996): 7B. Copyright © 1996, *USA Today*. Reprinted with permission.

new generation free of the psychological baggage of communism.

That process is happening, but slowly. "There is a cadre of trained executives, but they can't churn them out fast enough," says Phil Cronin, vice president in the Moscow office of A. T. Kearney, a U.S. consulting firm.

"The pool of talent is still very small, relative to the size of the Russian economy."

Levenchuk is more optimistic. "We *can* change because our past does not define our future. And it will not define the future of our country."

## For Discussion

**1.** What does Henri Fayol's work tell Russian managers about making the transition from the old Soviet system to modern capitalism?

**2.** What advice would Mary Parker Follett probably give Russia's managers?

**3.** What advice about building successful businesses would Chester I. Barnard probably offer to Russian managers?

**4.** If you were asked to make a guest presentation to a group of Russian managers, which of the eight attributes of excellence in Table 2.4 would you urge them to focus on when making the transition from communism to capitalism? Why?

**5.** Do you think it is a good idea for Russian managers to blend Western management practices with Russian techniques? Explain.

## chapter three

# The **Changing Environment** of **Management**

## Diversity, Global Economy and Technology

### CHAPTER OBJECTIVES

*When you finish studying this chapter you should be able to*

**1** **Identify** and briefly highlight seven major changes shaping the twenty-first-century workplace.

**2** **Summarize** the demographics of the new workforce.

**3** **Define** the term *managing diversity* and **explain** why it is particularly important today.

**4** **Discuss** how the changing political-legal environment is affecting the practice of management.

**5** **Discuss** why business cycles and the global economy are vital economic considerations for modern managers.

**6** **Describe** the three-step innovation process and **define** the term *intrapreneur*.

> **"** The best way to predict the future is to create it. **"**
>
> Alan Kaye

# Sweet Success for This Mexican-Born Entrepreneur

Handed a bunch of lemons, entrepreneurs do what resourceful people do—they make lemonade. Maria Sobrino made gelatin.

It was 1982, in Los Angeles. Sobrino watched in horror as the value of Mexican pesos plunged against the U.S. dollar, killing her travel business by making her services prohibitively expensive for a predominantly Mexican clientele. She scoured Los Angeles for a way to make a living.

But even after she fought her way into another venture—manufacturing gelatin snacks—Sobrino, 49, faced myriad new threats: The early-1990s recession. A failed marriage. The death of her father. Family members laughing at her entrepreneurial pursuits.

And . . . [in 2001, she faced] California's energy crisis. "Nothing is easy," Sobrino says, with bare-knuckled tenacity.

Indeed, her LuLu's Dessert in Vernon, Calif., has overcome all obstacles to become a leading maker of ready-to-eat gelatin—a staple in her native Mexico but a novelty when she introduced it in Southern California 20 years ago. With 100 workers, her company expects about $10 million in revenue this year on sales of 80 million cups.

Sobrino is a player in an economic wonder of the past 20 years: growth in Hispanic firms, especially those begun by Latinas. There are 1.2 million Hispanic firms nationwide, five times as many as when Sobrino started LuLu's, Census data show. And LuLu's is one of almost 400,000 firms owned by Hispanic women, a segment that's grown four times faster than all firms. . . .

She was supposed to be a lawyer.

That's what her father wanted, even though Sobrino never saw women attorneys when growing up in Mexico City. The oldest of four girls and a boy, Sobrino was expected to follow her father, a successful civil law attorney.

But the image of the newly opened Disneyland flickering on the family's black-and-white TV made her yearn for life in the USA. After graduating from Universidad Autonoma de Mexico with a business administration degree, she joined IBM's Mexico City office. She wanted to learn computer programming. But her boss told her: "This is only men's work," and pointed to the 17 other employees—all men.

Sobrino persisted, however, winning the right to enter an IBM training program. Although she didn't mind working for someone else, she quit IBM after 18 months and set out on her own. "It's the entrepreneurial spirit," she says. "You always want to start something and be your own boss."

The business she started—the first of three—was a flower shop in a large Mexico City hotel. She didn't have a business plan, and had only a vague idea of what she wanted to do. She learned a fundamental rule about start-ups: You don't get rich overnight.

The store morphed into her second start-up, a travel business, Turismo Copsa. Working her IBM connections, she branched into convention planning for corporations with Mexican operations.

By 1981, she'd opened an office in Los Angeles to serve clients who wanted to host meetings in the USA. One year later, the Mexican currency tanked after authorities devalued the peso. Travel costs for Mexicans soared, putting Sobrino out of business. She tried importing Mexican arts and crafts, but it didn't work out. Then one day, a neighbor watched her making the gelatin Sobrino's mother used to cook and suggested she do it for a living.

Sobrino had noticed that ready-to-eat gelatin—a ubiquitous dessert back home—wasn't available in Southern California despite a growing population of Mexican immigrants. It was sold almost exclusively in powder form by Kraft's Jell-O and others.

Sobrino rented a 700-square-foot store and started making 300 cups a day by hand. To expand sales, she offered a small grocery store the chance to stock her desserts on consignment. The owner called the moment she returned from making her first delivery, saying: "Señora, please come back; your gelatin is gone."

Sobrino had a winner. . . .

But back in Mexico City, her family said she was nuts. "They thought I was really selling my product in the streets because that's the way it was in Mexico," she says, still amazed. "They wanted me to go back!"

. . . Harvard University said it wants to include her in an exhibit devoted to Oprah Winfrey, Martha Stewart, and other women entrepreneurs.

Fred Dominguez, head of We Give Thanks, a charity that Sobrino supports, says she won't give up. "You fall down, you get up again. You fall down, you get up again," he says. "That shows determination."

*Source:* Jim Hopkins, "Childhood Treat Helps Sobrino Savor Sweet Success," *USA Today* (May 16, 2001): 10B. Copyright 2001, *USA Today*. Reprinted with permission.

Even though Maria Sobrino is now a successful businesswoman, she will continue to face a steady diet of change. Nothing new for her. Like many successful managers today, Sobrino has learned to do more than merely cope with change; she has learned to thrive on it. Consequently, present and future managers need to be aware of *how* things are changing in the world around them.

Ignoring the impact of general environmental factors on management makes about as much sense as ignoring the effects of weather and road conditions on high-speed driving. The general environment of management includes social, political-legal, economic, and technological dimensions. Changes in each area present managers with unique opportunities and obstacles that will shape not only the organization's strategic direction but also the course of daily operations. This challenge requires forward-thinking managers who can handle change and see the greater scheme of things.

The purpose of this chapter, then, is to prepare you for constant change and help you see the *big picture* by identifying key themes in the changing environment of management.

**1** Identify and briefly highlight seven major changes shaping the twenty-first-century workplace.

# The Twenty-First-Century Workplace: Seven Major Changes

Predictions about everything under the sun are plentiful with the new millennium at hand. Our immediate concern is how the workplace will change as the twenty-first century unfolds. After all, the workplace is where you will spend half (or more) of your nonsleep life in the years to come. Management consultant and futurist Robert Barner foresees seven major changes that promise to challenge managers and employees.[1] As a departure point for this chapter, let us highlight each of Barner's major workplace changes.

1. *The virtual organization.* Thanks to modern telecommunications and computer network technology, centralized workplaces where employees gather each workday for face-to-face interaction are being dispersed. Yes, many people will continue to commute to factories and offices. But many more will set up shop *wherever* they are—on a plane, at home, in a customer's office, or in a moving vehicle—and communicate with their coworkers via cellular phones, wireless e-mail, fax machines, and personal digital assistants. Virtual organizations will be faster and more flexible. Meanwhile, they will present managers with new challenges regarding information overload, organization structure, teamwork, communication, decision making, and career development. Barner notes: "To meet these challenges, workers will need to develop skills in network-based decision making, including the use of such specialized tools as group-decision-support software."[2]

2. *The just-in-time workforce.* The trends toward using part-time or temporary workers and outsourcing organizational tasks and functions to other companies will

*This version of the 21st-century virtual organization comes with some unusual hazards: gunfire and rocket attacks. Pictured here is photographer Oleg Nikishin filing his report from an Afghan military base near Mazar-i-Sharif as the war in Afghanistan was getting underway. Thanks to modern computer and satellite communication technology (and some very hardy photographers), Nikishin's employer, Getty Images, has up-to-the-minute news photos from far-flung corners of the world.*

pick up speed. But how can part-time employees be motivated to do their best and be committed employees? Human resource practices such as hiring, training, and compensation will need to be refined.

3. *The ascendancy of knowledge workers.* We are moving from an industrial economy to an information economy. Information-age technologies require sharp minds, not strong backs. Lifelong learning will be the key to fighting the rapid obsolescence of technical skills. According to Barner, "The rapid growth of knowledge workers will require organizations to rethink their traditional approaches to directing, coaching, and motivating employees." Instead of doing nothing but manage, " . . . managers will be expected to contribute technical expertise to their jobs and to be willing to roll up their sleeves and contribute when necessary."[3]

4. *Computerized coaching and electronic monitoring.* Computers will continue to be a mixed blessing in the workplace. Computer-assisted learning, decision making, and performance monitoring can trim costs and boost productivity. However, we can anticipate a backlash from employees who feel manipulated and deprived of their privacy rights.

5. *The growth of worker diversity.* Growing minority and immigrant populations will contribute to increased racial and ethnic diversity in North America. A multicultural and multilingual workforce will slowly evolve as managers learn how to compete in the global economy where cross-cultural dealings are constant. Products and services will be customized to accommodate individual tastes. Women and minorities will occupy a greater proportion of executive positions. Labor unions will attempt to exploit the proliferation of special-interest groups and technology-based grievances.

6. *The aging workforce.* As the leading edge of the post–World War II baby-boom generation reaches retirement age, our preoccupation with youth is giving way to greater sophistication, realism, and responsibility. College education is no longer just for the young. Older workers will be viewed as a vital and reliable economic resource. Early retirement in the United States will be discouraged as employees pay more into the Social Security retirement system, while collecting less at an older age.

7. *The birth of the dynamic workforce.* Information-age managers will question traditional assumptions about employees, organizations, competitors, and customers. Boundaries between the private (business) and public (government) sectors will blur as social problems such as educational reform and child care are tackled by business leaders. Whole new industries, such as the one surrounding the Internet, will emerge. As Barner sees it: "Managers will be increasingly judged on their ability to identify and implement improvements and to encourage innovative thinking from team members, while professionals will be judged on their ability to adapt quickly to widely different work environments."[4] Rapid redeployment of employees from one project team to another will be the norm.

These seven major changes promise to reshape our world significantly, both for better and for worse. Whether one likes or dislikes them is another matter. Progressive managers need to heed them as early warning signals of change in their social, political-legal, economic, and technological environments.

# The Social Environment

According to sociologists, society is the product of a constant struggle between the forces of stability and change. Cooperation promotes stability, whereas conflict and competition upset the status quo. The net result is an ever-changing society. Keeping this perspective in mind, we shall discuss four important dimensions of the social environment: demographics, the new social contract, inequalities, and managing diversity. Each presents managers with unique challenges.

**demographics**  *statistical profiles of population changes*

## Demographics of the New Workforce

**2**  Summarize the demographics of the new workforce.

**Demographics**—statistical profiles of population characteristics—are a valuable planning tool for managers. Foresighted managers who study demographics can make appropriate adjustments in their strategic, human resource, and marketing plans. Selected demographic shifts reshaping the U.S. workforce are presented in Figure 3.1. (Other countries have their own demographic trends.)[5] The projections in Figure 3.1 are not "blue sky" numbers. They are based on people already born, most of whom are presently working. In short, the U.S. workforce demonstrates the following trends:

■ *It is getting larger.* As in the previous two decades, the U.S. labor force will continue to grow at a faster rate than the national population. The resulting labor shortage will continue to be a magnet for legal and illegal immigration.

■ *It is getting increasingly female.* Employment opportunities for both men and women will grow, but at a faster rate for women.

■ *It is getting more racially and ethnically diverse.* As the white, non-Hispanic majority of the U.S. workforce continues to shrink, Hispanics will replace African-Americans as the second-largest segment by 2010. The "Asians and others" category is the fastest growing, but still the smallest, segment.

■ *It is getting older.* As the post–World War II baby-boom generation moves toward retirement, the median age of U.S. employees will continue to increase, with most vigorous growth for the 45-and-older groups. Interestingly, the trend toward an older workforce hides a significant exception. For the first time since the baby boomers were young, the 16–24 age group will grow, reflecting the so-called echo baby boom.

**3A**

## Back to the Opening Case

How does Maria Sobrino symbolize the "new" U.S. workforce? How is this changing the way America does business?

For further information about the interactive annotations in this chapter, visit our Web site (http://business.college. hmco.com/students).

## Figure 3.1 The Changing U.S. Workforce: 2000–2010

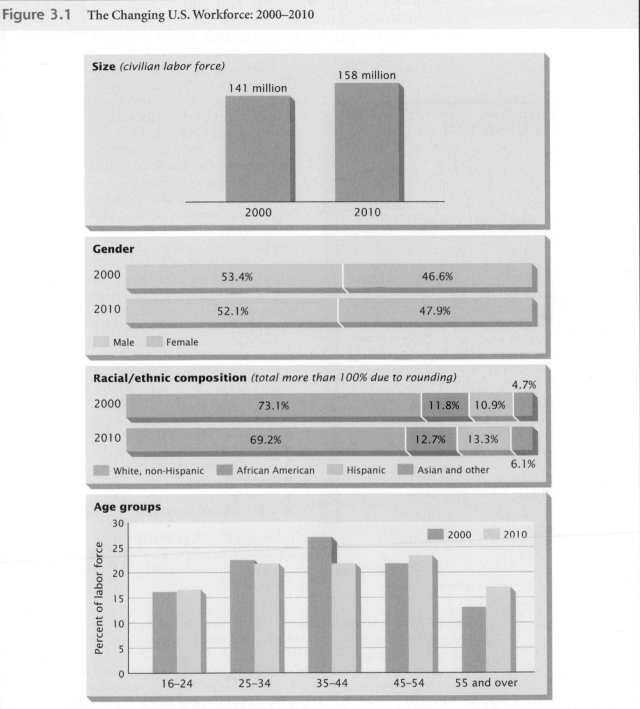

**Size** *(civilian labor force)*

141 million — 2000
158 million — 2010

**Gender**

2000: Male 53.4% / Female 46.6%
2010: Male 52.1% / Female 47.9%

☐ Male  ☐ Female

**Racial/ethnic composition** *(total more than 100% due to rounding)*

2000: 73.1% | 11.8% | 10.9% | 4.7%
2010: 69.2% | 12.7% | 13.3% | 6.1%

☐ White, non-Hispanic  ☐ African American  ☐ Hispanic  ☐ Asian and other

**Age groups**

Percent of labor force

(2000 and 2010 by age group: 16–24, 25–34, 35–44, 45–54, 55 and over)

*Source:* Data and bottom figure from U.S. Department of Labor, Bureau of Labor Statistics, "Tomorrow's Jobs," *Occupational Outlook Handbook,* 2002–2003 edition, **http://stats.bls.gov.**

**Needed: On-the-Job Remedial Education.**  While demographics foretell possible labor shortages in the near term, the picture for employers grows worse when the issue of labor force *quality* is put on the table. In the United States, the numbers are not encouraging. At present, the U.S. workforce is at a competitive disadvantage globally because of deficient reading, writing, science, and basic math skills.[6] According to the American Management Association, "More than a third of job applicants tested in reading and math in 2000 lacked the basic skills necessary to perform the jobs they sought,"[7] sharply up from 19 percent in 1997.

Experts say about 20 percent of working adults in the United States are *functionally illiterate,* meaning they have difficulty with basic life skills such as reading a newspaper, completing a job application, or interpreting a bus schedule. In other words, 23 to 27 million U.S. workers could not comprehend the paragraph you are now reading. Another 12 million would struggle to do so.[8] According to the National Jewish Coalition for Literacy: "illiteracy costs the USA about $225 billion a year in lost productivity."[9] Consequently, many businesses, often in partnership with local schools and colleges, have launched remedial education programs. A recent *Training* magazine survey of 1,652 companies with 100 or more employees found a broad corporate commitment to remedial education; the following skills were being taught at indicated percentages of the companies surveyed:

- Basic life/work skills (71 percent)
- English as a second language (41 percent)
- Remedial math (42 percent)
- Remedial reading (37 percent)
- Remedial writing (41 percent)
- Welfare-to-work transition (35 percent)[10]

These remedial programs typically involve an intensive schedule of small-group sessions emphasizing practical, work-related instruction. Knowledge is the entry ticket to today's computerized service economy.

---

### 3B  A Curious Educational System

Craig R. Barrett, CEO, Intel Corp., on the U.S. educational system:

*The educational system basically hasn't changed in the past century, and it hasn't recognized that there is international competition. It hasn't really recognized that our university system is popular with graduate students from foreign countries because it's the best university system in the world. More than 50% of the degrees in engineering are granted to foreign nationals. It hasn't recognized that, very methodically and consistently, what you are doing is dumbing down the U.S. citizenry and educating the rest of the globe. It hasn't fully recognized that the standard of living is going to be dependent on the quality of the workforce.*

**Source:** As quoted in "U.S. System Helps Educate the World, Yet Fails at Home," *USA Today* (November 8, 2001): 15A.

**Questions:** *How can a country with a supposedly weak K-through-12 educational system be a world leader in higher education? Do you agree or disagree with Barrett's "dumbing down" claim? What improvements need to be made?*

---

**Myths About Older Workers.**  As documented earlier, the U.S. workforce is getting older. Strengthening this tendency is a recent reversal in the long-standing trend toward early retirement. In 2000, "12.8 percent of people ages 65 and older were in the workforce, the most since 1979."[11] While we're on the subject, how old is old? According to a nationwide survey of 2,503 Americans between the ages of 18 and 75, the answer depends on how old *you* are! "Among those over 65, only 8 percent think of people under 65 as old, while 30 percent of those under 25 say 'old' is anywhere from 40 to 64."[12] Older workers, defined by the U.S. Department of Labor as those aged 55 and up, tend to be burdened by a negative image in America's youth-oriented culture.[13] Researchers have identified and disproved five stubborn myths about older workers:

*Myth:*  *Older workers are less productive than the average worker.*
*Fact:*  *Research shows that productivity does not decline with a worker's age. Older employees perform as well as younger workers in most jobs. Moreover, older workers meet the productivity expectations. . . .*

In our youth-obsessed culture, older people often are assumed to have obsolete skills and are pushed aside. That's not the case with 78-year-old Cecilia Bearchum from the Umatilla Indian Reservation in Oregon. A new Oregon law allows tribal elders who lack college degrees to teach Native American languages in public schools, using a special teaching permit. The idea is to revive interest in Native American languages. Ryan Branstetter, one-quarter Walla Walla Indian, appreciates Bearchum's teaching and wisdom.

Myth:   The costs of employee benefits outweigh any possible gain from hiring older workers.

Fact:   The costs of health insurance increase with age, but most other fringe benefits do not since they are tied to length of service and level of salary. A study at The Travelers Companies found that it was not safe to assume that older workers cost more or less than younger workers. . . .

Myth:   Older workers are prone to frequent absences because of age-related infirmities and above-average rates of sickness.

Fact:   Data show that workers age 65 and over have attendance records that are equal to or better than most other age groups of workers. Older people who are not working may have dropped out of the workforce because of their health. Older workers who stay in the labor force may well represent a self-selected healthier group of older people.

Myth:   Older workers have an unacceptably high rate of accidents at work.

Fact:   Data show that older workers account for only 9.7 percent of all workplace injuries while they make up 13.6 percent of the labor force. . . .

Myth:   Older workers are unwilling to learn new jobs and [are] inflexible about the hours they will work.

Fact:   The truth depends on the individual. Studies of older employees' interest in alternative work arrangements found that many were interested in altering their work hours and their jobs. They were particularly interested in part-time work.[14]

Enlightened employers view older workers as an underutilized and valuable resource in an aging society facing a labor shortage.[15] Like all employees, older workers need to be managed according to their individual abilities, not as members of a demographic group.

# A New Social Contract Between Employer and Employee

Between World War II and the 1970s there was an implicit cultural agreement, a social contract, in the United States between employers and employees: "Be loyal to the company and the company will take care of you until retirement." But then the 1980s and 1990s brought restructuring, downsizing, and layoffs. With the dawn of the twenty-first century came a recession that only made matters worse. In 2001, 2.5 million employees in the United States were put out of work by layoffs involving 50 or more people.[16] The traditional social contract between employers and employees had been broken. In its place is a new social contract, framed in these terms:

> *In short, the rules of the game have changed, and they go something like this: Your career depends on you, and you had better work at increasing your own long-term value, because nobody is going to do it for you. Employers, in turn, have accepted this reality: In the new marketplace for talent, we must provide opportunities, resources, and rewards for the continual development of our workforce or risk losing our greatest competitive asset.*[17]

**new social contract**
*assumption that employer-employee relationship will be a shorter-term one based on convenience and mutual benefit, rather than for life*

Thus, the **new social contract** is based not on the notion of lifetime employment with a single employer but rather on shorter-term relationships of convenience and mutual benefit.[18] The senior vice president of human resources at AT&T, Harold Burlingame, put it more bluntly:

> *There was a time when someone would come to the front door of AT&T and see an invisible sign that said, AT & T: A JOB FOR LIFE. . . . That's over. Now it's a shared kind of thing. Come to us. We'll invest in you, and you invest in us. Together, we'll face the market, and the degree to which we succeed will determine how things work out.*[19]

# Nagging Inequalities in the Workplace

Can the United States achieve full and lasting international competitiveness if a large proportion of its workforce suffers nagging inequalities? Probably not. Unfortunately, women, minorities, and part-timers often encounter barriers in the workplace. Let us open our discussion by focusing on women because their plight is shared by all minorities to varying degrees.

**Under the Glass Ceiling.**  As a large and influential minority, women are demanding—and getting—a greater share of workplace opportunities. Women occupy 47 percent of the managerial and administrative positions in the U.S. civilian workforce. Still, a large inequity remains. In 2001, the median weekly salary for those women managers was $706, compared with $1,060 for their male counterparts (a 33 percent shortfall).[20] Across all job categories—from top business executives to lawyers, physicians, and office workers—the same sort of gender pay gap can be found.[21] This gap has expanded and contracted at various times since the 1950s in the United States, with the shortfall actually *growing* for women managers between 1995 and 2000.[22] In the United States, the gender pay gap can be summed up in two words: *large* and *persistent*. Comparatively well-paid men can grasp the significance of the gender wage gap by pondering the impact on their standard of living of a 33 percent pay cut. Moreover, men who share household expenses with a woman wage earner are also penalized by the gender wage gap.

**glass ceiling**  *the transparent but strong barrier keeping women and minorities from moving up the management ladder*

In addition to suffering a wage gap, women (and other minorities) bump up against the so-called glass ceiling when climbing the managerial ladder.[23] "The **glass ceiling** is a concept popularized in the 1980s to describe a barrier so subtle that it is transparent, yet so strong that it prevents women and minorities from moving up in the management hierarchy."[24] It is not unique to the United States.

Consider the situation in 2002:

- The *Fortune* 500, America's largest corporations, were headed by 495 men (3 of them African American) and 5 women.[25]
- Women "held just 12% of all Standard & Poor's 500 corporate board seats."[26] (A sign of progress: 21 percent of the new board members in 2000 were women.)

Why is there a glass ceiling? According to *Working Woman* magazine, women are being held back by "the lingering perception of women as outsiders, exclusion from informal networks, male stereotyping and lack of experience."[27]

Another force is also at work here, siphoning off some of the best female executive talent part way up the corporate ladder. Many women are leaving the corporate ranks to start their own businesses. About 6.2 million businesses in the United States were owned by women in 2002, up 14 percent from five years earlier (double the growth rate for all companies).[28]

### Continuing Pressure for Equal Opportunity.

Persistent racial inequality is underscored by the fact that the unemployment rate for African Americans generally is about twice as high as that for whites during both good and bad economic times.[29] Women, African-Americans, Hispanics, Native Americans, the physically challenged, and other minorities who are overrepresented in either low-level, low-paying jobs or the unemployment line can be expected to press harder to become full partners in the world of work. Equal employment opportunity (EEO) and affirmative action are discussed in Chapter 11.

### Part-Timer Promises and Problems.

An increasing percentage of the U.S. labor force is now made up of **contingent workers.** Estimates vary widely. According to the U.S. Bureau of Labor Statistics, "using three alternative measures, contingent workers accounted for 1.7 percent to 4.0 percent of total employment in February 2001."[30] This "just-in-time" or "flexible" workforce includes a diverse array of part-timers, temporary workers, and self-employed contractors. "Their common denominator is that they do not have a long-term implicit contract with their ultimate employers, the purchasers of the labor and services they provide."[31] Employers are relying more on part-timers for two basic reasons. First, because they are paid at lower rates and often do not receive the full range of employer-paid benefits, part-timers are much less costly to employ than full-time employees.[32] Second, as a flexible workforce, they can be let go when times are bad, without the usual repercussions of a general layoff.

On the down side, research indicates that part-time employees tend to have more negative work attitudes than their full-time coworkers. In addition, part-timers express less organizational loyalty and quit more readily than full-timers.[33] Also, critics warn of the risk of creating a permanent underclass of employees. Indeed, retirement benefits are a rarity for contingent workers. While some highly skilled professionals enjoy good pay and greater freedom by working part time, most part-timers do not.

*. . . the fact is that contingent work dooms a great many people to a much lower standard of living than they enjoyed as core workers. Even discounting the lower wages that many of them earn and the fact that they have no fringe benefits, such as health care or disability insurance, to buoy them in case of disaster, the very precariousness of their work situation*

---

**3C**

### Is Race the Issue?

Kenneth Chenault, on being named CEO of American Express Corp.:

*From a societal standpoint, it's a big deal; I won't minimize it. . . . But I want them to say, "He's a terrific CEO," not "He's a terrific black CEO."*

**Source:** As quoted in Nelson D. Schwartz, "What's in the cards for AMEX?" *Fortune* (January 22, 2001): 60.

**Question:** *What is the real message here?*

---

**contingent workers** *part-timers and other employees who do not have a long-term implicit contract with their ultimate employers* *makes it hard for them to get ahead. A low-income worker, for instance, will find it especially hard to qualify for a home loan if he is employed on a contingent basis, subject to layoff at any time.*[34]

The plight of part-timers promises to become a major social and political issue worldwide in the years to come.[35]

# Managing Diversity

The United States, a nation of immigrants, is becoming even more racially and ethnically diverse. The evidence is compelling:

- Out of every 100 new U.S. residents, 64 are native born and 34 are *legal* immigrants.[36]
- "The country will become a nation of minorities. Whites accounted for about 71% of the population . . . [in 2000,] but by 2050, the number will drop to 53%, blacks will increase one percentage point (to 13.2%), Asians will more than double to 8.9% (from 3.9%), and Hispanics will jump to 24.3% (from 11.8%)."[37]
- "California joins New Mexico and half of the 100 largest U.S. cities, as well as numerous counties along the U.S.-Mexico border, where Caucasians do not constitute a clear majority."[38]
- *Sonia Perez, National Council of La Raza:* "A third of the Latinos are under 18, so this is going to be the future of the workforce in the U.S."[39]

**3** Define the term *managing diversity* and explain why it is particularly important today.

**managing diversity**
*process of helping all employees, including women and minorities, reach their full potential*

Accordingly, the U.S. workforce is becoming more culturally diverse. For example, the employees at some Marriott Hotels speak 30 different languages.[40] Some Americans decry what they consider to be an invasion of "their" national and organizational "territories." But many others realize that America's immigrants and minorities have always been a vitalizing, creative, hardworking force.[41] Progressive organizations are taking steps to better accommodate and more fully utilize America's more diverse workforce. **Managing diversity** is the process of creating an organizational culture that enables *all* employees, including women and minorities, to realize their full potential.[42]

**More than EEO.**    Managing diversity builds on equal employment opportunity (EEO) and affirmative action programs (discussed in Chapter 11). EEO and affirmative action are necessary to get more women and minorities into the workplace. But getting them in is not enough. Comprehensive diversity programs are needed to create more *flexible* organizations where *everyone* has a fair chance to thrive and succeed.[43] These programs need to include white males who have sometimes felt slighted or ignored by EEO and affirmative action; they, too, have individual differences (opinions, lifestyles, age, and schedules) that deserve fair accommodation. Managing diversity requires many of us to adjust our thinking. According to sociologist Jack McDevitt, "We don't want to have as a goal just tolerating people. We have to *value* them."[44] In addition to being the ethical course of action, managing diversity is a necessity; a nation cannot waste human potential and remain globally competitive.

**Promising Beginnings.**    Among the diversity programs in use today are the following:

**Be yourself.** Race. Ethnicity. Religion. Nationality. Gender. In the end, there's just one variety of human being. The individual. All six billion of us. **Be bullish.**

ml.com

Stock broker Merrill Lynch uses its famous Wall Street bull to give diversity a boost in this advertisement. (And there's only one race—the human race.)

- Teaching English as a second language.
- Creating mentor programs (an experienced employee coaches and sponsors a newcomer).
- Providing immigration assistance.
- Fostering the development of support groups for minorities.
- Training minorities for managerial positions.
- Training managers to value and skillfully manage diversity.
- Actively recruiting minorities.[45]

The scope of managing diversity is limited only by management's depth of commitment and imagination.[46] For example, a supervisor learns sign language to communicate with a hearing-impaired employee. Or a married male manager attends a diversity workshop and becomes aware of the difficulties of being a single working mother. Perhaps a younger manager's age bias is blunted after reading a research report documenting that older employees tend to be absent less often and have lower accident rates than younger ones.[47] Maybe other companies begin to follow Corning's diversity policy, whereby "new employees are no longer encouraged to adopt the dress, style, and social activities of the white male majority."[48] (See Managing Diversity.)

# Managing Diversity

## The New Look of Black Leadership

No one can pinpoint exactly when the ground shifted, when it became possible for a black American male to join the gods of the corporate universe. Like the moment when darkness yields to dawn, it crept up quietly, largely unperceived. We awakened and a new day had come. But if we must mark our awareness of that day's arrival, put down Jan. 1, 1999, the day Franklin Raines, former director of the federal Office of Management and Budget, took over as chairman and CEO of Fannie Mae, becoming the first African-American to head a major American corporation. Since then, few have fared as well. A. Barry Rand was named head of Avis in November 1999 but didn't survive the transfer of ownership in 2001. Lloyd Ward, named top man at Maytag, also in 1999, lasted little more than a year before walking away amid reports of conflict with his board. But [in 2001] the ground shifted again, and suddenly it became significantly less lonely at the top, as three black men prepared to take their place at the pinnacle of some of America's most important companies.

As miracles go, this corporate trifecta does not exactly rank with the parting of the sea. But that a group of talented executives who are also black could so nonchalantly take the reins of three huge companies says something important about the expansion of opportunity (at least for a few) in an arena that, until very recently, might as well have hung BLACKS NOT ALLOWED signs on the door. And it's not just the corporate world that is embracing authority figures who happen to be black. Washington has grown accustomed to seeing the president take foreign-policy lessons from two African-Americans. . . . Indeed, there is no major area of American life these days, from education to politics to religion, where society is not coming to terms with a new black leadership class—one

whose credentials, in many cases, have very little to do with their color, and one whose very existence raises questions about the continuing viability of the "black leadership" model of old.

Under the old model, a handful of leaders (virtually all male and generally preachers—but often politicians, educators, or some fusion of the three) supposedly represented the black community. Over the past several decades, as blacks have entered and conquered a host of previously forbidden realms, thanks in large measure to the civil-rights movement's storied successes, the very idea that one person (or handful of "leaders") could speak on all matters for entire racial groups has begun to seem increasingly silly. . . .

The confusion stems in part from uncertainty over just how to classify many of the members of this new leadership class. Are they "black leaders," or are they something else? Corporate leaders whose color is irrelevant? Political leaders who happen to have mostly black constituencies? And whom exactly do they speak for, other than themselves? . . .

Such questions miss an important point: that in this age of falling racial barriers our leaders will have to be as diverse as we are. Some will be preoccupied with the continuing battle for equality; some will focus primarily on other things. And we, of course, will judge them in line with our own particular preoccupations. For people who insist on seeing blacks as a monolith, the notion that blacks are as complicated and varied as whites may take some getting used to—but to argue otherwise would be to assume that we are lesser (more simple) human beings.

*Source:* Excerpted from Ellis Cose, "Rethinking Black Leadership." From *Newsweek* (January 28, 2002): 42–43. © 2002 Newsweek, Inc. All rights reserved. Reprinted by permission.

---

**4** Discuss how the changing political-legal environment is affecting the practice of management.

# The Political-Legal Environment

In its broadest terms, *politics* is the art (or science) of public influence and control. Laws are an outcome of the political process that differentiate good and bad conduct. An orderly political process is necessary because modern society is the product of an

*Reggie James, head of the Southwest Office of Consumer's Union, spends most of his time lobbying Texas state legislators and drafting bills on behalf of consumers. But he's also a manager who has an office to run. Here he leads a staff meeting at the Consumer's Union office in Austin. James and his staff must have all their facts straight before launching a lobbying campaign.*

evolving consensus among diverse individuals and groups, often with conflicting interests and objectives. Although the list of special-interest groups is long and still growing, not everyone can have his or her own way. The political system tries to balance competing interests in a generally acceptable manner.

Ideally, elected officials pass laws that, when enforced, control individual and collective conduct for the general good. Unfortunately, as we all know, variables such as hollow campaign promises, illegal campaign financing, and voter apathy throw sand into a democracy's political gears. A prime example is Russia's transition to democracy. In its 1993 multiparty election, the first since 1917, the combination of wild promises and low voter turnout helped give control of its parliament to radical antireformers.[49] Managers, as both citizens and caretakers of socially, politically, and economically powerful organizations, have a large stake in the political-legal environment. Two key pressure points for managers in this area are the politicization of management and increased personal legal accountability.

## The Politicization of Management

Prepared or not and willing or not, today's managers often find themselves embroiled in issues with clearly political overtones.[50] Just ask the Walt Disney Company. In 1994 Disney abandoned plans to build a history-oriented theme park in Virginia in the face of public outcry about dishonoring nearby Civil War battlefields.[51] Another political bombshell exploded in

**3D A Political Awakening on Campus?**

Results of a survey of 281,064 college freshmen at 421 schools:

*More U.S. college freshmen are politically liberal or "far left" than at any time since 1975, says an annual survey . . . that suggests a rebirth of interest in politics after decades of campus apathy. . . .*

*Some 30% of freshmen say they're liberals, compared with 21% in 1981. Popularity of the "liberal" label has increased for five consecutive years. . . . About 49% now are "middle-of-the-road" and 21% "conservative" or "far right."*

**Source:** Marilyn Elias, "Boomer Echo: College Freshmen Look Liberal," *USA Today* (January 28, 2002): 5D.

**Questions:** *In political terms, what do the labels "conservative" and "liberal" mean to you? Is the shift toward liberal politics among college students a good or bad thing? Why?*

1996. "The Southern Baptist Convention, 16 million members strong, threatened . . . to boycott Walt Disney's parks, movies and products to protest Disney's departure from its 'family-values image.' The chief complaint: Disney gives health benefits to companions of gay employees."[52] This time, Disney did not give in to pressure. Disney's official response: "We question any group that demands that we deprive people of health benefits."[53] This sort of political pressure has spurred the growth of a practice called *issues management.*

**issues management**

*ongoing process of identifying, evaluating, and responding to important social and political issues*

**Issues Management.**     **Issues management** (IM) is defined as the ongoing organizational process of identifying, evaluating, and responding to relevant and important social and political issues. According to a pair of experts on the subject:

> *The purpose of IM is twofold. First, it attempts to minimize "surprises" which accompany social and political change by serving as an early warning system for potential environment threats and opportunities. IM analyzes the past development of an issue and assesses its importance for the firm. Second, IM attempts to prompt more systematic and effective responses to particular issues by serving as a coordinating and integrating force within the corporation. Once the issue has been analyzed, IM constructs alternative responses to deal with competing internal and external demands.*[54]

IM is not an exact science. It has been carried out in various ways in the name of strategic planning, public relations, community affairs, and corporate communications, among others. IM's main contribution to good management is its emphasis on systematic preparedness for social and political action. With this background in mind, let us turn our attention to three general political responses and four specific political strategies.

**General Political Responses.**     The three general political responses available to management can be plotted on a continuum, as illustrated in Figure 3.2. Managers who are politically inactive occupy the middle neutral zone and have a "wait and see" attitude. But few managers today can afford the luxury of a neutral political stance. Those on the extreme left of the continuum are politically active in defending the status quo and/or fighting government intervention. In contrast, politically active managers on the right end of the continuum try to identify and respond constructively to emerging political/legal issues.

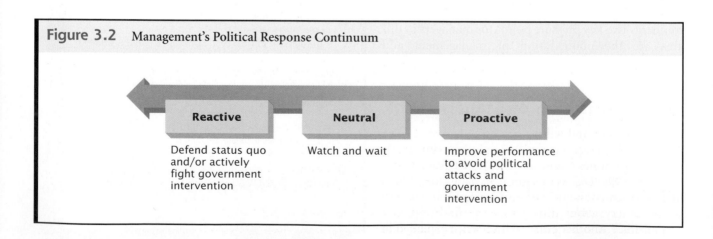

**Figure 3.2**     Management's Political Response Continuum

| Reactive | Neutral | Proactive |
|---|---|---|
| Defend status quo and/or actively fight government intervention | Watch and wait | Improve performance to avoid political attacks and government intervention |

In recent years, more and more business managers have swung away from being reactive and become proactive. Why? In short, they view prompt action as a way to avoid additional governmental regulation. The wisdom of choosing a proactive stance is clearly illustrated by the recent experiences of Microsoft and Intel. Both are dominant players in their respective fields of software and computer chips. According to *Harvard Business Review*:

> *For years now, Microsoft has been mired in court, facing charges of predatory behavior by the U.S. Department of Justice and the attorneys general of more than a dozen states. It has seen its name and business practices dragged through the mud, its senior executives distracted and embarrassed, and its very future as a single company thrown into doubt. . . .*
>
> *Intel, in stark contrast, has managed to avoid prolonged, high-profile antitrust cases. It's remained above the fray, its business focus largely undisturbed by trustbusters.*
>
> *Intel's success is not a matter of luck. It's a matter of painstaking planning and intense effort. The company's antitrust compliance program, refined over many years, may not receive a lot of attention from the press and the public, but it's been an integral element in the chip maker's business strategy.*[55]

**Specific Political Strategies.**    Whether acting reactively or proactively, managers can employ four major strategies.[56]

1. *Campaign financing.* Although federal law prohibits U.S. corporations from backing a specific candidate or party with the firm's name, funds, or free labor, a legal alternative is available. Corporations can form political action committees (PACs) to solicit volunteer contributions from employees biannually for the support of preferred candidates and parties.[57] Importantly, PACs are registered with the Federal Election Commission and are required to keep detailed and accurate records of receipts and expenditures. Some criticize corporate PACs for having too great an influence over federal politics. But legislators are reluctant to tamper with a funding mechanism that tends to favor those already in office.

2. *Lobbying.* Historically, lobbying has been management's most popular and successful political strategy. Secret and informal meetings between hired representatives and key legislators in smoke-filled rooms have largely been replaced by a more forthright approach. Today, formal presentations by well-prepared company representatives are the preferred approach to lobbying for political support.[58] Despite lobbying reform legislation from the U.S. Congress in response to abuses, loopholes, and weak penalties for inappropriate gifts, it is pretty much business as usual for corporate lobbyists.[59]

3. *Coalition building.* In a political environment of countless special-interest groups, managers are finding that coalitions built around common rallying points are required for political impact.

4. *Indirect lobbying.* Having learned a lesson from unions, business managers now appreciate the value of grassroots lobbying. Members of legislative bodies tend to be more responsive to the

**3E  Give 'til It Hurts!**

How executives responded to a survey about why U.S. businesses contribute to political campaigns:

| | |
|---|---|
| Support electoral process | 12% |
| Promote an ideology | 22% |
| Avoid negative legislation | 31% |
| Buy access for influence | 23% |
| Other | 12% |

**Source:**  Adapted from "Business of Campaign Contributions," *USA Today* (November 7, 2000): 1B.

**Questions:**  *Are corporate political contributions "good business" or "dirty business"? Explain. What changes, if any, need to be made in the system?*

desires of their constituents than to those of individuals who vote in other districts. Employee and consumer letter-writing, telephone, and e-mail campaigns have

**advocacy advertising**
*promoting a point of view along
with a product or service*

proved effective. **Advocacy advertising,** the controversial practice of promoting a point of view along with a product or service, is another form of indirect lobbying that has grown in popularity in recent years.[60]

## Increased Personal Legal Accountability

Recent changes in the political and legal climate have made it increasingly difficult for managers to take refuge in the bureaucratic shadows when a law has been broken. Managers in the United States who make illegal decisions stand a good chance of being held personally accountable in a court of law.

Things got even tougher in July 2002, when President George W. Bush signed into law a sweeping corporate fraud bill driven by an unusually high degree of bipartisan cooperation. The lawmakers were prodded into decisive action by public disgust over the fraud-tainted failures of corporate giants including Enron, Andersen, WorldCom, and Adelphia.

> The law, which passed the Senate by 99-0 and the House by 423-3, quadruples sentences for accounting fraud, creates a new felony for securities fraud that carries a 25-year prison term, places new restraints on corporate officers, and establishes a federal oversight board for the accounting industry.
>
> "No more easy money for corporate criminals, just hard time," the president said. "The era of low standards and false profits is over, no boardroom in America is above or beyond the law."[61]

This greatly increases the likelihood of managers being held *personally responsible* for the illegal actions of their companies. The trend is spreading to other countries as well.

Misguided folks who do not heed this warning can take some comfort in a new Dallas, Texas, consulting service.

> The company is the nation's only felon-run consulting service that preps newly convicted white-collar crooks on what to expect once they get to prison, coaching them about how to make their hard time easier—a sort of school for scoundrels. . . .
>
> [According to the consultant, a three-time loser for investment scams,] a lot of white-collar crooks, represented by some of the nation's best lawyers, were utterly clueless about life behind bars. . . .[62]

## Political-Legal Implications for Management

Managers will continue to be forced into becoming more politically astute, whether they like it or not. Support appears to be growing for the idea that managers can and should try to shape the political climate in which they operate. And the vigilant media and a wary public can be expected to keep a close eye on the form and substance of managerial politics to ensure that the public interest is served. Managers who abuse their political power and/or engage in criminal conduct while at work will increasingly be held accountable.

On the legal side, managers are attempting to curb the skyrocketing costs of litigation. Suing large companies with so-called deep pockets is common practice in the United States today. For example, consider the landslide of class-action lawsuits involving the tread separation/rollover issue facing Bridgestone/Firestone Inc. and Ford Motor Co.[63] *Business Week* recently tracked down the bill for all this litigation:

*Tillinghast-Towers Perrin, a management consultant with a specialty in insurance issues, estimates that the overall annual cost of the American tort system, including payments to injured people, legal fees, and administrative expenses, was at least $165 billion in 1999. That was about 2% of gross domestic product—twice as much as in most industrial countries.*[64]

Managers can better prepare their companies and hopefully avoid costly legal problems by performing legal audits. A **legal audit** reviews all aspects of a firm's operations to pinpoint possible liabilities and other legal problems.[65] For example, a company's job application forms need to be carefully screened by the human resources department to eliminate any questions that could trigger a discriminatory hiring lawsuit. Another approach, called **alternative dispute resolution** (ADR), strives to curb courtroom costs by settling disagreements out of court through techniques such as arbitration and mediation.

**legal audit**   *review of all operations to pinpoint possible legal liabilities or problems*

*The modern ADR phenomenon has led to much greater use of older methods such as arbitration and mediation, as well as the creation of many new methods such as mini-trial, summary jury trial, private judging, neutral evaluation, and regulatory negotiation. Variations and hybrids of these techniques are also commonly found today.*[66]

**alternative dispute resolution**   *avoiding courtroom battles by settling disputes with less costly methods, including arbitration and mediation*

As a technical point, a third-party arbitrator makes a binding decision, whereas a mediator helps the parties reach their own agreement.

# The Economic Environment

As stated in Chapter 1, there is a close relationship between economics and management. Economics is the study of how scarce resources are used to create wealth and how that wealth is distributed. Managers, as trustees of our resource-consuming productive organizations, perform an essentially economic function.

Three aspects of the economic environment of management deserving special consideration are jobs, business cycles, and the global economy.

## The Job Outlook in Today's Service Economy, Where Education Counts

As in other important aspects of life, you have no guarantee of landing your dream job. However, as you move through college and into the labor force, one assumption is safe: you will probably end up with a service-producing job. Why? "According to the [U.S.] Bureau of Labor Statistics, the service economy is expected to account for 19.1 million of the 19.5 million total new wage and salary jobs generated over the 1998–2008 period."[67]

The traditional notion of the service sector as a low-wage haven of nothing but hamburger flippers and janitors is no longer valid. Well-paid doctors, lawyers, airline pilots, engineers, scientists, consultants, and other professionals are all service-sector employees enjoying the fruits of a good education. Economists at the U.S. Bureau of Labor Statistics see it this way: "Occupations that require a bachelor's degree are projected to grow the fastest, nearly twice as fast as the average for all occupations. All of the 20 occupations with the highest earnings require at least a bachelor's degree. . . . Education is essential in getting a high paying job."[68]

# Coping with Business Cycles

**business cycle**   *the up-and-down movement of an economy's ability to generate wealth*

The **business cycle** is the up-and-down movement of an economy's ability to generate wealth; it has a predictable structure but variable timing. Historical economic data from industrialized economies show a clear pattern of alternating expansions and recessions. In between have been peaks and troughs of varying magnitude and duration. According to Nobel economist Paul Samuelson, the four phases are like the changing seasons: "Each phase passes into the next. Each is characterized by different economic conditions: for example, during expansion we find that employment, production, prices, money, wages, interest rates, and profits are usually rising, with the reverse true in recession."[69]

**5**  Discuss why business cycles and the global economy are vital economic considerations for modern managers.

**Cycle-Sensitive Decisions.**    Important decisions depend on the ebb and flow of the business cycle (see Figure 3.3). These decisions include ordering inventory, borrowing funds, increasing staff, and spending capital for land, equipment, and energy.

*Timing* is everything when it comes to making good cycle-sensitive decisions. Just as a baseball batter needs to start swinging before the ball reaches home plate, managers need to make appropriate cutbacks prior to the onset of a recession. Failure to do so, in the face of decreasing sales, leads to bloated inventories and idle productive resources—both costly situations. On the other hand, managers cannot afford to get caught short during a period of rapid expansion. Prices and wages rise sharply when everyone is purchasing inventories and hiring at the same time.

The trick is to stay slightly ahead of the pack. This is particularly true during recessions, when corporate strategy is tested to the fullest. According to a leading management consultant: "Successful players in a downturn place counterintuitive bets in order to dramatically transform their market positions, but these bets are not lucky gambles that miraculously win big against the odds. Instead they are rigorous and systematic moves that shift the odds in management's favor."[70] Consider the following example

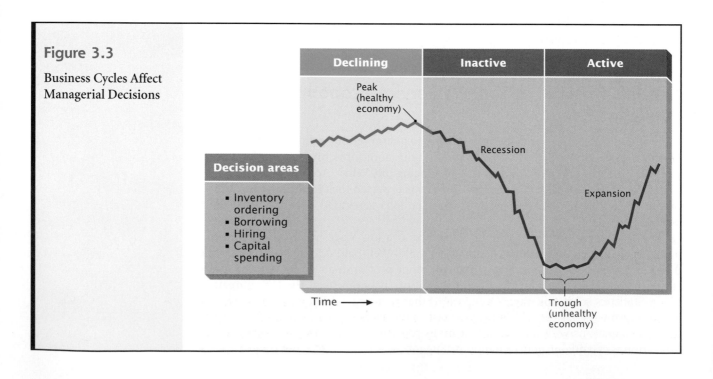

**Figure 3.3**

**Business Cycles Affect Managerial Decisions**

reported by *Business Week* after the September 11, 2001, terrorist attacks on the United States hammered an economy already in recession:

> While other hotel executives have been trekking to Washington seeking relief for their hard-hit sector, Hilton Hotels Chief Executive Stephen F. Bollenbach has taken a different tack. He has been spending liberally to renovate such top-of-the-line properties as the San Francisco Hilton & Towers. And instead of remodeling just a planned five floors at a time, he's overhauling 10 at a bound—taking advantage of slack occupancies at the 1,900-room site to replace everything from furniture to draperies.[71]

Bollenbach's strategy was simple: take market share from more timid competitors. Time will tell if it was a good cycle-sensitive move. As mentioned repeatedly in this text, successful managers are *foresighted* rather than hindsighted. Accurate economic forecasts can be very helpful in this regard.

**3F  The Economy: Surf's Up! Surf's Down!**

James Morgan, long-time CEO of Applied Materials, maker of equipment for computer chip manufacturers:

*. . . problems show up like the rocks in a bay when the tide is out. You can develop a navigation plan. When the water is up, you don't know where the rocks are. Use downturns to find areas that need to be improved. In an upturn you're responding to orders, meeting capacity, getting parts in. That's why when it starts to slow down, things unravel pretty quickly. I'm usually out of sync with the public. I'm focused on the next transition. I've developed the skill of anticipation.*

**Source:** Del Jones, "Use Recession to Plan for Next Level," *USA Today* (February 1, 2002): 6B.

**Question:** *Why does it take* bad *economic times to make a truly* good *manager?*

**Benefiting from Economic Forecasts.** In view of the fact that Congress's economic advisers accurately predicted the U.S. economy's output only one-third of the time between 1980 and 1994,[72] economic forecasting has come under fire lately.[73] One wit chided economic forecasters by claiming they have predicted eight out of the last four recessions! How can managers get some value from the hundreds of economic forecasts they encounter each year?

A pair of respected forecasting experts recommends a *consensus approach.*[74] They urge managers to survey a wide variety of economic forecasts, taking the forecasters' track records into consideration, and to look for a consensus or average opinion. Cycle-sensitive decisions can then be made accordingly, and slavish adherence to a single forecast avoided. One sure formula for failure is naively to assume that the future will simply be a replication of the past. In spite of their imperfection, professional economic forecasts are better than no forecasts at all. One economist puts it this way: "Forecasters are very useful, in fact indispensable, because they give you plausible scenarios to help you think about the future in an organized way."[75]

# The Challenge of a Global Economy

The global economy is expanding today as international trade increases. "International trade now accounts for almost 20% of global gross domestic product, up from just 10% a decade ago."[76] Each of us is challenged to understand the workings and implications of the global economy better in light of its profound impact on our lives and work.

**A Single Global Marketplace.**    Money spent on imported Japanese cars, French perfumes, Colombian coffee, New Zealand meat and produce, German beers, and Italian shoes may be evidence of an increasingly global economy. Deeper analysis, however, reveals more profound changes. First, according to John Naisbitt's and Patricia

*Although Sbarro, the Italian restaurant chain, has its corporate headquarters in Melville, New York, it does business around the world. Slices of its thick-crust pizza can be purchased just about anywhere— from New Zealand to Japan, from Kuwait to Chile. Unique challenges are presented by each different country and culture. This Sbarro restaurant in Israel, for example, does a brisk business despite a bomb attack in 2001.*

Aburdene's book *Megatrends 2000,* "The new global economy . . . must be viewed as the world moving from trade among countries to a single economy. One economy. One marketplace."[77] Both the North American Free Trade Agreement (NAFTA) among Mexico, Canada, and the United States and the 134-nation World Trade Organization (WTO) represent steps toward that single global marketplace. Second, the size of the global economy has expanded dramatically. *Fortune* explains why:

> *. . . the commercial world has been swelled by the former Soviet empire, China, India, Indonesia, and much of Latin America—billions of people stepping out from behind political and economic walls. This is the most dramatic change in the geography of capitalism in history.*[78]

Third, and an ominous sign to some, the business cycles of countries around the world show signs of converging in concert with the U.S. economy. International Monetary Fund economists recently documented this trend after studying 20 years of economic data from 170 countries: "They found that an increase of one percentage point in the growth of U.S. output per capita was associated with an increase of 0.8 to 1.0 percentage point in the average growth of other countries. Decreases in U.S. output likewise lowered growth elsewhere."[79] The prospect of global expansions and recessions gives new meaning to the old saying, "We're all in the same boat."

**Globalization Is Personal.**    Economic globalization is a huge concept, stretching the limits of the imagination. For instance, try to grasp what it means that more than $1 trillion moves through the global banking network in a single day![80] Ironically, globalization is also a very personal matter affecting where we work, how much we're paid, what we buy, and how much we pay. Let us explore two personal aspects of the global economy:

1. *Working for a foreign-owned company.* One of the most visible and controversial signs of a global economy is the worldwide trend toward foreign ownership. During the 1980s, for example, a Japanese spending spree for prime properties in the

United States caused alarm. Subsequently, with much less fanfare, most of those investments were sold at steep losses as Japan's economy began a decade-long dive in the 1990s. Now Europe's checkbook is out. (In fact, the Boston-based publisher of this textbook was bought by France's Vivendi Universal in 2001.)[81] From 1998 to 2000, European firms led the way as U.S. companies totaling $900 billion were bought by foreigners (as opposed to the $419 billion Americans spent buying foreign companies).[82] Has this increase in foreign-owned companies in the United States been a positive or a negative? Economists have found positive evidence:

> *Americans who work in the USA for foreign companies typically make about 10% more than those who work for U.S. companies, just as foreigners who work for U.S. companies abroad make 10% more than domestic workers there, says Gary Hufbauer, senior economist with the Institute for International Economics.*
>
> *The reason, Hufbauer says, is that companies with the might to expand globally are the most productive, want the best workers and are willing to pay a premium.*[83]

2. *Meeting world standards.* One does not have to work for a foreign-owned company to be personally impacted by the global economy. Many people today complain of having to work harder for the same (or perhaps less) money. Whether they realize it or not, they are being squeezed by two global economic trends: higher quality and lower wages. Only companies striking the right balance between quality and costs can be globally competitive.

---

**3G  Watch Out! Here Come the Cowboy Capitalists**

*Fortune* magazine:

> In the Business world, at least, globalization has meant Americanization.

*USA Today:*

> One idea enshrined in MBA curricula is the primacy of shareholder value: Students learn early that, as managers, their top priority will be to maximize value for shareholders.
>
> That smacks of "cowboy capitalism"—hostile takeovers, large-scale layoffs, golden parachutes—to many Europeans. But today, European corporations find themselves in the midst of an unprecedented frenzy of merger activity and cross-border investment as they scramble to stay competitive with their U.S. counterparts.

**Source:** Janet Guyon, "The American Way," *Fortune* (November 26, 2001): 114; and James Cox, "U.S. Success Draws Envy, Protests," *USA Today* (August 3, 2000): 2B.

**Question:** *Are you pleased or displeased with the economic globalization trend? Explain.*

---

# The Technological Environment

*Technology* is a term that ignites passionate debates in many circles these days. Some blame technology for environmental destruction and cultural fragmentation. Others view technology as the key to economic and social progress. No doubt there are important messages in both extremes. See Table 3.1 for technological shifts likely to have significant impacts on our lives in the future.

For our purposes, **technology** is defined as all the tools and ideas available for extending the natural physical and mental reach of humankind. A central theme in technology is the practical application of new ideas, a theme that is clarified by the following distinction between science and technology: "Science is the quest for more or less abstract knowledge, whereas technology is the application of organized knowledge to help solve problems in our society."[84] According to the following historical perspective, technology is facilitating the evolution of the industrial age into the information age, just as it once enabled the agricultural age to evolve into the industrial age.

**technology** *all the tools and ideas available for extending the natural physical and mental reach of humankind*

**Table 3.1    What Futurists Have to Say About Technological Change**

- Mundane commercial and service jobs, environmentally dangerous jobs, and assembly and repair of space-station components in orbit increasingly will be done by robots. Personal robots will appear in the home by 2010.

- Satellite-based telephone systems and Internet connections and other wireless links will simplify relocation of personnel, minimize delays in accomplishing new installations, and let terminals travel with the user instead of forcing the user to seek out the terminal.

- By 2005, [computerized] expert systems will permeate manufacturing, energy prospecting, automotive diagnostics, medicine, insurance underwriting, and law enforcement.

- Superconductors operating at or near room temperature will be in commercial use soon after 2015. Products will include supercomputers the size of three-pound coffee cans, electric motors 75% smaller and lighter than those of today, practical hydrogen-fusion power plants, electrical storage facilities with no heat loss, and noninvasive analyzers that can chart the interaction of brain cells.

- By 2010, "smart car" technologies will begin to reduce deaths due to auto accidents in the United States and Europe.

- All the technological knowledge we work with today will represent only 1% of the knowledge that will be available in 2050.

- Memory-enhancing drugs should reach clinical use by 2010.

- "Magic bullet" drug-delivery systems will make it possible to direct enormous doses of medication exactly where they are needed, sparing the rest of the body from possible side effects. This will improve therapeutic results in many conditions that require the use of powerful drugs.

- In the next 10 years, we expect to see more and better bionic limbs, hearts, and other organs; drugs that prevent disease rather than merely treating symptoms; and body monitors that warn of impending trouble.

- By 2010, most of the United States will be "wired" for high-speed data access. By 2015, most of the rest of the world will follow.

*Source:*  Originally published in the March-April 2001 issue of *The Futurist*. Used with permission from the World Future Society, 7910 Woodmont Avenue, Suite 450, Bethesda, Maryland 20814. Telephone: 301-656-8274; Fax: 301-951-0394; **http://www.wfs.org**.

*Stephen R. Barley, a professor at Cornell's School of Industrial and Labor Relations, builds on the work of others to argue that until recently, "the economies of the advanced industrial nations revolved around electrical power, the electric motor, the internal combustion engine, and the telephone." The development of these "infrastructural technologies" made possible the shift from an agricultural to a manufacturing economy, in the process precipitating "urbanization, the growth of corporations, the rise of professional management. . . ."*

*Now, Barley writes, the evidence suggests that another shift is taking place, with implications likely to be just as seismic: "Our growing knowledge of how to convert electronic and mechanical impulses into digitally encoded information (and vice versa) and how to transmit such information across vast distances is gradually enabling industry to replace its electromechanical infrastructure with a computational infrastructure."*[85]

Consequently, *information* has become a valuable strategic resource. Organizations using appropriate information technologies to get the right information to the right people at the right time will enjoy a competitive advantage (Internet strategies are discussed in Chapter 7).

Two aspects of technology with important implications for managers are the innovation process and intrapreneurship.

## The Innovation Process

Technology comes into being through the **innovation process,** defined as the systematic development and practical application of a new idea.[86] A great deal of time-consuming work is necessary to develop a new idea into a marketable product or service. And many otherwise good ideas do not become technologically feasible, let alone marketable and profitable. According to one innovation expert, "only one of every 20 or 25 ideas ever becomes a successful product—and of every 10 or 15 new products, only one becomes a hit."[87] A better understanding of the innovation process can help improve management's chances of turning new ideas into profitable goods and services.

**A Three-Step Process.**    The innovation process has three steps (see Figure 3.4). First is the conceptualization step, when a new idea occurs to someone. Development of a working prototype is the second step, called **product technology.** This involves actually creating a product that will work as intended. The third and final step is developing a production process to create a profitable quantity-quality-price relationship. This third step is labeled **production technology.** Successful innovation depends on the right combination of new ideas, product technology, and production technology. A missing or deficient step can ruin the innovation process.

**innovation process**    *the systematic development and practical application of a new idea*

**6** Describe the three-step innovation process and define the term *intrapreneur.*

**product technology**    *second stage of innovation process involving the creation of a working prototype*

**production technology**    *third stage of innovation process involving the development of a profitable production process*

---

**3H | A Slap Shot: "Disruptive Technologies"**

*As hockey great Wayne Gretzky used to say, the key to winning is getting first to where the puck is going next. The same could be said about succeeding in business. . . .*

*The pattern we observed arises out of a key tenet of the concept of "disruptive technologies"—that the pace of technological progress generated by established players inevitably outstrips customers' ability to absorb it, creating opportunity for up-starts to displace incumbents.*

**Source:** Clayton M. Christensen, Michael Raynor, and Matt Verlinden, "Skate to Where the Money Will Be," *Harvard Business Review,* 79 (November 2001): 73–74.

**Questions:** *What "disruptive" technologies, á la Napster's peer-to-peer music file sharing, do you see on the horizon? In other words, as a businessperson or an investor, what future profits would you skate to today?*

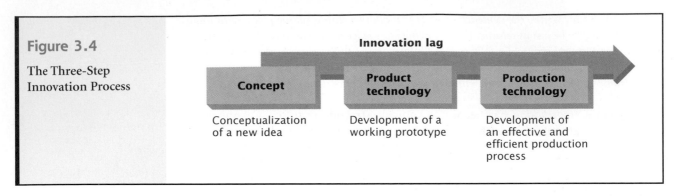

**Figure 3.4**

The Three-Step
Innovation Process

**Innovation lag**

| Concept | Product technology | Production technology |
|---|---|---|
| Conceptualization of a new idea | Development of a working prototype | Development of an effective and efficient production process |

**Innovation Lag.**    The time it takes for a new idea to be translated into satisfied demand is called **innovation lag.** The longer the innovation lag, the longer society must wait to benefit from a new idea. For example, fax machines came into wide use in the early 1990s. But the fax concept was patented by a Scottish clockmaker named Alexander Bain in 1843—an innovation lag of nearly a century and a half.[88] Over the years, the trend has been toward shorter innovation lags. For example, Britain's Imperial Chemical Industries has "slashed the time it takes to commercialize a technology from the industry norm of more than a decade to only five years."[89]

**Shortening Innovation Lag.**    Reducing innovation lags should be a high priority for modern managers. Innovative companies generally rely on two sound management practices: *goal setting* and *empowerment.* These practices create the sense of urgency necessary for speedier innovation. Medtronic, the Minnesota-based leader in manufacturing heart pacemakers, uses goal setting skillfully. A powerful message is sent to its 25,000-plus employees worldwide about promptly getting new ideas to market when top management restates the "annual goal of gathering 70% of its sales from products introduced within the past two years."[90] That is a bold commitment!

Empowerment, discussed in Chapter 15, involves pushing decision-making authority down to levels where people with the appropriate skills can do the most good. Software giant Microsoft is strong in this regard, as illustrated by the following story told by the firm's recently retired chief operating officer:

> *I was in a meeting where Bill Gates was quizzing a young manager—dressed in cutoffs, sandals, and a well-worn Microsoft T-shirt—about a new product proposal. After the meeting, I asked Bill, for whom this had been the first significant briefing on the product, what the next step would be. Would the manager prepare a memo summarizing the arguments, something top management could review before suggesting modifications to his proposal and granting final approval? Bill looked at me and smiled. "No, that's it. The key decisions got made," he said. "Now his group better hustle to implement things—or else."[91]*

Another step in the right direction is a practice called *concurrent engineering.* Also referred to as parallel design, **concurrent engineering** is a team approach to product design. This approach lets research, design, production, finance, and marketing specialists have a direct say in the product design process from the very beginning.[92] This contrasts with the traditional, and much slower, practice of having a product move serially from research to design, from design to manufacturing, and so on down the line toward the marketplace. The time to hear about possible marketing problems is while a product is still in the conceptualization stage, not after it has become a warehouse full of unsold goods.

# Promoting Innovation Through Intrapreneurship

When we hear someone called an entrepreneur, we generally think of a creative individual who has risked everything while starting his or her own business. Indeed, as we saw in Chapter 1, entrepreneurs are a vital innovative force in the economy. A lesser-known but no less important type of entrepreneur is the so-called intrapreneur.

Gifford Pinchot, author of the book *Intrapreneuring*, defines an **intrapreneur** as an employee who takes personal "hands-on responsibility" for pushing any type of innovative idea, product, or process through the organization. Pinchot calls intrapreneurs "dreamers who do." But unlike traditional entrepreneurs, who tend to leave the organizational confines to pursue their dreams, intrapreneurs strive for innovation *within* existing organizations.[93] Intrapreneurs tend to have a higher need for security than entrepreneurs, who strike out on their own. They pay a price for being employees rather than owners. Pinchot explains:

> *Corporate entrepreneurs [or intrapreneurs], despite prior successes, have no capital of their own to start other ventures. Officially, they must begin from zero by persuading management that their new ideas are promising. Unlike successful independent entrepreneurs, they are not free to guide their next ventures by their own intuitive judgments; they still have to justify every move.*[94]

Kathleen Synnott, a division marketing manager for Pitney Bowes Inc., is the classic intrapreneur. After seeing the potential of the versatile new Mail Center 2000, a computerized mail-handling and -stamping machine, Synnott became its enthusiastic champion. Just two things stood in her way: change-resistant managers and satisfied customers.

> *During the design process, for instance, Synnott helped protect the original blueprint from execs who wanted to break up the Mail Center 2000 and sell it as upgrading components to Pitney's existing mail-metering machines. She also guided it through a technical maze, insisting on 22 simulations to make sure potential customers liked what they saw. "There were naysayers who didn't think we were ready" for such a system, says Synnott. . . . "But they got religion."*[95]

If today's large companies are to achieve a competitive edge through innovation, they need to foster a supportive climate for intrapreneurs like Synnott. According to experts on the subject, an organization can foster intrapreneurship if it does four things:

- Focuses on results and teamwork
- Rewards innovation and risk taking
- Tolerates and learns from mistakes
- Remains flexible and change-oriented[96]

Our discussions of creativity, participative management, and organizational cultures in later chapters contain ideas about how to encourage intrapreneurship of all types.

**intrapreneur**   *an employee who takes personal responsibility for pushing an innovative idea through a large organization*

**31   Advice for Future Intrapreneurs**

Among Gifford Pinchot's ten commandments for intrapreneurs are the following:

- "Come to work each day willing to be fired."

- "Do any job needed to make your project work, regardless of your job description."

- "Remember it is easier to ask for forgiveness than for permission."

**Source:** Excerpted from Gifford Pinchot III, *Intrapreneuring: Why You Don't Have to Leave the Corporation to Become an Entrepreneur* (New York: Harper & Row, 1985), 22.

**Questions:** *How can these ideas enhance innovation in large organizations? Is this advice a formula for career success or sudden unemployment?*

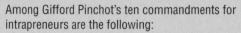

# Summary

1.  Seven major changes reshaping the workplace at the beginning of the twenty-first century are (1) *the virtual organization* with greater reliance on computer networks, (2) *the just-in-time workforce* with more part-timers, (3) *the ascendancy of knowledge workers* as we pursue lifelong learning in the information age, (4) *computerized coaching and electronic monitoring* with enhanced learning and decision making, as well as privacy concerns, (5) *the growth of worker diversity* in an evolving multicultural and multilingual workforce, (6) *the aging workforce* with a greater appreciation of older workers and less emphasis on early retirement, and (7) *the birth of the dynamic workforce* with an emphasis on innovation and adaptability.

2.  Demographically, the U.S. workforce is becoming larger, older, more culturally diverse, and increasingly female. Remedial education programs are needed to improve the quality of the U.S. workforce. Researchers have disproved persistent myths that older workers are less productive and more accident-prone than younger coworkers. A new social contract between employers and employees is taking shape because the tradition of lifetime employment with a single organization is giving way to shorter-term relationships of convenience and mutual benefit.

3.  The persistence of opportunity and income inequalities (and the so-called glass ceiling) among women and minorities is a strong stimulus for change. With part-timers playing a greater role in the U.S. workforce, there is genuine concern about creating a disadvantaged underclass of employees. Managing-diversity programs attempt to go a step beyond equal employment opportunity. The new goal is to tap *every* employee's *full* potential in today's diverse workforce.

4.  Because of government regulations and sociopolitical demands from a growing list of special-interest groups, managers are becoming increasingly politicized. More and more believe that if they are going to be affected by political forces, they should be more active politically. Some organizations rely on issues management to systematically identify, evaluate, and respond to important social and political issues. Managers can respond politically in three ways: by being reactive, neutral, or proactive. Four political strategies that managers have found useful for pursuing active or reactive political goals are campaign financing, lobbying, coalition building, and indirect lobbying. There is a strong trend toward managers being held personally accountable for the misdeeds of their organizations. Alternative dispute resolution tactics such as arbitration and mediation can help trim management's huge litigation bill.

5.  Managers can make timely decisions about inventory, borrowing, hiring, and capital spending during somewhat unpredictable business cycles by taking a consensus approach to economic forecasts. Business is urged to compete actively and creatively in the emerging global economy. By influencing jobs, prices, quality standards, and wages, the global economy affects virtually *everyone*.

6.  Including conceptualization, product technology, and production technology, a healthy innovation process is vital to technological development. Innovation lags must be shortened. An organizational climate that fosters intrapreneurship can help. An intrapreneur is an employee who champions an idea or innovation by pushing it through the organization.

**Terms to Understand**

## Skills & Tools

### How Business Leaders Can Help Women Break the Glass Ceiling

Businesses need as much leadership, talent, quality, competence, productivity, innovation, and creativity as possible as they face more effective worldwide competition. Following are ten actions companies can take to ensure maximum use of women's business capability:

1. **Provide feedback on job performance.** Give frequent and specific appraisals. Women need and want candid reviews of their work. Clearly articulated suggestions for improvement, standards for work performance and plans for career advancement will make women feel more involved in their jobs and help make them better employees.

2. **Accept women.** Welcome them as valued members of your management team. Include women in every kind of communication. Listen to their needs and concerns and encourage their contributions.

3. **Ensure equal opportunities.** Give women the same chances you give to talented men to grow, develop, and contribute to company profitability. Give them the responsibility to direct major projects, to plan and implement systems and programs. Expect them to travel and relocate and to make the same commitment to the company as do men who aspire to leadership positions.

4. **Provide career counseling.** Give women the same level of counseling on professional career advancement opportunities as you give to men.

5. **Identify potential.** Identify women as possible future managers early in their employment and encourage their advancement through training and other developmental activities.

6. **Encourage assertiveness.** Assist women in strengthening their assertion skills. Reinforce strategic career planning to encourage women's commitment to their careers and long-term career plans.

7. **Accelerate development.** Provide "fast track" programs for qualified women. Either formally or informally, these programs will give women the exposure, knowledge, and positioning they need for career advancement.

8. **Offer mentoring opportunities.** Give women the chance to develop mentoring relationships with other employees. The overall goal should be to provide advice, counsel, and support to promising female employees from knowledgeable, senior-level men and women.

9. **Encourage networking.** Promote management support systems and networks among employees of both genders. Sharing experiences and information with other men and women who are managers provides invaluable support to peers. These activities give women the opportunity to meet and learn from men and women in more advanced stages of their careers—a helpful way of identifying potential mentors or role models.

10. **Increase women's participation.** Examine the feasibility of increasing participation of women in company-sponsored planning retreats, use of company facilities, social functions, and so forth. With notable exceptions, men are still generally more comfortable with other men, and as a result, women miss many of the career and business opportunities that arise during social functions. In addition, women may not have access to information about the company's informal political and social systems. Encourage male managers to include women when socializing with other business associates.

*Source:* Excerpted from Rose Mary Wentling, "Breaking Down Barriers to Women's Success," *HRMagazine,* 40 (May 1995). Reprinted with the permission of *HRMagazine,* published by the Society for Human Resource Management, Alexandria, Virginia.

# Hands-On Exercise

## Crystal Ball Gazing

**Instructions**

Read these predictions from *The Futurist* magazine and rate how probable each is, according to the scale below. (*Note:* Use the year 2015 if a specific time frame is not mentioned.)

**No chance**                                                              **Virtually guaranteed**

| 0% | 10% | 20% | 30% | 40% | 50% | 60% | 70% | 80% | 90% | 100% |

| Prediction | Probability of occurrence |
|---|---|

**1. Globalization could make foods less safe to eat.** As more food is imported from far-flung local producers, national food-safety standards will become harder to enforce. Growing demand for fresh foods year-round makes refrigeration and other safe-transport issues more of a concern.

_____

**2. Falling language barriers could spur more travel.** Automated translation systems could enable most of the world's people to communicate directly with one another—each speaking and hearing in his or her own language—by about 2020.

_____

**3. No more textbooks?** Printed and bound textbooks may disappear as more interactive coursework goes online.

_____

**4. "Internet Universities" could lead to the demise of traditional institutions.** Web-linked education services that offer franchised software and "college-in-a-box" courses from superstar teachers could lead to educational monopolies. Such "virtual" universities would have rigidly standardized curricula that undersell traditional courses in brick-and-mortar institutions.

_____

**5. The era of cheap oil is NOT over.** Not only is the world not running out of oil, but prices are likely to fall again and remain around $20 per barrel for the next decade. Reason: The current high prices make intensive exploration and development of new oil sources more attractive, thus ultimately increasing supply and lowering prices.

_____

**6. Water shortages will become more frequent and severe.** Most of the major cities in the developing world will face severe water shortages in the next two decades, as will one-third of the population of Africa. By 2040, at least 3.5 billion people will run short of water—almost 10 times as many as in 1995—and by 2050, two-thirds of the world's population could be living in regions with chronic, widespread shortages of water.

_____

*(continued)*

| Prediction | Probability of occurrence |
|---|---|

**7. Tissue engineers may one day grow a "heart in a bottle."** Using a fibrous "scaffold" that is seeded with stem cells, researchers could coax the cells to grow into the needed organ. Skin and cartilage have already been grown this way. In the future, organ generation could help the tens of thousands of patients in need of organ transplants, predicts Vladimir Mironov, chief scientific officer with Cardiovascular Tissues Technology Inc.

_____

**8. Nanomachines will enhance our brains.** Nano-computers may soon be placed inside human brains to enhance memory, thinking ability, visualization, and other tasks, according to futurist consultant Michael Zey, author of *The Future Factor*. Technologies will also be developed that allow us to connect our brains to a computer and either download or upload data.

_____

**9. Touch-sensitive robots may make virtual reality more realistic.** The ability to collect and transmit tactile data—such as the way it feels to kick a soccer ball—could add to humans' ability to experience events.

_____

**10. Hardware will soften up.** Instead of pounding on hard, plastic keyboards to do your computing, you'll soon be able to gently caress soft electronic fabrics. Among potential applications for smart textiles: tablecloths with piano keyboards and furniture slipcovers with TV remote controls.

_____

*Source:* Originally published in the November–December 2001 issue of *The Futurist.* Used with permission from the World Future Society, 7910 Woodmont Avenue, Suite 450, Bethesda, Maryland 20814. Telephone: 301-656-8274; Fax: 301-951-0394; **http://www.wfs.org**.

**For Consideration/ Discussion**

**1.** When you compare your ratings with those of others, do you envision things changing faster or slower than they do? What is the implication for how you, as a manager, would tend to deal with organizational and external changes?

**2.** What, if any, potentially profitable business ideas do you see in any of these predictions? Explain.

**3.** What are two or three of your own ten-year predictions for our sociocultural, political-legal, economic, or technological futures?

**4.** What needs to be done now to prepare for two or three selected predictions from *The Futurist*'s list (or from your own predictions)?

# Internet Exercises

1. **Current events online:** Today's managers need to follow worldwide current events to track new markets, customer preferences, competitors, new technology, and investment opportunities. The Internet stands ready to fill this need 24 hours a day, seven days a week. For example, select one of the following three general news Web sites and search it for a news story that updates one of the topical areas in this chapter (social-demographic, political-legal, economic, and technological). Read the news story and be prepared to take a copy of it to class if your instructor requests.

   ■ Go to the home page of the Cable News Network (**www.cnn.com**) and select one or more of the following main menu items: "World," "Politics," "Business," or "Sci-Tech."

   ■ At the home page of MSNBC (**www.msnbc.com**), start by clicking on the last heading on the navigation bar: "Headlines." After that, you may want to move on to the "Business" and "Technology" pages.

   ■ The BBC, Britain's publicly funded and noncommercial radio, television, and Internet broadcaster (known in the U.K. as "The Beeb"), is a good source for news from around the world (**www.bbc.co.uk**). Alternative language versions— including Russian, Spanish, Arabic, and Hindi—are available at the click of a mouse. Select "BBC News" at the home page, and then "World," "Business," or "Sci/Tech" from the BBC News page.

2. **What does the job situation look like?** Getting (and keeping) the *right* job is a major quality-of-life issue for most of us. Thanks to the immense data-gathering capabilities of the U.S. Labor Department's Bureau of Labor Statistics (**stats.bls.gov**), you can put yourself on the right path toward a rewarding career. The idea is to prepare yourself with the right education and training for sectors of the economy with the greatest potential. A very useful and readable publication can be found online by going to the home page and selecting "Occupational Outlook Handbook" under the heading "Occupations." Then click on the tab titled "Tomorrow's Jobs."

   *Learning Points:* 1. Is your present program of study taking you in a fruitful direction for jobs? Explain. 2. Is the career you have in mind in a growing sector of the economy? Explain. 3. What are the most useful pieces of information you picked up from this handbook?

3. **Technology makes the world go 'round:** Technological developments are a window on tomorrow's world. For a general survey of what's new, go to **www.usatoday.com** and click on "Tech" and then "Tech briefs." Read one or two articles of personal interest. (*Note:* Be sure to print a hard copy if classroom discussion is planned.)

   *Learning Points:* 1. Will the technology you read about make the world a better or worse place? Explain. 2. What, if any, are the implications of this technology for modern managers? For the world in general? 3. What was the most interesting bit of knowledge you picked up during this Web search?

4. **Check it out:** A treasure chest of free career information is available at *The Wall Street Journal*'s Internet site (**www.careerjournal.com**). Be sure to review the helpful readings in the section tabs titled "Job-Hunting Advice" and "Managing Your Career."

For updates to these exercises, visit our Web site (**http://business.college.hmco.com/students**).

# Closing Case

## Welcome to the World of Younger Bosses and Older Workers

They're young corporate climbers, full of brash attitude and rogue ideas. And suddenly, they're in charge.

Better get used to it. As Generation X matures and job promotions no longer depend on seniority, the baby-faced boss is here to stay.

That means more managers are in their 20s or 30s and overseeing employees who are older, a twist on the typical manager-employee relationship. The age reversal is causing a shake-up. Employers are more vulnerable to age-discrimination lawsuits, and workers are facing generation gaps never before tackled on the job.

"We've always had older and younger workers, but they never mixed. You were ghettoized with your own age group," says Ron Zemke, co-author of . . . *Generations At Work*. "Now it's the first time they're together. It's a new kind of diversity and a new kind of challenge."

In a tight labor market, the trend has swept across industries. Youthful managers are cropping up in manufacturing plants and white-collar offices. When striking General Motors workers in Flint, Mich., took to the picket lines last year, many complained that supervisors were too young and inexperienced.

The discord is coming in part because the number of workers age 20–34 in the managerial category increased from 4.8 million in 1994 to 5.2 million last year, the Department of Labor reports.

The ranks of young bosses are expected to surge as the 52.4 million people who make up Generation X—born from 1965 through 1978—assume more supervisory roles. Already, 14% of top executives such as CEOs, presidents, and company owners are in their 30s or 20s, according to Dun & Bradstreet, which provides financial management services.

The age difference is bringing a values clash. Raised on a diet of MTV and video games, Generation X bosses are generally quick to roam from job to job, hungry for quick results, willing to do things differently and intolerant of technophobes. All this can be a bit bewildering to baby boomers widely considered more loyal to employers and less likely to bend rules.

"I say 'dude' a lot, which people have to get used to," says Ryan Deutsch, 27, vice president of operations at Sidney Printing Works in Cincinnati, who directs employees in their 40s. "The experience gap is the biggest challenge. You're never going to know or have as much experience as the people you work with, so it's important to give the proper respect."

Says Richard Autzen, 43, a plant manager and his employee: "I enjoy his energy. I get to explain a lot of things to him."

## A New Breed of Boss

More young bosses are coming in part because employers are seeking a different type of supervisor no longer molded solely by seniority and experience.

They want a new breed of boss who can provide strong leadership, handle technology, inspire teamwork, cope with constant change and handle never-ending uncertainty. Many older workers have such attributes. But such characteristics are widely considered to be traits learned in college business programs or picked up from employees who hop scotch from job to job—attributes strongly linked to younger workers and newly minted graduates.

And employers are willing to pay. Managers' salaries can range from the mid-$20,000 a year in the service sector on up into six figures. It's no longer safe to assume that the silver-haired worker earns more than a new hire. . . .

But making it work once they've started the job is easier said than done. Younger bosses can contend with plenty of resistance.

Older workers may think a young boss who is still single can't understand family demands. They may chafe at taking commands from someone with less job experience. And they can be less tolerant of a younger person's management mistakes.

*Source:* Excerpted from Stephanie Armour, "The Challenge: Mix Energy, Experience," *USA Today* (April 20, 1999): 1A–2A. Copyright 1999, *USA Today*. Reprinted with permission.

"There are huge value differences among generations," says Ben Rosen, a management professor at the University of North Carolina. "So many companies have focused on diversity, but they've overlooked age, and it's such a prevalent issue. There are potential problems."

No age group is immune from the friction. . . . even 20-something employees have found themselves dealing with younger supervisors.

"She was terrible," says Ali Friedman, 26, who once had a boss who was just out of college. Friedman now works for a record label in Boston. "When someone has no mentors, how are they supposed to mentor someone else? I had to manage her managing me.'" . . .

Some young workers burst onto the scene full of flashy new ideas without the experience or proof to back them up. . . .

But newer isn't necessarily better. Hagberg Consulting Group of Foster City, Calif., researched results of more than 3,000 executives who were rated by coworkers and found that as an executive's age increases, he or she becomes more thorough and better at planning.

## Stereotyping Problems

Blame many of the problems on stereotyping. Young workers may see their older counterparts as ill at ease with technology, unable to make snap decisions, and set in their ways.

"People tend to look on older people as if they can only do so much," says Mary Barbour, 73, an administrative assistant in Washington, D.C., whose supervisor is roughly 20 years younger. "But believe it or not, our memory does not leave us. You're never really too old to learn."

Older workers, on the other hand, may see their younger managers as inferior. They may doubt their loyalty to the company, think they're favored because of their youth.

"You have to work harder to prove yourself," says Lyle Lininger, 31, at Sandia National Laboratories in Albuquerque. "Especially when I was new in this job, it was really awkward to feel like I was giving instructions to someone as old as my parents. I just say, 'You know what, I don't have all the answers.'" . . .

And there is hope for younger managers and their older counterparts. Many such pairings work.

They've relied on patience, mutual understanding and an ability to look beyond age-defined stereotypes, drawing on each other's strengths instead [of] focusing on their differences.

Take Russ McFee, 40. He is a manager at GHS Strings, a company in Battle Creek Mich., that makes guitar strings. He says he doesn't let age become an issue.

"Age is irrelevant," McFee says. "It's the person."

It's a good thing he sees it that way. One of his employees, John Mally, is still working as an engineer at the age of 90.

"It's wonderful," Mally quips. "You never know what he's going to do next. It's a very big pleasure. He's a very nice fellow to work for."

## For Discussion

**1.** Some people do not like to have a group label attached to them. Are you opposed to terms such as *generation X, generation Y,* and *baby boomers*? Explain.

**2.** Honestly, how do you typically characterize older workers? How do you generally characterize younger workers?

**3.** Would you be uncomfortable reporting to a manager who is younger than you? Explain.

**4.** If you worked for Ryan Deutsch, the Sidney Printing Works vice president in Cincinnati, and he called you "dude" all the time, how would you respond?

**5.** What is an older employee entitled to at the end of a long career at the same company? Explain.

## chapter four

# International Management and Cross-Cultural Competence

## CHAPTER OBJECTIVES

*When you finish studying this chapter you should be able to*

**1** **Describe** the six-step internationalization process, and **explain** how to make an international joint venture a success.

**2** **Distinguish** between a global company and a transnational company.

**3** **Contrast** ethnocentric, polycentric, and geocentric attitudes toward foreign operations.

**4** **Explain** from a cross-cultural perspective the difference between high-context and low-context cultures, and **distinguish** between individualistic and collectivist cultures.

**5** **Discuss** what Geert Hofstede's research has to say about the applicability of American management theories in foreign cultures.

**6** **Identify** important comparative management lessons learned from William Ouchi's Theory Z research and international studies of work goals and leadership styles.

**7** **Discuss** the nature and importance of cross-cultural training in international management.

**8** **Summarize** the position of women on foreign assignments.

# Guess What, Mickey D? Yum! Is the World's Largest Restaurant Chain

In early October [2001], on the first Muslim holy day after American warplanes began the bombing campaign in Afghanistan, thousands of protesters spilled out onto the streets of Karachi. Armed with sticks and bats, intermittently chanting "Death to America," they made their way through the streets of Pakistan's largest city, smashing windows and setting fire to a bus and several cars along the way. The mob's objective was the U.S. consulate. But police barricades and tear gas turned them back. So they went looking for the next-best option: Colonel Sanders.

To the demonstrators, it didn't matter that the nearby KFC, one of 18 in Pakistan, was locally owned. The red, white, and blue KFC logo was justification enough. Though the owners of the restaurant had tried to cover the KFC signs in an attempt to protect their property, their effort was futile; the protesters set fire to the restaurant before being dispersed by police.

"You have no choice but to operate in a world shaped by globalization," Andy Grove wrote in *Fortune* in 1995. "Adapt or die." That maxim is truer today than ever, especially for companies like Coke, McDonald's, Gillette, and Kodak, companies that own the great, ubiquitous—but aging—American brands. Yum! Brands, Inc., which owns not only KFC but also Pizza Hut and Taco Bell, is another good example [Update: The company recently bought Long John Silver's and A&W restaurants.] For companies like these, growth in the U.S. is now measured in the low single digits—at best. So if they want to grow, they will have to go global.

As, indeed, they have. Look no further than KFC. Founded about 50 years ago as Kentucky Fried Chicken by the late Colonel Harland Sanders, the chain has around 5,000 U.S. restaurants—and 6,000 abroad. It has 158 franchises in Indonesia, which has the world's largest Muslim population. (Three were also looted in the days after Sept. 11.) It has a restaurant in the holy city of Mecca, Saudi Arabia. In all, KFC has stores in more than 80 countries, including Japan, Australia, Egypt, Mexico, Malaysia, and Swaziland. In China, where KFC has more than 500 restaurants, Yum! is opening, on average, ten new stores a month.

And it's not about to slow down, Sept. 11 or no. Just days after the Karachi incident, Yum! CEO David Novak reaffirmed to Wall Street analysts that overseas growth would continue unabated—and downplayed the potential impact of an anti-American backlash. As Novak sees it, the company's long-standing presence in so many countries makes it an accepted part of the landscape, and therefore less likely to be a major target. "We're going to have some radical situations," he told *Fortune*, "but not to the extent that we think it's going to alter our business plan." Then again, what choice does he have? As with so many U.S. companies, continued globalization is, quite simply, the key to Yum!'s future.

Tricon [Yum!'s original name] was born in 1997, when PepsiCo decided to spin off its restaurant division and refocus on its core beverage business. Prior to the spinoff, the fast-food business—which included the three chains Yum! now owns—had been a laggard; the assumption was that an executive team focused solely on restaurants would get better results. And it has. Margins are up—from 11.6% to just over 15%. Revenues ($1.7 billion in 2000) and profits ($860 million) have grown steadily. . . .

Clearly those good things have come about in large part because Yum! is committed to international growth. Since it was formed, Yum! has opened more than 5,100 restaurants—of which nearly 3,200 have been abroad. It plans to open more than 1,000 stores a year overseas for the foreseeable future. Indeed, its 30,000-plus outlets in more than 100 countries are the most of any restaurant company in the world. "A lot of people talk about being international, but they don't have the infrastructure to really get it done," says Novak, 49. "We now have the people, the brands, and the presence."

Like most successful global companies, Yum! believes that business, like politics, is local. As a practical matter, that means that Yum! can't just open restaurants based on the U.S. model and expect success. It has to adapt to local tastes and negotiate changing cultural and political climates. In Japan, for instance, KFC sells tempura crispy strips. In northern England, KFC stresses gravy and potatoes, while in Thailand it offers fresh rice with soy or sweet chili sauce. In Holland the company makes a potato-and-onion croquette. In France it sells pastries alongside chicken. And in China the chicken gets spicier the farther inland you travel. "Most companies are not really jumping up and down now and saying, 'We're an American company'," says Clayton Tolley, CEO of global-branding firm Addison Whitney. "More and more, if it's only an American brand without a regional appeal, it's going to be difficult to market. . . ."

During this tense time, Yum! is taking precautions to protect its employees. Executives have stopped wearing "logo-wear" identifying them as Yum! employees. The company monitors events through an international secu-rity service that allows them to stay one step ahead of the media when trouble flares up. Yum!'s international presi-dent Pete Bassi consults with franchisees in hot spots on a regular basis. When there's an incident, the company reviews its options but often defers to the judgment of the local businessmen. Right now Yum! is advising them to stay out of the spotlight.

Ultimately, though, there's not much Yum! can do except hope for the best. "I'm sure we'll have the ebbs and flows of the political climate as it evolves," says CEO Novak. But he's confident that KFC and Pizza Hut tran-scend nationalism. "I don't think we're viewed as a differ-ent culture; I think we're part of the culture."

**M**anagers, such as those at Yum! Brands, Inc., are moving from country to country as never before, meeting the challenges of international competi-tion. They are carrying on a business tradition dating back further than one might think:

> In the antique shops of Shanghai's old French quarter, amid the German cameras, Ameri-can radios, Russian crystal and other relics of a vanished past, lie tarnished reminders of just how long the world economy has been a global economy: rough-casts taels of South Ameri-can silver and smooth-worn Mexican silver dollars.
>
> It was in 1571 that modern global commerce began, argues Dennis O. Flynn, head of the economics department of the University of the Pacific in Stockton, Calif. That year, the Spanish empire founded the city of Manila in the Philippines to receive its silver-laden galleons that made their way across the vast Pacific Ocean from the New World. The metal was bound not for Spain, but for imperial China. For the first time, all of the world's popu-lated continents were trading directly—Asia with the Americas, Europe and Africa, and each with the others. They were highly interdependent: when silver depreciated in later decades, world-wide inflation ensued.
>
> "Some economists think the global economy is a post–World War II thing," says Prof. Flynn. "That just demonstrates an ignorance of history."[1]

Both air travel and modern information technology have made the world a seemingly smaller place. A third globe-shrinking force steadily gaining momentum is *corporate globalism*. By creating global organizations, this third force promises to be the main contributor to a smaller world with many similarities.

Striking evidence of the modern global marketplace is everywhere. Consider these recent examples:

- Vodafone, the British wireless phone company, has "100 million subscribers in 28 countries."[2]
- Every official Rawlings baseball used in Major League Baseball games is assembled and hand-sewn in Costa Rica ("the rubber-coated 'pill' or nucleus comes from Mississippi and the cowhide covers are made in Tennessee").[3]

- Germany's electronics and engineering giant Siemens operates in 192 countries, employs 90,000 Americans, and rings up the largest share ($16.2 billion) of its sales in the United States.[4]
- When a wave of patriotism swept the United States following the 2001 terrorist attacks, shelves were stocked with piles of American flags made in China.[5]

This dizzying array of international commerce is simply business as usual in our global economy, which is projected to grow from $26 trillion in 1994 to $48 trillion in 2010. Over the same period, world trade is expected to quadruple, from $4 trillion to $16.6 trillion![6]

Like any other productive venture, an international corporation must be effectively and efficiently managed. Consequently, **international management,** the pursuit of organizational objectives in international and intercultural settings, has become an important discipline. Indeed, Nancy Adler, a leading international management scholar at Canada's McGill University, sees it this way: "Managing the global enterprise and modern business management have become synonymous."[7] The purpose of this chapter is to define and discuss multinational and global corporations, stimulate global and cultural awareness, explore comparative management insights, and discuss the need for cross-cultural training.

**international management**
*pursuing organizational objectives in international and cross-cultural settings*

# Global Organizations for a Global Economy

Many labels have been attached to international business ventures over the years. They have been called international companies, multinational companies, global companies, and transnational companies. This section clarifies the terminology confusion by reviewing the six-stage internationalization process as a foundation for contrasting global and transnational companies.

## The Internationalization Process

There are many ways to do business across borders. At either extreme, a company may merely buy goods from a foreign source or actually buy the foreign company itself. In between is an internationalization process with identifiable stages. Companies may skip steps when pursuing foreign markets, so the following sequence should *not* be viewed as a lock step sequence.

**1** Describe the six-step internationalization process, and explain how to make an international joint venture a success.

**Stage 1: Licensing.**    Companies in foreign countries are authorized to produce and/or market a given product within a specified territory in return for a fee.[8] For example, under the terms of a ten-year licensing agreement, South Korea's Samsung Electronics will get to use Texas Instruments' patented semiconductor technology for royalty payments exceeding $1billion.[9]

**Stage 2: Exporting.**    Goods produced in one country are sold to customers in foreign countries. As documented in Chapter 3, exports amount to a large and growing slice of the U.S. economy.[10]

**4A**

## The Global Economy in Your Own Backyard

Team up with two or three other people and have a five-minute brainstorming session to come up with as many answers to the following question as possible.

**Question:** *What evidence of the global economy is there in your city, region, or state? Hint: Think of foreign-made products sold in local stores, foreign-owned companies, and local companies that export goods or services.*

For further information about the interactive annotations in this chapter, visit our Web site (http://business.college. hmco.com/students).

**Stage 3: Local Warehousing and Selling.**   Goods produced in one country are shipped to the parent company's storage and marketing facilities located in one or more foreign countries.

**Stage 4: Local Assembly and Packaging.**   Components, rather than finished products, are shipped to company-owned assembly facilities in one or more foreign countries for final assembly and sales.

**Stage 5: Joint Ventures.**   A company in one country pools resources with one or more companies in a foreign country to produce, store, transport, and market products with resulting profits/losses shared appropriately. Joint ventures, also known as *strategic alliances* or *strategic partnerships,* have become very popular in recent years.[11] Fuji Xerox is a prime example of a successful international joint venture.

> *Joint ventures are usually formed to ensure a fast and convenient entry into a complex foreign market. That's particularly the case in Japan, where convoluted distribution systems, tightly knit supplier relationships and close business-government cooperation have long encouraged foreign companies to link up with knowledgeable local partners.*
>
> *But in truth, these joint ventures don't often last long. And they sometimes flop, occasionally spectacularly. The reasons for failure can include disagreements over strategy, struggles over operational control or even simple spats over each partner's level of effort.*
>
> *But Fuji Xerox, a 34-year-old joint venture between Xerox Corp., Stamford, Conn., and Tokyo-based Fuji Photo Film Co., has avoided all that. In contrast to the turmoil at many other joint ventures, Fuji Xerox not only has been bedrock stable, but also has grown into a major strategic asset for both companies.[12]*

Indeed, the strength of the Fuji Xerox joint venture was underscored in 2001 when a financially struggling Xerox sold half of its 50 percent share to Fuji, while all other aspects of the venture remained intact.[13]

International joint ventures/strategic alliances have tended to be fruitful for Japanese companies but disappointing for American and European partners.

> *Gary Hamel, a professor at the London Business School, regards partnerships as "a race to learn": The partner that learns fastest comes to dominate the relationship and can then rewrite its terms. Thus, an alliance becomes a new form of competition. The Japanese excel at learning from others, Hamel says, while Americans and Europeans are not so good at it.[14]*

Experts offer the following recommendations for successful international joint ventures/strategic alliances. First, exercise *patience* when selecting and building trust with a partner that has compatible (but not directly competitive) products and markets. Second, *learn* as fast and as much as possible without giving away core technologies and secrets. Third, establish firm *ground rules* about rights and responsibilities at the outset.[15]

**Stage 6: Direct Foreign Investments.**   Typically, a company in one country produces and markets products through wholly owned subsidiaries in foreign countries. Global corporations are expressions of this last stage of internationalization.

*Cross-border mergers* are an increasingly popular form of direct foreign investment.[16] A cross-border merger occurs when a company in one country buys an entire company in another country. Unfortunately, cross-border mergers are not a quick and easy way to go global.

*When does e-mail stand for elephant mail? Perhaps in India, where outsourced software development has become a major industry. In today's global economy, many specialized software companies in the United States find plenty of talented and less expensive programming talent in far-flung places such as India, Russia, and China. Shortages of state-of-the-art computer technology in less-developed countries foster creative problem solving, yet another competitive advantage.*

*On top of the usual challenges of acquiring a company—paying a fair price, melding two management teams, and capturing the elusive "synergy" that's supposed to light up the bottom line—special risks and costs attach to cross-border mergers. They often involve wide differences in distance, language, and culture that can lead to serious misunderstandings and conflicts. . . .*

*According to a study of cross-border mergers among large companies by consultants McKinsey & Co., nearly 40% end in total failure, with the acquiring company never earning back its cost of capital.[17]*

## From Global Companies to Transnational Companies

The difference between these two types of international ventures is the difference between actual and theoretical. That is to say, transnational companies are evolving and represent a futuristic concept. Meanwhile, global companies, such as the giants in Table 4.1, do business in many countries simultaneously. They have global strategies for product design, financing, purchasing, manufacturing, and marketing. By definition, a **global company** is a multinational venture centrally managed from a specific country.[18] For example, even though Coca-Cola earns most of its profit outside the United States, it is viewed as a U.S. company because it is run from a powerful headquarters in Atlanta, Georgia.[19] The same goes for McDonald's, Ford, IBM, and Wal-Mart, with their respective U.S. headquarters.

A **transnational company,** in contrast, is a global network of productive units with a decentralized authority structure and no distinct national identity.[20] Transnationals rely on a blend of global and local strategies, as circumstances dictate. Local values and practices are adopted whenever possible because, in the end, all *customer contacts* are local. Ideally, managers of transnational organizations "think globally, but act locally." Managers of foreign operations are encouraged to interact freely with their colleagues from around the world. Once again, this type of international business venture exists mostly in theory, although some global companies are moving toward transnational-

**2** Distinguish between a global company and a transnational company.

**global company**
*a multinational venture centrally managed from a specific country*

**transnational company**
*a futuristic model of a global, decentralized network with no distinct national identity*

| Company | Home Country | Industry | 2001 Sales (U.S. $, billions) |
|---|---|---|---|
| Petrobrás | Brazil | Petroleum products | 25 |
| BP | Britain | Petroleum products | 174 |
| Nokia | Finland | Electronics | 28 |
| Vivendi Universal | France | Entertainment/Publishing | 51 |
| DaimlerChrysler | Germany | Motor vehicles | 137 |
| Fiat | Italy | Motor vehicles | 52 |
| Toyota Motor | Japan | Motor vehicles | 121 |
| Pemex | Mexico | Petroleum products | 39 |
| ING | Netherlands | Insurance | 83 |
| Samsung Electronics | South Korea | Electronics | 36 |
| Nestlé | Switzerland | Food products | 50 |
| General Electric | United States | Electrical equipment/ Financial services | 126 |

**Table 4.1**  Corporate Giants Worldwide

*Source:* Adapted from data in "The World's 500 Largest Corporations," *Fortune* (July 22, 2002): 144–147, F1–F13.

**4B**

**Back to the Opening Case**

Is Yum! Brands a global company or a transnational company? Explain.

ism. For example, consider L. M. Ericsson, the Swedish telecommunications equipment manufacturer. As reported in *Business Week*, "Ericsson . . . moved its European headquarters to London to escape Sweden's high personal-income taxes, and to be closer to investors and customers."[21] Ericsson's decision to relocate its headquarters was not constrained by national identity, but rather guided by business and financial considerations.

*Companies with a global presence are in a fishbowl when it comes to being scrutinized for ethical practices. For example, when the price of coffee beans plunged largely due to weather-related factors, Starbucks raised its prices and notched record sales. Observers cried foul, saying it was unfair for Starbucks to prosper while coffee bean farmers suffered. Starbucks countered by pointing out that coffee beans actually are a relatively small cost factor, far behind rents and payroll. Still, critics want Starbucks and other global companies to do more to improve conditions for small foreign suppliers.*

Significantly, many experts are alarmed at the prospect of immense "stateless" transnational companies because of unresolved political, economic, and tax implications. If transnational companies become more powerful than the governments of even the largest countries in which they do business, who will hold them accountable in cases of fraud, human rights violations, and environmental mishaps?[22]

# Toward Greater Global Awareness and Cross-Cultural Competence

Americans in general and American business students and managers in particular are often considered too narrowly focused for the global stage. Boris Yavitz, former dean of Columbia University's Graduate School of Business, observed that, "unlike European and Asian managers, who grow up expecting to see international service, U.S. executives are required to prepare only for domestic experience, with English as their only language."[23] This state of affairs is slowly changing amid growth of international business and economic globalization. To compete successfully in a dynamic global economy, present and future managers need to develop their international and cross-cultural awareness. In this section we distinguish between travelers and settlers, examine attitudes toward international operations, and explore key sources of cultural diversity.

## Travelers Versus Settlers

One or more short visits to a foreign country do not make a person competent to transact business deals there. Accordingly, cross-cultural management experts distinguish between travelers and settlers. Travelers visit foreign countries, whether for work or pleasure, on a short-term basis (a few days to several weeks). They tend to have limited knowledge of the local history, culture, and customs. Their local language skills typically vary from none to few. In contrast, settlers take foreign assignments lasting from two to five years or more.

> The Settler has to deal with a variety of challenges, starting from pre-departure training to the hassles of relocating, transitional challenges to acclimatization, to culture shock to re-entry shock . . . [because] the Settler must receive more in-depth insights into the host country's customs and culture. The language skills must be much more than conversational and a solid knowledge of the country's religion, politics, history, meaning of nature, morals, social structure, education, food and table manners, roles of man and woman, business ethics, negotiation techniques, humor and values is highly important. . . . The Settler should be extremely open-minded, flexible, friendly and honest . . . [and] adaptability is a valuable asset.[24]

## Contrasting Attitudes Toward International Operations

Can a firm's degree of internationalization be measured? Some observers believe it can, and they claim a true global company must have subsidiaries in at least six nations. Others say that, to qualify as a multinational or global company, a firm must have a certain percentage of its capital or operations in foreign countries. However, Howard Perlmutter insisted that these measurable guidelines tell only part of the story and suggested it is management's *attitude* toward its foreign operations that really counts.

**3** Contrast ethnocentric, polycentric, and geocentric attitudes toward foreign operations.

*The more one penetrates into the living reality of an international firm, the more one finds it is necessary to give serious weight to the way executives think about doing business around the world. The orientation toward "foreign people, ideas, resources," in headquarters and subsidiaries, and in host and home environments, becomes crucial in estimating the multi-nationality of a firm.[25]*

Perlmutter identified three managerial attitudes toward international operations, which he labeled ethnocentric, polycentric, and geocentric.[26] Each attitude is presented here in its pure form, but all three are likely to be found in a single multinational or global corporation (see Table 4.2). The key question is, "Which attitude predominates?"

**ethnocentric attitude**   *view that assumes the home country's personnel and ways of doing things are best*

**Ethnocentric Attitude.**   Managers with an **ethnocentric attitude** are home-country-oriented. Home-country personnel, ideas, and practices are viewed as inherently superior to those from abroad. Foreign nationals are not trusted with key decisions or technology. Home-country procedures and evaluation criteria are applied worldwide without variation. Proponents of ethnocentrism say that it makes for a simpler and more tightly controlled organization. Critics believe this attitude makes for poor planning and ineffective operations because of inadequate feedback, high turnover of subsidiary managers, reduced innovation, inflexibility, and social and political backlash.

**Table 4.2**    Three Different Attitudes Toward International Operations

| Organization design | Ethnocentric | Polycentric | Geocentric |
|---|---|---|---|
| **Identification** | Nationality of owner | Nationality of host country | Truly international company but identifying with national interests |
| **Authority; decision making** | High in headquarters | Relatively low in headquarters | Aim for a collaborative approach between headquarters and subsidiaries |
| **Evaluation and control** | Home standards applied for person and performance | Determined locally | Find standards that are universal and local |
| **Communication; information flow** | High volume to subsidiaries; orders, commands, advice | Little to and from headquarters; little between subsidiaries | Both ways and between subsidiaries; heads of subsidiaries part of management team |
| **Perpetuation (recruiting, staffing, development)** | Recruit and develop people of home country for key positions everywhere in the world | Develop people of local nationality for key positions in their own country | Develop best people everywhere in the world for key positions everywhere in the world |

*Source:* Excerpted from Howard V. Perlmutter, "The Tortuous Evolution of the Multinational Corporation," *Columbia Journal of World Business,* 4 (January–February 1969): 12. Used with permission.

In U.S.-Japanese business relations, ethnocentrism cuts both ways. Procter & Gamble failed to do its cultural homework when it ran a series of advertisements for Pampers in Japan. Japanese customers were bewildered by the ads, in which a stork carried a baby, because storks have no cultural connection to birth in Japan.[27] Similarly, Japanese companies operating in the United States seem to be out of touch with the expectations of American managers. In a survey of American managers employed by 31 such companies, the common complaint was too few promotions and too little responsibility.[28]

Ethnocentric attitudes can also cause problems in ethnically diverse countries, such as the United States, where Hispanics/Latinos are projected to be nearly one-quarter of the population by 2050[29] and 12 percent of the population presently speak Spanish.[30]

> *When it comes to Hispanic marketing, a little knowledge is a dangerous thing. . . . Tropicana advertised* jugo de china *in Miami.* China *means orange to Puerto Ricans, but Miami's Cubans thought it was juice from the Orient. Jack in the Box goofed with a commercial featuring a band of Mexican mariachis accompanying a Spanish flamenco dancer. "That's like having Willie Nelson sing while Michael Jackson does the moonwalk," says Bert Valencia, a marketing professor at the American Graduate School of International Management in Glendale, Arizona.*
>
> *Why do companies sometimes end up looking like* idiotas? *Because learning this market takes more than a few lessons at Berlitz. An occasional blunder is forgivable. But many companies are designing advertising for the nation's . . . [more than 35] million Hispanics without understanding the differences among Mexicans, Puerto Ricans, Cubans, and the rich array of the other nationalities that make up the U.S. Hispanic population.[31]*

In fact, U.S. Hispanics and Latinos trace their roots to 22 different countries (see Managing Diversity).

## Polycentric Attitude.
This host-country orientation is based on the assumption that, because cultures are so different, local managers know what is best for their operations. A **polycentric attitude** leads to a loose confederation of comparatively independent subsidiaries rather than to a highly integrated structure. Because foreign operations are measured in terms of ends (instead of means), methods, incentives, and training procedures vary widely from location to location.

On the negative side, wasteful duplication of effort occurs at the various units within the confederation precisely because they are independent. Such duplication can erode the efficiency of polycentric organizations. Moreover, global objectives can be undermined by excessive concern for local traditions and success. But there is a positive side: "The main advantages are an intensive exploitation of local markets, better sales since local management is often better informed, more local initiative for new products, more host-government support, and good local managers with high morale."[32]

**polycentric attitude** *view that assumes local managers in host countries know best how to run their own operations*

## Geocentric Attitude.
Managers with a **geocentric attitude** are world-oriented. "As Sue Evens, senior manager of international human resources consulting at KPMG, New York, says, thinking globally means 'taking the best other cultures have to offer and blending that into a third culture.' "[33] Skill, not nationality, determines who gets promoted or transferred to key positions around the globe. In geocentric companies, local and worldwide objectives are balanced in all aspects of operation. Collaboration between headquarters and subsidiaries is high, but an effort is made to maintain a balance between global standards and local discretion. Thus, a geocentric attitude is essential in the transnational model discussed earlier. Bausch & Lomb, the Rochester, New York, maker of Ray-Ban sunglasses, fosters a geocentric attitude by telling its managers to "think globally, but act locally." Says international division senior vice president Ronald Zarella: "What we try to do today is set strategic goals and let local

**geocentric attitude** *world-oriented view that draws upon the best talent from around the globe*

# Managing Diversity

## Hispanic Employees and Patients Fit in at This North Carolina Hospital

Hispanics will become the largest ethnic minority in the United States by 2005, according to the U.S. Census Bureau. For Sandra Stokes, the implications of that projection are already being felt where she lives and works.

Stokes, human resource development consultant at the University of North Carolina Health Care System in Chapel Hill, began to recognize several years ago that the composition of the workforce at her hospital and in her community was changing. She also astutely realized that the policies and culture at her organization had to change too....

The first time Stokes realized there was a specific need was during an orientation program for new employees. The Hispanic employees who didn't speak English, or did so with limited skill, had trouble understanding the orientation leader and could not read the materials provided—materials that explained important hospital policies that cover their rights, safety and benefits.

That's when Stokes took action. "We realized that we had a challenging opportunity to welcome employees from Spanish-speaking countries," Stokes recalls. "Our team committed to translating all written orientation materials into Spanish and ensuring that qualified interpreters be present during the orientation program."

The hospital now has paid part-time and full-time interpreters as well as volunteers who are made available for both employees and patients; the number of new Hispanic patients has doubled from 3,000 in 1995 to 6,000 in 1999. All interpreters must pass a proficiency test.

Stokes did not stop there. She realized that learning the language of Hispanic employees meant that she could not only communicate better with them, but also could build a bond and a trust that encouraged them to come to her with questions or concerns.

"Because I welcome Hispanic employees in their native language when they arrive for orientation, I often become the person they relate to over a long period," she explains. Stokes is quick to point out that she is not fluent in Spanish. But it's not important. "The Hispanic employees are so grateful that you make the effort to speak their language that we can work together to understand each other." . . .

Recognizing the importance of breaking down the language barrier between Hispanics and non-Hispanics at the hospital, the UNC HR department, through the interpreting department, began arranging English as a Second Language classes for Spanish-speaking employees. Also important, the Department of Human Resource Development offers Spanish-language classes to all employees on-site. . . .

Stokes and her team soon realized that language classes weren't enough. There were cultural divides that also needed to be addressed. She began reading about Hispanic culture and offering Hispanic culture classes as well.

What she learned—and what she is now teaching non-Hispanic employees—is that Hispanics have firm beliefs, especially when it comes to medicine. "Many Hispanic patients come in with babies wearing a pin or a cross to ward off evil spirits," she explains. "If a nurse tries to take it off, the patient becomes very upset." . . .

She also has learned that Hispanics are a patriarchal society and how that can affect the doctor-patient relationship. "Doctors need to know to talk to the man about medical decisions, even about birth control," she says.

Another trait that can be frustrating for a hospital running on a tight schedule is that Hispanics tend to be late for appointments. "But for them, it's rude to be on time," Stokes explains, "because they think, if you're on time, you're being selfish and taking all the time and medicine."

As for employees, Stokes says cultural differences can hinder the relationships between Hispanics and those not familiar with their culture. "Hispanics won't disagree with you," she says, "but it doesn't mean they will do what you tell them. You have to give a really good reason to do what you tell them. Some may not make eye contact because it shows disrespect."

*Source:* Excerpted from Adrienne Fox, "Southern Hospitality Assimilates Hispanic Workers," *HRMagazine,* 45 (December 2000): 56, 58. Reprinted with the permission of *HRMagazine,* published by the Society for Human Resource Management, Alexandria, VA.

management take advantage of nuances in their market."[34] This has enabled Bausch & Lomb to satisfy European demand for more styles and costly sunglasses than is typical in the United States. "In Asia the company redesigned them to better suit the Asian face—with its flatter bridge and higher cheek bones—and sales took off."[35]

Of these three contrasting attitudes, only a geocentric attitude can help management take a long step toward success in today's vigorously competitive global marketplace.

## The Cultural Imperative

Culture has a powerful impact on people's behavior. For example, consider the everyday activity of negotiating a business contract.

> *To Americans, a contract signals the conclusion of negotiations; its terms establish the rights, responsibilities, and obligations of the parties involved. However, to the Japanese, a company is not forever bound to the terms of the contract. In fact, it can be renegotiated whenever there is a significant shift in the company's circumstances. For instance, an unexpected change in governmental tax policy, or a change in the competitive environment, are considered legitimate reasons for contract renegotiation. To the Chinese, a signatory to an agreement is a partner with whom they can work, so to them the signing of a contract is just the beginning of negotiations.*[36]

Cross-cultural business negotiators who ignore or defy cultural traditions do so at their own risk. That means the risk of not making the sale or of losing a contract or failing to negotiate a favorable deal. Therefore, a sensitivity to cross-cultural differences is imperative for people who do business in other countries.

### 4C  A Corporate United Nations?

*USA Today identified CEOs of U.S. companies who were born in nearly 100 countries, from Bulgaria to Colombia to Tunisia to Vietnam. At least 14 of the Fortune 500 CEOs are foreign-born.*

**Source:** Del Jones, "Foreign-Born CEOs Cite U.S. Merit-Based System," *USA Today* (October 2, 2001): 2B.

**Question:** *Will this trend likely make American companies more ethnocentric or geocentric? Explain.*

*Are the people of the world becoming more alike or more different? The theory of* convergence *says we will become more similar than different, because of global business, travel, telecommunications, media, and entertainment. Oppositely, the theory of* divergence *points toward a world of expanding differences, because of cultural tribalization and the growing gap between rich and poor. A third perspective,* crossvergence, *says nations will evolve their own unique blends of domestic and foreign practices. This mobile-phone store in the West African country of Cote d'Ivoire illustrates convergence.*

In this section, we define the term *culture,* address the fear of an "Americanized" world culture, and discuss a cultural profile of U.S. managers. Then, drawing primarily from the work of pioneering cultural anthropologist Edward T. Hall, we explore key sources of cross-cultural differences.

**culture**    *a population's taken-for-granted assumptions, values, beliefs, and symbols that foster patterned behavior*

**Culture Defined.**     **Culture** is the pattern of taken-for-granted assumptions about how a given collection of people should think, act, and feel as they go about their daily affairs.[37] Regarding the central aspect of this definition—taken-for-granted assumptions—Hall noted:

> *Much of culture operates outside our awareness; frequently, we don't even know what we know. . . . This applies to all people. The Chinese or the Japanese or the Arabs are as unaware of their assumptions as we are of our own. We each assume that they're part of human nature. What we think of as "mind" is really internalized culture.[38]*

In Chapter 9, *organizational* culture is called the social glue binding members of an organization together. Similarly, at a broader level, societal culture acts as a social glue. That glue is made up of norms, values, attitudes, role expectations, taboos, symbols, heroes, beliefs, morals, customs, and rituals. Cultural lessons are imparted from birth to death via role models, formal education, religious teachings, and peer pressure.

Cultural undercurrents make international dealings immensely challenging. According to Fons Trompenaars and Charles Hampden-Turner, the Dutch and English authors of the landmark book *Riding the Waves of Culture:*

> *International managers have it tough. They must operate on a number of different premises at any one time. These premises arise from their culture of origin, the culture in which they are working, and the culture of the organization which employs them.*
>
> *In every culture in the world such phenomena as authority, bureaucracy, creativity, good fellowship, verification, and accountability are experienced in different ways. That we use the same words to describe them tends to make us unaware that our cultural biases and our accustomed conduct may not be appropriate, or shared.[39]*

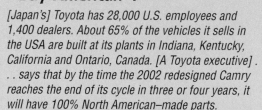

**4D   Is It Futile to Ask People in the United States to "Buy American"?**

*[Japan's] Toyota has 28,000 U.S. employees and 1,400 dealers. About 65% of the vehicles it sells in the USA are built at its plants in Indiana, Kentucky, California and Ontario, Canada. [A Toyota executive] . . . says that by the time the 2002 redesigned Camry reaches the end of its cycle in three or four years, it will have 100% North American–made parts.*

**Source:**  David Kiley, " 'Buying American' Takes Some American Know-How," *USA Today* (October 3, 2001): 6D.

**Question:**  *Is it a good idea to try to buy goods made in your own country? Why?*

**Are U.S. Global Corporations Turning the World into a Single "Americanized" Culture?** Protesters at World Trade Organization and global economic summit meetings in recent years have decried the growing global reach of McDonald's (in 120 countries) and other American corporate giants. They predict a homogenizing of the world's unique cultures into a so-called McWorld, where American culture prevails. Although emotionally appealing, these concerns are *not* supported by University of Michigan researchers who have been tracking cultural values in 65 societies for more than 20 years. Citing evidence from their ongoing World Values Survey, the researchers recently concluded:

> *The impression that we are moving toward a uniform "McWorld" is partly an illusion. The seemingly identical McDonald's restaurants that have spread throughout the world actually have different social meanings and fulfill different social functions in different cultural zones. Eating in*

a McDonald's restaurant in Japan is a different social experience from eating in one in the United States, Europe, or China.

>    *Likewise, the globalization of communication is unmistakable, but its effects may be overestimated. It is certainly apparent that young people around the world are wearing jeans and listening to U.S. pop music; what is less apparent is the persistence of underlying value differences.*
>
>    *In short, economic development will cause shifts in the values of people in developing nations, but it will not produce a uniform global culture. The future may look like McWorld, but it won't feel like one.[40]*

Cultural roots run deep, have profound impacts on behavior, and are not readily altered.

## A Cultural Profile of American Managers.

A good way to become more aware of cross-cultural differences is to look at oneself through the eyes of people from other cultures. One study based on interviews with 40 managers from many different countries has given American managers a revealing look in the cultural mirror.[41] All of the managers had professional experience in more than one country. Only three of the interviewees were American. Each manager was asked to characterize the "American style" of management. Results of the study are presented in Table 4.3.

Two sets of characteristics of the American style of managing turned out to be clearly positive. International managers generally like Americans' informality, creativity, open-mindedness, and related traits. At the other end of the scale, American managers were

**4D   Big Wide World? What World?**

*More than 75% of the [U.S.] public supports requiring students to take courses addressing global issues. But college coursework of that nature is, at best, uneven. One study indicates that less than 7% of college students meet even basic standards of global preparedness.*

**Source:** Mary Beth Marklein, "Colleges Lose Their Foreign Accent," *USA Today* (November 13, 2000): 7D.

**Questions:** *How do you rate your own awareness of global issues and preparedness to work in the global economy? How world-wise is your college coursework?*

**Table 4.3**   How Do International Managers Characterize American Managers?

| Frequently mentioned features that distinguish the U.S. from other nations | |
|---|---|
| **Positive** | **Negative** |
| Informal, frank, trustworthy | |
| Innovative, open-minded, objective, pragmatic, flexible | |
| Work harder than Europeans | But less than many Asians. Often "spinning wheels" |
| Impatient; get things done; hands-on mentality | Short-term orientation |
| Materialistic; profit-oriented; business is a valid, worthy profession | Judge person's worth by their wealth; shun low-pay manufacturing jobs |
| Individualistic; entrepreneurial | Loyal to division, not firm |
| Aggressive, hard-nosed, pragmatic | Overlook simpler, diplomatic means |
| | Not well rounded educationally; parochial |

*Source:* Ashok Nimgade, "American Management as Viewed by International Professionals," November–December 1989, Figure 4, p. 102. Reprinted from *Business Horizons,* November–December 1989. Copyright 1989 by the Foundation for the School of Business at Indiana University. Used with permission.

Question: *Where's the world's biggest Wal-Mart store? Hint: Notice the English and Spanish greeting cards. Answer: Laredo, Texas. This giant 151,900-square-foot store draws customers from a 150-mile radius covering big chunks of South Texas and Northeastern Mexico. Wal-Mart's low price strategy plays a big role in the success of this store. But so do shelves packed with culturally appropriate goods. A Wal-Mart in Japan wouldn't sell cards for your favorite* tia *or* sobrina.

roundly criticized for being educationally and professionally narrow. Between the extremes, representing a mix of positives and negatives, were five other sets of characteristics. In this middle zone, strengths such as impatience and individualism, when taken to extreme, became weaknesses. In sum, American managers have a lot going for themselves. But a number of their basic cultural tendencies can cause problems in cross-cultural dealings. Self-awareness and cultural adaptations are required.[42]

**4** Explain from a cross-cultural perspective the difference between high-context and low-context cultures, and distinguish between individualistic and collectivist cultures.

**high-context cultures**
*cultures in which nonverbal and situational messages convey primary meaning*

### High-Context and Low-Context Cultures.

People from European-based cultures typically assess people from Asian cultures such as China and Japan as quiet and hard to figure out. Conversely, Asians tend to view Westerners as aggressive, insensitive, and even rude.[43] True, language differences are a significant barrier to mutual understanding. But something more fundamental is involved, something cultural. Anthropologist Hall prompted better understanding of cross-cultural communication by distinguishing between high- and low-context cultures.[44] The difference centers on how much meaning one takes from what is actually said or written versus who the other person is.

In **high-context cultures,** people rely heavily on nonverbal and subtle situational messages when communicating with others. The other person's official status, place in society, and reputation say a great deal about the person's rights, obligations, and trustworthiness. In high-context cultures, people do not expect to talk about such "obvious" things. Conversation simply provides general background information about the other person. Thus, in high-context Japan, the ritual of exchanging business cards is a social necessity, and failing to read a card you have been given is a grave insult. The other person's company and position determine what is said and how. Arab, Chinese, and Korean cultures also are high-context.

People from **low-context cultures** convey essential messages and meaning primarily with words. Low-context cultures in Germany, Switzerland, Scandinavia, North America, and Great Britain expect people to communicate their precise intended meaning. While low-context people do read so-called body language, its messages are secondary to spoken and written words. Legal contracts with precisely worded expectations are important in low-context countries such as the United States. However, according to international communications experts, "in high-context cultures the process of forging a business relationship is as important as, if not more important than, the written details of the actual deal."[45] This helps explain why Americans tend to be frustrated with the apparently slow pace of business dealings in Japan. For the Japanese, the many rounds of meetings and social gatherings are necessary to collect valuable contextual information as a basis for judging the other party's character. For the schedule-driven American, anything short of actually signing the contract is considered a pointless waste of time. *Patience* is a prime virtue for low-context managers doing business in high-context cultures.

**low-context cultures**
*cultures in which words convey primary meaning*

## Other Sources of Cultural Diversity.

Managers headed for a foreign country need to do their homework on the following cultural variables to avoid awkwardness and problems.[46] There are no rights or wrongs here, only cross-cultural differences.

- *Individualism versus collectivism.* This is a distinction between "me" and "we" cultures. People in **individualistic cultures** focus primarily on individual rights, roles, and achievements. The United States and Canada are highly individualistic cultures. Meanwhile, people in **collectivist cultures**—such as Egypt, Mexico, India, and Japan—rank duty and loyalty to family, friends, organization, and country above self-interests. Group goals and shared achievements are paramount to collectivists; personal goals and desires are suppressed. Importantly, individualism and collectivism are extreme ends of a continuum, along which people and cultures are variously distributed and mixed. For example, in the United States, one can find pockets of collectivism among Native Americans and recent immigrants from Latin America and Asia. This helps explain why a top-notch engineer born in China would be reluctant to attend an American-style recognition dinner where individual award recipients are asked to stand up for a round of applause.

**individualistic cultures**
*cultures that emphasize individual rights, roles, and achievements*

**collectivist cultures** *cultures that emphasize duty and loyalty to collective goals and achievements*

- *Time.* Hall referred to time as a silent language of culture. He distinguished between monochronic and polychronic time.[47] **Monochronic time** is based on the perception that time is a unidimensional straight line divided into standard units, such as seconds, minutes, hours, and days. In monochronic cultures, including North America and Northern Europe, everyone is assumed to be on the same clock and time is treated as money. The general rule is to use time efficiently, be on time, and above all, do not waste time. In contrast, **polychronic time** involves the perception of time as flexible, elastic, and multidimensional. Latin American, Mediterranean, and Arab cultures are polychronic. Managers in polychronic cultures such as rural Mexico see no problem with loosely scheduled, overlapping office visits. A monochronic American, arriving 10 minutes early for an appointment with a regional Mexican official, resents having to wait another 15 minutes. The American perceives the Mexican official as slow and insensitive. The Mexican believes the American is self-centered and impatient.[48] Different perceptions of time are responsible for this collision of cultures.

**monochronic time** *a perception of time as a straight line broken into standard units*

**polychronic time** *a perception of time as flexible, elastic, and multidimensional*

- *Interpersonal space.* People in a number of cultures prefer to stand close when conversing. Both Arabs and Asians fall into this group. An interpersonal distance of only six inches is very disturbing to a Northern European or an American who is accustomed to conversing at arm's length. Cross-cultural gatherings in the Middle

## 4F  Foreign Language Skills

*Fact:* Senior executives in the Netherlands speak an average of 3.9 languages. Their counterparts in both the United Kingdom and the United States speak an average of 1.5 languages.

Learning a foreign language is easier for some than for others. International business experts say it is worth the time and effort in order to

- Enhance the traveler's sense of mastery, self-confidence, and safety.
- Show respect for foreign business hosts or guests.
- Help build rapport and trust with foreign hosts or guests.
- Improve the odds of a successful foreign business venture.
- Build a base of confidence for learning other languages.
- Promote a deeper understanding of other cultures.
- Help travelers obtain the best possible medical care during emergencies.
- Minimize culture shock and the frustrations of being an outsider.

**Sources:** Data from "Bilingual Business," *USA Today* (April 11, 2000): 1B; list adapted from Gary P. Ferraro, "The Need for Linguistic Proficiency in Global Business," *Business Horizons*, 39 (May–June 1996): 39–46.

**Questions:** *Could you conduct a business meeting in one or more foreign languages? What has been your experience with trying to learn foreign languages? How strong is your desire to speak a foreign language? Which language(s)? Why? Would a strong second language help you get a better job? Explain.*

East often involve an awkward dance as Arab hosts strive to get closer while their American and European guests shuffle backwards around the room to maintain what they consider to be a proper distance.

- *Language.* Foreign language skills are the gateway to true cross-cultural understanding. Translations are not an accurate substitute for conversational ability in the local language.[49] Consider, for example, the complexity of the Japanese language:

*Japanese is a situational language and the way something is said differs with the relationship between speaker, listener, or the person about whom they are speaking; their respective families, ages, professional statuses, and companies all affect the way they express themselves.*

*In this respect, Japanese isn't one language but a group of them, changing with a dizzying array of social conventions with which Americans have no experience. Japanese people are raised dealing with the shifting concepts of in group/out group, male and female speech patterns, appropriate politeness levels, and humble and honorific forms of speech. An unwary student, armed only with a few years of classroom Japanese, can pile up mistakes in this regard very quickly.[50]*

Foreign-language instructors who prepare Americans for foreign assignments have noted these recent trends: an increase in demand for Brazilian Portuguese and Mandarin Chinese and a decrease in demand for Japanese. Spanish remains the most widely studied foreign language, followed by French and German.[51]

- *Religion.* Awareness of a business colleague's religious traditions is essential for building a lasting relationship. Those traditions may dictate dietary restrictions, religious holidays, and Sabbath schedules, which are important to the devout and represent cultural minefields for the uninformed. For instance, the official day of rest in Iran is Thursday; in Kuwait and Pakistan it is Friday.[52] In Israel, where the official day off is Saturday, "Burger King restaurants—unlike McDonald's—do not offer cheeseburgers in order to conform to Jewish dietary laws forbidding mixing milk products and meat."[53]

# Comparative Management Insights

**comparative management**
*study of how organizational behavior and management practices differ across cultures*

**Comparative management** is the study of how organizational behavior and management practices differ across cultures. In this comparatively new field of inquiry, as in other fields, there is disagreement about theoretical frameworks and research methodologies.[54] Nevertheless, some useful lessons have been learned. In this section, we focus on (1) the applicability of American management theories in other cultures,

(2) Ouchi's Theory Z, which contrasts American and Japanese management practices, (3) a cross-cultural study of work goals, and (4) an international contingency model of leadership.

## Applying American Management Theories Abroad

The results of a unique study indicate that management theories may not be universally applicable. Geert Hofstede, a Dutch organizational behavior researcher, surveyed 116,000 IBM employees from 40 different countries.[55] Hofstede classified each of his 40 national samples according to four different cultural dimensions, each of which probed an important question about the prevailing culture:

- *Power distance.* How readily do individuals accept the unequal distribution of power in organizations and institutions?
- *Uncertainty avoidance.* How threatening are uncertain and ambiguous situations, and how important are rules, conformity, and absolute truths?
- *Individualism-collectivism.* Are people responsible for their own welfare within a loosely knit social framework, or does the group look out for individuals in exchange for loyalty?
- *Masculinity-femininity.* How important are masculine attitudes (assertiveness, money and possessions, and performance) versus feminine attitudes (concern for people, the quality of life, and the environment)?

Hofstede scored the 40 countries in his sample from low to high on each of the four cultural dimensions. The United States ranked moderately low (15 out of 40) on power distance, low (9 out of 40) on uncertainty avoidance, very high (40 out of 40) on individualism, and moderately high (28 out of 40) on masculinity.

The marked cultural differences among the 40 countries led Hofstede to recommend that American management theories should be adapted to local cultures rather than imposed on them. As we saw in Chapter 2, many popular management theories were developed within the U.S. cultural context. Hofstede believes that it is naive to expect those theories to apply automatically in significantly different cultures. For example, American-made management theories that reflect Americans' preoccupation with individualism are out of place in countries such as Mexico, Brazil, and Japan, where individualism is discouraged. Moreover, as Hofstede discovered, the need ranked highest differs from culture to culture (see Table 4.4).

Hofstede's research does not attempt to tell international managers *how* to apply various management techniques in different cultures. However, it does provide a useful cultural typology and presents a convincing case for the cultural adaptation of American management theory and practice.[56]

**5** Discuss what Geert Hofstede's research has to say about the applicability of American management theories in foreign cultures.

## Ouchi's Theory Z: The Marriage of American and Japanese Management

The work of UCLA management scholar William Ouchi highlighted a type of U.S. company that successfully melded the American way of managing with some aspects of management in another culture. Ouchi began his study by identifying the contrasting characteristics of Japanese and American companies.[57] During the course of his research, he discovered that certain then-successful U.S.-based companies—including IBM, Intel, Hewlett-Packard, Eastman Kodak, and Eli Lilly—exhibited a style of management that effectively combined the traits of typical American and Japanese

**6** Identify important comparative management lessons learned from William Ouchi's Theory Z research and international studies of work goals and leadership styles.

**Table 4.4     Top-Ranking Needs Vary from Country to Country**

| Security | Security and social | Social | Self-actualization |
|---|---|---|---|
| Switzerland | Iran | Singapore | Hong Kong** |
| Germany* | Thailand | Denmark | Great Britain |
| Austria | Taiwan | Sweden | India |
| Italy | Brazil | Norway | United States |
| Venezuela | Israel | Netherlands | Philippines |
| Mexico | France | Finland | Canada |
| Colombia | Spain | | New Zealand |
| Argentina | Turkey | | Australia |
| Belgium | Peru | | South Africa |
| Japan | Chile | | Ireland |
| Greece | Yugoslavia | | |
| Pakistan | Portugal | | |

*At the time of this study, East and West Germany were separate countries. East Germany was not one of the forty countries surveyed.
**Now reunited with China.

*Source:*  Paraphrased with permission from Geert Hofstede, "Motivation, Leadership, and Organization: Do American Theories Apply Abroad?" in *Organizational Dynamics*, 9, no. 1 (Summer 1980): 54–56. This article summarizes Dr. Hofstede's research published in the book *Culture's Consequences: International Differences in Work-Related Values* (Beverly Hills, Calif.: Sage Publications, 1980).

companies. He called these hybrid companies *Theory Z* organizations (see Figure 4.1). Interestingly, Ouchi's Theory Z companies did not simply imitate the Japanese. Instead, each firm's Theory Z qualities evolved from a desire to improve upon the typical American way of managing. Each Theory Z company was strictly American in origin, but American and Japanese in conduct and appearance.

The Japanese-like qualities of Theory Z organizations are identified as long-term employment, slower promotions, cross-functional career paths, greater emphasis on self-control, participative decision making, and a concern for the whole employee. Unlike Japanese organizations, Theory Z organizations emphasize *individual* responsibility, a distinctly American trait. Ouchi's work not only gives us a better understanding of Japanese management,[58] it also shows that American organizations can benefit from thoughtful incorporation of the experience of managers in other cultures.

Too much emphasis on one country's cultural management practices can cause problems. For example, *Business Week* described how the Japanese style of management has been a hindrance to change-minded leaders at Mitsubishi, Toshiba, and Toyota during Japan's prolonged recession:

> [They] are among the best corporate chiefs on the planet. But they have been cruelly misplaced in a Japan that cannot tolerate the unemployment and social upheaval that wholesale restructuring would entail. And because Japanese corporate culture places so much stress on building consensus and saving face, even world-class bosses often struggle vainly to impose their visions on the organizations they theoretically run.
>
> As competition grows increasingly global, these executives are at a huge disadvantage compared with rivals in America and Europe.[59]

The principal lesson from this example and from Hofstede's and Ouchi's research is clear. *Successful geocentric managers are not prisoners of their own culture.* They create

**4G**

## Ouch, That Hurts!

*Old Japanese saying:* "The nail that sticks out is hammered down."

**Source:** As quoted in Julie Schmit, "Japan Undergoes E-Makeover," *USA Today* (April 19, 2000): 2B.

**Questions:** *What implications does this have for would-be entrepreneurs in Japan? Does the "nail" ever get hammered down in the United States (or another country of your choice)? Explain.*

**Figure 4.1**    A Continuum of Social Responsibility Strategies

| Japanese Organizations | + American Organizations | = Theory Z Organizations |
|---|---|---|
| Lifetime employment | Short-term employment | **Long-term employment** *Large training investment encourages company to retain personnel through good and bad times.* |
| Slow evaluation and promotion | Rapid evaluation and promotion | **Relatively slow evaluation and promotion** *Promotions are tied to skills and contributions rather than to the calendar.* |
| Nonspecialized career paths | Specialized career paths | **Cross-functional career paths** *Companywide skills are acquired through varied and nonspecialized experience.* |
| Implicit control mechanisms *(self-control)* | Explicit control mechanisms *(control through policies and rules)* | **Balanced explicit and implicit control mechanisms** *Bureaucratic control is supplemented by personal judgments and feelings about what is right or wrong, appropriate or inappropriate.* |
| Collective decision making | Individual decision making | **Consensual, participative decision making** *Decisions are derived through democratic process involving all affected employees.* |
| Collective responsibility | Individual responsibility | **Individual responsibility** *Ultimate responsibility for decisions remains with relevant individuals.* |
| Holistic concern | Segmented concern | **Holistic concern for employees** *There is a willingness to deal with the "whole" person rather than fragmented organizational role players.* |

*Source:* From *Theory Z: How American Business Can Meet the Japanese Challenge* by William Ouchi. Copyright © 1981. Reprinted by permission of Perseus Books Publishers, a member of Perseus Books Publishers, a member of Perseus Books, L.L.C.

(and constantly update) a workable blend of management concepts and practices from around the world.

## A Cross-Cultural Study of Work Goals

What do people want from their work? A survey of 8,192 employees from seven countries found general disagreement about the relative importance of 11 different work goals.[60] Respondents to the survey represented a broad range of professions and all

**Table 4.5**    Work Goals Vary from Country to Country

| Work goals | Means rankings (by country) | | | | |
|---|---|---|---|---|---|
| | **U.S.** | **Britain** | **Germany\*** | **Israel** | **Japan** |
| **Interesting work** | 1 | 1 | 3 | 1 | 2 |
| **Pay** | 2 | 2 | 1 | 3 | 5 |
| **Job security** | 3 | 3 | 2 | 10 | 4 |
| **Match between person and job** | 4 | 6 | 5 | 6 | 1 |
| **Opportunity to learn** | 5 | 8 | 9 | 5 | 7 |
| **Variety** | 6 | 7 | 6\*\* | 11 | 9 |
| **Interpersonal relations** | 7 | 4 | 4 | 2 | 6 |
| **Autonomy** | 8 | 10 | 8 | 4 | 3 |
| **Convenient work hours** | 9 | 5 | 6\*\* | 7 | 8 |
| **Opportunity for promotion** | 10 | 11 | 10 | 8 | 11 |
| **Working conditions** | 11 | 9 | 11 | 9 | 10 |

\* Formerly West Germany.
\*\* Two goals tied for sixth rank.

*Source:*  Data from Itzhak Harpaz, "The Importance of Work Goals: An International Perspective," *Journal of International Business Studies,* 21 (First Quarter 1990): 81. Reprinted with permission.

levels of the organizational hierarchy. They were asked to rank 11 work goals. Those work goals are listed in Table 4.5, along with the average rankings for five countries. "Interesting work" got a consistently high ranking. "Opportunity for promotion" and "working conditions" consistently were at or very near the bottom of each country's rankings. Beyond those few consistencies, general disagreement prevailed.

The main practical implication of these findings is that managers need to adapt their motivational programs to local preferences.[61] Throughout this text, we consistently stress the importance of the contingency approach to management. In this case, an international contingency approach to motivation is called for. For instance, pay is relatively less important in Japan than in the other four countries. And job security is much less important to Israelis than it is to American, British, German, and Japanese employees.

## An International Contingency Model of Leadership

Like motivational programs, leadership styles must be adapted to the local culture. This conclusion is based on a new international contingency model of leadership, which is the product of two separate but overlapping studies. As indicated in Table 4.6, the four path-goal leadership styles have varying applicability in selected countries. (Refer to our discussion of path-goal leadership theory in Chapter 15 for definitions of the four styles.) Importantly, the model in Table 4.6 is intended to be a general guideline for international managers, not a set of hard-and-fast rules.

According to the model, participative leadership is the most broadly applicable style. Participative leadership is not necessarily the *best* style; it simply is culturally acceptable in many different countries. Interestingly, in a more recent study of employees in Russia's largest textile factory, participative leadership triggered a *decrease* in out-

**Table 4.6**   An International Contingency Model of Leadership: Culturally Appropriate Path-Goal Leadership Styles

| Country | Directive | Supportive | Participative | Achievement-oriented |
|---|---|---|---|---|
| Australia | | X | X | X |
| Brazil | X | | X | |
| Canada | | X | X | X |
| France | X | | X | |
| Germany | | X | X | X |
| Great Britain | | X | X | X |
| Hong Kong* | X | X | X | X |
| India | X | | X | X |
| Italy | X | X | X | |
| Japan | X | X | X | |
| Philippines | X | X | X | X |
| Sweden | | | X | X |
| Taiwan | X | X | X | |
| United States | | X | X | X |

*Now reunited with China.

*Sources:* Adapted from Carl A. Rodrigues, "The Situation and National Culture as Contingencies for Leadership Behavior: Two Conceptual Models," in *Advances in International Comparative Management*, 5, ed. S. Benjamin Prasad (Greenwich, Conn.: JAI Press, 1990), pp. 51–68; and Geert Hofstede and Michael Harris Bond, "The Confucius Connection: From Cultural Roots to Economic Growth," *Organizational Dynamics* (Spring 1988): 4–21.

put. Why? The researchers felt the Russians had a lack of faith in participative schemes found to be untrustworthy during the Communist era.[62] It takes time for people in new democracies to get used to participative management. For example, American entrepreneur Michael Smolens has taken it one step at a time at Danube Knitware Ltd., the textile mill he cofounded in Hungary. It has been a learning experience for all involved at the 950-employee company that recently opened a sewing factory in neighboring Romania.

*The first step was getting workers used to high Western production standards and motivating them to accept the company's priorities. Hungary's low wage base was seen as a big plus when the company was being formed, but absenteeism has been an ongoing problem. . . . Smolens realized he'd have to strengthen his wage structure to keep his workers from abandoning the company for the family farms or the black market. He also moved from awarding attendance bonuses to providing other job incentives—in particular, cultivating a more comfortable, open work environment.*

*"We're actively soliciting comments from the workers day to day," says [cofounder Phil] Lightly. "They know what the problems are, but because of the way things used to be in this country, they're not always comfortable sharing them."*

*"It's a good approach," Smolens adds, "and we do see progress. They're starting to realize that what they say is being taken seriously."*[63]

Relative to the countries listed in Table 4.6, directive leadership turned out to be the *least* appropriate leadership style.

**4H   Looking for the Right Stuff**

According to Robert Rosen, author and international management consultant, today's global businesses need leaders who:

- See the world's challenges and opportunities.
- Think with an international mindset.
- Act with fresh, global-centric leadership behaviors.
- Mobilize a world-class team and company.

**Source:** Ruth E. Thaler-Carter, "Whither Global Leaders?" *HRMagazine*, 45 (May 2000): 84.

**Questions:** *How do you measure up to this profile? Can you identify people you know personally who fit these requirements? Describe these people and assess their effectiveness.*

Hong Kong and the Philippines, probably because of their rich cultural diversity, are unique in their receptiveness to all four leadership styles. International managers need a full repertoire of leadership styles in a culturally diverse world.[64]

# Staffing Foreign Positions

In today's global economy, successful foreign experience is becoming a required stepping-stone to top management. *Fortune* magazine's Marshall Loeb observed, "An assignment abroad, once thought to be a career dead end, has become a ticket to speedy advance. And an increasingly necessary one."[65]

Unfortunately, owing largely to the sink-or-swim approach to foreign assignments, too many Americans find it very difficult to become competent global managers.[66] "According to the Centre for International Briefing, roughly 25 percent of American managers fail overseas. That's three to four times higher than failure rates experienced by European and Asian companies."[67] Failure in this context means that foreign-posted employees perform so poorly they are either fired or sent home early. This problem can be very costly in view of the following data: "Each year, U.S. firms send an estimated 100,000 Americans on foreign assignments. With an average stay of four years, the investment in an expatriate—including salary, housing allowances, and moving expenses—can easily run over $1 million."[68] Predeparture training for the employee and education allowances for children can drive the bill much higher. Managers are challenged not to waste this sort of investment. They need to do a much better job of preparing employees for foreign assignments. Toward that end, let us examine why a higher-than-average proportion of American managers fail abroad and what can be done about it.

## Why Is the U.S. Expatriate Failure Rate So High?

Although historically a term for banishment or exile to a foreign country, *expatriate* today refers to those who live and work abroad. A survey of 80 U.S.-based multinational companies uncovered some important facts about the reasons for corporate

*"Who wants to go to school when we can watch these guys." Maybe that's what these Indonesian schoolgirls are thinking as they study this odd airborne pair. What they actually are watching is Kentuckian Rusty Smith and his Indonesian coworker, Sodik, splicing fiber-optic cable. It's a productive cross-cultural partnership. Smith taught Sodik sophisticated technical skills and Sodik helps Smith navigate the Indonesian countryside and culture.*

| **Table 4.7**   Why U.S. Employees Fail in Foreign Assignments (in descending order of importance) |
| --- |
| 1. Inability of the manager's spouse to adjust to a different physical or cultural environment |
| 2. The manager's inability to adapt to a different physical or cultural environment |
| 3. Other family-related problems |
| 4. The manager's personality or emotional immaturity |
| 5. The manager's inability to cope with the responsibilities posed by overseas work |
| 6. The manager's lack of technical competence |
| 7. The manager's lack of motivation to work overseas |

*Source:* Ranking based on responses to a survey of 80 U.S. MNCs. Rosalie L. Tung, "Expatriate Assignments: Enhancing Success and Minimizing Failure," *Academy of Management Executive,* 1 (May 1987): 117. Reprinted by permission.

expatriate failures (see Table 4.7). *Family and personal adjustment problems* head the list, whereas technical incompetence ranks near the bottom. Expatriate American managers tend to be technically competent, but they and/or their families too often are at a disadvantage in cross-cultural settings.[69] This state of affairs is not surprising in view of the following:

> *[Research] underscores the woeful lack of preparation many U.S. executives receive for assignments overseas. Of some 100 high-level U.S. executives (average income $172,000) working in Western Europe, 84 percent received no corporate briefing on management practices in their host countries, and 77 percent didn't even get factual information on the new country. Only 15 percent received language training. And over 75 percent of the companies failed to communicate with their employee's spouses about the new assignments and to offer them job assistance overseas.[70]*

Twenty percent of the polled executives desired a transfer home, and 9 percent actually went home early.

## Cross-Cultural Training

In line with our earlier definition, culture is the unique system of values, beliefs, and symbols that foster patterned behavior in a given population. It is difficult to distinguish the individual from his or her cultural context. Consequently, people tend to be very protective of their cultural identity. Careless defiance of cultural norms or traditions by outsiders can result in grave personal insult and put important business dealings at risk. Cultural sensitivity can be learned, fortunately, through cross-cultural training.[71]

**7** Discuss the nature and importance of cross-cultural training in international management.

**cross-cultural training**
*guided experience that helps people live and work in foreign cultures*

**Specific Techniques.**   **Cross-cultural training** is defined as any form of guided experience aimed at helping people live and work comfortably in another culture. Following is a list of five basic cross-cultural training techniques, ranked in order of increasing complexity and cost.

- *Documentary programs.* Trainees read about a foreign country's history, culture, institutions, geography, and economics. Videotaped presentations also are often used.
- *Culture assimilator.* Cultural familiarity is achieved through exposure to a series of simulated intercultural incidents, or typical problem situations. This technique has

**41  Parlez vous Microsoft Excel?**

*Fact:* Mandarin Chinese is the world's most common language, spoken by 885 million people. Spanish is next with 332 million speakers, followed by English (322 million), Bengali (189 million), Hindi (182 million), Portuguese and Russian (170 million each), and Japanese (125 million).

*Opinion:* "Odds are more business-oriented Asians speak fluent Microsoft Excel than speak fluent English. Which fluency better helps their business?"

**Sources:**  Data from Julie Schmit, "Rough Translation: 'No English, No Job'—A Reality Many of Asia's Workers Face," *USA Today* (July 21, 2000): 1B; and Michael Schrage, "Beyond Babel: Why the Babble Below Will Matter Less," *Fortune* (March 19, 2001): 214.

**Question:**  *In today's high-tech world, with common software and promises of instant electronic translations, is learning a foreign language any less important than before? Explain.*

been used to quickly train those who are given short notice of a foreign assignment.

■ *Language instruction.* Conversational language skills are taught through a variety of methods. Months, sometimes years, of study are required to master difficult languages. But as a cross-cultural communications professor noted, "To speak more than one language is no longer a luxury, it is a necessity."[72] A good role model is Tupperware's top management team, made up of nine executives (all with foreign experience) who speak from two to four languages each.[73]

■ *Sensitivity training.* Experiential exercises teach awareness of the impact of one's actions on others.

■ *Field experience.* Extensive firsthand exposure to ethnic subcultures in one's own country or to foreign cultures heightens awareness.[74]

**Is One Technique Better than Another?**   A study of 80 (63 male, 17 female) managers from a U.S. electronics company attempted to compare the relative effectiveness of different training techniques.[75] A documentary approach was compared with an interpersonal approach. The latter combined sensitivity training and local ethnic field experience. Both techniques were judged equally effective at promoting cultural adjustment, as measured during the managers' three-month stay in South Korea. The researchers recommended a *combination* of documentary and interpersonal training. The importance of language training was diminished in this study because the managers dealt primarily with English-speaking Koreans.

Considering that 57 percent of U.S. companies have no formal expatriate training programs,[76] the key issue is not which type of training is better, but whether companies have any systematic cross-cultural training at all.

**An Integrated Expatriate Staffing System.**   Cross-cultural training, in whatever form, should not be an isolated experience. Rather, it should be part of an integrated, selection-orientation-repatriation process focused on a distinct career path.[77] The ultimate goal should be a positive and productive experience for the employee and his or her family and a smooth professional and cultural reentry back home.

During the selection phase, the usual interview should be supplemented with an orientation session for the candidate's family. This session gives everyone an opportunity to "select themselves out" before a great deal of time and money has been invested. Experience has shown that, upon arrival at the foreign assignment, family sponsors or assigned mentors are effective at reducing culture shock.[78] Sponsors and mentors ease the expatriate family through the critical first six months by answering naive but important questions and by serving as cultural translators.

Finally, repatriation should be a forethought rather than an afterthought.[79] Candidates for foreign assignments deserve a firm commitment from their organization that a successful tour of duty will lead to a step up the career ladder upon return. Expatriates who spend their time worrying about being leapfrogged while they are absent from headquarters are less likely to succeed.

## What About North American Women on Foreign Assignments?

Historically, companies in Canada and the United States have sent very few women on foreign assignments. Between the early 1980s and late 1990s, the representation of women among North American expatriates grew from 3 percent to a still small 14 percent.[80] Conventional wisdom—that women could not be effective because of foreign prejudice—has turned out to be a myth. Recent research and practical experience have given us these insights:

- North American women have enjoyed above-average success on foreign assignments.
- The greatest barriers to foreign assignments for North American women have been self-disqualification and prejudice among *home-country* managers. A recent survey led to this conclusion: "We found that American women in management and executive roles in foreign countries can do just as well as American men. Their biggest problem was convincing their companies to give them the assignments."[81]
- Culture is a bigger hurdle than gender. In other words, North American women on foreign assignments are seen as North Americans first and women second.[82]

Testimonial evidence suggests these last two factors are also true for African-Americans, many of whom report smoother relations abroad than at home.[83] Thus, the best career advice for *anyone* seeking a foreign assignment is this: carefully prepare yourself, *go for it,* and don't take "no" for an answer![84]

## Relying on Local Managerial Talent

In recent years, the expensive expatriate failure problem and general trends toward geocentrism and globalism have resulted in a greater reliance on managers from host countries. Foreign nationals already know the language and culture and do not require huge relocation expenditures.[85] In addition, host-country governments tend to look favorably on a greater degree of local control. On the negative side, local managers may have an inadequate knowledge of home-office goals and procedures. The staffing of foreign positions is necessarily a case-by-case proposition.

**8** Summarize the position of women on foreign assignments.

**4J**

### Back to the Opening Case

After reading this case, the material in this chapter, and the travel tips in the Skills & Tools feature at the end of the chapter, are you more or less motivated to seek a foreign assignment someday? Explain.

# Summary

**1.** The study of international management is more important than ever as the huge global economy continues to grow. Doing business internationally typically involves much more than importing and/or exporting goods. The six stages of the internationalization process are licensing, exporting, local warehousing and selling, local assembly and packaging, joint ventures, and direct foreign investments. There are three main guidelines for success in international joint ventures: (a) Be patient while building trust with a carefully selected partner; (b) learn as much and as fast as possible without giving away key secrets; and (c) establish clear ground rules for rights and responsibilities.

**2.** The main distinction between global companies and transnational companies is the difference between reality and a futuristic vision. A global company does business simultaneously in many countries but pursues global strategies administered from a strong home-country headquarters. In contrast, a transnational company is envisioned as a decentralized global network of productive units with no distinct national identity. There is growing concern about the economic and political power of these stateless enterprises as they eclipse the power and scope of their host nations.

**3.** Experts, noting that American managers generally are prepared only for domestic service, recommend that present and future managers begin to think globally and cross-culturally. According to Howard Perlmutter, management may have any of three general attitudes about international operations: an ethnocentric attitude (home-country-oriented), a polycentric attitude (host-country-oriented), or a geocentric attitude (world-oriented). Perlmutter claims that a geocentric attitude will lead to better product quality, improved use of resources, better local management, and more profit than the other attitudes.

**4.** Communication in high-context cultures such as Japan is based more on nonverbal and situational messages than it is in low-context cultures such as the United States. People in individualistic "me" cultures emphasize the individual's rights and goals, whereas loyalty and duty to the well-being of social units such as family and organization are primary in collectivist "we" cultures. People in monochronic time cultures perceive time to be linear and divided into standard units. They believe time should be used efficiently. In contrast, people in cultures based on polychronic time consider time to be flexible and multidimensional. International managers need to be aware of cultural differences in interpersonal space, agreements, language, and religion.

**5.** Comparative management is a new field of study concerned with how organizational behavior and management practices differ across cultures. A unique study by Geert Hofstede of 116,000 IBM employees in 40 nations classified each country by its prevailing attitude toward power distance, uncertainty avoidance, individualism-collectivism, and masculinity-femininity. In view of significant international differences on these cultural dimensions, Hofstede suggests that American management theory and practice be adapted to local cultures rather than imposed on them.

**6.** Ouchi's Theory Z describes a hybrid type of American company that exhibits a combination of typical American and Japanese characteristics. Theory Z firms rely heavily on Japanese-style consensus and participation during decision making. But Theory Z organizations prefer an American-style emphasis on individual responsibility. Cross-cultural studies of work goals and leadership styles uncovered a great deal of diversity. Thus international contingency approaches to motivation and leadership are recommended.

**7.** Compared with European and Japanese companies, U.S. multinationals have a much higher expatriate failure rate. Family and personal adjustment problems to foreign cultures, not lack of technical expertise, are the leading causes of this failure. Systematic cross-cultural training is needed to help solve this costly problem, though use of local managerial talent is also a possible solution, depending on the situation.

**8.** North American women fill a growing but still small share of foreign positions. The long-standing assumption that women will fail on foreign assignments because of foreigners' prejudice has turned out to be false. Women from the United States and Canada have been successful on foreign assignments but face two major hurdles at *home:* self-disqualification and prejudicial managers. Culture, not gender, is the primary challenge for women on foreign assignments. The situation for African Americans parallels that of women.

## Terms to Understand

International management (p. 111)

Global company (p. 113)

Transnational company (p. 113)

Ethnocentric attitude (p. 116)

Polycentric attitude (p. 117)

Geocentric attitude (p. 117)

Culture (p. 120)

High-context cultures (p. 122)

Low-context cultures (p. 123)

Individualistic cultures (p. 123)

Collectivist cultures (p. 123)

Monochronic time (p. 123)

Polychronic time (p. 123)

Comparative management (p. 124)

Cross-cultural training (p. 131)

## Skills & Tools

### Twelve Tips for Safe International Business Trips

1. Before leaving home, discuss with your family what to do in case of an emergency. Upon arrival at your destination, register with the U.S. Embassy or Consulate and inform them of your travel plans. This approach will enable a relative to find you quickly in an emergency. It will also enable State Department officials to quickly contact you if conditions in the country deteriorate and require evacuation of U.S. citizens.

2. Listen to the ubiquitous television commercials touting the benefits of traveler's checks. They're as good as cash in most places and much safer. If you don't have traveler's checks, convert as much money as possible into local currency to spend during your stay. Flashing Yankee dollars is a dead giveaway of your identity.

3. At the airport, keep hand luggage in sight at all times. Experienced thieves know carry-on bags are likely to contain valuables such as cameras, computers, jewelry, or cash.

4. Don't put a sign in your car window advertising yourself as a traveler. Tuck the car rental agreement into the glove compartment. It's like a beacon to drug addicts and petty thieves who assume you have money in your pocket, and expensive clothes, cameras, and other valuables in the trunk.

5. Stick to main roads when leaving the airport. Never take shortcuts or turnoffs unless you know exactly where they lead. Drive with the windows up and lock the doors.

6. Don't pull off the road or stop if another motorist attempts to alert you that something is wrong with your car. It's a favorite ruse of carjackers from Moscow to Miami. Also, don't get out of your car to examine the damage when a vehicle rear ends you. Drive to a busy, well-lighted intersection and wait for the police.

7. Take taxis instead of hiring limousines. Those big, block-long luxury liners attract the wrong kind of attention, particularly in countries where the poverty and crime rates are high. Cabdrivers know their way around and can park freely at stands near office buildings, stores, embassies, and concert halls without attracting the attention of panhandlers, pickpockets, and professional criminals.

8. When making a hotel reservation, book a room between the second and eighth floor because fire apparatus can't go higher and the first floor is usually an invitation to burglars. Check all valuables and keep your door locked at all times. Never admit anyone to your room who isn't expected—including room service. Also, be suspicious of a call from the front desk just after checking in requesting verification of your credit card number because the imprint was unreadable. A thief may have watched you enter the hotel and called from the guest phone in the lobby.

9. Travel with friends, colleagues, or an escort whenever possible. A lone person is always a more tempting target.

10. Stay away when you see trouble developing. Riots, civil disturbances, and political demonstrations are common in many foreign countries, and you can literally get run over or caught in the cross-fire. Travel security reports frequently can alert you to avoid certain unsafe areas based on advanced information about where and when dangerous demonstrations may occur.

11. Don't fight a "hostile takeover." If confronted by bandits or street thugs, surrender your valuables and/or vehicle without a struggle. Comply with instructions, act calm, keep your self-control, and hide your fear. Pleading for mercy, cringing, crying, or other actions that diminish your dignity in the eyes of your captors can actually provoke gratuitous violence.

12. Avoid fatal attractions. Stay away from districts known for gambling, pornography, or prostitution. Aside from the physical danger, your presence or an embarrassing photograph of you in an unsavory surrounding can lead to extortion attempts. When planning to visit historic or scenic locations, never hire street guides to show you the sites. Ask the hotel concierge to recommend a licensed tour agent.

By observing these simple precautions you'll greatly minimize the risks involved with international travel. So next time someone tells you to have a safe trip, smile and say "thanks."[86]

*Source:*  Excerpted from J. Antonio Tijerino, "12 Tips for Business Travel." Reprinted from *Management Review*, 85 (December 1995). © 1995 by American Management Association. Reproduced with permission of American Management Association in the textbook format via Copyright Clearance Center.

## Hands-On Exercise

## Look into the Cultural Mirror

**Instructions**

Culture, as defined in this chapter, involves *taken-for-granted* assumptions about how we should think, act, and feel (relative to both ourselves and the world in general). Here is an opportunity to bring those assumptions to the surface. Remember, there are no right or wrong answers. Moreover, because this exercise has no proven scientific validity, it is intended for instructional purposes only. The idea is to see where you stand in the world's rich mosaic of cultural diversity by rating yourself on the cultural variables discussed in this chapter.

Low context　　　　　　　　　　　　　　　High context
("Put it in writing.")　　　　　　　　　　　("The situation is more
　　　　　　　　　　　　　　　　　　　　important than words.")

　　　1 · · · · · · · · · · · · · 2 · · · · · · · · · · · · · 3 · · · · · · · · · · · · · 4 · · · · · · · · · · · · · 5

Individualistic　　　　　　　　　　　　　　Collectivist
("Me first.")　　　　　　　　　　　　　　　("It's all about us.")

　　　1 · · · · · · · · · · · · · 2 · · · · · · · · · · · · · 3 · · · · · · · · · · · · · 4 · · · · · · · · · · · · · 5

Monochronic
*("Do one thing at a time
and be on time.")*

Polychronic
*("There's a time to go fast and a
time to go slow. Do more than one
thing at a time.")*

1·················2·················3·················4·················5

Power Distance

Low
*("Leaders are no better
than anyone else.")*

High
*("Authority and power of
leaders should be respected.")*

1·················2·················3·················4·················5

Uncertainty Avoidance

Low
*("Take chances, bend
the rules.")*

High
*("Take no chances, follow
the rules.")*

1·················2·················3·················4·················5

Masculinity
*("Winning and material
wealth are what count.")*

Femininity
*("Relationships and quality of
life are what really matter.")*

1·················2·················3·················4·················5

**For Consideration/
Discussion**

**1.** Did this exercise help you better understand any of the cultural variables discussed in this chapter? Explain.

**2.** Does your cultural profile help you better understand some of your family's traditions, values, rituals, or customs?

**3.** How does your cultural profile compare with those of others (spouse, friends, classmates)? Could the seeds of conflict and misunderstanding grow from any cultural differences with them?

**4.** How do you match up with the cultural profile of American managers in Table 4.3? Which of your positive cultural traits could become a negative if taken to extremes?

# Internet Exercises

1. **Using the Internet to prepare for a foreign assignment (or travel adventure).** When your author was in graduate school, he was offered the chance to teach for six months in Micronesia. He accepted—and then ran to the university library to find out where Micronesia was (it turned out to be 2,200 islands in the Western Pacific, just north of the Equator). To make a long story short, he soon found himself standing at the airport in a pool of sweat on a tiny coral atoll in the Marshall Islands with his books, virtually no knowledge of the local culture, and a big lump in his throat. Six months, lots of mistakes and lessons, countless mosquito bites, and five islands later, he boarded a plane back to the United States, a grateful and wiser person. Thanks to the Internet, you can get to the grateful and wiser stage a lot more efficiently.

   Log on to the Internet and go to *The Wall Street Journal*'s online career publication (**www.careerjournal.com**). At the home page, find the heading "Related Sites" and click on "European Careers." Scroll to the bottom of the page and select "Country Profiles." Pick one of the 26 countries that you would like to visit, live and work in, or just learn more about. (*Note:* You may want to print a copy of your selected country profile for class discussion or future reference.)

   An excellent second source of national and cultural information about your selected country (or one not on the *Journal*'s list) comes from the publishers of the somewhat offbeat *Lonely Planet* travel guides (**www.lonelyplanet.com**). From the home page menu, click on "Worldguide." At the "Destinations" page, follow the prompts to tap into useful information about the country you have in mind.

   If the local language for your selected country is not your native language, the Internet can get you headed in the right direction. At the home page of **www.travlang.com,** scroll down to the bottom and select "Foreign Languages for Travelers" and then follow the two steps for your chosen language. Next, at your selected language page, click on the option "Basic Words." Practice your new vocabulary of essential greetings and questions. The quiz option is a good learning tool.

   *Learning Points:* 1. Does your selected country appear to be high-context or low-context? Individualistic or collectivist? Monochronic or polychronic? How can you tell? 2. How much culture shock are you likely to experience in your chosen country? Explain. 3. How well will your native language serve you? What language will you have to know to do business in your selected country? 4. If it is not your native language, how do you say "Yes," "No," "Hello," "Thank you," and "Goodbye" in the language of your selected country? 5. Based on your Internet studies, how strong is your desire to visit or work in the country you selected? Explain.

2. **Check it out:** After the 2001 terrorist attacks on America, foreign business travelers have a greater need than ever to know about potential trouble spots. At the home page of Air Security International (**www.airsecurity.com**), click on "Hotspots." Next, click on the "Current Issue" button for Hot Spots. You will find lots of up-to-date and useful information on travel alerts and trouble spots around the world. Featured countries are assigned a "country threat level" rating from 1 (reasonably safe) to 5 (high threat of physical harm). *Bon voyage!*

For updates to these exercises, visit our Web site (**http://business.college.hmco. com/students**).

# Closing Case

## Tell the Kids We're Moving to Kenya

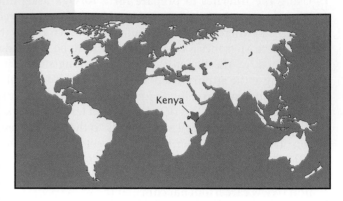

**D**ale Pilger, General Motors Corp.'s new managing director for Kenya, wonders if he can keep his Kenyan employees from interrupting his paperwork by raising his index finger.

"The finger itself will offend," warns Noah Midamba, a Kenyan. He urges that Mr. Pilger instead greet a worker with an effusive welcome, offer a chair and request that he wait. It can be even trickier to fire a Kenyan, Mr. Midamba says. The government asked one German auto executive to leave Kenya after he dismissed a man—whose brother was the East African country's vice president.

Mr. Pilger, his adventurous wife and their two teenagers, miserable about moving, have come to . . . [Boulder, Colorado,] for three days of cross-cultural training. The Cortland, Ohio, family learns to cope with being strangers in a strange land as consultants Moran, Stahl & Boyer International give them a crash immersion in African political history, business practices, social customs and nonverbal gestures. The training enables managers to grasp cultural differences and handle culture-shock symptoms such as self-pity.

Cross-cultural training is on the rise everywhere because more global-minded corporations moving fast-track executives overseas want to curb the cost of failed expatriate stints. . . .

But as cross-cultural training gains popularity, it attracts growing criticism. A lot of the training is garbage, argues Robert Bontempo, assistant professor of international business at Columbia University. Even customized family training offered by companies like Prudential Insurance Co. of America's Moran Stahl—which typically costs $6,000 for three days—hasn't been scientifically tested. "They charge a huge amount of money, and there's no evidence that these firms do any good" in lowering foreign-transfer flops, Prof. Bontempo contends.

"You don't need research," to prove that cross-cultural training works because so much money has been wasted on failed overseas assignments, counters Gary Wederspahn, director of design and development at Moran Stahl.

General Motors agrees. Despite massive cost cutting lately, the auto giant still spends nearly $500,000 a year on cross-cultural training for about 150 Americans and their families headed abroad. "We think this substantially contributes to the low [premature] return rate" of less than 1 percent among GM expatriates, says Richard Rachner, GM general director of international personnel. . . .

The Pilgers' experience reveals the benefits and drawbacks of such training. Mr. Pilger, a 38-year-old engineer employed by GM for 20 years, sought an overseas post but never lived abroad before. He finds the sessions "worthwhile" in readying him to run a vehicle-assembly plant that is 51 percent owned by Kenya's government. But he finds the training "horribly empty . . . in helping us prepare for the personal side of the move."

Dale and Nancy Pilger have just spent a week in Nairobi. But the executive's scant knowledge of Africa becomes clear when trainer Jackson Wolfe, a former Peace Corps official, mentions Nigeria. "Is that where Idi Amin was from?" Mr. Pilger asks. The dictator ruled Uganda. With a sheepish smile, Mr. Pilger admits, "We don't know a lot about the world."

The couple's instructors don't always know everything about preparing expatriates for Kenyan culture, either. Mr. Midamba, an adjunct international-relations professor at Kent State University and son of a Kenyan political leader, concedes that he neglected to caution Mr. Pilger's predecessor against holding business dinners at Nairobi restaurants.

*Source:* Republished with permission of *The Wall Street Journal*, from Joann S. Lublin, "Companies Use Cross-Cultural Training to Help Their Employees Adjust Abroad" (August 4, 1992): B1, B6. Permission conveyed by Copyright Clearance Center, Inc.

As a result, the American manager "got his key people to the restaurant and expected their wives to be there," Mr. Midamba recalls. But "the wives didn't show up." Married women in Kenya view restaurants "as places where you find prostitutes and loose morals," notes Mungai Kimani, another Kenyan trainer.

The blunder partly explains why Mr. Midamba goes to great lengths to teach the Pilgers the art of entertaining at home. Among his tips: Don't be surprised if guests arrive an hour early, an hour late, or announce their departure four times.

The Moran Stahl program also zeros in on the family's adjustment (though not to Mr. Pilger's satisfaction). A family's poor adjustment causes more foreign-transfer failures than a manager's work performance. That is the Pilgers' greatest fear because 14-year-old Christy and 16-year-old Eric bitterly oppose the move. The lanky, boyish-looking Mr. Pilger remembers Eric's tearful reaction as: "You'll have to arrest me if you think you're going to take me to Africa."

While distressed by his children's hostility, Mr. Pilger still believes living abroad will be a great growth experience for them. But he says he promised Eric that if "he's miserable" in Kenya, he can return to Ohio for his last year of high school next year.

To ease their adjustment, Christy and Eric receive separate training from their parents. The teens' activities include sampling Indian food (popular in Kenya) as well as learning how to ride Nairobi public buses, speak a little Swahili and juggle, of all things.

By the training's last day, both youngsters grudgingly accept being uprooted from friends, her swim team and his brand-new car. Going to Kenya "no longer seems like a death sentence," Christy says. Eric mumbles that he may volunteer at a wild-game reserve.

But their usually upbeat mother has become increasingly upset as she hears more about a country troubled by drought, poverty, and political unrest—where foreigners live behind walled fortresses. Now, at an international parenting session, she clashes with youth trainer Amy Kaplan over whether her offspring can safely ride Nairobi's public buses, even with Mrs. Pilger initially accompanying them.

"All the advice we've gotten is that it's deadly" to ride buses there, Mrs. Pilger frets. Ms. Kaplan retorts, "It's going to be hard" to let teenagers do their own thing in Kenya, but then they'll be less likely to rebel. The remark fails to quell Mrs. Pilger's fears that she can't handle life abroad. "I'm going to let a lot of people down if I blow this," she adds, her voice quavering with emotion.

## For Discussion

1. Does the Pilgers' son, Eric, seem to have an ethnocentric, polycentric, or geocentric attitude? Explain.

2. Would you label Kenya a monochronic or polychronic culture, based on the evidence in this case? Explain.

3. What were the positive and negative aspects of the Pilgers' predeparture training?

4. Do you think the Pilger family will end up having a productive and satisfying foreign assignment? Explain.

## chapter five

# Management's Social and Ethical Responsibilities

*"* I find a universal belief in fairness, kindness, dignity, charity, integrity, honesty, quality, and patience. *"*

Stephen R. Covey

# Is This Major Polluter Turning Green?

Jim Rogers is a 54-year-old Kentuckian with a friendly grin, a slow drawl, and a quirky way of introducing himself. It goes something like this: Hi, I'm Jim Rogers. I'm the CEO of Cinergy, an electric and gas supplier. I burn 30 million tons of coal a year, and I'm responsible for 1% of the world's manmade carbon dioxide. Now what was it you wanted to talk about?

Rogers has always been a maverick. He's been reaching out to green groups for more than a decade. Since 1998 he has used his position at the Edison Electric Institute, a power-company trade association, to argue that his fellow CEOs should begin talking about the once taboo subject of $CO_2$. And—in a move that burns up many within his industry—he favors compromise with environmentalists on legislation that would require power companies to spend billions of dollars to sharply reduce emissions of greenhouse gases and pollutants.

Congress is debating more stringent air-quality standards for coal-burning power plants. Besides restrictions on sulfur dioxide, nitrous oxide, and mercury, lawmakers are also considering—for the first time—limits on the emission of $CO_2$, a possibility that has split the energy sector into warring factions. Companies like Cinergy and American Electric Power, which are willing to compromise on $CO_2$ reductions, are facing off against coal companies and electricity generators like Atlanta's Southern Co. that fear that any limits will mean the beginning of the end for coal-fired power in America. No matter which side wins, the outcome will have far-reaching implications for U.S. energy policy, the environment, and the economy.

Most people think of coal as the fuel that fired the Industrial Revolution. Remarkably, however, it is still responsible for more than half of all electricity consumed in the U.S. It is cheap—$20 to $30 per megawatt of electricity produced, vs. $45 to $60 for natural gas—and plentiful. Last year 1.1 billion tons of coal were mined in the U.S., up 16% from a decade ago, and there are still at least 250 years' worth of reserves. That's a statistic the coal industry has been quick to point to since Sept. 11, amid renewed concerns about America's dependence on foreign oil. But coal is dirty. Burning it produces a toxic miasma that contributes to smog and acid rain. And no fuel emits more greenhouse gas. Each year America's coal-fired power plants pump about two billion tons of carbon dioxide into the atmosphere, more than twice the amount produced by cars.

Rogers considers himself an environmentalist. But he says hard business logic, not green sentiment, underlies his position on $CO_2$. His primary goal is to scrap what he calls "a death by 1,000 cuts" approach to regulation. Power plants are governed by 17 federal environmental programs, each with its own set of requirements and deadlines. Such conditions make long-term business planning nearly impossible. "No one wants to spend $1 billion to build a new coal-fired plant and discover ten years later that they have to spend another $500 million to meet new regulations," says Cinergy spokesman Steve Brash.

In return for regulatory certainty, Rogers would be willing to make steep reductions in $CO_2$. "If there is a way to put together a comprehensive approach that gives us certainty over the next ten to 15 years, then I am prepared to offer further emissions cuts," he says. "Because that allows me to plan whether I retrofit my plants, whether I convert them to gas, or whether I shut them down." Rogers knows he'll never get the legislation he wants if it addresses only sulfur dioxide, nitrous oxide, and mercury. "Clearly the environmentalists are not going to have that happen," he says. That's why he is offering concessions on $CO_2$; it's the ultimate bargaining chip in a high-stakes game of political poker. . . .

No cost-effective technology exists for removing $CO_2$ from power-plant exhaust; there is no such thing as a $CO_2$ scrubber. The simplest method to reduce $CO_2$ in the air is to plant trees. The resulting forests, called "carbon sinks," absorb the gas. Cinergy has worked with the Nature Conservancy to preserve woodlands in Ohio and rain forests in Belize. But carbon sinks only do so much. "They're maybe 10% to 15% of an effective response," says Mike Coda, who directs the Nature Conservancy's climate-change program.

Coal-mining and electric companies have teamed up to work on "clean coal" technologies (environmentalists insist the term is an oxymoron), the most promising of which involves turning coal into a gas before burning it. But plants that run on coal gas cost more to build than conventional ones. And there is still the problem of what to do with the $CO_2$ once it is removed from the coal gas. Experiments on carbon sequestration, which involve storing $CO_2$ underground or trapping it deep in the sea, have only begun. That's why Rogers would like more time—and government subsidies—for further research.

He may not get either. The energy industry has cried wolf over deadlines for emissions cuts so many times that environmentalists are understandably skeptical. "It doesn't surprise me to hear the industry say this is too much too soon," says Rebecca Stanfield, staff attorney at the U.S. Public Interest Research Group. "They have said that at every turn since the 1990 Clean Air Act. But study after study shows these are achievable and cost-effective targets."

If green groups object that Rogers' proposals don't go far enough fast enough, his opponents worry that he's about to give away the store. "Regulatory certainty in these agreements is an illusion," says Dwight Evans, Southern's head of external affairs. "There's no guarantee that the next day environmental groups won't be back to pressure you for even more." Southern and Peabody Energy, the world's largest coal-mining company, are digging in to keep $CO_2$ out of any emissions bill. To sway lawmakers, they paint doomsday scenarios about a U.S. economy hobbled by high electricity prices. They don't concede an inch, refusing even to acknowledge that $CO_2$ poses an environmental risk. "There is conflicting research," says Irl Englehardt, CEO of coal giant Peabody Energy and Rogers' bête noir. "We need a new scientific review." . . .

Unless carbon sequestration technology improves dramatically in the next decade, limits on $CO_2$ emissions will force power companies to begin switching to less-polluting natural gas or to renewable energy sources. That's why hard-liners in the energy sector can't understand Rogers' position. Privately they claim that he has sold out to the environmentalists in order to burnish his public image. But what's really happening is that the interests of electricity producers and coal companies are diverging. The Department of Energy predicts that coal will generate about 30% of America's electricity in 20 years, even if Congress mandates $CO_2$ cuts. While that's bad news for coal, it isn't necessarily bad for Rogers. After all, he's in the electricity business, not the coal-burning business. "At the end of the day we have to produce energy and fuel our economy on a sustainable basis," Rogers says. "In the long term that means weaning ourselves from fossil fuels."

**M**ajor changes are never easy, particularly when entrenched interests and huge capital investments are involved. Just ask Jim Rogers, who is attempting to walk a narrow tightrope between the interests of his industry and the demands of environmentalists. Meanwhile, important questions remain unanswered. Are Rogers's actions little more than a public relations gimmick to keep government regulators and the environmental camp at bay? Or is he wisely crafting a strategy for the long-term survival of his company? Is this sort of corporate social responsibility an expedient luxury or a nonnegotiable necessity? What is the appropriate balance between profits and the public good? This chapter will help you tackle these tough questions.

As the social, political, economic, and technological environments of management have changed, the practice of management itself has changed. This is especially true for managers in the private business sector. Today, in the wake of the Enron, Tyco, and WorldCom debacles, it is far less acceptable for someone in business to stand before the public and declare that his or her only job is to make as much profit as possible. The public is wary of the abuse of power and the betrayal of trust, and business managers—indeed, managers of all types of organizations—are expected to make a wide variety of economic and social contributions. Demands on business that would have been considered patently unreasonable 30 years ago have become normal today. The purpose of this chapter is to examine management's social and ethical responsibilities.

# Social Responsibility: Definition and Perspectives

When John D. Rockefeller was at the zenith of his power as the founder of Standard Oil Company, he handed out dimes to rows of eager children who lined the street. Rockefeller did this on the advice of a public relations expert who believed the dime campaign would counteract his widespread reputation as a monopolist who had ruthlessly eliminated his competitors in the oil industry. The dime campaign was not a complete success, however, because Standard Oil was broken up under the Sherman Antitrust Act of 1890.[1] Conceivably, Rockefeller believed he was fulfilling some sort of social responsibility by passing out dimes to hungry children. Since Rockefeller's time, the concept of social responsibility has grown and matured to the point where many of today's companies are intimately involved in social programs that have no direct connection with the bottom line. These programs include everything from support of the arts and urban renewal to environmental protection. But like all aspects of management, social responsibility needs to be carried out in an effective and efficient manner.

## What Does Social Responsibility Involve?

Social responsibility, as defined in this section, is a relatively new concern of the business community. Like a child maturing through adolescence on the way to adulthood, the idea of corporate social responsibility is evolving. Business writer Susan Gaines offered this perspective:

> *Analysts predict that what was once known as "the socially responsible business movement" will from this point forward grow more slowly as its appeal broadens and takes root in the mainstream business community. "The low-hanging fruit has already been picked for the most part," says Bill Shireman, CEO and president of California Futures, a research and consulting firm that helps resolve conflicts between the business and environmental communities. "The businesses that very easily and eagerly call themselves socially responsible are already in the arena. Mainstream businesses will get there, too, but they are very, very cautious." Eventually, most businesses will begin to understand that they are maximizing profits to pursue higher values, he adds.[2]*

A wide-ranging disagreement remains over the exact nature and scope of management's social responsibilities.

**Voluntary Action.**    One expert defined **corporate social responsibility** as "the notion that corporations have an obligation to constituent groups in society other than stockholders and beyond that prescribed by law or union contract."[3] A central feature of this definition is that an action must be *voluntary* to qualify as a socially responsible action. For example, consider Peter Levy's intriguing corporate spy story:

> *Reared in a small Indiana town by a banker and a school teacher, Levy graduated from Purdue University, then worked for Andersen Consulting. Stepping out on his own, he entered the decidedly unglamorous fastener industry by co-founding a paper-clip maker near New York City 13 years ago.*
>
> *But there he was in 1997: wielding a video camera as he tailed a truck to a prison in the city of Nanjing in eastern China, where slave laborers bloodied their fingers assembling metal clips for a competitor who exported them illegally to the United States.*

**1** Define corporate social responsibility and summarize the arguments for and against it.

**corporate social responsibility**    *idea that business has social obligations above and beyond making a profit*

*The black metal clips, used to bind thick documents, were costing Levy's company, Gem Office Products, millions in lost revenue.*

*The videotape that Levy, 40, made that spring day became critical evidence in a U.S. Customs Service investigation that resulted, . . . [in 2001,] in the first criminal conviction of a Chinese company in a prison labor case.*[4]

According to our definition and the ten commandments listed in Table 5.1, would you credit Levy with an act of corporate social responsibility? This could be open to debate because his actions, although voluntary, were clearly profit-motivated. But one fact remains: he helped strike a major blow to the prison slave-labor problem. Importantly, the notion of corporate social responsibility does *not* discard the profit motive. It simply challenges managers to *voluntarily* make the world a better place while pursuing a *legitimate* profit.

When lawsuits must be initiated or court orders issued before a company will respond to societal needs, that company is not being socially responsible. A classic example of this type of foot-dragging behavior was the manner in which Beech-Nut Nutrition Corporation, a subsidiary of Switzerland's Nestlé, responded to charges that it had adulterated its supposedly 100 percent apple juice for babies between 1981 and 1983.

*Federal and state officials later charged that Beech-Nut's strategy—executed very effectively—was to avoid publicity and stall their investigations until it could unload its $3.5 million inventory of tainted apple juice products. "They played a cat-and-mouse game with us," says one investigator. When the FDA [U.S. Food and Drug Administration] would identify a specific apple juice lot as tainted, Beech-Nut would quickly destroy it before the FDA could seize it, an act that could have created negative publicity.*[5]

In 1988, two top Beech-Nut officials who had pleaded guilty to 215 felony charges were sentenced to a year and a day in jail and fined $100,000 apiece.[6] Endless court battles and reluctant compliance do not exemplify corporate social responsibility; neither does the use of hollow public relations ploys in lieu of meaningful action.

**Table 5.1    Ten Commandments of Corporate Social Responsibility**

I. Thou Shall Take Corrective Action Before It Is Required.

II. Thou Shall Work with Affected Constituents to Resolve Mutual Problems.

III. Thou Shall Work to Establish Industrywide Standards and Self-Regulation.

IV. Thou Shall Publicly Admit Your Mistakes.

V. Thou Shall Get Involved in Appropriate Social Programs.

VI. Thou Shall Help Correct Environmental Problems.

VII. Thou Shall Monitor the Changing Social Environment.

VIII. Thou Shall Establish and Enforce a Corporate Code of Conduct.

IX. Thou Shall Take Needed Public Stands on Social Issues.

X. Thou Shall Strive to Make Profits on an Ongoing Basis.

*Source:* Excerpted from Larry D. Alexander and William F. Matthews, "The Ten Commandments of Corporate Social Responsibility," *Business and Society Review,* 50 (Summer 1984): 62–66.

*Meet Waldy Malouf and Tom Valenti. These Manhattan restaurant owner-chefs are standing at Ground Zero in New York City to make the point that seemingly small ideas, when acted upon with passion and persistence, can yield enormous social benefits.* The challenge: *help families of Windows on the World employees who were lost when the famous restaurant atop the north tower of the World Trade Center was destroyed on Sept. 11, 2001.* The plan of action: *recruit chefs from around the country to donate 10 percent of one day's receipts to a benefit fund.* The result: *4,000 restaurants and nearly a million diners helped raise over $4 million in aid.*

**An Emphasis on Means, Not Ends.**    Another key feature of this definition of corporate social responsibility is its emphasis on means rather than ends:

> *Corporate behavior should not, in most cases, be judged by the decisions actually reached, but by the process by which they were reached. Broadly stated, corporations need to analyze the social consequences of their decisions before they make them and take steps to minimize the social costs of these decisions when appropriate. The appropriate demand to be made of those who govern large corporations is that they incorporate into their decision-making process means by which broader social concerns are given full consideration. This is corporate social responsibility as a means, not as a set of ends.*[7]

Unfortunately, social consequences are too often shortchanged in the heat of competitive battle.

## What Is the Role of Business in Society?

Much of the disagreement over what social responsibility involves can be traced to a fundamental debate about the exact purpose of a business. Is a business an economic entity responsible only for making a profit for its stockholders? Or is it a socioeconomic entity obligated to make both economic and social contributions to society?[8] Depending on one's perspective, social responsibility can be interpreted either way.

**5A  Actor Paul Newman Sets the Standard in Corporate Social Responsibility**

*In 1982 Newman's Own, Inc. began with Mr. Newman's famous Oil & Vinegar Salad Dressing. Newman's Own now offers an expanded line of salad dressings, pasta sauces, popcorn, lemonade, ice cream, and steak sauce.*

*. . . he gives away all profits, after taxes, from the sale of the products to educational and charitable organizations, both in the U.S. and foreign countries where his products are sold.*

*Over 1,000 charities have received donations from Paul Newman as a result of the sale of Newman's Own products worldwide. $100 million has been donated since 1982.*

**Source:** Excerpted from "The Legend of Newman's Own®," **http://www.newmansown.com**.

**Questions:**  *Are you inspired by this case of corporate social responsibility? Explain. Should we be asking for more from our corporations and ourselves? Explain.*

For further information about the interactive annotations in this chapter, visit our Web site (http://business.college.hmco.com/students).

**The Classical Economic Model.**     The classical economic model can be traced to the eighteenth century, when businesses were owned largely by entrepreneurs or owner-managers. Competition was vigorous among small operations, and short-run profits were the sole concern of these early entrepreneurs. Of course, the key to attaining short-run profits was to provide society with needed goods and services. According to Adam Smith, father of the classical economic model, an "invisible hand" promoted the public welfare. Smith believed the efforts of competing entrepreneurs had a natural tendency to promote the public interest when each tried to maximize short-run profits. In other words, Smith believed the public interest was served by individuals pursuing their own economic self-interests.[9]

This model has survived into modern times. For example, *Business Week* quoted Robert J. Eaton, former chairman of Chrysler Corporation prior to the creation of DaimlerChrysler, as saying, "The idea of corporations taking on social responsibility is absolutely ridiculous. . . . You'll simply burden industry to a point where it's no longer competitive."[10] Thus, according to the classical economic model of business, short-run profitability and social responsibility are the same thing.

**The Socioeconomic Model.**     Reflecting society's broader expectations for business (for example, safe and meaningful jobs, clean air and water, charitable donations, safe products), many think the time has come to revamp the classical economic model, which they believe to be obsolete. Enron, the company that took a spectacular tumble from number 7 on the 2001 *Fortune* 500[11] list to a scandalous bankruptcy in 2002, has been cited as a prime case in point. Economist Robert Kuttner bluntly explained:

*The deeper scandal here is ideological. Enron epitomized an entire philosophy about the supposed self-cleansing nature of markets. . . .*

*Enron, as a trading enterprise, claimed to be the quintessence of a pure free market. In practice, it was up to its ears in cronyism, influence-peddling, rigging the rules to favor insiders, and undermining the transparency on which efficient markets depend. . . .*

*Enron is to the menace of market fundamentalism what September 11 was to the peril of global terror—a very costly wake-up call.*[12]

Enron's 21,000 former employees—most of whom lost their life savings along with their jobs—would likely agree.[13] According to the socioeconomic model proposed as an alternative to the classical economic model, business is just one subsystem among many in a highly interdependent society.

Advocates of the socioeconomic model point out that many groups in society besides stockholders have a stake in corporate affairs. Creditors, current and retired employees, customers, suppliers, competitors, all levels of government, the community, and society in general have expectations, often conflicting, for management. Some companies go so far as to conduct a **stakeholder audit**.[14] This growing practice involves systematically identifying all parties that could possibly be impacted by the company's performance (for an example, see Figure 5.1). According to the socioeconomic view, business has an obligation to respond to the needs of all stakeholders while pursuing a profit.

**stakeholder audit**
*identifying all parties possibly impacted by the organization*

## Arguments for and Against Corporate Social Responsibility

As one might suspect, the debate about the role of business has spawned many specific arguments both for and against corporate social responsibility.[15] A sample of four major arguments on each side reveals the principal issues.

**Arguments For.**    Convinced that a business should be more than simply a profit machine, proponents of social responsibility have offered these arguments:

1. *Business is unavoidably involved in social issues.* As social activists like to say, business is either part of the solution or part of the problem. There is no denying that private business shares responsibility for such societal problems as unemployment, inflation, and pollution. Like everyone else, corporate citizens must balance their rights and responsibilities.

**5B Jack Speaks**

General Electric's recently retired CEO, Jack Welch, when asked "How do you define 'social responsibility'?":

*Win. By winning, being highly profitable. Only then can you be a socially responsible company. If you are worried about your job, you can't give anything back.*

**Source:** As quoted in Del Jones and David Kiley, "Welch Gives Book Launch Another Try," *USA Today* (October 22, 2001): 7B.

**Questions:** *How does this align with the distinction between the classical economic and socioeconomic models of business? Do you agree or disagree with Welch? Explain.*

**Figure 5.1**

A Sample Stakeholder Audit for Wal-Mart, the World's Largest Retailer

Customers

Neighbors of stores and facilities (homeowner's associations)

Employees and contractors

Labor unions

All levels of domestic and foreign government

Consumer advocacy groups

**WAL–MART**

Domestic and foreign suppliers and distributors

Competitors

Stockholders

Financial community (bankers, brokers, and investors)

Public-at-large

Political parties

International and local press and news media

**5C**

**Back to the Opening Case**

Which arguments for and against corporate social responsibility are evident in this case? Explain with specific examples.

2. *Business has the resources to tackle today's complex societal problems.* With its rich stock of technical, financial, and managerial resources, the private business sector can play a decisive role in solving society's more troublesome problems. After all, without society's support, business could not have built its resource base in the first place.
3. *A better society means a better environment for doing business.* Business can enhance its long-run profitability by making an investment in society today. Today's problems can turn into tomorrow's profits.
4. *Corporate social action will prevent government intervention.* As evidenced by waves of antitrust, equal employment opportunity, and pollution-control legislation, government will force business to do what it fails to do voluntarily.

Arguments like the preceding four give business a broad socioeconomic agenda.

**Arguments Against.**    Remaining faithful to the classical economic model, opponents of corporate social responsibility rely on the first two arguments below. The third and fourth arguments have been voiced by those who think business is already too big and powerful.

1. *Profit maximization ensures the efficient use of society's resources.* By buying goods and services, consumers collectively dictate where assets should be deployed. Social expenditures amount to theft of stockholders' equity.
2. *As an economic institution, business lacks the ability to pursue social goals.* Gross inefficiencies can be expected if managers are forced to divert their attention from their pursuit of economic goals.

3. *Business already has enough power.* Considering that business exercises powerful influence over where and how we work and live, what we buy, and what we value, more concentration of social power in the hands of business is undesirable.

4. *Because managers are not elected, they are not directly accountable to the people.* Corporate social programs can easily become misguided. The market system effectively controls business's economic performance but is a poor mechanism for controlling business's social performance.

These arguments are based on the assumption that business should stick to what it does best—pursuing profit by producing marketable goods and services. Social goals should be handled by other institutions such as the family, school, religious organizations, or government.

# Toward Greater Social Responsibility

Is it inevitable that management will assume greater social responsibility? Some scholars believe so. It has been said that business is bound by an **iron law of responsibility,** which states that "in the long run, those who do not use power in a way that society considers responsible will tend to lose it."[16] This is an important concept, considering that cynicism about business runs deep today, despite a more probusiness political climate worldwide. In 2002, General Electric's new CEO, Jeffrey R. Immelt, observed: "The backlash is beginning. . . . Credibility and trust is everything [in business]. And because of the recession, because of Enron, that trust has evaporated."[17] The demand for business to act more responsibly is clear. If this challenge is not met voluntarily, government reform legislation will probably force business to meet it. In this section we look at four alternative social responsibility strategies and some contrasting expressions of corporate social responsibility.

**iron law of responsibility**
*those who do not use power in a socially responsible way will eventually lose it*

## Social Responsibility Strategies

Similar to management's political response continuum, discussed in Chapter 3, is its social responsibility continuum (see Figure 5.2), marked by four strategies: reaction, defense, accommodation, and proaction.[18] Each involves a distinctly different approach to demands for greater social responsibility.

**2** Identify and describe the four social responsibility strategies.

**Reaction.**   A business that follows a **reactive social responsibility strategy** will deny responsibility while striving to maintain the status quo. A case in point involves charges of "environmental racism" made by local residents against the many petrochemical plants along the Mississippi River near Baton Rouge, Louisiana. Their complaint centers on the fact that industrial pollution tends to be worst in the poorest, typically minority-populated neighborhoods. In response, a Louisiana Chemical Association spokesman said: "There has been a big emphasis on minority training, recruiting, and hiring. . . . We are trying to reach out to the minority community, to those who live near our plants, to find out what their concerns are. I just think we need to talk more and build up some trust."[19] Widespread mistrust in the affected minority communities presages a wave of lawsuits against the chemical companies.

**reactive social responsibility strategy**
*denying responsibility and resisting change*

**Defense.**   A **defensive social responsibility strategy** uses legal maneuvering and/or a public relations campaign to avoid assuming additional responsibilities. This strategy

**defensive social responsibility strategy**
*resisting additional responsibilities with legal and public relations tactics*

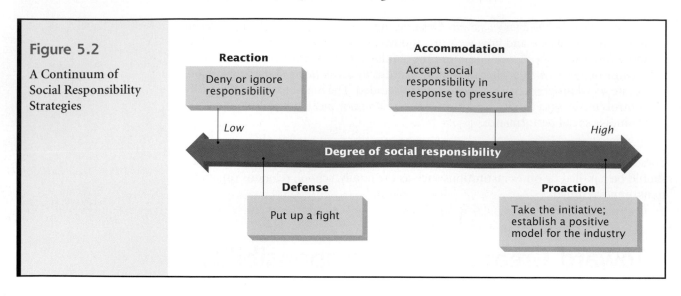

**Figure 5.2**

A Continuum of Social Responsibility Strategies

**Reaction**
Deny or ignore responsibility

**Accommodation**
Accept social responsibility in response to pressure

*Low*

**Degree of social responsibility**

*High*

**Defense**
Put up a fight

**Proaction**
Take the initiative; establish a positive model for the industry

has been a favorite one for the tobacco industry, intent on preventing any legal liability linkage between smoking and cancer. When European countries showed signs of adopting U.S.-style bans on secondhand smoke, Philip Morris launched a rather odd defensive strategy:

> *In a Western European ad campaign that backfired, Philip Morris suggested that inhaling secondhand smoke is less dangerous than eating a cookie or drinking milk. The campaign was banned from France after the National Union of Biscuit Makers and the National Committee Against Tobacco Use filed separate suits against Philip Morris.*[20]

**accommodative social responsibility strategy**
*assuming additional responsibilities in response to pressure*

**Accommodation.**    The organization must be pressured into assuming additional responsibilities when it follows an **accommodative social responsibility strategy.** Some outside stimulus, such as pressure from a special-interest group or threatened government action, is usually required to trigger an accommodative strategy. For example, consider this 2001 news item:

> *McDonald's buckled first. Then Burger King. Now, Wendy's has plans to bolster its animal welfare standards following intense pressure from an animal rights group.*
>
> *People for the Ethical Treatment of Animals (PETA) today will announce the end of its 2-month-old campaign against Wendy's. The move comes 1 day after the fast-food chain told PETA it would strengthen oversight of its suppliers and improve treatment of animals before and during slaughter.*
>
> *The campaign featured billboard images of a Wendy-like character holding a butcher knife dripping with blood. . . .*
>
> *"The Big Three have taken a bite out of their worst cruelties," says Ingrid Newkirk, PETA president. "Consumers don't want blatant animal abuse between the buns."*[21]

**proactive social responsibility strategy**
*taking the initiative with new programs that serve as models for the industry*

Was Wendy's accommodation necessary and appropriate? You be the judge.

**Proaction.**    A **proactive social responsibility strategy** involves formulating a program that serves as a role model for the industry. Proaction means aggressively taking the initiative. Consider, for example, Herman Miller's actions:

*. . . the furniture maker in Zeeland, Michigan, no longer uses tropical woods, such as rose-
wood, from endangered rain forests in its office desks and tables. Instead it uses cherry,
which does not come from the tropics. Says CEO Richard Ruch: "We thought first about the
environmental aspect and then wondered if the switch would impact sales." In fact, the
switch has not hurt sales. . . . And it has added more luster to Herman Miller's already fine
reputation. Inspired by Herman Miller's decision, the Business and Institutional Furniture
Manufacturers Association now urges all its members not to use tropical wood from endangered forests.*[22]

Such creative and trend-setting action qualifies as proactive social responsibility. But
because today's solution often becomes tomorrow's problem, furniture makers may
have to adjust once again if and when cherry trees become endangered.

Corporate social responsibility proponents would like to see proactive strategies
become management's preferred response in both good times and bad.[23]

> **5D**
>
> **Back to the
> Opening Case**
>
> Which of the four social
> responsibility strategies
> are evident in this case?
> Explain.

## Who Benefits from Corporate Social Responsibility?

Is social responsibility the old theory of home medicine, "It has to taste bad to be
good"? In other words, does social responsibility have to be a hardship for the organization? Those who answer *yes* believe that social responsibility should be motivated by
**altruism,** an unselfish devotion to the interests of others.[24] This implies that businesses
that are not socially responsible are motivated strictly by self-interest. In short-run
economic terms, Beech-Nut's cover-up saved it millions of dollars. In contrast, 3M's
decision to pull its popular Scotchgard fabric protector spray cans from the marketplace as soon as the company became aware of a possible health hazard actually cost
the company an estimated $500 million in annual sales.[25] On the basis of these cases
alone, one would be hard pressed to say that social responsibility pays. But research
paints a brighter picture.

**altruism**   *unselfish devotion to
the interests of others*

- A study of 243 companies for two years found a positive correlation between
  industry leadership in environmental protection/pollution control and profitability. The researchers concluded: "It pays to be green."[26]
- A second study found a good reputation for corporate social responsibility to be a
  competitive advantage in recruiting talented people.[27]

**Enlightened Self-Interest.**   **Enlightened self-interest,** the realization that business ultimately helps itself by helping to solve societal problems, involves balancing
short-run costs and long-run benefits. Advocates of enlightened self-interest contend
that social responsibility expenditures are motivated by profit. Research into **corporate
philanthropy,** the charitable donation of company resources ($11 billion in the United
States in 1999),[28] supports this contention.

After analyzing Internal Revenue Service statistics for firms in 36 industries,
researchers concluded that corporate giving is a form of *profit-motivated advertising.*
They went on to observe that "it would seem ill-advised to use philanthropy data to
measure altruistic responses of corporations."[29] This profit-motivated advertising the-
sis was further supported by a study of 130 large manufacturing firms in the United
States. Companies that had committed significant crimes but donated a good deal of
money had better responsibility ratings than companies that had committed no crimes
but donated very little money.[30] Still more evidence of corporate philanthropy being
profit-motivated advertising is the tactic called *cause-related marketing.* This is an off-
shoot of advocacy advertising, discussed in Chapter 3. Only in this instance, instead of

**3** Explain the role of
enlightened self-interest in
social responsibility.

**enlightened self-interest**   *a
business ultimately helping itself by
helping to solve societal problems*

**corporate philanthropy**
*charitable donation of company
resources*

*Some would call it shameless public relations, others would say it's "enlightened self-interest." By telling Lucy Bremond's story in advertisements, General Electric portrays itself as a socially responsible corporate citizen. So what's wrong with a little bragging, if others can be inspired to volunteer for community improvement programs?*

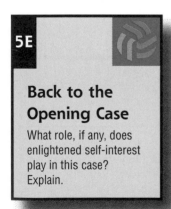

### 5E

### Back to the Opening Case

What role, if any, does enlightened self-interest play in this case? Explain.

promoting a point of view or opinion along with their products, advertisers support a worthy cause. Typically, customers are urged to buy a product or service because a portion of the proceeds will go to a specified charity. For example, "Use of American Express credit cards generated $22 million for Share Our Strength, a poverty-relief charity, over the four-year life of the Charge Against Hunger program."[31] Clearly, this win-win situation was an act of enlightened self-interest by American Express because it polished the company's reputation while fighting poverty.

**An Array of Benefits for the Organization.**    In addition to the advertising effect, other possible long-run benefits for socially responsible organizations include the following:

- Tax-free incentives to employees (such as buying orchestra tickets and giving them to deserving employees).
- Retention of talented employees by satisfying their altruistic motives.
- Help in recruiting talented and socially conscious personnel.
- Swaying public opinion against government intervention.
- Improved community living standards for employees.
- Attracting socially conscious investors.

# The Global Manager

## Ben Cohen, of Ben & Jerry's, Dips into "Venture Philanthropy"

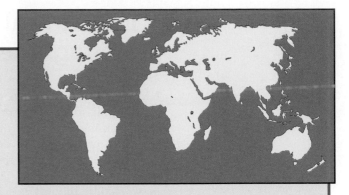

**B**en Cohen of Ben & Jerry's knows that if you add hot fudge to a scoop of good vanilla ice cream, it makes the ordinary extraordinary. He also knows that if you add Hot Fudge venture capital to a good business idea, it will do the same. That's why he set out in August 2000 to create the cutting-edge Hot Fudge Venture Fund as a "venture philanthropy" fund—a nonprofit community development venture capital fund, with the primary aim of building wealth among people who traditionally had no access to it. Its dual aim is to make a profit and serve society.

The fund received a one-time capital infusion of $5 million from Unilever, as part of the agreement when Unilever purchased Ben & Jerry's. The fund uses this capital to invest in small businesses in economically distressed communities, providing startup or first-round funding. As a venture philanthropy fund, Hot Fudge puts human returns before financial returns. It does not seek to forego capital returns, but neither does it seek to maximize them. Its goal is modest annual returns of between 8 and 12 percent.

This approach to returns is based on the model of Mondragon, which is a network of cooperative businesses in northern Spain. "It is the reverse of venture capital approaches here that start off with high-return expectations," said Pierre Ferrari, president of Hot Fudge and a former Coca-Cola executive. When businesses get in trouble, traditional venture capitalists make the next round of financing even more expensive, he explained. Mondragon does the opposite. If the company falters, it provides additional technical assistance, plus a new round of capital at a lower price. And, Ferrari adds, the new business success rate for Mondragon is 98 percent. . . .

In Atlanta, Hot Fudge invested in Scales Precision Sheet Metal Fabrication, a startup planning to offer internships and find jobs for disadvantaged youth, with the aim of increasing the economic self-sufficiency of families. Still another investment was in the Guayaki Yerba Maté Project (**http://www.guayaki.com**), part of the Guayaki Rainforest Reserve in Paraguay, where sustainable cultivation of yerba maté tea protects the rainforest as it provides long-term income to indigenous people.

Currently, Hot Fudge is investing $1.25 million in Team X, a startup company run by George Akers, a 25-year veteran of the apparel industry recognized as a leading expert in organic cotton clothing and sustainable manufacturing. In the mid-1990s, he ran the only fully sustainable manufacturing facilities in Los Angeles, which produced certified cotton knits under the brand "OWEAR." Akers' new venture, Team X, will produce the brand "Sweat X," a line of sweatshop-free clothing, made in factories that offer a progressive model for L.A., where two-thirds of garment factories are known to violate minimum wage laws and run unsafe operations. Team X will pay workers a living wage and allow them to form unions.

To build capital for future investments, Hot Fudge hopes to earn capital on its current investments, and to seek funding from corporations, foundations, and individuals. "Even though I'm going to try to earn around 10 percent, I've had a lot of interest from people coming in and expecting a return of 4 percent, just because of the mission," said Ferrari.

*Hot Fudge Venture Fund, 85 Peachtree Circle, Atlanta, GA 30309. Phone 404/255 5667.*

*Source:* Excerpted from Mary Miller, "Ben Cohen's Hot Fudge Venture Fund," *Business Ethics,* 16 (January–February 2002): 6. Reprinted with permission from *Business Ethics,* P.O. Box 8439, Minneapolis, Minn. 55408. 612-879-0695. **www.business-ethics.com**

■ A nontaxable benefit for employees in which company funds are donated to their favorite causes. Many companies match employees' contributions to their college alma maters, for example.

Social responsibility can be a win-win proposition; both society and the socially responsible organization can benefit in the long run.[32] (See the Global Manager.)

# The Ethical Dimension of Management

Highly publicized accounts of corporate misconduct in recent years have led to widespread cynicism about business ethics. First, we had long-time partners Ford and Firestone blaming each other for Ford Explorer rollover deaths and injuries. Later, we saw Enron executives hiding behind the Fifth Amendment while being scolded like naughty children by Congress.[33] Not surprisingly, according to a *Business Week*/Harris survey of Americans in 2002: "Only a third . . . feel large companies have ethical business practices and just 26% believe they are straightforward and honest in their dealings with consumers and employees."[34] Equally disturbing, a 1999 survey of 1,000 executives yielded this finding: "As many as one-third of U.S. senior-level executives lie on their résumés."[35] What sort of role models do these powerful people make? The subject of ethics certainly deserves serious attention in management circles these days.[36]

**ethics**   *study of moral obligation involving right versus wrong*

 **Ethics** is the study of moral obligation involving the distinction between right and wrong.[37] *Business ethics,* sometimes referred to as management ethics or organizational ethics, narrows the frame of reference to productive organizations.[38] But, as a pair of ethics experts noted, business ethics is not a simple matter:

> *Just being a good person and, in your own way, having sound personal ethics may not be sufficient to handle the ethical issues that arise in a business organization. Many people who have limited business experience suddenly find themselves making decisions about product quality, advertising, pricing, hiring practices, and pollution control. The values they learned from family, church, and school may not provide specific guidelines for these complex business decisions. For example, is a particular advertisement deceptive? Should a gift to a customer be considered a bribe, or is it a special promotional incentive? . . . Many business ethics decisions are close calls. Years of experience in a particular industry may be required to know what is acceptable.*[39]

With this realistic context in mind, we turn to a discussion of business ethics research, personal values, ethical principles, and steps that management can take to foster ethical business behavior.

**5F   A Bad Case of "Enronitis"?**

Survey results:

*[H]alf of adults say the practices of top Enron executives are the norm for at least some other large corporations. And one-fourth say they're the norm for most.*

**Source:** Thomas A. Fogarty, "Poll Finds Many Think Other Execs Act Like Enron's," *USA Today* (February 12, 2002): 1B.

**Questions:** *What is your general opinion about the present state of business ethics? Explain. What needs to be done to improve business ethics?*

## Practical Lessons from Business Ethics Research

Empirical research is always welcome in a socially relevant and important area such as business ethics.[40] It permits us to go beyond mere intuition and speculation to determine more precisely who, what, and why. On-the-job research of business ethics has produced three practical insights for managers: (1) ethical hot spots, (2) pressure from above, and (3) discomfort with ambiguity.

**Ethical Hot Spots.**   In a recent survey of 1,324 U.S. employees from all levels across several industries, 48 percent admitted to at least one illegal or unethical act (during the prior year) from a list of 25 questionable practices. The list included every-thing from calling in sick when feeling well to cheating on expense accounts, forging signatures, and giving or accepting kickbacks, to ignoring violations of environmental laws. Also uncovered in the study were the top ten workplace hot spots responsible for triggering unethical and illegal conduct:

- Balancing work and family
- Poor internal communications
- Poor leadership
- Work hours, workload
- Lack of management support
- Need to meet sales, budget, or profit goals
- Little or no recognition of achievements
- Company politics
- Personal financial worries
- Insufficient resources[41]

4 Summarize the three practical lessons from business ethics research.

**Pressure from Above.**   A number of studies have uncovered the problem of per-ceived pressure for results. As discussed later in Chapter 14, pressure from superiors can lead to blind conformity. How widespread is the problem? Very widespread, according to the ethical hot spots survey just discussed:

- Most workers feel some pressure to act unethically or illegally on the job (56 percent), but far fewer (17 percent) feel a high level of pressure to do so. . . .
- Mid-level managers most often reported a high level of pressure to act unethically or illegally (20 percent). Employees of large companies cited such pressure more than those at small businesses (21 percent versus 14 percent).
- High levels of pressure were reported more often by those with a high school diploma or less (21 percent) versus college graduates (13 percent).[42]

Location: *U.S.–Mexico border in Nogales, Arizona.* Problem: *The FBI wants to know how a U.S. Immigration and Naturalization Service (INS) officer earning $30,000 a year happens to have $300,000 in cash lying around the house. They claim three INS officers collected nearly $800,000 from smugglers for letting 20 tons of cocaine pass through.* Ethical dilemma: *Who is primarily to blame: overworked and underpaid public servants tempted by lottery-size payoffs or Americans who buy illegal drugs?*

By being aware of this problem of pressure from above, managers can (1) consciously avoid putting undue pressure on others and (2) prepare to deal with excessive organizational pressure.

A prime case in point is the overselling scandal at Sears, Roebuck & Company's automotive centers. According to investigations by the California attorney general's office and a U.S. Senate subcommittee, between 1990 and 1992 Sears systematically pressured auto customers to buy parts and services they didn't need. Many customers across the country complained of having paid hundreds of dollars for unnecessary repair work. Roy Liebman, a California deputy attorney general, told *Business Week,* "There was a deliberate decision by Sears management to set up a structure that made it totally inevitable that the customer would be oversold."[43] Indeed, former Sears employees claimed that intense pressure to boost revenue, a commission pay system tied to actual sales, and unrealistic sales goals forced them to oversell. Sears reworked the goal-setting and commission structure in its auto repair shops only to see similar problems crop up among overzealous bill collectors in its credit card operations. The situation led to a two-year FBI investigation and culminated in a record $60 million fine for bankruptcy fraud in 1999.[44] Excessive pressure to achieve results is a serious problem, because it can cause otherwise good and decent people to take ethical shortcuts just to keep their jobs. The challenge for managers is to know where to draw the line between motivation to excel and undue pressure.

**Ambiguous Situations.**   Surveys of purchasing managers and field sales personnel uncovered discomfort with ambiguous situations in which there are no clear-cut ethical guidelines. One result of this kind of research is the following statement: "A striking aspect of the responses to the questionnaire is the degree to which the purchasing managers desire a stated policy."[45] In other words, those who often face ethically ambiguous situations want formal guidelines to help sort things out. Ethical codes, discussed later, can satisfy this need for guidelines.

**A Call to Action.**   Corporate misconduct and the foregoing research findings underscore the importance of the following call to action. It comes from Thomas R. Horton, former president and chief executive officer of the American Management Association:

> *In my view, this tide can be turned only by deliberate and conscious actions of management at all levels. Each manager needs to understand his or her own* personal *code of ethics: what is* fair; *what is* right; *what is* wrong? *Where is the ethical line that* I *draw, the line beyond which* I *shall not go? And where is the line beyond which I shall not allow my organization to go?*[46]

Horton's call is *personal.* His words suggest each of us can begin the process of improving business ethics by looking in a mirror.[47]

## Personal Values as Ethical Anchors

Values are too often ignored in discussions of management. This oversight is serious because personal values play a pivotal role in managerial decision making and ethics.[48] Contemporary social observers complain that many managers lack character and have turned their backs on ethical values such as honesty. MIT management scholar Michael Schrage recently observed:

> *If there's a single issue that frightens me about the workplace future, it's the rising willingness of people to blame institutional imperatives for betraying their own values. . . . There's*

## 5G Where Do You Draw the Line?

Kevin Gibson, philosophy professor, Marquette University:

*Morality is not a question of counting heads, and opinion polls do not reflect moral correctness. The fact that most people in a company feel that mocking obese coworkers is morally acceptable will not make it morally correct.*

**Source:** Kevin Gibson, "Excuses, Excuses: Moral Slippage in the Workplace," *Business Horizons*, 43 (November–December 2000): 67.

**Questions:** *What instances of the majority being morally wrong have you observed lately? Do you have the courage to act on your convictions, or do you pretty much just go along with the crowd to avoid being seen as a troublemaker? Explain.*

*no shortage of talent and intelligence; character may be the scarcer and more valuable commodity. That's the one to watch.*[49]

Defined broadly, **values** are abstract ideals that shape an individual's thinking and behavior.[50] Let us explore two different types of values that act as anchors for our ethical beliefs and conduct.

**values** *abstract ideals that shape one's thinking and behavior*

**Instrumental and Terminal Values.** Each manager, indeed each person, values various means and ends in life. Recognizing this means-ends distinction, behavioral scientists have identified two basic types of values. An **instrumental value** is an enduring belief that a certain way of behaving is appropriate in all situations. For example, the time-honored saying, "Honesty is the best policy" represents an instrumental value. A person who truly values honesty will probably behave in an honest manner. A **terminal value,** in contrast, is an enduring belief that a certain end-state of existence is worth striving for and attaining.[51] Whereas one person may strive for eternal salvation, another may strive for social recognition and admiration. Instrumental values (modes of behavior) help achieve terminal values (desired end-states).

**5** Distinguish between instrumental and terminal values and explain their relationship to business ethics.

**instrumental value** *enduring belief in a certain way of behaving*

Because a person can hold a number of different instrumental and terminal values in various combinations, individual value systems are somewhat like fingerprints: each of us has a unique set. No wonder managers who face the same ethical dilemma often differ in their interpretations and responses.

**terminal value** *enduring belief in the attainment of a certain end-state*

**Identifying Your Own Values.** To help you discover your own set of values, refer to the Rokeach value survey in the Hands-On Exercise at the end of this chapter. Take a few moments now to complete this survey. (As a reality check between your intentions and your actual behavior, have a close friend or spouse evaluate you later with the Rokeach survey.)

If your results surprise you, it is probably because we tend to take our basic values for granted. We seldom stop to arrange them consciously according to priority. For the sake of comparison, compare your top five instrumental and terminal values with the value profiles uncovered in a survey of 220 eastern U.S. managers. On average, those managers ranked their instrumental values as follows: (1) honest, (2) responsible, (3) capable, (4) ambitious, and (5) independent. The most common terminal value rankings were (1) self-respect, (2) family security, (3) freedom, (4) a sense of accomplishment, and (5) happiness.[52] These managerial value profiles are offered for purposes of comparison only; they are not necessarily an index of desirable or undesirable priorities. When addressing specific ethical issues, managers need to consider each individual's personal values.

## General Ethical Principles

**6** Identify and describe at least four of the ten general ethical principles.

Like your highly personalized value system, your ethical beliefs have been shaped by many factors, including family and friends, the media, culture, schooling, religious instruction, and general life experiences.[53] This section brings taken-for-granted ethical beliefs, generally unstated, out into the open for discussion and greater understanding. It does so by exploring ten general ethical principles. Even though we may not necessarily know how ethics scholars label them, we use ethical principles both consciously and unconsciously when dealing with ethical dilemmas.[54] Each of the ten ethical principles is followed by a brief behavioral guideline.*

1. *Self-interests.* "Never take any action that is not in the *long-term* self-interests of yourself and/or of the organization to which you belong."
2. *Personal virtues.* "Never take any action that is not honest, open, and truthful and that you would not be proud to see reported widely in national newspapers and on television."
3. *Religious injunctions.* "Never take any action that is not kind and that does not build a sense of community, a sense of all of us working together for a commonly accepted goal."
4. *Government requirements.* "Never take any action that violates the law, for the law represents the minimal moral standards of our society."
5. *Utilitarian benefits.* "Never take any action that does not result in greater good than harm for the society of which you are a part."
6. *Universal rules.* "Never take any action that you would not be willing to see others, faced with the same or closely similar situation, also be free to take."
7. *Individual rights.* "Never take any action that abridges the agreed-upon and accepted rights of others."
8. *Economic efficiency.* "Always act to maximize profits subject to legal and market constraints, for maximum profits are the sign of the most efficient production."
9. *Distributive justice.* "Never take any action in which the least [fortunate people] among us are harmed in some way."
10. *Contributive liberty.* "Never take any action that will interfere with the right of all of us for self-development and self-fulfillment."[55]

Which of these ethical principles appeals most to you in terms of serving as a guide for making important

**5H  Does God Belong in the Workplace?**

Gregory F. A. Pearce, author of the book *Spirituality@Work:*

*Why would we want to look for God in our work. . . . The simple answer is most of us spend so much time working, it would be a shame if we couldn't find God there. A more complex answer is that there is a creative energy in work that is somehow tied to God's creative energy. If we can understand that connection, perhaps we can use it to transform the workplace into something remarkable.*

**Source:** As quoted in Marc Gunther, "God & Business," *Fortune* (July 9, 2001), 61.

**Questions:** *Is it time to change the traditional practice of keeping spirituality out of the workplace? Explain. What implications does your answer have for business ethics?*

---

*\*Source:* Excerpted from Hosmer, *Moral Leadership in Business*, pp. 39–41, © 1994, McGraw-Hill. Reprinted with permission of The McGraw-Hill Companies.

*What on earth could this cute little bundle of fur have to do with values and ethics? Lots, it turns out. This is Cc, the famous cloned house cat who is genetically identical (but not visually identical) to her biological mother. Ethics experts ask, how far should the technology of cloning be allowed to go? Will a manager's staffing request to "send me another programmer just like Jamie" someday mean a cloned duplicate? Should we clone great leaders and athletes? Should people be allowed to have cloned doubles they can use for replacement body parts?*

decisions? Why? The best way to test your ethical standards and principles is to consider a *specific* ethical question and see which of these ten principles is most likely to guide your *behavior*. Sometimes, in complex situations, a combination of principles would be applicable.

# Encouraging Ethical Conduct

Simply telling managers and other employees to be good will not work. Both research evidence and practical experience tell us that words must be supported by action. Four specific ways to encourage ethical conduct within the organization are ethics training, ethical advocates, ethics codes, and whistle-blowing. Each can make an important contribution to an integrated ethics program.

**7** Discuss what management can do to improve business ethics.

## Ethics Training

Managers lacking ethical awareness have been labeled *amoral* by ethics researcher Archie B. Carroll. **Amoral managers** are neither moral nor immoral, but indifferent to the ethical implications of their actions. Carroll contends that managers in this category far outnumber moral or immoral managers.[56] If his contention is correct, there is a great need for ethics training, a need that too often is not adequately met. According

**amoral managers** *managers who are neither moral nor immoral, but ethically lazy*

# Management Ethics

## A "Scared-Straight" Program for Business Students

CUMBERLAND, Md.—Before getting diplomas Wednesday night, the University of Maryland's MBA graduates got a lesson in life from distinguished alumnus Gerard Evans.

A lawyer renowned as the state's highest-paid lobbyist, he boasts deep ties to the university. He earned a master's degree at Maryland, taught there and served on the school's board of visitors. Currently, he is a doctoral candidate in the American studies program.

Evans does his doctoral work at a distance, though, because he also happens to be prisoner No. 33950-037 at the Federal Correctional Institution here.

A trip to prison is mandatory for second-year Maryland MBA students, part of an ethics class intended to puncture their sometimes sizable egos just weeks before they graduate and leap to the corporate world. Maryland officials describe the 1-day prison field trip as a kind of "scared-straight" program for MBAs. The purpose is to show them how smart, successful, business-savvy overachievers—people like them—can land in the slammer.

Murders, rapes, assaults, and other violent crimes have been declining across the USA over the past two decades. But rates for embezzlement, fraud, and other white-collar crimes have proved stubbornly resistant, remaining steady despite beefed-up law-enforcement efforts.

Experts say computers and cross-border commerce have made white-collar crimes easier to commit and easier to conceal. At the same time, the growing ranks of women in top jobs have led to a surge in the number of women convicted of embezzlement and other financial crimes, says the National White Collar Crime Center. . . .

"I felt that I could do no wrong," says inmate Monte Greenbaum, former CEO of a property-management firm now serving 18 months for fraud at the prison camp.

Greenbaum, who holds an accounting degree from Maryland, describes the networking skills that brought him wealth and got him elected president of the state board of public accounting. "I had everything. . . . I could have retired 5 years ago. We were looking at retirement properties in Arizona."

Retirement was off when he was nabbed shifting funds between buildings he owned and those he managed for the Department of Housing and Urban Development.

Greenbaum, 52, says he informed HUD of his moves and had every intention of eventually squaring accounts. "But if you rob a bank and put all the money back, you still robbed a bank," he says. . . .

Evans, Greenbaum, and convicted embezzler Greg Gamble, 49, sound other common themes. They say it's the little gray-area decisions that ultimately lead to more serious ethical and legal breaches.

"That got to me," student Patricia Martinez says later. "It made me think we're all just one decision away from the big decision that leads to trouble." . . .

Ethics educators at business schools say they have lots of ground to cover. MBA students are armed with sophisticated knowledge of finance, so it's vital they know the dangers of earnings manipulation, money laundering, price fixing, accounting fraud, intellectual property theft, and insider trading. They need to know how to recognize harassment and discrimination, and how to handle whistleblowers. And they need to consider the moral implications of polluting a community or closing a plant or firing a worker who's about to be vested [in the company's retirement fund].

*Source:* Excerpted from James Cox, "Inmates Teach MBA Students Ethics from Behind Bars," *USA Today* (May 24, 2001): 1B–2B. Copyright 2001, *USA Today*. Reprinted with permission.

to surveys by *Training* magazine, the use of ethics training programs (at least annually) has stalled at a disappointingly low level. For companies with more than 100 employees, figures for 1990, 1997, and 2001 were 37 percent, 46 percent, and 45 percent, respectively.[57]

Some say ethics training is a waste of time because ethical lessons are easily shoved aside in the heat of competition.[58] For example, Dow Corning's model ethics program included ethics training but did not keep the company from getting embroiled in charges of selling leaky breast implants.[59] Ethics training is often halfhearted and intended only as window dressing (for an interesting exception, see Management Ethics).[60] Hard evidence that ethics training actually improves behavior is lacking. Nonetheless, carefully designed and administered ethics training courses can make a positive contribution. Key features of effective ethics training programs include the following:

- Top-management support.
- Open discussion of realistic ethics cases or scenarios.
- A clear focus on ethical issues specific to the organization.
- Integration of ethics themes into all training.
- A mechanism for anonymously reporting ethical violations. (Companies have had good luck with e-mail and telephone hot lines.)
- An organizational climate that rewards ethical conduct.[61]

## Ethical Advocates

An **ethical advocate** is a business ethics specialist who sits as a full-fledged member of the board of directors and acts as the board's social conscience.[62] This person may also be asked to sit in on top-management decision deliberations. The idea is to assign someone the specific role of critical questioner (see Table 5.2 for recommended

**ethical advocate** *ethics specialist who plays a role in top-management decision making*

| **Table 5.2**  Twelve Questions for Examining the Ethics of a Business Decision |
|---|
| 1. Have you defined the problem accurately? |
| 2. How would you define the problem if you stood on the other side of the fence? |
| 3. How did this situation occur in the first place? |
| 4. To whom and to what do you give your loyalty as a person and as a member of the corporation? |
| 5. What is your intention in making this decision? |
| 6. How does this intention compare with the probable results? |
| 7. Whom could your decision or action injure? |
| 8. Can you discuss the problem with the affected parties before you make your decision? |
| 9. Are you confident that your position will be as valid over a long period of time as it seems now? |
| 10. Could you disclose without qualm your decision or action to your boss, your CEO, the board of directors, your family, society as a whole? |
| 11. What is the symbolic potential of your action if understood? If misunderstood? |
| 12. Under what conditions would you allow exceptions to your stand? |

*Source:* Reprinted by permission of the *Harvard Business Review.* Excerpt from "Ethics Without the Sermon," by Laura L. Nash (November–December 1981). Copyright © 1981 by Harvard Business School Publishing Corporation; all rights reserved.

questions). Problems with groupthink and blind conformity, discussed in Chapter 14, are less likely when an ethical advocate tests management's thinking about ethical implications during the decision-making process.

## Codes of Ethics

An organizational code of ethics is a published statement of moral expectations for employee conduct. Some codes specify penalties for offenders. As with the case of ethics training, growth in the adoption of company codes of ethics has stalled in recent years.

Recent experience has shown codes of ethics to be a step in the right direction, but not a cure-all.[63] To encourage ethical conduct, formal codes of ethics for organization members must satisfy two requirements. First, they should refer to specific practices such as kickbacks, payoffs, receiving gifts, record falsification, and misleading claims about products. For example, Xerox Corporation's 15-page ethics code says: "We're honest with our customers. No deals, no bribes, no secrets, no fooling around with prices. A kickback in any form kicks anybody out. Anybody."[64] General platitudes about good business practice or professional conduct are ineffective—they do not provide specific guidance and they offer too many tempting loopholes.

---

### 51   An Uphill Battle?

After a study of the ethical principles and ethical behavior of 674 business students at a U.S. university, a pair of researchers drew this rather somber conclusion:

> *While ethical behavior can be taught to our business students in the classroom, their resolve will be challenged on the job. Faced with pressure from above, platitudinous ethical codes, spotty enforcement, and no discernible link to the reward system, many will revert to expedience.*

News item:

> *When San Diego State University instructor Brian Cornforth received an anonymous tip in March that students were cheating in his undergraduate business-ethics course, he decided to make a case study of his own class. The tipster said students in one class had obtained answer keys for the multiple-choice quizzes from earlier test-takers, so Cornforth scrambled the questions for the later class. "I was horrified," Cornforth says: 25 of 75 students simply cribbed the pirated test key, even though many answers were clearly nonsense. Punishment came swiftly. He flunked all 25, and several management majors won't graduate until they retake the required course. "Students really want that piece of paper and apparently they are willing to do anything to get it," says Julie Logan, the school's judicial officer.*

**Sources:** Larry R. Watts and Joseph G. Ormsby, "Ethical Frameworks and Ethical Behavior: A Survey of Business Students," *International Journal of Value-Based Management*, 73, no. 3 (1994): 233; and Jamie Reno, "Need Someone in Creative Accounting?" *Newsweek* (May 17, 1999): 51.

---

**Questions:** *Is it a waste of time to teach business ethics to college students? Explain. How can colleges and universities do a better job of improving business ethics? What does the business community need to do to improve ethics in the workplace?*

The second requirement for an organizational code of ethics is that it be firmly supported by top management and equitably enforced through the reward-and-punishment system. Selective or uneven enforcement is the quickest way to kill the effectiveness of an ethics code. The effective development of ethics codes and monitoring of compliance are more important than ever in today's complex global economy.[65]

## Whistle-Blowing

Detailed ethics codes help managers deal swiftly and effectively with employee misconduct. But what should a manager do when a superior or an entire organization is engaged in misconduct? Yielding to the realities of organizational politics, many managers simply turn their backs or claim they were "just following orders." (Nazi war criminals who based their defense at the Nuremberg trials on the argument that they were following orders ended up with ropes around their necks.) Managers with leadership and/or political skills may attempt to work within the organizational system for positive change.[66] Still others will take the boldest step of all, whistle-blowing. **Whistle-blowing** is the practice of reporting perceived unethical practices to outsiders such as the news media, government agencies, or public-interest groups.[67] (See the Closing Case for a whistle-blower in action.)

**whistle-blowing** *reporting perceived unethical organizational practices to outside authorities*

Not surprisingly, whistle-blowing is a highly controversial topic among managers, many of whom believe that whistle-blowing erodes their authority and decision-making prerogatives. Because loyalty to the organization is still a cherished value in some quarters, whistle-blowing is criticized as the epitome of disloyalty. Consumer advocate Ralph Nader disagrees: "The willingness and ability of insiders to blow the whistle is the last line of defense ordinary citizens have against the denial of their rights and the destruction of their interests by secretive and powerful institutions."[68] Still, critics worry that whistle-blowers may be motivated by revenge.

*No doubt, it took ethical courage for CPA Sherron Smith Watkins to confront Enron's leadership with her concerns about accounting irregularities and questionable finanancial deals. She even passed her concerns along to the firm's auditor, Arthur Andersen, to little avail. Unfortunately, Enron soon unraveled and took Andersen with it. Although rightly praised in the popular media for being an honest "whistle-blower," Watkins technically wasn't a whistle-blower, as the term is defined in this chapter. Whistle-blowers report corporate misdeeds to outsiders such as the media and government watchdog agencies.*

Whistle-blowing generally means putting one's job and/or career on the line, even though the federal government and many states have passed whistle-blower protection acts.[69] The challenge for today's management is to create an organizational climate in which the need to blow the whistle is reduced. Constructive steps include the following:

- Encourage the free expression of controversial and dissenting viewpoints.
- Streamline the organization's grievance procedure so that problems receive a prompt and fair hearing.
- Find out what employees think about the organization's social responsibility policies and make appropriate changes.
- Let employees know that management respects and is sensitive to their individual consciences.
- Recognize that the harsh treatment of a whistle-blower will probably lead to adverse public opinion.[70]

In the final analysis, individual behavior makes organizations ethical or unethical. Organizational forces can help bring out the best in people by clearly identifying and rewarding ethical conduct.

## Summary

1. Corporate social responsibility is the idea that management has broader responsibilities than just making a profit. A strict interpretation holds that an action must be voluntary to qualify as socially responsible. Accordingly, reluctant submission to court orders or government coercion is not an example of social responsibility. The debate over the basic purpose of the corporation is long-standing. Those who embrace the classical economic model contend that business's social responsibility is to maximize profits for stockholders. Proponents of the socioeconomic model disagree, saying that business has a responsibility, above and beyond making a profit, to improve the general quality of life. The arguments *for* corporate responsibility say businesses are members of society with the resources and motivation to improve society and avoid government regulation. Those arguing *against* call for profit maximization because businesses are primarily economic institutions run by unelected officials who have enough power already.

2. Management scholars who advocate greater corporate social responsibility cite the iron law of responsibility. This law states that if business does not use its socioeconomic power responsibly, society will take away that power. A continuum of social responsibility includes four strategies: reaction, defense, accommodation, and proaction. The reaction strategy involves *denying* social responsibility, whereas the defense strategy involves actively *fighting* additional responsibility with political and public relations tactics. Accommodation occurs when a company must be *pressured into* assuming additional social responsibilities. Proaction occurs when a business *takes the initiative* and becomes a positive model for its industry.

**3.** In the short run, proactive social responsibility usually costs the firm money. But, according to the notion of enlightened self-interest, both society and the company will gain in the long run. Research indicates that corporate philanthropy actually is a profit-motivated form of advertising.

**4.** Business ethics research has taught these three practical lessons: (1) 48 percent of surveyed workers reported engaging in illegal or unethical practices; (2) perceived pressure from above can erode ethics; and (3) employees desire clear ethical standards in ambiguous situations. The call for better business ethics is clearly a *personal* challenge.

**5.** Managers cannot afford to overlook each employee's personal value system; values serve as anchors for one's beliefs and conduct. Instrumental values relate to desired behavior, whereas terminal values involve desired end-states. Values provide an anchor for one's ethical beliefs and conduct.

**6.** The ten general ethical principles that consciously and unconsciously guide behavior when ethical questions arise are self-interests, personal virtues, religious injunctions, government requirements, utilitarian benefits, universal rules, individual rights, economic efficiency, distributive justice, and contributive liberty.

**7.** The typical manager is said to be *amoral*—neither moral or immoral—just ethically lazy or indifferent. Management can encourage ethical behavior in the following four ways: conduct ethics training; use ethical advocates in high-level decision making; formulate, disseminate, and consistently enforce specific codes of ethics; and create an open climate for dissent in which whistle-blowing becomes unnecessary.

Corporate social responsibility (p. 145)

Stakeholder audit (p. 149)

Iron law of responsibility (p. 151)

Reactive social responsibility strategy (p. 151)

Defensive social responsibility strategy (p. 151)

Accommodative social responsibility strategy (p. 152)

Proactive social responsibility strategy (p. 152)

Altruism (p. 153)

Enlightened self-interest (p. 153)

Corporate philanthropy (p. 153)

Ethics (p. 156)

Values (p. 159)

Instrumental value (p. 159)

Terminal value (p. 159)

Amoral managers (p. 161)

Ethical advocate (p. 163)

Whistle-blowing (p. 165)

# Terms to Understand

# Skills & Tools

## An International Code of Ethics

Developed in 1994 by the Caux Round Table in Switzerland, these Principles for Business are believed to be the first international ethics code created from a collaboration of business leaders in Europe, Japan, and the United States.

**Principle 1.** *The Responsibility of Businesses: Beyond Shareholders Toward Stakeholders.* The value of a business to society is the wealth and employment it creates and the marketable products and services it provides to consumers at a reasonable price commensurate with quality. To create such value, a business must maintain its own economic health and viability, but survival is not a sufficient goal.

Businesses have a role to play in improving the lives of all their customers, employees, and shareholders by sharing with them the wealth they have created. Suppliers and competitors as well should expect businesses to honor their obligations in a spirit of honesty and fairness. As responsible citizens of the local, national, regional, and global communities in which they operate, businesses share a part in shaping the future of those communities.

**Principle 2.** *The Economic and Social Impact of Business: Toward Innovation, Justice, and World Community.* Businesses established in foreign countries to develop, produce, or sell should also contribute to the social advancement of those countries by creating productive employment and helping to raise the purchasing power of their citizens. Businesses also should contribute to human rights, education, welfare, and vitalization of the countries in which they operate.

Businesses should contribute to economic and social development not only in the countries in which they operate, but also in the world community at large, through effective and prudent use of resources, free and fair competition, and emphasis upon innovation in technology, production methods, marketing, and communications.

**Principle 3.** *Business Behavior: Beyond the Letter of Law Toward a Spirit of Trust.* While accepting the legitimacy of trade secrets, businesses should recognize that sincerity, candor, truthfulness, the keeping of promises, and transparency contribute not only to their own credibility and stability but also to the smoothness and efficiency of business transactions, particularly on the international level.

**Principle 4.** *Respect for Rules.* To avoid trade frictions and to promote freer trade, equal conditions for competition, and fair and equitable treatment for all participants, businesses should respect international and domestic rules. In addition, they should recognize that some behavior, although legal, may still have adverse consequences.

**Principle 5.** *Support for Multilateral Trade.* Businesses should support the multilateral trade systems of the World Trade Organization and similar international agreements. They should cooperate in efforts to promote the progressive and judicious liberalization of trade, and to relax those domestic measures that unreasonably hinder global commerce, while giving due respect to national policy objectives.

**Principle 6.** *Respect for the Environment.* A business should protect and, where possible, improve the environment, promote sustainable development, and prevent the wasteful use of natural resources.

**Principle 7.** *Avoidance of Illicit Operations.* A business should not participate in or condone bribery, money laundering, or other corrupt practices: indeed, it should seek cooperation with others to eliminate them. It should not trade in arms or other materials used for terrorist activities, drug traffic, or other organized crime.

*Source:* Excerpted from "Principles for Business," *Business Ethics*, 10 (May–June 1996): 16–17. Reprinted with permission from *Business Ethics*, P.O. Box 8439, Minneapolis, Minn. 55408, 612-879-0695. **www.business-ethics.com**

# Hands-On Exercise

## The Rokeach Value Survey

Study the two lists of values presented below. Then rank the instrumental values in order of importance to you (1 = most important, 18 = least important). Do the same with the list of terminal values.

**Instructions**

| **Instrumental values** | **Terminal values** |
|---|---|
| **Rank** | **Rank** |
| ___ Ambitious (hardworking, aspiring) | ___ A comfortable life (a prosperous life) |
| ___ Broadminded (open-minded) | ___ An exciting life (a stimulating active life) |
| ___ Capable (competent, effective) | ___ A sense of accomplishment (lasting contribution) |
| ___ Cheerful (lighthearted, joyful) | |
| ___ Clean (neat, tidy) | ___ A world at peace (free of war and conflict) |
| ___ Courageous (standing up for your beliefs) | ___ A world of beauty (beauty of nature and the arts) |
| ___ Forgiving (willing to pardon others) | ___ Equality (brotherhood, equal opportunity for all) |
| ___ Helpful (working for the welfare of others) | ___ Family security (taking care of loved ones) |
| ___ Honest (sincere, truthful) | ___ Freedom (independence, free choice) |
| ___ Imaginative (daring, creative) | ___ Happiness (contentedness) |
| ___ Independent (self-sufficient) | ___ Inner harmony (freedom from inner conflict) |
| ___ Intellectual (intelligent, reflective) | |
| ___ Logical (consistent, rational) | ___ Mature love (sexual and spiritual intimacy) |
| ___ Loving (affectionate, tender) | ___ National security (protection from attack) |
| ___ Obedient (dutiful, respectful) | |
| ___ Polite (courteous, well-mannered) | ___ Pleasure (an enjoyable, leisurely life) |
| ___ Responsible (dependable, reliable) | ___ Salvation (saved, eternal life) |
| ___ Self-controlled (restrained, self-disciplined) | ___ Self-respect (self-esteem) |
| | ___ Social recognition (respect, admiration) |
| | ___ True friendship (close companionship) |
| | ___ Wisdom (a mature understanding of life) |

*Source:* Copyright, 1967, by Milton Rokeach, and reproduced by permission of Halgren Tests, 873 Persimmon Avenue, Sunnyvale, Calif. 94087.

**For Consideration/
Discussion**

**1.** How does this value survey help you better understand yourself? Or others?

**2.** Do you believe that values drive behavior (including ethical and unethical behavior)? Explain.

**3.** Value *conflict* can make life troublesome in three ways. First, there can be incompatibility among one's highly ranked instrumental values (e.g., honest vs. polite; courageous vs. obedient). Second, it may be difficult to achieve one's top terminal values via one's highly ranked instrumental values (e.g., ambitious and responsible vs. happiness and an exciting life). Third, your important instrumental and terminal values may clash with those of significant others—such as friends, spouse, coworkers, or an organization. What sorts of potential or actual value conflict do you detect in your survey responses? Explain. What can you do to minimize these conflicts?

# Internet Exercises

**1. In search of socially responsible companies.** One of *Fortune* magazine's annual features is its list of "America's Most Admired Companies." Eight criteria, including "social responsibility," are used to screen candidates for the list. Our purpose here is to learn more about the top ten socially responsible companies in America. What makes them stand out from the crowd? To find out, go to *Fortune*'s home page (**www.fortune.com**) and click on "America's Most Admired" and then select the "Custom Ranking" option. For the "Basic" custom ranking, choose the attribute "Social Responsibility" for the top ten companies. Next, pick one of the companies, either at random or based on your interests, and find out more about it by clicking on the main tab heading "Company Profiles," going directly to the company's Web site, or doing a standard Internet search.

*Learning Points:* 1. What are the top ten socially responsible companies? Which one did you pick? Why? 2. What does this company do to earn its top ranking? 3. Is it a profitable company as well? 4. Does its high ranking in this category make you want to work for the company? Why or why not?

**2. Learning more about the world of corporate social responsibility (CSR).** *Business Ethics* magazine (**www.business-ethics.com**) calls the Business for Social Responsibility Web site (**www.bsr.org**) the best CSR site of all. This site has a wealth of information to inspire and challenge all of us to take CSR to new heights. First go to the home page and browse the "Headlines." Next, click on the home page "Library" tab and select "Topic Overviews." Browse one or more of the several topical areas, such as "Business Ethics," "Corporate Social Responsibility," or "Human Rights."

*Learning Points:* 1. What new and/or useful ideas did you acquire about CSR? 2. Do you like or dislike how encompassing the field of CSR has become? Explain. 3. What, if any, social responsibility spark (for making the world a better place) has been ignited in you? Explain.

**3. Check it out:** Many people believe today's large and powerful corporations need to be monitored carefully (and held accountable) to make sure they are behaving effectively, responsibly, and ethically. An excellent one-stop Web site for checking up on corporate saints and sinners alike is **www.corpwatch.org**. This is a must-see site for politically and socially conscious people who are out to "save the world."

For updates to these exercises, visit our Web site (**http://business.college.hmco.com/students**).

## Closing Case

# The Whistle-Blowing Nurse

In the spring of . . . [1999], Cherlynn Mathias was browsing the classifieds in the *Tulsa World* when she came across an ad that caught her eye: Wanted, it said, a research nurse at the University of Oklahoma. Mathias, a registered nurse with a limited background in clinical research, landed the job.

Now, a tumultuous year later, some officials in the College of Medicine in Tulsa surely wish they had never set eyes on her. It was Mathias, 44, a divorced mother of two teenage boys, who blew the whistle on a problem cancer study that brought scandal to the small campus in Tulsa.

Her allegations were simple but powerful: In June, she wrote federal health regulators that university researchers on the cancer trial repeatedly broke federal health rules, injected a potentially dangerous vaccine into patients, overstated the possible benefits of the experiment and sought to cover up the mess. She alleged that top officials in the College of Medicine ignored her warnings and failed to notify regulators.

Vindication came swiftly. Regulators shut down all government-funded research at the Tulsa campus and directed the university to fix the problem. The university suspended all research and, in a report to regulators this week, acknowledged that its researchers had violated safety rules. Officials pledged to restore public confidence in their tarnished program.

## "This Needed to Come to Light"

How all this all came about is a classic tale of a whistle-blower—a story of how an employee, troubled by what she saw, sought to force change within the system. When that failed, she went over the heads of her bosses to the only people she believed could effect change: health regulators in Washington.

Today, Mathias feels something like a skunk at the garden party, but she says she had to act. "I am upset about the suppression of information, the failure to comply with the safety rules, the lying to the patients and

*Source:* Edward T. Pound, "Nurse's Clues Shut Down Research," *USA Today* (July 13, 2000): 3A, Copyright 2000, *USA Today*. Reprinted with permission.

the lying (to federal health regulators)," she says.

She worries that she will be ostracized by the close-knit university community and that she might even lose her job in the Department of Surgery, which is located at St. John's Medical Center. Ken Lackey, president of the Tulsa campus, says she needn't worry: "I am personally happy she came forward with the information. This needed to come to light." . . .

The Tulsa oversight board is at the heart of the scandal. The 19-member board didn't adequately monitor a trial in which patients with melanoma, a deadly skin cancer, were injected with an experimental vaccine, officials say. The trial enrolled 98 patients. The board's chairman approved changes in the study without consulting other members, says a suspension letter issued June 29 by the Office for Human Research Protections, an HHS regulatory agency. The board failed to provide "substantive and meaningful" review, the letter says.

The university finally canceled [the] three-year melanoma trial in March—but only after Mathias pushed officials into having a private consulting firm review the trial. A nurse for 10 years, Mathias, by her own admission, is a bit of a firecracker. She clashed with Michael McGee, the sponsor and chief investigator on the cancer study, and some of his aides. She says she pressed McGee repeatedly to follow the study's safety rules. His response, she says, was that "I was simply background noise."

Mathias went to work at the university on June 1, 1999, as a study coordinator on the clinical trial. She had only three months' experience in clinical research and recalls initially being "overwhelmed by just the responsibility of injecting patients," some of whom were terminally ill.

In her complaint to the federal human research protections office, she said, "I became alarmed at what I found. Missing documentation, shipping of drugs to people's homes, allowing subjects to self-inject and numerous" deviations from the study's guidelines. McGee did not share her concerns, she wrote.

Mathias kept pressing. In October, she notified IRB officials about the safety issues. In December she met with officials in research and surgery, including McGee, and argued for bringing in a private outside company to evaluate the study. Her recommendation was accepted.

In March, the outside firm issued two reports sharply critical of the study. The firm said that the trial should be shut down because it was endangering patients. It urged the university to quarantine the remaining vaccine and label it, "Not for use in humans."

One major discovery: Patients were injected with the vaccine before it was tested on animals. Those tests are required by federal rules.

In April, McGee informed patients he was stopping the study because he had run out of vaccine. Mathias and federal regulators said the study was stopped because of safety problems.

She pressed top officials in Tulsa to report the consultants' findings to higher officials at Oklahoma City. She said Harold Brooks, dean of the Health Sciences Center in Tulsa, refused. She wrote federal regulators that he was worried that research would be shut down at Tulsa. According to her complaint, Brooks and Daniel Plunket, the board chairman, wanted "to put a positive spin on all information."

She wrote the federal protections office: "This is the reason I am reporting the information to you. I consider the suppression of the information as unethical."

## "Miss Marple" vs. the University

Brooks says that his actions were entirely proper and that he had kept higher officials informed. Plunket says the university is reviewing thoroughly all allegations. McGee declined to comment. Plunket and McGee remain on the university's payroll but have been removed from their administrative posts. McGee was vice chairman of the Department of Surgery, and Plunket was senior associate dean for clinical affairs.

The university says that 26 of the 98 people who participated in the melanoma trial had died, but that there is no evidence that the vaccine caused their deaths. Once problems emerged in the spring, the university says, the vaccine was tested and found not to have been contaminated with dangerous bacteria or viruses.

Looking back, Mathias says, "I kind of feel like Miss Marple," the heroine in detective novels by Agatha Christie. She says if she had to do it again, she would. If she needed any reminder that she had done the right thing, she says, a phone call cemented her belief:

"One of the subjects enrolled in the trial called me at home. He said, 'Thank you, thank you for being there for me and not allowing them to brush this away.' That makes it worth it to me. My whole goal was to protect the rights and welfare of the study's subjects. I was not going to abandon them."

## For Discussion

**1.** What was the major ethical breach in this case?

**2.** What situational factors increased the likelihood of unethical behavior in this case?

**3.** Would you attach primary blame for the unethical conduct to any single individual? Who? Why?

**4.** In terms of the constructive steps for reducing the need for whistle-blowing, discussed in this chapter, what should have been done at the University of Oklahoma College of Medicine to avoid this whistle-blowing event?

**5.** Putting yourself in Cherlynn Mathias's place, would you, as a divorced mother of two, have had the courage to blow the whistle? Explain. Would you have handled the problem differently than she did? Explain.

# Video Skill Builders

Born in Puerto Rico, Milton Rodriguez moved to the United States with his parents and grew up to embody the "American Dream." He invented an anti-theft labeling system for motor vehicles and built a thriving business for 15 years. Today, as co-owner of the Southington Chevrolet dealership in Southington, Connecticut, he is a positive and inspiring role model for his employees and customers. You will enjoy meeting Milton Rodriguez.

## 1A Milton Rodriguez, the Passionate Entrepreneur

### Learning Objective
To see how a start-from-nothing entrepreneur with a positive attitude energizes a business and its employees.

### Links to Textual Material
**Chapter 1:** Management defined; The twenty-first century manager; Managerial functions and roles; Small business management and entrepreneurship    **Chapter 14:** Teamwork    **Chapter 15:** Influence tactics; Leadership

### Discussion Questions

1. How does Milton Rodriguez exemplify the definition of management?

2. Which characteristics of the twenty-first century manager (see Table 1.1) are evident in this video profile?

3. Which of the eight managerial functions (Figure 1.3) and Mintzberg's ten managerial roles (Figure 1.4) are evident in this video case?

4. How well does Milton Rodriguez fit the entrepreneur trait profile in Table 1.4? Explain, trait by trait.

This New Hampshire maker of organic yogurt products has become a major player in the national marketplace. From its roots as a "three-cow" operation, Gary Hirshberg and his family have built a large business with an even bigger heart. Ten percent of each previous year's profits are donated to environmental causes. The firm's mission blends organic ingredients, environmental responsibility, and social responsibility with the quest for profits. Hirshberg recently extended this progressive business model to fast food, with the launching of the O'Naturals restaurant chain. (*Note:* see the Chapter 6 closing case for more on O'Naturals.)

## 1B Stonyfield Farm: "Yogurt on a Mission"

### Learning Objective
To see how one business attempts to make a profit in a socially responsible and environmentally friendly manner.

### Links to Textual Material
**Chapter 5:** The socioeconomic model of business; Proactive social responsibility strategy; Personal values and ethics; General ethical principles    **Chapter 15:** Transformational leaders; Servant leaders

### Discussion Questions

1. What does this video case say about the role of business in society?

2. Why does Stonyfield Farm's business model qualify as proactive social responsibility?

3. Why aren't more businesses run like Stonyfield Farm?

4. Using the Rokeach Value Survey (see the Hands-On Exercise following Chapter 5) as a guide, what are Gary Hirshberg's apparent top instrumental and top terminal values?

5. Which of the ten general ethical principles in Chapter 5 does Stonyfield Farm best exemplify? Explain.

# part two

# Planning and Decision Making

# chapter six

# The **Basics** of **Planning** and **Project Management**

> **"** Management is a balancing act between the short term and the long term, between different objectives at different times. **"**
>
> Peter F. Drucker

# In a Fast-Paced World, How Three Managers Plan on the Run

More than ever before, people in the business world are scrambling to control this elusive thing called time. The pace of marketplace change has become dizzying, making it difficult for executives to get beyond the day-to-day travails and grasp the bigger picture.

Indeed, the corporate world is experiencing the greatest calamity of its history as millions of corporate souls suffer from a phenomenon known as "time famine." It's not about having too little time to manage what you have to *do* on a daily basis; it is about not having time to *think* strategically. This inability to engage in long-range thinking affects the majority of executives today. They are in such a survival mode, always reacting to what's urgent, that they maneuver the bumps in the road rather than make decisions that will guide their company's futures. . . .

Name: Bobby Yazadani
Title: President and founder, Saba Software Inc., Redwood Shores, California

**Who has time to think?** "You have to create a business plan [for this]. It's something that not only I have to do, it's something my management team has to do. I have to manage the space for thinking."

**How do you find the space/time to think?** "I try to do two sets of disciplines for myself. One discipline is to communicate to the staff what they'll do and what I'll do. This communication truly empowers the executives; by doing that I have more space. I've done that in the past two years, and I have gained more and more time and space. I actually have time to follow research and spend time doing some planning work."

"Secondly, I am involved with the advisory board and board directors on a biweekly basis, so I can get away from my business. That has helped me to clear my mind, to make sound [decisions]."

Name: Maria D. Chevalier
Title: Director of special projects, HQ Global Workplaces, Atlanta, Georgia

**Who has time to think?** "I have the time to react but not enough time to spend on strategic planning. That is probably one of my biggest challenges and frustrations that I've ever had."

**How do you find the space/time to think?** "I have started to literally put it on my calendar and make it part of my tasks that I have scheduled. I find that's the only way I can do it because if not, the days and weeks get away from me. The best time I have found to think strategically is to come in as early as possible in the morning when it is quieter. I find that at the end of the day, you are too exhausted. And during the course of the day, too many things are occurring."

Name: Joe Crace
Title: Executive vice president and COO, Gaylord Entertainment Co., Nashville, Tennessee

**Who has time to think?** "You have to almost schedule time to think. Not only do you have to have time to think, but you have to have time where people are free to express their ideas and let their minds run without any restrictions."

**How do you find the space/time to think?** "From time to time, once or twice a quarter, Terry London, our CEO, and myself, or other key people in the management group, go off-site somewhere where everybody locks themselves indoors. There are no interruptions; we just schedule time to blend some fun and some time to sit and go through each of our businesses. We also think of any other distribution outlets, products or services, people and talent that we are not touching on."

*Source:* Excerpted from Cheryl Comeau-Kirschner and Louisa Wah, "Who Has Time to Think?" *Management Review,* (January 2000): 16-23. © 2000 American Management Association. Reprinted with permission of American Management Association in the format textbook via the Copyright Clearance Center.

n the age of Internet speed, more and more managers are finding they have a lot in common with Yazadani, Chevalier, and Crace. Small and large, public and private organizations are struggling to stay relevant and responsive. A standing joke among managers is that they are responsible for "doing the impossible by yesterday!" Indeed, virtually all of today's managers are asked to do a lot with limited budgets, resources, and time. All this takes thoughtful planning and a healthy dose of courage in the face of nerve-wracking uncertainty.

**planning**  *coping with uncertainty by formulating courses of action to achieve specified results*

**Planning** is the process of coping with uncertainty by formulating future courses of action to achieve specified results. Planning enables humans to achieve great things by envisioning a pathway from concept to reality. The greater the mission, the longer and more challenging the pathway. For example, imagine the challenges awaiting Walgreen, the drugstore chain, as it pursues its ambitious growth plan. As *Fortune* magazine recently reported: "The company's aim is to nearly double its stores, to around 6,000, within five years."[1] Planning is a never-ending process because of constant change, uncertainty, new competition, unexpected problems, and emerging opportunities.[2]

Because planning affects all downstream management functions (see Figure 6.1), it has been called the primary management function. With this model in mind, we shall discuss uncertainty, highlight five essential aspects of the planning function, and take a close look at management by objectives, project planning, and enterprise resource planning. We shall also introduce four practical tools (flow charts, Gantt charts, PERT networks, and break-even analysis).

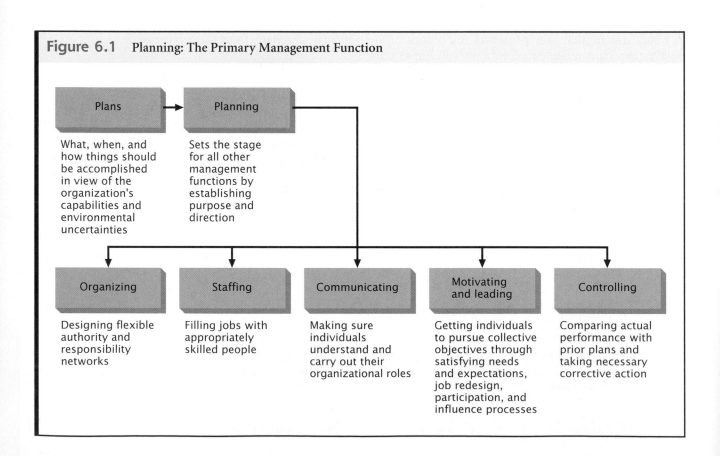

**Figure 6.1**    Planning: The Primary Management Function

Plans → Planning

**Plans**
What, when, and how things should be accomplished in view of the organization's capabilities and environmental uncertainties

**Planning**
Sets the stage for all other management functions by establishing purpose and direction

**Organizing**
Designing flexible authority and responsibility networks

**Staffing**
Filling jobs with appropriately skilled people

**Communicating**
Making sure individuals understand and carry out their organizational roles

**Motivating and leading**
Getting individuals to pursue collective objectives through satisfying needs and expectations, job redesign, participation, and influence processes

**Controlling**
Comparing actual performance with prior plans and taking necessary corrective action

# Coping with Uncertainty

Ben Franklin said the only sure things in life are death and taxes. Although this is a gloomy prospect, it does capture a key theme of modern life: We are faced with a great deal of uncertainty. Organizations, like individuals, are continually challenged to accomplish something in spite of general uncertainty. Organizations meet this challenge largely through planning. As a context for our discussion of planning in this and the following chapter, let us explore environmental uncertainty from two perspectives: (1) types of uncertainty and (2) organizational responses to environmental uncertainty.

## Three Types of Uncertainty

Through the years, *environmental uncertainty* has been a catch-all term among managers and researchers. However, research indicates that people actually perceive three types of environmental uncertainty: state uncertainty, effect uncertainty, and response uncertainty. **State uncertainty** occurs when the environment, or a portion of the environment, is considered unpredictable. A manager's attempt to predict the *effects* of specific environmental changes or events on his or her organization involves **effect uncertainty. Response uncertainty** relates to being unable to predict the *consequences* of a particular decision or organizational response.[3]

A simple analogy can help us conceptually sort out these three types of uncertainty. Suppose you are a golfer and on your way to the course you wonder whether it is going to rain; this is *state uncertainty*. Next, you experience *effect uncertainty* because you are not sure it will rain hard enough, if it does rain, to make you quit before finishing nine holes. You begin weighing your chances of making par if you have to adjust your choice of golf clubs to poor playing conditions; now you are experiencing *response uncertainty*. Each of the three types of perceived uncertainty could affect your golfing attitude and performance. Similarly, managers are affected by their different perceptions of environmental factors. Their degree of uncertainty may vary from one type of

> **1** Distinguish among state, effect, and response uncertainty.

> **state uncertainty**
> *unpredictable environment*

> **effect uncertainty**   *impacts of environmental changes are unpredictable*

> **response uncertainty**
> *consequences of decisions are unpredictable*

*Talk about uncertainty! Here's what happened the night before the Blue Smoke restaurant in New York City was set to open in March 2002: The water heater went on vacation, the computers crashed, and the fire alarm went off (followed by an apology to firefighters for a false alarm). A few more glitches and some fine tuning on opening day got the new eatery and jazz club off to a rousing start. Even the best laid plans can't eliminate unforeseen bumps in the road.*

**6A**

**Back to the Opening Case**

Which type of uncertainty—state, effect, or response—do you think these three managers find most difficult? Why?

For further information about the interactive annotations in this chapter, visit our Web site (http://business.college. hmco.com/students).

uncertainty to another. A manager may, for example, be unsure about the timing of a labor strike (state uncertainty) but very sure that a strike would ruin profits (effect uncertainty).[4]

## Organizational Responses to Uncertainty

Some organizations do a better job than others of planning amid various combinations of uncertainty. This is due in part to differing patterns of response to environmental factors beyond the organization's immediate control. As outlined in Table 6.1, organizations cope with environmental uncertainty by adopting one of four positions vis-á-vis the environment in which they operate. These positions are defenders, prospectors, analyzers, and reactors,[5] each with its own characteristic impact on planning.

**Defenders.**    A defender can be successful as long as its primary technology and narrow product line remain competitive. Defenders can become stranded on a dead-end road if their primary market seriously weakens. A prime example of a defender is Harley-Davidson, which sold its recreational vehicle division and other nonmotorcycle businesses to get back to basics. Harley-Davidson enjoys such fierce brand loyalty among Hog riders that many sport a tattoo of the company's logo. Can you imagine a

---

**Table 6.1    Different Organizational Responses to an Uncertain Environment**

| Type of organizational response | Characteristics of response |
|---|---|
| **1. Defenders** | Highly expert at producing and marketing a few products in a narrowly defined market |
| | Opportunities beyond present market not sought |
| | Few adjustments in technology, organization structure, and methods of operation because of narrow focus |
| | Primary attention devoted to efficiency of current operations |
| **2. Prospectors** | Primary attention devoted to searching for new market opportunities |
| | Frequent development and testing of new products and services |
| | Source of change and uncertainty for competitors |
| | Loss of efficiency because of continual product and market innovation |
| **3. Analyzers** | Simultaneous operations in stable and changing product market domains |
| | In relatively stable product/market domain, emphasis on formalized structures and processes to achieve routine and efficient operation |
| | In changing product/market domain, emphasis on detecting and copying competitors' most promising ideas |
| **4. Reactors** | Frequently unable to respond quickly to perceived changes in environment |
| | Make adjustments only when finally forced to do so by environmental pressures |

*Source:* Adapted from *Organizational Strategy, Structure, and Process,* by Raymond E. Miles and Charles C. Snow. Copyright © 1978, McGraw-Hill Book Company, p. 29. Used with permission of McGraw-Hill Book Company.

Coca-Cola or Wal-Mart tattoo? But Harley-Davidson runs the risk of having its narrow focus miss the mark in an aging America. Specifically, the median age of Harley buyers rose from 35 in 1987 to 46 in 2002. Harley-Davidson is therefore seeking to lure younger riders who prefer sleek bikes away from Honda and other Japanese rivals.[6]

**Prospectors.**     Prospector organizations are easy to spot because they have a reputation for aggressively making things happen rather than waiting for them to happen. But life is not easy for prospectors such as Capital One. The credit card issuer, with nearly 44 million customers worldwide,[7] has to run faster and faster to stay a step ahead of competitors:

> *Capital One scored some early victories in the credit-card game by changing the rules. Its founders invented the "teaser rate"—the banking equivalent of a cheap mortgage that gets adjusted up after a certain period. The teaser attracted millions of customers, and eventually competitors began to mimic the idea. The result was a merry-go-round of so-called teaser hoppers. People would move their balance to a low-introductory-rate card; as soon as the rate expired, they would switch to another card. Over time, Cap One was being eaten alive because of customer attrition.*
>
> *The lesson: Companies that thrive on change can never rest. Competitors are quick to copy good ideas. The way to compete on innovation is to keep innovating.*
>
> *That's the hard part. And that's why Capital One is so obsessed with making its own innovations obsolete.*[8]

Prospectors (or pioneers) traditionally have been admired for their ability to gain what strategists call a *first-mover advantage*. In other words, the first one to market wins. Following the Internet crash, when many dot-com pioneers were the first to go bank-

*The executive team at network equipment maker Zhone Technologies are true prospectors. When they needed a place to set up shop, they called on the mayor of Oakland, California, Jerry Brown (pictured center). Yes, the very same Jerry Brown who, as the Golden State's governor, was know as Governor Moonbeam for his unconventional ways. In very unMoonbeam-like fashion, Brown responded with his own bit of prospecting. Zhone Technologies got the land, permits, and access to roads and power they needed, all in record time. Along with 1,500 jobs, Oakland got 100,000 shares of Zhone stock. Now there's a real moon shot!*

rupt, the first-mover advantage was given a second look. Two researchers, one from the United States and the other from France, recently offered this finding about both industrial and consumer goods companies: " . . . we found that over the long haul, early movers are considerably *less* profitable than later entrants. Although pioneers do enjoy sustained revenue advantages, they also suffer from persistently *high* costs, which eventually overwhelm the sales gains."[9] Prospectors need to pick their opportunities very carefully, selecting those with the best combination of feasibility and profit potential. This is especially true for entrepreneurs starting small businesses.[10]

**Analyzers.**   An essentially conservative strategy of following the leader marks an organization as an analyzer. It is a "me too" response to environmental uncertainty. Analyzers let the market leader take expensive R&D risks and then imitate what works. This slower, more studied approach can pay off when the economy turns down and market leaders stumble. Verizon, the telephone company, is a good case in point:

> *Remember the tortoise and the hare? Sometimes slow and steady is better than fast and furious. A couple of years ago, industry observers cried that Verizon, weighed down by regulatory matters and merger pains, had missed the bandwidth wagon. But the Baby Bell's sluggishness turned out to be an asset: While other telecom companies are writing off billions, Verizon actually wins big as a result of the fiber glut.*
>
> > *Instead of building its own system a couple of years ago, Verizon is now cobbling together an international network that it is buying in bits and pieces from other fiber carriers at enormous discounts.*[11]

Although analyzers may not get a lot of respect, they can perform the important economic function of breaking up monopolistic situations. Customers appreciate the resulting lower prices.

**Reactors.**   The reactor is the exact opposite of the prospector. Reactors wait for adversity, such as declining sales, before taking corrective steps. They are slow to develop new products to supplement their tried-and-true ones. Their strategic responses to changes in the environment are often late. An interesting example in this area is Joseph E. Seagram & Sons, Inc. The Canadian firm grew into the world's largest distiller by specializing in brown liquors such as Seagram's 7 Crown. But drinking habits changed over the years. Consequently, white liquors such as Bacardi rum and Smirnoff vodka pushed Seagram's 7 Crown from first place to third. Moreover, with more North Americans drinking wine, the public outcry against drunk driving, and higher excise taxes on liquor, Seagram's sales dropped. By the time Seagram reacted by bolstering its wine business in the 1980s, the wine market was glutted because of European imports and overplanted vineyards in California.[12]

   According to one field study, reactors tended to be less profitable than defenders, prospectors, and analyzers.[13]

## Balancing Planned Action and Spontaneity in the Twenty-First Century

In the obsolete command-and-control management model, plans were considered destiny. Top management formulated exacting plans for every aspect of operations and then kept everything under tight control to "meet the plan." All too often, however, plans were derailed by unanticipated events and success was dampened by organizational inflexibility. Today's progressive managers see plans as general guidelines for action, based on imperfect and incomplete information. Planning is no longer the exclusive domain of top management; it now typically involves those who carry out the plans because they are closer to the customer. Planning experts say managers need to balance planned action with the flexibility to take advantage of surprise events and unexpected opportunities. A good analogy is to an improvisational comedy act.[14] The stand-up comic has a plan for the introduction, structure of the act, some tried-and-true jokes, and closing remarks. Within this planned framework, the comic will play off the audience's input and improvise as necessary. Accordingly, 3M Corporation had a plan for encouraging innovation that allowed it to capitalize on the spontaneous success of the Post-it note. Planning should be a springboard to success, not a barrier to creativity.

## 6B  The Chaos Theory of Planning

Andy Grove, chairman of Intel Corporation, the world's leading computer chip maker:

*You need to try to do the impossible, to anticipate the unexpected. And when the unexpected happens, you should double your efforts to make order from the disorder it creates in your life. The motto I'm advocating is, Let chaos reign, then rein in chaos. Does that mean that you shouldn't plan? Not at all. You need to plan the way a fire department plans. It cannot anticipate fires, so it has to shape a flexible organization that is capable of responding to unpredictable events.*

**Source:** Andrew S. Grove, "A High-Tech CEO Updates His Views on Managing and Careers," *Fortune* (September 18, 1995): 229.

**Questions:** *How well does Grove's approach to planning agree with what you just read about the need to balance planned action with creative spontaneity? Do either of these new perspectives of planning go against your assumptions about why or how companies should plan? What do you think of Grove's philosophy?*

# The Essentials of Planning

Planning is an ever-present feature of modern life, although there is no universal approach. Virtually everyone is a planner, at least in the informal sense. We plan leisure activities after school or work; we make career plans. Personal or informal plans give purpose to our lives. In a similar fashion, more formalized plans enable managers to mobilize their intentions to accomplish organizational purposes. A **plan** is a specific, documented intention consisting of an objective and an action statement. The objective portion is the end, and the action statement represents the means to that end. Stated another way, objectives give management targets to shoot at, whereas action statements provide the arrows for hitting the targets. Properly conceived plans tell *what, when,* and *how* something is to be done.

In spite of the wide variety of formal planning systems that managers encounter on the job, we can identify some essentials of sound planning. Among these common denominators are organizational mission, types of planning, objectives, priorities, and the planning/control cycle.

**plan** *an objective plus an action statement*

## Organizational Mission

To some, defining an organization's mission might seem an unnecessary exercise. But exactly the opposite is true. Some organizations drift along without a clear mission. Others lose sight of their original mission. Sometimes an organization, such as the U.S. Army Corps of Engineers, finds its original mission no longer acceptable to key stakeholders. In fact, the Corps is stepping back from its tradition of building dams and levees, in favor of more environmentally sensitive projects. It has tackled "a 30-year, $7.8 billion restoration of the Florida Everglades"[15] that will involve tearing down levees to restore the natural flow of the Kissimmee River. Periodically redefining an organization's mission is both common and necessary in an era of rapid change.

*If you want a Big Mac, fries, a chocolate shake, and a prayer of forgiveness, this is the man to see. He's the Reverend Joe Ratliff, senior pastor of the Brentwood Baptist Church in Houston, Texas. Reverend Ratliff saw McDonald's outlets popping up in unusual places such as gas stations, schools, and hospitals. So why not have one for the church's 10,000-member congregation? After all, on-site dining fit the church's mission of helping people and a restaurant fit nicely into the plans for a huge new multi-purpose building. "Good idea," said McDonald's, and the rest is history. Did you say, "Hold the onions?"*

A clear, formally written, and publicized statement of an organization's mission is the cornerstone of any planning system that will effectively guide the organization through uncertain times. The satirical definition by Scott Adams, the Dilbert cartoonist, tells us how *not* to write an organizational mission statement: "A Mission Statement is defined as a long, awkward sentence that demonstrates management's inability to think clearly."[16] This sad state of affairs, too often true, can be avoided by a well-written mission statement that does the following things:

1. *Defines* your organization for key stakeholders
2. Creates an *inspiring vision* of what the organization can be and can do
3. Outlines *how* the vision is to be accomplished
4. Establishes key *priorities*
5. States a *common goal* and fosters a sense of togetherness
6. Creates a *philosophical anchor* for all organizational activities
7. Generates *enthusiasm* and a "can do" attitude
8. *Empowers* present and future organization members to believe that *every* individual is the key to success[17]

A good mission statement provides a focal point for the entire planning process. When Vincent A. Sarni took the top job at PPG, the large glass and paint company, he created a document he called "Blueprint for the Decade." In it, he specified the company's mission and corporate objectives for such things as service, quality, and financial performance.

> *Sarni . . . trudged from plant to plant preaching the virtues in his Little Blue Book. "My first two or three years I always started with a discussion of the Blueprint," he says. "I don't have to do that anymore. The Blueprint's on the shop floor, and it has meaning."*[18]

## Types of Planning

Ideally, planning begins at the top of the organizational pyramid and filters down. The rationale for beginning at the top is the need for coordination. It is top management's job to state the organization's mission, establish strategic priorities, and draw up major policies. After these statements are in place, successive rounds of strategic, intermediate, and operational planning can occur. Figure 6.2 presents an idealized picture of the three types of planning, as carried out by different levels of management.

**2** Identify and define the three types of planning.

**Strategic, Intermediate, and Operational Planning.** **Strategic planning** is the process of determining how to pursue the organization's long-term goals with the resources expected to be available. A well-conceived strategic plan communicates much more than general intentions about profit and growth. It specifies *how* the organization will achieve a competitive advantage, with profit and growth as necessary by-products. **Intermediate planning** is the process of determining the contributions subunits can make with allocated resources. Finally, **operational planning** is the process of determining how specific tasks can best be accomplished on time with available resources. Each level of planning is vital to an organization's success and cannot effectively stand alone without the support of the other two levels.

**strategic planning**
*determining how to pursue long-term goals with available resources*

**intermediate planning**
*determining subunits' contributions with allocated resources*

**operational planning**
*determining how to accomplish specific tasks with available resources*

**Planning Horizons.** As Figure 6.2 illustrates, planning horizons vary for the three types of planning. The term **planning horizon** refers to the time that elapses between the formulation and the execution of a planned activity. As the planning process evolves from strategic to operational, planning horizons shorten and plans become increasingly specific. Naturally, management can be more confident and hence more specific about the near future than it can about the distant future.

**planning horizon** *elapsed time between planning and execution*

Notice, however, that the three planning horizons overlap, their boundaries being elastic rather than rigid. The trend today is toward involving employees from all levels in the strategic planning process. Also, it is not uncommon for top and lower managers to have a hand in formulating intermediate plans. Middle managers often help lower managers draw up operational plans as well. So, Figure 6.2 is an ideal instructional model with countless variations in the workplace.

## Objectives

Just as a distant port is the target or goal for a ship's crew, objectives are targets that organizational members steer toward. Although some theorists distinguish between goals and objectives, managers typically use the terms interchangeably. A goal or an

**6C  A Model Mission Statement?**

Alan Brunacini, the long-time chief of the Phoenix, Arizona, Fire Department, has a reputation as a great manager. He has boiled his department's mission down to five words: "Prevent harm, survive, be nice."

**Source:** As quoted in Jon Talton, "What in Blazes Has the Chief Done? Create a Model for Managers," *The Arizona Republic* (January 27, 2002): D1.

**Questions:** *Based on what you have just read, is this an effective organizational mission statement? Why or why not?*

**Figure 6.2**

Types of Planning

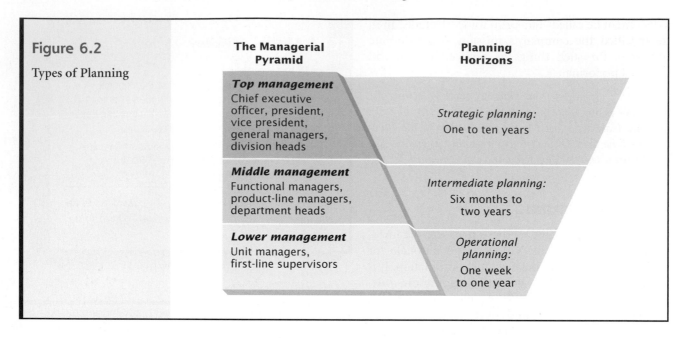

**The Managerial Pyramid**

*Top management*
Chief executive officer, president, vice president, general managers, division heads

*Middle management*
Functional managers, product-line managers, department heads

*Lower management*
Unit managers, first-line supervisors

**Planning Horizons**

*Strategic planning:* One to ten years

*Intermediate planning:* Six months to two years

*Operational planning:* One week to one year

---

**objective**  *commitment to achieve a measurable result within a specified period*

**objective** is defined as a specific commitment to achieve a measurable result within a given time frame. Many experts view objectives as the single most important feature of the planning process. They help managers and entrepreneurs build a bridge between their dreams, aspirations, and visions and an achievable *reality*. Dan Sullivan, a consultant for entrepreneurs, explains:

> [Objectives and goals] should be achievable by definition. If you are setting functional goals, at useful increments, they should be both *real* and *realizable*. The distance between where you actually are now and your goal can be measured objectively, and when you achieve your goal, you know it. Think of the distinction this way: no matter how fast you run toward the horizon, you'll never get there, but if you run more quickly toward a goalpost, you will get there faster. Sounds simplistic, but I'm constantly amazed at how many people—and entrepreneurs in particular—confuse their goals with their ideals.[19]

It is important for present and future managers to be able to write good objectives, to be aware of their importance, and to understand how objectives combine to form a means-ends chain.

**3**  Write good objectives and discuss the role of objectives in planning.

**Writing Good Objectives.**    An authority on objectives recommends that "as far as possible, objectives are expressed in quantitative, measurable, concrete terms, in the form of a written statement of desired results to be achieved within a given time period."[20] In other words, objectives represent a firm commitment to accomplish something specific. A well-written objective should state what is to be accomplished and when it is to be accomplished. In the following sample objectives, note that the desired results are expressed *quantitatively,* in units of output, dollars, or percentage of change.

■ To increase subcompact car production by 240,000 units during the next production year
■ To reduce bad-debt loss by $50,000 during the next six months
■ To achieve an 18 percent increase in Brand X sales by December 31 of the current year

For actual practice in writing good objectives and plans, see the Hands-On Exercise at the end of this chapter.

**The Importance of Objectives.**    From the standpoint of planning, carefully prepared objectives benefit managers by serving as targets and measuring sticks, fostering commitment, and enhancing motivation.[21]

- *Targets.* As mentioned earlier, objectives provide managers with specific targets. Without objectives, managers at all levels would find it difficult to make coordinated decisions. People quite naturally tend to pursue their own ends in the absence of formal organizational objectives.
- *Measuring sticks.* An easily overlooked, after-the-fact feature of objectives is that they are useful for measuring how well an organizational subunit or individual has performed. When appraising performance, managers need an established standard against which they can measure performance. Concrete objectives enable managers to weigh performance objectively on the basis of accomplishment rather than subjectively on the basis of personality or prejudice.
- *Commitment.* The very process of getting an employee to agree to pursue a given objective gives that individual a personal stake in the success of the enterprise. Thus objectives can be helpful in encouraging personal commitment to collective ends. Without individual commitment, even well-intentioned and carefully conceived strategies are doomed to failure.
- *Motivation.* Good objectives represent a challenge—something to reach for. As such, they have a motivational aspect. People usually feel good about themselves and what they do when they successfully achieve a challenging objective. Moreover, objectives give managers a rational basis for rewarding performance. Employees who believe they will be equitably rewarded for achieving a given objective will be motivated to perform well.

**The Means-Ends Chain of Objectives.**    Like the overall planning process, objective setting is a top-to-bottom proposition. Top managers set broader objectives with longer time horizons than do successively lower levels of managers. In effect, this downward flow of objectives creates a means-ends chain. Working from bottom to top in Figure 6.3, supervisory-level objectives provide the means for achieving middle-level objectives (ends) that, in turn, provide the means for achieving top-level objectives (ends).

**6D**

### Okay Now, Everybody S-t-r-e-t-c-h!

Jack Welch, retired General Electric CEO:

*In a stretch environment the . . . field team is asked to come in with "operating plans" that reflect their dreams—the highest numbers they think they have a shot at: their "stretch." The discussion revolves around new directions and growth, energizing stuff.*

**Source:** Jack Welch, *Jack: Straight from the Gut,* (New York: Warner Books, 2001), p. 386.

**Question:** *What are the positives and negatives of this approach to planning?*

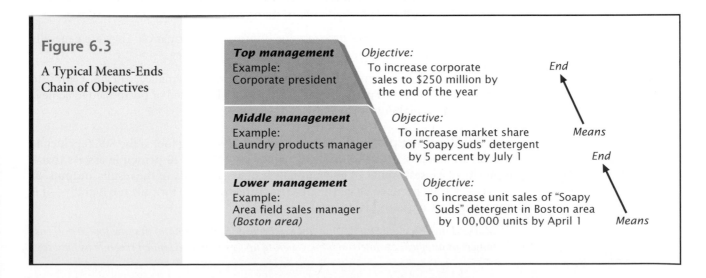

**Figure 6.3**

A Typical Means-Ends Chain of Objectives

The organizational hierarchy in Figure 6.3 has, of course, been telescoped and narrowed at the middle and lower levels for illustrative purposes. Usually, two or three layers of management would separate the president and the product-line managers. Another layer or two would separate product-line managers from area sales managers. But the telescoping helps show that lower-level objectives provide the means for accomplishing higher-level ends or objectives.

## Priorities

**priorities**  *ranking goals, objectives, or activities in order of importance*

Defined as a ranking of goals, objectives, or activities in order of importance, **priorities** play a special role in planning. By listing long-range organizational objectives in order of their priority, top management prepares to make later decisions regarding the allocation of resources. Limited time, talent, and financial and material resources need to be channeled proportionately into more important endeavors and away from other areas. Establishment of priorities is a key factor in managerial and organizational effectiveness. Strategic priorities give both insiders and outsiders answers to the questions, "Why does the organization exist?" and "How should it act and react during a crisis?" An inspiring illustration of the latter occurred for American Express after the September 11, 2001, terrorist attacks:

> *The hundreds of ad hoc decisions made by [new CEO Kenneth I.] Chenault and his team were guided by two overriding concerns: employee safety and customer service. AmEx helped 560,000 stranded cardholders get home, in some cases chartering airplanes and buses to ferry them across the country. It waived millions of dollars in delinquent fees on late-paying cardholders and increased credit limits to cash-starved clients. . . .*
>
> *Most telling, Chenault gathered 5,000 American Express employees at the Paramount Theater in New York on Sept. 20 for a highly emotional "town hall meeting." During the session, Chenault demonstrated . . . poise, compassion, and decisiveness.*[22]

### The A-B-C Priority System.

Despite time-management seminars, day planners, and computerized "personal digital assistants," establishing priorities remains a subjective process affected by organizational politics and value conflicts.[23] Although there is no universally acceptable formula for carrying out this important function, the following A-B-C priority system is helpful.

A: "Must do" objectives *critical* to successful performance. They may be the result of special demands from higher levels of management or other external sources.

B: "Should do" objectives *necessary* for improved performance. They are generally vital, but their achievement can be postponed if necessary.

C: "Nice to do" objectives *desirable* for improved performance, but not critical to survival or improved performance. They can be eliminated or postponed to achieve objectives of higher priority.[24]

### The 80/20 Principle.

**80/20 principle**  *a minority of causes, inputs, or effort tend to produce a majority of results, outputs, or rewards*

Another proven priority-setting tool is the 80/20 principle (or Pareto analysis, as mentioned in Chapter 2). "The **80/20 principle** asserts that a minority of causes, inputs, or effort usually lead to a majority of the results, outputs, or rewards."[25] Care needs to be taken not to interpret the 80/20 formula too literally—it is approximate. Consider this situation, for example:

> *Market Line Associates, an Atlanta financial consultancy, estimates that the top 20% of customers at a typical commercial bank generate up to six times as much revenue as they cost,*

*while the bottom fifth cost three to four times more than they make for the company.*[26]

For profit-minded banks and other businesses, all customers are not alike!

**Avoiding the Busyness Trap.** These two simple yet effective tools for establishing priorities can help managers avoid the so-called *busyness trap*.[27] In these fast-paced times, managers should not confuse being busy with being effective and efficient. *Results* are what really count. Activities and speed, without results, are an energy-sapping waste of time. By slowing down a bit, having clear priorities, and taking a strategic view of daily problems, busy managers can be successful *and* "get a life."

Finally, managers striving to establish priorities amid lots of competing demands would do well to heed management expert Peter Drucker's advice—that the most important skill for setting priorities and managing time is simply learning to say no.

**6E Meg Whitman Avoids the Busyness Trap by Getting Her Priorities Straight**

Margaret C. Whitman, CEO of eBay Inc., the online auction site:

> *Again, it's this notion of choosing what you're going to focus on. And I have this philosophy that you really need to do things 100 percent. Better to do five things at 100 percent than ten things at 80 percent. And while we have to move very, very fast, I think you are not well served by moving incredibly rapidly and not doing things that well.*

**Source:** As quoted in Linda Himelstein, "Meg Whitman: eBay," *Business Week* (May 31, 1999): 134.

**Questions:** *Are you caught in the busyness trap? How can you tell? What can you do to improve the situation?*

## The Planning/Control Cycle

To put the planning process in perspective, it is important to show how it is connected with the control function. Figure 6.4 illustrates the cyclical relationship between planning and control. Planning gets things headed in the right direction, and control keeps them headed in the right direction. (Because of the importance of the control func-

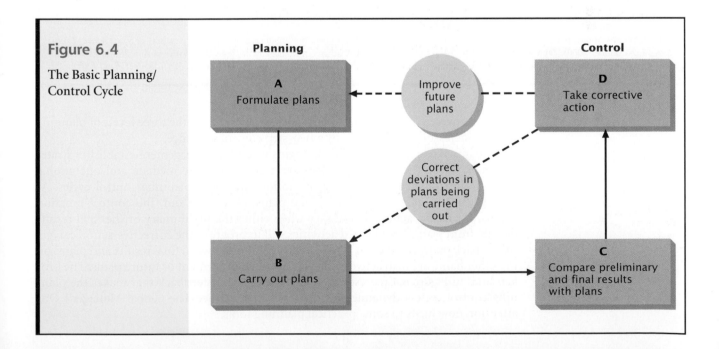

**Figure 6.4**

**The Basic Planning/Control Cycle**

Planning

**A** Formulate plans

Improve future plans

Control

**D** Take corrective action

Correct deviations in plans being carried out

**B** Carry out plans

**C** Compare preliminary and final results with plans

# The Global Manager

Culture Affects How Planning and
Control Are Perceived: Russian Versus
Western Views

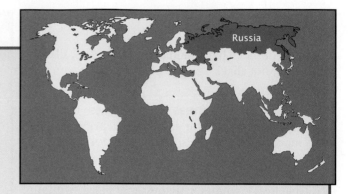

Russia

## Views of Planning in Organizations

| **Russians** | **Westerners** |
|---|---|
| The plan is an ultimate end-task. | The plan is only a starting point and articulates alternative courses of action. |
| The plan must be executed by all means in the way that it was initially defined. | The plan needs to be adjusted continuously. |
| Only short-term planning is meaningful. | Planning is a long-term activity. |
| Success is measured according to whether the plan has been executed. | In order to be successful, one needs to reassess and readjust the plan. |

## Views of Control in Organizations

| **Russians** | **Westerners** |
|---|---|
| Prefer the notion of control instead of feedback. | Prefer the notion of feedback instead of control. |
| Control is top-down. | Control is intrinsic to all organizational members' actions. |
| Control is focused on formalized bureaucracy. | Control is oriented toward involvement. |
| Control is exercised by using rewards and punishments. | Control is related to monitoring processes. |
| Control is a discrete activity. | Control is continuous. |

*Source:* Snejina Michailova, "Contrasts in Culture: Russian and Western Perspectives on Organizational Change," *Academy of Management Executive,* 14 (November 2000): Tables 3 and 4, pp. 106–107. Copyright 2000 by Academy of Management. Reproduced with permission of Academy of Management in the format textbook via the Copyright Clearance Center.

tion, it is covered in detail in Chapter 17.) Basically, each of the three levels of planning is a two-step sequence followed by a two-step control sequence.

The initial planning/control cycle begins when top management establishes strategic plans. When those strategic plans are carried out, intermediate and operational plans are formulated, thus setting in motion two more planning/control cycles. As strategic, intermediate, and operational plans are carried out, the control function begins. Corrective action is necessary when either the preliminary or the final results deviate from plans. For planned activities still in progress, the corrective action can get things back on track before it is too late. Deviations between final results and plans, on the other hand, are instructive feedback for the improvement of future plans. The broken lines in Figure 6.4 represent the important sort of feedback that makes the planning/control cycle a dynamic and evolving process. (See The Global Manager.) Our attention now turns to some practical planning tools.

# Management by Objectives and Project Planning

In this section we examine a traditional planning technique and a modern planning challenge. Valuable lessons about planning can be learned from each.

## Management by Objectives

**Management by objectives (MBO)** is a comprehensive management system based on measurable and participatively set objectives. MBO has come a long way since it was first suggested by Peter Drucker in 1954 as a way of promoting managerial self-control.[28] MBO theory[29] and practice subsequently mushroomed and spread around the world. In one form or another, and under various labels, MBO has been adopted by most public and private organizations of any significant size. For example, at Cypress Semiconductor Corporation, the San Jose, California, electronics firm, computerization paved the way for high-tech MBO. T. J. Rodgers, the company's founder and chief executive officer, explains:

> *All of Cypress's 1,400 employees have goals, which, in theory, makes them no different from employees at most other companies. What makes our people different is that every week they set their own goals, commit to achieving them by a specific date, enter them into a database, and report whether or not they completed prior goals. Cypress's computerized goal system is an important part of our managerial infrastructure. It is a detailed guide to the future and an objective record of the past. In any given week, some 6,000 goals in the database come due. Our ability to meet those goals ultimately determines our success or failure. . . .*
>
> *I developed the goal system long before personal computers existed. It has its roots in management-by-objectives techniques I learned in the mid-1970s at American Microsystems.*[30]

The common denominator that has made MBO programs so popular in both management theory and practice is the emphasis on objectives that are both *measurable* and *participatively set.*

**The MBO Cycle.**   Because MBO combines planning and control, the four-stage MBO cycle corresponds to the planning/control cycle outlined in Figure 6.4. Steps 1 and 2 make up the planning phase of MBO, and steps 3 and 4 are the control phase.

*Step 1: Setting objectives.* A hierarchy of challenging, fair, and internally consistent objectives is the necessary starting point for the MBO cycle and serves as the foundation for all that follows. All objectives, according to MBO theory, should be reduced to writing and put away for later reference during steps 3 and 4. Consistent with what was said earlier about objectives, objective setting in MBO begins at the top of the managerial pyramid and filters down, one layer at a time.

MBO's main contribution to the objective-setting process is its emphasis on the participation and involvement of people at lower levels. There is no place in MBO for the domineering manager ("Here are the objectives I've written for you") or for the passive manager ("I'll go along with whatever objectives you set"). MBO calls for a give-and-take negotiation of objectives between the manager and those who report directly to him or her.[31]

**management by objectives (MBO)**   *comprehensive management system based on measurable and participatively set objectives*

**4**   Describe the four-step management by objectives (MBO) process and explain how it can foster individual commitment and motivation.

*Step 2: Developing action plans.* With the addition of action statements to the participatively set objectives, the planning phase of MBO is complete. Managers at each level develop plans that incorporate objectives established in step 1. Higher managers are responsible for ensuring that their direct assistants' plans complement one another and do not work at cross-purposes.

*Step 3: Periodic review.* As plans turn into action, attention turns to step 3, monitoring performance. Advocates of MBO usually recommend face-to-face meetings between a manager and his or her people at three-, six-, and nine-month intervals. (Some organizations, such as Cypress, rely on shorter cycles.) These periodic checkups permit those who are responsible for a particular set of objectives to reconsider them, checking their validity in view of unexpected events—added duties or the loss of a key assistant—that could make them obsolete. If an objective is no longer valid, it is amended accordingly. Otherwise, progress toward valid objectives is assessed. Periodic checkups also give managers an excellent opportunity to give their people needed and appreciated feedback.

*Step 4: Performance appraisal.* At the end of one complete cycle of MBO, typically one year after the original goals were set, final performance is matched with the previously agreed-upon objectives. The pairs of superior and subordinate managers who mutually set the objectives one year earlier meet face to face once again to discuss how things have turned out. MBO emphasizes results, not personalities or excuses. The control phase of the MBO cycle is completed when success is rewarded with promotion, merit pay, or other suitable benefits and when failure is noted for future corrective action.

After one round of MBO, the cycle repeats itself, with each cycle contributing to the learning process. A common practice in introducing MBO is to start at the top and to pull a new layer of management into the MBO process each year. Experience has shown that plunging several layers of management into MBO all at once often causes confusion, dissatisfaction, and failure. In fact, even a moderate-sized organization usually takes five or more years to evolve a full-blown MBO system that ties together such areas as planning, control, performance appraisal, and the reward system. MBO programs can be facilitated by using off-the-shelf software programs. Such programs offer helpful spreadsheet formats for goal setting, timelines, at-a-glance status boards, and performance reports. MBO proponents believe that effective leadership and greater motivation—through the use of realistic objectives, more effective control, and self-control—are the natural by-products of a proper MBO system.[32]

**Strengths and Limitations of MBO.** Any widely used management technique is bound to generate debate about its relative strengths and weaknesses, and MBO is no exception.[33] Present and future managers will have more realistic expectations for MBO if they are familiar with both sides of this debate. The four primary strengths of MBO and four common complaints about it are compared in Figure 6.5.

This debate will probably not be resolved in the near future. Critics of MBO, such as the late quality expert W. Edwards Deming, point to both theoretical and methodological flaws.[34] Meanwhile, MBO advocates are quick to point out that the misapplication of MBO, not the MBO concept itself, leads to problems. In the final analysis, MBO will probably work when organizational conditions are favorable and will probably fail when those conditions are unfavorable. A favorable climate for MBO includes top-management commitment, openness to change, Theory Y management, and employees who are willing and able to shoulder greater responsibility.[35] Research justifies putting *top-management commitment* at the top of the list. In a review of 70 MBO studies,

**6F**

**Making MBO Work**

**Questions:** *What is your experience with MBO-type programs in the workplace? What was the program called? Was the program effective? Why or why not? Referring back to McGregor's Theory X and Theory Y distinction in Chapter 2, why does a Theory Y manager have a better chance of administering a successful MBO program?*

**Figure 6.5**

MBO's Strengths and Limitations

| Strengths | Limitations |
|---|---|
| ■ MBO blends planning and control into a rational system of management. | ■ MBO is too often sold as a cure-all. |
| ■ MBO forces an organization to develop a top-to-bottom hierarchy of objectives. | ■ MBO is easily stalled by authoritarian (Theory X) managers and inflexible bureaucratic policies and rules. |
| ■ MBO emphasizes end results rather than good intentions or personalities. | ■ MBO takes too much time and effort and generates too much paperwork. |
| ■ MBO encourages self-management and personal commitment through employee participation in setting objectives. | ■ MBO's emphasis on measurable objectives can be used as a threat by overzealous managers. |

researchers found that "when top-management commitment was high, the average gain in productivity was 56 percent. When commitment was low, the average gain in productivity was only 6 percent."[36] A strong positive relationship was also found between top-management commitment to MBO program success and employee job satisfaction.[37] The greater management's commitment, the greater the satisfaction.

## Project Planning and Management

Project-based organizations are becoming the norm today. Why? Drawing-board-to-market times are being honed to the minimum in today's technology-driven world.[38] Typically, cross-functional teams of people with different technical skills are brought together on a temporary basis to complete a specific project as swiftly as possible. According to the Project Management Institute, "A **project** is a temporary endeavor undertaken to achieve a particular aim."[39] Projects, like all other activities within the management domain, need to be systematically planned and managed. What sets project planning and management apart is the *temporary* nature of projects, as opposed to the typical ongoing or continuous activities in organizations. When the job is done, project members disband and move on to other projects or return to their usual work routines.[40]

**project** *a temporary endeavor undertaken to achieve a particular aim*

Project management is the usual thing on Hollywood movie sets and at construction companies building homes, roads, and skyscrapers. But it is new to manufacturers, banks, insurance companies, hospitals, and government agencies. Unfortunately, much of this Internet-age project management leaves a lot to be desired. For example, consider the dismal track record for information technology (IT) projects, typically involving conversion of an old computer system to new hardware, software, and work methods.

> *Most large IT projects are delivered late and over budget because they are inefficiently managed. A study by the Hackett Group, a Hudson, Ohio-based benchmarking firm, found that the average company completes only 37 percent of large IT projects on time and only 42 percent on budget.*[41]

A broader and deeper understanding of project management is in order.

*Effective project managers need to be able to focus on the little details and the big picture all at the same time. Chris Roome, vice president of engineering at Video Networks, only 26 at the time of this photo, has the right tools. His Gaithersburg, Maryland, employer designs and builds "war rooms" for the U.S. Department of Defense, among other clients. These sophisticated multi-media rooms are designed for simulations and to facilitate crisis-speed planning and control. As you might guess, Roome doesn't talk to his friends about his projects.*

Project managers face many difficult challenges. First and foremost, they work outside the normal organizational hierarchy or chain of command because projects are ad hoc and temporary. So they must rely on excellent "people management skills" instead of giving orders. Those skills include, but are not limited to, communication, motivation, leadership, conflict resolution, and negotiation[42] (see Chapters 12–16). Because projects are deadline-driven, they carry added pressures. High visibility increases the pressure. Imagine, for example, it is February 2001 and you're in charge of the Boeing project team responsible for moving the $51-billion-a-year company's headquarters from Seattle to a more strategically appropriate location. Oh, yes, and the move has to be completed before the transferred employees' children have to start school in September 2001. A heroic effort narrowed the search to Chicago, found the right building, and executed the move *on time.*[43]

Project *planning* deserves special attention in this chapter because project managers have the difficult job of being both intermediate/tactical and operational planners. They are responsible for both the big picture and the little details of their project. A project that is not well planned is a project doomed to failure. So let

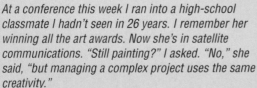

**6G    A Work of Art**

*At a conference this week I ran into a high-school classmate I hadn't seen in 26 years. I remember her winning all the art awards. Now she's in satellite communications. "Still painting?" I asked. "No," she said, "but managing a complex project uses the same creativity."*

**Source:** Thomas Petzinger Jr., "Some Thoughts on All I've Learned from You as New Fronts Beckon," *The Wall Street Journal* (May 21, 1999): B1.

**Question:**  *What do you think she meant?*

us take a look at the project life cycle, project management software, and guidelines for project managers.

**The Project Life Cycle.**    Every project, from developing a new breakfast cereal to staging a benefit rock concert, has a predictable four-stage life cycle. As shown in Figure 6.6, the four stages are conceptualization, planning, execution, and termination. Although equally spaced in Figure 6.6, the four stages typically involve varying periods of time. Sometimes the borders between stages blur. For example, project goal setting actually begins in the conceptualization stage and often carries over to the planning stage. During this stage project managers turn their attention to facilities and equip-

**5** Discuss project planning within the context of the project life cycle.

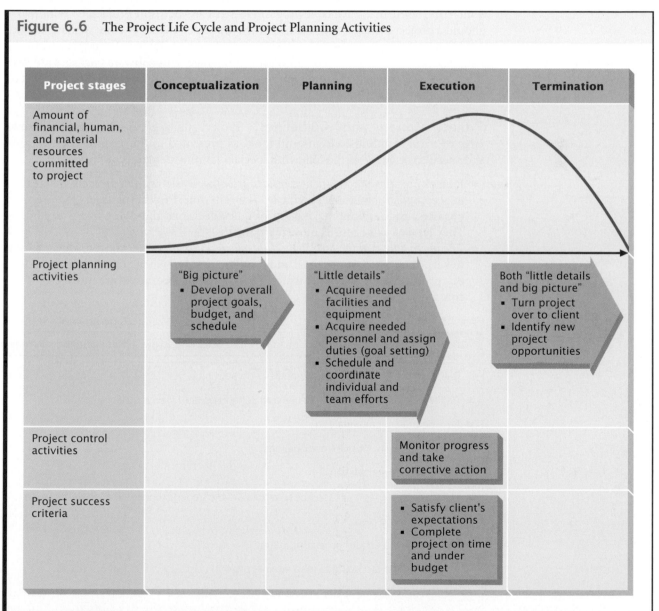

**Figure 6.6**    The Project Life Cycle and Project Planning Activities

| Project stages | Conceptualization | Planning | Execution | Termination |
|---|---|---|---|---|
| Amount of financial, human, and material resources committed to project | | | | |
| Project planning activities | "Big picture"<br>• Develop overall project goals, budget, and schedule | "Little details"<br>• Acquire needed facilities and equipment<br>• Acquire needed personnel and assign duties (goal setting)<br>• Schedule and coordinate individual and team efforts | Both "little details and big picture"<br>• Turn project over to client<br>• Identify new project opportunities | |
| Project control activities | | | Monitor progress and take corrective action | |
| Project success criteria | | | • Satisfy client's expectations<br>• Complete project on time and under budget | |

*Source:*  Adapted in part from Figure 1.2 and discussion in Jeffrey K. Pinto and O. P. Kharbanda, *Successful Project Managers: Leading Your Team to Success* (New York: Van Nostrand Reinhold, 1995), pp. 17–21.

ment, personnel and task assignments, and scheduling. Work on the project begins in the execution stage, and additional resources are acquired as needed. Budget demands are highest during the execution stage because everything is in motion. To some, the label "termination" in stage 4 might suggest a sudden end to the project. But more typically, the completed project is turned over to an end user (e.g., a new breakfast cereal is turned over to manufacturing) and project resources are phased out.[44]

**Project Management Software.**    Recall from our earlier discussion of the basic planning/control cycle (Figure 6.4) how planning and control are intertwined. One cannot occur without the other. The same is true for project planning. Making sure planned activities occur when and where appropriate and taking corrective action when necessary can be an overwhelming job for the manager of a complex project. Fortunately, a host of computer software programs can make the task manageable. But which one of the many available programs—such as Microsoft Project for Windows— should a project manager use? Thanks to **www.project-manager.com,** we have a handy list of screening criteria for selecting the right tool (see Table 6.2). Judging from this list, the overriding attributes of good project management software packages are *flexibility* and *transparency* (meaning quick and up-to-date status reports on all important aspects of the project).[45]

**Project Management Guidelines.**    Project managers need a working knowledge of basic planning concepts and tools, as presented in this chapter. Beyond that, they need to be aware of the following special planning demands of projects.[46]

- *Projects are schedule-driven and results-oriented.* By definition, projects are created to accomplish something specific by a certain time. Project managers require a positive attitude about making lots of quick decisions and doing things in a hurry. They tend to value results more than process.
- *The big picture and the little details are of equal importance.* Project managers need to keep the overall project goal and deadline in mind when attending to day-to-day problems and personnel issues. This is difficult because distractions are constant.

| **Table 6.2**   Ten Attributes to Consider when Selecting Project Management Software |
| --- |
| ■ Identify and ultimately schedule need-to-do activities |
| ■ Ability to dynamically shift priorities and schedules, and view resulting impact |
| ■ Provide critical path analysis |
| ■ Provide flexibility for plan modifications |
| ■ Ability to set priority levels |
| ■ Flexibility to manage all resources: people, hardware, environments, cash |
| ■ Ability to merge plans |
| ■ Management alerts for project slippage |
| ■ Automatic time recording to map against project |
| ■ Identification of time spent on activities |

*Source:* Excerpted from a list of 26 attributes in "4.1) Software Attributes," **www.project-manager.com.**

- *Project planning is a necessity, not a luxury.* Novice project managers tend to get swept away by the pressure for results and fail to devote adequate time and resources to project planning.
- *Project managers know the motivational power of a deadline.* A challenging (but not impossible) project deadline is the project manager's most powerful motivational tool. The final deadline serves as a focal point for all team and individual goal setting.[47]

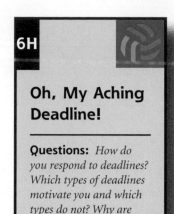

**6H**

## Oh, My Aching Deadline!

**Questions:** *How do you respond to deadlines? Which types of deadlines motivate you and which types do not? Why are deadlines such a powerful motivational tool?*

## Enterprise Resource Planning (ERP)

Ever since computers became a management tool, managers have longed for the time when a single, integrated computer system could help them plan and control the *entire* organization. Over the years, many promises about such systems have been made and broken. Typically, the reality is computer anarchy, with a maze of incompatible hardware, software, and databases. Today, leading software companies such as SAP, Oracle, and PeopleSoft claim to have the answer. While cautioning us not to "pronounce the term as a word that rhymes with 'burp,' say each letter: 'E-R-P,'" a technology writer recently offered this overview of ERP:

> *ERP software integrates the information used by an organization's many different functions and departments into a unified computing system. That means that instead of using isolated departmental databases to manage information, such as employee records, customer data, purchase orders, and inventory, everyone in the enterprise relies on the same database. This allows employees in different departments to look at the same information.*
>
> *The unified nature of an ERP system can lead to significant benefits, including fewer errors, improved speed and efficiency, and more complete access to information. With better access to information, employees and managers alike can gain a better understanding of what's going on in the enterprise so they make better business decisions.*
>
> *Although ERP projects are complex and expensive, properly implemented, they are nonetheless worthwhile. Meta Group found that once fully deployed, the median annual savings from a new ERP system was $1.6 million per year.[48]*

**6** Summarize the pros and cons of enterprise resource planning (ERP).

E-business applications of ERP include "customer relationship management" and "supply chain management." Unfortunately, ERP systems are very expensive and, according to most users, extremely difficult to implement. Before venturing into an area with an average total cost of $15 million,[49] strategic planners need to weigh the factors in Table 6.3.

# Graphic Planning/Scheduling/ Control Tools

Management science specialists have introduced needed precision to the planning/control cycle through graphics analysis. Three graphics tools for planning, scheduling, and controlling operations are flow charts, Gantt charts, and PERT networks. They can be found in project management software programs.

**Table 6.3    Pros and Cons of Enterprise Resource Planning (ERP)**

| In support of ERP . . . | Criticizing ERP . . . |
|---|---|
| ■ An ERP system is a solution panacea for all the IS [information system] woes of an enterprise and will be the only IS an enterprise needs to conduct its business. | ■ The application of an ERP system is the domain of only the very large companies. |
| ■ The ERP approach simplifies and standardizes systems across the enterprise, making it easier to upgrade systems in the future. | ■ ERP systems became popular solely because of the Y2K problem; with Y2K a distant memory, the future of ERP is bleak. |
| ■ An ERP system typically reduces the cost of IT operations and the number of personnel needed to maintain the organizational IS. | ■ An ERP system and its implementation are very expensive. The system needs extensive modifications, or the company needs to go through a major reengineering process to use it. |
| ■ An ERP system forces all processes to be integrated and a high level of data integrity to be achieved. | ■ Installed ERP systems are typically slow and cannot meet the transaction needs of most companies. |
| ■ ERP is an excellent decision support tool that will provide a competitive advantage. | ■ ERP systems have not provided the returns on investment that were originally predicted. |
| ■ ERP systems embed all the best practices for various processes, allowing a firm to configure the systems quickly and easily so as to minimize implementation costs. | ■ Many firms have gone out of business primarily because of the implementation of an ERP system. |
| ■ ERP systems allow for better global integration. | ■ ERP systems increase the IT costs and staff head counts. |
| | ■ Multiple additional systems are needed for smooth functioning, in spite of an ERP implementation. |

*Source:* Vincent A. Mabert, Ashok Soni, and M. A. Venkataramanan, "Enterprise Resource Planning: Common Myths Versus Evolving Reality." Reprinted with permission from *Business Horizons*, 44 (May–June 2001). Copyright 2001 by the Trustees at Indiana University, Kelley School of Business.

**7** Compare and contrast flow charts and Gantt charts, and discuss the value of PERT networks.

## Sequencing with Flow Charts

Flow charts have been used extensively by computer programmers for identifying task components and by TQM (total quality management) teams for *work simplification* (eliminating wasted steps and activities). Beyond that, flow charts are a useful sequencing tool with broad application.[50] Sequencing is simply arranging events in the order of their actual or desired occurrence. For instance, this book had to be purchased before it could be read. Thus the event "purchase book" would come before the event "read book" in flow-chart sequence.

A sample flow chart is given in Figure 6.7. Notice that the chart consists of boxes and diamonds in addition to the start and stop ovals. Each box contains a major event, and each diamond contains a yes-or-no decision.

Managers at all levels and in all specialized areas can identify and properly sequence important events and decisions with flow charts of this kind. User-friendly computer programs make flow-charting fun and easy today. Flow charts force people to consider all relevant links in a particular endeavor as well as their proper sequence. This is an advantage because it encourages analytical thinking. But flow charts have two disadvantages. First, they do not indicate the time dimension, that is, the varying amounts of time required to complete each step and make each decision. Second, flow charts are not practical for complex endeavors in which several activities take place at once.

**Figure 6.7** A Sample Flow Chart

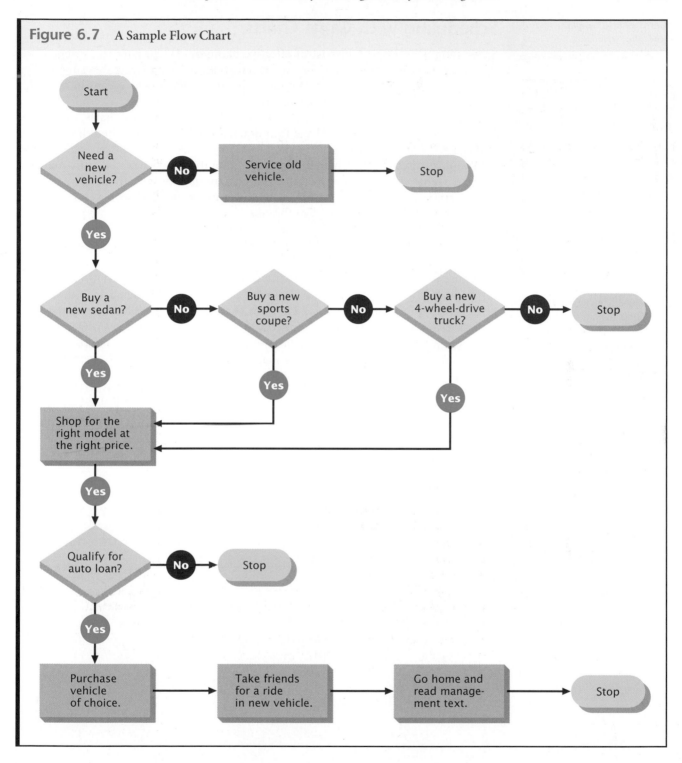

**Gantt chart** *graphic scheduling technique*

**61**

## Gantt Chart Exercise

Construct a Gantt chart for a project you are presently working on or might be working on soon. For example, a Gantt chart can help you plan for a major school project such as a term paper or team project. Workplace projects are fair game, too.

# Scheduling with Gantt Charts

Scheduling is an important part of effective planning. When later steps depend on the successful completion of earlier steps, schedules help managers determine when and where resources are needed. Without schedules, inefficiency creeps in as equipment and people stand idle. Also, like any type of plan or budget, schedules provide management with a measuring stick for corrective action. Gantt charts, named for Henry L. Gantt, who developed the technique, are a convenient scheduling tool for managers.[51] Gantt worked with Frederick W. Taylor at Midvale Steel beginning in 1887 and, as discussed in Chapter 2, helped refine the practice of scientific management. A **Gantt chart** is a graphic scheduling technique historically used in production operations. Things have changed since Gantt's time, and so have Gantt chart applications. Updated versions like the one in Figure 6.8 are widely used today for planning and scheduling all sorts of organizational activities. They are especially useful for large projects such as moving into a new building or installing a new computer network.[52]

Figure 6.8 also shows how a Gantt chart can be used for more than just scheduling the important steps of a job. By filling in the timelines of completed activities, *actual* progress can be assessed at a glance. Like flow charts, Gantt charts force managers to be analytical as they reduce jobs or projects to separate steps. Moreover, Gantt charts improve on flow charts by allowing the planner to specify the time to be spent on each activity. A disadvantage Gantt charts share with flow charts is that overly complex endeavors are cumbersome to chart.

**Figure 6.8    A Sample Gantt Chart**

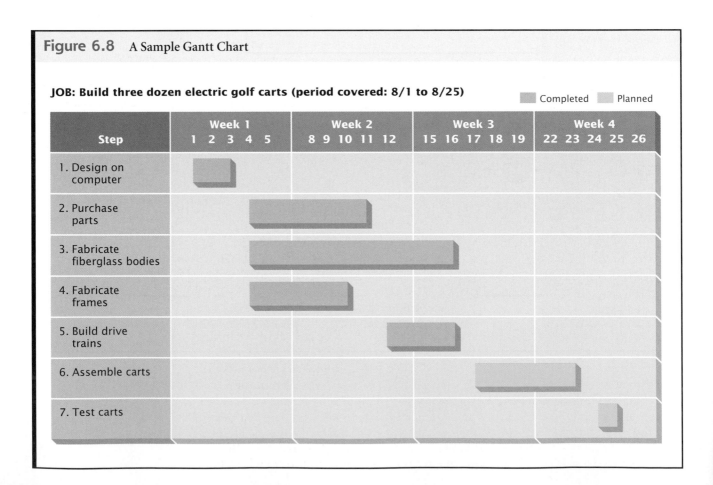

# PERT Networks

The more complex the project, the greater the need for reliable sequencing and scheduling of key activities. Simultaneous sequencing and scheduling amounts to programming. One of the most widely recognized programming tools used by managers is a technique referred to simply as PERT. An acronym for **Program Evaluation and Review Technique, PERT** is a graphic sequencing and scheduling tool for large, complex, and nonroutine projects.

**PERT (Program Evaluation and Review Technique)**
*graphic sequencing and scheduling tool for complex projects*

**History of PERT.**    PERT was developed in 1958 by a team of management consultants for the U.S. Navy Special Projects Office. At the time, the navy was faced with the seemingly insurmountable task of building a weapon system that could fire a missile from the deck of a submerged submarine. PERT not only contributed to the development of the Polaris submarine project but was also credited with helping to bring the system to combat readiness nearly two years ahead of schedule. News of this dramatic administrative feat caught the attention of managers around the world. But, as one user of PERT reflected, "No management technique has ever caused so much enthusiasm, controversy, and disappointment as PERT."[53] Realizing that PERT is not a panacea, but rather a specialized planning and control tool that can be appropriately or inappropriately applied, helps managers accept it at face value.[54]

**PERT Terminology.**    Because PERT has its own special language, four key terms must be understood.

- *Event.* A **PERT event** is a performance milestone representing the start or finish of some activity. Handing in a difficult management exam is an event.

  **PERT event**   *performance milestone; start or finish of an activity*

- *Activity.* A **PERT activity** represents work in process. Activities are time-consuming jobs that begin and end with an event. Studying for a management exam and taking the exam are activities.

  **PERT activity**   *work in process*

- *Time.* **PERT times** are estimated times for the completion of PERT activities. PERT times are weighted averages of three separate time estimates: (1) *optimistic time* ($T_o$)—the time an activity should take under the best of conditions; (2) *most likely time* ($T_m$)—the time an activity should take under normal conditions; and (3) *pessimistic time* ($T_p$)—the time an activity should take under the worst possible conditions. The formula for calculating estimated PERT time ($T_e$) is:

  **PERT times**   *weighted time estimates for completion of PERT activities*

$$T_e = \frac{T_o + 4T_m + T_p}{6}$$

- *Critical path.* The **critical path** is the most time-consuming chain of activities and events in a PERT network. In other words, the longest path through a PERT network is critical because if any of the activities along it are delayed, the entire project will be delayed accordingly.[55]

  **critical path**   *most time-consuming route through a PERT network*

**PERT in Action.**    A PERT network is shown in Figure 6.9. The task in this example, the design and construction of three dozen customized golf carts for use by physically challenged adults, is relatively simple for instructional purposes. PERT networks are usually reserved for more complex projects with hundreds or even thousands of activities. PERT events are coded by circled letters, and PERT activities, shown by the arrows connecting the PERT events, are coded by number. A PERT time ($T_e$) has been calculated and recorded for each PERT activity.

See if you can pick out the critical path in the PERT network in Figure 6.9. By calculating which path will take the most time from beginning to end, you will see that

## Figure 6.9    A Sample PERT Network

**TASK: Build three dozen customized golf carts for use by physically challenged adults**

| PERT events |
| --- |
| A. Receive contract |
| B. Begin construction |
| C. Receive parts |
| D. Bodies ready for testing |
| E. Frames ready for testing |
| F. Drive trains ready for testing |
| G. Components ready for assembly |
| H. Carts assembled |
| I. Carts ready for shipment |

### PERT activities and times

| Activities | $T_o$ | $T_m$ | $T_p$ | $T_e^*$ |
| --- | --- | --- | --- | --- |
| 1. Prepare final design | 3 | 4 | 6 | $4^1/_4$ |
| 2. Purchase parts | 4 | 5 | 12 | 6 |
| 3. Fabricate bodies | 5 | $7^1/_2$ | 9 | $7^1/_4$ |
| 4. Fabricate frames | $2^1/_2$ | 3 | 4 | 3 |
| 5. Build drive trains | $1^1/_2$ | 2 | 3 | 2 |
| 6. Test bodies | $^1/_2$ | 1 | $1^1/_2$ | 1 |
| 7. Test frames | $^1/_2$ | 1 | $1^1/_2$ | 1 |
| 8. Test drive trains | 1 | $1^1/_2$ | 5 | 2 |
| 9. Assemble carts | 3 | 5 | 9 | $5^1/_4$ |
| 10. Test carts | 1 | 2 | 5 | $2^1/_4$ |

*Rounded to nearest $^1/_4$ workday*

the critical path turns out to be A-B-C-F-G-H-I. This particular chain of activities and events will require an estimated 21.75 workdays to complete. The overall duration of the project is dictated by the critical path, and a delay in any of the activities along this critical path will delay the entire project.

**Positive and Negative Aspects of PERT.**   During the nearly 50 years that PERT has been used in a wide variety of settings, both its positive and negative aspects have become apparent.

On the plus side, PERT is an excellent scheduling tool for large, nonroutine projects, ranging from constructing an electricity generation station to launching a space vehicle. PERT is a helpful planning aid because it forces managers to envision projects in their entirety. It also gives them a tool for predicting resource needs, potential problem areas, and the impact of delays on project completion. If an activity runs over or under its estimated time, the ripple effect of lost or gained time on downstream activities can be calculated. PERT also gives managers an opportunity, through the calculation of optimistic and pessimistic times, to factor in realistic uncertainties about planning horizons.

On the minus side, PERT is an inappropriate tool for repetitive assembly-line operations in which scheduling is dictated by the pace of machines. PERT also shares with other planning and decision-making aids the disadvantage of being only as good as its underlying assumptions. False assumptions about activities and events and miscalculations of PERT times can render PERT ineffective. Despite the objective impression of numerical calculations, PERT times are derived rather subjectively. Moreover, PERT's critics say it is too time-consuming: a complex PERT network prepared by hand may be obsolete by the time it is completed, and frequent updates can tie PERT in knots. Project management software with computerized PERT routines is essential for complex projects because it can greatly speed the graphic plotting process and updating of time estimates.

# Break-Even Analysis

In well-managed businesses, profit is a forethought rather than an afterthought. A widely used tool for projecting profits relative to costs and sales volume is break-even analysis. In fact, break-even analysis is often referred to as cost-volume-profit analysis. By using either the algebraic method or the graphic method, planners can calculate the **break-even point,** the level of sales at which the firm neither suffers a loss nor realizes a profit. In effect, the break-even point is the profit-making threshold. If sales are below that point, the organization loses money. If sales go beyond the break-even point, it makes a profit. Break-even points, as discussed later, are often expressed in units. For example, Airbus Industrie, based in France, is moving forward on its plan to build a huge 555-passenger commercial airliner. Airbus had 62 orders for the A380 by mid-2001 but needed to sell 200 more to break even.[56]

From a procedural standpoint, a critical part of break-even analysis is separating fixed costs from variable costs.

**8** Explain how break-even points can be calculated.

**break-even point**   *level of sales at which there is no loss or profit*

*Fily and Madeline Keita run a successful African art and clothing shop in an exclusive location in Marina del Rey, California. Factored into their break-even calculation for their store, Fara Fina Collection, are some high fixed costs. Three times each year, Fily travels to his native Mali and other African nations such as Cameroon, Tanzania, and Zimbabwe to buy native art, crafts, and fabrics. Annual travel expenses approaching $20,000 are an unavoidable cost of doing business first-hand with village crafts-people. Of course, the love they have for their business is incalculable.*

## Fixed Versus Variable Costs

**fixed costs**   *contractual costs that must be paid regardless of output or sales*

**variable costs**   *costs that vary directly with production and sales*

Some expenses, called fixed costs, must be paid even if a firm fails to sell a single unit. Other expenses, termed variable costs, are incurred only as units are produced and sold. **Fixed costs** are contractual costs that must be paid regardless of the level of output or sales. Typical examples include rent, utilities, insurance premiums, managerial and professional staff salaries, property taxes, and licenses. **Variable costs** are costs that vary directly with the firm's production and sales. Common variable costs include costs of production (such as labor, materials, and supplies), sales commissions, and product delivery expenses. As output and sales increase, fixed costs remain the same but variable costs accumulate. Looking at it another way, fixed costs are a function of *time* and variable costs are a function of *volume*. You can now calculate the break-even point.

## The Algebraic Method

Relying on the following labels,

$$FC = \text{total fixed costs}$$
$$P = \text{price (per unit)}$$
$$VC = \text{variable costs (per unit)}$$
$$BEP = \text{break-even point}$$

the formula for calculating break-even point (in units) is

$$BEP \text{ (in units)} = \frac{FC}{P - VC}$$

**contribution margin**   *selling price per unit minus variable costs per unit*

The difference between the selling price $P$ and per unit variable costs $VC$ is referred to as the **contribution margin.** In other words, the contribution margin is the portion of the unit selling price that falls above and beyond the variable costs and that can be applied to fixed costs. Above the break-even point, the contribution margin contributes to profits.

Variable costs are normally expressed as a percentage of the unit selling price. As a working example of how the break-even point (in units) can be calculated, assume that a firm has total fixed costs of $30,000, a unit selling price of $7, and variable costs of 57 percent (or $4 in round numbers):

$$BEP \text{ (in units)} = \frac{30,000}{7 - 4} = 10,000$$

This calculation shows that 10,000 units must be produced and sold at $7 each if the firm is to break even on this particular product.

**Price Planning.**   Break-even analysis is an excellent "what-if" tool for planners who want to know what impact price changes will have on profit. For instance, what would the break-even point be if the unit selling price were lowered to match a competitor's price of $6?

$$BEP \text{ (in units)} = \frac{30,000}{6 - 4} = 15,000$$

In this case, the $1 drop in price to $6 means that 15,000 units must be sold before a profit can be realized.

**Profit Planning.**   Planners often set profit objectives and then work backward to determine the required level of output. Break-even analysis greatly assists such planners. The modified break-even formula for profit planning is:

$$BEP \text{ (in units)} = \frac{FC + \text{desired profit}}{P - VC}$$

Assuming that top management has set a profit objective for the year at $30,000 and that the original figures above apply, the following calculation would result:

$$BEP \text{ (in units)} = \frac{30,000 + 30,000}{7 - 4} = 20,000$$

To meet the profit objective of $30,000, the company would need to sell 20,000 units at $7 each.

## The Graphic Method

If you place the dollar value of costs and revenues on a vertical axis and unit sales on a horizontal axis, you can calculate the break-even point by plotting fixed costs, total costs (fixed + variable costs), and total revenue. As illustrated in Figure 6.10, the break-even point is where the total costs and the total sales revenue lines intersect. Although the algebraic method does the same job as the graphic method, some planners prefer the graphic method because it presents in a convenient visual aid the various cost-volume-profit relationships at a glance.

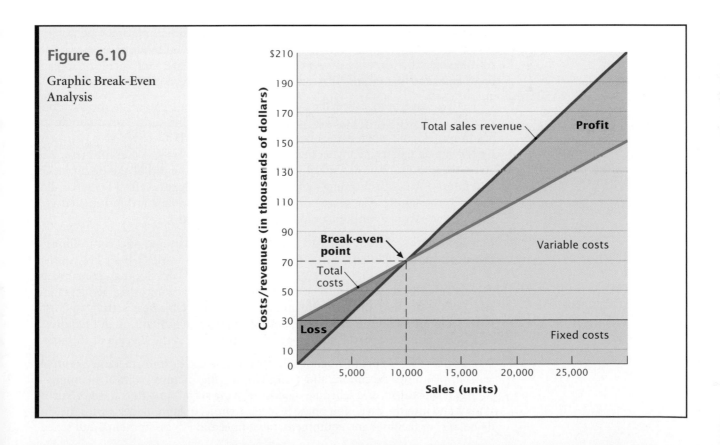

**Figure 6.10**

Graphic Break-Even Analysis

## Break-Even Analysis: Strengths and Limitations

Like the other planning tools discussed in this chapter, break-even analysis is not a cure-all. It has both strengths and limitations.

On the positive side, break-even analysis forces planners to interrelate cost, volume, and profit in a realistic way. All three variables are connected such that a change in one sends ripples of change through the other two. As mentioned earlier, break-even analysis allows planners to ask what-if questions concerning the impact of price changes and varying profit objectives.

The primary problem with break-even analysis is that a neat separation of fixed and variable costs can be very difficult. General managers should get the help of accountants to isolate relevant fixed and variable costs. Moreover, because of complex factors in supply and demand, break-even analysis is not a good tool for setting prices. It serves better as a general planning and decision-making aid.

## Summary

1. Planning has been labeled the primary management function because it sets the stage for all other aspects of management. Along with many other practical reasons for planning, managers need to plan in order to cope with an uncertain environment. Three types of uncertainty are state uncertainty ("What will happen?"), effect uncertainty ("What will happen to our organization?"), and response uncertainty ("What will be the outcome of our decisions?"). To cope with environmental uncertainty, organizations can respond as defenders, prospectors, analyzers, or reactors.

2. A properly written plan tells what, when, and how something is to be accomplished. A clearly written organizational mission statement tends to serve as a useful focus for the planning process. Strategic, intermediate, and operational plans are formulated by top-, middle-, and lower-level management, respectively.

3. Objectives have been called the single most important feature of the planning process. Well-written objectives spell out in measurable terms what should be accomplished and when it is to be accomplished. Good objectives help managers by serving as targets, acting as measuring sticks, encouraging commitment, and strengthening motivation. Objective setting begins at the top of the organization and filters down, thus forming a means-ends chain. Priorities affect resource allocation by assigning relative importance to objectives. Plans are formulated and executed as part of a more encompassing planning/control cycle.

4. Management by objectives (MBO), an approach to planning and controlling, is based on measurable and participatively set objectives. MBO basically consists of four steps: (1) setting objectives participatively, (2) developing action plans, (3) periodically reevaluating objectives and plans and monitoring performance, and (4) conducting annual performance appraisals. Objective setting in MBO flows from top to bottom. MBO has both strengths and limitations and requires a supportive climate favorable to change, participation, and the sharing of authority.

5. Project planning occurs throughout the project life cycle's four stages: conceptualization, planning, execution, and termination. "Big-picture" tactical planning—project goal, budget, and schedule—occurs during stage 1 and into stage 2. During stage 2 and into the execution phase in stage 3, project planning deals with the "little details" of facilities and equipment, personnel and job assignments, and sched-

uling. Starting near the end of stage 3 and carrying into the termination stage, both little-details and big-picture planning are required to pass the project along and identify new project opportunities. Planning is central to project success because projects are schedule-driven and results-oriented. Project planners need to keep constantly abreast of both the big picture and the little details. Novice project managers too often shortchange planning. Challenging but realistic project deadlines are project managers' most powerful motivational tool.

**6.** Enterprise resource planning (ERP) creates a unified computer information system for all business functions—from customer orders to inventory control to employee records. ERP systems have a reputation for being very expensive and hard to implement. An effective ERP system can save money, provide decision support, and enhance global integration. Critics say ERP systems are only for the largest companies, are too expensive, do not live up to promises, have high operating costs, and are not an ultimate solution.

**7.** Flow charts, Gantt charts, and PERT networks, found in project management software packages, are three graphics tools for more effectively planning, scheduling, and controlling operations. Flow charts visually sequence important events and yes-or-no decisions. Gantt charts, named for Frederick W. Taylor's disciple Henry L. Gantt, are a graphic scheduling technique used in a wide variety of situations. Both flow charts and Gantt charts have the advantage of forcing managers to be analytical. But Gantt charts realistically portray the time dimension, whereas flow charts do not. PERT, which stands for Program Evaluation and Review Technique, is a sequencing and scheduling tool appropriate for large, complex, and nonroutine projects. Weighted PERT times enable management to factor in their uncertainties about time estimates.

**8.** Break-even analysis, or cost-volume-profit analysis, can be carried out algebraically or graphically. Either way, it helps planners gauge the potential impact of price changes and profit objectives on sales volume. A major limitation of break-even analysis is that specialized accounting knowledge is required to identify relevant fixed and variable costs.

## Terms to Understand

Planning (p. 178)
State uncertainty (p. 179)
Effect uncertainty (p. 179)
Response uncertainty (p. 179)
Plan (p. 183)
Strategic planning (p. 185)
Intermediate planning (p. 185)
Operational planning (p. 185)
Planning horizon (p. 185)
Objective (p. 186)
Priorities (p. 188)
80/20 principle (p. 188)

Management by objectives (MBO) (p. 191)
Project (p. 193)
Gantt chart (p. 200)
PERT (Program Evaluation and Review Technique) (p. 201)
PERT event (p. 201)
PERT activity (p. 201)
PERT times (p. 201)
Critical path (p. 201)
Break-even point (p. 203)
Fixed costs (p. 204)
Variable costs (p. 204)
Contribution margin (p. 204)

## Skills & Tools

### Ten Common Errors to Avoid When Writing a Plan for a New Business

Here are errors in business-plan preparation[57] that almost certainly will result in denial of a loan application by a bank:

- Submitting a "rough copy," perhaps with coffee stains on the pages and crossed-out words in the text, tells the banker that the owner doesn't take his idea seriously.

- Outdated historical financial information or industry comparisons will leave doubts about the entrepreneur's planning abilities.

- Unsubstantiated assumptions can hurt a business plan; the business owner must be prepared to explain the "whys" of every point in the plan.

- Too much "blue sky"—a failure to consider prospective pitfalls—will lead the banker to conclude that the idea is not realistic.

- A lack of understanding of the financial information is a drawback. Even if an outside source is used to prepare the projections, the owner must fully comprehend the information.

- Absence of any consideration of outside influences is a gap in a business plan. The owner needs to discuss the potential impact of competitive factors as well as the economic environment prevalent at the time of the request.

- No indication that the owner has anything at stake in the venture is a particular problem. The lender will expect the entrepreneur to have some equity capital invested in the business.

- Unwillingness to personally guarantee any loans raises a question: If the business owner isn't willing to stand behind his or her company, then why should the bank?

- Introducing the plan with a demand for unrealistic loan terms is a mistake. The lender wants to find out about the viability of the business before discussing loan terms.

- Too much focus on collateral is a problem in a business plan. Even for a cash-secured loan, the banker is looking toward projected profits for repayment of the loan. The emphasis should be on cash flow.

*Source:* J. Tol Broome Jr., "Mistakes to Avoid in Drafting a Plan," *Nation's Business,* 81 (February 1993): 30. Reprinted by permission, *Nation's Business,* February 1993. Copyright 1993, U.S. Chamber of Commerce.

# Hands-On Exercise

## How to Write Good Objectives and Plans
## (Plan = What + When + How)

Well-written objectives are the heart of effective planning. An objective should state **Instructions**
*what* is to be accomplished (in measurable terms) and *when* it will be accomplished.
An objective becomes a plan when the *how* is added. Here is an everyday example of a
well-written plan: "I will ("what?") lose 5 pounds ("when?") in 30 days ("how?") by
not eating desserts and walking a mile four days a week."

Remember this handy three-way test to judge how well your plans are written:

- Test 1: Does this plan specify *what* the intended result is and is it stated in *measurable* terms?
- Test 2: Does this plan specify *when* the intended result is to be accomplished?
- Test 3: Does this plan specify *how* the intended result is to be accomplished?

Write a plan that passes all three tests for each of the following areas of your life:

Self-improvement plan:    What? _____

When? _____

How? _____

Work-related plan:           What? _____

When? _____

How? _____

Community-service plan: What? _____

When? _____

How? _____

**1.** In terms of the above three-way test, which of your plans is the best? Why? Which is    **For Consideration/**
the worst? Why?    **Discussion**

**2.** What is the hardest part of writing good plans? Explain.

**3.** From a managerial standpoint, why is it important to have plans written in measurable terms?

**4.** What is the managerial value of formally written plans, as opposed to verbal commitments?

**5.** Why would some employees resist writing plans according to the specifications in this exercise? Explain.

# Internet Exercises

1. **All about project management.** Project management software, as covered in this chapter, belongs in virtually every modern manager's tool kit. The purpose of this exercise is to explore the different features of the most widely used project management software package: Microsoft Project. The journey begins at Microsoft Project's Web page (**www.microsoft.com/office/project**), where you first need to click on "Features List" under the heading "Discover Microsoft Project 2000." Browse the features list to get a feel for how this software can help managers plan and control a project. Next, go back and select the major topic heading "See Microsoft Project 2000 in Action." Take the six-step tour. (*Note:* By the time you read this, a new version of Microsoft Project may have been released. In that case, simply follow the prompts to view the material mentioned above.)

    *Learning Points:* 1. Have you ever used project management software? Was it Microsoft Project? If you used something else, does Microsoft Project appear to be superior or inferior? Explain. 2. If you have never used project management software, which of the features of Microsoft Project do you like best? Why? 3. Why is project management software essential for today's complex projects?

2. **How to write a business plan.** Got a great new product or service idea? Thinking of starting your own business? You need a plan, not only to sharpen your focus but to obtain financing as well. *Inc.* magazine's Web site (**www.inc.com**) offers an excellent selection of resources for both future and present small-business owners. At the home page, find the menu heading "Getting Started" and click on "Writing a Business Plan." A good place to begin your self-education trip is at the heading "Build a Strong Business Plan, Section by Section." Your time availability and interest level will determine how many of the additional useful topics you access.

    *Learning Points:* 1. Is there a lot more to a basic business plan than you first thought? Explain. 2. Which part of the business plan would be the most difficult for you to prepare? Why? The easiest part? Why? 3. Does this exercise make you more or less interested in starting your own business? Explain.

3. **Check it out.** What sort of contributor can you be in today's team/project-oriented workplaces? This interesting and fun 24-question self-assessment quiz will tell you if you are a Pioneer, Innovator, Craftsman, or Adapter. Practical advice is offered for each category. Go to **www.project-manager.com** and select the box "Direct to P-M's Site Map." Scroll down the Map Page to the topical list and click on "3.0) Personal Skills." Choose the link "Quiz 2" and proceed with the exercise.

For updates to these exercises, visit our Web site (**http://business.college.hmco. com/students**).

# Closing Case

## Healthy Fast Food? That's the Plan?

Americans spent $112 billion on fast food last year, including an average of $53 million a month on McDonald's Happy Meals. The total fat count alone—never mind all those plastic toys rattling around under car seats—is enough to make Gary Hirshberg cringe. Hirshberg is betting that a significant percentage of American consumers share his disdain for typical takeout fare. Hence O'Naturals, a proposed chain of natural/organic fast-food restaurants aiming for a share of the nearly $20-billion natural-foods market.

Hirshberg, president and CEO of Stonyfield Farm, a Londonderry, N.H., yogurt company, conceived of O'Naturals four years ago on a family drive up the Pacific Coast. He had assumed that health-conscious California would offer meal choices beyond greasy burgers and fries. Wrong. "We were hostages to limited choices on the road," he says.

Now Hirshberg, who is O'Naturals' chairman, and a cadre of private investors are set to expand the fast-food universe with three or four O'Naturals restaurants in wealthy New England locales in the next three years. The first O'Naturals opened its doors last May [2001] in tony Falmouth, Maine, a town near Portland that typifies the target demographic: on-the-go, highly educated, upper-income families craving fast, tasty, healthful food. The Falmouth store is already posting daily average revenues of $2,000 to $3,000, roughly on par with the typical Burger King.

"I don't think anyone has tried to put together something that is family-friendly, tasty, natural, and organic fast-food," says O'Naturals cofounder and president Mac McCabe. D'Lites, a chain of restaurants that stressed low-fat, reduced-calorie offerings, bombed in the 1980s partly because it didn't deliver on taste. McCabe promises that O'Naturals won't make the same mistake. The restaurant offers flatbread sandwiches (made with bread baked on the premises), Asian-style noodles, soups, and salads, as well as macaroni and cheese, baked chicken nuggets, and tortilla dogs for the kids. And it's leveraging Stonyfield's brand recognition with fruit and yogurt shakes. The average register ring is between $5 and $8—higher than the big chains but well within the typical range for premium fast food.

For now Hirshberg and McCabe are sticking to a grassroots marketing strategy. They're lining up environmental groups, youth museums, and other nonprofits to run on-site programs for children and adults. And they're playing up the restaurant's environmental mission big-time: according to the company's job application, even kitchen assistants are expected to "become passionate around the recycling program of O'Naturals."

McCabe says those values—along with the company's $7-an-hour starting wage—are attracting topflight employees. "We're getting extraordinary kids from the best high schools," he says. Hirshberg is optimistic that the softer real estate market will ease the company's planned move into other Northeast locations. Once those restaurants are operating, O'Naturals will roll out the concept nationwide. But Hirshberg is in no hurry. "We're trying to find that fine line between seizing the opportunity and not growing so fast that we burn ourselves out."

## For Discussion

1. On a scale of *1 = a sure flop* to *10 = a sure winner*, how would you rate the probable success of O'Naturals? Explain.

2. Is O'Naturals a defender, prospector, analyzer, or reactor? Why? Is this a strategic advantage or disadvantage? Explain.

3. How would you rate O'Naturals' mission statement (you can find it at **www.onaturals.com**) relative to the eight criteria for a well-written mission statement presented in this chapter? Explain.

4. Will Hirshberg and McCabe need to engage in any project planning/management? Explain.

5. Making reasonable assumptions, what will be the major fixed and variable costs when O'Naturals' managers attempt to calculate a break-even point?

## chapter seven

# Strategic Management

## Planning for Long-Term Success

*When you finish studying this chapter you should be able to*

**1** **Define** the term *strategic management* and **explain** its relationship to strategic planning, implementation, and control.

**2** **Explain** the concept of synergy and identify four kinds of synergy.

**3** **Describe** Porter's model of generic competitive strategies.

**4** **Identify** and **explain** the major contribution the business ecosystems model makes to strategic thinking.

**5** **Identify** and **discuss** at least four e-business lessons from the Internet revolution.

**6** **Identify** and **describe** the four steps in the strategic management process.

**7** **Explain** the nature and purpose of a SWOT analysis.

**8** **Describe** the three types of forecasts.

> **"** The only sustainable competitive advantage any business has is its reputation. **"**
>
> **Laurel Cutler**

# Michael Dell: From Dorm Room to Personal Computer King

Over the years I've spent a fair amount of time hanging out with Michael Dell, and what I noticed during my latest visit with him in Austin is how things have changed. Yes, he is still unflappable. And yes, he greets me in his new glossy offices with the same Stepford Wife–like grin he has always had. But he appears thinner now, as if he's lost baby fat. While he's still slow-moving, as if he's conserving energy, he now cuts to the quick in conversation. And when he zeroes in on the point he wants to make, when he reiterates why Dell Computer is in a better position than any other PC maker in the world, you realize that the 36-year-old has lost what was once one of his greatest advantages: No one underestimates him anymore.

Instead, Michael Dell looms over the PC landscape like a giant, casting a shadow over all his unfortunate competitors. This is a terrible time in a difficult business. PC sales were down for the first time last year. Dell's sales will be down, too, also for the first time. Yet even with that, even with recession, even with the threat of a Hewlett-Packard/Compaq Goliath, this is the only PC maker you can count on to grow and grow and grow. Almost single-handedly, Dell is forcing this industry to consolidate. Could this mean "game over" in the PC biz? Not even the ambitious CEO buys that. "Game over?" he looks back at me incredulously. "No way. We only have 14% global market share."

The Dellites may not admit to "game over" aspirations, but clearly they are thinking of a kind of domination never seen before among PC makers. "We think 40% market share is possible," says Dell's No. 2, Kevin Rollins. That's a remarkable goal; what's more remarkable is that it really is attainable. Don't look for Dell to hit that kind of number anytime soon. Rather, the company's growth will come from grinding out gains on several existing fronts, while shrewdly expanding into new target markets. But the growth *will* come—just ask Oracle CEO Larry Ellison, who has watched Dell take great chunks out of the market for Windows servers, which are essentially high-powered PCs that can help manage Web sites or data on corporate networks. "If you want to be in the PC business, you have to compete against Dell," says Ellison, "and that is very, very difficult."

The reason is simple: There's no better way to make, sell, and deliver PCs than the way Dell does it, and nobody executes that model better than Dell. By now most business people can recite the basic tenets of Dell's direct-sales model. Dell machines are made to order and delivered directly to the customer. There is no middleman. The customer gets the exact machine he wants cheaper than he can get it from the competition. The company gets paid by the customer weeks before it pays suppliers. Given all that, the company that famously started in Austin out of a University of Texas dorm room now dominates the northern side of this city the way giant steelworks once lorded over old mill towns. Dell has some 24 facilities in and near Austin and employs more than 18,000 local workers. Dell did over $30 billion in sales in 2000, ranking 48th on the FORTUNE 500, ahead of names like Walt Disney, Johnson & Johnson, and Du Pont. Michael is the richest man under 40 in the world, worth $16 billion.

Two facts show how well the Dell model is working, even in tough times: Dell is on track to *earn* over $1.7 billion in 2001, taking almost every single dollar of profit among makers of Windows-based PCs. (Intel and Microsoft, of course, earn good money too—but they extract profits *from* the PC makers.) And Dell is gaining market share. That's not true for any other major PC maker.

Quite the contrary. The others are going *splat* for the same reason Dell is succeeding: commoditization. The desktop PC has become a commodity. That's great for consumers, who get standardized, easy-to-use, cheap PCs. But it's horrible for all but one manufacturer. As prices plummet, CEOs of most PC makers find it so hard to make a dime that they must justify to shareholders staying in the business at all. Commoditization relentlessly drives consolidation. And so it is no surprise when

213

# Thinking Strategically (Including E-Business Strategies)

Effective strategic management involves more than just following a few easy steps. It requires *every* employee, on a daily basis, to consider the "big picture" and think strategically about gaining and keeping a competitive edge.[11] A pair of experts on the subject recently framed the issue in terms of *innovation*:

> *Strategy innovation is not simply about extending a product line or pouring money into long-term, theoretical R&D projects. It is about rethinking the basis of competition for any company in any industry. Innovation cannot be a one-time event in the race to the future; it must be a continuous theme that extends throughout the entire company. . . .*
>
> *It is a deliberate process by which daring companies question the business model that may have brought them success in the first place. Although obviously needed when the economic chips are down, this type of thinking is equally critical for companies riding a wave of success. That's precisely when they may feel exempt from the need for radical innovation. "Why tinker," the reasoning goes, "with a proven formula?" . . .*
>
> *What's needed is a built-in capacity to challenge orthodoxies, develop foresight, build innovation-oriented processes, and continuously regenerate the strategy.[12]*

This section presents four alternative perspectives for thinking innovatively about strategy in today's fast-paced global economy: synergies, Porter's generic strategies, business ecosystems, and e-business strategies.

## Synergy

**2** Explain the concept of synergy and identify four kinds of synergy.

**synergy**   *the concept that the whole is greater than the sum of its parts*

Although not necessarily a familiar term, *synergy* is a well-established and valuable concept. **Synergy** occurs when two or more variables (for example, chemicals, drugs, people, organizations) interact to produce an effect greater than the sum of the effects of any of the variables acting independently. Some call this the $1 + 1 = 3$ effect; others prefer to say that with synergy, the whole is greater than the sum of its parts. Either definition is acceptable as long as one appreciates the bonus effect in synergistic relationships. In strategic management, managers are urged to achieve as much *market, cost, technology*, and *management synergy*[13] as possible when making strategic decisions. Those decisions may involve mergers, acquisitions, new products, new technology or production processes, or executive replacement. When Germany's Daimler Benz and Detroit's Chrysler merged in 1998 to form DaimlerChrysler, executives trumpeted the potential synergies. The merger now seems to be bearing some fruit. One result is the Crossfire, a sporty two-seat coupe, scheduled for market in 2003. According to *Business Week*: "It has a sleek Chrysler look, while many of the components under the hood are borrowed from Mercedes."[14]

**Market Synergy.**   When one product or service fortifies the sales of one or more other products or services, market synergy has been achieved. Examples of market synergy are common in the business press. For example, consider this scenario inspired by Vivendi Universal, the French entertainment and broadcasting giant:

> *The ultimate synergistic dream is to take a hit such as* American Pie *(the movie), spin it into* American Pie *(the TV series) that runs endlessly on USA Network, and then maybe crank out several* American Pie *soundtracks and create an* American Pie *attraction at the Universal Studios theme parks.[15]*

**7B**

### Tasty Synergy

Some people think Reese's Peanut Butter Cups are a great example of synergy.

**Questions:** *Why would they say that? Are they right? Explain.*

*In 1977, Steve Demos (on the left) founded his company White Wave in Boulder, Colorado, with a curious mission: get Americans to eat healthy soy products. Unfortunately, quivering blobs of tofu didn't come to mind when Americans were hungry. After a couple of decades of experimentation in the kitchen and tireless marketing, he developed his Silk brand of organic soymilk. Thanks to a good-tasting product and management synergy among the members of his multitalented leadership team, Silk soymilk has become a staple in grocery store dairy cases nationwide.*

**Cost Synergy.**   This second type of synergy can occur in almost every dimension of organized activity. When two or more products can be designed by the same engineers, produced in the same facilities, distributed through the same channels, or sold by the same salespeople, overall costs will be lower than if each product received separate treatment. In an interesting example of cost synergy, major hotels are trying to squeeze more value from their costly real estate. "At Miami Airport, Marriott has three hotels on the same plot of land. There's the Marriott Hotel, a full-service hotel. Behind the hotel are a Courtyard by Marriott, a midprice hotel, and a Fairfield Inn, an economy brand."[16]

Cost synergy also can be achieved by recycling by-products and hazardous wastes that would normally be thrown away. Human imagination is the only limit to creating cost synergies through recycling. For example, chicken farms in the Shenandoah valley region of Virginia annually produce half a million tons of manure. Harmony Products, in Harrisonburg, Virginia, has found a way to make high-quality fertilizer pellets for golf courses from the chicken waste. Even better, Harmony burns some of the manure to produce heat for its drying process, thereby saving $500,000 a year on natural gas.[17] Cost synergy through waste recycling is good business ethics, too.

**Technological Synergy.**   The third variety of synergy involves transferring technology from one application to another, thus opening up new markets. For example,

again. A great deal of work is needed in this area, considering the results of a recent study: two-thirds of the visitors to online stores did not return within a year.[42]

> *E-business strategy lesson.* Even though e-retailing might appear to be a quick-and-easy and impersonal process, loyal customers still expect a personal touch and some "hand holding" when they have questions, problems, or suggestions.

**Bricks and Mortar Must Earn Their Keep.**    Popular accounts of e-business conjure up visions of "virtual organizations" where an entrepreneur and a handful of employees run a huge business with little more than an Internet hookup and a coffee maker. Everything—including product design, production, marketing, shipping, billing, and accounting—is contracted out. As discussed in Chapter 10, these network or virtual organizations *do* exist, but they are more the exception than the rule. More typically, companies with bricks-and-mortar facilities such as factories, warehouses, retail stores, and showrooms are blending the Internet into their traditional business models. For example, some traditional retailers are using "the concept of 'three-tailing,' in which retailers such as J. C. Penney use multiple channels—stores, Web site and catalogs—to reach consumers."[43] Expect to see many more so-called *clicks*-and mortar combinations in the future.

> *E-business strategy lesson.* Strategists need to identify their company's core competencies to determine which assets and tasks give them a distinct competitive advantage. No one can afford the luxury of inefficient or unproductive assets in the Internet age. For example, why own a fleet of trucks and warehouses when FedEx or United Parcel Service can handle your shipments faster, better, and less expensively?[44]

**Cannibalism Can Pay.**    Over the years, one article of faith in management classrooms and offices has been that you should never get into a line of business or sell a product that cannibalizes your present sales. One early lesson from the e-business front directly contradicts this rule. However, as David Pottruck discovered at Charles Schwab, this e-business strategy is not for the faint-hearted:

> *In 1996 the co-CEO of discount broker Charles Schwab established a separate online unit, e.Schwab, with its own staff, own offices, and own sense of mission. Then he did the unthinkable: He let e.Schwab eat Schwab.*
>
> *The moment of truth came in late 1997, just as demand for e.Schwab's $29.95 online trades was booming beyond anyone's expectations. Problem was, customers with Charles Schwab's traditional brokerage still had to pay an average of $65 per trade. The two-tiered pricing system was clearly awkward: Some customers were keeping small sums of money with Charles Schwab to maintain access to live brokers, then executing their trades through e.Schwab. So Pottruck came to a radical decision: All trades would be priced at $29.95. In essence, all of Schwab would become e.Schwab.*
>
> *Employees in the company's branch offices were skittish. "All of them thought they would have no more business and were going to lose their jobs," Pottruck says. "It attacked our old business." Schwab's board had its doubts too. The price cut would shave an estimated $125 million off revenues, and the company's stock would clearly take a pummeling. Even Pottruck himself wasn't quite sure of what he was doing. "I can't tell you honestly that I didn't lose a lot of sleep about it," he says now. . . .*
>
> *In January 1998 the price cut took effect. Schwab's stock lost almost a third of its value. But the short-term pain yielded outsized long-term gain: Total accounts climbed from three million to 6.2 million; the stock recovered; $51 billion in new assets poured in during the first six months of [1999].[45]*

*E-business strategy lesson.* E-business sometimes requires a quick revolution, rather than slow evolution. A separate e-business unit can start with a blank sheet of paper when building a new business model, as opposed to encountering the stubborn resistance to change found in existing business units. Managers and employees are typically reluctant to turn their backs on comfortably familiar assumptions, tools, techniques, facilities, and work habits.

**E-Business Partnering Should Not Dilute Strategic Control or Ethical Standards.** If uncompetitive assets are sold and tasks contracted out, care needs to be taken to maintain ethical and quality standards. Do both domestic and foreign subcontractors follow applicable labor laws and ethical labor practices, or do sweatshop conditions prevail? Are subcontractors ruining the natural environment to reduce costs? Is a product designed properly before it is manufactured by an outside contractor? Are product quality standards faithfully met? These ethical and technical questions can be answered only through systematic monitoring and strategic oversight. Tough sanctions are also needed.[46]

*E-business strategy lesson.* Increasingly, informed consumers are holding the sellers of goods and services to higher standards. And in doing so, they include a company's *entire* supply chain, foreign and domestic. Sweatshop-produced goods sold via sophisticated e-business networks are still dirty business.

# The Strategic Management Process

Strategic plans are formulated during an evolutionary process with identifiable steps. In line with the three-level planning pyramid covered in Chapter 6, the strategic management process is broader and more general at the top and filters down to narrower and more specific terms. Figure 7.2 outlines the four major steps of the strategic management process: (1) formulation of a grand strategy, (2) formulation of strategic plans, (3) implementation of strategic plans, and (4) strategic control. Corrective action based on evaluation and feedback takes place throughout the entire strategic management process to keep things headed in the right direction.

> **6** Identify and describe the four steps in the strategic management process.

It is important to note that this model represents an ideal approach for instructional purposes. Because of organizational politics, as discussed in Chapter 14, and different planning orientations among managers, a somewhat less systematic process typically results. Nevertheless, it is helpful to study the strategic management process as a systematic and rational sequence to better understand what it involves. Although noting that rational strategic planning models should not be taken literally, Henry Mintzberg acknowledged their profound instructional value. They teach necessary vocabulary and implant the notion "that strategy represents a fundamental congruence between external opportunity and internal capability."[47]

## Formulation of a Grand Strategy

As pointed out in Chapter 6, a clear statement of organizational mission serves as a focal point for the entire planning process. Key stakeholders inside and outside the organization are given a general idea of why the organization exists and where it is headed. Working from the mission statement, top management formulates the

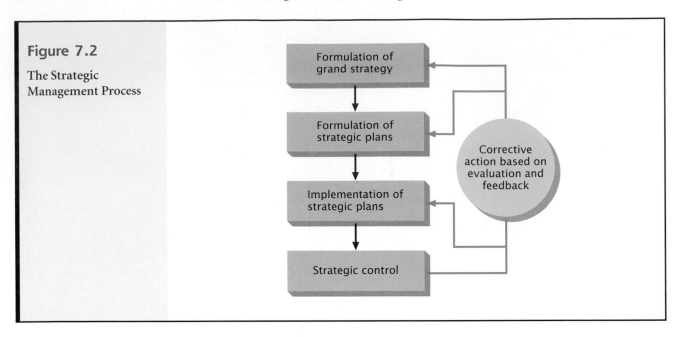

**Figure 7.2**

The Strategic Management Process

---

**grand strategy** *how the organization's mission will be accomplished*

organization's **grand strategy,** a general explanation of *how* the organization's mission is to be accomplished. Grand strategies are not drawn out of thin air. They are derived from a careful *situational* analysis of the organization and its environment. A clear vision of where the organization *is* headed and where it *should be* headed is the gateway to competitive advantage.[48]

**situational analysis** *finding the organization's niche by performing a SWOT analysis*

**Situational Analysis.**    A **situational analysis** is a technique for matching organizational strengths and weaknesses with environmental opportunities and threats to determine the organization's right niche (see Figure 7.3). Many strategists refer to this process as a SWOT analysis. SWOT stands for *Strengths, Weaknesses, Opportunities,* and *Threats.* (Perform an actual SWOT analysis in the Hands-On Exercise at the end of this chapter.) Every organization should be able to identify the purpose for which it is best suited. But this matching process is more difficult than it may at first appear. Strategists are faced not with snapshots of the environment and the organization but with a movie of rapidly changing events. As one researcher said: "The task is to find a match between opportunities that are still unfolding and resources that are still being acquired."[49] For example, Citibank, whose headquarters are in New York City, has set its strategic sights on a greater share of emerging Asian markets:

**7** Explain the nature and purpose of a SWOT analysis.

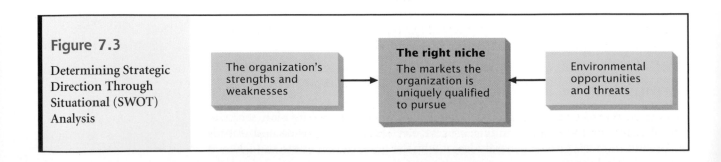

**Figure 7.3**

**Determining Strategic Direction Through Situational (SWOT) Analysis**

*. . . most foreign banks still shy away from developing countries such as India, Indonesia, and Thailand. Their rationale is that these markets are too small and that consumers lack experience in handling personal debt. . . .*

*Citi, however, is gambling that such Asian economies won't remain backward. Consider India, with a population of [over 1 billion]. . . . The growing middle class still rides mopeds. But within a decade, Citi bets they'll be buying BMWs. To take advantage of that possibility, Citi has positioned itself as one of the country's leading moped-loan originators.*[50]

Forecasting techniques, such as those reviewed later in this chapter, help managers cope with uncertainty about the future while conducting situational analyses.

Strategic planners, whether top managers, key operating managers, or staff planning specialists, have many ways to scan the environment for opportunities and threats. They can study telltale shifts in the economy, recent innovations, growth and movement among competitors, market trends, labor availability, and demographic shifts.

Unfortunately, according to a survey of executives at 100 U.S. corporations, not enough time is spent looking outside the organization: "Respondents said they spend less than half of their planning time (44 percent) evaluating external factors—competition and markets—compared with 48 percent on internal analysis—budget, organizational factors, human resources. 'That's the corporate equivalent of contemplating one's navel,' "[51] says the researcher.

Environmental opportunities and threats need to be sorted out carefully. A perceived threat may turn out to be an opportunity, or vice versa. Steps can be taken to turn negatives into positives.[52]

> ### 7G  Back to the Opening Case
>
>
>
> Based on the facts of this case and any reasonable assumptions you might make about Dell Computer, what would a situational (SWOT) analysis suggest Dell's strategic direction should be? *Hint:* First arrange your evidence under these four headings: organizational strengths, organizational weaknesses, environmental opportunities, and environmental threats.

**Capability Profile.**   After scanning the external environment for opportunities and threats, management's attention turns inward to identifying the organization's strengths and weaknesses.[53] This subprocess is called a **capability profile.** The following are key capabilities for today's companies:

**capability profile**
*identifying the organization's strengths and weaknesses*

- Quick response to market trends
- Rapid product development
- Rapid production and delivery
- Continuous cost reduction
- Continuous improvement of processes, human resources, and products
- Greater flexibility of operations[54]

Diversity initiatives are an important way to achieve continuous improvement of human resources (for example, see Managing Diversity). Also, notice the clear emphasis on *speed* in this list of key organizational capabilities.

**The Strategic Need for Speed.**   Speed has become an important competitive advantage. Warren Holtsberg, a Motorola corporate vice president, recently offered this perspective:

*I find the impatience of the new economy refreshing. The concept that fast is better than perfect bodes well, particularly for the technology industry. At Motorola, we used to be able to introduce a cellular telephone, and it would have a life expectancy in the marketplace of about two years. Now we face cycle times of four to six months. People continue to demand new things. They demand change. They're impatient. Bringing that into a big corporation is invigorating.*[55]

# Managing Diversity

## Diversity Boosts Allstate's Bottom Line

A number of progressive companies that had a head start in elevating diversity to a strategic priority are starting to see the results, from better customer satisfaction to increased sales. Allstate Insurance Co. is one of those leaders (**www.allstate.com**). Since 1993, the Northbrook, Illinois, insurance company has been managing diversity as a central business issue closely connected to its overall corporate objectives. The focus is to drive greater levels of employee and customer satisfaction by taking an integrated approach to diversity in the workplace and the market.

Joan Crockett, senior vice president for human resources at Allstate, stresses that the company's diversity initiative isn't a nice-to-do, social conscience program. "It's a compelling business strategy," she says. . . .

## An Integrated Approach

For Allstate, the concept of diversity is not limited to ethnicity and gender. It is based on a wider perspective that includes diversity in age, religion, sexual orientation, disability, etc.

Diversity at Allstate is rooted in the company's culture, which has embodied inclusiveness and equal opportunity since the 1960s. But it wasn't until 1993 that it became a strategic initiative. Carlton Yearwood, director of diversity management, says that programs in the 1960s and 1970s were geared toward assimilating cultural differences into Allstate's culture. Today, the focus is on accepting these differences. The question thus becomes: "How do you take this workforce of differences and bring them together in a more powerful way so that it can impact business results?" asks Yearwood.

The answer was to incorporate differences into all business processes, such as decision making and product innovation. Once Allstate began this process, it started to see an increase in its customer base and greater levels of customer satisfaction as well.

"Diversity has become an initiative that has clear business outcomes," Yearwood says. "If you start by having customers say they want to interact with knowledge workers who are like themselves, that gives the customers

absolute best services and products. . . . Through the diversity initiative, we demonstrate our commitment to a diverse marketplace."

Just as a company would inject financial goals in its daily operations, Allstate is resolved to penetrate its day-to-day functions with the concept of diversity. A number of processes have been established to bring the concept and strategy alive. These processes go beyond recruiting a diverse mix of employees to encompass a proactive retention strategy, ongoing training and education, a rigorous feedback mechanism, and community outreach. . . .

## Sensitivity to Customers

Allstate's leading position in market share among minorities reflects its commitment to local communities consisting of many ethnic backgrounds. The key to success is that local agents, with backing from Allstate's relationship marketing managers and staff, have learned over the years how to relate to the specific needs of their respective communities.

Allstate's director of relationship marketing, Andre Howell, says that learning from customers is the best way to develop products and services which serve their specific needs. "Education, education and education will be my primary lead," he says. "We need to be continuously in a learning mode from customers."

Howell works with a team of six to create community outreach programs whose ultimate aim is to capture a larger market share. These programs include financial and expert contributions to ethnic, local, and other organizations.

The company also works with community groups and homeowner associations to accelerate urban revitalization projects through its Neighborhood Partnership Program (NPP). There are currently 33 NPPs operating in 26 cities, including Chicago, Cleveland, Los Angeles, New York, and Philadelphia. By establishing a good relationship with residents of the communities, Allstate has been able to accelerate its customer acquisitions. In many cases, the company's businesses in inner cities that used to lose money are now profitable, says Ron McNeil, senior vice president for product operations.

"Our diverse workforce has allowed us to establish relationships in communities and allowed us to shorten the acquisition curves for new customers," he says. The partnership program in Philadelphia, for example, boosted Allstate's market share in the city from 7.3 percent in 1993 to 33 percent in 1997.

*Source:* Excerpted from Louisa Wah, "Diversity at Allstate: A Competitive Weapon." Reprinted from *Management Review,* July–August 1999. © 1999 American Management Association in the format textbook via the Copyright Clearance Center.

Accordingly, the new strategic emphasis on speed involves more than doing the same old things, only faster. It calls for rethinking and radically redesigning the entire business cycle, a process called **reengineering**[56] (see Skills & Tools). The idea is to have cross-functional teams develop a whole new—and better—production process, one that does not let time-wasting mistakes occur in the first place. (The related topic of horizontal organizations is covered in Chapter 10.)

## Formulation of Strategic Plans

In the second major step in the strategic management process, general intentions are translated into more concrete and measurable strategic plans, policies, and budget allocations.[57] This translation is the responsibility of top management, though input from staff planning specialists and middle managers is common. From our discussion in the last chapter we recall that a well-written plan consists of both an objective and an action statement. Plans at all levels need to specify who, what, when, and how things are to be accomplished and for how much. Many managers prefer to call these specific plans "action plans" to emphasize the need to turn good intentions into action. Even though strategic plans may have a time horizon of one or more years, they must meet the same criteria that shorter-run intermediate and operational plans meet. They should do the following:

1. Develop clear, results-oriented objectives in measurable terms.
2. Identify the particular activities required to accomplish the objectives.
3. Assign specific responsibility and authority to the appropriate personnel.
4. Estimate times to accomplish activities and their appropriate sequencing.
5. Determine resources required to accomplish the activities.
6. Communicate and coordinate the above elements and complete the action plan.[58]

All of this does not happen in a single quick-and-easy session. Specific strategic plans usually evolve over a period of months as top management consults with key managers in all areas of the organization to gather their ideas and recommendations and, one hopes, to win their commitment.

---

**7H   How Fast Is Too Fast?**

*Speed is one of the great themes of our time, and the big lesson is that you're like a sailboat: Unless you're moving faster than the water around you, you can't control your direction. And the water is moving faster every day. Your competitors, customers, suppliers, and capital providers have continuous, global, real-time information about virtually everything that affects your business, and they act on it quickly.*

*Source:* Geoffrey Colvin, "Mr. Big, Don't Get Too Cozy," *Fortune* (December 10, 2001): 64.

**Questions:** *What do you like or dislike about the sailboat metaphor? Is there too much emphasis on speed today? Explain.*

---

**reengineering**   *radically redesigning the entire business cycle for greater strategic speed*

# Strategic Implementation and Control

As illustrated earlier in Figure 7.2, the third and fourth stages of the strategic management cycle involve implementation and control. The entire process is only as strong as these two traditionally underemphasized areas.

## Implementation of Strategic Plans

Because strategic plans are too often shelved without adequate attention to implementation, top managers need to do a better job of facilitating the implementation process and building middle-manager commitment.[59]

**A Systematic Filtering-Down Process.**    Strategic plans require further translation into successively lower-level plans. Top-management strategists can do some groundwork to ensure that the filtering-down process occurs smoothly and efficiently. Planners need answers to four questions, each tied to a different critical organizational factor:

1. *Organizational structure.* Is the organizational structure compatible with the planning process, with new managerial approaches, and with the strategy itself?
2. *People.* Are people with the right skills and abilities available for key assignments, or must attention be given to recruiting, training, management development, and similar programs?
3. *Culture.* Is the collective viewpoint on "the right way to do things" compatible with strategy, must it be modified to reflect a new perspective, or must top management learn to manage around it?
4. *Control systems.* Is the necessary apparatus in place to support the implementation of strategy and to permit top management to assess performance in meeting strategic objectives?[60]

*In the car business, they call it "moving the metal." In early 2001, as indicated in this photo, the metal wasn't moving for DaimlerChrysler. Finished cars backed up by the thousands at the firm's Sterling Heights, Michigan, factory. So strategic control efforts were taken via layoffs and plant closings. Though painful for all involved, these moves helped the German-owned car company get back on the road to profitability.*

Strategic plans that successfully address these four questions have a much greater chance of helping the organization achieve its intended purpose than those that do not. In addition, field research indicates the need to *sell* strategies to all affected parties. New strategies represent change, and people tend to resist change for a variety of reasons. "The strategist thus faces a major selling job; that is, trying to build and maintain support among key constituencies for a plan that is freshly emerging."[61] This brings us to the challenge of obtaining commitment among middle managers.

**Building Middle-Manager Commitment.**    Resistance among middle managers can kill an otherwise excellent strategic management program. A study of 90 middle managers who wrote 330 reports about instances in which they had resisted strategic decisions documented the scope of this problem. It turned out that, to protect their own self-interests, the managers in the study frequently derailed strategies. This finding prompted the researchers to conclude as follows:

> *If general management decides to go ahead and impose its decisions in spite of lack of commitment, resistance by middle management can drastically lower the efficiency with which the decisions are implemented, if it does not completely stop them from being implemented. Particularly in dynamic, competitive environments, securing commitment to the strategy is crucial because rapid implementation is so important.[62]*

Participative management (see Chapter 13) and influence tactics (see Chapter 15) can foster middle-management commitment.[63]

## Strategic Control

Strategic plans, like our more informal daily plans, can go astray. But a formal control system helps keep strategic plans on track. Software programs (such as eWorkbench by PerformaWorks)[64] that synchronize and track all contributors' goals in real time are indispensable today. Importantly, strategic control systems need to be carefully designed ahead of time, not merely tacked on as an afterthought.[65] Before strategies are translated downward, planners should set up and test channels for information on progress, problems, and strategic assumptions about the environment or organization that have proved to be invalid. If a new strategy varies significantly from past ones, new production, financial, or marketing reports will probably have to be drafted and introduced.

The ultimate goal of a strategic control system is to detect and correct downstream problems in order to keep strategies updated and on target, without stifling creativity and innovation in the process. A survey of 207 planning executives found that in high-performing companies there was no tradeoff between strategic control and creativity. Both were delicately balanced.[66]

## Corrective Action Based on Evaluation and Feedback

As illustrated in Figure 7.2, corrective action makes the strategic management process a dynamic cycle. A rule of thumb is that negative feedback should prompt corrective action at the step immediately before. Should the problem turn out to be more deeply rooted, then the next earlier step also may require corrective action. The key is to detect problems and initiate corrective action, such as updating strategic assumptions, reformulating plans, rewriting policies, making personnel changes, or modifying budget allocations, as soon as possible. In the absence of prompt corrective action, problems can rapidly worsen.

Let us turn to forecasting. Without the ability to obtain or develop reliable environmental forecasts, managerial strategists have a minimal chance of successfully negotiating their way through the strategic management process.

# Forecasting

**forecasts**    *predictions, projections, or estimates of future situations*

An important aspect of strategic management is anticipating what will happen. **Forecasts** may be defined as predictions, projections, or estimates of future events or conditions in the environment in which the organization operates.[67] Forecasts may be little more than educated guesses or may be the result of highly sophisticated statistical analyses. They vary in reliability. (Consider the track record of television weather forecasters!)[68] They may be relatively short run—a few hours to a year—or long run—five or more years. A combination of factors determines a forecast's relative sophistication, time horizon, and reliability. These factors include the type of forecast required, management's knowledge of forecasting techniques, and the money that management is willing to invest.[69]

## Types of Forecasts

**8**  Describe the three types of forecasts.

There are three types of forecasts: (1) event outcome forecasts, (2) event timing forecasts, and (3) time series forecasts.[70] Each type answers a different general question (see Table 7.4). **Event outcome forecasts** are used when strategists want to predict the outcome of highly probable future events. For example: "How will an impending strike affect output?"

**event outcome forecasts**
*predictions of the outcome of highly probable future events*

**Event timing forecasts** predict when, if ever, given events will occur. Strategic questions in this area might include, "When will the prime interest rate begin to fall?" or, "When will our primary competitor introduce a certain product?" Timing questions like these typically can be answered by identifying leading indicators that historically have preceded the events in question. For instance, a declining inflation rate often prompts major banks to lower their prime interest rate, or a competitor may flag the introduction of a new product by conducting market tests or ordering large quantities of a new raw material.

**event timing forecasts**
*predictions of when a given event will occur*

---

**Table 7.4**    Types of Forecasts

| Type of forecast | General question | Example |
|---|---|---|
| 1. Event outcome forecast | "What will happen when a given event occurs?" | "Who will win the next World Series?" |
| 2. Event timing forecast | "When will a given event occur?" | "When will a human set foot on Mars?" |
| 3. Time series forecast | "What value will a series of periodic data have at a given point in time?" | "What will the closing Dow Jones Industrial Average be on January 5, 2007?" |

**Time series forecasts** seek to estimate future values in a sequence of periodically recorded statistics. A common example is the sales forecast for a business. Sales forecasts need to be as accurate as possible because they impact decisions all along the organization's supply chain. As learned the hard way by Cisco Systems, sales forecasts based on poor input can be very costly.

**time series forecasts**
*estimates of future values in a statistical sequence*

> *In May 2001, Cisco Systems announced the largest inventory write-down in history: $2.2 billion erased from its balance sheet for components it ordered but couldn't use. . . .*
>
> *To lock in supplies of scarce components during the [Internet] boom, Cisco ordered large quantities well in advance, based on demand projections from the company's sales force. What the forecasters didn't notice, however, was that many of their projections were inflated artificially. With network gear hard to come by, many Cisco customers also ordered similar equipment from Cisco's competitors, knowing that they'd ultimately make just one purchase—from whoever could deliver the goods first.*[71]

## Forecasting Techniques

Modern managers may use one or a combination of four techniques to forecast future outcomes, timing, and values. These techniques are informed judgment, scenario analysis, surveys, and trend analysis.

**Informed Judgment.**   Limited time and money often force strategists to rely on their own intuitive judgment when forecasting. Judgmental forecasts are both fast and inexpensive, but their accuracy depends greatly on how well informed the strategist is. Frequent visits with employees—in sales, purchasing, and public relations, for example—who regularly tap outside sources of information are a good way of staying informed. A broad reading program to stay in touch with current events and industry trends and refresher training through management development programs are also helpful. Additionally, customized news clipping services (delivered by e-mail), spreadsheet forecasting software, and a competitive intelligence-gathering operation[72] can help keep strategic decision makers up to date.

**71  A Thin Line Between Corporate Intelligence and Espionage**

*Competitive intelligence involves legal methods of data collection and analysis, from scouring securities filings and news reports to database research to schmoozing with representatives of rival companies at trade shows. That's different from corporate espionage—the theft of trade secrets through illegal means such as wiretaps, bribery, and cyberintrusions.*

**Source:** Louis Lavelle, "The Case of the Corporate Spy," *Business Week* (November 26, 2001): 56.

**Questions:** *How widespread do you think illegal corporate espionage is today? Explain. What needs to be done to keep corporate intelligence from crossing into illegal territory?*

The hugely profitable Pokémon craze traces to this intuitive approach to making important decisions:

> *In 1997, Nintendo of America President Minoru Arakawa made the biggest bet of his career. Everyone said he was nuts to import a strange Japanese video game featuring 150 tiny collectible monsters. Research showed that American kids hated it, and employees dismissed the game as too confusing. But Arakawa persisted—and hit the Pokémon jackpot.*[73]

Of course, informed judgment is no panacea. It generally needs to be balanced with data from other forecasting techniques.

**Scenario Analysis.**    This technique also relies on informed judgment, but it is more systematic and disciplined than the approach just discussed. **Scenario analysis** (also called scenario planning) is the preparation and study of written descriptions of *alternative* but *equally likely* future conditions.[74] Scenarios are visions of what "could be." The late futurist Herman Kahn is said to have first used the term *scenario* in conjunction with forecasting during the 1950s. The two types of scenarios are longitudinal and cross-sectional. **Longitudinal scenarios** describe how the present is expected to evolve into the future. **Cross-sectional scenarios,** the most common type, simply describe possible future situations at a given time.

While noting that *multiple forecasts* are the cornerstone of scenario analysis, one researcher offered the following perspective:

> *Scenario writing is a highly qualitative procedure. It proceeds more from the gut than from the computer, although it may incorporate the results of quantitative models. Scenario writing is based on the assumption that the future is not merely some mathematical manipulation of the past, but the confluence of many forces, past, present and future that can best be understood by simply thinking about the problem.*[75]

The same researcher recommends developing two to four scenarios (three being optimal) for narrowly defined topics.[76] Likely candidates for scenario analysis are specific products, industries, or markets. For example, a grain-exporting company's strategists might look five years into the future by writing scenarios for three different likely situations: (1) above-average grain harvests, (2) average harvests, and (3) below-average harvests. These scenarios could serve as focal points for strategic plans concerning construction of facilities, staffing and training, and so on. As the future unfolds, the strategies accompanying the more realistic scenario would be followed.

This approach has been called "no surprise" strategic planning. As *Business Week* explained while offering up scenarios for the twenty-first century:

> *If you envision multiple versions of the future and think through their implications, you will be better prepared for whatever ends up happening. In effect, you won't be seeing the future for the first time. You'll be remembering it. The alternative won't cut it: Those who cannot remember the future are condemned to be taken by surprise.*[77]

The key to good scenario writing is to focus on the few readily identifiable but unpredictable factors that will have the greatest impact on the topic in question. Because scenarios look far into the future, typically five or more years, they need to be written in general and rather imprecise terms.[78]

**Surveys.**    Surveys are a forecasting technique involving face-to-face or telephone interviews and mailed, fax, or e-mail questionnaires. They can be used to pool expert opinion or fathom consumer tastes, attitudes, and opinions. When carefully constructed and properly administered to representative samples, surveys can give management comprehensive and fresh information. They suffer the disadvantages, however, of being somewhat difficult to construct, time-consuming to administer and

**scenario analysis** *preparing written descriptions of equally likely future situations*

**longitudinal scenarios** *describing how the future will evolve from the present*

**cross-sectional scenarios** *describing future situations at a given point in time*

interpret, and expensive. Although costs can be trimmed by purchasing an off-the-shelf or "canned" survey, standardized instruments too often either fail to ask precisely the right questions or ask unnecessary questions.[79]

**Trend Analysis.** Essentially, a **trend analysis** is the hypothetical extension of a past pattern of events or time series into the future. An underlying assumption of trend analysis is that past and present tendencies will continue into the future.[80] Of course, surprise events such as the September 11, 2001, terrorist attacks can destroy that assumption. Trend analysis can be fickle and cruel to reactive companies. As a case in point, Chrysler's commitment to fuel-efficient, four-cylinder cars in the early 1980s was based on the assumption that the 1970s trend toward higher gas prices would continue. However, when the price of gasoline stabilized during the 1980s, Chrysler came up short as U.S. car buyers demanded more horsepower.[81] By the time Chrysler had geared up its production of more powerful V-6 engines, Iraq's 1990 invasion of Kuwait sent the price of gasoline skyward and car buyers scrambling for four-cylinder cars. Again Chrysler tripped over a faulty trend analysis. If sufficient valid historical data are readily available, trend analysis can, barring disruptive surprise events, be a reasonably accurate, fast, and inexpensive strategic forecasting tool. An unreliable or atypical database, however, can produce misleading trend projections.

Each of these forecasting techniques has inherent limitations. Consequently, strategists are advised to cross-check one source of forecast information with one or more additional sources.

**trend analysis** *hypothetical extension of a past series of events into the future*

# Summary

1. Strategic management sets the stage for virtually all managerial activity. Managers at all levels need to think strategically and to be familiar with the strategic management process for three reasons: farsightedness is encouraged, the rationale behind top-level decisions becomes more apparent, and strategy formulation and implementation are more decentralized today. Strategic management is defined as the ongoing process of ensuring a competitively superior fit between the organization and its ever-changing environment. Strategic management effectively merges strategic planning, implementation, and control.

2. Strategic thinking, the ability to look ahead and spot key organization-environment interdependencies, is necessary for successful strategic management and planning. Four perspectives that can help managers think strategically are synergy, Porter's model of competitive strategies, the concept of business ecosystems, and e-business strategic signposts. Synergy has been called the $1 + 1 = 3$ effect because it focuses on situations where the whole is greater than the sum of its parts. Managers are challenged to achieve four types of synergy: market synergy, cost synergy, technological synergy, and management synergy.

3. According to Porter's generic competitive strategies model, four strategies are (1) cost leadership, (2) differentiation, (3) cost focus, and (4) focused differentiation. Porter's model helps managers create a profitable organization-environment "fit."

4. Contrary to the traditional assumption that strategy automatically equates to competition, the business ecosystems model emphasizes that organizations need to be as good at *cooperating* as they are at competing. By balancing competition and cooperation, competitors can *coevolve* into a dominant economic community (or business ecosystem).

**5.** The Internet is a disruptive technology that has managers scrambling to create successful e-business strategies. E-business pioneers have taught us these eight lessons: (1) a solid business model, not technology, should drive decisions about using the Internet; (2) evolving technologies will reshape the Internet and e-business opportunities; (3) new dot-com companies and established companies need different Internet strategies; (4) ways to make money on the Web include subscriptions, advertising space, sales to businesses and consumers, transaction fees, and commissions; (5) reliable brand names and sticky Web sites, integrated with a personal touch and hand holding, are required to build customer loyalty; (6) existing bricks-and-mortar assets such as factories and stores are useful in the Internet age only if they relate to core competencies that provide a competitive advantage; (7) contrary to the traditional rule against cannibalizing one's own sales, e-business sometimes requires a strategic revolution; and (8) informed consumers will not tolerate the use of sophisticated e-business partnerships, either domestic or foreign, to mask unethical labor practices and poor product quality.

**6.** The strategic management process consists of four major steps: (1) formulation of grand strategy, (2) formulation of strategic plans, (3) implementation of strategic plans, and (4) strategic control. Corrective action based on evaluation of progress and feedback helps keep the strategic management process on track. Results-oriented strategic plans that specify what, when, and how are then formulated and translated downward into more specific and shorter-term intermediate and operational plans. Participative management can build needed middle-manager commitment during implementation. Problems encountered along the way should be detected by the strategic control mechanism or by ongoing evaluation and subjected to corrective action.

**7.** Strategists formulate the organization's grand strategy after conducting a SWOT analysis. The organization's key capabilities and appropriate niche in the marketplace become apparent when the organization's strengths (S) and weaknesses (W) are cross-referenced with environmental opportunities (O) and threats (T). Strategic speed has become an important capability today, sometimes necessitating radical reengineering of the entire business cycle.

**8.** Event outcome, event timing, and time series forecasts help strategic planners anticipate and prepare for future environmental circumstances. Popular forecasting techniques among today's managers are informed judgment, scenario analysis, surveys, and trend analysis. Each technique has its own limitations, so forecasts need to be cross-checked against one another.

## Terms to Understand

**Strategic management (p. 216)**
**Strategy (p. 217)**
**Synergy (p. 218)**
**Differentiation (p. 220)**
**Business ecosystem (p. 222)**
**Grand strategy (p. 228)**
**Situational analysis (p. 228)**
**Capability profile (p. 229)**
**Reengineering (p. 231)**

**Forecasts (p. 234)**
**Event outcome forecasts (p. 234)**
**Event timing forecasts (p. 234)**
**Time series forecasts (p. 235)**
**Scenario analysis (p. 236)**
**Longitudinal scenarios (p. 236)**
**Cross-sectional scenarios (p. 236)**
**Trend analysis (p. 237)**

## Skills & Tools

### Reengineering: Strong Medicine for Strategic Ills

Reengineering, a.k.a. process innovation and core process redesign, is the search for, and implementation of, radical change in business processes to achieve breakthrough results. Its chief tool is a clean sheet of paper. Most change efforts start with what exists and fix it up. Reengineering, adherents emphasize, is not tweaking old procedures and certainly not plain-vanilla downsizing. Nor is it a program for bottom-up continuous improvement. Reengineers start from the future and work backward, as if unconstrained by existing methods, people, or departments. In effect they ask, "If we were a new company, how would we run this place?" Then, with a meat ax and sandpaper, they conform the company to their vision.

That's how GTE looks at its telephone operations, which account for four-fifths of the company's $20 billion in annual revenues. Facing new competitive threats, GTE figured it had to offer dramatically better customer service. Rather than eke out steady gains in its repair, billing, and marketing departments, the company examined its operations from the outside in. Customers, it concluded, wanted one-stop shopping—one number to fix an erratic dial tone, question a bill, sign up for call waiting, or all three, at any time of day.

GTE set up its first pilot "customer care center" in Garland, Texas, late last year and began to turn vision into fact. The company started with repair clerks, whose job had been to take down information from a customer, fill out a trouble ticket, and send it on to others who tested lines and switches until they found and fixed the problem. GTE wanted that done while the customer was still on the phone—something that happened just once in 200 calls. The first step was to move testing and switching equipment to the desks of the repair clerks—now called "front-end technicians"—and train them to use it. GTE stopped measuring how fast they handled calls and instead tracked how often they cleared up a problem without passing it on. Three out of ten now, and GTE is shooting for upward of seven.

The next step was to link sales and billing with repair, which GTE is doing with a push-button phone menu that allows callers to connect directly to any service. It has given operators new software so their computers can get into databases that let the operators handle virtually any customer request. In the process, says GTE vice president Mark Feighner, "we eliminated a tremendous amount of work—in the pilots, we've seen a 20 percent or 30 percent increase in productivity so far."

GTE's rewired customer-contact process—one of eight similar efforts at the company—displays most of the salient traits of reengineering: It is occurring in a dramatically altered competitive landscape; it is a major change, with big results; it cuts across departmental lines; it requires hefty investment in training and information technology; and layoffs result. . . .

It ain't cheap, and it ain't easy. At Blue Cross of Washington and Alaska, where redesigning claims processing raised labor productivity 20 percent in 15 months, CEO Betty Woods says the resource she drew on most was courage: "It was more difficult than we ever imagined, but it was worth it."

Therein lies the most important lesson from business's experience with reengineering: Don't do it if you don't have to. Says Thomas H. Davenport, head of research for Ernst & Young: "This hammer is incredibly powerful, but you can't use it on everything." Don't reengineer your buggy whip business; shut it. If you're in decent shape but struggling with cost or quality problems or weak brand recognition, by all means juice up your quality program and fire your ad agency, but don't waste money and energy on reengineering. Save reengineering for big processes that really matter, like new-product development or customer service, rather than test the technique someplace safe and insignificant.

*Source:* Excerpted from Thomas A. Stewart, "Reengineering: The Hot New Management Tool," *Fortune* (August 23, 1993): 41–42. © Time, Inc. All rights reserved.

# Hands-On Exercise

## Thinking Strategically: A SWOT Analysis

**Instructions**

This exercise is suitable for either an individual or a team. First, pick an organization as the focal point of the exercise. It can be a large company, a unit of a large company, a small business, or a nonprofit organization such as a college, government agency, or religious organization. Next, look inward and list the organization's strengths and weaknesses. Turning the analysis outward, list opportunities and threats in the organization's environment. Finally, envision workable strategies for the organization by cross-referencing the two sets of factors. Be sure to emphasize organizational strengths that can exploit environmental opportunities and neutralize or overcome outside threats. Also think about what needs to be done to correct organizational weaknesses. The general idea is to create the best possible fit between the organization and its environment (the "right niche").

*Note:* A SWOT analysis also can be a powerful career guidance tool. Simply make *yourself* the focus of the exercise and go from there.

Organization or Unit: _____

Organization (Unit)

| Strengths | Weaknesses |
|---|---|

Environment (Unit's Situation)

| Opportunities | Threats |
|---|---|

**1.** Which of the four elements—strengths, weaknesses, opportunities, threats— turned out to be the most difficult to develop? Why? Which the easiest? Why?

**2.** What valuable insights about your focal organization did you gain during your SWOT analysis?

**3.** Why should every manager know how to do a SWOT analysis?

**4.** What "right niche" did your SWOT analysis yield?

**5.** How can a personal SWOT analysis improve your career prospects?

## Internet Exercises

**1.** **Get the BIG Picture with BIG Ideas:** Strategic management is all about looking forward and thinking big. Busy students and managers can stretch their minds and jump-start their imaginations by going online. A good place to begin is at *Fast Company* magazine's excellent Web site. Any article published in paper by the magazine can be found in its Internet archive. Go to **www.fastcompany.com** and select "Themes" under the main menu heading "Magazine." At the "Themes" page, select a category such as "The Internet in Business" or "Strategy." (*Note:* If these listings have changed, simply select one or more relating to the topics in this chapter on strategic management.) Read two or three of the articles you have selected to identify a BIG idea about strategic management and/or making sense of an uncertain future. Your instructor may want you to print a hard copy of your key article if it is part of a formal assignment or class presentation.

   *Learning Points:* 1. What is the BIG idea you selected and how is it relevant to strategic management? 2. How should managers respond appropriately to your BIG idea (understand, exploit, avoid, etc.)? 3. Is your BIG idea a threat or opportunity? Explain. 4. Does your BIG idea represent an opportunity to start a new business? Explain.

**2.** **Check it out:** Go to the home page of the World Future Society (**www.wfs.org**) and search for forecasts and predictions. The main menu lists good search options. Make sure you click on the society's publication, *The Futurist,* to scan article titles past and present.

For updates to these exercises, visit our Web site (**http://business.college.hmco. com/students**).

# Closing Case

## The Oracles of Oil

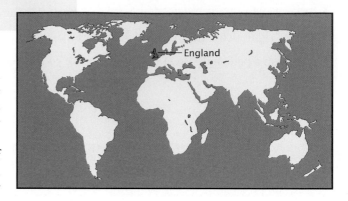

England

**D**own the hall from Ged Davis's 21st-floor office in Royal Dutch/Shell's London headquarters, there is a clear view of the enormous high-tech Ferris wheel known as the London Eye. Cantilevered out over the Thames River, the Eye is supported by two giant leaning pylons anchored, in turn, by four massive cables of braided steel. It is a spectacular feat of engineering—and yet it looks as if it might topple into the river at any moment.

Sounds a lot like the oil and gas business—a vast and complex structure that appears vulnerable to disaster at many points. Upheaval appears inevitable: OPEC's reign is crumbling, new oil and gas demand is shifting to Asia, and worries about global warming are forcing hard choices on governments and businesses. And since Sept. 11, it has become impossible to ignore the deeply anti-Western psychology that festers above the world's richest oil deposits.

Davis, a soft-spoken, rapier-slim Briton with a master's in engineering from Stanford University and one in economics from the London School of Economics, is the person responsible for helping Shell managers grapple with all this uncertainty. The head of Shell's fabled scenario-planning group, Davis leads a 12-person team in developing "scenarios," or alternative visions of the future based on broad economic and political developments. Rather than making forecasts, which tend to extrapolate the future from the past, scenario planners create hypothetical stories of how the future *might* turn out. "Scenarios are plausible, pertinent, and consistent alternative stories about the future that aim at changing the policy and strategy agenda," Davis explains. If physical plant security, insurance management, and IT [information technology] safeguards are the applied mechanics of risk management, scenario planning is its quantum physics.

Many other companies, including UPS, Daimler-Chrysler, and Zurich Financial Services, now use scenario planning, but no one has practiced it longer or in a more sophisticated fashion than Shell. Every year Davis's group devises 5- to 10-year scenarios for at least a dozen countries. Every three years, they construct a pair of grand, global scenarios that trace the implications of long-term social or economic trends.

Shell's scenario movement began with a notable success. In 1972, a scenario called "Energy Crisis"—one of seven developed that year—walked through what would happen if Western oil companies lost control of world supply. When OPEC shut the spigot the next year, Shell was the only major oil company positioned to withstand the shock. The company was also prepared when prices reversed direction a decade later. "When the price collapsed in the mid-1980s," recalls Peter Schwartz, who headed Shell's scenario group during that period, "we spent $3.5 billion [buying up oil fields at depressed prices] and locked in a 20-year price advantage."

Consultants like Global Business Network, founded by Schwartz after he left Shell, . . . can help companies create scenarios without an in-house department like Shell's. Outsourced or not, scenarios must promote unconventional thinking. "A scenario practitioner has to look outside, almost with the eyes of a child, to see things anew," Davis says. To expand his own group's perspective, Davis has brought jugglers, artists, and musicians into scenario-planning workshops.

Planners say the best use of the technique is to challenge a company's strategic assumptions by pointing out that completely different outcomes are equally plausible. When scenario planning doesn't work, it's often because companies expect an immediate impact on decision-making. Shell's experience in 1972 notwithstanding, the lag between the creation of a scenario and its strategic payoff is usually years.

Shell's most recent energy scenarios, released in October [2001], show just how wide a range of outcomes planners need to assess. One, called "Dynamics as Usual," considers the implications should energy suppliers evolve gradually toward renewable forms such as solar, wind, and hydro. If this is the future, the planners conclude, oil would remain the dominant source of energy for the bulk of the 21st century. A second scenario, "Spirit of the Coming Age," envisions revolutionary technologies sparking a much faster shift toward renewable forms. In this scenario, oil is overtaken by gases, particularly hydrogen fuel cells, by 2050.

Davis's group is also putting the finishing touches on Shell's latest triennial global scenarios. . . . One premise of the scenario called "People and Connections" is that nation-states are ceding influence to networks that owe allegiance to no particular government. These include not only multinational businesses but also organized crime webs and loosely knit "communities of shared values," like the anti-globalization movement and, unfortunately, al Qaeda. Businesses and governments alike have to recognize these new constituencies, Davis warns, or they'll face consequences.

In summarizing the risks at this moment, Davis draws on a whitewater-rafting analogy that Shell planners have used before. "We are in a global 'rapids' now," he says. "With all the transitions going on—demographic, technological, geopolitical, environmental—we will be truly tested in the years ahead. Looking back, people may label this period 'childhood's end.'"

## For Discussion

1. Which of Porter's four generic competitive strategies would be most profitable for Royal Dutch/Shell? Why?

2. Using your imagination and making reasonable assumptions, what opportunities and threats (the O and T portions of a SWOT analysis) can you envision for Shell?

3. Why is scenario analysis (referred to in this chapter as a "no surprise" approach to strategic planning) particularly useful for a global oil company such as Royal Dutch/Shell?

4. Which scenario do you think is more likely to come true: "Dynamics as Usual" or "Spirit of the Coming Age"? Why? (*Note:* Be sure to visit **www.shell.com** and check out the instructive and interesting material under the heading "Global Scenarios.")

## chapter eight

# Decision Making and Creative Problem Solving

> **"** If your instinct is to wait, ponder, and perfect, then you're dead. In practice, that means that leaders have to hit the undo key without flinching. **"**
>
> Ruthann Quindlen

*When you finish studying this chapter you should be able to*

**1** **Specify** at least five sources of decision complexity for modern managers.

**2** **Explain** what a *condition of risk* is and what managers can do to cope with it.

**3** **Define** and **discuss** the three decision traps: framing, escalation of commitment, and overconfidence.

**4** **Discuss** why programmed and non-programmed decisions require different decision-making procedures and **distinguish** between the two types of knowledge in knowledge management.

**5** **Explain** the need for a contingency approach to group-aided decision making.

**6** **Identify** and briefly **describe** five of the ten "mental locks" that can inhibit creativity.

**7** **List** and **explain** the four basic steps in the creative problem-solving process.

**8** **Describe** how causes of problems can be tracked down with fishbone diagrams.

# A Trend-Spotter Helps Drive Hallmark's Creativity

Marita Wesely-Clough went shopping in Manhattan the other day, hitting 16 stores in less than six hours. She was serious about her mission, sweeping in and out of shops, touching merchandise, chatting up sales clerks.

And though all she picked up on her spree was $26.14 worth of colored thread and beads at Toho Shoji on Sixth Avenue, she considered the marathon a success, mainly because she wasn't really looking to buy anything. She was looking for the future.

Wesely-Clough is the trends expert at what many think of as staid and conservative Hallmark Cards. . . .

"It's like mixing a stew," she says of her mission. "I hope I come away with two, maybe three, ingredients or insights today. I don't always come back with answers, but I always come back with questions." Much of her life, she says, is spent looking at the fringe. "You have to get out of your own head to let other ideas in."

The first stop of the day is Takashimiya, the definitive less-is-more Japanese boutique on Fifth Avenue. Wesely-Clough says she likes to begin her semiannual outings to New York there "because of the *experience*. You can walk out of there renewed and refreshed and not having bought a thing."

There were a couple of possible trend sightings, however: coral-colored peonies—"Oh, my God, *look* at that color!"—and brightly colored rugs that she runs her hands across.

She likes the store's use of limited colors, its quietness.

"One of the tricks (of good design) is how to be clean without being cold," she says. "That's where texture is important."

So what's all this got to do with a greeting card? Well, for one, Takashimiya epitomizes the trend toward simplicity, the Zen influences of China and the East. The look already is reflected in a line of Hallmark cards.

Wesely-Clough writes up a brief trip report when she returns home to Kansas City, but, more important, she and her team of five trend spotters meet with a variety of groups at Hallmark, from artists, writers, and designers to the licensing people and the Hall family itself.

Their stacks of items and information, everything from emerging design looks to edgy products to current colors, are displayed in what they call Hallmark's "trend room." It all helps shape not only greeting cards, but also merchandising, store environments and advertising. In short: "The trick is to get people's creative juices going," she says, luring Hallmark staffers into the room with whatever trinkets she brings home. . . .

Wesely-Clough's team scans everything from TV ads to magazines to see what's up and if certain trends are continuing. . . .

A trend can make it onto a card and into the marketplace in just four weeks, if it's that hot and timely. That happened with the arrival of Viagra and Ricky Martin's hit song *Livin' la Vida Loca.*

But more often, it's not that simple or straightforward a process.

"We might take some of the concepts and trends that Marita brings back and work early with them to see if it's a good idea. We go to moms with kids, for instance, and ask if this is going to work for their lives," says Jay Dittmann, Hallmark's vice president of research.

Or, as Hallmark's creative director Linda Smith says, "Marita gathers in trends, ideas bubble up, then Jay's group will test to validate them."

Trend spotting is a 24-hour-a-day job. Back home, Wesely-Clough often rides the bus just to hear what people are talking about, what's being said on the street these days.

Some of her research is done even closer to home.

Her 15-year-old daughter, Sara, might just be the most scrutinized teen in America. . . . "I have to admit, I look at her, her friends, what she's wearing, what they're wearing." . . .

Wesely-Clough, who has held a variety of roles at Hallmark for 27 years, likes to think of herself as a walking catalyst, making dozens of exploratory trips a year.

"I like to see people express themselves in our products; I enjoy provoking ideas," she says. "It's about finding ways to say things differently." . . .

"What she's doing is trying to connect the dots," adds Irma Zandl, president of New York's Zandl Group, a trend-spotting company.

"What are kids seeing on TV? What Web sites are they going to?" asks Paul Barker, Hallmark's senior vice president for creative product development. "We have to look at that, pull out the common threads. Like humor, for instance. It's taking a slightly different angle these days, toward more grossness or authenticity. How do we use that humor thread to include in a kid's product so it speaks to them? It's almost like vapors we're pulling out of this, but it's a careful analysis to link those vapors to a product."

But Hallmark has been wrong on occasion.

Divorce cards, for instance.

"It was too early when we first introduced them in 1973. People didn't want to talk about it," Wesely-Clough says.

"But, oh, it's the right time now. We have a nice array."

But they've been right more often. Hallmark's 1997 "Out of the Blue" line of 99-cent cards, for example, has been extremely successful, because they're inexpensive and research showed consumers like sending cards for absolutely no reason. . . .

"If we're good students of consumer behavior, we can be right there at the right time with the right product," Barker says. "Our success is when people say, 'You had to be spying on me!'" . . .

Why Wesely-Clough most often heads to New York is because, well, it's New York.

"I find anywhere there's a port, there's good trend possibilities," she says. "Wherever you get layer upon layer of people, it makes for a certain richness. New York. San Francisco. Seattle. But New York is the richest."

Are there days she feels she's seen it all, touched it all?

"There's always something new to be seen. Really!" she says as she passes an East Village street market, more fertile ground. "You can find surprises anywhere. It's like being married to someone for a long time and finding out years later that their favorite color is pink."

*Source:* Craig Wilson, "Hallmark Hits the Mark," *USA Today* (June 14, 2001): 1D-2D. Copyright 2001, *USA Today*. Reprinted with permission.

**decision making**  *identifying and choosing alternative courses of action*

**D**ecision making is the process of identifying and choosing alternative courses of action in a manner appropriate to the demands of the situation. The act of choosing implies that alternative courses of action must be weighed and weeded out. Many choices face Hallmark's product development team members as they strive to turn trends into profitable products amid lots of change and uncertainty. They will need to make important decisions at a rapid pace, despite incomplete information. Reason and judgment are required. Thus judgment and discretion are fundamental to decision making. This chapter highlights major challenges for decision makers, introduces a general decision-making model, discusses group-aided decision making, and examines creativity and problem solving.

# Challenges for Decision Makers

Though decision making has never been easy, it is especially challenging for today's managers. In an era of accelerating change, the pace of decision making also has accelerated. According to a recent survey of 479 managers, 77 percent reported making *more decisions* during the previous three years and 43 percent said they had *less time* to make each of those decisions.[1] In addition to having to cope with this acceleration, today's decision makers face a host of tough challenges. Ones we will discuss here include (1) complex streams of decisions, (2) uncertainty, (3) information-processing styles, and (4) perceptual and behavioral decision traps.

## Dealing with Complex Streams of Decisions

Above all else, today's decision-making contexts are not neat and tidy. A pair of experts lent realism to the subject by using the analogy of a stream:

*If decisions can be viewed as streams—streams containing countless bits of information, events, and choices—then how should decision makers be viewed? . . . The streams flowing through the organization do not wait for them; they flow around them. The streams do not serve up problems neatly wrapped and ready for choice. Rather, they deliver the bits and pieces, the problems and choices, in no particular order. . . .*

*In short, decision makers in an organization are floating in the stream, jostled capriciously by problems popping up, and finding anchors through action at a given time in a given place.*[2]

Importantly, the foregoing is a recognition of complexity, *not* an admission of hopelessness. A working knowledge of eight intertwined factors contributing to decision complexity can help decision makers successfully navigate the stream (see Figure 8.1). They include the following:

1.  *Multiple criteria.* Typically, a decision today must satisfy a number of often conflicting criteria representing the interests of different groups. For example, the new Denver International Airport was designed and built with much more than airplanes in mind:

    *Denver's is the first airport to be built for maximum accessibility for the disabled. During construction, the city took blind people, deaf people and those who use wheelchairs and canes through the terminal and concourses to road-test the layout.*

    *"They wanted to make sure a sign wasn't too low or a drinking fountain sticking out too far," says Thom Walsh, project manager at Fentress Bradburn. "It's a completely accessible building and uses Braille and voice paging."*[3]

Identifying stakeholders and balancing their conflicting interests is a major challenge for today's decision makers.

2.  *Intangibles.* Factors such as customer goodwill, employee morale, increased bureaucracy, and aesthetic appeal (for example, a billboard on a scenic highway), although difficult to measure, often determine decision alternatives.

3.  *Risk and uncertainty.* Along with every decision alternative goes the chance that it will fail in some way. Poor choices can prove costly. Yet the right decision, as illustrated in this legendary example, can open up whole new worlds of opportunity:

    *In 1967, seven dry holes on Alaska's harsh North Slope had left Atlantic Richfield Chairman Robert O. Anderson facing a costly choice. Should he try one more? The consummate wildcatter, Anderson pushed ahead, making one of the strategic decisions in U.S. oil history.*

    *The day after Christmas, oil historian Daniel Yergin recounts, a sound like four jumbo jets flying just overhead announced a plume of spewing natural gas. Prudhoe Bay turned out to be the largest petroleum discovery ever in North America.*[4]

Because of the importance of this particular aspect of decision complexity, we shall devote special attention to it in the next section.

---

**8A   How Decisiveness Pumped New Life into Procter & Gamble**

*Background:* Alan G. Lafley was named CEO in June 2000, capping a 25-year career at P&G.

*"I had to come up with something quickly to get people focused. I didn't want everyone sitting around worrying that our stock price had dropped in half," he says. Within days he set his plan. . . .*

*"The fact that we were in crisis made it easier to make changes," he says. "In a crisis, people accept change faster." . . .*

*So Lafley refocused the company on its big brands. He chose P&G's then ten best-sellers—the brands that each generated over $1 billion in sales and which combined made up more than half of total revenues.*

**Source:** Katrina Brooker, "The Un-CEO," *Fortune* (September 16, 2002): 92.

---

**Questions:** *What would have happened if Lafley was not as decisive, preferring instead to thoroughly study the situation and patiently build broad support for P&G's turnaround strategy?*

For further information about the interactive annotations in this chapter, visit our Web site (http://business.college.hmco.com/students).

---

**1** Specify at least five sources of decision complexity for modern managers.

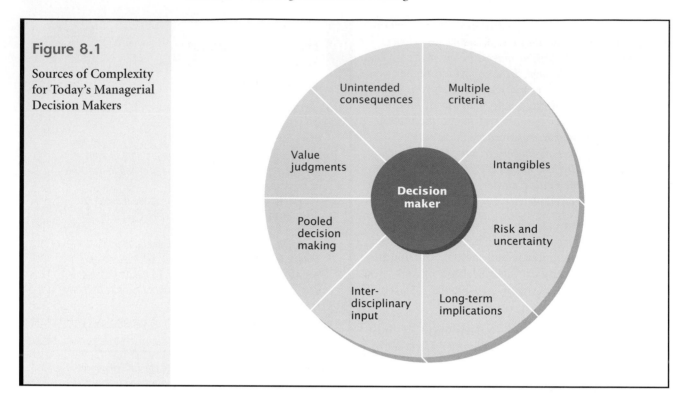

**Figure 8.1**

**Sources of Complexity for Today's Managerial Decision Makers**

4. *Long-term implications.* Major decisions generally have a ripple effect, with today's decisions creating the need for later rounds of decisions. For example, remember the proposed 555-seat A380 jetliner mentioned in Chapter 6? Consider these long-term implications for the world's largest commercial airplane now on the drawing board in Europe:

> The Airbus A380 is so large that it cannot park at a terminal designed for a row of Boeing 747s. It is so long that it will handle some taxiways like a tractor-trailer truck turning into a suburban driveway. It is so heavy that it cannot taxi across some culverts and bridges.
>
> Its engines are spaced so far apart that their exhaust could fry a runway's guide lights. Its body is so wide and tall that tower controllers may have to ban aircraft from nearby runways and taxiways before the plane lands or takes off.[5]

Airports will have to be significantly redesigned to accommodate the A380. We expect some lively debate on this issue.

5. *Interdisciplinary input.* Decision complexity is greatly increased when technical specialists such as lawyers, consumer advocates, tax advisers, accountants, engineers, and production and marketing experts are consulted before making a decision. This also is a time-consuming process.

6. *Pooled decision making.* Rarely is a single manager totally responsible for the entire decision process. For example, consider the approach of Brian Ruder, the successful president of Heinz's U.S. unit:

> [He] has collected a number of mentors and advisers over the course of his career. Ruder, in fact, has elected a group of people, including his father, to a personal board of directors. He canvasses them whenever he's faced with a major decision, such as introducing plastic ketchup bottles. . . . "I rely on them," he says, "for total frankness and objectivity." Obviously, it's helped.[6]

**8B**

**Back to the Opening Case**

How many of the eight sources of decision complexity are evident in this case? Explain.

# Management Ethics

## Toxic Waste: An Unintended Consequence of the Electronics Age

Pressure is building on computer and electronics makers to recycle old equipment to curb toxic electronics waste. . . .

[A state legislator], from Los Angeles, is expected to propose legislation to force manufacturers to take back used PCs, televisions and other high-tech junk for recycling. So-called e-waste, which often contains toxic chemicals, is clogging U.S. landfills and, environmental groups say, polluting Third World countries.

But recycling is expensive: about $20 per PC. And manufacturers say they'll have little choice but to pass the cost on to consumers, which could hurt sales. . . .

E-waste is a growing problem; about 1.8 million tons were created in the USA in 1999, according to the latest Environmental Protection Agency data. . . .

Europe and Japan have led with laws requiring manufacturers to recycle their products. No such law exists in the USA. And PC and electronics makers have been slow to launch U.S. recycling programs. Hewlett-Packard and IBM have them, but they charge consumers a fee that runs about $20 per PC.

PC makers say they cannot recycle for free without putting themselves at a competitive disadvantage. . . .

Environmental groups . . . say that 50% to 80% of e-waste collected for recycling in the USA is exported to countries such as China, Pakistan and India. The report by five groups, including the Basel Action Network and Silicon Valley Toxics Coalition, alleges that much of that waste is dismantled by hand. That's a problem because the chemicals inside electronics—including lead, cadmium and mercury—can poison groundwater and cause damage to the nervous and reproductive systems. The EPA "is not aware of a broad problem overseas" but is in talks with industry and state legislators to come up with an e-waste platform, says EPA assistant administrator Michael Shapiro.

The report focuses on electronics recycling in one region in China, where an estimated 100,000 workers handle e-waste. The environmentalists witnessed tons of e-waste being dumped along rivers, in open fields and in irrigation canals, the report says.

*Source:* Excerpted from Michelle Kessler, "PC Makers Soon May Be Forced to Recycle," *USA Today* (February 26, 2002): 1B. Copyright 2002, *USA Today*. Reprinted with permission.

---

After pooled input, complex decisions wind their way through the organization, with individuals and groups interpreting, modifying, and sometimes resisting. Minor decisions set the stage for major decisions, which in turn are translated back into local decisions. Typically, many people's fingerprints are on final decisions in the organizational world.

7. *Value judgments.* As long as decisions are made by people with differing backgrounds, perceptions, aspirations, and values, the decision-making process will be marked by disagreement over what is right or wrong, good or bad, and ethical or unethical.[7]

8. *Unintended consequences.* The **law of unintended consequences,** according to an expert on the subject, "states that you cannot always predict the results of purposeful action."[8] In other words, there can be a disconnect between intentions and actual results. Although unintended consequences can be positive, negative ones are most troublesome and have been called the Frankenstein monster effect.[9] For example, did the designers of motor vehicle airbags, in their quest to save lives, adequately anticipate how lethal the devices would be for small children and frail adults? Evidently not. And therein lies the crux of the problem of unintended consequences. Namely, *hurried decision makers typically give little or no consideration to*

**law of unintended consequences** *results of purposeful actions are often difficult to predict*

*the broader consequences of their decisions* (see Management Ethics). Unintended consequences cannot be eliminated altogether in today's complex world. Still, they can be moderated to some extent by giving them creative and honest consideration when making important decisions.

## Coping with Uncertainty

Among the valuable contributions of decision theorists are classification schemes for types and degrees of uncertainty. (Recall our discussion in Chapter 6 about state, effect, and response uncertainty.) Unfortunately, life is filled with varying degrees of these types of uncertainties. Managers are continually asked to make the best decisions they can, despite uncertainties about both present and future circumstances. Imagine yourself as a manager in Canada's pulp and paper industry facing this complex web of uncertainties, as described by a business writer during the 1990s:

> *Battered by slack demand and production overcapacity, hounded by environmentalists, and hit with regulations forcing costly new pollution controls, Canada's paper manufacturers are under siege. . . .*
>
> *To the recession, add unfavorable exchange rates, tougher competition abroad, and a shift toward recycled newsprint in the crucial United States market. . . .*[10]

Managers who are able to assess the degrees of certainty in a situation—whether conditions are certain, risky, or uncertain—are able to make more effective decisions. As illustrated in Figure 8.2, there is a negative correlation between uncertainty and the decision maker's confidence in a decision. In other words, the more uncertain a man-

*Most of us have never heard of glassy-winged sharpshooters. Grape farmers sure have in recent years, adding yet another major uncertainty to farming. This Florida native somehow infested vineyards in Southern California. Now it threatens to move northward into prime wine grape country, spreading Pierce's disease, caused by a fatal bacterium that strangles grapevines. Unlike their situation in Florida, the sharpshooters have no natural enemies in California. It promises to be an all-out battle for the wineries.*

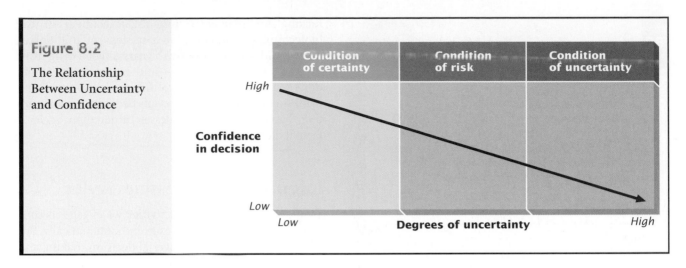

**Figure 8.2**

The Relationship Between Uncertainty and Confidence

ager is about the principal factors in a decision, the less confident he or she will be about the successful outcome of that decision. The key, of course, lies not in eliminating uncertainty, which is impossible, but rather in learning to work within an acceptable range of uncertainty.[11]

**Certainty.**   A **condition of certainty** exists when there is no doubt about the factual basis of a particular decision and its outcome can be predicted accurately. Much like the economic concept of pure competition, the concept of certainty is useful mainly as a theoretical anchor point for a continuum. In a world filled with uncertainties, certainty is relative rather than absolute. For example, the decision to order more rivets for a manufacturing firm's fabrication department is based on the relative certainty that the current rate of use will exhaust the rivet inventory on a specific date. But even in this case, uncertainties about the possible misuse or theft of rivets creep in to reduce confidence. Because nothing is truly certain, conditions of risk and uncertainty are the general rule for managers, not the exception.

**condition of certainty** *solid factual basis allows accurate prediction of decision's outcome*

**2** Explain what a *condition of risk* is and what managers can do to cope with it.

**Risk.**   A **condition of risk** is said to exist when a decision must be made on the basis of incomplete but reliable factual information.[12] Reliable information, though incomplete, is still useful to managers coping with risk because they can use it to calculate the probability that a given event will occur and then to select a decision alternative with favorable odds.

The two basic types of probabilities are objective and subjective. **Objective probabilities** are derived mathematically from reliable historical data, whereas **subjective probabilities** are estimated from past experience or judgment. Decision making based on probabilities is common in all areas of management today. For instance, laundry product manufacturers would not think of launching a new detergent without determining its probability of acceptance by means of consumer panels and test marketing. A number of inferential statistical techniques can help managers objectively cope with risks.[13]

**condition of risk** *decision made on basis of incomplete but reliable information*

**objective probabilities** *odds derived mathematically from reliable data*

**subjective probabilities** *odds based on judgment*

**Uncertainty.**   A **condition of uncertainty** exists when little or no reliable factual information is available. Still, judgmental or subjective probabilities can be estimated. Decision making under conditions of uncertainty can be both rewarding and nerve-

**condition of uncertainty** *no reliable factual information available*

## 8C  Hmmm. You've Got Me!

Research finding:

*It turns out that people working for managers who openly express uncertainty and who seek employee input in resolving ambiguous challenges are more satisfied with their jobs, more committed to and less cynical about their organizations, and more likely to identify with the companies they work for.*

**Source:** Kate Sweetman, "When in Doubt . . ." *Training,* 39 (February 2002): 24.

**Question:** *We are told over and over that employees hate uncertainty. So how do you explain this research finding?*

## 8D  How Intuitive Are You? A Quiz

Rate yourself on each item with the following 1 to 5 scale. The higher your total score, the more intuitive you are.

Not at all like me  1—2—3—4—5  Very much like me

1. You can identify something you haven't seen clearly.
2. You can time three-minute eggs without a clock.
3. You are good at generating images spontaneously.
4. You look at a cloud and many images come to mind.
5. You always know when it's the ideal time to strike.
6. You're good at hunches.
7. You're good at detective work; you know what elements fit together.

Total score: _____

**Source:** Questionnaire items excerpted from Daniel Cappon, "The Anatomy of Intuition," *Psychology Today,* 26 (May–June 1993): 42–43.

**Questions:** *How intuitive are you? Would your close friends and relatives agree with your score? How do others tend to react to your level of intuition? How can your intuition (or lack of it) help or hinder you as a manager?*

racking for managers. Just ask executives in the biotechnology industry: "It costs tens of millions of dollars and can take five to 15 years to get a drug from the test tube to the clinic—and many drugs simply don't make it."[14] Decision confidence is lowest when a condition of uncertainty prevails because decisions are then based on educated guesses rather than on hard factual data.

## Information-Processing Styles

Thinking is one of those activities we engage in constantly yet seldom pause to examine systematically. But within the context of managerial decision making and problem solving, it is important that one's thinking does not get into an unproductive rut. The quality of our decisions is a direct reflection of how we process information.

Researchers have identified two general information-processing styles: the thinking style and the intuitive style.[15] One is not superior to the other. Both are needed during organizational problem solving. Managers who rely predominantly on the *thinking* style tend to be logical, precise, and objective. They prefer routine assignments requiring attention to detail and systematic implementation. Conversely, managers who are predominantly *intuitive* find comfort in rapidly changing situations in which they can be creative and follow their hunches and visions. Intuitive managers see things in complex patterns rather than as logically ordered bits and pieces.[16] Of course, not everyone falls neatly into one of these two categories; many people process information through a combination of the two styles. For example, Bonnie Reitz, a senior vice president for sales at Continental Airlines, recently said: "I believe in unshakable facts. Get as many facts as you can. Don't spend forever on it, but if you have enough facts and the gut intuition, you're going to get it right most of the time."[17] (See Figure 8.3.)

The important thing to recognize here is that managers approach decision making and problem solving in very different ways, depending on their information-processing styles.[18] It is a matter of diversity. Their approaches, perceptions, and recommendations vary because their minds work differently. In traditional pyramid work organizations, where the thinking style tends to prevail, intuitive employees may be criticized for being imprecise and rocking the boat. A concerted effort needs to be made to tap the creative skills of "intuitives" and the implementation abilities of "thinkers." An appreciation for alternative information-processing styles needs to be cultivated because they complement one another.

**Figure 8.3**   Two General Information-Processing Styles

| Brain skill emphasized | Type of organization where predominant | Task preference | Problem-solving/ decision-making style | Example applications | Sample occupational specialty |
|---|---|---|---|---|---|
| **Thinking** | • Traditional<br>• Pyramid | • Routine<br>• Precision<br>• Detail<br>• Implementation<br>• Repetitive | • Deductive<br>• Objective<br>• Prefers solving problems by breakdown into parts, then approaching the problem sequentially using logic. | • Model building<br>• Projection | • Planning<br>• Management science<br>• Financial management<br>• Engineering<br>• Law enforcement<br>• Military |
| **Intuitive** | • Open<br>• Temporary<br>• Rapidly changing | • Nonroutine<br>• Broad issues<br>• General policy options<br>• Constant new assignments | • Inductive<br>• Subjective<br>• Prefers solving problems by looking at the whole, then approaching the problem through hunches. | • Brainstorming<br>• Challenging traditional assumptions | • Personnel<br>• Marketing<br>• Organization development<br>• Intelligence |

*Source:* Weston H. Agor, "Managing Brain Skills: The Last Frontier," *Personnel Administrator*, 32 (October 1987): 58, Figure 1. Used with permission.

## Avoiding Perceptual and Behavioral Decision Traps

Behavioral scientists have identified some common human tendencies capable of eroding the quality of decision making. Three well-documented ones are framing, escalation, and overconfidence. Awareness and conscious avoidance of these traps can give decision makers a competitive edge.

**Framing Error.**   One's judgment can be altered and shaped by how information is presented or labeled. In other words, labels create frames of reference with the power to bias our interpretations. **Framing error** is the tendency to evaluate positively presented information favorably and negatively presented information unfavorably.[19] Those evaluations, in turn, influence one's behavior. A study with 80 male and 80 female University of Iowa students documented the framing-interpretation-behavior linkage. Half of each gender group was told about a cancer treatment with a 50 percent success rate. The other two groups heard about the same cancer treatment but were told it had a 50 percent failure rate. The researchers summed up results of the study as follows:

> *Describing a medical treatment as having a 50 percent success rate led to higher ratings of perceived effectiveness and higher likelihood of recommending the treatment to others, including family members, than describing the treatment as having a 50 percent failure rate.*[20]

**3**   Define and discuss the three decision traps: framing, escalation of commitment, and overconfidence.

**framing error**   *how information is presented influences one's interpretation of it*

Framing thus influenced both interpretations and intended behavior. Given the importance of the information in this study (cancer treatment), ethical questions arise about the potential abuse of framing error.

In organizations, framing error can be used constructively or destructively. Advertisers, for instance, take full advantage of this perceptional tendency when attempting to sway consumers' purchasing decisions. A leading brand of cat litter boasts of being 99 percent dust free. Meanwhile, a shampoo claims to be fortified with 1 percent natural protein. Thanks to framing error, we tend to perceive very little dust in the cat litter and a lot of protein in the shampoo. Managers who couch their proposals in favorable terms hope to benefit from framing error. And who can blame them? On the negative side, prejudice and bigotry thrive on framing error. A male manager who believes women can't manage might frame interview results so that John looks good and Mary looks bad.

**Escalation of Commitment.**    Why are people slow to write off bad investments? Why do companies stick to unprofitable strategies? And why has the U.S. government typically continued to fund over-budget and behind-schedule programs? Escalation of commitment is a possible explanation for these diverse situations.[21] **Escalation of commitment** is the tendency of individuals and organizations to get locked into losing courses of action because *quitting is personally and socially difficult.* This decision-making trap has been called the "throwing good money after bad" dilemma. Those victimized by escalation of commitment are often heard talking about "sunk costs" and "too much time and money invested to quit now." Within the context of management, psychological, social, and organizational factors conspire to encourage escalation of commitment[22] (see Figure 8.4).

**escalation of commitment**
*people get locked into losing courses of action to avoid embarrassment of quitting or admitting error*

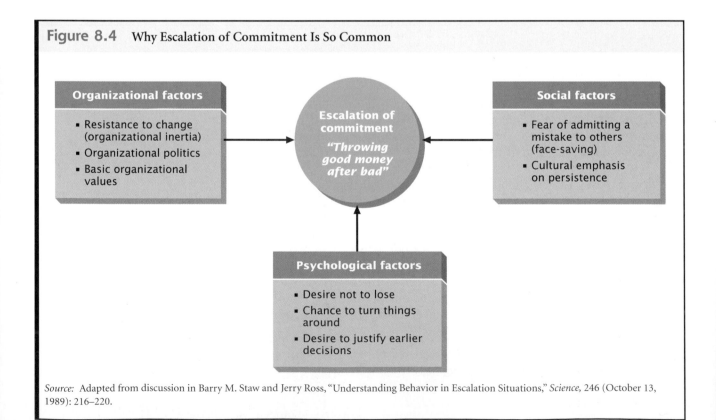

**Figure 8.4    Why Escalation of Commitment Is So Common**

*Source:* Adapted from discussion in Barry M. Staw and Jerry Ross, "Understanding Behavior in Escalation Situations," *Science,* 246 (October 13, 1989): 216–220.

The model in Figure 8.4 can be brought to life by using it to analyze a highly unusual decision by the Pentagon in 1991. Two giant defense contractors, McDonnell Douglas and General Dynamics, were under contract to design and build the A-12 attack plane. All told, 620 of the aircraft carrier–based bombers were to be built for the U.S. Navy at a cost of $60 billion. With the A-12 program 18 months behind schedule and $2.7 billion over budget, then–Secretary of Defense Dick Cheney terminated the contract. It was the Pentagon's biggest cancellation ever. An appreciation of the contributing factors shown in Figure 8.4 underscores how truly unusual Cheney's decision was. Psychologically, his termination decision flew in the face of three possible motives for throwing good money after bad. Cheney went against the social grain as well by publicly admitting the Defense Department's mistake and doing something culturally distasteful to Americans, giving up. (American folk heroes tend to be persistent to the bitter end.) Finally, Cheney had to overcome bureaucratic resistance in the defense establishment. He also had to withstand political opposition from the contractors about their having to lay off 8,000 A-12 project employees. Nevertheless, despite many pressures to continue the program, Cheney refused to let the forces of escalation carry the day.

Reality checks, in the form of comparing actual progress with effectiveness and efficiency standards, are the best way to keep escalation in check.[23] In Cheney's case, he concluded: "No one can tell me exactly how much more it will cost to keep this [A-12] program going. And I do not believe that a bailout is in the national interest. If we cannot spend the taxpayers' money wisely, we will not spend it."[24] This is an instructive lesson for all potential victims of escalation.

**Overconfidence.**    The term *overconfidence* is commonplace and requires no formal definition. We need to comprehend the psychology of overconfidence because it can expose managers to unreasonable risks. For instance, overconfidence proved costly for Boeing in 1998. As *Business Week* reported at the time:

> *Boeing's prized new Delta III rocket blew up on its maiden flight on Aug. 26, taking with it a $225 million PanAmSat Corp. satellite. Overconfidence lured Boeing into taking the risky step of carrying a live payload on the maiden voyage.*[25]

Ironically, researchers have found a positive relationship between overconfidence and task difficulty. In other words, the more difficult the task, the greater the tendency for people to be overconfident.[26] Easier and more predictable situations foster confidence, but generally not unrealistic overconfidence. People may be overconfident about one or more of the following: accuracy of input data; individual, team, or organizational ability; and the probability of success. There are various theoretical explanations for this research evidence. One likely reason is that overconfidence is often necessary to generate the courage needed to tackle difficult situations.[27]

As with the other decision traps, managerial awareness of this problem is the important first step toward avoiding it. Careful analysis of situational factors, critical thinking about decision alternatives, and honest input from stakeholders can help managers avoid overconfidence.[28]

---

**8E  I Think I'll Sleep on It**

*It's good to be cautious, but mulling over a decision usually boosts confidence without actually improving accuracy. Unless you expect to get fresh information, it rarely helps to "sleep on it," particularly given the human tendencies to focus on confirming information and to discount contrary facts.*

**Source:** J. Wesley Hutchinson and Joseph W. Alba, "When Business Is a Confidence Game," *Harvard Business Review,* 79 (June 2001): 21.

---

**Question:** *People in the United States have a reputation for hasty decision making. How can they strike the right balance between speed and the overconfidence trap described here?*

# Making Decisions

**4** Discuss why programmed and non-programmed decisions require different decision-making procedures and distinguish between the two types of knowledge in knowledge management.

It stands to reason that if the degree of uncertainty varies from situation to situation, there can be no single way to make decisions.[29] A second variable with which decision makers must cope is the number of times a particular decision is made. Some decisions are made frequently, perhaps several times a day. Others are made infrequently or just once. Consequently, decision theorists have distinguished between programmed and nonprogrammed decisions.[30] Each of these types of decisions requires a different procedure.

## Making Programmed Decisions

**programmed decisions**
*repetitive and routine decisions*

**Programmed decisions** are those that are repetitive and routine. Examples include hiring decisions, billing decisions in a hospital, supply reorder decisions in a purchasing department, consumer loan decisions in a bank, and pricing decisions in a university bookstore. Managers tend to devise fixed procedures for handling these everyday decisions. Most decisions made by the typical manager on a daily basis are of the programmed variety.

**decision rule**  *tells when and how programmed decisions should be made*

At the heart of the programmed decision procedure are decision rules. A **decision rule** is a statement that identifies the situation in which a decision is required and specifies how the decision will be made. Behind decision rules is the idea that standard, recurring problems need to be solved only once. Decision rules permit busy managers to make routine decisions quickly without having to go through comprehensive problem solving over and over again. Generally, decision rules should be stated in "if-then" terms. A decision rule for a consumer loan officer in a bank, for example, might be: *If* the applicant is employed, has no record of loan default, and can put up 20 percent collateral, *then* a loan not to exceed $10,000 can be authorized." Carefully conceived decision rules can streamline the decision-making process by allowing lower-level managers to shoulder the responsibility for programmed decisions and freeing higher-level managers for relatively more important, nonprogrammed decisions.

## Making Nonprogrammed Decisions

**nonprogrammed decisions**
*decisions made in complex and nonroutine situations*

**Nonprogrammed decisions** are those made in complex, important, and nonroutine situations, often under new and largely unfamiliar circumstances. This kind of decision is made much less frequently than are programmed decisions. Examples of nonprogrammed decisions include deciding whether to merge with another company, how to replace an executive who died unexpectedly, whether a foreign branch should be opened, and how to market an entirely new kind of product or service. The following six questions need to be asked prior to making a nonprogrammed decision:

1. What decision needs to be made?
2. When does it have to be made?
3. Who will decide?
4. Who will need to be consulted prior to the making of the decision?
5. Who will ratify or veto the decision?
6. Who will need to be informed of the decision?[31]

The decision-making process becomes more sharply focused when managers take the time to answer these questions.

*Ice build-up on an aircraft's wings can add tons of dangerous weight. Consequently, a de-icing solution is sprayed on prior to take-off, as pictured here during a record snowstorm at Hartsfield Atlanta International Airport. This critical procedure cannot be left to chance or haphazard guesswork. Programmed decision making with precise decision rules specify when and how de-icing should take place.*

One respected decision theorist has described nonprogrammed decisions as follows: "There is no cut-and-dried method for handling the problem because it hasn't arisen before, or because its precise nature and structure are elusive or complex, or because it is so important that it deserves a custom-tailored treatment."[32]

Nonprogrammed decision making calls for creative problem solving. The four-step problem-solving process introduced later in this chapter helps managers make effective and efficient nonprogrammed decisions.

## A General Decision-Making Model

Although different decision procedures are required for different situations, it is possible to construct a general decision-making model. Figure 8.5 shows an idealized, logical, and rational model of organizational decision making. Importantly, it describes how decisions can be made, but it does not portray how managers actually make decisions.[33] In fact, on-the-job research found managers did not follow a rational and logical series of steps when making decisions.[34] Why, then, should we even consider a rational, logical model? Once again, as in the case of the strategic management process in Chapter 7, a rational descriptive model has instructional value because it identifies key components of a complex process. It also suggests a better way of doing things.

The first step, a scan of the situation, is important, although it is often underemphasized or ignored altogether in discussions of managerial decision making. Scanning answers the question "How do I know a decision should be made?" More than 60 years ago, Chester I. Barnard gave one of the best answers to this question, stating that "the occasions for decision originate in three distinct fields: (a) from authoritative communications from superiors; (b) from cases referred for decision by subordinates; (c) from cases originating in the initiative of the [manager] concerned."[35] In addition to signaling when a decision is required, scanning reveals the degree of uncertainty and provides necessary information for pending decisions.[36]

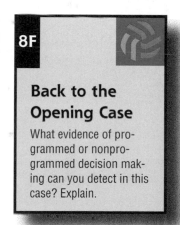

**8F**

### Back to the Opening Case

What evidence of programmed or nonprogrammed decision making can you detect in this case? Explain.

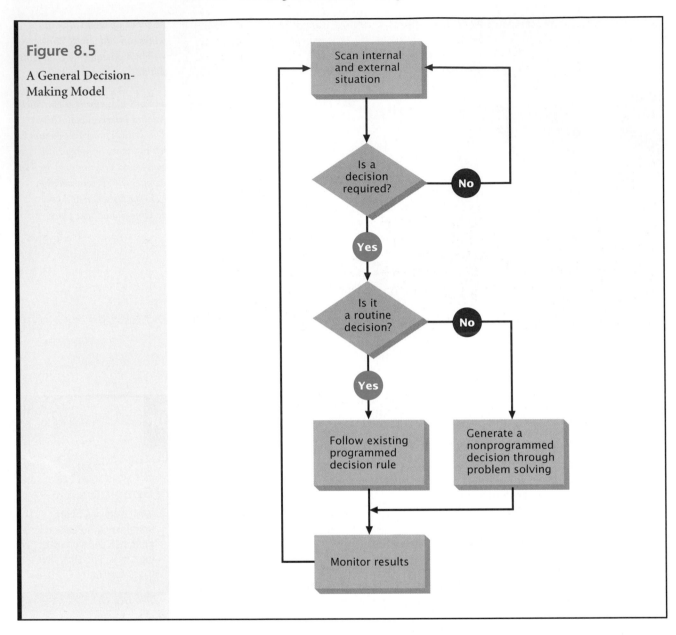

**Figure 8.5**

A General Decision-
Making Model

When the need for a decision has been established, the manager must determine whether the situation is routine. If it is routine and there is an appropriate decision rule, the rule is applied. But if it turns out to be a new situation demanding a nonprogrammed decision, comprehensive problem solving begins. In either case, the results of the final decision need to be monitored to see if any follow-up action is necessary.

## Knowledge Management: A Tool for Improving the Quality of Decisions

An army of academics, consultants, and managers have rallied around the concept of knowledge management during the last decade. While some may dismiss it as a passing fad, knowledge management is a powerful and robust concept deserving a permanent place in management theory and practice.[37] Authorities on the subject define **knowledge management** (KM) as "the development of tools, processes, systems, structures, and cultures explicitly to improve the creation, sharing, and use of knowledge critical for decision-making."[38] KM is at the heart of *learning organizations,* discussed in the next chapter. Our purpose here is to explore the basics of KM, with an eye toward better organizational decisions. After all, decisions are only as good as the information on which they are based.

**knowledge management**
*developing a system to improve the creation and sharing of knowledge critical for decision making*

**Two Types of Knowledge.**   KM specialists draw a fundamental distinction between two types of knowledge: tacit knowledge and explicit knowledge (see Figure 8.6). **Tacit knowledge** is personal, intuitive, and undocumented information about how to skillfully perform tasks, solve problems, and make decisions. People who are masters of their craft have tacit knowledge and more often than not have difficulty explaining how they actually do things. They simply "do" the task; they have a "feel" for the job; they know when they are in the "zone." For example, ask really good golfers how they swing their clubs.[39] Meanwhile, **explicit knowledge** is readily sharable information because it is in verbal, textual, visual, or numerical form. It can be found in presentations and lectures, books and magazines (both hard copy and online), policy manuals, technical specifications, training programs, databases, and software programs. In short, explicit knowledge is public (to varying degrees), whereas tacit knowledge is private.

**tacit knowledge**   *personal, intuitive, and undocumented information*

**explicit knowledge**
*documented and sharable information*

**Improving the Flow of Knowledge.**   As indicated in Figure 8.6, knowledge flows in four basic directions. Each is important in its own way. Each needs to be carefully cultivated. But flow number one—the flow of constructive tacit knowledge between coworkers—is a top priority. Organizational support is needed to help individuals feel comfortable about giving and receiving useful task-related knowledge on demand.[40]

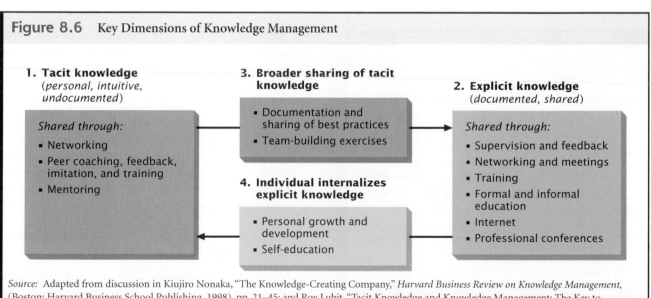

**Figure 8.6**   Key Dimensions of Knowledge Management

**1. Tacit knowledge**
(*personal, intuitive, undocumented*)

*Shared through:*
- Networking
- Peer coaching, feedback, imitation, and training
- Mentoring

**3. Broader sharing of tacit knowledge**
- Documentation and sharing of best practices
- Team-building exercises

**4. Individual internalizes explicit knowledge**
- Personal growth and development
- Self-education

**2. Explicit knowledge**
(*documented, shared*)

*Shared through:*
- Supervision and feedback
- Networking and meetings
- Training
- Formal and informal education
- Internet
- Professional conferences

*Source:*  Adapted from discussion in Kiujiro Nonaka, "The Knowledge-Creating Company," *Harvard Business Review on Knowledge Management,* (Boston: Harvard Business School Publishing, 1998), pp. 21–45; and Roy Lubit, "Tacit Knowledge and Knowledge Management: The Key to Sustainable Competitive Advantage," *Organizational Dynamics,* 29 (Winter 2001): 164–178.

*In the oil and gas business there are the "majors" and "independents." Majors, like Exxon Mobil and Shell, do everything from drilling to refining to selling at the pump. Independents, on the other hand, are the gunslingers of the business—they just explore and drill. Houston-based Anadarko has become the leading independent by boldly looking for gas and oil in places ignored by others. President John Seitz, a geologist by training, knows the strategic value of both tacit and explicit knowledge. After all, it takes superior knowledge management to drill in the right places.*

## 8G   Wow! What a Great Mistake!

Alberto Alessi, Italy's leading product designer:

*"Revel in your glorious failures. Dance on the border-line between success and disaster. Because that's where your next big breakthrough will come from."*

*It's the duds that enjoy center stage in the company's private museum, where Alessi summons his designers weekly to discuss new projects.*

**Source:** As quoted in Ian Wylie, "Failure Is Glorious," *Fast Company*, no. 51 (October 2001): 36.

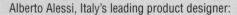

**Question:** *How well does this perspective mesh with knowledge management? Explain.*

Sophisticated new KM software is proving very useful and cost-effective in large organizations for the second type of knowledge flow—sharing of explicit knowledge.

*For example, Deloitte Consulting uses a KM system based on a search engine from Verity, along with an Oracle database and content management software from BroadVision, to provide its nearly 20,000 employees with access to a repository of more than 250,000 documents. Deloitte chief information officer Larry Quinlan says the $2 million system provides an "essential" means of sharing information about consulting practices. "Deloitte is all over the world," he says. "Without [the KM system], we just wouldn't be able to function."*[41]

According to KM advocates, it is important to know what you know, what you don't know, and know how to find what you need to know. The result: better and more timely decisions.

You will encounter many topics in this book to improve the various knowledge flows. Among them are organizational learning, organizational cultures, training, communication, empowerment, participative management, virtual teams, transformational leadership, and mentoring.

# Group-Aided Decision Making: A Contingency Perspective

Decision making, like any other organizational activity, does not take place in a vacuum. Typically, decision making is a highly social activity with committees, study groups, review panels, or project teams contributing in a variety of ways.

## Collaborative Computing

Computer networks, the Internet, and the advent of **collaborative computing** guarantee even broader participation in the decision-making process.

> *Collaborative computing is a catchphrase for a new body of software and hardware that helps people work better together. A collaborative system creates an environment in which people can share information without the constraints of time and space.*
>
> *Network groupware applications link workgroups across a room or across the globe. The software gives the group a common, online venue for meetings, and it lets all members labor on the same data simultaneously.*
>
> *Collaborative applications include calendar management, video teleconferencing, computer teleconferencing, integrated team support, and support for business meetings and group authoring. Messaging and e-mail systems represent the most basic type of groupware.*[42]

**collaborative computing**
*teaming up to make decisions via a computer network programmed with groupware*

Unfortunately, according to research, groupware is typically plagued by low-quality implementation. Sixty-five percent of the survey respondents used it simply as a communication tool, to send and receive e-mail, which is analogous to using a personal computer for word processing only. Groupware users need to be taught how to *collaborate* via computer (for instance, jointly identifying and solving problems). "When implemented correctly, the benefits are astounding. Groupware had twice the impact on individual job performance and nearly three times the impact on customer satisfaction at the organizations with the highest-quality implementation compared with the organization with the lowest."[43]

## Group Involvement in Decisions

Whether the situation is a traditional face-to-face committee meeting or a global e-meeting, at least five aspects of the decision-making process can be assigned to groups:

1. *Analyzing the problem*
2. *Identifying components of the decision situation*
3. *Estimating components of the decision situation [for example, determining probabilities, feasibilities, time estimates, and payoffs]*
4. *Designing alternatives*
5. *Choosing an alternative*[44]

## 8H What Does Consensus Mean?

*A consensus requires unity but not unanimity and concurrence but not consistency. . . .*

*A consensus is reached when all members can say they either agree with the decision or have had their "day in court" and were unable to convince the others of their viewpoint. In the final analysis, everyone agrees to support the outcome. It is not a majority because that implies a vote, and voting is* verboten *[taboo] for teams using the consensus method. Voting tends to split the group into winners and losers, thereby creating needless divisions. Consensus does not require unanimity since members may still disagree with the final result but are willing to work toward its success. This is the hallmark of a team player.*

**Source:** Glenn M. Parker, *Team Players and Teamwork: The New Competitive Business Strategy* (San Francisco: Jossey-Bass, 1990), p. 44.

**Questions:** *Are you surprised by any of this information? Why is it so important not to submit an issue to a vote when trying to reach a consensus? In today's organizations, why is it often better to strive for a consensus rather than insist upon unanimous support? What are the major drawbacks of the consensus approach?*

Assuming that two (or more) heads may be better than one and that managers can make better use of their time by delegating various decision-making chores, there is a strong case for turning to groups when making decisions. But before bringing others into the decision process, managers need to be aware of the problem of dispersed accountability and consider the tradeoff between the advantages and disadvantages of group-aided decision making. In view of these problems and of research evidence comparing individual and group performance, a contingency approach is recommended.

## The Problem of Dispersed Accountability

There is a critical difference between group-aided decision making and group decision making. In the first instance, the group does everything except make the final decision. In the second instance, the group actually makes the final decision. Managers who choose the second route face a dilemma. Although a decision made by a group will probably reflect the collective experience and wisdom of all those involved, personal accountability is lost. Blame for a joint decision that fails is too easily passed on to others. For example, Robert Palmer, hired to turn Digital Equipment around, inherited the following situation: "This was a company run by committee, by consensus. No one actually made a decision. When things went well, there would be a number of people willing to take credit. But when things went wrong, it was impossible to fix responsibility on anyone."[45] This legacy of dispersed accountability proved too much for Palmer, and Digital was sold to Compaq Computer.

The traditional formula for resolving this problem is to make sure that a given manager is personally accountable for a decision when the responsibility for it has to be traced. According to this line of reasoning, even when a group is asked to recommend a decision, the responsibility for the final outcome remains with the manager in charge. For managers who want to maintain the integrity of personal accountability, there is no such thing as group decision making; there is only group-*aided* decision making. There are three situations in which individual accountability for a decision is necessary.

- The decision will have significant impact on the success or failure of the unit or organization.
- The decision has legal ramifications (such as possible prosecution for price-fixing, antitrust, or product safety violations).
- A competitive reward is tied to a successful decision. (For example, only one person can get a promotion.)

In less critical areas, the group itself may be responsible for making decisions.[46]

*Nina Niu-Ok, employed by health-care provider Kaiser Permanente, appreciates the power of group-aided decision making. During this session in Palo Alto, California, she successfully tapped the creative energy of a mix of coworkers ranging from doctors to administrators. The idea was to map out scenarios to guide future strategy and decision making at Kaiser Permanente. Typically a six-month ordeal, this intense cooperative effort got the job done in three days. Cooperation and participation—just what the doctor ordered for these turbulent times in health care.*

## Advantages and Disadvantages of Group-Aided Decision Making

Various combinations of positive and negative factors are encountered when a manager brings others into the decision-making process. The advantages and disadvantages are listed in Table 8.1. If there is a conscious effort to avoid or at least minimize the disadvantages, managers can gain a great deal by sharing the decision-making process with peers, outside consultants, and team members.[47] However, some important contingency factors need to be taken into consideration.

## A Contingency Approach Is Necessary

Are two or more heads actually better than one? The answer depends on the nature of the task, the ability of the contributors, and the form of interaction (see Figure 8.7). An analysis of dozens of individual-versus-group performance studies conducted over a 61-year period led one researcher to the following conclusions: (1) groups tend to do quantitatively and qualitatively better than the *average* individual; and (2) *exceptional*

**5** Explain the need for a contingency approach to group-aided decision making.

**Table 8.1**    Advantages and Disadvantages of Group-Aided Decision Making and Problem Solving

**Advantages**

1. **Greater pool of knowledge.** A group can bring much more information and experience to bear on a decision or problem than can an individual acting alone.

2. **Different perspectives.** Individuals with varied experience and interests help the group see decision situations and problems from different angles.

3. **Greater comprehension.** Those who personally experience the give-and-take of group discussion about alternative courses of action tend to understand the rationale behind the final decision.

4. **Increased acceptance.** Those who play an active role in group decision making and problem solving tend to view the outcome as "ours" rather than "theirs."

5. **Training ground.** Less experienced participants in group action learn how to cope with group dynamics by actually being involved.

**Disadvantages**

1. **Social pressure.** Unwillingness to "rock the boat" and pressure to conform may combine to stifle the creativity of individual contributors.

2. **Domination by a vocal few.** Sometimes the quality of group action is reduced when the group gives in to those who talk the loudest and longest.

3. **Logrolling.** Political wheeling and dealing can displace sound thinking when an individual's pet project or vested interest is at stake.

4. **Goal displacement.** Sometimes secondary considerations such as winning an argument, making a point, or getting back at a rival displace the primary task of making a sound decision or solving a problem.

5. **"Groupthink."** Sometimes cohesive "in groups" let the desire for unanimity override sound judgment when generating and evaluating alternative courses of action. (Groupthink is discussed in Chapter 14.)

individuals tend to outperform the group, particularly when the task is complex and the group is made up of relatively low-ability people.[48]

Consequently, busy managers need to delegate aspects of the decision-making process (specified earlier) according to the contingencies in Figure 8.7. More is said about delegation in Chapter 10.

**Figure 8.7**

Individual Versus Group Performance: Contingency Management Insights from 61 Years of Research

| Nature of task | Insights from research |
|---|---|
| Problem-solving task | Individuals are faster, but groups tend to produce better results |
| Complex task | Best results achieved by polling the contributions of individuals working alone |
| Brainstorming task | Same as for complex task |
| Learning task | Groups consistently outperform individuals |
| Concept mastery/ creative task | Contributions from average-ability group members tend to improve when they are teamed with high-ability group members |

*Source:* Based in part on research conclusions found in Gayle W. Hill, "Group Versus Individual Performance: Are N + 1 Heads Better than One?" *Psychological Bulletin*, 91 (May 1982): 517–539.

# Managerial Creativity

Demands for creativity and innovation make the practice of management endlessly exciting (and often extremely difficult).[49] Nearly all managerial problem solving requires a healthy measure of creativity as managers mentally take things apart, rearrange the pieces in new and potentially productive configurations, and look beyond normal frameworks for new solutions. This process is like turning the kaleidoscope of one's mind. Thomas Edison used to retire to an old couch in his laboratory to do his creative thinking. Henry Ford reportedly sought creative insights by staring at a blank wall in his shop. Although the average manager's attempts at creativity may not be as dramatically fruitful as Edison's or Ford's, workplace creativity needs to be understood and nurtured.[50] As a steppingstone for the next section on creative problem solving, this section defines creativity, discusses the management of creative people, and identifies barriers to creativity.

## What Is Creativity?

Creativity is a rather mysterious process known chiefly by its results and is therefore difficult to define. About as close as we can come is to say that **creativity** is the reorganization of experience into new configurations.[51] According to a management consultant specializing in creativity:

> *Creativity is a function of knowledge, imagination, and evaluation. The greater our knowledge, the more ideas, patterns, or combinations we can achieve. But merely having the knowledge does not guarantee the formation of new patterns; the bits and pieces must be shaken up and interrelated in new ways. Then, the embryonic ideas must be evaluated and developed into usable ideas.*[52]

**creativity**  *the reorganization of experience into new configurations*

Creativity is often subtle and may not be readily apparent to the untrained eye. But the combination and extension of seemingly insignificant day-to-day breakthroughs lead to organizational progress.

Identifying general types of creativity is easier than explaining the basic process. One pioneering writer on the subject isolated three overlapping domains of creativity: art, discovery, and humor.[53] These have been called the "ah!" reaction, the "aha!" reaction, and the "haha!" reaction, respectively.[54]

The discovery ("aha!") variation is the most relevant to management. Entirely new businesses can spring from creative discovery. A prime example is Donald L. Beaver Jr.'s low-tech discovery that grew into a thriving multimillion-dollar business.[55] He found that nylon stockings stuffed with ground-up corncobs could soak up oil and grease spills faster than any known technique and at much less cost. Machine shops and gas stations, where slippery oil spills are a costly occupational hazard, clamored for Beaver's new product. Beaver's creativity did not stop there. It extended to the company's name: New PIG Corp. According to Beaver, PIG stands for "Partners in Grime." Creative ideas can spring from unexpected places and unlikely people.

## Workplace Creativity: Myth and Modern Reality

Recent research has shattered a long-standing myth about creative employees. According to the myth, creative people are typically nonconformists. But Alan Robinson's field research paints a very different picture:

*"We went to 450 companies in 13 countries and spoke to 600 people who'd done highly creative things, from big new innovations to tiny improvements," he explains. Only three out of the 600 were true nonconformists. The rest were more like your average corporate Joe, much more "plodding and cautious" than most managers would expect. Other creativity studies have had similar results, he says.*

*One reason for the mismatch between popular perception and reality, he believes, is that so many steps are needed to bring most new ideas to fruition. Those who succeed must be able to build support for the idea among other team members, and they sometimes need a lot of patience as well. Corporate nonconformists may not have a great deal of either.[56]*

Thus, creative self-expression through unconventional dress and strange behavior does not necessarily translate into creative work.

Today's managers are challenged to create an organizational culture and climate capable of surfacing the often hidden creative talents of *every* employee. In the Internet age, where intellectual capital is the number one resource, the emphasis is on having fun in high-energy work environments. For example, Theresa Garza, a vice president and general manager at Dell Computer, seeks to make the workplace "hum":

*Not the whirling white noise emanating from your computer, but the very tangible sense of fully engaged people, channeling unbounded energy into their work. "You know it as soon as you enter a building," says Garza, general manager of Dell's large corporate-accounts group. "You can tell when a company feels dead just by walking through its halls. We try to create the hum. It's people who have momentum, who are working hard, and who are excited to be here."*

*To get hum, Garza has flung herself onto Velcro walls and had fellow employees dunk her in a water tank—all in the name of generating enthusiasm and encouraging accessibility.[57]*

*Pixar Animation Studios, birthplace of the films* Toy Story, A Bug's Life, *and* Monsters Inc., *looks like just another old factory in Emeryville, California. A trip inside, however, reveals something akin to a carnival fun house, complete with animators zipping around on scooters. Hallways serve as an art gallery for employees' handiwork. Because the company encourages employees to decorate their offices as they please, the creative juices flow at Pixar. Here, Jason Topolski sits in his "natural habitat" office. Other offices feature a Hawaiian Tiki village and a disco. What else would you expect from the people who gave us talking bugs?*

## Learning to Be More Creative

Some people naturally seem to be more creative than others. But that does not mean that those who feel the need cannot develop their creative capacity. It does seem clear that creative ability can be learned, in the sense that our creative energies can be released from the bonds of convention, lack of self-confidence, and narrow thinking. We all have the potential to be more creative.

The best place to begin is by trying consciously to overcome what creativity specialist Roger von Oech calls *mental locks*. The following mental locks are attitudes that get us through our daily activities but tend to stifle our creativity:

1. *Looking for the "right" answer.* Depending on one's perspective, a given problem may have several right answers.
2. *Always trying to be logical.* Logic does not always prevail, given human emotions and organizational inconsistencies, ambiguity, and contradictions.
3. *Strictly following the rules.* If things are to be improved, arbitrary limits on thinking and behavior need to be questioned.
4. *Insisting on being practical.* Impractical answers to "what-if" questions can become steppingstones to creative insights.
5. *Avoiding ambiguity.* Creativity can be stunted by too much objectivity and specificity.
6. *Fearing and avoiding failure.* Fear of failure can paralyze us into not acting on our good ideas. This is unfortunate because we learn many valuable and lasting lessons from our mistakes.[58]
7. *Forgetting how to play.* The playful experimentation of childhood too often disappears by adulthood.
8. *Becoming too specialized.* Cross-fertilization of specialized areas helps in defining problems and generating solutions.
9. *Not wanting to look foolish.* Humor can release tensions and unlock creative energies. Seemingly foolish questions can enhance understanding.
10. *Saying "I'm not creative."* By nurturing small and apparently insignificant ideas we can convince ourselves that we are indeed creative.[59] (Try the creativity exercise in the Hands-On Exercise at the end of this chapter.)

If these mental locks are conquered, the creative problem-solving process discussed in the next section can be used to its full potential.

**6** Identify and briefly describe five of the ten "mental locks" that can inhibit creativity.

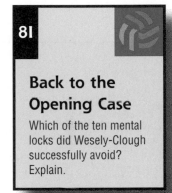

**81**

### Back to the Opening Case

Which of the ten mental locks did Wesely-Clough successfully avoid? Explain.

# Creative Problem Solving

We are all problem solvers. But this does not mean that all of us are good problem solvers or even, for that matter, that we know how to solve problems systematically. Most daily problem solving is done on a haphazard, intuitive basis. A difficulty arises, we look around for an answer, jump at the first workable solution to come along, and move on to other things. In a primitive sense, this sequence of events qualifies as a problem-solving process, and it works quite well for informal daily activities. But in the world of management, a more systematic problem-solving process is required for tackling difficult and unfamiliar nonprogrammed decision situations. In the context of

**7** List and explain the four basic steps in the creative problem-solving process.

**problem solving** *conscious process of closing the gap between actual and desired situations*

management, **problem solving** is the conscious process of bringing the actual situation closer to the desired situation.[60] Managerial problem solving consists of a four-step sequence: (1) identifying the problem, (2) generating alternative solutions, (3) selecting a solution, and (4) implementing and evaluating the solution (see Figure 8.8).

## Identifying the Problem

As strange as it may seem, the most common problem-solving difficulty lies in the identification of problems. Busy managers have a tendency to rush into generating and selecting alternative solutions before they have actually isolated and understood the real problem. According to Peter Drucker, a respected management scholar, "the most common source of mistakes in management decisions is emphasis on finding the right answers rather than the right questions."[61] As problem finders, managers should probe for the right questions.[62] Only then can the right answers be found.

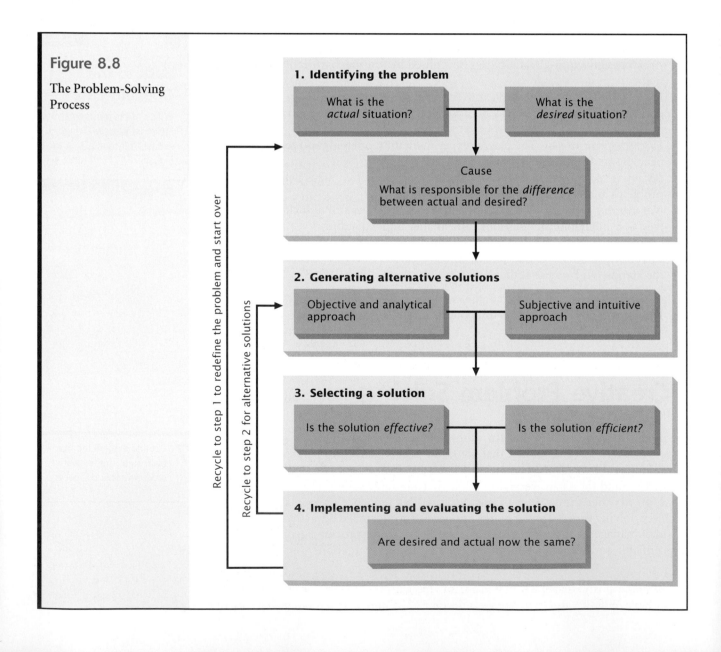

**Figure 8.8**

The Problem-Solving Process

Problem finding can be a great career booster, too, as Michael Iem discovered. It all started with his love of tough challenges.

*This bricklayer's son has no formal job title and no office, but his career at Tandem Computers is on a tear. He personifies the advice that executive recruiter Robert Horton offers all who want to advance: "Find the biggest business problem your employer faces for which you and your skills are the solution." . . . [Iem's problem-solving ability] made him known throughout Tandem, bringing promotions and a doubling of his $32,000 starting salary. . . . The company lets him decide what projects to take on, making him the youngest of perhaps a dozen employees with the broad mandate.*[63]

**What Is a Problem?**   Ask half a dozen people how they identify problems and you are likely to get as many answers. Consistent with the definition given earlier for problem solving, a **problem** is defined as the difference between an actual state of affairs and a desired state of affairs. In other words, a problem is the gap between where one is and where one wants to be. Problem solving is meant to close this gap. For example, a person in New York who has to make a presentation in San Francisco in 24 hours has a problem. The problem is not being in New York (the actual state of affairs), nor is it presenting in San Francisco in 24 hours (the desired state of affairs). Instead, the problem is the distance between New York and San Francisco. Flying would be an obvious solution. But, thanks to modern communications technology such as videoconferencing, there are ways to overcome the 2,934-mile gap without having to travel.

Managers need to define problems according to the gaps between the actual and the desired situations. A production manager, for example, would be wise to concentrate on the gap between the present level of weekly production and the desired level. This focus is much more fruitful than complaining about the current low production or wishfully thinking about high production. The challenge is discovering a workable alternative for closing the gap between actual and desired production.[64]

**problem**   *the difference between actual and desired states of affairs*

**Stumbling Blocks for Problem Finders.**   There are three common stumbling blocks for those attempting to identify problems:

1. *Defining the problem according to a possible solution.* One should be careful not to rule out alternative solutions in the way one states a problem. For example, a manager in a unit plagued by high absenteeism who says, "We have a problem with low pay," may prevent management from discovering that tedious and boring work is the real cause. By focusing on how to close the gap between actual and desired attendance, instead of simply on low pay, management stands a better chance of finding a workable solution.
2. *Focusing on narrow, low-priority areas.* Successful managers are those who can weed out relatively minor problems and reserve their attention for problems that really make a difference. Formal organizational goals and objectives provide a useful framework for determining the priority of various problems. Don't be concerned with waxing the floor when the roof is caving in.
3. *Diagnosing problems in terms of their symptoms.* As a short-run expedient, treating symptoms rather than underlying causes may be appropriate. Buying a bottle of aspirin is cheaper than trying to find a less stressful job, for example. In the longer run, however, symptoms tend to reappear and problems tend to get worse. There is a two-way test for discovering whether one has found the cause of a problem: "If I *introduce* this variable, will the problem (the gap) disappear?" or "If I *remove* this variable, will the problem (the gap) disappear?" **Causes** are variables that, because

**causes**   *variables responsible for the difference between actual and desired conditions*

of their presence in or absence from the situation, are primarily responsible for the difference between the actual and the desired conditions. For example, the *absence* of a key can cause a problem with a locked door, and the *presence* of a nail can cause a problem with an inflated tire.[65]

**8** Describe how causes of problems can be tracked down with fishbone diagrams.

**Pinpointing Causes with Fishbone Diagrams.**   Fishbone diagrams, discussed in Chapter 17 as a TQM process improvement tool, are a handy way to track down causes of problems. They work especially well in group problem-solving situations. Construction of a fishbone diagram begins with a statement of the problem (the head of the fish skeleton). "On the bones growing out of the spine one lists possible causes of . . . problems, in order of possible occurrence. The chart can help one see how various separate problem causes might interact. It also shows how possible causes occur with respect to one another, over time, helping start the problem-solving process."[66] (A sample fishbone diagram is illustrated in Skills & Tools at the end of this chapter.)

## Generating Alternative Solutions

After the problem and its most probable cause have been identified, attention turns to generating alternative solutions. This is the creative step in problem solving. Unfortunately, as the following statement points out, creativity is often shortchanged.

> *The natural response to a problem seems to be to try to get rid of it by finding an answer—often taking the first answer that occurs and pursuing it because of one's reluctance to spend the time and mental effort needed to conjure up a rich storehouse of alternatives from which to choose.*[67]

It takes time, patience, and practice to become a good generator of alternative solutions: a flexible combination of analysis and intuition is helpful. A good sense of humor can aid the process as well. Several popular and useful techniques can stimulate individual and group creativity. Among them are the following approaches:

- *Brainstorming*. This is a group technique in which any and all ideas are recorded, in a *nonjudgmental* setting, for later critique and selection.[68] Computerized brainstorming on computer network systems is proving worthwhile now that sophisticated groupware is available.[69]
- *Free association*. Analogies and symbols are used to foster unconventional thinking. For example, think of your studies as a mountain requiring special climbing gear and skills.
- *Edisonian*. Named for Thomas Edison's tedious and persistent search for a durable light bulb filament, this technique involves trial-and-error experimentation.

**8J   Something to Think About**

Joey Reiman, an Atlanta-based creativity consultant:

*Coming up with an idea requires investigation, incubation, illumination and illustration. We always forget about incubation. . . . Business is full of people who are crashing and burning because there is a tremendous pressure to constantly be producing. If you're just sitting at your desk thinking when someone asks what you are doing, what do you say? 'I was just thinking.' People devalue themselves by apologizing for thinking. . . .*

*Yet incubation is the most important step in the idea process. It's no surprise that great ideas come to us at unexpected times: when you go for a run, when you're in the shower. Those are some of the rare times in most people's busy days when their minds are free to explore. Great thinking is always simmering just below the surface.*

**Source:** As quoted in Echo Montgomery Garrett, "Joey Reiman, Idea Man," *Management Review*, 88 (October 1999): 64.

**Questions:** *When and where do you usually do most of your creative thinking? How could you do a better job of "incubating" creative ideas?*

- *Attribute listing.* Ideal characteristics of a given object are collected and then screened for useful insights.
- *Scientific method.* Systematic hypothesis testing, manipulation of variables, situational controls, and careful measurement are the essence of this rigorous approach.
- *Creative leap.* This technique involves thinking up idealistic solutions to a problem and then working back to a feasible solution.

## Selecting a Solution

Simply stating that the best solution should be selected in step 3 (refer to Figure 8.8) can be misleading. Because of time and financial constraints and political considerations, *best* is a relative term. Generally, alternative solutions should be screened for the most appealing balance of effectiveness and efficiency in view of relevant constraints and intangibles. Russell Ackoff, a specialist in managerial problem solving, contends that three things can be done about problems: they can be resolved, solved, or dissolved.[70]

**Resolving the Problem.**   When a problem is resolved, a course of action that is good enough to meet the minimum constraints is selected. The term **satisfice** has been applied to the practice of settling for solutions that are good enough rather than the best possible.[71] A badly worn spare tire may satisfice as a replacement for a flat tire for the balance of the trip, although getting the flat repaired is the best possible solution. According to Ackoff, most managers rely on problem resolving. This nonquantitative, subjective approach is popular because managers claim they do not have the necessary information or time for the other approaches. Satisficing, however, has been criticized as a shortsighted and passive technique emphasizing expedient survival instead of improvement and growth.

> **satisfice**  to settle for a solution that is good enough

**Solving the Problem.**   A problem is solved when the best possible solution is selected. Managers are said to **optimize** when through scientific observation and quantitative measurement they systematically research alternative solutions and select the one with the best combination of benefits.

> **optimize**  to systematically identify the solution with the best combination of benefits

**Dissolving the Problem.**   A problem is dissolved when the situation in which it occurs is changed, so that the problem no longer exists. Problem dissolvers are said to **idealize** because they actually change the nature of the system in which a problem resides. Managers who dissolve problems rely on whatever combination of nonquantitative and quantitative tools is needed to get the job done. The replacement of automobile assembly-line welders with robots, for instance, has dissolved the problem of costly absenteeism among people in that job category.

> **idealize**  to change the nature of a problem's situation

Whatever approach a manager chooses, the following advice from Ackoff should be kept in mind: "Few if any problems . . . are ever permanently resolved, solved, or dissolved; every treatment of a problem generates new problems."[72] A Japanese manager at the General Motors–Toyota joint venture auto plant in California put it this way: "No problem is a problem."[73] However, as pointed out by the cofounder of a successful import business, an administrative life made up of endless problems is cause for optimism, not pessimism: "Spare yourself some grief. Understand that, in business, you will always have problems. They are where the opportunities lie."[74] Hence the need for continuous improvement.

## Implementing and Evaluating the Solution

Time is the true test of any solution. Until a particular solution has had time to prove its worth, the manager can rely only on his or her judgment concerning its effectiveness and efficiency. Ideally, the solution selected will completely eliminate the difference between the actual and the desired in an efficient and timely manner. Should the gap fail to disappear, two options are open. If the manager remains convinced that the problem has been correctly identified, he or she can recycle to step 2 to try another solution that was identified earlier. This recycling can continue until all feasible solutions have been given a fair chance or until the nature of the problem changes to the extent that the existing solutions are obsolete. If the gap between actual and desired persists in spite of repeated attempts to find a solution, then it is advisable to recycle to step 1 to redefine the problem and engage in a new round of problem solving.

## Summary

**1.** Decision making is a fundamental part of management because it requires choosing among alternative courses of action. In addition to having to cope with an era of accelerating change, today's decision makers face the challenges of dealing with complexity, uncertainty, the need for flexible thinking, and decision traps. Seven factors contributing to decision complexity are multiple criteria, intangibles, risk and uncertainty, long-term implications, interdisciplinary input, pooled decision making, and value judgments.

**2.** Managers must learn to assess the degree of certainty in a situation—whether conditions are certain, risky, or uncertain. Confidence in one's decisions decreases as uncertainty increases. Managers can respond to a condition of risk—incomplete but reliable factual information—by calculating objective or subjective probabilities. Today's managers need to tap the creative potential of intuitive employees and the implementation skills of those who process information as thinkers.

**3.** Researchers have identified three perceptual and behavioral decision traps that can hamper the quality of decisions. Framing error occurs when people let labels and frames of reference sway their interpretations. People are victimized by escalation of commitment when they get locked into losing propositions for fear of quitting and looking bad. Oddly, researchers find overconfidence tends to grow with the difficulty of the task.

**4.** Decisions, generally, are either programmed or nonprogrammed. Because programmed decisions are relatively clear-cut and routinely encountered, fixed decision rules can be formulated for them. In contrast, nonprogrammed decisions require creative problem solving because they are novel and unfamiliar. Decision making can be improved with a knowledge management (KM) program. KM is a systematic approach to creating and sharing critical information throughout the organization. Two types of knowledge are *tacit* (personal, intuitive, and undocumented) and *explicit* (documented and sharable).

**5.** Managers may choose to bring other people into virtually every aspect of the decision-making process. However, when a group rather than an individual is responsible for making the decision, personal accountability is lost. Dispersed accountability is undesirable in some key decision situations. Group-aided decision making has both advantages and disadvantages. Because group performance does not always exceed individual performance, a contingency approach to group-aided decision making is advisable.

**6.** Creativity requires the proper combination of knowledge, imagination, and evaluation to reorganize experience into new configurations. The domains of creativity may be divided into art, discovery (the most relevant to management), and humor. Contrary to myth, researchers have found a weak link between creativity and nonconformity. A fun and energizing workplace climate can tap *every* employee's creativity. By consciously overcoming ten mental locks, we can become more creative.

**7.** The creative problem-solving process consists of four steps: (1) identifying the problem, (2) generating alternative solutions, (3) selecting a solution, and (4) implementing and evaluating the solution. Inadequate problem finding is common among busy managers. By seeing problems as gaps between an actual situation and a desired situation, managers are in a better position to create more effective and efficient solutions. Depending on the situation, problems can be resolved, solved, or dissolved. It is important to remember that today's solutions often become tomorrow's problems.

## Terms to Understand

Decision making (p. 246)

Law of unintended consequences (p. 249)

Condition of certainty (p. 251)

Condition of risk (p. 251)

Objective probabilities (p. 251)

Subjective probabilities (p. 251)

Condition of uncertainty (p. 251)

Framing error (p. 253)

Escalation of commitment (p. 254)

Programmed decisions (p. 256)

Decision rule (p. 256)

Nonprogrammed decisions (p. 256)

Knowledge management (p. 259)

Tacit knowledge (p. 259)

Explicit knowledge (p. 259)

Collaborative computing (p. 261)

Creativity (p. 265)

Problem solving (p. 268)

Problem (p. 269)

Causes (p. 269)

Satisfice (p. 271)

Optimize (p. 271)

Idealize (p. 271)

## Skills & Tools

### How to Construct a Fishbone Diagram

#### Tips

- Reduce complex web of problems to a distinct, high-priority problem.
- Create fishbones for main categories of causes.
- Chart most recent causes nearest the head (problem).
- Fill in specific causes.

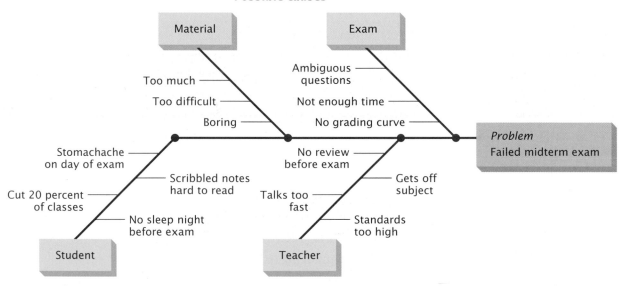

## Hands-On Exercise

### How Creative Are You?

**Instructions**

This exercise is for both individuals and teams. Assume that a steel pipe is embedded in the concrete floor of a bare room as shown below. The inside diameter is .06" larger than the diameter of a ping-pong ball (1.50") which is resting gently at the bottom of the pipe. You are one of a group of six people in the room, along with the following objects:

- 100′ of clothesline
- Carpenter's hammer
- Chisel
- Box of Wheaties
- File
- Wire coat hanger
- Monkey wrench
- Light bulb

List as many ways you can think of (in five minutes) to get the ball out of the pipe without damaging the ball, tube, or floor.

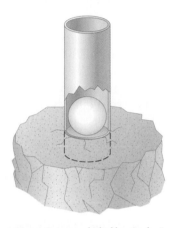
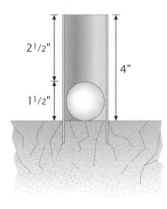

*Source:* From *Conceptual Blockbusting* by James L. Adams. © 1986 by James L. Adams. Reprinted by permission of Perseus Books Publishers, a member of Perseus Books, L.L.C.

**1.** In terms of the definition in this chapter, what is the "problem" here?

**2.** What assumptions did you make about any of the objects?

**3.** How would you rate your creativity on this exercise on a scale of
1 = low to 10 = high?

**4.** How many of the eight resource objects did you manage to employ? Which was the most useful? Why?

**5.** How many solutions did you develop? Which one is the "best"? Why?

**For Consideration/ Discussion**

# Internet Exercises

**1. Creativity in action:** 3M Company enjoys a worldwide reputation as an innovative company. Among its thousands of products are familiar items such as Scotch tape and Post-it notes as well as less familiar ones like surgical staplers and traffic signal lenses. According to the firm's cultural values, creativity generates new ideas and innovation turns those ideas into reality. The purpose of this exercise is to learn how 3M creates and exploits new ideas. 3M has prospered from new ideas in some interesting and unexpected ways.

Go to 3M's home page (**www.mmm.com**) and click on "About 3M." On the next two pages, select "Pioneers" and then "Innovation Chronicles." From the collection of 33 short stories about 3M innovators, find a product category that interests you and read the story. You may want to read three or four different stories to find a particularly interesting and/or instructive one. Three recommended stories are "Dick Drew and the invention of masking tape," "Art Fry and the invention of Post-it notes," and "How Harry Heltzer and his glass beads produced 3M's first reflective sheeting." As you read your selected stories, keep the following questions in mind.

*Learning Points:* 1. What was the creative idea that got things going? 2. What barriers or obstacles did the innovator encounter? How were they avoided or overcome? 3. Did the innovator get help from others? What sorts of help? 4. How did 3M foster a good climate for creativity and innovation? 5. How important was plain old persistence? Explain.

**2. Check it out:** Sometimes our creativity needs a boost and our inspiration needs a jump start. A good departure point is **www.queendom.com,** a richly stocked Web site created by and for women, but equally valuable to men. Get your creativity cranked up by selecting the section "Brain Tools" from the main menu. Among the fun and challenging mind-stretching exercises are lots of trivia quizzes, jigsaw puzzles, and puzzles. *Note:* This Internet resource also has a great selection of automatically scored self-assessment and personality tests under the main menu heading "Tests and Profiles. . . ."

For updates to these exercises, visit our Web site (**http://business.college.hmco.com/students**).

# Closing Case

## Honeywell's Ozone Busters

Torrance, Calif.—The engineers who created a device to remove ozone from aircraft cabin air describe it as being shaped like a genie's bottle. Then they talk about the wish that came true.

Their hope was to fix a troublesome ozone converter used on Boeing 777s that was wearing out less than a year into its expected three-year life span. They reengineered it into an industry leader.

Their efforts not only salvaged a $20 million enterprise; the new device has proved so effective, it's now used on other types of aircraft, creating another $10 million in business.

"Instead of just getting themselves in condition to win a race, they went out and won the Olympics," says

Jack ReVelle, one of the judges who chose Honeywell's Ozone Busters Team for the 2000 RIT/USA TODAY Quality Cup for manufacturing.

The challenge revolved around the design of a cylinder-shaped object called the ozone converter. The device converts the ozone-heavy outside air found at high altitudes into breathable air for the cabin.

When it was discovered that the units were being used up faster than expected in service, the team was created from engineers and experts at the aerospace environmental controls division headquarters here, at Boeing's commercial division in Everett, Wash., and Honeywell's technical center in Des Plaines, Ill.

First, they figured out how to clean the gunk off the used-up units and get them back into service faster. After trying 32 different methods, some as simple as dishwashing liquid, they struck on a formula that worked and cut turnaround time from a month to a week.

*Source:* Chris Woodyard, "Revamped Tool Helps Fliers Breathe Easier, *USA Today,* (May 5, 2000): 7B. Copyright 2000, *USA Today,* Reprinted with permission.

By recycling the units faster, the team had time to find a permanent solution. Jonathan Nunag, an engineer for United Airlines, arranged for a Boeing 777 to crisscross the skies over Oakland, Calif., for six hours to evaluate the problem. A pair of Honeywell senior project engineers, Todd Funston and Andy Hamelynck, put in up to 18 hours a day testing ozone converters.

"We probably learned more about ozone contamination than anyone else in the world," says Keith Wong, Honeywell's Boeing 777 ozone converter program manager.

All the time, Boeing was kept informed of the ongoing tests through Honeywell's Jon Edgar, who worked with Boeing contacts Kevin Gahagan, Mike Freese, Jean Ray, and Ed Silverman.

"They did an incredible job," says Boeing buyer Gahagan. "Honeywell has become the model for problem resolution at Boeing."

In the end, it turned out the converters were wearing out early because much of the contamination was coming from dirty air on the ground at airports and from other jets' exhaust.

The team beefed up the unit to allow it to eliminate more ozone. A pair of scientists, Peter Michalakos and Di Jia Lui, arranged to have test results turned around overnight at the Des Plaines facility to speed the process.

Now the unit is expected to last more than three years.

The team also improved testing methods so that only a few units from a batch need extensive testing rather than each one.

"We got more consistency," says Robert Koukol, a senior staff engineer.

As a result, Honeywell has been able to expand its market for the converters into certain models of Boeing 757s and 767s and some Fairchild Dornier regional jets.

The company succeeded in the face of tough odds. "This is one where most people have given up," says Jorge Alvarez, director of heat transfer technology.

## For Discussion

1. Was the team's temporary solution for cleaning the dirty ozone converters a case of problem resolving, solving, or dissolving? Explain.

2. How did the Ozone Busters apparently avoid the three common stumbling blocks for problem *finders?*

3. The team's problem-solving approach most closely resembled which of the six creativity techniques (discussed under the heading Generating Alternative Solutions)?

4. Would a fishbone diagram have proven useful for the Ozone Busters? Explain.

5. Which of the group-aided decision advantages in Table 8.1 likely played a role in this case? Explain.

6. What, if any, evidence of knowledge management can you detect in this case? Explain.

7. Everything considered, why is this a "textbook case" for on-the-job problem solving?

# Video Skill Builders

Since 1982, when Mary Guerrero-Pelzel became a general contractor in Austin, Texas, Pelzel Construction has faced lots of tough challenges. Heavy construction historically has been a male-dominated field, but Guerrero-Pelzel has thrived because her suppliers, subcontractors, and customers trust her to get the job done properly and on time. She earned that trust by carefully watching costs, keeping her employee teams motivated, and maintaining tight control.

## 2A Mary Guerrero-Pelzel, Contractor

### Learning Objectives
To learn more about the marriage of planning and control. To appreciate how a project manager needs to balance the little details and the big picture.

### Links to Textual Material
**Chapter 6:** Planning/control cycle; Project planning   **Chapter 7:** Porter's generic competitive strategies   **Chapter 8:** Decision complexity

### Discussion Questions

1. Using Figure 6.4 as a guide, how is the planning/control cycle demonstrated in this video case?

2. Relative to Figure 6.6, why is Guerrero-Pelzel an effective project manager?

3. Which of Porter's generic competitive strategies (see Figure 7.1) is Pelzel Construction using?

4. Which sources of decision complexity (see Figure 8.1) are evident in this video case? Explain your choices.

Cuddly teddy bears come in all sizes and shapes, especially at Build-A-Bear Workshops, where customers literally create their own stuffed animals. Founder and CEO Maxine Clark explains how she blended everything she ever learned about what customers want to create her do-it-yourself teddy bear factories. Build-A-Bear's happy customers seem to agree with Clark that people want a high-tech/high-touch experience and an opportunity for creative expression.

## 2B Build-A-Bear: Creativity in Action

### Learning Objective
To show how creativity often involves doing something extraordinary with ordinary things.

### Links to Textual Material
**Chapter 1:** Entrepreneurs   **Chapter 6:** Organizational responses to uncertainty   **Chapter 7:** Synergy; Porter's generic competitive strategies   **Chapter 8:** What is creativity?; Learning to be more creative

### Discussion Questions

1. What entrepreneurial traits (see Table 1.4) does Clark exemplify? Explain.

2. Using Table 6.1 as a guide, would you call Clark a defender, prospector, analyzer, or reactor? Explain.

3. What synergies can you detect in this video case? Explain.

4. Which of Porter's generic competitive strategies (see Figure 7.1) does Clark appear to be following? Explain.

5. How does Build-A-Bear exemplify the definition of creativity in Chapter 8? Explain.

6. Which of the ten "mental locks" on creativity in Chapter 8 did Clark apparently have to overcome to create Build-A-Bear? Explain.

# part three

# Organizing, Managing Human Resources, and Communicating

# chapter nine

# Organizations

## Structure, Effectiveness, and Cultures

**"** Equip people to make decisions by clearly defining the culture. **"**

Kevin and Jackie Freiberg

# A Country Called Microsoft

I spent several weeks trying to learn what it was like to work at Microsoft. I visited the company, and, at Microsoft's invitation, I spent time with the teams working on electronic books, or eBooks, and on the TabletPC, a flat pen-based computer that might be the Holy Grail of computer design and is a pet project of Bill Gates. I also spoke to researchers and programmers in other parts of the company, to so-called temporary workers, and to former employees as well. . . .

Over and over people there told me a story that I came to think of as the story of the secret garden: Once I was lost, they said; I did not fit in; then I found the key to the magical garden of Microsoft, where I had belonged in the first place.

"The reason I hated Florida," says Alex Loeb, general manager of the TabletPC group and a 12-year Microsoft employee, "was that I was seen as an upstart young woman who wasn't old enough or male enough to make decisions. Microsoft just took me as me." For a huge corporation, Microsoft is highly accepting of nonconformity, and there are a lot of people at Microsoft for whom being there is the key to being themselves. This is certainly true of the software tester I spoke with who comes to work every day dressed in extravagant Victorian outfits, and of the star programmer who keeps his given name a secret from colleagues and insists that he be called simply J. Microsoft's a tesseract; behind the door is a whole big world of similarly smart people, many of whom have made the decision that Being Microsoft trumps all. Says Bill Hill, a researcher who left Scotland six years ago to work at Microsoft: "Microsoft is a country. I moved here, and it is home to me."

Saying that Microsoft is a country might be going a little far, but only a little. It still lacks its own language, but it undoubtedly has its own mores and values, all of which stem from the conviction of its citizens that they are part of a new, very special secular elect. Behind the door to the secret garden is a place designed to constantly reinforce the belief in its employees—in a way in which few corporations bother to anymore—that they are different. Almost all of Microsoft's employees have their own office, and the company can feel hushed in the way

that one imagines the dusty hallways of the State Department must be hushed—only more so, because in this e-mail culture, the phones never ring. The public atriums are hung with contemporary paintings—not overly soothing "corporate" art or inspirational art, but real art that gets loaned to real museums. It is also, surprisingly, a place with a collegial (or, better, collegiate) sense of fun. When people go off on vacation, their colleagues take the trouble to welcome them back by filling their office with Styrofoam peanuts, covering it with spider webs, or even (as in one fairly recent Microsoft escapade) converting it into a miniature farm complete with potbellied pig.

All this emphasizes the distinction of working at Microsoft as opposed to working at either stodgy old-economy companies or the new-economy riffraff that happily pack their workers into "open offices," where they brush elbows as if at a crowded formal dinner. And yet strangely none of this veneer is central. It's just the icing on the cake of what anybody who spends much time at Microsoft, or talking in depth to people who work there, will recognize as the Microsoft way of thinking. . . .

"Bill" is famous for telling people that whatever they just told him is the stupidest thing he ever heard. This is pretty much the opposite of how the rest of Microsoft actually works. Microsoft managers do occasionally tell stories of pounding a table to get their way, but the intent of the tale is cautionary. More often—actually, incessantly—they talk of getting "buy-in," Microsoft slang for the cooperation of their colleagues. They argue and cajole. They publish white papers. They use sneaky tricks; when the eBooks team was getting started, the new managers set up a Website on the company intranet describing the project. By secretly tracking the e-mail addresses of visitors they compiled a list of Microsofters they could recruit. In these ways they do get buy-in, because if they don't, their projects just fall flat. . . .

It turns out that the more you talk to people at Microsoft, the more you find that these people who seem so spectacularly different on the surface all share a distinct ethos that transcends stock options or hours spent on their office couches or practical jokes. . . . And, yup, this ethos is even more important to Microsoft than the average IQ of its employees. It embodies a few very big concepts about work and life. It's this set of values that is the key to understanding life in the innermost sanctum of the Information Age. And it's the evolution of these values that will define what Microsoft will become in the future.

The cornerstone of the Microsoft ethos is the unwavering belief in *the moral value of zapping bugs and shipping products.* Like other Brahmin societies, Microsoft (certainly *the* Brahmin society of the Information Age) puts a premium on doing things that are hard, and doing them the hard way; this makes one a better person and justifies one's place in the privileged class. The American upper class used to send its youth on freezing swims and mountaineering expeditions to build moral character. At Microsoft, moral fiber is believed to grow out of interminable discussion of the smallest details of software features, painful rounds of compromise, and unbelievably tedious sessions of categorizing hundreds of software bugs. Going through this process strengthens the intellect, hones the passions, and fortifies character.

The primary currency of prestige at Microsoft is the SHIP-IT plaque, given to every member of a team that has successfully shipped a product to the market. Outsiders who notice this—and virtually everyone does, in part because Microsoft's PR machinery points it out—generally use it as evidence of Microsoftian drive, resolve, go-getterhood, and all that good stuff.

That's true, but there's more to it than that. The reality of software development in a huge corporation like Microsoft is that a substantial portion of the work involves days of boredom punctuated by hours of tedium. For instance, anybody who observes a "triage" session, in which developers and testers (the lowest rung in the Microsoft hierarchy) convene to enumerate and evaluate hundreds of bugs and potential bugs, quickly sees that the level of gut-wrenching excitement falls as the lines of code rise. In the powerhouse applications group, whole teams are charged with missions like getting Microsoft Word to start three seconds faster. This is not the heady air of pure, research-driven science. Says Jim Gray, a Microsoft engineer who spent time at the University of California, Berkeley, "The attitude at Berkeley is primarily focused on creating ideas. Microsoft has some of that, but it's much more focused on the 99% perspiration."

That 99% perspiration isn't intuitively appealing, but in the world-view of the Microsoft Brahmin, perspiration is the vehicle of moral uplift. Even Bert Keely, the prime technical visionary behind the TabletPC, sitting in an office filled with ebony cubes engraved with the titles of patents he's applied for at Microsoft, pooh-poohs the significance of the creative spark that other organizations value so highly. "Creativity is highly regarded for a very short time, but that's not how people rank each other," says Keely. "The primary thing is to ship a product. Before you've done it, you're suspect. It involves taking this passion of yours and running it through a humiliating, exhausting process. You can't believe how many ego-deflating compromises people have to make to get it out. Some have quit. Others have made lifelong enemies." We can safely assume that the ones who quit are, in the Microsoft cosmology, *losers.*

---

**O**rganizations are an ever-present feature of modern society. We look to organizations for food, clothing, education, employment, entertainment, health care, transportation, and protection of our basic rights. Nearly every aspect of modern life is influenced in one way or another by organizations. As the relentless push for growth and improvement by Microsoft's 40,000+ employees demonstrates, the management of modern organizations requires bold and imaginative action.

In Chapter 1 we said the purpose of the management process is to achieve *organizational* objectives in an effective and efficient manner. Organizations are social entities enabling people to work together to achieve objectives they normally could not achieve alone. This chapter explores the organizational context in which managers operate. It serves as an introduction, laying the foundation for the discussion of organization design alternatives in Chapter 10. Specifically, this chapter defines the term *organization* and discusses different types of organizations and organization charts. It contrasts traditional and modern (open-system) views in the evolution of organization theory and explores the concept of learning organizations. The chapter also examines organizational effectiveness as a backdrop for a discussion of organizational decline. Finally, it looks at organizational cultures.

# What Is an Organization?

An **organization** is defined as a cooperative social system involving the coordinated efforts of two or more people pursuing a shared purpose.[1] In other words, when people gather and formally agree to combine their efforts for a common purpose, an organization is the result.

There are exceptions, of course, as when two individuals team up to push a car out of a ditch. This task is a one-time effort based on temporary expediency. But if the same two people decide to pool their resources to create a towing service, an organization would be created. The "coordinated efforts" portion of our definition, which implies a degree of formal planning and division of labor, is present in the second instance but not in the first.

**organization** *cooperative and coordinated social system of two or more people with a common purpose*

## Common Characteristics of Organizations

According to Edgar Schein, a prominent organizational psychologist, all organizations share four characteristics: (1) coordination of effort, (2) common goal or purpose, (3) division of labor, and (4) hierarchy of authority.[2]

**1** Identify and describe four characteristics common to all organizations.

**Coordination of Effort.**   As discussed in the last chapter, two heads are sometimes better than one. Individuals who join together and coordinate their mental and/or physical efforts can accomplish great and exciting things. Building the great pyramids, conquering polio, sending manned flights to the moon—all these achievements far exceeded the talents and abilities of any single individual. Coordination of effort multiplies individual contributions.

**Common Goal or Purpose.**   Coordination of effort cannot take place unless those who have joined together agree to strive for something of mutual interest. A common goal or purpose gives the organization focus and its members a rallying point.

**Division of Labor.**   By systematically dividing complex tasks into specialized jobs, an organization can use its human resources efficiently. Division of labor permits each organization member to become more proficient by repeatedly doing the same specialized task. (But, as is discussed in Chapter 13, overspecialized jobs can cause boredom and alienation.)

The advantages of dividing labor have been known for a long time. One of its early proponents was the pioneering economist Adam Smith. While touring an eighteenth-century pin-manufacturing plant, Smith observed that a group of specialized laborers could produce 48,000 pins a day. This was an astounding figure, considering that each laborer could produce only 20 pins a day when working alone.[3]

**Hierarchy of Authority.**   According to traditional organization theory, if anything is to be accomplished through formal collective effort, someone should be given the authority to see that the intended goals are carried out effectively and efficiently. Organization theorists have defined **authority** as the right to direct the actions of others. Without a clear hierarchy of authority, coordination of effort is difficult, if not impossible, to achieve. Accountability is also enhanced by having people serve in what is often called, in military language, the *chain of command*. For instance, a grocery store manager has authority over the assistant manager, who has authority over the produce

**authority** *right to direct the actions of others*

*One characteristic of all organizations is division of labor. People with specialized skills contribute toward a common goal or purpose. For example, anthropologist Ellen Brown worked with local inhabitants in Chad on behalf of her employer, Exxon Mobil. During a recent drilling project in the Central African country, Brown put her knowledge of the local culture to work to achieve cross-cultural understanding. She became known as Madame Sacrifice because occasionally she had to spend the company's money on ritual chicken sacrifices. Her expense reports must have been interesting reading.*

## 9A    Avoiding Authority Disease

Donald G. Smith, retired manager:

*One of the most difficult things that a new boss must do is to back off and leave things alone. For people who are actively engaged in climbing the corporate ladder, it means they must do battle with their own ambition. I have seen such people make the most superficial of unnecessary changes: rearranging the furniture, making lateral personnel switches. Employees recognize these silly charades for what they are, namely futile exercises in demonstrating authority.*

**Source:**  Donald G. Smith, "Fighting the Ego Monster," *Training*, 36 (February 1999): 84.

**Questions:**  *Why do new managers often get carried away with their authority? What sort of response do authoritarian managers generally get in today's workplaces? Explain. How do effective managers handle their authority?*

For further information about the interactive annotations in this chapter, visit our Web site (http://business.college.hmco.com/students).

department head, who in turn has authority over the employees in the produce department. Without such a chain of command, the store manager would have the impossible task of directly overseeing the work of every employee in the store.

The idea of hierarchy has many critics, particularly among those who advocate flatter organizations with fewer levels of management.[4] An organization theorist answered those critics as follows:

*At first glance, hierarchy may seem difficult to praise. Bureaucracy is a dirty word even among bureaucrats, and in business there is a widespread view that managerial hierarchy kills initiative, crushes creativity, and has therefore seen its day. Yet 35 years of research have convinced me that managerial hierarchy is the most efficient, the hardiest, and in fact the most natural structure ever devised for large organizations. Properly structured, hierarchy can release energy and creativity, rationalize productivity, and actually improve morale.*[5]

**Putting All the Pieces Together.**    All four of the foregoing characteristics are necessary before an organization can be said to exist. Many well-intentioned attempts to create organizations have failed because something was missing. In 1896, for example, Frederick Strauss, a boyhood friend of Henry Ford, helped Ford set up a machine shop, supposedly to produce gasoline-powered engines. But while Strauss was busy carrying out his end of the bargain by machining needed parts, Ford was secretly building a horse-less carriage in a workshop behind his house.[6] Although Henry Ford eventually went on to become an automobile-industry giant, his first attempt at organization failed because not all of the pieces of an organization were in place. Ford's and his partner's efforts were not coordinated, they worked at cross-purposes, their labor was vaguely divided, and they had no hierarchy of authority. In short, they had organizational intentions, but no organization.

## Classifying Organizations

Because organizations are created to pursue particular purposes, they can be classified accordingly. The classification by organizational purpose discussed here has four categories: business, nonprofit service, mutual-benefit, and commonweal organizations.[7] Some of today's large and complex organizations overlap categories. For example, religious organizations are both nonprofit service organizations and mutual-benefit organizations. Nevertheless, classifying organizations by their purpose helps clarify the variety of roles they play in society and the similar problems shared by organizations with similar purposes (see Table 9.1).

**Business Organizations.**   Business organizations such as General Mills, Southwest Airlines, and the Washington Post all have one underlying purpose: to make a profit in a socially acceptable manner. Businesses cannot survive, let alone grow, without earning a profit, and profits are earned by efficiently satisfying demand for products and services. This economic production function is so important to society that many think immediately of business when the word *management* is mentioned.

**Table 9.1**   Classifying Organizations by Their Intended Purpose

| Purpose | Primary beneficiary | Common examples | Overriding management problem |
|---|---|---|---|
| **Business** | Owners | Computer manufacturers<br>Newspapers<br>Railroads<br>Fast-food restaurant chains | Must make a profit |
| **Nonprofit service** | Clients | Universities<br>Welfare agencies<br>Hospitals (nonprofit) | Must selectively screen large numbers of potential clients |
| **Mutual-benefit** | Members | Unions<br>Clubs<br>Political parties<br>Trade associations<br>Cooperatives | Must satisfy members' needs |
| **Commonweal** | Public at large | U.S. Postal Service<br>Police departments<br>Fire departments<br>Public schools | Must provide standardized services to large groups of people with diverse needs |

*Habitat for Humanity International is a nonprofit service organization run in businesslike fashion. Founded by successful businessman Millard Fuller over a quarter-century ago, Habitat's mission is to combine donated resources and volunteer labor (as pictured here) to build decent, affordable houses. In the true spirit of sweat equity, future owners must donate hundreds of hours, alongside volunteers from the community, helping to build both their own and others' homes. They also must meet strict selection criteria, such as being employed. Habitat for Humanity volunteers are improving the world one nail at a time (to find out how you can help, go to* **www.habitat.org***).*

### Nonprofit Service Organizations.

Unlike businesses, many organizations survive and even grow, without making any profits at all. They need to be solvent, of course, but they measure their success not in dollars and cents but by how well they provide a specific service for some segment of society. The American Heart Association, Notre Dame University, and Massachusetts General Hospital are examples of nonprofit service organizations. Because the services of such organizations are usually in great demand, one of their biggest problems lies in screening large numbers of applicants to determine who qualifies for service. Another problem for most nonprofit service organizations is securing a reliable stream of funds through fees, donations, grants, or appropriations. Given today's limited resources, both private-sector and public-sector nonprofit service organizations are under pressure to operate more efficiently.[8]

### Mutual-Benefit Organizations.

Often, as in the case of labor unions or political parties, individuals join together strictly to pursue their own self-interests. In other cases—the National Association of Manufacturers, for example—organizations may feel compelled to join together in an umbrella organization. Mutual-benefit organizations, like all other types of organizations, need to be effectively and efficiently managed if they are to survive. In this instance, survival depends on satisfying members' needs.

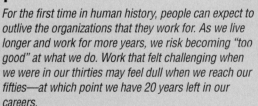

## 9B  Peter Drucker Sees a Nonprofit in Your Future

*For the first time in human history, people can expect to outlive the organizations that they work for. As we live longer and work for more years, we risk becoming "too good" at what we do. Work that felt challenging when we were in our thirties may feel dull when we reach our fifties—at which point we have 20 years left in our careers.*

*So we need new ways to manage the "second half" of our work lives. That might mean retraining yourself for a different kind of job. It might mean developing a "parallel career"—for example, working in a nonprofit organization that interests you while cutting back on your regular job. It might mean doing the same kind of work that you've done, but in a different setting.*

**Source:** "Peter Drucker," *Fast Company*, no. 27 (September 1999): 112.

**Questions:** *What particular nonprofit organization would likely offer you new challenge and meaning later in your career? Explain. Does Drucker's concept of a parallel career appeal to you? Explain.*

**Commonweal Organizations.**   Like nonprofit service organizations, commonweal organizations offer public services without attempting to earn a profit. But unlike nonprofit service organizations, which serve some *segment* of society, a **commonweal organization** offers standardized service to *all* members of a given population. The Canadian Army, for example, protects everyone within Canada's borders, not just a select few. The same can be said for local police and fire departments. Commonweal organizations are generally large, and their great size makes them unwieldy and difficult to manage. The U.S. federal government, for example, has 2.7 million civilian employees.[9] Competing demands from a diverse array of clients also complicate matters. Members of the New York City Fire Department, for example, stand ready to do everything from fighting fires to administering emergency medical treatment to disaster assistance to rescuing pets.[10]

> **commonweal organization**
> *nonprofit organization serving all members of a given population*

# Organization Charts

An **organization chart** is a diagram of an organization's official positions and formal lines of authority. In effect, an organization chart is a visual display of an organization's structural skeleton. With their familiar pattern of boxes and connecting lines, these charts (called tables by some) are a useful management tool because they are an organizational blueprint for deploying human resources.[11] Organization charts are common in both profit and nonprofit organizations.

> **organization chart**   *visual display of organization's positions and lines of authority*

## Vertical and Horizontal Dimensions

Every organization chart has two dimensions, one representing *vertical hierarchy* and one representing *horizontal specialization*. Vertical hierarchy establishes the chain of command, or who reports to whom. Horizontal specialization establishes the division of labor. A short case tracing the growth of a new organization helps demonstrate the relationship between vertical hierarchy and horizontal specialization.

> **2**   Identify and explain the two basic dimensions of organization charts.

## A Case Study: The Growth of an Organization

For years, George Thomas was an avid trout fisherman.[12] The sight of George loading up his old camper with expensive fly-casting gear and heading out to the nearest trout stream was familiar to his family and neighbors. About six years ago, George tried his hand at the difficult task of tying his own trout flies. Being a creative individual and a bit of a handyman, George soon created a fly that trout seemingly fought over to bite. Word spread rapidly among local and regional fishing enthusiasts. Eventually, George was swamped with orders for his newly patented Super Flies at $3.50 each. What had started out as a casual hobby turned into a potentially lucrative business bringing in roughly $500 per week. George no longer found any time to fish; all his time was taken up tying and selling Super Flies. An organization chart at that point would have looked like the one in Figure 9.1A. George was the entire operation, and technically, an organization did not yet exist. There was no vertical hierarchy or horizontal specialization at that early stage.

George soon found it impossible to tie more than a couple hundred flies a week and still visit fishing-tackle retailers who might carry his Super Flies. To free up some time, George hired and trained a family friend named Amy to help him run the operation in

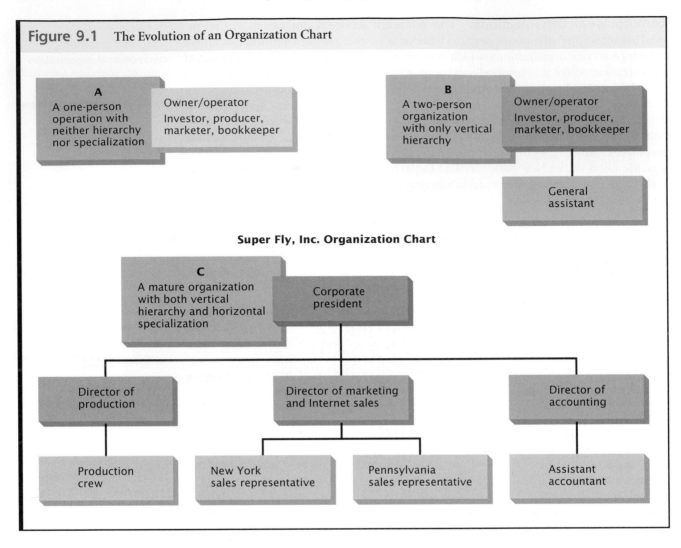

**Figure 9.1**    The Evolution of an Organization Chart

a small building he had leased. An organization chart could have been drawn up at that time because an organization came into existence when Amy was hired. (Remember that it takes at least two people to make an organization.) The chart would have resembled the one in Figure 9.1B. Vertical hierarchy had been introduced since Amy was George's subordinate. However, there still was no horizontal specialization because Amy did many different things.

As business picked up, George had to hire and train four full-time employees to work under Amy tying flies. He also hired Fred, a computer salesman and an old fishing buddy, to head the marketing operation, recruit and train two regional sales representatives, and create a Web site. Shortly afterward, an accountant was brought into the organization to set up and keep the books. Today, Super Fly, Inc., is recording annual sales in excess of $2.5 million. George has finally gotten around to formally organizing the company he built in patchwork fashion through the years. His current organization chart is displayed in Figure 9.1C.

Notice that the company now has three layers in the vertical hierarchy and three distinct forms of horizontal specialization. The three specialized directors now do separately what George used to do all by himself. George's job of general management will become progressively more difficult as additional vertical layers and horizontal specialists are added. Coordination is essential; the "right hand" must operate in concert with the "left hand." *Generally, specialization is achieved at the expense of coordination when designing organizations.* A workable balance between specialization and coordination can be achieved through contingency design, as discussed in the next chapter.

# Contrasting Theories of Organization

The study of organization theory is largely a twentieth-century development. As one organization theorist philosophically observed, "The study of organizations has a history but not a pedigree."[13] This history is marked by disagreement rather than uniformity of thinking. A useful way of approaching the study of organization theory is to contrast the traditional view with a modern view, two very different ways of thinking about organizations.

    In the traditional view, the organization is characterized by closed-system thinking. This view assumes the surrounding environment is fairly predictable and uncertainty within the organization can be eliminated through detailed planning and strict control. An organization's primary goal is seen to be economic efficiency. In contrast, a prevailing modern view characterizes the organization as an open system interacting continuously with an uncertain environment. Both the organization and its surrounding environment are assumed to be filled with variables that are difficult to predict or control. As the open-system theorists see it, the organization's principal goal is survival in an environment of uncertainty and surprise. These contrasting approaches are summarized in Table 9.2.

**3**   Contrast the traditional and modern views of organizations.

**Table 9.2**   Contrasting Theories of Organization

|  | **Traditional view** | **Modern view** |
|---|---|---|
| **General perspective** | Closed-system thinking | Open-system thinking |
| **Primary goal of organization** | Economic efficiency | Survival in an environment of uncertainty and surprise |
| **Assumption about surrounding environment** | Predictable | Generally uncertain |
| **Assumptions about organizations** | All causal, goal-directed variables are known and controllable. Uncertainty can be eliminated through planning and controlling. | The organizational system has more variables than can be comprehended at one time. Variables often are subject to influences that cannot be controlled or predicted. |

*Source:* Adapted, by permission, from James D. Thompson, *Organizations in Action* (New York: McGraw-Hill, 1967), pp. 4–7.

# The Traditional View

Let us explore the evolution of traditional organization theory by first reviewing the contributions of the early management writers and Max Weber's concept of bureaucracy. Then a look at challenges to these traditional models will prepare the way for our examination of the modern open-system model of organizations.

**The Early Management Writers.**    Early contributors to management literature, such as Henri Fayol and Frederick W. Taylor, treated organizing as a subfield of management. You will recall from Chapter 1 that organizing was among Fayol's five universal functions of management. Taylor's narrow task definitions and strict work rules implied a tightly structured approach to organization design.

In general, Fayol and the other pioneering management writers who followed in his footsteps endorsed closely controlled authoritarian organizations. For instance, managers were advised to have no more than six immediate subordinates. Close supervision and obedience were the order of the day. Emphasis in these organizations was on the unrestricted downward flow of authority in the form of orders and rules. Four traditional principles of organization that emerged were (1) a well-defined hierarchy of authority, (2) unity of command,[14] (3) authority equal to responsibility, and (4) downward delegation of authority but not of responsibility (see Table 9.3).

**Max Weber's Bureaucracy.**    Writing more than a hundred years ago, a German sociologist named Max Weber described what he considered to be the most rationally efficient form of organization, to which he affixed the label **bureaucracy.** According to Weber's model, bureaucracies are efficient because of the following characteristics: (1) division of labor, (2) hierarchy of authority, (3) a framework of rules, and (4) impersonality.[15] By *impersonality,* Weber meant hiring and promoting people on the basis of *what* they know, not *who* they know. It is important to realize that Weber's ideas about organizations were shaped by prevailing circumstances. In the late 1800s, Germany was a semifeudal state struggling to adjust to the pressures of the Industrial Revolution. Weber was appalled at the way public administrators relied on subjective

**bureaucracy**   *Weber's model of a rationally efficient organization*

---

**Table 9.3**   Traditional Principles of Organization

1. **A well-defined hierarchy of authority.** This principle was intended to ensure the coordinated pursuit of organizational goals by contributing individuals.

2. **Unity of command.** It was believed that the possibility of conflicting orders, a serious threat to the smooth flow of authority, could be avoided by making sure that each individual answered to only one superior.

3. **Authority equal to responsibility.** *Authority* was defined as the right to get subordinates to accomplish something. *Responsibility* was defined as the obligation to accomplish something. The traditionalists cautioned against holding individuals ultimately accountable for getting something done unless they were given formal authority to get it done.

4. **Downward delegation of authority but not of responsibility.** Although a superior with the requisite authority and responsibility can pass along the *right* to get something accomplished to subordinates, the *obligation* for getting it done remains with the superior. This arrangement was intended to eliminate the practice of "passing the buck."

judgment, emotion, fear tactics, and nepotism (the hiring and promotion of one's relatives) rather than on sound management practices.[16] He used the widely respected and highly efficient Prussian army as the model for his bureaucratic form of organization.

In theory, Weber's bureaucracy was supposedly the epitome of efficiency. But experience with bureaucracies has shown that they can be slow, insensitive to individual needs, and grossly inefficient.[17] Today, the term *bureaucracy* has a strongly negative connotation. According to Jack Welch, the recently retired head of General Electric: "Bureaucracy frustrates people, distorts their priorities, limits their dreams and turns the face of the enterprise inward."[18] This bureaucratic paradox can be reconciled somewhat by viewing bureaucracy as a matter of degree.

Every systematically managed organization, regardless of its size or purpose, is to some extent a bureaucracy. Bureaucratic characteristics are simply more pronounced or advanced in some organizations than in others.[19] Trying to eliminate bureaucracy is impractical. The real challenge is keeping bureaucratic characteristics within functional limits. As Table 9.4 indicates, a moderate degree of bureaucratization can enhance organizational

## 9C  Unruly Rules

Fire Chief Alan Brunacini, Phoenix, Arizona:

*"When I got here, all our rules were the size of a bushel," he says. "Now they're on one sheet of paper. How many rules do you need? It only takes 10 to get into heaven."*

**Source:** As quoted in Jon Talton, "What in Blazes Has the Chief Done? Create a Model for Managers," *The Arizona Republic* (January 27, 2002): D1.

**Questions:** *Do today's organizations have too many rules? Explain. Which rules should stay and which should go?*

**Table 9.4**   Functional Versus Dysfunctional Bureaucracy: A Matter of Degree

| | Indications of functional bureaucracy | Symptoms of dysfunctional bureaucracy |
|---|---|---|
| **Degree of bureaucratization** | Moderate | High |
| **Division of labor** | More work, of higher quality, can be completed faster because complex tasks are separated into more readily mastered jobs. | Grievances, absenteeism, and turnover increase as a result of overly fragmented jobs that people find boring and dehumanizing. Poor-quality performance leads to customer complaints. |
| **Hierarchy of authority** | A generally accepted chain of command serves to direct individuals' efforts toward organizational goal accomplishment. | Due to a fear of termination, a climate of blind obedience to authority, whether right or wrong, exists. |
| **Framework of rules** | Individual contributions to the collective effort are directed and coordinated by rules that answer important procedural questions. | Pursuit of the organization's mission is displaced by the practice of formulating and enforcing self-serving rules that protect, create unnecessary work, hide, or disperse accountability. |
| **Impersonality** | Hiring, promotion, and other personnel decisions are made on the basis of objective merit rather than favoritism or prejudice. | Employees and clients complain about being treated like numbers by bureaucrats who fail to respond to the full range of human needs. |

efficiency, but, taken too far, each dimension of bureaucracy can hinder efficiency. Managers who learn to read and retreat from the symptoms of dysfunction can reap the benefits of functional bureaucracy.[20]

## Challenges to the Traditional View of Organizations

Because the traditionalists' rigid recommendations for organizing and managing did not work in all situations, their recommendations were eventually challenged. Prescriptions for machinelike efficiency that worked in military units and simple shop operations often failed to work in complex organizations. Fayol's universal functions and principles turned out to be no guarantee of success. Similarly, experience proved that organizing was more than just the strict obedience to authority that Taylor had emphasized. In spite of Weber's rationally efficient organizational formula, bureaucracy in practice often became the epitome of inefficiency. In addition, challenges to traditional thinking about organizations arose from two other sources.

**Bottom-Up Authority.**    Traditionalists left no doubt about the origin of authority in their organizational models. Authority was inextricably tied to property ownership and therefore naturally flowed from the top of the organization to the bottom. In businesses, those farthest removed from the ownership of stock were entitled to the least amount of authority. Naturally, this notion appealed strongly to those interested in maintaining the power base of society's more fortunate members. But when Chester I. Barnard described organizations as cooperative systems, he questioned the traditional assumption about the automatic downward flow of authority. Instead, he proposed a more democratic **acceptance theory of authority.** According to Barnard's acceptance theory, a leader's authority is determined by his or her subordinates' willingness to comply with it. Barnard believed that a subordinate recognizes a communication from above as being authoritative and decides to comply with it only when all of the following conditions apply:

**acceptance theory of authority**  *Barnard's theory that authority is determined by subordinates' willingness to comply*

1. The message is understood.
2. The subordinate believes it is consistent with the organization's purpose.
3. It serves the subordinate's interest.
4. The subordinate is able to comply.[21]

Barnard's acceptance theory opened the door for a whole host of ideas, such as upward communication and the informal organization that is based on friendship rather than work rules. Prior to Barnard's contribution, such concepts had been discussed only by human relationists. In effect, Barnard humanized organization theory by characterizing workers as active controllers of authority, not mere passive recipients. Interestingly, Barnard's empowerment theme has resulted in a distaste for the term *subordinate*, regarded by many today as a demeaning label.

**Environmental Complexity and Uncertainty.**    Although traditionalists liked to believe that rigid structure and rational management were important to organizational effectiveness and efficiency, environmental complexity and uncertainty often intervened to upset them. As Charles Perrow observed in writing about the history of organization theory, "The increasing complexity of markets, variability of products, increasing number of branch plants, and changes in technology all required more adaptive organizations."[22] Plans usually have to be made on the basis of incomplete or imperfect information and, consequently, things do not always work out according to plan. Similarly, many of the traditional principles of organization, such as the number of people a manager can effectively manage, have proved to be naive.

The net result of these and other challenges to traditional thinking was a desire to look at organizations in some new ways. When open-system thinking appeared on the management horizon, as discussed in Chapter 2, many eagerly embraced it because it emphasized the need for flexibility and adaptability in organization structure.

## Organizations as Open Systems: A Modern View

Open-system thinking fosters a more realistic view of the interaction between an organization and its environment.[23] Traditional closed-system perspectives—such as Fayol's universal process approach, scientific management, and bureaucracy—largely ignored environmental influences. Today's managers cannot afford that luxury. Intense competition in a fast-changing world prompted Andy Grove, chairman of Intel Corp., to offer this view: "A corporation is a living organism, and it has to continue to shed its skin."[24]

Organizations are systems made up of interacting subsystems. Organizations are themselves subsystems that interact with larger social, political-legal, and economic systems. Those who take an open-system perspective realize that system-to-system interactions are often as important as the systems themselves. Among these interactions are movements of people in and out of the labor force (for example, unemployment), movements of capital (for example, stock exchanges and corporate borrowing), and movements of goods and services (for example, international trade). A highly organized and vigorously interactive world needs realistically dynamic models. In this area, particularly, open-system thinking can make a contribution to organization theory.

**Some Open-System Characteristics.**   According to general systems theory, all open systems—whether the human body, an organization, a society, or the solar system—share certain characteristics. At the same time, the theory recognizes significant differences among the various kinds of open systems. Four characteristics that emphasize the adaptive and dynamic nature of all open systems are (1) interaction with the environment, (2) synergy, (3) dynamic equilibrium, and (4) equifinality.

*According to the open-system concept of equifinality, there is more than one way to get the job done. Dramatic evidence of equifinality was spotted by race fans in 1989 at the Golden Gate Fields track in Albany, California. As Nate Hubbard, a 19-year-old apprentice jockey, guided Sweetwater Oak into the final stretch, the filly stumbled on the muddy track and Hubbard lurched out of the saddle, holding on to the horse's mane. Hubbard finished second. Officials declared it a legal ride because the jockey remained aboard the horse.*

- *Interaction with the environment.* Open systems have permeable boundaries, whereas closed systems do not. Open systems, like the human body, are not self-sufficient. Life-sustaining oxygen, nutrients, and water must be imported from the surrounding environment, and waste must be exported. Similarly, organizations depend on the environment for survival.

- *Synergy.* As discussed in Chapter 7, synergy is the $1 + 1 = 3$ effect. In other words, an open system adds up to more than the sum of its parts. A winning athletic team is more than its players, coaches, plays, and equipment. Only when all parts are in place and working in concert can the winning edge be achieved. Likewise, a successful business is more than the traditional factors of production—land, labor, and capital. Synergistic thinking emphasizes that a firm's competitive edge is dictated as much by how the factors of production are mobilized as by what those factors are.

**dynamic equilibrium**
*process whereby an open system maintains its own internal balances with help from its environment*

- *Dynamic equilibrium.* In open systems, **dynamic equilibrium** is the process of maintaining the internal balance necessary for survival by importing needed resources from the environment.[25] Proper blood chemistry in the human body is maintained through dynamic equilibrium. When a person's blood sugar drops below normal, a craving for sugar prompts the ingestion of something sweet, thus increasing the blood-sugar level. Similarly, management can take out a loan when operations have drained the organization's cash reserves.

**equifinality**   *open systems can achieve similar ends through different means*

- *Equifinality.* Open systems are made up of more than fixed cause-and-effect linkages. **Equifinality** means reaching the same result by different means. In their landmark book *Organization and Management*, Fremont Kast and James Rosenzweig summarize: "The concept of equifinality suggests that the manager can utilize a varying bundle of inputs into the organization, can transform them in a variety of ways, and can achieve satisfactory output."[26] For example, Nucor, a rapidly growing and highly profitable steel producer, is almost totally unlike traditional steel companies. Nucor builds its own mills, avoids debt, makes steel from scrap rather than ore, uses the latest energy-saving technology, and ties its nonunion employees' weekly bonuses to productivity.[27] Whereas America's steel giants have had to retrench in the face of stiff foreign competition, Nucor has thrived because of equifinality. In short, Nucor found a different (and better) way of getting the job done.

**4**  Describe a business organization in terms of the open-system model.

**Developing an Open-System Model.**    An open-system model encourages managers to think about organization-environment interaction (see Figure 9.2). A business must acquire various *inputs*: capital, either through selling stock or borrowing; labor, through hiring people; raw materials, through purchases; and market information, through research. On the *output* side of the model, goods and services are marketed, profits (or losses) are realized, and waste materials are discarded (if not recycled).[28] There are other inputs and outputs as well. This open-system model, although descriptive of a business organization, readily generalizes to all types of organizations.

By using the open-system premise that systems are made up of interacting subsystems, we can identify three prominent organizational subsystems: technical, boundary-spanning, and managerial. Sometimes called the production function, the technical subsystem physically transforms raw materials into finished goods and services. But the ability to turn out a product does not in itself guarantee organizational survival. Other supporting subsystems working in concert are also needed.

Whereas technical subsystems may be viewed as being at an organization's very core, boundary-spanning subsystems are directed outward toward the general environment. Most boundary-spanning jobs, or interface functions, as they are sometimes

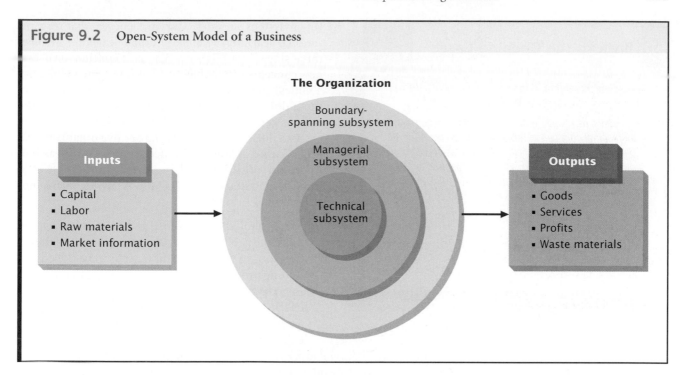

**Figure 9.2**   Open-System Model of a Business

called, are easily identified by their titles. Purchasing and supply-chain specialists are responsible for making sure the organization has a steady and reliable flow of raw materials and subcomponents. Public relations staff are in charge of developing and maintaining a favorable public image of the organization. Strategic planners have the responsibility of surveying the general environment for actual or potential opportunities and threats. Sales personnel probe the environment for buyers for the organization's goods or services. Purchasing agents, public relations staff, strategic planners, and sales personnel have one common characteristic: they all facilitate the organization's interaction with its environment. Each, so to speak, has one foot inside the organization and one foot outside.

Although the technical and boundary-spanning subsystems are important and necessary, one additional subsystem is needed to tie the organization together. As Figure 9.2 indicates, the managerial subsystem serves as a bridge between the other two subsystems. The managerial subsystem controls and directs the other subsystems in the organization. It is within this subsystem that the subject matter of this book is practiced as a blend of science and art.

### Extending the Open-System Model: The Learning Organization.
The idea of organizational learning, as it relates to the topic of knowledge management discussed in Chapter 8, dates back to the 1970s.[29] It took Peter Senge's 1990 best-seller, *The Fifth Discipline,* to popularize this extension of open-system thinking.[30] Many management writers and consultants then jumped on the bandwagon and confusion prevailed.

Fortunately, Harvard's David A. Garvin did a good job of sorting things out. According to Garvin, "A **learning organization** is an organization skilled at creating, acquiring, and transferring knowledge, and at modifying its behavior to reflect new knowledge and insights."[31] One could view Garvin and the others as having extended the open-system model of organizations by putting a human head on the biological

**5** Explain the term *learning organization*.

**learning organization**
*one that turns new ideas into improved performance*

## 9D   Back to the Opening Case

Jim Collins, co-author of the best-selling book, *Built to Last: Successful Habits of Visionary Companies*:

> . . . sadly, as we add years to our lives, it becomes increasingly difficult to remain dedicated learners. We become experts in our field and cease asking as many questions. We're all born as learning people, but most of us lose our innate curiosity and love of learning as we age. The more we know, the less we learn.

**Source:** Jim Collins, "The Learning Person," *Training*, 36 (March 1999): 84.

**Question:** *How does Microsoft keep the learning spark alive?*

(open-system) model. Garvin believes that organizational learning, just like human learning, involves three stages (see Figure 9.3): (1) cognition (learning new concepts), (2) behavior (developing new skills and abilities), and (3) performance (actually getting something done). All three stages are required to erase the famous gap between theory and practice.

Also illustrated in Figure 9.3 are five organizational skills Garvin claims are needed to turn new ideas into improved organizational performance. Each skill is important if today's organizations are to *thrive*, not just survive.

- *Solving problems.* Problems, as discussed in Chapter 8, are the gap between actual and desired situations. Everyone in the organization needs to be skilled at finding problems and creatively solving them.
- *Experimenting.* W. Edwards Deming's plan-do-check-act (PDCA) cycle, covered in Chapter 17, is an excellent tool for learning through systematic experimentation.
- *Learning from organizational experience/history.* Role models and often-told stories of success and failure embedded in the organization's culture teach vital lessons. Also, as recently pointed out, creating an organization "that can concurrently harness innovation, initiative, and competence-building is a difficult task that often requires significant 'unlearning' of previous organizational practices."[32]
- *Learning from others.* Two prime sources of valuable knowledge in this regard are benchmarking, also discussed in Chapter 17, and customer input and feedback.
- *Transferring and implementing.* All the other skills are for naught if actions are not taken to make the organization perform better. Training (Chapter 11) and effective communication (Chapter 12) are key bridges spanning the gap between ideas and skills and superior organizational performance.

The concept of learning organizations is a valuable addition to organization theory because it explains how managers can deal with today's only certainty—*change*.[33] (For more, see Skills & Tools and the Closing Case at the end of this chapter.)

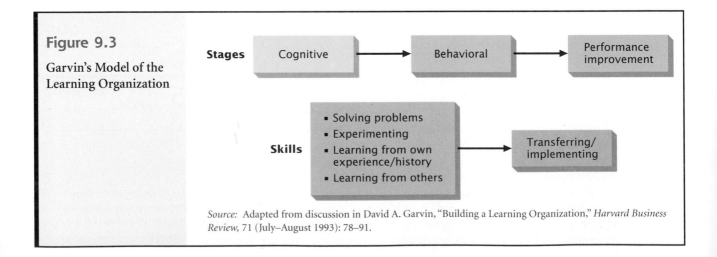

**Figure 9.3**

**Garvin's Model of the Learning Organization**

**Stages**   Cognitive → Behavioral → Performance improvement

**Skills**
- Solving problems
- Experimenting
- Learning from own experience/history
- Learning from others

→ Transferring/implementing

*Source:* Adapted from discussion in David A. Garvin, "Building a Learning Organization," *Harvard Business Review*, 71 (July–August 1993): 78–91.

# Organizational Effectiveness

The practice of management, as defined in Chapter 1, challenges managers to use organizational resources effectively and efficiently. Effectiveness is a measure of whether or not organizational objectives are accomplished. In contrast, efficiency is the relationship between outputs and inputs. Only monopolies can get away with being effective but not efficient. Moreover, in an era of diminishing resources and increasing concern about civil rights, society is reluctant to label "effective" any organization that wastes scarce resources or tramples on civil rights. Management's definition of organizational effectiveness therefore needs to be refined. The related issue of organizational decline also needs to be understood and skillfully managed.

## No Silver Bullet

According to one management scholar, "no single approach to the evaluation of effectiveness is appropriate in all circumstances or for all organizational types."[34] More and more, the effectiveness criteria for modern organizations are being prescribed by society in the form of explicit expectations, regulations, and laws. In the private sector, profitability is no longer the sole criterion of effectiveness.[35] Winslow Buxton, CEO of Pentair, Inc., a Minnesota manufacturing company with $2 billion in annual revenue and 10,000 employees, recently offered this perspective:

> One of the most challenging aspects of my job is balancing the differing expectations of employees, management, customers, financial analysts, and investors. The common denominator for all these groups is growth. But this seemingly simple term has different connotations for each constituency, and a successful company must satisfy all of those meanings.[36]

*Historically, most African-Americans have been reluctant to invest in the stock market. Mellody Hobson wants to change that. She wants to make the stock market a standard dinner-table topic in black households. By doing so, she believes she can help erase long-standing wealth inequalities. As president of a Chicago-based mutual fund, Ariel Capital Management, Hobson is in a good position to make changes. The effectiveness of her company can be measured in many ways: including number of customers, asset growth, capital gains, wealth accumulated by clients, and dreams realized.*

Moreover, today's managers are caught up in an enormous web of laws and regulations covering employment practices, working conditions, job safety, pensions, product safety, pollution, and competitive practices. To be truly effective, today's productive organizations need to strike a generally acceptable balance between organizational and societal goals. Direct conflicts, such as higher wages for employees versus lower prices for customers, are inevitable. Therefore, the process of determining the proper weighting of organizational effectiveness criteria is an endless one requiring frequent review and updating.[37]

## A Time Dimension

**6** Explain the time dimension of organizational effectiveness.

To build a workable definition of organizational effectiveness, we shall introduce a time dimension. As indicated in Figure 9.4, the organization needs to be effective in the near, intermediate, and distant future. Consequently, **organizational effectiveness** can be defined as meeting organizational objectives and prevailing societal expectations in the near future, adapting and developing in the intermediate future, and surviving into the distant future.[38]

**organizational effectiveness**
*being effective, efficient, satisfying, adaptive and developing, and ultimately surviving*

Most people think only of the near future. It is in the near future that the organization has to produce goods or render services, use resources efficiently, and satisfy both insiders and outsiders with its activity. But this is just the beginning, not the end. To grow and be effective, an organization must adapt to new environmental demands and mature and learn in the intermediate future (two to four years).[39]

## Organizational Decline

Prior to the mid-1970s, North American managers sped along a one-way street to growth. Fueled by strong demand, corporations mushroomed in size and diversity of

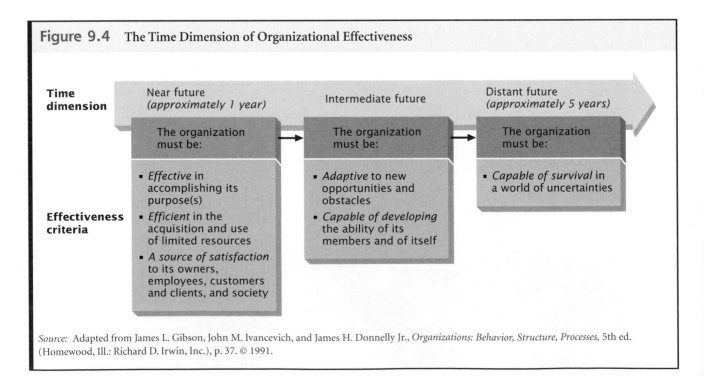

**Figure 9.4     The Time Dimension of Organizational Effectiveness**

| Time dimension | Near future *(approximately 1 year)* | Intermediate future | Distant future *(approximately 5 years)* |
|---|---|---|---|
| | The organization must be: | The organization must be: | The organization must be: |
| **Effectiveness criteria** | ▪ *Effective* in accomplishing its purpose(s)<br>▪ *Efficient* in the acquisition and use of limited resources<br>▪ *A source of satisfaction* to its owners, employees, customers and clients, and society | ▪ *Adaptive* to new opportunities and obstacles<br>▪ *Capable of developing* the ability of its members and of itself | ▪ *Capable of survival* in a world of uncertainties |

*Source:* Adapted from James L. Gibson, John M. Ivancevich, and James H. Donnelly Jr., *Organizations: Behavior, Structure, Processes*, 5th ed. (Homewood, Ill.: Richard D. Irwin, Inc.), p. 37. © 1991.

operations as they achieved ever-greater market shares. In recent years, however, unsteady economic growth, resource shortages, mismanagement, global competition, and the end of the Cold War have taken their toll among industrial giants. Layoffs, retrenchments, cutbacks, and plant closings have become commonplace in the United States. During the last decade, the figures have been stunning, in both good times and bad. In 2001, for example, 1,040,466 employees were laid off by just the *Fortune* 500 companies.[40]

Turnaround specialists, hired to restore companies to health, have come to use terms like *downsizing, demassing*, and *reengineering* when shrinking and breaking up companies. This organizational revolution points up a fundamental shortcoming of modern management theory and practice: We know a lot about striving for growth when times are good, but precious little about retreating when times are bad. Logic says what goes up must come down. According to a pair of experts on the subject, "Corporate performance almost always declines following a period of success."[41] These experts believe that *management complacency* is largely responsible for turning success into decline (see Figure 9.5).

**7** Explain the role of complacency in organizational decline and discuss the ethics of downsizing.

If allowed to persist, organizational decline can mean failure and bankruptcy. As the Enron debacle demonstrated, organizational decline can be remarkably swift and brutal. In January 2001, Enron was number 7 on the *Fortune* 500 list, number 22 on *Fortune*'s "One Hundred Best Companies" list, and its stock was selling for $83 a share. Just one year later, the company was bankrupt and its stock fetched a mere 67 cents a share before being delisted.[42] Worse yet, tens of thousands of people were left to deal with unemployment and worthless retirement accounts. Today's managers must be adept at expanding, remaking, and sometimes shrinking their organizations, as conditions warrant.

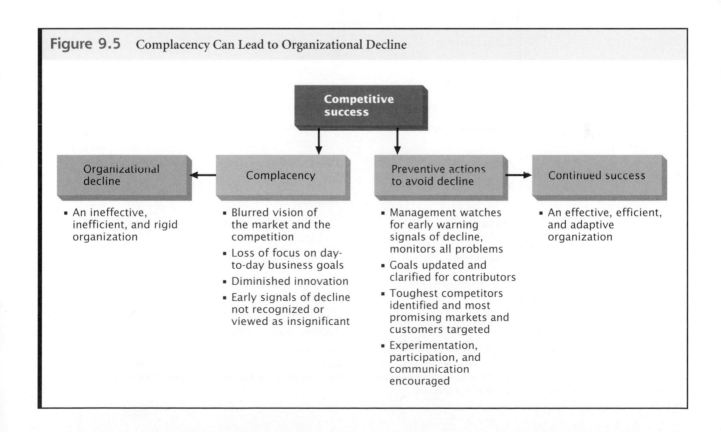

**Figure 9.5**   **Complacency Can Lead to Organizational Decline**

**organizational decline**
*organization is weakened by resource or demand restrictions and/or mismanagement*

**Organizational decline** is a weakened condition resulting from resource or demand restrictions and/or mismanagement. It typically involves a reduction in the size or scope of the organization.[43] For example, Lee Iacocca's turnaround team had to reduce Chrysler's size by 50 percent during its 1979–1981 brush with bankruptcy. Because that management era was preoccupied with growth, Iacocca had no textbook models, research base, or collection of proven techniques from which to learn. Thanks to recent interest in the management of organizational decline, an instructive body of theory, research, and practice is taking shape. Let us review that body of knowledge to better understand how managers can steer their organizations through the bad times that typically follow the good times.

## Characteristics of Organizational Decline

What are the characteristics or indicators of an organization in decline? A partial answer to this question came from a survey of 3,406 administrators at 334 four-year colleges in the United States.[44] Kim Cameron and his colleagues used six years of revenue data to divide the schools into three categories: growing, stable, and declining. They found that nine attributes (listed in Table 9.5) were statistically significant characteristics of organizational decline. The researchers were surprised to find that the same characteristics were associated with stable organizations, suggesting that all organizations are actually in one of two phases—either growth or decline. In short, an organization that has entered a period of stability has taken the first step toward decline.

**Table 9.5**   Nine Characteristics of Organizational Decline

| Characteristic | Description |
|---|---|
| Centralization | Decision making is passed upward, participation decreases, control is emphasized. |
| No long-term planning | Crisis and short-term needs drive out strategic planning. |
| Innovation curtailed | No experimentation, risk aversion, and skepticism about noncore activities. |
| Scapegoating | Leaders are blamed for the pain and uncertainty. |
| Resistance to change | Conservatism and turf protection lead to rejection of new alternatives. |
| Turnover | The most competent leaders tend to leave first, causing leadership anemia. |
| Low morale | Few needs are met, and infighting is predominant. |
| Nonprioritized cuts | Attempts to ameliorate conflict lead to attempts to equalize cutbacks. |
| Conflict | Competition and in-fighting for control predominate when resources are scarce. |

*Source:* Characteristics and descriptions excerpted from Kim S. Cameron, David A. Whetten, and Myung U. Kim, "Organizational Dysfunction of Decline," *Academy of Management Journal,* 30 (March 1987): 128. Reprinted by permission.

**Decline Dilemmas.**    Of the nine characteristics of organizational decline presented in Table 9.5, five particularly troublesome dilemmas emerge. First, the leaders most needed by the organization tend to be the first to leave. For example, Lucent Technologies lost many key players during its 2001–2002 slump.[45] Second, control is achieved at the expense of employee participation and morale. Third, when management needs to take long-term risks, short-term thinking and risk avoidance prevail. Fourth, conflict intensifies when teamwork is most needed. Finally, at precisely the time when changes are required, resistance to change is the greatest. Organizational decline is a cycle that feeds on itself and only gets worse if left unmanaged.

**9E    Any Slackers Here?**

Nina Disesa, CEO of the New York advertising agency McCann-Erickson:

*When you step into a turnaround situation, you can safely assume four things: Morale is low, fear is high, the good people are halfway out the door, and the slackers are hiding.*

**Source:** Regina Fazio Maruca, "Unit of One: Nina Disesa," *Fast Company,* no. 45 (April 2001): 82.

**Question:** *As the new head of an organization in decline, what would be your top priorities and first moves?*

**Decline Is a Never-Ending Challenge.**    More research is required in this important area.[46] Meanwhile, to avoid being caught by surprise, managers need to anticipate and counteract the characteristics of decline (refer again to Figure 9.5). Seeds of decline are sown during periods of success, when management is most likely to become overconfident, arrogant, and complacent. At these times, Peter Drucker actually recommends stirring things up.

> *One strategy is practically infallible: Refocus and change the organization when you are successful. When everything is going beautifully. When everybody says, "Don't rock the boat. If it ain't broke, don't fix it." At that point, let's hope, you have some character in the organization who is willing to be unpopular by saying, "Let's improve it." If you don't improve it, you will go downhill pretty fast.*[47]

*Kaizen,* the Japanese philosophy of continuous improvement, is the best weapon against organizational decline.[48] Just ask the people at Boeing, the world's number-one manufacturer of commercial jet aircraft. The president of Boeing's Commercial Airplane Group is clear about the challenge: "We are dedicated to not doing what IBM, Sears Roebuck, and General Motors have done—which is to get to the top, be the best, and then get fat and lazy."[49] Boeing is reinventing itself by shortening product development cycles, shrinking inventories, and training *every* employee to be a world-class competitor.

## Downsizing: An Ethical Perspective

**Downsizing** has been defined simply as "the planned elimination of positions or jobs."[50] While generally associated with organizations in decline, mergers and acquisitions also can prompt downsizing, especially when jobs and/or facilities become redundant. For example, when Bank of America merged with neighboring Security Pacific Bank, unnecessary branches had to be closed.[51] Whether due to decline or merger, the net result is the same—people lose their jobs. Ethical implications abound.

**downsizing**    *planned elimination of positions or jobs*

**Does Downsizing Work?**    According to researchers, the short answer is: *not nearly as well as expected.* An analysis of annual nationwide surveys by the American Management Association revealed the following:

# Management Ethics

## Discount Stockbroker Charles Schwab Dug Deep After Laying Off 10 percent of His Employees During the 2001 Recession

Q. You and your wife set up a $10 million fund, out of your own money, to help people who were laid off.

SCHWAB: Yes, out of our Schwab Foundation, we set up money for tuition reimbursement. If laid-off employees want to go back to school, we are helping them to the extent of $10,000 a year for two years.

Q. Why?

SCHWAB: I feel a responsibility to those people. And I wanted to deliver the message that we as a company know that, in time, we are going to grow into needing many of these people back. And maybe they will consider coming back.

*Source:* Excerpted from Charles Fishman, "You Can Quote Him," *Fast Company,* no. 48 (July 2001): 68.

---

*. . . only 30 percent of companies implementing job cuts since 1990 reported an increase in worker productivity over the next year, and only 40 percent report an increase in subsequent years.*

*Similarly, just 45 percent of job-cutters experienced a rise in operating profits in either the year following a workforce reduction or over the longer term.[52]*

Another survey of 1,000 companies found that downsizings yielded the expected savings only 34 percent of the time. This was the case because the companies tended to go through cycles of overstaffing, laying off, overstaffing, laying off, and so on.[53] If this scenario reminds you of the unhealthy weight control strategy of overeating and then crash dieting, you understand the problem.

Critics remind us that layoffs are traumatic for *everyone*—those who lose their jobs, the managers who must decide who stays and who goes, the community, and the survivors.[54] Managers who see their employees as a commodity to be hired when times are good and fired when times are bad are rightfully criticized for being shortsighted and unethical. The preferred model today views employees as valuable human resources requiring careful nurturing and career assistance in the event of a last-resort layoff[55] (see Management Ethics).

**Making Layoffs a Last Resort.**    Managers who view employees as valuable human resources have several progressive alternatives to sudden, involuntary layoffs.

- *Redeployment.* Displaced employees are retrained and/or transferred. This approach amounts to a recycling program for human resources.
- *Downgrading.* To prevent a layoff, the organization moves displaced employees to unstaffed, lower-level jobs, avoiding pay cuts if possible.[56]
- *Work sharing.* Instead of laying off a portion of its workforce, management divides the available work among all employees, who take proportional cuts in hours and pay. This approach has been called "share the gain, share the pain."[57]
- *Job banks.* Work that would normally be outsourced is kept in-house for employees caught in a downturn. For example, Harman International Industries, the Washington, D.C., maker of JBL and Infinity audio systems, calls its job bank pro-

gram Off-Line Enterprises (OLÉ). At any time, a total of 15 to 20 jobs are available through OLÉ in four general categories:

1. Manufacturing products usually purchased by external suppliers
2. Providing services such as security, which usually is contracted out
3. Converting waste by-products into marketable products, such as making clocks from scrap wood
4. Training and employing plant employees in Harman's nearby retail outlet[58]

■ *Employee sharing.* This unique approach to redeployment involves finding temporary jobs for laid-off employees with another company. For example, consider this situation reported in mid-2001: "About 12 employees at MLT Vacations' call center in Minot, N.D., are working on loan to Sykes, a computer support firm in the area. The MLT employees work several months for Sykes, which pays MLT for the use of its workers."[59]

■ *Voluntary early retirement and voluntary layoffs.* Employees are induced to leave the organization with offers of accelerated retirement benefits, severance pay, bonuses, and/or prepaid health insurance. This tactic can backfire if valued employees leave and poor performers stay. For example, "Eastman Kodak had to scurry to refill the jobs of 2,000 of the 8,300 workers who unexpectedly took its 1991 buyout offer."[60]

■ *Early warning of facility closings.* Imagine the pain of an unsuspecting employee who goes to work only to find a permanently locked gate. Several state legislatures in the United States have passed laws requiring companies to provide employees with some sort of advance warning of factory or office closings.[61] The Worker Adjustment and Retraining Notification Act, a federal law that went into effect in 1989, requires U.S. companies with 100 or more employees to give 60 days' notice of a closing or layoff.[62] Early warnings give displaced employees time to prepare financially and emotionally for a job change.

■ *Outplacement.* The practice of **outplacement** involves helping laid-off workers polish their job-seeking skills to increase their chances of finding suitable employment promptly.[63] This ethical practice can be costly.

**outplacement** *the ethical practice of helping displaced employees find new jobs*

■ *Helping layoff survivors.* The needs of these people have traditionally been ignored because, after all, they are the "lucky ones who still have their jobs." But research indicates that layoff survivors are stressed by overwork, uncertainty about future layoffs, and guilt over not suffering the same fate as their friends. Psychological and career counseling and retraining are appropriate and ethical options.[64]

---

Our discussions of organizational structure, effectiveness, and decline teach valuable lessons about the functioning of modern organizations. But the picture is not complete. A more subtle yet influential dimension of organizations remains to be explored. Managers who ignore this key dimension of organizations have little chance of success. So let's turn our attention to the interesting topic of organizational cultures to see what makes otherwise static structures come alive.

---

### 9F Is Training the Secret to Improving Productivity After a Layoff?

According to a 1998 survey by the American Management Association, companies that increase long-term training activity after downsizing are

■ 80 percent more likely to increase worker productivity.

■ More than twice as likely to report improvements in quality.

■ 75 percent more likely to increase operating profits.

■ 80 percent more likely to increase the value of their stock.

Unfortunately, training budgets typically are among the first items to be cut when times get tough.

**Source:** Marc Adams, "Training Employees as Partners," *HRMagazine,* 44 (February 1999): 66.

**Questions:** *Based on this information and what you have just read about the ethics of downsizing, what would you say to a top executive who is thinking about resorting to a big layoff?*

## 9G Loyalty Is a Two-Way Street

*Nucor, a Charlotte, N.C.-based steel manufacturer, hasn't laid off any employees due to lack of work since it entered the industry in the 1960s. The firm has more than 7,000 employees. Cutbacks have included work schedules and travel restrictions but no job cuts.*
*"A lot of our mills are in rural communities, and you can decimate the communities by laying those workers off," CEO Dan DiMicco says. "How can you build loyalty when you pat people on the back when times are good and when times are tough, you show them the door?"*

**Source:** Stephanie Armour, "Some Companies Choose No-Layoff Policy," *USA Today* (December 17, 2001): 1B.

**Question:** *Why aren't corporate no-layoff policies more common?*

# Organizational Cultures

**organizational culture**
*shared values, beliefs, and language that create a common identity and sense of community*

The notion of organizational culture is rooted in cultural anthropology.[65] **Organizational culture** is the collection of shared (stated or implied) beliefs, values, rituals, stories, myths, and specialized language that foster a feeling of community among organization members.[66] Culture, although based largely on taken-for-granted or "invisible" factors, exerts a powerful influence on behavior. For example, a six-year study of more than 900 newly hired college graduates found significantly lower turnover among those who joined public accounting firms with cultures emphasizing respect for people and teamwork. New hires working for accounting firms whose cultures emphasized detail, stability, and innovation tended to quit 14 months sooner than their counterparts in the more people-friendly organizations. According to the researcher's estimate, the companies with people-friendly cultures saved $6 million in human resources expenses because of lower turnover rates.[67]

Some call organizational (or corporate) culture the "social glue" that binds an organization's members together. Accordingly, this final section binds together all we have said about organizations in this chapter. Without an appreciation for the cultural aspect, an organization is just a meaningless collection of charts, tasks, and people. An anthropologist-turned-manager offered these cautionary words:

*Corporate culture is not an ideological gimmick to be imposed from above by management or management consulting firms but a stubborn fact of human social organization that can scuttle the best of corporate plans if not taken into account.[68]*

**8** Describe at least three characteristics of organizational cultures and explain the cultural significance of stories.

## Characteristics of Organizational Cultures

Given the number of variables involved, organizational cultures can vary widely from one organization to the next. Even so, authorities on the subject have identified six common characteristics.[69] Let us briefly examine these common characteristics to gain a fuller understanding of organizational cultures.

*Don't just sit there. Get up and dance! That's the scene once a week for employees at Mango's Tropical Cafe in Miami, Florida. Weekly dance classes are one way the organization gets its employees to embrace the look and feel of the company's culture, one of fun and multicultural celebration. It also builds friendships, trust, and a common bond. Okay, now—one, two, three, kick!*

1. *Collective.* Organizational cultures are *social* entities. While an individual may exert a cultural influence, it takes collective agreement and action for an organization's culture to take on a life of its own. Organizational cultures are truly synergistic (1 + 1 = 3). Jeffrey R. Immelt offered this companywide perspective soon after becoming the new head of General Electric: "We run a multibusiness company with common cultures, with common management . . . where the whole is always greater than the sum of its parts. Culture counts."[70]

2. *Emotionally charged.* People tend to find their organization's culture a comforting security blanket that enables them to deal with (or sometimes mask) their insecurities and uncertainties. Not surprisingly, people can develop a strong emotional attachment to their cultural security blanket. They will fight to protect it, often refusing to question its basic values. Corporate mergers often get bogged down in culture conflicts.[71]

3. *Historically based.* Shared experiences, over extended periods of time, bind groups of people together. We tend to identify with those who have had similar life experiences. Trust and loyalty, two key components of culture, are earned by consistently demonstrating predictable patterns of words and actions.

4. *Inherently symbolic.* Actions often speak louder than words. Memorable symbolic actions are the lifeblood of organizational culture. For instance, when Bob Moffat was put in charge of IBM's money-losing personal computer business in 2000, he wanted to shake things up a bit and set the tone for a fresh new direction. *Fast Company* magazine followed the action:

   *When Moffat took over the PC division, he publicly promised his bosses profits. But he promised staff members in Raleigh, North Carolina something else: a beer party for all 5,000 of them. "People kept telling me that we couldn't have a beer party at IBM," Moffat says. "I just kept asking, Why can't we?" The result: a beer party in the quadrangle behind Moffat's building—and a symbol of the boss's determination to change things in a way that everyone remembers.*[72]

**9H**

**Back to the Opening Case**

How many of the six characteristics of organizational cultures are evident in the Microsoft case? Explain.

Culturally, the beer party wasn't what really mattered. What really mattered was a new boss who kept his word, who was believable and credible to his people.

5. *Dynamic.* In the long term, organizational cultures promote predictability, conformity, and stability. Just beneath this apparently stable surface, however, change boils as people struggle to communicate and comprehend subtle cultural clues. A management trainee who calls the president by her first name after being invited to do so may be embarrassed to learn later that "no one actually calls the president by her first name, even if she asks you to."

6. *Inherently fuzzy.* Ambiguity, contradictions, and multiple meanings are fundamental to organizational cultures. Just as a photographer cannot capture your typical busy day in a single snapshot, it takes intense and prolonged observation to capture the essence of an organization's culture.

## Forms and Consequences of Organizational Cultures

Figure 9.6 lists major forms and consequences of organizational cultures. To the extent that people in an organization share symbols, a common language, stories, and practices, they will tend to experience the four consequences. The degree of sharing and intensity of the consequences determine whether the organization's culture is strong or weak.

Shared values stand out as a pivotal factor in Figure 9.6. Unlike instrumental and terminal values, discussed in Chapter 5 as *personal* beliefs, **organizational values** are *shared* beliefs about what the organization stands for.[73] For example, prior to its merger with EarthLink in 2000, Internet service provider MindSpring took great pride in superior customer service. MindSpring's founder, Charles Brewer, drove home his customer service ethic with strong corporate values. As reported at the time:

**organizational values**
*shared beliefs about what the organization stands for*

> *MindSpring has nine "core values and beliefs" that govern how it operates. The principles are posted on office walls and on the backs of business cards. MindSpringers even recite them before their weekly all-hands meeting. "Work is an important part of life," declares one principle, "and it should be fun. Being a good business person does not mean being stuffy and boring." Another declares, "We make commitments with care, and then live up to them."[74]*

**Figure 9.6**

Forms and Consequences of Organizational Cultures

**Cultural forms**
- Symbols (*shared values, objects, and heroes*)
- Language (*shared jargon, slogans, and humor*)
- Stories (*shared legends and myths*)
- Practices (*shared rituals, ceremonies, and activities*)

**Cultural consequences**
- Sense of identity for the individual
- Individual commitment to organization's mission
- Organizational stability
- Organization makes sense to the individual

*Source:* Forms adapted from Harrison M. Trice and Janice M. Beyer, *The Cultures of Work Organizations* (Englewood Cliffs, N.J.: Prentice-Hall, 1993), pp. 77–128. Consequences adapted from Linda Smircich, "Concepts of Culture and Organizational Analysis," *Administrative Science Quarterly,* 28 (September 1983): 339–358.

A recent visit to Earthlink's Web site found no sign of Brewer, but his corporate values (plus a new one) were definitely alive and well (see Internet Exercise 2 at the end of this chapter for directions to the complete list).

# The Organizational Socialization Process

**Organizational socialization** is the process through which outsiders are transformed into accepted insiders.[75] In effect, the socialization process shapes newcomers to fit the organizational culture.

**organizational socialization**
*process of transforming outsiders into accepted insiders*

> *The culture asserts itself when the taken-for-granted cultural assumptions are in some way violated by the uninitiated and provoke a response. As the uninitiated bump into one after another taken-for-granted assumption, more acculturated employees respond in a variety of ways (tell stories, offer advice, ridicule, lecture, shun, and so forth) that serve to mold the way in which the newcomer thinks about his or her role and about "how things are done around here."*[76]

**Orientations.**   *Orientation programs*—in which newly hired employees learn about their organization's history, culture, competitive realities, and compensation and benefits—are an important first step in the socialization process. Too often today, however, orientations are hurried or nonexistent and new employees are left to "sink or swim." This is a big mistake, according to recent workplace research:

> *One study at Corning Glass Works (in Corning, New York) found that new employees who went through a structured orientation program were 69 percent more likely to be with the company after three years than those who were left on their own to sort out the job. A similar two-year study at Texas Instruments concluded that employees who had been carefully oriented to both the company and their jobs reached full productivity two months sooner than those who weren't.*[77]

**Storytelling.**   *Stories* deserve special attention here because, as indicated in Figure 9.6, they are a central feature of organizational socialization and culture. Company stories about heroic or inspiring deeds let newcomers know what "really counts."[78] For example, 3M's eleventh commandment—"Thou shalt not kill a new product idea"—has been ingrained in new employees through one inspiring story about the employee who invented transparent cellophane tape.

> *According to the story, an employee accidentally discovered the tape but was unable to get his superiors to buy the idea. Marketing studies predicted a relatively small demand for the new material. Undaunted, the employee found a way to sneak into the board room and tape down the minutes of board members with his transparent tape. The board was impressed enough with the novelty to give it a try and experienced incredible success.*[79]

Upon hearing this story, a 3M newcomer has believable, concrete evidence that innovation and persistence pay off at 3M. It has been said that stories are "social roadmaps" for employees, telling them where to go and where not to go and what will happen when they get there. Moreover, stories are remembered longer than abstract facts or rules and regulations. How many times have you recalled a professor's colorful story but forgotten the rest of the lecture?

## 91  What Is Your **Unlearning** Agenda?

Edgar H. Schein, pioneering organizational psychologist:

*Clearly, when we speak of cultural change in organizations, we are referring to transformational learning. The current fads include creating an environment of genuine trust and openness; building flat organizations where employees are truly empowered; and creating self-managed teams. Change of this magnitude requires people to give up long-held assumptions and to adopt radically new ones. . . . [T]his kind of process of unlearning and relearning is unbelievably painful and slow.*

**Source:**  As quoted in Diane L. Coutu, "The Anxiety of Learning," *Harvard Business Review,* 80 (March 2002): 106.

**Question:**  *Generally speaking, what do today's managers need to unlearn and/or relearn to make our organizations more effective?*

## Strengthening Organizational Cultures

Given the inherent fuzziness of organizational cultures, how can managers identify cultural weak spots needing improvement? Symptoms of a weak organizational culture include the following:

■ *Inward focus.* Have internal politics become more important than real-world problems and the marketplace?
■ *Morale problems.* Are there chronic unhappiness and high turnover?
■ *Fragmentation/inconsistency.* Is there a lack of "fit" in the way people behave, communicate, and perceive problems and opportunities?
■ *Ingrown subcultures.* Is there a lack of communication among subunits?
■ *Warfare among subcultures.* Has constructive competition given way to destructive conflict?
■ *Subculture elitism.* Have organizational units become exclusive "clubs" with restricted entry? Have subcultural values become more important than the organization's values?[80]

Evidence of these symptoms may encourage a potential recruit to look elsewhere. Each of these symptoms of a weak organizational culture can be a formidable barrier to organizational effectiveness. Organizations with strong cultures do a good job of avoiding these symptoms.[81]

# Summary

1. Organizations need to be understood and intelligently managed because they are an ever-present feature of modern life. Whatever their purpose, all organizations have four characteristics: (1) coordination of effort, (2) common goal or purpose, (3) division of labor, and (4) hierarchy of authority. If even one of these characteristics is absent, an organization does not exist. One useful way of classifying organizations is by their intended purpose. Organizations can be classified as business, nonprofit service, mutual-benefit, or commonweal.

2. Organization charts are helpful visual aids for managers. Representing the organization's structural skeleton, organization charts delineate vertical hierarchy and horizontal specialization. Vertical hierarchy is the so-called chain of command. Horizontal specialization involves the division of labor.

3. There are both traditional and modern views of organizations. Traditionalists such as Fayol, Taylor, and Weber subscribed to closed-system thinking and ignored the impact of environmental forces. Modern organization theorists tend to prefer open-system thinking because it realistically incorporates organizations' environmental dependency. Early management writers proposed tightly controlled authoritarian organizations. Max Weber, a German sociologist, applied the label

*bureaucracy* to his formula for the most rationally efficient type of organization. When bureaucratic characteristics, which are present in all organizations, are carried to an extreme, efficiency gives way to inefficiency. Chester I. Barnard's acceptance theory of authority and growing environmental complexity and uncertainty questioned traditional organization theory.

**4.** Open-system thinking became a promising alternative because it was useful in explaining the necessity of creating flexible and adaptable rather than rigid organizations. Although the analogy between natural systems and human social systems (organizations) is imperfect, there are important parallels. Organizations, like all open systems, are unique because of their (1) interaction with the environment, (2) synergy, (3) dynamic equilibrium, and (4) equifinality. In open-system terms, business organizations are made up of interdependent technical, boundary-spanning, and managerial subsystems.

**5.** Harvard's David A. Garvin characterizes learning organizations as those capable of turning new ideas into improved performance. Five skills required to do this are (1) solving problems, (2) experimenting, (3) learning from organizational experience and history, (4) learning from others, and (5) transferring and implementing knowledge for improved performance.

**6.** Because there is no one criterion for organizational effectiveness, for-profit as well as nonprofit organizations need to satisfy different effectiveness criteria in the near, intermediate, and distant future. Effective organizations are effective, efficient, and satisfying in the near term. They are adaptive and developing in the intermediate term. Ultimately, in the long term, effective organizations survive.

**7.** The management of organizational decline has only recently received the attention it deserves. Decline is often attributable to managerial complacency. The characteristics of decline are interlocking dilemmas that foster organizational self-destruction. To avoid decline as much as possible, or at least lessen its frequency, organizations should adopt preventive safeguards that counteract complacency. Continuous improvement is the primary tool for fighting decline. Downsizing tends to yield disappointing results. Among the ethical alternatives to layoffs are redeployment and work sharing.

**8.** Organizational culture is the "social glue" binding people together through shared symbols, language, stories, and practices. Organizational cultures can commonly be characterized as collective, emotionally charged, historically based, inherently symbolic, dynamic, and inherently fuzzy (or ambiguous). Diverse outsiders are transformed into accepted insiders through the process of organizational socialization. Orientations and stories are powerful and lasting socialization techniques. Systematic observation can reveal symptoms of a weak organizational culture.

## Terms to Understand

Organization (p. 283)

Authority (p. 283)

Commonweal organization (p. 287)

Organization chart (p. 287)

Bureaucracy (p. 290)

Acceptance theory of authority (p. 292)

Dynamic equilibrium (p. 294)

Equifinality (p. 294)

Learning organization (p. 295)

Organizational effectiveness (p. 298)

## Skills & Tools

### How to Build Your Organization's Learning Capability

"**Learning capability** represents the capacity of managers within an organization to generate and generalize ideas with *impact*."

## Managerial Actions to Ensure Learning Capability

**Step 1: Build a commitment to learning capability.**

- Make learning a visible and central element of the strategic intent.
- Invest in learning.
- Publicly talk about learning.
- Measure, benchmark, and track learning.
- Create symbols of learning.

**Step 2: Work to generate ideas with impact.**

- Continuous improvement (improve it).
- Competence acquisition (buy or hire it).
- Experimentation (try it).
- Boundary spanning (adapt it).

**Step 3: Work to generalize ideas with impact.**

- Teach leaders to coach.
- Teach leaders to facilitate.
- Select leaders who teach.
- Select leaders with vision.
- Walk the talk.

*Source:* Adapted from Dave Ulrich, Todd Jick, and Mary Ann Von Glinow, "High-Impact Learning: Building and Diffusing Learning Capability." Reprinted from *Organizational Dynamics*, Autumn 1993. © 1993 American Management Association. Reproduced with permission of the American Management Association in the format textbook via the Copyright Clearance Center.

# Hands-On Exercise

## An Organizational X-Ray: Capturing the "Feel" of an Organization's Culture

Either working alone or as part of a team, select an organization you are personally familiar with (e.g., your college or university, a place of present or past employment). Alternatively, you may choose to interview someone about an organization of their choice. The key is to capture a knowledgeable "insider's" perspective. Complete Parts A and B of this exercise with your target organization in mind. (*Notes:* This instrument is for instructional purposes only because it has not been scientifically validated. Also, you may want to disguise the organization in any class discussion if your cultural profile could offend someone or is strongly negative.)

**Instructions**

**Part A:** Circle one number for each of the following adjective pairs that best describes the "feel" of the organization and then calculate a sum total:

| | | |
|---|---|---|
| Rejecting | 1····2····3····4····5····6····7····8····9····10 | Accepting |
| Destructive | 1····2····3····4····5····6····7····8····9····10 | Constructive |
| Uncomfortable | 1····2····3····4····5····6····7····8····9····10 | Comfortable |
| Unfair | 1····2····3····4····5····6····7····8····9····10 | Fair |
| Unsupportive | 1····2····3····4····5····6····7····8····9····10 | Supportive |
| Demeaning | 1····2····3····4····5····6····7····8····9····10 | Empowering |
| Dishonest | 1····2····3····4····5····6····7····8····9····10 | Honest |
| Dull, boring | 1····2····3····4····5····6····7····8····9····10 | Challenging |
| Declining | 1····2····3····4····5····6····7····8····9····10 | Improving |
| Untrustworthy | 1····2····3····4····5····6····7····8····9····10 | Trustworthy |

Total score = \_\_\_\_\_

*Interpretive scale*
10–39 = Run for your life!
40–69 = Needs a culture transplant.
70–100 = Warm and fuzzy!

**Part B:** Write a brief statement for each of the following:

1. What are the organization's key values (as enacted, not simply written or stated)?
2. What story (or stories) best conveys what the organization is "really" like?
3. Does the organization have legends or heroes that strongly influence how things are done? Describe.
4. What traditions, practices, or symbols make the organization's culture stronger?
5. Does the organization have a larger-than-life reputation or mythology? Explain.

**For Consideration/ Discussion**

**1.** Is the organization's culture strong or weak? How can you tell?

**2.** Is the organization's culture people-friendly? Explain.

**3.** Does the strength (or weakness) of the culture help explain why the organization is thriving (or suffering)? Explain.

**4.** Will the organization's culture attract or repel high-quality job applicants? Explain.

**5.** What can or should be done to improve the organization's culture?

# Internet Exercises

**1. Applying organizational effectiveness criteria:** (*Note:* This is a variation of the Internet exercise for Chapter 5.) Organizational effectiveness criteria can be used by job seekers, customers, and investors for making important decisions. The point of this exercise is to give you a Web-based tool for evaluating U.S. (and global) corporate giants. *Fortune* magazine's online version of its annual "America's Most Admired Companies" survey can be found at **www.fortune.com**. From the "Companies" menu, select "America's Most Admired" and scan the overall top ten list. (Alternatively, you may want to choose "Global Most Admired.") Next, explore the top ten and bottom ten companies for each of the eight effectiveness criteria by clicking on "Key Attributes." To give your search a personal touch, create your own ranking for the eight attributes from most important to least important. You may want to click on some of the companies (and/or do a Web search) to learn more about them. Remember to print copies of the various lists if there will be a class discussion.

    *Learning Points:*  1. Are you surprised by the top-ranked company? Why? Are you surprised a particular company is *not* in your top ten?  2. What is your rationale for the overall rankings you gave the eight attributes?  3. How do your attribute rankings compare with your classmates?  4. Do you like/dislike *Fortune*'s list of corporate attributes as effectiveness criteria? How would you amend their list?

**2. Earthlink's down-to-earth corporate values:** As mentioned in our discussion of organizational cultures, Internet service provider Earthlink has a published list of corporate values. You can view them at **www.earthlink.com** by scrolling to the bottom of the home page and clicking on "About Earthlink." Select "Our Values" and then "Core Values and Beliefs." Read the single-page proclamation of the company's mission, purpose, and core values and beliefs.

    *Learning Points:*  1. What do you like or dislike about these values?  2. Is this type of corporate-values statement a good way to improve individual and company performance, or just a useful public relations ploy? Explain.  3. Does reading this list make you more or less likely to be an Earthlink customer and/or apply for a job there? Explain.  4. What do Earthlink's managers need to do to make the corporate values become business-as-usual?

**3. The power of organizational stories:** As discussed in this chapter, stories can be a powerful way to socialize newcomers and reinforce the organization's cultural values. Giant retailer Wal-Mart's Web site (**www.walmart.com**) contains some entertaining and insightful company stories. At the very bottom of the home page, click on "Company Information" and then choose "About Wal-Mart." All the material in the "The Wal-Mart Culture" section is worth reading, but be sure to focus on "Sundown Rule," "Ten Foot Rule," "Pricing Philosophy," and "The Wal-Mart Cheer" for interesting stories. ("Sam's Rules for Building a Business" are must reading for any one who wants to succeed in business.) Remember to print copies if this exercise will be discussed in class.

   *Learning Points:* 1. What specific cultural values are communicated by the Wal-Mart stories you read?  2. Would reading these stories help socialize a new Wal-Mart employee? Explain.  3. Have you heard any stories about Wal-Mart that create a different impression?  4. Why is a well-told story such a powerful cultural tool?

**4. Check it out:** Follow the instructions in exercise 1 to get to *Fortune*'s annual survey of the 100 Best Companies to Work For under the heading "Best to Work For." By clicking on that feature, you will uncover lots of interesting bits of corporate culture information about many highly respected companies. Who knows . . . you may even find your next employer.

For updates to these exercises, visit our Web site (**http://business.college.hmco.com/students**).

## Closing Case

# How Great Harvest Bread Company Cooked Up a Learning Organization

## The First Step

Marian Cihacek had an idea. It came to her as she sat in a makeshift classroom with her husband, Dennis, in Dillon, Mont. The Cihaceks were being trained to run the Great Harvest Bread bakery franchise that the couple had just bought back in Omaha. Great Harvest chief operating officer Tom McMakin was talking to the group of new franchisees about marketing. He had been in the midst of describing the company's belief in "giving generously," in "winning hearts in the community," in "bread-in-mouth" promotions, when Marian Cihacek got an idea for how a bakery could practice meaningful local philanthropy and at the same time get potential new customers to taste its product. What if—she wondered aloud—we chose a needy group in our community, opened the bakery on a Sunday (when Great Harvests are normally closed), donated the ingredients and labor, and handed over the day's sales as charity? The community group would promote the event, help staff it, and bring attention and new people to the store. The program could be called "Baker for the Day."

   "Great idea," said McMakin. "Great."

And there the idea sat. Except that Scott Creevy, an experienced franchisee who was in Dillon to help out with the training, liked the idea enough that without comment he simply went back to his 10-year-old bakery in Boulder, Colo., and tried it.

And Baker for the Day worked. Just as Cihacek had imagined it might.

That the idea worked, however, that it turned out to be good, is not what matters here. What matters—the lesson of Great Harvest—is in what happened to it next.

## A 'Learning Community'

What happened is that the idea traveled. But before we look at how it traveled, and why, and what that means for other organizations, ask yourself this: Is there anything more important to a business these days than making good ideas spread?

Well, maybe. There's the life-or-death need to come up with good ideas in the first place (new insights, solutions to problems, breakthroughs of all kinds that move a company forward). Understood.

But what if making sure ideas spread is the secret to making sure an organization comes up with them in the first place? Imagine capturing the brainspills of each employee and exposing them to the collectively breathed air, enabling each notion to prompt whatever reactions it will, to spark rounds of fresh thoughts by other employees, which in turn prompt fresh reactions. Thus would even the smallest ideas evolve. The weakest would get better, and the best would ultimately alter—in Darwinian fashion—a company's very genes. At least that's what the theorists say. They'd call a place where that occurred a "learning organization"—an organization where innovation happens organically, irrepressibly, and without any particular genius from leaders at the top. Such a company would almost run itself (goes the hypothesis), mutating naturally and in charmed sync with the market's demands. Really, it would be a beautiful thing, a business like that. Now if only somebody could find one.

Which brings us back to Montana. It would be too large a claim to say that the Great Harvest Bread Co. is the learning organization incarnate. Its practices, taken one by one, seem too humble for that. Still, by watching a single idea—Cihacek's Baker for the Day—bounce like a pinball across the fragmented and loosely knit company, one begins to see how to build a self-improving, self-managing organization out of nothing more than a handful of commonsense tools and one bold philosophical commitment.

Great Harvest is a franchisor of retail bread bakeries (137 in all). As Marian and Dennis Cihacek learned in their training class several years ago, the basic business looks simple: bake and sell bread from milled-in-the-shop Montana wheat. (Great Harvest claims that milling wheat on site just prior to baking is what makes its bread not only taste superior but also stay fresh for 12 days on a kitchen shelf.) It isn't the hard-crust, faux-European bread that's become so popular over the past decade, but the American kind—big, soft loaves, perfect for sandwiches and toast. It's a grocery item, not the sort of thing waiters bring to candlelit dinner tables with a side of olive oil. Loaves go for $3 or so apiece, and a franchisee has to sell a lot of them to gross the $450,000 that the typical Great Harvest bakery takes in each year. . . .

The Cihaceks, like all the other new franchisees who've passed through Dillon, learned this: what Great Harvest does isn't franchising as we know it.

While most franchisors dictate everything about their franchisees' operations in order to ensure a predictable experience for customers everywhere, Great Harvest doesn't even require that its franchisees use the same bread recipes. Or paint their stores the same colors. Or use the same promotions. Instead, Great Harvest sets its franchisees free after a one-year apprenticeship to run their stores in the time-honored mom-and-pop way. Be unique, the company tells them; be yourselves, and experiment. And therein is Great Harvest's fundamental philosophical principle: the conviction that command-and-control is wrong, that the company's real product is its offer of freedom to run a bakery as the owner sees fit—but with "handrails," as McMakin calls the help that's available if wanted. Further, in Great Harvest's view it's only by putting freedom first—including the freedom to *fail*—that an organization can fully tap the magic of human creativity.

In other words, Great Harvest says to its bakery owners, *Do whatever you want.* Except in one respect, which makes all the difference: Every owner in the chain is encouraged to be part of Great Harvest's "learning community." Those who join (and most have) must share information, financial results, observations, and ideas. If asked questions, they must give answers. They must keep no secrets. They must, as McMakin describes it, "let things go." The result is what academics would call an intentionally created "complex adaptive system." A learning organization.

An organization, that is to say, that responded to Marian Cihacek's idea in the way that it does to any new information: it picked it up and took it for a ride.

## How Ideas Spread Informally

Creevy, at his shop in Boulder, got exactly what he wanted from Baker for the Day. He turned over more than $2,000 to the charity that his customers had chosen by ballot to help—a rape crisis center—at a cost to his business of about $600 in ingredients and payroll, and his bakery benefited immediately from the novel and highly positive publicity.

When he told all of that to Sally Weissman, a Great Harvest franchisee in Minneapolis he kept in touch with, she decided to try the program herself. Same happy result. Weissman in turn told the story of her good experience to Linda Hanick, owner of the Great Harvest franchise in Kansas City, prompting Hanick to try the program, too. When it worked for Hanick, she not only spread the word informally to other bakery owners, just as Creevy and Weissman had done, but also brought it to a one-step-more-routinized forum: the Great Harvest marketing group, a committee consisting of five bakery owners and Lisa Allen, who was then the company's corporate marketing director. "This is a great idea," the group told Allen. "You should do materials to support it." . . .

So what happened to Baker for the Day? It traveled into the bloodstream of the entire Great Harvest system, pumped along by the Breadboard [the internal Web site] and all the company's other methods of capturing and communicating ideas—printed newsletters, personal visits to bakeries by field reps from Dillon, and gatherings of owners at annual Great Harvest conferences and training sessions. Along the way it was steadily refined, as it continues to be. Successive bakery owners figured out nuances about how to select charity partners, what kinds of publicity draw the most attention, how best to involve the bakery's workforce, and more. A template is being developed, and a cadre of experienced guides can help newcomers understand it.

Of course, this being Great Harvest with all its libertarian zeal, franchisees are free to use the template or not—or to use any part of it and deviate from there—just as they choose. "The currency of innovation is use," says McMakin. "If a new idea's good, it gets adopted fast." If it's bad, it doesn't.

In this free marketplace of ideas, Marian Cihacek's little notion has passed the test. This year 40% of Great Harvest's 137 franchisees are planning Baker for the Day promotions of their own.

## For Discussion

1. What role, if any, does enlightened self-interest, as covered in Chapter 5, play in this case?

2. How has Garvin's model of the learning organization, in Figure 9.3, been brought to life at Great Harvest?

3. What roles do Great Harvest's organizational structure and culture play in this case? Explain.

4. What lessons can managers of today's large organizations learn from this case?

5. Would you like to own and run a Great Harvest Bread franchise? Why or why not?

## chapter ten

# Organizing in the Twenty-First Century

*When you finish studying this chapter you should be able to*

**1**   **Explain** the concept of contingency organization design.

**2**   **Distinguish** between mechanistic and organic organizations.

**3**   **Discuss** the roles that differentiation and integration play in organization structure.

**4**   **Identify** and briefly **describe** the five basic departmentalization formats.

**5**   **Describe** how a highly centralized organization differs from a highly decentralized one.

**6**   **Define** the term *delegation* and **list** at least five common barriers to delegation.

**7**   **Explain** how the traditional pyramid organization is being reshaped.

**"** . . . You have to think small to grow big. **"**

Sam Walton

# A CEO's Kindergarten Lessons

Standing in the kitchen at Eze Castle Software, CEO Sean McLaughlin watches as one of his programmers sets milk and cookies on a table. It's 2:30 on a Wednesday afternoon. "Hang on, Parvathy," McLaughlin says to the employee as he opens the refrigerator door and pulls out an apple pie. "Put this out, too." When Parvathy is done in the kitchen, she flips some switches, and the lights flicker all over the fifth floor. Almost instantly, programmers leave their cubicles and make a beeline for the kitchen.

Then Parvathy jogs up a staircase and flashes the lights on the sixth floor. Account managers, salespeople, and assorted techies come downstairs and join their colleagues in the kitchen. When they arrive, McLaughlin is at the center of the steadily building crowd, dishing out the pie. Around him conversations spring up between colleagues who work in different departments. The topics range from work to social life to politics. Ten minutes later the lights flash again and it's back to work for the 90 employees in the Boston office of Eze.

What's so remarkable about the staff of a developer of securities-trading software with $13 million in revenues taking daily milk-and-cookie breaks? Not much—until you consider that the practice is part of a cultural shift engineered by the CEO, a shift that has profoundly changed the way he and his employees relate to one another. Perhaps more significant, the changes have affected how employees deal with the myriad little details that keep the six-year-old company grounded.

Eze's transformation began last year, when McLaughlin realized to his chagrin that his once small and collegial company had—because of accelerated growth—begun acting like a large corporation. His employees no longer knew one another, and he himself was increasingly vague about who some of the new faces were. "In the early days I could get to know everyone," says McLaughlin. . . .

But . . . [in 2001] two things happened that spurred McLaughlin to make some changes.

First, the Boston office lost both of its administrative assistants. One assistant quit and the other left a few weeks later. The two had stocked the supply room, sorted the mail, and welcomed visitors. The dual departures wreaked havoc. "The kitchen was out of milk, we didn't have any pens in the supply cabinet, the reception area looked like crap," McLaughlin says.

Then came the World Trade Center attacks. Though McLaughlin had long been brooding on how to reverse Eze's fat-cat habits, he had yet to act. He says that 9-11, and the "what are my priorities" thinking it engendered, "created an environment where it was easy for me to initiate a change."

The change he had in mind was inspired by a visit to his daughter's kindergarten class. There he saw how the teacher divided the cleanup tasks among the children by posting a rotating "chore wheel." McLaughlin thought the wheel was just the thing to clean up the mess and teach his employees a little corporate responsibility. But he also wanted to institute something that would help improve camaraderie. That's where another kindergarten institution, the milk-and-cookie breaks, came in. "I wanted to build relationships among the employees, to make them feel more company morale," he says.

Rather than posting an actual wheel in the office, McLaughlin had chief operating officer Tom Gavin post the tasks—and the names of the employees who were responsible for them—on the company intranet and on a board in the kitchen. There are eight tasks in all: stocking the kitchen with food and drinks, cleaning and organizing the dishes, maintaining the supply closet, sorting and distributing the mail, tidying the kitchen, overseeing the reception area, arranging and setting up the snack breaks, and acting as ombudsperson. Each employee (plus a backup) is assigned a particular task for a week. Any disputes or questions go to the ombudsperson, who also handles miscellaneous tasks, such as changing lightbulbs and fixing the printer.

In explaining the new system to his crew, McLaughlin faced an uphill battle. Many employees were already putting in 12-hour days. "Everyone here is so driven, so consumed with what they do," says Kristine O'Brien, a marketing-department staffer. "My first reaction was, 'I have to do all this stuff plus the dishes?'"

To gain buy-in, McLaughlin himself did kitchen cleanup during the first week. Gavin took supply-closet

317

duty. McLaughlin then announced that of the $100,000 he saved in salaries and benefits by not replacing either of the administrative assistants, $20,000 would go to the employees. A portion of the money would go to the food fund. Another portion would finance the activities of two committees to be staffed by volunteers: one devoted to internal culture and the other to community service.

When he first gathered the employees together to explain the chore system, McLaughlin told them: "There's not one person here, including myself, who doesn't spend 20 to 30 minutes a day messing around on the Internet. Just give us back half that time every few months." Sure enough, employees found that the tasks were welcome breaks that took fewer than 15 minutes a

day. And dividing eight tasks among 90 employees meant that each person had only one assignment every three months.

Results came quickly. Programmer Matt Taylor, the first ombudsperson, suddenly became the name on everyone's lips. He requested a replacement for the company's outdated elevator certificate and changed lightbulbs. "People came looking for me who normally would never have come to find me," he says. The assignment system, it turned out, was great for what business-school professors call "team-building." O'Brien built a rapport with Amish Patel in IT because he served as her backup one week on milk-and-cookies duty. Now they both have one more person to talk to each day at 2:30.

**W**e've probably all been to picnics where everyone brings a bottle of ketchup but no one brings the mustard. Although too much of one thing and too little of another may be laughable at a picnic, such disorganized situations can spell disaster for an organization that needs to manage human and material resources effectively and efficiently in order to survive. In the case of Eze Castle Software, simple steps to make the Boston office at least *look* more organized actually created a stronger, more team-oriented organization.

**organizing**   *creating a coordinated authority and task structure*

**Organizing** is the structuring of a coordinated system of authority relationships and task responsibilities. By spelling out who does what and who reports to whom, organizational structure can translate strategy into an ongoing productive operation. Structure always follows strategy in well-managed organizations. Tasks and interrelationships cannot be realistically and systematically defined without regard for the enterprise's overall direction. Furthermore, strategy determines the required technologies and the resources likely to be available.[1]

Unfortunately, as pointed out recently in the *Harvard Business Review*, the current state of organization structure and design leaves a lot to be desired:

> *Organizational structures rarely result from systematic, methodical planning. Rather, they evolve over time, in fits and starts, shaped more by politics than by policies. The haphazard nature of the resulting structures is a source of constant frustration to senior executives. Strategic initiatives stall or go astray because responsibilities are fragmented or unclear. Turf wars torpedo collaboration and knowledge sharing. Promising opportunities die for lack of managerial attention. Overly complex structures, such as matrix organizations, collapse because of lack of clarity about responsibilities.*[2]

The modern open-system view, with its emphasis on organization-environment interaction and learning organizations, has helped underscore the need for more flexible organization structures. These more flexible organizations are adaptable to sudden changes and are also interesting and challenging for employees. Traditional principles of organization are severely bent or broken during the design of flexible and adaptive organizations, and managers need new formulas for drawing up these designs. This is where the contingency approach enters the picture. The contingency approach permits the custom tailoring of organizations to meet unique external and internal situational demands.[3]

In this chapter we introduce and discuss organizational design alternatives that enhance situation appropriateness and, hence, organizational effectiveness. We also explore the dramatic reshaping of today's organizations.

# Contingency Design

Recall from our discussion in Chapter 2 that contingency thinking amounts to situational thinking. Specifically, the contingency approach to organizing involves taking special steps to make sure the organization fits the demands of the situation. In direct contrast to traditional bureaucratic thinking, contingency design is based on the assumption that there is no single best way to structure an organization. **Contingency design** is the process of determining the degree of environmental uncertainty and adapting the organization and its subunits to the situation. This does not necessarily mean that all contingency organizations will differ from each other. Instead, it means that managers who take a contingency approach select from a number of standard design alternatives to create the most situationally effective organization possible. Contingency managers typically start with the same basic collection of design alternatives but end up with unique combinations of them as dictated by the demands of their situations.

The contingency approach to designing organizations boils down to two questions: (1) How much environmental or state uncertainty is there? (See Table 10.1 for a handy way to answer this question.) (2) What combination of structural characteristics is most appropriate? We will examine two somewhat different contingency models to establish the validity of the contingency approach. Each model presents a scheme for systematically matching structural characteristics with environmental demands.

## The Burns and Stalker Model

Tom Burns and G. M. Stalker, both British behavioral scientists, proposed a useful typology for categorizing organizations by structural design.[4] They distinguished between mechanistic and organic organizations. **Mechanistic organizations** tend to be

**1** Explain the concept of contingency organization design.

**contingency design**
*fitting the organization to its environment*

**2** Distinguish between mechanistic and organic organizations.

**mechanistic organizations**
*rigid bureaucracies*

| **Table 10.1**   Determining Degree of Environmental Uncertainty | | | |
|---|---|---|---|
| | **Low** | **Moderate** | **High** |
| 1. How strong are social, political, and economic pressures on the organization? | Minimal | Moderate | Intense |
| 2. How frequent are technological breakthroughs in the industry? | Infrequent | Occasional | Frequent |
| 3. How reliable are resources and supplies? | Reliable | Occasional, predictable shortages | Unreliable |
| 4. How stable is the demand for the organization's product or service? | Highly stable | Moderately stable | Unstable |

---

**Table 10.2**    Mechanistic Versus Organic Organizations

| Characteristic | Mechanistic organizations | Organic organizations |
|---|---|---|
| 1. Task definition for individual contributors | Narrow and precise | Broad and general |
| 2. Relationship between individual contribution and organization purpose | Vague | Clear |
| 3. Task flexibility | Low | High |
| 4. Definition of rights, obligations, and techniques | Clear | Vague |
| 5. Reliance on hierarchical control | High | Low (reliance on self-control) |
| 6. Primary direction of communication | Vertical (top to bottom) | Lateral (between peers) |
| 7. Reliance on instructions and decisions from superior | High | Low (superior offers information and advice) |
| 8. Emphasis on loyalty and obedience | High | Low |
| 9. Type of knowledge required | Narrow, technical, and task-specific | Broad and professional |

*Source:* Adapted from Tom Burns and G. M. Stalker, *The Management of Innovation* (London: Tavistock, 1961), pp. 119–125. Reprinted by permission.

---

**organic organizations**
*flexible, adaptive organization structures*

rigid in design and have strong bureaucratic qualities. In contrast, **organic organizations** tend to be quite flexible in structure and adaptive to change. Actually, these two organizational types are the extreme ends of a single continuum. Pure types are difficult to find, but it is fairly easy to check off the characteristics listed in Table 10.2 to determine whether a particular organization (or subunit) is relatively mechanistic or relatively organic. It is notable that a field study found distinctly different communication patterns in mechanistic and organic organizations. Communication tended to be the formal command-and-control type in the mechanistic factory and participative in the organic factory.[5]

**Telling the Difference.**    Here is a quick test of how well you understand the distinction between mechanistic and organic organizations. Read the following description of how an Emeryville, California, company maximizes the security of its clients' Web site data and attach a mechanistic or organic label.

> *SiteROCK employees . . . are required to read through several three-inch-thick binders of standard operating procedures before they can work in the command center. As each shift turns over, the staff must shuffle through 90 minutes of paperwork before handing over the keys. "Not everyone would be able to do this job. You have to be able to follow directions and follow the processes," says Lori Perrine, a customer-support specialist at siteROCK.[6]*

If you said mechanistic, you're right. Using Table 10.2 as a guide, we see evidence of precise task definition, low task flexibility, clear definition of techniques, and high emphasis on obedience. Indeed, siteROCK is staffed mostly by former military personnel and is run with military precision. An organic organization would have exactly the opposite characteristics.

**Situational Appropriateness.** Burns and Stalker's research uncovered distinct organization-environment patterns indicating the relative appropriateness of both mechanistic and organic organizations. They discovered that *successful organizations in relatively stable and certain environments tended to be mechanistic.* Conversely, they also discovered that *relatively organic organizations tended to be the successful ones when the environment was unstable and uncertain.*

For practical application, this means that mechanistic design is appropriate for environmental stability, and organic design is appropriate for high environmental uncertainty. Today, the trend necessarily is toward more organic organizations because uncertainty is the rule. *Management Review* recently summed up the situation this way:

*Products, companies, and industries all have shorter life cycles, which means that product launches, corporate realignments, and other initiatives may take place in months rather than years. The global span of today's companies, which have employees, customers, and suppliers throughout the*

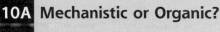 

## 10A Mechanistic or Organic?

Among its many products, Delaware-based W. L. Gore is best known for its Gore-Tex fabric used in outdoor gear. Here is a brief description of one of its five Scottish factories, where all employees are called associates:

*Associates are always encouraged to join a team with particular responsibilities, but they also have the opportunity—and encouragement—to pursue ideas and projects of their own choosing, particularly those which might lead to new applications and markets for the product. Much of the company's growth has come from finding new uses for their applications.*

**Source:** Tom Lester, "The Gores' Happy Family" *Management Today* (February 1993): 66.

**Questions:** *Does this illustrate a mechanistic or organic organization? Explain. What problems could this type of organization likely have? What could be done to avoid those problems? Would you like to work for this sort of organization? Why or why not?*

For further information about the interactive annotations in this chapter, visit our Web site (http://business.college.hmco.com/students).

This is not your grandfather's Cadillac. General Motors hopes its sportier CTS model Cadillacs will appeal to younger drivers. Assembly-line operations such as the one pictured here require mechanistic structure, complete with detailed product design specifications and uniform work methods, to ensure high product quality and safety standards. Administratively, GM has tried to become a bit more organic to be a more responsive and flexible company.

*world, also multiplies the complexities of change. And let us not forget another complicator—technology. Companies must constantly upgrade systems, evaluate new technology, and adopt new ways of doing business.*[7]

This is not to say that organic is good and mechanistic is bad. Mechanistic organizations do have their appropriate places. SiteROCK's mechanistic structure, for example, makes it highly resistant to human error, technical failures, and attacks by hackers and terrorists.

**Woodward's Study.**    Since Burns and Stalker's pioneering study, several different contingency models have been proposed. Some, such as Joan Woodward's study of the relationship among technology, structure, and organizational effectiveness, focused on a single environmental variable rather than on general environmental certainty-uncertainty. Applying her own scale of technological complexity to 100 British firms, Woodward found distinctly different patterns of structure in effective and ineffective organizations. When technological complexity was either low or high, Woodward found that effective organizations tended to have organic structure. Mechanistic structure was associated with effectiveness when technological complexity was moderate.[8] In spite of criticism of weak methodology, Woodward's study added to the case against the traditional notion of a universally applicable organization design.

## The Lawrence and Lorsch Model

**differentiation**   *tendency of specialists to think and act in restricted ways*

**integration**   *collaboration needed to achieve a common purpose*

### Back to the Opening Case

Using Figure 10.1 as a guide, what evidence of organizational integration can you find at Eze Castle Software?

Paul R. Lawrence and Jay W. Lorsch, researchers from Harvard University, made a valuable contribution to contingency design theory by documenting the relationship between two opposing structural forces and environmental complexity. The opposing forces they isolated were labeled *differentiation* and *integration*. **Differentiation** is the tendency among specialists to think and act in restricted ways. This structural force results from division of labor and technical specialization. Differentiation tends to fragment and disperse the organization (see Figure 10.1). **Integration,** in opposition to differentiation, is the collaboration among specialists that is needed to achieve a common purpose.[9] Integration can be partially achieved through a number of mechanisms, including hierarchical control, standard policies and procedures, departmentalization, computer networks, cross-functional teams and committees, better human relations, and liaison individuals and groups. As illustrated in Figure 10.1, integration is a unifying and *coordinating* force.

According to Lawrence and Lorsch, every organization requires an appropriate *dynamic equilibrium* (an open-system term) between differentiation and integration. Moreover, their comparison of successful and unsuccessful firms in three different industries demonstrated that in the successful firms *both differentiation and integration increased as environmental complexity increased*. These findings applied not only to the overall organization but also to organizational subunits such as departments or divisions. Lawrence and Lorsch also found that "the more differentiated an organization, the more difficult it is to achieve integration."[10]

These findings suggest that organizational failure in the face of environmental complexity probably results from a combination of high differentiation and inadequate integration.[11] Under these conditions, specialists in different areas within the organization work at cross-purposes and get embroiled in counterproductive jurisdictional conflicts. Greater integration (coordination) certainly was on the minds of 360 senior executives in the United States during a recent survey. Among the four key ways to boost profits, according to the executives, was to: "Implement cross-functional coor-

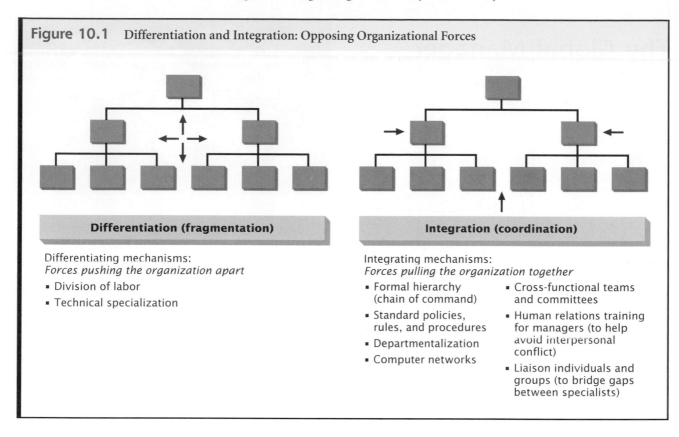

**Figure 10.1**   Differentiation and Integration: Opposing Organizational Forces

**Differentiation (fragmentation)**

Differentiating mechanisms:
*Forces pushing the organization apart*
- Division of labor
- Technical specialization

**Integration (coordination)**

Integrating mechanisms:
*Forces pulling the organization together*

- Formal hierarchy (chain of command)
- Standard policies, rules, and procedures
- Departmentalization
- Computer networks

- Cross-functional teams and committees
- Human relations training for managers (to help avoid interpersonal conflict)
- Liaison individuals and groups (to bridge gaps between specialists)

dination throughout the organization to increase customer retention."[12] Such action could prove fruitful because, in another study of 39 companies, productivity increased when organizational integration was improved. One source of improvement involved increased contact and coordination between product design and manufacturing specialists.[13] These research findings should ring true for Motorola. The one-time global leader in mobile phones has sustained huge losses while being pushed aside by Finland's Nokia. According to *Business Week:*

> *Costs rose because of a "skunk works" approach, in which as many as 15 teams of 20 people developed different phones. The teams often used different parts, making manufacturing and purchasing an expensive headache. [In 2000,] . . . Motorola had 128 different phone types and used a staggering 550 different silicon pieces on the circuit boards inside the handsets.[14]*

Meanwhile, efficient and profitable Nokia had only ten basic phone types. In Lawrence and Lorsch's terms, Motorola had too much differentiation and not enough integration in its product design area—a costly problem it is now correcting.

Although contingency design models may differ in perspective and language, two conclusions stand out. First, research has proved time and time again that *there is no single best organization design.* Second, research generally supports the idea that the more uncertain the environment, the more flexible and adaptable the organization structure must be.[15] (See The Global Manager.) With this contingency perspective in mind, we now consider five basic structural formats.

# The Global Manager

## A Globe-Trotting Organizational Thinker Looks at the Future of Work Organizations

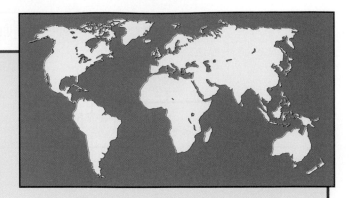

**A**bout Charles Handy: A native of Dublin, Ireland, he is the author of well-regarded books such as *The Age of Unreason* and, more recently, *The Hungry Spirit*. His diverse background includes being the executive of an oil company and a London Business School professor. He and his wife, a professional photographer, shuttle between residences in England and Italy.

Here are excerpts from an interview by Barbara Ettorre, senior editor of *Management Review:*

Q. The corporation as we know it is approximately 100 years old. Will it survive the twenty-first century?

HANDY: Not in its present form. The twentieth century will be known as the century of the organization. The next one will not be known as that. We are seeing the withering of the employment organization. It won't totally disappear, but it will be reduced to an organizing core. Organizations will live up to the name—they will organize. [They won't] have to employ everybody being organized, only the organizers. So my formula is half-by-two-by-three: Half the workers paid twice as well, producing three times as much.

The other half will be outside the organization. And because those on the inside are working very hard to be paid twice as well, they will have short lives in the organization, 20 or 30 years, instead of 50 years. It could be 15. It's a hell of a reduction. I try not to frighten people too much. But I would say 15 to 20.

This upper half of society, those with competent skills, will become independent workers, selling back into the organization for the most part, but also into several organizations at the same time. At the bottom level you will still need people because most of the jobs for the less skilled will be in the service world, giving people food and drink, keeping places clean, [taking care of old] folks. They will probably be organized by what I call intermediary employers.

Q. If the future consists of virtual corporations, portfolio workers, and knowledge as the competitive edge, what of the vast majority that cannot be a part of this? Are we creating an even larger underclass, large groups without salable portfolios?

HANDY: To some extent, there's no way out of that. Wealth doesn't trickle down as it used to. If you don't make the poor rich, the rich are not going to have any customers before long.

# Basic Structural Formats

**departmentalization**
*grouping related jobs or processes into major organizational subunits*

As we noted earlier, differentiation occurs in part through division of labor. When labor is divided, complex processes are reduced to distinct and less complex jobs. But because differentiation tends to fragment the organization, some sort of integration must be introduced to achieve the necessary coordination. Aside from the hierarchical chain of command, one of the most common forms of integration is departmentalization. It is through **departmentalization** that related jobs, activities, or processes are grouped into major organizational subunits. For example, all jobs involving staffing activities such as recruitment, hiring, and training are often grouped into a human resources department. Grouping jobs through the formation of departments, according to management author James D. Thompson, "permits coordination to be handled in the least costly manner."[16] A degree of coordination is achieved through departmentalization because members of the department work on interrelated tasks, obey the same departmental rules, and report to the same department head. It is important to note that although the term *departmentalization* is used here, it does not always literally apply; managers commonly use labels such as *division, group,* or *unit* in large organizations.

Five basic types of departmentalization are functional departments, product-service departments, geographic location departments, customer classification departments, and work flow process departments.[17]

**4** Identify and briefly describe the five basic departmentalization formats.

## Functional Departments

Functional departments categorize jobs according to the activity performed. Among profit-making businesses, variations of the functional production-finance-marketing arrangement in Figure 10.2A are the most common forms of departmentalization. Functional departmentalization is popular because it permits those with similar technical expertise to work in a coordinated subunit. Of course, functional departmentalization is not restricted to profit-making businesses. Functional departments in a nonprofit hospital might be administration, nursing, housekeeping, food service, laboratory and x-ray, admission and records, and accounting and billing.

A negative aspect of functional departmentalization is that it creates "technical ghettos," in which local departmental concerns and loyalties tend to override strategic organizational concerns. For example, look what Bruce L. Claflin, head of IBM's new mobile computing division, ran into when he called a planning meeting for the Think-Pad 700C.

**10C  Pumping Some Life into the Research and Development (R&D) Function**

In an attempt to instill a sense of vitality and harmony in its designs, Haworth formed a radically new type of R&D department in 1996. Christened the "Ideation Group" and commissioned to explore possibilities for future office environments, this unconventional group quickly added zest to Haworth through its revolutionary designs.

To visitors, the Ideation Group appears to be part consulting firm, part think tank, and part "skunk works." . . . Although the group is perceived as slightly irreverent in its behavior and somewhat eccentric in its approach to design, it has given Haworth a leading-edge design capability for its office furniture and systems.

**Source:** Excerpted from Janis R. Evink and Henry H. Beam, "Just What Is an Ideation Group?" *Business Horizons,* 42 (January–February 1999): 73.

**Question:** *Why was this reorganization successful?*

> *Everybody cared more about how their own area—say, marketing—would fare than for what was best for IBM. The marketing people knew [the 700C] would be competitive, but they had made commitments to sell only 6,000 worldwide. They didn't believe the development*
group would build it anyway. The development people knew they could design it, but they said, "Well, marketing won't sell it, and anyway, manufacturing can't build it." And manufacturing figured it would never be developed. It was complete gridlock.[18]

Situations like this prompted a major overhaul of IBM.[19]

## Product-Service Departments

Because functional departmentalization has been criticized for encouraging differentiation at the expense of integration, a somewhat more organic alternative has evolved. It is called product-service departmentalization because a product (or service), rather than a functional category of work, is the unifying theme. As diagrammed in Figure 10.2B, the

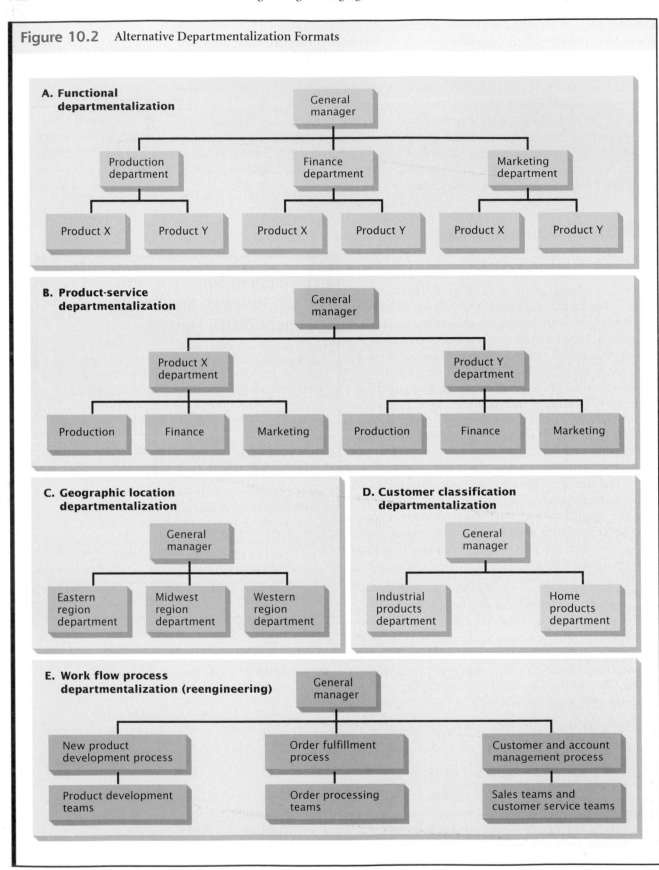

**Figure 10.2**    Alternative Departmentalization Formats

product-service approach permits each of, say, two products to be managed as semiautonomous businesses. Organizations rendering a service instead of turning out a tangible product might find it advantageous to organize around service categories. For example, reflecting its greater interest in the fast-growing casino gambling area, Hilton Hotels Corp. reorganized its worldwide operations into two units: gaming and lodging.[20] Ideally, those working in this sort of product-service structure have a broad "business" orientation rather than a narrow functional perspective. As Figure 10.2B shows, it is the general manager's job to ensure that these minibusinesses work in a complementary fashion.

## Geographic Location Departments

Sometimes, as in the case of organizations with nationwide or worldwide markets, geography dictates structural format (see Figure 10.2C). Geographic dispersion of resources (for example, mining companies), facilities (for example, railroads), or customers (for example, chain supermarkets) may encourage the use of a geographic format to put administrators "closer to the action." One can imagine that drilling engineers in a Houston-based petroleum firm would be better able to get a job done in Alaska if they actually went there. Similarly, a department-store marketing manager would be in a better position to judge consumer tastes in Florida if working out of a regional office in Orlando rather than a home office in Salt Lake City or Toronto.

Long lines of communication among organizational units have traditionally been a limiting factor with geographically dispersed operations. But space-age telecommunications technology has created some interesting regional advantages. One interesting case in point is Omaha, Nebraska. Its central location, along with the absence of a distinct regional accent among Nebraskans, has made Omaha the 1-800 capital of the country. Every major hotel chain and most of the big telemarketers have telephone service centers in Omaha.[21]

Global competition is pressuring managers to organize along geographical lines. This structure allows multinational companies to serve local markets better.

*Sometimes, circumstances dictate a certain structural format for a business. In the case of online grocer Peapod, a geographic location structure is necessary. Customers in Boston, for example, don't want perishable grocery items such as milk and produce shipped in from Peapod's headquarters in Skokie, Illinois. So Peapod has regional distribution centers serving each of its six major markets around the United States.*

## Customer Classification Departments

A fourth structural format centers on various customer categories (see Figure 10.2D). Aircraft maker Boeing, for example, was reorganized in 1998 into three units: commercial, defense, and space.[22] The rationale was to better serve the distinctly different needs of those three sets of customers. Customer classification departmentalization shares a weakness with the product-service and geographic location approaches: all three can create costly duplication of personnel and facilities. Functional design is the answer when duplication is a problem.

## Work Flow Process Departments in Reengineered Organizations

In Chapter 7, we introduced the concept of reengineering, which involves starting with a clean sheet of paper and radically redesigning the organization into cross-functional teams that speed up the entire business process. The driving factors behind reengineering are lower costs, better quality, greater speed, better use of modern information technology, and improved customer satisfaction.[23] Organizations with work flow process departments are called *horizontal organizations* because emphasis is on the smooth and speedy horizontal flow of work between two key points: (1) identifying customer needs and (2) satisfying the customer.[24] This is a distinct *outward* focus, as opposed to the inward focus of functional departments. Here is what happens inside the type of organization depicted in Figure 10.2E:

> Rather than focusing single-mindedly on financial objectives or functional goals, the horizontal organization emphasizes customer satisfaction. Work is simplified and hierarchy flattened by combining related tasks—for example, an account-management process that subsumes the sales, billing, and service functions—and eliminating work that does not add value. Information zips along an internal superhighway. The knowledge worker analyzes it, and technology moves it quickly across the corporation instead of up and down, speeding up and improving decision making.[25]

Each of the preceding design formats is presented in its pure form, but in actual practice hybrid versions occur frequently. For example, Coca-Cola created a mix of three geographic location units and a functional unit in 2001 to make the global company more responsive to both customers and product trends. The four units: "Americas, Asia, Europe/Africa, and New Business Ventures."[26] From a contingency perspective, the five design formats are useful starting points rather than final blueprints for organizers. A number of structural variations show how the basic formats can be adapted to meet situational demands.

**10D    How Reengineering Got a Bad Name**

A manager reportedly told James Champy, co-author of the landmark book on reengineering:

*We don't really know how to do reengineering in our company; so what we do is, we regularly downsize and leave it to the three people who are left to figure out how to do their work differently.*

**Source:** As quoted in "Anything Worth Doing Is Worth Doing from Scratch," *Inc.* (20th Anniversary Issue), 21 (May 18, 1999): 51–52.

**Questions:** *Does the term* reengineering *have a positive or negative connotation for you? Explain. How often do you think misapplication or misinterpretation gives otherwise sound management practices a bad name? Explain.*

# Contingency Design Alternatives

Contingency design requires managers to select from a number of situationally appropriate alternatives instead of blindly following fixed principles of organization.[27] Managers who face a relatively certain environment can enhance their effectiveness by drawing on comparatively mechanistic alternatives. Those who must cope with high uncertainty will do better to select organic alternatives. Design alternatives include span of control, decentralization, line and staff, and matrix design.

## Span of Control

The number of people who report directly to a manager represents that manager's **span of control.** (Some scholars and managers prefer the term *span of management.*) Managers with a narrow span of control oversee the work of a few people, whereas those with a wide span of control have many people reporting to them (see Figure 10.3). Generally, narrow spans of control foster tall organizations (many levels in the hierarchy). In contrast, flat organizations (few hierarchical levels) have wide spans of control. Everything else being equal, it stands to reason that an organization with narrow spans of control needs more managers than one with wide spans. Management theorists and practitioners have devoted a good deal of time and energy through the years attempting to answer the question, "What is the ideal span of control?"[28] Ideally, the right span of control strikes an efficient balance between too little and too much supervision, important considerations in the era of lean organizations.

**Is There an Ideal Span of Control?**   Early management theorists confidently specified exactly how many individuals should be in a manager's span of control. In the words of one early management scholar, "No superior can supervise directly the work of more than five or, at the most, six subordinates whose work interlocks."[29]

As time went by, research results began to supersede strictly intuitive judgments and evidence supported wider spans of control. James C. Worthy, a vice president of Sears, Roebuck and Co., reported that his company had gotten good results with spans

**10F  Wider Is Better, for the Head of Cisco Systems**

Says John Chambers, CEO of Cisco Systems Inc.: "I learned a long time ago that a team will always defeat an individual. And if you have a team of superstars, then you have a chance to create a dynasty." That's one reason Chambers has two to three times as many people reporting to him as does the average executive in his company: It forces him to empower those directly under him with greater autonomy, because he can't possibly keep up with every detail of their work.

**Source:**  John Byrne, "The Global Corporation Becomes the Leaderless Corporation," *Business Week* (August 30, 1999): 90.

**Question:**  *What is the key to making Chambers's wide span of control work?*

> **span of control**  *number of people who report directly to a given manager*

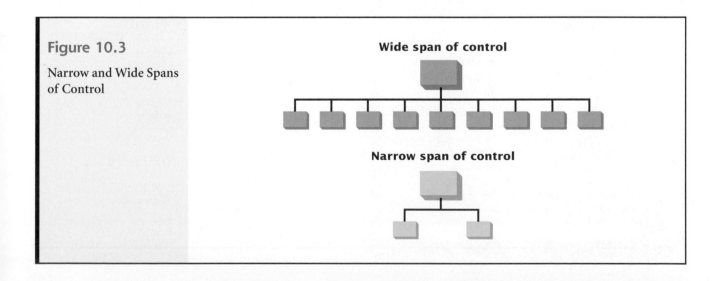

**Figure 10.3**

Narrow and Wide Spans of Control

**Wide span of control**

**Narrow span of control**

of control far in excess of six. Specifically, Worthy found morale and effectiveness were higher in one department store in which 36 department managers reported to a single manager than in a second store in which the span of control averaged only five.[30]

Today's emphasis on contingency organization design, combined with evidence that wide spans of control can be effective, has made the question of an ideal span obsolete. The relevant question is no longer how wide spans of control *should* be but instead, "How wide *can* one's span of control be?" Wider spans of control mean less administrative expense and more self-management, both popular notions today.

**The Contingency Approach to Spans of Control.**   Both overly narrow and overly wide spans of control are counterproductive. Overly narrow spans create unnecessarily tall organizations plagued by such problems as oversupervision; long lines of communication; slow, multilevel decision making; limited initiative due to minimal delegation of authority; restricted development among managers who devote most of their time to direct supervision; and increased administrative cost.[31] In contrast, overly wide spans can erode efficiency and inflate costs due to workers' lack of training, behavioral problems among inadequately supervised workers, and lack of coordination. Clearly, a rationale is needed for striking a workable balance.

Situational factors such as those listed in Figure 10.4 are a useful starting point. The narrow, moderate, and wide span of control ranges in Figure 10.4 are intended to be illustrative benchmarks rather than rigid limits. Each organization must do its own on-the-job experimentation. At Federal Express, for example, the span of control varies with different areas of the company. Departments that employ many people doing the same

**Figure 10.4**    Situational Determinants of Span of Control

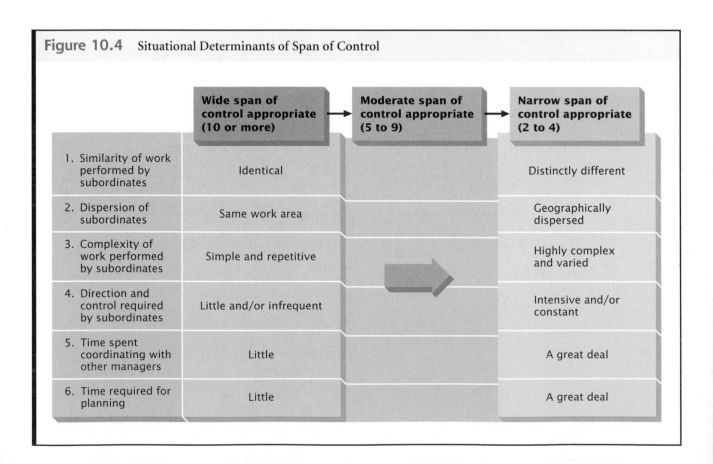

| | Wide span of control appropriate (10 or more) | Moderate span of control appropriate (5 to 9) | Narrow span of control appropriate (2 to 4) |
|---|---|---|---|
| 1. Similarity of work performed by subordinates | Identical | | Distinctly different |
| 2. Dispersion of subordinates | Same work area | | Geographically dispersed |
| 3. Complexity of work performed by subordinates | Simple and repetitive | | Highly complex and varied |
| 4. Direction and control required by subordinates | Little and/or infrequent | | Intensive and/or constant |
| 5. Time spent coordinating with other managers | Little | | A great deal |
| 6. Time required for planning | Little | | A great deal |

or very similar jobs—such as customer service agents, handlers/sorters, and couriers— usually have a span of control of 15 to 20 employees per manager. Groups performing multiple tasks, or tasks that require only a few people, are more likely to have spans of control of five or fewer.[32] No ideal span of control exists for all kinds of work.

## Centralization and Decentralization

Where are the important decisions made in an organization? Are they made strictly by top management or by middle- and lower-level managers? These questions are at the heart of the decentralization design alternative. Centralization is at one end of a continuum and at the other end is decentralization. **Centralization** is defined as the relative retention of decision-making authority by top management. Almost all decision-making authority is retained by top management in highly centralized organizations. In contrast, **decentralization** is the granting of decision-making authority by management to lower-level employees. Decentralization increases as the degree, importance, and range of lower-level decision making *increases* and the amount of checking up by top management *decreases* (see Figure 10.5).

**The Need for Balance.**    When we speak of centralization or decentralization, we are describing a comparative degree, not an absolute. The challenge for managers, as a management consultant observed, is to strike a workable balance between two extremes.

**5** Describe how a highly centralized organization differs from a highly decentralized one.

**centralization**    *the retention of decision-making authority by top management*

**decentralization**    *management shares decision-making authority with lower-level employees*

---

**Figure 10.5**    Factors in Relative Centralization/Decentralization

| | Highly centralized organization | Highly decentralized organization |
|---|---|---|
| How many decisions are made at lower levels in the hierarchy? | Very few, if any | Many or most |
| How important are the decisions that are made at lower levels (*i.e., do they impact organizational success or dollar values*)? | Not very important | Very important |
| How many different functions (*e.g., production, marketing, finance, human resources*) rely on lower-level decision making? | Very few, if any | All or most |
| How much does top management monitor or check up on lower-level decision making? | A great deal | Very little or not at all |

| **Table 10.3**    Advantages and Disadvantages of Matrix Organizations | |
| --- | --- |
| **Advantages** | **Disadvantages** |
| **Efficient use of resources:** Individual specialists as well as equipment can be shared across projects. | **Power struggles:** Conflict occurs because boundaries of authority and responsibility overlap. |
| **Project integration:** There is a clear and workable mechanism for coordinating work across functional lines. | **Heightened conflict:** Competition over scarce resources occurs especially when personnel are being shared across projects. |
| **Improved information flow:** Communication is enhanced both laterally and vertically. | **Slow reaction time:** Heavy emphasis on consultation and shared decision making retards timely decision making. |
| **Flexibility:** Frequent contact between members from different departments expedites decision making and adaptive responses. | **Difficulty in monitoring and controlling:** Multidiscipline involvement heightens information demands and makes it difficult to evaluate responsibility. |
| **Discipline retention:** Functional experts and specialists are kept together even though projects come and go. | **Excessive overhead:** Double management by creating project managers. |
| **Improved motivation and commitment:** Involvement of members in decision making enhances commitment and motivation. | **Experienced stress:** Dual reporting relations contribute to ambiguity and role conflict. |

*Source:* From Erik W. Larson and David H. Gobeli, "Matrix Management: Contradictions and Insights." Copyright © 1987 by the Regents of the University of California. Reprinted from the *California Management Review*, vol. 29, no. 4. By permission of the Regents.

## 10G    Philips Flips the Switch on Matrix

*In the 1990s, Dutch electronics giant Philips experimented with matrix management, which organizes the company along product lines and country sector. But the scheme sparked too much conflict. "We killed the matrix. It was too slow—it put the management board in a referee role," says Jan Oosterveld, board member in charge of strategy at Philips. Now Philips is trying something more flexible: Managers of individual businesses have primary global responsibility, while regional bosses or global account managers for key clients play a role as well.*

**Source:** Gail Edmondson, "See the World, Erase Its Borders," *Business Week* (August 28, 2000): 114.

**Questions:** *Why would matrix design be especially difficult for a huge global corporation? What arguments could you present in favor of a well-run matrix design for Philips? Does Philips's new arrangement sound good to you? Explain.*

**Advantages.**    Increased *coordination* is the overriding advantage of matrix design. The matrix format places a project manager in a good position to coordinate the many interrelated aspects of a particular project, both inside and outside the organization.[46] In mechanistic organizations, the various aspects of a project normally would be handled in a fragmented fashion by functional units, such as production and marketing, with no single person being in charge of the project.

Improved information flow, the third advantage listed in Table 10.3, needs to be interpreted carefully. Research has found that matrix design increases the *quantity* of communication but decreases its *quality*.[47]

**Disadvantages.**    First and foremost, matrix design flagrantly violates the traditional unity-of-command principle. A glance at Figure 10.7 reveals that an engineer, for instance, actually has two supervisors at the same time. This special arrangement can and sometimes does cause power struggles and conflicts of interest. Only frequent and comprehensive communication between functional and project managers (integration) can minimize unity-of-command problems. A corollary of the unity-of-command problem is the "authority gap" facing project managers who must complete projects in spite of a lack of formal line authority. Research has shown that project managers tend to use negotiation, persuasive ability, technical competence, and the exchange of favors to compensate for their lack of authority.[48] All of these challenges might explain why project managers, in a recent study of a matrix organization, reported significantly higher job satisfaction than did their line-manager colleagues.[49]

Finally, matrix organizations have turned out to be too complex and cumbersome for some organizations. After years of serving as a model for matrix design, Texas Instruments scrapped its complex matrix structure in favor of a more decentralized arrangement approximating strategic business units.[50] However, to conclude that matrix design was a passing fad of the 1970s and early 1980s, as some have done, would be a mistake. According to a study reported in the late 1980s, 89 percent of 387 U.S. and Canadian companies with matrix management experience said they would continue using it.[51]

# Effective Delegation

**6** Define the term *delegation* and list at least five common barriers to delegation.

Delegation is an important common denominator that runs through virtually all relatively organic design alternatives. It is vital to successful decentralization. Formally defined, **delegation** is the process of assigning various degrees of decision-making authority to lower-level employees.[52] As this definition implies, delegation is not an all-or-nothing proposition. There are at least five different degrees of delegation[53] (see Figure 10.8).

A word of caution about delegation is necessary because there is one thing it does *not* include. Former President Harry Truman is said to have had a little sign on his White House desk that read, "The Buck Stops Here!"[54] Managers who delegate should keep this idea in mind because, although authority may be passed along to people at lower levels, ultimate responsibility cannot be passed along. Thus delegation is the sharing of authority, not the abdication of responsibility. Chrysler's former CEO Lee Iacocca admittedly fell victim to this particular lapse:

**delegation** *assigning various degrees of decision-making authority to lower-level employees*

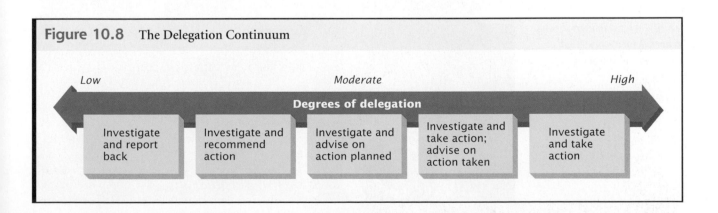

**Figure 10.8    The Delegation Continuum**

*When the company started to make money, it spent its cash on stock buybacks and acquisitions. For his part, Iacocca was distracted by nonautomotive concerns.*

*[Iacocca] concedes that while he kept his finger on finance and marketing, he should have paid closer attention to new model planning. "If I made one mistake," he says now, "it was delegating all the product development and not going to one single meeting."*[55]

Iacocca corrected this mistake prior to his retirement, and customers liked Chrysler's bold new designs.

## The Advantages of Delegation

Managers stand to gain a great deal by adopting the habit of delegating. By passing along well-defined tasks to lower-level people, managers can free more of their time for important chores like planning and motivating. Regarding the question of exactly *what* should be delegated, Intel's chairman, Andy Grove, made the following recommendation: "Because it is easier to monitor something with which you are familiar, if you have a choice you should delegate those activities you know best."[56] Grove cautions that delegators who follow his advice will experience some psychological discomfort because they will quite naturally want to continue doing what they know best.

In addition to freeing valuable managerial time,[57] delegation is also a helpful management training and development tool. Moreover, lower-level managers who desire more challenge generally become more committed and satisfied when they are given the opportunity to tackle significant problems. Conversely, a lack of delegation can stifle initiative. Consider the situation of a California builder:

*President George W. Bush knows how to delegate. His job is simply too big to do alone. When a complex web of national security issues boiled to the surface after 9/11, the President tapped former Pennsylvania governor Tom Ridge to assume the new position of Director of Homeland Security. Ridge's job is to coordinate national security–related matters among many federal agencies that might otherwise work at cross-purposes.*

*[The founder and chairman] personally negotiates every land deal. Visiting every construction site repeatedly, he is critical even of details of cabinet construction. "The building business is an entrepreneurial business," he says. "Yes, you can send out people. But you better follow them. You have to manage your managers."*

*Says one former . . . executive: "The turnover there's tremendous. He hires bright and talented people, but then he makes them eunuchs. He never lets them make any decisions."*[58]

Perfectionist managers who avoid delegation have problems in the long run when they become overwhelmed by minute details.

## Barriers to Delegation

There are several reasons why managers generally do not delegate as much as they should:

- Belief in the fallacy, "If you want it done right, do it yourself"
- Lack of confidence and trust in lower-level employees
- Low self-confidence
- Fear of being called lazy
- Vague job definition
- Fear of competition from those below
- Reluctance to take the risks involved in depending on others
- Lack of controls that provide early warning of problems with delegated duties
- Poor example set by bosses who do not delegate[59]

**10H  Two Types of Delegation?**

*There are two types of delegating that managers need to consider before passing the workload to their employees: delegating for results and delegating for employee development.*

**Source:** Sharon Gazda, "The Art of Delegating," *HRMagazine,* 47 (January 2002): 75.

**Questions:** *What do you like or dislike about this distinction? How can a manager effectively blend the two types of delegation?*

Managers can go a long way toward effective delegation by recognizing and correcting these tendencies both in themselves and in their fellow managers.[60] Since successful delegation is habit forming, the first step usually is the hardest. Properly trained and motivated people who know how to take initiative in challenging situations (see Skills & Tools at the end of this chapter) often reward a delegator's trust with a job well done.[61]

Once managers have developed the habit of delegating, they need to remember this wise advice from Peter Drucker: "Delegation . . . requires that delegators follow up. They rarely do—they think they have delegated, and that's it. But they are still accountable for performance. And so they have to follow up, have to make sure that the task gets done—and done right."[62]

# The Changing Shape of Organizations

Management scholars have been predicting the death of traditional pyramid-shaped bureaucracies for nearly 40 years.[63] Initial changes were slow in coming and barely noticeable. Observers tended to dismiss the predictions as naive and exaggerated. However, the pace and degree of change has picked up dramatically since the 1980s. All of the social, political-legal, economic, and technological changes discussed in Chapter 3

**7** Explain how the traditional pyramid organization is being reshaped.

threaten to make traditional organizations obsolete. Why? Because they are too slow, unresponsive, uncreative, costly, and hard to manage. It is clear today that no less than a reorganization revolution is under way. Traditional pyramid organizations, though still very much in evidence, are being questioned as never before. General Electric's legendary CEO Jack Welch put it this way:

> *The old organization was built on control, but the world has changed. The world is moving at such a pace that control has become a limitation. It slows you down. You've got to balance freedom with some control, but you've got to have more freedom than you ever dreamed of.*[64]

Consequently, to be prepared for tomorrow's workplace, we need to take a look at how organizations are being reshaped.

## Characteristics of the New Organizations

Three structural trends, already well established, are paving the way for new and different organizations. Layers are being eliminated, teamwork is becoming the norm, and size is being compartmentalized. Let us explore each of these exciting and sometimes troublesome trends.

**Fewer Layers.**    As documented in the last chapter, the dramatic downsizing of large U.S. businesses continues. Well-paid middle managers have been particularly hard hit. The plain truth is that companies can no longer afford layer upon layer of costly managerial talent in today's global economy. *Fortune* magazine offered this instructive historical perspective:

> *Middle managers have always handled two main jobs: supervising people, and gathering, processing, and transmitting information. But in growing numbers of companies, self-managed teams are taking over such standard supervisory duties as scheduling work, maintaining quality, even administering pay and vacations. Meanwhile, the ever-expanding power and dwin-*

*Video-conferences, such as the one going on here among employees of Polycom, are a key tool in today's virtual organizations. Improved technology has made video-conferencing very affordable. Time commitments and travel expenses are cut significantly when teams hook up electronically to get the job done. Still, researchers tell us that members of virtual work units need to have occasional face-to-face interaction to build social bonds and trust.*

*dling cost of computers have transformed information handling from a difficult, time-consuming job to a far easier and quicker one. Zap! In an instant, historically speaking, the middle manager's traditional functions have vaporized.*

*That's bad enough. At the same time, competition is forcing many companies to squeeze costs without mercy. Guess who looks like a big, fat target?[65]*

The so-called delayering of corporate America during the past decade has been remarkable. General Electric stripped away six layers of management, from ten to four.[66] America's second biggest copper company, Asarco, compressed 13 layers of management down to only five, thus helping to save the company $100 million.[67] Does delayering mean that hierarchies are unnecessary? According to motivation expert Edward Lawler, hierarchies are necessary, but less hierarchy is better:

*Hierarchies perform some very important organizational functions that must be done in some way if coordinated, organized behavior is to take place. On the other hand, if an organization design is adopted that includes work teams, new reward systems, extensive training, and . . . various other practices . . . , organizations can operate effectively with substantially less hierarchy.[68]*

Some organizations have already proved Lawler's point. Federal Express, for example, created a whole new overnight delivery industry with only five layers of management.[69]

**More Teams.**    Envisioning tomorrow's organizations, Peter Drucker mentions three characteristics: they will have fewer layers, be information-based, and be structured around teams.[70] Common team formats include project teams, quality circles, cross-functional teams, and self-managed teams. We pay close attention to each of these in later chapters. Greater emphasis on teamwork demands more effective communication, greater interpersonal trust, negotiating skills, and efficient conflict management. These topics also are discussed in later chapters.

**Smallness Within Bigness.**    When it comes to organizations, how big is too big? Is small beautiful? Is bigger better? These questions continue to stir lively debate in management circles. Research has not produced clear-cut answers.[71] Today, however, many have come to realize the issue is not the size of the organization. Rather, *complexity* seems to be the key issue. As organizations grow, they tend to become more complex and unmanageable. The trick for managers is to strike a balance to jointly reap the benefits of large size and small scale. A prime example is Cleveland's Parker Hannifin Corporation, the successful maker of hydraulics and other heavy equipment.

**10I  You Call That Teamwork?**

Michael Schrage, author of the book, *No More Teams!*:

*Somehow, we have to get past this idea that all we have to do is join hands and sing Kum Ba Yah and say, 'We've moved to teamwork.' . . . It's just not that easy. Anyone who's ever been on a team knows that. . . .*

**Source:** As quoted in Ellen Neuborne, "Companies Save, but Workers Pay," *USA Today* (February 25, 1997): 1B.

**Questions:** *Does Schrage have a good point or is he being overly negative? Explain. What is your own experience with teamwork? What does management have to do to promote real teamwork?*

*"When a division gets to a point where its general manager can't know and understand the business and be close to the customer, we split it off," says [now retired] Chief Executive Paul G. Schloemer. Typically, that means plants of 300 to 400 workers, but there is no hard-and-fast rule on size. It has more to do with how well managers can deal with the organization's complexity. Parker Hannifin now has more than 200 plants in some 80 divisions.[72]*

We can expect to see many attempts to create entrepreneurial units within the financial security blanket of big companies in the years ahead. General Electric's Jack Welch observed: "Well, in the end, that's what it's all about, trying to create a small-company soul in a big-company body. If you can do that and use the leverage and power, the global reach and human resources of a big company, you can create massive amounts of opportunity."[73]

## New Organizational Configurations

Figure 10.9 illustrates three different ways in which the traditional pyramid organization is being reshaped.[74] They are the hourglass organization, the cluster organization, and the virtual organization. In various combinations, these three configurations embody the characteristics just discussed. They also may overlap, as when an hourglass organization relies extensively on teams. The new structures have important implications for both the practice of management and the quality of work life. Let us examine them and take an imaginary peek into the not-too-distant future of work organizations.

**hourglass organization**

*a three-layer structure with a constricted middle layer*

**Hourglass Organizations.**    The **hourglass organization** consists of three layers, with the middle layer distinctly pinched. A strategic elite is responsible for formulating a vision for the organization and making sure it becomes reality. A significantly shrunken middle-management layer carries out a coordinating function for diverse lower-level activities. Thanks to computer networks that flash information directly from the factory floor or retail outlet to the executive suite and back again, middle managers are no longer simply conduits for warmed-over information. Also unlike traditional middle managers, hourglass middle managers are generalists rather than narrow specialists. They are comfortable dealing with complex interfunctional problems. A given middle manager might deal with an accounting problem one day, a product design issue the next, and a marketing dilemma the next—all within cross-functional team settings.

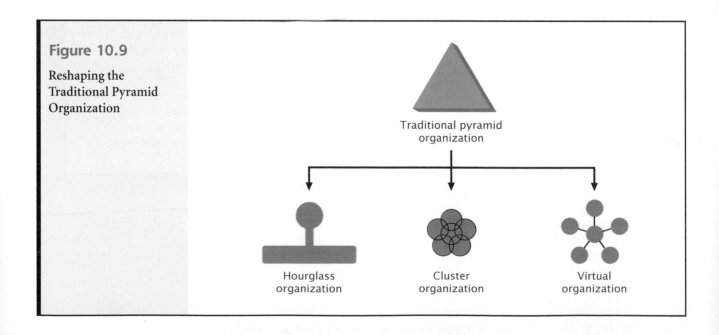

**Figure 10.9**

**Reshaping the Traditional Pyramid Organization**

Traditional pyramid organization

Hourglass organization

Cluster organization

Virtual organization

At the bottom of the hourglass is a broad layer of technical specialists who act as their own supervisors much of the time. Consequently, the distinction between supervisors and rank-and-file personnel is blurred. Employees at this operating level complain about a very real lack of promotion opportunities. Management tries to keep them motivated with challenging work assignments, lateral transfers, skill-training opportunities, and pay-for-performance schemes. Union organizers attempt to exploit complaints about employees "having to act like managers, but not being paid like managers."

**Cluster Organizations.**    Another new configuration shown in Figure 10.9 is the **cluster organization.** This label is appropriate because teams are the primary structural unit.[75]

> *For instance, Oticon Inc., a Danish hearing-aid manufacturer that also has operations in Somerset, NJ, abolished its formal organizational structure several years ago as part of a strategic turnaround. The old way of doing things has been replaced with a flexible work environment and project-based work processes. Self-directed teams have become the defining unit of work, disbanding and forming again as the work requires. Oticon typically has 100 projects running at any time, and most of its 1,500 employees work on several projects at once.[76]*

Imagining ourselves working in a cluster organization, we see multiskilled people moving from team to team as projects dictate. Pay for knowledge is a common practice. Motivation seems to be high, but some complain about a lack of job security because things are constantly changing. Stress levels rise when the pace of change quickens. Special training efforts, involving team-building exercises, are aimed at enhancing everyone's communication and group involvement skills.[77]

**Virtual Organizations.**    From the time of the Industrial Revolution until the Internet age, the norm was to build an organization capable of designing, producing, and marketing products. Bigger was assumed to be better. And this approach worked as long as large batches of look-alike products were acceptable to consumers. But along came the Internet, e-business, and mass customization, discussed in Chapters 1 and 7. *Speed*—in the form of faster market research, faster product development, faster production, and faster delivery—became more important than size. Meanwhile, global competition kept a lid on prices. Suddenly, consumers realized they could get exactly what they wanted, at a good price, and fast. Many lumbering organizational giants of the past were not up to the task. Enter **virtual organizations,** flexible networks of

**cluster organization**
*collaborative structure in which teams are the primary unit*

**virtual organizations**
*Internet-linked networks of value-adding subcontractors*

---

**10J    A Radical Approach to Virtual Organizations**

Advice from management guru Michael Hammer:

> *See your business not as a self-contained company but as part of an extended enterprise of companies that work together to create customer value.*

**Source:** Michael Hammer, *The Agenda: What Every Business Must Do to Dominate the Decade* (New York: Crown Business, 2001), p. 221.

**Questions:** *But what about quaint notions such as loyalty and company pride? How prepared are you to work in this sort of fluid and uncertain environment? Explain.*

PUBLISHED IN HARVARD BUSINESS REVIEW, JUNE 2001.

value-adding subcontractors, linked by the Internet, e-mail, fax machines, and tele-phones.[78] *Business Week* offered this perspective:

> *The sea change flowing from the Net is so profound that owning a factory is increasingly regarded as a liability. Hewlett-Packard, IBM, Silicon Graphics, and others have sold plants to contract producers such as Solectron, SCI Systems, Flextronics, and Celestica—then signed up these manufacturing specialists as suppliers. Some experts imagine that many enterprises will ultimately become tripartite virtual partnerships. One arm will handle product development and engineering, another will take care of marketing, and the third will do the production chores.[79]*

From a personal perspective, life in virtual organizations is *hectic.* Everything moves at Internet speed. Change and learning are constant. Cross-functional teams are the norm, and job reassignments are frequent. Project specialists rarely see a single project to completion because they are whisked off to other projects. Unavoidable by-products of constant change are stress and burnout. Unexpectedly, the need for face-to-face con-tact increases as geographically dispersed team members communicate via e-mail, instant messaging, groupware, and voice mail. Only face-to-face interaction, both on and off the job, can build the rapport and trust necessary to get something done quickly with people you rarely see. The growing gap between information haves and have-nots produces resentment and alienation among low-paid workers employed by factory, data-processing, and shipping subcontractors.

# Summary

1. Contingency organization design has grown in popularity as environmental complexity has increased. The idea behind contingency design is structuring the organization to fit situational demands. Consequently, contingency advocates contend that there is no one best organizational setup for all situations. Diagnosing the degree of environmental uncertainty is an important first step in contingency design. Field studies have validated the assumption that organization structure should vary according to the situation.

2. Burns and Stalker discovered that mechanistic (rigid) organizations are effective when the environment is relatively stable and that organic (flexible) organizations are best when unstable conditions prevail.

3. Lawrence and Lorsch found that differentiation (division of labor) and integration (cooperation among specialists) increased in successful organizations as environmental complexity increased. Today's organizations tend to suffer from excessive differentiation and inadequate integration.

4. There are five basic departmentalization formats, each with its own combination of advantages and disadvantages. Functional departmentalization is the most common approach. The others are product-service, geographic location, customer classification, and work flow process departmentalization. In actual practice, these pure types of departmentalization are usually combined in various ways.

5. Design variables available to organizers are span of control, decentralization, line and staff, and matrix. As organizers have come to realize that situational factors dictate how many people a manager can directly supervise, the notion of an ideal span of control has become obsolete. Decentralization, the delegation of decision authority to lower-level managers, has been praised as being democratic and criticized for reducing top management's control. Strategic business units foster a high degree of decentralization. Line and staff organization helps balance specialization and unity of command. Functional authority serves to make line and staff organizations more organic by giving staff specialists temporary and limited line authority. Matrix organizations are highly organic because they combine vertical and horizontal lines of authority to achieve coordinated control over complex projects.

6. Delegation of authority, although generally resisted for a variety of reasons, is crucial to decentralization. Effective delegation permits managers to tackle higher-priority duties while helping train and develop lower-level managers. Although delegation varies in degree, it never means abdicating primary responsibility. Successful delegation requires plenty of initiative from lower-level managers.

7. Many factors, with global competition leading the way, are forcing management to reshape the traditional pyramid bureaucracy. These new organizations are characterized by fewer layers, extensive use of teams, and manageably small subunits. Three emerging organizational configurations are the hourglass organization, the cluster organization, and virtual organizations. Each has its own potentials and pitfalls.

## Terms to Understand

Organizing (p. 318)

Contingency design (p. 319)

Mechanistic organizations (p. 319)

Organic organizations (p. 320)

Differentiation (p. 322)

Integration (p. 322)

Departmentalization (p. 324)

Span of control (p. 329)

Centralization (p. 331)

Decentralization (p. 331)

Strategic business unit (p. 332)

Line and staff organization (p. 333)

Functional authority (p. 334)

Matrix organization (p. 334)

Delegation (p. 337)

Hourglass organization (p. 342)

Cluster organization (p. 343)

Virtual organizations (p. 343)

## Skills & Tools

### If You Want to Be Delegated Important Duties, Then Demonstrate a Lot of *Initiative*

*Instructions:* Assess yourself with this checklist for taking initiative. What areas need improvement?

## Going Beyond the Job

- I make the most of my present assignment.
- I do more than I am asked to do.
- I look for places where I might spot problems and fix them.
- I fix bugs that I notice in programs or at least tell someone about them.
- I look for opportunities to do extra work to help the project move along more quickly.

## New Ideas and Follow-Through

- I try to do some original work.
- I look for places where something that's already done might be done better.
- I have ideas about new features and other technical projects that might be developed.
- When I have an idea, I try to make it work and let people know about it.

- I try to document what my idea is and why it's a good idea.

- I think about and try to document how my idea would save the company money or bring in new business.

- I seek advice from people who have been successful in promoting ideas.

- I construct a plan for selling my idea to people in the company.

## Dealing Constructively with Criticism

- I tell colleagues about my ideas to get their reactions and criticisms.

- I use their comments and criticisms to make my ideas better.

- I consult the sources of criticisms to help find solutions.

- I continue to revise my ideas to incorporate my colleagues' concerns.

## Planning for the Future

- I spend time planning what I'd like to work on next.

- I look for other interesting projects to work on when my present work gets close to the finish line.

- I talk to people to find out what projects are coming up and will need people.

*Source:* Reprinted by permission of *Harvard Business Review*. An exhibit from "How Bell Labs Creates Star Performers," by Robert Kelley and Janet Caplan, 71 (July–August 1993). Copyright © 1993 by the Harvard Business School Publishing Corporation; all rights reserved.

# Hands-On Exercise

## A Field Study: Sizing up an Organization's Structure and Design

This exercise is designed to help you better understand organization design by getting you out into the real world to interview a manager. (*Note:* If you *are* a manager— meaning you are responsible for directly overseeing the work of others in a formal organization—simply complete the exercise yourself.) Higher-level managers are best for this exercise because their perspective will tend to be broader and more strategic. If you interview a first-line supervisor, on the other hand, be sure to remind him or her to respond from an organizationwide perspective. The only materials you will need are photocopies of Table 10.1, Table 10.2, Figure 10.4, Figure 10.5, and Figure 10.8 to share with your interviewee to explain the questions.

    If the manager you interview works for a large organization, the unit of analysis can be a division, group, department, or stand-alone facility such as a factory, bank, restaurant, or store. Otherwise, the focus should be on the whole organization. (*Tip:* This exercise can give you a better feel for an organization where you might want to apply for a job.)

**Instructions**

A. *What is the degree of environmental uncertainty?* (Table 10.1)

> Low　1····2····3····4····5····6····7····8····9····10　High

B. *Is the organization relatively mechanistic or organic?* (Table 10.2)

> Mechanistic　1····2····3····4····5····6····7····8····9····10　Organic

C. *How wide is the typical span of control?* (Figure 10.4)

> _____ Narrow (2 to 4)　_____ Moderate (5 to 9)　_____ Wide (10 or more)

D. *How centralized or decentralized is the organization?* (Figure 10.5)

> Highly Centralized　1····2····3····4····5····6····7····8····9····10　Highly Decentralized

E. *What is the typical degree of delegation?* (Figure 10.8)

> Low　1····2····3····4····5····6····7····8····9····10　High

F. *How effective is the organization* (profitability and/or customer satisfaction)?

> Not effective　1····2····3····4····5····6····7····8····9····10　Effective

G. *How strong is employee morale and job satisfaction?*

> Weak　1····2····3····4····5····6····7····8····9····10　Strong

**For Consideration/ Discussion**

1. According to Burns and Stalker's research findings about mechanistic and organic organizations, is this organization appropriately structured for its environment? Explain.

2. What sort of connection do you see between this organization's design and its overall effectiveness?

3. What sort of connection do you see between this organization's design and employee morale and job satisfaction?

4. How were the degree of centralization/decentralization and the degree of delegation related in this study?

5. In your opinion, is the design of this organization a strategic strength or weakness?

6. Would you like to work for this organization (if you don't already)? Why?

7. What was the most interesting, useful, or important thing you learned from this exercise?

# Internet Exercises

1. **Let's get really organic:** Safe to say, there's probably no other company quite like W. L. Gore & Associates (**www.gore.com**). The maker of Gore-Tex fabrics, popular among sportspeople, consistently makes *Fortune*'s "100 Best Companies to Work for in America" list. This exercise gives you a peek inside an extraordinarily organic organization. Select the main menu heading "About Gore" and then click on "Profile." Do a quick tour of "Fast Facts" and then go back and select "Corporate

Culture." At the bottom of that page you will find a link to a presentation on Gore's unique "lattice organization."

*Learning Points:* 1. Using Table 10.2 as a guide, try to figure out what organic organization features are evident at Gore. 2. What types of people would and would not be comfortable working at W. L. Gore? Would you like to work at Gore? 3. What are the main risks of being too organic?

**2. Check it out:** *Fast Company* magazine (**www.fastcompany.com**) always has interesting and provocative ideas for modern managers. At the home page, under the tab "Magazine," click on the submenu item "Dynamic Archives." Starting with the most recent issue of *Fast Company,* scan the contents of three or four issues for a topic relevant to this chapter. Read the full text of an article or two. Chances are very good you'll find something instructive and interesting about the design and management of today's organizations.

For updates to these exercises, visit our Web site (**http://business.college.hmco. com/students**).

## Closing Case

## Bean Counters' Revenge: "Tear Down the Walls"

Anton Hendler, a certified public accountant, is deep into a phone conversation with a longtime client whose $10-million textile business unexpectedly found itself without a controller a couple of days ago. Hendler speedily dispatched a fellow accountant to fill in for a while, and now his client is going into raptures over the way the arrangement's working out. "That's wonderful news," Hendler booms into the telephone. "WON-DAH-FULL!" Half a dozen heads whirl around as his baritone reverberates like a sonic wave through the wide-open work environment (there are no private offices, no cubicles, no secrets) owned and occupied by Lipschultz, Levin & Gray, Certified Public Accountants, in Northbrook, Illinois, just north of Chicago.

If LLG were your basic run-of-the-mill CPA practice, Hendler would be squirreled away in a sound-sucking windowless warren of bank-teller-size cubes near the elevators. Happy news straight from paying customers would never reach him or any other staff accountant unless it had been vetted by senior heavyweights and handed down the chain of command in dignified order. No, Hendler would be as far removed as possible from real live clients and unfiltered feedback, until the day he finally hit the big time and moved up into the lonely grandeur and complex networks of privileged communication that mark partnership territory.

Then again, Lipschultz, Levin & Gray (or "The Bean Counters," as the firm likes to be called) is way out of the range of what anyone who's halfway familiar with accounting firms is used to. Not one of the firm's 26 employees (called "team members") or five partners (called "members") has an office or a desk to call his or her own—or even a regular location. Instead, everyone who works there is part of a nomadic tribe of people who tote their gear (files, phones, laptops) to a new spot every day, a chore made easier than it sounds because each piece of furniture is mounted on casters and locomotes at a touch.

The foundation of LLG's novel approach is everywhere you look in this building: evidence of versatility, comfort, and eccentricity in a fizzy, constantly metamorphosing space that makes even a hot new concept like "flexible workplace" seem drab and worn-out. True, the top people had to give up some executive ego candy, like private offices and reserved parking and pinstriped suits, but in exchange for roughing it, they got this jaw dropper of an office, as beautiful as it is revolutionary.

The firm's nickname is really what started it. In the early 1990s, when LLG surveyed its clients to find out what they thought of accountants in general, the thing that kept turning up was the phrase *bean counter*, the rude but ubiquitous term that disses accountants as uncommunicative, shortsighted penny pinchers who are obsessed with the smallest of financial details. Maybe these accountants couldn't do much to alter the negative perceptions that dogged their whole profession—which, as everybody kept telling them, is as boring as airline food—but that didn't stop them from poking fun at it. Why not liberate themselves from the confines of the green-eyeshade mentality to pursue a bigger, zippier way of working, where souped-up skills and distinctive service to clients are far more important than the size of partners' offices?

The Bean Counters have since unleashed a whole slew of changes that are wonderfully entrepreneurial and also sort of nuts. Every telltale remnant of dreary CPA-ness has been purged. Today the firm still delivers traditional accounting, audit, and tax services, but it also has just launched four new business-consulting offshoots. Income has tripled and client referrals have doubled over the past ten years. More than anything else, LLG has paid careful attention to developing the creativity, talent, and diversity of its staffers so that new knowledge can be acquired and passed around without getting hung up on the thorns of reporting relationships or stuck in out-of-the-way corner offices. That is an accomplishment that could be brought about only by time, a deep and durable dissatisfaction with the way things were, accidental discoveries, and the kind of leader who is bold and funny and idealistic and a natural at figuring stuff out....

"We always followed the pattern of the big firms," says Steve Siegel, LLG's 47-year-old managing member, a CPA/lawyer who joined the firm full-time in 1976 and was named to his current post in 1991. "We threw more and more people at problems and built big offices and a big wonderful pyramid," he says. Ask Siegel about the business preoccupation back then, and he gets a little hyper. "Why aren't we making any money? Where's our money?' That was it," he says, chuckling.

He can laugh about it now, but back in those dark pre–Bean Counter megapyramid days, it was no joke.

LLG employed some 55 people, who occupied nearly 17,000 square feet of standard-issue chopped-up office space. The firm spent a fortune on salaries and most of the rest of its revenues on rent. Partners, whose take-home pay is traditionally about a third of a firm's profits, were making about one-sixth of LLG's profits....

Since new clients weren't exactly clamoring for LLG's services, the firm didn't kick up enough work to keep everybody busy. Staffers—bored, discouraged, and underpaid—headed for the green in other pastures. Recruiting new people became a regular, though dismal, feature of life at the firm. "We kept saying we wanted top-notch people, but who the hell would come to us? So we ended up with everybody else's dregs," says Siegel. ...

Siegel's eyes were opened when he cornered Scottish-born-and-trained partner Bill Finestone. "Are you a really good accountant in Scotland?" he wanted to know, and, "Are there others of you?" When Finestone replied he thought that among Scottish accountants he was about average, it came as a shock. Here was this Scot who'd scored in the top 100 in the United States when he sat for his CPA exam, who is everything you'd want in a partner and an accountant—and he says, well, I'm about average. That convinced Siegel he should look outside the United States for talent, a search that has paid off handsomely. Of the 26 current team members, four are from Scotland, two are English, two are South Africans, one is Russian, and one is from France.

## For Discussion

1. Using Table 10.2 as a guide, is LLG a mechanistic or organic organization? Cite specific supporting evidence.

2. Would you call LLG a centralized or decentralized organization? Explain.

3. Is LLG a good or bad climate for delegation? Explain.

4. Which of the new organizational configurations—hourglass, cluster, or virtual—apparently fits LLG? Explain.

## chapter eleven

# Human Resource Management

> **" Great vision without great people is irrelevant. "**
>
> Jim Collins

## CHAPTER OBJECTIVES

*When you finish studying this chapter you should be able to*

**1** **Explain** what human resource management involves.

**2** **Define** the term *human capital* and **identify** at least four of Pfeffer's people-centered practices.

**3** **Identify** and briefly **explain** the seven steps in the PROCEED model of employee selection.

**4** **Distinguish** among equal employment opportunity, affirmative action, and managing diversity.

**5** **Explain** how managers can be more effective interviewers.

**6** **Discuss** how performance appraisals can be made legally defensible.

**7** **Compare** and **contrast** the ingredients of good training programs for both skill and factual learning.

**8** **Specify** the essential components of an organization's policies for dealing with sexual harassment and alcohol and drug abuse.

# Welfare-to-Work Works for T. J. Maxx

Back in May 1997, Ben Cammarata went to the White House and pledged to hire 5,000 people from the welfare rolls by the year 2000. At the time, moving people from welfare to work was more hope than reality, and nobody, including Cammarata, really knew what to expect. Moreover, he hadn't worked out all the details. For one thing, the CEO of the TJX Cos., parent of off-price clothing retailers T. J. Maxx and Marshalls, wondered whether the new workers would be able to adjust to the workplace. What if they made attrition worse? Another big question Cammarata asked himself: "How do we find these people?" For a company with over a thousand stores in 47 states, the answer was not obvious.

Cammarata is the first to admit that his motives in making that pledge weren't purely charitable. He was desperate. Unemployment in the spring of 1997 stood at just 5%, and TJX was feeling the pinch. Turnover is endemic to retail, and the company was used to turning over 100% of its store jobs in a year. But the lowest unemployment rates in decades had created intense competition for workers. Cammarata says his managers talked a lot about the $8-an-hour signs in McDonald's windows—and how TJX was losing people because it paid less. With the company in the midst of an ambitious expansion plan, TJX needed lots of bodies.

Fast-forward three years: Instead of taking on 5,000 people from welfare, the Framingham, Mass., company has hired 16,000. Like many companies in the non-profit Welfare to Work Partnership, TJX reaped great benefits from hiring former welfare recipients. Instead of exacerbating the stores' retention problems, the new hires are helping to solve them, even as the labor market has continued to tighten. TJX says 61% of the employees it hired from welfare are still there after a year, well above the 43% retention rate for traditional hires. Retail stores typically attract people looking for short-term and part-time work, but Ted English, TJX's new CEO (founder Cammarata continues as chairman), says these new hires are looking for something more: "The welfare-to-work associates we're hiring are looking for a little bit more stability and a little bit more of a long-term relationship," he says. "It's worked out great for us."

How did TJX make this work? First it had to figure out how to find the new workers. To that end, the company pays an Indianapolis outfit called CIC Enterprises $200,000 a year to create and run a job hot line tied to agencies that help prepare welfare recipients for work. CIC set up the network so that a store manager for a T. J. Maxx or Marshalls in any city could call an 800 number day or night to request candidates for a job opening. Within 24 hours, job descriptions are dispatched to social service agencies in the store's area. The results have been stunning: For every ten calls made to the hot line, eight have produced a candidate who's been hired. (And TJX gets another benefit for hiring them—tax credits, which came to $2 million last year.) Now the phone networks are being expanded to recruit older workers, with plans to reach immigrants and people with developmental disabilities.

Store managers don't necessarily know if job applicants walking in the door have been dispatched through the job hot line—they could just as easily be responding to a HELP WANTED sign. TJX brass wanted the new hires coming from welfare to be treated just like anybody else, with no special training.

While that approach worked for thousands, it became apparent early on that some people needed extra help. Betsy Shortell was an assistant manager at the Marshalls store in the Dorchester section of Boston in 1998 when local residents who told her they were losing their welfare benefits started applying for jobs. Sometimes they showed up for interviews in halter tops or ripped blue jeans; one filled in an application in purple crayon.

To reach people like the applicant with the purple crayon—those with little or no work experience—and no high school diploma—TJX started a pilot program in partnership with Morgan Memorial Goodwill Industries in Boston. Called First Step, the program—now in three cities—gives welfare recipients three weeks of classroom training, followed by an internship at a T. J. Maxx, Marshalls, or Goodwill store. Goodwill handles the training, which is funded with federal dollars. Those who complete the internship are guaranteed jobs at a TJX or Goodwill store.

A First Step case manager follows up on graduates for at least a year, helping solve breakdowns in child care and transportation, and a store liaison is available to both the manager and the employee to nip any performance problems in the bud. That support system helped take some of the pressure off Shortell when she hired First Step graduates. Shortell, who is now a store manager in Quincy, Mass., says working with First Step helped her manage better. In the past, if an employee missed a couple of days, she'd be fired. Now Shortell is more inclined to say, "We're having a problem—what can we do?" . . .

But First Step is no panacea. [Store Manager John] D'Amico says that of the six First Step graduates hired at his store, only two are still there.

One, however, is an unqualified success: in 18 months, Vicki Glover has had three promotions and is on track to begin training to be an assistant manager within the next few years (she wants to get her GED first). Not bad for someone who got pregnant at 17 and dropped out of high school, and whose previous work experience was limited to some temp assignments doing light assembly. An energetic 37-year-old with an engaging smile, Glover's clearly suited to her current assignment, trying to give the store's once neglected kids' department some TLC. "I'm like a magnet when it comes to people," she says.

But as much as Glover loves her work, she still has trouble making ends meet. She earns $8.50 an hour, which puts her above the poverty level for a family of four (she has three sons, ages 4, 11, and 19), but not by much. She's back on food stamps after being turned down twice, and sometimes has to choose between paying the rent and paying the phone bill. Every little victory seems to be accompanied by a new challenge: She recently got a voucher to help pay the day-care bill for her youngest, but her rent just went up.

Ted English knows TJX can't do everything for everybody. He says the company is doing its part by offering jobs and an opportunity to advance. Beyond that, he thinks the government needs to help out. Of course, the government has helped TJX too—by pushing welfare recipients into the labor force, offering tax credits, and subsidizing training. But TJX isn't likely to boost its entry-level wages by much: "In order for us to exist, we have to be a low-cost operator," CEO English says. And as he likes to remind people, he started his career as a stock boy.

**1** Explain what human resource management involves.

**human resource management** *acquisition, retention, and development of human resources*

Staffing has long been an integral part of the management process. Like other traditional management functions, such as planning and organizing, the domain of staffing has grown throughout the years. This growth reflects increasing environmental complexity and greater organizational sophistication, as the T. J. Maxx case clearly illustrates. Early definitions of staffing focused narrowly on hiring people for vacant positions. Today, the traditional staffing function is just one part of the more encompassing human resource management process. **Human resource management** involves the acquisition, retention, and development of human resources necessary for organizational success. This broader definition underscores the point that people are valuable *resources* requiring careful nurturing. In fact, what were once called personnel departments are now called human resource departments. In a more folksy manner, the top human resources executive at Wal-Mart is called the "senior vice president of people."[1] This people-centered human resource approach emphasizes the serious moral and legal issues involved in viewing labor simply as a commodity to be bought, exploited to exhaustion, and discarded when convenient. Moreover, global opportunities and competitive pressures have made the skillful management of human resources more important than ever.[2]

Progressive and successful organizations treat all employees as valuable human resources. A prime example is Southwest Airlines, the growing and consistently profitable company with a no-layoff policy. New CEO Jim Parker says: "We're people-focused. . . . We treat our employees with respect. We prize loyalty."[3] Field research indicates that employees tend to return the favor when they are treated with dignity and respect. For instance, one study compared steel mills with either "control" or "commitment" human resource systems. Emphasis at the control-oriented steel mills was on cost cutting, rule compliance, and efficiency. Meanwhile, the other steel mills encouraged psychological commitment to the company with a climate of trust and participation. "The mills with commitment systems had higher productivity, lower scrap rates, and lower employee turnover than those with control systems."[4]

Figure 11.1 presents a model for the balance of this chapter; it reflects this strategic orientation. Notice how a logical sequence of human resource management activities— human resource strategy, recruiting, selection, performance appraisal, and training—all derive from organizational strategy and structure. Without a strategic orientation, the management of people becomes haphazardly inefficient and ineffective. Also, as indicated in Figure 11.1, an ongoing process following the hiring decision involves identifying and solving human resource problems. Two contemporary human resource problems, explored in the last section of this chapter, are discouraging sexual harassment and controlling alcohol and drug abuse.

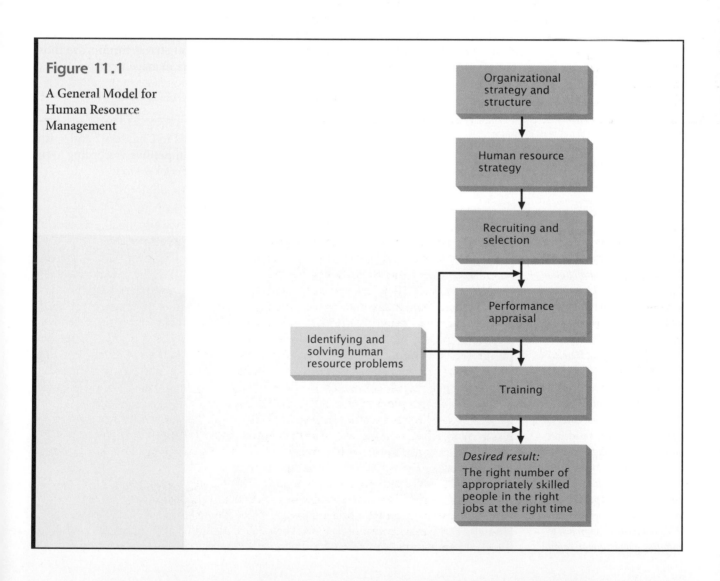

**Figure 11.1**

A General Model for
Human Resource
Management

# Human Resource Strategy: A People-Centered Approach

Conventional wisdom about how employees should be perceived and managed has evolved greatly over the last 50 years. The pendulum has swung from reactive to proactive. Following World War II, personnel departments filled hiring requisitions and handled disciplinary problems submitted by managers. During the 1970s and 1980s, human resource (HR) departments became the norm and a more encompassing approach evolved. HR departments attempted to forecast labor supply and demand, recruit and hire, manage payrolls, and conduct training and development programs. Too often, however, HR was treated as a support-staff function with only an indirect link to corporate strategy. Today, in well-managed companies, HR is embedded in organizational strategy and many traditional HR functions are decentralized throughout the enterprise.[5] But the transition is far from complete, as indicated by this recent observation: "Some business pundits have likened the current status of HR to an awkward adolescent. The profession is just beginning to come of age but isn't quite sure where it's heading."[6] In fact, in a survey of senior HR managers, 37 percent said they "always" participated in corporate strategic planning. Another 42 percent said they "sometimes" had a hand in company strategy.[7] This section strives to improve those numbers by outlining a strategic agenda for human resource management.

**2** Define the term *human capital* and identify at least four of Pfeffer's people-centered practices.

## The Age of Human Capital

This perspective requires open-system thinking, as discussed in Chapters 2 and 9. It is a "big picture" approach to managing people and staying competitive. According to the authors of *The HR Scorecard: Linking People, Strategy, and Performance:*

*Mexico's President Vicente Fox applies straightforward logic to the issue of illegal immigration of Mexicans into the United States. Create more (and better-paying) employment opportunities south of the border and the appeal of El Norte will diminish. Here, 27-year-old Armando Bernabe wields a fabric cutter in a garment factory southeast of Mexico City. Bernabe owes this opportunity to Fox's padrino program (Spanish for Godfather) in which 100 wealthy Mexicans living in the U.S. have invested in businesses and public works projects back in their hometowns. This is a creative approach to building global human capital.*

*We're living in a time when a new economic paradigm—characterized by speed, innovation, short cycle times, quality, and customer satisfaction—is highlighting the importance of intangible assets, such as brand recognition, knowledge, innovation, and particularly human capital.*[8]

The term **human capital** encompasses all present and future workforce participants and emphasizes the need to develop their fullest potential for the benefit of the global economy. Central to this perspective is the assumption that every employee is a valuable asset, not merely an expense item.[9] This broad concern for possible *future* employees is a marked departure from traditional "employees-only" perspectives.

**human capital** *the need to develop to their fullest potential all present and future employees*

Intel, the Santa Clara, California–based maker of computer microprocessors, is committed to developing human capital. The company adopts primary and secondary schools—providing computers, teaching talent, and money—and encourages its employees to help. "For every 20 hours workers volunteer at local schools, Intel donates $200."[10] As might be expected from a high-tech company, the emphasis is on math and science. Additionally, Intel matches employees' donations to their college alma maters up to $10,000 a year and awards $1,250,000 in school grants and scholarships each year to winners in a national science competition for high school seniors. Most of those who benefit from these initiatives will *not* end up working for Intel. That's what developing the *world's* human capital is all about—thinking big! (For more, see the Internet Exercises at the end of this chapter.)

**11A**

**Back to the Opening Case**

What role does the concept of "human capital" play in the T. J. Maxx case?

For further information about the interactive annotations in this chapter, visit our Web site (http://business.college.hmco.com/students).

## People-Centered Organizations Enjoy a Competitive Advantage

In an era of nonstop layoffs, the often-heard slogan "Employees are our most valuable asset" rings hollow. In fact, Dilbert cartoonist Scott Adams calls that statement "The First Great Lie of Management."[11] But such cynicism can be put aside by looking at how leading companies build a bridge from progressive human resource practices to market success. Once again, we turn to Southwest Airlines. Cofounder and chairman Herb Kelleher told *Fortune* magazine: "My mother taught me that your employees come first. If you treat them well, then they treat the customers well, and that means your customers come back and your shareholders are happy."[12] Well, Herb's mom was right! Solid research support for this approach comes from Stanford's Jeffrey Pfeffer, who reported a strong connection between *people-centered practices* and higher profits and lower employee turnover. Pfeffer identified these seven people-centered practices:

- Protection of job security (including a no-layoff policy)
- Rigorous hiring process
- Employee empowerment through decentralization and self-managed teams
- Compensation linked to performance
- Comprehensive training
- Reduction of status differences
- Sharing of key information

Pfeffer sees these practices as an integrated package and cautions against implementing them piecemeal. Unfortunately, according to Pfeffer's calculations, only about 12 percent of today's organizations qualify as

**11B What About Loyalty?**

*U.S. corporations lose half their customers in five years, half their employees in four, and half their investors in less than one. By fostering loyalty, companies can boost productivity, customer retention and referrals, and attract talented staff.*

**Source:** Mara Der Hovanesian, "When Loyalty Erodes, So Do Profits," *Business Week* (August 13, 2001): 8.

**Question:** *What are the linkages between people-centered practices and employee, customer, and investor loyalty?*

being systematically people-centered.[13] Thus, we have a clear developmental agenda for human resource management. Ideas about how to enact people-centered practices can be found throughout the balance of this book.

# Recruitment and Selection

Jim Collins, in his best-seller *Good to Great: Why Some Companies Make the Leap and Others Don't*, uses the metaphor of a bus when referring to the organization and its employees.[14] He believes a busload of great people can go just about anywhere it wants. But a bus filled with confused and unruly passengers is destined for the ditch. A recent survey of CEOs reinforces the importance of getting the right people on the bus and keeping them there. When asked what they likely will look back on five years from now as the key to their success, the number one response was "Getting and retaining talent."[15] This section deals with that important challenge.

## Recruiting for Diversity

The ultimate goal of recruiting is to generate a pool of qualified applicants for new and existing jobs. Everyday recruiting tactics include internal job postings, referrals by present and past employees, campus recruiters, newspaper ads, Web sites, public and private employment agencies, so-called headhunters, job fairs, temporary-help agencies, and union halls. Meanwhile, an underlying reality makes today's recruiting extremely challenging. Namely, applicant pools need to be demographically representative of the population at large if diversity is to be achieved. A casual review of today's recruiting ads reveals abundant evidence of corporate diversity initiatives. Monica Reed, at Prudential in Newark, New Jersey, explains the rationale:

> *Our corporate culture is diverse, because that brings a variety of new ideas and perspectives into the company. We also want to sell to a diverse audience, and someone who sees a recruitment ad that focuses on diversity may also become a customer.*[16]

Companies strive hard to make *Fortune*'s annual "America's 50 Best Companies for Minorities" list so that they can cite the honor in their recruiting ads. Among the major names on the most recent list are McDonald's, Xerox, BellSouth, and PepsiCo.[17]

Recent research holds a major surprise about recruiting for diversity (see Table 11.1). Importantly, the study turned the tables and took a *job hunter's* perspective. Within the top five categories of search methods, corporate Web sites had the distinction of being the most frequently used but *least successful* job-hunting method. Referrals turned out to be the best way to land a job. So we have one word of advice for job hunters in all walks of life: *network*.

> *Especially in a tough economy, networking is the key. Resume-deluged employers are posting job openings only as a last resort, says Kirsten Watson, president of HireTopTalent. Rather, job leads come from "a friend who had a friend who had an uncle." . . .*

## 11C  Cool Tattoo!

*About 42 percent of managers polled by Vault.com said they would lower their opinions of someone with tattoos or body piercings. Fifty-eight percent said they would be less likely to offer them a job in the first place.*

**Source:** Michael Rosenwald, "Tattoo Wearers Cover Up at Work," *The Arizona Republic* (June 3, 2001): D2.

**Question:** *Are tattoos and body piercings fair game for discrimination in hiring or are they a matter of diversity? Explain.*

| Table 11.1   How Diverse Candidates Search for and Find Jobs | |
|---|---|
| **Top 5 Search Methods** | |
| 1. Corporate web sites | 70% |
| 2. General job-listing sites | 67 |
| 3. Classified ads | 53 |
| 4. Referrals | 52 |
| 5. Headhunters/agencies | 35 |
| **Top 5 Ways Candidates Found Jobs** | |
| 1. Referrals | 25% |
| 2. General job-listing sites | 17 |
| 3. Headhunters/agencies | 17 |
| 4. Classified ads | 15 |
| 5. Corporate web sites | 6 |

*Source:* Reprinted with the permission of *HRMagazine* from Ruth E. Thaler-Carter, "Diversify Your Recruitment Advertising," *HRMagazine*, 46 (June 2001): 99, published by the Society for Human Resource Management, Alexandria, VA.

*To network effectively, start with friends, family, and others who know you well and can help present your case, says Bob Critchley, executive VP for global relationships at outplacement firm Drake Beam Morin.*[18]

## The Selection Process: An Overview

HR experts commonly compare the screening and selection process to a hurdle race. Equal employment opportunity (EEO) legislation in the United States and elsewhere attempts to ensure a fair and unprejudiced race for all job applicants.[19] The first two hurdles are résumé screening and reference checking; both are very important because an estimated "40% of job applications include false information."[20] Background checks for criminal records and citizenship/immigration status are more essential than ever in an age of workplace violence and international terrorism. Consider this: "Between January 1998 and October 2000, American Background Information Services Inc. (ABI), based in Winchester, Va., found undisclosed criminal backgrounds on 12.6 percent of the people it screened."[21] Other hurdles may include psychological tests, physical examinations, interviews, work-sampling tests, and drug tests.

Del J. Still, a respected author and trainer, summarizes the overall employee selection process with the acronym PROCEED, with each letter representing one of the seven steps involved (see Table 11.2). This model encourages managers to take a systems perspective, all the way from preparation to the final hiring decision. Before examining key elements of the PROCEED model in depth, we need to clarify what is involved in the first three action items for step 1. This is where job analysis and job descriptions come into play. **Job analysis** is the process of identifying basic task and skill requirements for specific jobs by studying superior performers. A **job description** is a concise document outlining the role expectations and skill requirements for a specific job. Although some say they have become obsolete in today's fast-paced world, up-to-date job descriptions foster discipline in selection and performance appraisal by offering a formal measuring stick.[22]

**3** Identify and briefly explain the seven steps in the PROCEED model of employee selection.

**job analysis**  *identifying task and skill requirements for specific jobs by studying superior performers*

**job description**  *document outlining role expectations and skill requirements for a specific job*

**Table 11.2    The Employee Selection Process: Still's PROCEED Model**

**Step 1: PREPARE**

- Identify existing superior performers
- Create a job description for the position
- Identify the competencies or skills needed to do the job
- Draft interview questions

**Step 2: REVIEW**

- Review questions for legality and fairness

**Step 3: ORGANIZE**

- Select your interview team and your method of interviewing
- Assign roles to your team and divide the questions

**Step 4: CONDUCT**

- Gather data from the job candidate

**Step 5: EVALUATE**

- Determine the match between the candidate and the job

**Step 6: EXCHANGE**

- Share data in a discussion meeting

**Step 7: DECIDE**

- Make the final decision

*Source:* Del J. Still, *High Impact Hiring: How to Interview and Select Outstanding Employees,* 2nd ed., rev. (Dana Point, Calif.: Management Development Systems, 2001), pp. 43–44. Reprinted by permission.

**4** Distinguish among equal employment opportunity, affirmative action, and managing diversity.

# Equal Employment Opportunity

Although earlier legislation selectively applies, the landmark EEO law in the United States is Title VII of the Civil Rights Act of 1964. Subsequent amendments, presidential executive orders, and related laws have expanded EEO's coverage. EEO law now provides a broad umbrella of employment protection for certain categories of disadvantaged individuals:

> *The result of this legislation has been that in virtually all aspects of employment, it is unlawful to discriminate on the basis of race, color, sex, religion, age, national origin, . . . [disabilities], being a disabled veteran, or being a veteran of the Vietnam Era.*[23]

What all this means is that managers cannot refuse to hire, promote, train, or transfer employees simply on the basis of the characteristics listed above. Nor can they lay off or discharge employees on these grounds. Sexual preference has been added to the list in some local jurisdictions.[24] Selection and all other personnel decisions must be made solely on the basis of objective criteria such as ability to perform or seniority. Lawsuits and fines by agencies such as the Equal Employment Opportunity Commission

(EEOC) are powerful incentives to comply with EEO laws. In fact, racial discrimination settlements cost Texaco $176 million in 1996 and Coca-Cola $192.5 million in 2000.[25]

**Affirmative Action.**   A more rigorous refinement of EEO legislation is affirmative action. An **affirmative action program (AAP)** is a plan for actively seeking out, employing, and developing the talents of those groups traditionally discriminated against in employment.[26] Affirmative action amounts to a concerted effort to make up for *past* discrimination. EEO, in contrast, is aimed at preventing *future* discrimination. Typical AAPs attack employment discrimination with the following four methods: (1) *active* recruitment of women and minorities, (2) elimination of prejudicial questions on employment application forms, (3) establishment of specific goals and timetables for minority hiring, and (4) statistical validation of employment testing procedures.

> **affirmative action program (AAP)** *making up for past discrimination by actively seeking and employing minorities*

   Like any public policy with legal ramifications, the EEO/AAP area is fraught with complexity.[27] Varying political and legal interpretations and inconsistent court decisions have sometimes frustrated and confused managers.[28] Researchers have uncovered both negative and positive findings about affirmative action. On the negative side, "people believed to be hired through affirmative action programs carry a stigma of incompetence no matter how qualified they are for the job."[29] On the positive side, a study based on nationwide U.S. Census Bureau data found that affirmative action had helped the promotion opportunities of black workers in both government and business organizations. In fact, according to the researcher, "with the exception of women in the public sector, women and blacks enjoyed better promotion opportunities than equally qualified and situated white male workers."[30] These findings disturb some white males, who claim to be the victims of "reverse discrimination."[31] At the same time, some minority employees complain of swapping one injustice for another when they take advantage of affirmative action. Legislated social change, however necessary or laudable, is not without pain. Much remains to be accomplished to eliminate the legacy of unfair discrimination in the workplace.

**From Affirmative Action to Managing Diversity.**   As discussed in Chapter 3, the "managing-diversity" movement promises to raise the discussion of equal employment opportunity and affirmative action to a higher plane. One authority on the subject, R. Roosevelt Thomas Jr., put it this way:

> *Managers usually see affirmative action and equal employment opportunity as centering on minorities and women, with very little to offer white males. The diversity I'm talking about includes not only race, gender, creed, and ethnicity but also age, background, education, function, and personality differences. The objective is not to assimilate minorities and women into a dominant white male culture but to create a dominant heterogeneous culture.*[32]

In short, diversity advocates want to replace all forms of bigotry, prejudice, and intolerance with tolerance and, ideally, *appreciation* of interpersonal differences.[33] They also want to broaden the focus on minorities to include recruitment *and retention*. Don Richards, senior vice president and director of human resource development at Leo Burnett Company, the Chicago-based advertising agency, offered this hopeful perspective of managing diversity:

> *"As an African-American, when I was graduated from college in 1960, there was little effort made by private industries to recruit minority students," Richards said. "I'm encouraged by the changes I've seen in the past 30 years. We have a long way to go, but my hope is that one day diversity will not be a special effort but the norm—just part of doing business."*[34]

*The world changed for Carmen Jones when a car accident during her junior year at Virginia's Hampton University left her in a wheelchair for life. After months of painful rehabilitation, an inspiring boost from the University's president helped her eliminate deep self-doubts and earn a marketing degree with honors. It's been onward and upward ever since. Now she's the founding president of Solutions Marketing Group in Arlington, Virginia. The company helps businesses reach and better serve disabled people—a group Jones believes is seriously underserved. For Jones, the key word in disability is "ability."*

Periodically, as in the cases of Texaco and Coca-Cola, we are reminded of just how much remains to be done.

### Accommodating the Needs of People with Disabilities.

From the perspective of someone in a wheelchair, the world can be a very unfriendly place. Curbs, stairways, and inward-swinging doors in small public toilet stalls all symbolically say, "You're not welcome here; you don't fit in." Human disabilities vary widely, but historically, disabled people have had one thing in common—unemployment. Consider these telling statistics:

> *Today, more than 54 million Americans are disabled, nearly 20 percent of the U.S. population. One in five disabled adults has not graduated from high school, and more than 70 percent of disabled people between ages 18 and 55 are unemployed.[35]*

**11D    The Word "Ability" Is the Most Important Part of Disability**

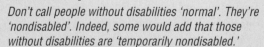

*Don't call people without disabilities 'normal'. They're 'nondisabled'. Indeed, some would add that those without disabilities are 'temporarily nondisabled.'*

**Source:** Marc Hequet, "ADA Etiquette," *Training*, 30 (April 1993): 33.

**Questions:** *What are the implications of these statements for people with disabilities? What sort of accommodations to disabled people have you observed recently? How do any of these accommodations affect your life?*

Reducing the unemployment rate for people with disabilities is not just about jobs and money. It is about self-sufficiency, hopes, and dreams.[36] With enactment of the Americans with Disabilities Act of 1990 (ADA), disabled Americans hoped to get a real chance to take their rightful place in the workforce.[37] But according to recent data, this hope remains unfulfilled. In fact, added government regulation reportedly has discouraged some employers from hiring disabled people. The disappointing findings: "analysis of Census Bureau survey data from 1987 to 1996 indicates that the act's impact on employment of the disabled was negative."[38]

The ADA, enforced by the EEOC, requires employers to make *reasonable* accommodations to the needs of present and future employees with physical and mental disabilities. As the ADA was being phased in to cover nearly all employers, many feared their businesses would be saddled with burdensome expenses and many lawsuits. But a 1998 White House–sponsored survey "determined that the mean cost of helping disabled workers to overcome their impairments was a mere $935 per person."[39]

New technology is also making accommodation easier.[40] Large-print computer screens for the partially blind, braille keyboards and talking computers for the blind, and telephones with visual readouts for the deaf are among today's helpful technologies. Here are some general policy guidelines for employers:

- Audit all facilities, policies, work rules, hiring procedures, and labor union contracts to eliminate barriers and bias.
- Train all managers in ADA compliance and all employees in how to be sensitive to coworkers and customers with disabilities.
- Do not hire anyone who cannot safely perform the basic duties of a particular job with reasonable accommodation.

With lots of low-tech ingenuity, a touch of high tech, and support from coworkers, millions of disabled people can help their employers win the battle of global competition (see Managing Diversity).

## Employment Selection Tests

EEO guidelines in the United States have broadened the definition of an **employment selection test** to include any procedure used as a basis for an employment decision. This means that, in addition to traditional pencil-and-paper tests, numerous other procedures qualify as tests, such as unscored application forms; informal and formal interviews; performance tests; and physical, educational, or experience requirements.[41] This definition of an employment test takes on added significance when you realize that in the United States the federal government requires all employment tests to be statistically valid and reliable predictors of job success.[42] Historically, women and minorities have been victimized by invalid, unreliable, and prejudicial employment selection procedures. Similar complaints have been voiced about the use of personality tests, polygraphs, drug tests, and AIDS and DNA screening during the hiring process[43] (see Table 11.3).

**employment selection test**
*any procedure used in the employment decision process*

## Effective Interviewing

Interviewing warrants special attention here because it is the most common employee selection tool. Line managers at all levels are often asked to interview candidates for job openings and promotions and should be aware of the weaknesses of the traditional unstructured interview. The traditional unstructured or informal interview, which has no fixed question format or systematic scoring procedure, has been criticized on grounds such as the following:

**5** Explain how managers can be more effective interviewers.

- It is highly susceptible to distortion and bias.
- It is highly susceptible to legal attack.
- It is usually indefensible if legally contested.
- It may have apparent validity, but no real validity.
- It is rarely totally job-related and may incorporate personal items that infringe on privacy.
- It is the most flexible selection technique, thereby being highly inconsistent.

# Managing Diversity

## Interviewing and Employing Blind and Visually Impaired People

### Interviewing Applicants Who Are Blind or Visually Impaired

If you know that an applicant is blind or visually impaired, you may be concerned about what questions you are allowed to ask during an interview. Relax, and use the following suggestions to guide you.

- Remember that a blind or visually impaired person is a "person" first. Lack of vision is just one aspect or characteristic and doesn't define a person any more than hair color does.
- Visual impairment does not equate to helplessness. When you greet an applicant, you may want to ask if he or she needs assistance. Some people with visual impairments will want to take your arm while others will prefer to follow your verbal directions.
- When you enter the interview room, it may be helpful to describe the setting to the applicant. For instance, "We are going to sit at a round table. Your chair is on your left, and I will sit across the table from you."
- Focus on the person's qualifications to do the job that you are seeking to fill. Matters that are not job related such as how or when an applicant lost his or her sight are not relevant to the interview.
- Never pet a dog guide. A dog guide is a working animal. While some of these dogs are indeed beautiful and friendly, lengthy discussion about the dog during the interview takes time away from discussing the applicant's qualifications.
- Don't be afraid to use terms like "see you later" or "do you see what I mean?" Blind and visually impaired people use them, too.

### How People Who Are Blind or Visually Impaired Do Their Jobs

Employees need tools to do their jobs effectively and environments conducive to their efforts. Two people doing the same job may use different tools, and work in very different settings. Blind or visually impaired employees can accomplish their jobs using non-traditional tools or by working in a modified environment. These modifi-

cations to the job or job site are referred to as reasonable accommodations.

An accommodation is a modification or adjustment that allows a qualified applicant or employee with a disability to participate in an application process or to perform a job's essential functions. No specific accommodation list exists, since each job situation differs. However, the following are examples of accommodations that have proven effective and affordable:

- Reduce glare or adjust lighting by removing or replacing bulbs; adding portable lamps; installing rheostats; or adjusting drapes, blinds, or shades.
- Rather than sending handwritten notes between supervisors and employees or among colleagues, voice or e-mail messages can usually be sent, or if neither of these is available, an inexpensive tape recorder can be used.
- For a job that requires the use of a computer, affordable software programs are readily available that convert the text on the screen to speech, large print, or braille, depending on the user's specific needs and preferences. Computers can also be equipped with scanners that convert printed materials to speech or braille.
- For a job that requires measuring, weighing, or calculations, many different kinds of measuring and calculating devices are available that "talk." These include calipers, scales, tape measures, thermometers, blood pressure cuffs, watches, calculators, money identifiers, and cash registers.
- For a job that requires travel, a person who is blind may travel with a long cane, a dog guide, or by using electronic travel aids. Some people with low vision use special telescopes to read signs when traveling. Independent travel to a variety of destinations and even remote areas without public transportation is usually possible. People who are blind or visually impaired are often experienced at finding creative travel solutions.

*Source:* Reprinted with permission from the American Foundation for the Blind. From "Are You Looking for a Few Good Workers?" © 2000. All rights reserved.

| **Table 11.3**   Employment Testing Techniques: An Overview | | |
|---|---|---|
| **Type of test** | **Purpose** | **Comments** |
| **Pencil-and-paper psychological and personality tests** | Measure attitudes and personality characteristics such as emotional stability, intelligence, and ability to deal with stress. | Renewed interest based on claims of improved validity. Can be expensive when scoring and interpretations are done by professionals. Validity varies widely from test to test. |
| **Pencil-and-paper honesty tests (integrity testing)** | Assess candidate's degree of risk for engaging in dishonest behavior. | Inexpensive to administer. Promising evidence of validity. Growing in popularity since recent curtailment of polygraph testing. Women tend to do better than men. |
| **Job skills tests (clerical and manual dexterity tests, math and language tests, assessment centers, and simulations)** | Assess competence in actual "hands-on" situations. | Generally good validity if carefully designed and administered. Assessment centers and simulations can be very expensive. |
| **Polygraph (lie detector) tests** | Measure physical signs of stress, such as rapid pulse and perspiration. | Growing use in recent years severely restricted by federal (Employee Polygraph Protection Act of 1988), state, and local laws. Questionable validity. |
| **Drug tests** | Check for controlled substances through urine, blood, or hair samples submitted to chemical analysis. | Rapidly growing in use despite strong employee resistance and potentially inaccurate procedures. |
| **Handwriting analysis (graphoanalysis)** | Infer personality characteristics and styles from samples of handwriting. | Popular in Europe and growing in popularity in United States. Sweeping claims by proponents leave validity in doubt. |
| **AIDS/HIV antibody tests** | Find evidence of AIDS virus through blood samples. | An emerging area with undetermined legal and ethical boundaries. Major confidentiality issue. |
| **Genetic/DNA screening** | Use tissue or blood samples and family history data to identify those at risk of costly diseases. | Limited but growing use strongly opposed on legal and moral grounds. Major confidentiality issue. |

- There is a tendency for the interviewer to look for qualities he or she prefers, and then to justify the hiring decision based on these qualities.
- Often the interviewer does not hear about the selection mistakes.
- There is an unsubstantiated confidence in the traditional interview.[44]

**The Problem of Cultural Bias.**   Traditional unstructured interviews are notorious for being culturally insensitive. Evidence of this problem surfaced in a study of the interviewing practices of 38 general managers employed by nine different fast-food chains. According to the researcher:

*Considering the well-known demographics of today's workforce, it's amazing that 9 percent of those receiving a negative hiring decision are turned down for inappropriate eye contact. To give a firm handshake and look someone straight in the eyes is a very important lesson taught by Dad to every middle-class male at a tender age. Not only do nonmainstream*

## 11E    Asking for Trouble

Research fact:

*Job seekers asked an illegal interview question per-taining to race, age, marital status, religion, ethnicity: 39 percent.*

**Source:** "Footnotes," *Business Week* (May 10, 1999): 8.

**Questions:** *What inappropriate and/or illegal interview questions have you ever been asked? How did it make you feel about the interviewer and the organization? Explain.*

groups miss the lesson from Dad, some are taught that direct eye contact is rude or worse. Girls are frequently taught that direct eye contact is unbecoming in a female. In reality, having averted or shifty eyes may indicate mostly that the job applicant is not a middle-class male.[45]

Managers can be taught, however, to be aware of and to overcome cultural biases when interviewing. This is particularly important in today's era of managing diversity and greater sensitivity to disabled people.

**Structured Interviews.**    Structured interviews are the recommended alternative to traditional unstructured or informal interviews.[46] A **structured interview** is defined as a set of job-related questions with standardized answers applied consistently across all interviews for a specific job.[47] Structured interviews are constructed, conducted, and scored by a committee of three to six members to try to eliminate individual bias. The systematic format and scoring of structured interviews eliminate the weaknesses inherent in unstructured interviews. Four types of questions typically characterize structured interviews: (1) situational, (2) job knowledge, (3) job sample simulation, and (4) worker requirements (see Table 11.4).

> **structured interview**    *a set of job-related questions with standardized answers*

**Behavioral Interviewing.**    Behavioral scientists tell us past behavior is the best predictor of future behavior. We are, after all, creatures of habit. Situational-type interview questions can be greatly strengthened by anchoring them to actual past behavior (as opposed to hypothetical situations).[48] Structured, job-related, behaviorally specific interview questions keep managers from running afoul of the problems associated with unstructured interviews, as listed above.

> **behavior-based interview**    *detailed questions about specific behavior in past job-related situations*

*In a* **behavior-based interview,** *candidates are asked to recall specific actions they have taken in past job-related situations and describe them in detail. . . .*

*Behavior-based interviews are rich with verifiable data. Candidates are required to include details such as names, dates, times, locations, and numbers.*

*Candidates are reminded to use the word "I" rather than using "we" or "they" as they describe past experiences. This helps the candidate remain focused on their role in each situation and helps the interviewer evaluate the presence or absence of specific competencies.*[49]

If the questions are worded appropriately, the net result should be a good grasp of the individual's relevant skills, initiative, problem-solving ability, and ability to recover from setbacks and learn from mistakes.[50] (For practice, see the Hands-On Exercise at the end of the chapter.)

# Performance Appraisal

Annual performance appraisals are such a common part of modern organizational life that they qualify as a ritual. As with many rituals, the participants repeat the historical pattern without really asking the important questions—"Why?" and "Is there a better way?" Both appraisers and subjects tend to express general dissatisfaction with per-

| **Table 11.4** | Types of Structured Interview Questions | | |
| --- | --- | --- | --- |
| **Type of question** | **Method** | **Information sought** | **Sample question** |
| **Situational** | Oral | Can the applicant handle difficult situations likely to be encountered on the job? | "What would you do if you saw two of your people arguing loudly in the work area?" |
| **Job knowledge** | Oral or written | Does the applicant possess the knowledge required for successful job performance? | "Do you know how to do an Internet search?" |
| **Job sample simulation** | Observation of actual or simulated performance | Can the applicant actually do essential aspects of the job? | "Can you show us how to compose and send an e-mail message?" |
| **Worker requirements** | Oral | Is the applicant willing to cope with job demands such as travel, relocation, or hard physical labor? | "Are you willing to spend 25 percent of your time on the road?" |

*Source:* Updated from "Structured Interviewing: Avoiding Selection Problems," by Elliott D. Pursell, Michael A. Campion, and Sarah R. Gaylord, copyright November 1980. Reprinted with permission of *Personnel Journal,* Costa Mesa, California; all rights reserved.

formance appraisals. In fact, nearly 75 percent of the companies responding to a survey expressed major dissatisfaction with their performance appraisal system.[51] This is not surprising, in view of the following observation:

> *The annual performance review process, touted by some as the gateway to future prosperity, is, in reality for many companies, nothing more than a fill-in-the-blank, form-completing task that plots an individual's performance against a sanitized list of often generic corporate expectations and required competencies.*[52]

Considering that experts estimate the average cost of a *single* performance appraisal to be $1,500, the waste associated with poorly administered appraisals is mind boggling![53]

Performance appraisal can be effective and satisfying if systematically developed and implemented techniques replace haphazard methods. For our purposes, **performance appraisal** is the process of evaluating individual job performance as a basis for making objective personnel decisions.[54] This definition intentionally excludes occasional coaching, in which a supervisor simply checks an employee's work and gives immediate feedback. Although personal coaching is fundamental to good management, formally documented appraisals are needed both to ensure equitable distribution of opportunities and rewards and to avoid prejudicial treatment of protected minorities.[55]

**performance appraisal**
*evaluating job performance as a basis for personnel decisions*

In this section, we will examine two important aspects of performance appraisal: (1) legal defensibility and (2) alternative techniques.

## Making Performance Appraisals Legally Defensible

Lawsuits challenging the legality of specific performance appraisal systems and resulting personnel actions have left scores of human resource managers asking themselves, "Will my organization's performance appraisal system stand up in court?" From the standpoint of limiting legal exposure, it is better to ask this question when developing

 **6** Discuss how performance appraisals can be made legally defensible.

a formal appraisal system rather than after it has been implemented. Managers need specific criteria for legally defensible performance appraisal systems. Fortunately, researchers have discerned some instructive patterns in court decisions.

After studying the verdicts in 66 employment discrimination cases in the United States, one pair of researchers found that employers could successfully defend their appraisal systems if they satisfied four criteria:

1.  A *job analysis* was used to develop the performance appraisal system.
2.  The appraisal system was *behavior-oriented,* not trait-oriented.
3.  Performance evaluators followed *specific written instructions* when conducting appraisals.
4.  Evaluators *reviewed the results* of the appraisals with the ratees.[56]

Each of these conditions has a clear legal rationale. Job analysis, discussed earlier relative to employee selection, anchors the appraisal process to specific job duties, not to personalities. Behavior-oriented appraisals properly focus management's attention on *how* the individual actually performed his or her job.[57] Performance appraisers who follow specific written instructions are less likely to be plagued by vague performance standards and/or personal bias. Finally, by reviewing performance appraisal results with those who have been evaluated, managers provide the feedback necessary for learning and improvement. Managers who keep these criteria for legal defensibility and the elements in Table 11.5 in mind are better equipped to select a sound appraisal system from alternative approaches and techniques.

## Alternative Performance Appraisal Techniques

The list of alternative performance appraisal techniques is long and growing. Appraisal software programs also are proliferating. Unfortunately, many are simplistic, invalid, and unreliable. In general terms, an *invalid* appraisal instrument does not accurately measure what it is supposed to measure. *Unreliable* instruments do not measure criteria in a consistent manner. Many other performance appraisal techniques are so complex that they are impractical and burdensome to use. But armed with a working knowledge of the most popular appraisal techniques, a good manager can distinguish the strong from the weak. Once again, the strength of an appraisal technique is gauged by its conformity to the criteria for legal defensibility discussed previously. Following are some of the techniques used through the years:

**Table 11.5** Elements of a Good Performance Appraisal

Appraisals can be used to justify merit increases, document performance problems or simply "touch base" with employees. Experts say HR first must decide what it wants the appraisal to accomplish, then customize the form and the process to meet that goal.

Elements to consider include:
1. Objectives set by the employee and manager at the last appraisal.

2. List of specific competencies or skills being measured, with examples of successful behaviors.

3. Ratings scale appropriate to the organization.

4. Space for employee's self-appraisal.

5. Space for supervisor's appraisal.

6. Space for specific comments from the supervisor about the employee's performance.

7. Suggestions for employee development.

8. Objectives to meet by the next appraisal date.

*Source:* Carla Joinson, "Making Sure Employees Measure Up," *HRMagazine*, 46 (March 2001): 39. Copyright 2001 by Society for Human Resource Management. Reprinted with the permission of *HRMagazine* published by the Society for Human Resource Management, Alexandria, VA.

- *Goal setting.* Within an MBO framework, performance is typically evaluated in terms of formal objectives set at an earlier date. This is a comparatively strong technique if desired outcomes are clearly linked to specific behavior. For example, a product design engineer's "output" could be measured in terms of the number of product specifications submitted per month.
- *Written essays.* Managers describe the performance of employees in narrative form, sometimes in response to predetermined questions. Evaluators often criticize this technique for consuming too much time. This method is also limited by the fact that some managers have difficulty expressing themselves in writing.
- *Critical incidents.* Specific instances of inferior and superior performance are documented by the supervisor when they occur. Accumulated incidents then provide an objective basis for evaluations at appraisal time. The strength of critical incidents is enhanced when evaluators document specific behavior in specific situations and ignore personality traits.[58]
- *Graphic rating scales.* Various traits or behavior are rated on incremental scales. For example, "initiative" could be rated on a 1(= low)—2—3—4—5(= high) scale. This technique is among the weakest when personality traits are employed. However, **behaviorally anchored rating scales (BARS),** defined as performance rating scales divided into increments of observable job behavior determined through job

**11F Straight Talk**

Dick Brown, CEO of Dallas-based EDS:

> *. . . people inherently want to do a good job. As long as what you say is well intentioned and constructive— if it helps them improve their performance—people will accept what you have to say, even if it's candid, even if it's kind of hard to swallow.*

**Source:** As quoted in "Personal Histories: Leaders Remember the Moments and People That Shaped Them," *Harvard Business Review* (Special Issue: Breakthrough Leadership), 79 (December 2001): 37.

**Questions:** *Do you agree? Why or why not? Can how a manager comments on your performance be more important than the content of the message? Explain.*

**behaviorally anchored rating scales (BARS)**
*performance appraisal scales with notations about observable behavior*

analysis, are considered to be one of the strongest performance appraisal techniques (see Figure 11.2). For example, managers at credit card issuer Capital One use performance rating scales with behavioral anchors such as: "Do you get things done well through other people? Do you play well as a team member?"[59]

- *Weighted checklists.* Evaluators check appropriate adjectives or behavioral descriptions that have predetermined weights. The weights, which gauge the relative importance of the randomly mixed items on the checklist, are usually unknown to the evaluator. Following the evaluation, the weights of the checked items are added or averaged to permit interpersonal comparisons. As with the other techniques, the degree of behavioral specificity largely determines the strength of weighted checklists.

- *Rankings/comparisons.* Coworkers in a subunit are ranked or compared in head-to-head fashion according to specified accomplishments or job behavior. A major shortcoming of this technique is that the absolute distance between ratees is unknown. For example, the employee ranked number one may be five times as effective as number two, who in turn is only slightly more effective than number three. Rankings/comparisons are also criticized for causing resentment among lower-ranked, but adequately performing, coworkers. *Fortune* recently offered this update:

  > *In companies across the country, from General Electric to Hewlett-Packard, such grading systems—in which all employees are ranked against one another and grades are distributed along some sort of bell curve—are creating a firestorm of controversy. In the past 15 months employees have filed class-action suits against Microsoft and Conoco as well as Ford, claiming that the companies discriminate in assigning grades. In each case, a different group of disaffected employees is bringing the charges: older workers at Ford, blacks and women at Microsoft, U.S. citizens at Conoco.*[60]

  Ford has since dropped its forced ranking system.[61] This technique can be strengthened by combining it with a more behavioral technique, such as critical incidents or BARS.

- *Multirater appraisals.* This is a general label for a diverse array of nontraditional appraisal techniques involving more than one rater for the focal person's performance. The rationale for multirater appraisals is that "two or more heads are less

---

**11G  Appraising "Rank-and-Yank" Appraisals**

Jack Welch's approach when he headed General Electric:

> The top 20% should be "rewarded in the soul and wallet because they are the ones who make magic happen. Losing one of these people must be held up as a leadership sin," Welch says.
>
> The middle 70% should be energized to improve; the rest should be shown the door.
>
> Not getting rid of the 10% early "is not only a management failure, but false kindness as well—a form of cruelty," Welch says. They will wind up being fired eventually and "stranded" in midcareer.

**Source:** Del Jones, "Welch: Nurture Best Workers, Lose Bottom 10%," *USA Today* (February 27, 2001): 2B.

---

**Question:** *Do you agree or disagree with Welch's approach? Explain.*

biased than one." One approach enjoying faddish popularity in recent years is 360-degree feedback. In a **360 degree review**, a manager is evaluated by his or her boss, peers, and subordinates. The results may or may not be statistically pooled and are generally fed back anonymously.[62] Although 360-degree feedback is best suited for use in management development programs, some companies have turned it into a performance appraisal tool, with predictably mixed results.[63] If 360-degree appraisals are to be successful, they need to be carefully designed and skillfully implemented.

**360-degree review**   *pooled, anonymous evaluation by one's boss, peers, and subordinates*

---

**Figure 11.2**   A Sample Behaviorally Anchored Rating Scale for a College Professor

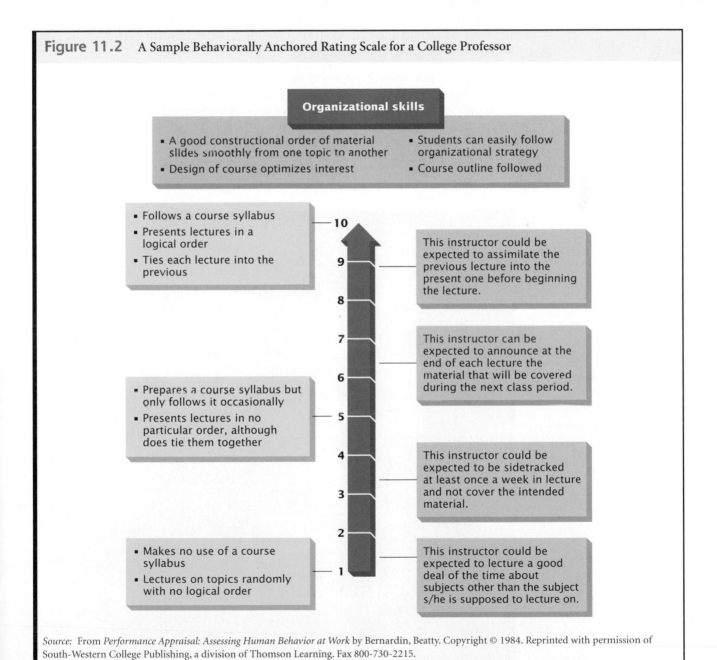

# Training

No matter how carefully job applicants are screened and selected, typically a gap remains between what employees *do* know and what they *should* know. Training is needed to fill in this knowledge gap. In 2001, U.S. companies with 100 or more employees spent nearly $56.8 billion on training, according to *Training* magazine's annual industry survey.[64] Huge as this number sounds, it still is not nearly enough. How the $56.8 billion was spent is also a problem. Most of it was spent by big companies training already well-educated managers and professionals.

Clearly, American managers need to rethink the country's training priorities. Remedial education and basic skills training for nonmanagement personnel are good for both the employer and the employee.

> At Borden Foodservice, 71 percent of those who received basic skills certification remained employed five years later, despite downsizing and the sale of the company. Of those who received other training, but not basic skills, only 54 percent are still with the company. In the same period and among the same groups of employees, 21 percent of basic-skills trainees were promoted, while not a single promotion was made from among those who had not received the training.[65]

*Field sales representatives at electronic billing specialist Convergys know the traditional dilemma of training. Time spent in training sessions is time lost with customers. Mary Kay Nedrich, the firm's director of sales training and development, had a better idea. In May, everyone gathers for a traditional sales training meeting. Each week, during the rest of the year, two or three Web-based training sessions synchronized with conference calls are available on demand. The result: more training, less irritation.*

*someone to ride horseback. How would you do it? It basically must entail telling someo specifically what you want them to do (goal setting), showing them how you want them do it (modeling), giving them the opportunity to try out what you have told them a shown them (practice), and then telling them what they are doing correctly (feedback).[70]*

When factual learning is involved, the same sequence is used, except that in step "meaningful presentation of the materials" is substituted for modeling. Keep in mi that the object of training is *learning*. Learning requires thoughtful preparation, car fully guided exposure to new ideas or behavior, and motivational support.[71] Let us tu our attention to modern human resource management problems that have seriou implications for the well-being of today's organizations and employees.

# Contemporary Human Resource Challenges and Problems

Modern organizations are a direct reflection of society in general. People take societa influences to work (such as attitudes toward the opposite sex). Along with these pre dispositions, they take their social, emotional, behavioral, and health-related problem to work. Like it or not and prepared or not, managers face potential problems such a sexual harassment and alcohol and drug abuse. Today's challenge to deal effectively with human resource problems of this nature cannot be ignored because organiza tional competitiveness is at stake.

## Discouraging Sexual Harassment

A great deal of misunderstanding surrounds the topic of sexual harassment because of sexist attitudes, vague definitions, and inconsistent court findings. **Sexual harassment,** defined generally as unwanted sexual attention or conduct, has both behavioral and legal dimensions (see Table 11.6). Important among these are the following:

- Although typically it is female employees who are the victims of sexual harass-ment, both women and men (in the United States) are protected under Title VII of the Civil Rights Act of 1964.
- Sexual harassment includes, but is not limited to, unwanted physical contact. Ges-tures, displays, joking, and language also may create a sexually offensive or intimi-dating work environment.
- It is the manager's job to be aware of and correct cases of sexual harassment. Igno-rance of such activity is not a valid legal defense.[72]

Research evidence indicates that sexual harassment is commonplace. In a nationwide survey of 2,765 employees, "45 percent of women and 19 percent of men said they have been sexually harassed at work."[73] Employees using e-mail systems must also contend with problems of sexual harassment in the form of rape threats and obscene words and graphics. In 2000, "Dow Chemical fired 50 employees and disciplined 200 others after an e-mail investigation turned up hard-core pornography and violent subject matter. . . .'This sort of activity creates a harassment environment that we can't tolerate,' [said a company official]."[74] Sexual harassment begins early, with

Given that 47 percent of all American adults are not literate enough to read this page, the need for more extensive worker training is inescapable,[66]

Formally defined, **training** is the process of changing employee behavior and/or attitudes through some type of guided experience. We now focus on the content and delivery of modern training, the ingredients of a good training program, and the important distinction between skill and factual learning.

**training** *using guided experience to change employee behavior/attitudes*

## Today's Training: Content and Delivery

*Training* magazine's 2001 survey of companies with at least 100 employees gives us a revealing snapshot of current training practices.[67] The top portion of Figure 11.3 lists the ten most common types of training. How that training was delivered in both 2000 and 2001 is displayed in the bottom portion of Figure 11.3. Surprisingly, despite all we read and hear about computer-based training and e-learning over the Internet, the vast bulk of today's training is remarkably low-tech. One likely explanation for the small shift back to traditional training methods between 2000 and 2001 was the recession at the time. We anticipate growth of e-learning and other nontra-ditional methods as the economy strengthens.[68] Meanwhile, the old standbys—classroom presenta-tions, workbooks/manuals, videotapes, and seminars —are still the norm. For better or for worse, the typi-cal college classroom is still a realistic preview of what awaits you in the world of workplace training.

Which instructional method is best? There are probably as many answers to this question as there are trainers. Given variables such as interpersonal differ-ences, budget limitations, and instructor capabilities, it is safe to say that there is no one best training tech-nique. For example, the lecture method, though widely criticized for being dull and encouraging learner passivity, is still on top in the study just discussed. Whatever method is used, trainers need to do their absolute best because they are key facilitators for people's hopes and dreams.

**11H Subject: Sleeping in Class**

Professor Roger Schank, Carnegie Mellon University, Pittsburgh, identifies three major training flaws that dampen motivation:

*One, it's boring. . . .Second, it's not obvious why you need what you're being trained to do. And third, you're being trained in what you need, but not when you need it.*

**Source:** As quoted in Dianne Molvig, "Yearning for Learning," *HRMagazine*, 47 (March 2002): 68.

**Question:** *Drawing on your many years of being a "consumer" of classroom instruction, what would you do as a trainer to avoid these three flaws?*

## The Ingredients of a Good Training Program

Although training needs and approaches vary, managers can get the most out of their training budgets by following a few guidelines. According to two training specialists, every training program should be designed along the following lines to maximize retention and transfer learning to the job:

1. Maximize the similarity between the training situation and the job situation.
2. Provide as much experience as possible with the task being taught.
3. Provide for a variety of examples when teaching concepts or skills.
4. Label or identify important features of a task.
5. Make sure that general principles are understood before expecting much transfer.
6. Make sure that the trained behaviors and ideas are rewarded in the job situation.
7. Design the training content so that the trainees can see its applicability.
8. Use adjunct questions to guide the trainee's attention.[69]

## Figure 11.3   The Content and Delivery of Today's Training

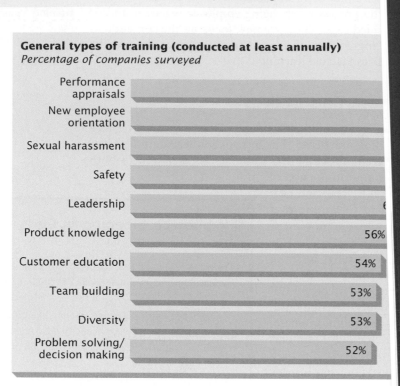

**General types of training (conducted at least annually)**
*Percentage of companies surveyed*

- Performance appraisals
- New employee orientation
- Sexual harassment
- Safety
- Leadership   6
- Product knowledge   56%
- Customer education   54%
- Team building   53%
- Diversity   53%
- Problem solving/ decision making   52%

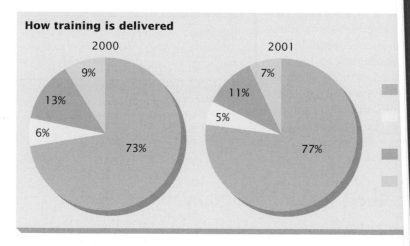

**How training is delivered**

2000
- 9%
- 13%
- 6%
- 73%

2001
- 7%
- 11%
- 5%
- 77%

*Source:* Data from top portion and figure in bottom portion republished with permission of *Training* from Ta...
*Training,* 38 (October 2001): 54, 66; permission conveyed through Copyright Clearance Center.

## Skill Versus Factual Learning

The ingredients of a good training program vary accordi...
factual learning is involved.

> *Effective skill learning should incorporate four essentia...*
> *(2) modeling, (3) practice, and (4) feedback. Let's take as...*

---

5. **Always follow up.** Write and mail a follow-up letter to the interviewer within 12 to 24 hours of your meeting, with a copy to any other executives who are involved in the decision. [An e-mail can get lost in the clutter.]

Your letter should state:
- What you liked most about the company.
- The assets you'd bring to the position.
- Your availability and enthusiasm.
- Your hope of meeting other decision-makers as soon as possible.

*Source:* Excerpted from "Interview Success Tips from an Old Pro," by Milton Gralla. *The College Edition of the National Employment Weekly* (Winter/Spring 1997). Copyright 1999 by Dow Jones & Co Inc. Reproduced with permission of Dow Jones & Co. Inc. in the format textbook via Copyright Clearance Center.

# Hands-On Exercise

## Writing Behavioral Interview Questions

**Instructions**

Either working alone or as a member of a team, select a specific job and write *two* behavioral interview questions for at least *five* of these categories.

- Being a self-starter and demonstrating initiative
- Being a leader
- Being an effective communicator
- Being ethical
- Being able to make a hard decision
- Being a team player
- Ability to handle conflict
- Ability to handle a setback, disappointment, or failure

*Tips:* If you pick a higher-level job, this exercise will be easier because people at higher levels have more responsibility and engage in a broader range of behavior. Be sure to prepare by rereading the Behavioral Interviewing section in this chapter.

**For Consideration/ Discussion**

1. How well will each of your questions uncover *actual past job-related behavior?*

2. Would any of your questions put the candidate at a disadvantage because of his or her gender, race, ethnicity, religion, disability, marital status, or sexual preference?

3. When others hear your questions, are they judged to be *fair* questions?

4. Which question is your absolute best? Why? Which is the weakest? Why?

5. What do you like or dislike about behavioral interviews?

# Internet Exercises

1. **A case study in diversity:** Dell Computer Corp. takes diversity very seriously. It is of major strategic importance to the company's success. At Dell's home page (**www.dell.com**), click on "About Dell." Next, select "Diversity Programs" and read the message from Michael Dell. Then browse the categories "Definition/Mission," "Workforce Development," "Diversity Events," and "Access to Technology" while keeping the following questions in mind.

    *Learning Points:* 1. How embedded is diversity in Dell's overall corporate strategy? How can you tell? 2. Which particular diversity initiative or program appeals most to you? Why? 3. If you were on Dell's diversity program staff, how would you justify the firm's diversity efforts to Dell stockholders? 4. Would you like to work for Dell Computer? Why or why not?

2. **Intel is very serious about human capital:** The investment Intel is making in students and educational programs around the world is amazing. At Intel's home page (**www.intel.com**), select "Intel Innovation in Education" under the heading "About Intel." Explore Intel's various human capital programs while keeping the following questions in mind.

    *Learning Points:* 1. Putting yourself in the place of the company's CEO, how would you justify the huge expenditure of time and money on people who probably will end up working somewhere else? 2. In your view, which of Intel's investments in human capital is the best? Why? Which is the most questionable? Why? 3. Thinking back to what you read in Chapter 5, what is the role of "enlightened self-interest" in Intel's investment in education? 4. Would you like to work at Intel? Why or why not?

3. **Check it out:** The popular Internet job site **www.monster.com** has lots of great stuff to help you prepare for the job-hunting experience. Click on "Career Center" at the home page and explore from there. Recommended stops include the "Resume Center" and the "Interview Center." You also can use this site to check out employment opportunities in foreign countries.

For updates to these exercises, visit our Web site (**http://business.college.hmco. com/students**).

# Closing Case

## Training Pays Off at Paychex

There's no need for the latest e-learning course or enhanced multimedia facility at Rochester, N.Y.–based Paychex, where employees are trained the "old-fashioned" way. "We still get the most impact out of the basic Socratic method with an instructor, close mentoring and things that involve personal contact," says Paychex's vice president, William Kuchta.

Old-fashioned or not, Paychex is reaping the rewards of its training program and sticking to founder Tom Galisano's basic belief that if you train people properly to do their job, they will do a better job.

Paychex opened for business in 1971 as a payroll, tax-pay and employee services provider to small businesses. It filed a successful IPO (in 1983) and followed this with

10 consecutive years of 30-plus percent earnings and profit growth. And one of the keys to its fiscal prosperity: continual training and employee development.

Consider: in the last fiscal year alone, nearly 5,000 employees were trained at the University of Paychex, 750,000 additional hours were spent doing field-based testing and ongoing training, and more than half of the 30 programs offered at the corporate university receive college-level certification.

So what does the University of Paychex hold that's so special, besides your future paycheck? The same old good stuff just done better and better, according to Kuchta (and no, "old good stuff" does not yet mean online). Every Paychex employee undergoes an intensive orientation program held at the 15-year-old corporate university. The program—a two-week, eight-hours-a-day event—is exclusively confined to a classroom setting. And upon the program's completion, trainees must pass a senior exam. Rigorous and boring, you say? Read on.

Before entering Paychex U, employees train for training, so to speak. For four weeks prior to the two-week orientation session, employees go through an induction of sorts, learning the basics of the company through a series of exercises. Each employee is assigned to a mentor who aids the trainee in preparing for his or her training.

Once through orientation, training still does not end. Employees return to their branch or department and enter a seven-step, self-paced learning process—largely consisting of workbook assignments and a small amount of online exercises—that can take anywhere from eight to 14 months. That, alone, could potentially equate to 15 months of initial training.

Training, though, really never ends for Paychex employees. Every Friday, employees gather in a classroom session at each of the company's 77 branches for refresher training on new products, services or software. "If you have a new product, many companies simply hand out big binders, and employees are supposed to go home and read them," says Kuchta. "We never do that. The whole culture here is one that if there's ever a new product or a new process, it is trained into the organization. It's not just sent out."

## Maintaining Interest

Despite the long hours and follow-up assignments, the motivation to learn at Paychex is high, with the company's 50 professional trainers instrumental in ensuring trainees are fully engaged during the eight-hour sessions. "There is not much time for goofing around," Kuchta explains. "Training is a formal process for us—it's a route to promotion—plus trainees get a nice watch and lots of recognition."

"We just use a lot of good classic classroom, good trainer modality. We mix up the delivery," Kuchta says. This includes limiting each discussion or activity to no more than an hour, using two to three trainers per course, and giving trainees ample opportunity to take comfort breaks. "We use some AV in most of our classes, and on the payroll side, trainees do a lot of work on the computer, so it's very hands-on with a lot of application," explains Kuchta. He is quick to point out, however, that this is not online learning. Rather, the trainees are learning how to use specific systems, like payroll, for example, on an "almost live, dummy system." Using technology to deliver other forms of training accounts for less than 5 percent of the company's employee development programs.

Several unique aspects of the payroll sales training course made the "learning experience enjoyable as well as educational," explains Dawn Wilcox, a recent graduate of the University of Paychex and now manager of employment and employee relations. "The use of different activities such as group exercises, lectures, hands-on work, pre-shadowing pre-work and homework provided an opportunity for me to learn in a manner that was effective for me."

Some activities are actually held off campus as well, allowing students to observe real work situations. For example, Wilcox's class visited the National Sales Support Center, which enabled her to work one-on-one with a phone representative, listening in on how the rep handled each call. "The opportunity to listen in on phone conversations provided me with a clear understanding of how NSS interacts with our clients and supports the sales organization within Paychex."

Before beginning official work at Paychex, Wilcox was required to attend the two-week orientation session even though she was entering a managerial position. "Although it was designed for new sales representatives, I found it extremely beneficial as the manager of employment and employee relations," Wilcox admits. "It provided me with an in-depth understanding of our products and services, and now I can use this knowledge when acquiring talent for our company."

It is clear, though, that the trainers must have a particularly challenging job to keep students such as Wilcox interested and motivated to learn. Enter continuous train-the-trainer sessions, in which the 50 instructors attend meetings and workshops to critique each other, evaluate the effectiveness of each class and discuss possible improvements. Such ongoing sessions are paramount to the overall success of Paychex, since the company operates in a highly regulated government business. Every time tax laws or regulations change, so must Paychex. Consequently, the Paychex trainers end up rewrit-

ing 15 to 25 percent of the curriculum each year, which is why more than 25 of the trainers are technically writers.

Kuchta and his staff firmly believe in the personal contact benefit that classroom training affords. "The trainers take ownership to ensure that each participant understands the material and can use the newly acquired skills immediately on the job," says Wilcox. "For individuals who are having difficulty learning a certain aspect, the trainers make themselves available before and after class, each day, for private tutoring. Teamwork and camaraderie are definitely a part of the learning environment."

Ongoing assessments—both of the trainees and trainers—are crucial to the success of any training session, says Kuchta. "We're rigorous about our evaluation methodology," he explains. Upon conclusion of the two-week training session, for example, each trainee fills out a lengthy survey of the course. The training instructor then compiles and analyzes each survey and distributes them to other people in the department, including Kuchta, for comments. "I read every one of them," he says. "So does the training center director—every evaluation from every course."

Not only are the surveys analyzed to make sure the sessions are well received, but Kuchta and his staff also receive an added benefit: They are able to get a better handle on the learning style of each individual. "We actually give our trainees, not in every class, but in most of them, a pre-training learning styles instrument that is then reviewed by the trainer on the first day," Kuchta explains. "The instructor goes through it and says, 'Do you realize what this means to you? How do you play to your strengths when you're in a modality that is in your weakness area? How do you get over that?'"

The second part of the assessment process is a survey conducted by trainers and executives who travel to the individual branches over the course of 30 to 60 days following training. "We have developed a list of key questions working with the sales department to say, 'How are we going to know if these people are really using what they learn, and is it actually making an impact? Has this person used tool A, B or C in his or her sales presentations? Have you seen them doing this?'" Kuchta explains.

The managers rate the employees, and once the results are in, they are distributed so "we can monitor that on a very regular basis by class. We actually physically go out and use, what some would call, a levels-of-use tool."

Lastly, the trainers regularly call the branch managers asking if the programs worked, whether or not they have seen any changes, and if the payroll specialists are returning to work better or worse than they used to be. "It's very much the day-to-day feedback from the line that helps evaluate how well we are doing," says Kuchta. Programs also are evaluated by tracking the number of employees who return to the training center. "We bring them back," Kuchta proudly affirms. "Our head of sales training is a person who started in sales, came into the training center as a sales trainer, went back out into the field as a district sales manager and just recently came back in to be the manager of sales training. That's terrific for the company." Also, knowing the trainers have returned to teach after having "been there and done that" out in the field does wonders for the trainees, Kuchta says.

"There's a lot of evidence that just reading a book, or nowadays just going online, isn't anywhere near as effective as good teaching," Kuchta says. "I'm sure someone would label me as a reactionary, but for all the stuff we put into training, I don't think it's changed much at all."

## For Discussion

1. Is the concept of "human capital" evident in this case? Explain.

2. Would Jeffrey Pfeffer likely call Paychex a people-centered company? Why or why not?

3. Why not just put the entire University of Paychex curriculum online to eliminate all the travel and classroom time?

4. What are the keys to success for the University of Paychex?

5. How could Paychex improve its training program?

## chapter twelve

# Communicating in the Internet Age

## CHAPTER OBJECTIVES

*When you finish studying this chapter you should be able to*

**1**   **Identify** each major link in the communication process.

**2**   **Explain** the concept of media richness and the Lengel-Daft contingency model of media selection.

**3**   **Identify** the five communication strategies and **specify** guidelines for using them.

**4**   **Discuss** why it is important for managers to know about grapevine and nonverbal communication.

**5**   **Explain** ways in which management can encourage upward communication.

**6**   **Identify** and **describe** four barriers to communication.

**7**   **List** two practical tips for each of the three modern communication technologies (e-mail, cell phones, and videoconferences) and **summarize** the pros and cons of telecommuting.

**8**   **List** at least three practical tips for improving each of the following communication skills: listening, writing, and running a meeting.

> **"It is a luxury to be understood."**
>
> Ralph Waldo Emerson

# Swedish CEO of U.S. Company Faces Communication Challenges

**B**ackground: Lars Nyberg, born and educated in Sweden, is fluent in Swedish, English, and Dutch and speaks some German. Yet this multilingual executive has found American-style communication and figures of speech perplexing. When he left Royal Philips Electronics in the Netherlands in 1995 to take over at NCR, the former computer division of AT&T was a big money loser. Nyberg since has gotten NCR back on an even keel by dumping the PC business and focusing on data warehousing. Here are some of Nyberg's comments from a recent interview:

Q. Do you have to stop being a Swede to run a U.S. company?

A. I don't know what I consider myself. My wife and I have had that discussion quite regularly the last couple of years. I was more European coming here. You lose your roots and you don't know where you belong. We're very comfortable in the U.S., but all four of our children live in Sweden. I'm a citizen of Sweden, but I could become a U.S. citizen. I don't really care, to be quite honest. There are different cultures and languages, but the fundamental drivers of business are the same.

Q. What is the biggest adjustment foreign-born CEOs must make?

A. My biggest adjustment was when I moved from Sweden to the (United Kingdom). The Swedish management style is consensus-based. The CEO spends a lot of time trying to get agreement. Swedish executives are never surprised by a CEO decision. When I came to the UK, I called the guys in, and they said: "You're the boss, you decide. You get paid for making sensitive decisions." If it's wrong, it's my fault. At the end of the day, the captain makes the decision. You can't say, "I'm Swedish, and therefore I'm different."

Q. How is it different being a CEO here vs. other countries?

A. Direct communication in Japan is considered rude. In the U.S. and Europe, it's very direct. Americans pay attention to how well you communicate, while in Europe, they key on what you say and are more forgiving if you don't deliver the message in the most eloquent way. When I came to NCR, I did not imagine the public relations I would have to do. I do interviews, CNN live, the whole Wall Street thing with analysts. I make keynote addresses. I was forced to learn on the job. I've made a quarterly video to employees for the last 6 years. The first time, I had to do 20 retakes, I was so nervous.

Q. Why do you think NCR didn't hire an American?

A. That one's simple. Nobody in this country wanted the job. The (AT&T board) said only a Swede wouldn't understand where the Midwest is and would understand the challenge. I knew NCR was in trouble, but it was deeper than I thought. Four weeks after I was hired, AT&T spun off NCR and Lucent. I was never told AT&T would be broken up when I was hired. I didn't sleep well the night I was told. That's water under the bridge. I have no hard feelings, no complaints, no regrets. When I started NCR was losing $2 million a day. Revenues have fallen, but NCR is actually making some money now.

Q. That makes it sound like foreign executives are being hired as a last resort. Doesn't a U.S. multinational company with a foreign CEO have a competitive advantage?

A. There are advantages and disadvantages. I understand European markets, and maybe Asian-Pacific markets. On the other hand, I wasn't raised here. The first time I heard the word diversity, I didn't know what it meant. I had to discuss affirmative action and, as a foreigner, I needed time to understand and come to grips with the issue. American companies, because of Wall Street, are more short-term oriented, although European companies are following suit very quickly.

Q. Have you experienced any resentment from employees, customers or suppliers who think it is a little un-American for you to be in charge of a U.S. company?

A. Never. Never. NCR had burned through four CEOs before I arrived. I was a new face with a funny accent, and the employees thought I would be going away soon, too. That had nothing to do with my nationality, and after a month or two, I felt very supported.

Q. Some U.S. executives are taking CEO jobs with companies based in the UK, Australia and South Africa.

What advice can you offer someone with ambitions to run a company abroad?

A. Sometime early in their career they should go to China, Taiwan, Indonesia, Singapore, maybe pick up the language. That would improve their understanding. The United States is huge, but if you go half the distance between Texas and Ohio in Europe you find a country with a language you don't understand. . . .

Q. You certainly are fluent in English.

A. I felt extremely comfortable speaking English in Europe. When I came here, I was really concerned. The Americans have so many expressions, most of them related to sports. People would say, "I want to tee this up with you." Home runs. Strikeouts. I never played baseball, I didn't follow baseball. An American CEO who knew Swedish would run into the same thing.

One of the most difficult challenges for management is getting individuals to understand and voluntarily pursue organizational objectives. Effective communication, of the sort Lars Nyberg is striving to achieve, is vital to meeting this challenge. Organizational communication takes in a great deal of territory—virtually every management function and activity can be considered communication in one way or another. Planning and controlling require a good deal of communicating, as do organization design and development, decision making and problem solving, leadership, and staffing. Organizational cultures would not exist without communication. Studies have shown that both organizational and individual performance improve when managerial communication is effective.[1] Given today's team-oriented organizations where things need to be accomplished with and through people over whom a manager has no direct authority, communication skills are more important than ever.[2]

Thanks to modern technology, we can communicate more quickly and less expensively. But the ensuing torrent of messages (see Figure 12.1) has proved to be a mixed blessing for managers and nonmanagers alike. Complaints of information overload are common today.[3] Worse yet, managers have a growing suspicion that more communication is not necessarily better. Research validates this suspicion: "Executives say 14 percent of each 40-hour workweek is wasted because of poor communication between staff and managers. . . .

## 12A   Attention, Please!

*[Microsoft vice president Linda] Stone is a creative thinker who has coined the term* continuous partial attention *to describe the way we cope with the barrage of communication coming at us. It's not the same as multitasking, Stone says; that's about trying to accomplish several things at once. With continuous partial attention, we're scanning incoming alerts for the best thing to seize upon:* "How can I tune in in a way that helps me sync up with the most interesting, or important, opportunity?"

**Source:** Jill Hecht Maxwell, "Stop the Net, I Want to Get Off," *Inc.,* 24 (January 2002): 93.

**Question:** *What are the pros and cons of this technique relative to communicating in the workplace?*

For further information about the interactive annotations in this chapter, visit our Web site (http://business.college.hmco.com/students).

**Figure 12.1**

The World of Communication Overload (average daily number of messages sent and received by office workers)

| | United States | United Kingdom | Germany |
|---|---|---|---|
| Telephone | 52 | 46 | 50 |
| E-mail | 36 | 27 | 20 |
| Voice mail | 23 | 11 | 6 |
| Postal mail | 18 | 19 | 26 |
| Interoffice mail | 18 | 15 | 27 |
| Fax | 14 | 11 | 15 |
| Cell phone | 4 | 9 | 10 |
| TOTAL | 165 | 138 | 154 |

*Source:* Data from "Message Overload?" *USA Today* (September 13, 1999): 1B.

That amounts to a staggering seven workweeks of squandered productivity a year."[4] The challenge to improve this situation is both immense and immediate. But before managers, or anyone else for that matter, can become more effective communicators, they need to appreciate that communication is a complex process subject to a great deal of perceptual distortion and many problems. This is especially true for the apparently simple activity of communicating face to face.

# The Communication Process

**1** Identify each major link in the communication process.

**communication**
*interpersonal transfer of information and understanding*

Management scholar Keith Davis defined **communication** as "the transfer of information and understanding from one person to another person."[5] Communication is inherently a social process. Whether one communicates face to face with a single person or with a group of people via television, it is still a social activity involving two or more people. By analyzing the communication process, one discovers that it is a chain made up of identifiable links (see Figure 12.2). Links in this process include sender, encoding, medium, decoding, receiver, and feedback.[6] The essential purpose of this chainlike process is to send an idea from one person to another in a way that will be understood by the receiver. Like any other chain, the communication chain is only as strong as its weakest link.[7]

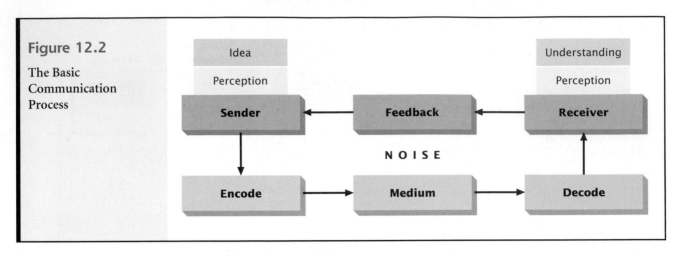

**Figure 12.2**

The Basic
Communication
Process

## Encoding

Thinking takes place within the privacy of your brain and is greatly affected by how you perceive your environment. But when you want to pass along a thought to someone else, an entirely different process begins. This second process, communication, requires that you, the sender, package the idea for understandable transmission. Encoding starts at this point. The purpose of encoding is to translate internal thought patterns into a language or code the intended receiver of the message will probably understand.

Managers usually rely on words, gestures, or other symbols for encoding. Their choice of symbols depends on several factors, one of which is the nature of the message itself. Is it technical or nontechnical, emotional or factual? Perhaps it could be expressed better with colorful PowerPoint slides than with words, as in the case of a budget report. To express skepticism, merely a shrug might be enough. More fundamentally, will the encoding help get the attention of busy and distracted people?[8]

Greater cultural diversity in the workplace also necessitates careful message encoding. Trudy Milburn, an American Management Association program coordinator, offers this perspective:

> *Communication . . . becomes problematic when organizations adopt a narrow perspective of communication that focuses on a single normative standard. Some African-American employees, for example, may be discouraged from speaking in a dialect defined as "black English" and may be mandated to adopt proper business grammar. When companies deem their standard to be the only acceptable one, they will not be able to appreciate different ways of interacting.[9]*

In the global marketplace, where language barriers hamper communication, e-mail translation programs promise to make the encoding process a bit easier.

## Selecting a Medium

Managers can choose among a number of media: face-to-face conversations, telephone calls, e-mails, memos, letters, computer reports and networks, photographs, bulletin boards, meetings, organizational publications, and others. Communicating with those outside the organization opens up further possibilities, such as news releases, press conferences, and advertising on television and radio or in magazines, in newspapers, and on the Internet.

*Modern communication media are a boon to both business and education. Just ask the seventh graders in Brandon Lloyd's civics class at the SEED Public Charter School in Washington, D.C. Thanks to a partnership with Microsoft, this school is linked with many others across the nation in a sophisticated digital network. The world is just a click away for today's Internet-savvy students.*

**Media Selection in Cross-Cultural Settings.** The importance of selecting an appropriate medium is magnified when one moves from internal to cross-cultural dealings. Recalling the distinction we made in Chapter 4, managers moving from low-context cultures to high-context cultures need to select communication media with care.

> *The United States, Canada, and northern European nations are defined as low-context cultures, meaning that the verbal content of a message is more important than the medium—the setting through which the message is delivered. In such cultures, a videoconference or an e-mail is usually accepted as an efficient substitute for an in-person meeting.*
>
> *But in other countries—including many in Asia and the Middle East—context, or setting, with its myriad nonverbal cues, can convey far more meaning than the literal words of a given message. In such high-context cultures, business transactions are ritualized, and the style in which the rituals are carried out matters more than the words. A high value is placed on face-to-face interaction, and after-hours socialization with customers and colleagues is almost a daily occurrence.*[10]

**A Contingency Approach.** A contingency model for media selection has been proposed by Robert Lengel and Richard Daft.[11] It pivots on the concept of media richness. **Media richness** describes the capacity of a given medium to convey information and promote learning. As illustrated in the top portion of Figure 12.3, media vary in richness from high (or rich) to low (or lean). Face-to-face conversation is a rich medium because it (1) simultaneously provides *multiple information cues,* such as message content, tone of voice, facial expressions, and so on; (2) facilitates immediate *feedback;* and (3) is *personal* in focus. In contrast, bulletins and general computer reports are lean media, that is, they convey limited information and foster limited learning. Lean media, such as general e-mail bulletins, provide a single cue, do not facilitate immediate feedback, and are impersonal.

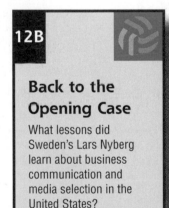

**12B**

**Back to the Opening Case**
What lessons did Sweden's Lars Nyberg learn about business communication and media selection in the United States?

**2** Explain the concept of media richness and the Lengel-Daft contingency model of media selection.

**media richness** *a medium's capacity to convey information and promote learning*

**Figure 12.3**   The Lengel-Daft Contingency Model of Media Selection

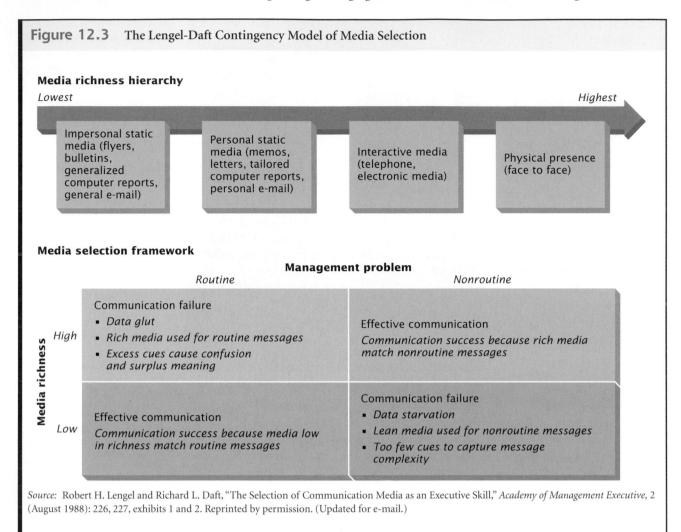

**Media richness hierarchy**

*Lowest* → *Highest*

| Impersonal static media (flyers, bulletins, generalized computer reports, general e-mail) | Personal static media (memos, letters, tailored computer reports, personal e-mail) | Interactive media (telephone, electronic media) | Physical presence (face to face) |

**Media selection framework**

**Management problem**

|  |  | *Routine* | *Nonroutine* |
|---|---|---|---|
| **Media richness** | **High** | Communication failure<br>• *Data glut*<br>• *Rich media used for routine messages*<br>• *Excess cues cause confusion and surplus meaning* | Effective communication<br>*Communication success because rich media match nonroutine messages* |
|  | **Low** | Effective communication<br>*Communication success because media low in richness match routine messages* | Communication failure<br>• *Data starvation*<br>• *Lean media used for nonroutine messages*<br>• *Too few cues to capture message complexity* |

*Source:*  Robert H. Lengel and Richard L. Daft, "The Selection of Communication Media as an Executive Skill," *Academy of Management Executive*, 2 (August 1988): 226, 227, exhibits 1 and 2. Reprinted by permission. (Updated for e-mail.)

Management's challenge, indicated in the bottom portion of Figure 12.3, is to match media richness with the situation. Nonroutine problems are best handled with rich media such as face-to-face, telephone, or video interactions.[12] Lean media are appropriate for routine problems. Examples of mismatched media include reading a corporate annual report at a stockholders' meeting (data glut) or announcing a massive layoff with an impersonal e-mail (data starvation).

## Decoding

Even the most expertly fashioned message will not accomplish its purpose unless it is understood. After physically receiving the message, the receiver needs to comprehend it. If the message has been properly encoded, decoding will take place rather routinely. But perfect encoding is nearly impossible to achieve in our world of many languages and cultures.[13] (In fact, India alone has 17 official languages!)[14] The receiver's willingness to receive the message is a principal prerequisite for successful decoding. Successful decoding is more likely if the receiver knows the language and terminology used in the message. It helps, too, if the receiver understands the sender's purpose and background situation. Effective listening is given special attention later in this chapter.

## Feedback

Some sort of verbal or nonverbal feedback from the receiver to the sender is required to complete the communication process. Appropriate forms of feedback are determined by the same factors governing the sender's encoding decision. Without feedback, senders have no way of knowing whether their ideas have been accurately understood. Knowing whether others understand us significantly affects both the form and content of our follow-up communication.

Employee surveys consistently underscore the importance of timely and personal feedback from management. For example, one survey of 500,000 employees from more than 300 firms contrasted satisfaction with "coaching and feedback from boss" for two groups of employees: (1) committed employees who planned to stay with their employer for at least five years and (2) those who intended to quit within a year. Satisfaction with coaching and feedback among the committed employees averaged 64 percent, while it dropped to 34 percent among those ready to quit.[15]

## Noise

Noise is not an integral part of the chainlike communication process, but it may influence the process at any or all points. As the term is used here, **noise** is any interference with the normal flow of understanding from one person to another. This is a very broad definition. Thus, a speech impairment, garbled technical transmission, negative attitudes, lies,[16] misperception, illegible print or pictures, telephone static, partial loss of hearing, and poor eyesight all qualify as noise.[17] Understanding tends to diminish as noise increases. In general, the effectiveness of organizational communication can be improved in two ways. Steps can be taken to make verbal and written messages more understandable. At the same time, noise can be minimized by foreseeing and neutralizing sources of interference.[18]

**noise**  *any interference with the normal flow of communication*

### 12C  You Want the Truth?

Employees often say they wish the organization would demonstrate "open and honest" communication. But because of the inherent unpredictability of interpersonal confrontation, they, themselves, avoid telling the truth, ducking personal responsibility for the change they advocate. Those who want to build an open and honest atmosphere should first take the emotional risk of telling the truth themselves.

**Source:** Bill Treasurer, "How Risk-Taking Really Works," *Training*, 37 (January 2000): 44.

**Questions:** *Do you agree or disagree? Why? Is it appropriate to call lying "noise" in the communication process? How much lying do you observe on a daily basis? Explain.*

# Dynamics of Organizational Communication

As a writer on the subject pointed out, "civilization is based on human cooperation and without communication, no effective cooperation can develop."[19] Accordingly, effective communication is essential for cooperation within productive organizations. At least four dynamics of organizational communication—communication strategies, the grapevine, nonverbal communication, and upward communication—largely determine the difference between effectiveness and ineffectiveness in this important area.

*Nowhere is precise communication more important than in health care. Medical histories, medications, and current symptoms all need to be kept straight. UnitedHealth Group, the largest health-care provider in the United States, relies on high-tech communication to get the job done. Here, an employee at a UnitedHealth nursing home updates a patient's records with a laptop computer. Because nurses and doctors now review all relevant information from an Internet database prior to visiting patients, UnitedHealth has cut down on unnecessary and costly hospitalizations.*

## Communication Strategies

A good deal of effort goes into plotting product development, information technology, financial, and marketing strategies these days. Much less, if any, attention is devoted to organizational communication strategies. Hence, organizational communication tends to be haphazard and often ineffective. A more systematic approach is needed. This section introduces five basic communication strategies, with an eye toward improving the overall quality of communication.

**3** Identify the five communication strategies and specify guidelines for using them.

**A Communication Continuum with Five Strategies.**    A team of authors led by communication expert Phillip G. Clampitt created the useful communication strategy continuum shown in Figure 12.4. Communication effectiveness is the vertical dimension of the model, ranging from low to high. A message communicated via any of the media discussed earlier is effective if one's intended meaning is conveyed fully and accurately to the receiver. The horizontal dimension of Clampitt's model is the amount of information transmitted, ranging from great to little. Plotted on this quadrant are five common communication strategies. Let us examine each one more closely.

- *Spray & Pray.* This is the organizational equivalent of a large lecture section where passive receivers are showered with information in the hopes that some of it will stick. Managers employing the Spray & Pray strategy assume "more is better." Unfortunately, as employees who are swamped by corporate e-mail directives and announcements will attest, more is *not* necessarily better. This strategy suffers from being one-way, impersonal, and unhelpful because it leaves receivers to sort out what is actually important or relevant.
- *Tell & Sell.* This strategy involves communicating a more restricted set of messages and taking time to explain the importance and relevance. Top executives often rely on Tell & Sell when introducing new strategies, merger plans, and reorganizations. A potentially fatal flaw arises when more time is spent polishing the presentation than assessing the receivers' actual needs.

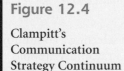

**Figure 12.4**

Clampitt's
Communication
Strategy Continuum

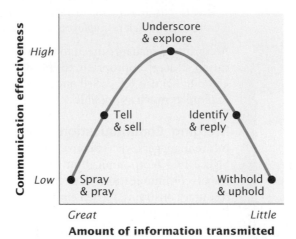

*Source:* Phillip G. Clampitt, Robert J. DeKoch, and Thomas Cashman, "A Strategy for Communicating About Uncertainty," *Academy of Management Executive,* 14 (November 2000): 48. Copyright 2000 by Academy of Management. Reproduced with permission of the Academy of Management in the format textbook via the Copyright Clearance Center.

- *Underscore & Explore.* Key information and issues closely tied to organizational success are communicated with this give-and-take strategy. Priorities are included and justifications are offered. Unlike the first two strategies, this one is two-way. Receivers are treated as active rather than passive participants in the process. Feedback is generated by "allowing employees the creative freedom to explore the implications of those ideas in a disciplined way."[20] Listening, resolving misunderstandings, building consensus and commitment, and addressing actual or potential obstacles are fundamental to success with the Underscore & Explore strategy.
- *Identify & Reply.* This is a reactive and sometimes defensive strategy. Employee concerns about prior communications are the central focus here. Employees are not only viewed as active participants; they essentially drive the process because they are assumed to know the key issues. According to Clampitt and his colleagues, "Employees set the agenda, while executives respond to rumors, innuendoes, and leaks."[21] Those using the Identify & Reply strategy need to be good listeners.
- *Withhold & Uphold.* With this communication strategy, you tell people what you think they need to know only when you believe they need to know it. Secrecy and control are paramount. Because information is viewed as power, it is rationed and restricted. Those in charge uphold their rigid and narrow view of things when challenged or questioned. If you think this sounds like the old Theory X command-and-control style of management, you're right. The Withhold & Uphold communication strategy virtually guarantees rumors and resentment.

In organizational life, one can find hybrid combinations of these five strategies. But usually there is a dominant underlying strategy that may or may not be effective.

**Seeking a Middle Ground.** Both ends of the continuum in Figure 12.4 are problematic.

*On one extreme, employees receive all the information they could possibly desire, while at the other, they are provided with little or no communication. Strategies at the extremes have a similar quality: employees have difficulty framing and making sense out of organizational events. Discovering salient information, focusing on core issues, and creating the proper memories are left to employees' personal whims.*[22]

Accordingly, managers need to follow this set of guidelines when selecting a communication strategy appropriate to the situation: (1) avoid Spray & Pray and Withhold & Uphold; (2) use Tell & Sell and Identify & Reply sparingly; and (3) use Underscore & Explore as much as possible.

**Merging Communication Strategies and Media Richness.**     Present and future managers who effectively blend lessons from Figure 12.3 (media selection) and Figure 12.4 (communication strategies) are on the path toward improved organizational communication. The trick is to select the richest medium possible (given resource constraints) when employing the Tell & Sell, Identify & Reply, and Underscore & Explore strategies.

# The Grapevine

In every organization, large or small, there are actually two communication systems, one formal and the other informal. Sometimes these systems complement and reinforce each other; at other times they come into direct conflict. Although theorists have found it convenient to separate the two, distinguishing one from the other in real life can be difficult. Information required to accomplish official objectives is channeled throughout the organization via the formal system. Official or formal communication by definition flows in accordance with established lines of authority and structural boundaries. Media for official communication include all of those discussed earlier. But superimposed on this formal network is the **grapevine,** the unofficial and informal communication system. The term *grapevine* can be traced back to Civil War days, when vinelike telegraph wires were strung from tree to tree across battlefields.

**Grapevine Patterns.**     An authority on grapevine communication has offered the following vivid description:

> *The grapevine operates fast and furiously in almost any work organization. It moves with impunity across departmental lines and easily bypasses superiors in chains of command. It flows around water coolers, down hallways, through lunch rooms, and wherever people get together in groups. It performs best in informal social contacts, but it can operate almost as effectively as a sideline to official meetings. Wherever people congregate, there is no getting rid of the grapevine. No matter how management feels about it, it is here to stay.*[23]

Since this description originally was written, computer networks and e-mail have become commonplace in the workplace. These new electronic grapevines, along with the more traditional telephone, have made grapevine communication more vibrant than ever.[24]

Regardless of the medium used, an important point needs to be made about grapevine communication. It is not a formless, haphazard process: close study has uncovered definite orderly patterns (see Figure 12.5), the most common of which is the cluster configuration. When the cluster pattern is operating, only select individuals repeat what they hear; others do not.[25] Those who consistently pass along what they hear to others serve as grapevine liaisons or gatekeepers.

> *About 10 percent of the employees on an average grapevine will be highly active participants. They serve as liaisons with the rest of the staff members who receive information but*

## 12D

**Back to the Opening Case**

Which communication strategies are evident in the NCR case? Explain. Were they used appropriately? Explain.

---

**4**   Discuss *why* it is important for managers to know about grapevine and nonverbal communication.

---

**grapevine**   *unofficial and informal communication system*

*spread it to only a few other people. Usually these liaisons are friendly, outgoing people who are in positions that allow them to cross departmental lines. For example, secretaries tend to be liaisons because they can communicate with the top executive, the janitor, and everyone in between without raising eyebrows.*[26]

Alert managers can keep abreast of grapevine communication by regularly conversing with known gatekeepers.

**Managerial Attitudes Toward the Grapevine.**    One survey of 341 participants in a management development seminar uncovered predominantly negative feelings among managers toward the grapevine. Moreover, first-line supervisors perceived the grapevine to be more influential than did middle managers. This second finding led the researchers to conclude that "apparently the grapevine is more prevalent, or at least more visible, at lower levels of the managerial hierarchy where supervisors can readily feel its impact."[27] Finally, the survey found that employees of relatively small organizations (fewer than 50 people) viewed the grapevine as less influential than did those from larger organizations (more than 100 people). A logical explanation for this last finding is that smaller organizations are usually more informal.

In spite of the negative attitude that many managers have toward it, the grapevine does have a positive side. In fact, experts estimate that grapevine communication is about 75 percent accurate.[28] Though the grapevine has a reputation among managers as a bothersome source of inaccurate information and gossip, it helps satisfy a natural desire to know what is really going on and gives employees a sense of belonging. The grapevine also serves as an emotional outlet for employee fears and apprehensions.[29] Consider, for example, what happened when investor Laurence A. Tisch became chairman of CBS:

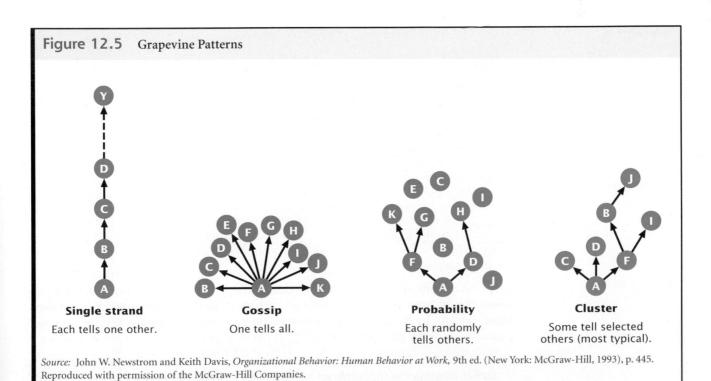

**Figure 12.5    Grapevine Patterns**

**Single strand**
Each tells one other.

**Gossip**
One tells all.

**Probability**
Each randomly tells others.

**Cluster**
Some tell selected others (most typical).

*Source:* John W. Newstrom and Keith Davis, *Organizational Behavior: Human Behavior at Work,* 9th ed. (New York: McGraw-Hill, 1993), p. 445. Reproduced with permission of the McGraw-Hill Companies.

*Tisch's reputation as a ferocious cost cutter, which he despises, forces him to watch every word and gesture. Simple questions—such as why a department needs so many people—are sometimes interpreted as orders to slash. One day Tisch and [the CBS News department head] were talking outside CBS's broadcast center on Manhattan's West 57th Street when Tisch pointed to a tower atop the building, asking what it was. Apparently staffers at a window saw him pointing in their general direction, and the next day newspaper reporters called CBS checking out a rumor that Tisch planned to sell the building.*[30]

Nevertheless, grapevine communication can carry useful information through the organization with amazing speed. Moreover, grapevine communication can help management learn how employees truly feel about policies and programs.[31]

**Coping with the Grapevine.** Considering how the grapevine can be an influential and sometimes negative force, what can management do about it? First and foremost, the grapevine *cannot be extinguished.* In fact, attempts to stifle grapevine communication may serve instead to stimulate it. Subtly monitoring the grapevine and officially correcting or countering any potentially damaging misinformation is about all any management team can do.[32] "Management by walking around" is an excellent way to monitor the grapevine in a nonthreatening manner. Some managers selectively feed information into the grapevine. For example, a health care administrator has admitted: "Sure, I use the grapevine. Why not? The employees sure use it. It's fast, reaches everyone, and employees believe it—no matter how preposterous. I limit its use, though."[33] Rumor-control hotlines and Web sites have proved useful for neutralizing disruptive and inaccurate rumors and grapevine communication.[34]

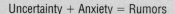

## 12E  Have You Heard About the Rumor Formula?

Uncertainty + Anxiety = Rumors

**Source:** Inspired by discussion in Nicholas Difonzo, Prashant Bordia, and Ralph L. Rosnow, "Reining in Rumors," *Organizational Dynamics,* 23 (Summer 1994): 47–62.

**Questions:** *What does this formula tell you about how organizational grapevine rumors get started? What does it suggest managers can do to avoid destructive rumors?*

## Nonverbal Communication

In today's hurried world, our words often have unintended meanings. Facial expressions and body movements that accompany our words can worsen matters. This nonverbal communication, sometimes referred to as **body language,** is an important part of the communication process.[35] In fact, one expert contends that only 7 percent of the impact of our face-to-face communication comes from the words we utter; the other 93 percent comes from our vocal intonations, facial expressions, posture, and appearance.[36] Even periods of silence can carry meaning. Consider this recent advice:

**body language** *nonverbal communication based on facial expressions, posture, and appearance*

*Your job as a manager is to learn to hear not only what people are saying, but also what they may not be saying in a conversation. So the next time you encounter someone's silence during an interview or a meeting, don't interrupt unless the person is clearly anxious or having a hard time responding.*[37]

Silence may indicate doubt, lack of understanding, or polite disagreement. Even the whole idea of "dressing for success" is an attempt to send a desired nonverbal message about oneself. Image consultants have developed a thriving business helping aspiring executives look the part:

*Vanda Sachs had a problem. The 35-year-old senior marketing executive for a well-known fashion magazine had her sights set on the publisher's office. Her trouble? Projecting enough authority to be considered for the job. "I'm petite and blonde and I'm baby-faced," she says,*

*Nice fit. Looks great! Bring on the job interviews. Geanetta Gary knows that dressing for success is an important aspect of nonverbal communication. As an unemployed mother of ten, Gary is grateful for assistance from The Working Wardrobe in Philadelphia. The nonprofit organization specializes in outfitting women in business clothes. In addition to making a good first impression, a sharp business outfit also tends to boost one's self-esteem and confidence.*

*"none of which goes over very well in a world of 45-year-old men who are 6-foot-2." Being short, in particular, is a "major liability," she adds, "more so than being a woman."*

*Beyond wearing high heels, Sachs (a pseudonym) couldn't do much about her height, but she decided she could improve on her appearance. The first step was to hire a personal image consultant. Her choice: Emily Cho, founder of New Image, a respected New York City personal-image shopping service that for 19 years has been helping women choose clothes compatible with their private and professional aspirations. Four days and $3,000 later, Sachs had a knockout wardrobe and a newly acquired savvy that would help her look the part of a publisher. "Like it or not," she explains, "we're a society that's built on first impressions."[38]*

**Types of Body Language.**   There are three kinds of body language: facial, gestural, and postural.[39] Without the speaker or listener consciously thinking about it, seemingly insignificant changes in facial expressions, gestures, and posture send various messages. A speaker can tell whether a listener is interested by monitoring a combination of nonverbal cues, including an attentive gaze, an upright posture, and confirming or agreeing gestures. Unfortunately, many people in positions of authority—parents, teachers, and managers—ignore or misread nonverbal feedback. When this happens, they become ineffective communicators.

**Receiving Nonverbal Communication.**   Like any other interpersonal skill, sensitivity to nonverbal cues can be learned (see Table 12.1). Listeners need to be especially aware of subtleties, such as the fine distinctions between an attentive gaze and a glaring stare and between an upright posture and a stiff one. Knowing how to interpret a nod, a grimace, or a grin can be invaluable to managers.[40] If at any time the response seems inappropriate to what one is saying, it is time to back off and reassess one's approach. It may be necessary to explain things more clearly, adopt a more patient manner, or make other adjustments.

Nonverbal behavior can also give managers a window on deep-seated emotions. For example, consider the situation Michael C. Ruettgers encountered shortly after joining EMC Corp., a leading manufacturer of computer data storage equipment:

| Table 12.1 | Reading Body Language |

| Unspoken message | Behavior |
| --- | --- |
| "I want to be helpful." | Uncrossing legs<br>Unbuttoning coat or jacket<br>Unclasping hands<br>Moving closer to other person<br>Smiling face<br>Removing hands from pockets<br>Unfolding arms from across chest |
| "I'm confident." | Avoiding hand-to-face gestures and head scratching<br>Maintaining an erect stance<br>Keeping steady eye contact<br>Steepling fingertips below chin |
| "I'm nervous." | Clearing throat<br>Expelling air (such as "Whew!")<br>Placing hand over mouth while speaking<br>Hurried cigarette smoking |
| "I'm superior to you." | Peering over tops of eyeglasses<br>Pointing a finger<br>Standing behind a desk and leaning palms down on it<br>Holding jacket lapels while speaking |

*Source:* Adapted from William Friend, "Reading Between the Lines," *Association Management,* 36 (June 1984): 94–100. Reprinted by permission of the publisher.

*Four months into Ruettgers' new job as head of operations and customer service, EMC's product quality program erupted into a full-blown crisis. Every piece of equipment the company sold was crashing because EMC engineers [had] failed to detect faulty disk drives supplied by NEC Corp. Ruettgers made a series of marathon swings across the country to meet personally with customers. In Denver and Salt Lake City, he came face to face with the scope of the catastrophe when managers broke down in tears because their computer operations were in shambles. "Nothing can really prepare you for that," Ruettgers says.*[41]

After his promotion to CEO, Ruettgers helped make EMC a leader in product quality. No doubt his face-to-face interaction with frustrated customers, who conveyed powerful nonverbal emotional messages, drove home the need for improvement.

**Giving Nonverbal Feedback.** What about the nonverbal feedback that managers give rather than receive? A research study carried out in Great Britain suggests that nonverbal feedback from authority figures significantly affects employee behavior. Among the people who were interviewed, those who received nonverbal approval from the interviewers in the form of smiles, positive head nods, and eye contact behaved quite differently from those who received nonverbal disapproval through frowns, head shaking, and avoidance of eye contact. Those receiving positive nonverbal feedback were judged by neutral observers to be significantly more relaxed, more friendly, more talkative, and more successful in creating a good impression.[42]

Positive nonverbal feedback to and from managers is a basic building block of good interpersonal relations. A smile or nod of the head in the appropriate situation tells the individual that he or she is on the right track and to keep up the good work (see Managing Diversity). Such feedback is especially important for managers, who must avoid participating in the subtle but powerful nonverbal discrimination experienced by women in leadership positions.[43] When samples of men and women leaders in one study offered the same arguments and suggestions in a controlled setting, the women leaders received more negative and less positive nonverbal feedback than did the men.[44] Managing-diversity workshops target this sort of "invisible barrier" to women and minorities. Similarly, cross-cultural training alerts employees bound for foreign assignments to monitor their nonverbal gestures carefully. For example, the familiar thumbs-up sign tells American employees to keep up the good work. Much to the embarrassment of poorly informed expatriates, that particular nonverbal message does not travel well. The same gesture would be a vulgar sign in Australia, would say "I'm winning" in Saudi Arabia, and would signify the number one in Germany and the number five in Japan. Malaysians use the thumb, instead of their forefinger, for pointing.[45]

Two other trends in nonverbal communication are etiquette classes for students and management trainees[46] and teaching sign language to coworkers of deaf employees.

**12F Is This a Joke?**

Research finding:

*"A little corporate horseplay goes right to the bottom line. A gag to take the edge off a busted project, a funny story to bring people around to your point of view, a good laugh—any and all relieve stress, fuel creativity, and contribute to better performance. . . . In short, good managers are funny managers."*

**Source:** "Get Funny, Make Money," *Training*, 33 (July 1996): 14–15.

**Questions:** *Do you believe that managers should try to be funny? Explain. What sort of humorous communication should managers* not *use in today's organizations?*

## Upward Communication

As used here, the term **upward communication** refers to a process of systematically encouraging employees to share their feelings and ideas with management. Upward communication has become increasingly important in recent years as employees have demanded—and, in many cases, received—a greater say in their work lives. *The Wall Street Journal* recently reported this example:

**upward communication**
*encouraging employees to share their feelings and ideas with management*

John Much, CEO of HNC Software, San Diego, says he often uncovers the most important information during informal conversations with employees. "As a leader, you need a network of people from the highest to the lowest levels who can be your trusted advisers, and who know that you are open to hearing any message, bad as well as good, that they may send you," he says. He holds weekly Java with John coffee sessions open to the first 20 employees who sign up, and encourages those who attend to talk about problems they see at work.[47]

At least seven different options are open to managers who want to improve upward communication.

**5** Explain ways in which management can encourage upward communication.

**Formal Grievance Procedures.** When unions represent rank-and-file employees, provisions for upward communication are usually spelled out in the collective bargaining agreement. Typically, unionized employees utilize a formal grievance procedure for contesting managerial actions and oversights. Grievance procedures usually consist of a series of progressively more rigorous steps. For example, union members who have been fired may talk with their supervisor in the presence of the union steward. If the issue is not resolved at that level, the next step may be a meeting with the department head. Sometimes the formal grievance process includes as many as five or six steps, with a third-party arbitrator as the last resort. Formal grievance procedures are also found in nonunion situations.

# Managing Diversity

## To Touch or Not to Touch? That Is the Question.

Female supervisors have more liberty to touch their workers, which for them can create an atmosphere of trust, warmth and professionalism, according to researchers.

Men, on the other hand, consider themselves largely boxed into the formality of a handshake.

Women have long had more freedom to give a hug of support to another woman. But a paper published last year in the *Applied Communication Research* journal indicates that women are freer to emphasize a point with other forms of non-sexual touch to the forearm of a man or woman.

Women were seen as particularly composed and confident when they used touch once considered masculine, such as a playful mock push to a man's shoulder. And, women can even place a firm hand on a man's shoulder to signal, if necessary, who is in charge, says University of Arizona communications expert Judee Burgoon.

A man putting the same firm hand on a woman's shoulder would likely come off as condescending, "like correcting a child," Burgoon says. "Touch isn't always there to give warm fuzzies."

The paper, *Types of Touch in Cross-Sex Relationships Between Coworkers*, used videotapes of workers of different sexes. The non-sexual touch they used ranged from handshakes to face touching to an arm around the waist, to a pat on the shoulder. After viewing the videotapes, focus groups rated the female touchers as more affectionate, trusting, happy and composed than the men.

Burgoon warns that touch by any supervisor remains fraught with potential misunderstanding. Women especially run the risk of appearing flirtatious.

Not all female bosses are convinced they have an advantage. Melissa Stevens, president of a small public

relations firm, uses an orchestra of touch ranging from comforting hugs to congratulatory high-fives. But her four employees are women. If she employed a man, "I'd have to be very, very careful," she says.

Men are being advised almost universally to keep hands off. "Maybe we're conservative, but touching can be potentially offensive to anyone," says Steve Harvey of human resources firm OI Consultants, which gives the same advice to female supervisors.

That might be the best legal advice, but it is contrary to the best managerial practices. It also goes against the grain of bosses such as Carmine Sprio, chef and owner of an Albany, N.Y., restaurant. With customers, he thinks nothing of putting a friendly hand on the shoulder of a man or a hand on the arm of a woman.

It's good for business, he says, and waiters and waitresses have long known that they receive bigger tips when they touch customers.

In Sprio's crowded all-male kitchen, touch is important when he has a hot pan and must step around someone with a sharp knife. And he gives the kitchen staff bear hugs for a job well done.

But when he's out front among waitresses and other female employees, he is mostly hands off, even though his instincts tell him that proper, respectful touch would also build trust with the women.

Michaela Rodeno, CEO of St. Supéry winery, says touch is commonplace in the wine business, but "I'm also a director on a bank board, where touch doesn't happen."

*Source:* Del Jones, "Female Bosses Can Touch More Freely," *USA Today* (February 19, 2002): 9B. Copyright 2002, *USA Today.* Reprinted with permission.

A promising alternative to the traditional grievance process is the *peer review* program. Originally developed in the early 1980s by General Electric at its Appliance Park factory in Columbia, Maryland, peer reviews have been adopted by a growing number of organizations. At GE, the three specially trained coworkers and two managers on the panel listen to the grievance, conduct a majority-rule secret ballot, and render a final decision. Certain issues, including those involving work rules, performance appraisal results, and pay rates, are not handled by GE's peer review panels. GE created this process as a union-avoidance tactic.[48]

**Employee Attitude and Opinion Surveys.**   Both in-house and commercially prepared surveys can bring employee attitudes and feelings to the surface. Thanks to commercial software packages, time-saving and paperless electronic surveys are popular in today's workplaces.[49] Employees will usually complete surveys if they are convinced meaningful changes will result. Du Pont, for example, took the right approach:

> Du Pont surveyed 6,600 of its people, including some at Towanda, [Pennsylvania,] and found that flexible work hours were a top priority. Working mothers and single parents said it was hard to cope with the kids while keeping to a rigid plant schedule. A team at Towanda got together and devised a novel solution: Take vacation time by the hour. During slack times when three of the four [task] team members could easily handle the job, one could take off a few hours in the afternoon to go to a school play or bring a sick kid to the doctor. Today other Du Pont workers and managers visit Towanda to learn about flextime. A few have already borrowed it for their own plants.[50]

Surveys with no feedback or follow-up action tend to alienate employees, who feel they are just wasting their time.[51] On the other hand, a researcher found unionized companies conducting regular attitude surveys were less likely to experience a labor strike than companies failing to survey their employees.[52]

**Suggestion Systems.**   Who knows more about a job than someone who performs that job day in and day out? This rhetorical question is the primary argument for suggestion systems. Fairness and prompt feedback are keys to successful suggestion systems. Monetary incentives can help, too. For example, consider this success story at Winnebago Industries, the recreational vehicle maker in Forest City, Iowa:

> The program works because employees take it seriously. All reasonable suggestions submitted—an impressive 10,355 since the program began in 1991—are investigated by two full-time employees. The company has ended up implementing fully a third of these ideas, and employees have won more than $500,000 (they receive 10 percent of what the company saves in the first year). Winnebago says the program's first-year savings have added up to $5.8 million.[53]

**12G  Fair Play with Employee Suggestions**

**Situation:** Jodie Kavanagh, a paint shop employee at one of Honda's Ohio facilities, suggested a design modification in the bumpers of the Honda Civic to reduce painting time. She persisted and prevailed, after an initial disappointing response. "Honda's annual savings: $1.2 million in the U.S. alone."

**Source:** Edith Hill Updike and David Woodruff, "Honda's Civic Lesson," *Business Week* (September 18, 1995): 76.

**Questions:** *What would be a fair reward for Jodie? What are the implications of your decision for Jodie's coworkers?*

Nice return on investment! A study of U.S. government employees found a positive correlation between suggestions and productivity.[54]

**Open-Door Policy.**   The open-door approach to upward communication has been both praised and criticized. Proponents say problems can be nipped in the bud when managers keep their doors open and employees feel free to walk in at any time and talk with them. But critics contend that an open-door policy encourages employees to leapfrog the formal chain of command (something that happens a lot these days because of e-mail). They argue further that it is an open invitation to annoying interruptions when managers can least afford them. A limited open-door policy—afternoons only, for example—can effectively remedy this last objection.

**Informal Meetings.**   Employees may feel free to air their opinions and suggestions if they are confident management will not criticize or penalize them for being frank.[55] Our earlier example of the 20-person coffee session with the CEO of HNC Software is an excellent case in point.

**Internet Chat Rooms.**    In the Internet age, a convenient way for management to get candid feedback is to host a meeting place on the Web. These so-called "virtual water coolers" give employees unprecedented freedom of speech. Dave Barram, head of the huge General Services Administration (GSA) in Washington, D.C., offered this assessment:

> . . . GSA has set up a Web-based "chat line," in which employees exchange uncensored thoughts and ideas. "If we have honest conversations about what's working and what isn't, we can become really good," Barram says. "If we don't, we'll never help each other."[56]

This approach takes lots of managerial courage, if the rough-and-tumble "cyberventing" on unauthorized Web sites aimed at specific companies is any indication.[57]

**Exit Interviews.**    An employee leaving the organization, for whatever reason, no longer fears possible recrimination from superiors and so can offer unusually frank and honest feedback, obtained in a brief, structured **exit interview.**[58] On the other hand, exit interviews have been criticized for eliciting artificially negative feedback because the employee may have a sour-grapes attitude toward the organization. Research finds the use of exit interviews to be spotty and haphazard, although many employers claim to use them. "If done well, managers and consultants said, exit interviews can show trends and point to potential problems that need to be addressed."[59] Systematic use of exit interviews is recommended.

   In general, attempts to promote upward communication will be successful only if employees truly believe that their contributions will have a favorable impact on their employment. Halfhearted or insincere attempts to get employees to open up and become involved will do more harm than good.

**exit interview**  *brief structured interview with a departing employee*

# Communication Problems and Promises in the Internet Age

Because communication is a complex, give-and-take process, problems will occur. Managers who are aware of common barriers to communication and who are sensitive to the problems of sexist and racist communication are more likely to be effective communicators. In addition, managers who want to be effective communicators need to be aware of opportunities and obstacles in Internet-age communication systems.

## Barriers to Communication

Do intended messages actually have the desired impact on employee behavior? This is the true test of organizational communication. Emerson Electric, the successful maker of electric motors, has a simple but effective way of testing how well its organizational communication is working. According to the head of the company:

> As a measure of communication at Emerson, we claim that every employee can answer four essential questions about his or her job:
>
> 1.  What cost reduction are you currently working on?
> 2.  Who is the "enemy" (who is the competition)?
> 3.  Have you met with your management in the past six months?
> 4.  Do you understand the economics of your job?

*When I repeated to a business journalist the claim that every employee can answer these questions, he put it to the test by randomly asking those questions of different employees at one of our plants. Each employee provided clear and direct answers, passing both the journalist's test and ours.*[60]

Emerson Electric evidently has done a good job of overcoming the four main types of communication barriers: (1) process barriers, (2) physical barriers, (3) semantic barriers, and (4) psychosocial barriers.

**6** Identify and describe four barriers to communication.

**Process Barriers.**   Every step in the communication process is necessary for effective communication. Blocked steps become barriers. Consider the following situations:

- *Sender barrier.* A management trainee with an unusual new idea fails to speak up at a meeting for fear of criticism.
- *Encoding barrier.* This is a growing problem in today's culturally diverse workplace:

    *William D. Fleet, human-resources director at the Seattle Marriott, where employees speak 17 languages, once fired a Vietnamese kitchen worker for wrongly accusing a chef of assault. Only after another employee was attacked by a kitchen worker did Fleet figure out that the Vietnamese employee had used the word "chef" to refer to all kitchen workers with white uniforms. The misunderstanding had led to the firing of a good staffer and delayed the arrest of a dangerous one. . . .*

    *That's why . . . [Fleet] instituted a comprehensive ESL [English as a second language] program for staffers to take on company time. After all, workers who know English interact better with guests.*[61]

- *Medium barrier.* After getting no answer three times and a busy signal twice, a customer concludes that a store's consumer hot line is a waste of time.
- *Decoding barrier.* A restaurant manager does not understand unfamiliar computer jargon during a sales presentation for laptop computers.
- *Receiver barrier.* A manager who is preoccupied with the preparation of a budget asks a team member to repeat an earlier statement.
- *Feedback barrier.* During on-the-job training, the failure of the trainee to ask any questions causes a manager to wonder if any real understanding has taken place.

The complexity of the communication process itself is a potentially formidable barrier to communication. Malfunctions anywhere along the line can singly or collectively block the transfer of understanding.

**Physical Barriers.**   Sometimes a physical object blocks effective communication. For example, a riveter who wears ear protectors probably could not hear someone yelling "Fire!" Distance is another physical barrier. Thousands of miles and differing time zones traditionally made international business communication difficult. So today's global managers appreciate how the Internet and modern telecommunications technology have made the planet a seemingly smaller place. Although people often take physical barriers for granted, they can sometimes be removed. Perhaps an inconveniently positioned wall in an office can be torn out. Architects and office layout specialists called "organizational ecologists" are trying to redesign buildings and offices with more effective communication in mind. An interesting example is Timex's eye-catching new headquarters building in Middlebury, Connecticut:

*All of the 275 employees—including the CEO—work in a single, open room roughly the size of a football field: No walls, no partitions, no cubes divide them. . . .*

*By opening up space, Timex hopes to promote all of the usual behavior expected from workspace design these days: collaboration, interaction, spontaneous meetings.*[62]

**semantics** *study of the meaning of words*

### Semantic Barriers.

Formally defined, **semantics** is the study of the meaning of words. Words are indispensable, though they can cause a great deal of trouble. In a well-worn army story, a growling drill sergeant once ordered a frightened recruit to go out and paint his entire jeep. Later, the sergeant was shocked to find that the private had painted his *entire* jeep, including the headlights, windshield, seats, and dashboard gauges. Obviously, the word *entire* meant something different to the recruit than it did to the sergeant.

In today's highly specialized world, managers and professionals in such fields as accounting, computer science, advertising, medicine, and law may become so accustomed to their own technical language that they forget that people outside their field may not understand them. Unexpected reactions or behavior by others may signal a semantic barrier. It may become necessary to reencode the message using more familiar terms. Sometimes, if the relationship among specialists in different technical fields is an ongoing one, remedial steps can be taken. For example, hospital administrators often take a special course in medical terminology so that they can better understand the medical staff.

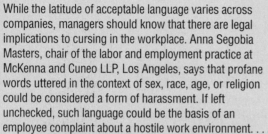

**12H Watch Your #@~*&$% Language!**

While the latitude of acceptable language varies across companies, managers should know that there are legal implications to cursing in the workplace. Anna Segobia Masters, chair of the labor and employment practice at McKenna and Cuneo LLP, Los Angeles, says that profane words uttered in the context of sex, race, age, or religion could be considered a form of harassment. If left unchecked, such language could be the basis of an employee complaint about a hostile work environment. . . .

To minimize the risks of lawsuits, Masters suggests creating a written policy stating that harassment can be verbal and establishing procedures for employees who want to seek corrective action.

**Source:** Excerpted from Louisa Wah, "Profanity in the Workplace," *Management Review,* 88 (June 1999): 8.

**Questions:** *Do you hear more profanity in the workplace today? Is it a problem? Does it create a hostile work environment? Explain.*

### Psychosocial Barriers.

Psychological and social barriers are probably responsible for more blocked communication than any other type of barrier.[63] People's backgrounds, perceptions, values, biases, needs, and expectations differ. Childhood experiences may result in negative feelings toward authority figures (such as supervisors), racial prejudice, distrust of the opposite sex, or lack of self-confidence. Family and personal problems, including poor health, alcoholism, lack of sleep, and emotional strain, may be so upsetting that an employee is unable to concentrate on work. Experience on present or past jobs may have created anger, distrust, and resentment that speak more loudly in the employee's mind than any work-related communication. Sincere sensitivity to the receiver's needs and personal circumstances goes a long way toward overcoming psychosocial barriers to communication.

## Sexist and Racist Communication

In recent years the English language has been increasingly criticized for being sexist and racist. Words like *he, chairman, brotherhood, mankind,* and the like have traditionally been used in reference to both men and women. The usual justification is that everyone understands that these words refer to both sexes, and it is simpler to use the masculine form. Critics maintain that wholly masculine wording subtly denies women a place and image worthy of their equal status and importance in society.[64] This criticism is largely based on psychological and sociological considerations. Calling the human race *mankind,* for instance, is seldom a real barrier to understanding. But a Stanford University researcher found that "males appear to use 'he' in response to male-related imagery, rather than in response to abstract or generic notions of humanity."[65] In other words, *he* is commonly interpreted to mean literally *he* (a man), not *they* (men and women).

These same cautions carry over to the problem of racist communication for both ethical and legal reasons.

*Words spoken at work that aren't literally racist—such as "you people," "poor people," and "that one in there"—now can be grounds for employment discrimination lawsuits [in the United States].*

*They're called "code words."* . . .

*It's not just the words, says Herman Cain, the black CEO of Godfather's Pizza and author of Leadership Is Common Sense.* "It's body language. Tone of voice. How people talk to you. Over the years you can develop a sixth sense."[66]

Progressive and ethical managers are weeding sexist and racist language out of their vocabularies and correspondence to eliminate both intentional and inadvertent demeaning of women and racial minorities.[67]

## Communicating in the Online Workplace

Computers speak a simple digital language of 1s and 0s. Today, every imaginable sort of information is being converted into a digital format, including text, numbers, still and moving pictures, and sound. This process means nothing short of a revolution for the computer, telecommunications, consumer electronics, publishing, and entertainment industries. Organizational communication, already significantly reshaped by computer technology, is undergoing its own revolutionary change. This section does *not* attempt the impossible task of describing all the emerging communication technologies, ranging from speech recognition computers to online full-motion video to virtual reality.[68] Rather, it explores the impact of some established Internet-age technologies on workplace communications. Our goal is to more effectively use the technologies we have and prepare for those to come.

**Getting a Handle on E-Mail.**    E-mail via the Internet has precipitated a communication revolution akin to those brought about by the printing press, telephone, radio, and television. If you are on the Internet, you are ultimately linked to each of hundreds of millions of people on Earth capable of sending and receiving e-mail. Both on and off the job, e-mail is more than a way of communication—it is a lifestyle! Jim Keyes, CEO of the 7-Eleven convenience store chain, "burns three to four hours of his day on 200 e-mails and is such a heavy user that if a top field executive or licensee were to phone him, he might not recognize the voice."[69] Shifting the focus from individual to organization, we run into astonishing numbers. After discovering that many of its 88,000 employees worldwide were spending about 2 1/2 hours each day exchanging 3 million e-mails, Intel decided to act:

*The chipmaker recently started classes on how to manage e-mail. Some tips: Put short messages in the subject line so recipients don't have to open it to read the note. Intel also is asking workers to sparingly use graphics and attachments and get off unnecessary distribution lists.*

*"We're not discouraging e-mail use, just better use," spokesman Chuck Mulloy says.*[70]

Meanwhile, IBM is responding to e-mail overload by encouraging the use of instant messaging, because it is faster and less of a burden on the network.[71] E-mail is a two-headed beast: easy and efficient, while at the same time grossly abused and mismanaged. By properly managing e-mail, the organization can take a big step toward properly using the Internet. An organizational e-mail policy, embracing these recommendations from experts, can help:

**7** List two practical tips for each of the three modern communication technologies (e-mail, cell phones, and videoconferences) and summarize the pros and cons of telecommuting.

- The e-mail system belongs to the company, which has the legal right to monitor its use. (*Never* assume privacy with company e-mail.)[72]
- Workplace e-mail is for business purposes only.
- Harassing and offensive e-mail will not be tolerated.
- E-mail messages should be concise (see Table 12.2). As in all correspondence, grammar and spelling count because they reflect on your diligence and credibility. Typing in all capital letters makes the message hard to read and amounts to SHOUTING in cyberspace. (All capital letters can be appropriate, for contrast purposes, when adding comments to an existing document.)
- Lists of bullet items (similar to the format you are reading now) are acceptable because they tend to be more concise than paragraphs.
- Long attachments defeat the quick-and-easy nature of e-mail.
- Recipients should be told when a reply is *unnecessary*.
- An organization-specific priority system should be used for sending and receiving all e-mail. *Example:* "At Libit, a company in Palo Alto, Calif., that makes silicon products for the cable industry, e-mail is labeled as either informational or action items to avoid time wasting."[73]
- "Spam" (unsolicited and unwanted e-mail) that gets past filters should be deleted without being read.
- To avoid file clutter, messages unlikely to be referred to again should not be saved.[74]

**Hello! Can We Talk About Cell Phone Etiquette?**   Cell phones are in wide use in the United States, with a market penetration rate of 48 percent in 2001. Other countries have much higher rates: 85 percent in Hong Kong and over 86 percent in Italy.[75] Like e-mail, cell phones have proved to be both a blessing and a curse. Offsetting the mobility and convenience are concerns about distracted drivers and loud and obnoxious phone conversations in public places.[76] Managers need to be particularly sensitive to the risk of inadvertently broadcasting proprietary company information, names, and numbers. Competitors could be standing in the same airport line or sitting in the next restaurant booth. Table 12.3 offers some practical tips to help make the use of cell phones more effective, secure, and courteous.

**Table 12.2    How to Compose a CLEAR E-Mail Message**

**Concise.** A brief message in simple conversational language is faster for you to write and more pleasant for your readers to read.

**Logical.** A message in logical steps, remembering to include any context your readers need, will be more easily understood.

**Empathetic.** When you identify with your readers, your message will be written in the right tone and in words they will readily understand.

**Action-oriented.** When you remember to explain to your readers what you want them to do next, they are more likely to do it.

**Right.** A complete message, with no important facts missing, with all the facts right, and with correct spelling, will save your readers having to return to you to clarify details.

*Source:* Joan Tunstall, *Better, Faster Email: Getting the Most Out of Email* (St. Leonards, Australia: Allen & Unwin, 1999), p. 37. Reprinted by permission.

**Table 12.3    Cell Phone Etiquette**

The technology may be modern, but cell phone etiquette is mainly good old-fashioned manners: Respect others. Don't curse on the phone or carry on about private matters. And don't talk with your mouth full.

The rudest offenders, Palm Beach manners maven Jacqueline Whitmore says, seem unaware that once-private phone calls are now gratingly public. Cell phones aren't the wisest choice when talking about your troubled teenagers or sizzling sex life.

And remember, even though we can't see you chewing, we can hear you on the other end. A similar rule applies equally—if not more so—to ill-advised calls from a toilet stall. Some tips:

- Turn off your phone—or set it to vibrate—in public places such as theaters, restaurants and places of worship. If you must make or take a call, move outside or to a secluded area.

- Alert others at social or business gatherings if you're expecting a call. Excuse yourself when it comes, and be brief. It's rude to give the cell phone call precedence over people you're with.

- Speak softly, in a conversational tone. "Cell yell" is alarmingly widespread, despite being technologically unnecessary. You're not Alexander Graham Bell, shouting into the first phone ever invented.

- Polite responses to annoying cell phone users can be tricky. Whitmore says moving away may be easiest. Finding a theater or café manager to intervene is another option. Be courteous and not angry if you're asking a caller to lower his or her voice or to end a call.

*Source:*  Deborah Sharp, "Be Polite, Be Discreet, Be Quiet," *USA Today* (September 4, 2001): 4A. Copyright 2001, *USA Today.* Reprinted with permission.

**Videoconferences.**    A **videoconference** is a live television or broadband Internet video exchange between people in different locations. The decreasing cost of steadily improving videoconferencing technologies and the desire to reduce costly travel time have fostered wider use of this approach to organizational communication.[77] The September 11, 2001, terrorist attacks gave videoconferencing a boost because of greater reluctance to fly. As a sample of what is available, it now is possible to go to one of 150 Kinko's stores and rent a videoconferencing room for either a meeting or a "virtual interview."[78] Moreover, "companies turned off by the $30,000 bulky systems of a decade ago can outfit a broadband-connected conference room for $5,000."[79]

Communication pointers for videoconference participants include the following:

- Test the system before the meeting convenes.
- Dress for the occasion. The video image is distorted by movement of wild patterns and flashy jewelry. Solid white clothing tends to "glow" on camera.
- Make sure everyone is introduced.
- Check to make sure everyone can see and hear the content of the meeting.
- Do not feel compelled to direct your entire presentation to the camera or monitor. Directly address those in the same room.
- Speak loudly and clearly. Avoid slang and jargon in cross-cultural meetings where translations are occurring.
- Avoid exaggerated physical movements that tend to blur on camera.
- Adjust your delivery to any transmission delay, pausing longer than usual when waiting for replies.

**videoconference**  *live television or broadband Internet video exchange between people in different locations*

*"On the Internet, nobody knows you're a dog."*

### 12I | Proper Supervision or Questionable "Snoopervision" for Telecommuters?

A sampling of new technologies:

- **Block Internet sites.** *Employers may restrict remote workers from visiting Web sites devoted to non-business topics, such as shopping.*

- **Monitor where remote workers go online.** *Employees working remotely who connect through company servers may find their Web surfing monitored. Companies can compile a profile on each user based on where they're going online.*

- **Read employees' e-mail.** *Employers in many cases can read e-mail containing certain words . . . .*

- **Count keystrokes.** *Companies that have large numbers of customer-service representatives working at home are using technology that allows them to measure keystrokes to ensure work is actually being done.*

**Source:** Excerpted from Stephanie Armour, "More Bosses Keep Tabs on Telecommuters," *USA Today* (July 24, 2001): 1B.

**Questions:** *Is privacy an issue here? Explain. Is this good management practice? Explain. Does this make you more or less likely to want to telecommute at least three or four days a month? Explain.*

- Avoid side conversations, which are disruptive.
- Do not nervously tap the table or microphone or shuffle papers.[80]

**Telecommuting.**    Futurist Alvin Toffler used the term *electronic cottage* to refer to the practice of working at home on a personal computer connected—typically by telephone—to an employer's place of business. More recently, this practice has been labeled **telecommuting** because work, rather than the employee, travels between a central office and the employee's home, reaching the computer via telephone or cable modem. The advent of overnight delivery services, low-cost facsimile (fax) machines, e-mail, and high-speed modems, combined with traditional telephone communication, has broadened the scope of telecommuting. According to a recent U.S. General Accounting Office study, "an estimated 16.5 million employees in the United States telecommute at least once a month and 9.3 million employees telecommute at least once a week.[81] The growth of telecommuting has slowed to a crawl. Despite some compelling advantages, telecommuting has enough drawbacks to make it unsuitable for many employees as well as employers (see Table 12.4). Telecommuting seriously disrupts the normal social and communication patterns in the workplace. Telecommuting will not become the prevailing work mode anytime soon, but it certainly is more than a passing fad.[82]

| **Table 12.4** Telecommuting: Promises and Problems |
|---|

| Promises | Potential problems |
|---|---|
| 1. Significantly boosts individual productivity. | 1. Can cause fear of stagnating at home. |
| 2. Saves commuting time and travel expenses (lessens traffic congestion). | 2. Can foster sense of isolation, due to lack of social contact with coworkers. |
| 3. Taps broader labor pool (such as mothers with young children, disabled and retired persons, and prison inmates). | 3. Can result in competition or interference with family duties, thus causing family conflict. |
| 4. Eliminates office distractions and politics. | 4. Can disrupt traditional manager-employee relationship. |
| 5. Reduces employer's cost of office space. | 5. Can cause fear of being "out of sight, out of mind" at promotion time. |

**telecommuting** *sending work to and from one's office via computer modem while working at home*

# Becoming a Better Communicator

Three communication skills as important as ever in today's highly organized world are listening, writing, and running meetings. Managers who master these skills usually have relatively few interpersonal relations problems. Moreover, effective communicators tend to move up the hierarchy faster than poor ones do. According to *Fortune* magazine:

> *Management experts say that communicating often and clearly with workers will be among every manager's key skills in coming years, while in an interconnected world, skillful communication outside one's company becomes steadily more important. Yet just as these trends take hold, many managers are becoming worse communicators.*[83]

**8** List at least three practical tips for improving each of the following communication skills: listening, writing, and running a meeting.

## Effective Listening

Almost all training in oral communication in high school, college, and management development programs is in effective speaking. But what about listening, the other half of the communication equation? Listening is the forgotten stepchild in communication skills training. This is unfortunate because the most glowing oration is a waste of time if it is not heard. Interestingly, a Cornell University researcher asked 827 employees in the hospitality industry to rate their managers' listening ability. Managers considered to be good listeners by employees tended to be female, under 45 years of age, and relatively new to their position.[84]

Listening takes place at two steps in the verbal communication process. First, the receiver must listen in order to decode and understand the original message. Then the sender becomes a listener when attempting to decode and understand subsequent feedback. Identical listening skills come into play at both ends.

We can hear and process information much more quickly than the normal speaker can talk. According to researchers, our average rate of speaking is about 125 words per minute, whereas we are able to listen to about 400 to 600 words a minute.[85] Thus, listeners have up to 75 percent slack time during which they can daydream or

*Listen to this! Native American tradition calls for giving each person in a "talking circle" an uninterrupted opportunity to speak. It is referred to as "passing the rock." The person holding the object speaks without interference, then passes the rock and shifts into a listening mode. Here a group of Xerox employees in Rochester, New York, pass the rock in their talking circle. Of course, you don't have to work for Xerox to copy this tradition.*

alternatively analyze the information and plan a response. Effective listeners know how to put that slack time to good use. Here are some practical tips for more effective listening:

- Tolerate silence. Listeners who rush to fill momentary silences cease being listeners.
- Ask stimulating, open-ended questions, ones that require more than merely a yes-or-no answer.
- Encourage the speaker with attentive eye contact, alert posture, and verbal encouragers such as "umhum," "yes," and "I see." Occasionally repeating the speaker's last few words also helps.
- Paraphrase. Periodically restate in your own words what you have just heard.
- Show emotion to demonstrate that you are a sympathetic listener.
- Know your biases and prejudices and attempt to correct for them.
- Avoid premature judgments about what is being said.
- Summarize. Briefly highlight what the speaker has just finished saying to bring out possible misunderstandings.[86]

Wal-Mart has developed an admired "culture of listening." All of Wal-Mart's senior managers, including the CEO, try to devote two days each week to visiting stores across the United States and listening to employees' concerns.[87] The valuable information gathered more than makes up for the Wal-Mart managers' hectic travel schedules.

## Effective Writing

Managers often complain about college graduates' poor writing skills.[88] Writing difficulties stem from an educational system that requires students to do less and less writing. Essay tests have given way in many classes to the multiple-choice variety, and term papers are being pushed aside by team activities and projects. Quick-and-dirty computer e-mail correspondence at home, school, and the workplace also has contributed to the erosion of writing quality in recent years. Moreover, computerized "spell checkers" used by those who compose at the computer keyboard do nothing to improve grammar. (There is no substitute for careful proofreading.) As a learned skill, effective writing is the product of regular practice.[89] Students who do not get the necessary writing practice in school are at a disadvantage when they step up to the managerial firing line.

Good writing is clearly part of the encoding step in the basic communication process. If it is done skillfully, potentially troublesome semantic and psychosocial barriers can be surmounted. Caterpillar's publications editor offered four helpful reminders:

### 12J  Do You Have the "Write" Stuff?

In a survey of college professors, 81 percent rated high school graduates only "fair" or "poor" on *writing clearly*. Seventy-eight percent were rated only "fair" or "poor" in *grammar/spelling*.

**Source:** Data from "Much to Learn, Professors Say," *USA Today* (July 5, 2001): 8D.

**Questions:** *Should this be a matter of concern for managers in the Internet age? Explain.*

1. *Keep words simple.* Simplifying the words you use will help reduce your thoughts to essentials; keep your readers from being "turned off" by the complexity of your letter, memo, or report; and make it more understandable.
2. *Don't sacrifice communication to rules of composition.* Most of us who were sensitized to the rules of grammar and composition in school never quite recovered from the process. As proof, we keep trying to make our writing conform to rigid rules and customs without regard to style or the ultimate purpose of the communication. (Of course, managers need to be sensitive to the stylistic preferences of their bosses.)
3. *Write concisely.* This means expressing your thoughts, opinions, and ideas in the fewest number of words consistent with composition and smoothness. But don't confuse conciseness with mere brevity; you may write briefly without being clear or complete.
4. *Be specific.* Vagueness is one of the most serious flaws in written communication because it destroys accuracy and clarity, leaving the reader to wonder about your meaning or intent.[90]

Also, avoid irritating your readers with useless phrases such as "to be perfectly honest," "needless to say," "as you know," and "please be advised that."[91]

## Running a Meeting

Meetings are an ever-present feature of modern organizational life. Whether they are convened to find facts, devise alternatives, or pass along information, meetings typically occupy a good deal of a manager's time. This is particularly true in the United States, where employees in general have an average of 7.2 face-to-face meetings and 2.1 telephone conferences a week. Those figures were the highest among five countries in a recent study, including Canada, the United Kingdom, Germany, and France (listed in diminishing order of meeting frequency).[92] Meetings are the principal format for committee action. Too often, as illustrated by this research insight, meetings are a waste of valuable time. "The typical professional attends more than 60 meetings per month—and more than one-third are rated unproductive."[93] Whatever the reason for a meeting, managers who chair meetings owe it to themselves and their organization to use everyone's time and talent efficiently. Some useful pointers for conducting successful meetings are the following:*

- Prepare ahead of time.
- Have a reason for the meeting. Don't get together just because of tradition.

---

*Stephanie Armour, "Team Efforts, Technology Add New Reasons to Meet," *USA Today* (December 8, 1997): 2A. Copyright 1997, *USA Today*. Reprinted with permission.

- Distribute an agenda to participants before the meeting.
- Give participants at least one day's notification.
- Participants should ask themselves what is expected of them, what they can read to prepare.
- Limit attendance and designate a leader.
- Keep a clock in the meeting room and have a specific start and end time.
- Encourage everyone to talk while keeping with the agenda.
- Foster rigorous debate and brainstorming while respecting each person's opinion.
- Use visual aids. Presentations with visual aids are 43 percent more persuasive than those without such presentations.
- Follow up. Meeting leader should let participants know any outcome.[94]

With practice, these guidelines will become second nature. Running a meeting brings into focus all the components of the communication process, including coping with noise and barriers. Effective meetings are important to organizational communication and, ultimately, to organizational success.

# Summary

1. Modern technology has made communicating easier and less costly, with the unintended side effect of information overload. Managers are challenged to improve the *quality* of their communication because it is a core process for everything they do. Communication is a social process involving the transfer of information and understanding. Links in the communication process include sender, encoding, medium, decoding, receiver, and feedback. Noise is any source of interference.

2. According to the Lengel-Daft contingency model, media richness is determined by the amount of information conveyed and learning promoted. Rich media such as face-to-face communication are best for nonroutine problems. Lean media such as impersonal bulletins are suitable for routine problems.

3. Organizational communication is typically too haphazard. Clampitt's communication continuum indicates how the five basic strategies are not equally effective. The Spray & Pray and Withhold & Uphold strategies are generally ineffective and should be avoided. The Tell & Sell and Identify & Reply strategies should be used sparingly. Managers need to use the Underscore & Explore strategy as much as possible. Media richness needs to be as high as possible if the preferred communication strategies are to be effective.

4. The unofficial and informal communication system that sometimes complements and sometimes disrupts the formal communication system has been labeled the grapevine. A sample of managers surveyed had predominantly negative feelings toward it. Recognizing that the grapevine cannot be suppressed, managers are advised to monitor it constructively. Nonverbal communication, including facial, gestural, and postural body language, accounts for most of the impact of face-to-face communication. Managers can become more effective communicators by doing a better job of receiving and giving nonverbal communications.

5. Upward communication can be stimulated by using formal grievance procedures, employee attitude and opinion surveys, suggestion systems, an open-door policy, informal meetings, Internet chat rooms, and exit interviews.

**6.** Managers need to identify and overcome four barriers to communication. Process barriers can occur at any one of the basic links in the communication process. Physical barriers, such as walls and distance between two points, can block the transfer of understanding. Semantic barriers are encountered when there is confusion about the meaning of words. Psychosocial barriers to communication involve the full range of human perceptions, prejudices, and attitudes that can block the transfer of understanding. Care needs to be taken to eliminate subtle forms of sexist and racist communication.

**7.** E-mail, supposedly a real time saver, has quickly become a major time waster. Organizations need to create and enforce a clear e-mail policy to improve message quality and curb abuses. Cell phone users need to be discreet and courteous to avoid broadcasting privileged information and/or offending others. Videoconferencing restricts how people communicate because televised contacts are more mechanical than face-to-face meetings. While telecommuting can reduce travel time and expense and offer employment to nontraditional employees, it severely restricts normal social contact and face-to-face communication in the workplace.

**8.** Listening does not get sufficient attention in communications training. Active, cooperative listening is to be encouraged. Writing skills are no less important in the computer age. Written messages need to be specific, simply worded, and concise. Meetings, an ever-present feature of organizational life, need to be agenda-driven if time is to be used wisely.

**Terms to Understand**

Communication (p. 389)
Media richness (p. 391)
Noise (p. 393)
Grapevine (p. 396)
Body language (p. 398)

Upward communication (p. 401)
Exit interview (p. 404)
Semantics (p. 406)
Videoconference (p. 409)
Telecommuting (p. 411)

## Skills & Tools

### Harvard's Sarah McGinty Tells How to Develop Your Speaking Style

Popular discussion of communication style in recent years has centered on differences between the sexes. The subject has been fodder for TV talk shows, corporate seminars, and best-sellers, notably Deborah Tannen's *You Just Don't Understand* and John Gray's *Men Are from Mars, Women Are from Venus.* But Sarah McGinty, a teaching supervisor at Harvard University's School of Education, believes language style is based more on power than on gender—and that marked differences distinguish the powerful from the powerless loud and clear. As a consultant, she is often called on to help clients develop more effective communication styles. *Fortune*'s Justin Martin spoke with McGinty about her ideas:

## What style of speaking indicates that someone possesses power?

A person who feels confident and in control will speak at length, set the agenda for conversation, stave off interruptions, argue openly, make jokes, and laugh. Such a person is more inclined to make statements, less inclined to ask questions. They are more likely to offer solutions or a program or a plan. All this creates a sense of confidence in listeners.

## What about people who lack power? How do they speak?

The power deficient drop into conversations, encourage other speakers, ask numerous questions, avoid argument, and rely on gestures such as nodding and smiling that suggest agreement. They tend to offer empathy rather than solutions. They often use unfinished sentences. Unfinished sentences are a language staple for those who lack power.

## How do you figure out what style of communication you lean toward?

It's quite hard to do. We're often quite ignorant about our own way of communicating. Everyone comes home at night occasionally and says, "I had that idea, but no one heard me, and everyone thinks it's Harry's idea." People like to pin that on gender and a lot of other things as well. But it's important to find out what really did happen. Maybe it was the volume of your voice, and you weren't heard. Maybe you overexplained, and the person who followed up pulled out the nugget of your thought.

But it's important to try to get some insight into what your own language habits are so that you can be analytical about whether you're shooting yourself in the foot. You can tape your side of phone calls, make a tape of a meeting, or sign up for a communications workshop. That's a great way to examine how you conduct yourself in conversations and in meetings.

## Does power language differ from company to company?

Certainly. The key is figuring out who gets listened to within your corporate culture. That can make you a more savvy user of language. Try to sit in on a meeting as a kind of researcher, observing conversational patterns. Watch who talks, who changes the course of the discussion, who sort of drops in and out of the conversation. Then try to determine who gets noticed and why.

One very effective technique is to approach the person who ran the meeting a couple of days after the fact and ask for an overall impression. What ideas were useful? What ideas might have a shot at being implemented?

## How can you get more language savvy?

You can start by avoiding bad habits, such as always seeking collaboration in the statements you make. Try to avoid "as Bob said" and "I pretty much agree with Sheila." Steer clear of disclaimers such as "I may be way off base here, but  . . . " All these serve to undermine the impact of your statements.

The amount of space you take up can play a big part in how powerful and knowledgeable you appear. People speaking before a group, for instance, should stand with their feet a little bit apart and try to occupy as much space as possible. Another public-speaking tip: Glancing around constantly creates a situation in which nobody really feels connected to what you're saying.

Strive to be bolder. Everyone tends to worry that they will offend someone by stating a strong opinion. Be bold about ideas, tentative about people. Saying "I think you're completely wrong" is not a wise strategy. Saying "I have a plan that I think will solve these problems" is perfectly reasonable. You're not attacking people. You're being bold about an idea.

*Source:*  Justin Martin, "How to Speak Shows Where You Rank," *Fortune* (February 2, 1998): 156. © 1998 Time Inc. Reprinted by permission.

## Hands-On Exercise

### Oh, No! What Have I Done?

**Situation**

It's almost 6 P.M. and you're back at your office putting the finishing touches on next week's annual presentation to top management. Your stomach is churning, partly from hunger and partly from the stress of having missed another one of your twins' soccer matches. As the corporate director of product design at a large multinational company, you don't need to be reminded about the importance of next week's presentation. Between 3 P.M. and a few minutes ago, you had hidden out in a remote conference room fine-tuning it. Your cell phone was with you but had a dead battery, as you just noticed.

Right now, you are staring in disbelief at an e-mail message on your computer screen. The three-word message "WHERE WERE YOU!" burns into your mind. This particular e-mail is from your firm's director of marketing. She e-mailed an hour ago from her home after a late-afternoon meeting with two executives from a company that has been a customer for over ten years. During a quick chat in the hallway yesterday, you had promised the marketing director you'd attend today's meeting to provide technical support. This customer is one of your smaller accounts, but there is potential for a big jump in business this year. The marketing director's idea was to have a brief "let's explore possibilities" meeting.

The plain truth is you simply forgot about the meeting. You've been on major overload. You never bothered to put it on your electronic calendar because the commitment was made just yesterday and you thought you'd surely remember it. Well, you didn't!

Your mind races, weighing the situation and what to do about it. Losing this customer would be very bad for your career because your CEO is a table-pounder about customer service. Whom should you contact first—the marketing director, your boss, the customer, your family? And how should you communicate with them? It's dinner-time now. What about calling later tonight? Can everything but your family wait until tomorrow? What about e-mails? You know both your boss and the marketing director check their e-mails later each evening at home. Should you stop by anybody's home tonight to delivery a personal apology and explanation? What should you do? What should you say? How should you say it? Your stomach tightens a couple more notches.

**Instructions**

Either working alone or as a member of a team, quickly develop a communication plan for this awkward situation. Your plan should involve (1) specifying your assumptions and objectives, (2) choosing an appropriate medium for each message (face-to-face, cell phone, telephone/voice mail, or e-mail), and (3) composing messages to relevant parties in this situation.

**For Consideration/ Discussion**

**1.** What assumptions did you make in this case? How did they influence your response?

**2.** What were your priorities in this situation? How did they influence your actions?

**3.** Whom did you contact first? How and why?

**4.** How did you communicate with each party? Why that way?

**5.** What practical lessons about communication did you learn from this exercise? Explain.

# Internet Exercises

**1.** **Assessing your communication style and skills:** Communication is such an everyday activity we seldom pause to review how we're actually doing. Here's an opportunity to systematically evaluate your communication style and skills, with the goal of becoming a more effective communicator. Once again, as we did in Chapter 8, let's visit QueenDom's unique Web site (**www.queendom.com**) and take advantage of the excellent collection of free self-assessment questionnaires. At the home page, select the main menu category "Tests & Profiles." At the "tests, tests, tests" page, select "Communication Skills" under the Heading "top tests." Next, click on the "GO!" button under the heading "non-members take the test." (*Note:* You do not have to register or purchase anything to take the communication skills test. Also, if the site has been revised by the time you read this, simply search the site for the free communication skills test. It is well worth the effort.) This 34-item assessment instrument is designed to take about 15 to 20 minutes to complete. It is self-paced, so you might complete it in less time. Score the test and read the brief free interpretation.

*Learning Points:* 1. Are you surprised by the result of this assessment test? Explain. 2. What are your communication strengths? 3. What are your communication weaknesses or limitations? 4. What do you need to do to improve? 5. How motivated are you to improve your communication skills? Explain.

**2.** **Some timeless advice on good writing:** Most literary scholars say the best primer on English composition ever written was William Strunk Jr.'s *The Elements of Style*. This masterful little book was originally published in 1918. Eighty-five years later, after revision by E. B. White and countless reprintings, it is still essential reading for college students. The current 105-page paperback version is William Strunk Jr. and E. B. White, *The Elements of Style*, 4th ed. (Boston: Allyn & Bacon, 1999.) Thanks to the Internet, the original version is available free online. Go to (**www.bartleby. com**), click on the tab "Reference," scroll down the list of authors and titles, and click on Strunk (under the heading "English Usage: Language, Style, and Composition"). Browse through the topics in Part III, Elementary Principles of Composition, with the objective of answering the following questions.

*Learning Points:* 1. Is this 85-year-old book instructive for e-mail users? How? 2. According to Strunk's standards, which principles of composition are your strengths? 3. What elements of composition do you need to improve? 4. How important are writing skills in the Internet age? Explain.

3. **Check it out:** Public speaking can be a dreadful experience for those who are unprepared. On the other hand, a well-delivered oral presentation is a very gratifying accomplishment. Next time you are preparing an oral presentation, be sure to tap the extensive collection of resources at the Advanced Public Speaking Institute's Web site (**www.public-speaking.org**). You will find lots of practical tips on everything from handouts and humor to room setup and stage fright.

For updates to these exercises, visit our Web site (**http://business.college.hmco. com/students**).

## Closing Case

# The Case of the Errant Messenger

*The following case study has been reported by Robert I. Stevens, a systems consultant and writer.*

Whenever anyone on the executive floor wanted to tease Henry Reeves, they would ask him, "Are you sure you don't have any messages for me from the president?" Hank would become somewhat flustered and ignore the question. This byplay, which lasted for a year or so, was the result of the following incident—known by many, but not including the president.

The president of the company was a grizzled, dour army veteran who ran the operation as if he was still commanding a unit in the service. He made all major decisions and was almost always right in his judgment. I had seen him join a meeting of top staff just after a policy decision had been reached and ask a few big questions that resulted in a complete reversal of the original deci-

*Source:* "The Case of the Errant Messenger," *Journal of Systems Management,* 35 (July 1984): 42. Reprinted by permission of the author, Robert I. Stevens.

sion. The only executive who contested the president, usually at meetings where the president was not present, was vice president James Dubler, who was almost always wrong.

The president believed in "seeing what the troops were doing" and spent a good portion of his time visiting the many dispersed locations of the company. . . . Whenever the president wanted to inform an officer of the company who was not present of a decision, request for information, or at times a reprimand, he would turn to a member of his traveling party and give him an oral message to deliver to the appropriate person. Usually, the selected messenger was Henry Reeves, a shy, introverted MBA, recently hired.

On one trip that I attended just before Reeves was hired, a situation developed that displeased the president. He turned to me and said, "You tell Jim Dubler, he better get this problem corrected before it blows up in his face." Although I was only a senior analyst, it would never have occurred to me to question the president's order to deliver such a message to a vice president.

When I delivered the president's message to Mr. Dubler, he became very agitated and gave me the type of verbal thrashing that a vice president can give an analyst. I finally blurted out, "Mr. Dubler, I'm only the messenger." He immediately calmed down and told me to leave.

From what we pieced together later, the first time Hank Reeves delivered a message to Mr. Dubler, he received the same type of tongue-lashing from Dubler without being able to withdraw from the confrontation. Evidently, the occasion so traumatized Reeves that when the president gave him other messages to be relayed to Dubler, he never delivered them. The situation of Reeves not delivering the president's messages to Dubler went on for several months without Reeves telling anyone about his problem. During that time, the president was heard to grumble about Dubler not reacting too fast to various situations.

Then one Friday afternoon the president asked Reeves to get Dubler to prepare a report over the weekend that he wanted on his desk Monday morning. Reeves again did not deliver the message. Monday morning, when the president arrived at his office and no report was present, he checked with his secretary if Dubler had left a message as to why he had not finished the report. He muttered to me (I had just entered his office as requested), "Well, this is the last straw." He then called the personnel office on the phone and said, "Fire Dubler. Give him whatever severance benefits you think he should have, but get him off the property—and I don't want him coming up to see me."

As in most corporations, such situations become common knowledge in short order—and that's why Reeves was asked occasionally if he had any messages to deliver from the president.

## For Discussion

**1.** Who is primarily to blame for Dubler's firing: the president, Reeves, or Dubler himself? Why?

**2.** Did the grapevine have a positive or negative impact in this case? Explain.

**3.** Considering what you now know about organizational communication, what advice would you give the president? Reeves? Dubler?

# Video Skill Builders

This brief overview employs a gardening metaphor and classic Hollywood film clips to explain how organizations are structured. Structure necessarily follows strategy. Donna Van Fleet, V. P. Line Management at IBM Corporation, defines an organization and walks the viewer through four basic structural formats for organizations: functional, product, customer, and geographical location. Goals, buyers, and skills need to be considered when designing organizations.

## 3A Organizing for Success

### Learning Objective
To provide a real-world context for organizational structure concepts covered in the text.

### Links to Textual Material
**Chapter 9:** Definition of an organization; Common characteristics of organizations; Organizational effectiveness   **Chapter 10:** Contingency design; Basic structural formats/departmentalization

### Discussion Questions

1. Why should organizational structure always follow strategy?

2. How important is a common goal to organizational effectiveness? Explain.

3. What are the main pros and cons of the four structural formats covered in this video (functional, product, customer, and geographical location)?

4. How can a poor structure doom an organization to failure?

Founded in 1969, the New England Aquarium hosts 1.3 million visitors a year. Maureen C. Hentz, Director of Volunteer Programs, tells viewers how her organization has firmly embraced the concept of diversity for its 1,000 volunteers. The overriding goal is to have the volunteer staff reflect the rich diversity of the aquarium's visitors. Emphasis is not only on attracting a diverse pool of volunteer candidates, but also on changing the culture to make everyone feel comfortable.

## 3B Diversity at the New England Aquarium

### Learning Objective
To show how a role-model organization has taken diversity from concept to practice.

### Links to Textual Material
**Chapter 3:** Demographics of the new workforce; Nagging inequalities in the workplace; Managing diversity   **Chapter 11:** The age of human capital; Recruiting and selection; From affirmative action to managing diversity

### Discussion Questions

1. Why is managing diversity important for a non-profit organization like the New England Aquarium?

2. What part of the aquarium's diversity program impressed you most? Why?

3. How could the aquarium's diversity program be improved?

4. What role does the concept of "human capital" play in this video case? Explain.

5. What are the practical implications of this comment by Hentz? "There isn't a formula."

# part four

# Motivating and Leading

# Motivating Job Performance

> *There are no simple, cookbook formulas for working with people.*
>
> **Keith Davis**

# Medtronic's Employees Find Fulfillment in Making Life-Saving Products

Visitors to corporate headquarters in Fridley, Minn., a pastel-bungalow suburb of Minneapolis, are met by a statue of Earl Bakken, the engineer who co-founded Medtronic in 1949 with his brother-in-law, Palmer Hermundslie. Bakken is depicted in late middle age, wearing a baggy suit, squinting through a pair of aviator-frame glasses, and clutching in one hand a spookily banal box with a screwed-on faceplate, an on-off switch, and a dial for revving up the pulse rate—the primitive pacemaker that made Medtronic famous. The box looks like something straight out of Dr. Frankenstein's laboratory, which is appropriate, for according to company legend, proudly recounted on the timeline in the lobby, it was the film version of *Frankenstein,* released in 1931, that awakened in young Earl Bakken a lifelong fascination with the role of electricity in medicine.

Bakken, 76, lives in Hawaii now but returns to Fridley often. He shows up at ceremonies to present new hires with their Medtronic medallions—keepsakes inscribed with an excerpt from the mission statement (ALLEVIATE PAIN, RESTORE HEALTH AND EXTEND LIFE). And he never misses the holiday party, Medtronic's annual rite of corporate renewal, where people whose bodies function thanks to Medtronic devices come to give testimonials. It's a teary, communal reminder that what goes on here day after day is not the same as making VCRs. "We have patients who come in who would be dead if it wasn't for us," says Karen McFadzen, a production supervisor. "I mean, they sit right up there and they tell us what their lives are like. You don't walk away from them not feeling anything."

If ever a company had a built-in advantage in the motivating-the-worker department, Medtronic is it. And its leaders know the power of playing to that advantage. But even making lifesaving medical devices is, ultimately, just a job. It takes constant care and feeding of corporate legend (remember *Frankenstein*) and mission (those medallions) to imbue Medtronic employees with a sense of satisfaction in their jobs day after day. In the employee surveys that help determine *Fortune*'s 100 Best Companies to Work For, 86% of Medtronic employees said their work had special meaning; 94% felt pride in what they accomplished. You can get more shared satisfaction than that, but not much.

But keeping workers motivated takes much more than a mission. Spend time with people at Medtronic, and you begin to understand why people keep working at the 100 Best Companies. They don't stay for on-site gyms or free dry cleaning—although those things may have attracted them in the first place. The ones who are lucky enough to get stock options and big bonuses might stay to get a payout, but they could just as easily leave afterwards. The real reasons people stay are more personal and come down to something pretty basic: fulfillment.

Imagine someone walking up to you and saying, "Your work helped save my life." Medtronic's employees are fortunate to enjoy such gratifying feedback—as are medical doctors, firefighters, and police officers. The truth is, however, most of us are employed in far less heroic circumstances. Accordingly, the complex combinations of factors motivating our work efforts are as varied as our occupations. As used here, the term **motivation** refers to the psychological process that gives behavior purpose and direction. By appealing to this process, managers attempt to get individuals to willingly pursue organizational objectives. Motivation theories are generalizations about the "why" and "how" of purposeful behavior.[1]

**motivation** *psychological process giving behavior purpose and direction*

Figure 13.1 is an overview model for this chapter. The final element in this model, job performance, is the product of a combination of an individual's motivation and ability. Both are necessary. All the motivation in the world, for example, will not enable a computer-illiterate person to sit down and create a computer spreadsheet. Ability and skills, acquired through training and/or on-the-job experience, are also required. The individual's motivational factors—needs, satisfaction, expectations, and goals—are affected by challenging work, rewards, and participation.[2] We need to take a closer look at each key element in this model. A review of four basic motivation theories is a good starting point.

# Motivation Theories

**1** Explain the motivational lessons taught by Maslow's theory, Herzberg's theory, and expectancy theory.

Although there are dozens of different theories of motivation, four have emerged as the most influential: Maslow's needs hierarchy theory, Herzberg's two-factor theory, expectancy theory, and goal-setting theory. Each approaches the motivation process from a different angle, each has supporters and detractors, and each teaches important lessons about motivation to work.

## Maslow's Needs Hierarchy Theory

In 1943 psychologist Abraham Maslow proposed that people are motivated by a predictable five-step hierarchy of needs.[3] Little did he realize at the time that his tentative proposal, based on an extremely limited clinical study of neurotic patients, would become one of the most influential concepts in the field of management. Perhaps because it is so straightforward and intuitively appealing, Maslow's theory has strongly influenced those interested in work behavior. Maslow's message was simply this: people always have needs, and when one need is relatively fulfilled, others emerge in a predictable sequence to take its place. From bottom to top, Maslow's needs hierarchy includes physiological, safety, love, esteem, and self-actualization needs (see Figure 13.2). According to Maslow, most individuals are not consciously aware of these needs; yet we all supposedly proceed up the hierarchy of needs, one level at a time.

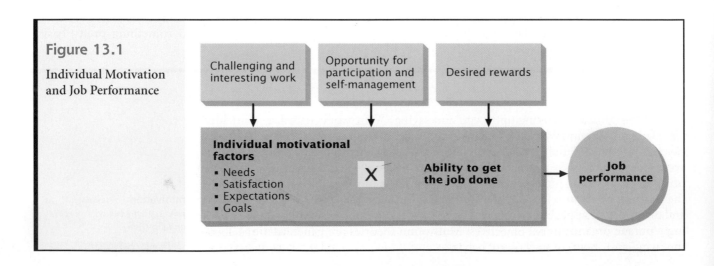

**Figure 13.1**

Individual Motivation and Job Performance

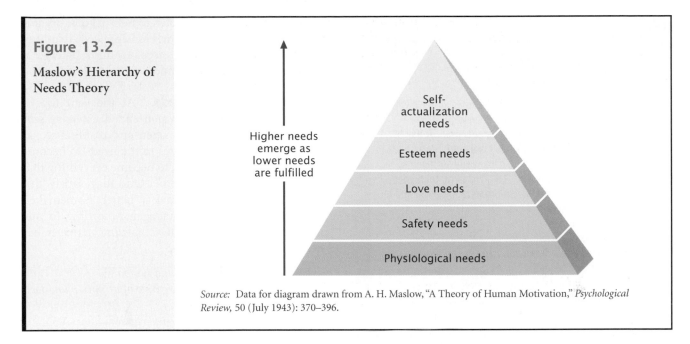

**Figure 13.2**

Maslow's Hierarchy of Needs Theory

Higher needs emerge as lower needs are fulfilled

Self-actualization needs

Esteem needs

Love needs

Safety needs

Physiological needs

*Source:* Data for diagram drawn from A. H. Maslow, "A Theory of Human Motivation," *Psychological Review,* 50 (July 1943): 370–396.

**Physiological Needs.** At the bottom of the hierarchy are needs based on physical drives, including the need for food, water, sleep, and sex. Fulfillment of these lowest-level needs enables the individual to survive, and nothing else is important when these bodily needs have not been satisfied. As Maslow observed, "It is quite true that man lives by bread alone—when there is no bread."[4] But today the average employee experiences little difficulty in satisfying physiological needs. Figuratively speaking, the prospect of eating more bread is not motivating when one has plenty of bread to eat.

**Safety Needs.** After our basic physiological needs have been relatively well satisfied, we next become concerned about our safety from the elements, enemies, and other threats. Most modern employees, by earning a living, achieve a high degree of fulfillment in this area. Unemployment assistance is a safety net for those between jobs. Insurance also helps fulfill safety needs, a point not lost on Coca-Cola Femsa, Mexico's primary bottler of Coke:

*Many of the store owners in Mexico, Coke's second-biggest market, turned out to be single mothers and retirees who couldn't afford health insurance. Armed with that intelligence, Femsa was able to create an incentive program that rewards shopkeepers who sell enough Cokes with access to group insurance—a move that helped boost Coke's sales volume in Mexico 13 percent last year.[5]*

**Love Needs.** A physiologically satisfied and secure person focuses next on satisfying needs for love and affection. This category is a powerful motivator of human behavior. People typically strive hard to achieve a sense of belonging with others. As with the first two levels of needs, relative satisfaction of love needs paves the way for the emergence of the next, higher level.

**Esteem Needs.** People who perceive themselves as worthwhile are said to possess high self-esteem.[6] Self-respect is the key to esteem needs. Much of our self-respect, and therefore our esteem, comes from being accepted and respected by others. It is impor-

## 13A   Billionaire Investor Warren Buffett on Self-Actualization

"I can certainly define happiness, because happy is what I am," Buffett told students at the University of Washington. "I get to do what I like to do every single day of the year. I get to do it with people I like, and I don't have to associate with anybody who causes my stomach to churn. I tap-dance to work . . . I'd advise you that when you go out to work, work for an organization of people you admire, because it will turn you on. I always worry about people who say, 'I'm going to do this for ten years; I really don't like it very well. And then I'll do this . . . ' That's a little like saving up sex for your old age. Not a very good idea."

**Source:** Steve Nearman, "The Simple Billionaire," *Selling Power,* 19 (June 1999): 48.

**Questions:** *How do you interpret Buffett's remarks to the students? What would it take to help you achieve self-actualization? Is it possible that once you reach your "mountaintop" you will set your sights on a higher peak? Explain.*

For further information about the interactive annotations in this chapter, visit our Web site (http://business.college.hmco.com/students).

tant for those who are expected to help achieve organizational objectives to have their esteem needs relatively well fulfilled. But esteem needs cannot emerge if lower-level needs go unattended.

**Self-Actualization Needs.** At the very top of Maslow's hierarchy is the open-ended category *self-actualization needs.* It is open-ended because, as Maslow pointed out, it relates to the need "to become more and more what one is, to become everything that one is capable of becoming."[7] One may satisfy this need by striving to become a better homemaker, plumber, rock singer, or manager. According to one management writer, the self-actualizing manager has the following characteristics:

1. *Has warmth, closeness, and sympathy.*
2. *Recognizes and shares negative information and feelings.*
3. *Exhibits trust, openness, and candor.*
4. *Does not achieve goals by power, deception, or manipulation.*
5. *Does not project own feelings, motivations, or blame onto others.*
6. *Does not limit horizons; uses and develops body, mind, and senses.*
7. *Is not rationalistic; can think in unconventional ways.*
8. *Is not conforming; regulates behavior from within.*[8]

Granted, this is a rather tall order to fill. It has been pointed out that "a truly self-actualized individual is more of an exception than the rule in the organizational context."[9] Whether productive organizations need more self-actualized individuals is subject to debate. On the positive side, self-actualized employees might help break down barriers to creativity and steer the organization in

*Self-actualization, becoming all that one can become, sometimes means getting reacquainted with one's cultural heritage. David Rocky Mountain, a 13-year-old Lakota, surveys a traditional campsite constructed by troubled teens from the Cheyenne River Sioux tribe in South Dakota. This "spiritual boot camp" bonds the youngsters with their elders who offer many valuable life lessons. Funding is provided by the Robert Wood Johnson Foundation.*

new directions. On the negative side, too many unconventional nonconformists could wreak havoc with the typical administrative setup dedicated to predictability.

**Relevance of Maslow's Theory for Managers.**    Behavioral scientists who have attempted to test Maslow's theory in real life claim it has some deficiencies.[10] Even Maslow's hierarchical arrangement has been questioned. Practical evidence points toward a two-level rather than a five-level hierarchy. In this competing view, physiological and safety needs are arranged in hierarchical fashion, as Maslow contends. But beyond that point, any one of a number of needs may emerge as the single most important need, depending on the individual. Edward Lawler, a leading motivation researcher, observed, "Which higher-order needs come into play after the lower ones are satisfied and in which order they come into play cannot be predicted. If anything, it seems that most people are simultaneously motivated by several of the same-level needs."[11]

Although Maslow's theory has not stood up well under actual testing, it teaches managers one important lesson: a *fulfilled* need does not motivate an individual. For example, the promise of unemployment benefits may partially fulfill an employee's need for economic security (the safety need). But the added security of additional unemployment benefits will probably not motivate fully employed individuals to work any harder. Effective managers anticipate each employee's personal need profile and provide opportunities to fulfill *emerging* needs. Because challenging and worthwhile jobs and meaningful recognition tend to enhance self-esteem, the esteem level presents managers with the greatest opportunity to motivate better performance.

## Herzberg's Two-Factor Theory

During the 1950s, Frederick Herzberg proposed a theory of employee motivation based on satisfaction.[12] His theory implied that a satisfied employee is motivated from within to work harder and that a dissatisfied employee is not self-motivated. Herzberg's research uncovered two classes of factors associated with employee satisfaction and dissatisfaction (see Table 13.1). As a result, his concept has come to be called Herzberg's two-factor theory.

**Dissatisfiers and Satisfiers.**    Herzberg compiled his list of dissatisfiers by asking a sample of about 200 accountants and engineers to describe job situations in which they felt exceptionally bad about their jobs. An analysis of their responses revealed a consistent pattern. Dissatisfaction tended to be associated with complaints about the job context or factors in the immediate work environment.

Herzberg then drew up his list of satisfiers, factors responsible for self-motivation, by asking the same accountants and engineers to describe job situations in which they had felt exceptionally good about their jobs. Again, a patterned response emerged, but this time different factors were described: the opportunity to experience achievement, receive recognition, work on an interesting job, take responsibility, and experience advancement and growth. Herzberg observed that these satisfiers centered on the nature of the task itself. Employees appeared to be motivated by *job content*—that is, by what they actually did all day long. Consequently, Herzberg concluded that enriched jobs were the key to self-motivation. The work itself—not pay, supervision, or some other environmental factor—was the key to satisfaction and motivation.

**Implications of Herzberg's Theory.**    By insisting that satisfaction is not the opposite of dissatisfaction, Herzberg encouraged managers to think carefully about what actually motivates employees. According to Herzberg, "the opposite of job satis-

| **Table 13.1**    Herzberg's Two-Factor Theory of Motivation | |
|---|---|
| **Dissatisfiers:**<br>**Factors mentioned most often by dissatisfied employees** | **Satisfiers:**<br>**Factors mentioned most often by satisfied employees** |
| 1. Company policy and administration | 1. Achievement |
| 2. Supervision | 2. Recognition |
| 3. Relationship with supervisor | 3. Work itself |
| 4. Work conditions | 4. Responsibility |
| 5. Salary | 5. Advancement |
| 6. Relationship with peers | 6. Growth |
| 7. Personal life | |
| 8. Relationship with subordinates | |
| 9. Status | |
| 10. Security | |

*Source:* Adapted and reprinted by permission of the *Harvard Business Review.* An exhibit from "One More Time: How Do You Motivate Employees?" by Frederick Herzberg (January–February 1968). Copyright © 1968 by the Harvard Business School Publishing Corporation; all rights reserved.

## 13B  Is Everybody Happy?

. . . Do happy workers improve corporate performance? The Gallup Organization recently surveyed 55,000 workers in an attempt to match employee attitudes with company results. The survey found that four attitudes, taken together, correlate strongly with higher profits. The attitudes: Workers feel they are given the opportunity to do what they do best every day; they believe their opinions count; they sense that their fellow workers are committed to quality; and they've made a direct connection between their work and the company's mission.

**Sources:** Linda Grant, "Happy Workers, High Returns," *Fortune* (January 12, 1998): 81. Also see Del Jones, "Rule-Breaking Turns into Boss-Training," *USA Today* (February 20, 2002): 1B–2B.

**Questions:** *What would Herzberg likely say about this evidence? Is your own job performance affected by your job satisfaction? Explain.*

faction is not job dissatisfaction, but rather *no* job satisfaction; and similarly, the opposite of job dissatisfaction is not job satisfaction, but *no* dissatisfaction,"[13] Rather, the dissatisfaction-satisfaction continuum contains a zero midpoint at which both dissatisfaction and satisfaction are absent. An employee stuck on this midpoint, though not dissatisfied with pay and working conditions, is not particularly motivated to work hard because the job itself lacks challenge. Herzberg believes that the most managers can hope for when attempting to motivate employees with pay, status, working conditions, and other contextual factors is to reach the zero midpoint. But the elimination of dissatisfaction is not the same as truly motivating an employee. To satisfy and motivate employees, an additional element is required: meaningful, interesting, and challenging work. Herzberg believed that money is a weak motivational tool because, at best, it can only eliminate dissatisfaction.

Like Maslow, Herzberg triggered lively debate among motivation theorists. His assumption that job performance improves as satisfaction increases has been criticized for its weak empirical basis. For example, one researcher, after reviewing 20 studies that tested this notion, concluded that the relationship, though positive, was too weak to have any theoretical or practical significance.[14] Others have found that one person's dissatisfier may be another's satisfier (for example, money).[15] Nonetheless, Herzberg made a useful contribution to motivation theory by emphasizing the motivating potential of enriched work. (Job enrichment is discussed in detail in the next section.)

## Expectancy Theory

Both Maslow's and Herzberg's theories have been criticized for making unsubstantiated generalizations about what motivates people. Practical experience shows that people are motivated by lots of different things. Fortunately, expectancy theory, based largely on Victor H. Vroom's 1964 classic *Work and Motivation,* effectively deals with the highly personalized rational choices individuals make when faced with the prospect of having to work to achieve rewards. Individual perception, though secondary in the Maslow and Herzberg models, is central to expectancy theory. Accordingly, **expectancy theory** is a motivation model based on the assumption that motivational strength is determined by perceived probabilities of success. The term **expectancy** refers to the subjective probability (or expectation) that one thing will lead to another. Work-related expectations, like all other expectations, are shaped by ongoing personal experience. For instance, an employee's expectation of a raise, diminished after being turned down, later rebounds when the supervisor indicates a willingness to reconsider the matter.

**expectancy theory**   *model that assumes motivational strength is determined by perceived probabilities of success*

**expectancy**   *one's belief or expectation that one thing will lead to another*

**A Basic Expectancy Model.**   Although Vroom and other expectancy theorists developed their models in somewhat complex mathematical terms, the descriptive model in Figure 13.3 is helpful for basic understanding. In this model, one's motivational strength increases as one's perceived effort-performance and performance-reward probabilities increase. All this is not as complicated as it sounds. For example, estimate your motivation to study if you expect to do poorly on a quiz no matter how hard you study (low effort-performance probability) and you know the quiz will not be graded (low performance-reward probability). Now contrast that estimate with your motivation to study if you believe that you can do well on the quiz with minimal study (high effort-performance probability) and that by doing well on the quiz your course grade will significantly improve (high performance-reward probability). Like students, employees are motivated to expend effort when they believe it will ultimately lead to rewards they themselves value. This expectancy approach not only appeals strongly to common sense; it also has received encouraging empirical support from researchers.[16]

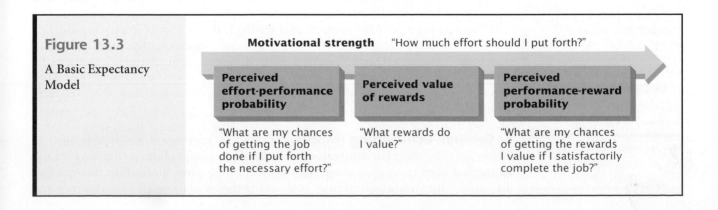

**Figure 13.3**

A Basic Expectancy Model

## 13C  What Did You Expect?

Results of a *Fast Company* Roper Starch online survey of 1,122 college-educated employees:

**When you started to work for your current employer, did you think that your job would be . . . ?**

| | |
|---|---|
| Mostly just a way to make money | 12% |
| Meaningful, but not as meaningful as the rest of your life | 37% |
| Just as meaningful as family life and other activities | 46% |
| The most meaningful thing in your life | 5% |

**Think about your job *today.* Do you think that your job is . . . ?**

| | |
|---|---|
| Mostly just a way to make money | 18% |
| Meaningful, but not as meaningful as the rest of your life | 52% |
| Just as meaningful as family life and other activities | 26% |
| The most meaningful thing in your life | 4% |

**Overall, do you think that your job has . . . ?**

| | |
|---|---|
| Exceeded your expectations | 16% |
| Met your expectations | 52% |
| Fallen short of your expectations | 28% |
| Been completely disappointing | 4% |

**Source:** Excerpted from "FC Roper Starch Survey," *Fast Company,* no. 29 (November 1999): 214–222.

**Question:** *How do your met and unmet job expectations influence your job performance?*

### Relevance of Expectancy Theory for Managers.

According to expectancy theory, effort → performance → reward expectations determine whether motivation will be high or low. Although these expectations are in the mind of the employee, they can be influenced by managerial action and organizational experience. Training, combined with challenging but realistic objectives, helps give people the idea they can get the job done if they put forth the necessary effort. But perceived effort-performance probabilities are only half the battle. Listening skills enable managers to discover each individual's perceived performance-reward probabilities. Employees tend to work harder when they believe they have *a good chance* of getting *personally meaningful* rewards. Both sets of expectations require managerial attention. Each is a potential barrier to work motivation.

## Goal-Setting Theory

Think of the three or four most successful people you know personally. Their success may have come via business or professional achievement, politics, athletics, or community service. Chances are they got where they are today by being goal-oriented. In other words, they committed themselves to (and achieved) progressively more challenging goals in their professional and personal affairs.[17] A prime example is Noël Forgeard, who has helped put France-based Airbus on an equal footing with Boeing in the commercial airliner business. According to one of his former colleagues:

> *He appears low-key, but can be very tough, and when he has set a goal, nothing can distract him from it. He has an impressive ability to set priorities, to focus on his goals, and then set up a very strong team to achieve those goals.*[18]

Biographies and autobiographies of successful people in all walks of life generally attest to the virtues of goal setting. Accordingly, goal setting is acknowledged today as a respected and useful motivation theory.

Within an organizational context, **goal setting** is the process of improving individual or group job performance with formally stated objectives, deadlines, or quality standards.[19] Management by objectives (MBO), discussed in Chapter 6, is a specific application of goal setting that advocates participative and measurable objectives. Also, recall from Chapter 6 how managers tend to use the terms *goal* and *objective* interchangeably.

**goal setting**  *process of improving performance with objectives, deadlines, or quality standards*

**2**  Describe how goal setting motivates performance.

### A General Goal-Setting Model.

Thanks to motivation researchers such as Edwin A. Locke, there is a comprehensive body of knowledge about goal setting.[20] Goal setting has been researched more rigorously than the three motivation theories just discussed.[21] Important lessons from goal-setting theory and research are incorporated

*Carin Knickel, general manager of Conoco's Rocky Mountain region, knows the petroleum business from one end to the other. When she inherited a slow-moving unit, she got things going by creating a "climate of inspiration." The key was getting each of her key people to present detailed goals each month in front of their peers, who were instructed to act as coaches. It worked. Now she's steering everyone toward what she terms "breakthrough goals." That's really stepping on the gas!*

in the general model in Figure 13.4. This model shows how properly conceived goals trigger a motivational process that improves performance. Let us explore the key components of this goal-setting model.

**Personal Ownership of Challenging Goals.**   In Chapter 6, the discussion of MBO and writing good objectives stressed how goal effectiveness is enhanced by *specificity, difficulty*, and *participation*. Measurable and challenging goals encourage an individual or group to stretch while trying to attain progressively more difficult levels of achievement. For instance, parents who are paying a college student's tuition and expenses are advised to specify a challenging grade point goal rather than to simply tell

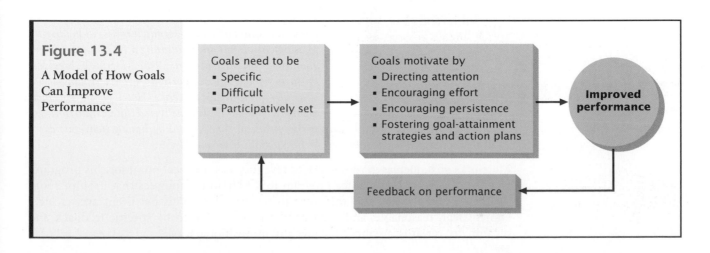

**Figure 13.4**

**A Model of How Goals Can Improve Performance**

Goals need to be
- Specific
- Difficult
- Participatively set

Goals motivate by
- Directing attention
- Encouraging effort
- Encouraging persistence
- Fostering goal-attainment strategies and action plans

**Improved performance**

Feedback on performance

their son or daughter, "Just do your best." Otherwise, the student could show up at the end of the semester with two Cs and three Ds, saying, "Well, I did my best!" It is important to note that goals need to be difficult enough to be challenging but not impossible. Impossible goals hamper performance; they are a handy excuse for not even trying.[22]

Participation in the goal-setting process gives the individual *personal ownership.* From the employee's viewpoint, it is "something I helped develop, not just my boss's wild idea." Feedback on performance operates in concert with well-conceived goals. Feedback lets the person or group know if things are on track or if corrective action is required to reach the goal. An otherwise excellent goal-setting program can be compromised by lack of timely and relevant feedback from managers. Researchers have documented the motivational value of matching *specific goals* with *equally specific feedback.*[23] Sam Walton, the founder of Wal-Mart, was a master of blending goals and feedback. For example, consider this exchange between Sam Walton and an employee during one of his regular visits:

> *A manager rushes up with an associate in tow.*
>
> *"Mr. Walton, I want you to meet Renee. She runs one of the top ten pet departments in the country."*
>
> *"Well, Renee, bless your heart. What percentage of the store [sales] are you doing?"*
>
> *"Last year it was 3.1 percent," Renee says, "but this year I'm trying for 3.3 percent."*
>
> *"Well, Renee, that's amazing," says Sam. "You know our average pet department only does about 2.4 percent. Keep up the great work."*[24]

**How Do Goals Actually Motivate?**  Goal-setting researchers say goals perform a motivational function by doing the four things listed in the center of Figure 13.4. First, a goal is an exercise in selective perception because it directs one's *attention* to a specific target. Second, a goal encourages one to exert *effort* toward achieving something specific. Third, because a challenging goal requires sustained or repeated effort, it encourages *persistence.* Fourth, because a goal creates the problem of bridging the gap between actual and desired, it fosters the creation of *strategies and action plans.* Consider, for example, how all these motivational components were activated by the following program at Marriott's hotel chain.

> *For years, Marriott's room-service business didn't live up to its potential. But after initiating a 15-minute-delivery guarantee for breakfast in 1985, Marriott's breakfast business—the biggest portion of its room-service revenue—jumped 25 percent. [Hotel guests got their breakfast free if it was delivered late.] Marriott got employees to devise ways to deliver the meals on time, including having deliverers carry walkie-talkies so they [could] receive instructions more quickly.*[25]

Marriott's goal, increased room-service revenue, was the focal point for this program. In effect, the service-guarantee program told Marriott employees that prompt room service was important, and they rose to the challenge with persistent and creative effort. Clear, reasonable, and challenging goals, reinforced by specific feedback and meaningful rewards, are indeed a powerful motivational tool.[26]

**13D    Are You Aiming Too Low?**

Gary Hamel, management author and consultant:

*No company outperforms its aspirations. If most of your colleagues believe you are in a 5% or 10% growth business, you are.*

*In most companies the majority of individuals believe that there is some preordained, uninspiring industry growth rate. . . . The beliefs of your employees set the upper limit on what's possible.*

**Source:** Gary Hamel, "Reinvent Your Company," *Fortune* (June 12, 2000): 100.

**Questions:** *How often in your school work and/or on the job have you penalized yourself by aiming too low? Which of your goals need to be adjusted upward? Is it possible to aim too high? Explain.*

**Practical Implications of Goal-Setting Theory.**     Because the model in Figure 13.4 is a generic one, the performance environment may range from athletics to academics to the workplace. The motivational mechanics of goal setting are the same, regardless of the targeted performance. If you learn to be an effective goal setter in school, that ability will serve you faithfully throughout life.

Anyone tempted to go through life without goals should remember the smiling Cheshire Cat's good advice to Alice when she asked him to help her find her way through Wonderland:

> *"Would you tell me, please, which way I ought to walk from here?"*
> *"That depends a good deal on where you want to get to," replied the Cat.*
> *"I don't much care where—" said Alice.*
> *"Then it doesn't matter which way you walk," said the Cat.*
> *"—so long as I get somewhere," Alice added as an explanation.*
> *"Oh, you're sure to do that," said the Cat, "if you only walk long enough."*[27]

# Motivation Through Job Design

A job serves two separate but related functions. It is a productive unit for the organization and a career unit for the individual. Thus **job design,** the delineation of task responsibilities as dictated by organizational strategy, technology, and structure, is a key determinant of individual motivation and ultimately of organizational success. Considering that the average adult spends about half of his or her waking life at work, jobs are a central feature of modern existence. A challenging and interesting job can add zest and meaning to one's life. Boring and tedious jobs, on the other hand, can become a serious threat to one's motivation to work hard, not to mention the effect on one's physical and mental health.[28] Concern about uneven productivity growth, product quality, and declining employee satisfaction has persuaded managers to consider two job design strategies.[29]

**job design**   *creating task responsibilities based upon strategy, technology, and structure*

## Strategy One: Fitting People to Jobs

For technological or economic reasons, work sometimes must be divided into routine and repetitive tasks. Imagine, for example, doing Paula Villalta's job at Chung's Gourmet Foods in Houston, Texas:

> *Quickly wrapping one egg roll after another, Paula Villalta becomes rapt herself.*
>
> *Her fingers move with astonishing speed, placing a glutinous vegetable mixture on a small sheet of pastry before rolling it closed in one smooth stroke. But the secret to her swiftness lies not just in her nimble hands.*
>
> *The real key, says Ms. Villalta, pointing to her head, is staying completely focused throughout an eight-hour shift. . . .*
>
> *The results are stunning. The average wrapper at Chung's Gourmet churns out about 4,000 shrimp, pork, vegetable, or chicken egg rolls per shift. Ms. Villalta typically tops 6,000.*[30]

**3**  Discuss how managers can improve the motivation of routine-task personnel.

In routine-task situations, steps can be taken to avoid chronic dissatisfaction and bolster motivation.[31] Three proven alternatives include realistic job previews, job rotation, and limited exposure. Each involves adjusting the person rather than the job in the person-job equation. Hence, each entails creating a more compatible fit between an

"WHOSE TURN IS IT TO LICK THE VAT?"

individual and a routine or fragmented job. (In line with this approach is the use of mentally disadvantaged workers, often in sheltered workshops.)

### Realistic Job Previews.

Unrealized expectations are a major cause of job dissatisfaction, low motivation, and turnover. Managers commonly create unrealistically high expectations in job applicants to entice them to accept a position. This has proved particularly troublesome with regard to routine tasks. Dissatisfaction too often sets in when lofty expectations are brought down to earth by dull or tedious work. **Realistic job previews** (RJPs), honest explanations of what a job actually entails, have been successful in helping to avoid employee dissatisfaction resulting from unrealized expectations. On-the-job and laboratory research have demonstrated the practical value of giving a realistic preview of both positive and negative aspects to applicants for highly specialized and/or difficult jobs.

A recent statistical analysis of 40 different RJP studies revealed these patterns: fewer dropouts during the recruiting process, lower initial expectations, and lower turnover and higher performance once on the job. The researcher recommended a contingency approach regarding the form and timing of RJPs. *Written* RJPs are better for reducing the dropout rate during the recruiting process, whereas *verbal* RJPs more effectively reduce post-hiring turnover (quitting). "RJPs given just *before* hiring are advisable to reduce attrition [dropouts] from the recruitment process and to reduce . . . turnover, but organizations wishing to improve employee performance should provide RJPs *after* job acceptance, as part of a realistic socialization effort."[32]

### Job Rotation.

As the term is used here, **job rotation** involves periodically moving people from one specialized job to another. Such movement prevents stagnation.

**realistic job previews** *honest explanations of what a job actually entails*

**job rotation** *moving people from one specialized job to another*

Other reasons for rotating personnel include compensating for a labor shortage, safety, training, and preventing fatigue.[33] *Carpal tunnel syndrome* and other painful and disabling injuries stemming from repetitive motion tasks can be reduced significantly through job rotation.[34] (The FBI rotates its agents off the drug squad periodically to discourage corruption.[35]) If highly repetitious and routine jobs are unavoidable, job rotation, by introducing a modest degree of novelty, can help prevent boredom and resulting alienation. Of course, a balance needs to be achieved—people should be rotated often enough to fight boredom and injury but not so often that they feel unfairly manipulated or disoriented.

**Limited Exposure.**    Another way of coping with the need to staff a highly fragmented and tedious job is to limit the individual's exposure to it. A number of organizations have achieved high productivity among routine-task personnel by allowing them to earn an early quitting time.[36] This technique, called **contingent time off** (CTO) or earned time off, involves establishing a challenging yet fair daily performance standard, or quota, and letting employees go home when it is reached. The following CTO plan was implemented at a large manufacturing plant where the employees were producing about 160 units a day with 10 percent rejects:

> *If the group produced at 200 units with three additional good units for each defective unit, then they could leave the work site for the rest of the day. Within a week of implementing this CTO intervention, the group was producing 200+ units with an average of 1.5 percent rejects. These employees, who had formerly put in an 8-hour day, were now working an average of 6.5 hours per day and, importantly, they increased their performance by 25 percent.*[37]

Some employees find the opportunity to earn eight hours of pay for six hours of steady effort extremely motivating.

Companies using contingent time off report successful results. Impressive evidence comes from a large-scale survey of 1,598 U.S. companies employing about 10 percent of the civilian workforce. Among nine nontraditional reward systems, "earned time off" ranked only eighth in terms of use (5 percent of the companies). But among those using it, earned time off ranked *second* in terms of positive impact on job performance—an 85 percent approval rating.[38] Thus, the use of contingent time off has not yet reached its excellent potential as a motivational tool.

## Strategy Two: Fitting Jobs to People

The second job-design strategy calls for managers to consider changing the job instead of the person. Two job-design experts have proposed that managers address the question, "How can we achieve a fit between persons and their jobs that fosters *both* high work productivity and a high-quality organizational experience for the people who do the work?"[39] Two techniques for moving in this direction are job enlargement and job enrichment.

**13E    A Production Ballet at Honda**

As a nearly completed StepWGN moves down the line, a worker jumps into the front compartment and pats carpeting into place around the front console. Then he uses an electric screwdriver to bolt the back seats to the floor, first fastening screws in front of the seat, then scurrying around to the back to fasten two more. Finally, he hops out of the vehicle again to affix two plastic pieces to the rear taillights and glues the nameplate onto the tailgate. This incredible ballet takes him all of 60 seconds—and if he's doing his job properly, he repeats it 60 times an hour.

**Source:** Alex Taylor III, "The Man Who Put Honda Back on Track," *Fortune* (September 9, 1996): 98, 100.

**Questions:** *How can management effectively motivate this repetitive-task employee? What would motivate you to accept this job at Honda?*

**contingent time off**
*rewarding people with early time off when they get the job done*

**job enlargement** *combining two or more specialized tasks to increase motivation*

### Job Enlargement.

As used here, **job enlargement** is the process of combining two or more specialized tasks in a work flow sequence into a single job. Aetna used this technique to give some of its office employees a measure of relief from staring at a video display terminal (VDT) all day:

> *Aetna Life & Casualty in Hartford . . . reorganized its payroll department to combine ten full-time data-entry jobs with ten jobs that involve paperwork and telephoning. Now nobody in the department spends more than 70 percent of [the] day on a VDT. Morale and productivity have gone up dramatically since the change, says Richard Assunto, Aetna's payroll services manager.[40]*

A moderate degree of complexity and novelty can be introduced in this manner. But critics claim that two or more potentially boring tasks do not necessarily make one challenging job. Furthermore, organized labor has criticized job enlargement as a devious ploy for getting more work for the same amount of money. But if pay and performance are kept in balance, boredom and alienation can be pushed aside a bit by job enlargement.

**job enrichment** *redesigning jobs to increase their motivational potential*

**4** Explain how job enrichment can be used to enhance the motivating potential of jobs.

### Job Enrichment.

In general terms, **job enrichment** is redesigning a job to increase its motivating potential.[41] Job enrichment increases the challenge of one's work by reversing the trend toward greater specialization. Unlike job enlargement, which merely combines equally simple tasks, job enrichment builds more complexity and depth into jobs by introducing planning and decision-making responsibility normally carried out at higher levels. Thus, enriched jobs are said to be *vertically loaded,* whereas enlarged jobs are *horizontally loaded.* Managing an entire project can be immensely challenging and motivating due to vertical job loading. Scott Nichols, a home construction foreman, had this to say about his job:

> *I find it very rewarding. Just building something, creating something, and actually seeing your work. . . . You start with a bare, empty lot with grass growing up and then you build a house. A lot of times you'll build a house for a family, and you see them move in, that's pretty gratifying. . . . I'm proud of that.[42]*

Jobs can be enriched by upgrading five core dimensions of work: (1) skill variety, (2) task identity, (3) task significance, (4) autonomy, and (5) job feedback. Each of these core dimensions deserves a closer look.

- *Skill variety.* The degree to which the job requires a variety of different activities in carrying out the work, involving the use of a number of different skills and talents of the person
- *Task identity.* The degree to which the job requires completion of a "whole" and identifiable piece of work; that is, doing a job from beginning to end with a visible outcome
- *Task significance.* The degree to which the job has a substantial impact on the lives of other people, whether those people are in the immediate organization or in the world at large
- *Autonomy.* The degree to which the job provides substantial freedom, independence, and discretion to the individual in scheduling the work and in determining the procedures to be used in carrying it out
- *Job feedback.* The degree to which carrying out the work activities required by the job provides the individual with direct and clear information about the effectiveness of his or her performance[43]

Figure 13.5 shows the theoretical connection between enriched core job characteristics and high motivation and satisfaction. At the heart of this job-enrichment model are

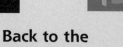

**13F**

### Back to the Opening Case

Which of the five core dimensions of work is most evident in the Medtronic case? How much does it probably impact employee motivation? Explain.

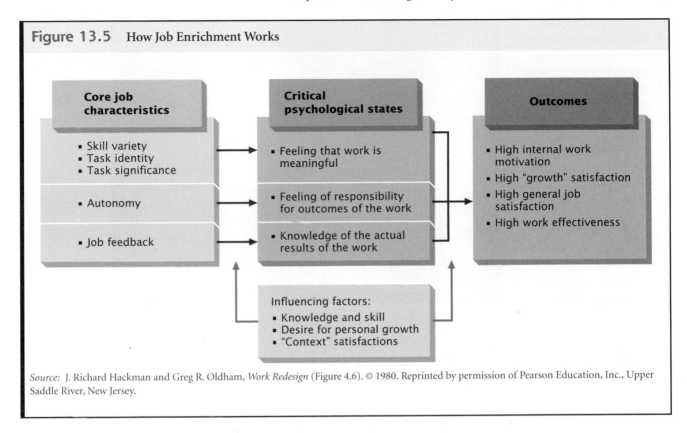

**Figure 13.5    How Job Enrichment Works**

*Source:* J. Richard Hackman and Greg R. Oldham, *Work Redesign* (Figure 4.6). © 1980. Reprinted by permission of Pearson Education, Inc., Upper Saddle River, New Jersey.

three psychological states that highly specialized jobs usually do not satisfy: meaningfulness, responsibility, and knowledge of results.

It is important to note that not all employees will respond favorably to enriched jobs. Personal traits and motives influence the connection between core job characteristics and desired outcomes. Only those with the necessary knowledge and skills plus a desire for personal growth will be motivated by enriched work. Furthermore, in keeping with Herzberg's two-factor theory, dissatisfaction with factors such as pay, physical working conditions, or supervision can neutralize enrichment efforts. Researchers have reported that fear of failure, lack of confidence, and lack of trust in management's intentions can stand in the way of effective job enrichment. But job enrichment can and does work when it is carefully thought out, when management is committed to its long-term success, and when employees desire additional challenge.[44]

# Motivation Through Rewards

All workers, including volunteers who donate their time to worthy causes, expect to be rewarded in some way for their contributions. **Rewards** may be defined broadly as the material and psychological payoffs for performing tasks in the workplace. Managers have found that job performance and satisfaction can be improved by properly administered rewards. Today, rewards vary greatly in both type and scope, depending on one's employer and geographical location. In fact, a popular book among managers is titled *1001 Ways to Reward Employees.*[45]

**rewards** *material and psychological payoffs for working*

*As a fighter of wildfires, Sean Hendrix, seen here checking in on his radio while battling a huge Oregon fire, puts it all on the line. The question is why? It's dangerous and exhausting work, hours are long, base-camp food and sleeping quarters are primitive, and the pay is barely adequate. Sean and his coworkers walk away from each fire with a mix of intrinsic and extrinsic rewards. Intrinsic payoffs—such as satisfaction from having faced a tough situation and triumphed—are what keep people like Sean coming back each wildfire season.*

**5** Distinguish extrinsic rewards from intrinsic rewards and list four rules for administering extrinsic rewards effectively.

**extrinsic rewards** *payoffs, such as money, that are granted by others*

**intrinsic rewards** *self-granted and internally experienced payoffs, such as a feeling of accomplishment*

In this section, we distinguish between extrinsic and intrinsic rewards, review alternative employee compensation plans, and discuss the effective management of extrinsic rewards.

## Extrinsic Versus Intrinsic Rewards

There are two different categories of rewards. **Extrinsic rewards** are payoffs granted to the individual by other people. Examples include money, employee benefits, promotions, recognition, status symbols, and praise. The second category is called **intrinsic rewards,** which are self-granted and internally experienced payoffs. Among intrinsic rewards are a sense of accomplishment, self-esteem, and self-actualization.[46] Usually, on-the-job extrinsic and intrinsic rewards are intermingled. For instance, employees often experience a psychological boost when they complete a big project in addition to reaping material benefits. Harvard Business School's Abraham Zaleznik recently offered this perspective:

> *I think a paycheck buys you a baseline level of performance. But one thing that makes a good leader is the ability to offer people intrinsic rewards, the tremendous lift that comes from being aware of one's own talents and wanting to maximize them.*[47]

## Employee Compensation

Compensation deserves special attention at this point because money is the universal extrinsic reward.[48] Moreover, since "labor costs are about two-thirds of total business expenses,"[49] compensation practices need to be effective and efficient. Employee compensation is a complex area fraught with legal and tax implications. Although an exhaustive treatment of employee compensation plans is beyond our present purpose, we can identify major types. Table 13.2 lists and briefly describes ten different pay plans. Two are nonincentive plans, seven qualify as incentive plans, and one plan is in a category of its own. Each type of pay plan has advantages and disadvantages. Therefore, there is no single best plan suitable for all employees. Indeed, two experts at the

U.S. Bureau of Labor Statistics say the key words in compensation for the next 25 years will be "flexible" and "varied."[50] A diverse workforce will demand an equally diverse array of compensation plans.

## Improving Performance with Extrinsic Rewards

Extrinsic rewards, if they are to motivate job performance effectively, need to be administered in ways that (1) satisfy operative needs, (2) foster positive expectations, (3) ensure equitable distribution, and (4) reward results. Let us see how these four criteria can be met relative to the ten different pay plans in Table 13.2.

### Rewards Must Satisfy Individual Needs.

Whether it is a pay raise or a pat on the back, a reward has no motivational impact unless it satisfies an operative need. Not all people need the same things, and one person may need different things at different times. Money is a powerful motivator for those who seek security through material wealth. But the promise of more money may mean little to a financially secure person who seeks ego gratification from challenging work. People's needs concerning when and how they want to be paid also vary.

**13G   Kiss a Frog? For How Much?**

*Would you kiss a stranger for $200? Of those surveyed, 37% said no. But 75% would kiss a frog for $50. Only 20% would fight a heavyweight boxer for $100,000. Fifty-nine percent would shave their heads for $10,000. Nearly a quarter of us would give up a friend's secret for $3,000. . . .*

*And for a million bucks? Sixty-five percent of us would live on a deserted island for a year. . . .*

**Source:** Amy Wilson, "Pricing Our Values," *Money*, 31 (February 2002): 24.

**Questions:** *Some management theorists say, "money isn't a motivator?" How does this survey evidence affect that theory? What about values and ethics? What are the practical management lessons here?*

*Research tells us profit sharing is one of the keys to successful employee participation programs. The concept behind profit-sharing is to give employees a sense of ownership and, hopefully, a motivational boost. Valassis, where these Durham, North Carolina, printing press operators work, has a generous profit-sharing plan that can increase an employee's paycheck by as much as 25 percent. Of course, profit sharing loses its motivational punch when profits dry up. A share of Valassis stock dropped from $45 a share to $20 during the last recession. Now we know why some call profit sharing "share the gain, share the pain."*

**Table 13.2**   Guide to Employee Compensation Plans

| Pay plan | Description/calculation | Main advantage | Main disadvantage |
|---|---|---|---|
| *Nonincentive* | | | |
| **Hourly wage** | Fixed amount per hour worked | Time is easier to measure than performance | Little or no incentive to work hard |
| **Annual salary** | Contractual amount per year | Easy to administer | Little or no incentive to work hard |
| *Incentive* | | | |
| **Piece rate** | Fixed amount per unit of output | Pay tied directly to personal output | Negative association with sweatshops and rate-cutting abuses |
| **Sales commission** | Fixed percentage of sales revenue | Pay tied directly to personal volume of business | Morale problem when sales personnel earn more than other employees |
| **Merit pay** | Bonus granted for outstanding performance | Gives salaried employees incentive to work harder | Fairness issue raised when tied to subjective appraisals |
| **Profit sharing** | Distribution of specified percentage of bottom-line profits | Individual has a personal stake in firm's profitability | Profits affected by more than just performance (for example, by prices and competition) |
| **Gain sharing** | Distribution of specified percentage of productivity gains and/or cost savings | Encourages employees to work harder *and* smarter | Calculations can get cumbersome |
| **Pay-for-knowledge** | Salary or wage rates tied to degrees earned or skills mastered | Encourages lifelong learning | Tends to inflate training and labor costs |
| **Stock options** | Selected employees earn right to acquire firm's stock free or at a discount | Gives individual a personal stake in firm's financial performance | Can be resented by ineligible personnel; morale tied to stock price |
| *Other* | | | |
| **Cafeteria compensation (life-cycle benefits)** | Employee selects personal mix of benefits from an array of options | Tailored benefits package fits individual needs | Can be costly to administer |

**cafeteria compensation**

*plan that allows employees to select their own mix of benefits*

Because cafeteria compensation is rather special and particularly promising, we shall examine it more closely. **Cafeteria compensation** (also called life-cycle benefits) is a plan that allows each employee to determine the makeup of his or her benefit package.[51] Because today's nonwage benefits are a significant portion of total compensation, the motivating potential of such a privilege can be sizable.

*Under these plans, employers provide minimal "core" coverage in life and health insurance, vacations, and pensions. The employee buys additional benefits to suit [his or her] own needs, using credit based on salary, service, and age.*

*The elderly bachelor, for instance, may pass up the maternity coverage he would receive, willy-nilly, under conventional plans and "buy" additional pension contributions instead. The mother whose children are covered by her husband's employee health insurance policy may choose legal and dental care insurance instead.*[52]

Although some organizations have balked at installing cafeteria compensation because of added administrative expense, the number of programs in effect in the United States has grown steadily. Cafeteria compensation enhances employee satisfaction, according to at least one study,[53] and represents a revolutionary step toward fitting rewards to people, rather than vice versa.

**Employees Must Believe Effort Will Lead to Reward.**  According to expectancy theory, an employee will not strive for an attractive reward unless it is perceived as being attainable. For example, the promise of an expenses-paid trip to Hawaii for the leading salesperson will prompt additional efforts at sales only among those who feel they have a decent chance of winning. Those who believe they have little chance of winning will not be motivated to try any harder than usual. Incentive pay plans, especially merit pay, profit sharing, gain sharing, and stock options, need to be designed and communicated in a way that will foster believable effort-reward linkages.[54]

**Rewards Must Be Equitable.**  Something is equitable if people perceive it to be fair and just. Each of us carries in our head a pair of scales upon which we weigh equity.[55] Figure 13.6 shows one scale for *personal equity* and another for *social equity*. The personal equity scale tests the relationship between effort expended and rewards received. The social equity scale, in contrast, compares our own effort-reward ratio with that of someone else in the same situation. We are motivated to seek personal and social equity and to avoid inequity.[56] An interesting aspect of research on this topic has demonstrated that inequity is perceived by those who are *overpaid* as well as by those who are underpaid.[57] Since perceived inequity is associated with feelings of dissatisfaction and anger, jealousy, or guilt, inequitable reward schemes tend to be counterproductive and are ethically questionable. Record-setting executive pay in recent years of painful downsizings and massive layoffs has been roundly criticized as inequitable and unfair.[58]

**Rewards Must Be Linked to Performance.**  Ideally, there should be an if-then relationship between task performance and extrinsic rewards. Traditional hourly wage and annual salary pay plans are weak in this regard. They do little more than reward the person for showing up at work. Managers can strengthen motivation to work by making sure that those who give a little extra get a little extra. In addition to piece-rate and sales-commission plans, merit pay, profit sharing, gain sharing, and stock option plans are popular ways of linking pay and performance.[59] The concept of team-based incentive pay as a way of rewarding teamwork and cooperation has been slow to take hold in the United States for two reasons: (1) it goes against the grain of an individualistic culture; and (2) poorly conceived and administered plans have given team-based pay a bad reputation.[60]

**Figure 13.6    Personal and Social Equity**

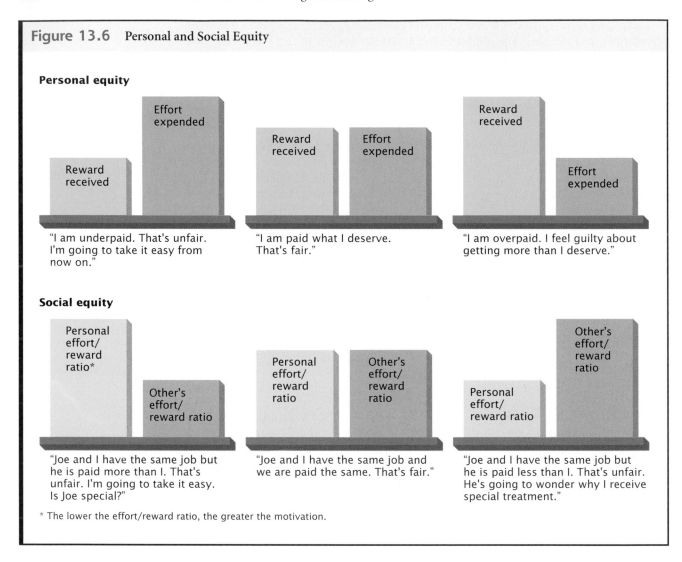

**Personal equity**

Reward received | Effort expended

"I am underpaid. That's unfair. I'm going to take it easy from now on."

Reward received | Effort expended

"I am paid what I deserve. That's fair."

Reward received | Effort expended

"I am overpaid. I feel guilty about getting more than I deserve."

**Social equity**

Personal effort/ reward ratio* | Other's effort/ reward ratio

"Joe and I have the same job but he is paid more than I. That's unfair. I'm going to take it easy. Is Joe special?"

Personal effort/ reward ratio | Other's effort/ reward ratio

"Joe and I have the same job and we are paid the same. That's fair."

Personal effort/ reward ratio | Other's effort/ reward ratio

"Joe and I have the same job but he is paid less than I. That's unfair. He's going to wonder why I receive special treatment."

* The lower the effort/reward ratio, the greater the motivation.

All incentive pay plans should be carefully conceived because undesirable behavior may inadvertently be encouraged. Consider, for example, what the head of Nucor Corporation, a successful minimill steel company, had to say about his firm's bonus system:

> *[Nucor's] bonus system . . . is very tough. If you're late even five minutes, you lose your bonus for the day. If you're late more than 30 minutes, or you're absent because of sickness or anything else, you lose your bonus for the week. Now, we do have what we call four "forgive-ness" days during the year when you can be sick or you have to close on a house or your wife is having a baby. But only four. We have a melter, Phil Johnson, down in Darlington, and one of the workers came in one day and said that Phil had been in an automobile accident and was sitting beside his car off of Route 52, holding his head. So the foreman asked, "Why didn't you stop and help him?" And the guy said, "And lose my bonus?"*[61]

Like goals, incentive plans foster selective perception.[62] Consequently, managers need to make sure goals and incentives point people in ethical directions.

# Motivation Through Employee Participation

While noting that the term *participation* has become a "stewpot" into which every conceivable kind of management fad has been tossed, one management scholar has helpfully identified four key areas of participative management. Employees may participate in (1) setting goals, (2) making decisions, (3) solving problems, and (4) designing and implementing organizational changes.[63] Thus, **participative management** is defined as the process of empowering employees to assume greater control of the workplace.[64] When personally and meaningfully involved, above and beyond just doing assigned tasks, employees are said to be more motivated and productive. In fact, a recent study of 164 New Zealand companies with at least 100 employees found lower employee turnover and higher organizational productivity among firms using participative management practices.[65]

**participative management**
*empowering employees to assume greater control of the workplace*

This section focuses on three approaches to participation. They are quality control circles, open-book management, and self-managed teams. After taking a closer look at each, we consider four keys to successful employee participation programs.

## Quality Control Circles

Developed in Japan during the early 1960s, this innovation took the U.S. industrial scene by storm during the late 1970s and early 1980s. Today, thousands of quality control circles can be found in hundreds of North American and European companies. **Quality control circles,** commonly referred to as QC circles or simply quality circles, are voluntary problem-solving groups of five to ten employees from the same work area who meet regularly to discuss quality improvement and ways to reduce costs.[66] A weekly one-hour meeting, during company time, is common practice. By relying on *voluntary* participation, QC circles attempt to tap the creative potential every employee possesses. Although QC circles do not work in every situation, benefits such as direct cost savings, improved worker-management relations, and greater individual commitment have been reported.[67]

**quality control circles**
*voluntary problem-solving groups committed to improving quality and reducing costs*

QC circles should be introduced in evolutionary fashion rather than by management edict. Training, supportive supervision, and team building are all part of this evolutionary development. The idea is to give those who work day in and day out at a specific job the tools, group support, and opportunity to have a say in nipping quality problems in the bud. Each QC circle is responsible not only for recommending solutions but also for actually implementing and evaluating those solutions. According to one observer, "The invisible force behind the success of QC's is its ability to bring the psychological principles of Maslow, McGregor, and Herzberg into the workplace through a structured process."[68]

**6** Explain how quality control circles, open-book management, and self-managed teams promote employee participation.

## Open-Book Management

**Open-book management** (OBM) involves "opening a company's financial statements to all employees and providing the education that will enable them to understand how the company makes money and how their actions affect its success and bottom line."[69] Clearly, this is a bold break from traditional management practice. Many companies claim to practice OBM, but few actually do.[70] Why? OBM asks managers to correct three typical shortcomings by (1) displaying a high degree of trust in employees,

**open-book management**
*sharing key financial data and profits with employees who are trained and empowered*

(2) having a deep and unwavering commitment to employee training, and (3) being patient when waiting for results.[71]

A four-step approach to OBM is displayed in Figure 13.7. The STEP acronym stands for *share, teach, empower,* and *pay.* Skipping or inadequately performing a step virtually guarantees failure. A systematic process is needed. Experts tell us it takes at least two complete budget cycles (typically two years) to see positive results. In step 1, employees are exposed to eye-catching public displays of key financial data. Sales, expense, and profit data for both the organization and relevant business units are shared in hallways, cafeterias, and on internal Web sites. Of course, without step 2, step 1 would be meaningless. Comprehensive, ongoing training gives *all* employees a working knowledge of the firm's business model. Here is what Jelly Belly Candy Co. does:

> *Through Jelly Belly University, employees from the upper-most management level to administrative support personnel learn the art of candymaking, evaluate the results and conduct product evaluations, production scheduling and inventory control.[72]*

Thus, Jelly Belly's employees not only learn how to make great jelly beans; they also learn what it takes to make a profit in the process. In OBM companies, finance specialists teach other employees how to read and interpret basic financial documents such as profit-loss statements. Entertaining and instructive business board games and computer simulations have proved effective. Remedial education is provided when needed.

**Figure 13.7    The Four S.T.E.P. Approach to Open-Book Management**

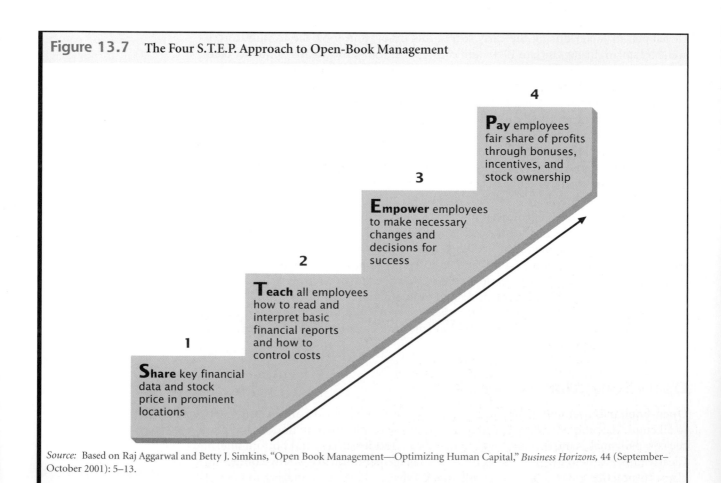

*Source:* Based on Raj Aggarwal and Betty J. Simkins, "Open Book Management—Optimizing Human Capital," *Business Horizons,* 44 (September–October 2001): 5–13.

Armed with knowledge about the company's workings and financial health, employees are ready for step 3. Managers find it easier to trust empowered employees to make important decisions when the employees are adequately prepared. (More on empowerment in Chapter 15.) In step 4, employees enjoy the fruits of their efforts by sharing profits and/or receiving bonuses and incentive compensation. There is no magic to OBM. It simply involves doing *important* things in the *right* way.[73]

## Self-Managed Teams

According to the logic of this comprehensive approach to participation, self-management is the best management because it taps people's full potential. Advocates say self-management fosters creativity, motivation, and productivity. **Self-managed teams,** also known as autonomous work groups or high-performance work teams, take on traditional managerial tasks as part of their normal work routine.[74] They can have anywhere from 5 to more than 30 members, depending on the job. Unlike QC circles, which are staffed with volunteers, employees are assigned to self-managed teams. Cross-trained team members typically rotate jobs as they turn out a complete product or service. Any supervision tends to be minimal, with managers acting more as *facilitators* than as order givers.

**self-managed teams** *high-performance teams that assume traditional managerial duties such as staffing and planning*

**Vertically Loaded Jobs.**    In the language of job enrichment, team members' jobs are vertically loaded. This means nonmanagerial team members assume duties traditionally performed by managers. But specifically which duties? A survey of industry practices in *Training* magazine answered this question. The profile of traditional managerial duties performed by self-managing teams in Figure 13.8 was derived from a sample of 1,456 U.S. companies with 100 or more employees. Significantly, the researchers observed: "For all the talk of self-directed teams, fewer than one-third

---

## 13H Lessons from Social Insects (Ants, Bees, and Termites)

*. . . we believe that social insects have been so successful—they are almost everywhere in the ecosphere—because of three characteristics:*

- flexibility (the colony can adapt to a changing environment);
- robustness (even when one or more individuals fail, the group can still perform its tasks); and
- self-organization (activities are neither centrally controlled nor locally supervised).

*Business executives relate readily to the first two attributes, but they often balk at the third, which is perhaps the most intriguing. Through self-organization, the behavior of the group emerges from the collective interactions of all the individuals.*

**Source:** Eric Bonabeau and Christopher Meyer, "Swarm Intelligence: A Whole New Way to Think About Business," *Harvard Business Review,* 79 (May 2001): 108.

---

**Question:** *What can this metaphor teach us about making self-managed teams more effective? Why do managers generally resist the concepts of self-organization and self-management?*

**Figure 13.8**    Research Insight: What Do Self-Managed Teams Manage?

**Organizations with self-directed teams**
*Percentage indicating that teams perform these functions on their own*

*Source:* "1996 Industry Report: What Self-Managing Teams Manage." Reprinted with permission from the October 1996 issue of *Training* magazine. Copyright 1996. Lakewood Publications, Minneapolis, Minn. All rights reserved. Not for resale.

[31 percent] of our respondents say they let teams call the shots."[75] Thus, self-managed teams are still in the early growth stage.

General Mills has extended the idea of self-managed teams to the point that the night shift in its cereal plant in Lodi, California, runs with no managers at all. Other progressive organizations such as General Foods, Texas Instruments, Corning, General Electric, Boeing, Procter & Gamble, and Volvo have operations built around self-managed teams. *Fortune* quoted the head of Texas Instruments as saying, "No matter what your business, these teams are the wave of the future"[76] (see The Global Manager).

**Managerial Resistance.**    Not surprisingly, managerial resistance is the number one barrier to self-managed teams. More than anything else, self-managed teams represent *change*, and lots of it.

> *Adopting the team approach is no small matter; it means wiping out tiers of managers and tearing down bureaucratic barriers between departments. Yet companies are willing to undertake such radical changes to gain workers' knowledge and commitment—along with productivity gains that exceed 30 percent in some cases.*[77]

Traditional authoritarian supervisors view autonomous teams as a threat to their authority and job security. For this reason, *new* facilities built around the concept of

# The Global Manager

## Culturally Adapting Self-Managed Teams in Mexico

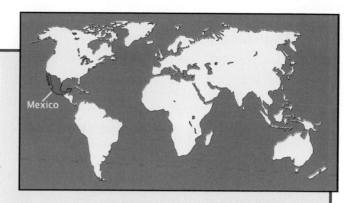

### Background

During a management seminar, Spanish-language versions of a self-managed teams survey were completed by 243 Mexican executives, jointly responding in 32 discussion groups.

| Self-Managed Teams | Mexican Business Culture |
|---|---|
| **Norms** | **Value Expectations** |
| *Individualism* | *Collectivism* |
|   Personal accountability |   Shared responsibility |
|   Individual responsibility |   Moral obligation |
|   Confidence in ability |   Paternalistic management |
|   Confrontation and debate |   Harmony |
| *Low uncertainty avoidance* | *High uncertainty avoidance* |
|   Take self-initiative |   Resist change |
| *Low power distance* | *High power distance* |
|   Self-leadership |   Respect status roles |
|   Bottom-up decision making |   Top-down hierarchical structure |
| **Required Behaviors** | **Expected Behaviors** |
| Team members solve problems, resolve conflicts, set goals, assess performance, initiate change, and communicate upward. Managers delegate, provide information, and encourage open communication. | Workers follow instructions, respect managers, receive feedback, avoid conflict and criticism, and save face. Managers make decisions, direct, control, and discipline. |

### Contrasting Cultures

"Although a team-based work design would seem to appeal to the collectivist values of the Mexican culture, the behavioral requirements of the North American concept of teamwork reflect individualist values, as well as value placed on low power distance and individual risk tolerance."

*Source:* Excerpted and adapted with permission of *Academy of Management Executive* from "Taking Self-Managed Teams to Mexico," by Chantell E. Nicholls, Henry W. Lane, and Mauricio Brehm Brechu, August 1999, pp. 15–25. Copyright 1999 Academy of Management. Reproduced with permission of Academy of Management in the format textbook via Copyright Clearance Center.

### Conclusions

" . . . it would be feasible to implement self-managed teams in Mexico, but the process of implementation will take longer than expected; training will be required for more basic skills necessary for effective work teams (e.g., holding meetings, setting goals, and solving problems) than would be required in Canada or the United States; and clear instruction and endorsement from the top will be necessary to legitimize changes, even those involving a participatory style of work design."

## 13l  Transparent Organizations

Peter Janson, CEO of AGRA Inc., a Canadian construction services company, says the three keys to excellence are speed, simplicity, and transparency:

> *Transparency is the atmosphere of openness and trust that helps turn a simple, speedy organization into an excellent company. It means letting go of command-and-control methods. It also means addressing problems openly so that they can be identified, analyzed, and dealt with early on. In a transparent culture, relevant information is shared with customers, employees, and shareholders, enabling these essential decision makers to make good, informed decisions.*

**Source:** Peter Janson, "Three Keys to Excellence," *Management Review*, 88 (September 1999): 9.

**Questions:** *What does transparency have to do with participative management and open-book management? What are the major positives and negatives of organizational transparency?*

self-managed teams, so-called greenfield sites, tend to fare better than reworked existing operations.

Managers who take the long view and switch to self-managed teams are finding it well worth the investment of time and money. Self-managed teams even show early promise of boosting productivity in the huge service sector.[78] (Teamwork is discussed in the next chapter.)

## Keys to Successful Employee Participation Programs

According to researchers, four factors build the *employee* support necessary for any sort of participation program to work:

1. A profit-sharing or gain-sharing plan
2. A long-term employment relationship with good job security
3. A concerted effort to build and maintain group cohesiveness
4. Protection of the individual employee's rights[79]

Working in combination, these factors help explain motivational success stories such as that of Norsk Hydro in the chapter Closing Case.

It should be clear by now that participative management involves more than simply announcing a new program, such as open-book management. To make sure a supportive climate exists, a good deal of background work often needs to be done.[80] This is particularly important in view of the conclusion drawn by researchers who analyzed 41 participative management studies:

> *Participation has . . . [a positive] effect on both satisfaction and productivity, and its effect on satisfaction is somewhat stronger than its effect on productivity. . . . Our analysis indicates specific organizational factors that may enhance or constrain the effect of participation. For example, there is evidence that a participative climate has a more substantial effect on workers' satisfaction than participation in specific decisions.[81]*

In the end, effective participative management is as much a managerial attitude about sharing power as it is a specific set of practices. In some European countries, such as Germany, the supportive climate is reinforced by government-mandated participative management.[82]

# Other Motivation Techniques for a Diverse Workforce

**7** Explain how companies are striving to motivate an increasingly diverse workforce.

Workforce diversity has made "flexibility" a must for managers today. This chapter concludes with a look at ways of accommodating emerging employee needs. For example, a big concern these days involves striking a proper life balance between work and leisure.[83] By meeting these needs in creative ways, such as flexible work schedules, family support services, wellness programs, and sabbaticals, managers hope to enhance motivation and job performance.

## Flexible Work Schedules

The standard 8 A.M. to 5 P.M., 40-hour workweek has come under fire as dual-income families, single parents, and others attempt to juggle hectic schedules. Taking its place is **flextime,** a work-scheduling plan that allows employees to determine their own arrival and departure times within specific limits.[84] All employees must be present during a fixed core time (see the center portion of Figure 13.9). If an eight-hour day is required, as in Figure 13.9, an early bird can put in the required eight hours by arriving at 7:00 A.M., taking half an hour for lunch, and departing at 3:30 P.M. Alternatively, a late starter can come in at 9:00 A.M. and leave at 5:30 P.M. When given the choice of "flexible work hours" versus an "opportunity to advance" in a recent survey, 58 percent of the women opted for flexible hours. Forty-three percent of the men chose that option.[85] The growing use of flextime and other alternative work arrangements, such as telecommuting, is partly due to employer self-interest. Employers want to cut the cost of unscheduled absenteeism. A 2001 survey found the average annual cost for each employee's unscheduled absenteeism (68 percent of which was *not* for illness) to be $775.[86] Flextime can also be used to accommodate the special needs of disabled employees.[87]

> **flextime** *allows employees to choose their own arrival and departure times within specified limits*

**Benefits.**   In addition to many anecdotal reports citing the benefits of flextime, research studies have uncovered promising evidence. Flextime has several documented benefits:

- Better employee-supervisor relations
- Reduced absenteeism
- Selective positive impact on job performance (e.g., a 24 percent improvement for computer programmers over a two-year period but no effect on the performance of data-entry workers).[88]

Flextime, though very popular among employees because of the degree of freedom it brings, is not appropriate for all situations. Problems reported by adopters include greater administrative expense, supervisory resistance, and inadequate coverage of jobs.

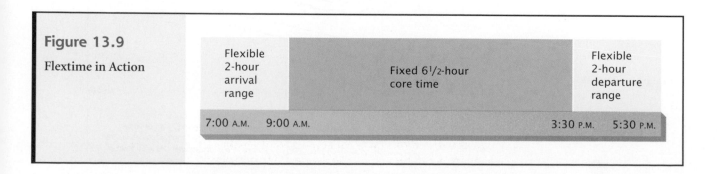

**Figure 13.9**

**Flextime in Action**

Flexible 2-hour arrival range | Fixed 6½-hour core time | Flexible 2-hour departure range

7:00 A.M.    9:00 A.M.          3:30 P.M.    5:30 P.M.

## 13J    In Search of a Balanced Life

*In 1975, 48 percent of respondents rated work as "the important thing" versus 36 percent for leisure. By 2000 the numbers had reversed—43 percent chose leisure and 34 percent work.*

*"It's the movement from the work ethic to the fun ethic," says Thomas Riehle of Ipsos-Reid, a survey firm. But, as Riehle notes, the work ethic is not collapsing so much as the boundaries between work and leisure are blurring—a combination that often produces stress and confusion.*

**Source:** Robert J. Samuelson, "Fun Ethic vs. Work Ethic?" *Newsweek* (September 10, 2001): 43.

**Question:** *What relative weights do you apply to work and leisure in your life? What sort of rebalancing do you need for a less stressful life? How?*

**Alternatives.**    Other work-scheduling innovations include *compressed workweeks* (40 or more hours in fewer than five days)[89] and *permanent part-time* (workweeks with fewer than 40 hours). *Job sharing* (complementary scheduling that allows two or more part-timers to share a single full-time job), yet another work-scheduling innovation, is growing in popularity among employers of working parents.[90]

A recent European study suggests employees may be paying a price for the freedom of flexible work scheduling. Compared with a control group of employees on fixed schedules, employees with compressed workweeks, rotating shifts, irregular schedules, and part-time jobs experienced significantly more health, psychological, and sleeping problems.[91]

## Family Support Services

With dual-income families and single parents caught between obligations to family and the job, both the government and companies are coming to the rescue. On the federal government front, the Family and Medical Leave Act (FMLA) took effect in the United States in 1993 after years of political debate.[92] As indicated in Table 13.3, FMLA has significant holes and limitations. First, only companies with 50 or more employees are required to comply with the law mandating up to 12 weeks of

"... AM I INTERESTED IN AN ALTERNATIVE WORK ARRANGEMENT?,... YES,... I'D LIKE TO TELECOMMUTE FROM A COMPUTER EQUIPPED HOT TUB ON FLEX TIME..."

| **Table 13.3**   The 1993 Family and Medical Leave Act (FMLA) in Brief |
|---|

The Federal Family and Medical Leave Act:

- Guarantees workers up to 12 weeks a year off, unpaid, for births, adoptions, the care of sick children, spouses or parents, or to recover from an illness themselves.
- Affects businesses with 50 or more workers living within a 75-mile radius of work.
- Covers employees who have spent at least 1,250 hours on the job the last 12 months.
- Allows employers to exclude the top-paid 10 percent of their employees.
- Allows employers to require workers to use vacation or other leave first.
- Allows companies to restrict couples employed at the same place to 12 weeks total leave a year.
- Requires workers to provide employers with 30 days' notice when practical, such as for birth or adoption.
- Requires employers to continue to provide health insurance during an employee's leave.
- Guarantees workers the same or equivalent job upon return.
- Affects 5 percent of U.S. employers and 57 percent of workers.

Companies found in violation of the family leave act can be found liable for back wages, reinstatement, promotions, and monetary damages. Damage claims must be filed within two years of the alleged violation, unless state law says otherwise.

The family leave law doesn't overrule state laws with more generous provisions, such as a state statute providing for more than 12 weeks of unpaid leave.

*Source:* Mimi Hall and Blair S. Walker, "Federal Family Leave Act: Provisions at a Glance," *USA Today* (August 5, 1993): 2B. Copyright 1993, *USA Today*. Reprinted with permission.

unpaid leave per year for family events such as births, adoptions, or sickness. Because the vast majority of U.S. businesses (95 percent) employ fewer than 50 people, millions of working Americans (43 percent) are left unprotected by FMLA. Second, employees can be required by their employer to exhaust their sick leave and vacation allotments before taking FMLA leave. Fortunately, states and businesses can plug some of the holes in FMLA.

At least 35 states have equivalent or more generous parental and family leave laws. Eligible employees can choose the more generous option when both federal and state laws apply.[93] Meanwhile, on the business front, a few companies go so far as to grant *paid* parental and family sickness leaves. Many other exciting corporate family support service initiatives are cropping up. A growing but still very small number of companies in the United States (11 percent in 1999) provide on-site day-care facilities. About 15 percent provide emergency child-care services.[94] Elder-care centers, for employees' elderly relatives who cannot be left home alone, are starting to appear.[95] Some companies have banded together to form reduced-rate day-care cooperatives for their employees. Emergency child care is a welcome corporate benefit for working parents.

## Wellness Programs

Stress and burnout are inevitable consequences of modern work life.[96] (See the Skills & Tools box at the end of this chapter.) Family-versus-work conflict, long hours, overload, hectic schedules, deadlines, frequent business travel, and accumulated work-place irritations are taking their toll. Progressive companies are coming to the rescue with *wellness programs* featuring a wide range of offerings. Among them are stress reduction, healthy eating and living clinics, quit-smoking and weight-loss programs, exercise facilities, massage breaks, behavioral health counseling, and health screenings. The ultimate objective is to help employees achieve a sustainable balance between their personal lives and work lives, with win-win benefits all around.

> *For example, Citibank experienced decreases in health risks and savings of between $4.56 and $4.73 for each dollar spent on its health education and awareness program. In another example, Glaxo Wellcome's health promotion program saved the company an estimated $1 million in 1998, and has reduced medical leaves of absence by 20,000 workdays since 1996.*[97]

## Sabbaticals

Several companies, including IBM, Wells Fargo, 3Com, and McDonald's, give selected employees paid sabbaticals after a certain number of years of service. Two to six months of paid time off gives the employee time for family, recreation, and travel. Intel offers an eight-week break with pay every seven years. The idea is to refresh long-term employees and hopefully bolster their motivation and loyalty in the process.[98]

# Summary

1. Maslow's five-level needs hierarchy, although empirically criticized, makes it clear to managers that people are motivated by emerging rather than fulfilled needs. Assuming that job satisfaction and performance are positively related, Herzberg believes that the most that wages and working conditions can do is eliminate sources of dissatisfaction. According to Herzberg, the key to true satisfaction, and hence motivation, is an enriched job that provides an opportunity for achievement, responsibility, and personal growth. Expectancy theory is based on the idea that the strength of one's motivation to work is the product of perceived probabilities of acquiring personally valued rewards. Both effort-performance and performance-reward probabilities are important to expectancy theory.

2. Goals can be an effective motivational tool when they are specific, difficult, participatively set, and accompanied by feedback on performance. Goals motivate performance by directing attention, encouraging effort and persistence, and prompting goal-attainment strategies and action plans.

3. Managers can counteract the boredom associated with routine-task jobs through realistic job previews, job rotation, and limited exposure. This third alternative involves letting employees earn early time off.

4. Job enrichment vertically loads jobs to meet individual needs for meaningfulness, responsibility, and knowledge of results. Personal desire for growth and a supportive climate must exist for job enrichment to be successful.

**5.** Both extrinsic (externally granted) and intrinsic (self-granted) rewards, when properly administered, can have a positive impact on performance and satisfaction. There is no single best employee compensation plan. A flexible and varied approach to compensation will be necessary in the coming years because of workforce diversity. The following rules can help managers maximize the motivational impact of extrinsic rewards: (1) rewards must satisfy individual needs, (2) one must believe that effort will lead to reward, (3) rewards must be equitable, and (4) rewards must be linked to performance. Gain-sharing plans have great motivational potential because they emphasize participation and link pay to actual productivity.

**6.** Participative management programs foster direct employee involvement in one or more of the following areas: goal setting, decision making, problem solving, and change implementation. Quality control circles are teams of volunteers who meet regularly on company time to discuss ways to improve product/service quality. The S.T.E.P. model of open-book management encourages employee participation when managers (1) *share* key financial data with all employees, (2) *teach* employees how to interpret financial statements and control costs, (3) *empower* employees to make improvements and decisions, and (4) *pay* a fair share of profits to employees. Employees assigned to self-managed teams participate by taking on tasks traditionally performed by management. Profit sharing or gain sharing, job security, cohesiveness, and protection of employee rights are keys to building crucial employee support for participation programs.

**7.** A diverse workforce requires diverse motivational techniques. Flextime, a flexible work-scheduling scheme that allows employees to choose their own arrival and departure times, has been effective in improving employee-supervisor relations while reducing absenteeism. Employers are increasingly providing family support services such as child care, elder care, parental leaves, and adoption benefits. Employee wellness programs and sabbaticals are offered by some companies.

## Terms to Understand

# Skills & Tools

## Stress Management 101

Feeling burned out? You're not alone. According to a survey of 7,000 senior executives in the United States and 12 other countries, burnout is on the rise in the executive ranks, and many companies fail to handle the problem properly.

"All leaders are at risk for burnout, but too often companies are embarrassed by the phenomenon and have no idea how to address it," says Andrew Kakabadse, director of the survey and professor of management at the Cranfield University School of Management, Bedford, UK.

Even if companies aren't addressing the issue of burnout, there are some steps individuals can take on their own. Lois Tamir, vice president of Personnel Decisions International in Minneapolis, Minnesota, offers a number of suggestions for the busy executive who needs to stay focused during a tough time (see list). In a nutshell, managers can reduce stress by thinking big and treating themselves better.

### How to Avoid Burnout

**Pace yourself.** Don't put in extra hours because you probably won't get much done anyway.

**Laugh more.** Humor relieves a great deal of physiological and psychological stress.

**Be good to yourself.** Do something that you enjoy, such as going to the movies.

**Keep it simple.** Separate your work into small tasks that can be accomplished easily. It's important to feel a sense of achievement.

**Stay true to your values.** Think about the larger values in your work and personal life. Integrity, family priorities, and kindness to others will keep you grounded and put things in perspective.

**Keep expectations in check.** Forget about changing the world or achieving your greatest goal at work. Some things will have to be postponed until you are better equipped to handle your own situation.

**Don't try to be perfect.** Everyone experiences difficult times in his or her professional and personal life.

*Source:* Cheryl Comeau-Kirschner, "Stress Management 101." Reprinted from *Management Review,* 88 (November 1999): 9. © 1999 American Management Association. Reproduced with permission of American Management Association in the format textbook via Copyright Clearance Center.

# Hands-On Exercise

## Quality-of-Work-Life Survey

**Instructions**

Think of your present job, or one you had in the past, and circle one number for each of the following items. Add the circled numbers to get a total quality-of-work-life score. Alternatively, you can use this survey to interview another jobholder to determine his or her quality of work life. (*Note:* This survey is for instructional purposes only because it has not been scientifically validated.)

*General Job Satisfaction*

■ Most of the time, my job satisfaction is

Very low                                                                    Very high
1·············2·············3·············4·············5·············6·············7

*Quality of Supervision*

■ The person I report to respects me, listens to me, and supports me.

Never                                                                        Always
1·············2·············3·············4·············5·············6·············7

*Quality of Communication*

■ The organization keeps me well informed about its mission and pending changes.

Never                                                                        Always
1·············2·············3·············4·············5·············6·············7

*Organizational Climate*

■ My workplace generally feels like

A cold, rainy day                                              A warm, sunny day
1·············2·············3·············4·············5·············6·············7

*Job Design*

■ The work I do is

Routine and boring                                        Varied and challenging
1·············2·············3·············4·············5·············6·············7

Unimportant                                                                Important
1·············2·············3·············4·············5·············6·············7

*Feedback and Compensation*

■ I am given timely and constructive feedback.

False                                                                            True
1·············2·············3·············4·············5·············6·············7

■ I am paid fairly for what I do.

False                                                                            True
1·············2·············3·············4·············5·············6·············7

*Coworkers*

■ My coworkers are

Negative and unfriendly                                      Positive and friendly
1·············2·············3·············4·············5·············6·············7

*Work Hours and Schedules*

■ My work hours and schedules are flexible and accommodate my lifestyle.

Never                                                                      Always
1·············2·············3·············4·············5·············6·············7

*Organizational Identification*

■ I have a strong sense of commitment and loyalty to my work organization.

False                                                                        True
1·············2·············3·············4·············5·············6·············7

*Stress*

■ The degree of unhealthy stress in my workplace is

Very high                                                                Very low
1·············2·············3·············4·············5·············6·············7

Total quality-of-work-life score = _____

Scale

12–35 = Warning—this job could be
        hazardous to your health
36–60 = Why spend half your waking
        life settling for average?
61–84 = T.G.I.M. (Thank goodness it's *Monday*)

**For Consideration/ Discussion**

**1.** Which of these various quality-of-work-life factors is of overriding importance to you? Why? Which are least important? Why?

**2.** How strongly does your quality-of-work-life score correlate with the amount of effort you put into your job? Explain the connection.

**3.** How helpful would this survey be in your search for a better job? Explain.

**4.** How much does your total score reflect your attitude about life in general?

**5.** What should your managers do to improve the quality-of-work-life scores for you and your coworkers?

**6.** How important is quality of work life to your overall lifestyle and happiness? Explain.

# Internet Exercises

**1. More on open-book management (OBM):** As discussed in this chapter, OBM is an underused way to reap the benefits of participative management. It requires managers to rethink some of their assumptions about managing people. A good place to begin is with a free tutorial at **www.bizcenter.com.** At the home page, click on the box "Open-Book Mgmt." Read the one-page introduction and, at the bottom of the page, click on "To Book Excerpt." Read the clear and concise four-page overview of OBM.

*Learning Points:* 1. Name two or three useful insights about OBM you gained from this tutorial. 2. Does OBM appeal to you? Explain. 3. Do you believe OBM has great promise in the business world? Why or why not? 4. What are the major stumbling blocks for OBM in today's typical organizations? How can they be overcome?

**2. Getting the upper hand on stress and heart disease:** According to the American Heart Association, "nearly 62 million Americans have some form of cardiovascular disease, and nearly 1 million die from it each year. . . . Heart disease ranks as the No. 1 killer in the USA, although one-third of those deaths could be prevented if people ate better diets and exercised more."[99] Stress also is a risk factor in this heart disease epidemic. A good place to start your personal battle against heart disease is with a risk assessment. You can do that for free online, thanks to the Medical University of South Carolina **www.musc.edu.** Click on the tab "Search" at the home page. Enter the words "stress quiz" in the search box and click on "Submit." Select "AA Week 1999 Stress Quiz" and complete and score the ten-item quiz. For a heart disease risk assessment, go back and follow the same procedure, entering the words "risk of heart disease" in the search box. From the list of resources, select "Your Risk of Heart Disease: Quiz." Score your heart disease risk and read about the risk factors you can and cannot control.

*Learning Points:* 1. What do you need to do to improve your stress score? (*Tip:* Consult the Skills & Tools box at the end of this chapter for advice on managing stress.) 2. What do you need to do to lower your risk of heart disease?

**3. Check it out:** Are you underpaid? Need supporting evidence to ask for a raise? Want to know how much you could make if you switched jobs or careers? Like to know how much someone else makes? Go online to **www.salary.com** and put the Salary Wizard to work.

For updates to these exercises, visit our Web site (**http://business.college.hmco.com/students**).

# Closing Case

## Seeking Proper Balance at Norway's Norsk Hydro

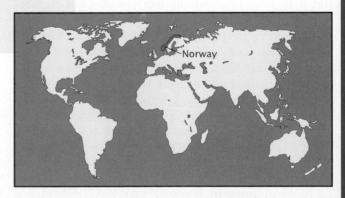

On the surface, Norway seems to be a moderate place. The climate can be intemperate, but the people and the lifestyle are just the opposite—the picture of restraint and judiciousness. Oh, there are some unassuming little oddities: Norwegians eat fish for breakfast, and often for lunch and for dinner. Caviar is so common that it comes in tubes, just like toothpaste. Very few people are overweight.

All of which seems charmingly unusual—but hardly alien.

The workplace, too, seems familiar: computers, cubicles, bullet-point slides. Familiar, that is, until you look more closely.

Every weekday at 6:10 A.M., Morten Lingelem boards a train at Sandefjord for the 90-minute ride to his job in Oslo. Lingelem, 42, a process-technology manager, has a standing reservation in the train's "office car," where he can power up his laptop and work in quiet comfort. That office car serves a purpose that's exactly the opposite of what it would be in the United States: It enables Lingelem to hold down a demanding engineering-management job, to spend more than three hours a day commuting, and still to be home by 6 P.M.

Atle Taerum, a colleague of Lingelem's, lives on a farm 90 minutes west of Oslo. And, two days a week, that's where he is, taking care of his 10-month-old daughter. Taerum is never without his cell-phone. On those days, customers—perhaps calling from Africa or from the Middle East—often reach him while he's plowing his fields, or chaperoning his son's kindergarten class.

Norway is, in fact, a sort of alternative universe of work. The inhabitants, the setting, the language, and the profit imperative all seem familiar. But Norwegians have a very different attitude about work—and a singular view of what work can become.

That vision is rooted in the notion that balance is healthy. The argument: work can be redesigned to promote balance. More than that, balance can become a source of corporate and national competitive advantage. Working less can, in fact, mean working better.

Norsk Hydro, the company that employs both Lingelem and Taerum, is one of Norway's dominant institutions. It's the world's second-largest producer of oil from the Norwegian North Sea, and the single-largest salmon farmer. Hydro fertilizer feeds Florida tomatoes and Arizona golf courses. Hydro metals toughen Cadillac Seville bumpers and Nokia cell-phones.

Hydro operates in 70 countries and employs 39,000 people, many of whom live and work outside of Norway. But it remains emphatically Norwegian—an organization not easily understood in American terms. As excess defines American culture, so balance shapes life for Norwegians, who long ago discovered sane responses to the tension between work and family. Norway is a place, after all, where people typically leave work between 4 P.M. and 4:30 P.M. Working women get at least 38 weeks of paid maternity leave; men get as many as 4 weeks of paid leave. Norway's answer to "How much is enough?" is found in the way the nation operates. Balance is the place where conversations about work and life begin.

In its 94 years of operation, "Hydro has created and nurtured industry in Norway," says Roald Nomme, a consultant and former manager at Hydro. "What is deep in the culture of Hydro is to think in the long term, to think more holistically—to think about the connections between employees, the company, and society."

Now Hydro is reexamining these connections. In a series of experiments across the company, it is testing a much more ambitious vision of balance. The two-year-old project, known as Hydroflex, has given hundreds of employees varying combinations of flexible hours, home offices, new technology, and redesigned office space.

What has Hydro learned?

Hydro believes that it can help employees find a better balance by redesigning physical work spaces—and by redesigning work itself. It can free people from old restrictions on where and when they work. That flexibility makes workers more productive and jobs more appealing, and more appealing jobs attract more talented people.

Linked to the push for flexibility are new notions of diversity. Hydro believes that diversity goes beyond race or gender. Diversity has to do with *perspective*—and it exists *within* individuals: each of us is many different people at different times in our lives. Cultivate that diversity, and greater creativity will follow.

These workplace initiatives come at a critical time for Hydro. Because of weak commodity and oil prices, profits dropped by 4 percent between 1994 and 1998, even as revenues increased by 40 percent. In most American companies, such performance would be enough to end any grand experiments in work redesign, diversity, and balance. But at Hydro, those projects persist and even thrive—because, to Hydro, these initiatives are not indulgences. They are critical strategic elements for survival.

Yes, Hydro must go head-to-head with competitors in the United States—and in Germany, in Singapore, and in Mexico. As it fights these global battles, Hydro is up against relentless freneticism. We Americans pay lip service to sanity, but when the going gets tough, we readily abandon balance and work even harder.

Norwegians believe that such mania is not sustainable. In the end, they say, balance will win out. . . .

Indeed, Norwegian culture—the prism through which Hydro's efforts at balance must be viewed—takes some fundamental American attitudes about work and turns them upside down.

In the United States, for instance, working long hours is seen as admirable, even heroic. At Hydro, the standard workday, even for professionals, is seven and a half hours. If you're still sitting at your desk at 6 P.M., people wonder why you can't get your work done.

Work in Norway is also shaped by a tradition of cooperation between unions and management that's unheard of in the United States. Labor and management typically work together to change processes and structures for greater efficiency. Unions believe that higher productivity brings more jobs and higher pay. Management wants higher profits—but satisfied employees aren't bad either.

All this allows—and perhaps requires—Norwegians to consider balance in fundamental terms. A rich life is a diverse collection of compelling experiences, some of which involve work. Work that is all-consuming is unhealthy—for the individual, for the organization, and for the community. Time spent away from work is restorative. More to the point: Time spent outside work fuels work itself.

## For Discussion

**1.** How does Herzberg's two-factor theory enter into this case? Explain.

**2.** How well do you think open-book management would work at Norsk Hydro? Explain.

**3.** Do you like Norsk Hydro's attempts to promote better work/life balance? Why? How well would this approach work in the United States (or another country of your choice)?

**4.** What role does work play in your life? What are you doing (or do you plan to do) to achieve a decent balance in your life?

## chapter fourteen

# Group Dynamics and Teamwork

*"* There's no substitute for people who have a common vision and passion. *"*

Amy Williams

# How Political Infighting Helped Bring Down Enron

*Note:* This is an unpleasant story about a dysfunctional organization. We normally prefer upbeat, positive success stories to inspire and challenge today's and tomorrow's managers. However, so many people were hurt by the Enron debacle—honest employees, their families, customers, and stockholders—that the story must be told to illustrate how *not* to run a business. This is a story of powerful managers who put themselves first and engaged in ruinous organizational politics in a climate of fear and deceit.

The Enron scandal has been told as a kind of Greek tragedy, a cautionary tale of hubris, even a battle of the sexes. But it can perhaps be best understood as a brutal competition. The miracle of the marketplace is supposed to be that competition is healthy—that the struggle to create something better, faster and cheaper benefits nearly everyone. That's the theory, at least, that some people use to explain why greed is good. But throw in pride (and lust), and sometimes the game goes out of control. This is the story of how Jeff Skilling and Rebecca Mark took their rivalry and drove it—and a multibillion-dollar company, its employees and its stockholders—right off the edge of a cliff.

While the drama played out, Enron founder Ken Lay seemed more interested in schmoozing Washington and going to charity events in Houston than running the company day to day. The two young dynamos vying for his favor offered competing models of the future. To Mark, the road to riches lay in building ever-grander castles, massive energy infrastructures. But to Skilling, tangible assets like power plants were just toys. The real money, he argued, was in the action—the trading, buying and selling. They each had an enormous interest in justifying their respective visions.

Inside Enron, Mark was sometimes known as "Mark the Shark." Blond and tall and toned, she was sleek and fast and knew how to bite. When she entered the utility business in the early '80s, it was populated with frumpy males in baggy suits and short-sleeved shirts with pocket protectors. Mark wore stiletto heels and tightly tailored size-6 Escada suits. She was a builder. Her job was to create and develop power plants and sell the electricity they made. In the sleepy, once tightly regulated world of power companies she was regarded as both a curiosity and a whirlwind, able to use her femininity and no-nonsense manner to disarm, then buffalo the men sitting across the table. By the mid-'90s, she had constructed or acquired five plants in the United States and was on her way to buying or building well in excess of 15 in Europe, Asia, South America and the Middle East.

But inside her own company, she had competition. Like her, Jeff Skilling had been born middle class and Middle Western, gone to college in Texas and to Harvard Business School. They both turned 40 in 1993; both were clearly on track for the top jobs at Enron. But Skilling saw himself as the true visionary. Buying power plants and selling their product—that was Old Think, argued Skilling. In the new, wired, free-for-all economy, the greatest rewards would go to those who made markets, who bought and sold—but didn't actually own much of anything. Constructing and running power plants was for chumps: it required huge capital investments and never produced the return on investment he was after. Anyone could build a factory, Skilling said. But it took a special genius—a whiz kid who had not just been a Harvard Business School grad but a high-ranking Baker scholar—to manipulate all the pieces, to make them add up to more than the sum of their parts. (As it turned out, it also took creative and possibly fraudulent accounting that masked losses and debts and recorded projected and far-from-certain future profits as present earnings.) And why stop at gas and electricity? Why not trade water or broadband capacity? By the time Skilling was done, Enron would be trading securities based on weather data.

Skilling was aggressive and brash, not so much articulate and smooth as cunning and willful. He thrived on one-upmanship and didn't mind trying to embarrass the less-quick-witted or anyone who challenged him. In one conference call with Wall Street analysts he dismissed one nagging questioner as an "a--hole." Skilling wanted to stomp not just Enron's competitors in the corporate world but any potential rival within Enron. In 1993 he persuaded his boss—Ken Lay—to cut him a piece of Mark's business. Skilling was given control of Enron's power plants in the United States; he promptly sold these assets in order to have more cash for his plans. (Skilling's spokeswoman says he never considered Mark a direct rival.) At first, Mark was baffled by Skilling's raid on her turf—especially since it was a sneak attack. She had never been given a chance to make her case. She regarded Skilling as a flashy consultant type who had never done the hard work of building anything.

Rather than pout, Mark just pushed herself harder. She became a world traveler, ranging round the globe buying and building plants. She lived high and, in retrospect, paid too much, especially for a $3 billion plant in India that immediately became enmeshed in local political intrigue. But she wanted to prove that her way was the golden road. As she flew around in her corporate jet and smart suits, she began to get noticed. She worked with Henry Kissinger to lobby the Chinese prime minister on the need for Western-built pipelines and plants. She spoke on the phone to the Israeli prime minister and raised the gender awareness of a high-ranking official in Qatar. At first, the Qatari official refused to address her directly, but by the end of three hours, he was gushing, "It's a shame you haven't been here before. We would have resolved the issues a long time ago."

In foreign capitals, Enron was no longer being confused with Exxon. Mark had every reason to believe her bosses would be pleased with her efforts to extend and enshrine the Enron brand. She was, like other Enron executives, showered in stock options. But she didn't get quite the glory she anticipated. Perhaps because Lay saw himself as Enron's pitchman, he didn't seem to welcome Mark's high profile.

Lay's boy, it soon became clear, was Skilling. While Mark globe-trotted, Skilling was filling headquarters with his own troops. He was not looking for "fuzzy skills," a former employee recalls. His recruits talked about a socialization process called "Enronizing." Family time? Quality of life? Forget it. Anybody who did not embrace the elbows-out culture "didn't get it." They were "damaged goods" and "shipwrecks," likely to be fired by their bosses at blistering annual job reviews known as rank-and-yank sessions. The culture turned paranoid: former CIA and FBI agents were hired to enforce security. Using "sniffer" programs, they would pounce on anyone e-mailing a potential competitor. The "spooks," as the former agents were called, were known to barge into offices and confiscate computers.

Some employees found the cultural revolution troubling. The Rev. James Nutter of Palmer Memorial Epis-

copal Church heard from so many unhappy Enron souls that he penned a letter to Skilling: "These people don't belong to you," Nutter recalls writing. "They belong to God." But many Enronites worshiped Mammon instead. The real status symbol at Enron was not a new Ferrari but one of the company's half-dozen parking spaces monitored by security cameras. Skilling would take his favorites, "The Mighty Man Force," as one employee called them, on macho adventure trips. They raced across Mexico on a 1,000-mile bike tour. While tearing through the rugged Australian Outback, the overexuberant Mighty Men trashed several expensive SUVs they'd rented.

Enron parties were suitably imperial, with Tiffany glassware as door prizes and waiters standing by at all times with flutes of champagne. Some of the informal partying was less classy. . . .

Sex suffused the Enron atmosphere. Skilling divorced his wife and became engaged to an Enron secretary, whom he promoted to a $600,000 job and whom insiders immediately dubbed "Va Voom!" One top executive, Lou Pai, divorced his wife and married a former stripper. Several women who were believed to be sleeping with their bosses were called "The French Lieutenants' Women." Staffers fearful of the next rank-and-yank session worried that these women were acting as spies. The most celebrated affair was between two top executives, Ken Rice and Amanda Martin. Their affection, described by Enron staffers to *Newsweek* as "touchy feely" and "obscene," was visible through the windows of Martin's office.

Mark apparently had her own intramural affair. In the late '80s, after she was divorced, she had a relationship with an Enron consultant, John Wing. Some of Mark's colleagues believed their relationship continued after Wing joined Enron. Some employees found the office romances and salacious gossip so disturbing that they proposed the company adopt a formal policy against fraternization, according to a former personnel executive. The company let the suggestion drop.

Mark was not above ostentatious revelry. At a party to celebrate the development of the Enron power plant in India, she brought a small elephant into a resort outside Houston (at the same party, dressed in leather, she rode in on the back of a Harley-Davidson). But for the most part, she remained outside the Lay-Skilling in-crowd, working in a separate building downtown. She failed to fully realize how hard Skilling was working to undermine her.

In 1997, Skilling was given another chunk of Mark's territory—energy development in parts of Europe. Too late, Mark realized that Skilling was playing for keeps. The two had a "short and extremely acrimonious" discussion, she says. But by 1998, Skilling was Enron's chief operating officer. Mark was made vice chairman, a fancy title for a position described by Enron insiders as "the ejection seat."

Mark had one last play. That same year she took over a small water company called Azurix spun off by Enron. Mark had grand plans for Azurix: essentially to control as much of the world's drinking water as possible and sell it for a profit. Yet lacking adequate financing from Enron, she took the company public before it was ready. But the stock quickly crashed. Azurix invested heavily in an English company—but again was ensnared in local politics, and the project turned out to be a loser. To help her make deals, she brought in the hard-charging Amanda Martin, who, like Mark, was stylish and well educated. But she had misgivings about Martin. Some of her colleagues suspected that Martin was a spy for Skilling. Martin dismisses the notion, but says she understands why some people believed it. "I was one of the few people coming out of Jeff's camp," she says.

Mark left herself open to attack. When she tried to buy a company that provided services to water utilities, there were grumbles that she was overpaying. As it turned out, the services company was run by her fiancé. An employee urged Enron's general counsel to look into Mark's potential conflict of interest. The whistle-blower? Martin. The deal was scuttled. According to a person close to Mark, it was Mark herself who decided to kill it.

By August 2000 it was time to go, and Mark was forced out. In terms of her own finances, the timing was fortunate. Mark sold her stock at a big profit [$56 million, total]. Outsiders, including Enron shareholders, were kept in the dark, but Skilling's empire was already starting to rot from within. Desperate to keep the price of the stock climbing, Enron's management was creating hundreds of off-the-books "entities," some of which served to hide or disguise heavy debts and losses. By 2001, the stock price was beginning to slide. Skilling won the ultimate prize—he succeeded Ken Lay as CEO in January 2001. But by August he was gone, claiming "personal reasons" for his early retirement.

*Source:* Excerpted from "Enron's Dirty Laundry," by Johnnie L. Roberts and Evan Thomas, from *Newsweek* (March 11, 2002): 22–28. © 2002 Newsweek, Inc. All rights reserved. Reprinted by permission.

A s in daily life itself, relationships rule in modern organizations. The more managers know about building and sustaining good working relationships, the better. A management consultant recently put it this way:

> At the end of the day, a company's only sustainable competitive advantage is its relationships with customers, business partners, and employees. After all, we provide products and services to people, not to companies. A commitment to developing effective relationships strengthens the fabric of the organization in the long run.[1]

What is involved here is a new concept called *social capital*.[2] In line with our discussion of human capital in Chapter 11, managers need to build social capital by working on strong, constructive, and mutually beneficial relationships. Precisely the opposite happened at Enron prior to its slide into bankruptcy. The purpose of this chapter is to build a foundation of understanding about how groups and teams function in today's organizations.

# Fundamental Group Dynamics

According to one organization theorist, "All groups may be collections of individuals, but all collections of individuals are not groups."[3] This observation is more than a play on words; mere togetherness does not automatically create a group. Consider, for example, this situation. Half a dozen people who worked for different companies in the same building often shared the same elevator in the morning. As time passed, they introduced themselves and exchanged pleasantries. Eventually, four of the elevator riders discovered that they all lived in the same suburb. Arrangements for a car pool were made, and they began to take turns picking up and delivering one another. A group technically came into existence only when the car pool was formed. To understand why this is so, we need to examine the definition of the term *group*.

## What Is a Group?

**1**  Define the term *group*.

**group**  *two or more freely interacting individuals with a common identity and purpose*

From a sociological perspective, a **group** can be defined as two or more freely interacting individuals who share a common identity and purpose.[4] Careful analysis of this definition reveals four important dimensions (see Figure 14.1). First, a group must be made up of two or more people if it is to be considered a social unit. Second, the individuals must freely interact in some manner. An organization may qualify as a sociological group if it is small and personal enough to permit all its members to interact regularly with each other. Generally, however, larger organizations with bureaucratic tendencies are made up of many overlapping groups. Third, the interacting individuals must share a common identity. Each must recognize himself or herself as a member of the group. Fourth, interacting individuals who have a common identity must also have a common purpose. That is, there must be at least a rough consensus on why the group exists.

**14A  An Uphill Battle?**

Max De Pree, former CEO of Herman Miller, the Michigan office furniture maker:

*In our group activities, intimacy is betrayed by such things as politics, short-term measurements, arrogance, superficiality, and an orientation toward self rather than toward the good of the group.*

**Source:** Max De Pree, *Leadership Is an Art* (New York: Dell, 1989), p. 56.

**Questions:** *Which of the various barriers to effective group action mentioned by De Pree is the most difficult for managers to overcome? Why? Is De Pree being too negative, or just being realistic? Explain.*

For further information about the interactive annotations in this chapter, visit our Web site (http://business.college.hmco.com/students).

## Types of Groups

Human beings belong to groups for many different reasons. Some people join a group as an end in itself. For example, an accountant may enjoy the socializing that is part of belonging to a group at a local health club. That same accountant's membership in a work group is a means to a professional end. Both the exercise group and the work group satisfy the sociological definition of a group, but they fulfill very different needs. The former is an informal group, and the latter is a formal group.

**Informal Groups.**  As Abraham Maslow pointed out, a feeling of belonging is a powerful motivator. People generally have a great need to fit in, to be liked, to be one of the gang. Whether the group meets at

### Figure 14.1

**What Does It Take to Make a Group?**

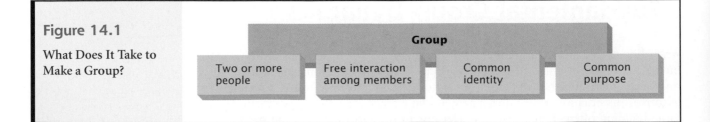

| Group | | | |
|---|---|---|---|
| Two or more people | Free interaction among members | Common identity | Common purpose |

work or during leisure time, it is still an **informal group** if the principal reason for belonging is friendship.[5] Informal groups usually evolve spontaneously. They serve to satisfy esteem needs because one develops a better self-image when accepted, recognized, and liked by others. Sometimes, as in the case of a group of friends forming an investment club, an informal group may evolve into a formal one.

    Managers cannot afford to ignore informal groups because grassroots social networks can either advance or threaten the organization's mission.[6] As experts on the subject explained:

> *These informal networks can cut through formal reporting procedures to jump-start stalled initiatives and meet extraordinary deadlines. But informal networks can just as easily sabotage companies' best-laid plans by blocking communication and fomenting opposition to change unless managers know how to identify and direct them. . . .*
>
>     *If the formal organization is the skeleton of a company, the informal is the central nervous system driving the collective thought processes, actions, and reactions of its business units. Designed to facilitate standard modes of production, the formal organization is set up to handle easily anticipated problems. But when unexpected problems arise, the informal organization kicks in. Its complex web of social ties form[s] every time colleagues communicate and solidif[ies] over time into surprisingly stable networks. Highly adaptive, informal networks move diagonally and elliptically, skipping entire functions to get work done.[7]*

**Formal Groups.**    A **formal group** is a group created for the purpose of doing productive work. It may be called a team, a committee, or simply a work group. Whatever its name, a formal group is usually formed for the purpose of contributing to the success of a larger organization. Formal groups tend to be more rationally structured and less fluid than informal groups. Rather than joining formal task groups, people are assigned to them according to their talents and the organization's needs. One person normally is granted formal leadership responsibility to ensure that the members carry out their assigned duties. Informal friendship groups, in contrast, generally do not have officially appointed leaders, although informal leaders often emerge by popular demand. For the individual, the formal group and an informal group at the place of

**informal group** *collection of people seeking friendship*

**formal group** *collection of people created to do something productive*

*Come on, let's see what you got! This basketball team of middle-agers in Boston is ready to rumble. It is an informal group consisting of a company president, two lawyers, a photographer, and a psychologist. After-work and week-end sports are a great way for today's busy professionals to stay in shape, polish their team skills, and make contacts. Come to think of it, this could be the ultimate dream team. A president to call the plays, a photographer to capture the action, two lawyers to argue the calls, and a psychologist to console the losers.*

employment may or may not overlap. In other words, one may or may not be friends with one's coworkers.

## Attraction to Groups

**2** Explain the significance of cohesiveness, roles, norms, and ostracism in regard to the behavior of group members.

**cohesiveness**  *tendency of group to stick together*

What attracts a person to one group but not to another? And why do some groups' members stay whereas others leave? Managers who can answer these questions can take steps to motivate others to join and remain members of a formal work group. Individual commitment to either an informal or formal group hinges on two factors. The first is *attractiveness,* the outside-looking-in view.[8] A nonmember will want to join a group that is attractive and will shy away from a group that is unattractive. The second factor is **cohesiveness,** the tendency of group members to follow the group and resist outside influences. This is the inside-looking-out view. In a highly cohesive group, individual members tend to see themselves as "we" rather than "I." Cohesive group members stick together.[9]

Factors that either enhance or destroy group attractiveness and cohesiveness are listed in Table 14.1. It is important to note that each factor is a matter of degree. For example, a group may offer the individual little, moderate, or great opportunity for prestige and status. Similarly, group demands on the individual may range from somewhat disagreeable to highly disagreeable. What all this means is that both the decision to join a group and the decision to continue being a member depend on a net balance of the factors in Table 14.1. Naturally, the resulting balance is colored by one's perception and frame of reference, as it was in the case of Richard Dale, a former manager of distribution at Commodore International, during his first meeting with the company's founder, Jack Tramiel:

> *Dale's first meeting with Tramiel began with a summons to appear at Tramiel's office. Dale flew from his office in Los Angeles to Santa Clara . . . , only to find that Tramiel had decided to visit him instead.*
>
> *Terrified, Dale caught a plane back to find his secretary shaking in her shoes and the burly Tramiel sitting at his desk. For an hour Tramiel grilled Dale on his philosophy of*

---

**Table 14.1**    **Factors That Enhance or Detract from Group Attractiveness and Cohesiveness**

| Factors that enhance | Factors that detract |
|---|---|
| 1. Prestige and status | 1. Unreasonable or disagreeable demands on the individual |
| 2. Cooperative relationship | 2. Disagreement over procedures, activities, rules, and the like |
| 3. High degree of interaction | 3. Unpleasant experience with the group |
| 4. Relatively small size | 4. Competition between the group's demands and preferred outside activities |
| 5. Similarity of members | 5. Unfavorable public image of the group |
| 6. Superior public image of the group | 6. Competition for membership by other groups |
| 7. A common threat in the environment | |

*Source:* Table adapted from *Group Dynamics: Research and Theory,* 2nd ed., by Dorwin Cartwright and Alvin Zander. New York: HarperCollins Publishers, Inc.

*business, pronounced it all wrong, and suggested a tour of the warehouse. When they passed boxes of . . . [computers] waiting for shipment, recalls Dale, Tramiel seemed to "go crazy," pounding the boxes with his fists and yelling, "Do you think this is bourbon? Do you think it gets better with age?"*[10]

Dale's departure within a few months of this episode is not surprising in view of the fact that Tramiel's conduct destroyed work group attractiveness and cohesiveness.

## Roles

According to Shakespeare, "All the world's a stage, and all the men and women merely players." In fact, Shakespeare's analogy between life and play-acting can be carried a step further—to organizations and their component formal work groups. Although employees do not have scripts, they do have formal positions in the organizational hierarchy, and they are expected to adhere to company policies and rules. Furthermore, job descriptions and procedure manuals spell out how jobs are to be done. In short, every employee has one or more organizational roles to play. An organization that is appropriately structured, in which everyone plays his or her role(s) effectively and efficiently, will have a greater chance for organizational success.

A social psychologist has described the concept of *role* as follows:

*The term role is used to refer to (1) a set of expectations concerning what a person in a given position must, must not, or may do, and (2) the actual behavior of the person who occupies the position. A central idea is that any person occupying a position and filling a role behaves similarly to anyone else who could be in that position.*[11]

A **role,** then, is a socially determined prescription for behavior in a *specific* position. Roles evolve out of the tendency for social units to perpetuate themselves, and roles are socially enforced. Role models are a powerful influence. They are indispensable to those trying to resolve the inherent conflicts between work and family roles, for example.[12]

**role** *socially determined way of behaving in a specific position*

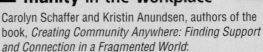

### 14B Toward a Sense of Community in the Workplace

Carolyn Schaffer and Kristin Anundsen, authors of the book, *Creating Community Anywhere: Finding Support and Connection in a Fragmented World*:

*Community is a dynamic whole that emerges when a group of people:*

- *Participate in common practices;*
- *Depend upon one another;*
- *Make decisions together;*
- *Identify themselves as part of something larger than the sum of their individual relationships; and*
- *Commit themselves for the long term to their own, one another's, and the group's well-being.*

**Source:** Quoted in Ron Zemke, "The Call of Community," *Training*, 33 (March 1996): 27.

**Questions:** *How important is it to build this sense of community in today's work groups and organizations? Explain. What is your personal experience with a genuine feeling of community? Are we naive to expect a sense of community in today's hurried and rapidly changing workplace? Explain.*

## Norms

Norms define "degrees of acceptability and unacceptability."[13] More precisely, **norms** are general standards of conduct that help individuals judge what is right or wrong or good or bad in a given social setting (such as work, home, play, or religious organization). Because norms are culturally derived, they vary from one culture to another. For example, public disagreement and debate, which are normal in Western societies, are often considered rude in Eastern countries such as Japan.

Norms have a broader influence than do roles, which focus on a specific position. Although usually unwritten, norms influence behavior enormously.[14]

**norms** *general standards of conduct for various social settings*

**14C**

## Back to the Opening Case

What role expectations and norms paved the way for Enron's failure?

Every mature group, whether informal or formal, generates its own pattern of norms that constrains and directs the behavior of its members. Norms are enforced for at least four different reasons:

1. To facilitate survival of the group
2. To simplify or clarify role expectations
3. To help group members avoid embarrassing situations (protect self-images)
4. To express key group values and enhance the group's unique identity[15]

As illustrated in Figure 14.2, norms tend to go above and beyond formal rules and written policies. Compliance is shaped with social reinforcement in the form of attention, recognition, and acceptance.[16] Those who fail to comply with the norm may be criticized or ridiculed. For example, consider the pressure Gwendolyn Kelly experienced in medical school:

> The word among students is that if you've got any brains, "tertiary" medicine—which involves complex diagnostic procedures and comprehensive care—is where it's at. Instructors often refer to the best students as "future surgeons" and belittle the family-practice specialty. These attitudes trickle down. I've heard my peers say the reason so many women choose pediatrics is that "they want to be mommies." And students who take a family-practice residency may be maligned by colleagues who say the choice is a sign of subpar academic credentials.[17]

Reformers of the U.S. health care system, who want to increase the number of primary care (family practice) doctors from one-third to one-half, need to begin by altering medical school norms.

**ostracism** *rejection from a group*

Worse than ridicule is the threat of being ostracized. **Ostracism,** or rejection from the group, is figuratively the capital punishment of group dynamics. Informal groups

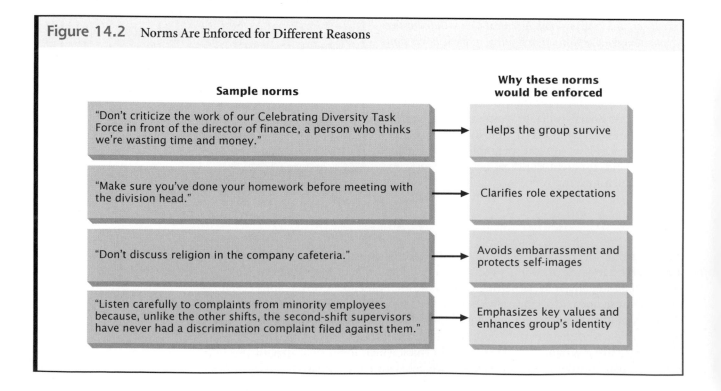

**Figure 14.2    Norms Are Enforced for Different Reasons**

| Sample norms | Why these norms would be enforced |
|---|---|
| "Don't criticize the work of our Celebrating Diversity Task Force in front of the director of finance, a person who thinks we're wasting time and money." | Helps the group survive |
| "Make sure you've done your homework before meeting with the division head." | Clarifies role expectations |
| "Don't discuss religion in the company cafeteria." | Avoids embarrassment and protects self-images |
| "Listen carefully to complaints from minority employees because, unlike the other shifts, the second-shift supervisors have never had a discrimination complaint filed against them." | Emphasizes key values and enhances group's identity |

derive much of their power over individuals through the ever-present threat of ostracism. Thus, informal norms play a pivotal role in on-the-job ethics.[18] Police officers, for example, who honor the traditional "code of silence" norm that demands *total* loyalty to one's fellow officers, face a tough moral dilemma.

# Group Development

Like inept youngsters who mature into talented adults, groups undergo a maturation process before becoming effective. We have all experienced the uneasiness associated with the first meeting of a new group, be it a class, club, or committee. Initially, there is little mutual understanding, trust, and commitment among the new group members, and their uncertainty about objectives, roles, and leadership doesn't help. The prospect of cooperative action seems unlikely in view of defensive behavior and differences of opinion about who should do what. Someone steps forward to assume a leadership role, and the group is off and running toward eventual maturity (or perhaps premature demise). A working knowledge of the characteristics of a mature group can help managers envision a goal for the group development process.

*For Procter & Gamble's Tide brand laundry detergent, a seemingly small one percentage point gain in market share in the U. S. alone translates into an additional $60 million in sales. So Craig Bahner (left) assembled a team to broaden the brand's exposure. Here, they pose with a Tide-sponsored race car. Just as the car's pit crew had to do, Bahner had to develop his task group into a winning team. And it's Tide, by a car length!*

# Management Ethics

## Building Social Capital Through Compassion

**W**hen people think of compassion, the first thing that comes to mind for many is empathy. But while empathy can be comforting, it does not engender a broader response and therefore has limited capacity for organizational healing. Instead, our research shows that compassionate leadership involves taking some form of public action, however small, that is intended to ease people's pain—and that inspires others to act as well.

TJX president and CEO Edmond English, who lost seven employees aboard one of the planes that hit the World Trade Center, gathered his staff together shortly after the attacks to confirm the names of the victims. He called in grief counselors the very same day and chartered a plane to bring the victims' relatives from Canada and Europe to the company's headquarters in Framingham, Massachusetts. He personally greeted the families when they arrived in the parking lot at midnight on September 15. Although told by English that they could take some time off after the attacks, most employees opted to come in to work, as English himself had done, and support one another in the early days following the tragedy. . . .

In vivid contrast, immediately following the terrorist attacks in New York City, leaders at a publishing company close to ground zero refused to disrupt business as usual. The company held regularly scheduled meetings the day after the attacks and provided little or no support for people to share and express their pain. One editor told us she'd gotten a call at home early on the morning of September 12, just as she was trying to help her eight-year-old daughter to make sense of what had happened the day before, demanding to know why she was late for a meeting. She went to work and sat through a four-hour conference call but was present in body only. Because she was given no opportunity to connect with her family, friends, and colleagues and was offered little organizational comfort in the face of a terrifying and confusing sequence of events, she felt her loyalty to the company eroding with every passing minute.

*Source:* Reprinted by permission of *Harvard Business Review.* Excerpt from *"Leading in Times of Trauma,"* by Jane E. Dutton, Peter J. Frost, Monica C. Worline, Jacoba M. Lilius, and Jason M. Kanov. January 2002. Copyright © 2002 by the Harvard Business School Publishing Corporation; all rights reserved.

## Characteristics of a Mature Group

If and when a group takes on the following characteristics, it can be called a mature group:

1. *Members are aware of their own and each other's assets and liabilities vis-à-vis the group's task.*
2. *These individual differences are accepted without being labeled as good or bad.*
3. *The group has developed authority and interpersonal relationships that are recognized and accepted by the members.*
4. *Group decisions are made through rational discussion. Minority opinions and dissension are recognized and encouraged. Attempts are not made to force decisions or a false unanimity.*
5. *Conflict is over substantive group issues such as group goals and the effectiveness and efficiency of various means for achieving those goals. Conflict over emotional issues regarding group structure, processes, or interpersonal relationships is at a minimum.*
6. *Members are aware of the group's processes and their own roles in them.*[19]

Effectiveness and productivity should increase as the group matures. Recent research with groups of school teachers found positive evidence in this regard. The researchers concluded: "Faculty groups functioning at higher levels of development have students who perform better on standard achievement measures."[20] This finding could be fruitful for those seeking to reform and improve the American education system.

A hidden but nonetheless significant benefit of group maturity is that individuality is strengthened, not extinguished.[21] Protecting the individual's right to dissent is particularly important in regard to the problem of blind obedience, which we shall consider later in this chapter. Also, as indicated in the fifth item on the list above, members of mature groups tend to be emotionally mature.[22] This paves the way for building much-needed social capital (for example, see Management Ethics).

## Six Stages of Group Development

Experts have identified six distinct stages in the group development process[23] (see Figure 14.3). During stages 1 through 3, attempts are made to overcome the obstacle of uncertainty over power and authority. Once this first obstacle has been surmounted, uncertainty over interpersonal relations becomes the challenge. This second obstacle must be cleared during stages 4 through 6 if the group is to achieve maturity. Each stage confronts the group's leader and contributing members with a unique combination of problems and opportunities.

**3** Identify and briefly describe the six stages of group development.

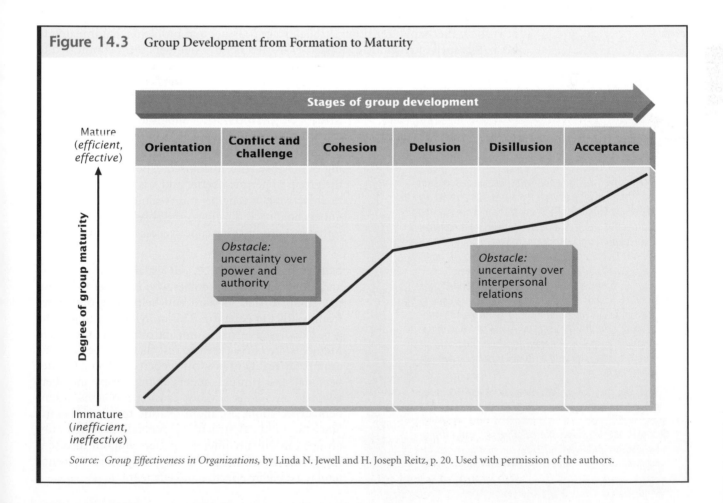

**Figure 14.3**   Group Development from Formation to Maturity

*Source: Group Effectiveness in Organizations,* by Linda N. Jewell and H. Joseph Reitz, p. 20. Used with permission of the authors.

### Stage 1: Orientation.

Attempts are made to "break the ice." Uncertainty about goals, power, and interpersonal relationships is high. Members generally want and accept any leadership at this point. Emergent leaders often misinterpret this "honeymoon period" as a mandate for permanent control.

### Stage 2: Conflict and Challenge.

As the emergent leader's philosophy, objectives, and policies become apparent, individuals or subgroups advocating alternative courses of action struggle for control. This second stage may be prolonged while members strive to clarify and reconcile their roles as part of a complete redistribution of power and authority. Many groups never continue past stage 2 because they get bogged down due to emotionalism and political infighting. Committees within the organization often bear the brunt of jokes because their frequent failure to mature beyond stage 2 prevents them from accomplishing their goals. (As one joke goes, a camel is a horse designed by a committee.)

### Stage 3: Cohesion.

The shifts in power started in stage 2 are completed, under a new leader or the original leader, with a new consensus on authority, structure, and procedures. A "we" feeling becomes apparent as everyone becomes truly involved. Any lingering differences over power and authority are resolved quickly. Stage 3 is usually of relatively short duration. If not, the group is likely to stall.

### Stage 4: Delusion.

A feeling of "having been through the worst of it" prevails after the rather rapid transition through stage 3. Issues and problems that threaten to break this spell of relief are dismissed or treated lightly. Members seem committed to fostering harmony at all costs. Participation and camaraderie run high as members believe that all the difficult emotional problems have been solved.

### Stage 5: Disillusion.

Subgroups tend to form as the delusion of unlimited goodwill wears off, and there is a growing disenchantment with how things are turning out. Those with unrealized expectations challenge the group to perform better and are prepared to reveal their personal strengths and weaknesses if necessary. Others hold back. Tardiness and absenteeism are symptomatic of diminishing cohesiveness and commitment.

### Stage 6: Acceptance.

It usually takes a trusted and influential group member who is concerned about the group to step forward and help the group move from conflict to cohesion. This individual, acting as the group catalyst, is usually someone other than the leader. Members are encouraged to test their self-perceptions against the reality of how others perceive them. Greater personal and mutual understanding helps members adapt to situations without causing problems. Members' expectations are more realistic than ever before. Since the authority structure is generally accepted, subgroups can pursue different matters without threatening group cohesiveness. Consequently, stage 6 groups tend to be highly effective and efficient.

---

**14D**  **The Business of Golf**

*Ask people why they golf with business associates, and the answer is always the same: It's a great way to build relationships. They say this far more about golf than about going to dinner or attending a baseball game, and for good reason. Indeed, this may be the central fact about corporate golf, though it's rarely said: When people golf together, they see one another humiliated. At least 95% of all golfers are terrible, which means that in 18 holes everyone in the foursome will hit a tree, take three strokes in one bunker, or four-putt, with everyone else watching. Bonding is simply a matter of people jointly going through adversity, and a round of golf will furnish plenty of it.*

**Source:** Geoffrey Colvin, "Why Execs Love Golf," *Fortune* (April 30, 2001): 46.

---

**Questions:** *Why does shared adversity foster strong relationships and bonding? How can managers get task group members to bond like this without playing golf?*

Time-wasting problems and inefficiencies can be minimized if group members are consciously aware of this developmental process. Just as it is impossible for a child to skip being a teenager on the way to adulthood, committees and other work groups will find there are no short cuts to group maturity. Some emotional stresses and strains are inevitable along the way.[24]

# Organizational Politics

Only in recent years has the topic of organizational politics (also known as impression management) begun to receive serious attention from management theorists and researchers.[25] But as we all know from practical experience, organizational life is often highly charged with political wheeling-and-dealing. For example, consider this recent complaint:

> *I've been working at my current job as a marketing manager for about a year now, and one thing is bugging me. Every time I propose a strategy or a solution in a meeting, someone else at the table repeats it, in somewhat altered form—and ends up getting the credit for having thought of it. This is no trivial problem, since in my department, year-end bonuses are based on how many of each person's ideas have been put into (profitable) practice.[26]*

Workplace surveys reveal that organizational politics can hinder effectiveness and be an irritant to employees. A recent three-year study of 46 companies attempting to establish themselves on the Internet "found that poor communication and political infighting were the No. 1 and No. 2 causes, respectively, for slowing down change."[27] Meanwhile, 44 percent of full-time employees and 60 percent of independent contractors listed "freedom from office politics" as extremely important to their job satisfaction.[28]

Whether politically motivated or not, managers need to be knowledgeable about organizational politics because their careers will be affected by it.[29] New managers, particularly, should be aware of the political situation in their organization. As "new kids on the job" they might be more easily taken advantage of than other more experienced managers. Certain political maneuvers also have significant ethical implications[30] (see Table 14.2).

**4** Define *organizational politics* and summarize relevant research insights.

**Table 14.2    How Do You Feel About "Hard Ball" Organizational Politics?**

Circle one number for each item, total your responses, and compare your score with the scale below:

|  | *Unacceptable attitude/conduct* | | | | *Acceptable attitude/conduct* |
|---|---|---|---|---|---|
| 1. The boss is always right. | 1 | 2 | 3 | 4 | 5 |
| 2. If I were aware that an executive in my company was stealing money, I would use that information against him or her in asking for favors. | 1 | 2 | 3 | 4 | 5 |
| 3. I would invite my boss to a party in my home even if I didn't like that person. | 1 | 2 | 3 | 4 | 5 |
| 4. Given a choice, take on only those assignments that will make you look good. | 1 | 2 | 3 | 4 | 5 |
| 5. I like the idea of keeping a "blunder (error) file" about a company rival for future use. | 1 | 2 | 3 | 4 | 5 |
| 6. If you don't know the correct answer to a question asked by your boss, bluff your way out of it. | 1 | 2 | 3 | 4 | 5 |
| 7. Why go out of your way to be nice to any employee in the company who can't help you now or in the future? | 1 | 2 | 3 | 4 | 5 |
| 8. It is necessary to lie once in a while in business in order to look good. | 1 | 2 | 3 | 4 | 5 |
| 9. Past promises should be broken if they stand in the way of one's personal gain. | 1 | 2 | 3 | 4 | 5 |
| 10. If someone compliments you for a task that is another's accomplishment, smile and say thank you. | 1 | 2 | 3 | 4 | 5 |

*Scale*
10–20 = Straight arrow with solid ethics.
21–39 = Closet politician with elastic ethics.                                    Total score = _____
40–50 = Hard ball politician with no ethics.

*Source:* From *Winning Office Politics* by Andrew Dubrin. Copyright © 1990. Reprinted with permission of Prentice-Hall Direct.

# What Does Organizational Politics Involve?

**organizational politics** *the pursuit of self-interest in response to real or imagined opposition*

As the term implies, self-interest is central to organizational politics. In fact, **organizational politics** has been defined as "the pursuit of self-interest at work in the face of real or imagined opposition."[31] Political maneuvering is said to encompass all self-serving behavior above and beyond competence, hard work, and luck.[32] Although the term organizational politics has a negative connotation, researchers have identified both positive and negative aspects:

> *Political behaviors widely accepted as legitimate would certainly include exchanging favors, "touching bases," forming coalitions, and seeking sponsors at upper levels. Less legitimate behaviors would include whistle-blowing, revolutionary coalitions, threats, and sabotage.*[33]

Recall our discussion of whistle-blowing in Chapter 5.

Employees resort to political behavior when they are unwilling to trust their career solely to competence, hard work, or luck. One might say that organizational politicians help luck along by relying on political tactics. Whether employees will fall back on political tactics has a lot to do with an organization's climate or culture. A culture that presents employees with unreasonable barriers to individual and group success tends to foster political maneuvering. Consider this situation, for example: "A cadre of Corvette lovers inside General Motors lied, cheated, and stole to keep the legendary sports car from being eliminated during GM's management turmoil and near-bankruptcy in the late 1980s and early 1990s."[34] The redesigned Corvette finally made it to market in 1997, thanks in part to the Corvette team giving high-level GM executives thrilling unauthorized test rides in the hot new model.

**14E** **Is TV's Survivor a Metaphor for Worklife?**

*"The same games are being played in the office," . . . says Rutgers University anthropologist Helen Fisher. "That is why we like the show. We are trying to figure out if we could play the game."*

*"People are built to constantly size up the costs and benefits of their behavior, to decide when to be the good Samaritan and when to cheat, when to form coalitions and when to be honest and when to be dishonest." says Fisher. "This is part of the survival of the fittest."*

**Source:** Karen S. Peterson, "'Survivor' Tactics Could Become Norm," *USA Today* (February 8, 2001): 1D.

**Questions:** *Is it really that brutal in today's workplace? Explain. How do you plan to be a survivor in the organizational jungle?*

## Research on Organizational Politics

Researchers in one widely cited study of organizational politics conducted structured interviews with 87 managers employed by 30 electronics firms in southern California. Included in the sample were 30 chief executive officers, 28 middle managers, and 29 supervisors. Significant results included the following:

- The higher the level of management, the greater the perceived amount of political activity.
- The larger the organization, the greater the perceived amount of political activity.
- Personnel in staff positions were viewed as more political than those in line positions.
- People in marketing were the most political; those in production were the least political.
- "Reorganization changes" reportedly prompted more political activity than any other type of change.
- A majority (61 percent) of those interviewed believed organizational politics helps advance one's career.
- Forty-five percent believed that organizational politics distracts from organizational goals.[35]

Regarding the last two findings, it was clear that political activities were seen as helpful to the individual. On the other hand, the interviewed managers were split on the question of the value of politics to the organization. Managers who believed political behavior had a positive impact on the organization cited the following reasons: "gaining visibility for ideas, improving coordination and communication, developing teams and groups, and increasing *esprit de corps.* . . ."[36] As listed above, the most-often-cited negative effect of politics was its distraction of managers from organizational goals. Misuse of resources and conflict were also mentioned as typical problems.

## Political Tactics

As defined earlier, organizational politics takes in a lot of behavioral territory. The following six political tactics are common expressions of politics in the workplace:

- *Posturing.* Those who use this tactic look for situations in which they can make a good impression. "One-upmanship" and taking credit for other people's work are included in this category.
- *Empire building.* Gaining and keeping control over human and material resources is the principal motivation behind this tactic. Those with large budgets usually feel more safely entrenched in their positions and believe they have more influence over peers and superiors.
- *Making the supervisor look good.* Traditionally referred to as "apple polishing," this political strategy is prompted by a desire to favorably influence those who control one's career ascent. Anyone with an oversized ego is an easy target for this tactic.
- *Collecting and using social IOUs.* Reciprocal exchange of political favors can be done in two ways: (1) by helping someone look good or (2) by preventing someone from looking bad by ignoring or covering up a mistake. Those who rely on this tactic feel that all favors are coins of exchange rather than expressions of altruism or unselfishness.
- *Creating power and loyalty cliques.* Because there is power in numbers, the idea here is to face superiors and competitors as a cohesive group rather than alone.
- *Engaging in destructive competition.* As a last-ditch effort, some people will resort to character assassination through suggestive remarks, vindictive gossip, or outright lies. This tactic also includes sabotaging the work of a competitor.[37]

Obvious illegalities notwithstanding, one's own values and ethics as well as organizational sanctions are the final arbiters of whether or not these tactics are acceptable. (See Table 14.3 for a practicing manager's advice on how to win at office politics.)

## Antidotes to Political Behavior

Each of the foregoing political tactics varies in degree. The average person will probably acknowledge using at least one of these strategies. But excessive political maneuvering can become a serious threat to productivity when self-interests clearly override the interests of the group or organization. Organizational politics can be kept within reasonable bounds by applying the following five tips:

- Strive for a climate of openness and trust.
- Measure performance results rather than personalities.
- Encourage top management to refrain from exhibiting political behavior that will be imitated by employees.
- Strive to integrate individual and organizational goals through meaningful work and career planning.[38]
- Practice job rotation to encourage broader perspectives and understanding of the problems of others.[39]

**14F**

**Back to the Opening Case**

Which political tactics are most evident in the Enron case? Explain. How could the destructive political infighting been avoided or minimized at Enron?

# Conformity and Groupthink

**conformity** *complying with prevailing role expectations and norms*

**Conformity** means complying with the role expectations and norms perceived by the majority to be appropriate in a particular situation. Conformity enhances predictability, generally thought to be good for rational planning and productive enterprise. How

| **Table 14.3**  One Manager's Rules for Winning at Office Politics |
|---|

1. Find out what the boss expects.

2. Build an information network. Knowledge is power. Identify the people who have power and the extent and direction of it. Title doesn't necessarily reflect actual influence. Find out how the grapevine works. Develop good internal public relations for yourself.

3. Find a mentor. This is a trusted counselor who can be honest with you and help train and guide you to improve your ability and effectiveness as a manager.

4. Don't make enemies without a very good reason.

5. Avoid cliques. Keep circulating in the office.

6. If you must fight, fight over something that is really worth it. Don't lose ground over minor matters or petty differences.

7. Gain power through allies. Build ties that bind. Create IOUs, obligations, and loyalties. Do not be afraid to enlist help from above.

8. Maintain control. Don't misuse your cohorts. Maintain the status and integrity of your allies.

9. Mobilize your forces when necessary. Don't commit your friends without their approval. Be a gracious winner when you do win.

10. Never hire a family member or a close friend.

*Source:* Adapted from David E. Hall, "Winning at Office Politics," *Credit & Financial Management,* 86 (April 1984): 23. Reprinted with permission from *Credit & Financial Management,* copyright April 1984, published by the National Association of Credit Management, 475 Park Avenue South, New York, NY 10016.

can anything be accomplished if people cannot be counted on to perform their assigned duties? On the other hand, why do so many employees actively participate in or passively condone illegal and unethical organizational practices involving discrimination, environmental degradation, accounting fraud, and unfair competition?[40] The answers to these questions lie along a continuum with anarchy at one end and blind conformity at the other. Socially responsible management is anchored to a point somewhere between them.

## Research on Conformity

Social psychologists have discovered much about human behavior by studying individuals and groups in controlled laboratory settings. One classic laboratory study conducted by Solomon Asch was designed to answer the question, How often will an individual take a stand against a unanimous majority that is obviously wrong?[41] Asch's results were both intriguing and unsettling.

**The Hot Seat.**  Asch began his study by assembling groups of seven to nine college students, supposedly to work on a perceptual problem. Actually, though, Asch was studying conformity. All but one member of each group were Asch's confederates, and Asch told them exactly how to behave and what to say. The experiment was really concerned with the reactions of the remaining student—called the naive subject—who didn't know what was going on.

All the students in each group were shown cards with lines similar to those in Figure 14.4. They were instructed to match the line on the left with the one on the right that was closest to it in length. The differences in length among the lines on the right

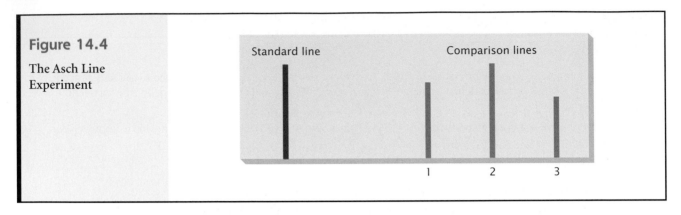

**Figure 14.4**

The Asch Line Experiment

Standard line        Comparison lines

1        2        3

were obvious. Each group went through 12 rounds of the matching process, with a different set of lines for every round. The researcher asked one group member at a time to announce to the group his or her choice. Things proceeded normally for the first two rounds as each group member voiced an opinion. Agreement was unanimous. Suddenly, on the third round only one individual, the naive subject, chose the correct pair of lines. All the other group members chose a different (and obviously wrong) pair. During the rounds in which there was disagreement, all of Asch's confederates conspired to select an incorrect pair of lines. It was the individual versus the rest of the group.

**Following the Immoral Majority.**    Each of the naive subjects was faced with a personal dilemma. Should he or she fight the group or give in to the obviously incorrect choice of the overwhelming majority? Among 31 naive subjects who made a total of 217 judgments, two-thirds of the judgments were correct. The other one-third were incorrect; that is, they were consistent with the majority opinion. Individual differences were great, with some subjects yielding to the incorrect majority opinion more readily than others. *Only 20 percent of the naive subjects remained entirely independent in their judgments.* All the rest turned their backs on their own perceptions and went along with the group at least once. In other words, 80 percent of Asch's subjects knuckled under to the pressure of group opinion at least once, even though they knew the majority was dead wrong.

Replications of Asch's study in the Middle East (Kuwait) and in Japan have demonstrated that this tendency toward conformity is not unique to American culture.[42] Indeed, a recent statistical analysis of 133 Asch conformity studies across 17 countries concluded that blind conformity is a greater problem in collectivist ("we") cultures than in individualist ("me") cultures. Japan is strongly collectivist, whereas the United States and Canada are highly individualistic cultures.[43] (You may find it instructive to ponder how you would act in such a situation.)

Because Asch's study was a contrived laboratory experiment, it failed to probe the relationship between cohesiveness and conformity. Asch's naive subjects were outsiders. But more recent research on "groupthink" has shown that a cohesive group of insiders can fall victim to blind conformity.

**5**  Explain how groupthink can lead to blind conformity.

**groupthink**  *Janis's term for blind conformity in cohesive in-groups*

## Groupthink

After studying the records of several successful and unsuccessful American foreign policy decisions, psychologist Irving Janis uncovered an undesirable by-product of group cohesiveness. He labeled this problem **groupthink** and defined it as a "mode of thinking that people engage in when they are deeply involved in a cohesive in-group, when the members' strivings for unanimity override their motivation to realistically appraise alternative courses of action."[44] Groupthink helps explain how intelligent policymakers, in both government and business, can sometimes make incredibly unwise decisions.

One dramatic result of groupthink in action was the Vietnam War. Strategic advisers in three successive administrations unwittingly rubber-stamped battle plans laced with false assumptions. Critical thinking, reality testing, and moral judgment were temporarily shelved as decisions to escalate the war were enthusiastically railroaded through. Although Janis acknowledges that cohesive groups are not inevitably victimized by groupthink, he warns group decision makers to be alert for the signs of groupthink—the risk is always there.

### Symptoms of Groupthink.
According to Janis, the onset of groupthink is foreshadowed by a definite pattern of symptoms. Among these are excessive optimism, an assumption of inherent morality, suppression of dissent, and an almost desperate quest for unanimity.[45] Given such a decision-making climate, the probability of a poor decision is high. Managers face a curious dilemma here. While a group is still in stage 1 or stage 2 of development, its cohesiveness is too low to get much accomplished because of emotional and time-consuming power struggles. But by the time the group achieves enough cohesiveness in stage 3 to make decisions promptly, the risk of groupthink is high. The trick is to achieve needed cohesiveness without going to the extreme of groupthink.

### Preventing Groupthink.
According to Janis, one of the group members should periodically ask, "Are we allowing ourselves to become victims of groupthink?"[46] More fundamental preventive measures include the following:

- Avoiding the use of groups to rubber-stamp decisions that have already been made by higher management.[47]
- Urging each group member to be a critical evaluator.
- Bringing in outside experts for fresh perspectives.
- Assigning someone the role of devil's advocate to challenge assumptions and alternatives.[48]
- Taking time to consider possible side effects and consequences of alternative courses of action.[49]

Ideally, decision quality improves when these steps become second nature in cohesive groups. But groupthink remains a constant threat in management circles. One major area ripe for abuse is corporate governance. Corporate boards of directors are supposed to represent the interests of stockholders and hold top executives accountable for results. Too often, however, domineering CEOs and pliable boards create the perfect environment for groupthink. For instance, consider the situation at Advanced Micro Devices (AMD), as reported by *Fortune* magazine:

> *AMD's board appears to work not for the shareholders but for CEO and founder Walter Jeremiah Sanders III. Many in Silicon Valley think he should have been replaced long ago; instead the board has given him a remarkable 33-page employment contract. Among many other provisions, it obligates AMD to repay up to $3.5 million Sanders might borrow from anyone for any reason and guarantees him a performance bonus after he's dead.*[50]

Disturbing? Yes. Unusual? Not really, especially when groupthink prevails.

Managers who cannot imagine themselves being victimized by blind conformity are prime candidates for groupthink.[51] Dean Tjosvold of Canada's Simon Fraser University recommends "cooperative conflict" (see Skills & Tools at the end of this chapter). The constructive use of conflict is discussed further in Chapter 16.

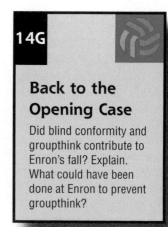

**14G**

**Back to the Opening Case**

Did blind conformity and groupthink contribute to Enron's fall? Explain. What could have been done at Enron to prevent groupthink?

# Teams, Teamwork, and Trust

Ask Gordon Bethune, CEO of Continental Airlines, about the secret to success in his highly competitive industry today and he zeros in on *teamwork:*

> *Running an airline is the biggest team sport there is. It's not an approach, it's not reorganization, and it's not a daily team plan. We are like a wristwatch—lots of different parts, but the whole has value only when we all work together. It has no value when any part fails. So we are not a cross-functional team, we're a company of multi functions that has value when we all work cooperatively—pilots, flight attendants, gate agents, airport agents, mechanics, reservation agents. And not to understand that about doing business means you're going to fail. Lots of people failed because they don't get it.*[52]

Thus, teams and teamwork are vital group dynamics in the modern workplace.[53] Unfortunately, team skills in today's typical organization tend to lag far behind technical skills.[54] It is one thing to be a creative software engineer, for example. It is quite another for that software specialist to be able to team up with other specialists in accounting, finance, and marketing to beat the competition to market with a profitable new product. In this final section, we explore teams and teamwork by discussing cross-functional teams, virtual teams, a model of team effectiveness, and the importance of trust.

## Cross-Functional Teams

**cross-functional team**    *task group staffed with a mix of specialists pursuing a common objective*

A **cross-functional team** is a task group staffed with a mix of specialists focused on a common objective. This structural innovation deserves special attention here because cross-functional teams are becoming commonplace.[55] They may or may not be self-managed, although self-managed teams generally are cross-functional. Cross-

*Talk about teamwork and trust! Lives of the crews and passengers of this Bombardier business jet will depend on how well this Canadian-made cockpit and Irish-made fuselage come together in a Wichita, Kansas, factory. Oh, and let's not forget the other parts shipped in from Austria, Japan, Taiwan, Australia, and Phoenix, Arizona. Teams of engineers from each supplier met with teams of Bombardier's engineers in Montreal, Canada, to develop and refine this incredible global manufacturing puzzle. Excluding the rivets, it takes only a dozen major parts to create a plane, fewer than you'll find in a model airplane kit.*

functional teams are based on assigned rather than voluntary membership. Quality control (QC) circles made up of volunteers, discussed in Chapter 13, technically are in a different category. Cross-functional teams stand in sharp contrast to the tradition of lumping specialists into functional departments, thereby creating the problem of integrating and coordinating those departments. Boeing, for example, relies on cross-functional teams to integrate its various departments to achieve important strategic goals. The giant aircraft manufacturer thus accelerated its product development process for the Boeing 777 jetliner. Also, Boeing engineer Grace Robertson turned to cross-functional teams for faster delivery of a big order of customized jetliners to United Parcel Service:

> When UPS ordered 30 aircraft, Boeing guaranteed that it could design and build a new, all-cargo version of the 767 jet in a mere 33 months—far faster than the usual cycle time of 42 months. The price it quoted meant slashing development costs dramatically.
>
> Robertson's strategy has been to gather all 400 employees working on the new freighter into one location and organize them into "cross-functional" teams. By combining people from the design, planning, manufacturing, and tooling sectors, the teams speed up development and cut costs by enhancing communication and avoiding rework.[56]

## 14H  No Team is an Island

Martha Rogers, partner, Peppers and Rogers Group, Bowling Green, Ohio:

*You can't say, "teams work because of this" or "teams don't work because of that"—because it depends. But if you're looking for one quality that most good teams share, I'd have to say that it's the culture of the company in which the team exists. Is the culture one that rewards groups? Is it one that rewards individuals? Or is it a culture where no one gets rewarded? Look around. Watch how people act and interact, regardless of whether they're on a team. Do people do things for one another? Do they pick up coffee for others when they're going out? If the culture is full of give and take—if it's supportive and trusting—there's a good chance that you'll see successful teams at work.*

**Source:** As quoted in Regina Fazio Maruca, "What Makes Teams Work?" *Fast Company*, no. 40 (November 2000): 109. **www.fastcompany.com.**

**Questions:** *Do you agree? Explain. How can management build a supportive and trusting organizational culture?*

*You want the finest hand-tailored Italian suit? Ciro Paone, founder of Kiton in Naples, Italy, has the right formula. A team of master tailors + 24 hours of labor + lots of passion + love + the finest materials = one suit costing up to $5,000. World-class quality takes incredible talent, teamwork, and dedication to craft. And in this case, it doesn't come cheap!*

This teamwork approach helped Robertson's group stay on schedule and within its budget, both vitally important achievements in Boeing's quest to remain the world's leading aircraft maker.

Cross-functional teams have exciting potential. But they present management with the immense challenge of getting technical specialists to be effective boundary spanners.

## Virtual Teams

**6** Define and discuss the management of virtual teams.

**virtual team**  *task group members from dispersed locations who are electronically linked*

Along with the move toward virtual organizations, discussed in Chapter 10, have come virtual teams. A **virtual team** is a physically dispersed task group linked electronically.[57] Face-to-face contact is usually minimal or nonexistent. E-mail, voice mail, videoconferencing, Web-based project software, and other forms of electronic interchange allow members of virtual teams from anywhere on the planet to accomplish a common goal.[58] It is commonplace today for virtual teams to have members from different organizations, different time zones, and different cultures.[59] Because virtual organizations and teams are so new, paced as they are by emerging technologies, managers are having to learn from the school of hard knocks rather than from established practice.

---

**Table 14.4    It Takes More than E-Mail to Build a Virtual Team**

Teams need a structure to work successfully across time and distance. In *Mastering Virtual Teams: Strategies, Tools, and Techniques That Succeed,* authors Deborah Duarte and Nancy Tennant Snyder list six steps for creating a virtual team, of which each acts as a support beam that helps uphold the structure.

1. **Identify the team's sponsors, stakeholders, and champions.** These are the people who connect the team to the power brokers within the organizations involved.
2. **Develop a team charter that includes its purpose, mission, and goals.** The authors say it's best to do this in a face-to-face meeting that includes the team's leader, management, and other stakeholders.
3. **Select team members.** Most virtual teams have at least three types of members: *core* members who regularly work on the project; *extended* members who provide support and advice; and *ancillary* members who review and approve work.
4. **Contact team members and introduce them to each other.** During this initial meeting, team leaders should make sure members understand why they've been selected, use computers that are compatible, and have a forum in which to ask and get answers to questions. Duarte says leaders should use this time to find out what other projects members are working on. "It's easy to put people on a team when you can't see them," she says. "People don't say 'no,' but then they find themselves on five or six teams and don't have time for any of them."
5. **Conduct a team-orientation session.** This is one of the most important steps. Duarte says an eyeball-to-eyeball meeting is essential, unless team members are working on a very short task or have worked together in another capacity and know each other. "This forms the basis for more natural dialogue later if problems arise," she says. At this getting-to-know-you session, which often includes some type of team-building activity, the leader should provide an overview of the team's charter so members understand the task they are charged with and their roles in achieving it.

   Leaders also should provide guidance in developing team norms. This includes discussing telephone, audio- and videoconference etiquette; establishing guidelines for sending and replying to e-mail and returning phone calls; determining which meetings members must attend in person and which can be done by audio- or videoconference; outlining how work will be reviewed; and discussing how meetings will be scheduled.

   Team leaders also can use this session to decide which technologies the team will use and discuss how members will communicate with each other, with the leader, and with management.
6. **Develop a team process.** Leaders should explain how the team's work will be managed, how information will be stored and shared, and who will review documents and how often.

Duarte says teams that follow these steps often have a better sense of clarity about their goals, the roles of each member, how the work will get done, and how the team will communicate. "They don't feel as though they've been left floating."

---

*Source:*  Kim Kiser, "Building a Virtual Team," *Training,* 36 (March 1999): 34. Reprinted with permission from the March 1999 issue of *Training* magazine. Copyright 1999, Bill Communications, Minneapolis, Minn. All rights reserved. Not for resale.

As discussed in Chapter 10 relative to virtual organizations, one reality of managing virtual teams is clear. *Periodic face-to-face interaction, trust building, and team building are more important than ever when team members are widely dispersed in time and space.* While faceless interaction may work in Internet chat rooms, it can doom a virtual team with a crucial task and pressing deadline. Additionally, special steps need to be taken to clearly communicate role expectations, performance norms, goals, and deadlines (see Table 14.4). Virtual teamwork may be faster than the traditional face-to-face kind, but it is by no means easier[60] (see the Closing Case).

## What Makes Workplace Teams Effective?

Widespread use of team formats—including QC circles, self-managed teams, cross-functional teams, and virtual teams—necessitates greater knowledge of team effectiveness.[61] A model of team effectiveness criteria and determinants is presented in Figure 14.5. This model is the product of two field studies involving 360 new product-development managers employed by 52 high-tech companies.[62] Importantly, it is a generic model, applying equally well to all workplace teams.[63]

**7** Discuss the criteria and determinants of team effectiveness.

The five criteria for effective team performance in the center of Figure 14.5 parallel the criteria for organizational effectiveness discussed in Chapter 9. Thus, team effectiveness feeds organizational effectiveness. For example, if the Boeing 777 product development teams had not been effective, the entire corporation could have stumbled.

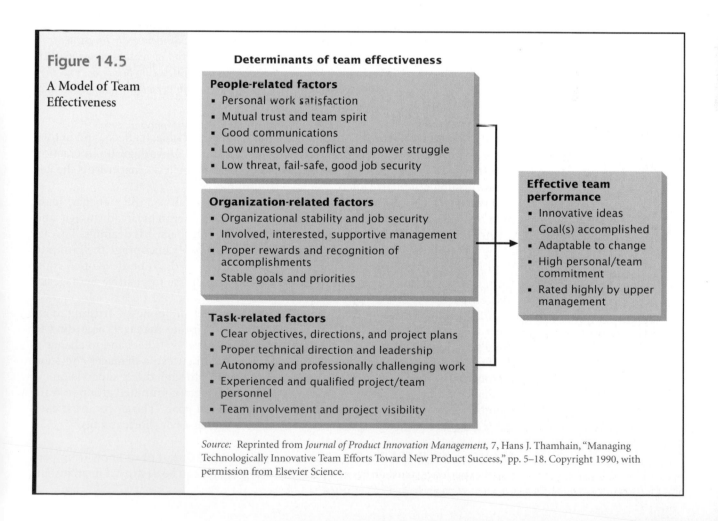

**Figure 14.5**

A Model of Team Effectiveness

**Determinants of team effectiveness**

**People-related factors**
- Personal work satisfaction
- Mutual trust and team spirit
- Good communications
- Low unresolved conflict and power struggle
- Low threat, fail-safe, good job security

**Organization-related factors**
- Organizational stability and job security
- Involved, interested, supportive management
- Proper rewards and recognition of accomplishments
- Stable goals and priorities

**Task-related factors**
- Clear objectives, directions, and project plans
- Proper technical direction and leadership
- Autonomy and professionally challenging work
- Experienced and qualified project/team personnel
- Team involvement and project visibility

**Effective team performance**
- Innovative ideas
- Goal(s) accomplished
- Adaptable to change
- High personal/team commitment
- Rated highly by upper management

*Source:* Reprinted from *Journal of Product Innovation Management*, 7, Hans J. Thamhain, "Managing Technologically Innovative Team Efforts Toward New Product Success," pp. 5–18. Copyright 1990, with permission from Elsevier Science.

Determinants of team effectiveness, shown in Figure 14.5, are grouped into people-, organization-, and task-related factors. Considered separately, these factors involve rather routine aspects of good management. But the collective picture reveals each factor to be part of a complex and interdependent whole. Managers cannot maximize just a few of them, ignore the rest, and hope to have an effective team. In the spirit of the Japanese concept of *kaizen,* managers and team leaders need to strive for "continuous improvement" on all fronts. Because gains on one front will inevitably be offset by losses in another, the pursuit of team effectiveness and teamwork is an endless battle with no guarantees of success.[64]

Let us focus on trust, one of the people-related factors in Figure 14.5 that can make or break work teams.

## Trust: A Key to Team Effectiveness

**trust**  *belief in the integrity, character, or ability of others*

**Trust,** a belief in the integrity, character, or ability of others, is essential if people are to achieve anything together in the long run.[65] Participative management programs are very dependent on trust.[66] Sadly, trust is not one of the hallmarks of the current U.S. business scene. "The distrust is widespread. Only 10% of adults surveyed think corporations can be trusted a great deal to look out for the interests of their employees, according to a *USA Today*/CNN/Gallup poll."[67] To a greater extent than they may initially suspect, managers determine the level of trust in the organization and its component work groups and teams. Experts in the area of social capital tell us:

> No one can manufacture trust or mandate it into existence. When someone says, "You can trust me," we usually don't, and rightly so. But leaders can make deliberate investments in trust. They can give people reasons to trust one another instead of reasons to watch their backs. They can refuse to reward successes that are built on untrusting behavior. And they can display trust and trustworthiness in their own actions, both personally and on behalf of the company.[68]

**8**  Explain why trust is a key ingredient of teamwork and discuss what management can do to build trust.

**Zand's Model of Trust.**    Trust is not a free-floating variable. It affects, and in turn is affected by, other group processes. Dale E. Zand's model of work group interaction puts trust into proper perspective (see Figure 14.6). Zand believes that trust is the key to establishing productive interpersonal relationships.[69]

Primary responsibility for creating a climate of trust falls on the manager. Team members usually look to the manager, who enjoys hierarchical advantage and greater access to key information, to set the tone for interpersonal dealings. Threatening or intimidating actions by the manager will probably encourage the group to bind together in cohesive resistance. Therefore, trust needs to be developed right from the beginning, when team members are still receptive to positive managerial influence.

Trust is initially encouraged by a manager's openness and honesty. Trusting managers talk *with* their people rather than *at* them. A trusting manager, according to Zand's model, demonstrates a willingness to be influenced by others and to change if the facts indicate a change is appropriate. Mutual trust between a manager and team members encourages *self-control,* as opposed to control through direct supervision.

Paradoxically, managerial control actually expands when committed group or team members enjoy greater freedom in pursuing consensual goals. Those who trust each other generally avoid taking advantage of others' weaknesses or shortcomings.[70]

**Six Ways to Build Trust.**    Trust is a fragile thing. As most of us know from personal experience, trust grows at a painfully slow pace yet can be destroyed in an instant

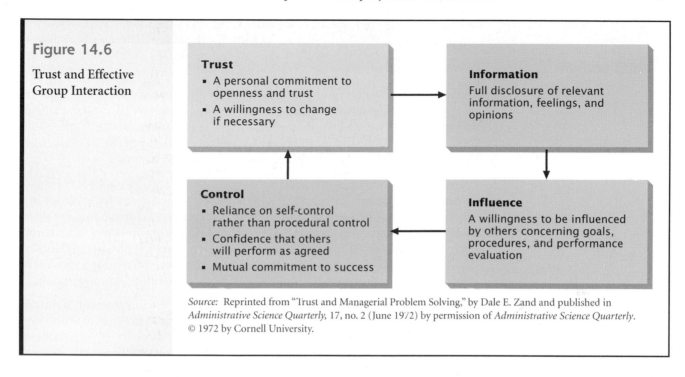

**Figure 14.6**

Trust and Effective Group Interaction

**Trust**
- A personal commitment to openness and trust
- A willingness to change if necessary

**Information**
Full disclosure of relevant information, feelings, and opinions

**Control**
- Reliance on self-control rather than procedural control
- Confidence that others will perform as agreed
- Mutual commitment to success

**Influence**
A willingness to be influenced by others concerning goals, procedures, and performance evaluation

*Source:* Reprinted from "Trust and Managerial Problem Solving," by Dale E. Zand and published in *Administrative Science Quarterly*, 17, no. 2 (June 1972) by permission of *Administrative Science Quarterly*. © 1972 by Cornell University.

with a thoughtless remark. Mistrust can erode the long-term effectiveness of work teams and organizations. According to management professor and consultant Fernando Bartolomé, managers need to concentrate on six areas: communication, support, respect, fairness, predictability, and competence.

- *Communication.* Keep your people informed by providing accurate and timely feedback and explaining policies and decisions. Be open and honest about your own problems. Do not hoard information or use it as a political device or reward.
- *Support.* Be an approachable person who is available to help, encourage, and coach your people. Show an active interest in their lives and be willing to come to their defense.
- *Respect.* Delegating important duties is the sincerest form of respect, followed closely by being a good listener.
- *Fairness.* Evaluate your people fairly and objectively and be liberal in giving credit and praise.
- *Predictability.* Be dependable and consistent in your behavior and keep all your promises.
- *Competence.* Be a good role model by exercising good business judgment and being technically and professionally competent.[71]

Managers find that trust begets trust. In other words, those who feel they are trusted tend to trust others in return.[72]

**14I   The Truth About Trust**

*A few weeks ago I asked a group of consumer affairs professionals two questions: Do you trust the organization you work for? What can your leadership do to repair your confidence in themselves and the organization?*

*To the first query, as you might expect, the news wasn't good. Trust, they said, is sea-floor low. To the second question, their answers were more encouraging than I'd expected. "Tell the truth," one piped up—to a chorus of agreement.*

*"Talk to us, communicate, level with us," another offered—to more "Amens."*

**Source:** Ron Zemke, "Trust Inspires Trust," *Training*, 39 (January 2002): 10.

**Questions:** *So why don't managers follow this commonsense advice to "simply tell the truth"? What steps need to be taken to improve the situation?*

# Summary

1. Managers need a working understanding of group dynamics because groups are the basic building blocks of organizations. Generating social capital through strong, constructive, and win-win relationships is essential to success today. Both informal (friendship) and formal (work) groups are made up of two or more freely interacting individuals who have a common identity and purpose.

2. After someone has been attracted to a group, cohesiveness—a "we" feeling—encourages continued membership. Roles are social expectations for behavior in a specific position, whereas norms are more general standards for conduct in a given social setting. Norms are enforced because they help the group survive, clarify role expectations, protect self-images, and enhance the group's identity by emphasizing key values. Compliance with role expectations and norms is rewarded with social reinforcement; noncompliance is punished by criticism, ridicule, and ostracism.

3. Mature groups are characterized by mutual acceptance, encouragement of minority opinion, and minimal emotional conflict. They are the product of a developmental process with identifiable stages. During the first three stages—orientation, conflict and challenge, and cohesion—power and authority problems are resolved. Groups are faced with the obstacle of uncertainty over interpersonal relations during the last three stages—delusion, disillusion, and acceptance. Committees have a widespread reputation for inefficiency and ineffectiveness because they tend to get stalled in an early stage of group development.

4. Organizational politics centers on the pursuit of self-interest. Research shows greater political activity to be associated with higher levels of management, larger organizations, staff and marketing personnel, and reorganizations. Political tactics such as posturing, empire building, making the boss look good, collecting and using social IOUs, creating power and loyalty cliques, and engaging in destructive competition need to be kept in check if the organization is to be effective.

5. Although a fairly high degree of conformity is necessary if organizations and society in general are to function properly, blind conformity is ultimately dehumanizing and destructive. Research shows that individuals have a strong tendency to bend to the will of the majority, even if the majority is clearly wrong. Cohesive decision-making groups can be victimized by groupthink when unanimity becomes more important than critical evaluation of alternative courses of action.

6. Teams are becoming the structural format of choice. Today's employees generally have better technical skills than team skills. Cross-functional teams are particularly promising because they enable greater strategic speed. Although members of virtual teams by definition collaborate via electronic media, there is still a need for periodic face-to-face interaction and team building. Three sets of factors—relating to people, organization, and task—combine to determine the effectiveness of a work team.

7. Trust, a key ingredient of effective teamwork, is disturbingly low in the American workplace today. When work group members trust one another, there will be a more active exchange of information, more interpersonal influence, and hence greater self-control. Managers can build trust through communication, support, respect (primarily in the form of delegation), fairness, predictability, and competence.

# Skills & Tools

## How to Use *Cooperative Conflict* to Avoid Groupthink

### Guides for Action

- Elaborate positions and ideas.
- List facts, information, and theories.
- Ask for clarification.
- Clarify opposing ideas.
- Search for new information.
- Challenge opposing ideas and positions.
- Reaffirm your confidence in those who differ.
- Listen to all ideas.
- Restate opposing arguments that are unclear.
- Identify strengths in opposing arguments.
- Change your mind only when confronted with good evidence.
- Integrate various information and reasoning.
- Create alternative solutions.
- Agree to a solution responsive to several points of view.
- Use a new round of cooperative conflict to develop and refine the solution.

### Pitfalls to Avoid

- Assume your position is superior.
- Prove your ideas are right and must be accepted.

- Interpret opposition to your ideas as a personal attack.

- Refuse to admit weaknesses in your position.

- Pretend to listen.

- Ridicule to weaken the others' resolve to disagree.

- Try to win over people to your position through charm and exaggeration.

- See accepting another's ideas as a sign of weakness.

*Source:* Reprinted from *Learning to Manage Conflict: Getting People to Work Together Productively* by Dean Tjosvold. Copyright © 1993 Dean Tjosvold. First published by Lexington Books. All rights reserved. All correspondence should be sent to Lexington Books, 4720 Boston Way, Lanham, Md., 20706.

## Hands-On Exercise

### Management Teamwork Survey

**Instructions**

Think of your present job (or a past one) and check one box for each of the following 10 questions. Alternatively, you can ask a manager to complete this survey. The idea is to assess the organization's commitment to building cooperation and teamwork among managers. This instrument also pinpoints weak spots needing attention.

| TO WHAT EXTENT DO ... | Never | To a Limited Extent | To a Great Extent | Always |
|---|---|---|---|---|
| **1.** Our managers pursue common goals that focus on our customers and profitability? | ☐ | ☐ | ☐ | ☐ |
| **2.** We have team-based performance measurements and feedback devices? | ☐ | ☐ | ☐ | ☐ |
| **3.** Our top managers demonstrate and foster cooperation in their approach to leadership? | ☐ | ☐ | ☐ | ☐ |
| **4.** We provide incentives and rewards that encourage management cooperation? | ☐ | ☐ | ☐ | ☐ |
| **5.** We engage in ongoing team building activities and skill development among our managers? | ☐ | ☐ | ☐ | ☐ |
| **6.** We identify and resolve problems/ conflicts among managers in a timely fashion? | ☐ | ☐ | ☐ | ☐ |
| **7.** We create management team ownership of decision processes and outcomes? | ☐ | ☐ | ☐ | ☐ |

**8.** We clarify each manager's roles and goals to each other? ☐ ☐ ☐ ☐

**9.** We integrate planning, problem-solving, and communication activities among managers? ☐ ☐ ☐ ☐

**10.** We build consensus and understanding around work processes and systems? ☐ ☐ ☐ ☐

**Interpretation**

Scores in Columns 1 and 2 represent areas that damage management cooperation and teamwork; these areas should be systematically addressed to enhance organizational performance. Scores in Columns 3 and 4 represent practices that can and should be continued and improved to increase management cooperation and teamwork.

**For Consideration/Discussion**

**1.** Why are cooperation and teamwork among managers so important today?

**2.** Overall, how does this organization measure up in terms of fostering managerial cooperation and teamwork?

**3.** Which areas are strongest? How can they be made even stronger?

**4.** Which areas are weakest and what needs to be done?

**5.** Which factors in this survey are most critical to organizational success today? Explain.

*Source:* Clinton O. Longenecker and Mitchell Neubert, "Barriers and Gateways to Management Cooperation and Teamwork," reprinted with permission from *Business Horizons*, 43 (September–October 2000). Copyright 2000 by the Trustees of Indiana University, Kelley School of Business.

# Internet Exercises

**1. What's new with teams and teamwork?** Things are changing rapidly in this area because teams have become such an important part of organizational life. Lots of new ideas can be found on the Internet for those willing to search a bit. Here is a way to jump-start your Web search for updates on teams and teamwork. Go to *Fast Company* magazine's excellent Web site (**www.fastcompany.com**) and click on "Themes" under the main menu tab "Magazine." At the Themes page, select the category "Teamwork." Read at least two of the full-text articles, with the goal of picking up at least three good ideas about managing workplace teams. You may have to select and read additional articles if you don't find enough good ideas right away. *Note:* You may want to make hard copies of the articles you selected and notes of your good ideas for possible class discussion.

*Learning Points:* 1. Why did you select those particular articles? 2. Among your "good ideas" about managing teams, which idea stands out as the best? Why? 3. Did other class members tend to focus on the same (or different) articles and ideas as you? 4. When comparing notes with your classmates, which of their "good ideas" are superior to the ones on your list?

**2.** **Getting "street smart" about organizational politics:** Ethical managers today play clean in the game of business but are street smart enough to avoid getting hurt by those who fight dirty. For good background reading, go back to *Fast Company* magazine's home page and click on "Dynamic Archives" under the "Magazine" tab. Scroll down to the April–May 1998 issue (no. 14). From the table of contents for that issue, select and read the articles titled "The Bad Guy's (and Gal's) Guide to Office Politics" and "The Good Guy's (and Gal's) Guide to Office Politics." Also look up Polly LaBarre's article, "The New Face of Office Politics," in the October 1999 issue (no. 28). While you're in *Fast Company*'s online archives, you may want to search recent issues for articles relating to organizational and office politics.

    *Learning Points:* 1. Why is it fair to say organizational politics can be both good and bad? 2. What new ideas or useful tips did you learn about workplace politics? 3. Is political maneuvering an inescapable part of life on the job? Explain. 4. Is organizational politics a fun (or distasteful) aspect of organizational life for you? Explain. 5. Why is it important to know about political tactics in the workplace even if you don't enjoy engaging in them?

**3.** **Check it out:** Are you a team player or a solo act? Which of your team skills need polishing? Find out by taking the free 8-item quiz at **www.project-manager.com.** At the home page, click on the box "Direct to P-M's Site Map" and then scroll down to the heading "3.0) PERSONAL SKILLS." Click on that heading and then select the link "*Quiz 1.*" Simply follow the instructions and scoring procedure.

For updates to these exercises, visit our Web site (**http://business.college.hmco. com/students**).

# Closing Case

## Thirteen Time Zones Can't Keep Lucent's Virtual Team from Succeeding

Imagine designing the most complex product in your company's history. You need 500 engineers for the job. They will assemble the world's most delicate hardware and write more than a million lines of code. In communicating, the margin for error is minuscule.

Now, scatter those 500 engineers over 13 time zones. Over three continents. Over five states in the United States alone. The Germans schedule to perfection. The Americans work on the fly. In Massachusetts, they go to work early. In New Jersey, they stay late.

*Source:* Republished with permission of *The Wall Street Journal* from "With the Stakes High, a Lucent Duo Conquers Distance and Culture," by Thomas Petzinger Jr., *The Wall Street Journal* (April 23, 1999). Permission conveyed through Copyright Clearance Center, Inc.

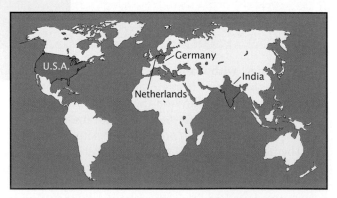

Now you have some idea of what Bill Klinger and Frank Polito have been through in the past 18 months. As top software-development managers in Lucent Technologies' Bell Labs division, they played critical roles in creating a new fiber-optic phone switch called the Bandwidth Manager, which sells for about $1 million. . . . The high-stakes development was Lucent's most complex undertaking by far since its spin-off from AT&T in 1996.

Managing such a far-flung staff ("distributed development," it's called) is possible only because of technology. But as the two Lucent leaders painfully learned, distance still magnifies differences, even in a high-tech age. "You lose informal interaction—going to lunch, the water cooler," Mr. Klinger says. "You can never discount how many issues get solved that way."

The product grew as a hybrid of exotic, widely dispersed technologies: "lightwave" science from Lucent's Merrimack Valley plant, north of Boston, where Mr. Polito works; "cross-connect" products here in New Jersey, where Mr. Klinger works; timing devices from the Netherlands; and optics from Germany.

Development also demanded multiple locations because Lucent wanted a core model as a platform for special versions for foreign and other niche markets. Involving overseas engineers in the flagship product would speed the later development of spin-offs and impress foreign customers.

And rushing to market meant tapping software talent wherever it was available—ultimately at Lucent facilities in Colorado, Illinois, North Carolina, and India. "The scary thing, scary but exciting, was that no one had really pulled this off on this scale before," says Mr. Polito.

Communication technology was the easy part. Lashing together big computers in different cities assured everyone was working on the same up-to-date software version. New project data from one city were instantly available on Web pages everywhere else. Test engineers in India could tweak prototypes in New Jersey. The project never went to sleep.

Technology, however, couldn't conquer cultural problems, especially acute between Messrs. Klinger's and Polito's respective staffs in New Jersey and Massachusetts. Each had its own programming traditions and product histories. Such basic words as "test" could mean different things. A programming chore requiring days in one context might take weeks in another. Differing work schedules and physical distance made each location suspect the other of slacking off. "We had such clashes," says Mr. Klinger.

Personality tests revealed deep geographic differences. Supervisors from the sleek, glass-covered New Jersey office, principally a research facility abounding in academics, scored as "thinking" people who used cause-and-effect analysis. Those from the old, brick facility in Massachusetts, mainly a manufacturing plant, scored as "feeling" types who based decisions on subjective, human values. Sheer awareness of the differences ("Now I know why you get on my nerves!") began to create common ground.

Amid much cynicism, the two directors hauled their technical managers into team exercises—working in small groups to scale a 14-foot wall and solve puzzles. It's corny, but such methods can accelerate trust building when time is short and the stakes are high. At one point Mr. Klinger asked managers to show up with the product manuals from their previous projects—then, in a ritualistic break from technical parochialism, instructed everyone to tear the covers to pieces.

More than anything else, it was sheer physical presence—face time—that began solidifying the group. Dozens of managers began meeting fortnightly in rotating cities, socializing as much time as their technical discussions permitted. (How better to grow familiar than over hot dogs, beer, and nine innings with the minor league Durham Bulls?) Foreign locations found the direct interaction especially valuable. "Going into the other culture is the only way to understand it," says Sigrid Hauenstein, a Lucent executive in Nuremberg, Germany. "If you don't have a common understanding, it's much more expensive to correct it later."

Eventually the project found its pace. People began wearing beepers to eliminate time wasted on voice-mail tag. Conference calls at varying levels kept everyone in the loop. Staffers posted their photos in the project's Web directory. Many created personal pages. "It's the ultimate democracy of the Web," Mr. Klinger says.

The product is now shipping—on schedule, within budget, and with more technical versatility than Lucent expected. Distributed development "paid off in spades," says Gerry Butters, Lucent optical-networking chief.

Even as it helps build the infrastructure of a digitally connected planet, Lucent is rediscovering the importance of face-to-face interaction. All the bandwidth in the world can convey only a fraction of what we are.

## For Discussion

1. Which team effectiveness criteria in Figure 14.5 are apparent in this case?

2. How big a problem do you suppose organizational politics was during this project? Explain.

3. What practical lessons does this case teach managers about managing a virtual team?

4. Would you be comfortable working on this sort of global virtual team? Explain.

## chapter fifteen

# Influence Processes and Leadership

> *"* The leader now is someone who con-
> nects, informs, and engages people. *"*
>
> Mary Boone
>
> *"* The role of a leader is to define reality
> and to give hope. *"*
>
> Kenneth I. Chenault

## CHAPTER OBJECTIVES

*When you finish studying this chapter you should be able to*

**1** **Identify** and **describe** eight generic influence tactics used in modern organizations.

**2** **Identify** the five bases of power and **explain** what it takes to make empowerment work.

**3** **Explain** the concept of emotional intelligence in terms of Goleman's four leadership traits.

**4** **Summarize** what the Ohio State model and the Leadership Grid® have taught managers about leadership.

**5** **Describe** the path-goal theory of leadership and **explain** how the assumption on which it is based differs from the assumption on which Fiedler's contingency theory is based.

**6** **Explain** Greenleaf's philosophy of the servant leader.

**7** **Identify** the two key functions that mentors perform and **explain** how a mentor can develop a junior manager's leadership skills.

**8** **Explain** the management of antecedents and consequences in behavior modification.

# Pat Carmichael, a Mentor You Can Bank On

Companies have tried all sorts of things to improve corporate life for minority employees. Many efforts fail, but one approach has proved so successful that it should be a staple at every concerned firm: mentoring. Why are mentors effective? For starters, employees of color have a crying need for the guidance senior people can provide. A study by Korn/Ferry International and the Columbia Business School found that 80% of high-level minority executives lack formal mentors to help chart their careers; nearly a third don't even have informal guides—and these are minority executives who have "made it."

To find out how mentoring can be effective in retaining and promoting minorities, we got to know Pat Carmichael at banking giant J. P. Morgan Chase. J. P. Morgan and Chase both had mentoring programs before their merger, and now every business unit at the combined company sponsors several. Carmichael has mentored hundreds, both formally and informally, over her 30-year banking career. Currently she boasts a roster of about ten "mentees"—people she talks to at least once a month. She's worked with people of all races—including whites. One of her current charges, John Imperiale, is a 25-year-old white assistant branch manager from Glendale, N.Y.

We'll get back to Imperiale in a moment. First, a few reasons Carmichael, 48, is such a terrific mentor. For one, she has an important job—she is a senior vice president overseeing Chase branches in Queens and Long Island. That alone makes her a role model. And she has three decades of experience to draw on when she counsels minorities. Carmichael advises them to ask for tough assignments—and feedback. "Minority employees have to take the initiative and say to their bosses, 'What do I need to do to grow?'" she says. All too often, Carmichael says, bosses hesitate to give constructive criticism for fear of appearing biased.

Carmichael is also a consummate networker, introducing her protégés to key executives—especially other minorities. "Pat has increased my access to other African Americans in senior roles such that I don't ever need to make a cold call," says Dinah Moore, a 43-year-old senior vice president in one of the bank's technology groups. How powerful has mentoring been for Moore? "[It's] one of the components that has kept me at Chase," she says.

Carmichael started as a teller at Chemical Bank (later purchased by Chase) in the early 1970s. It's no surprise, given the era, that her own mentors were white males. She speaks fondly of Bob Como, now a vice president in J. P. Morgan Chase's middle-markets group. When she started as Como's deputy, Carmichael was "a shy, skinny kid" who sat in the back during meetings. Como pushed her to voice her ideas and lead discussions.

That's part of the reason Carmichael now mentors a number of nonminorities, include Imperiale. Her motives aren't entirely colorblind. "My hope is that the exposure John has to me will give him insights when he's managing a diverse group of employees," she says. But there's more to the relationship than race: It was Carmichael who encouraged Imperiale—a quiet young man who feels most comfortable analyzing numbers—to broaden his experience with a stint managing a bank branch.

For all her efforts to be inclusive, Carmichael still feels a special obligation toward minorities. "When you go to meetings and don't see people who look like you, you start to wonder why that is," she says. "And how do I get involved so that when I leave, that isn't the case?" Thanks to her work—and the bank's support—it's changing already.

W hat do the following situations have in common?

- A magazine editor praises her supervisor's new outfit shortly before asking for the afternoon off.
- A milling-machine operator tells a friend that he will return the favor if his friend will watch out for the supervisor while he takes an unauthorized cigarette break.
- An office manager attempts to head off opposition to a new Internet-use policy by carefully explaining how it will be fair and will increase productivity.

Aside from the fact that all of these situations take place on the job, the common denominator is "influence." In each case, someone is trying to get his or her own way by influencing someone else's behavior. J. P. Morgan Chase's Pat Carmichael is an inspiring role model for the skillful and responsible use of influence, power, and leadership.

**influence** *any attempt to change another's behavior*

   **Influence** is any attempt by a person to change the behavior of superiors, peers, or lower-level employees. Influence is not inherently good or bad. As the foregoing situations illustrate, influence can be used for purely selfish reasons, to subvert organizational objectives, or to enhance organizational effectiveness. Managerial success is firmly linked to the ability to exercise the right sort of influence at the right time.[1]

   The purpose of this chapter is to examine different approaches to influencing others. We focus specifically on influence tactics, power, leadership, mentoring, and behavior modification.

*You might say Jamaican-born Michael Lee-Chin is a world-class expert on influence. After all, he turned a $150,000 investment in AIC Ltd., a Canadian mutual fund company, into a financial services giant with $9.5 billion under management. His personal net worth has grown to $1.1 billion. He is a master at earning people's trust; enough trust to have them turn over their life savings to be managed by AIC. If Lee-Chin can't win over new clients, then perhaps the two parrots in his corporate lobby can do the trick. They've been trained to say "Buy" and "Hold."*

# Influence Tactics in the Workplace

A replication and refinement of an earlier groundbreaking study provides useful insights about on-the-job influence.[2] Both studies asked employees basically the same question: "How do you get your boss, coworker, or subordinate to do something you want?" The following eight generic influence tactics emerged:

1. *Consultation.* Seeking someone's participation in a decision or change
2. *Rational persuasion.* Trying to convince someone by relying on a detailed plan, supporting information, reasoning, or logic
3. *Inspirational appeals.* Appealing to someone's emotions, values, or ideals to generate enthusiasm and confidence
4. *Ingratiating tactics.* Making someone feel important or good before making a request; acting humble or friendly before making a request
5. *Coalition tactics.* Seeking the aid of others to persuade someone to agree
6. *Pressure tactics.* Relying on intimidation, demands, or threats to gain compliance or support
7. *Upward appeals.* Obtaining formal or informal support of higher management
8. *Exchange tactics.* Offering an exchange of favors; reminding someone of a past favor; offering to make a personal sacrifice[3]

These influence tactics are *generic* because they are used by various organizational members to influence lower-level employees (downward influence), peers (lateral influence), or superiors (upward influence). Table 15.1 indicates what the researchers found out about patterns of use for the three different directions of influence. Notice how consultation, rational persuasion, and inspirational appeals were the three most popular tactics, regardless of the direction of influence. Meanwhile, pressure tactics, upward appeals, and exchange tactics consistently were the least used influence tactics. Ingratiating and coalition tactics fell in the midrange of use. This is an encouraging

**1** Identify and describe eight generic influence tactics used in modern organizations.

**Table 15.1**    Use of Generic Organizational Influence Tactics

| Tactic | Downward | Lateral | Upward |
|---|---|---|---|
| Consultation | 1 | 1 | 2 |
| Rational persuasion | 2 | 2 | 1 |
| Inspirational appeals | 3 | 3 | 3 |
| Ingratiating tactics | 4 | 4 | 5 |
| Coalition tactics | 5 | 5 | 4 |
| Pressure tactics | 6 | 7 | 7 |
| Upward appeals | 7 | 6 | 6 |
| Exchange tactics | 8 | 8 | 8 |

Rank order (by direction of influence)

*Source:* Adapted from discussion in Gary Yukl and Cecilia M. Falbe, "Influence Tactics and Objectives in Upward, Downward, and Lateral Influence Attempts," *Journal of Applied Psychology,* 75 (April 1990): 132–140.

## 15A   Are You a Control Freak?

*The theme song of the control freak should be* I Did It My Way (and You Will, Too) *[author Les] Parrott says. . . .*

*Readers wrote him tales about their least-favorite type: the control freak. . . .*

*They object to what Parrott calls the tools of the control trade: "showing false friendliness, giving expensive gifts, making empty promises, sulking, shouting, nagging, being chronically late, withholding affection, bullying, badgering, or just plain bossing the people around them."*

**Source:** Karen S. Peterson, "In Charge . . . and Out of Control," *USA Today* (July 31, 2000): 6D.

**Questions:** *Sound like anyone you know? What lessons about influence do control freaks need to learn?*

For further information about the interactive annotations in this chapter, visit our Web site (http://business.college.hmco.com/students).

pattern from the standpoint of getting things done through problem solving rather than through intimidation and conflict.

Do women and men tend to rely on different influence tactics? Available research evidence reveals no systematic gender-based differences relative to influencing others.[4] In contrast, influence tactics used by employees to influence their bosses were found to vary with different leadership styles. Employees influencing authoritarian managers tended to rely on ingratiating tactics and upward appeals. Rational persuasion was used most often to influence participative managers.[5]

# Power

Power is inevitable in modern organizations. According to one advocate of the positive and constructive use of power:

> *Power must be used because managers must influence those they depend on. Power also is crucial in the development of managers' self-confidence and willingness to support subordinates. From this perspective, power should be accepted as a natural part of any organization. Managers should recognize and develop their own power to coordinate and support the work of subordinates; it is powerlessness, not power, that undermines organizational effectiveness.[6]*

As a manager, if you understand power, its bases, and empowerment, you will have an advantage when it comes to getting things accomplished with and through others.[7]

## What Is Power?

**power**   *ability to marshal resources to get something done*

**Power** is "the ability to marshal the human, informational, and material resources to get something done."[8] Power affects organizational members in the following three areas:

1. *Decisions.* A packaging engineer decides to take on a difficult new assignment after hearing her boss's recommendations.
2. *Behavior.* A hospital lab technician achieves a month of perfect attendance after receiving a written warning about absenteeism from his supervisor.
3. *Situations.* The productivity of a product design group increases dramatically following the purchase of project management software.[9]

Another instructive way of looking at power is to distinguish between "power over" (ability to dominate), "power to" (ability to act freely), and "power from" (ability to resist the demands of others).[10]

By emphasizing the word *ability* in our definition and discussion of power, we can contrast power with authority. As defined in Chapter 9, authority is the "right" to direct the activities of others.[11] Authority is an officially sanctioned privilege that may or may not get results. In contrast, power is the demonstrated *ability* to get results. As illustrated in Figure 15.1, one may possess authority but have no power, possess no authority yet have power, or possess both authority and power. The first situation, authority

## 15B  Authority to Do What?

*The secret of today's most successful power players: They are candid about what their formal authority is, bring it out into the open, and give it away.*

**Source:** Thomas A. Stewart, "Get with the *New* Power Game," *Fortune* (January 13, 1997): 60.

**Questions:** *How does this perspective differ from traditional beliefs about managerial power? Why wouldn't a manager who adopted this approach to power be considered weak and ineffective?*

but no power, was experienced by Albanian police in 1997, when Europe's poorest nation fell into anarchy over dissatisfaction with a corrupt government. According to *Newsweek,* "An angry mob surrounded one group of police, stripped them to their underpants, and burned their gear."[12] At the other end of the model in Figure 15.1, power but no authority can occur. For example, employees may respond to the wishes of the supervisor's spouse.[13] Finally, a manager who gets employees to work hard on an important project has both authority and power.

## The Five Bases of Power

Essential to the successful use of power in organizations is an understanding of the various bases of power. One widely cited classification of power bases identifies five types of power: reward, coercive, legitimate, referent, and expert.[14]

**2** Identify the five bases of power and explain what it takes to make empowerment work.

**Reward Power.**   One's ability to grant rewards to those who comply with a command or request is the key to **reward power.** Management's reward power can be strengthened by linking pay raises, merit pay, and promotions to job performance. Sought-after expressions of friendship or trust also enhance reward power.

**reward power**  *gaining compliance through rewards*

**Coercive Power.**   Rooted in fear, **coercive power** is based on threatened or actual punishment. For example, a manager might threaten a habitually tardy employee with a demotion if he or she is late one more time.

**coercive power**  *gaining compliance through threats or punishment*

**Figure 15.1**

The Relationship Between Authority and Power

**Authority but no power**
The *right* but not the *ability* to get subordinates to do things

**Authority plus power**
The *right* and the *ability* to get subordinates to do things

**Power but no authority**
The *ability* but not the *right* to get other people to do things

**legitimate power**  *compliance based on one's formal position*

## Legitimate Power.

**Legitimate power** is achieved when a person's superior position alone prompts another person to act in a desired manner. This type of power closely parallels formal authority, as discussed above. Parents, teachers, religious leaders, and managers who demand obedience by virtue of their superior social position are attempting to exercise legitimate power. Note, however, the following warning about legitimate power:

> *Trying to control others solely by directing them and on the basis of the power associated with one's position simply will not work—first, because managers are always dependent on some people over whom they have no formal authority, and second, because virtually no one in modern organizations will passively accept and completely obey a constant stream of orders from someone just because he or she is the "boss."*[15]

One might reasonably conclude that legitimate power has been eroded by its frequent abuse (or overuse) through the years.[16]

**referent power**  *compliance based on charisma or personal identification*

## Referent Power.

An individual has **referent power** over those who identify with him or her if they comply on that basis alone. Personal attraction is an elusive thing to define, let alone consciously cultivate. *Charisma* is a term often used in conjunction with referent power. Although leaders with the personal magnetism of Abraham Lincoln, John Kennedy, or Martin Luther King Jr., are always in short supply, charisma in the workplace can be problematic. *Fortune* magazine offered this perspective:

> *Used wisely, it's a blessing. Indulged, it can be a curse. Charismatic visionaries lead people ahead—and sometimes astray. They can be impetuous, unpredictable, and exasperating to work for, like [media mogul Ted] Turner. [Donald] Trump. Steve Jobs. Ross Perot. Lee*

"Of course, that's only a suggestion. You're all free to ignore it and resign."

*Iacocca. "Often what begins as a mission becomes an obsession," says John Thompson, president of Human Factors, a leadership consulting service in San Rafael, California. "Leaders can cut corners on values and become driven by self-interest. Then they may abuse anyone who makes a mistake."*

*Like pornography, charisma is hard to define. But you know it when you see it. And you don't see much of it in the* Fortune 500.[17]

Still, as we will see in our discussion of transformational leadership later in this chapter, charisma does have its positive side.

**Expert Power.** Those who possess and can dispense valued information generally exercise **expert power** over those in need of such information. Information technology experts, for instance, are in a position today to wield a great deal of expert power. Anyone who has ever been taken advantage of by an unscrupulous automobile mechanic knows what expert power in the wrong hands can mean.

**expert power** *compliance based on ability to dispense valued information*

# Empowerment

**Empowerment** occurs when employees are adequately trained, provided with all relevant information and the best possible tools, fully involved in key decisions, and fairly rewarded for results.[18] Those who endorse this key building block of progressive management view power as an unlimited resource. Frances Hesselbein, a widely respected former head of the Girl Scouts of the USA, offered this perspective: "The more power you give away, the more you have."[19] This can be a difficult concept to grasp for traditional authoritarian managers who see empowerment as a threat to their authority and feeling of being in control. Today, the issue is not empowerment versus no empowerment. Rather, the issue is how empowerment should take place. As indicated in Skills & Tools at the end of this chapter, employee empowerment is like a seed requiring favorable growing conditions (see The Global Manager). Much of the burden for successful empowerment falls on the *individual*. No amount of empowerment and supportive management can overcome dishonesty, untrustworthiness, selfishness, and inadequate skills.[20] Moreover, as we learned in the Enron case, empowerment without proper oversight can lead to very bad consequences.

**15C Empowerment in Action**

Ron Ferner, former Campbell's Soup Co. vice president:

*One time a packaging team in Sacramento was having problems with boxes breaking. Some of us managers started talking to them about what the problems were and realized they really had a good handle on what was wrong. So we said, "Why don't you guys call the supplier?" Then we called the supplier to tell them they would be hearing from our crew, and they said, "Why not have them talk directly to our hourly employees?"*

*If the managers alone had tried to solve this problem, it would have gone on forever. Instead, we rented a van, sent our people over, and solved the whole thing. Afterward, we had a party. It gave the workers great confidence.*

**Source:** As quoted in Thea Singer, "Share It All with Employees, Soup to Nuts," *Inc.* Tech, no. 1 (1999): 48.

**Questions:** *Why do many managers who say they believe in empowering employees fail to do it? Can empowerment be carried too far? Explain.*

*Young people, many just out of undergraduate or MBA programs, were handed extraordinary authority, able to make $5 million decisions without higher approval. . . .*

*At Enron, however, the pressure to make the numbers often overwhelmed the pretext of "tight" controls. "The environment was ripe for abuse," says a former manager in Enron's energy services unit. "Nobody at corporate was asking the right questions. It was completely hands-off management. A situation like that requires tight controls. Instead, it was a runaway train."[21]*

**empowerment** *making employees full partners in the decision-making process and giving them the necessary tools and rewards*

# The Global Manager

## Lessons in Empowerment from Germany's Siemens

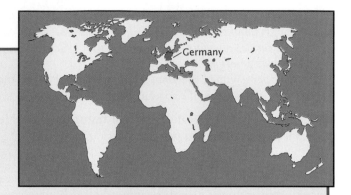

A start-up company that needs entrepreneurial managers can go out and hire them as it builds its organization. By contrast, established companies like Siemens, a worldwide provider of everything from mobile phones to gas turbines, already have tens of thousands of managers around the world and have no choice but to find ways to make its old managers into new ones. So collaboration became the central goal of an in-house management development program at Siemens. The program was created for all managers in the late 1990s.

Many companies have established "active learning" curricula focused on the study of cases and other real-life problems. But we realized that changing people's behavior is less about intellectual learning than it is about blasting them loose from nearly impenetrable, self-imposed—and often company-rewarded—boundaries. We started our people off with some classroom teaching, but the bulk of the program put them in teams working on actual projects.

These "business impact projects" had to show measurable results and typically lasted about four months. It wasn't enough for a team to recommend a new marketing strategy or propose a new procedure for product development. We didn't want the end result to be a paper no one would read. Instead, we wanted people to get their hands dirty in the real work of organizational maneuvering and achievement.

Once a team settled on an opportunity to pursue, they had to recruit a "coach," usually a high-level executive in the business area that the team was focusing on. Execu-

tives were free to decline these requests; some teams had to try several times before landing their coaches....

In each case, it helped that the teams consisted of people from different product areas, functions, and geographies. But diverse teammates and their existing contact networks weren't enough; the projects wouldn't work without each team figuring out how to win support from people who had little interest in—or who even feel threatened by—the team's efforts.

In interviews after the projects ended, nearly all the participants reported a new perspective on their organizational comfort zones.

At first, they said, they had felt liberated by their status in the program—as though they were immune from risk. But in retrospect, they came to understand that the program conferred no special status on them at all; their previous hesitation toward risk-taking had been largely self-imposed. The management program had given them the unique sense of "permission" to venture that they had actually had all along.

*Source:* Reprinted by permission of *Harvard Business Review*. Excerpt from "Freeing Managers to Innovate," by Matthias Bellmann and Robert H. Schaffer, June 2001. Copyright © 2001 by the Harvard Business School Publishing Corporation; all rights reserved.

Once again, rigorous employee selection and training and ethics training, as discussed in Chapters 5 and 11, come to the forefront.

# Leadership

Leadership has fascinated people since the dawn of recorded history. The search for good leaders has been a common thread running through human civilization.[22] In view of research evidence that effective leadership is associated with both better performance and more ethical performance, the search for ways to identify (or develop) good leaders needs to continue.[23]

## Leadership Defined

Research on leadership has produced many definitions of the term. Much of the variation is semantic; the definition offered here is a workable compromise. **Leadership** is the process of inspiring, influencing, and guiding others to participate in a common effort.[24] To encourage participation, leaders supplement any authority and power they possess with their personal attributes, visions, and social skills. Colin Powell, an admired leader in both military and civilian situations, offers his own definition: "Leadership is the art of accomplishing more than the science of management says is possible."[25]

**leadership**   *social influence process of inspiring and guiding others in a common effort*

## Formal Versus Informal Leaders

Experts on leadership distinguish between formal and informal leadership. **Formal leadership** is the process of influencing relevant others to pursue official organizational objectives. **Informal leadership,** in contrast, is the process of influencing others to pursue unofficial objectives that may or may not serve the organization's interests. Formal leaders generally have a measure of legitimate power because of their formal authority, whereas informal leaders typically lack formal authority. Beyond that, both types rely on expedient combinations of reward, coercive, referent, and expert power. Informal leaders who identify with the job to be done are a valuable asset to an organization. Conversely, an organization can be brought to its knees by informal leaders who turn cohesive work groups against the organization.

**formal leadership**   *the process of influencing others to pursue official objectives*

**informal leadership**   *the process of influencing others to pursue unofficial objectives*

Like the study of management, the study of leadership has evolved as theories were developed and refined by successive generations of researchers.[26] Something useful has been learned at each stage of development. We now turn to significant milestones in the evolution of leadership theory by examining the trait, behavioral styles, situational, and transformational approaches (see Figure 15.2).

## Trait Theory

During most of recorded history the prevailing assumption was that leaders are born and not made. Leaders such as Alexander the Great, Napoleon Bonaparte, and George Washington were said to have been blessed with an inborn ability to lead. This so-called

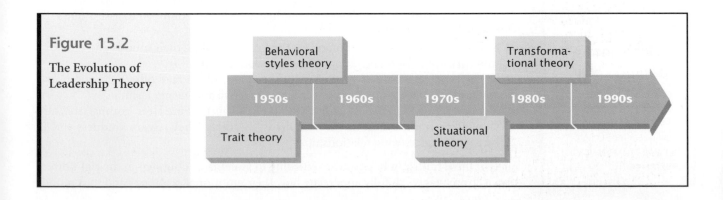

**Figure 15.2**

**The Evolution of Leadership Theory**

great-man approach to leadership[27] eventually gave way to trait theory. According to one observer, "under the influence of the behavioristic school of psychological thought, the fact was accepted that leadership traits are not completely inborn but can also be acquired through learning and experience. Attention turned to the search for universal traits possessed by leaders."[28]

As the popularity of the trait approach mushroomed during the second quarter of the twentieth century, literally hundreds of physical, mental, and personality traits were said to be the key determinants of successful leadership. Unfortunately, few theorists agreed on the most important traits of a good leader. The predictive value of trait theory was severely limited because traits tend to be a chicken-and-egg proposition: Was George Washington a good leader because he had self-confidence, or did he have self-confidence because he was thrust into a leadership role at a young age? In spite of inherent problems, trait profiles provide a useful framework for examining what it takes to be a good leader.

**An Early Trait Profile.**    Not until 1948 was a comprehensive review of competing trait theories conducted. After comparing more than 100 studies of leader traits and characteristics, the reviewer uncovered moderate agreement on only five traits. In the reviewer's words, "the average person who occupies a position of leadership exceeds the average member of his group in the following respects: (1) intelligence, (2) scholarship, (3) dependability in exercising responsibilities, (4) activity and social participation, and (5) socioeconomic status."[29]

**A Modern Trait Profile: Leaders with Emotional Intelligence.**    Daniel Goleman's 1995 book, *Emotional Intelligence,* popularized a concept psychologists had talked about for years.[30] Whereas standard intelligence (IQ) deals with thinking and reasoning, emotional intelligence (EQ) deals more broadly with building social relationships and controlling one's emotions. **Emotional intelligence** has been defined as:

> . . . *good old street smarts—knowing when to share sensitive information with colleagues, laugh at the boss's jokes or speak up in a meeting. In more scientific terms, . . . [emotional intelligence] can be defined as an array of noncognitive skills, capabilities and competencies that influence a person's ability to cope with environmental demands and pressures.*[31]

**emotional intelligence**    *the ability to monitor and control one's emotions and behavior in complex social settings*

Higher EQ scores indicate more polished social skills and greater emotional maturity (try the Hands-On Exercise at the end of this chapter). Interestingly, Goleman says emotional intelligence should be evaluated by others because it is difficult to be objective about oneself in such an important domain.

Goleman and his colleagues recently cast emotional intelligence in terms of four leadership traits:

**3**    Explain the concept of emotional intelligence in terms of Goleman's four leadership traits.

- *Self-awareness.* This essential component of emotional intelligence involves the ability to read one's own emotions and hence be better equipped to assess one's strengths and limitations.
- *Self-management.* Those who possess this trait do not let their moods and emotions disrupt honest and straightforward relationships.
- *Social awareness.* Those who possess this trait are able to read others' emotions and reactions and subsequently adapt in a constructive and caring fashion.
- *Relationship management.* Leaders who possess this trait are clear, enthusiastic, and convincing communicators who can defuse conflicts. They rely on kindness and humor to build strong relationships.[32]

**15D**

**Back to the Opening Case**

How would you rate Pat Carmichael's emotional intelligence? Explain. How does her EQ help her as a manager, leader, and mentor?

Each of these traits can be learned, according to Goleman. A big step in the right direction is for managers to fully appreciate how their emotional outbursts and foul moods can poison the work environment. Leaders and followers alike need to exhibit greater emotional intelligence in order to build social capital in today's hectic and often stressful workplaces.

**The Controversy over Female and Male Leadership Traits.**  A second source of renewed interest in leadership traits is the ongoing debate about female versus male leadership traits. In an often-cited survey by Judy B. Rosener, female leaders were found to be better at sharing power and information than were their male counterparts.[33] Critics have chided Rosener for reinforcing this traditional feminine stereotype.[34] Actually, a comprehensive review of 162 different studies found *no significant difference* in leadership styles exhibited by women and men. In real-life organizational settings, women did *not* fit the feminine stereotype of being more relationship-oriented and men did *not* fit the masculine stereotype of being more task-oriented.[35] As always, it is bad practice to make prejudicial assumptions about individuals based on their membership in some demographic category.

## Behavioral Styles Theory

During World War II, the study of leadership took on a significant new twist. Rather than concentrating on the personal traits of successful leaders, researchers working with the military began turning their attention to patterns of leader behavior (called leadership styles). In other words, attention turned from who the leader was to how the leader actually behaved. One early laboratory study of leader behavior demonstrated that followers overwhelmingly preferred managers who had a democratic style to those with an authoritarian style or a laissez-faire (hands-off) style.[36] An updated review of these three classic leadership styles can be found in Table 15.2.

For a number of years, theorists and managers hailed democratic leadership as the key to productive and happy employees. Eventually, however, their enthusiasm was dampened when critics noted how the original study relied on children as subjects and

**Table 15.2**  The Three Classic Styles of Leadership

|  | Authoritarian | Democratic | Laissez-faire |
|---|---|---|---|
| **Nature** | Leader retains all authority and responsibility | Leader delegates a great deal of authority while retaining ultimate responsibility | Leader grants responsibility and authority to group |
|  | Leader assigns people to clearly defined tasks | Work is divided and assigned on the basis of participatory decision making | Group members are told to work things out themselves and do the best they can |
|  | Primarily a downward flow of communication | Active two-way flow of upward and downward communication | Primarily horizontal communication among peers |
| **Primary strength** | Stresses prompt, orderly, and predictable performance | Enhances personal commitment through participation | Permits self-starters to do things as they see fit without leader interference |
| **Primary weakness** | Approach tends to stifle individual initiative | Democratic process is time-consuming | Group may drift aimlessly in the absence of direction from leader |

virtually ignored productivity. Although there is a general agreement that these basic styles exist, debate has been vigorous over their relative value and appropriateness. Practical experience has shown, for example, that the democratic style does not always stimulate better performance. Some employees prefer to be told what to do rather than to participate in decision making.[37]

**4** Summarize what the Ohio State model and the Leadership Grid® have taught managers about leadership.

**The Ohio State Model.**    While the democratic style of leadership was receiving attention, a slightly different behavioral approach to leadership emerged. This second approach began in the late 1940s when a team of Ohio State University researchers defined two independent dimensions of leader behavior.[38] One dimension, called "initiating structure," was the leader's efforts to get things organized and get the job done. The second dimension, labeled "consideration," was the degree of trust, friendship, respect, and warmth that the leader extended to subordinates. By making a matrix out of these two independent dimensions of leader behavior, the Ohio State researchers identified four styles of leadership (see Figure 15.3).

This particular scheme proved to be fertile ground for leadership theorists, and variations of the original Ohio State approach soon appeared.[39] Leadership theorists began a search for the "one best style" of leadership. The high-structure, high-consideration style was generally hailed as the best all-around style. This "high-high" style has intuitive appeal because it embraces the best of both categories of leader behavior. But one researcher cautioned in 1966 that, although there seemed to be a positive relationship between consideration and employee satisfaction, a positive link between the high-high style and work group performance had not been proved conclusively.[40]

**The Leadership Grid®.**    Developed by Robert R. Blake and Jane S. Mouton, and originally called the Managerial Grid®, the Leadership Grid® is a trademarked and widely recognized typology of leadership styles.[41] Today, amid the growing popularity of situational and transformational leadership theories, Blake's followers remain convinced that there is one best style of leadership.[42] As we will see, they support this claim with research evidence.

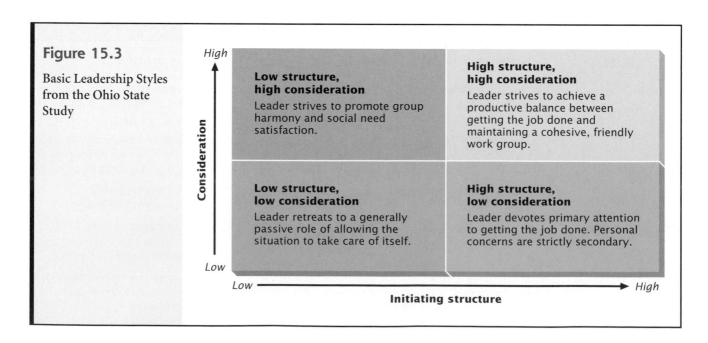

**Figure 15.3**

Basic Leadership Styles from the Ohio State Study

**Low structure, high consideration**
Leader strives to promote group harmony and social need satisfaction.

**High structure, high consideration**
Leader strives to achieve a productive balance between getting the job done and maintaining a cohesive, friendly work group.

**Low structure, low consideration**
Leader retreats to a generally passive role of allowing the situation to take care of itself.

**High structure, low consideration**
Leader devotes primary attention to getting the job done. Personal concerns are strictly secondary.

Consideration — High / Low

Initiating structure — Low / High

As illustrated in Figure 15.4, the Leadership Grid® has "concern for production" on the horizontal axis and "concern for people" on the vertical axis. Concern for production involves a desire to achieve greater output, cost-effectiveness, and profits in profit-seeking organizations. Concern for people involves promoting friendship, helping coworkers get the job done, and attending to things that matter to people, like pay and working conditions. By scaling each axis from 1 to 9, the grid is highlighted by five major styles:

*9,1 style:* primary concern for production; people secondary

*1,9 style:* primary concern for people; production secondary

*1,1 style:* minimal concern for either production or people

*5,5 style:* moderate concern for both production and people to maintain the status quo

*9,9 style:* high concern for both production and people as evidenced by personal commitment, mutual trust, and teamwork

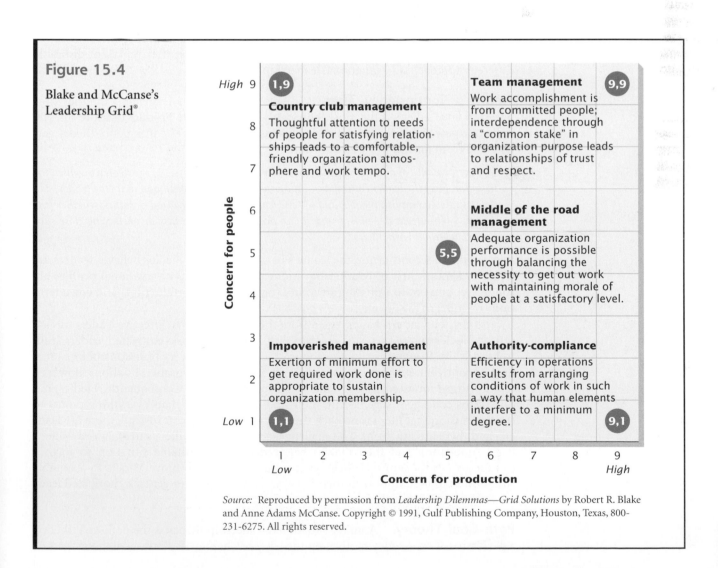

**Figure 15.4**

Blake and McCanse's Leadership Grid®

*Source:* Reproduced by permission from *Leadership Dilemmas—Grid Solutions* by Robert R. Blake and Anne Adams McCanse. Copyright © 1991, Gulf Publishing Company, Houston, Texas, 800-231-6275. All rights reserved.

**15E**

## Back to the Opening Case

Where would you plot Pat Carmichael on Blake and McCanse's Leadership Grid®? Why? Is this particular style the best for her present situation? Why or why not?

Although they stress that managers and leaders need to be versatile enough to select the courses of action appropriate to the situation, Blake and his colleagues contend that a 9,9 style correlates positively with better results, better mental and physical health, and effective conflict resolution. They believe there *is* one best leadership style. As they see it, the true 9,9 style has never been adequately tested by the situationalists. In a more recent study by Blake and Mouton, 100 experienced managers overwhelmingly preferred the 9,9 style, regardless of how the situation varied.[43] Consequently, Blake's management training and organization development programs were designed to help individuals and entire organizations move into the 9,9 portion of the Leadership Grid®.

## Situational Theory

Convinced that no one best style of leadership exists, some management scholars have advocated situational or contingency thinking. Although a number of different situational-leadership theories have been developed, they all share one fundamental assumption: successful leadership occurs when the leader's style matches the situation. Situational-leadership theorists stress the need for flexibility. They reject the notion of a universally applicable style. Research is under way to determine precisely when and where various styles of leadership are appropriate. Fiedler's contingency theory and the path-goal theory are introduced and discussed here because they represent distinctly different approaches to situational leadership.

**Fiedler's Contingency Theory.**　Among the various leadership theories proposed so far, Fiedler's is the most thoroughly tested. It is the product of more than 30 years of research by Fred E. Fiedler and his associates. Fiedler's contingency theory gets its name from the following assumption:

> The performance of a leader depends on two interrelated factors: (1) the degree to which the situation gives the leader control and influence—that is, the likelihood that [the leader] can successfully accomplish the job; and (2) the leader's basic motivation—that is, whether [the leader's] self-esteem depends primarily on accomplishing the task or on having close supportive relations with others.[44]

Regarding the second factor, the leader's basic motivation, Fiedler believes leaders are either task-motivated or relationship-motivated. These two motivational profiles are roughly equivalent to initiating structure (or concern for production) and consideration (or concern for people).

A consistent pattern has emerged from the many studies of effective leaders carried out by Fiedler and others.[45] As illustrated in Figure 15.5, task-motivated leaders seem to be effective in extreme situations when they have either very little control or a great deal of control over situational variables. In moderately favorable situations, however, relationship-motivated leaders tend to be more effective. Consequently, Fiedler and one of his colleagues summed up their findings by noting that "everything points to the conclusion that there is no such thing as an ideal leader."[46] Instead, there are leaders, and there are situations. The challenge, according to Fiedler, is to analyze a leader's basic motivation and then match that leader with a suitable situation to form a productive combination. He believes it is more efficient to move leaders to a suitable situation than to tamper with their personalities by trying to get task-motivated leaders to become relationship-motivated, or vice versa.

**Path-Goal Theory.**　Another situational leadership theory is the path-goal theory, a derivative of expectancy motivation theory (see Chapter 13). Path-goal theory gets its

**Figure 15.5**   Fiedler's Contingency Theory of Leadership

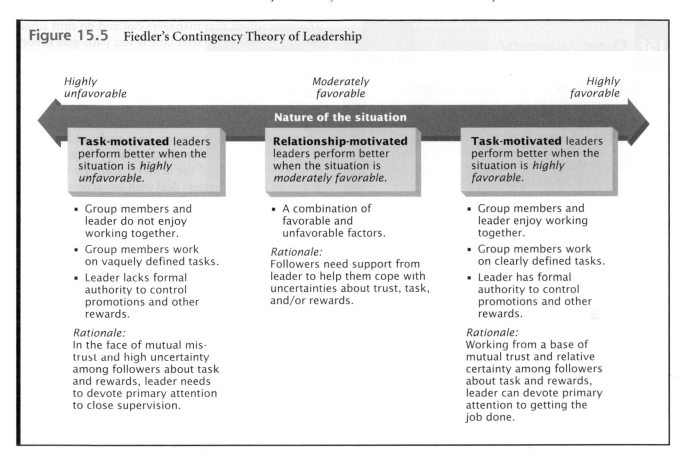

*Highly unfavorable*                          *Moderately favorable*                          *Highly favorable*

**Nature of the situation**

**Task-motivated** leaders perform better when the situation is *highly unfavorable*.

- Group members and leader do not enjoy working together.
- Group members work on vaguely defined tasks.
- Leader lacks formal authority to control promotions and other rewards.

*Rationale:*
In the face of mutual mistrust and high uncertainty among followers about task and rewards, leader needs to devote primary attention to close supervision.

**Relationship-motivated** leaders perform better when the situation is *moderately favorable*.

- A combination of favorable and unfavorable factors.

*Rationale:*
Followers need support from leader to help them cope with uncertainties about trust, task, and/or rewards.

**Task-motivated** leaders perform better when the situation is *highly favorable*.

- Group members and leader enjoy working together.
- Group members work on clearly defined tasks.
- Leader has formal authority to control promotions and other rewards.

*Rationale:*
Working from a base of mutual trust and relative certainty among followers about task and rewards, leader can devote primary attention to getting the job done.

name from the assumption that effective leaders can enhance employee motivation by (1) clarifying the individual's perception of work goals, (2) linking meaningful rewards with goal attainment, and (3) explaining how goals and desired rewards can be achieved. In short, leaders should motivate their followers by providing clear goals and meaningful incentives for reaching them. Path-goal theorists believe that motivation is essential to effective leadership.

According to two path-goal theorists, leaders can enhance motivation by "increasing the number and kinds of personal payoffs to subordinates for work-goal attainment and making paths to these payoffs easier to travel by clarifying the paths, reducing road blocks and pitfalls, and increasing the opportunities for personal satisfaction en route."[47] Personal characteristics of employees, environmental pressures, and demands on employees will all vary from situation to situation. Thus, path-goal proponents believe managers need to rely contingently on four different leadership styles:

- *Directive:* Tell people what is expected of them and provide specific guidance, schedules, rules, regulations, and standards.[48]
- *Supportive:* Treat employees as equals in a friendly manner while striving to improve their well-being.
- *Participative:* Consult with employees to seek their suggestions and then seriously consider those suggestions when making decisions.
- *Achievement-oriented:* Set challenging goals, emphasize excellence, and seek continuous improvement while maintaining a high degree of confidence that employees will meet difficult challenges in a responsible manner.[49]

**5** Describe the path-goal theory of leadership and explain how the assumption on which it is based differs from the assumption on which Fiedler's contingency theory is based.

# Mentoring

In spite of mountains of leadership research, much remains to be learned about why some people are good leaders whereas many others are not.[59] One thing is clear, though: mentors can make an important difference. Let us explore this interesting process whereby leadership skills are acquired by exposure to role models.

## Learning from a Mentor

The many obstacles and barriers blocking the way to successful leadership make it easy to understand why there is no simple formula for developing leaders. Abraham Zaleznik, a respected sociologist, insists that leaders must be nurtured under the wise tutelage of a mentor. A **mentor** is an individual who systematically develops another person's abilities through intensive tutoring, coaching, and guidance.[60] Zaleznik explains the nature of this special relationship:

**mentor**   *someone who develops another person through tutoring, coaching, and guidance*

> *Mentors take risks with people. They bet initially on talent they perceive in [junior] people. Mentors also risk emotional involvement in working closely with their juniors. The risks do not always pay off, but the willingness to take them appears crucial in developing leaders.*[61]

A survey of 246 health care industry managers found higher satisfaction, greater recognition, and more promotion opportunities among managers with mentors than among those without.[62] Other research suggests that *informal* relationships that arise naturally work better than formally structured pairings.[63] Wal-Mart prefers the structured approach. In the following example, notice how the world's number one retailer has integrated formal mentors into a comprehensive human resources program:

> *. . . the company has modified its human resources philosophy from "getting, keeping, and growing" employees to "keeping, growing, and getting" them. The shift isn't just semantics, says Coleman Peterson, senior vice president of Wal-Mart's people division. It indicates an increased emphasis on retaining and developing the talent Wal-Mart already has, rather than the "hire, hire, hire" strategy Peterson says characterized the company in the past.*

*A good mentor can be very helpful to one's career. They can provide both career advice and social support. Pictured here in Washington, D.C., are Wanda Lopes and her mentor Gus Crosetto, Director of Training at Fannie Mae, the $50 billion-a-year financial services company. Fannie Mae encourages mentoring with a formal program.*

*To that end, Wal-Mart focuses intensively on how employees adapt during their first 90 days with the company. To make sure new hires don't feel lost at the mammoth company, they are assigned veteran employees as mentors. They are also assessed on their progress at the 30-, 60-, and 90-day marks. These efforts have helped reduce attrition rates by 25 percent. Wal-Mart employees who exhibit leadership potential are sent for training to the Sam Walton Development Center, at company headquarters in Bentonville, Arkansas.*[64]

## Dynamics of Mentoring

According to Kathy Kram, who conducted intensive biographical interviews with both members in 18 different senior manager–junior manager mentor relationships, mentoring fulfills two important functions: (1) a career enhancement function and (2) a psychological support function (see Table 15.5). Mentor relationships were found to average about five years in length.[65] Thus a manager might have a series of mentors during the course of an organizational career.

Interestingly, the junior member of a mentor relationship is not the only one to benefit. Mentors often derive great intrinsic pleasure from seeing their protégés move up through the ranks and conquer difficult challenges. Moreover, by passing along their values and technical and leadership skills to promising junior managers, mentors can wield considerable power. Mentor relationships do sometimes turn sour. A mentor can become threatened by a protégé who surpasses him or her. Also, cross-gender[66] and cross-race mentor relationships can be victimized by bias and social pressures.[67]

## Behavior Modification

This last approach to influencing behavior can be traced to two psychologists, John B. Watson and Edward L. Thorndike, who did their work in the early twentieth century. From Watson came the advice to concentrate on observable behavior. Accordingly, the philosophy of **behaviorism** says that observable behavior is more important than hypothetical inner states such as needs, motives, or expectations.[68] From Thorndike came an appreciation of the way in which consequences control behavior. According to

**7** Identify the two key functions that mentors perform and explain how a mentor can develop a junior manager's leadership skills.

**15H**

## Back to the Opening Case

Which of the mentor functions in Table 15.5 are evident in this case? Explain. Why is Pat Carmichael an especially good mentor?

**behaviorism** *belief that observable behavior is more important than inner states*

---

**Table 15.5** Mentors Serve Two Important Functions

| Career functions* | Psychosocial functions** |
|---|---|
| Sponsorship | Role modeling |
| Exposure and visibility | Acceptance and confirmation |
| Coaching | Counseling |
| Protection | Friendship |
| Challenging assignments | |

\* Career functions are those aspects of the relationship that primarily enhance career advancement.
\*\* Psychosocial functions are those aspects of the relationship that primarily enhance a sense of competence, clarity of identity, and effectiveness in the managerial role.

*Source:* Kathy E. Kram, "Phases of the Mentor Relationship," *Academy of Management Journal,* 26 (December 1983): 614 (Exhibit 1). Reprinted by permission.

*When Julius Walls Jr. was growing up in Brooklyn, he aspired to be a Catholic priest. As things turned out, he studied business in college and ended up working for Greyston Bakery. The bakery was started by a Zen Buddhist in 1982 to bring hope to a depressed area of Yonkers, N.Y. Walls introduced business discipline to the venture that employs former substance abusers and ex-convicts to produce gourmet baked goods. Walls may not be a priest, but his "enlightened capitalism" that calls for helping others while pursuing a profit (that Greyston donates to the needy) has answered many prayers. His core theme of making employees responsible for their own actions has taken lots of behavior modification.*

Thorndike's classic law of effect, favorable consequences encourage behavior, whereas unfavorable consequences discourage behavior.[69] However, it remained for B. F. Skinner, the late Harvard psychologist, to integrate Watson's and Thorndike's contributions into a precise technology of behavior change.

## What Is Behavior Modification?

Skinner was the father of *operant conditioning,* the study of how behavior is controlled by the surrounding environment.[70] Although some find Skinner's substitution of environmental control for self-control repulsive and dehumanizing,[71] few deny that operant conditioning actually occurs. Indeed, much of our behavior is the product of environmental shaping. Rather, the debate centers on whether or not natural shaping processes should be systematically managed to alter the course of everyday behavior.[72] Advocates of behavior modification in the workplace believe they should be.[73]

**behavior modification**
*systematic management of the antecedents and consequences of behavior*

Behavior modification is the practical application of Skinnerian operant-conditioning techniques to everyday behavior problems. **Behavior modification** (B. Mod.) involves systematically managing environmental factors to get people to do the right things more often and the wrong things less often. This is accomplished by managing the antecedents and/or consequences of observable behavior.

## Managing Antecedents

**antecedent**    *an environmental cue for a specific behavior*

An **antecedent** is an environmental cue that prompts an individual to behave in a given manner. Antecedents do not automatically *cause* an individual to behave in a predictable manner, as a hot stove causes you to withdraw your hand reflexively when you touch it. Rather, we learn through experience to interpret antecedents as signals telling us it is time to behave in a certain way if we are to get what we want or to avoid what we do not want. This process is sometimes referred to as *cue control.* Domino's Pizza Inc. makes effective use of cue control for maintaining product quality.

> *[Every Domino's] features a myriad of strategically placed, visually appealing posters displaying helpful, job-related tips and reminders. . . .*
>
> *Centrally located, particularly for the benefit of the oven tender who slices and boxes the just-baked pizza, are two photos, one of "The Perfect Pepperoni" pizza, the other showing a pizza with ten common flaws, one per slice.*[74]

Although often overlooked, the management of antecedents is a practical and simple way of encouraging good performance. As Table 15.6 indicates, there are two ways to manage antecedents. Barriers can be removed, and helpful aids can be offered. These steps ensure that the path to good performance is clearly marked and free of obstacles (which meshes with the path-goal theory of leadership).

**8** Explain the management of antecedents and consequences in behavior modification.

## Managing Consequences

Managing the consequences of job performance is more complex than dealing strictly with antecedents because there are four different classes of consequences. Each type of consequence involves a different process. Positive reinforcement and negative reinforcement both encourage behavior, but they do so in different ways. Extinction and punishment discourage behavior, but again, in different ways. These four terms have precise meanings that are often confused by casual observers.

**Table 15.6**  Managing Antecedents

| Barriers: remove barriers that prevent or hinder the completion of a good job. For example: | Aids: provide helpful aids that enhance the opportunity to do a good job. For example: |
|---|---|
| Unrealistic objectives, plans, schedules, or deadlines | Challenging yet attainable objectives |
| Uncooperative or distracting coworkers | Clear and realistic plans |
| Training deficiencies | Understandable instructions |
| Contradictory or confusing rules | Constructive suggestions, hints, or tips |
| Inadequate or inappropriate tools | Clear and generally acceptable work rules |
| Conflicting orders from two or more managers | Realistic schedules and deadlines |
| | Friendly reminders |
| | Posters or signs with helpful tips |
| | Easy-to-use forms |
| | Nonthreatening questions about progress |
| | User-friendly computer software and hardware |

**positive reinforcement**
*encouraging a behavior with a pleasing consequence*

**Positive Reinforcement.**    **Positive reinforcement** encourages a specific behavior by immediately following it with a consequence the individual finds pleasing. For example, a machine operator who maintains a clean work area because he or she is praised for doing so has responded to positive reinforcement. As the term implies, positive reinforcement reinforces or builds behavior in a positive way.

**Negative Reinforcement.**    *Negative reinforcement* encourages a specific behavior by immediately withdrawing or terminating something a particular person finds displeasing. Children learn the power of negative reinforcement early in life when they discover that the quickest way to get something is to cry and scream until their parents give them what they want. In effect, the parents are negatively reinforced for complying with the child's demand by the termination of the crying and screaming. In other words, the termination or withdrawal of an undesirable state of affairs (for example, the threat of being fired) has an incentive effect. In a social context, negative reinforcement amounts to blackmail. "Do what I want, or I will continue to make your life miserable" are the bywords of the person who relies on negative reinforcement to influence behavior.

**Extinction.**    Through *extinction,* a specific behavior is discouraged by ignoring it. For example, managers sometimes find that the best way to keep employees from asking redundant questions is simply not to answer them. Just as a plant will wither and die without water, behavior will fade away without occasional reinforcement.

**Punishment.**    *Punishment* discourages a specific behavior by the immediate presentation of an undesirable consequence or the immediate removal of something desirable. For example, a manager may punish a tardy employee by either assigning the individual to a dirty job or docking the individual's pay.

It is important to remember that positive and negative reinforcement, extinction, and punishment all entail the manipulation of the *immediate* or *direct* consequences of a desired or undesired behavior. If action is taken before the behavior, behavior control is unlikely. For instance, if a manager gives an employee a cash bonus *before* a difficult task is completed, the probability of the task being completed declines because the incentive effect has been removed. In regard to managing consequences, behavior modification works only when there is a contingent ("if . . . then") relationship between a specific behavior and a given consequence.

**15I  Zap 'Em!**

Catherine Muther, who retired early in the mid-1990s from Cisco Systems with millions of dollars in company stock:

*In that male-dominated company, Muther pushed for a change. She gave other executives electronic "zappers" with flashing red lights. They were used to make a buzzing sound whenever someone made a sexist remark during management meetings, says Cisco Chairman John Morgridge. "She certainly was a major factor in bringing the gender issue to Cisco," he says.*

**Source:** Jim Hopkins, "Philanthropist Nurtures Tech Start-Ups by Women," *USA Today* (January 22, 2002): 12B.

**Questions:** *Which behavior modification tactic did Muther use? Explain. Why was it apparently effective?*

## Positively Reinforce What Is Right About Job Performance

Behavior modification proponents prefer to build up desirable behaviors rather than tear down undesirable ones. Every undesirable behavior has a desirable counterpart that can be reinforced. For example, someone who comes in late once a week actually comes in on time four days a week. To encourage productive behaviors, managers are advised to focus on the positive aspects of job performance when managing consequences. Thus, positive reinforcement is the preferred consequence strategy.[75] This positive approach was effectively taken to heart by Preston Trucking, a Maryland shipping company:

> *Preston, years ago, had terrible relations between management and labor. Then, one day, top management resolved to bury the hatchet. All sorts of reforms were announced, including the Four-to-One Rule: For every criticism a manager made about a driver's performance, he had to give him four compliments. You can imagine how this went over. "It was like a . . . like a* marriage encounter," *says Teamster Nick Costa, rolling his eyes. Eventually, though, drivers discovered that the rule really did reflect a change of heart.[76]*

This positive approach to modifying behavior is the central theme in the best-selling book *The One Minute Manager,* which extols the virtues of "catching people doing something *right!"[77]*

## Schedule Positive Reinforcement Appropriately

Both the type and the timing of consequences are important in successful B. Mod. When a productive behavior is first tried out by an employee, a continuous schedule of reinforcement is appropriate. Under **continuous reinforcement** every instance of the desired behavior is reinforced. For example, a bank manager who is training a new loan officer to handle a difficult type of account should praise the loan officer after every successful transaction until the behavior is firmly established. After the loan officer seems able to handle the transaction, the bank manager can switch to a schedule of intermittent reinforcement. As the term implies, **intermittent reinforcement** calls for reinforcing some, rather than all, of the desired responses.

**continuous reinforcement**
*every instance of a behavior is rewarded*

**intermittent reinforcement**
*rewarding some, but not all, instances of a behavior*

The more unpredictable the payoff schedule is, the better the results will be. One way to appreciate the power of intermittent reinforcement is to think of the enthusiasm with which people play slot machines; these gambling devices pay off on an unpredictable intermittent schedule. In the same way, occasional reinforcement of established productive behaviors with meaningful positive consequences is an extremely effective management technique.[78] (Now go do something nice for yourself as positive reinforcement for reading this chapter.)

# Summary

1. Influence is fundamental to management because individuals must be influenced to pursue collective objectives. In addition to motivation, important influence processes include power, leadership, mentoring, and behavior modification. Recent research has identified eight generic influence tactics used on the job: consultation, rational persuasion, inspirational appeals, ingratiating tactics, coalition tactics, pressure tactics, upward appeals, and exchange tactics.

2. The five bases of power are reward, coercive, legitimate, referent, and expert. Empowerment cannot work without a supporting situation such as a skilled individual, an organizational culture of empowerment, an emotionally mature individual with a well-developed character, and empowerment opportunities such as delegation, participation, and self-managed teams.

**3.** Formal leadership is influencing relevant others to voluntarily pursue organizational objectives. Informal leadership can work for or against the organization. Leadership theory has evolved through four major stages: trait theory, behavioral styles theory, situational theory, and transformational theory. A promising trait approach is based on Goleman's four dimensions of emotional intelligence: self-awareness, self-management, social awareness, and relationship management. Researchers who differentiated authoritarian, democratic, and laissez-faire styles concentrated on leader behavior rather than personality traits. Leadership studies at Ohio State University isolated four styles of leadership based on two categories of leader behavior: initiating structure and consideration. According to Blake and his colleagues, a 9,9 style (high concern for both production and people) is the best overall style.

**4.** Situational-leadership theorists believe there is no single best leadership style; rather, different situations require different styles. Many years of study led Fiedler to conclude that task-motivated leaders are more effective in either very favorable or very unfavorable situations, whereas relationship-motivated leaders are better suited to moderately favorable situations. The favorableness of a situation is dictated by the degree of the leader's control and influence in getting the job done. Path-goal leadership theory, an expectancy perspective, assumes that leaders are effective to the extent that they can motivate followers by clarifying goals and clearing the paths to achieving those goals and valued rewards. Unlike Fiedler, path-goal theorists believe that managers can and should adapt their leadership style to the situation.

**5.** In contrast to transactional leaders who maintain the status quo, transformational leaders are visionary, charismatic leaders dedicated to change. Greenleaf's philosophy of the servant leader helps aspiring leaders integrate what they have learned about leadership. The servant leader is motivated to serve rather than lead. Clear goals, trust, good listening skills, positive feedback, foresight, and self-development are the characteristics of a servant leader.

**6.** Mentors help develop less experienced people by fulfilling career and psychosocial functions. Mentors engage in intensive tutoring, coaching, and guiding. Mentors are role models for aspiring leaders.

**7.** Behavior modification (B. Mod.) is the practical application of Skinner's operant conditioning principles. B. Mod. involves managing antecedents and consequences to strengthen desirable behavior and weaken undesirable behavior. Proponents of B. Mod. prefer to shape behavior positively through positive reinforcement in lieu of negative reinforcement, extinction, and punishment. Continuous reinforcement is recommended for new behavior and intermittent reinforcement for established behavior.

## Terms to Understand

Influence (p. 496)

Power (p. 498)

Reward power (p. 499)

Coercive power (p. 499)

Legitimate power (p. 500)

Referent power (p. 500)

Expert power (p. 501)

Empowerment (p. 501)

Leadership (p. 503)

Formal leadership (p. 503)

Informal leadership (p. 503)

Emotional intelligence (p. 504)

## Skills & Tools

### Putting the Empowerment Puzzle Together

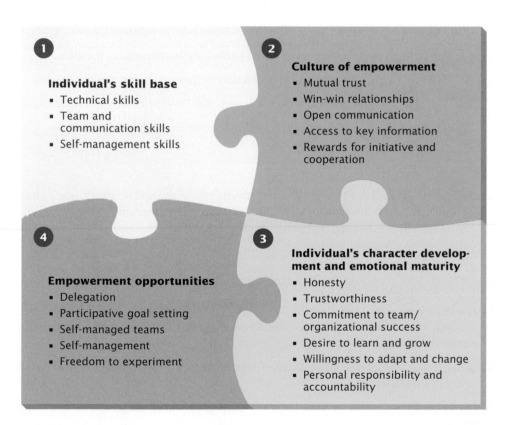

**1 Individual's skill base**
- Technical skills
- Team and communication skills
- Self-management skills

**2 Culture of empowerment**
- Mutual trust
- Win-win relationships
- Open communication
- Access to key information
- Rewards for initiative and cooperation

**4 Empowerment opportunities**
- Delegation
- Participative goal setting
- Self-managed teams
- Self-management
- Freedom to experiment

**3 Individual's character development and emotional maturity**
- Honesty
- Trustworthiness
- Commitment to team/organizational success
- Desire to learn and grow
- Willingness to adapt and change
- Personal responsibility and accountability

*Source:* Adapted in part from discussion in Stephen R. Covey, *Principle-Centered Leadership* (New York: Simon & Schuster, 1991), pp. 212–216.

## Hands-On Exercise

## What Is Your Emotional Intelligence (EQ)?[79]

**Instructions**

Evaluate each statement about your emotional intelligence on a scale of 1 = "not at all like me" to 10 = "very much like me." Try to be objective by viewing yourself through the eyes of key people in your life such as family members, close friends, coworkers, and classmates. (Note: This instrument is for instructional purposes only because it was derived from a 25-item survey of unknown validity.)

___ **1.** I usually stay composed, positive, and unflappable in trying situations.

___ **2.** I am able to admit my own mistakes.

___ **3.** I usually or always meet commitments and keep promises.

___ **4.** I hold myself accountable for meeting my goals.

___ **5.** I can smoothly handle multiple demands and changing priorities.

___ **6.** Obstacles and setbacks may delay me a little, but they don't stop me.

___ **7.** I seek fresh perspectives, even if that means trying something totally new.

___ **8.** My impulses or distressing emotions don't often get the best of me at work.

___ **9.** I usually don't attribute setbacks to a personal flaw (mine or somebody else's).

___**10.** I operate from an expectation of success rather than a fear of failure.

Total = _____

**Interpretation**

A score below 70 indicates a need for improvement. With sincere effort, one's emotional intelligence can be improved. It is part of a natural process of "growing up" and becoming mature in challenging social situations. People with low EQ scores are like porcupines—they're hard to hug.

**For Consideration/ Discussion**

**1.** What do you like or dislike about the concept of emotional intelligence?

**2.** Have you ever worked with or for someone who had high emotional intelligence? If so, describe them and rate their effectiveness. Do the same for someone with low emotional intelligence.

**3.** What, if any, connection do you see between the concepts of emotional intelligence and servant leader? Explain.

**4.** How could you improve your emotional intelligence, in terms of the items on this test?

# Internet Exercises

1. **More on social influence:** Robert B. Cialdini, author of the book *Influence: The Science of Persuasion,* says we are exposed to countless good and evil influence tactics every day of our lives. As a researcher, he knows the power of social influence and fears that power is often abused. A combination Web and library search will provide instructive details and practical insights. First, go to his Web site (**www.influenceatwork.com**) and take the short quiz by clicking on "What's Your Influence Quotient (NQ)?" Next, read Cialdini's ideas about the six principles of influence in the following article: Robert B. Cialdini, "Harnessing the Science of Persuasion," *Harvard Business Review,* 79 (October 2001): 72–79.

   *Learning Points:* 1. Are you surprised at how pervasive influence is in modern life? 2. Generally speaking, do you view social influence as a positive or negative aspect of modern life? Explain. 3. What useful lessons did you learn from this exercise? 4. Are you better equipped to handle unwanted influence attempts after completing this exercise? Explain. 5. How can and should managers use influence ethically?

2. **More on emotional intelligence:** Did you find the coverage of Goleman's four dimensions of emotional intelligence (EQ) and the Hands-On Exercise interesting? If so, and you want to know more, go to **www.fortune.com** and click on the main menu tab "Careers." Under the heading "Quizzes," select "What's Your EQ at Work?" You will find the complete 25-item survey from which the Hands-On Exercise was excerpted. This longer version is more job-oriented. Complete the survey and submit your responses for scoring. Alternatively, you may find it instructive to have a relative or close acquaintance evaluate your emotional intelligence with this survey.

   *Learning Points:* 1. Is it really possible to take an objective outsider's view of yourself and your behavior with this type of instrument? Explain. 2. How useful is Goleman's concept of emotional intelligence within a management context? 3. If you would like to improve your EQ, what is your plan for doing so? 4. What is your personal experience with leaders who were high or low on emotional intelligence? What impact did their EQ have on their effectiveness?

3. **Check it out:** The Women's Organization for Mentoring Education and Networking, sponsored by WOMEN Unlimited Inc., is dedicated to enhancing diversity and achieving gender parity in the workplace. For instructive resources and readings on mentoring and related topics, go to the organization's home page at **www.women-unlimited.com** and click on "Press Room" and "Resources." Both women and men can pick up useful career tips from this Web site.

For updates to these exercises, visit our Web site (**http://business.college.hmco.com/students**).

## Closing Case

# Can David Neeleman Pilot JetBlue Airways to Success?

Preparing to meet JetBlue Airways CEO David Neeleman—by all accounts the most successful, innovative airline founder to hit the scene since Southwest Airlines founder Herb Kelleher—I'm thinking I'll encounter a certain swagger. A kick-ass attitude. A guy who's going to knock me off my feet. I guess I'm expecting Herb II, to be honest.

What I find when I actually interview him, in Syracuse, N.Y., catches me completely off guard. Neeleman has just completed a rather low-key press conference marking the inauguration of JetBlue's daily service into the town, and he sits at an airport gate that's teeming with passengers, airport employees, kids, politicians, local newspapermen. Neeleman mentions something about his "philosophy of life." I ask him what he means, and he mumbles something about customer service. Neeleman's gaze shifts across the gate area, where one of his executives is fumbling with her purse. "She is so funny," he says, perking up and waving at her. I try asking him another question. Seeing a friend, he jumps out of his seat and walks away.

Neeleman, 41, has told some people that he thinks he has an attention deficit disorder. To me, he has mentioned merely that he gets "easily distracted." Whatever his deal is, he hardly seems like the kind of outrageous extrovert who can make an airline fly—the kind of leader who, through the sheer force of his personality and the example of his dedication, can inspire employees and customers to turn a business that's fundamentally flawed into a money-making machine. Neeleman's no Kelleher. He's a college dropout, not a hotshot lawyer; a Mormon with nine kids who won't sip coffee, much less chain-smoke cigarettes and toss back the Wild Turkey. He doesn't have much time for partying, and he says his only pastime—other than hanging out with his kids—is reading history books (he's particularly interested in the "post-Christ" period). But you shouldn't be fooled. David Neeleman wants to one-up Southwest. And in his own idiosyncratic way, he may very well pull it off.

By anyone's measure, Neeleman's JetBlue, which has been flying [only a short time], is a runaway success. It operates out of New York City, the largest market in the country, sending planes to five destinations in Florida, four in the Northeast, and five out west. Like Southwest, JetBlue offers low-fare service. It flies mostly in secondary markets. It keeps its costs low. It "turns" its aircraft quickly, keeping them in the air and earning money. Unlike most startups, which buy cheap, old planes, Neeleman's airline flies new Airbus A320s. JetBlue doesn't serve meals, but it lets passengers pick their own seats, has leather upholstery and free satellite TV, and will soon introduce a frequent-flier program.

"Customers have gone berserk for this," says Miami airline consultant Stuart Klaskin. Michael Lazarus, a partner at the San Francisco venture firm (and JetBlue backer) Weston Presidio, says he's had people thank *him* after they've flown on the airline. "We don't spend tens of millions of dollars telling people how cool we are," Neeleman says. "We put low fares out there and let them tell us." JetBlue estimates that 74% of its first-time passengers choose the airline because of good word of mouth. . . .

JetBlue is Neeleman's third successful airline startup. Back in the early '80s he was co-founder with June Morris of Morris Air, a low-cost carrier based in Salt Lake City. The company was on the brink of an IPO when Southwest snatched it up for $130 million. (Neeleman, who was 33 at the time, reportedly made $20 million on the deal.) He signed on with Southwest but found the place too regimented (!) and left within five months.

Kelleher made Neeleman sign a five-year noncompete agreement, so the younger man went to Canada to help start another airline, WestJet. Neeleman also founded a company called OpenSkies, which makes software for airline reservations systems.

"He's a genius entrepreneur," says Kevin Murphy, a friend and airline analyst at Morgan Stanley. Agrees Dave Barger, Neeleman's No. 2 at JetBlue: "He has an uncanny knack for knowing when an opportunity's right." Like Kelleher, Neeleman takes notions that others dismiss outright and implements them so impeccably that in hindsight their value seems obvious. ("I love being contrarian!" he says.) Neeleman is widely credited with coming up with electronic ticketing (Morris Air first offered the service in 1993). He also recognized early the benefits of telecommuting: as far back as 1992 he encouraged Morris Air reservations agents to take calls in their homes.

At JetBlue, Neeleman's brilliant insight was to base his airline at J.F.K., the black sheep of New York airports. Low-cost carriers had always avoided New York City, the country's largest air market, because (1) flying out of LaGuardia and Newark is expensive, and (2) conventional wisdom had long held that you couldn't run domestic service out of Kennedy, which is farther from Manhattan than LaGuardia or Newark and, at certain times of the day, is choked with international flights. Neeleman saw things differently. If you hit J.F.K. right, he realized, you could pretty much sail through without delays. And Neeleman thought the convenience complaints were ridiculous. "Kennedy is only eight miles away from LaGuardia. It's like eight miles is 800 miles to some people," he says.

Convinced that he could run a Southwest-like airline profitably out of J.F.K., he set about pursuing partners who could make it happen. His track record served him well. Neeleman recruited Continental's Barger, who had turned around operations at Newark, to be president and COO [chief operating officer]. He raised $160 million from A-list investors: Weston Presidio Capital, J. P. Morgan Partners, Soros Private Equity Partners. Neeleman courted the right people in government too. By promising to provide jet service to Buffalo, Rochester, and Syracuse, he persuaded New York Senator Charles Schumer to help him get slots at Kennedy. Neeleman's partners all say they were blown away by his pitch. "I went in with enormous skepticism about investing in an airline," says Neal Moszkowski, a partner at Soros and a member of JetBlue's board. "But his presence, coupled with the strength of the team, was staggering."

So what gives with the distraction, the opacity I encountered in Neeleman when I tried to talk with him in Syracuse? I'm not the only one who senses it—even people who know him well often paint Neeleman in bland brush strokes. "He's low-key, and he's totally directed, and he has great faith, being a Mormon," Schumer says. "He's a nut job, but he's a focused nut job," grins JetBlue government affairs director Robert Land, without further explanation.

But Neeleman, I learn, has all the depth and force of personality I'd looked for at the start. He and Kelleher aren't polar opposites; they're different actors tackling the same part. The same day I meet Neeleman in Syracuse, he lets me tag along to an employee orientation where he plans to give a talk on airline economics. Standing at the front of the room, Magic Marker in hand, he talks with his new colleagues—baggage handlers from Buffalo, check-in agents from Oakland—calmly, naturally, explaining how JetBlue can make money when the big guys don't. He answers personal questions. He doesn't lose his concentration. You can imagine what Moszkowski saw when Neeleman arrived at his office looking for money. The man can be completely, utterly riveting.

But can he be the next Kelleher? If he can stay focused, the answer seems to be yes. JetBlue has big plans. . . .

Neeleman's hunkering down. He has moved his giant family east from Utah; talking to the Syracuse crowd, he asks the audience to "visit us in New York City." Will he be there 35 years, as long as Kelleher has been at Southwest? "Oh, I don't know—that's a long time, and I'm young," he says. "But once you've seen the bright lights of New York, starting an airline, what else are you going to do? Run a widget factory?"

## For Discussion

1. Which of the eight generic influence tactics are evident in this case? Explain.

2. What are Neeleman's primary and secondary power bases? Explain.

3. How would you rate Neeleman's emotional intelligence (EQ) in terms of Goleman's four leadership traits? Explain.

4. Where would you plot Neeleman's leadership style on the Leadership Grid®?

5. Is Neeleman more of a transformational leader, a servant leader, or some combination of the two? Explain.

6. How you rate Neeleman's chances for success at JetBlue? Explain.

# Change, Conflict, and Negotiation

## CHAPTER OBJECTIVES

*When you finish studying this chapter you should be able to*

**1** **Identify** and **describe** four types of organizational change according to the Nadler-Tushman model.

**2** **Explain** how people tend to respond differently to changes they like and those they dislike.

**3** **List** at least six reasons why employees resist change and **discuss** what management can do about resistance to change.

**4** **Describe** how the unfreezing-change-refreezing analogy applies to organization development (OD).

**5** **Describe** tempered radicals and **identify** the 5Ps in the checklist for grassroots change agents.

**6** **Contrast** the competitive and cooperative conflict styles.

**7** **Identify** and **describe** five conflict resolution techniques.

**8** **Identify** and **describe** the elements of effective negotiation and **explain** the advantage of added value negotiating (AVN).

# No Revolutionary Change for Switzerland's Nestlé

## An Interview with CEO Peter Brabeck

Background: Founded in 1867 in Vevey, Switzerland, to sell infant formula, the company grew quickly through an aggressive campaign of acquisitions that continues today. Nestlé now operates in every country on earth, selling thousands of products, from Nescafé instant coffee to Perrier bottled water to Friskies cat food.

The company employs 230,000 people and operates more than 500 factories as well as 17 research and development facilities with a combined budget of close to $600 million a year. The corporate inertia caused by such complexity prompted Brabeck's charismatic predecessor, Helmut Maucher, to restructure and streamline the company's operations throughout the 1990s. So it was a revitalized, vastly more nimble company that Brabeck inherited nearly four years ago.

He was no stranger to the organization. The Austrian-born Brabeck joined Nestlé in 1968 as an ice-cream and frozen-food salesman, after studying economics at the University of World Trade in Vienna. Over the next three decades, Brabeck followed the typical Nestlé management track, running operations around the world, including those in Chile, Ecuador, and Venezuela. In 1987, he moved to headquarters in Vevey to direct the company's culinary products division and then, in 1992, its strategy-making units, marketing, and communications. He spoke to *Harvard Business Review* in his office overlooking Lake Geneva.

Q. *What's wrong with radical change?*
A. What is so good about it?

Q. *Not good, but necessary. The markets are constantly changing. So are consumers. And so is technology. One could make a strong case—and many management theorists and executives do—that companies today have to embrace radical change just to keep up.*
A. Big, dramatic change is fine for a crisis. If you come in as CEO and a turnaround is necessary, then fine, have a revolution. In that situation, change is relatively easy because the whole organization understands that, just to survive, you need to do things differently. They are prepared for change. They understand when you say, "The cancer is here, where do I cut?"

But not every company in the world is in crisis all the time. Many companies are like us—not as big, of course—but they are performing well. Growing, innovating, and so forth—good and fit. Why should we manufacture dramatic change? Just for change's sake? To follow some sort of fad without logical thinking behind it? We are very skeptical of any kind of fad and of the self-appointed gurus you hear from all the time, making pronouncements. It is easy to be dogmatic when you don't actually have to run a business. When you run a business, you must be pragmatic. Big, disruptive change programs are anything but that. You cannot underestimate the traumatic impact of abrupt change, the distraction it causes in running the business, the fear it provokes in people, the demands it makes on management's time.

And frankly, you could make the case that any kind of onetime change program is actually a very worrisome warning—it's a bad sign that a company's leaders have had to make such an intervention. Think of medicine again. If you take preventive care of your health, and you've taken the time for check-ups, you won't wake up one day to find you have to cut off your leg. That is why we see adapting, improving, and restructuring as a continuous process. . . .

Q. *Then what's the business case for being a company that performs like a reasonably robust 40-year-old jogger?*
A. Look, Nestlé caters to billions of consumers around the world. In our business—food and drink—more perhaps than in others, we need a relationship of trust to be successful. Can anyone trust a company that reinvents itself every few years? Sure, we will act swiftly to change our products and our business methods if need be, and we do our best to improve all aspects of the company each day. But we will never allow our value system, or our focus on quality and safety, to deteriorate. Trust is our most important asset. We must always defend it.

# Managing Diversity

## Tempered Radicals as Everyday Leaders

In the course of their daily actions and interactions, tempered radicals teach important lessons and inspire change. In so doing, they exercise a form of leadership within organizations that is less visible than traditional forms—but just as important.

The trick for organizations is to locate and nurture this subtle form of leadership. Consider how Barry Coswell, a conservative, yet open-minded lawyer who headed up the securities division of a large, distinguished financial services firm, identified, protected, and promoted a tempered radical within his organization. Dana, a left-of-center, first-year attorney, came to his office on her first day of work after having been fingerprinted—a standard practice in the securities industry. The procedure had made Dana nervous: What would happen when her new employer discovered that she had done jail time for participating in a 1960s-era civil rights protest? Dana quickly understood that her only hope of survival was to be honest about her background and principles. Despite the difference in their political proclivities, she decided to give Barry the benefit of the doubt. She marched into his office and confessed to having gone to jail for sitting in front of a bus.

"I appreciate your honesty," Barry laughed, "but unless you've broken a securities law, you're probably okay." In return for her small confidence, Barry shared stories of his own about growing up in a poor county and about his life in the military. The story swapping allowed them to put aside ideological disagreements and to develop a deep respect for each other. Barry sensed a budding leader in Dana. Here was a woman who operated on the strength of her convictions and was honest about it but was capable of discussing her beliefs without self-righteousness. She didn't pound tables. She was a good conversationalist. She listened attentively. And she was able to elicit surprising confessions from him.

Barry began to accord Dana a level of protection, and he encouraged her to speak her mind, take risks, and most important, challenge his assumptions. In one instance, Dana spoke up to defend a female junior lawyer who was being evaluated harshly and, Dana believed, inequitably. Dana observed that different standards were being applied to male and female lawyers, but her colleagues dismissed her "liberal" concerns. Barry cast a glance at Dana, then said to the staff, "Let's look at this and see if we are being too quick to judge." After the meeting, Barry and Dana held a conversation about double standards and the pervasiveness of bias. In time, Barry initiated a policy to seek out minority legal counsel, both in-house and at outside legal firms. And Dana became a senior vice president.

In Barry's ability to recognize, mentor, and promote Dana there is a key lesson for executives who are anxious to foster leadership in their organizations. It suggests that leadership development may not rest with expensive external programs or even with the best intentions of the human resources department. Rather it may rest with the open-minded recognition that those who appear to rock the boat may turn out to be the most effective of captains.

*Source:* Reprinted by permission of *Harvard Business Review.* Excerpt from "Radical Change the Quiet Way," Debra E. Meyerson, October 2001. Copyright © 2001 by the Harvard Business School Publishing Corporation; all rights reserved.

Meyerson's research has found many "square pegs in round holes" who identify powerfully with her concept of the tempered radical. They tend to work quietly yet relentlessly to advance their vision of a better organization. If progressive managers are to do a good job of managing diversity, then they need to handle their tempered radicals in win-win fashion (see Managing Diversity). Too often those with different ideas are marginalized and/or trivialized. When this happens, the organization's intellectual and social capital suffer greatly.

Four practical guidelines for tempered radicals stem from Meyerson's research:

1. *Think small for big results.* Don't try to change the organization's culture all at once. Start small and build a string of steadily larger victories. Learn as you go. Encourage small, nonthreatening experiments. Trust and confidence in you and your ideas will grow with the victories.
2. *Be authentic.* Base your actions on your convictions and thoughtful preparation, not on rash emotionalism. Anger, aggression, and arrogance give people an easy excuse to dismiss you and your ideas.
3. *Translate.* Build managerial support by explaining the business case for your ideas.
4. *Don't go it alone.* Build a strong support network of family, friends, and coworkers to provide moral support and help advance your cause.[32]

**16F  Celebrating the Unexpected**

Legendary management writer and consultant Peter F. Drucker:

*If you start out by looking at change as threats, you will never innovate. Don't dismiss something simply because this is not what you had planned. The unexpected is often the best source of innovation.*

**Source:** As quoted in James Daly, "Sage Advice," *Business 2.0*, 1 (August 22, 2000): 142.

**Question:** *What does this perspective teach us about dealing with tempered radicals?*

### The 5P Checklist for Grassroots Change Agents (Turning Ideas into Action).

The 5P model consists of an easy-to-remember list for anyone interested in organizational change: *preparation, purpose, participation, progress,* and *persistence* (see Figure 16.5). The model is generic, meaning it applies to all levels in profit and nonprofit organizations of all sizes. Let us examine each item more closely.

**5** Describe tempered radicals and identify the 5Ps in the checklist for grassroots change agents.

- *Preparation:* Is the concept or problem clearly defined? Has adequate problem *finding* taken place? Are underlying assumptions sound? Will the end result be worth the collective time, effort, and expense? Can the change initiative be

---

**Figure 16.5**

The 5P Checklist for Change Agents

| Key action steps | |
| --- | --- |
| ✓ **P**reparation | Develop concept; test assumptions; weigh costs and benefits; identify champion or driver. |
| ✓ **P**urpose | Specify measurable objectives, milestones, deadlines. |
| ✓ **P**articipation | Refine concept while building broad and powerful support. |
| ✓ **P**rogress | Keep things moving forward despite roadblocks. |
| ✓ **P**ersistence | Foster realistic expectations and a sense of urgency while avoiding impatience. |

harnessed to another change effort with a high probability of success, or should it stand alone? Does the proposed change have a *champion* or a *driver* who has the passion and persistence to see the process through to completion?

- *Purpose:* Can the objective or goal of the change initiative be expressed in clear, measurable terms? Can it be described quickly to busy people? What are the specific progress milestones and critical deadlines?
- *Participation:* Have key people been involved in refining the change initiative to the extent of having personal ownership and willingness to fight for it? Have potential or actual opponents been offered a chance to participate? Have powerful people in the organization been recruited as advocates and defenders?
- *Progress:* Are performance milestones and intermediate deadlines being met? If not, why? Is support for the initiative weakening? Why? Have unexpected roadblocks been encountered? How can they be removed or avoided?
- *Persistence:* Has a reasonable sense of urgency been communicated to all involved? (*Note:* extreme impatience can fray relationships and be stressful.) Has the change team drifted away from the original objective as time passed? Does everyone on the team have realistic expectations about how long the change process will take?

With situational adjustments for unique personalities and circumstances, the 5P approach can help ordinary employees create extraordinary change.[33] So sharpen your concept and take your best shot!

# Managing Conflict

Conflict is intimately related to change and interpersonal dealings. Harvard's Abraham Zaleznik offered this perspective:

> *Because people come together to satisfy a wide array of psychological needs, social relations in general are awash with conflict. In the course of their interactions, people must deal with differences as well as similarities, with aversions as well as affinities. Indeed, in social relations, Sigmund Freud's parallel of humans and porcupines is apt: like porcupines, people prick and injure one another if they get too close; they will feel cold if they get too far apart.[34]*

The term *conflict* has a strong negative connotation, evoking words such as *opposition, anger, aggression,* and *violence.*[35] But conflict does not have to be a negative experience. Based on research evidence that most organizational conflict occurs within a cooperative context, Dean Tjosvold offered this more positive definition: "**Conflict** involves incompatible behaviors; one person interfering, disrupting, or in some other way making another's actions less effective."[36] This definition paves the way for an important distinction between *competitive* (or destructive) conflict and *cooperative* (or constructive) conflict. Cooperative conflict is based on the win-win negotiating attitude discussed later in this chapter. Also, recall our discussion of cooperative conflict in Chapter 14 as a tool for avoiding groupthink.

**conflict** *incompatible behaviors that make another person less effective*

## Dealing with the Two Faces of Conflict

**6** Contrast the competitive and cooperative conflict styles.

Tjosvold contrasts competitive and cooperative conflict as follows:

> *The assumption that conflict is based on opposing interests leads to viewing conflict as a struggle to see whose strength and interests will dominate and whose will be subordinated. We must fight to win, or at least not lose. The assumption that you have largely cooperative*

*Students who want to argue for a higher grade may not want to tackle this particular professor. He's Bruce Patton, who teaches conflict management seminars in Harvard Law School's Program on Negotiation. For better or for worse, he calls conflict "a growth industry." He advises managers to not waste their time minimizing conflict, but rather to harness it in creative and constructive ways. Now, about that grade.*

*goals leads to viewing the conflict as a common problem to be solved for mutual benefit, which in turn makes it more likely that the conflict will be constructive and that people will improve their abilities to deal with conflict.*[37]

Figure 16.6 graphically illustrates the difference between competitive and cooperative conflict. In the competitive mode, the parties pursue directly opposite goals. Each mistrusts the other's intentions and disbelieves what the other party says. Both parties actively avoid constructive dialogue and have a win-lose attitude. Unavoidably, the disagreement persists and they go their separate ways.[38] Does this self-defeating cycle sound familiar? Probably, because most of us at one time or another have suffered through a broken relationship or destructive conflict with someone else.

In sharp contrast, the *cooperative* conflict cycle in Figure 16.6 is a mutually reinforcing experience serving the best interests of both parties. Cooperative conflict is standard practice at Anheuser-Busch, brewer of Budweiser beer:

*When the policy committee of that company considers a major move—getting into or out of a business, or making a big capital expenditure—it sometimes assigns teams to make the case for each side of the question. There may be two teams or even three. Each is knowledgeable about the subject; each has access to the same information. Occasionally someone in favor of the project is chosen to lead the dissent, and an opponent to argue for it. Pat Stokes, who heads the company's beer empire, describes the result: "We end up with decisions and alternatives we hadn't thought of previously," sometimes representing a synthesis of the opposing views. "You become a lot more anticipatory, better able to see what might happen, because you have thought through the process."*[39]

As a skill-building exercise, you might want to use the cooperative conflict model in Figure 16.6 to salvage a personal relationship mired in competitive conflict. Show the

**Figure 16.6    Competitive Versus Cooperative Conflict**

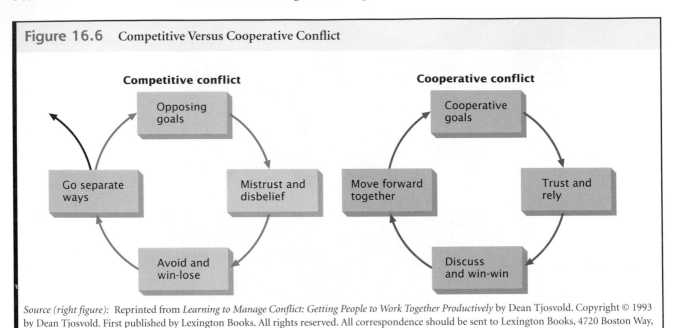

Source (right figure): Reprinted from *Learning to Manage Conflict: Getting People to Work Together Productively* by Dean Tjosvold. Copyright © 1993 by Dean Tjosvold. First published by Lexington Books. All rights reserved. All correspondence should be sent to Lexington Books, 4720 Boston Way, Lanham, Md. 20706.

**conflict trigger**   *any factor that increases the chances of conflict*

cooperative model to the other party and suggest starting over with a new set of ground rules. Cooperative goals are the necessary starting point. This process can be difficult, yet very rewarding. Win-win conflict is not just a good idea; it is one of the keys to a better world. (See Skills & Tools at the end of this chapter for tips on how to express anger.)

There are two sets of tools available for managing conflict.[40] The first we call conflict triggers, for stimulating conflict; the second involves conflict resolution techniques, used when conflict becomes destructive.

## Conflict Triggers

A **conflict trigger** is a circumstance that increases the chances of intergroup or interpersonal conflict. As long as a conflict trigger appears to stimulate constructive conflict, it can be allowed to continue. But as soon as the symptoms of destructive conflict[41] become apparent, steps need to be taken to remove or correct the offending conflict trigger. Major conflict triggers include the following:

- *Ambiguous or overlapping jurisdictions.* Unclear job boundaries often create competition for resources and control. Reorganization can help to clarify job boundaries if destructive conflict becomes a problem (refer to the organization design alternatives discussed in Chapter 10).

- *Competition for scarce resources.* As the term is used here, *resources* include funds, personnel, authority,

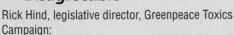

**16G    Greenpeace Disagrees Without Being Disagreeable**

Rick Hind, legislative director, Greenpeace Toxics Campaign:

*At Greenpeace, we are often in conflict with PVC manufacturers. The big users of plastics don't need to use PVC—but they don't know that yet. We start out by being reasonable. For example, we met with the whole toy industry before we made a public campaign against vinyl toys. When two meetings resulted in foot-dragging and stonewalling, we began to publicize toy additives. After two years of such publicity, companies became interested in talking with us privately.*

**Source:** As quoted in "Disagree—Without Being Disagreeable," *Fast Company,* no. 29 (November 1999): 58.

**Questions:** *Why is it so difficult for people to avoid competitive and destructive conflict? Why is it important for environmentalists at Greenpeace to engage in cooperative conflict?*

power, and valuable information. In other words, anything of value in an organizational setting can become a competitively sought-after scarce resource. Sometimes, as in the case of money and people, destructive competition for scarce resources can be avoided by enlarging the resource base (such as increasing competing managers' budgets or hiring additional personnel).[42]

- *Communication breakdowns.* Because communication is a complex process beset by many barriers, these barriers often provoke conflict. It is easy to misunderstand another person or group of people if two-way communication is hampered in some way. The battle for clear communication never ends.

- *Time pressure.* Deadlines and other forms of time pressure can stimulate prompt performance or trigger destructive emotional reactions. When imposing deadlines, managers should consider individuals' ability to cope.

- *Unreasonable standards, rules, policies, or procedures.* These triggers generally lead to dysfunctional conflict between managers and the people they manage. The best remedy is for the manager to tune into employees' perceptions of fair play and correct extremely unpopular situations before they mushroom.

- *Personality clashes.* It is very difficult to change one's personality on the job. Therefore the practical remedy for serious personality clashes is to separate the antagonistic parties by reassigning one or both to a new job.

- *Status differentials.* As long as productive organizations continue to be arranged hierarchically, this trigger is unavoidable. But managers can minimize dysfunctional conflict by showing a genuine concern for the ideas, feelings, and values of lower-level employees.

- *Unrealized expectations.* Dissatisfaction grows when expectations are not met. Conflict is another by-product of unrealized expectations. Destructive conflict can be avoided in this area by taking time to discover, through frank discussion, what people expect from their employment. Unrealistic expectations can be countered before they become a trigger for dysfunctional conflict.

Managers who understand these conflict triggers will be in a much better position to manage conflict in a systematic and rational fashion. Those who passively wait for things to explode before reacting will find conflict managing them.

**16H  Please, Let's Be More Respectful. Thank You.**

*We are not, sad to say, born kind and tolerant. Survival instincts still push us to fight or flee, dominate or submit. Just watch children at play. The good news is we're trainable. We learn our behaviors. We can develop different ways of interacting. We can be taught to play nice. . . .*

*Learning to develop respectful relationships at work is perhaps the most important work-related skill we can develop. Our successes will be a measure of how far we've come as a society. Our failures will end up as headlines in the morning newspaper.*

**Source:** Robert Rosell, "The Respectful Workplace," *Training,* 38 (November 2001): 80.

**Questions:** *Do you think standards of social conduct have declined in recent years? Examples? Are disrespect and incivility conflict triggers in the workplace? Explain. What can managers (and you) do to improve the situation?*

## Resolving Conflict

Even the best managers sometimes find themselves in the middle of destructive conflict, whether it is due to inattention or to circumstances beyond their control. In such situations, they may choose to do nothing, called an *avoidance* strategy by some, or try one or more of the following conflict resolution techniques.[43]

**7** Identify and describe five conflict resolution techniques.

**Problem Solving.**  When conflicting parties take the time to identify and correct the source of their conflict, they are engaging in problem solving. This approach is based on the assumption that causes must be rooted out and attacked if anything is really to change. Problem solving (refer to our discussion of creative problem solving in Chapter 8) encourages managers to focus their attention on causes, factual information, and promising alternatives rather than on personalities or scapegoats. The major shortcoming of the problem-solving approach is that it takes time, but the investment of extra time can pay off handsomely when the problem is corrected instead of ignored and allowed to worsen.

**Superordinate Goals.**    "Superordinate goals are highly valued, unattainable by any one group [or individual] alone, and commonly sought."[44] When a manager relies on superordinate goals to resolve destructive conflict, he or she brings the conflicting parties together and, in effect, says, "Look, we're all in this together. Let's forget our differences so we can get the job done." For example, a company president might remind the production and marketing department heads who have been arguing about product design that the competition is breathing down their necks. Although this technique often works in the short run, the underlying problem tends to crop up later to cause friction once again.

**Compromise.**    This technique generally appeals to those living in a democracy. Advocates of compromise say everyone wins because it is based on negotiation, on give-and-take.[45] However, as discussed in the next section, most people do not have good negotiating skills. They approach compromise situations with a win-lose attitude. So compromises tend to be disappointing, leaving one or both parties feeling cheated. Conflict is only temporarily suppressed when people feel cheated. Successful compromise requires skillful negotiation.

**Forcing.**    Sometimes, especially when time is important or a safety issue is involved, management must simply step into a conflict and order the conflicting parties to handle the situation in a certain manner. Reliance on formal authority and the power of a superior position is at the heart of forcing. As one might suspect, forcing does not resolve the conflict and, in fact, may serve to compound it by hurting feelings and/or fostering resentment and mistrust.

**Smoothing.**    A manager who relies on smoothing says to the conflicting parties something like, "Settle down. Don't rock the boat. Things will work out by themselves." This approach may tone down conflict in the short run, but it does not solve the underlying problem. As with each of the other conflict resolution techniques, smoothing has its place. It can be useful when management is attempting to hold things together until a critical project is completed or when there is no time for problem solving or compromise and forcing is deemed inappropriate.

Problem solving and skillfully negotiated compromises are the only approaches that remove the actual sources of conflict. They are the only resolution techniques capable of improving things in the long run. The other approaches amount to short-run, stopgap measures. And managers who fall back on an avoidance strategy are simply running away from the problem. Nonetheless, as mentioned, problem solving and full negotiation sessions can take up valuable time, time managers may not be willing or able to spend at the moment. When this is the case, management may choose to fall back on superordinate goals, forcing, or smoothing, whichever seems most suitable.[46]

# Negotiating

Negotiating is a fact of everyday life. Our negotiating skills are tested when we begin a new job, rent an apartment, live with a roommate, buy a house, buy or lease a car, ask for a raise or promotion, live with a spouse, divorce a spouse, or fight for custody of a child. Managers have even more opportunities to negotiate. Salespeople, employees, labor unions, other managers, and customers all have wishes the organization may not be able to grant without some give-and-take. Sadly, most of us are rather poor negotiators. Negotiating skills, like any other crucial communication skill, need to be developed through diligent study and regular practice.[47] In fact, subjects in a study who had been trained in negotiating tactics negotiated more favorable outcomes than did those with no such training.[48]

Experts from Northwestern University define **negotiation** as "a decision-making process among interdependent parties who do not share identical preferences." They go on to say, "It is through negotiation that the parties decide what each will give and take in their relationship."[49] The scope of negotiations spans all levels of human interaction, from individuals to organizations to nations. Two common types of negotiation are *two-party* and *third-party*. This distinction is evident in common real estate transactions. If you sell your home directly to a buyer after settling on a mutually agreeable price, that is a two-party negotiation. It becomes a third-party negotiation when a real estate agent acts as a go-between for seller and buyer. Regardless of the type of negotiation, the same basic negotiating concepts apply. This final section examines three elements of effective negotiation and introduces a useful technique called *added value negotiating.*

**negotiation** *decision-making process among interdependent parties with different preferences*

*When Ford Motor Company and Firestone began negotiating with lawyers representing rollover accident victims, they must have felt like they were hit by a giant truck themselves. Actually, what they encountered was the work of an obscure nonprofit organization in Birmingham, Alabama, called Attorneys Information Exchange Group (AIEG). By collecting relevant documentation from its 600 members, AIEG was able to build a 400,000-page case against Ford and Firestone before the rollover problem made headlines and attracted the attention of Congress. The object lesson: do your homework prior to any negotiation.*

3. *Design alternative deal packages.* Rather than tying the success of the negotiation to a single win-win offer, create a number of alternatives from various combinations of value items. This vital step, which distinguishes AVN from other negotiation strategies, fosters *creative agreement.*

4. *Select a deal.* Each party tests the various deal packages for value, balance, and fit. Feasible deals are then discussed jointly and a *mutually acceptable deal* selected.

5. *Perfect the deal.* Unresolved details are hammered out by the negotiators. Agreements are put in writing. *Relationships* are strengthened for future negotiations. Added value negotiating, according to the Albrechts, "is based on openness, flexibility, and a mutual search for the successful exchange of value. It allows you to build strong relationships with people over time."[59]

# Summary

1. Managers need to do a much better job of managing the process of change. Nadler and Tushman's model identifies four types of organizational change by cross-referencing anticipatory and reactive change with incremental and strategic change. Four resulting types of change are tuning, adaptation, re-orientation, and re-creation.

2. People who like a change tend to go through three stages: unrealistic optimism, reality shock, and constructive direction. When someone fears or dislikes a change, a more complex process involving five stages tends to occur: getting off on the wrong track, laughing it off, experiencing growing self-doubt, buying in, and moving in a constructive direction. Managers are challenged to help employees deal effectively with reality shock and self-doubt.

3. Inevitable resistance to change must be overcome if the organization is to succeed. Employees resist change for many different reasons, including (but not limited to) inertia, lack of trust, fear of failure, and competing commitments. Modern managers facing resistance to change can select from several strategies, including education and communication, participation and involvement, facilitation and support, negotiation and agreement, manipulation and co-optation, and explicit and implicit coercion.

4. Organization development (OD) is a systematic approach to planned organizational change. The principal objectives of OD are increased trust, better problem solving, more effective communication, improved cooperation, and greater willingness to change. The typical OD program is a three-phase process of unfreezing, change, and refreezing.

5. Unofficial and informal grassroots change can be initiated by tempered radicals, who quietly follow their convictions when trying to change the dominant organizational culture. Four guidelines for tempered radicals are (1) think small for big results, (2) be authentic, (3) translate, and (4) don't go it alone. The 5P checklist for grassroots change agents—*preparation, purpose, participation, progress,* and *persistence*—

is a generic model for people at all levels in all organizations. Ordinary employees can achieve extraordinary changes by having a clear purpose, a champion or driver for the change initiative, a measurable objective, broad and powerful support achieved through participation, an ability to overcome roadblocks, and a persistent sense of urgency.

**6.** Competitive conflict is characterized by a destructive cycle of opposing goals, mistrust and disbelief, and avoidance and a win-lose attitude. Oppositely, cooperative conflict involves a constructive cycle of cooperative goals, trust and reliance, and discussion and a win-win attitude.

**7.** Conflict triggers can cause either constructive or destructive conflict. Destructive conflict can be resolved through problem solving, superordinate goals, compromise, forcing, or smoothing.

**8.** Three basic elements of effective negotiations are a win-win attitude, a BATNA (best alternative to a negotiated agreement) to serve as a negotiating standard, and the calculation of a bargaining zone to identify overlapping interests. Added value negotiating (AVN) improves on standard negotiation strategies by fostering a creative range of possible solutions.

## Terms to Understand

Anticipatory changes (p.530)

Reactive changes (p.530)

Incremental changes (p.530)

Strategic changes (p.530)

Organization development (OD) (p.539)

Unfreezing (p.540)

Refreezing (p.540)

Tempered radicals (p.541)

Conflict (p.544)

Conflict trigger (p.546)

Negotiation (p.549)

Bargaining zone (p.551)

Added value negotiating (p.551)

# Skills & Tools

## How to Express Anger

Although not every angry feeling should be expressed to the person held accountable, this approach is direct and has the most potential to initiate a productive conflict. There are several rules to keep in mind when expressing anger.

- **Check assumptions.** No matter how convinced employees are that someone has deliberately interfered and tried to harm them, they may be mistaken. People can ask questions and probe. It may be that the other person had no intention and was unaware that others were frustrated. The incident may just dissolve into a misunder-standing.

- **Be specific.** People find being the target of anger stressful and anxiety provoking. They fear insults and rejection. The more specific the angry person can be, the less threatening and less of an attack on self-esteem the anger is. Knowing what angered the other can give the target of the anger concrete ways to make amends.

- **Be consistent.** Verbal and nonverbal messages should both express anger. Smiling and verbally expressing anger confuses the issue.

- **Take responsibility for anger.** Persons expressing anger should let the target know that they are angry and the reasoning and steps they took that made them feel unjustly frustrated.

- **Avoid provoking anger.** Expressing anger through unfair, insinuating remarks ("I can't believe someone can be as stupid as you!") can make the target of the anger angry too. Such situations can quickly deteriorate.

- **Watch for impulsivity.** Anger agitates and people say things they later regret.

- **Be wary of self-righteousness.** People can feel powerful, superior, and right; angry people can play, "Now I got ya and you will pay." But anger should be used to get to the heart of the matter and solve problems, not for flouting moral superiority.

- **Be sensitive.** People typically underestimate the impact their anger has on others. Targets of anger often feel defensive, anxious, and worried. It is not usually necessary to repeat one's anger to get people's attention.

- **Make the expression cathartic.** Anger generates energy. Telling people releases that energy rather than submerges it. Anger is a feeling to get over, not to hang on to.

- **Express positive feelings.** Angry people depend upon and usually like people they are angry with. People expect help from people who have proved trustworthy, and are angry when it is not forthcoming.

- **Move to constructive conflict management.** Feeling affronted, personally attacked, and self-righteous should not side-track you from solving the underlying problems. Use the anger to create positive conflict.

- **Celebrate joint success.** Anger tests people's skills and their relationship. Be sure to celebrate the mutual achievement of expressing and responding to anger success-fully.

*Source:* Dean Tjosvold, *The Conflict-Positive Organization* (pp. 133–134). © 1991. Reprinted by permission of Pearson Education, Inc., Upper Saddle River, New Jersey.

# Hands-On Exercise

## Putting Conflict on Ice[60]

**Instructions**

Working alone or as a member of a team, read the following material on the iceberg of conflict. As instructed in the reading, focus on a specific conflict and then answer the seven sets of questions. Alternatively, both parties in a conflict can complete this exercise and then compare notes to establish interconnections and move toward resolution.

### The Iceberg of Conflict

One way of picturing the hidden layers and complexities of conflict is through the metaphor of the iceberg, as depicted in the following chart. You may want to identify additional layers besides the ones we cite, to reveal what is below the surface for you.

**Iceberg of conflict**

Issues

Personalities

Emotions

Interests, needs, and desires

Self-perceptions and self-esteem

Hidden expectations

Unresolved issues from the past

**Awareness of interconnection**

### Exploring Your Iceberg

Each level of the iceberg represents something that does not appear on the surface, yet adds weight and immobility to our arguments when we are in conflict. Beneath the iceberg, the chart identifies an "awareness of interconnection," meaning that we all have the capacity, when we go deep enough and are not stuck on the surface of our conflicts, to experience genuine empathy and awareness of our interconnection with each other—including the person who is upsetting us.

To understand the deeper layers of your iceberg and get to an awareness of interconnection, consider a conflict in which you are now engaged. Try to identify the specific issues, problems, and feelings that exist for you at each level of the iceberg. As you probe deeper, notice whether your definition of the conflict changes, and how it evolves. Become aware of any emotions that emerge as you look deeper. Fear or resistance to these feelings can keep the conflict locked in place and block you from reaching deeper levels. Allow yourself to experience these feelings, whatever they are, and identify them to yourself or to someone you trust, so you can let them go. Try to answer the following questions for yourself and your opponent:

- *Issues:* What issues appear on the surface of your conflict?

- *Personalities:* Are differences between your personalities contributing to misunderstanding and tension? If so, what are they and how do they operate?

- *Emotions:* What emotions are having an impact on your reactions? How are they doing so? Are you communicating your emotions responsibly, or suppressing them?

- *Interests, needs, desires:* How are you proposing to solve the conflict? Why is that your proposal? What deeper concerns are driving the conflict? What do you really want? Why? What needs or desires, if satisfied, would enable you to feel good about the outcome? Why is that important? What does getting what you want have to do with the conflict?

- *Self-perceptions and self-esteem:* How do you feel about yourself and your behavior when you are engaged in the conflict? What do you see as your strengths and weaknesses?

- *Hidden expectations:* What are your primary expectations of your opponent? Of yourself? Have you clearly, openly, and honestly communicated your expectations to the other person? What would happen if you did? How might you release yourself from false expectations?

- *Unresolved issues from the past:* Does this conflict remind you of anything from your past relationships? Are there any unfinished issues remaining from the past that keep you locked in this conflict? Why?

*Source:* Kenneth Cloke and Joan Goldsmith, *Resolving Conflicts at Work: A Complete Guide for Everyone on the Job* (San Francisco: Jossey-Bass, 2000), pp. 114–116. Copyright © 2000 by Kenneth Cloke and Joan Goldsmith. This material is used by permission of Jossey-Bass, Inc., a subsidiary of John Wiley & Sons, Inc.

**For Consideration/ Discussion**

1. Did the issues and your perception of the conflict change as you worked through the iceberg? Explain.

2. Was there more (or less) to this conflict than you initially thought? Explain.

3. Which level of the iceberg was the most difficult to address? Why? Which was the easiest? Why?

4. What interconnections surfaced? How can they be used as a foundation for resolving the conflict?

5. How will this exercise affect the way you try to understand and resolve (or avoid) conflicts in the future?

# Internet Exercises

1. **Ready, set, change:** This practical application exercise has three parts: (a) think of an organizational change you would like to champion at your present or past place of work; (b) draw up an action plan based on the 5P checklist in Figure 16.5; and (c) search the Internet for good ideas about being an effective change agent. (*Note:* an alternative approach in the first step is to "borrow" a change proposal from a manager you know.) To jump-start your Internet search, go to **www.fastcompany. com** and click on the submenu "Dynamic Archives" under the tab "Magazine." From there, scroll down to issue number 5 (October–November 1996) and read Nicholas Morgan's short article "9 Tips for Change Agents." Return to the archives page, scroll up to recent issues of *Fast Company* magazine, and find and read two or three more articles dealing with change.

    *Learning Points:* 1. Is your proposed change realistic? What do others think about it?  2. What sort of "unfreezing" will need to be done?  3. What sort of resistance will likely be encountered? From whom?  4. How can the resistance to your change be avoided or neutralized?  5. Which powerful people do you need to recruit for your change team? How will you recruit them?  6. What helpful tips and guidelines about being a change agent did you acquire from your Internet search?

2. **Building your tool kit for handling conflict:** Society suffers and our general quality of life is eroded because of poor conflict management skills. Daily reports in the news media about domestic and workplace violence, road rage, school violence, and international warfare attest to the need for peaceful ways of resolving conflicts. The National Crime Prevention Council has a very useful Web site (**www.ncpc.org/ 1safe5dc.htm**) offering advice and resources for dealing with conflict. Read "Making Peace—Tips on Managing Conflict" and then explore the links "Help your children manage conflict" and "stopping school violence."

    *Learning Points:* 1. What was the best piece of advice you acquired?  2. What was the most unusual bit of advice you read?  3. What proportion of the material you read dealt with cooperative, as opposed to competitive, conflict (refer back to Figure 16.6)?  4. How would you rate your ability to handle interpersonal conflict between yourself and someone else? Between two other people?  5. What do you need to do to improve your conflict-handling skills?

3. **Check it out:** In discussing the political implications for managers back in Chapter 3, we introduced the practice of *alternative dispute resolution* (ADR). Two common forms of ADR are arbitration and mediation. In arbitration, a third party gathers information from disputing parties and renders a binding decision, much like an informal court. Mediation, on the other hand, occurs when a third party facilitates a constructive dialogue between conflicting parties, who then create their own settlement. Both approaches can save time and money and avoid further clogging the court system. Being an effective mediator is a key conflict-handling skill for managers. To learn more about mediation, visit the Web site sponsored by Stephen R. Marsh (**www.adrr.com**), a lawyer and mediator from Dallas, Texas. In the section "Mediation Essays" (volume one), be sure to read the material under the headings "What Is Mediation?" and "Negotiation in Mediation."

For updates to these exercises, visit our Web site (**http://business.college.hmco. com/students**).

## Closing Case

# The Unstoppable Entrepreneur

"**W**e've never done it that way before." In these hypercompetitive times, it's hard to believe people utter such words. Yet Bob Schmonsees hears that excuse with maddening frequency.

His small software firm, WisdomWare Inc. has developed a slick tool that makes salespeople better informed and more efficient. But it requires them—and their bosses—to do things just a little bit differently, and the wall of resistance looms high. "The good news is we've got something that's truly visionary," he says. "That's also the bad news."

But Mr. Schmonsees, 51 years old, as you'll soon see, has plenty of experience scaling huge obstacles. And although his story is intensely personal, it holds lessons for anyone facing an uphill climb in business.

As a high-tech sales manager in the 1970s, Mr. Schmonsees made a priority of protecting salespeople from the endless white papers, binders, and other epistles churned out by marketing types. Each quarter, he condensed a mountain of documents into a pocket-sized booklet that crisply summarized what a sales rep needed to know about the product, the market, and the competition.

Then came disaster. A contender in mixed-doubles tennis and a former football star, Mr. Schmonsees was standing near a ski lift when an out-of-control skier rammed him. His legs were paralyzed. He would spend the rest of his life in a wheelchair.

Fortunately, he discovered a formula for his different world: figure out the new rules for any activity, then take as many small steps as necessary to master those rules. After learning the physics of a tennis swing on wheels and the geometry of playing a second bounce (standard rules), he became the world's top wheelchair player over age 40.

No number of steps, however, could change the behavior of others. The sudden wariness of his former colleagues drove him from the company he loved. Then came many crushing job rejections. But after landing in a junior supervisory position in software sales, he climbed

to top marketing management. Later, switching to software vendor Legent Corp., he became global sales chief. "Finally, I was back to where I should have been," he says, though once again it had taken many small steps.

As always, he worked to keep his sales staff informed but not inundated. This was a losing battle by the 1990s, with electronic libraries of marketing material growing like digital kudzu. Pondering this problem one day in the shower, he thought back to those little leatherbound digests he used to hand out.

Why not put something like that online? Even more important, why not enable every piece of information to link with any other piece? That way, salespeople could assemble just the right combination of facts necessary for the task of the moment.

Moving forward with an engineering team, Mr. Schmonsees created the interactive equivalent of Cliffs Notes. While planning a call, a sales rep makes a few menu choices to identify the customer, the product, and the like. One click creates the most up-to-date qualifying questions, another reveals how the competition stacks up, another reports the most common objections, still another suggests an "elevator speech" for precisely those circumstances. Though only a few concise sentences pop on the screen, detailed reports are just a click away.

Mr. Schmonsees left Legent in late 1995. But in his own effort at selling the new product, he ran smack into a powerful objection.

The issue wasn't training; that takes five minutes. Nor was it compatibility; WisdomWare works seamlessly with other front-office software. Neither has any customer winced at the price of $500 and up per user.

The problem was culture. WisdomWare requires marketing managers to write snappy summaries in addition to (or instead of) their beloved white papers. "We've never done it that way!" came the reply.

"When this becomes part of your culture, it's a real competitive advantage," says Dan Gillis, president of SAGA Software, which embraces WisdomWare. "But it takes a real commitment."

The culture of the field force is another hurdle. Users love the encapsulated, up-to-date information that comes to the screen. But WisdomWare depends on those same users to provide intelligence from the field: what

*Source:* Republished with permission of *The Wall Street Journal* from "Bob Schmonsees Has a Tool for Better Sales, and It Ignores Excuses," by Thomas Petzinger Jr., *The Wall Street Journal* (March 26, 1999). Permission conveyed through Copyright Clearance Center, Inc.

the competition is up to, for instance, and which pitches are getting the best and worst results. Sharing information? "We've never had to do *that* before!" came the cry.

Platinum Technology, for one, equipped its sales force of 1,000 with WisdomWare in January [1999]. And although efficiencies are already evident, too few salespeople are giving back information. Platinum's Glenn Shimkus is now searching for ways to reward contributors. "We have to change the culture so that power and rewards come from sharing information, not from hoarding it," he says.

With 20 employees, Mr. Schmonsees is grinding out orders one at a time, counting 10 customers to date. And despite the slow takeoff, the company's venture-capital backers are about to step up for another round. Eventually, the product will run on a hand-held, wireless device that sales reps will consult on their way into sales calls—then use to submit feedback on their way out.

Mr. Schmonsees concedes that the business, for now, is behind his expectations. "It's going to take some time to change the world," he says. But as a metaphor for busi-

ness, his personal life encourages him. "I take pride in taking a lot of little steps toward a long-term vision," he says.

## For Discussion

**1.** Why is Schmonsees uniquely qualified to fight resistance to change?

**2.** Which of the reasons discussed in this chapter that account for employees' resistance to change are evident in this case? Explain.

**3.** Using Table 16.2 as a guide, which strategy (or strategies) should Schmonsees use to overcome resistance to WisdomWare? Explain.

**4.** What lessons from OD apply to this case? Explain.

**5.** What lessons from the 5P checklist for change agents apply to this case? Explain.

# Video Skill Builders

Partners L. D. Dabney, President, and Niva Patel, Senior V. P., grew Regional Health Supply, Inc. from nothing into a thriving business employing over 40 people. They try to hire self-starters and self-motivated people who, in Dabney's words, will put in "a day's work for a day's pay." Because the company competes on customer service rather than price, a multi-faceted motivation program is used. Empowerment, flextime, and timely rewards are key features of the motivation program.

## 4A Employee Motivation at RHS

### Learning Objective
To discover how to motivate employees in a growing business.

### Links to Textual Material
**Chapter 12:** Communication strategies     **Chapter 13:** Motivation theories; Flexible work schedules     **Chapter 14:** What makes work teams effective; Trust: a key to team effectiveness     **Chapter 15:** Empowerment; Behavior modification/positive reinforcement

### Discussion Questions

1. Which of Clampitt's five communication strategies (see Figure 12.4) seem to be most prevalent at RHS? Explain.

2. What would Maslow and Herzberg likely say about RHS's approach to employee motivation?

3. Why is flextime a good motivator?

4. Relative to the six ways to build trust, presented in Chapter 14, how is trust strengthened at RHS?

5. What evidence of empowerment do you find in this video case?

6. What evidence of positive reinforcement do you detect in this video case?

This inspiring 11-minute video introduces Jayson Goltz, president of Artist's Frame Service, based in Chicago, Illinois, and documents how an entrepreneur's leadership style must grow with the business.

## 4B Entrepreneurial Leadership

### Learning Objectives
To demonstrate how modern leaders need to constantly learn and adapt to meet new challenges. To illustrate why successful inspirational leaders are not cookie-cutter imitations, but unique individuals who dare to be different.

### Links to Textual Material
**Chapter 1:** Entrepreneurship     **Chapter 12:** Communication     **Chapter 13:** Motivating     **Chapter 15:** Influence tactics; Power; Leadership     **Chapter 16:** Managing change     **Chapter 17:** Product/service quality

### Discussion Questions

1. How well does Jayson Goltz fit the entrepreneur trait profile in Table 1.4? Explain.

2. What influence tactics, as discussed in Chapter 15, are evident in this case?

3. Which path-goal leadership style, as covered in Chapter 15, does Goltz seem to rely on the most?

4. Would you label Goltz a transactional or transformational leader (see Table 15.4)? Explain.

5. Is Goltz a good leader? Explain. Would you like to work for him? Why or why not?

# part five

# Organizational Control Processes

# Organizational Control and Quality Improvement

> **"** You can't go wrong if you keep the customer in mind. **"**
>
> Linda Sanford

*When you finish studying this chapter you should be able to*

**1** **Identify** three types of control and the components common to all control systems.

**2** **Discuss** organizational control from a strategic perspective.

**3** **Identify** the four key elements of a crisis management program.

**4** **Identify** five types of product quality.

**5** **Explain** how providing a service differs from manufacturing a product and **list** the five service-quality dimensions.

**6** **Define** *total quality management (TQM)* and **discuss** the basic TQM principles.

**7** **Describe** at least three of the seven TQM process improvement tools.

**8** **Explain** how Deming's PDCA cycle can improve the overall management process.

**9** **Specify** and **discuss** at least four of Deming's famous 14 points.

# Supply-Chain Hero

Ask most Americans for their personal recollections of Sept. 11, and they'll tell you where they were when they heard of the attack, what time it was, who broke the news, and so on. But if you ask Gus Pagonis, head of logistics at retail giant Sears Roebuck, what you'll get is a minute-by-minute recounting of the odyssey of thousands of washing machines, Craftsman tools, and palletloads of flannel pajamas.

September's terrorist attacks posed one of the most serious challenges ever to the just-in-time delivery systems that many inventory-dependent companies have relied on for nearly 20 years. Closures at bridges, tunnels, and airports triggered unprecedented delays throughout the supply chain for weeks. Heavily outsourced manufacturing industries such as automobiles, electronics, and computers were among the hardest hit, creating situations that supply-chain software simply wasn't prepared to handle.

Sears, which has millions of dollars' worth of material on the move on a typical business day, came in for its share of disruption during the crisis. Yet it's possible that no company in America was better prepared, a fact largely attributable to one man: William "Gus" Pagonis. A former three-star Army general, Pagonis served as the chief of logistics for U.S. military operations during the 1991 Gulf War. Now an executive vice president at Sears, he oversees the systems the retailer depends on to make 5,000 home deliveries per day and move 250,000 truckloads of goods every year. With 30 large distribution centers and 90 smaller outlets, it's Pagonis's job to supply 100,000-plus products to more than 2,000 Sears stores.

The Gulf War was a revolution in military logistics. During the peak of the military buildup, 5,000 troops arrived on the front each day. Using GPS technology to track the movement of supplies, Pagonis made sure that each soldier was properly fed, sheltered, and equipped for desert combat.

Pagonis joined Sears in October of 1993. Two months later he emulated military practice by establishing contingency plans and creating a dedicated disaster operations center. When a crisis strikes the United States—hurricane, earthquake, snowstorm, flood—Pagonis and his team fall back on predetermined procedures to solve problems quickly and minimize losses.

On the morning of Sept. 11, Pagonis received a call from his wife, who told him that a plane had struck the World Trade Center. When the second plane hit, he realized that a coordinated attack was under way.

Pagonis immediately launched the first stage of his disaster planning program: activating an operational contingency cell. The cell consists of one or two employees who serve as focal points for communication during disasters. After setting up on Sept. 11, the cell began to receive calls from truck drivers who reported that Sears's logistical problems were concentrated in the Northeast.

As reports of additional transportation glitches poured in, Pagonis decided to activate the disaster operations center, located in a dedicated room in Sears headquarters in Hoffman Estates, Ill. The center's walls are covered with system status charts, and computers in the facility track home deliveries, vendor shipments, and trucks. One team uses software that monitors when containers are off-loaded. Another tracks the flow of products en route. Another receives orders from the field.

When delays began to increase at U.S. borders, Pagonis and his crew developed contingency plans to minimize the damage. Shipping containers were prioritized as they came off ships and trucks; those filled with advertised promotional items were given priority, to ensure that stores had the inventory they needed most.

On the morning of Sept. 12, Pagonis held a meeting with 12 company vice presidents to craft additional contingency plans. Handing out index cards describing a variety of possible situations—truck bombs, national days of mourning, and public panic, for example—he instructed the team to craft solutions to each scenario.

The Sears disaster operations center stayed open for 30 days. The company continues to monitor its supply chain closely, and Pagonis is confident that his team is prepared to deal with future uncertainty. "If soldiers are well trained, they'll function even in the heat of battle," the former general says. "It's the same thing in business. If you train well enough, it pays off when you need it."

Pagonis is now working hard to strike a balance between minimizing inventory overhead and having enough goods on hand to keep store shelves stocked. "You can't depend on just-in-time," he says. "You have to have inventory in the system that you can control: World-class companies will figure out how to do it without creating excessive safety stock. Inventory visibility is now just as important as just-in-time."

Meanwhile, Pagonis continues to reevaluate both Sears's response to Sept. 11 and the company's ongoing level of preparedness. "It's too expensive to keep overreacting," Pagonis warns. "You need to say, 'OK, we did this during an emergency. Now how can we make it more cost-effective if we have to continue doing it?'"

In wartime, it is said, amateurs debate tactics, but professionals worry about logistics. Ironically, war has once again placed Pagonis in the spotlight. "Logistics is reaching a new plateau," he says. "The supply chain is the last frontier—the last place where you can take out cost, improve service, and tip the balance on a P&L statement." Who says an old warhorse can't learn a few new tricks?

G us Pagonis's inspiring story teaches us an important management lesson. Strategies and plans, no matter how well conceived, are no guarantee of organizational success. Those plans need to be carried out by skilled and motivated employees amid changing circumstances and an occasional crisis. Adjustments and corrective action are inevitable. This final chapter helps present and future managers put this lesson to work by introducing fundamentals of organizational control, discussing crisis management, and exploring product and service quality.

# Fundamentals of Organizational Control

**control** *taking preventive or corrective actions to keep things on track*

The word *control* suggests the operations of checking, testing, regulation, verification, or adjustment. As a management function, **control** is the process of taking the necessary preventive or corrective actions to ensure that the organization's mission and objectives are accomplished as effectively and efficiently as possible. Objectives are yardsticks against which actual performance can be measured. If actual performance is consistent with the appropriate objective, things will proceed as planned. If not, changes must be made. Successful managers detect (and even anticipate) deviations from desirable standards and make appropriate adjustments.[1] Those adjustments can range from ordering more raw materials to overhauling a production line; from discarding an unnecessary procedure to hiring additional personnel; from containing an unexpected crisis to firing a defrauder. Although the possible adjustments exercised as part of the control function are countless, the purpose of the control function is always the same: *get the job done despite environmental, organizational, and behavioral obstacles and uncertainties.*

## Types of Control

**1** Identify three types of control and the components common to all control systems.

Every open system processes inputs from the surrounding environment to produce a unique set of outputs. Natural open systems, such as the human body, are kept in life-sustaining balance through automatic feedback mechanisms. In contrast, artificial open systems, such as organizations, do not have automatic controls. Instead, they require constant monitoring and adjustment to control for deviations from standards. Figure 17.1 illustrates the control function. Notice the three different types of control: feedforward, concurrent, and feedback.

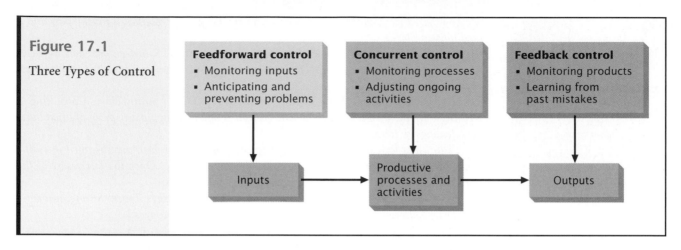

**Figure 17.1**

Three Types of Control

**Feedforward control**
- Monitoring inputs
- Anticipating and preventing problems

**Concurrent control**
- Monitoring processes
- Adjusting ongoing activities

**Feedback control**
- Monitoring products
- Learning from past mistakes

Inputs → Productive processes and activities → Outputs

**Feedforward Control.** According to two early proponents of feedforward control, "the only way [managers] can exercise control effectively is to see the problems coming in time to do something about them."[2] **Feedforward control** is the active anticipation of problems and their timely prevention, rather than after-the-fact reaction. Carpenters have their own instructive version of feedforward control: "Measure twice, cut once." It is important to note that planning and feedforward control are two related but different processes. Planning answers the question, "Where are we going and how will we get there?" Feedforward control addresses the issue, "What can we do ahead of time to help our plan succeed?" *Preventive maintenance* on machinery and equipment and *due diligence* also qualify as feedforward control. Consider this recent example of due diligence:

**feedforward control** *active anticipation and prevention of problems, rather than passive reaction*

*If ever there was a need for feedforward control, this is it! Malden Mills' giant circular knitting machine in Lawrence, Massachusetts, produces tubes of polyester fabric used to make Polartec garments for rugged outdoor wear. Feedforward control, the anticipation and prevention of problems, is required to make sure the automatic equipment is maintained and loaded properly. If not, costly batches of scrap material would pile up quickly.*

*Moscow-based Itera Group has the world's fourth-largest gas reserves, a murky past and a credibility problem.*

*Many Russians think its assets were stolen from the state. U.S. law-enforcement agencies suspect it of money laundering. Western energy companies wonder if it's safe to do business with Itera.*

*To prove to the world that it's clean, Itera said . . . it hired Strang Hayes Consulting, a New York private investigative firm. The gumshoes' job is to dig up any proof of illicit business dealings by Itera.*

*It's unusual for companies to want their own integrity probed, but so-called due diligence investigations are becoming increasingly commonplace. Once the last resort of the paranoid, they're now routine in major corporate transactions.*

*"It's standard practice for most deals over $25 million," says Robert Strang, a former U.S. Drug Enforcement Agency agent and president of Strang Hayes.*[3]

On a more personal level, think of due diligence as refusing to go on a blind date without first researching the person's background and reputation.

Of the three types of control, American managers tend to do the poorest job with feedforward control. Longer-term thinking and better cross-functional communication could remedy this situation.

**concurrent control**
*monitoring and adjusting ongoing activities and processes*

**Concurrent Control.**    This second type of control might well be called real-time control because it deals with the present rather than the future or past. **Concurrent control** involves monitoring and adjusting ongoing activities and processes to ensure compliance with standards. When you are using a bread toaster, for instance, you can set the automatic control mechanism and run the risk of ending up with a piece of charcoal. Because toaster control mechanisms often malfunction, they are not a very reliable form of feedforward control. To compensate, you can exercise concurrent control by keeping an eye on the toasting process and ejecting your toast by hand when it reaches just the right shade. So, too, construction supervisors engage in concurrent control when they help carpenters and plumbers with difficult tasks at the building site.

**feedback control**    *checking a completed activity and learning from mistakes*

**Feedback Control.**    **Feedback control** is gathering information about a completed activity, evaluating that information, and taking steps to improve similar activities in the future. Feedback control permits managers to use information on past performance to bring future performance in line with planned objectives and acceptable standards. For example, by monitoring complaints from discharged patients about billing errors, a hospital's comptroller learns about problems in the billing process. Critics of feedback control say it is like closing the gate after the horse is gone. Because corrective action is taken after the fact, costs tend to pile up quickly, and problems and deviations persist.

On the positive side, feedback control tests the quality and validity of objectives and standards. Objectives found to be impossible to attain should be made more reasonable. Those that prove too easy need to be toughened. A bank's loan officer, for example, may discover that too much potentially profitable business is being turned away because the criteria for granting credit are too strict. By exercising feedback control—loosening the credit standards loan applicants must meet—the bank's lending operation can be made more profitable. Of course, if this adjustment leads to a default rate that eats up the additional profits, the credit criteria may need yet another round of feedback control.

In summary, a successful manager must exercise all three types of control in today's complex organizations. Feedforward control helps managers avoid mistakes in the first place; concurrent control enables them to catch mistakes as they are being made; feedback control keeps them from repeating past mistakes. Interaction and a workable balance among the three types of control are desirable.

## Components of Organizational Control Systems

The owner-manager of a small business such as a dry-cleaning establishment can keep things under control by personally overseeing operations and making necessary adjustments. An electrician can be called in to fix a broken pressing machine, poor workmanship can be improved through coaching, a customer's complaint can be handled immediately, or a shortage of change in the cash register can be remedied. A small organization directed by a single, highly motivated individual with expert knowledge of all aspects of the operation represents the ideal control situation.[4] Unfortunately, the size and complexity of most productive organizations have made firsthand control by a single person obsolete. Consequently, multilevel, multidimensional organizational control systems have evolved.

A study of nine large companies in different industries sheds some needed light on the mechanics of complex organizational control systems.[5] After interviewing dozens of key managers, the researchers identified six distinct control subsystems:

**17B  EMC, Call Home**

A quiz to see if you're paying attention: Which kind of control is this?

*EMC [a Massachusetts data storage company] likes to call it "service and support mind reading." Sensors that are built into its storage systems monitor things such as temperature, vibration, and tiny fluctuations in power, as well as unusual patterns in the way data is being stored and retrieved—over 1,000 diagnostics in all. Every two hours, an EMC system checks its own state of health. If everything is running smoothly, the log file is stored away. If the machine spots something that it doesn't like, it "phones home" to customer service over a line dedicated for that purpose.*

*Every day, an average of 3,500 calls for help reach EMC's call center in Hopkinton. But it's not people who are calling in to ask for help—it's machines.*

**Source:** Paul C. Judge, "EMC Corporation," *Fast Company*, no. 47 (June 2001): 144.

**Question:** *Is this feedforward, concurrent, or feedback control? Explain.*

1. *Strategic plans.* Qualitative analyses of the company's position within the industry
2. *Long-range plans.* Typically, five-year financial projections
3. *Annual operating budgets.* Annual estimates of profit, expenses, and financial indicators
4. *Statistical reports.* Quarterly, monthly, or weekly nonfinancial statistical summaries of key indicators such as orders received and personnel surpluses or shortages
5. *Performance appraisals.* Evaluation of employees through the use of management by objectives (MBO) or rating scales
6. *Policies and procedures.* Organizational and departmental standard operating procedures referred to on an as-needed basis

A seventh organizational control subsystem is *cultural control.*[6] As discussed in Chapter 9, stories and company legends have a profound impact on how things are done in specific organizations. Employees who deviate from cultural norms are promptly straightened out with glances, remarks, or ridicule.

Complex organizational control systems such as these help keep things on the right track because they embrace three basic components, common to all organizational control systems: objectives, standards, and an evaluation-reward system.[7]

**Objectives.**    In Chapter 6, we defined an *objective* as a target signifying what should be accomplished and when. Objectives are an indispensable part of any control system because they provide measurable reference points for corrective action. In 2000,

Sweden's Volvo announced the ambitious objective of a 50 percent increase in worldwide car sales by 2004.[8] Yearly milestones will let Volvo's managers know if they are on target or if corrective actions, such as creating a new advertising campaign, are necessary.

### Standards.
Whereas objectives serve as measurable targets, standards serve as guideposts on the way to reaching those targets. Standards provide feedforward control by warning people when they are off the track.[9] Golfers use par as a standard for gauging the quality of their game. When the objective is to shoot par, a golfer who exceeds par on a hole is warned that he or she must improve on later holes to achieve the objective. Universities exercise a degree of feedforward control over student performance by establishing and following admission standards for grades and test scores. Businesses rely on many different kinds of standards, including those in purchasing, engineering, time, safety, accounting, and quality.

**benchmarking** *identifying, studying, and building upon the best practices of organizational role models*

A proven technique for establishing challenging standards is **benchmarking,** that is, identifying, studying, and imitating the best *practices* of market leaders.[10] The central idea in benchmarking is to be competitive by striving to be as good as or better than the *best* in the business. The search for benchmarks is not restricted to one's own industry. Consider, for example, United Airlines' recent benchmarking efforts in Marina Del Rey, California:

> In a bid to boost the quality of its overseas service, United Airlines is bringing some of its attendants to the best hotels, such as the Ritz-Carlton here, to learn the fine points of catering to the needs of the well-heeled.
>
> "They are very much recognized name-wise for a higher level of service," explains United trainer Christine Swanstrom. "The clientele we're trying to attract in international is the clientele that would stay at a Ritz."[11]

### An Evaluation-Reward System.
Because employees do not get equal results, some sort of performance review is required to document individual and/or team contributions to organizational objectives. Extrinsic rewards need to be tied equitably to documented results and improvement. A carefully conceived and clearly communi-

*When Alicia Compusto performs a quality check on a printed circuit board at the Cisco Systems factory in San Jose, California, she compares it to precise standards. In effect, the quality standards give her a measuring stick for determining if a unit's quality is acceptable or unacceptable. If it is unacceptable, adjustments can be made in the manufacturing process to improve product quality. Her job is vital to success at the maker of Internet switches and routers because a faulty circuit board can compromise the quality of the expensive piece of equipment it is to built into.*

cated evaluation-reward scheme can shape favorable effort-reward expectancies, hence motivating better performance.

When integrated systematically, objectives, standards, and an equitable evaluation-reward system constitute an invaluable control mechanism.

## Strategic Control

Managers who fail to complement their strategic planning with strategic control, as recommended in Chapter 7, will find themselves winning some battles but losing the war.[12] The performance pyramid in Figure 17.2 illustrates the necessarily tight linkage between planning and control. It is a strategic model because everything is oriented toward the strategic peak of the pyramid. Objectives based on the corporate vision (or mission) are translated downward during planning. As plans become reality, control measures of activities and results are translated up the pyramid. The flow of objectives and measures requires a good information system.

External effectiveness and internal efficiency criteria are distinguished in Figure 17.2 by color coding. Significantly, all of the external effectiveness areas are focused on the marketplace in general and on the *customer* in particular. According to the performance pyramid, control measures are needed for cycle time, waste, flexibility, productivity, and financial results. *Cycle time* is the time it takes for a product to be transformed from raw materials or parts into a finished good. Notice how *flexibility* relates to both effectiveness and efficiency. A garden tractor manufacturer, for example, needs to be externally flexible in adapting to changing customer demands and internally flexible in training employees to handle new technology.

**2** Discuss organizational control from a strategic perspective.

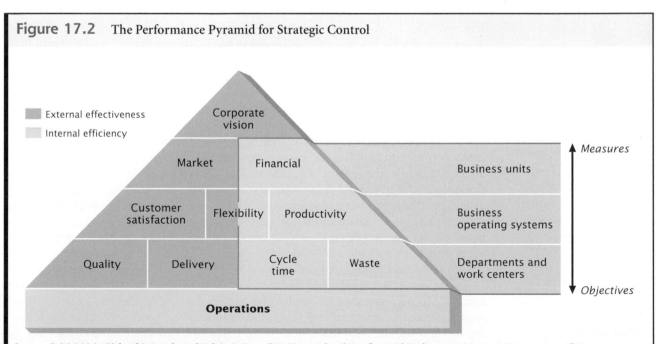

**Figure 17.2    The Performance Pyramid for Strategic Control**

*Source:* C. J. McNair, Richard L. Lynch, and Kelvin F. Cross, "Do Financial and Nonfinancial Performance Measures Have to Agree?" *Management Accounting* published by the Institute of Management Accountants, Montvale, N.J., 72 (November 1990): 30. Copyright by Institute of Management Accountants. Reprinted by permission.

## 17C  Who's in Charge Here?

Avram Miller, high-tech consultant, offers this advice for doing business at Internet speed:

*Give up control. Or the illusion of control. Companies no longer determine the success of products and markets—if they ever did. Customers do. Control is an illusion, and the Internet has completely shattered that illusion. Nobody is in charge anymore.*

**Source:** As quoted in Katharine Mieszkowski, "The Power of the Internet Is That You Can Experiment," *Fast Company,* no. 30 (December 1999): 160.

**Questions:** *What does Miller mean? Does he think managers should throw up their hands and abandon all forms of organizational control? Explain.*

# Identifying Control Problems

Control problems have a way of quietly snowballing into overwhelming proportions. Progressive managers can take constructive steps to keep today's complex operations under control.[13] Two very different approaches are executive reality checks and internal auditing.

### Executive Reality Check.
The **executive reality check** occurs when top-level managers periodically work in the trenches to increase their awareness of operations. Consider this interesting variation of Peters and Waterman's "management by wandering around," discussed in Chapter 2:

> *Thanks to Robert Thirkell, customers at British supermarket giant Sainsbury's push smaller shopping carts. . . .*
>
> *Thirkell isn't a consultant or a noted business-school professor. As the creative director at the British Broadcasting Corp. (BBC), he has figured out how to turn business into good TV—and how to use TV to make business better.*

**executive reality check**  *top managers periodically working at lower-level jobs to become more aware of operations*

*Thirkell's secret? Most executives are worried about climbing to the top of the ladder. But with his hit series* Back to the Floor, *he persuades CEOs to do just the opposite, dispatching them to the bottom rung of their organizations to spend a week as trash collectors, paramedics, baggage handlers, or waiters. The goal: to find out what's really going on at their companies and make them better. In the process, Thirkell has made traditional business-on-television fare (all talking heads and market quotes) look bankrupt.*[14]

Executive reality checks not only alert top managers to control problems, they also foster empathy for lower-level employees' problems and concerns. In addition to first-hand reality checks, an internal audit can identify weak spots and problems in the organizational control system.

### Internal Audits.
There are two general types of auditing, external and internal. External auditing, generally performed by certified public accountants (CPAs), is the verification of an organization's financial records and reports. In the United States, the protection of stockholders' interests is the primary rationale for objective external audits. Of course, the Internal Revenue Service (IRS) and the Securities and Exchange Commission (SEC) also benefit from external auditors' watchdog function. Ideally, external auditors help keep organizations honest by double-checking to see if reported financial results are derived through generally accepted accounting principles and are based on material fact, not fiction. Thanks to the Enron/Arthur Andersen scandal, external auditing has been put under the microscope and needed reforms are under way.[15]

**internal auditing**  *independent appraisal of organizational operations and systems to assess effectiveness and efficiency*

Internal auditing differs from external auditing in a number of ways. First, and most obviously, it is performed by an organization's staff rather than by outsiders. General Electric, for example, employs 500 internal auditors.[16] Second, internal auditing is intended to serve the interests of the organization as a whole. Also, as the following definition illustrates, internal auditing tends to be more encompassing than the external variety: "**Internal auditing** is the independent appraisal of the various operations and systems control within an organization to determine whether acceptable policies and procedures are followed, established standards are met, resources are used efficiently and economically, planned missions are accomplished effectively, and the organization's objectives are being achieved."[17]

The product of internal auditing is called a *process audit* by some and a *management audit* by others. To strengthen the objectivity of internal auditing, experts recommend that internal auditors report directly to the top person in the organization. In organization development terms, some "unfreezing" needs to be done to quiet the common complaint that internal auditing is a ploy used by top management for snooping and meddling. Timely and valid internal audits are a primary safeguard against organizational decline, as discussed in Chapter 9, as well as against theft and fraud.[18]

### Symptoms of Inadequate Control.

When a comprehensive internal audit is not available, a general checklist of symptoms of inadequate control can be a useful diagnostic tool. While every situation has some unusual problems, certain symptoms are common:

- An unexplained decline in revenues or profits
- A degradation of service (customer complaints)
- Employee dissatisfaction (complaints, grievances, turnover)
- Cash shortages caused by bloated inventories or delinquent accounts receivable
- Idle facilities or personnel
- Disorganized operations (workflow bottlenecks, excessive paperwork)
- Excessive costs
- Evidence of waste and inefficiency (scrap, rework)[19]

Problems in one or more of these areas may be a signal that things are getting out of control.

# Crisis Management

The September 11, 2001, terrorist attacks on America were more costly than most people would imagine. Beyond the immediate costs in lives (over 3,000), destroyed property, and lost productivity, *Fortune* magazine estimates the *annual* cost of those attacks for the foreseeable future to be $151 billion. Included in that admittedly rough estimate are higher costs for insurance, changes in supply-chain and inventory practices, transportation delays for goods and people, security systems, and backup computer systems.[20] In short, business-as-usual permanently changed. Central to the new, more costly business reality is a firm commitment to more skillful crisis management and disaster recovery.[21]

Today, the diversity and scope of organizational crises stretch the imagination. Experts on the subject define an *organizational crisis* this way:

> *An organizational crisis is a low-probability, high-impact event that threatens the viability of the organization and is characterized by ambiguity of cause, effect, and means of resolution, as well as by belief that decisions must be made swiftly.*[22]

Clearly, managers need to "manage the unthinkable" in a foresighted, systematic, and timely manner.[23] Enter the emerging discipline known as *crisis management*.

*This is not the usual Winter Olympics sports gear. However, as a sign of the times, it certainly was when Salt Lake City, Utah, hosted the 2002 winter games. Crisis management experts from around the world helped create a terror-free zone for 2,500 athletes from 80 nations and 70,000 spectators a day. Every conceivable precaution, from tamper-proof ID badges and surveillance cameras to metal detectors and 15,000 security troops, was put to work. By systematically thinking about the unthinkable, Olympic officials were able to avoid the unthinkable. That deserves a gold medal.*

## Crisis Management Defined

Traditionally, crisis management was viewed negatively, as "managerial firefighting"—waiting for things to go wrong and then scurrying to limit the damage. More recently, the term has taken on a more precise and proactive meaning. In fact, a body of theory and practice is evolving around the idea that managers should think about the unthinkable and expect the unexpected.[24] **Crisis management** is the systematic anticipation of and preparation for internal and external problems that seriously threaten an organization's reputation, profitability, or survival. Importantly, crisis management involves much more than an expedient public relations ploy or so-called spin control to make the organization look good amid bad circumstances. This new discipline is intertwined with strategic control.

**crisis management**
*anticipating and preparing for events that could damage the organization*

## Developing a Crisis Management Program

**3** Identify the four key elements of a crisis management program.

As illustrated in Figure 17.3, a crisis management program is made up of four elements. Disasters need to be anticipated, contingency plans need to be formulated, and crisis management teams need to be staffed and trained. Finally, the program needs to be perfected through realistic practice. Let us examine each of these elements.

**Conducting a Crisis Audit.**    A crisis audit is a systematic way of seeking out trouble spots and vulnerabilities. Disaster scenarios become the topic of discussion as managers ask a series of "What if?" questions. Lists such as the one in Table 17.1 can

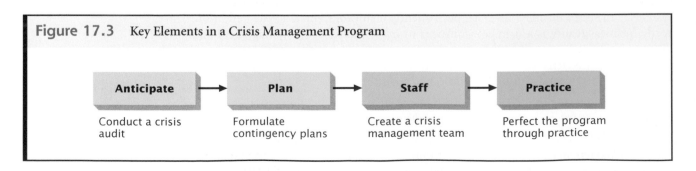

**Figure 17.3     Key Elements in a Crisis Management Program**

**Anticipate** → **Plan** → **Staff** → **Practice**

Conduct a crisis audit | Formulate contingency plans | Create a crisis management team | Perfect the program through practice

## Table 17.1  An Organizational Crisis Can Come in Many Different Forms

- Extortion
- Hostile takeover
- Product tampering
- Vehicular fatality
- Copyright infringement
- Environmental spill
- Computer tampering
- Security breach
- Executive kidnapping
- Product/service boycott
- Work-related homicide
- Malicious rumor
- Natural disaster that disrupts a major product or service
- Natural disaster that destroys organizational information base
- Bribery
- Information sabotage
- Workplace bombing
- Terrorist attack
- Plant explosion
- Sexual harassment
- Escape of hazardous materials
- Personnel assault
- Assault of customers
- Product recall
- Counterfeiting
- Natural disaster that destroys corporate headquarters
- Natural disaster that eliminates key stakeholders

*Source:* From "Reframing Crisis Management," by Christine M. Pearson and Judith A. Clair, 23 (January 1998): Table 1. p. 60. Copyright 1998 by *Academy of Management*. Reproduced with permission of Academy of Management in the format textbook via Copyright Clearance Center.

be useful during this stage. Some crises, such as the untimely death of a key executive, are universal and hence readily identified. Others are industry-specific. For example, crashes are an all-too-real disaster scenario for passenger airline companies.[25]

**Formulating Contingency Plans.**  A **contingency plan** is a backup plan that can be put into effect when things go wrong.[26] Whenever possible, each contingency plan should specify early warning signals, actions to be taken, and expected consequences of those actions.

> Attention to detail is a crucial component of most contingency plans. Dow has produced a 20-page program for communicating with the public during a disaster, right down to such particulars as who is going to run the copy machines. Many companies designate a single corporate spokesperson to field all inquiries from the press. A list may be drawn up of those executives to be notified in emergency situations, and the late-night phone numbers of local radio and television stations may be kept posted on office walls.[27]

**contingency plan**  *a backup plan for emergencies*

Both crisis audits and related contingency plans need to be updated at least annually and, if changing conditions dictate, more often.

**Creating a Crisis Management Team.**  Organizational crisis management teams have been likened to SWAT teams that police departments use for extraordinary situations such as hostage takings. Crisis management teams necessarily represent different specialties, depending on the likely crisis. For example, an electrical utility company might have a crisis management team made up of a media relations expert, an electrical engineer, a consumer affairs specialist, and a lawyer. As the case of Dow Chemical Canada illustrates, quick response and effective communication are the hallmarks of an effective crisis management team:

> Dow Chemical Canada decided to improve its crisis plans after a railroad car carrying a Dow chemical derailed near Toronto in 1979, forcing the evacuation of 250,000 residents. Since then, Dow Canada has prepared information kits on the hazards of its products and trained executives in interview techniques.
>
> . . . Another accident [years later] spilled toxic chemicals into a river that supplies water for several towns. Almost immediately, Dow Canada's emergency-response team arrived at the site and set up a press center to distribute information about the chemicals. They also recruited a neutral expert—the regional public health officer—to speak about the hazards and how to deal with them. The result: officials praised Dow's response.[28]

Although an exact figure is not available, many companies have crisis management teams in place today.

**Perfecting the Program Through Practice.**   Like athletic teams, crisis management teams can gain the necessary teamwork, effectiveness, and speed of response only through diligent practice. Simulations, drills, and mock disasters provide this invaluable practice. Top-management support of such exercises is essential to provide good role models and create a sense of importance. Moreover, reinforcing employee efforts in this area with an effective reward system can encourage serious practice.

Experts say management's two biggest mistakes regarding organizational crises are (1) ignoring early warning signs and (2) denying the existence of a problem when disaster strikes. These mistakes cost Ford Motor Company "about $3 billion to replace 10.6 million Firestone tires. . . . More than 250 people were killed and hundreds more injured in accidents involving Bridgestone/Firestone tires."[29] Arthur Andersen also was faulted for not responding appropriately to the Enron debacle.[30] A good crisis management program effectively eliminates these self-defeating mistakes.

## The Quality Challenge

Not long ago, North American industry was roundly criticized for paying inadequate attention to the quality of goods and services. Today, many organizations have achieved a dramatic turnaround.[31] There is even a national trophy for quality in the United States that means prestige and lots of free media exposure for winners: the Malcolm Baldrige National Quality Award. Named for a former U.S. Secretary of Commerce, it was launched by Congress in 1987 to encourage and reward world-class quality.[32] Some observers claim the drive for quality was a passing fad. Tom Peters, the well-known management writer and consultant, offered this instructive perspective in a recent question-and-answer session:

> Q: Do you think the bloom is off the quality movement?
> A: I think it's in the genes. The quality movement has gone from hype to something people do. The average American manager, whether she or he is in accounting or purchasing or engineering, takes for granted that quality is a major thing you think about in life. You can't compete with shabby products.[33]

**17D**

### Back to the Opening Case

Former New York City Mayor Rudolph Giuliani:

*If I can give one singular piece of advice, it's to be honest, to be up front, to be in front of the crisis rather than having the crisis drive you.*

**Source:** Interview response on PBS *Nightly Business Report*, **www.nbr.com**, January 15, 2002.

**Questions:** *What would Giuliani probably say about Sears's crisis management program? How would you rate the program? Explain.*

The balance of this chapter builds a foundation of understanding about quality. The following questions will be answered: How are product and service quality defined? What does total quality management (TQM) involve? What is Deming management?

## Defining Quality

According to quality expert Philip Crosby, the basic definition of **quality** is "conformance to requirements."[34] But whose requirements? The sound quality of a CD player may seem flawless to its new owner, adequate to the engineer who helped design it, and terrible to an accomplished musician. In regard to *service* quality, being put on hold for 30 seconds when calling a computer company's hotline may be acceptable for one person but very irritating for another. Because quality is much more than a simple either/or proposition, both product and service quality need to be analyzed. To do this, we will explore five types of product quality, the unique challenges faced by service organizations, and the ways in which consumers judge service quality.

**quality**   *conformance to requirements*

## Five Types of Product Quality

Other specialists in the field have refined Crosby's general perspective by identifying at least five different types of product quality: transcendent, product-based, user-based, manufacturing-based, and value-based.[35] Each represents a unique and useful perspective on product quality.

**4**  Identify five types of product quality.

**Transcendent Quality.**   Inherent value or innate excellence is apparent to the individual. Observing people's varied reactions to pieces of art in a museum is a good way to appreciate the subjectiveness of this type of quality. Beauty, as they say, is in the eye of the beholder.

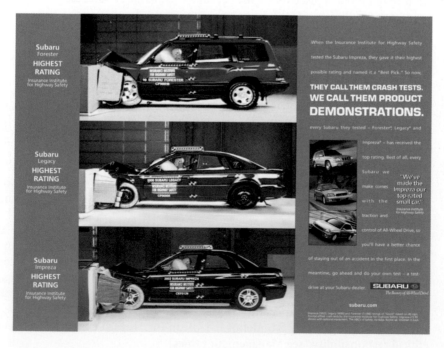

*It's a hard life being a crash-test dummy. Thanks to the constant abuse they take, each of us is safer. Why? Feedback from the annual crash tests motivated auto and truck manufacturers to design and build the safest and highest-quality motor vehicles ever. In fact, when the Insurance Institute for Highway Safety (IIHS) began its tests in 1995, many vehicles performed so poorly the dummies had to be cut out of the mangled wrecks. By 2002, every vehicle tested by IIHS achieved at least a "good" rating, for the first time ever. Now that's product quality we all can live with!*

**Product-Based Quality.**    The presence or absence of a given product attribute is the primary determinant of this type of quality. Soft tissues, rough sandpaper, flawless glass, sweet candy, and crunchy granola signify product-based quality in very different ways.

**User-Based Quality.**    Here, the quality of a product is determined by its ability to meet the user's expectations. Does it get the job done? Is it reliable? Customer satisfaction surveys conducted by *Consumer Reports* magazine[36] give smart shoppers valuable input about user-based quality.

**Manufacturing-Based Quality.**    How well does the product conform to its design specifications or blueprint? The closer the match between the intended product and the actual one, the higher the quality. Car doors designed to close easily, quietly, and snugly are high quality if they do so. This category corresponds to Crosby's "conformance to requirements" definition of quality.

**Value-Based Quality.**    When you hear someone say, "I got a lot for my money," the speaker is describing value-based quality. Cost-benefit relationships are very subjective because they derive from human perception and personal preferences. About value, *Fortune* magazine observed: "The concept can be nebulous because each buyer assesses value individually. In the end, value is simply giving customers what they want at a price they consider fair."[37] Wal-Mart's "everyday low price" strategy very successfully exploits this important type of product quality.

---

**17E    Do You Take Quality for Granted?**

The dramatic improvement in the quality of most products over the past decade or so helped create the new psychology of value. As manufacturers everywhere have improved goods, buyers' expectations have soared. The Japanese call this *atarimae hinshitsu,* which means "quality taken for granted."

**Source:** Stratford Sherman, "How to Prosper in the Value Decade," *Fortune* (November 30, 1992): 91.

**Questions:** *Think of three or four products and/or services you have regularly purchased during the last five years. Has the quality of any of these goods or services gradually improved to the point where you now take for granted certain characteristics that once were in doubt? Which characteristics? What has this done to your expectations for the quality of these same goods or services in the future?*

---

## Unique Challenges for Service Providers

Services are a rapidly growing and increasingly important part of today's global economy. Startling evidence of this appeared in the 2002 *Fortune* 500 list of the largest U.S. companies by sales revenue. In the number one spot was Wal-Mart. A pure service business finally topped the list long dominated by petroleum refiners and automobile companies. Wal-Mart, with annual revenues approaching $220 billion, has 1,383,000 employees.[38] (If Wal-Mart were a city, it would rank among the 10 largest ones in the United States.) Indeed, the vast majority of the U.S. labor force now works in the service sector.

Because services are customer-driven, pleasing the customer is more important than ever.[39] Experts say it costs five times more to win a new customer than it does to keep an existing one.[40] Still, U.S. companies lose an average of about 20 percent of their customers each year.[41] Service-quality strategists emphasize that it is no longer enough simply to satisfy the customer. The strategic service challenge today is to *anticipate* and *exceed* the customer's expectations. Many managers of service operations, following the lead of the legendary founder of L. L. Bean Inc., regard customer satisfaction as an ethical responsibility (see Management Ethics).

# Management Ethics

## Leon Leonwood Bean Wrote the Book on Good Service

The first product Leon Bean ever sold was a disaster. It was 1912, and Bean, a 40-year-old hunter and fisherman, had concocted for his own use a hybrid hunting boot with a leather top and a rubber bottom. He liked his invention so much he started selling the boots through the mail to fellow sportsmen, promising refunds if customers weren't satisfied. They weren't—90 of his first 100 pairs fell apart and were returned.

What did Leon do? Yes, he kept his word and refunded the full price, but then what? Did he stop promising refunds? No. Bean went in the other direction: He borrowed $400—a lot of money for a partner in a small-town clothing store in Maine—and used it to perfect the boot. Then he perfected the guarantee. His credo: "No sale is really complete until the product is worn out, and the customer is satisfied."

That kind of service set the tone for one of retailing's most unique enterprises, L. L. Bean. Today the [$1.2 billion a year] mail-order company continues to replace or repair faulty goods, sometimes years after they were sold. . . .

With his own savings, [Bean] paid his way through private high school. He then joined his older brother,

Otho, who ran a clothing store near Freeport, Maine, the current home of L. L. Bean. . . .

He started selling his boots the same year the U.S. Post Office began parcel post service. To tap the big out-of-state market, he acquired the names and addresses of sportsmen who weren't residents but who held Maine hunting licenses, and mailed his catalogue to them. When his brother, Guy, became postmaster, Leon set up his factory on the second floor over the post office and connected the two with a series of chutes and elevators.

He never lost his touch. Knowing that hunters from out of state often drove through Freeport in the middle of the night on their way to some hunting camp in the far wilds, Bean opened for business 24 hours a day. Night customers found a doorbell and a sign that read: "Push once a minute until clerk appears."

Leon Bean ran the company until his death in 1967. He was 94.

*Source:* Excerpted from Peter Nulty, "The National Business Hall of Fame," *Fortune,* April 5, 1993, 112, 114. © 1993 Time Inc. All rights reserved.

---

To varying extents, virtually every organization is a service organization. Pure service organizations such as day-care centers and manufacturers providing delivery and installation services face similar challenges. Specifically, they need to understand and manage five distinctive service characteristics:[42]

**5** Explain how providing a service differs from manufacturing a product and list the five service-quality dimensions.

1. *Customers participate directly in the production process.* Although people do not go to the factory to help build the cars and refrigerators they eventually buy, they do need to be present when their hair is styled or a broken bone is set.
2. *Services are consumed immediately and cannot be stored.* Hairstylists cannot store up a supply of haircuts in the same way electronics manufacturer Intel can amass an inventory of computer chips.
3. *Services are provided where and when the customer desires.* McDonald's does more business by building thousands of restaurants in convenient locations than it would if everyone had to travel to its Oakbrook, Illinois, headquarters to get a Big Mac and fries. Accommodating customers' sometimes odd schedules is a fact of life for service providers. Insurance salespersons generally work evenings and weekends during their clients' leisure periods.
4. *Services tend to be labor-intensive.* Although skilled labor has been replaced by machines such as automatic bank tellers in some service jobs, most services are

**17F** **Capitalizing on Customer Impatience and Irritation**

*So how can you stop wasting your customers' time? A simple process can help you get started. First, map the time your customers spend engaged with you or your product. Focus on finding those "points of impatience" when a little bit of a customer's time wasted causes disproportionate irritation. Consider what a customer's highest expectations are at any given moment during an engagement with you.*

**Source:** Christopher Meyer, "While Customers Wait, Add Value," *Harvard Business Review,* 79 (July–August 2001): 26.

**Questions:** *How much waiting have you done recently (in line or on the phone) while being served? How did you feel and respond? Aside from reducing the waiting period, what could have been done to reduce the stress and irritation of waiting?*

provided by people to customers face to face. Consequently, the morale and social skills of service employees are vitally important. In fact, customer service has been called a *performing art* requiring a good deal of "emotional labor."[43] It isn't easy to look happy and work hard for an angry customer when you're having a bad day; but good customer service demands it.

5. *Services are intangible.* Objectively measuring an intangible service is more difficult than measuring a tangible good, but nonetheless necessary. For example, this is how a Pennsylvania electrical parts maker measures key services. During one observation period, the company reportedly shipped 93 percent of its orders on time and averaged a delay of 3.5 seconds in answering phone calls from customers.[44]

Because customers are more intimately involved in the service-delivery process than in the manufacturing process, we need to go directly to the customer for service-quality criteria. As service-quality experts tell us:

> *Quality control of a service entails watching a process unfold and evaluating it against the consumer's judgment. The only completely valid standard of comparison is the customer's level of satisfaction. That's a perception—something appreciably more slippery to measure than the physical dimensions of a product.*[45]

So how do consumers judge service quality?

## Defining Service Quality

Researchers at Texas A&M University uncovered valuable insights about customer perceptions of service quality.[46] They surveyed hundreds of customers of various types of service organizations. The following five service-quality dimensions emerged: *reliability, assurance, tangibles, empathy,* and *responsiveness* (*Learning tip:* remember them with the acronym RATER).[47] Customers apparently judge the quality of each service transaction in terms of these five dimensions. (To better understand each dimension and to gauge your own service-quality satisfaction, take a moment now to complete the Hands-On Exercise at the end of this chapter.)

Which of the five RATER dimensions is most important to you? In the Texas A&M study, *reliability* was the most important dimension of service quality, regardless of the type of service involved. Anyone who has waited impatiently for an overdue airplane knows firsthand the central importance of service reliability.[48]

Specific ways to improve product and service quality are presented throughout the balance of this chapter.

# An Introduction to Total Quality Management (TQM)

Definitions of TQM are many and varied, which is not surprising for an area subject to intense discussion and debate in recent years.[49] For our present purposes, **total quality management (TQM)** is defined as creating an organizational culture committed to the continuous improvement of skills, teamwork, processes, product and service quality, and customer satisfaction.[50] Consultant Richard Schonberger's shorthand definition calls TQM "continuous, customer-centered, employee-driven improvement."[51]

Our definition of TQM is anchored to *organizational culture* because successful TQM is deeply embedded in virtually every aspect of organizational life. As discussed in detail in Chapter 9, an organization's culture encompasses all the assumptions its employees take for granted about how people should think and act. In other words, personal commitment to systematic continuous improvement needs to become an everyday matter of "that's just the way we do things here." For example, Dr. Frank P. Carrubba, chief technical officer at Philips, the huge Dutch electronics firm, believes it is never too early to get people thinking about quality:

> "It is not good enough to invent something new," he says. "An elegant result that is not strategic or reproducible in a reliable, high-quality way is not worth much to the customer. Quality has to begin in research. We have to invent in an environment that reflects the same quality we want to achieve throughout the company."[52]

As might be expected with a topic that received so much attention in a relatively short period of time, some unrealistic expectations were created. Unrealistic expectations inevitably lead to disappointment and the need for a new quick fix.[53] However, managers with realistic expectations about the deep and long-term commitment necessary for successful TQM can make it work. TQM can have a positive impact if managers understand and enact these four principles of TQM:

1. Do it right the first time.
2. Be customer-centered.
3. Make continuous improvement a way of life.
4. Build teamwork and empowerment.[54]

Let us examine each of these TQM principles.

## 1. Do It Right the First Time

As mentioned in Chapter 1, the trend in quality has been toward designing and building quality into the product. This approach is much less costly than fixing or throwing away substandard parts and finished products. Ford Motor Company has learned the first lesson of TQM the hard way, not only in the Firestone tire situation, but in this recent case as well: "Ford Motor must replace defective ignition devices on 2 million [California] vehicles prone to stalling, a judge ruled. . . . The order could cost Ford $300

**6** Define *total quality management (TQM)* and discuss the basic TQM principles.

**total quality management (TQM)** *creating an organizational culture committed to continuous improvement in every regard*

million."[55] Schonberger, who has studied many Japanese and U.S. factories firsthand, contends that "errors, if any, should be caught and corrected at the source, i.e., where the work is performed."[56] Comprehensive training in TQM tools and statistical process control is essential if employees are to accept personal responsibility for quality improvement.

## 2. Be Customer-Centered

**internal customer** *anyone in your organization who cannot do a good job unless you do a good job*

Everyone has one or more customers in a TQM organization. They may be internal or external customers. **Internal customers** are other members of the organization who rely on *your* work to get *their* job done.[57] For example, a corporate lawyer employed by Marriott does not directly serve the hotel chain's customers by changing beds, serving meals, or carrying luggage. But that lawyer has an internal customer when a Marriott manager needs to be defended in court. Walt Disney Company serves its internal customers by providing "employees round-the-clock referrals for medical care and housing, discounts at restaurants and a video-rental service."[58]

**customer-centered** *satisfying the customer's needs by anticipating, listening, and responding*

Regarding external customers, TQM requires all employees who deal directly with outsiders to be customer-centered. Being **customer-centered** means: (1) anticipating the customer's needs, (2) listening to the customer, (3) learning how to satisfy the customer, and (4) responding appropriately to the customer. Listening to the customer is a major stumbling block for many companies. But at profitable Southwest Airlines, listening to the customer is practically a religion. "Frequent fliers sit in with personnel managers to interview and evaluate prospective flight attendants. They also participate in focus groups to help gauge response to new services or solicit ideas for improving old ones."[59] Appropriate responses depend upon the specific nature of the business.[60] For example, Table 17.2 lists good and bad customer service behaviors at an eastern U.S. supermarket chain. Notice how service-quality training led to very different patterns of behavior for the different jobs.

Vague requests to "be nice to the customer" are useless in TQM organizations. *Behavior*, not good intentions, is what really matters. As discussed in Chapter 15 in relation to behavior modification, desirable behavior needs to be strengthened with *positive reinforcement*. A good role model in this regard is Internet equipment giant

### 17G The Customers Wanted Green Ketchup

Take ketchup, a staple in 90% of U.S. households. Heinz discovered its 50% market share foundering among core ketchup users: the 6- to 12-year-old kids who Heinz says use 60% more than adults. To spur consumption, Heinz developed EZ Squirt, which sports a shortened bottle made from easy-to-squeeze plastic and needle-shaped nozzle that lets small hands use it to decorate food.

What's with the green?

"We asked kids what else could we do to make ketchup fun. They said it would be cool if we could make it a different color," says Casey Keller, managing director of Heinz ketchup, condiments and sauces. "So we made it green."

**Source:** Gary Strauss, "Squeezing New from Old," *USA Today* (January 4, 2001): 2B.

**Questions:** *Figuratively speaking, what is your "green ketchup"? In other words, what changes or improvements would you like to see in the goods and services you buy?*

> **Table 17.2**   Turning a Supermarket into a Customer-Centered Organization

| Employees | Behaviors before the change | Behaviors after the change |
|---|---|---|
| Bag packers | Ignore customers<br>Lack of packing standards | Greet customers<br>Respond to customers<br>Ask for customers' preference |
| Cashiers | Ignore customers<br>Lack of eye contact | Greet customers<br>Respond to customers<br>Assist customers<br>Speak clearly<br>Call customers by name |
| Shelf stockers | Ignore customers<br>Don't know store | Respond to customers<br>Help customers with correct product location information<br>Knowledgeable about product location |
| Department workers | Ignore customers<br>Limited knowledge | Respond to customers<br>Know products<br>Know store |
| Department managers | Ignore customers<br>Ignore workers | Respond to customers<br>Reward employees for responding to customers |
| Store managers | Ignore customers<br>Stay in booth | Respond to customers<br>Reward employees for service<br>Appraise employees on customer service |

*Source:* Randall S. Schuler, "Strategic Human Resource Management: Linking the People with the Strategic Needs of the Business." Reprinted from *Organizational Dynamics,* (Summer 1992): Exhibit 4. Copyright 1992, with permission from Elsevier Science.

Cisco Systems. CEO John T. Chambers sets the tone by giving his personal telephone number to *all* customers and taking calls in the middle of the night. As for the positive reinforcement, "all the company's top execs have their bonuses tied to customer-satisfaction ratings."[61] No surprise, then, that Cisco Systems gets high marks for customer service.

## 3. Make Continuous Improvement a Way of Life

The Japanese word for "continuous improvement" is **kaizen,** which means improving the overall system by constantly improving the little details. TQM managers dedicated to *kaizen* are never totally happy with things. *Kaizen* practitioners view quality as an endless journey, not a final destination. They are always experimenting, measuring, adjusting, and improving. Rather than naively assuming that zero defects means perfection, they search for potential and actual trouble spots.

**kaizen**   *a Japanese word meaning "continuous improvement"*

There are four general avenues for continuous improvement:

- Improved and more consistent product and service *quality*
- Faster *cycle times* (in cycles ranging from product development to order processing to payroll processing)

**17H   Taking TQM to Heart**

Medtronic pacemakers are implanted in about 250,000 people every year, and the technology has proved remarkably able to evolve with the times. The basic idea is still to supplement the body's electrical system, yet just about everything else about the product has changed. It has shrunk to the size of a small stopwatch—and packs uncanny intelligence, which lets it sense when your heart is doing fine on its own and when it needs help. It can be fully implanted in the body yet does not require major surgery. A surgeon cuts a four-inch slit under the clavicle bone, creating a pocket for the pacemaker. Then an insulated wire with a silicon tip is fed through the subclavian vein to the inner wall of the heart.

**Source:** Bethany McLean, "How Smart Is Medtronic Really?" *Fortune* (October 25, 1999): 176.

**Question:** *Why is it appropriate to call TQM a quality-of-life issue, not only for pacemaker patients, but for every one of us?*

- Greater *flexibility* (for example, faster response to changing customer demands and new technology)
- Lower *costs* and less *waste* (for example, eliminating needless steps, scrap, rework, and non–value-adding activities)[62]

Significantly, these are not tradeoffs, as traditionally believed. In other words, TQM advocates reject the notion that a gain on one front necessitates a loss on another. Greater quality, speed, and flexibility have to be achieved at lower cost and with less waste. This is an "all things are possible" approach to management. It requires diligent effort and creativity.[63]

## 4. Build Teamwork and Empowerment

Earlier, we referred to TQM as employee-driven. In other words, it empowers employees at all levels in order to tap their full creativity, motivation, and commitment. *Empowerment,* as defined in Chapter 15, occurs when employees are adequately trained, provided with all relevant information and the best possible tools, fully involved in key decisions, and fairly rewarded for results.[64] TQM advocates prefer to reorganize the typical hierarchy into teams of people from different specialties. For a prime example, consider how Chrysler Corporation reinvented itself prior to becoming part of DaimlerChrysler:

> *Gone are the days when the development of a new vehicle plodded through a rigid set of sequential "chimneys"—from design to engineering to procurement and supply to manufacturing to marketing and sales—until, seven or eight years later, the new model turned up in the customer's driveway. Today Chrysler is organized into four streamlined platform teams: large car, small car, minivan, and Jeep/truck. Each team is composed of product and manufacturing engineers, planners and buyers, marketers, designers, financial analysts, and outside suppliers, and each is responsible for getting their vehicles to market.*
>
> *"It's not the old way: an engineer finishing his piece of the car and tossing the plan over the fence to the next guy up the line," says [retired] chairman Lee A. Iacocca. "Platform teams are about everybody working together. The result is better quality, lower cost, and a reduction in the time it takes to get a product to market."[65]*

In earlier chapters you encountered many ways to promote teamwork and employee involvement: suggestion systems (Chapter 12), quality control circles and self-managed teams (Chapter 13), teamwork and cross-functional teams (Chapter 14), and participative leadership (Chapter 15). Each can be a valuable component of TQM.

## The Seven Basic TQM Process Improvement Tools

Continuous improvement of productive processes in factories, offices, stores, hospitals, hotels, and banks requires lots of measurement. Skilled TQM managers have a large repertoire of graphical and statistical tools at their disposal. The beginner's set consists of the seven tools displayed in Figure 17.4. A brief overview of each will help promote awareness and a foundation for further study.

**Flow Chart.**   A **flow chart** is a graphic representation of a sequence of activities and decisions. Standard flow-charting symbols include boxes for events or activities, diamonds for key decisions, and ovals for start and stop points. Flow charts show, for instance, how a property damage claim moves through an insurance company. By knowing who does what to the claim, and in which sequence, management can streamline the process by eliminating unnecessary steps or delays. Chapter 6 shows a sample flow chart as a planning and control tool. TQM teams have found flowcharting to be a valuable tool for increasing efficiency, reducing costs, and eliminating waste.

**7** Describe at least three of the seven TQM process improvement tools.

**flow chart**   *graphic display of a sequence of activities and decisions*

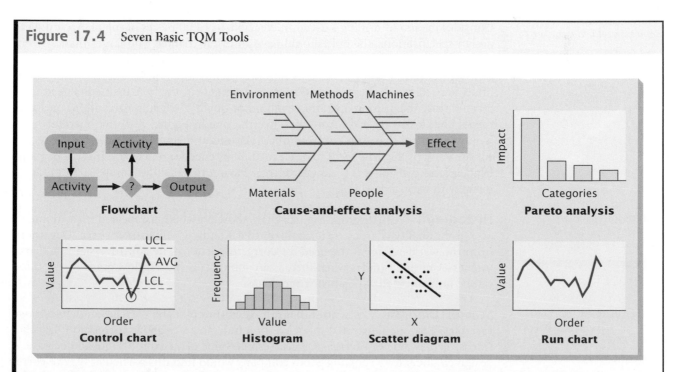

**Figure 17.4**    Seven Basic TQM Tools

*Source:*  Arthur R. Tenner and Irving J. DeToro, *Total Quality Management* (Figure 9.2, p. 113). © 1992 by Addison-Wesley Publishing Company, Inc. Reprinted by permission of Pearson Education, Inc.

## Cause-and-Effect Analysis.

The **fishbone diagram,** named for its rough resemblance to a fish skeleton, helps TQM teams visualize important cause-and-effect relationships. (Some refer to fishbone diagrams as Ishikawa diagrams, in tribute to the Japanese quality pioneer mentioned in Chapter 2.) For example, did a computer crash because of an operator error, an equipment failure, a power surge, or a software problem? A TQM team can systematically track down a likely cause by constructing a fishbone diagram. An illustrative fishbone diagram is presented in Skills & Tools at the end of Chapter 8.

## Pareto Analysis.

This technique, popularized by quality expert Joseph M. Juran and discussed in Chapter 6, is named for the Italian economist Vilfredo Pareto (1848–1923). Pareto detected the so-called 80/20 pattern in many worldly situations: relatively few people or events (about 20 percent) account for most of the results or impacts (about 80 percent). It is thus most efficient to focus on the few things (or people) that make the biggest difference. The next time you are in class, for example, notice how relatively few students offer the great majority of the comments in class. Likewise, a few students account for most of the absenteeism during the semester. In TQM, a **Pareto analysis** involves constructing a bar chart by counting and tallying the number of times significant quality problems occur. The tallest bar on the chart, representing the most common problem, demands prompt attention. In a newspaper printing operation, for example, the most common cause of printing press stoppages for the week might turn out to be poor-quality paper. A quick glance at a Pareto chart would tell management to demand better quality from the paper supplier.

## Control Chart.

*Statistical process control* of repetitive operations helps employees keep key quality measurements within an acceptable range. A **control chart** is used to monitor actual versus desired quality measurements during repetitive operations. Consider the job of drilling a 2-centimeter hole in 1,000 pieces of metal. According to design specifications, the hole should have an inside diameter no larger than 2.1 centimeters and no smaller than 1.9 centimeters. These measurements are the upper control limit (UCL) and the lower control limit (LCL). Any hole diameters within these limits are acceptable quality. Random measurements of the hole diameters need to be taken during the drilling operation to monitor quality. When these random measurements are plotted on a control chart, like the one in Figure 17.4, the operator has a handy visual aid that flags control limit violations and signals the need for corrective action. Perhaps the drill needs to be cleaned, sharpened, or replaced. This sort of statistical process control is less expensive than having to redrill or scrap 1,000 pieces of metal with wrong-sized holes.

## Histogram.

A **histogram** is a bar chart showing whether repeated measurements of a given quality characteristic conform to a standard bell-shaped curve. Deviations from the standard signal the need for corrective action. The controversial practice of teachers "curving" grades when there is an abnormally high or low grade distribution can be implemented with a histogram.

## Scatter Diagram.

A **scatter diagram** is used to plot the correlation between two variables. The one illustrated in Figure 17.4 indicates a negative correlation. In other words, as the value of variable X increases, the value of variable Y tends to decrease. A design engineer for a sporting goods company would find this particular type of correlation while testing the relationship between various thicknesses of fishing rods and flexibility. The thicker the rod, the lower the flexibility.

**Run Chart.**   Also called a time series or trend chart, a **run chart** tracks the frequency or amount of a given variable over time. Significant deviations from the norm signal the need for corrective action. Hospitals monitor vital body signs such as temperature and blood pressure with daily logs, actually run charts. TQM teams can use them to spot "bad days." For example, automobiles made in U.S. factories on a Friday or Monday historically have had more quality defects than those assembled on a Tuesday, Wednesday, or Thursday.

**run chart**   *a trend chart for tracking a variable over time*

Before we move on to Deming management, an important point needs to be made. As experts on the subject remind us, "Tools are necessary but not sufficient for TQM."[66] Successful TQM requires a long-term, organizationwide drive for continuous improvement. The appropriate time frame is *years,* not days or months. Tools such as benchmarking and control charts are just one visible feature of that process. Invisible factors—such as values, learning, attitudes, motivation, and personal commitment—dictate the ultimate success of TQM.

**17I  Which TQM Tool?**

**Situation:** A mutual fund company raised its minimum initial investment from zero to $2,500. Why? Smaller accounts are just too expensive. "About 41 percent of all our phone calls were from people with account balances of less than $1,000," said a company official.

**Source:**  John Waggoner, "Twentieth Century Plans for Millennium," *USA Today* (August 11, 1994): 8B.

**Question:**  *This line of thinking is best explained by which of the seven basic TQM tools? Explain your reasoning.*

# Deming Management

It is hard to overstate the worldwide impact of W. Edwards Deming's revolutionary ideas about management. His ideas have directly and indirectly created better and more productive work environments for countless millions of people. This section builds upon the historical sketch in Chapter 2 by examining basic principles of Deming management and Deming's famous 14 points.

## Principles of Deming Management

**Deming management** is the application of W. Edwards Deming's ideas to revitalize productive systems by making them more responsive to the customer, more democratic, and more efficient. This approach qualifies as a revolution because, when first proposed by Deming in the 1950s, it directly challenged the legacy of Taylor's scientific management.[67] Scientific management led to rigid and autocratic organizations unresponsive to customers and employees alike. Deming management proposed essentially the opposite. Some of the principles discussed below may not seem revolutionary today because Deming management has become ingrained in everyday *good* management.

**Deming management**
*application of W. Edwards Deming's ideas for more responsive, more democratic, and less wasteful organizations*

### Quality Improvement Drives the Entire Economy.   Higher quality eventually means more jobs. Deming's simple yet convincing logic is presented in Figure 17.5. Quality improvement is a powerful engine driving out waste and inefficiency. Quality also powers higher productivity, greater market share, and new business and employment opportunities. In short, everybody wins when quality improves.[68]

**The Customer Always Comes First.**    In his influential 1986 text, *Out of the Crisis,* Deming wrote: "The consumer is the most important part of the production line. Quality should be aimed at the needs of the consumer, present and future."[69] Of course, these are just inspirational words until they are enacted faithfully by individuals on the job. Skip Tobey, who joined America West Airlines when it first started flying, embodies the Deming management spirit:

> *"I'm not just an aircraft cleaner," the 36-year-old Phoenix native said. "That's my title, but that's not the end of my job."*
>
> *Tobey said he looks for ways to help passengers, lending a hand to young families maneuvering strollers through narrow aircraft aisles and assisting elderly travelers.*
>
> *"My satisfaction is tied into quality, helping the passengers," he said. "No matter what it takes, if it means going to the furthest extreme, I'll do it."*[70]

Casual observers might dismiss the importance of Tobey's job, but his contribution was critical as America West fought its way out of bankruptcy in the mid-1990s.

**Don't Blame the Person, Fix the System.**    Deming management chides U.S. managers for their preoccupation with finding someone to blame rather than fixing problems. His research convinced him that "the system"—meaning management, work rules, technology, and the organization's structure and culture—typically is responsible for upwards of 85 percent of substandard quality. People can and will turn out superior quality, *if* the system is redesigned to permit them to do so. Deming management urges managers to treat employees as internal customers, listening and responding to their ideas and suggestions for improvement. After all, who knows more about a particular job—the person who performs it for 2,000 hours a year or a manager who stops by now and again?

**PDCA cycle**  *Deming's plan-do-check-act cycle that relies on observed data for continuous improvement of operations*

**Plan-Do-Check-Act.**    Deming's approach calls for making informed decisions on the basis of hard data. His recommended tool for this process is what is popularly known as the **PDCA cycle** (plan-do-check-act). Deming preferred the term *Shewhart cycle,*[71] in recognition of the father of statistical quality control, Walter A. Shewhart, mentioned in Chapter 2. (Japanese managers call it the Deming cycle.) Whatever the

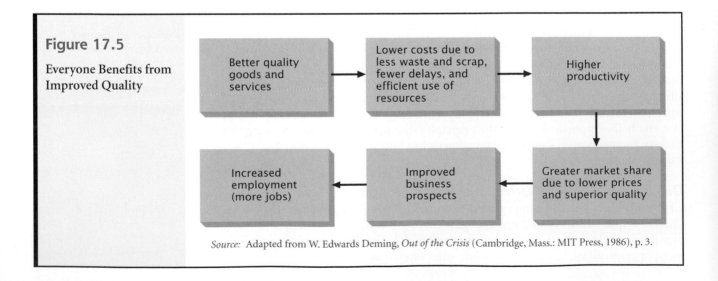

**Figure 17.5**

**Everyone Benefits from Improved Quality**

*Source:*  Adapted from W. Edwards Deming, *Out of the Crisis* (Cambridge, Mass.: MIT Press, 1986), p. 3.

label, the PDCA cycle reminds managers to focus on what is really important, use observed data, start small and build upon accumulated knowledge, and be research-oriented in observing changes and results (see Figure 17.6). The influence of Deming management was obvious at Intel when CEO Craig Barrett recently met with division heads:

**8** Explain how Deming's PDCA cycle can improve the overall management process.

> *He has told them to make sure they are following the fundamentals of decision-making: plan, do, check, act. And he has tied bonuses to performance in each group. "My job is to refresh in everyone's mind: This is how we do projects. These are the exact steps you go through. Don't take shortcuts," he says.*[72]

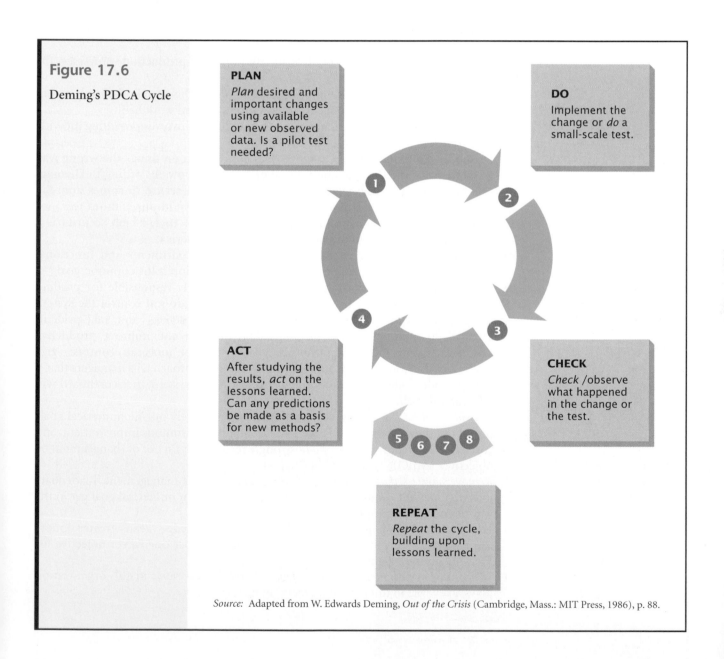

**Figure 17.6**

Deming's PDCA Cycle

**PLAN**
*Plan* desired and important changes using available or new observed data. Is a pilot test needed?

**DO**
Implement the change or *do* a small-scale test.

**ACT**
After studying the results, *act* on the lessons learned. Can any predictions be made as a basis for new methods?

**CHECK**
*Check* /observe what happened in the change or the test.

**REPEAT**
*Repeat* the cycle, building upon lessons learned.

*Source:* Adapted from W. Edwards Deming, *Out of the Crisis* (Cambridge, Mass.: MIT Press, 1986), p. 88.

# Deming's 14 Points

Deming formulated his 14 points to transform U.S. industry from what he considered to be its backward ways. Here is a summary of the 14 points constituting the heart and soul of Deming management:[73]

**9** Specify and discuss at least four of Deming's famous 14 points.

1. *Constant purpose.* Strive for continuous improvement in products and services to remain competitive.
2. *New philosophy.* Western management needs to awaken to the realities of a new economic age by demanding wiser use of all resources.
3. *Give up on quality by inspection.* Inspecting for faulty products is unnecessary if quality is built in from the very beginning.
4. *Avoid the constant search for lowest-cost suppliers.* Build long-term, loyal, and trusting relationships with single suppliers.
5. *Seek continuous improvement.* Constantly improve production processes for greater productivity and lower costs.
6. *Train everyone.* Make sure people have a clear idea of how to do their job. Informally learning a new job from coworkers entrenches bad work habits.
7. *Provide real leadership.* Leading is more than telling. It involves providing individualized help.
8. *Drive fear out of the workplace.* Employees continue to do things the wrong way when they are afraid to ask questions about why and how. According to Deming, "No one can put in his best performance unless he feels secure. *Se* comes from the Latin, meaning without, *cure* means fear or care. *Secure* means without fear, not afraid to express ideas, not afraid to ask questions."[74] Lack of job security is a major stumbling block for quality improvement in America.
9. *Promote teamwork.* Bureaucratic barriers between departments and functional specialists need to be broken down. Customer satisfaction is the common goal.
10. *Avoid slogans and targets.* Because the *system* is largely responsible for product quality, putting pressure on individuals who feel they do not control the system breeds resentment. Posters with slogans such as "zero defects" and "take pride in quality" do nothing to help the individual measure and improve productive processes. Control charts and other process-control tools, in contrast, give employees direction and encouragement. Deming's approach tells managers that if they provide leadership and continually improve the system, the scoreboard will take care of itself.
11. *Get rid of numerical quotas.* When employees aggressively pursue numerical goals or quotas, they too often take their eyes off quality, continuous improvement, and costs. Hence, Deming management strongly rejects the practice of management by objectives (MBO),[75] discussed in Chapter 6.
12. *Remove barriers that stifle pride in workmanship.* Poor management, inadequate instruction, faulty equipment, and pressure to achieve a numerical goal get in the way of continuous improvement.
13. *Education and self-improvement are key.* Greater knowledge means greater opportunity. Continuous improvement should be the number one career objective for everyone in the organization.
14. *"The transformation is everyone's job."*[76] Virtually *everyone* in the organization plays a key role in implementing Deming management.

# Summary

**1.** Feedforward control is preventive in nature, whereas feedback control is based on the evaluation of past performance. Managers engage in concurrent control when they monitor and adjust ongoing operations to keep them performing to standard. The three basic components of organizational control systems are objectives, standards, and an evaluation-reward system.

**2.** According to the performance pyramid, strategic control involves the downward translation of objectives and upward translation of performance measures. Both external effectiveness and internal efficiency criteria need to be achieved.

**3.** The four elements of a crisis management program are: (a) *anticipate* (conduct a crisis audit), (b) *plan* (formulate contingency plans), (c) *staff* (create a crisis management team), and (d) *practice* (perfect the program through practice).

**4.** Product quality involves much more than the basic idea of "conformance to requirements." Five types of product quality are transcendent, product-based, user-based, manufacturing-based, and value-based.

**5.** Service providers face a unique set of challenges that distinguish them from manufacturers. Because we live in a predominantly service economy, it is important to recognize these challenges: (1) direct customer participation, (2) immediate consumption of services, (3) provision of services at customers' convenience, (4) tendency of services to be more labor-intensive than manufacturing, and (5) intangibility of services, making them harder to measure. Consumer research uncovered five service-quality dimensions: reliability, assurance, tangibles, empathy, and responsiveness (RATER). Consumers consistently rank *reliability* number one.

**6.** Total quality management (TQM) involves creating a culture dedicated to customer-centered, employee-driven continuous improvement. The four TQM principles are

- Do it right the first time.
- Be customer-centered.
- Make continuous improvement a way of life.
- Build teamwork and empowerment.

**7.** Seven basic TQM process improvement tools are flow charts, fishbone diagrams, Pareto analysis, control charts, histograms, scatter diagrams, and run charts.

**8.** Deming's plan-do-check-act (PDCA) cycle forces managers to make decisions and take actions on the basis of observed and carefully measured data. This procedure removes quality-threatening guesswork. The PDCA cycle also helps managers focus on what is really important. PDCA work never ends, because lessons learned from one cycle are incorporated into the next.

**9.** Deming's famous 14 points seek to revolutionize Western management practices. In summary, they urge managers to seek continuous improvement through extensive training, leadership, teamwork, and self-improvement. The points call for *doing away with* mass quality inspections, selecting suppliers only on the basis of low cost, fear, slogans and numerical quotas, and barriers to pride in workmanship. The transformation, according to Deming, is *everyone's* job.

## Terms to Understand

Control (p.564)
Feedforward control (p.565)
Concurrent control (p.566)
Feedback control (p.566)
Benchmarking (p.568)
Executive reality check (p.570)
Internal auditing (p.570)
Crisis management (p.572)
Contingency plan (p.573)
Quality (p.575)
Total quality management (TQM) (p.579)
Internal customer (p.580)

Customer-centered (p.580)
*Kaizen* (p.581)
Flow chart (p.584)
Fishbone diagram (p.584)
Pareto analysis (p.584)
Control chart (p.584)
Histogram (p.584)
Scatter diagram (p.584)
Run chart (p.585)
Deming management (p.585)
PDCA cycle (p.586)

# Skills & Tools

## How to Avoid a Public Relations Nightmare in a Crisis

1. **Prepare written organizational policies,** including:
   - an employee handbook
   - policies for screening potential employees (including volunteers)
   - antidiscrimination and harassment policies
   - financial control systems
   - an ethics policy

2. **Be sure all employees** (including volunteers) understand the organization's policies.

3. **Create a written crisis plan,** clearly stating what will be done and who will do it in case of a crisis. Make sure your plan includes:
   - names and contact numbers of people to contact in an emergency
   - a list of questions you're likely to be asked by the media and other stakeholders in a crisis
   - forms to record the details of what happens in a crisis
   - details on who will communicate what to whom
   - your goals for effective crisis communications—the outcomes you hope for and how you will measure success.

4. **Build trust and respect** with local media representatives.

5. **Appoint someone to communicate** with the media and someone to meet with victims' families in case of an emergency. Choose these people *before* a crisis occurs. They should know what's expected and be ready to swing into action at the first hint of a problem.

6. **Keep communication lines open** between your organization and its stakeholders at all times.

7. **Hold frequent brainstorming and roleplaying sessions.** Encourage all staff to participate, and be open to all their ideas.

8. **Accept the blame** when your organization makes an error. Let the public know what you're doing to be sure the problem isn't repeated.

9. **Always tell the truth.**

10. **Don't wait till a crisis occurs** before implementing these ideas. Begin today to prevent the preventable and prepare for the inevitable.

*Source:* Lolita Hendrix, "Will You Be Ready When Disaster Strikes," *Nonprofit World,* 18 (May–June 2000): 37. Reprinted by permission.

## Hands-On Exercise

### Measuring Service Quality

Think of the kind of treatment you have received in service establishments recently. Pick a specific restaurant, hairstyling salon, bank, airline, hospital, government agency, auto repair shop, department store, bookstore, or other service organization and rate the kind of customer service you received, using the following five RATER factors. Circle one response for each factor and total them.

**Instructions**

**R**   1. *Reliability:* ability to perform the desired service dependably, accurately, and consistently.

Very poor                                                          Very good
  1        2        3        4        5        6        7        8        9        10

**A**   2. *Assurance:* employees' knowledge, courtesy, and ability to convey trust and confidence.

Very poor                                                          Very good
  1        2        3        4        5        6        7        8        9        10

**T**   3. *Tangibles:* physical facilities, equipment, appearance of personnel.

Very poor                                                          Very good
  1        2        3        4        5        6        7        8        9        10

**E**   4. *Empathy:* provision of caring, individualized attention to customers.

Very poor                                                          Very good
  1        2        3        4        5        6        7        8        9        10

**R**   5. *Responsiveness:* willingness to provide prompt service and help customers.

Very poor                                                          Very good
  1        2        3        4        5        6        7        8        9        10

Total score = _____

**Scoring Key**

  5–10  Cruel and unusual punishment.
11–20  You call this service?
21–30  Average, but who wants average service?
31–40  Close only counts in horseshoes.
41–50  Service hall-of-fame candidate.

**For Consideration/
Discussion**

**1.** If your service encounter was good (or bad), how many other people have you told about it? Why do people tend to pass along more stories about bad service than they do about good service?

**2.** Which of the five service-quality criteria was a major problem in the specific service situation you chose? What corrective actions should management take?

**3.** In the service situation you selected, which of the five criteria was most important to you? Why? Did you walk away satisfied? Why or why not?

**4.** If your present (or most recent) job involves rendering a service, how would you score yourself on the RATER factors? What needs to be done to improve your total score?

**5.** Does the most important RATER factor change for various types of service (for instance, a visit to the doctor versus flying on a commercial airliner)? Explain, with specific examples.

**6.** Generally speaking, which of the RATER factors is the weak link for today's service organizations? What remedies do you recommend?

# Internet Exercises

**1. An Internet search for higher-quality customer service:** For the vast majority of today's employees who work in the service sector, service quality has two faces: *providing* services and *paying for and receiving* services. Hence, learning more about service quality can have a double benefit as we become better both as service providers and as consumers. Customer service expert John Tschohl's Web site (**www.customer-service.com**) for the Service Quality Institute he founded and heads is an excellent resource. At the home page, click on "Media." Under the heading "Review Past Articles," select and read at least three of the brief tutorials. (*Note:* the reading "Want Better Service?" offers great tips on how to complain about bad service.)

    *Learning Points:*  1. What was the most useful thing you learned about customer service? Explain.  2. If you presently have a service job, what did Tschohl teach you about providing better service?  3. What did Tschohl teach you about demanding and getting better customer service?

**2. Check it out:** Many crisis management experts see the Internet as the next major battleground in the war on terrorism. At stake are countless private records containing everything from names, addresses, Social Security numbers, and credit card numbers to school, health, and criminal records. Corporate trade secrets and intellectual property are also at risk. Malicious hacking and identity theft via the Internet already are huge and costly problems. The Web site for Internet security company Telenisus (**www.telenisus.com**) offers excellent free advice on how to improve Internet security. Follow the paths to the following two readings: "Don't Wait: 12 Actions You Should Start Today to Tighten Business Security" and "12 Principles for a Secure Business." If you know someone who is a high-level manager, be sure to give them a copy of the "12 Principles." Remember, *prevention* is the best way to handle a crisis.

For updates to these exercises, visit our Web site (**http://business.college.hmco. com/students**).

# Closing Case

## "For a Customer Service Representative, Press 1 . . . "

I am in the belly of the beast. I have risen early, traveled far, and overcome lines, rudeness, and indifference. Now, heedless of my chances of coming back without serious psychological or physical injury, I am journeying into a swamp that has become a source of boundless irritation, frustration, confusion—even fury—for tens of millions of Americans. I open the door and step into a customer-service call center. And not just any call center either—one that is exclusively devoted to handling problems with cell-phones. It's cool inside and fairly well lit, for a swamp. I am carrying the very tool itself: a Sprint PCS cell-phone. I love my Sprint PCS cell-phone. But God help me when I have to call Sprint PCS. I have sometimes called this very building in Fort Worth, Texas. Often, I'm not even sure that the customer-care advocate I finally speak with after I've been waiting on hold for 17 minutes even knows what a cell-phone is.

I have come here at the beginning of a long journey—really, a quest of the sort that was common in antiquity—during which I will cross the continent several times and seek out both oracles and common folk. I am determined to unravel a central mystery of life in modern America: Why is customer service so terrible?

At the Sprint PCS call center, I am soon teamed up with customer-care advocate Chad Ehrlich, a gracious 29-year-old with years of experience delivering service by phone. Chad takes a call from a businessman in Lubbock, Texas. The man is upset about his bill: It was run-ning $60 to $100 a month. Suddenly, it has shot up to $1,600. "I'm not going to pay it!" the man declares.

Chad is reserved. "Let me take a look at that bill," he says. Chad whirls through screens of information. "Hold on a moment for me, sir, I'm going to get a representative from the fraud department on the line." Chad puts Lubbock on hold and dials Sprint PCS's fraud department, where he reaches a familiar recorded message and is put on hold. Lubbock is on hold for customer-service rep Chad, and customer-service rep Chad is on hold for more customer service.

A female fraud rep takes Chad's call. She can see from Lubbock's history that he's complained about this problem before. The conversation between Chad and his colleague in fraud is frisky.

Fraud: "He thought he was cloned, but he wasn't."

Chad: "His bills did go from almost nothing to sky-high . . ."

Fraud: "We can send him to a cloning specialist and make it 'official' if you want . . ."

Chad: "He's denying that he made or received the calls."

The impatient woman from fraud dials the Sprint PCS cloning customer-care department and . . . is put on hold.

Do you ever wonder what's going on while you're waiting on hold for customer service? Really, you couldn't even imagine.

Chad, Lubbock's customer-care advocate, is talking to a woman who is Chad's customer-care advocate. She has called *her* customer-care advocate, who is busy on another call. So now we have two customer-care advocates on hold waiting for a third customer-care advocate. Meanwhile, a fuming customer from Lubbock (who may or may not be trying to rip Sprint off for $1,600) waits. On hold.

That, right there, is customer service in the new economy. It has become a slow, dissatisfying tangle of telephones, computers, Web sites, email, and people that wastes time at a prodigious rate, produces far more aggravation than service, and, most often, leaves you feeling impotent. What's even worse is that this situation is a kind of betrayal. It wasn't supposed to be this way. One of the promises of the new economy was that the customer would finally be in charge. We weren't supposed to need to call customer care—but if we did, then someone would take our call quickly. (Why not? No one else would be calling.) A customer-service rep would understand our problem practically before we mentioned it, and all would be made right. Everyone believes in delighting the customer. . . .

I didn't begin my journey through the service jungle at Sprint PCS by accident, or because I think that the company would be a good target for mockery. Sprint PCS is a pure new-economy company. It offers nothing but service—and it's digital wireless service to boot. The company's only product is moving voices through the air. The first time that you could have made a Sprint PCS call was December 1996. From a standing start, in four years, the company has grown to 28,328 employees (10,000 in customer care), 9.8 million customers, and annual revenues of roughly $6 billion. Sprint PCS signs up 10,000 new customers each day.

The company has access to every conceivable technological helper: the Net, automated phone services, and the most-sophisticated call centers. And yet, my own experience dealing with Sprint PCS has been consistently aggravating. In eight years of having BellSouth provide our home phone service, I've only had occasion to talk to them three or four times. I've talked to Sprint PCS more than that since Halloween—always with unhappy results.

Sprint PCS knows the right thing to do. It just can't do it. Faerie Kizzire, 51, senior vice president for Sprint PCS, is in charge of customer service for the company. She's a veteran: She spent nine years at Sprint managing customer service for the long-distance business, then managed customer service for a health-insurance company, and was wooed back to Sprint to create customer care for wireless.

I tell her the story of a call I have just listened to with Chad: Marlene in Ohio has had to call three times just to get a credit for charges that shouldn't have been on her bill in the first place. Before Chad, two customer-care advocates dealt with Marlene by simply telling her that she was wrong. As Chad discovers, Marlene was in fact improperly charged. So why did that happen? Why did two customer-service reps argue with Marlene, rather than credit her? Why does Marlene know more about her calling plan than customer care does?

Kizzire is disappointed. "The complexity of the product and the variations in the product can make that kind of problem very difficult," she says. "We do see some of our people falling on the side of 'I'm right' versus 'I'm going to make it right.'"

Sprint PCS looks as if it's doing all of the right things. The company's training program for reps is 6 to 10 weeks long. Across the call center are exhortations to good service: "Did you dazzle your customers today?" Says Kizzire: "It is true that people who have a little bit of knowledge can be dangerous. We always say, Don't try to dazzle the customer with what you know. These days, many customers have years of experience."

And therein lies a clue to what's really happening to customer service—and why. The secret about customer service in the new economy isn't that it's bad—everyone *knows* it's bad. The secret is that it's harder to deliver good customer service than ever before. Why? Technology, especially in its early days, is always hard. No surprise there. Why would we expect companies that can't figure out how to run a phone center—talking to real people about problems in their own business—to be really good at using advanced technology to automate the process of taking care of us?

And customers are more demanding. We want good service, quickly. We don't wait at gas pumps, we're antsy in ATM lines, and we pay FedEx . . . to avoid standing in line at the post office. Companies have created, nursed, and benefited from this impatience. We are victims of it in our own lives. They are victims of it too. It makes providing customer service brutally unforgiving.

Technology has, in fact, made some things quicker and easier, and it has allowed us to take care of ourselves. I can plunge through the details of my online bank statement more thoroughly in 50 seconds than any automated voice-mail system could permit in 50 minutes, or than even the most patient phone operator would tolerate. This means that when we talk to someone in person, either things are really screwed up, or we are really angry and want to share that anger with a person. Or both. Technology has made the actual person-to-person customer service of big companies much more complicated and demanding.

Despite all of the consultants, gurus, and outsource providers, customer service is hard to deliver in a mass economy. I wasn't on the phones at Sprint PCS for more than a couple of hours, and I can see that the real problem isn't customer service or even culture. No, the real problem is more fundamental: Sprint PCS offers a simple service that is really very complicated. Best tip-off? It takes someone 15 minutes to sell me a phone and a calling plan in a Sprint PCS store. It takes Faerie Kizzire 6 weeks—240 hours—to teach a phone rep to handle any problems that I might have with that phone.

## For Discussion

1. Okay, so why is customer service so poor today?

2. As a *customer,* what can *you* do to improve the quality of service you receive over the phone, via regular mail, or via e-mail?

3. How should Sprint PCS measure the quality of its call-center service?

4. How could Sprint PCS use the four principles of TQM to improve its customer service?

5. What sort of advice would an advocate of Deming management give Sprint PCS's service department?

6. What is your own formula for improving customer service in general?

# Video Skill Builders

New York-based Quick International Courier is a survivor in the highly competitive specialty courier industry. Quick, according to CEO Robert Mitzman, uses commercial air carriers to ship very critical, very time-sensitive customized shipments. An Internet-based information system is central to the 24/7 operation. There is no room for error when shipping such vital things as bone marrow.

## 5A Control at Quick International Courier

### Learning Objective
To demonstrate the importance of organizational control processes.

### Links to Textual Material
**Chapter 17:** Types of control; Components of organizational control systems; Identifying control problems

### Discussion Questions

1. What forms of feedforward control could be used in this case?

2. What forms of feedback control could Quick use to be successful?

3. How could objectives, standards, and an evaluation-reward system help keep things under control at Quick?

4. How would Mitzman and his managers know if things were getting out of control at Quick?

Quality is king at Gulfstream Aircraft Company, where customers' lives are on the line with each of its $30-million corporate jets. Gulfstream's success formula combines a strong customer focus with cross-functional teamwork and a dedication to world-class quality.

## 5B Gulfstream Aircraft Flies on Quality

### Learning Objective
To demonstrate how to achieve world-class product quality.

### Links to Textual Material
**Chapter 14:** Cross-functional teamwork    **Chapter 17:** Feedforward control; Total quality management; Deming management

### Discussion Questions

1. Why is cross-functional teamwork a key part of Gulfstream's success?

2. How does Gulfstream achieve feedforward control over product quality and customer satisfaction?

3. Which of the four principles of total quality management (TQM) are evident in this video case?

4. Which of Deming's 14 points are evident in this video case?

# References

## Chapter 1

**Opening Quotation**  As quoted in David Whitford, "A Human Place to Work," *Fortune* (January 8, 2001): 118.

**Opening Case**  Excerpted from Katrina Brooker, "It Took a Lady to Save Avon," *Fortune* (October 15, 2001): 202–208.

**Closing Case**  Excerpted from Emily Barker, "Start with . . . Nothing," *Inc.* (February 2002): 66–73. *Inc:* The Magazine for Growing Companies. Copyright 2002 by Bus. Innovator Group Resources/Inc. Reproduced with permission of Bus. Innovator Group Resources/Inc. in the format textbook via Copyright Clearance Center.

1. For a futuristic look at a day in the life of a manager in the year 2020, see Nanette Byrnes, "The Boss in the Web Age," *Business Week* (August 28, 2000): 102–108.

2. Anne B. Fisher, "Morale Crisis," *Fortune* (November 18, 1991): 76, 80.

3. Alan Farnham, "Who Beats Stress Best—And How," *Fortune* (October 7, 1991): 76. Also see "Boss Horribilus," *Fortune* (November 13, 2000): 460.

4. Ellen Van Velsor and Jean Brittain Leslie, "Why Executives Derail: Perspectives Across Time and Cultures," *Academy of Management Executive,* 9 (November 1995): 63. For a related study, see Frank Shipper and John E. Dillard Jr., "A Study of Impending Derailment and Recovery of Middle Managers Across Career Stages," *Human Resource Management,* 39 (Winter 2000): 331–345.

5. For related research, see Bennett J. Tepper, "Consequences of Abusive Supervision," *Academy of Management Journal,* 43 (April 2000): 178–190.

6. Linda Grant, "Rambos in Pinstripes: Why So Many CEOs Are Lousy Leaders," *Fortune* (June 24, 1996): 147.

7. For a complete background, see Carlos Ghosn, "Saving the Business Without Losing the Company," *Harvard Business Review* (January 2002): 37–45. Also see "Carlos Ghosn," *Business Week* (January 8, 2001): 66.

8. James R. Healey, "Renault Has No Plans for USA Beyond Nissan," *USA Today* (January 8, 2002): 5B.

9. See Del Jones and Barbara Hansen, "A Who's Who of Productivity," *USA Today* (August 30, 2001): 1B, 3B.

10. Christine Tierney, "Volkswagen," *Business Week* (July 23, 2001): 65.

11. Data from Evelyn L. Wright, "Cracks in the Greenhouse?" *Business Week* (July 26, 1999): 74, 76; and Jon Talton, "Real Price of Crude Oil Adds Up to More than Dollars on the Barrel," *The Arizona Republic* (January 1, 2002): D1.

12. Data from "Population Grows by the Hour," *USA Today* (April 30, 2001): 1A. U.S. population projections can be found in Rick Hampson, "1990s Boom Reminiscent of 1890s," *USA Today* (April 2, 2001): 3A.

13. Data from Margie Mason, "World Populace Will Max Out, Study Finds," *USA Today* (August 2, 2001): 8D.

14. See Gary S. Becker, "How Rich Nations Can Defuse the Population Bomb," *Business Week* (May 28, 2001): 28; and Laura D'Andrea Tyson, "It's Time to Step Up the Global War on Poverty," *Business Week* (December 3, 2001): 26.

15. Diane Brady, "Wanted: Eclectic Visionary with a Sense of Humor," *Business Week* (August 28, 2000): 143.

16. Profiles of future managers and leaders can be found in Michael A. Hitt, "The New Frontier: Transformation of Management for the New Millennium," *Organizational Dynamics,* 28 (Winter 2000): 7–17; Tom Peters, "The New Wired World of Work," *Business Week* (August 28, 2000): 172, 174; and Paul C. Judge, "Provocation 101," *Fast Company,* no. 54 (January 2002): 108–111.

17. Data from "Taking on the World," *USA Today* (July 11, 2001): 1B.

18. Data from Nelson D. Schwartz, "Breaking OPEC's Grip," *Fortune* (November 12, 2001): 78–88.

19. Nelson D. Schwartz, "Will Tech Earnings Ever Recover?" *Fortune* (June 25, 2001): 96.

20. Data from "AMA Global Survey on Key Business Issues," *Management Review,* 87 (December 1998): 27–38.

21. James Sloan Allen, "Capitalism Globe Trots with Jordan," *USA Today* (August 16, 1999): 6B. Also see Aaron Bernstein, "Backlash: Behind the Anxiety over Globalization," *Business Week* (April 24, 2000): 38–44; Sara Terry, "Free Trade Isn't Fair," *Fast Company,* no. 38 (September 2000): 250–258; and James Cox, "Think Tank Study Assails Globalization," *USA Today* (December 4, 2000): 5B.

22. "Peter Brabeck," *Business Week* (June 11, 2001): 78.

23. A good historical overview of the quality movement can be found in R. Ray Gehani, "Quality Value-Chain: A Meta-Synthesis of Frontiers of Quality Movement," *Academy of Management Executive,* 7 (May 1993): 29–42.

24. For more, see Kee Young Kim, Jeffrey G. Miller, and Janelle Heineke, "Mastering the Quality Staircase, Step by Step," *Business Horizons,* 40 (January–February 1997): 17–21; and Chun Hui, Simon S. K. Lam, and John Schaubroeck, "Can Good Citizens Lead the Way in Providing Quality Service? A Field Quasi Experiment," *Academy of Management Journal,* 44 (October 2001): 988–995.

25. See Kenneth R. Thompson, "Confronting the Paradoxes in a Total Quality Environment," *Organizational Dynamics,* 26 (Winter 1998): 62–74; and Thomas J. Douglas and William Q. Judge Jr., "Total Quality Management Implementation and Competitive Advantage: The Role of Structural Control and Exploration," *Academy of Management Journal,* 44 (February 2001): 158–169.

26. See Gail Whiteman and William H. Cooper, "Ecological Embeddedness," *Academy of Management Journal,* 43 (December 2000): 1265–1282.

27. See Pratima Bansal and Kendall Roth, "Why Companies Go Green: A Model of Ecological Responsiveness," *Academy of Management Journal,* 43 (August 2000): 717–736.

28. See Murray Weidenbaum, Christopher Douglass, and Michael Orlando, "How to Achieve a Healthier Environment *and a Stronger Economy,*" *Business Horizons,* 40 (January–February 1997): 9–16; John Carey, "Look Who's Thawing on Global Warming," *Business Week* (November 9, 1998): 103–104; and Al Gore, "Finding a Third Way," *Newsweek* (November 23, 1998): 58.

29. Data from Gene Koretz, "On Wall Street, Green Is Golden," *Business Week* (January 8, 2001): 30.

30. Data from James K. Kouzes and Barry Z. Posner, "The Credibility Factor: What Followers Expect from Their Leaders," *Management Review,* 79 (January 1990): 29–33.

31. Julie Amparano, "As Ethics Crisis Grows, Businesses Take Action," *The Arizona Republic* (November 24, 1996): D9.

32. See Janet Kornblum, "First U.S. Web Page Went Up 10 Years Ago," *USA Today* (December 11, 2001): 3D.

33. Data from David Kirkpatrick, "The Internet Is Dead—Long Live the Internet," *Fortune* (December 20, 2001): 239–242.

34. See Kevin Maney, "In the Future, You'll Pluck Your Info from Thin Air," *USA Today* (July 20, 2001): 1B–2B; Charles C. Mann, "Taming the Web," *Technology Review,* 104 (September 2001): 44–51; and Jon Swartz, "Experts Fear Cyberspace Could Be Terrorists' Next Target," *USA Today* (October 9, 2001): 1B–2B.

35. Data from Eric Hellweg, "Excite.com—99.85% Off!!!" *Business 2.0,* 3 (January 2002): 18. More dot-com wreckage is reported in Jon Swartz, "Dot-Commers Buy Back Start-Ups at Bargain Prices," *USA Today* (January 22, 2002): 1B.

36. See "The Website Is the Business," *Fortune* Tech Guide (Winter 2001): 144–150; J. William Gurley, "Unlearning Lessons of Internet Mania," *Fortune* (December 10, 2001): 244; and Brian Caulfield, "Toward a More Perfect (and Realistic) E-Business," *Business 2.0,* 3 (January 2002): 77–84.

37. As quoted in Cheryl Dahle, "Putting Its Chips on the Net," *Fast Company,* no. 48 (July 2001): 154.

38. For related research, see Frank Shipper, "A Study of the Psychometric Properties of the Managerial Skill Scales of the Survey of Management Practices," *Educational and Psychological Measurement,* 55 (June 1995): 468–479; Frank Shipper and Charles S. White, "Mastery, Frequency, and Interaction of Managerial Behaviors Relative to Subunit Effectiveness," *Human Relations,* 52 (January 1999): 49–66; and Frank Shipper, and Jeanette Davy, "A Model and Investigation of Managerial Skills, Employees' Attitudes, and Managerial Performance," *The Leadership Quarterly,* 13, no. 2 (2002): 95–120.

39. See Henri Fayol, *General and Industrial Management,* trans. Constance Storrs (London: Isaac Pitman & Sons, 1949).

40. Henry Mintzberg, "The Manager's Job: Folklore and Fact," *Harvard Business Review,* 53 (July–August 1975): 49.

41. Ibid., p. 54. For Mintzberg's recent thoughts about managing, see Henry Mintzberg, "The Yin and Yang of Managing," *Organizational Dynamics,* 29 (Spring 2001): 306–312.

42. As quoted in Alan Deutschman, "The CEO's Secret of Managing Time," *Fortune* (June 1, 1992): 136. Also see Steve Kaye, "How to Handle Interruptions that Steal Your Time," *Canadian Manager,* 24 (Summer 1999): 25–26; and Richard E. S.

Boulton, Barry D. Libert, and Steve M. Samek, "Learning to Juggle," *Business 2.0,* 1 (June 27, 2000): 250–263.

43. See Henry Mintzberg, "Managerial Work: Analysis from Observation," *Management Science,* 18 (October 1971): B97–B110.

44. See Scott Adams, *The Dilbert Principle* (New York: Harper-Business, 1996); and Lisa A. Burke and Jo Ellen Moore, "Contemporary Satire of Corporate Managers: Time to Cut the Boss Some Slack?" *Business Horizons,* 42 (July–August 1999): 63–67.

45. "AMA Research," *Management Review,* 85 (July 1996): 10. Also see Jenny C. McCune, "Brave New World," *Management Review,* 86 (October 1997): 11–14; and Robert J. Samuelson, "Why I Am Not a Manager," *Newsweek* (March 22, 1999): 47.

46. For glimpses into top executives' lives *off* the job, see Rifka Rosenwein, "Frank Tucker's Downtime," *Inc.,* 23 (September 2001): 74; and Rifka Rosenwein, "Jeanne Lambert, Home Alone," *Inc.,* 23 (October 2001): 52.

47. See Martin M. Broadwell and Carol Broadwell Dietrich, "Culture Clash: How to Turn Blue-Collar Workers into Good Supervisors," *Training,* 37 (March 2000): 34–36.

48. Adapted from Earnest R. Archer, "Things You Lose the Right to Do When You Become a Manager," *Supervisory Management,* 35 (July 1990): 8–9.

49. Trends in higher education are discussed in Michael Schrage, "Brave New World for Higher Education," *Technology Review,* 104 (October 2001): 90–91; and William C. Symonds, "Giving It the Old Online Try," *Business Week* (December 3, 2001): 76–80.

50. See Ron Zemke, "The Honeywell Studies: How Managers Learn to Manage," *Training,* 22 (August 1985): 46–51.

51. Adapted from Robin Snell, "Graduating from the School of Hard Knocks?" *Journal of Management Development,* 8, no. 5 (1989): 23–30. For a humorous view of the school of hard knocks, see Ray W. Cooksey, G. Richard Gates, and Hilary Pollock, "'Unsafe' Business Acts and Outcomes: A Management Lexicon," *Business Horizons,* 41 (May–June 1998): 41–49.

52. John Beeson, "Succession Planning: Building the Management Corps," *Business Horizons,* 41 (September–October 1998): 61–66; "Nicholas Negroponte on Following Your Passion," *Training,* 37 (May 2000): 25; and Beth Alexrod, Helen Handfield-Jones, and Ed Michaels, "A New Game Plan for C Players," *Harvard Business Review,* 80 (January 2002): 80–88.

53. Data from Jim Hopkins, "Small Businesses Not Making Full Use of the Web," *USA Today* (August 28, 2001): 1B.

54. Data from Jim Hopkins, "Small Businesses Hold Off on Big Purchases," *USA Today* (October 16, 2001): 1B.

55. Data from Jim Hopkins, "New Bosses Should Develop Management Skills," *USA Today* (September 12, 2001): 9B; and Jim Hopkins, "Micro-Businesses Targeted as Source of Sales Revenue," *USA Today* (April 3, 2001): 1B.

56. See George Gendron, "The Failure Myth," *Inc.,* (January 2001): 13.

57. See David R. Francis, "Spiking Stereotypes About Small Firms," *The Christian Science Monitor* (May 7, 1993): 9; Gene Koretz, "A Surprising Finding on New-Business Mortality

Rates," *Business Week* (June 14, 1993): 22; and James Aley, "Debunking the Failure Fallacy," *Fortune* (September 6, 1993): 21. For related reading, see Sydney Finkelstein, "The Myth of Managerial Superiority in Internet Startups: An Autopsy," *Organizational Dynamics*, 30 (Fall 2001): 172–185.

58. Data from Larry Light, "Small Business: The Job Engine Needs Fuel," *Business Week* (March 1, 1993): 78.

59. Data from Charles Burck, "Where Good Jobs Grow," *Fortune* (June 14, 1993): 22. Also see Gene Koretz, "Where the New Jobs Are," *Business Week* (March 20, 1995): 24.

60. For more on Birch's research, see Alan Webber, "Business Race Isn't Always to the Swift, but Bet That Way," *USA Today* (February 3, 1998): 15A. Also see "The Gazelle Theory," *Inc.*, 23 (May 29, 2001): 28–29.

61. For data on pay in big companies versus small companies, see Michael Mandel, "Big Players Offer Better Pay," *Business Week* (August 30, 1999): 30.

62. See Conrad S. Ciccotello and C. Terry Grant, "LLCs and LLPs: Organizing to Deliver Professional Services," *Business Horizons*, 42 (March–April 1999): 85–91.

63. See Surinder Tikoo, "Assessing the Franchise Option," *Business Horizons*, 39 (May–June 1996): 78–82; and Yvette Armendariz, "Fast Food, Fast Profits," *The Arizona Republic* (July 1, 2001): D1, D10.

64. See recent issues of *Inc.* and *Fast Company* magazines for inspiring small-business success stories.

65. Howard H. Stevenson and J. Carlos Jarillo, "A Paradigm of Entrepreneurship: Entrepreneurial Management," *Strategic Management Journal*, 11 (Summer 1990): 23 (emphasis added).

66. See Gene Koretz, "What Makes an Entrepreneur," *Business Week* (December 9, 1996): 32; John B. Miner, "The Expanded Horizon for Achieving Entrepreneurial Success," *Organizational Dynamics*, 25 (Winter 1997): 54–67; Edward O. Welles, "True Grit," *Inc.*, (July 2000): 43–44; and Edward O. Welles, "The Billionaire Next Door," *Inc.*, (May 2001): 80–85.

67. Stephanie Armour, "UBUBU Boldly Launches Start-Up in Cyberspace," *USA Today* (June 19, 2000): 3B. Also see Laura Cohn, "Are VC Startups Run Better?" *Business Week* (February 26, 2001): 24.

68. Steven Berglas, "G is for Guts," *Inc.*, 22 (May 2000): 45.

69. For instructive reading, see Eric G. Flamholtz, *How to Make the Transition from an Entrepreneurship to a Professionally Managed Firm* (San Francisco: Jossey-Bass, 1986); Richard L. Osborne, "Second Phase Entrepreneurship: Breaking Through the Growth Wall," *Business Horizons*, 37 (January–February 1994): 80–86; and Rita Gunther McGrath, "Falling Forward: Real Options Reasoning and Entrepreneurial Failure," *Academy of Management Review*, 24 (January 1999): 13–30.

## Chapter 2

**Opening Quotation**   John W. Gardner, *Self-Renewal: The Individual and the Innovative Society* (New York: Harper & Row, 1964), Chap. 11.

**Opening Case**   Donna Fenn, "Rescuing Tradition," *Inc.*, 23 (August 2001): 48–49. *Inc:* The Magazine for Growing Com-

panies. Copyright 2002 by Bus. Innovator Group Resources/Inc. Reproduced with permission of Bus. Innovator Group Resources/Inc. in the format textbook via Copyright Clearance Center.

**Closing Case**   Bill Montague, "Russia's New Management Style," *USA Today* (August 12, 1996): 7B. Copyright 1996, *USA Today*. Reprinted with permission.

1. A brief but instructive historical perspective on modern management can be found in Richard S. Tedlow, "The Making of the Modern Company," *Business Week* (August 28, 2000): 98–99.

2. Alonzo L. McDonald, as quoted in Alan M. Kantrow, ed., "Why History Matters to Managers," *Harvard Business Review*, 64 (January–February 1986): 82.

3. Barbara S. Lawrence, "Historical Perspective: Using the Past to Study the Present," *Academy of Management Review*, 9 (April 1984): 307.

4. For a discussion in this area, see "How Business Schools Began," *Business Week* (October 19, 1963): 114–116. Also see John Trinkaus, "Urwick on the Business Academy," *Business Horizons*, 35 (September–October 1992): 25–29.

5. The top ten most influential management thinkers of the twentieth century, as selected by the readers of *Business Horizons* magazine, are discussed in Dennis W. Organ, "And the Winners Are . . . ," *Business Horizons*, 43 (March–April 2000): 1–3.

6. See Marian M. Extejt and Jonathan E. Smith, "The Behavioral Sciences and Management: An Evaluation of Relevant Journals," *Journal of Management*, 16 (September 1990): 539–551. For a list of 40 management-oriented periodicals, see Jonathan L. Johnson and Philip M. Podsakoff, "Journal Influence in the Field of Management: An Analysis Using Salancik's Index in a Dependency Network," *Academy of Management Journal*, 37 (October 1994): 1392–1407.

7. For advice on dealing with information overload, see Suzy Wetlaufer, "Thanks for Asking," *Harvard Business Review*, 80 (February 2002): 10.

8. See the instructive timeline in "Management Ideas Through Time," *Management Review*, 87 (January 1998): 16–19. Also see Daniel A. Wren and Ronald G. Greenwood, *Management Innovators: The People and Ideas That Shaped Modern Business* (New York: Oxford University Press, 1998).

9. An interesting call for the reintegration of management theory may be found in Max S. Wortman Jr., "Reintegrating and Reconceptualizing Management: A Challenge for the Future," *Review of Business and Economic Research*, 18 (Spring 1983): 1–8.

10. See Henri Fayol, *General and Industrial Management*, trans. Constance Storrs (London: Isaac Pitman & Sons, 1949). An interesting review by Nancy M. Carter of Fayol's book can be found in Allen C. Bluedorn, ed., "Special Book Review Section on the Classics of Management," *Academy of Management Review*, 11 (April 1986): 454–456.

11. Stephen J. Carroll and Dennis J. Gillen, "Are the Classical Management Functions Useful in Describing Managerial Work?" *Academy of Management Review*, 12 (January 1987): 48.

12. Frank B. Copley, *Frederick W. Taylor: Father of Scientific Management* (New York: Harper & Brothers, 1923), I: 3. Also see the brief profile of Taylor in "Taylorism," *Business Week*: 100 Years of Innovation (Summer 1999): 16.

13. For expanded treatment, see Frank B. Copley, *Frederick W. Taylor: The Principles of Scientific Management* (New York: Harper & Brothers, 1911). A good retrospective review of Taylor's classic writings may be found in Bluedorn, ed., "Special Book Review Section on the Classics of Management," pp. 443–447. Robert Kanigel's *One Best Way,* a modern biography of Taylor, is reviewed in Alan Farnham, "The Man Who Changed Work Forever," *Fortune* (July 21, 1997): 114.

14. For an interesting update on Taylor, see Christopher Farrell, "Micromanaging from the Grave," *Business Week* (May 15, 1995): 34.

15. George D. Babcock, *The Taylor System in Franklin Management,* 2nd ed. (New York: Engineering Magazine Company, 1917), p. 31.

16. Taylor's seminal 1911 book, *The Principles of Scientific Management,* was recently selected by a panel of management experts as the most influential management book of the twentieth century: See Arthur G. Bedeian and Daniel A. Wren, "Most Influential Management Books of the 20th Century," *Organizational Dynamics,* 29 (Winter 2001): 221–225. Also see Oswald Jones, "Scientific Management, Culture and Control: A First-Hand Account of Taylorism in Practice," *Human Relations,* 53 (May 2000): 631–653.

17. For an alternative perspective and detailed critique of Taylor's pig iron handling–experiments, see Charles D. Wrege and Richard M. Hodgetts, "Frederick W. Taylor's 1899 Pig Iron Observations: Examining Fact, Fiction, and Lessons for the New Millennium," *Academy of Management Journal,* 43 (December 2000): 1283–1291.

18. Frederick W. Taylor, *Shop Management* (New York: Harper & Brothers, 1911), p. 22.

19. Frank B. Gilbreth and Lillian M. Gilbreth, *Applied Motion Study* (New York: Sturgis & Walton, 1917), p. 42. A retrospective review of the Gilbreths' writings, by Daniel J. Brass, can be found in Bluedorn, ed., "Special Book Review Section on the Classics of Management," pp. 448–451.

20. See Frank B. Gilbreth Jr., and Ernestine Gilbreth Carey, *Cheaper by the Dozen* (New York: Thomas Y. Crowell, 1948).

21. For example, see the Gantt chart on p. 64 of Tom D. Conkright, "So You're Going to Manage a Project," *Training,* 35 (January 1998): 62–67.

22. For detailed coverage of Gantt's contributions, see H. L. Gantt, *Work, Wages, and Profits,* 2nd ed. (New York: Engineering Magazine Company, 1913). An interesting update on Gantt's contributions can be found in Peter B. Peterson, "Training and Development: The Views of Henry L. Gantt (1861–1919)," *SAM Advanced Management Journal,* 52 (Winter 1987): 20–23.

23. Good historical overviews of the quality movement are Ron Zemke, "A Bluffer's Guide to TQM," *Training,* 30 (April 1993): 48–55; R. Ray Gehani, "Quality Value-Chain: A Meta-Synthesis of Frontiers of Quality Movement," *Academy of Manage-ment Executive,* 7 (May 1993): 29–42; and Sangit Chatterjee and Mustafa Yilmaz, "Quality Confusion: Too Many Gurus, Not Enough Disciples," *Business Horizons,* 36 (May–June 1993): 15–18.

24. Mary Walton, *Deming Management at Work* (New York: Putnam, 1990), p. 13. See John Hillkirk, "World-Famous Quality Expert Dead at 93," *USA Today* (December 21, 1993): 1B–2B; Peter Nulty, "The National Business Hall of Fame: W. Edwards Deming," *Fortune* (April 4, 1994): 124; Keki R. Bhote, "Dr. W. Edwards Deming—A Prophet with Belated Honor in His Own Country," *National Productivity Review,* 13 (Spring 1994): 153–159; Anne Willette, "Deming Legacy Gives Firms Quality Challenge," *USA Today* (October 19, 1994): 2B; and M. R. Yilmaz and Sangit Chatterjee, "Deming and the Quality of Software Development," *Business Horizons,* 40 (November–December 1997): 51–58.

25. See Jack Gordon, "An Interview with Joseph M. Juran," *Training,* 31 (May 1994): 35–41.

26. Zemke, "A Bluffer's Guide to TQM," p. 51. Also see Joseph M. Juran, "Made in U.S.A.: A Renaissance in Quality," *Harvard Business Review,* 71 (July–August 1993): 42–50.

27. See Armand V. Feigenbaum, "How Total Quality Counters Three Forces of International Competitiveness," *National Productivity Review,* 13 (Summer 1994): 327–330. More Feigenbaum ideas can be found in Del Jones, "Employers Going for Quality Hires, Not Quantity," *USA Today* (December 11, 1997): 1B.

28. Crosby's more recent ideas may be found in Philip B. Crosby, *Completeness: Quality for the 21st Century* (New York: Dutton, 1992).

29. Edwin A. Locke, "The Ideas of Frederick W. Taylor: An Evaluation," *Academy of Management Review,* 7 (January 1982): 22–23. Also see David H. Freedman, "Is Management Still a Science?" *Harvard Business Review,* 70 (November–December 1992): 26–38.

30. See Donald W. Fogarty, Thomas R. Hoffman, and Peter W. Stonebraker, *Production and Operations Management* (Cincinnati: South-Western Publishing Co., 1989), pp. 7–8; and Vincent A. Mabert, "Operations in the American Economy: Liability or Asset," *Business Horizons,* 35 (July–August 1992): 3–5.

31. The Hawthorne studies are discussed in detail in F. J. Roethlisberger and William J. Dickson, *Management and the Worker* (Cambridge, Mass.: Harvard University Press, 1939). Dennis W. Organ's review of this classic book, in which he criticizes the usual textbook treatment of it, can be found in Bluedorn, ed., "Special Book Review Section on the Classics of Management," pp. 459–463.

32. See Ellen S. O'Connor, "The Politics of Management Thought: A Case Study of the Harvard Business School and the Human Relations School," *Academy of Management Review,* 24 (January 1999): 117–131.

33. See Henry C. Metcalf and L. Urwick, *Dynamic Administration: The Collected Papers of Mary Parker Follett* (New York: Harper & Brothers, 1942); Mary Parker Follett, *Freedom and Coordination* (London: Management Publications Trust, 1949). A review by Diane L. Ferry of *Dynamic Administration* can be

found in Bluedorn, ed., "Special Book Review Section on the Classics of Management," pp. 451–454.

34. See L. D. Parker, "Control in Organizational Life: The Contribution of Mary Parker Follett, " *Academy of Management Review,* 9 (October 1984): 736–745; Albie M. Davis, "An Interview with Mary Parker Follett, " *Negotiation Journal,* 5 (July 1989): 223–225; and Dana Wechsler Linden, "The Mother of Them All," *Forbes* (January 16, 1995): 75–76.

35. For a recent case study of a military leader's transition from a Theory X style to a Theory Y style, see D. Michael Abrashoff, "Retention Through Redemption," *Harvard Business Review,* 79 (February 2001): 136–141.

36. An interesting and instructive timeline of human resource milestones can be found in "Training and Development in the 20th Century," *Training,* 35 (September 1998): 49–56.

37. For a statistical interpretation of the Hawthorne studies, see Richard Herbert Franke and James D. Kaul, "The Hawthorne Experiments: First Statistical Interpretation," *American Sociological Review,* 43 (October 1978): 623–643. Also see Stephen R. G. Jones, "Worker Interdependence and Output: The Hawthorne Studies Reevaluated," *American Sociological Review,* 55 (April 1990): 176–190.

38. Russell L. Ackoff, "Science in the Systems Age: Beyond IE, OR, and MS," *Operations Research,* 21 (May–June 1973): 664.

39. Charles J. Coleman and David D. Palmer, "Organizational Application of System Theory," *Business Horizons,* 16 (December 1973): 77.

40. Chester I. Barnard, *The Functions of the Executive* (Cambridge, Mass.: Harvard University Press, 1938), p. 65.

41. Ibid., p. 82. A retrospective review, by Thomas L. Keon, of Barnard's *The Functions of the Executive* can be found in Bluedorn, ed., "Special Book Review Section on the Classics of Management," pp. 456–459.

42. For details, see Lori Verstegen Ryan and William G. Scott, "Ethics and Organizational Reflection: The Rockefeller Foundation and Postwar 'Moral Deficits,' 1942–1954," *Academy of Management Review,* 20 (April 1995): 438–461.

43. Ludwig von Bertalanffy, "The History and Status of General Systems Theory," *Academy of Management Journal,* 15 (December 1972): 411.

44. For an example of an economic/industrial hierarchy of organizations, see Figure 2 (p. 774) in Philip Rich, "The Organizational Taxonomy: Definition and Design," *Academy of Management Review,* 17 (October 1992): 758–781.

45. Susan Albers Mohrman and Allan M. Mohrman Jr., "Organizational Change and Learning," in *Organizing for the Future: The New Logic for Managing Complex Organizations,* eds. Jay R. Galbraith, Edward E. Lawler III, and Associates (San Francisco: Jossey-Bass, 1993), p. 89. For an excellent overview of organizational learning, see David A. Garvin, "Building a Learning Organization," *Harvard Business Review,* 71 (July–August 1993): 78–91. Also see Robert Aubrey and Paul M. Cohen, *Working Wisdom: Timeless Skills and Vanguard Strategies for Learning Organizations* (San Francisco: Jossey-Bass, 1995); and Timothy T. Baldwin and Camden C. Danielson, "Building a Learning Strategy at the Top: Interviews with

Ten of America's CLOs," *Business Horizons,* 43 (November–December 2000): 5–14.

46. For an excellent collection of readings, see *Harvard Business Review on Knowledge Management* (Boston: Harvard Business School Publishing, 1998).

47. For example, see Gary Weiss, "Chaos Hits Wall Street—The Theory, That Is," *Business Week* (November 2, 1992): 138–140.

48. See Benyamin Bergmann Lichtenstein, "Self-Organized Transitions: A Pattern amid the Chaos of Transformative Change," *Academy of Management Executive,* 14 (November 2000): 128–141; and Polly LaBarre, "Organize Yourself," *Fast Company,* no. 50 (September 2001): 60.

49. Fred Luthans, *Introduction to Management: A Contingency Approach* (New York: McGraw-Hill, 1976), p. 28. Also see Henry L. Tosi Jr. and John W. Slocum Jr., "Contingency Theory: Some Suggested Directions," *Journal of Management,* 10 (Spring 1984): 9–26.

50. Y. K. Shetty, "Contingency Management: Current Perspective for Managing Organizations," *Management International Review,* 14, no. 6 (1974): 27.

51. See Joseph W. McGuire, "Management Theory: Retreat to the Academy," *Business Horizons,* 25 (July–August 1982): 37.

52. Data from John A. Byrne, "How the Best Get Better," *Business Week* (September 14, 1987): 98–99.

53. *Business Week* listed *In Search of Excellence* among ten indispensable business books. See John A. Byrne, "A Classic Business Bookshelf," *Business Week* (March 5, 1990): 10, 12.

54. Information about the sample in this study may be found in Thomas J. Peters and Robert H. Waterman Jr., *In Search of Excellence* (New York: Harper & Row, 1982), pp. 19–26.

55. Ibid., pp. 16–17.

56. Daniel T. Carroll, "A Disappointing Search for Excellence," *Harvard Business Review,* 61 (November–December 1983): 88.

57. "Who's Excellent Now?" *Business Week* (November 5, 1984): 76–78. 3M Company's troubles since being an "excellent" company are chronicled in De'Ann Weimer, "3M: The Heat Is on the Boss," *Business Week* (March 15, 1999): 82–84.

58. See Michael A. Hitt and R. Duane Ireland, "Peters and Waterman Revisited: The Unended Quest for Excellence," *Academy of Management Executive,* 1 (May 1987): 91–98. Also see James N. Vedder, "How Much Can We Learn from Success?" *Academy of Management Executive,* 6 (February 1992): 56–66.

59. For more, see Paula Phillips Carson, Patricia A. Lanier, Kerry David Carson, and Brandi N. Guidry, "Clearing a Path Through the Management Fashion Jungle: Some Preliminary Trailblazing," *Academy of Management Journal,* 43 (December 2000): 1143–1158; Jane Whitney Gibson and Dana V. Tesone, "Management Fads: Emergence, Evolution, and Implications for Managers," *Academy of Management Executive,* 15 (November 2001): 122–133; and Leigh Buchanan, "Managing from A to Z," *Inc.,* 24 (January 2002): 63–69.

60. Peters and Waterman, *In Search of Excellence,* p. 13.

61. For recent controversy about the "excellence" research methodology, see Tom Peters, "Tom Peters's True Confessions," *Fast Company,* no. 53 (December 2001): 78–92; David Lieberman, "Author: Data on Successful Firms 'Faked' But Still

Valid," *USA Today* (November 19, 2001): 6B; and John A. Byrne, "The Real Confessions of Tom Peters," *Business Week* (December 3, 2001): 46.

62. See Susan Albers Mohrman, Cristina B. Gibson, and Allan M. Mohrman Jr., "Doing Research That Is Useful to Practice: A Model and Empirical Exploration," *Academy of Management Journal,* 44 (April 2001): 357–375.

63. Excerpted from Amy Cortese, "Weapons of Mass Disruption," *Business 2.0* (January 2002): 44.

## Chapter 3

**Opening Quotation**   As quoted in R. Stanley Williams, "You Ain't Seen Nothin' Yet," *Business 2.0* (September 26, 2000): 168.

**Opening Case**   Excerpted from Jim Hopkins, "Childhood Treat Helps Sobrino Savor Sweet Success," *USA Today* (May 16, 2001): 10B. Copyright 2001, *USA Today*. Reprinted with permission.

**Closing Case**   Excerpted from Stephanie Armour, "The Challenge: Mix Energy, Experience," *USA Today* (April 20, 1999): 1A–2A. Copyright 1999, *USA Today*. Reprinted with permission.

1. This section adapted from Robert Barner, "The New Millennium Workplace: Seven Changes That Will Challenge Managers—and Workers," *The Futurist,* 30 (March–April 1996): 14–18. Also see James Daly, "Interview with Alvin Toffler," *Business 2.0,* 1 (September 26, 2000): 110–116; Joel Kotkin, "The Future Is Here! But Is It Shocking?" *Inc.,* 22 (December 2000): 108–114; Julie Wallace, "How to Be a Futurist," *HRMagazine,* 46 (January 2001): 184; "The 2001 HBR List: Breakthrough Ideas for Today's Business Agenda," *Harvard Business Review,* 79 (April 2001): 123–128; and Marvin J. Cetron and Owen Davies, "Trends Now Changing the World," *The Futurist,* 35 (January–February 2001): 30–43.

2. Barner, "The New Millennium Workplace," p. 15.

3. Ibid., p. 16.

4. Ibid., p. 18.

5. For example, see William Echikson, "Unsung Heroes," *Business Week* (March 6, 2000): 92–100; Gene Koretz, "Europe Faces a Retiree Crisis," *Business Week* (May 15, 2000): 38; Bill Powell, "Is Saudi Arabia Headed for a Fall?" *Fortune* (December 10, 2001): 193–200; and "The World's 'Oldest' Countries," *USA Today* (January 10, 2002): 1A.

6. See Tamara Henry, "Report: Mixed Progress in Math," *USA Today* (August 3, 2001): 4A.

7. "One Third of Tested Job Applicants Flunked in Basic Literacy and Math, American Management Association Survey Finds," *Business Horizons,* (July–August 2001): 84.

8. Data from Troy Segal, "When Johnny's Whole Family Can't Read," *Business Week* (July 20, 1992): 68–70.

9. "Illiteracy Still a Problem," *USA Today* (November 29, 2000): 1A.

10. Data from Tammy Galvin, "2001 Industry Report," *Training,* 38 (October 2001): 40–75.

11. Leigh Strope, "Older Workers Stay on Job," *The Arizona Republic* (June 10, 2001): D1. Also see Stephanie Armour, "More Firms Ask Retirees to Remain," *USA Today* (January 4, 2001): 1B.

12. Mark Clements, "What We Say About Aging," *Parade Magazine* (December 12, 1993): 4. Also see Roy Hoffman, "Working Past 90" *Fortune* (November 13, 2000): 364–384; and Peter Coy, "Older Now—and Steadier," *Business Week* (November 5, 2001): 32.

13. For good discussions, see Ellen Neuborne, "Generation Y," *Business Week* (February 15, 1999): 80–88; Alison Wellner, "Get Ready for Generation NEXT," *Training,* 36 (February 1999): 42–48; Brian O'Reilly, "Meet the Future" *Fortune* (July 24, 2000): 144–168; and Julie Wallace, "After X Comes Y" *HRMagazine,* 46 (April 2001): 192.

14. Excerpted from Paul Mayrand, "Older Workers: A Problem or the Solution?" *Proceedings: Textbook Authors' Conference* (AARP: Washington, D.C., October 21, 1992), pp. 28–29. Reprinted by permission of AARP. For more, see Allison Kindelan, "Older Workers Can Alleviate Labor Shortages," *HRMagazine,* 43 (September 1998): 200; Alison Stein Wellner, "Workplace 2018: Retirement Boom or Bust?" *Training,* 36 (August 1999): 54–59; and Anne Field, "Work Still Does a Body Good," *Business Week* (December 10, 2001): 98–99.

15. See Glenn M. McEvoy and Mary Jo Blahna, "Engagement or Disengagement? Older Workers and the Looming Labor Shortage," *Business Horizons,* 44 (September–October 2001): 46–52.

16. Data from "Mass Layoffs in USA Idle 2.5 Million in 2001," *USA Today* (January 30, 2002): 1B.

17. Robert Aubrey and Paul M. Cohen, *Working Wisdom: Timeless Skills and Vanguard Strategies for Learning Organizations* (San Francisco: Jossey-Bass, 1995), p. 29.

18. See Michelle Conlin, "And Now, the Just-in-Time Employee," *Business Week* (August 28, 2000): 168–170.

19. John Huey, "Where Managers Will Go," *Fortune* (January 27, 1992): 51.

20. Data from U.S. Bureau of Labor Statistics, February 2002, **http://stats.bls.gov**.

21. For specific data, see Louis Lavelle, "For Female CEOs, It's Stingy at the Top," *Business Week* (April 23, 2001): 70–71; "Female Lawyers' Pay Lags Behind Males," *USA Today* (April 27, 2001): 3A; "The Business World Is Still a Man's World," *USA Today* (April 11, 2001): 1B; and "Female Office Workers' Pay Trails Men's," *USA Today* (November 5, 2001): 1B.

22. Data from "Female Managers Still Earn Less, GAO Says," *USA Today* (January 24, 2002): 1B.

23. See Juliette Fairley, "Play Game Like a Man to Get Ahead," *USA Today* (May 8, 2000): 6B; Gene Koretz, "She's a Woman, Offer Her Less," *Business Week* (May 7, 2001): 34; Susan J. Wells, "A Female Executive Is Hard to Find," *HRMagazine,* 46 (June 2001): 40–49; and Patricia Sellers, "Patient but Not Passive," *Fortune* (October 15, 2001): 188–193.

24. Ann M. Morrison and Mary Ann Von Glinow, "Women and Minorities in Management," *American Psychologist,* 45 (February 1990): 200 (emphasis added).

25. See Del Jones, "Cinda Hallman: Need for Outsourcing Grows," *USA Today* (November 27, 2001): 7b; Noelle Knox, "Merrill

Lynch Names New President, COO," *USA Today* (July 25, 2001): 3B; Ellis Cose, "It's a Watershed Moment," *Newsweek* (December 17, 2001): 46; and Johnnie L. Roberts, "The Race to the Top," *Newsweek* (January 28, 2002): 44–49.

26. Toddi Gutner, "Wanted: More Diverse Directors," *Business Week* (April 30, 2001): 134. Also see Elisabeth Malkin, "Cracks in Mexico's Glass Ceiling," *Business Week* (July 10, 2000): 166.

27. As quoted in Rhonda Richards, "More Women Poised for Role as CEO," *USA Today* (March 26, 1996): 2B. Also see Marta M. Elvira and Lisa E. Cohen, "Location Matters: A Cross-Level Analysis of the Effects of Organizational Sex Composition on Turnover," *Academy of Management Journal*, 44 (June 2001): 591–605.

28. Data from "Growth Surges for Female-Led Businesses," *USA Today* (December 5, 2001): 1B.

29. For specifics, see George Hager, "More Black Workers Face Joblessness," *USA Today* (April 9, 2001): 1B; Aaron Bernstein, "Already, a Crush at the Soup Kitchens," *Business Week* (November 26, 2001): 74; and Stephanie Armour, "Minority Job Losses Shrink Gains Made in '90s," *USA Today* (January 14, 2002): 1B.

30. U.S. Bureau of Labor Statistics, "Contingent and Alternative Employment Arrangements, February 2001," p. 1, **http://stats.bls.gov/news.release/**.

31. Gene Koretz, "Taking Stock of the Flexible Work Force," *Business Week* (July 24, 1989): 12. Also see Vivien Corwin, Thomas B. Lawrence, and Peter J. Frost, "Five Strategies of Successful Part-Time Work," *Harvard Business Review*, 79 (July–August 2001): 121–127; Peter Coy, "Hourly Wages Are Up. So What?" *Business Week* (January 28, 2002): 26; and Peter F. Drucker, "They're not Employees, They're People," *Harvard Business Review*, 80 (February 2002): 70–77.

32. See Bill Leonard, "Recipes for Part-Time Benefits," *HRMagazine*, 45 (April 2000): 56–62.

33. These research results drawn from Robert P. Vecchio, "Demographic and Attitudinal Differences Between Part-Time and Full-Time Employees," *Journal of Occupational Behaviour*, 5 (July 1984): 213–218. Also see Daniel C. Feldman, Helen I. Doerpinghaus, and William H. Turnley, "Employee Reactions to Temporary Jobs," *Journal of Managerial Issues*, 7 (Summer 1995): 127–141.

34. Beverly Geber, "The Flexible Work Force," *Training*, 30 (December 1993): 27.

35. For more, see Courtney von Hippel, Stephen L. Mangum, David B. Greenberger, Robert L. Heneman, and Jeffrey D. Skoglind, "Temporary Employment: Can Organizations and Employees Both Win?" *Academy of Management Executive*, 11 (February 1997): 93–104; Bill Leonard, "Part-Time Jobs a Dead End for Some," *HRMagazine*, 43 (November 1998): 24; Aaron Bernstein, "When Is a Temp Not a Temp?" *Business Week* (December 7, 1998): 90, 92; and Monica Roman, "At Microsoft, a Consolation Prize," *Business Week* (December 25, 2000): 60.

36. Data from Maria Puente, "Birth Rate in U.S. at a Record Low," *USA Today* (February 10, 1998): 4A.

37. Tamara Henry, "Societal Shifts Could Alter Education by Mid-century," *USA Today* (February 26, 2001): 6D.

38. Dave Patel, "Minority Rules," *HRMagazine*, 46 (July 2001): 168.

39. As quoted in Stephanie Armour, "Welcome Mat Rolls Out for Hispanic Workers," *USA Today* (April 12, 2001): 2B.

40. Data from Del Jones, "Setting Diversity's Foundation in the Bottom Line," *USA Today* (October 15, 1996): 4B.

41. See Jerry Adler, "Sweet Land of Liberties," *Newsweek* (July 10, 1995): 18–23; and Robert J. Samuelson, "Immigration and Poverty," *Newsweek* (July 15, 1996): 43.

42. For good background information, see R. Roosevelt Thomas Jr., "From Affirmative Action to Affirming Diversity," *Harvard Business Review*, 68 (March–April 1990): 107–117; Marc Adams, "Building a Rainbow, One Stripe at a Time," *HRMagazine*, 43 (August 1998): 72–79; Patricia Digh, "Coming to Terms with Diversity," *HRMagazine*, 43 (November 1998): 117–120; Louisa Wah, "Diversity at Allstate: A Competitive Weapon," *Management Review*, 88 (July–August 1999): 24–30; and Mike Hofman, "It Takes All Kinds," *Inc.*, 23 (July 2001): 70–75.

43. For example, see Roy S. Johnson, "The 50 Best Companies for Asians, Blacks, and Hispanics," *Fortune* (August 3, 1998): 94–97.

44. Jack McDevitt, "Are We Becoming a Country of Haters?" *USA Today* (September 2, 1992): 9A.

45. Adapted from Sheryl Hilliard Tucker and Kevin D. Thompson, "Will Diversity = Opportunity + Advancement for Blacks?" *Black Enterprise*, 21 (November 1990): 50–60. Also see Jennifer Reingold, "B-Schools That Look Like America," *Business Week* (June 21, 1999): 92, 94.

46. For example, see Dottie Enrico, "Not Just a Policy: A Personal Commitment," *USA Today* (April 27, 1998): 8B.

47. Research support can be found in Joseph J. Martocchio, "Age-Related Differences in Employee Absenteeism: A Meta-Analysis," *Psychology and Aging*, 4 (December 1989): 409–414.

48. Douglas T. Hall and Victoria A. Parker, "The Role of Workplace Flexibility in Managing Diversity," *Organizational Dynamics*, 22 (Summer 1993): 8.

49. Based on Jack Kelley, "Russian Radical Threatens 'New Hiroshimas,'" *USA Today* (December 15, 1993): 8A.

50. See, for example, Stephanie Armour, "No-Smoking Zones Reach Outside," *USA Today* (July 6, 2001): 1A; and Richard Willing, "Lawsuits Follow Growth Curve of Wal-Mart," *USA Today* (August 14, 2001): 1A–2A.

51. See Michael D. Eisner, "Critics of Disney's America on Wrong Track," *USA Today* (July 12, 1994): 10A; and Steve Marshall and Carrie Dowling, "Disney Abandons Va. Site," *USA Today* (September 29, 1994): 1A.

52. Julie Schmit, "Baptists Threaten to Boycott Disney," *USA Today* (June 13, 1996): 1A.

53. Ibid.

54. Steven L. Wartick and Robert E. Rude, "Issues Management: Corporate Fad or Corporate Function?" *California Management Review*, 29 (Fall 1986): 124–140. Also see Andrew J. Hoffman, "Institutional Evolution and Change: Environmentalism and the U.S. Chemical Industry," *Academy of Management Journal*, 42 (August 1999): 351–371.

55. David B. Yoffie and Mary Kwak, "Playing by the Rules," *Harvard Business Review,* 79 (June 2001): 119–120.

56. Drawn from S. Prakash Sethi, "Serving the Public Interest: Corporate Political Action for the 1980s," *Management Review,* 70 (March 1981): 8–11.

57. For example, see Amy Borrus, "Silicon Valley Keeps on Giving," *Business Week* (December 17, 2001): 12.

58. See Ginger L. Graham, "The Leader as Lobbyist," *Harvard Business Review,* 79 (June 2001): 24–26; and "Kent Kresa: Northrop Grumman," *Business Week* (January 14, 2002): 59.

59. See David A. Andelman, "Capital Crises," *Management Review,* 87 (May 1998): 49–51; Jeffrey H. Birnbaum, "Capitol Clout: A Buyer's Guide," *Fortune* (October 26, 1998): 177–184; Jeffrey H. Birnbaum, "The Influence Merchants," *Fortune* (December 7, 1998): 134–152; and Mica Schneider, "The Color of Clout," *Business Week* (April 12, 1999): 6.

60. An instructive historical perspective of advocacy advertising may be found in Roland Marchand, "The Fitful Career of Advocacy Advertising: Political Protection, Client Cultivation, and Corporate Morale," *California Management Review,* 29 (Winter 1987): 128–156.

61. Sandra Sobiera, "Bush Signs Corporate Fraud Crackdown Bill," **www.azcentral.com** (July 31, 2002): 1. Also see Howard Fineman and Michael Isikoff, "Laying Down the Law," *Newsweek,* (August 5, 2002): 20–23.

62. Michelle Conlin, "If the Pardon Doesn't Come Through . . . ," *Business Week* (April 2, 2001): 64–65.

63. See Joann Muller, "Ford vs. Firestone: A Corporate Whodunit," *Business Week* (June 11, 2001): 46–47; and David Welch, "Firestone: Is This Brand Beyond Repair?" *Business Week* (June 11, 2001): 48.

64. Mike France, "The Litigation Machine," *Business Week* (January 29, 2001): 116.

65. Marianne M. Jennings and Frank Shipper, *Avoiding and Surviving Lawsuits* (San Francisco: Jossey-Bass, 1989), p. 118. Also see David Silverstein, "The Litigation Audit: Preventive Legal Maintenance for Management," *Business Horizons,* 31 (November–December 1988): 34–42; Paul J. H. Schoemaker and Joyce A. Schoemaker, "Estimating Environmental Liability: Quantifying the Unknown," *California Management Review,* 37 (Spring 1995): 29–61; and Milton Bordwin, "Twice Burned: Premises Liability," *Management Review,* 84 (December 1995): 9–11.

66. John R. Allison, "Easing the Pain of Legal Disputes: The Evolution and Future of Reform," *Business Horizons,* 33 (September–October 1990): 15. For more, see Stephanie Armour, "Workers' Right to Sue Can Be Forfeited," *USA Today* (March 22, 2001): 1A; and Carolyn Hirschman, "Order in the Hearing," *HRMagazine,* 46 (July 2001): 58–64.

67. Dave Patel, "Location, Location, Location," *HRMagazine,* 46 (November 2001): 168.

68. Data from 1998–1999 *Occupational Outlook Handbook,* September 1999 (**stats.bls.gov/oco/oco2003.htm**). Also see Kristine Ellis, "Mind the Gap" *Training,* 39 (January 2002): 30–35.

69. Paul A. Samuelson, *Economics,* 10th ed. (New York: McGraw-Hill, 1976), p. 253. Also see Jon Gertner, "The Economist," *Money,* 30 (November 2001): 98–102.

70. Darrell Rigby, "Moving Upward in a Downturn," *Harvard Business Review,* 79 (June 2001): 100. Also see "Smarter Moves for Tougher Times," *Fast Company,* no. 55 (February 2002): 58–63; and Geoffrey Colvin, "Smile! It's Recession Time!" *Fortune* (October 29, 2001): 48.

71. Julie Forster, "Making Hay While It Rains," *Business Week* (January 14, 2002): 32.

72. Data from Gene Koretz, "A D+ for Dismal Scientists," *Business Week* (September 25, 1995): 25.

73. See Gene Koretz, "Pollyanna Projections," *Business Week* (June 26, 2000): 34; Owen Ullmann, "Expert Sweats Big Government," *USA Today* (February 12, 2001): 4B; Michael J. Mandel, "If They Were Wrong in 1990 . . . ," *Business Week* (February 12, 2001): 28; and Robert J. Samuelson, "Optimists—Or Just Dreamers?" *Newsweek* (January 14, 2002): 39.

74. For an informative discussion of the value of economic forecasting, see Peter L. Bernstein and Theodore H. Silbert, "Are Economic Forecasters Worth Listening To?" *Harvard Business Review,* 62 (September–October 1984): 32–40. Also see Margaret Popper, "No Confidence in These Indexes," *Business Week* (January 28, 2002): 26.

75. Lawrence S. Davidson, "Knowing the Unknowable," *Business Horizons,* 32 (September–October 1989): 7.

76. David Fairlamb, "Hurting in Lockstep," *Business Week* (October 22, 2001): 30.

77. John Naisbitt and Patricia Aburdene, *Megatrends 2000* (New York: William Morrow, 1990), p. 21.

78. Thomas A. Stewart, "Welcome to the Revolution," *Fortune* (December 13, 1993): 67. Also see Janet Guyon, "The American Way," *Fortune* (November 26, 2001): 114–120.

79. Michael J. Mandel, "From America: Boom—and Bust," *Business Week* (January 28, 2002): 26.

80. Data from Tom Martin and Deborah Greenwood, "The World Economy in Charts," *Fortune* (July 26, 1993): 88–94.

81. See Devin Leonard, "Mr. Messier Is Ready for His Close-Up," *Fortune* (September 3, 2001): 136–150.

82. Data from Del Jones, "Foreign Firms Snap Up U.S. Rivals," *USA Today* (March 7, 2001): 6B.

83. Ibid.

84. Jerome B. Wiesner, "Technology and Innovation," in *Technological Innovation and Society,* ed. Dean Morse and Aaron W. Warner (New York: Columbia University Press, 1966), p. 11.

85. Walter Kiechel III, "How We Will Work in the Year 2000," *Fortune* (May 17, 1993): 39. Also see Willem F. G. Mastenbroek, "Organizational Innovation in Historical Perspective: Change as Duality Management," *Business Horizons,* 39 (July–August 1996): 5–14.

86. For good reading on innovation, see Eryn Brown, "In Search of the Silver Bullet," *Fortune* (May 14, 2001): 166–178; Vijay Govindarajan and Anil K. Gupta, "Strategic Innovation: A Conceptual Road Map," *Business Horizons,* 44 (July–August 2001): 3–12; Paul C. Judge, "Disrupter: Akira Ishikawa," *Fast Company,* no. 52 (November 2001): 146–148; and Clayton M. Christensen, Michael Raynor, and Matt Verlinden, "Skate to Where the Money Will Be," *Harvard Business Review,* 79 (November 2001): 72–81.

87. Brian Dumaine, "Closing the Innovation Gap," *Fortune* (December 2, 1991): 57.

88. Based on Stratford Sherman, "When Laws of Physics Meet Laws of the Jungle," *Fortune* (May 15, 1995): 193–194.

89. Joseph Weber, "Quick, Save the Ozone," *Business Week* (May 17, 1993): 78. For a graphic snapshot of how long it takes consumers to adopt new electronic technologies, see "New Technologies Take Time," *Business Week* (April 19, 1999): 8.

90. David Whitford, "A Human Place to Work," *Fortune* (January 8, 2001): 110. Also see Michael Arndt, "3M: A Lab for Growth?" *Business Week* (January 21, 2002): 50–51.

91. Robert J. Herbold, "Inside Microsoft: Balancing Creativity and Discipline," *Harvard Business Review*, 80 (January 2002): 73–74.

92. See Morgan L. Swink, J. Christopher Sandvig, and Vincent A. Mabert, "Adding 'Zip' to Product Development: Concurrent Engineering Methods and Tools," *Business Horizons*, 39 (March–April 1996): 41–49; and Bob Filipczak, "Concurrent Engineering: A Team by Any Other Name?" *Training*, 33 (August 1996): 54–59.

93. See Timothy D. Schellhardt, "David and Goliath," *The Wall Street Journal* (May 23, 1996): R14; and Saj-Nicole A. Joni, C. Gordon Bell, and Heidi Mason, "Innovations from the Inside," *Management Review*, 86 (September 1997): 49–53.

94. See Gifford Pinchot III, *Intrapreneuring* (New York: Harper & Row, 1985), p. xvii.

95. Tim Smart, "Kathleen Synnott: Shaping the Mailrooms of Tomorrow," *Business Week* (November 16, 1992): 66.

96. Vince Luchsinger and D. Ray Bagby, "Entrepreneurship and Intrapreneurship: Behaviors, Comparisons, and Contrasts," *SAM Advanced Management Journal*, 52 (Summer 1987): 12. Also see related articles on intrapreneurship in the same issue. For intrapreneurs in action, see Christine Canabou, "Free to Innovate," *Fast Company*, no. 52 (November 2001): 60–62.

## Chapter 4

**Opening Quotation** As quoted in Saren Starbridge, "Anita Roddick: Fair Trade," *Living Planet*, no. 3 (spring 2001): 92.

**Opening Case** From Brian O'Keefe, "Global Brands," *Fortune* (November 26, 2001): 104, 110. Copyright © 2001, *Time Inc.* Reprinted by permission. Update information from "The Corporate Name Game," *Busines Week* (July 29, 2002): 12.

**Closing Case** From "Companies Use Cross-Cultural Training to Help Their Employees Adjust Abroad," *The Wall Street Journal*, Eastern Edition by Joann S. Lublin, August 4, 1992; Copyright 1992 by Dow Jones & Co., Inc. Reproduced with permission of Dow Jones & Co., Inc. in the format textbook via Copyright Clearance Center.

1. From "Echoes of the Past," 9/26/96, *Wall Street Journal*, Eastern Edition by Marcus W. Brauchli. Copyright 1996 by Dow Jones & Co. Inc. Reproduced with permission of Dow Jones & Co. Inc. in the format textbook via Copyright Clearance Center.

2. Janet Guyon, "Why Big Is Better for Vodaphone," *Fortune* (February 18, 2002): 132.

3. "Executives Confirm Baseballs Are Hand-Stitched," *USA Today* (May 23, 2000): 6C.

4. Data from James Cox, "Siemens Cultivates American Accent," *USA Today* (March 5, 2001): 1B–2B.

5. Based on Theresa Howard, "Not All Patriotic Goods U.S. Made," *USA Today* (December 5, 2001): 6B.

6. Data from "Snapshots of the Next Century," *Business Week: 21st Century Capitalism* (Special Issue, 1994): 194. See the world trade data in James Cox, "U.S. Slowdown Would Ripple Around Globe," *USA Today* (January 22, 2001): 1B–2B; and "World Watches U.S. Drama Play Out," *USA Today* (January 22, 2001): 3B.

7. Nancy J. Adler, *International Dimensions of Organizational Behavior*, 4th ed. (Cincinnati: Thomson Learning, 2002), p. 3.

8. See Sandra Mottner and James P. Johnson, "Motivations and Risks in International Licensing: A Review and Implications for Licensing to Transitional and Emerging Economies," *Journal of World Business*, 35 (Summer 2000): 171–188.

9. Data from "Chip Licensing Deal," *USA Today* (November 27, 1996): 1B. *Note:* This six-step sequence is based on Alan M. Rugman, "A New Theory of the Multinational Enterprise: Internationalization Versus Internalization," *Columbia Journal of World Business*, 15 (Spring 1980): 23–29. Also see Roland Calori, Leif Melin, Tugrul Atamer, and Peter Gustavsson, "Innovative International Strategies," *Journal of World Business*, 35 (Winter 2000): 333–354; Anil K. Gupta and Vijay Govindarajan, "Managing Global Expansion: A Conceptual Framework," *Business Horizons*, 43 (March–April 2000): 45–54; Joseph A. Monti and George S. Yip, "Taking the High Road When Going International," *Business Horizons*, 43 (July–August 2000): 65–72; and Walter Kuemmerle, "Go Global—or No?" *Harvard Business Review*, 79 (June 2001): 37–49.

10. See William McCarty, Mark Kasoff, and Doug Smith, "The Importance of International Business at the Local Level," *Business Horizons*, 43 (May–June 2000): 35–42.

11. For related discussion, see Jeffrey J. Reuer and Michael J. Leiblein, "Downside Risk Implications of Multinationality and International Joint Ventures," *Academy of Management Journal*, 43 (April 2000): 203–214; Dennis A. Rondinelli and Sylvia Sloan Black, "Multinational Strategic Alliances and Acquisitions in Central and Eastern Europe: Partnerships in Privatization," *Academy of Management Executive*, 14 (November 2000): 85–98; and Patricia M. Norman, "Are Your Secrets Safe? Knowledge Protection in Strategic Alliances," *Business Horizons*, 44 (November–December 2001): 51–60.

12. David P. Hamilton, "United It Stands," *The Wall Street Journal* (September 26, 1996): R19.

13. Data from **www.xerox.com/online** fact book.

14. Jeremy Main, "Making Global Alliances Work," *Fortune* (December 17, 1990): 121–126.

15. Adapted from ibid. and David Lei and John W. Slocum Jr., "Global Strategic Alliances: Payoffs and Pitfalls," *Organizational Dynamics*, 19 (Winter 1991): 44–62. Also see John B. Cullen, Jean L. Johnson, and Tomoaki Sakano, "Success Through Commitment and Trust: The Soft Side of Strategic Alliance Management," *Journal of World Business*, 35 (Fall 2000): 223–240; John Child, "Trust—The Fundamental Bond

in Global Collaboration," *Organizational Dynamics,* 29 (Spring 2001): 274–288; and Paul Davidson, "AT&T, British Telecom Unplug Joint Concert," *USA Today* (October 17, 2001): 3B.

16. See David A. Andelman, "Merging Across Borders," *Management Review,* 87 (June 1998): 44–46.

17. Joan Warner, "The World Is Not Always Your Oyster," *Business Week* (October 30, 1995): 132. Also see Ping Deng, "WFOEs: The Most Popular Entry Mode in China," *Business Horizons,* 44 (July–August 2001): 63–72; and Julian Birkinshaw and Neil Hood, "Unleash Innovation in Foreign Subsidiaries," *Harvard Business Review,* 79 (March 2001): 131–137.

18. For example, see Michael Hickins, "Creating a Global Team," *Management Review,* 87 (September 1998): 6; Bruce Kogut, "What Makes a Company Global?" *Harvard Business Review,* 77 (January–February 1999): 165–170; and Thomas A. Stewart, "Getting Real About Going Global," *Fortune* (February 15, 1999): 170, 172.

19. See Patricia Sellers, "Who's in Charge Here?" *Fortune* (December 24, 2001): 76–86.

20. Based on Fons Trompenaars and Charles Hampden-Turner, *Riding the Waves of Culture: Understanding Cultural Diversity in Global Business,* 2nd ed. (New York: McGraw-Hill, 1998), pp. 191–192; Marie-Claude Boudreau, Karen D. Loch, Daniel Robey, and Detmar Straud, "Going Global: Using Information Technology to Advance the Competitiveness of the Virtual Transnational Organization," *Academy of Management Executive,* 12 (November 1998): 120–128; and Anil K. Gupta and Vijay Govindarajan, "Converting Global Presence into Global Competitive Advantage," *Academy of Management Executive,* 15 (May 2001): 45–56.

21. Stanley Reed, "Busting Up Sweden Inc.," *Business Week* (February 22, 1999): 52, 54.

22. For example, see Louisa Wah, "Treading the Sacred Ground," *Management Review,* 87 (July–August 1998): 18–22; and Tatiana Kostova and Srilata Zaheer, "Organizational Legitimacy Under Conditions of Complexity: The Case of the Multinational Enterprise," *Academy of Management Review,* 24 (January 1999): 64–81.

23. "Amidst Stiffer International Competition, U.S. Managers Need a Broader Perspective," *Management Review,* 69 (March 1980): 34. Also see Adler, *International Dimensions of Organizational Behavior,* pp. 11–15.

24. C. Bremmer, "The Global Manager—Insights in Succeeding the Challenge," unpublished paper, 1994, as quoted in Philip R. Harris and Robert T. Moran, *Managing Cultural Differences,* 4th ed. (Houston: Gulf Publishing, 1996), pp. 4–5.

25. Howard V. Perlmutter, "The Tortuous Evolution of the Multinational Corporation," *Columbia Journal of World Business,* 4 (January–February 1969): 11.

26. Perlmutter and a colleague later added "regiocentric attitude" to their typology. Such an attitude centers on a regional identification (North America, Europe, and Asia, for example). See David A. Heenan and Howard V. Perlmutter, *Multinational Organization Development* (Reading, Mass.: Addison-Wesley, 1979).

27. Drawn from Brian Dumaine, "The New Turnaround Champs," *Fortune* (July 16, 1990): 36–44.

28. See Amy Borrus, "Can Japan's Giants Cut the Apron Strings?" *Business Week* (May 14, 1990): 105–106.

29. Data from Brook Larmer, "Latino America," *Newsweek* (July 12, 1999): 48–51.

30. Data from Kitty Bean Yancey, "Learning Like There's No Mañana," *USA Today* (June 22, 2001): 1D–2D.

31. Julia Lieblich, "If You Want a Big, New Market . . . " *Fortune* (November 21, 1988): 181. Population update from Daniel J. Vargas, "M&M Candies Going Latin with a New Caramel Flavor," *The Oregonian* (August 13, 2001): C1, C3.

32. Perlmutter, "The Tortuous Evolution of the Multinational Corporation," p. 16.

33. Gail Dutton, "Building a Global Brain," *Management Review,* 88 (May 1999): 34–38.

34. Rahul Jacob, "Trust the Locals, Win Worldwide," *Fortune* (May 4, 1992): 76.

35. Ibid.

36. Arvind V. Phatak and Mohammed M. Habib, "The Dynamics of International Business Negotiations," *Business Horizons,* 39 (May–June 1996): 34.

37. For more, see Adler, *International Dimensions of Organizational Behavior,* pp. 16–34.

38. As quoted in "How Cultures Collide," *Psychology Today,* 10 (July 1976): 69.

39. Trompenaars and Hampden-Turner, *Riding the Waves of Culture,* p. 3.

40. Ronald Inglehart and Wayne E. Baker, "Modernization's Challenge to Traditional Values: Who's Afraid of Ronald McDonald?" *The Futurist,* 35 (March–April 2001): 18, 21.

41. Based on Ashok Nimgade, "American Management as Viewed by International Professionals," *Business Horizons,* 32 (November–December 1989): 98–105. Also see Carol Hymowitz, "Cultural Gap in Global Business," *The Arizona Republic* (August 28, 2000): D1, D4.

42. See Joyce S. Osland and Allan Bird, "Beyond Sophisticated Stereotyping: Cultural Sensemaking in Context," *Academy of Management Executive,* 14 (February 2000): 65–77.

43. Contrasting Chinese and American traits are presented in Jack Scarborough, "Comparing Chinese and Western Cultural Roots: Why 'East Is East and . . . ,' " *Business Horizons,* 41 (November–December 1998): 15–24. Also see Christopher B. Meek, "*Ganbatte*: Understanding the Japanese Employee," *Business Horizons,* 42 (January–February 1999): 27–36; and Tibbett L. Speer, "Avoid Gift-Giving and Cultural Blunders in Asian Locales," *USA Today* (March 16, 1999): 3E.

44. See "How Cultures Collide," pp. 66–74, 97; Edward T. Hall, *The Hidden Dimension* (Garden City, N.Y.: Doubleday, 1996); and Mary Munter, "Cross-Cultural Communication for Managers," *Business Horizons,* 36 (May–June 1993): 69–78.

45. Ronald E. Dulek, John S. Fielden, and John S. Hill, "International Communication: An Executive Primer," *Business Horizons,* 34 (January–February 1991): 21.

46. This list is based on Edward T. Hall, "The Silent Language in Overseas Business," *Harvard Business Review,* 38 (May–June

1960): 87–96; Rose Knotts, "Cross-Cultural Management: Transformations and Adaptations," *Business Horizons,* 32 (January–February 1989): 29–33; and Adler, *International Dimensions of Organizational Behavior,* pp. 27–28.

47. For detailed discussion, see Allen C. Bluedorn, Carol Felker Kaufman, and Paul M. Lane, "How Many Things Do You Like to Do at Once? An Introduction to Monochronic and Polychronic Time," *Academy of Management Executive,* 6 (November 1992): 17–26. For interesting reading on *time,* see Heath Row, "A (Really) Brief History of Time," *Fast Company,* no. 35 (June 2000): 58, 60.

48. See Gregory K. Stephens and Charles R. Greer, "Doing Business in Mexico: Understanding Cultural Differences," *Organizational Dynamics,* 24 (Summer 1995): 39–55; Mike Johnson, "Untapped Latin America," *Management Review,* 85 (July 1996): 31–34; and Yongsun Paik and J. H. Derick Sohn, "Confucius in Mexico: Korean MNCs and the Maquiladoras," *Business Horizons,* 41 (November–December 1998): 25–33.

49. See Karl Albrecht, "Lost in the Translation," *Training,* 33 (June 1996): 66–70; Daniel Pianko, "Smooth Translations," *Management Review,* 85 (July 1996): 10; and Rebecca Ganzel, "Universal Translator? Not Quite," *Training,* 36 (April 1999): 22, 24.

50. Jerry Shine, "More US Students Tackle Japanese," *The Christian Science Monitor* (November 25, 1991): 14.

51. Based on Kathryn Tyler, "Targeted Language Training Is Best Bargain," *HRMagazine,* 43 (January 1998): 61–64; and "When in Rio . . . ," *Training,* 35 (December 1998): 25.

52. Based on Figure 2 in Gary Bonvillian and William A. Nowlin, "Cultural Awareness: An Essential Element of Doing Business Abroad," *Business Horizons,* 37 (November–December 1994): 44–50.

53. "Burger Boost," *USA Today* (October 11, 1995): 1B. Also see Michael Arndt, "A Misguided Beef with McDonald's," *Business Week* (May 21, 2001): 14.

54. See P. Christopher Earley and Harbir Singh, "International and Intercultural Management Research: What's Next?" *Academy of Management Journal,* 38 (April 1995): 327–340; Mary B. Teagarden et al., "Toward a Theory of Comparative Management Research: An Idiographic Case Study of the Best International Human Resources Management Project," *Academy of Management Journal,* 38 (October 1995): 1261–1287; Abraham Sagie and Dov Elizur, "Taking Another Look at Cross-Cultural Research: Rejoinder to Lachman (1997)," *Journal of Organizational Behavior,* 19 (July 1998): 421–427; and Mark Easterby-Smith and Danusia Malina, "Cross-Cultural Collaborative Research: Toward Reflexivity," *Academy of Management Journal,* 42 (February 1999): 76–86.

55. See Geert Hofstede, *Culture's Consequences: International Differences in Work-Related Values,* abridged edition (Newbury Park, Calif.: Sage Publications, 1984); and Geert Hofstede, "Motivation, Leadership, and Organization: Do American Theories Apply Abroad?" *Organizational Dynamics,* 9 (Summer 1980): 42–63. Also see Geert Hofstede, "Cultural Constraints in Management Theories," *Academy of Management Executive,* 7 (February 1993): 81–94; and Richard Hodgetts, "A

Conversation with Geert Hofstede," *Organizational Dynamics,* 21 (Spring 1993): 53–61.

56. An extension of Hofstede's original work can be found in Geert Hofstede and Michael Harris Bond, "The Confucius Connection: From Cultural Roots to Economic Growth," *Organizational Dynamics,* 16 (Spring 1988): 4–21. Also see Peter B. Smith, Shaun Dugan, and Fons Trompenaars, "National Culture and the Values of Organizational Employees: A Dimensional Analysis Across 43 Nations," *Journal of Cross-Cultural Psychology,* 27 (March 1996): 231–264; James P. Johnson and Tomasz Lenartowicz, "Culture, Freedom and Economic Growth: Do Cultural Values Explain Economic Growth?" *Journal of World Business,* 33 (Winter 1998): 332–356; Geert Hofstede, "Problems Remain, but Theories Will Change: The Universal and the Specific in 21st-Century Global Management," *Organizational Dynamics,* 28 (Summer 1999): 34–44. Sang M. Lee and Suzanne J. Peterson, "Culture, Entrepreneurial Orientation, and Global Competitiveness," *Journal of World Business,* 35 (Winter 2000): 401–416; and Ashleigh Merritt, "Culture in the Cockpit: Do Hofstede's Dimensions Replicate?" *Journal of Cross-Cultural Psychology,* 31 (May 2000): 283–301.

57. See William G. Ouchi, *Theory Z: How American Business Can Meet the Japanese Challenge* (Reading, Mass.: Addison-Wesley, 1981). Also see David M. Hunt and Donald S. Bolon, "A Review of Five Versions of Theory Z: Does Z Have a Future?" in *Advances in International Comparative Management,* vol. 4, ed. S. Benjamin Prasad (Greenwich, Conn.: JAI Press, 1989), pp. 201–220; and William G. Ouchi and Raymond L. Price, "Hierarchies, Clans, and Theory Z: A New Perspective on Organization Development," *Organizational Dynamics,* 21 (Spring 1993): 62–70.

58. See Richard J. Schmidt, "Japanese Management, Recession Style," *Business Horizons,* 39 (March–April 1996): 70–76; and P. C. Chu, Eric E. Spires, and Toshiyuki Sueyoshi, "Cross-Cultural Differences in Choice Behavior and Use of Decision Aids: A Comparison of Japan and the United States," *Organizational Behavior and Human Decision Processes,* 77 (February 1999): 147–170.

59. Brian Bremner, "The President Has a Will—But No Way," *Business Week* (March 15, 1999): 92. Also see Ryoji Itoh and Till Vestring, "Buying into Japan Inc.," *Harvard Business Review,* 79 (November 2001): 26, 28; and "Hiroyuki Yoshino," *Business Week* (January 14, 2002): 70.

60. See Itzhak Harpaz, "The Importance of Work Goals: An International Perspective," *Journal of International Business Studies,* 21 (First Quarter 1990): 75–93. Also see David A. Ralston, David J. Gustafson, Priscilla M. Elsass, Fanny Cheung, and Robert H. Terpstra, "Eastern Values: A Comparison of Managers in the United States, Hong Kong, and the People's Republic of China," *Journal of Applied Psychology,* 77 (October 1992): 664–671.

61. See Bodil Jones, "What Future European Recruits Want," *Management Review,* 87 (January 1998): 6; Bill Leonard, "Workers' Attitudes Similar Worldwide," *HRMagazine,* 43

(December 1998): 28, 30; and Cheryl Comeau Kirschner, "It's a Small World," *Management Review,* 88 (March 1999): 8.

62. Data from Dianne H. B. Welsh, Fred Luthans, and Steven M. Sommer, "Managing Russian Factory Workers: The Impact of U.S.-Based Behavioral and Participative Techniques," *Academy of Management Journal,* 36 (February 1993): 58–79. For related reading, see Dong I. Jung and Bruce J. Avolio, "Effects of Leadership Style and Followers' Cultural Orientation on Performance in Group and Individual Task Conditions," *Academy of Management Journal,* 42 (April 1999): 208–218.

63. Kristin Dunlap Godsey, "Thread by Thread," *Success,* 43 (April 1996): 8.

64. See Ruth E. Thaler-Carter, "Whither Global Leaders?" *HRMagazine,* 45 (May 2000): 82–88.

65. Marshall Loeb, "The Real Fast Track Is Overseas," *Fortune* (August 21, 1995): 129. For more, see Andrea C. Poe, "Destination Everywhere," *HRMagazine,* 45 (October 2000): 67–75; Mason A. Carpenter, Wm. Gerard Sanders, and Hal B. Gregersen, "Building Human Capital with Organizational Content: The Impact of International Assignment Experience on Multicultural Firm Performance and CEO Pay," *Academy of Management Journal,* 44 (June 2001): 493–511; and "International Experience Aids Career," *USA Today* (January 28, 2002): 1B.

66. An excellent background article is J. Stewart Black and Hal B. Gregersen, "The Right Way to Manage Expats," *Harvard Business Review,* 77 (March–April 1999): 52–63.

67. "Don't Be an Ugly-American Manager," *Fortune* (October 16, 1995): 225.

68. John R. Engen, "Coming Home," *Training,* 32 (March 1995): 37.

69. See Marilyn Richey, "Global Families: Surviving an Overseas Move," *Management Review,* 85 (June 1996): 57–61; and Adler, *International Dimensions of Organizational Behavior,* ch. 9.

70. Gene Koretz, " . . . But It Could Be Cold Comfort for U.S. Companies There," *Business Week* (January 22, 1990): 20.

71. See Mansour Javidan and Robert J. House, "Cultural Acumen for the Global Manager: Lessons from Project GLOBE," *Organizational Dynamics,* 29 (Spring 2001): 289–305; and Joel Schettler, "Mariano Bernardez," *Training,* 38 (November 2001): 48.

72. Robert Moran, "Children of Bilingualism," *International Management,* 45 (November 1990): 93. Also see Wayne T. Price, "Learning the Language Is Critical," *USA Today,* (September 14, 1993): 6E.

73. Based on Joann S. Lublin, "An Overseas Stint Can Be a Ticket to the Top," *The Wall Street Journal* (January 29, 1996): B1, B5.

74. Adapted from Rosalie L. Tung, "Selection and Training of Personnel for Overseas Assignments," *Columbia Journal of World Business,* 16 (Spring 1981): 68–78. Also see Vesa Suutari and Chris Brewster, "Making Their Own Way: International Experience Through Self-Initiated Foreign Assignments," *Journal of World Business,* 35 (Winter 2000): 417–436; and Lyn Glanz, Roger Williams, and Ludwig Hoeksema, "Sensemaking in Expatriation—A Theoretical Basis," *Thunderbird International Business Review,* 43 (January–February 2001): 101–119.

75. See P. Christopher Earley, "Intercultural Training for Managers: A Comparison of Documentary and Interpersonal Methods," *Academy of Management Journal,* 30 (December 1987): 685–698. Also see J. Stewart Black and Mark Mendenhall, "Cross-Cultural Training Effectiveness: A Review and a Theoretical Framework for Future Research," *Academy of Management Review,* 15 (January 1990): 113–136.

76. Data from Joann S. Lublin, "Companies Use Cross-Cultural Training to Help Their Employees Adjust Abroad," *The Wall Street Journal* (August 4, 1992): B1, B6.

77. An excellent resource book is J. Stewart Black, Hal B. Gregersen, and Mark E. Mendenhall, *Global Assignments: Successfully Expatriating and Repatriating International Managers* (San Francisco: Jossey-Bass, 1992). Also see Linda K. Stroh and Paula M. Caligiuri, "Increasing Global Competitiveness Through Effective People Management," *Journal of World Business,* 33 (Spring 1998): 1–16; and Juan I. Sanchez, Paul E. Spector, and Cary L. Cooper, "Adapting to a Boundaryless World: A Developmental Expatriate Model," *Academy of Management Executive,* 14 (May 2000): 96–106.

78. See Elisabeth Marx, *Breaking Through Culture Shock: What You Need to Succeed in International Business* (London: Nicholas Brealey Publishing, 2001); and Barbara A. Anderson, "Expatriate Management: An Australian Tri-Sector Comparative Study," *Thunderbird International Business Review,* 43 (January–February 2001): 33–51.

79. See Andrea C. Poe, "Welcome Back," *HRMagazine,* 45 (March 2000): 94–105; and Jeff Barbian, "Return to Sender," *Training,* 39 (January 2002): 40–43.

80. Data from Rosalie L. Tung, "American Expatriates Abroad: From Neophytes to Cosmopolitans," *Journal of World Business,* 33 (Summer 1998): 125–144.

81. David Stauffer, "No Need for Inter-American Culture Clash," *Management Review,* 87 (January 1998): 8. Also see Arup Varma, Linda K. Stroh, and Lisa B. Schmitt, "Women and International Assignments: The Impact of Supervisor-Subordinate Relationships," *Journal of World Business,* 36 (Winter 2001): 380–388.

82. See Louisa Wah, "Surfing the Rough Sea," *Management Review,* 87 (September 1998): 25–29; and Paula M. Caligiuri and Wayne F. Cascio, "Can We Send Her There? Maximizing the Success of Western Women on Global Assignments," *Journal of World Business,* 33 (Winter 1998): 394–416.

83. See Lynette Clemetson, "Soul and Sushi," *Newsweek* (May 4, 1998): 38–41.

84. For helpful tips, see Linda K. Stroh, Arup Varma, and Stacey J. Valy-Durbin, "Why Are Women Left Home: Are They Unwilling to Go on International Assignments?" *Journal of World Business,* 35 (Fall 2000): 241–255.

85. For more, see Jennifer Smith, "Southeast Asia's Search for Managers," *Management Review,* 87 (June 1998): 9; Brock Stout, "Interviewing in Japan," *HRMagazine,* 43 (June 1998): 71–77; and David Ahlstrom, Garry Bruton, and Eunice S. Chan, "HRM of Foreign Firms in China: The Challenge of Managing Host Country Personnel," *Business Horizons,* 44 (May–June 2001): 59–68.

86. For more, see Frank Jossi, "Buying Protection from Terrorism," *HRMagazine,* 46 (June 2001): 155–160; and Gene Sloan, "Take a Security Expert's Advice to Avoid Travel Theft," *USA Today* (September 7, 2001): 4D.

## Chapter 5

**Opening Quotation** Stephen R. Covey, *Principle-Centered Leadership* (New York: Simon & Schuster, 1991), p. 95.

**Opening Case** Jeremy Kahn, "Stop Me Before I Pollute Again," *Fortune* (January 21, 2002): 87–90. Copyright 2002, Time Inc. Reprinted by permission.

**Closing Case** Edward T. Pound, "Nurse's Clues Shut Down Research," *USA Today* (July 13, 2000): 3A. Copyright 2000, *USA Today.* Reprinted with permission.

1. For an interesting look back at Rockefeller, see Jerry Useem, "Entrepreneur of the Century," *Inc.* Twentieth anniversary issue, 21 (May 18, 1999): 159–173.

2. Susan Gaines, "Growing Pains," *Business Ethics,* 10 (January–February 1996): 20.

3. Thomas M. Jones, "Corporate Social Responsibility Revisited, Redefined," *California Management Review,* 22 (Spring 1980): 59–60. Also see Abagail McWilliams and Donald Siegel, "Corporate Social Responsibility: A Theory of the Firm Perspective." *Academy of Management Review,* 26 (January 2001): 117–127; and Homer H. Johnson, "Corporate Social Audits—This Time Around," *Business Horizons,* 44 (May–June 2001): 29–36.

4. Jim Hopkins, "Paper Clip King Uncovers Slave Labor," *USA Today* (April 18, 2001): 8B.

5. Chris Welles, "What Led Beech-Nut Down the Road to Disgrace," *Business Week* (February 22, 1988): 128.

6. See Joe Queenan, "Juice Men," *Barron's* (June 20, 1988): 37–38.

7. Jones, "Corporate Social Responsibility Revisited," p. 65.

8. This distinction between the economic and the socioeconomic models is based partly on the discussion in Courtney C. Brown, *Beyond the Bottom Line* (New York: Macmillan, 1979), pp. 82–83.

9. See the discussion in Art Wolfe, "We've Had Enough Business Ethics," *Business Horizons,* 36 (May–June 1993): 1–3. Also see Robert J. Samuelson, "The Spirit of Adam Smith," *Newsweek* (December 2, 1996): 63; and Geoffrey Colvin, "Capitalists: Savor This Moment," *Fortune* (July 24, 2000): 64; and Anthony Bianco, "The Enduring Corporation," *Business Week* (August 28, 2000): 198–204.

10. As quoted in Keith H. Hammonds, "Writing a New Social Contract," *Business Week* (March 11, 1996): 60.

11. Data from "Fortune 5 Hundred Largest U.S. Corporations," *Fortune* (April 16, 2001): F1.

12. Robert Kuttner, "Enron: A Powerful Blow to Market Fundamentals," *Business Week* (February 4, 2002): 20.

13. For more, see Daniel McGinn, "The Ripple Effect," *Newsweek* (February 18, 2002): 29–32; Jayne O'Donnell and Gary Strauss, "Enron Investigator Blasts Senior Managers," *USA Today* (February 5, 2002): 1B; and John Ellis, "Life After Enron's Death," *Fast Company,* no. 56 (March 2002): 118, 120.

14. See Paul Vogelheim, Denise D. Schoenbachler, Geoffrey L. Gordon, and Craig C. Gordon, "The Importance of Courting the Individual Investor," *Business Horizons,* 44 (January–February 2001): 69–76; I. A. Jawahar and Gary L. McLaughlin, "Toward a Descriptive Stakeholder Theory: An Organizational Life Cycle Approach," *Academy of Management Review,* 26 (July 2001): 397–414; and Marjorie Kelly, "The Incredibly Unproductive Shareholder," *Harvard Business Review,* 80 (January 2002): 18, 20.

15. These arguments have been adapted in part from Jones, "Corporate Social Responsibility Revisited," p. 61; and Keith Davis and William C. Frederick, *Business and Society: Management, Public Policy, and Ethics,* 5th ed. (New York: McGraw-Hill, 1984), pp. 28–41.

16. Davis and Frederick, *Business and Society,* p. 34.

17. As quoted in Aaron Bernstein, "Bracing for a Backlash," *Business Week* (February 4, 2002): 34.

18. Drawn from Ian Wilson, "What One Company Is Doing About Today's Demands on Business," in *Changing Business-Society Interrelationships,* ed. George A. Steiner (Los Angeles: UCLA Graduate School of Management, 1975).

19. Gary Boulard, "Combating Environmental Racism," *The Christian Science Monitor* (March 17, 1993): 8. For updates, see Dennis Cauchon, "Racial, Economic Divide in La.," *USA Today* (September 9, 1997): 3A; Paul Hoversten, "EPA Puts Plant on Hold in Racism Case," *USA Today* (September 11, 1997): 3A; Traci Watson, "La. Town Successful in Stopping Plastics Plant," *USA Today* (September 18, 1998): 7A; and Lorraine Woellert, "Dumping on the Poor?" *Business Week* (November 19, 2001): 120–121.

20. Mike France, "The World War on Tobacco," *Business Week* (November 11, 1996): 100. Also see John Carey, "Big Tobacco Blows Some Smoke," *Business Week* (August 14, 2000): 8; and Paul Raeburn, "Blowing Smoke over Ventilation," *Business Week* (May 7, 2001): 72–73.

21. Bruce Horovitz, "Wendy's Steps Up Animal Welfare Standards," *USA Today* (September 6, 2001): 2B. Also see Theresa Howard, "Burger King Adopts Animal-Treatment Standards," *USA Today* (June 29, 2001): 2B.

22. Susan Caminiti, "The Payoff from a Good Reputation," *Fortune* (February 10, 1992): 75.

23. See Thomas S. Bateman, and J. Michael Crant, "Proactive Behavior: Meaning, Impact, Recommendations," *Business Horizons,* 42 (May–June 1999): 63–70.

24. See Vincent Jeffries, "Virtue and the Altruistic Personality," *Sociological Perspectives,* 41, no. 1 (1998): 151–166.

25. Based on Joseph Weber, "3M's Big Cleanup," *Business Week* (June 5, 2000): 96–98.

26. Data from Michael V. Russo and Paul A. Fouts, "A Resource-Based Perspective on Corporate Environmental Performance and Profitability," *Academy of Management Journal,* 40 (June 1997): 534–559.

27. Based on Daniel B. Turban and Daniel W. Greening, "Corporate Social Performance and Organizational Attractiveness to Prospective Employees," *Academy of Management Journal,* 40 (June 1996): 658–672.

28. Data from Christopher H. Schmitt, "Corporate Charity: Why It's Slowing," *Business Week* (December 18, 2000): 164, 166.

29. Louis W. Fry, Gerald D. Keim, and Roger E. Meiners, "Corporate Contributions: Altruistic or For-Profit?" *Academy of Management Journal,* 25 (March 1982): 105.

30. For complete details, see Richard E. Wokutch and Barbara A. Spencer, "Corporate Saints and Sinners: The Effects of Philanthropic and Illegal Activity on Organizational Performance," *California Management Review,* 29 (Winter 1987): 62–77. Also see Kimberly D. Elsbach and Robert I. Sutton, "Acquiring Organizational Legitimacy Through Illegitimate Actions: A Marriage of Institutional and Impression Management Theories," *Academy of Management Journal,* 35 (October 1992): 699–738.

31. Thomas A. Fogarty, "Corporations Use Causes for Effect," *USA Today* (November 10, 1997): 7B.

32. See Thea Singer, "Can Business Still Save the World?" *Inc.,* 23 (April 2001): 58–71.

33. See James R. Healey, "Firestone Leaves an Indelible Mark," *USA Today* (December 26, 2000): 1B–2B; David Kiley, "Bridgestone/Firestone to Pay $41.5M," *USA Today* (November 8, 2001): 1B; "Enron Officials: We Didn't Know," *USA Today* (February 8, 2002): 3B; Adam Shell and Donna Leinwand, "Missing U.S. Trader Accused of Defrauding Irish Bank," *USA Today* (February 7, 2002): 1B; and Matt Krantz, "Nortel CFO, Accused of Insider Trading, Quits," *USA Today* (February 12, 2002): 1B.

34. As quoted in Bernstein, "Bracing for a Backlash," p. 34.

35. Louisa Wah, "Lies in the Executive Wing," *Management Review,* 88 (May 1999): 9.

36. An excellent resource book is LaRue Tone Hosmer, *Moral Leadership in Business* (Burr Ridge, Ill.: Irwin, 1994).

37. See Rushworth M. Kidder, "Tough Choices: Why It's Getting Harder to Be Ethical," *The Futurist,* 29 (September–October 1995): 29–32.

38. See W. Edward Stead, Dan L. Worrell, and Jean Garner Stead, "An Integrative Model for Understanding and Managing Ethical Behavior in Business Organizations," *Journal of Business Ethics,* 9 (March 1990): 233–242; Robert Elliott Allinson, "A Call for Ethically Centered Management," *Academy of Management Executive,* 9 (February 1995): 73–76; and Dawn-Marie Driscoll, "Don't Confuse Legal and Ethical Standards," *Business Ethics,* 10 (July–August 1996): 44.

39. O. C. Ferrell and John Fraedrich, *Business Ethics: Ethical Decision Making and Cases* (Boston: Houghton Mifflin, 1991), pp. 10–11. Also see Barbara Ettorre, "Temptation of Big Money," *Management Review,* 85 (February 1996): 13–17; and "The Ethical Dilemma," *Selling Power* (March 1996): 32, 34.

40. Business ethics research findings are reviewed in Phillip V. Lewis, "Defining 'Business Ethics': Like Nailing Jell-O to a Wall," *Journal of Business Ethics,* 4 (October 1985): 377–383. Also see William A. Kahn, "Toward an Agenda for Business Ethics Research," *Academy of Management Review,* 15 (April 1990): 311–328; and Gene R. Laczniak, Marvin W. Berkowitz, Russell G. Brooker, and James P. Hale, "The Ethics of Business: Improving or Deteriorating?" *Business Horizons,* 38 (January–February 1995): 39–47.

41. Del Jones, "48% of Workers Admit to Unethical or Illegal Acts," *USA Today* (April 4, 1997): 1A.

42. Ibid., p. 2A.

43. As quoted in Julia Flynn, "Did Sears Take Other Customers for a Ride?" *Business Week* (August 3, 1992): 24.

44. Based on Kelley Holland, "Sears Settles Up with the Feds," *Business Week* (February 22, 1999): 45; and John McCormick, "The Sorry Side of Sears," *Newsweek* (February 22, 1999): 36–39.

45. William Rudelius and Rogene A. Buchholz, "Ethical Problems of Purchasing Managers," *Harvard Business Review,* 57 (March–April 1979): 12. Also see Alan J. Dubinsky, Eric N. Berkowitz, and William Rudelius, "Ethical Problems of Field Sales Personnel," *MSU Business Topics,* 28 (Summer 1980): 11–16; James R. Davis, "Ambiguity, Ethics, and the Bottom Line," *Business Horizons,* 32 (May–June 1989): 65–70; and "Cheating Hearts," *USA Today* (February 15, 2001): 1B.

46. Thomas R. Horton, "The Ethics Crisis Continues: What to Do?" *Management Review,* 75 (November 1986): 3. Derek Bok, former president of Harvard University, calls for greater civic mindedness in Derek Bok, "A Great Need of the '90s, *The Christian Science Monitor* (May 22, 1992): 18.

47. See Kevin Gibson, "Excuses, Excuses: Moral Slippage in the Workplace," *Business Horizons,* 43 (November–December 2000): 65–72.

48. For good management-oriented discussions of values, see Barry Z. Posner and Warren H. Schmidt, "Values and the American Manager: An Update Updated," *California Management Review,* 34 (Spring 1992): 80–94.

49. Michael Schrage, "I Wasn't Fired," *Fortune* (January 21, 2002): 128.

50. For excellent treatment of values, see Milton Rokeach, *Beliefs, Attitudes, and Values* (San Francisco: Jossey-Bass, 1968), p. 124; and Milton Rokeach and Sandra J. Ball-Rokeach, "Stability and Change in American Value Priorities, 1968–1981," *American Psychologist,* 44 (May 1989): 775–784. Also see Gregory R. Maio and James M. Olson, "Values as Truisms: Evidence and Implications," *Journal of Personality and Social Psychology,* 74 (February 1998): 294–311.

51. Rokeach, *Beliefs, Attitudes, and Values,* p. 124.

52. See Rick Wartzman, "Nature or Nurture? Study Blames Ethical Lapses on Corporate Goals," *The Wall Street Journal* (October 9, 1987): 27. Two other Rokeach scale studies are reported in Maris G. Martinsons and Aelita Brivins Martinsons, "Conquering Cultural Constraints to Cultivate Chinese Management Creativity and Innovation," *Journal of Management Development,* 15, no. 9 (1996): 18–35; and Ralph A. Rodriguez, "Challenging Demographic Reductionism: A Pilot Study Investigating Diversity in Group Composition," *Small Group Research,* 29 (December 1998): 744–759. Also see Shalom H. Schwartz and Galit Sagie, "Value Consensus and Importance: A Cross-National Study," *Journal of Cross-Cultural Psychology,* 31 (July 2000): 465–497.

53. Marc Gunther, "God & Business," *Fortune* (July 9, 2001): 58–80; and Gary R. Weaver and Bradley R. Agle, "Religiosity and Ethical Behavior in Organizations: A Symbolic Interactionist Perspective," *Academy of Management Review,* 27 (January 2002): 77–97.

54. See Edward Soule, "Managerial Moral Strategies—In Search of a Few Good Principles," *Academy of Management Review,* 27 (January 2002): 114–124.

55. Excerpted from Hosmer, *Moral Leadership in Business,* pp. 39–41. © 1994, McGraw-Hill. Reprinted with the permission of the McGraw-Hill Companies.

56. See Archie B. Carroll, "In Search of the Moral Manager," *Business Horizons,* 30 (March–April 1987): 7–15.

57. Data from Brad Lee Thompson, "Ethics Training Enters the Real World," *Training,* 27 (October 1990): 82–94; "1997 Industry Report: Specific Types of Training," *Training,* 34 (October 1997): 55; and Tammy Galvin, "2001 Industry Report," *Training,* 38 (October 2001): 54.

58. For example, see Dawn Blalock, "Study Shows Many Execs Are Quick to Write Off Ethics," *The Wall Street Journal* (March 26, 1996): C1, C22; and Liz Simpson, "Taking the High Road," *Training,* 39 (January 2002): 36–38.

59. For details, see John A. Byrne, "The Best-Laid Ethics Programs . . . " *Business Week* (March 9, 1992): 67–69.

60. See Paul C. Judge, "Ethics for Hire," *Business Week* (July 15, 1996): 26–28; and Louisa Wah, "Lip-Service Ethics Programs Prove Ineffective," *Management Review,* 88 (June 1999): 9. Promising ethics training programs are discussed in Julie Appleby, "Drugmakers Bankroll Ethics Guidelines on 'Freebies,'" *USA Today* (April 27, 2001): 1B; and Mikhail V. Gratchev, "Making the Most of Cultural Differences," *Harvard Business Review,* 79 (October 2001): 28, 30.

61. Based on discussion in Thompson, "Ethics Training Enters the Real World." For reasons why ethics programs fail, see Judge, "Ethics for Hire."

62. For informative reading on ethical advocates, see Theodore V. Purcell, "Electing an 'Angel's Advocate' to the Board," *Management Review,* 65 (May 1976): 4–11; Theodore V. Purcell, "Institutionalizing Ethics into Top Management Decisions," *Public Relations Quarterly,* 22 (Summer 1977): 15–20; Beverly Geber, "The Right and Wrong of Ethics Offices," *Training,* 32 (October 1995): 102–109; and Susan Gaines, "Who Are These Ethics Experts Anyway?" *Business Ethics,* 10 (March–April 1996): 26–30.

63. See Dale Kurschner, "Ethics Programs and Personal Values Are Still Not Enough," *Business Ethics,* 10 (May–June 1996): 12; Gary R. Weaver, Linda Klebe Treviño, and Philip L. Cochran, "Corporate Ethics Programs as Control Systems: Influences of Executive Commitment and Environmental Factors," *Academy of Management Journal,* 42 (February 1999): 41–57; and Louisa Wah, "Ethics Linked to Financial Performance," *Management Review,* 88 (July–August 1999): 7.

64. "Business' Big Morality Play," *Dun's Review* (August 1980): 56.

65. See Ruth E. Thaler-Carter, "Social Accountability 8000," *HRMagazine,* 44 (June 1999): 106–112.

66. See Richard P. Nielsen, "Changing Unethical Organizational Behavior," *Academy of Management Executive,* 3 (May 1989): 123–130. Relative to the Enron case, see Wendy Zellner, "A Hero—And a Smoking-Gun Letter," *Business Week* (January 28, 2002): 34–35; and Greg Farrell and Jayne O'Donnell, "Watkins Testifies Skilling, Fastow Duped Lay, Board," *USA Today* (February 15, 2002): 1B–2B.

67. See Blake Morrison, "Whistle-Blowing on Rise," *USA Today* (December 24, 2001): 1A.

68. Ralph Nader, "An Anatomy of Whistle Blowing," in *Whistle Blowing,* ed. Ralph Nader, Peter Petkas, and Kate Blackwell (New York: Bantam, 1972), p. 7. For interesting case studies of whistle-blowers, see William McGowan, "The Whistleblowers Hall of Fame," *Business and Society Review,* 52 (Winter 1985): 31–36.

69. The federal Whistleblowers Protection Act of 1989 is discussed in David Israel and Anita Lechner, "Protection for Whistleblowers," *Personnel Administrator,* 34 (July 1989): 106. Also see Marshall Loeb, "When to Rat on the Boss," *Fortune* (October 2, 1995): 183; Tom Lowry, "Whistle-Blower Now Fighting Former Allies," *USA Today* (November 9, 1998): 15B; and "The Gadfly of Trinity Place," *Business Week* (April 26, 1999): 110, 112.

70. Adapted from Kenneth D. Walters, "Your Employees' Right to Blow the Whistle," *Harvard Business Review,* 53 (July–August 1975): 26–34, 161–162. Also see Janet P. Near and Marcia P. Miceli, "Effective Whistle-Blowing," *Academy of Management Review,* 20 (July 1995): 679–708; and Kate Walter, "Ethics Hot Lines Tap into More than Wrongdoing," *HRMagazine,* 40 (September 1995): 79–85.

## Chapter 6

**Opening Quotation** As quoted in Brent Schlender, "Peter Drucker Takes the Long View," *Fortune* (September 28, 1998): 170.

**Opening Case** Excerpted from Cheryl Comeau-Kirschner and Louisa Wah, "Who Has Time to Think?" *Management Review,* 89 (January 2000): 16–23. © 2000 American Management Association. Reprinted with permission of American Management Association in the format textbook via the Copyright Clearance Center.

**Closing Case** Donna Fenn, "Veggie-Burger Kings," *Inc.,* 23 (November 30, 2001): 42, 44. *Inc:* The Magazine for Growing Companies. Copyright 2001 by Bus. Innovator Group Resources/Inc. Reproduced with permission of Bus. Innovator Group Resources/Inc. in the format textbook via Copyright Clearance Center.

1. Herb Greenberg, "Prescription for Recovery," *Fortune* (July 23, 2001): 252.

2. See Toby Tetenbaum, "To Plan or Not to Plan," *Management Review,* 87 (October 1998): 70; and Andrew Campbell, "Tailored, Not Benchmarked: A Fresh Look at Corporate Planning," *Harvard Business Review,* 77 (March–April 1999): 41–50.

3. Based on discussion in Frances J. Milliken, "Three Types of Perceived Uncertainty About the Environment: State, Effect, and Response Uncertainty," *Academy of Management Review,* 12 (January 1987): 133–143. Also see Hugh Courtney, *20/20 Foresight: Crafting Strategy in an Uncertain World* (Boston: Harvard Business School Press, 2001): Ch. 2.

4. For example, see Marilyn Adams, "United, Mechanics Dodge Walkout," *USA Today* (February 19, 2002): 1B.

5. See Raymond E. Miles and Charles C. Snow, *Organizational Strategy, Structure, and Process* (New York: McGraw-Hill,

1978), p. 29. A validation of the Miles and Snow model can be found in Stephen M. Shortell and Edward J. Zajak, "Perceptual and Archival Measures of Miles and Snow's Strategic Types: A Comprehensive Assessment of Reliability and Validity," *Academy of Management Journal,* 33 (December 1990): 817–832.

6. Data from Joseph Weber, "Harley Investors May Get a Wobbly Ride," *Business Week* (February 11, 2002): 65.

7. Data from **www.capitalone.com**.

8. "What's the Hard Part? Innovation Never Ends," *Fast Company,* no. 24 (May 1999): 212. Other prospectors are discussed in Christopher Palmeri, "His Venice Isn't Sinking," *Business Week* (October 23, 2000): 86, 90; and Stephen Baker, "Is Nokia's Star Dimming?" *Business Week* (January 2, 2001): 66–72.

9. William Boulding and Markus Christen, "First-Mover Disadvantage," *Harvard Business Review,* 79 (October 2001): 20–21 (emphasis added). Also see Jim Collins, "Best Beats First," *Inc.,* 22 (August 2000): 48–52; and Kevin Maney, "Impregnable 'First Mover Advantage' Philosophy Suddenly Isn't," *USA Today* (July 18, 2001): 3B.

10. See John B. Miner, "The Expanded Horizon for Achieving Entrepreneurial Success," *Organizational Dynamics,* 25 (Winter 1997): 54–66.

11. Christine Y. Chen, "The Last-Mover Advantage," *Fortune* (July 9, 2001): 84. Another 'analyzer' is profiled in Edward O. Welles, "The Next Starbucks," *Inc.,* 23 (January 2001): 48–53.

12. See "How Seagram Is Scrambling to Survive 'The Sobering of America,'" *Business Week* (September 3, 1984): 94–95; Andrea Rothman, "The Maverick Boss at Seagram," *Business Week* (December 18, 1989): 90–98; Laura Zinn, "Edgar Jr.'s Not So Excellent Ventures," *Business Week* (January 16, 1995): 78–79; and David Jones and Caroline Brothers, "Diageo, Pernod Buy Seagram Division," *USA Today* (December 20, 2000): 3B.

13. For details, see Jeffrey S. Conant, Michael P. Mokwa, and P. Rajan Varadarajan, "Strategic Types, Distinctive Marketing Competencies and Organizational Performance: A Multiple Measures Based Study," *Strategic Management Journal,* 11 (September 1990): 365–383. Also see Shaker A. Zahra and John A. Pearce II, "Research Evidence on the Miles-Snow Typology," *Journal of Management,* 16 (December 1990): 751–768.

14. Based on Mary M. Crossan, Henry W. Lane, Roderick E. White, and Leo Klus, "The Improvising Organization: Where Planning Meets Opportunity," *Organizational Dynamics,* 24 (Spring 1996): 20–35.

15. "$1.4B Authorized to Restore Everglades," *USA Today* (December 12, 2000): 15A.

16. Scott Adams, "Dilbert's Management Handbook," *Fortune* (May 13, 1996): 104.

17. Based on R. Duane Ireland and Michael A. Hitt, "Mission Statements: Importance, Challenge, and Recommendations for Development," *Business Horizons,* 35 (May–June 1992): 34–42. Also see Christopher K. Bart, "Sex, Lies, and Mission Statements," *Business Horizons,* 40 (December 1997): 9–18; James R. Lucas, "Anatomy of a Vision Statement," *Management Review,* 87 (February 1998): 22–26; and Jeffrey Pfeffer

and Robert I. Sutton, "The Smart-Talk Trap," *Harvard Business Review,* 77 (May–June 1999): 135–142.

18. Bill Saporito, "PPG: Shiny, Not Dull," *Fortune* (July 17, 1989): 107.

19. Dan Sullivan, "The Reality Gap," *Inc.,* 21 (March 1999): 119.

20. Anthony P. Raia, *Managing by Objectives* (Glenview, Ill.: Scott, Foresman, 1974), p. 24.

21. For an excellent and comprehensive treatment of goal setting, see Edwin A. Locke and Gary P. Latham, *Goal Setting: A Motivational Technique That Works!* (Englewood Cliffs, N.J.: Prentice-Hall, 1984). Also see Robert D. Pritchard, Philip L. Roth, Steven D. Jones, Patricia J. Galgay, and Margaret D. Watson, "Designing a Goal-Setting System to Enhance Performance: A Practical Guide," *Organizational Dynamics,* 17 (Summer 1988): 69–78.

22. John A. Byrne and Heather Timmons, "Tough Times for a New CEO," *Business Week* (October 29, 2001): 66.

23. For example, see Edward C. Baig, "Secretaries for the Rest of Us," *Business Week* (November 16, 1998): 146; Ed Brown, "Stephen Covey's New One-Day Seminar," *Fortune* (February 1, 1999): 138, 140; and Donna J. Abernathy, "A Get-Real Guide to Time Management," *Training & Development,* 53 (June 1999): 22–26.

24. Raia, *Managing by Objectives,* p. 54.

25. Richard Koch, *The 80/20 Principle: The Secret of Achieving More with Less* (New York: Currency Doubleday, 1998), p. 4.

26. Diane Brady, "Why Service Stinks," *Business Week* (October 23, 2000): 126.

27. See Barbara Moses, "The Busyness Trap," *Training,* 35 (November 1998): 38–42; and Stephen Bertman, "Hyper Culture," *The Futurist,* 32 (December 1998): 18–23.

28. See Peter F. Drucker, *The Practice of Management* (New York: Harper & Row, 1954).

29. As an indication of the widespread interest in MBO, more than 700 books, articles, and technical papers had been written on the subject by the late 1970s. For a brief history of MBO, see George S. Odiorne, "MBO: A Backward Glance," *Business Horizons,* 21 (October 1978): 14–24. An excellent collection of readings on MBO may be found in George Odiorne, Heinz Weihrich, and Jack Mendleson, *Executive Skills: A Management by Objectives Approach* (Dubuque, Iowa: Wm. C. Brown, 1980). Also see Henry H. Beam, " George Odiorne, " *Business Horizons,* 39 (November–December 1996): 73–76.

30. T. J. Rodgers, "No Excuses Management," *Harvard Business Review,* 68 (July–August 1990): 87, 89.

31. For related reading, see Philippe Haspeslagh, Tomo Noda, and Fares Boulos, "It's Not Just About the Numbers," *Harvard Business Review,* 79 (July–August 2001): 65–73.

32. For example, see Jan P. Muczyk and Bernard C. Reimann, "MBO as a Complement to Effective Leadership," *Academy of Management Executive,* 3 (May 1989): 131–139.

33. An interesting study of the positive and negative aspects of MBO may be found in Robert C. Ford and Frank S. McLaughlin, "Avoiding Disappointment in MBO Programs," *Human Resource Management,* 21 (Summer 1982): 44–49. Positive research evidence is summarized in Robert Rodgers and John

E. Hunter, "Impact of Management by Objectives on Organizational Productivity," *Human Resource Management,* 76 (April 1991): 322–336.

34. For a critical appraisal of MBO core assumptions, see David Halpern and Stephen Osofsky, "A Dissenting View of MBO," *Public Personnel Management,* 19 (Fall 1990): 321–330. Deming's critical comments may be found in W. Edwards Deming, *Out of the Crisis* (Cambridge, Mass.: MIT Press, 1986), pp. 23–96. Dennis W. Organ, "The Editor's Chair," *Business Horizons,* 39 (November–December 1996): 1.

35. See Richard Babcock and Peter F. Sorensen Jr., "An MBO Check-List: Are Conditions Right for Implementation?" *Management Review,* 68 (June 1979): 59–62.

36. Robert Rodgers and John E. Hunter, "Impact of Management by Objectives on Organizational Productivity," *Journal of Applied Psychology,* 76 (April 1991): 322.

37. See Robert Rodgers, John E. Hunter, and Deborah L. Rogers, "Influence of Top Management Commitment on Management Program Success," *Journal of Applied Psychology,* 78 (February 1993): 151–155.

38. See Jeffrey K. Pinto and Om P. Kharbanda, "Lessons for an Accidental Profession," *Business Horizons,* 38 (March–April 1995): 41–50. For an excellent resource book, see Jeffrey K. Pinto and O. P. Kharbanda, *Successful Project Managers: Leading Your Team to Success* (New York: Van Nostrand Reinhold, 1995).

39. Project Management Institute, "What Is a Project?" **www.pmi.org,** p. 1.

40. See Tom D. Conkright, "So You're Going to Manage a Project," *Training,* 35 (January 1998): 62–67.

41. Louisa Wah, "Most IT Projects Prove Inefficient," *Management Review,* 88 (January 1999): 7. Also see Nadim Matta and Sandy Krieger, "From IT Solutions to Business Results," *Business Horizons,* 44 (November–December 2001): 45–50.

42. For more, see Susan G. Turner, Dawn R. Utley, and Jerry D. Westbrook, "Project Managers and Functional Managers: A Case Study of Job Satisfaction in a Matrix Organization," *Project Management Journal,* 29 (September 1998): 11–19; Peg Thoms and Jeffrey K. Pinto, "Project Leadership: A Question of Timing," *Project Management Journal,* 30 (March 1999): 19–26; Gerben van der Vegt, Ben Emans, and Evert van de Vliert, "Effects of Interdependencies in Project Teams," *The Journal of Social Psychology,* 139 (April 1999): 202–214; and Timothy J. Kloppenborg and Joseph A. Petrick, "Leadership in Project Life Cycle and Team Character Development," *Project Management Journal,* 30 (June 1999): 8–13.

43. For details, see Andrea Ovans, "Inside Boeing's Big Move," *Harvard Business Review,* 79 (October 2001): 22–23. Also see Fred Bayles, "Boston's 'Big Dig' Deeper in Hole," *USA Today* (February 16, 2000): 5A; and Margaret Young, "Wired at Webcor," *Business Week e.biz* (November 20, 2000): EB59–EB62.

44. See Jennifer E. Jenkins, "Moving Beyond a Project's Implementation Phase," *Nursing Management,* 27 (January 1996): 48B, 48D.

45. See Terry L. Fox and J. Wayne Spence, "Tools of the Trade: A Survey of Project Management Tools," *Project Management Journal,* 29 (September 1998): 20–27.

46. Based partly on discussion in Pinto and Kharbanda, *Successful Project Managers,* p. 147.

47. See Mary J. Waller, Jeffrey M. Conte, Cristina B. Gibson, and Mason A. Carpenter, "The Effect of Individual Perceptions of Deadlines on Team Performance," *Academy of Management Review,* 26 (October 2001): 586–600.

48. Adrian Mello, "ERP Fundamentals," **http://techupdate.zdnet.com** (February 7, 2002).

49. Data from ibid. For more, see Darnell Little, "Even the Supervisor Is Expendable," *Business Week* (July 23, 2001): 78.

50. One example of a flow-chart application is Sharon M. McKinnon, "How Important Are Those Foreign Operations? A Flow-Chart Approach to Loan Analysis," *Financial Analysts Journal,* 41 (January–February 1985): 75–78.

51. For examples of early Gantt charts, see H. L. Gantt, *Organizing for Work* (New York: Harcourt, Brace and Howe, 1919), Ch. 8.

52. Gantt chart applications can be found in Conkright, "So You're Going to Manage a Project," p. 64; and Andrew Raskin, "Task Masters," *Inc. Tech* 1999, no. 1 (1999): 62–72.

53. Ivars Avots, "The Management Side of PERT," *California Management Review,* 4 (Winter 1962): 16–27.

54. Additional information on PERT can be found in Nancy Madlin, "Streamlining the PERT Chart," *Management Review,* 75 (September 1986): 67–68; Eric C. Silverberg, "Predicting Project Completion," *Research Technology Review,* 34 (May–June 1991): 46–49; Robert L. Armacost and Rohne L. Jauernig, "Planning and Managing a Major Recruiting Project," *Public Personnel Management,* 20 (Summer 1991): 115–126; T. M. Williams, "Practical Use of Distributions in Network Analysis," *Journal of the Operational Research Society,* 43 (March 1992): 265–270; and Hooshang Kuklan, "Effective Project Management: An Expanded Network Approach," *Journal of Systems Management,* 44 (March 1993): 12–16.

55. Adapted in part from John Fertakis and John Moss, "An Introduction to PERT and PERT/Cost Systems," *Managerial Planning,* 19 (January–February 1971): 24–31.

56. Data from "John Leahy," *Business Week* (June 11, 2001): 80.

57. For more, see Jill Andresky Fraser, "Do I Need to Plan Differently for a Dot-Com Business?" *Inc.,* 22 (July 2000): 142–143; Jim Hopkins, "Chart Your Firm's Route Before Hitting the Road," *USA Today* (November 9, 2000: 7B; and Emily Barker, "The Bullet-Proof Business Plan," *Inc.,* 23 (October 2001): 102–104.

## Chapter 7

**Opening Quotation** Laurel Cutler is vice chairman of FCB/Leber Katz Partners, an advertising agency in New York City. Quoted in Susan Caminiti, "The Payoff from a Good Reputation," *Fortune* (February 10, 1992): 74.

**Opening Case** Excerpted from Andy Serwer, "Dell Does Domination," *Fortune* (January 21, 2002): 70–75. Copyright © 2002, Time Inc. Reprinted by permission.

**Closing Case** Richard Martin, "The Oracles of Oil," *Business 2.0,* 3 (January 2002): 46–47. Reprinted by permission.

1. For Michael Dell's thoughts on starting a business, see Thea Singer, "What Business Would You Start?" *Inc.,* 24 (March 2002): 68, 71.

2. Data from "Fortune 1,000 Ranked Within Industries," *Fortune* (April 16, 2001): F-49.

3. See Bryan W. Barry, "A Beginner's Guide to Strategic Planning," *The Futurist*, 32 (April 1998): 33–36; R. Duane Ireland and Michael A. Hitt, "Achieving and Maintaining Strategic Competitiveness in the 21st Century: The Role of Strategic Leadership," *Academy of Management Executive*, 13 (February 1999): 43–57; Danny Miller and John O. Whitney, "Beyond Strategy: Configuration as a Pillar of Competitive Advantage," *Business Horizons*, 42 (May–June 1999): 5–17. Gregory G. Dess and Joseph C. Picken, "Changing Roles: Leadership in the 21st Century," *Organizational Dynamics*, 28 (Winter 2000): 18–34; and Brian Huffman, "What Makes a Strategy Brilliant?" *Business Horizons*, 44 (July–August 2001): 13–20.

4. Data from C. Chet Miller and Laura B. Cardinal, "Strategic Planning and Firm Performance: A Synthesis of More than Two Decades of Research," *Academy of Management Journal*, 37 (December 1994): 1649–1665.

5. For related discussion, see Rosabeth Moss Kanter, "Managing for Long-Term Success," *The Futurist*, 32 (August–September 1998): 43–45; Sheila M. Puffer, "Global Executive: Intel's Andrew Grove on Competitiveness," *Academy of Management Executive*, 13 (February 1999): 15–24; and Richard E. S. Boulton, Barry D. Libert, and Steve M. Samek, "Learning to Juggle," *Business 2.0*, 1 (June 27, 2000): 250–263.

6. John A. Byrne, "Strategic Planning," *Business Week* (August 26, 1996): 52.

7. Based on a definitional framework found in David J. Teece, "Economic Analysis and Strategic Management," *California Management Review*, 26 (Spring 1984): 87. An alternative view calls for supplementing the notion of "fit" with the concept of "stretch," thus better accommodating situations in which a company's aspirations exceed its present resource capabilities. See Gary Hamel and C. K. Prahalad, "Strategy as Stretch and Leverage," *Harvard Business Review*, 71 (March–April 1993): 75–84.

8. Based on discussion in Donald C. Hambrick and James W. Fredrickson, "Are You Sure You Have a Strategy?" *Academy of Management Executive*, 15 (November 2001): 48–59. For related research, see Mason A. Carpenter and James D. Westphal, "The Strategic Context of External Network Ties: Examining the Impact of Director Appointments on Board Involvement in Strategic Decision Making," *Academy of Management Journal*, 44 (August 2001): 639–660.

9. See Michael A. Hitt, Barbara W. Keats, and Samuel M. DeMarie, "Navigating in the New Competitive Landscape: Building Strategic Flexibility and Competitive Advantage in the 21st Century," *Academy of Management Executive*, 12 (November 1998): 22–42.

10. Ronald Henkoff, "How to Plan for 1995," *Fortune* (December 31, 1990): 70.

11. For example, see Takashi Kiuchi, "Business Lessons from the Rain Forest," *The Futurist*, 32 (January–February 1998): 50–53; Jenny C. McCune, "The Game of Business," *Management Review*, 87 (February 1998): 56–58; and Louisa Wah, "The Dear Cost of 'Scut Work,'" *Management Review*, 88 (June 1999): 27–31.

12. Linda Yates and Peter Skarzynski, "How Do Companies Get to the Future First?" *Management Review*, 88 (January 1999): 18. Also see Joseph C. Picken and Gregory G. Dess, "Right Strategy—Wrong Problem," *Organizational Dynamics*, 27 (Summer 1998): 35–49; Adrian J. Slywotzky, Kevin A. Mundt, and James A. Quella, "Pattern Thinking," *Management Review*, 88 (June 1999): 32–37; and Henk W. Volberda, Frans A. J. van den Bosch, Bert Flier, and Eric R. Gedajlovic, "Following the Herd or Not? Patterns of Renewal in the Netherlands and the U.K." *Long Range Planning*, 34 (April 2001): 209–229.

13. See William R. King and David I. Cleland, *Strategic Planning and Policy* (New York: Van Nostrand Reinhold, 1978), pp. 180–183; Laura Landro, "Giants Talk Synergy but Few Make It Work," *The Wall Street Journal* (September 25, 1995): B1–B2; and Thomas Osegowitsch, "The Art and Science of Synergy: The Case of the Auto Industry," *Business Horizons*, 44 (March–April 2001): 17–24.

14. Joann Muller, "Daimler and Chrysler Have a Baby," *Business Week* (January 14, 2002): 36. Also see Micheline Maynard, "Amid the Turmoil, a Rare Success at DaimlerChrysler," *Fortune* (January 22, 2001): 112[C]–112[P].

15. David Lieberman, "Vivendi, Universal Try to Milk Merger," *USA Today* (December 18, 2001): 3B.

16. "Hotels Developing Multiple Personalities," *USA Today* (September 10, 1996): 4B.

17. Based on Ian Mount, "Ashes to Ashes, Poop to Power," *Business 2.0*, 2 (December 2001): 42.

18. "Alfa-Laval: Updating Its Knowhow for the Biotechnology Era," *Business Week* (September 19, 1983): 80.

19. See Michael E. Porter, *Competitive Strategy* (New York: Free Press, 1980), p. 35; and Michael E. Porter, *The Competitive Advantage of Nations* (New York: Free Press, 1990), p. 39. For updates, see James Surowiecki, "The Return of Michael Porter," *Fortune* (February 1, 1999): 135–138; and Richard M. Hodgetts, "A Conversation with Michael E. Porter: A 'Significant Extension' Toward Operational Improvement and Positioning," *Organizational Dynamics*, 28 (Summer 1999): 24–33.

20. Porter, *The Competitive Advantage of Nations*, p. 37. Also see Keith H. Hammonds, "Michael Porter's Big Ideas," *Fast Company*, no. 44 (March 2001): 150–156.

21. See Mary Jo Hatch and Majken Schultz, "Are the Strategic Stars Aligned for Your Corporate Brand?" *Harvard Business Review*, 79 (February 2001): 128–134; and John Deighton, "How Snapple Got Its Juice Back," *Harvard Business Review*, 80 (January 2002): 46–53.

22. Ron Zemke and Dick Schaaf, *The Service Edge* (New York: New American Library, 1989), p. 360.

23. As quoted in Bruce Horovitz and Theresa Howard, "With Image Crumbling, Kmart Files Chapter 11," *USA Today* (January 23, 2002): 1B.

24. See Shelly Branch, "The Brand Builders," *Fortune* (May 10, 1999): 132–134. Also see Chris Lederer and Sam Hill, "See Your Brands Through Your Customer's Eyes," *Harvard Business Review*, 79 (June 2001): 125–133.

25. Data from Mark Ivey, "Does Compaq's Formula Still Compute?" *Business Week* (May 13, 1991): 100, 104.

26. Adrienne Carter, "Foot Locker," *Money*, 31 (January 2002): 69.

27. For details, see Luis Ma. R. Calingo, "Environmental Determinants of Generic Competitive Strategies: Preliminary Evidence from Structured Content Analysis of *Fortune* and *Business Week* Articles (1983–1984)," *Human Relations*, 42 (April 1989): 353–369. For related research, see Praveen R. Nayyar, "Performance Effects of Three Foci in Service Firms," *Academy of Management Journal*, 35 (December 1992): 985–1009.

28. James F. Moore, *The Death of Competition: Leadership and Strategy in the Age of Business Ecosystems* (New York: Harper-Business, 1996), p. 25. For relevant background material, see Warren Boeker, "Organizational Strategy: An Ecological Perspective," *Academy of Management Journal*, 34 (September 1991): 613–635; and James F. Moore, "Predators and Prey: A New Ecology of Competition," *Harvard Business Review*, 71 (May–June 1993): 75–86. Also see Eric Bonabeau and Christopher Meyer, "Swarm Intelligence: A Whole New Way to Think About Business," *Harvard Business Review*, 79 (May 2001): 106–114; and Seth Godin, "Survival Is Not Enough," *Fast Company*, no. 54 (January 2002): 90–94.

29. See Courtney Shelton Hunt and Howard E. Aldrich, "The Second Ecology: Creation and Evolution of Organizational Communities," in *Research in Organizational Behavior*, vol. 20, eds. Barry M. Staw and L. L. Cummings (Greenwich, Conn.: JAI Press, 1998), pp. 267–301.

30. For more, see Andy Reinhardt, "The Wintel of Their Discontent," *Business Week* (November 23, 1998): 57; Cliff Edwards, "Microsoft and Intel: Moving in on PC Makers' Turf," *Business Week* (January 15, 2001): 41; and Brent Schlender, "Intel Unleashes Its Inner Attila," *Fortune* (October 15, 2001): 168–184.

31. Moore, *The Death of Competition*, p. 228. Also see Kathy Rebello, "Inside Microsoft," *Business Week* (July 15, 1996): 56–67; and Jim Kerstetter and Spencer E. Ante, "IBM vs. Oracle: It Could Get Bloody," *Business Week* (May 28, 2001): 65–66.

32. For example, see James A. Belohlav, "The Evolving Competitive Paradigm," *Business Horizons*, 39 (March–April 1996): 11–19; and Raymond W. Smith, "Business as War Game: A Report from the Battlefront," *Fortune* (September 30, 1996): 190–193.

33. Moore, *The Death of Competition*, p. 61.

34. See Stephanie N. Mehta, "How to Get Broadband Moving Again," *Fortune* (December 10, 2001): 207–212.

35. See David Kirkpatrick, "The New Player," *Fortune* (April 17, 2000): 162–168.

36. As quoted in Bill Breen, "Banker's Hours," *Fast Company*, no. 52 (November 2001): 200, 202.

37. For more, see "The New Technology Crib Sheet: Basic Training," *Inc.* Technology, 23 (September 2001): 194–202. Also see Adrian J. Slywotzky and David J. Morrison, *How Digital Is Your Business?* (New York: Crown Business, 2000); and John Hagel III and John Seely Brown, "Your Next IT Strategy," *Harvard Business Review*, 79 (October 2001): 105–113.

38. Michael E. Porter, "Strategy and the Internet," *Harvard Business Review*, 79 (March 2001): 76. Also see Anthony K. Tjan, "Finally, a Way to Put Your Internet Portfolio in Order," *Harvard Business Review*, 79 (February 2001): 76–85; Michael J. Mandel and Robert D. Hof, "Rethinking the Internet," *Business Week* (March 26, 2001): 116–122; Leyland Pitt, "Total E-Clipse: Five New Forces for Strategy in the Digital Age," *Journal of General Management*, 26 (Summer 2001): 1–15; and Jerry Useem, "Our 10 Principles of the New Economy, Slightly Revised," *Business 2.0*, 2 (August–September 2001): 85.

39. Spencer E. Ante and Ira Sager, "IBM's New Boss" *Business Week* (February 11, 2002): 68. For more on IBM, see David Kirkpatrick, "The Future of IBM," *Fortune* (February 18, 2002): 60–68.

40. Based on Heather Green, "Throw Out Your Old Business Model," *Business Week e.biz* (March 22, 1999): EB 22–EB 23.

41. Based on Leyland Pitt, Pierre Berthon, and Richard T. Watson, "Cyberservice: Taming Service Marketing Problems with the World Wide Web," *Business Horizons*, 42 (January–February 1999): 11–18; Chris Charuhas, "How to Train Web-Site Builders," *Training*, 36 (August 1999): 48–53; and John R. Graham, "How Can We Get More Visitors to Our Web Site?" *Canadian Manager*, 25 (Fall 2000): 16–17.

42. Data from Jon Swartz, "E-Tailers Ring Up a Record Holiday Week," *USA Today* (December 27, 2001): 3B. Also see Jeanette Brown, "Shoppers Are Beating a Path to the Web," *Business Week* (December 24, 2001): 41.

43. Jon Swartz, "Retailers Discover Leap to Web's a Doozy," *USA Today* (December 18, 2001): 3B.

44. See Ann Harrington, "Customer Service: FedEx," *Fortune* (May 24, 1999): 124.

45. Jerry Useem, "Internet Defense Strategy: Cannibalize Yourself," *Fortune* (September 6, 1999): 124, 126. © 1999 Time Inc. Reprinted by permission. For an update, see Fred Vogelstein, "Can Schwab Get Its Mojo Back?" *Fortune* (September 17, 2001): 93–98.

46. See Jeffrey L. Seglin, "It's Not That Easy Going Green," *Inc.*, 21 (May 1999): 28–32; Aaron Bernstein, "Sweatshop Reform: How to Solve the Standoff," *Business Week* (May 3, 1999): 186, 188, 190; "Helping the Private Sector Embrace Human Rights," *Business Ethics*, 13 (May–June 1999): 16; and William Echikson, "It's Europe's Turn to Sweat About Sweatshops," *Business Week* (July 19, 1999): 96.

47. Henry Mintzberg, "The Design School: Reconsidering the Basic Premises of Strategic Management," *Strategic Management Journal*, 11 (March–April 1990): 192.

48. See Gail Dutton, "What Business Are We In?" *Management Review*, 86 (September 1997): 54–57; and Eric M. Olson, Rachael Cooper, and Stanley F. Slater, "Design Strategy and Competitive Advantage," *Business Horizons*, 41 (March–April 1998): 55–61.

49. Richard F. Vancil, "Strategy Formulation in Complex Organizations," *Sloan Management Review*, 17 (Winter 1976): 18. Also see Robert E. Linneman and John L. Stanton Jr., "Mining for Niches," *Business Horizons*, 35 (May–June 1992): 43–51.

50. Pete Engardio, "For Citibank, There's No Place Like Asia," *Business Week* (March 30, 1992): 66.

51. "Is Your Company an Extrovert?" *Management Review*, 85 (March 1996): 7. Also see Ruth C. May, Wayne H. Stewart Jr., and Robert Sweo, "Environmental Scanning Behavior in a Transnational Economy: Evidence from Russia," *Academy of Management Journal*, 43 (June 2000): 403–427; and M. Carl Drott, "Personal Knowledge, Corporate Information: The Challenges for Competitive Intelligence," *Business Horizons*, 44 (March–April 2001): 31–37.

52. See Thea Singer, "Comeback Markets," *Inc.*, 23 (May 2001): 53–54; and Prithviraj Chattopadhyay, William H. Glick, and George P. Huber, "Organizational Actions in Response to Threats and Opportunities," *Academy of Management Journal*, 44 (October 2001): 937–955.

53. See Jay B. Barney, "Looking Inside for Competitive Advantage," *Academy of Management Executive*, 9 (November 1995): 49–61; W. Jack Duncan, Peter M. Ginter, and Linda E. Swayne, "Competitive Advantage and Internal Organizational Assessment," *Academy of Management Executive*, 12 (August 1998): 6–16; and Leyland F. Pitt, Michael T. Ewing, and Pierre Berthon, "Turning Competitive Advantage into Customer Equity," *Business Horizons*, 43 (September–October 2000): 11–18; and Bernard L. Rosenbaum, "Seven Emerging Sales Competencies," *Business Horizons*, 44 (January–February 2001): 33–36.

54. Adapted from Andrew Bartmess and Keith Cerny, "Building Competitive Advantage Through a Global Network of Capabilities," *California Management Review*, 35 (Winter 1993): 78–103. Also see David A. Nadler and Michael L. Tushman, "The Organization of the Future: Strategic Imperatives and Core Competencies for the 21st Century," *Organizational Dynamics*, 28 (Summer 1999): 45–60; and Louisa Wah, "Thriving on Diversification," *Management Review*, 88 (July–August 1999): 8. Strategic flexibility is discussed in M. B. (Buff) Lawson, "In Praise of Slack: Time Is of the Essence," *Academy of Management Executive*, 15 (August 2001): 125–135.

55. As quoted in Alan Webber, "The Old Economy Meets the New Economy," *Fast Company*, no. 51 (October 2001): 74. For more on strategic speed, see "Stephen W. Sanger: General Mills," *Business Week* (January 8, 2001): 67; Christopher Meyer, "The Second Generation of Speed," *Harvard Business Review*, 79 (April 2001): 24–25; and Laura Riolli-Saltzman and Fred Luthans, "After the Bubble Burst: How Small High-Tech Firms Can Keep in Front of the Wave," *Academy of Management Executive*, 15 (August 2001): 114–124.

56. For essential reading in this area, see Michael and James Champy, *Reengineering the Corporation: A Manifesto for Business Revolution* (New York: HarperBusiness, 1993); and James Champy, *Reengineering Management: The New Mandate for Leadership* (New York: HarperBusiness, 1995).

57. According to Henry Mintzberg, there are four reasons why organizations need strategies: (1) to set direction, (2) to focus effort of contributors, (3) to define the organization, and (4) to provide consistency. For more, see Henry Mintzberg, "The Strategy Concept II: Another Look at Why Organizations Need Strategies," *California Management Review*, 30 (Fall 1987): 25–32.

58. Waldron Berry, "Beyond Strategic Planning," *Managerial Planning*, 29 (March–April 1981): 14.

59. See Eric Beaudan, "The Failure of Strategy," *Ivey Business Journal*, 65 (January–February 2001): 64–86.

60. Charles H. Roush Jr. and Ben C. Ball Jr., "Controlling the Implementation of Strategy," *Managerial Planning*, 29 (November–December 1980): 4.

61. Donald C. Hambrick and Albert A. Cannella Jr., "Strategy Implementation as Substance and Selling," *Academy of Management Executive*, 3 (November 1989): 282–283. Another good discussion of strategic implementation may be found in Orit Gadiesh and James L. Gilbert, "Transforming Corner-Office Strategy into Frontline Action," *Harvard Business Review*, 79 (May 2001): 72–79.

62. William D. Guth and Ian C. Macmillian, "Strategy Implementation Versus Middle Management Self-Interest," *Strategic Management Journal*, 7 (July–August 1986): 321.

63. See Christopher McDermott and Kenneth K. Boyer, "Strategic Consensus: Marching to the Beat of a Different Drummer?" *Business Horizons*, 42 (July–August 1999): 21–28; and Adelaide Wilcox King, Sally W. Fowler, and Carl P. Zeithaml, "Managing Organizational Competencies for Competitive Advantage: The Middle-Management Edge," *Academy of Management Executive*, 15 (May 2001): 95–106.

64. See Gary Meyer, "eWorkbench: Real-Time Tracking of Synchronized Goals," *HRMagazine*, (April 2001): 115–118. (**www. performaworks.com**)

65. See Michael Goold and John J. Quinn, "The Paradox of Strategic Controls," *Strategic Management Journal*, 11 (January 1990): 43–57; and Georg Kellinghusen and Klaus Wubbenhorst, "Strategic Control for Improved Performance," *Long Range Planning*, 23 (June 1990): 30–40.

66. See Vasudevan Ramanujan and N. Venkatraman, "Planning and Performance: A New Look at an Old Question," *Business Horizons*, 30 (May–June 1987): 19–25.

67. See Andy Hines, "A Checklist for Evaluating Forecasts," *The Futurist*, 29 (November–December 1995): 20–24.

68. See Peter Bishop, "Thinking like a Futurist," *The Futurist*, 32 (June–July 1998): 39–42; and Mark A. Moon, John T. Mentzer, Carlo D. Smith, and Michael S. Garver, "Seven Keys to Better Forecasting," *Business Horizons*, 41 (September–October 1998): 44–52.

69. An excellent overview of forecasting techniques may be found in David M. Georgoff and Robert G. Murdick, "Manager's Guide to Forecasting," *Harvard Business Review*, 64 (January–February 1986): 110–120.

70. Based on C. W. J. Granger, *Forecasting in Business and Economics* (New York: Academic Press, 1980), pp. 6–10.

71. Paul Kaihla, "Inside Cisco's $2 Billion Blunder," *Business 2.0*, 3 (March 2002): 88–89.

72. See Louis Lavelle, "The Case of the Corporate Spy," *Business Week* (November 26, 2001): 56, 58.

73. "Pokémon Patriarch," *Business Week* (January 10, 2000): 70.

74. See Steven Schnaars and Paschalina (Lilia) Ziamou, "The Essentials of Scenario Writing," *Business Horizons*, 44 (July–August 2001): 25–31; and Hugh Courtney, "Scenario

Planning," *20-20 Foresight: Crafting Strategy in an Uncertain World* (Boston: Harvard Business School Press, 2001), pp. 160–165.

75. Steven P. Schnaars, "How to Develop and Use Scenarios," *Long Range Planning,* 20 (February 1987): 106.

76. For example, see Kathy Moyer, "Scenario Planning at British Airways—A Case Study," *Long Range Planning,* 29 (April 1996): 172–181. Interesting scenarios for the U.S. Social Security system are presented in Peter Coy, "Social Security: The Long View," *Business Week* (January 14, 2002): 24.

77. Peter Coy and Neil Gross, "21 Ideas for the 21st Century," *Business Week* (August 30, 1999): 82.

78. For more, see Charles M. Perrottet, "Scenarios for the Future," *Management Review,* 85 (January 1996): 43–46; Michel Godet and Fabrice Roubelat, "Creating the Future: The Use and Misuse of Scenarios," *Long Range Planning,* 29 (April 1996): 164–171; James M. Kouzes and Barry Z. Posner, "Envisioning Your Future: Imagining Ideal Scenarios," *The Futurist,* 30 (May–June 1996): 14–19; and Robert Baldock, "5 Futures," *Management Review,* 88 (October 1999): 52–55.

79. For interesting reading about Internet surveys, see Bruce Horovitz, "High Level of Comfort Leads to Truthful Research Worth a Mint," *USA Today* (May 17, 1999): 1A–2A. Also see "Do Americans Trust Media Polls?" *USA Today* (May 18, 1999): 1A.

80. See Nancy Chambers, "The Really Long View," *Management Review,* 87 (January 1998): 10–15; Karen Thomas, "Fashion Understatement: That's So 5 Minutes Ago," *USA Today* (March 23, 1999): 1D–2D; and H. Donald Hopkins, "Using History for Strategic Problem-Solving: The Harley-Davidson Effect," *Business Horizons,* 42 (March–April 1999): 52–60.

81. See Wendy Zellner, "Chrysler's Next Generation," *Business Week* (December 19, 1988): 52–57.

## Chapter 8

**Opening Quotation** "Ruthann Quindlen," *Fast Company,* no. 25 (June 1999): 104.

**Opening Case** Craig Wilson, "Hallmark Hits The Mark," *USA Today* (June 14, 2001): 1D–2D. Copyright 2001, *USA Today.* Reprinted with permission.

**Closing Case** Chris Woodyard, "Revamped Tool Helps Fliers Breathe Easier," *USA Today* (May 5, 2000): 7B. Copyright 2001, *USA Today.* Reprinted with permission.

1. Data from "Hurry Up and Decide!" *Business Week* (May 14, 2001): 16.

2. Morgan W. McCall Jr. and Robert E. Kaplan, *Whatever It Takes: The Realities of Managerial Decision Making,* 2nd ed. (Englewood Cliffs, N.J.: Prentice-Hall, 1990), p. 5.

3. Paul Hoversten, "Backers Hope Amenities Will Quiet Critics," *USA Today* (February 22, 1995): 2A.

4. Michael Parrish, "Former Arco Chief Still Gambling on Oil Strikes," *Los Angeles Times* (September 21, 1993): D1.

5. Matthew L. Ward, "Airports Must Make Way for Airbus' Gigantic A380," *The Arizona Republic* (February 11, 2001): D1.

6. Justin Martin, "Tomorrow's CEOs," *Fortune* (June 24, 1996): 90.

7. See, for example, Thomas F. O'Boyle, "Profit at Any Cost," *Business Ethics,* 13 (March–April 1999): 13–16.

8. Steven M. Gillon, "Unintended Consequences: Why Our Plans Don't Go According to Plan," *The Futurist,* 35 (March–April 2001): 49.

9. See Edward Tenner, *Why Things Bite Back: Technology and the Revenge of Unintended Consequences* (New York: Vintage Books, 1996), ch. 1; and Peter Eisler, "Fallout Likely Caused 15,000 Deaths," *USA Today* (February 28, 2002): 1A.

10. Mark Clayton, "The Ink Is Red at Canadian Mills," *The Christian Science Monitor* (March 11, 1992): 7.

11. For related reading, see Mark C. Maletz and Nitin Nohria, "Managing in the Whitespace," *Harvard Business Review,* 79 (February 2001): 102–111; and Eric Bonabeau, "Predicting the Unpredictable," *Harvard Business Review,* 80 (March 2002): 109–116.

12. See Elke U. Weber, Christopher K. Hsee, and Joanna Sokolowska, "What Folklore Tells Us About Risk and Risk Taking: Cross-Cultural Comparisons of American, German, and Chinese Proverbs," *Organizational Behavior and Human Decision Processes,* 75 (August 1998): 170–186; Robert Simons, "How Risky Is Your Company?" *Harvard Business Review,* 77 (May–June 1999): 85–94; and Gerry McNamara and Philip Bromiley, "Risk and Return in Organizational Decision Making," *Academy of Management Journal,* 42 (June 1999): 330–339.

13. See Bill Treasurer, "How Risk-Taking Really Works," *Training,* 37 (January 2000): 40–44.

14. Paul Raeburn, "A Biotech Boom with a Difference," *Business Week* (December 31, 2001): 52. Also see "Alex Matter: Head of Oncology Research, Novartis," *Business Week* (June 11, 2001): 68.

15. For an informative discussion see Weston H. Agor, "Managing Brain Skills: The Last Frontier," *Personnel Administrator,* 32 (October 1987): 54–60.

16. See Bill Breen, "What's Your Intuition?" *Fast Company,* no. 38 (September 2000): 290–300; Joshua Hyatt, "The Death of Gut Instinct," *Inc.,* 23 (January 2001): 38–44; and Alden M. Hayashi, "When to Trust Your Gut," *Harvard Business Review,* 79 (February 2001): 59–65.

17. As quoted in Keith H. Hammonds, "Continental's Turnaround Pilot," *Fast Company,* no. 53 (December 2001): 100.

18. For research on decision styles, see Susanne G. Scott and Reginald A. Bruce, "Decision-Making Style: The Development and Assessment of a New Measure," *Educational and Psychological Measurement,* 55 (October 1995): 818–831; and Stacey M. Whitecotton, D. Elaine Sanders, and Kathleen B. Norris, "Improving Predictive Accuracy with a Combination of Human Intuition and Mechanical Decision Aids," *Organizational Behavior and Human Decision Processes,* 76 (December 1998): 325–348.

19. See Beverly Geber, "A Quick Course in Decision Science," *Training,* 25 (April 1988): 54–55; Alan E. Singer, Steven Lysonski, Ming Singer, and David Hayes, "Ethical Myopia: The Case of 'Framing' by Framing," *Journal of Business Ethics,* 10 (January 1991): 29–36; and Glen Whyte, "Decision Failures: Why They Occur and How to Prevent Them," *Academy of Management Executive,* 5 (August 1991): 23–31.

20. Irwin P. Levin, Sara K. Schnittjer, and Shannon L. Thee, "Information Framing Effects in Social and Personal Decisions," *Journal of Experimental Social Psychology,* 24 (November 1988): 527. For additional research evidence, see Michael J. Zickar and Scott Highhouse, "Looking Closer at the Effects of Framing on Risky Choice: An Item Response Theory Analysis," *Organizational Behavior and Human Decision Processes,* 75 (July 1998): 75–91; and Vikas Mittal and William T. Ross Jr., "The Impact of Positive and Negative Affect and Issue Framing on Issue Interpretation and Risk Taking," *Organizational Behavior and Human Decision Processes,* 76 (December 1998): 298–324.

21. For good background reading, see Barry M. Staw and Jerry Ross, "Knowing When to Pull the Plug," *Harvard Business Review,* 65 (March–April 1987): 68–74; and Barry M. Staw and Jerry Ross, "Understanding Behavior in Escalation Situations," *Science,* 246 (October 13, 1989): 216–220. Also see William S. Silver and Terence R. Mitchell, "The Status Quo Tendency in Decision Making," *Organizational Dynamics,* 18 (Spring 1990): 34–46.

22. See Joel Brockner, "The Escalation of Commitment to a Failing Course of Action: Toward Theoretical Progress," *Academy of Management Review,* 17 (January 1992): 39–61; Beth Dietz-Uhler, "The Escalation of Commitment in Political Decision-Making Groups: A Social Identity Approach," *European Journal of Social Psychology,* 26 (July–August 1996): 611–629; Jennifer L. DeNicolis and Donald A. Hantula, "Sinking Shots and Sinking Costs? Or, How Long Can I Play in the NBA?" *Academy of Management Executive,* 10 (August 1996): 66–67; and Marc D. Street and William P. Anthony, "A Conceptual Framework Establishing the Relationship Between Groupthink and Escalating Commitment Behavior," *Small Group Research,* 28 (May 1997): 267–293.

23. For related research evidence, see Itamar Simonson and Barry M. Staw, "Deescalation Strategies: A Comparison of Techniques for Reducing Commitment to Losing Courses of Action," *Journal of Applied Psychology,* 77 (August 1992): 419–426.

24. As quoted in "Navy Cancels Contract for Attack Planes," *The Christian Science Monitor* (January 9, 1991): 3. Also see Russell Mitchell, "Desperately Seeking an Attack Bomber," *Business Week* (January 21, 1991): 35. Another good case study of escalation can be found in Jerry Ross and Barry M. Staw, "Organizational Escalation and Exit: Lessons from the Shoreham Nuclear Power Plant," *Academy of Management Journal,* 36 (August 1993): 701–732.

25. Andy Reinhardt, "A Space Venture That's Sputtering," *Business Week* (November 9, 1998): 156.

26. For an interesting exercise, see J. Edward Russo and Paul J. H. Schoemaker, "The Overconfidence Quiz," *Harvard Business Review,* 68 (September–October 1990): 236–237.

27. See Mark Simon, "Man, I'm Smart About How Stupid I Am!" *Business Horizons,* 44 (July–August 2001): 21–24.

28. Decision traps and personal investing are instructively covered in Jonathan Clements, "Your Ego Can Cost You Plenty in Investing," *The Wall Street Journal Sunday/The Arizona Republic* (February 4, 2001): D6; and Jason Zweig, "Do You Sabotage Yourself?" *Money,* 30 (May 2001): 74–78.

29. An excellent resource book is James G. March, *A Primer on Decision Making: How Decisions Happen* (New York: Free Press, 1994). Also see Catherine A. Maritan, "Capital Investment as Investing in Organizational Capabilities: An Empirically Grounded Process Model," *Academy of Management Journal,* 44 (June 2001): 513–531.

30. For example, see Herbert A. Simon, *The New Science of Management Decision,* rev. ed. (Englewood Cliffs, N.J.: Prentice-Hall, 1977), p. 40. Also see James W. Dean Jr. and Mark P. Sharfman, "Does Decision Process Matter? A Study of Strategic Decision-Making Effectiveness," *Academy of Management Journal,* 39 (April 1996): 368–396; Jerre L. Stead, "Whose Decision Is It, Anyway?" *Management Review,* 88 (January 1999): 13; Anna Muoio, "All the Right Moves," *Fast Company,* no. 24 (May 1999): 192–200; and Brian Palmer, "Click Here for Decisions," *Fortune* (May 10, 1999): 153–156.

31. Andrew S. Grove, *High Output Management* (New York: Random House, 1983), p. 98.

32. Simon, *The New Science of Management Decision,* p. 46.

33. See David R. A. Skidd, "Revisiting Bounded Rationality," *Journal of Management Inquiry,* 1 (December 1992): 343–347; and March, *A Primer on Decision Making,* pp. 8–9.

34. See Charles R. Schwenk, "The Use of Participant Recollection in the Modeling of Organizational Decision Processes," *Academy of Management Review,* 10 (July 1985): 496–503. Also see the discussion of "adaptive decision making" in Amitai Etzioni, "Humble Decision Making," *Harvard Business Review,* 67 (July–August 1989): 122–126; and Janet Barnard, "Successful CEOs Talk About Decision Making," *Business Horizons,* 35 (September–October 1992): 70–74.

35. Chester I. Barnard, *The Functions of the Executive* (Cambridge, Mass.: Harvard University Press, 1938), p. 190. Also see Susan S. Kirschenbaum, "Influence of Experience on Information-Gathering Strategies," *Journal of Applied Psychology,* 77 (June 1992): 343–352.

36. See Stuart F. Brown, "Making Decisions in a Flood of Data," *Fortune* (August 13, 2001): 148[B]–148[H].

37. For good background reading, see *Harvard Business Review on Knowledge Management* (Boston: Harvard Business School Publishing, 1998); and Thomas A. Stewart, "The Case Against Knowledge Management," *Business 2.0,* 3 (February 2002): 80–83.

38. David W. De Long and Patricia Seemann, "Confronting Conceptual Confusion and Conflict in Knowledge Management," *Organizational Dynamics,* 29 (Summer 2000): 33.

39. For more on tacit knowledge, see Roy Lubit, "Tacit Knowledge and Knowledge Management: The Keys to Sustainable Competitive Advantage," *Organizational Dynamics,* 29 (Winter 2001): 164–178.

40. See David W. De Long and Liam Fahey, "Diagnosing Cultural Barriers to Knowledge Management," *Academy of Management Executive,* 14 (November 2000): 113–127; and Rob Cross, Andrew Parker, Laurence Prusak, and Stephen P. Borgatti, "Knowing What We Know: Supporting Knowledge Cre-

ation and Sharing in Social Networks," *Organizational Dynamics,* 30 (Fall 2001): 100–120.

41. Dylan Tweney, "How to Beat Corporate Alzheimer's," *Business 2.0,* 2 (October 2001): 114.

42. Jeffrey Hsu and Tony Lockwood, "Collaborative Computing," *Byte,* 18 (March 1993): 113. Also see Anthony M. Townsend, Michael E. Whitman, and Anthony R. Hendrickson, "Computer Support System Adds Power to Group Processes," *HRMagazine,* 40 (September 1995): 87–91.

43. Catherine Romano, "The Power of Collaboration: Untapped," *Management Review,* 86 (January 1997): 7. See Jennifer Hedlund, Daniel R. Ilgen, and John R. Hollenbeck, "Decision Accuracy in Computer-Mediated Versus Face-to-Face Decision-Making Teams," *Organizational Behavior and Human Decision Processes,* 76 (October 1998): 30–47; Kevin Maney, "Software Genius Gets into Groove," *USA Today* (February 12, 2001): 1B–2B; and Alison Overholt, "Virtually There?" *Fast Company,* no. 56 (March 2002): 108–114.

44. George P. Huber, *Managerial Decision Making* (Glenview, Ill.: Scott, Foresman, 1980), pp. 141–142. Also see Michael Pacanowsky, "Team Tools for Wicked Problems," *Organizational Dynamics,* 23 (Winter 1995): 36–51.

45. As quoted in Ronald Henkoff, "A Whole New Set of Glitches for Digital's Robert Palmer," *Fortune* (August 19, 1996): 193.

46. See Steven G. Rogelberg, Janet L. Barnes-Farrell, and Charles A. Lowe, "The Stepladder Technique: An Alternative Group Structure Facilitating Effective Group Decision Making," *Journal of Applied Psychology,* 77 (October 1992): 730–737; Steven W. Floyd and Bill Wooldridge, "Managing Strategic Consensus: The Foundation of Effective Implementation," *Academy of Management Executive,* 6 (November 1992): 27–39; James R. Larson Jr., Caryn Christensen, Timothy M. Franz, and Ann S. Abbott, "Diagnosing Groups: The Pooling, Management, and Impact of Shared and Unshared Case Information in Team-Based Medical Decision Making," *Journal of Personality and Social Psychology,* 75 (July 1998): 93–108; and Daniel P. Forbes and Francis J. Milliken, "Cognition and Corporate Governance: Understanding Boards of Directors as Strategic Decision-Making Groups," *Academy of Management Review,* 24 (July 1999): 489–505.

47. See Priscilla M. Elsass and Laura M. Graves, "Demographic Diversity in Decision-Making Groups: The Experiences of Women and People of Color," *Academy of Management Review,* 22 (October 1997): 946–973; and Katherine Hawkins and Christopher B. Power, "Gender Differences in Questions Asked During Small Decision-Making Group Discussions," *Small Group Research,* (April 1999): 235–256.

48. See Gayle W. Hill, "Group Versus Individual Performance: Are N + 1 Heads Better than One?" *Psychological Bulletin,* 91 (May 1982): 517–539. Also see John P. Wanous and Margaret A. Youtz, "Solution Diversity and the Quality of Group Decisions," *Academy of Management Journal,* 29 (March 1986): 149–158; and Warren Watson, Larry K. Michaelsen, and Walt Sharp, "Member Competence, Group Interaction, and Group Decision Making: A Longitudinal Study," *Journal of Applied Psychology,* 76 (December 1991): 803–809.

49. See William L. Shanklin, "Creatively Managing for Creative Destruction," *Business Horizons,* 43 (November–December 2000): 29–35; Stefan Thomke, "Enlightened Experimentation: The New Imperative for Innovation," *Harvard Business Review,* 79 (February 2001): 66–75; George Anders, "Roche's New Scientific Method," *Fast Company,* no. 54 (January 2002): 60–67; and George Anders, "How Intel Puts Innovation Inside," *Fast Company,* no. 56 (March 2002): 122, 124.

50. A good historical perspective of creativity can be found in Michael Michalko, "Thinking like a Genius," *The Futurist,* 32 (May 1998): 21–25. Also see Kerrie Unsworth, "Unpacking Creativity," *Academy of Management Review,* 26 (April 2001): 289–297.

51. Based on discussion in N. R. F. Maier, Mara Julius, and James Thurber, "Studies in Creativity: Individual Differences in the Storing and Utilization of Information," *The American Journal of Psychology,* 80 (December 1967): 492–519.

52. Sidney J. Parnes, "Learning Creative Behavior," *The Futurist,* 18 (August 1984): 30–31. Also see Liz Simpson, "Fostering Creativity," *Training,* 38 (December 2001): 54–57; and Polly LaBarre, "Weird Ideas That Work," *Fast Company,* no. 54 (January 2002): 68–73.

53. See Arthur Koestler, *The Act of Creation* (London: Hutchinson, 1969), p. 27.

54. See James L. Adams, *Conceptual Blockbusting* (San Francisco: Freeman, 1974), p. 35.

55. See Charles R. Day Jr., "What a Dumb Idea," *Industry Week* (January 2, 1989): 27–28; and "In Search of Oink," *Management Review,* 88 (January 1999): 32–36.

56. Minda Zetlin, "Nurturing Nonconformists," *Management Review,* 88 (October 1999): 30. Also see Diane L. Coutu, "Genius at Work," *Harvard Business Review,* 79 (October 2001): 63–68; and Ryan Mathews and Watts Wacker, "Deviants, Inc.," *Fast Company,* no. 56 (March 2002): 70–80.

57. John Byrne, "The Search for the Young and Gifted," *Business Week* (October 4, 1999): 108. Also see "Offices that Spark Creativity," *Business Week* (August 28, 2000): 158–160.

58. See Ian Wylie, "Failure Is Glorious," *Fast Company,* no. 51 (October 2001): 35–38.

59. List adapted from Roger von Oech, *A Whack on the Side of the Head,* Warner Books, 1983. Reprinted by permission.

60. Huber, *Managerial Decision Making,* p. 12. Also see Brent Roper, "Sizing Up Business Problems," *HRMagazine,* 46 (November 2001): 50–56.

61. Peter F. Drucker, *The Practice of Management* (New York: Harper & Row, 1954), p. 531.

62. A good typology of business problems is discussed in Tom Kramlinger, "A Trainer's Guide to Business Problems," *Training,* 30 (March 1993): 47–50.

63. Louis S. Richman, "How to Get Ahead in America," *Fortune* (May 16, 1994): 48.

64. For an empirical classification of organizational problems, see David A. Cowan, "Developing a Classification Structure of Organizational Problems: An Empirical Investigation," *Academy of Management Journal,* 33 (June 1990): 366–390.

65. Adapted from Huber, *Managerial Decision Making,* pp. 13–15.

66. Marshall Sashkin and Kenneth J. Kiser, *Total Quality Management* (Seabrook, Md.: Ducochon Press, 1991), p. 133.

67. Adams, *Conceptual Blockbusting*, p. 7.

68. See Michael Schrage, "Playing Around with Brainstorming," *Harvard Business Review,* 79 (March 2001): 149–154.

69. For related research, see John J. Sosik, Bruce J. Avolio, and Surinder S. Kahai, "Inspiring Group Creativity: Comparing Anonymous and Identified Electronic Brainstorming," *Small Group Research,* 29 (February 1998): 3–31.

70. See Russell L. Ackoff, "The Art and Science of Mess Management," *Interfaces,* 11 (February 1981): 20–26. Also see Russell L. Ackoff, *Management in Small Doses* (New York: Wiley, 1986), pp. 102–103.

71. See March, *A Primer on Decision Making,* p. 18; and Gina Imperato, "When Is 'Good Enough' Good Enough?" *Fast Company,* no. 26 (July–August 1999): 52.

72. Ackoff, "The Art and Science of Mess Management," p. 22.

73. As quoted in James B. Treece, "Shaking Up Detroit," *Business Week* (August 14, 1989): 78.

74. Paul Hawken, "Problems, Problems," *Inc.,* 9 (September 1987): 24.

## Chapter 9

**Opening Quotation**   Kevin Freiberg and Jackie Freiberg, *Nuts! Southwest Airlines' Crazy Recipe for Business and Personal Success* (Austin, Texas: Bard Press, 1996), p. 155.

**Opening Case**   Excerpted from Mark Gimein, "Smart Is Not Enough," *Fortune* (January 8, 2001): 124–136. Copyright © 2001 Time Inc. Reprinted by permission.

**Closing Case**   Excerpted from Michael Hopkins, "Zen and the Art of the Self-Managing Company," *Inc.,* 22 (November 2000): 54–63. *Inc:* The Magazine for Growing Companies. Copyright 2000 by Bus. Innovator Group Resources/Inc. Reproduced with permission of Bus. Innovator Group Resources/Inc. in the format textbook via Copyright Clearance Center.

1. See B. J. Hodge, William P. Anthony, and Lawrence M. Gales, *Organization Theory: A Strategic Approach,* 5th ed. (Upper Saddle River, N.J.: Prentice-Hall, 1996), p. 10.

2. Adapted from Edgar H. Schein, *Organizational Psychology,* 3rd ed. (Englewood Cliffs, N.J.: Prentice-Hall, 1980), pp. 12–15.

3. See Adam Smith, *The Wealth of Nations* (New York: Modern Library, 1937), p. 7.

4. For example, see Jay R. Galbraith and Edward E. Lawler III, "Effective Organizations: Using the New Logic of Organizing," in *Organizing for the Future: The New Logic for Managing Complex Organizations,* eds. Jay R. Galbraith, Edward E. Lawler III, and Associates (San Francisco: Jossey-Bass, 1993), pp. 293–294. Related research is reported in Kees van den Bos, Henk A. M. Wilke, and E. Allan Lind, "When Do We Need Procedural Fairness? The Role of Trust in Authority," *Journal of Personality and Social Psychology,* 75 (December 1998): 1449–1458.

5. Elliot Jaques, "In Praise of Hierarchy," *Harvard Business Review,* 68 (January–February 1990): 127.

6. For an interesting biography of Henry Ford, see Ann Jardim, *The First Henry Ford: A Study in Personality and Business Leadership* (Cambridge, Mass.: MIT Press, 1970), p. 40.

7. This classification scheme is adapted from Peter M. Blau and William R. Scott, *Formal Organizations* (San Francisco: Chandler, 1962).

8. See Elliott Alvarado, "Nonprofit or Not-for-Profit—Which Are You?" *Nonprofit World,* 18 (November–December 2000): 6–7.

9. Data from "Working for the Federal Government," *USA Today* (January 22, 2002): 1B.

10. For related reading, see Gary Strauss, "Catastrophe Suspends Business as Usual in USA," *USA Today* (September 12, 2001): 1B–2B; Michelle Conlin, "When the Office Is the War Zone," *Business Week* (November 19, 2001): 38; and James Lardner, "Be Prepared!" *Business 2.0,* 3 (January 2002): 41–52.

11. See Marc Cecere, "Drawing the Lines," *Harvard Business Review,* 79 (November 2001): 24.

12. For real-life versions of this story, see Lynn Henning, "Catau Still Enjoys Tying One On," *The Detroit News* (July 4, 1999): 8D; and Alan R. Kamuda, "Local Manufacturer's Lures Catch On with Fishermen," *Detroit Free Press* (March 30, 2000): 6D.

13. James G. March, *Handbook of Organizations* (Chicago: Rand McNally, 1965), p. ix.

14. For more recent research, see Sydney Finkelstein and Richard A. D'Aveni, "CEO Duality as a Double-Edged Sword: How Boards of Directors Balance Entrenchment Avoidance and Unity of Command," *Academy of Management Journal,* 37 (October 1994): 1079–1108.

15. Drawn from Max Weber, *The Theory of Social and Economic Organization,* trans. A. M. Henderson and Talcott Parsons (New York: Oxford University Press, 1947). A critique based on the claim that Weber's work was mistranslated can be found in Richard M. Weiss, "Weber on Bureaucracy: Management Consultant or Political Theorist?" *Academy of Management Review,* 8 (April 1983): 242–248.

16. For a more detailed discussion, consult Warren G. Bennis, *Changing Organizations* (New York: McGraw-Hill, 1966), pp. 4–5.

17. For an excellent critique of modern bureaucracies, see Ralph P. Hummel, *The Bureaucratic Experience,* 3rd ed. (New York: St. Martin's Press, 1987).

18. Del Jones, "Welch: Nurture Best Workers, Lose Bottom 10%," *USA Today* (February 27, 2001): 2B.

19. See Paul Jarley, Jack Fiorito, and John Thomas Delaney, "A Structural Contingency Approach to Bureaucracy and Democracy in U.S. National Unions," *Academy of Management Journal,* 40 (August 1997): 831–861.

20. See, for example, Brian Dumaine, "The Bureaucracy Busters," *Fortune* (June 17, 1991): 36–50. Also see Craig J. Cantoni, "Eliminating Bureaucracy—Roots and All," *Management Review,* 82 (December 1993): 30–33; Gifford Pinchot and Elizabeth Pinchot, "Beyond Bureaucracy," *Business Ethics,* 8 (March–April 1994): 26–29; and Oren Harari, "Let the Computers Be the Bureaucrats," *Management Review,* 85 (September 1996): 57–60.

21. Chester I. Barnard, *The Functions of the Executive* (Cambridge, Mass.: Harvard University Press, 1938), p. 165.

22. Charles Perrow, "The Short and Glorious History of Organizational Theory," *Organizational Dynamics*, 2 (Summer 1973): 4. Also see Joseph Ofori-Dankwa and Scott D. Julian, "Complexifying Organizational Theory: Illustrations Using Time Research," *Academy of Management Review*, 26 (July 2001): 415–430.

23. See Alan P. Brache and Geary A. Rummler, "Managing an Organization as a System," *Training*, 34 (February 1997): 68–74; Toby J. Tetenbaum, "Shifting Paradigms: From Newton to Chaos," *Organizational Dynamics*, 26 (Spring 1998): 21–32; and Rosabeth Moss Kanter, "Managing for Long-Term Success," *The Futurist*, 32 (August–September 1998): 43–45.

24. Stratford Sherman, "Andy Grove: How Intel Makes Spending Pay Off," *Fortune* (February 22, 1993): 58. Also see Alan M. Webber, "How Business Is a Lot Like Life," *Fast Company*, no. 45 (April 2001): 130–136; and John Child and Rita Gunther McGrath, "Organizations Unfettered: Organizational Form in an Information-Intensive Economy," *Academy of Management Journal*, 44 (December 2001): 1135–1148.

25. For related reading, see Marianne W. Lewis, "Exploring Paradox: Toward a More Comprehensive Guide," *Academy of Management Review*, 25 (October 2000): 760–776.

26. Fremont E. Kast and James E. Rosenzweig, *Organization and Management: A Systems and Contingency Approach*, 3rd ed. (New York: McGraw-Hill, 1979), p. 103. An excellent glossary of open-system terms can be found on page 102 of this source.

27. See Stephen Baker, "The Minimill That Acts like a Biggie," *Business Week* (September 30, 1996): 100, 104; and Dean Foust, "Nucor: Meltdown in the Corner Office," *Business Week* (June 21, 1999): 37.

28. See V. Daniel R. Guide Jr. and Luk N. Van Wassenhove, "The Reverse Supply Chain," *Harvard Business Review*, 80 (February 2002): 25–26.

29. See Chris Argyris, "The Executive Mind and Double-Loop Learning," *Organizational Dynamics*, 11 (Autumn 1982): 4–22; and Chris Argyris, "Teaching Smart People How to Learn," *Harvard Business Review*, 69 (May–June 1991): 99–109.

30. See Peter M. Senge, *The Fifth Discipline: The Art and Practice of the Learning Organization* (New York: Doubleday, 1990); Barry Sugarman, "A Learning-Based Approach to Organizational Change: Some Results and Guidelines," *Organizational Dynamics*, 30 (Summer 2001): 62–75; Martin Schulz, "The Uncertain Relevance of Newness: Organizational Learning and Knowledge Flows," *Academy of Management Journal*, 44 (August 2001): 661–681; and Diane L. Coutu, "The Anxiety of Learning," *Harvard Business Review*, 80 (March 2002): 100–106.

31. David A. Garvin, "Building a Learning Organization, *Harvard Business Review*, 71 (July–August 1993): 78–91. For an extension, see Rob Cross, Andrew Parker, Laurence Prusak, and Stephen P. Borgatti, "Knowing What We Know: Supporting Knowledge Creation and Sharing in Social Networks," *Organizational Dynamics*, 30 (Fall 2001): 100–120.

32. David Lei, John W. Slocum, and Robert A. Pitts, "Designing Organizations for Competitive Advantage: The Power of Unlearning and Learning," *Organizational Dynamics*, 27 (Winter 1999): 30. For a different perspective, see "Dee W. Hock," *Fast Company*, no. 26 (July–August 1999): 90.

33. For learning organizations in action, see Jack Welch, *Straight from the Gut* (New York: Warner Books, 2001), pp. 181–184; Robert Buderi, "Intel Revamps R&D," *Technology Review*, 104 (October 2001): 24–25; and "Grow or Die," *Training*, 39 (January 2002): 17.

34. Kim Cameron, "Critical Questions in Assessing Organizational Effectiveness," *Organizational Dynamics*, 9 (Autumn 1980): 70.

35. See Raj Aggarwal, "Using Economic Profit to Assess Performance: A Metric for Modern Firms," *Business Horizons*, 44 (January–February 2001): 55–60.

36. Winslow Buxton, "Growth from Top to Bottom," *Management Review*, 88 (July–August 1999): 11.

37. Detailed discussions of alternative models of organizational effectiveness may be found in Kishore Gawande and Timothy Wheeler, "Measures of Effectiveness for Governmental Organizations," *Management Science*, 45 (January 1999): 42–58; and Edward V. McIntyre, "Accounting Choices and EVA," *Business Horizons*, 42 (January–February 1999): 66–72.

38. See Jeffrey Pfeffer, "When It Comes to 'Best Practices'—Why Do Smart Organizations Occasionally Do Dumb Things?" *Organizational Dynamics*, 25 (Summer 1996): 33–44; and Michael Beer, "How to Develop an Organization Capable of Sustained High Performance: Embrace the Drive for Results-Capability Development Paradox," *Organizational Dynamics*, 29 (Spring 2001): 233–247.

39. It is instructive to ponder why companies fall from grace over the years. One tracking device is *Fortune* magazine's annual list of "America's Most Admired Corporations." For example, see Matthew Boyle, "The Shiniest Reputations in Tarnished Times," *Fortune* (March 4, 2002): 70–82.

40. Data from "Layoff Count," *Fortune* (January 7, 2000): 24.

41. Peter Lorange and Robert T. Nelson, "How to Recognize—and Avoid—Organizational Decline," *Sloan Management Review*, 28 (Spring 1987): 41. Also see "Gordon Eubanks," *Fast Company*, no. 45 (April 2001): 92; "Charlie Feld," *Fast Company*, no. 45 (April 2001): 93; Katherine M. Hudson, "Transforming a Conservative Company: One Laugh at a Time," *Harvard Business Review*, 79 (July–August 2001): 45–53; George C. Mueller, William McKinley, Mark A. Mone, and Vincent L. Barker III, "Organizational Decline—A Stimulus for Innovation?" *Business Horizons*, 44 (November–December 2001): 25–34; and David N. James, "The Trouble I've Seen," *Harvard Business Review*, 80 (March 2002): 42–49.

42. Data from "*Fortune* 500 Largest U.S. Corporations," *Fortune* (April 16, 2001): F1; "The 100 Best Companies," *Fortune* (January 8, 2001): 152; and Greg Farrell, "Accounting Firm Destroyed Enron Records," *USA Today* (January 11, 2002): 1B. Also see Wendy Zellner and Stephanie Anderson Forest, "The Fall of Enron," *Business Week* (December 17, 2001): 30–36; Bethany McLean, "Why Enron Went Bust," *Fortune* (December

24, 2001): 58–68; and Greg Farrell and Del Jones, "How Did Enron Come Unplugged?" *USA Today* (January 14, 2002): 1B–2B.

43. See Robert I. Sutton and Thomas D'Aunno, "Decreasing Organizational Size: Untangling the Effects of Money and People," *Academy of Management Review,* 14 (April 1989): 194–212.

44. See Kim S. Cameron, David A. Whetten, and Myung U. Kim, "Organizational Dysfunctions of Decline," *Academy of Management Journal,* 30 (March 1987): 126–138.

45. See Stephanie N. Mehta, "Lessons from the Lucent Debacle," *Fortune* (February 5, 2001): 143–148.

46. See Mark A. Mone, William McKinley, and Vincent L. Barker III, "Organizational Decline and Innovation: A Contingency Framework," *Academy of Management Review,* 23 (January 1998): 115–132; Arthur G. Bedeian and Achilles A. Armenakis, "The Cesspool Syndrome: How Dreck Floats to the Top of Declining Organizations," *Academy of Management Executive,* 12 (February 1998): 58–63; Donald N. Sull, "Why Good Companies Go Bad," *Harvard Business Review,* 77 (July–August 1999): 42–52; and Walter J. Ferrier, Ken G. Smith, and Curtis M. Grimm, "The Role of Competitive Action in Market Share Erosion and Industry Dethronement: A Study of Industry Leaders and Challengers," *Academy of Management Journal,* 42 (August 1999): 372–388.

47. Peter F. Drucker, *Managing the Non-Profit Organization* (New York: HarperCollins, 1990), p. 66.

48. The battle against complacency is discussed in Tim Smart, "GE's Welch: 'Fighting Like Hell to Be No. 1,'" *Business Week* (July 8, 1996): 48; and John P. Kotter, "Kill Complacency," *Fortune* (August 5, 1996): 168–170. Also see Ronald Henkoff, "Growing Your Company: Five Ways to Do It Right!" *Fortune* (November 25, 1996): 78–88.

49. As quoted in Dori Jones Yang and Andrea Rothman, "Reinventing Boeing," *Business Week* (March 1, 1993): 61.

50. Wayne F. Cascio, "Downsizing: What Do We Know? What Have We Learned?" *Academy of Management Executive,* 7 (February 1993): 95. Three downsizing strategies are discussed in Kim S. Cameron, Sarah J. Freeman, and Aneil K. Mishra, "Best Practices in White-Collar Downsizing: Managing Contradictions," *Academy of Management Executive,* 5 (August 1991): 57–73. Also see Charles R. Eitel, "The Ten Disciplines of Business Turnaround," *Management Review,* 87 (December 1998): 13; James R. Morris, Wayne F. Cascio, and Clifford E. Young, "Downsizing After All These Years: Questions and Answers About Who Did It, How Many Did It, and Who Benefited from It," *Organizational Dynamics,* 27 (Winter 1999): 78–87; and Bo Burlingham, "The Downsizer's Dilemma," *Inc.,* 23 (December 2001): 106–107.

51. See Michael Arndt, "How Companies Can Marry Well: European-U.S. Mergers Pay Off," *Business Week* (March 4, 2002): 28.

52. Gene Koretz, " . . . And How It Is Paying Off," *Business Week* (November 25, 1996): 30. For an alternative view, see Gene Koretz, "Big Payoffs from Layoffs," *Business Week* (February 24, 1997): 30.

53. Based on Elizabeth Lesly and Larry Light, "When Layoffs Alone Don't Turn the Tide," *Business Week* (December 7, 1992): 100–101. Also see Stephanie Armour, "Morale, Performance Slump After Layoffs," *USA Today* (July 30, 2001): 1B; and Louis Lavelle, "Swing That Ax with Care," *Business Week* (February 11, 2002): 78.

54. See Janina C. Latack, Angelo J. Kinicki, and Gregory E. Prussia, "An Integrative Process Model of Coping with Job Loss," *Academy of Management Review,* 20 (April 1995): 311–342; and Stephanie Armour, "Managers Forced to Make Layoffs Can Feel Demoralized, Guilty, Depressed," *USA Today* (May 10, 2001): 3B.

55. For example, see Paul Falcone, "A Scripted Layoff," *HRMagazine,* 47 (February 2002): 89–91; and Daniel Roth, "How to Cut Pay, Lay Off 8,000 People, and Still Have Workers Who Love You," *Fortune* (February 4, 2002): 62–68.

56. See Stephanie Armour, "Employers Reassign Workers to Save Jobs," *USA Today* (December 26, 2001): 1B.

57. See, for example, Stephanie Armour, "Workers Take Pay Cuts over Pink Slips," *USA Today* (April 13, 2001): 1B; and "Take the Road Less Traveled," *HRMagazine,* 46 (July 2001): 46–51.

58. Michelle Neely Martinez, "To Have and to Hold," *HRMagazine,* 43 (September 1998): 130–139.

59. Stephanie Armour, "Companies Get Creative to Avoid Layoffs," *USA Today* (September 5, 2001): 1B.

60. Eric Schine, "Take the Money and Run—Or Take Your Chances," *Business Week* (August 16, 1993): 28. Also see Pat Wechsler, "AT&T Managers Rush out the Door," *Business Week* (June 15, 1998): 53.

61. Plant-closing legislation and programs are discussed in Angelo Kinicki, Jeffrey Bracker, Robert Kreitner, Chris Lockwood, and David Lemak, "Socially Responsible Plant Closings," *Personnel Administrator,* 32 (June 1987): 116–128.

62. For a good overview, see "Closing Law's Key Provisions," *Nation's Business* (January 1989): 58, 60. Also see Richard A. Starkweather and Cheryl L. Steinbacher, "Job Satisfaction Affects the Bottom Line," *HRMagazine,* 43 (September 1998): 110–112.

63. See Nancy Hatch Woodward, "Spousal Support," *HRMagazine,* 46 (December 2001): 79–83.

64. See Shari Caudron, "Teach Downsizing Survivors How to Thrive," *Personnel Journal,* 75 (January 1996): 38–48; and Marc Adams, "Training Employees as Partners," *HRMagazine,* 44 (February 1999): 64–70. For a positive discussion of layoff survivors, see Stephanie Armour, "Layoff Survivors Climb Ladder Faster," *USA Today* (September 10, 2001): 1B:

65. See David M. Slipy, "Anthropologist Uncovers Real Workplace Attitudes," *HRMagazine,* 35 (October 1990): 76–79; and David A. Kaplan, "Studying the Gearheads," *Newsweek* (August 3, 1998): 62.

66. This definition is based in part on Linda Smircich, "Concepts of Culture and Organizational Analysis," *Administrative Science Quarterly,* 28 (September 1983): 339–358. For excellent discussions of organizational cultures, see Daniel R. Denison, "What *Is* the Difference Between Organizational Culture and Organizational Climate? A Native's Point of View on a Decade

of Paradigm Wars," *Academy of Management Review,* 21 (July 1996): 619–654; Byron Sebastian, "Integrating Local and Corporate Cultures," *HRMagazine,* 41 (September 1996): 114–121; and David W. Young, "The Six Levers for Managing Organizational Culture," *Business Horizons,* 43 (September–October 2000): 19–28.

67. Data from John E. Sheridan, "Organizational Culture and Employee Retention," *Academy of Management Journal,* 35 (December 1992): 1036–1056. For parallel findings, see Shelly Branch, "The 100 Best Companies to Work for in America," *Fortune* (January 11, 1999): 118–144.

68. Peter C. Reynolds, "Imposing a Corporate Culture," *Psychology Today,* 21 (March 1987): 38.

69. Based on Harrison M. Trice and Janice M. Beyer, *The Cultures of Work Organizations* (Englewood Cliffs, N.J.: Prentice-Hall, 1993), pp. 5–8.

70. As quoted in Stephen B. Shepard, "A Talk with Jeff Immelt," *Business Week* (January 28, 2002): 103.

71. See, for example, Beverly Geber, "100 Days of Training," *Training,* 36 (January 1999): 62–66; Peter Troiano, "Post-Merger Challenges," *Management Review,* 88 (January 1999): 6; and Robert J. Grossman, "Irreconcilable Differences," *HRMagazine,* 44 (April 1999): 42–48.

72. Charles Fishman, "Leader Bob Moffat," *Fast Company,* no. 52 (November 2001): 102.

73. See David Dorsey, "The New Spirit of Work," *Fast Company,* no. 16 (August 1998): 125–134; and Jim Collins, "When Good Managers Manage Too Much," *Inc.,* 21 (April 1999): 31–32.

74. Gina Imperato, "MindSpring Does a Mind-Flip," *Fast Company,* no. 22 (February–March 1999): 40.

75. See Steve Rosenbush, "Braced to Best Microsoft, Others," *USA Today* (February 17, 1999): 3B; Ron Lieber, "First Jobs Aren't Child's Play," *Fast Company,* no. 25 (June 1999): 155–171; and Tammy D. Allen, Stacy E. McManus, and Joyce E. A. Russell, "Newcomer Socialization and Stress: Formal Peer Relationships as a Source of Support," *Journal of Vocational Behavior,* 54 (June 1999): 453–470.

76. Alan L. Wilkins, "The Culture Audit: A Tool for Understanding Organizations," *Organizational Dynamics,* 12 (Autumn 1983): 34–35.

77. Rebecca Ganzel, "Putting Out the Welcome Mat," *Training,* 35 (March 1998): 54. Also see Noel M. Tichy, "No Ordinary Boot Camp," *Harvard Business Review,* 79 (April 2001): 63–70; and Jeff Barbian, "Mark Spear," *Training,* 38 (October 2001): 34–38.

78. For the full story, see Robert F. Dennehy, "The Executive as Storyteller," *Management Review,* 88 (March 1999): 40–43; Beverly Kaye and Betsy Jacobson, "True Tales and Tall Tales: The Power of Organizational Storytelling," *Training & Development,* 53 (March 1999): 45–50; and Cathy Olofson, "To Transform Culture, Tap Emotion," *Fast Company,* no. 23 (April 1999): 54.

79. Alan L. Wilkins, "The Creation of Company Cultures: The Role of Stories and Human Resource Systems," *Human Resource Management,* 23 (Spring 1984): 43.

80. Adapted from Terrence E. Deal and Allan A. Kennedy, *Corporate Cultures: The Rites and Rituals of Corporate Life* (Reading, Mass.: Addison-Wesley, 1982), pp. 136–139. Also see Haidee E. Allerton, "Dysfunctional Checklist," *Training & Development,* 53 (June 1999): 10; and Jenny C. McCune, "Sorry, Wrong Executive," *Management Review,* 88 (October 1999): 16–21.

81. Eight tips for maintaining the strength of an organization's culture are presented in Trice and Beyer, *Cultures of Work Organizations,* pp. 378–391. Also see David W. De Long and Liam Fahey, "Diagnosing Cultural Barriers to Knowledge Management," *Academy of Management Executive,* 14 (November 2000): 113–127; Carol Lavin Bernick, "When Your Culture Needs a Makeover," *Harvard Business Review,* 79 (June 2001): 53–61; Lea Soupata, "Managing Culture for Competitive Advantage at United Parcel Service," *Journal of Organizational Excellence,* 20 (Summer 2001): 19–26; and Bill Munck, "Changing a Culture of Face Time," *Harvard Business Review,* 79 (November 2001): 125–131.

## Chapter 10

**Opening Quotation** "Sam Walton in His Own Words," *Fortune* (June 29, 1992): 104.

**Opening Case** Excerpted from Ilan Mochari, "It's All in the Details," *Inc.,* 24 (March 2002): 120–122. *Inc:* The Magazine for Growing Companies. Copyright 2002 by Bus. Innovator Group Resources/Inc. Reproduced with permission of Bus. Innovator Group Resources/Inc. in the format textbook via Copyright Clearance Center.

**Closing Case** Excerpted from Nancy K. Austin, "Tear Down the Walls," *Inc.,* 21 (April 1999), pp. 66–76. *Inc:* The Magazine for Growing Companies. Copyright 1999 by Bus. Innovator Group Resources/Inc. Reproduced with permission of Bus. Innovator Group Resources/Inc. in the format textbook via Copyright Clearance Center.

1. For research support, see Terry L. Amburgey and Tina Dacin, "As the Left Foot Follows the Right? The Dynamics of Strategic and Structural Change," *Academy of Management Journal,* 37 (December 1994): 1427–1452.

2. Michael Goold and Andrew Campbell, "Do You Have a Well-Designed Organization?" *Harvard Business Review,* 80 (March 2002): 117.

3. An interesting overview is Robert W. Keidel, "Rethinking Organizational Design," *Academy of Management Executive,* 8 (November 1994): 12–30. Also see D. Harold Doty, William H. Glick, and George P. Huber, "Fit, Equifinality, and Organizational Effectiveness: A Test of Two Configurational Theories," *Academy of Management Journal,* 36 (December 1993): 1196–1250.

4. See Tom Burns and G. M. Stalker, *The Management of Innovation* (London: Tavistock, 1961), Ch. 5.

5. See John A. Courtright, Gail T. Fairhurst, and L. Edna Rogers, "Interaction Patterns in Organic and Mechanistic Systems," *Academy of Management Journal,* 32 (December 1989): 773–802.

6. Ben Elgin, "Running the Tightest Ship on the Net," *Business Week* (January 29, 2001): 126.

7. Jenny C. McCune, "The Change Makers," *Management Review,* 88 (May 1999): 17. Also see Peter F. Drucker, "Change Leaders," *Inc.,* 21 (June 1999): 65–72.

8. For a complete summary of Woodward's findings, see Joan Woodward, *Industrial Organization: Theory and Practice* (London: Oxford University Press, 1965), Ch. 4.

9. Adapted from Paul R. Lawrence and Jay W. Lorsch, *Organization and Environment* (Homewood, Ill.: Irwin, 1967), p. 11. One new approach to organizational integration is presented in Eileen M. Van Aken, Dominic J. Monetta, and D. Scott Sink, "Affinity Groups: The Missing Link in Employee Involvement," *Organizational Dynamics,* 22 (Spring 1994): 38–54. Also see Anthony Lee Patti and James Patrick Gilbert, "Collocating New Product Development Teams: Why, When, Where, and How?" *Business Horizons,* 40 (November–December 1997): 59–64; and Gail Edmondson, "Where Science Is More Than Skin Deep," *Business Week* (June 28, 1999): 75.

10. Lawrence and Lorsch, *Organization and Environment,* p. 157.

11. A good update on integration is Susan Albers Mohrman, "Integrating Roles and Structure in the Lateral Organization," in *Organizing for the Future: The New Logic for Managing Complex Organizations,* eds. Jay R. Galbraith, Edward E. Lawler III, et al. (San Francisco: Jossey-Bass, 1993), pp. 109–141.

12. Cheryl Comeau-Kirschner, "The Push for Profits," *Management Review,* 88 (February 1999): 7.

13. For details, see John E. Ettlie and Ernesto M. Reza, "Organizational Integration and Process Innovation," *Academy of Management Journal* (October 1992): 759–827.

14. Roger O. Crockett, "Chris Galvin Shakes Things Up—Again," *Business Week* (May 28, 2001): 39.

15. See Marco Iansiti, "Shooting the Rapids: Managing Product Development in Turbulent Environments," *California Management Review,* 38 (Fall 1995): 37–58; and David A. Morand, "The Role of Behavioral Formality and Informality in the Enactment of Bureaucratic Versus Organic Organizations," *Academy of Management Review,* 20 (October 1995): 831–872.

16. James D. Thompson, *Organizations in Action* (New York: McGraw-Hill, 1967), p. 59.

17. Based in part on Jay R. Galbraith, *Designing Organizations: An Executive Briefing on Strategy, Structure, and Process* (San Francisco: Jossey-Bass, 1995): pp. 24–37.

18. Catherine Arnst, "A Freewheeling Youngster Named IBM," *Business Week* (May 3, 1993): 136.

19. IBM's turnaround is honored in Stuart Crainer, "The 50 Best Management Saves," *Management Review,* 88 (November 1999): 16–23.

20. Drawn from David W. Myers, "Hilton Shifts Focus to Gaming Operations," *Los Angeles Times* (May 12, 1993): D2.

21. Adapted from "Dial 800, Talk to Omaha," *Fortune* (January 29, 1990): 16; Rhonda Richards, "Technology Makes Omaha Hotel-Booking Capital," *USA Today* (April 7, 1994): 4B; and Robert D. Kaplan, *An Empire Wilderness: Travels into America's Future* (New York: Random House, 1998), p. 59.

22. Based on Andy Reinhardt and Seanna Browder, "Fly, Damn It, Fly," *Business Week* (November 9, 1998): 150–156. Also see Wim G. Biemans, "Marketing in the Twilight Zone," *Business Horizons,* 41 (November–December 1998): 69–76.

23. For more, see Michael Hammer and James Champy, *Reengineering the Corporation: A Manifesto for Business Revolution* (New York: HarperCollins, 1993); James Champy, *Reengineering Management: The Mandate for New Leadership* (New York: HarperBusiness, 1995); Dutch Holland and Sanjiv Kumar, "Getting Past the Obstacles to Successful Reengineering," *Business Horizons,* 38 (May–June 1995): 79–85; and Rob Duboff and Craig Carter, "Reengineering from the Outside In," *Management Review,* 84 (November 1995): 42–46.

24. See John A. Byrne, "The Horizontal Corporation," *Business Week* (December 20, 1993): 76–81; and Susan Sonnesyn Brooks, "Managing a Horizontal Revolution," *HRMagazine,* 40 (June 1995): 52–58.

25. Rahul Jacob, "The Struggle to Create an Organization for the 21st Century," *Fortune* (April 3, 1995): 91. For related reading, see Michael H. Martin, "Smart Managing," *Fortune* (February 2, 1998): 149–151; and David Stamps, "Enterprise Training: This Changes *Everything,*" *Training,* 36 (January 1999): 40–48.

26. David Kiley, "Coke Reorganizes; President Resigns," *USA Today* (March 5, 2001): 2B.

27. A sample of contingency design research is Richard A. D'Aveni and Anne Y. Ilinitch, "Complex Patterns of Vertical Integration in the Forest Products Industry: Systematic and Bankruptcy Risks," *Academy of Management Journal,* 35 (August 1992): 596–625.

28. For an extensive bibliography on this subject, see David D. Van Fleet and Arthur G. Bedeian, "A History of the Span of Management," *Academy of Management Review,* 2 (July 1977): 356–372.

29. L. Urwick, *The Elements of Administration* (New York: Harper & Row, 1944), pp. 52–53.

30. For details of this study, see James C. Worthy, "Organizational Structure and Employee Morale," *American Sociological Review,* 15 (April 1950): 169–179.

31. Drawn from C. W. Barkdull, "Span of Control—A Method of Evaluation," *Michigan Business Review,* 15 (May 1963): 25–32.

32. William H. Wagel, "Keeping the Organization Lean at Federal Express," *Personnel,* 64 (March 1987): 4–12.

33. Paul Kaestle, "A New Rationale for Organizational Structure," *Planning Review,* 18 (July–August 1990): 22. Also see Robert W. Keidel, "Triangular Design: A New Organizational Geometry," *Academy of Management Executive,* 4 (November 1990): 21–37.

34. William C. Symonds, "The Most Aggressive CEO," *Business Week* (May 28, 2001): 77.

35. For example, see Jeffrey Schmidt, "Breaking Down Fiefdoms," *Management Review,* 86 (January 1997): 45–49; and Michael E. Raynor and Joseph L. Bower, "Lead from the Center: How to Manage Divisions Dynamically," *Harvard Business Review,* 79 (May 2001): 92–100.

36. For a comprehensive research summary on centralization and organizational effectiveness, see George P. Huber, C. Chet Miller, and William H. Glick, "Developing More Encompassing Theories About Organizations: The Centralization-Effectiveness Relationship as an Example," *Organization Science,* 1 (1990): 11–40.

37. Based on William E. Rothschild, "How to Ensure the Continued Growth of Strategic Planning," *Journal of Business Strategy,* 1 (Summer 1980): 11–18.

38. Louise Lee, "Nordstrom Cleans Out Its Closets," *Business Week* (May 22, 2000): 105.

39. For complete details, see Anil K. Gupta, "SBU Strategies, Corporate-SBU Relations, and SBU Effectiveness in Strategy Implementation," *Academy of Management Journal,* 30 (September 1987): 477–500. Also see V. Govindarajan and Joseph Fisher, "Strategy, Control Systems, and Resource Sharing: Effects on Business-Unit Performance," *Academy of Management Journal,* 33 (June 1990): 259–285.

40. For details, see Meni Koslowsky, "Staff/Line Distinctions in Job and Organizational Commitment," *Journal of Occupational Psychology,* 63 (June 1990): 167–173. Also see Hillel Schmid, "Staff and Line Relationships Revisited: The Case of Community Service Agencies," *Public Personnel Management,* 19 (Spring 1990): 71–83.

41. Jay R. Galbraith and Edward E. Lawler III, "Challenges to the Established Order," in Galbraith, Lawler, et al., *Organizing for the Future,* p. 6. Also see Thomas A. Stewart, "Yikes! Deadwood Is Creeping Back," *Fortune* (August 18, 1997): 221–222; and "Are You a Partner with Line Management?" *Training,* 36 (January 1999): 26–27.

42. See Louis A. Allen, "The Line-Staff Relationship," *Management Record,* 17 (September 1955): 346–349, 374–376.

43. Ibid., p. 348.

44. See David I. Cleland, "Why Project Management?" *Business Horizons,* 7 (Winter 1964): 81–88. For a discussion of how project management evolved into matrix management, see David I. Cleland, "The Cultural Ambience of the Matrix Organization," *Management Review,* 70 (November 1981): 24–28, 37–39; and David I. Cleland, "Matrix Management (Part II): A Kaleidoscope of Organizational Systems," *Management Review,* 70 (December 1981): 48–56.

45. See Thomas A. Stewart, "The Corporate Jungle Spawns a New Species: The Project Manager," *Fortune,* (July 10, 1995): 179–180.

46. For a good overview, see Christopher A. Bartlett and Sumantra Ghoshal, "Matrix Management: Not a Structure, a Frame of Mind," *Harvard Business Review,* 68 (July–August 1990): 138–145.

47. An informative description of a successful matrix organization may be found in Ellen Kolton, "Team Players," *Inc.* (September 1984): 140–144.

48. See William F. Joyce, "Matrix Organization: A Social Experiment," *Academy of Management Journal,* 29 (September 1986): 536–561.

49. Drawn from Richard M. Hodgetts, "Leadership Techniques in the Project Organization," *Academy of Management Journal,* 11 (June 1968): 211–219. Also see Jeffrey K. Pinto and O. P. Kharbanda, *Successful Project Management: Leading Your Team to Success* (New York: Van Nostrand Reinhold, 1995).

50. Drawn from Susan G. Turner, Dawn R. Utley, and Jerry D. Westbrook, "Project Managers and Functional Managers: A Case Study of Job Satisfaction in a Matrix Organization," *Project Management Journal,* 29 (September 1998): 11–19.

51. See "An About-Face in TI's Culture," *Business Week* (July 5, 1982): 77.

52. Data from Erik W. Larson and David H. Gobeli, "Matrix Management: Contradictions and Insights," *California Management Review,* 29 (Summer 1987): 126–138. Also see Lawton R. Burns and Douglas R. Wholey, "Adoption and Abandonment of Matrix Management Programs: Effects of Organizational Characteristics and Interorganizational Networks," *Academy of Management Journal,* 36 (February 1993): 106–138; and Richard E. Anderson, "Matrix Redux," *Business Horizons,* 37 (November–December 1994): 6–10.

53. See Larry Bossidy, "The Job No CEO Should Delegate," *Harvard Business Review,* 79 (March 2001): 46–49; and Sharon Gazda, "The Art of Delegating," *HRMagazine,* 47 (January 2002): 75–78.

54. Adapted from Marion E. Haynes, "Delegation: There's More to It Than Letting Someone Else Do It!" *Supervisory Management,* 25 (January 1980): 9–15. Three types of delegation—incremental, sequential, and functional—are discussed in William R. Tracey, "Deft Delegation: Multiplying Your Effectiveness," *Personnel,* 65 (February 1988): 36–42. Also see Pinto and Kharbanda, *Successful Project Management,* pp. 103–107.

55. Delegation styles of selected U.S. presidents are examined in Edward J. Mayo and Lance P. Jarvis, "Delegation 101: Lessons from the White House," *Business Horizons,* 31 (September–October 1988): 2–12.

56. Alex Taylor III, "Iacocca's Time of Trouble," *Fortune* (March 14, 1988): 79, 81.

57. Andrew S. Grove, *High Output Management* (New York: Random House, 1983), p. 60. Also see Wilson Harrell, "Your Biggest Mistake," *Success,* 43 (March 1996): 88.

58. For interesting facts about delegating, see "Top Dogs," *Fortune* (September 30, 1996): 189; and Bill Leonard, "Good Assistants Make Managers More Efficient," *HRMagazine,* 44 (February 1999): 12.

59. "How Conservatism Wins in the Hottest Market," *Business Week* (January 17, 1977): 43.

60. Adapted from William H. Newman, "Overcoming Obstacles to Effective Delegation," *Management Review,* 45 (January 1956): 36–41; and from Eugene Raudsepp, "Why Supervisors Don't Delegate," *Supervision,* 41 (May 1979): 12–15. Also see Gary Yukl and Ping Ping Fu, "Determinants of Delegation and Consultation by Managers," *Journal of Organizational Behavior,* 20 (March 1999): 219–232.

61. Practical tips on delegation can be found in Douglas Anderson, "Supervisors and the Hesitate to Delegate Syndrome," *Supervision,* 53 (November 1992): 9–11; and Michael C. Dennis, "Only Superman Didn't Delegate," *Business Credit,* 95 (February 1993): 41.

62. For more on initiative, see Michael Frese, Wolfgang Kring, Andrea Soose, and Jeanette Zempel, "Personal Initiative at Work: Differences between East and West Germany," *Academy of Management Journal,* 39 (February 1996): 37–63; and Alan L. Frohman, "Igniting Organizational Change from Below: The Power of Personal Initiative," *Organizational Dynamics,* 25 (Winter 1997): 39–53.

63. Peter F. Drucker, *Managing the Non-Profit Organization* (New York: HarperCollins, 1990), p. 117. Also see Jim Holt, "Management Master," *Management Review,* 88 (November 1999): 15.

64. See, for example, Warren G. Bennis, *Changing Organizations* (New York: McGraw-Hill, 1966).

65. As quoted in Noel M. Tichy and Stratford Sherman, *Control Your Destiny or Someone Else Will: How Jack Welch Is Making General Electric the World's Most Competitive Corporation* (New York: Doubleday, 1993), p. 21. Also see Peter Coy, "The 21st Century Corporation: The Creative Economy," *Business Week* (August 28, 2000): 76–82.

66. Brian Dumaine, "The New Non-Manager Managers," *Fortune* (February 22, 1993): 80. Also see Leonard R. Sayles, "Doing Things Right: A New Imperative for Middle Managers," *Organizational Dynamics,* 21 (Spring 1993): 5–14.

67. Data from Joseph Weber, "Farewell, Fast Track," *Business Week* (December 10, 1990): 192–200.

68. Data from Ricardo Sookdeo, "Why to Buy Big in Bad Times," *Fortune* (July 27, 1992): 96.

69. Edward E. Lawler III, "Substitutes for Hierarchy," *Organizational Dynamics,* 17 (Summer 1988): 15. For a good critique of hierarchy and teams, see "The Team Troubles That Won't Go Away," *Training,* 31 (August 1994): 25–34.

70. Data from David Woodruff, "Ford Has a Better Idea: Let Someone Else Have the Idea," *Business Week* (April 30, 1990): 116–117. Also see Wendy Zellner, "Go-Go Goliaths," *Business Week* (February 13, 1995): 64–70.

71. See Peter F. Drucker, "The Coming of the New Organization," *Harvard Business Review,* 66 (January–February 1988): 45–53. Teams are also discussed in Lynda McDermott, Bill Waite, and Nolan Brawley, "Putting Together a World-Class Team," *Training & Development,* 53 (January 1999): 47–51; Kim Kiser, "Building a Virtual Team," *Training,* 36 (March 1999): 34; and Donald Gerwin, "Team Empowerment in New Product Development," *Business Horizons,* 42 (July–August 1999): 29–36.

72. See Richard Z. Gooding and John A. Wagner III, "A Meta-Analytic Review of the Relationship Between Size and Performance: The Productivity and Efficiency of Organizations and Their Subunits," *Administrative Science Quarterly,* 30 (December 1985): 462–481; Edward E. Lawler III, "Rethinking Organization Size," *Organizational Dynamics,* 26 (Autumn 1997): 24–35; Charles Handy, *The Hungry Spirit* (New York: Broadway Books, 1998), pp. 107–108; and Oren Harari, "Too Big for Your Own Good?" *Management Review,* 87 (November 1998): 30–32.

73. John A. Byrne, "Is Your Company Too Big?" *Business Week* (March 27, 1989): 92. For more on Parker Hannifin, see Christopher Palmeri, "A Process That Never Ends," *Forbes* (December 21, 1992): 52–55. Small units with Dell Computer Corp. are discussed in Carla Joinson, "Moving at the Speed of Dell," *HRMagazine,* 44 (April 1999): 50–56.

74. As quoted in Marshall Loeb, "Jack Welch Lets Fly on Budgets, Bonuses, and Buddy Boards," *Fortune* (May 29, 1995): 145.

75. See Gregory G. Dess, Abdul M. A. Rasheed, Kevin J. McLaughlin, and Richard L. Priem, "The New Corporate Architecture," *Academy of Management Executive,* 9 (August 1995): 7–20; Alan Hurwitz, "Organizational Structures for the 'New World Order,'" *Business Horizons,* 39 (May–June 1996): 5–14; and James Brian Quinn, Philip Anderson, and Sydney Finkelstein, "Leveraging Intellect," *Academy of Management Executive,* 10 (August 1996): 7–27.

76. See Anthony M. Townsend, Samuel M. DeMarie, and Anthony R. Hendrickson, "Virtual Teams: Technology and the Workplace of the Future," *Academy of Management Executive,* 12 (August 1998): 17–29; and Russ Forrester and Allan B. Drexler, "A Model for Team-Based Organization Performance," *Academy of Management Executive,* 13 (August 1999): 36–49.

77. Toby Tetenbaum and Hilary Tetenbaum, "Office 2000: Tear Down the Walls," *Training,* 37 (February 2000): 60.

78. A good resource book is William G. Dyer, *Team Building: Current Issues and New Alternatives,* 3rd ed. (Reading, Mass.: Addison-Wesley, 1995).

79. See Gary Hamel and Jeff Sampler, "The E-Corporation," *Fortune* (December 7, 1998): 80–92; Randall J. Alford, "Going Virtual, Getting Real," *Training & Development,* 53 (January 1999): 34–44; William B. Werther Jr., "Structure-Driven Strategy and Virtual Organization Design," *Business Horizons,* 42 (March–April 1999): 13–18; Steve Hamm, "E-Biz: Down But Hardly Out," *Business Week* (March 26, 2001): 126–130; Melissa A. Schilling and H. Kevin Steensma, "The Use of Modular Organizational Forms: An Industry-Level Analysis," *Academy of Management Journal,* 44 (December 2001): 1149–1168; and John A. Byrne and Ben Elgin, "Cisco: Behind the Hype," *Business Week* (January 21, 2002): 54–61.

80. Otis Port, "Customers Move into the Driver's Seat," *Business Week* (October 4, 1999): 104, 106.

## Chapter 11

**Opening Quotation**   Jim Collins, *Good to Great: Why Some Companies Make the Leap and Others Don't* (New York: HarperBusiness, 2001), p. 42.

**Opening Case**   Ann Harrington, "How Welfare Worked for T. J. Maxx," *Fortune* (November 13, 2000): 453–456. Copyright © 2000 Time Inc. Reprinted by permission.

**Closing Case**   Republished with permission of *Training* from Heather Johnson, "Training Pays Off at Paychex," *Training,* 38 (December 2001): 50–53. Permission conveyed through Copyright Clearance Center.

1. Drawn from "Peterson Thrives on HR Challenges," *HRMagazine,* 43 (September 1998): 98, 100.

2. See Fred Luthans, Paul A. Marsnik, and Kyle W. Luthans, "A Contingency Matrix Approach to IHRM," *Human Resource Management,* 36 (Summer 1997): 183–199; and Johngseok Bae and John J. Lawler, "Organizational and HRM Strategies in Korea: Impact on Firm Performance in an Emerging Economy," *Academy of Management Journal,* 43 (June 2000): 502–517.

3. As quoted in Shaun McKinnon, "New Faces, Old Methods," *The Arizona Republic* (July 29, 2001): D11.

4. Jeffrey B. Arthur, "Effects of Human Resource Systems on Manufacturing Performance and Turnover," *Academy of Management Journal,* 37 (June 1994): 670.

5. Gerald R. Ferris, ed., *Research in Personnel and Human Resources Management: Strategic Human Resources Management in the Twenty-First Century* (Stamford, Conn.: JAI Press, 1999); Denise M. Rousseau and Michael B. Arthur, "The Boundaryless Human Resource Function: Building Agency and Community in the New Economic Era," *Organizational Dynamics,* 27 (Spring 1999): 7–18; and Frank Jossi, "Taking the E-HR Plunge," *HRMagazine,* 46 (September 2001): 96–103.

6. Bill Leonard, "Straight Talk," *HRMagazine,* 47 (January 2002): 46–51. Also see Carla Joinson, "HR's Seat on the Selection Committee," *HRMagazine,* 45 (April 2000): 82–90.

7. Data from Lin Grensing-Pophal, "Taking Your Seat 'At the Table,'" *HRMagazine,* 44 (March 1999): 90–96. Also see Lin Grensing-Pophal, "What's Your HR Creed?" *HRMagazine,* 46 (June 2001): 145–153.

8. Brian E. Becker, Mark A. Huselid, and Dave Ulrich, *The HR Scorecard: Linking People, Strategy, and Performance* (Boston: Harvard Business School Press, 2001): p. 4.

9. For more see David Stamps, "Measuring Minds," *Training,* 37 (May 2000): 76–84.

10. "The 100 Best Companies to Work For," *Fortune* (February 4, 2002): 84. For more stories about companies helping schools, see George Anders, "The *Reeducation of Silicon Valley," Fast Company,* no. 57 (April 2002): 100–108.

11. Scott Adams, "Dilbert's Management Handbook," *Fortune* (May 13, 1996): 99, 108.

12. As quoted in John Huey, "Outlaw Flyboy CEOs," *Fortune* (November 13, 2000): 246.

13. Data from Jeffrey Pfeffer, *The Human Equation: Building Profits by Putting People First* (Boston: Harvard Business School Press, 1998); and Jeffrey Pfeffer and John F. Veiga, "Putting People First for Organizational Success," *Academy of Management Executive,* 13 (May 1999): 37–48. Also see James P. Guthrie, "High-Involvement Work Practices, Turnover, and Productivity: Evidence from New Zealand," *Academy of Management Journal,* 44 (February 2001): 180–190; and Becker, Huselid, and Ulrich, *The HR Scorecard,* Table 1-3, pp. 16–17.

14. See Collins, *Good to Great;* and Jim Collins, "Good to Great," *Fast Company,* no. 51 (October 2001): 90–104.

15. Based on "What Are CEOs Thinking?" *USA Today* (May 3, 2001): 1B. Also see Alison Stein Wellner, "Employers Join Forces to Recruit," *HRMagazine,* 46 (January 2001): 86–96; Peter Cappelli, "Making the Most of On-Line Recruiting," *Harvard Business Review,* 79 (March 2001): 139–146; Jeffrey Pfeffer, "Fighting the War for Talent Is Hazardous to Your Organization's Health," *Organizational Dynamics,* 29 (Spring 2001): 248–259; and Jim Meade, "Recruiting Software Can Streamline Hiring Process," *HRMagazine,* 46 (September 2001): 139–140.

16. As quoted in Ruth E. Thaler-Carter, "Diversify Your Recruitment Advertising," *HRMagazine,* 46 (June 2001): 95.

17. See "America's 50 Best Companies for Minorities," *Fortune* (July 9, 2001): 122–128; or click on "Best for Minorities," at **www.fortune.com.**

18. Ann Harrington, "Make That Switch," *Fortune* (February 4, 2002): 1 at **www.fortune.com/careers.** For more job-hunting tips, see Alison Overholt, "Job Search 101," *Fast Company,* no. 57 (April 2002): 122–125.

19. For more, see Timothy S. Bland and Sue S. Stalcup, "Build a Legal Employment Application," *HRMagazine,* 44 (March 1999): 129–133. For an update on EEO in Japan, see Emily Thornton, "Make Way for Women with Welding Guns," *Business Week* (April 19, 1999): 54.

20. Jim Hopkins, "Small Businesses Take Steps to Protect Themselves," *USA Today* (November 14, 2001): 6B. Also see Alynda Wheat, "Your Ears Are Burning," *Fortune* (March 4, 2002): 226.

21. Merry Mayer, "Background Checks in Focus," *HRMagazine,* 47 (January 2002): 59. Also see Stephanie Armour, "Employers Scrutinize Workers More Closely," *USA Today* (October 18, 2001): 3B; and Ann Davis, "Employers Dig Deep into Workers' Pasts, Citing Terrorism Fears," *The Wall Street Journal* (March 12, 2002): A1, A12.

22. See Sharon Leonard, "The Demise of Job Descriptions," *HRMagazine,* 45 (August 2000): 184; and Carla Joinson, "Refocusing Job Descriptions," *HRMagazine,* 46 (January 2001): 66–72.

23. David A. Brookmire and Amy A. Burton, "A Format for Packaging Your Affirmative Action Program," *Personnel Journal,* 57 (June 1978): 294. Also see Karen C. Cash and George R. Gray, "A Framework for Accommodating Religion and Spirituality in the Workplace," *Academy of Management Executive,* 14 (August 2000): 124–133; and Michael Barrier, "An Age-Old Problem," *HRMagazine,* 47 (March 2002): 34–37.

24. See Marc Hequet, "Out at Work," *Training,* 32 (June 1995): 53–58; Dale Kurschner, "The Right to Be Oneself," *Business Ethics,* 10 (May–June 1996): 29; and Kenneth A. Kovach and Peter E. Millspaugh, "Employment Nondiscrimination Act: On the Cutting Edge of Public Policy," *Business Horizons,* 39 (July–August 1996): 65–73.

25. Data from Theresa Howard, "Coke Settles Bias Lawsuit for $192.5M," *USA Today* (November 17, 2000): 1B; and Stephanie Armour, "Bias Suits Put Spotlight on Workplace Diversity," *USA Today* (January 10, 2001): 1B–2B. Also see Gerald E. Calvasina, Richard V. Calvasina and Eugene J. Calvasina, "Management and the EEOC," *Business Horizons,* 43 (July–August 2000): 3–7; and Nancy Hatch Woodward, "Help from the EEOC?" *HRMagazine,* 46 (September 2001): 123–128.

26. See Charlene Marmer Solomon, "Frequently Asked Questions About Affirmative Action," *Personnel Journal,* 74 (August 1995): 61; and Catherine Yang and Mike McNamee, "A Hand Up, but Not a Handout," *Business Week* (March 27, 1995): 70, 72.

27. For instructive reading on EEO/AAP, see Jere W. Morehead and Peter J. Shedd, "Civil Rights and Affirmative Action: Revolution or Fine-Tuning?" *Business Horizons,* 33 (September–October 1990): 53–60; James P. Pinkerton, "Why Affirmative Action Won't Die," *Fortune* (November 13, 1995): 191–198; and Teresa Brady, "A New Twist on the 'Old' Age Discrimination Act," *Management Review,* 85 (December 1996): 38–39.

28. For related discussion, see Reginald D. Dickson, "The Business of Equal Opportunity," *Harvard Business Review,* 70 (January–February 1992): 46–53; "Debate: Can Equal Opportunity Be Made More Equal?" *Harvard Business Review,* 70 (March–April 1992): 138–158; Jonathan Alter, "Affirmative Ambivalence," *Newsweek* (March 27, 1995): 26; and Joanne D. Leck, David M. Saunders, and Micheline Charbonneau, "Affirmative Action Programs: An Organizational Justice Perspective," *Journal of Organizational Behavior,* 17 (January 1996): 79–89.

29. Julia Lawlor, "Study: Affirmative-Action Hires' Abilities Doubted," *USA Today* (August 31, 1992): 3B. The complete study is reported in Madeline E. Heilman, Caryn J. Block, and Jonathan A. Lucas, "Presumed Incompetent? Stigmatization and Affirmative Action Efforts," *Journal of Applied Psychology,* 77 (August 1992): 536–554. Also see Beverly L. Little, William D. Murry, and James C. Wimbush, "Perceptions of Workplace Affirmative Action Plans," *Group & Organization Management,* 23 (March 1998): 27–47.

30. Yehouda Shenhav, "Entrance of Blacks and Women into Managerial Positions in Scientific and Engineering Occupations: A Longitudinal Analysis," *Academy of Management Journal,* 35 (October 1992): 897. Also see Mike McNamee, "The Proof Is in Performance," *Business Week* (July 15, 1996): 22. A female executive's view can be found in "Helayne Spivak," *Fast Company,* no. 27 (September 1999): 113.

31. For example, see Jonathan Kaufman, "White Men Shake Off That Losing Feeling on Affirmative Action," *The Wall Street Journal* (September 5, 1996): A1, A4.

32. R. Roosevelt Thomas Jr., "From Affirmative Action to Affirming Diversity," *Harvard Business Review,* 68 (March–April 1990): 114. For an interview with R. Roosevelt Thomas, see Ellen Neuborne, "Diversity Challenges Many Companies," *USA Today* (November 18, 1996): 10B. Also see William Atkinson, "Bringing Diversity to White Men," *HRMagazine,* 46 (September 2001): 76–83.

33. For more on diversity, see Jim Adamson, "How Denny's Went from Icon of Racism to Diversity Award Winner," *Journal of Organizational Excellence,* 20 (Winter 2000): 55–68; Robert J. Grossman, "Is Diversity Working?" *HRMagazine,* 45 (March 2000): 46–50; Alison Wellner, "How Do You Spell Diversity?" *Training,* 37 (April 2000): 34–38; Cora Daniels, "Too Diverse for Our Own Good?" *Fortune* (July 9, 2001): 116; Lin Grensing-Pophal, "A Balancing Act on Diversity Audits," *HRMagazine,* 46 (November 2001): 87–95; and Jennifer Merritt, "Wanted: A Campus That Looks Like America," *Business Week* (March 11, 2002): 56, 58.

34. Carol Kleiman, "'New Diversity' Is Nothing New to Chicago Advertising Firm," *The Arizona Republic* (May 16, 1993): F2. Also see Jeremy Kahn, "Diversity Trumps the Downturn," *Fortune* (July 9, 2001): 114–116; and Orlando C. Richard, "Racial Diversity, Business Strategy, and Firm Performance: A Resource-Based View," *Academy of Management Journal,* 43 (April 2000): 164–177.

35. Joel Schettler, "Equal Access to All," *Training,* 39 (January 2002): 44.

36. For an inspiring case study of a blind sports reporter, see Robert Davis, "Friends 'Know of Nothing He Can't Do,'" *USA Today* (October 25, 1999): 10A. Also see Sandra Block, "Deaf Investors Make Themselves Heard," *USA Today* (December 6, 2000): 3B.

37. For more, see Cheryl Comeau-Kirschner, "New ADA Guidelines," *Management Review,* 88 (April 1999): 6; Robert H. Schwartz, Frederick R. Post, and Jack L. Simonetti, "The ADA and the Mentally Disabled: What Must Firms Do?" *Business Horizons,* 43 (July–August 2000): 52–58; and Eric V. Neumann and Brian H. Kleiner, "How to Accommodate Disabilities Under ADA," *Nonprofit World,* 18 (September–October 2000): 29–33.

38. Gene Koretz, "Dubious Aid for the Disabled," *Business Week* (November 9, 1998): 30. Also see David C. Baldridge and John F. Veiga, "Toward a Greater Understanding of the Willingness to Request an Accommodation: Can Requesters' Beliefs Disable the Americans with Disabilities Act?" *Academy of Management Review,* 26 (January 2001): 85–99; and Susan J. Wells, "Is the ADA Working?" *HRMagazine,* 46 (April 2001): 38–46.

39. Susan B. Garland, "Protecting the Disabled Won't Cripple Business," *Business Week* (April 26, 1999): 73.

40. See John Williams, "Enabling Technologies," *Business Week* (March 20, 2000): 68, 70; and Otis Port, "Artificial Eyes, Turbine Hearts," *Business Week* (March 20, 2000): 72–73.

41. See Michael P. Cronin, "This Is a Test," *Inc.,* 15 (August 1993): 64–68; Stephanie Armour, "Test? Forget the Test—You're Hired," *USA Today* (August 8, 2000): 1B; Matt Murray, "More Help, More Security, Less Testing," *The Wall Street Journal Sunday* (May 27, 2001): D7; and Dave Patel, "Testing, Testing, Testing," *HRMagazine,* 47 (February 2002): 112.

42. See Scott B. Parry, "How to Validate an Assessment Tool," *Training,* 30 (April 1993): 37–42.

43. See Deniz S. Ones, Chockalingam Viswesvaran, and Frank L. Schmidt, "Comprehensive Meta-Analysis of Integrity Test Validities: Findings and Implications for Personnel Selection and Theories of Job Performance," *Journal of Applied Psychology,* 78 (August 1993): 679–703; Kevin R. Murphy, "Why Pre-Employment Alcohol Testing Is Such a Bad Idea," *Business Horizons,* 38 (September–October 1995): 69–74; and Jenny C. McCune, "Testing, Testing 1—2—3," *Management Review,* 85 (January 1996): 50–52; Deniz S. Ones and Chockalingam Viswesvaran, "Gender, Age, and Race Differences on Overt Integrity Tests: Results Across Four Large-Scale Job Applicant Data Sets," *Journal of Applied Psychology,* 83 (February 1998): 35–42; Kevin Johnson, "Government Agencies See Truth in Polygraphs," *USA Today* (April 5, 1999): 11A; Bronwyn Fryer, "DNA: Handle with Care," *Harvard Business Review,* 79 (April 2001): 30, 32; Steve Bates, "Science Friction," *HRMagazine,* 46 (July 2001): 34–44; and Steve Bates, "Personality Counts," *HRMagazine,* 47 (February 2002): 28–34.

44. "Structured Interviewing: Avoiding Selection Problems," by Elliott D. Pursell, Michael A. Campion, and Sarah R. Gaylord, copyright November 1980. Reprinted with permission of *Personnel Journal,* Costa Mesa, Calif.; all rights reserved.

45. Barbara Whitaker Shimko, "New Breed Workers Need New Yardsticks," *Business Horizons,* 33 (November–December 1990): 35–36. For related research, see Allen I. Huffcutt and Philip L. Roth, "Racial Group Differences in Employment Interview Evaluations," *Journal of Applied Psychology,* 83 (April 1998): 179–189.

46. Practical tips on interviewing can be found in "12 Ways to Keep Good People," *Training,* 36 (April 1999): 19; Claudio Fernandez-Araoz, "Hiring Without Firing," *Harvard Business Review,* 77 (July–August 1999): 109–120; and Jim Kennedy, "What to Do When Job Applicants Tell Tales of Invented Lives," *Training,* 36 (October 1999): 110–114.

47. Based on Pursell et al., "Structured Interviewing."

48. Based on Bruce Bloom, "Behavioral Interviewing: The Future Direction and Focus of the Employment Interview." Paper presented to the Midwest Business Administration Association, Chicago (March 27, 1998). Also see Stephanie Armour, "Job Seekers Get Put Through the Wringer," *USA Today* (August 17, 2001): 1B.

49. Del J. Still, *High Impact Hiring: How to Interview and Select Outstanding Employees,* 2nd ed., rev. (Dana Point, Calif.: Management Development Systems, 2001), pp. 53–54 (emphasis added).

50. Other interview techniques are discussed in Martha Frase-Blunt, "Games Interviewers Play," *HRMagazine,* 46 (January 2001): 106–112; Mike Frost, "Video Interviewing: Not Yet Ready for Prime Time," *HRMagazine,* 46 (August 2001): 93–98; and Martha Frase-Blunt, "Peering into an Interview," *HRMagazine,* 46 (December 2001): 71–77.

51. Data from David Stamps, "Performance Appraisals: Out of Sync and as Unpopular as Ever," *Training,* 32 (August 1995): 16. Also see Tom Coens and Mary Jenkins, *Abolishing Performance Appraisals: Why They Backfire and What to Do Instead* (San Francisco: Berrett-Koehler, 2000).

52. Tammy Galvin, "The Weakest Link," *Training,* 38 (December 2001): 8. Also see Lin Grensing-Pophal, "Motivate Managers to Review Performance," *HRMagazine,* 46 (March 2001): 44–48.

53. Data from "What to Do with an Egg-Sucking Dog?" *Training,* 33 (October 1996): 17–21.

54. See Karen McKirchy, *Powerful Performance Appraisals: How to Set Expectations and Work Together to Improve Performance* (Franklin Lakes, N.J.: Career Press, 1998); and Carla Joinson, "Making Sure Employees Measure Up," *HRMagazine,* 46 (March 2001): 36–41.

55. For EEOC guidelines during performance appraisal, see William S. Swan and Philip Margulies, *How to Do a Superior Performance Appraisal* (New York: Wiley, 1991).

56. Adapted from Hubert S. Field and William H. Holley, "The Relationship of Performance Appraisal System Characteristics to Verdicts in Selected Employment Discrimination Cases," *Academy of Management Journal,* 25 (June 1982): 392–406. A more recent analysis of 51 cases that derived similar criteria can be found in Gerald V. Barrett and Mary C. Kernan, "Performance Appraisal and Terminations: A Review of Court Decisions Since *Brito v. Zia* with Implications for Personnel Practices," *Personnel Psychology,* 40 (Autumn 1987): 489–503.

57. For more, see Dick Grote, "Painless Performance Appraisals Focus on Results, Behaviors," *HRMagazine,* 43 (October 1998): 52–58.

58. For related research, see Todd J. Maurer, Jerry K. Palmer, and Donna K. Ashe, "Diaries, Checklists, Evaluations, and Contrast Effects in Measurement of Behavior," *Journal of Applied Psychology,* 78 (April 1993): 226–231.

59. Alan M. Webber, "How Business Is a Lot Like Life," *Fast Company,* no. 45 (April 2001): 135.

60. Matthew Boyle, "Performance Reviews: Perilous Curves Ahead," *Fortune* (May 28, 2001): 187. Also see Del Jones, "More Firms Cut Workers Ranked at Bottom to Make Way for Talent," *USA Today* (May 30, 2001): 1B–2B.

61. See David Kiley and Del Jones, "Ford Alters Worker Evaluation Process," *USA Today* (July 11, 2001): 1B; and Earle Eldridge, "Ford Settles 2 Lawsuits by White Male Workers," *USA Today* (December 19, 2001): 3B.

62. See Jai Ghorpade, "Managing Five Paradoxes of 360-Degree Feedback," *Academy of Management Executive,* 14 (February 2000): 140–150; Angelo S. DeNisi and Avraham N. Kluger, "Feedback Effectiveness: Can 360-Degree Appraisals Be Improved?" *Academy of Management Executive,* 14 (February 2000): 129–139; John Day, "Simple, Strong Team Ratings," *HRMagazine,* 45 (September 2000): 159–161; and Suzanne G. Scott and Walter O. Einstein, "Strategic Performance Appraisal in Team-Based Organizations: One Size Does Not Fit All," *Academy of Management Executive,* 15 (May 2001): 107–116.

63. See David A. Waldman, Leanne E. Atwater, and David Antonioni, "Has 360 Degree Feedback Gone Amok?" *Academy of Management Executive,* 12 (May 1998): 86–94; and Dennis E. Coates, "Don't Tie 360 Feedback to Pay," *Training,* 35 (September 1998): 68–78.

64. Data from Tammy Galvin, "2001 Industry Report," *Training,* 38 (October 2001): 42.

65. Frederick Kuri, "Basic-Skills Training Boosts Productivity," *HRMagazine,* 41 (September 1996): 77.

66. Data from a U.S. Department of Education literacy study of 13,600 people age 16 and older, as cited in Anna Mulrine, "Can You Read This Story? Half of All U.S. Adults Can't," *The Christian Science Monitor* (September 10, 1993): 2.

67. See Galvin, "2001 Industry Report," pp. 40–75.

68. See Lynn Miller, "Six Signs of Successful E-Learning Initiatives," *HRMagazine,* 46 (October 2001): 12; and Kathryn Tyler, "Take E-Learning to the Next Step," *HRMagazine,* 47 (February 2002): 56–61.

69. Kenneth N. Wexley and Gary P. Latham, *Developing and Training Human Resources in Organizations* (Glenview, Ill.: Scott, Foresman, 1981): 75–77.

70. Ibid., p. 77. Also see Diana Hird, "What Makes a Training Program Good?" *Training,* 37 (June 2000): 48–52.

71. Training program evaluation is covered in "Why Training Doesn't Work," *Training,* 35 (February 1998): 24; Donna J. Abernathy, "Thinking Outside the Evaluation Box," *Training & Development,* 53 (February 1999): 19–23; Dean R. Spitzer, "Embracing Evaluation," *Training,* 36 (June 1999): 42–47; Steve Thomas, "ROK Science," *Training,* 38 (December 2001):

72; and Liz Simpson, "Great Expectations," *Training,* 39 (February 2002): 40–44.

72. See Susan Crawford, "A Brief History of Sexual Harassment Law," *Training,* 31 (August 1994): 46–49; Kenneth M. Jarin and Ellen K. Pomfret, "New Rules for Same Sex Harassment," *HRMagazine,* 43 (June 1998): 114–123; Gerald L. Maatman Jr., "A Global View of Sexual Harassment," *HRMagazine,* 45 (July 2000): 151–158; and Nathan W. Janove, "Sexual Harassment and the Three Big Surprises," *HRMagazine,* 46 (November 2001): 123–130.

73. "Sex by the Numbers," *Time* (March 8, 1993): 21.

74. "Dow Chemical Fires 50 for Porno E-Mail," *USA Today* (July 28, 2000): 1B.

75. Data from Tamara Henry, "Sexual Harassment Pervades Schools, Study Says," *USA Today* (July 23, 1996): 8B. Also see John Tuohy, "Sex Discrimination Infects Med Schools," *USA Today* (June 7, 2000): 8D.

76. For a list of verbal and nonverbal forms of general harassment, see R. Bruce McAfee and Diana L. Deadrick, "Teach Employees to Just Say 'No!'" *HRMagazine,* 41 (February 1996): 86–89.

77. For details, see David E. Terpstra and Douglas D. Baker, "Outcomes of Federal Court Decisions on Sexual Harassment," *Academy of Management Journal,* 35 (March 1992): 181–190. Also see Jonathan A. Segal, "HR as Judge, Jury, Prosecutor and Defender," *HRMagazine,* 46 (October 2001): 141–154.

78. Sexual harassment training videos are reviewed in Kathryn Gravdal, "Screening for Harassment," *HRMagazine,* 45 (May 2000): 114–124.

79. Data from Brian O'Reilly, "In a Dry Era You Can Still Be Trapped by Drinking," *Fortune* (March 6, 1995): 167–177; and Marilyn Chase, "Finding Ways to Reach an Alcoholic Who Has Elaborate Defenses," *The Wall Street Journal* (October 23, 1995): B1.

80. "Volunteers to Test Alcoholism Treatments," *USA Today* (April 11, 2001): 7D. Also see Lauren M. Bernardi, "Alcohol and Employees: Risks and Responsibilities," *Canadian Manager,* 26 (Summer 2001): 17–18.

81. James A. Belohlav and Paul O. Popp, "Employee Substance Abuse: Epidemic of the Eighties," *Business Horizons,* 26 (July–August 1983): 29.

82. Matthew Boyle, "The New E-Workplace," *Fortune* (October 1, 2001): 176.

83. Data from Robert Davis, "Demands, Isolation of Dentistry Open Gates to Drug Addiction," *USA Today* (April 15, 1999): 1A–2A; and Laura Meckler, "Seven in Ten Drug Users Work Full-Time," **womenconnect.com** (September 9, 1999).

84. Based on Janice Castro, "Battling the Enemy Within," *Time* (March 17, 1986): 52–61; and Peter Corbett, "Bush on Drug War: 'Failure Not Option,'" *The Arizona Republic* (April 9, 1999): E1, E3.

85. Data from Aja Whitaker, "Tight Labor Market Could Mean More Drug Abuse," *Management Review,* 88 (October 1999): 8. Also see Donna Leinwand, "Study: Drugs Cost U.S. $400B," *USA Today* (March 9, 2001): 10A.

86. See Jonathan A. Segal, "Drugs, Alcohol and the ADA," *HRMagazine,* 37 (December 1992): 73–76.

87. Janet Deming, "Drug-Free Workplace Is Good Business," *HRMagazine,* 35 (April 1990): 61.

88. See Louisa Wah, "Treatment vs. Termination," *Management Review,* 87 (April 1998): 8.

89. Ruby M. Yandrick, "The EAP Struggle: Counselors or Referrers?" *HRMagazine,* 43 (August 1998): 90–96; Jane Easter Bahls, "Handle with Care," *HRMagazine,* 44 (March 1999): 60–66; Lin Grensing-Pophal, "Workplace Chaplains," *HRMagazine,* 45 (August 2000): 54–62; and Bill Leonard, "EAPs Pushed to the Limit Following the Terrorist Attacks," *HRMagazine,* 46 (December 2001): 25.

90. Stuart Feldman, "Today's EAPs Make the Grade," *Personnel,* 68 (February 1991): 3.

## Chapter 12

**Opening Quotation**  Laurence J. Peter, *Peter's Quotations* (New York: Bantam, 1977), p. 100.

**Opening Case**  Excerpted from Del Jones, "Ideas Can Get Lost in the Translation," *USA Today* (October 2, 2001): 6B. Copyright 2001, *USA Today.* Reprinted with permission.

**Closing Case**  Robert I. Stevens, "The Case of the Errant Messenger," *Journal of Systems Management,* 35 (July 1984): 42. Reprinted by permission of the author, Robert I. Stevens.

1. For example, see Mary Young and James E. Post, "Managing to Communicate, Communicating to Manage: How Leading Companies Communicate with Employees," *Organizational Dynamics,* 22 (Summer 1993): 31–43; and Ale Smidts, Ad Th. H. Pruyn, and Cees B. M. van Riel, "The Impact of Employee Communication and Perceived External Prestige on Organizational Identification," *Academy of Management Journal,* 49 (October 2001): 1051–1062.

2. See Laurence Prusak and Don Cohen, "How to Invest in Social Capital," *Harvard Business Review,* 79 (June 2001): 86–93.

3. For a brief look at how one executive avoids communication overload, see "Bix Norman," *Fast Company,* no. 34 (May 2000): 129.

4. Stephanie Armour, "Failure to Communicate Costly for Companies," *USA Today* (September 30, 1998): 1B.

5. Keith Davis, *Human Behavior at Work: Organizational Behavior,* 6th ed. (New York: McGraw-Hill, 1981), p. 399.

6. For an instructive distinction between one-way (the arrow model) and two-way (the circuit model) communication, see Phillip G. Clampitt, *Communicating for Managerial Effectiveness* (Newbury Park, Calif.: Sage, 1991), pp. 1–24.

7. For interesting reading, see Harriet Rubin, "The Power of Words," *Fast Company,* no. 21 (January 1999): 142–151.

8. See Thomas H. Davenport and John C. Beck, *The Attention Economy: Understanding the New Currency of Business* (Boston: Harvard Business School Press, 2001).

9. Trudy Milburn, "Bridging Cultural Gaps," *Management Review,* 86 (January 1997): 27. Also see Linda Kathryn Larkey, "Toward a Theory of Communicative Interactions in Culturally Diverse Workgroups," *Academy of Management Review,* 21 (April 1996): 463–491; and Jack L. Mendleson and C. Dianne Mendleson, "An Action Plan to Improve Difficult Communication," *HRMagazine,* 41 (October 1996): 118–126.

10. Ernest Gundling, "How to Communicate Globally," *Training & Development,* 53 (June 1999): 30.

11. See Robert H. Lengel and Richard L. Daft, "The Selection of Communication Media as an Executive Skill," *Academy of Management Executive,* 2 (August 1988): 225–232. For a research update, see John R. Carlson and Robert W. Zmud, "Channel Expansion Theory and the Experiential Nature of Media Richness Perceptions," *Academy of Management Journal,* 42 (April 1999): 153–170.

12. See Colin Mitchell, "Selling the Brand Inside," *Harvard Business Review,* 80 (January 2002): 99–105.

13. See Karl Albrecht, "Lost in the Translation," *Training,* 33 (June 1996): 66–70; and Jean-Anne Jordon, "Clear Speaking Improves Career Prospects," *HRMagazine,* 41 (June 1996): 75–82.

14. Drawn from Manjeet Kripalani, "Investing in India: Not for the Fainthearted," *Business Week* (August 11, 1997): 46–47.

15. Data from Louisa Wah, "An Ounce of Prevention," *Management Review,* 87 (October 1998): 9. Also see Ronda Roberts Callister, Michael W. Kramer, and Daniel B. Turban, "Feedback Seeking Following Career Transitions," *Academy of Management Journal,* 42 (August 1999): 429–438; and Robert Kegan and Lisa Laskow Lahey, "More Powerful Communication: From the Language of Prizes and Praising to the Language of Ongoing Regard," *Journal of Organizational Excellence,* 20 (Summer 2001): 11–17.

16. See Bella M. DePaulo, Deborah A. Kashy, Susan E. Kirkendol, Melissa M. Wyer, and Jennifer A. Epstein, "Lying in Everyday Life," *Journal of Personality and Social Psychology,* 70 (May 1996): 979–995; and Deborah A. Kashy and Bella M. DePaulo, "Who Lies?" *Journal of Personality and Social Psychology,* 70 (May 1996): 1037–1051.

17. "Backward, Chopped-Up Speech Can't Trip Up the Brain," *USA Today* (April 29, 1999): 10D.

18. For discussion of the communication process in modern organizations, see Nick Durutta, *IABC Communication World,* 12 (October 1995): 15–19.

19. Frank Snowden Hopkins, "Communication: The Civilizing Force," *The Futurist,* 15 (April 1981): 39.

20. Phillip G. Clampitt, Robert J. DeKoch, and Thomas Cashman, "A Strategy for Communicating About Uncertainty," *Academy of Management Executive,* 14 (November 2000): 48.

21. Ibid.

22. Ibid.

23. Keith Davis, "Grapevine Communication Among Lower and Middle Managers," *Personnel Journal,* 48 (April 1969): 269.

24. See Prashant Bordia, Nicholas DiFonzo, and Artemis Chang, "Rumor as Group Problem Solving: Development Patterns in Informal Computer-Mediated Groups," *Small Group Research,* 30 (February 1999): 8–28.

25. For more extensive discussion, see the classic article: Keith Davis, "Management Communication and the Grapevine," *Harvard Business Review,* 31 (September–October 1953): 43–49.

26. Hugh B. Vickery III, "Tapping into the Employee Grapevine," *Association Management,* 36 (January 1984): 59–60.

27. John W. Newstrom, Robert E. Monczka, and William E. Reif, "Perceptions of the Grapevine: Its Value and Influence," *Journal of Business Communication,* 11 (Spring 1974): 12–20.

28. See Roy Rowan, "Where Did *That* Rumor Come From?" *Fortune* (August 13, 1979): 130–137.

29. See Nicholas Difonzo, Prashant Bordia, and Ralph L. Rosnow, "Reining in Rumors," *Organizational Dynamics,* 23 (Summer 1994): 47–62; and Nancy B. Kurland and Lisa Hope Pelled, "Passing the Word: Toward a Model of Gossip and Power in the Workplace," *Academy of Management Review,* 25 (April 2000): 428–438.

30. Patricia Sellers, "Lessons from TV's New Bosses," *Fortune* (March 14, 1988): 115, 118. For an update on Tisch, see Kimberly Weisul, "One Bear Doesn't Make It a Picnic," *Business Week* (March 25, 2002): 8.

31. See Alan Zaremba, "Working with the Organizational Grapevine," *Personnel Journal,* 67 (July 1988): 38–41.

32. See "Patrolling the Online Rumor Mill," *Training,* 37 (June 2000): 29; and Chris Woodyard, "Lurker Prowls Web to Clarify Issues, Answer Questions," *USA Today* (February 6, 2001): 6B.

33. "Executives Favor Plucking the Fruits from Employee Grapevine," *Association Management,* 36 (April 1984): 105.

34. A comprehensive discussion of rumors and rumor control can be found in Ralph L. Rosnow, "Inside Rumor: A Personal Journey," *American Psychologist,* 46 (May 1991): 484–496. Also see Lin Grensing-Pophal, "Got the Message?" *HRMagazine,* 46 (April 2001): 74–79.

35. See Jack Griffin, "The Body's Language," in *How to Say It from the Heart* (Paramus, N.J.: Prentice-Hall Press, 2001), pp. 13–25.

36. See Albert Mehrabian, "Communication Without Words," *Psychology Today,* 2 (September 1968): 53–55. For a discussion of the nonverbal origins of language, see Sharon Begley, "Talking from Hand to Mouth," *Newsweek* (March 15, 1999): 56–58.

37. Pierre Mornell, "The Sounds of Silence," *Inc.,* 23 (February 2001): 117.

38. Excerpt from Brian Hickey, "People Packaging," *America West Airlines Magazine,* 5 (September 1990): 61. Reprinted by permission of the author. Also see Bill Leonard, "Casual Dress Policies Can Trip Up Job Applicants," *HRMagazine,* 46 (June 2001): 33, 35.

39. This three-way breakdown comes from Dale G. Leathers, *Nonverbal Communication Systems* (Boston: Allyn & Bacon, 1976), ch. 2. Also see James M. Carroll and James A. Russell, "Facial Expressions in Hollywood's Portrayal of Emotion," *Journal of Personality and Social Psychology,* 72 (January 1997): 164–176.

40. For details see Mac Fulfer, "Nonverbal Communication: How To Read What's Plain as the Nose . . . or Eyelid . . . or Chin . . . on Their Faces," *Journal of Organizational Excellence,* 20 (Spring 2001): 19–27.

41. Paul C. Judge, "High Tech Star," *Business Week* (March 15, 1999): 75.

42. Based on A. Keenan, "Effects of the Non-Verbal Behaviour of Interviewers on Candidates' Performance," *Journal of Occupational Psychology,* 49, no. 3 (1976): 171–175. Also see Stanford

W. Gregory Jr. and Stephen Webster, "Nonverbal Signal in Voices of Interview Partners Effectively Predicts Communication Accommodation and Social Status Perceptions," *Journal of Personality and Social Psychology,* 70 (June 1996): 1231–1240; Jeff Mowatt, "Making Connections: How to Create Rapport with Anyone in Under 30 Seconds," *Canadian Manager,* 25 (Fall 2000): 26, 29; and Nick Morgan, "The Kinesthetic Speaker: Putting Action into Words," *Harvard Business Review,* 79 (April 2001): 112–120.

43. See Linda L. Carli, Suzanne J. LaFleur, and Christopher C. Loeber, "Nonverbal Behavior, Gender, and Influence," *Journal of Personality and Social Psychology,* 68 (June 1995): 1030–1041.

44. For details, see Dore Butler and Florence L. Geis, "Nonverbal Affect Responses to Male and Female Leaders: Implications for Leadership Evaluations," *Journal of Personality and Social Psychology,* 58 (January 1990): 48–59.

45. Based on Ben Brown, "Atlanta Out to Mind Its Manners," *USA Today* (March 14, 1996): 7C.

46. See Andrea C. Poe, "Mind Their Manners," *HRMagazine,* 46 (May 2001): 75–80; and Noelle Knox, "Expert: Mind Your Manners, It's Good Business," *USA Today* (June 28, 2001): 7B.

47. Carol Hymowitz, "How CEOs Can Keep Informed Even as Work Stretches Across Globe," *The Wall Street Journal* (March 12, 2002): B1. Also see Lin Grensing-Pophal, "Talk to Me," *HRMagazine,* 45 (March 2000): 66–74.

48. For details, see Dick Grote and Jim Wimberly, "Peer Review," *Training,* 30 (March 1993): 51–55.

49. See Jack Welch, *Jack: Straight from the Gut* (New York: Warner Business Books, 2001), pp. 393–394; and Palmer Morrel-Samuels, "Getting the Truth into Workplace Surveys," *Harvard Business Review,* 80 (February 2002): 111–118.

50. Brian Dumaine, "Creating a New Company Culture," *Fortune* (January 15, 1990): 130.

51. See Brad Fishel, "A New Perspective: How to Get the Real Story from Attitude Surveys," *Training,* 35 (February 1998): 91–94.

52. See Robert J. Aiello, "Employee Attitude Surveys: Impact on Corporate Decisions," *Public Relations Journal* (March 1983): 21.

53. Paul Keegan, "Please, Just Don't Call Us Cheap," *Business 2.0,* 3 (February 2002): 51.

54. See James S. Larson, "Employee Participation in Federal Management," *Public Personnel Management,* 18 (Winter 1989): 404–414. Also see John Tschohl, "Be Bad," *Canadian Manager,* 23 (Winter 1998): 23–24; Stephanie Armour, "Firms Tap Employees for Cost-Saving Suggestions," *USA Today* (January 26, 1999): 1B; and Dale K. DuPont, "Eureka! Tools for Encouraging Employee Suggestions," *HRMagazine,* 44 (September 1999): 134–143.

55. See Michael Warshaw, "Open Mouth. Lose Career?" *Fast Company,* no. 20 (December 1998): 240–251; and Cheryl Dahle, "What Are You Complaining About?" *Fast Company,* no. 46 (May 2001): 66, 68.

56. Curtis Sittenfeld, "Here's How GSA Changed Its Ways," *Fast Company,* no. 25 (June 1999): 88.

57. For more, see Bill Leonard, "Cyberventing," *HRMagazine,* 44 (November 1999): 34–39; and John Simons, "Stop Moaning About Gripe Sites and Log On," *Fortune* (April 2, 2001): 181–182.

58. For more, see Paul W. Barada, "Before You Go . . . ," *HRMagazine,* 43 (December 1998): 99–102; and "Questions for Exiting Employees," *Training,* 36 (October 1999): 28.

59. "Exit Interviews Used Irregularly," *The Arizona Republic* (February 25, 2001): D2.

60. Charles F. Knight, "Emerson Electric: Consistent Profits, Consistently," *Harvard Business Review,* 70 (January–February 1992): 60.

61. Catherine Yang, "Low-Wage Lessons," *Business Week* (November 11, 1996): 114.

62. Ron Lieber, "Timex Resets Its Watch," *Fast Company,* no. 52 (November 2001): 48.

63. See Bob Filipczak, "Obfuscation Resounding: Corporate Communication in America," *Training,* 32 (July 1995): 29–36.

64. For a brief discussion of male versus female communication styles, see Deborah Tannen, "The Power of Talk: Who Gets Heard and Why," *Harvard Business Review,* 73 (September–October 1995): 138–148.

65. Wendy Martyna, "What Does 'He' Mean? Use of the Generic Masculine," *Journal of Communication,* 28 (Winter 1978): 138. A later study with similar results is Janet A. Sniezek and Christine H. Jazwinski, "Gender Bias in English: In Search of Fair Language," *Journal of Applied Social Psychology,* 16, no. 7 (1986): 642–662. Also see Patricia C. Kelley, "Can Feminist Language Change Organizational Behavior? Some Research Questions," *Business & Society,* 35 (March 1996): 84–88.

66. Del Jones, "'Code Words' Cloud Issue of Discrimination at Work," *USA Today* (October 1, 1996): 1B–2B.

67. See Deirdre Donahue, "Explosive, 'Troublesome' N-Word Gets an Airing," *USA Today* (January 10, 2002): 6D.

68. See Graham T. T. Molitor, "5 Forces Transforming Communications," *The Futurist,* 35 (September–October 2001): 32–37; Steven Levy, "Living in a Wireless World," *Newsweek* (December 10, 2001): 57–60; Dylan Tweney, "Don't Press Zero!!" *Business 2.0,* 3 (January 2002): 86–87; and Peter McGrath, "3G, Phone Home!" *Newsweek* (March 18, 2002): 38F–38H.

69. Del Jones, "E-Mail Avalanche Even Buries CEOs," *USA Today* (January 4, 2002): 1A.

70. Jon Swartz, "E-Mail Overload Taxes Workers and Companies," *USA Today* (June 26, 2001): 1A. Also see Alison Overholt, "Intel Fast-Forwards," *Fast Company,* no. 54 (January 2002): 24.

71. Based on Swartz, "E-Mail Overload Taxes Workers and Companies." Also see Paul Davidson, "More Businesses Turn to Instant Messaging," *USA Today* (October 23, 2000): 1B.

72. See Ann Therese Palmer, "Workers, Surf at Your Own Risk," *Business Week* (June 11, 2001): 14; and Janet Kornblum, "The Boss Is Tracking Moves of a Third of Online Workers," *USA Today* (July 10, 2001): 3D.

73. Stephanie Armour, "You Have (Too Much) E-mail," *USA Today* (March 2, 1999): 3B.

74. Drawn from Eryn Brown, "You've Got Mail. :-o," *Fortune* (December 7, 1998): 36, 40; Joan Tunstall, *Better, Faster Email: Getting the Most Out of Email* (St. Leonards, Australia: Allen & Unwin, 1999); and Donna J. Abernathy, "You've Got Email," *Training & Development,* 53 (April 1999): 18; and Andrea C. Poe, "Don't Touch That 'Send' Button!" *HRMagazine,* 46 (July 2001): 74–80.

75. Data from Michelle Kessler, "18% See Cellphones as Their Main Phones," *USA Today* (February 1, 2002): 1B.

76. See Deborah Sharp, "Cellphones Reveal Screaming Lack of Courtesy," *USA Today* (September 4, 2001): 4A; and Nigel Holmes, "Why Talking and Driving Don't Mix," *Business 2.0,* 3 (March 2002): 27.

77. See Sarah Fister, "Videoconferencing: Good, Fast *and* Cheap," *Training,* 37 (April 2000): 30–32; Eric Krell, "Videoconferencing Gets the Call," *Training,* 38 (December 2001): 36–42; "The Next Best Thing to Being There," *Inc.,* 24 (January 2002): 75; and Andrea Bennett, "Beam Yourself into a Meeting," *Fortune* (January 21, 2002): 128.

78. Data from Stephanie Armour, "Videoconferencing Takes Off as Job Interviews Go Remote," *USA Today* (January 22, 2002): 3B.

79. "Video Conferencing Gains New Appeal," *The Arizona Republic* (September 23, 2001): D1.

80. Tips adapted in part from Michael Emery and Margaret Schubert, "A Trainer's Guide to Videoconferencing," *Training,* 30 (June 1993): 59–63. Also see "Tips for the Photophobic," *Training,* 35 (October 1998): 26.

81. "Few Employers Are Embracing Telecommuting," *HRMagazine,* 46 (September 2001): 33.

82. Charlotte Garvey, "Teleworking HR," *HRMagazine,* 46 (August 2001): 56–60; Kimberlianne Podlas, "Reasonable Accommodation or Special Privilege? Flex-Time, Telecommuting, and the ADA," *Business Horizons,* 44 (September–October 2001): 61–65; and Susan J. Wells, "Making Telecommuting Work," *HRMagazine,* 46 (October 2001): 34–45.

83. Stratford P. Sherman, "America Won't Win Till It Reads More," *Fortune* (November 18, 1991): 202. For useful communication tips, see Jo Condrill and Bennie Bough, *101 Ways to Improve Your Communication Skills Instantly* (Palmdale, Calif.: Goal-Minds, 1999; "Effective Managers Must Learn the Eight 'Cs' of Good Communication," *Canadian Manager,* 25 (Fall 2000): 27; and Urs Bender, "Stand, Deliver and Lead," *Canadian Manager,* 26 (Summer 2001): 14–16, 27.

84. Data from Judi Brownell, "Perceptions of Effective Listeners: A Management Study," *Journal of Business Communication,* 27 (Fall 1990): 401–415.

85. Data from Cynthia Hamilton and Brian H. Kleiner, "Steps to Better Listening," *Personnel Journal,* 66 (February 1987): 20–21. Also see Madelyn Burley-Allen, "Listen Up," *HRMagazine,* 46 (November 2001): 115–120.

86. This list has been adapted from John F. Kikoski, "Communication: Understanding It, Improving It," *Personnel Journal,* 59 (February 1980): 126–131; John L. DiGaetani, "The Business of Listening," *Business Horizons,* 23 (October 1980): 40–46; P. Slizewski, "Tips for Active Listening," *HR Focus* (May 1995): 7; and Griffin, "10 Ways to Become a Better Listener," in *How to Say It from the Heart,,* pp. 39–42.

87. See Wendy Zellner, "O.K., So He's Not Sam Walton," *Business Week* (March 16, 1992): 56–58.

88. See "Wanted: Great Communicators," *The Christian Science Monitor* (June 22, 1990): 8.

89. See Larry R. Smeltzer and Jeanette W. Gilsdorf, "How to Use Your Time Efficiently When Writing," *Business Horizons,* 33 (November–December 1990): 61–64; and Tom Ehrenfeld, "A Ghost Speaks," *Harvard Management Communication Letter,* 2 (August 1999): 10–11.

90. Robert F. DeGise, "Writing: Don't Let the Mechanics Obscure the Message," *Supervisory Management,* 21 (April 1976): 26–28. Also see Kenneth W. Davis, "What Writing Training Can– and Can't—Do," *Training,* 32 (August 1995): 60–63; David A. Bates, "When Good Writing Goes Bad," *Internal Auditor,* 53 (February 1996): 36–38; and Jeffrey Marshall, "How to Write a Perfectly Good Memo," *Harvard Management Communication Letter,* 2 (July 1999): 4–6.

91. See "Give the Boot to Hackneyed Phrases," *Training,* 27 (August 1990): 10. Also see Herschell Gordon Lewis, "100 of the Easiest Ways to Begin an Effective Sales Letter," *Direct Marketing,* 56 (February 1994): 32–34.

92. Data from "How Workers Communicate," *USA Today* (January 3, 2001): 1B.

93. "Meeting 'Mania' Squanders Time and Money," *HRMagazine,* 43 (August 1998): 24, 26.

94. Stephanie Armour, "Team Efforts, Technology Add New Reasons to Meet," *USA Today* (December 8, 1997): 2A. Copyright 1997, *USA Today.* Reprinted with permission. Also see Kevin Maney, "Armed with PowerPoint, Speakers Make Pests of Themselves," *USA Today.* (May 12, 1999): 3B; Fred Niederman and Roger J. Volkema, "The Effects of Facilitator Characteristics on Meeting Preparation, Set Up, and Implementation," *Small Group Research,* 30 (June 1999): 330–360; Kathryn Tyler, "The Gang's All Here . . . " *HRMagazine,* 45 (May 2000): 104–113; Paul Falcone, "Reinventing the Staff Meeting," *HRMagazine,* 45 (August 2000): 143–146; and Ram Charan, "Conquering a Culture of Indecision," *Harvard Business Review,* 79 (April 2001): 74–82.

## Chapter 13

**Opening Quotation**   Keith Davis, *Human Behavior at Work: Organizational Behavior,* 6th ed. (New York: McGraw-Hill, 1981), p. 2.

**Opening Case**   Excerpted from David Whitford, "A Human Place to Work," *Fortune* (January 8, 2001): 108–122. Copyright © 2001 Time Inc. Reprinted by permission.

**Closing Case**   Excerpted from Charles Fishman, "The Way to Enough," *Fast Company,* no. 26 (July–August 1999): 160–174. Copyright 1999 by Bus. Innovator Group Resources/Inc. Reproduced with permission of Bus. Innovator Group Resources/Inc. in the format textbook by Copyright Clearance Center.

1. For an excellent historical and conceptual treatment of basic motivation theory, see the collection of readings in Chapter 2 of Richard M. Steers, Lyman W. Porter, and Gregory A. Bigley, *Motivation and Leadership at Work,* 6th ed. (New York: McGraw-Hill, 1996).

2. See Jon R. Katzenbach and Jason A. Santamaria, "Firing Up the Front Line," *Harvard Business Review,* 77 (May–June 1999): 107–117; Thad Green, "Three Steps to Motivating Employees," *HRMagazine,* 45 (November 2000): 155–158; and Woodruff Imberman, "Why Engineers Strike—The Boeing Story," *Business Horizons,* 44 (November–December 2001): 35–44.

3. See A. H. Maslow, "A Theory of Human Motivation," *Psychological Review,* 50 (July 1943): 370–396; Ron Zemke, "Maslow for a New Millennium," *Training,* 35 (December 1998): 54–58; and Robin Marantz Henig, "Basic Needs Met? Next Comes Happiness," *USA Today* (January 2, 2001): 11A.

4. Maslow, "A Theory of Human Motivation," p. 375.

5. Dean Foust, "Man on the Spot," *Business Week* (May 3, 1999): 142–143.

6. For more, see Gene Koretz, "The Vital Role of Self-Esteem," *Business Week* (February 2, 1998): 26; Donald G. Gardner and Jon L. Pierce, "Self-Esteem and Self-Efficacy Within the Organizational Context: An Empirical Investigation," *Group & Organization Management,* 23 (March 1998): 48–70; and Perry Pascarella, "It All Begins with Self-Esteem," *Management Review,* 88 (February 1999): 60–61.

7. Maslow, "A Theory of Human Motivation," p. 382.

8. George W. Cherry, "The Serendipity of the Fully Functioning Manager," *Sloan Management Review,* 17 (Spring 1976): 73. Also see Deirdre Donahue, "Live Your Best Life, with Oprah," *USA Today* (July 2, 2001): 1D–2D.

9. Vance F. Mitchell and Pravin Moudgill, "Measurement of Maslow's Need Hierarchy," *Organizational Behavior and Human Performance,* 16 (August 1976): 348. Self-actualizing executives are profiled in Keith H. Hammonds, "The Mission," *Business Week* (March 22, 1999): 97–107; and Micheline Maynard, "Lutz Gets a Charge out of New Career," *USA Today* (June 1, 1999): 12B.

10. For example, see Ellen L. Betz, "Two Tests of Maslow's Theory of Need Fulfillment," *Journal of Vocational Behavior,* 24 (April 1984): 204–220.

11. Edward E. Lawler, *Motivation in Work Organizations* (Monterey, Calif.: Brooks/Cole, 1973), p. 34.

12. See Frederick Herzberg, Bernard Mausner, and Barbara Bloch Snyderman, *The Motivation to Work,* 2nd ed. (New York: Wiley, 1959). For a marketing application of Herzberg's theory, see Earl Naumann and Donald W. Jackson Jr., "One More Time: How Do You Satisfy Customers?" *Business Horizons,* 42 (May–June 1999): 71–76.

13. Frederick Herzberg, "One More Time: How Do You Motivate Employees?" *Harvard Business Review,* 46 (January–February 1968): 56. For another view, see Dennis W. Organ, "The Happy Curve," *Business Horizons,* 38 (May–June 1995): 1–3. Herzberg's methodology is replicated in Susan G. Turner, Dawn R. Utley, and Jerry D. Westbrook, "Project Managers and Functional Managers: A Case Study of Job Satisfaction in a Matrix Organization," *Project Management Journal,* 29 (September 1998): 11–19.

14. For details, see Victor H. Vroom, *Work and Motivation* (New York: Wiley, 1964), p. 186. A positive correlation between job satisfaction and job level is reported in Chet Robie, Ann Marie Ryan, Robert A. Schmieder, Luis Fernando Parra, and Patricia C. Smith, "The Relation Between Job Level and Job Satisfaction," *Group & Organization Management,* 23 (December 1998): 470–495.

15. See Robert J. House and Lawrence A. Wigdor, "Herzberg's Dual-Factor Theory of Job Satisfaction and Motivation: A Review of the Evidence and a Criticism," *Personnel Psychology,* 20 (1967): 369–389.

16. For example, see Peter W. Hom, "Expectancy Prediction of Reenlistment in the National Guard," *Journal of Vocational Behavior,* 16 (April 1980): 235–248; John P. Wanous, Thomas L. Keon, and Janina C. Latack, "Expectancy Theory and Occupational/Organizational Choices: A Review and Test," *Organizational Behavior and Human Performance,* 32 (August 1983): 66–86; Alan W. Stacy, Keith F. Widaman, and G. Alan Marlatt, "Expectancy Models of Alcohol Use," *Journal of Personality and Social Psychology,* 58 (May 1990): 918–928; and Anne S. Tsui, Susan J. Ashford, Lynda St. Clair, and Katherine R. Xin, "Dealing with Discrepant Expectations: Response Strategies and Managerial Effectiveness," *Academy of Management Journal,* 38 (December 1995): 1515–1543.

17. See Bill Leonard, "College Students Confident They Will Reach Career Goals Quickly," *HRMagazine,* 46 (April 2001): 27.

18. "Noël Forgeard," *Business Week* (January 8, 2001): 76.

19. For example, see Jim Collins, "Turning Goals into Results: The Power of Catalytic Mechanisms," *Harvard Business Review,* 77 (July–August 1999): 71–82.

20. See, for example, Edwin A. Locke and Gary P. Latham, *Goal Setting: A Motivational Technique That Works!* (Englewood Cliffs, N.J.: Prentice-Hall, 1984).

21. See, for example, Edwin A. Locke, Keryll N. Shaw, Lise M. Saari, and Gary P. Latham, "Goal Setting and Task Performance: 1969–1980," *Psychological Bulletin,* 90 (July 1981): 125–152; Anthony J. Mento, Robert P. Steel, and Ronald J. Karren, "A Meta-Analytic Study of the Effects of Goal Setting on Task Performance: 1966–1984," *Organizational Behavior and Human Decision Processes,* 39 (February 1987): 52–83; and Don VandeWalle, Steven P. Brown, William L. Cron, and John W. Slocum Jr., "The Influence of Goal Orientation and Self-Regulation Tactics on Sales Performance: A Longitudinal Field Test," *Journal of Applied Psychology,* 84 (April 1999): 249–259.

22. "Stretch goals" are discussed in Shawn Tully, "Why Go for Stretch Targets," *Fortune* (November 14, 1994): 145–158; Strat Sherman, "Stretch Goals: The Dark Side of Asking for Miracles," *Fortune* (November 13, 1995): 231–232; and Kenneth R. Thompson, Wayne A. Hochwarter, and Nicholas J. Mathys, "Stretch Targets: What Makes Them Effective?" *Academy of Management Executive,* 11 (August 1997): 48–60.

23. See Christopher Earley, Gregory B. Northcraft, Cynthia Lee, and Terri R. Lituchy, "Impact of Process and Outcome Feedback on the Relation of Goal Setting to Task Performance," *Academy of Management Journal,* 33 (March 1990): 87–105.

24. John Huey, "America's Most Successful Merchant," *Fortune* (September 23, 1991): 50. For an update, see "H. Lee Scott Jr.: Wal Mart Stores," *Business Week* (January 14, 2002): 71.

25. Stephen Phillips and Amy Dunkin, "King Customer," *Business Week* (March 12, 1990): 91.

26. For more on goal setting, see Charlotte Garvey, "Goalsharing Scores," *HRMagazine,* 45 (April 2000): 99–106; Gerard H. Seijts, "Setting Goals: When Performance Doesn't Matter," *Ivey Business Journal,* 65 (January–February 2001): 40–44; and Don VandeWalle, "Goal Orientation: Why Wanting to Look Successful Doesn't Always Lead to Success," *Organizational Dynamics,* 30 (Fall 2001): 162–171.

27. Lewis Carroll, *Alice's Adventures in Wonderland* (Philadelphia: The John C. Winston Company, 1923), p. 57.

28. See Marilyn Elias, "Routine Job May Take Toll on Heart," *USA Today* (September 25, 1995): 1D; Jia Lin Xie and Gary Johns, "Job Scope and Stress: Can Job Scope Be Too High?" *Academy of Management Journal,* 38 (October 1995): 1288–1309; and "Stranger in Blue-Collar Land," *Training,* 36 (August 1999): 20.

29. Adapted from J. Richard Hackman, "The Design of Work in the 1980s," *Organizational Dynamics,* 7 (Summer 1978): 3–17. An instructive four-way analysis of job design may be found in Michael A. Campion and Paul W. Thayer, "Job Design: Approaches, Outcomes, and Trade-Offs," *Organizational Dynamics,* 15 (Winter 1987): 66–79.

30. Rick Wartzman, "Houston Turns Out to Be the Capital of the Egg Roll," *The Wall Street Journal* (December 7, 1995): A1. Also see Bob Filipczak, "I, Telemarketus," *Training,* 33 (March 1996): 48–56.

31. For an interesting discussion of people who do society's "dirty work," see Blake E. Ashforth and Glen E. Kreiner, "'How Can You Do It?' Dirty Work and the Challenge of Constructing a Positive Identity," *Academy of Management Review,* 24 (July 1999): 413–434.

32. Jean M. Phillips, "Effects of Realistic Job Previews on Multiple Organizational Outcomes: A Meta-Analysis," *Academy of Management Journal,* 41 (December 1998): 686. Also see Peter W. Hom, Roger W. Griffeth, Leslie E. Palich, and Jeffrey S. Bracker, "Revisiting Met Expectations as a Reason Why Realistic Job Previews Work," *Personnel Psychology,* 52 (Spring 1999): 97–112.

33. See James M. Mehring, "Flexibility Is No Key to Stability," *Business Week* (March 5, 2001): 30; and Martha Frase-Blunt, "Ready, Set, Rotate!" *HRMagazine,* 46 (October 2001): 46–53.

34. See Kathryn Tyler, "Sit Up Straight," *HRMagazine,* 43 (September 1998): 123–128.

35. See Lee Smith, "The FBI Is a Tough Outfit to Run," *Fortune* (October 9, 1989): 133–140. Also see Michael A. Campion, Lisa Cheraskin, and Michael J. Stevens, "Career-Related Antecedents and Outcomes of Job Rotation," *Academy of Management Journal,* 37 (December 1994): 1518–1542. For a condensed version of the foregoing study, see Susan Stites-Doe, "The New Story About Job Rotation," *Academy of Management Executive,* 10 (February 1996): 86–87.

36. See M. A. Howell, "Time Off as a Reward for Productivity," *Personnel Administration,* 34 (November–December 1971): 48–51.

37. Fred Luthans and Robert Kreitner, *Organizational Behavior Modification and Beyond: An Operant and Social Learning Approach* (Glenview, Ill.: Scott, Foresman, 1985), p. 192. Also see Diane L. Lockwood and Fred Luthans, "Contingent Time Off: A Nonfinancial Incentive for Improving Productivity," *Management Review,* 73 (July 1984): 48–52. The case for a six-hour workweek is presented in "That's Why They Call It 'Work,'" *Fast Company,* no. 29 (November 1999): 194.

38. Data from Carla O'Dell and Jerry McAdams, "The Revolution in Employee Rewards," *Management Review,* 76 (March 1987): 30–33. For a recent example of CTO in action, see Thomas Petzinger Jr., "They Keep Workers Motivated to Make Annoying Phone Calls," *The Wall Street Journal* (September 20, 1996): B1.

39. J. Richard Hackman and Greg R. Oldham, *Work Redesign* (Reading, Mass.: Addison-Wesley, 1980), p. 20. Also see Michael A. Campion and Michael J. Stevens, "Neglected Questions in Job Design: How People Design Jobs, Task-Job Predictability, and Influence of Training," *Journal of Business and Psychology,* 6 (Winter 1991): 169–191; and Gary Johns, Jia Lin Xie, and Yongqing Fang, "Mediating and Moderating Effects in Job Design," *Journal of Management,* 18 (December 1992): 657–676.

40. David Kirkpatrick, "How Safe Are Video Terminals?" *Fortune* (August 29, 1988): 71. For related research, see Michael A. Campion and Carol L. McClelland, "Interdisciplinary Examination of the Costs and Benefits of Enlarged Jobs: A Job Design Quasi-Experiment," *Journal of Applied Psychology,* 76 (April 1991): 186–198.

41. See J. Barton Cunningham and Ted Eberle, "A Guide to Job Enrichment and Redesign," *Personnel,* 67 (February 1990): 56–61; Roger E. Herman and Joyce L. Gioia, "Making Work Meaningful: Secrets of the Future-Focused Corporation," *The Futurist,* 32 (December 1998): 24–38; and Donna Fenn, "Redesign Work," *Inc.,* 21 (June 1999): 74–84.

42. As quoted in John Bowe, Marisa Bowe and Sabin Streeter, eds., *Gig: Americans Talk About Their Jobs at the Turn of the Millennium* (New York: Crown Publishers, 2000), p. 30.

43. Hackman and Oldham, *Work Redesign,* pp. 78–80. Also see John W. Medcof, "The Job Characteristics of Computing and Non-Computing Work Activities," *Journal of Occupational and Organizational Psychology,* 69 (June 1996): 199–212; and Joan R. Rentsch and Robert P. Steel, "Testing the Durability of Job Characteristics as Predictors of Absenteeism over a Six-Year Period," *Personnel Psychology,* 51 (Spring 1998): 165–190.

44. See Deborah J. Dwyer and Marilyn L. Fox, "The Moderating Role of Hostility in the Relationship Between Enriched Jobs and Health," *Academy of Management Journal,* 43 (December 2000): 1086–1096; and Amy Wrzesniewski and Jane E. Dutton, "Crafting a Job: Revisioning Employees as Active Crafters of

Their Work," *Academy of Management Review,* 26 (April 2001): 179–201.

45. See Bob Nelson, *1001 Ways to Reward Employees* (New York: Workman, 1994).

46. See Sheena S. Iyengar and Mark R. Lepper, "Rethinking the Value of Choice: A Cultural Perspective on Intrinsic Motivation," *Journal of Personality and Social Psychology,* 76 (March 1999): 349–366; and Bob Urichuck, "Employee Recognition and Praise," *Canadian Manager,* 24 (Summer 1999): 27–29.

47. As quoted in Roundtable, "All in a Day's Work," *Harvard Business Review* (Special Issue: Breakthrough Leadership), 79 (December 2001): 62.

48. See Pamela Kruger, "Money—Is That What You Want?" *Fast Company,* no. 24 (May 1999): 48–50.

49. James C. Cooper and Kathleen Madigan, "The Second Half Should Be Healthier," *Business Week* (August 13, 2001): 26.

50. See Stephen Kerr, "Organizational Rewards: Practical, Cost-Neutral Alternatives That You May Know, but Don't Practice," *Organizational Dynamics,* 28 (Summer 1999): 61–70; and Michelle Conlin, "The Software Says You're Just Average," *Business Week* (February 25, 2002): 126.

51. See Bill Leonard, "Perks Give Way to Life-Cycle Benefits Plans," *HRMagazine,* 40 (March 1995): 45–48; and Robert Kuttner, "Pensions: How Much Risk Should Workers Have to Bear?" *Business Week* (April 16, 2001): 23.

52. "Companies Offer Benefits Cafeteria-Style," *Business Week* (November 13, 1978): 116. Also see Michael Hickins, "Creative 'Get-a-Life' Benefits," *Management Review,* 88 (April 1999): 7.

53. For complete details, see Alison E. Barber, Randall B. Dunham, and Roger A. Formisano, "The Impact of Flexible Benefits on Employee Satisfaction: A Field Study," *Personnel Psychology,* 45 (Spring 1992): 55–75.

54. See David Fiedler, "Should You Adjust Your Sales Compensation?" *HRMagazine,* 47 (February 2002): 79–82.

55. For more, see David A. Bowen, Stephen W. Gilliland, and Robert Folger, "HRM and Service Fairness: How Being Fair with Employees Spills Over to Customers," *Organizational Dynamics,* 27 (Winter 1999): 7–23; and Matt Bloom, "The Performance Effects of Pay Dispersion on Individuals and Organizations," *Academy of Management Journal,* 42 (February 1999): 25–40.

56. A good overview of equity theory can be found in Robert P. Vecchio, "Models of Psychological Inequity," *Organizational Behavior and Human Performance,* 34 (October 1984): 266–282.

57. See J. Stacy Adams and Patricia R. Jacobsen, "Effects of Wage Inequities on Work Quality," *Journal of Abnormal and Social Psychology,* 69 (1964): 19–25; Jerald Greenberg and Suzyn Ornstein, "High Status Job Title as Compensation for Underpayment: A Test of Equity Theory," *Journal of Applied Psychology,* 68 (May 1983): 285–297.

58. For examples, see Carol J. Loomis, "This Stuff Is Wrong," *Fortune* (June 25, 2001): 72–84; Gary Strauss, "Coke CEO's Pay Package: $200M," *USA Today* (February 5, 2002): 2B; and Gary Strauss, "Why Are These CEOs Smiling? Must Be Payday," *USA Today* (March 25, 2002): 1B–2B.

59. See Nina Gupta and Jason D. Shaw, "Let the Evidence Speak: Financial Incentives *Are* Effective!!" *Compensation & Benefits Review,* 30 (March–April 1998): 26–32; Alfred Rappaport, "New Thinking on How to Link Executive Pay with Performance," *Harvard Business Review,* 77 (March–April 1999): 91–101; Roger Plachy and Sandra Plachy, "Rewarding Employees Who Truly Make a Difference," *Compensation & Benefits Review,* 31 (May–June 1999): 34–39; Robert Berner, "The Economy's Bonus Setback," *Business Week* (January 14, 2002): 24; Marc Knez and Duncan Simester, "Making Across-the-Board Incentives Work," *Harvard Business Review,* 80 (February 2002): 16–17; and Steve Bates, "Now, the Downside of Pay for Performance," *HRMagazine,* 47 (March 2002): 10.

60. See Peter V. LeBlanc and Paul W. Mulvey, "How American Workers See the Rewards of Work," *Compensation & Benefits Review,* 30 (January–February 1998): 24–28; and Louisa Wah, "Rewarding Efficient Teamwork," *Management Review,* 88 (February 1999): 7.

61. George Gendron, "Steel Man: Ken Iverson," *Inc.* (April 1986): 47–48.

62. The case *against* incentives is presented in Alfie Kohn, "Why Incentive Plans Cannot Work," *Harvard Business Review,* 71 (September–October 1993): 54–63. Also see Peter Nulty, "Incentive Pay Can Be Crippling," *Fortune* (November 13, 1995): 23; Robert Eisenberger and Judy Cameron, "Detrimental Effects of Reward," *American Psychologist,* 51 (November 1996): 1153–1166; and Alfie Kohn, "Challenging Behaviorist Dogma: Myths About Money and Motivation," *Compensation & Benefits Review,* 30 (March–April 1998): 27, 33–37.

63. Employee involvement is thoughtfully discussed in Jay R. Galbraith, Edward E. Lawler III, et al., *Organizing for the Future: The New Logic for Managing Complex Organizations* (San Francisco: Jossey-Bass, 1993), ch. 6 and 7. Also see William G. Lee, "The Society Builders," *Management Review,* 88 (September 1999): 52–57.

64. See W. Alan Randolph, "Navigating the Journey to Empowerment," *Organizational Dynamics,* 23 (Spring 1995): 19–32; Robert C. Ford and Myron D. Fottler, "Empowerment: A Matter of Degree," *Academy of Management Executive,* 9 (August 1995): 21–31; Gretchen M. Spreitzer, "Social Structural Characteristics of Psychological Empowerment," *Academy of Management Journal,* 39 (April 1996): 483–504. Another view is presented in Martin M. Broadwell, "Why Command & Control Won't Go Away," *Training,* 32 (September 1995): 62–68.

65. For details see James P. Guthrie, "High-Involvement Work Practices, Turnover, and Productivity: Evidence from New Zealand," *Academy of Management Journal,* 44 (February 2001): 180–190. Also see "Can the Workers Run the Firm?" *Business Ethics,* 15 (September–October 2001): 13.

66. See Edward E. Lawler III and Susan A. Mohrman, "Quality Circles: After the Honeymoon," *Organizational Dynamics,* 15 (Spring 1987): 42–54; and Gerald E. Ledford Jr., Edward E. Lawler III, and Susan A. Mohrman, "The Quality Circle and Its Variations," in *Productivity in Organizations,* eds. John P. Campbell, Richard J. Campbell, et al. (San Francisco: Jossey-Bass, 1988), pp. 255–294.

67. Evidence of a positive long-term impact on productivity may be found in Mitchell L. Marks, Philip H. Mirvis, Edward J. Hackett, and James F. Grady Jr., "Employee Participation in a Quality Circle Program: Impact on Quality of Work Life, Productivity, and Absenteeism," *Journal of Applied Psychology,* 71 (February 1986): 61–69. Also see Everett E. Adam Jr., "Quality Circle Performance," *Journal of Management,* 17 (March 1991): 25–39.

68. Frank Shipper, "Tapping Creativity," *Quality Circles Journal,* 4 (August 1981): 12. Also see Amal Kumar Naj, "Some Manufacturers Drop Effort to Adopt Japanese Techniques," *The Wall Street Journal* (May 7, 1993): A1.

69. Raj Aggarwal and Betty J. Simkins, "Open Book Management—Optimizing Human Capital," *Business Horizons,* 44 (September–October 2001): 5.

70. For more on OBM, see Tim R. V. Davis, "Open-Book Management: Its Promise and Pitfalls," *Organizational Dynamics,* 25 (Winter 1997): 7–20. Also see John Case, "HR Learns How to Open the Books," *HRMagazine,* 43 (May 1998): 70–76; Perry Pascarella, "Open the Books to Unleash Your People," *Management Review,* 87 (May 1998): 58–60; and "July Poll Results: Open-Book Management," *HRMagazine,* 43 (September 1998): 18.

71. See W. Alan Randolph, "Rethinking Empowerment: Why Is It So Hard to Achieve?" *Organizational Dynamics,* 29 (Fall 2000): 94–107; Laurence Prusak and Don Cohen, "How to Invest in Social Capital," *Harvard Business Review,* 79 (June 2001): 86–93; Christopher A. Bartlett and Sumantra Ghoshal, "Building Competitive Advantage Through People," *MIT Sloan Management Review,* 43 (Winter 2002): 34–41; and Ginger L. Graham, "If You Want Honesty, Break Some Rules," *Harvard Business Review,* 80 (April 2002): 42–47.

72. Heather Johnson, "Out With the Belly Flops," *Training,* 38 (December 2001): 22.

73. For related reading, see Noel M. Tichy, "No Ordinary Boot Camp," *Harvard Business Review,* 79 (April 2001): 63–70; Philippe Haspeslagh, Tomo Noda, and Fares Boulos, "It's Not Just About the Numbers," *Harvard Business Review,* 79 (July–August 2001): 65–73; and "Grow or Die," *Training,* 39 (January 2002): 17.

74. For more, see Ruth Wageman, "Critical Success Factors for Creating Superb Self-Managing Teams," *Organizational Dynamics,* 26 (Summer 1997): 49–61; Milan Moravec, Odd Jan Johannessen, and Thor A. Hjelmas, "The Well-Managed SMT," *Management Review,* 87 (June 1998): 56–58; Bradley L. Kirkman and Benson Rosen, "Beyond Self-Management: Antecedents and Consequences of Team Empowerment," *Academy of Management Journal,* 42 (February 1999): 58–74; Gary Dessler, "How to Earn Your Employees' Commitment," *Academy of Management Executive,* 13 (May 1999): 58–67; Carla Joinson, "Teams at Work," *HRMagazine,* 44 (May 1999): 30–36; and Bradley L. Kirkman and Debra L. Shapiro, "The Impact of Cultural Values on Job Satisfaction and Organizational Commitment in Self-Managing Work Teams: The Mediating Role of Employee Resistance," *Academy of Management Journal,* 44 (June 2001): 557–569.

75. "1996 Industry Report: What Self-Managing Teams Manage," *Training,* 33 (October 1996): 69.

76. Brian Dumaine, "Who Needs a Boss?" *Fortune* (May 7, 1990): 52. Also see Rudy M. Yandrick, "A Team Effort," *HRMagazine,* 46 (June 2001): 136–141.

77. John Hoerr, "The Payoff from Teamwork," *Business Week* (July 10, 1989): 57.

78. See John Hoerr, "Work Teams Can Rev Up Paper-Pushers, Too," *Business Week* (November 28, 1988): 64–72; and Beverly Geber, "Can TQM Cure Health Care?" *Training,* 29 (August 1992): 25–34.

79. Adapted from David I. Levine, "Participation, Productivity, and the Firm's Environment," *California Management Review,* 32 (Summer 1990): 86–100.

80. For good advice, see Robert C. Liden, Sandy J. Wayne, and Lisa Bradway, "Connections Make the Difference," *HRMagazine,* 41 (February 1996): 73–79; and Michael Donovan, "The First Step to Self-Direction is NOT Empowerment," *Journal for Quality and Participation,* 19 (June 1996): 64–66.

81. Katherine I. Miller and Peter R. Monge, "Participation, Satisfaction, and Productivity: A Meta-Analytic Review," *Academy of Management Journal,* 29 (December 1986): 748.

82. For example, see Adolph Haasen, "Opel Eisenach GMBH—Creating a High-Productivity Workplace," *Organizational Dynamics,* 24 (Spring 1996): 80–85.

83. See Pete Wakeman, "The Good Life & How to Get It," *Inc.,* 23 (February 2001): 44–54.

84. See Karen S. Kush and Linda K. Stroh, "Flextime: Myth or Reality?" *Business Horizons,* 37 (September–October 1994): 51–55; David Stamps, "Taming Time with Flexible Work," *Training,* 32 (May 1995): 60–66; Elizabeth Sheley, "Flexible Work Options: Beyond 9 to 5," *HRMagazine,* 41 (February 1996): 52–58; and Genevieve Capowski, "The Joy of Flex," *Management Review,* 85 (March 1996): 12–18.

85. Data from "More Women Value Flex Time," *USA Today* (August 1, 2000): 1B.

86. Data from Heather Johnson, "Roll Call," *Training,* 39 (March 2002): 16.

87. See Kimberlianne Podlas, "Reasonable Accommodation or Special Privilege? Flextime, Telecommuting, and the ADA," *Business Horizons,* 44 (September–October 2001): 61–65.

88. Data from V. K. Narayanan and Raghu Nath, "A Field Test of Some Attitudinal and Behavioral Consequences of Flextime," *Journal of Applied Psychology,* 67 (April 1982): 214–218; David A. Ralston, William P. Anthony, and David J. Gustafson, "Employees May Love Flextime, but What Does It Do to the Organization's Productivity?" *Journal of Applied Psychology,* 70 (May 1985): 272–279; and Charles S. Rodgers, "The Flexible Workplace: What Have We Learned?" *Human Resources Management,* 31 (Fall 1992): 183–199.

89. See Jon L. Pierce and Randall B. Dunham, "The 12-Hour Work Day: A 48-Hour, Eight-Day Week," *Academy of Management Journal,* 35 (December 1992): 1086–1098; and Dominic Bencivenga, "Compressed Weeks Fill an HR Niche," *HRMagazine,* 40 (June 1995): 71–74.

90. See Elizabeth Sheley, "Job Sharing Offers Unique Challenges," *HRMagazine,* 41 (January 1996): 46–49; Carla Joinson, "Time Share," *HRMagazine,* 43 (December 1998): 104–112; "Is It Nature or Nurture?" *Inc.,* 21 (April 1999): 103; "In Praise of the Six-Hour Day," *Inc.,* 23 (January 2001): 103; and Rosalind Chait Barnett and Douglas T. Hall, "How to Use Reduced Hours to Win the War for Talent," *Organizational Dynamics,* 29 (Winter 2001): 192–210.

91. Data from M. F. J. Martens, F. J. N. Nijhuis, M. P. J. Van Boxtel, and J. A. Knottnerus, "Flexible Work Schedules and Mental and Physical Health. A Study of a Working Population with Non-Traditional Working Hours," *Journal of Organizational Behavior,* 20 (January 1999): 35–46.

92. For more, see Eric Paltell, "FMLA: After Six Years, a Bit More Clarity," *HR Magazine,* 44 (September 1999): 144–150; Gene Koretz, "Did Maternity Leave Law Help?" *Business Week* (April 17, 2000): 36; Steve Bates, "Whirlwind of Change," *HRMagazine,* 46 (August 2001): 62–66; and Kathryn Tyler, "All Present and Accounted For?" *HRMagazine,* 46 (October 2001): 101–109.

93. See Michele Galen, "Sure, 'Unpaid Leave' Sounds Simple, but . . ." *Business Week* (August 9, 1993): 32–33.

94. Data from Ann Therese Palmer, "Who's Minding the Baby? The Company," *Business Week* (April 26, 1999): 32. Also see Stephanie Armour, "Watching the Kids on the Boss' Dime," *USA Today* (August 25, 1999): 3B; and Nancy Hatch Woodward, "Child Care to the Rescue," *HRMagazine,* 44 (August 1999): 82–88.

95. See Stephanie Armour, "Employees Stepping Up in Elder Care," *USA Today* (August 3, 2000): 3B; Susan J. Wells, "The Elder Care Gap," *HRMagazine,* 45 (May 2000): 38–46; and Rudy M. Yandrick, "Elder Care Grows Up," *HRMagazine,* 46 (November 2001): 72–77.

96. See Debra L. Nelson and Ronald J. Burke, "Women Executives: Health, Stress, and Success," *Academy of Management Executive,* 14 (May 2000): 107–121; William Atkinson, "When Stress Won't Go Away," *HRMagazine,* 45 (December 2000): 104–110; Merry Mayer, "Breaking Point," *HRMagazine,* 46 (October 2001): 111–116; and Richard Boyatzis, Annie McKee, and Daniel Goleman, "Reawakening Your Passion for Work," *Harvard Business Review,* 80 (April 2002): 87–94.

97. Bill Leonard, "Health Care Costs Increase Interest in Wellness Programs," *HRMagazine,* 46 (September 2001): 37. Also see Christopher P. Neck and Kenneth H. Cooper, "The Fit Executive: Exercise and Diet Guidelines for Enhancing Performance," *Academy of Management Executive,* 14 (May 2000): 72–83; and Leslie Brokaw, "Pat Croce's Bottom Line," *Inc.,* 24 (January 2002): 42.

98. See Stephanie Armour, "Workers View Sabbaticals as Two-Edged Sword," *USA Today* (September 8, 1997): 3B; Michelle Conlin, "Give a Geek a Break," *Business Week* (July 10, 2000): 102, 104; and Toddi Gutner, "The Pause That Refreshes," *Business Week* (November 19, 2001): 138.

99. "Heart Disease Claims a Million Lives," *USA Today* (January 2, 2002): 6D.

## Chapter 14

**Opening Quotation**    Amy Williams, vice president, finance and planning, Allstate Insurance Co., as quoted in Alan Webber, "The Old Economy Meets the New Economy," *Fast Company,* no. 51 (October 2001): 74.

**Opening Case**    Excerpted from "Enron's Dirty Laundry," by Johnnie L. Roberts and Evan Thomas. From *Newsweek* (March 11, 2002): 22–28. © 2000 Newsweek, Inc. All rights reserved. Reprinted by permission.

**Closing Case**    From "With the Stakes High, a Lucent Duo Conquers Distance and Culture," by Thomas Petzinger, Jr., *The Wall Street Journal* (April 23, 1999). Copyright 1999 by Dow Jones & Co., Inc. Reproduced with permission of Dow Jones & Co. Inc. in the format textbook via Copyright Clearance Center.

1. James P. Masciarelli, "Are You Managing Your Relationships?" *Management Review,* 87 (April 1998): 41.

2. See Laurence Prusak and Don Cohen, "How to Invest in Social Capital," *Harvard Business Review,* 79 (June 2001): 86–93; and Paul S. Adler and Seok-Woo Kwon, "Social Capital: Prospects for a New Concept," *Academy of Management Review,* 27 (January 2002): 17–40.

3. Joseph A. Litterer, *The Analysis of Organizations,* 2nd ed. (New York: Wiley, 1973), p. 231.

4. For an excellent elaboration of this definition, see David Horton Smith, "A Parsimonious Definition of 'Group': Toward Conceptual Clarity and Scientific Utility," *Sociological Inquiry,* 37 (Spring 1967): 141–167. The importance of social skills in today's workplace is discussed in Robert A. Baron and Gideon D. Markman, "Beyond Social Capital: How Social Skills Can Enhance Entrepreneurs' Success," *Academy of Management Executive,* 14 (February 2000): 106–116.

5. For related research, see Priti Pradhan Shah, "Who Are Employees' Social Referents? Using a Network Perspective to Determine Referent Others," *Academy of Management Journal,* 41 (June 1998): 249–268; and Ajay Mehra, Martin Kilduff, and Daniel J. Brass, "At the Margins: A Distinctiveness Approach to the Social Identity and Social Networks of Underrepresented Groups," *Academy of Management Journal,* 41 (August 1998): 441–452.

6. For example, see Del Jones, "Employees Rally 'Round the Copier," *USA Today,* (November 16, 1995): 4B; and Thomas A. Stewart, "The Invisible Key to Success," *Fortune* (August 5, 1996): 173–176.

7. David Krackhardt and Jeffrey R. Hanson, "Informal Networks: The Company Behind the Chart," *Harvard Business Review,* 71 (July–August 1993): 104.

8. See Cathy Olofson, "Let Outsiders In, Turn Your Insiders Out," *Fast Company,* no. 22 (February–March 1999): 46.

9. For more, see Naomi Ellemers, Russell Spears, and Bertjan Doosje, "Sticking Together or Falling Apart: In-Group Identification as a Psychological Determinant of Group Commitment Versus Individual Mobility," *Journal of Personality and Social Psychology,* 72 (March 1997): 617–626; Hank Rothgerber, "External Intergroup Threat as an Antecedent to Perceptions of In-Group and Out-Group Homogeneity," *Journal of*

*Personality and Social Psychology,* 73 (December 1997): 1206–1212; and Bertjan Doosje, Nyla R. Branscombe, Russell Spears, and Antony S. R. Manstead, "Guilty by Association: When One's Group Has a Negative History," *Journal of Personality and Social Psychology,* 75 (October 1998): 872–886.

10. Peter Nulty, "Cool Heads Are Trying to Keep Commodore Hot," *Fortune* (July 23, 1984): 38, 40.

11. Albert A. Harrison, *Individuals and Groups: Understanding Social Behavior* (Monterey, Calif.: Brooks/Cole, 1976), p. 16. Also see Elizabeth Wolfe Morrison, "Role Definitions and Organizational Citizenship Behavior: The Importance of the Employee's Perspective," *Academy of Management Journal,* 37 (December 1994): 1543–1567; Richard G. Netemeyer, Scott Burton, and Mark W. Johnston, "A Nested Comparison of Four Models of the Consequences of Role Perception Variables," *Organizational Behavior and Human Decision Processes,* 61 (January 1995): 77–93; and Linn Van Dyne and Jeffrey A. LePine, "Helping and Voice Extra-Role Behaviors: Evidence of Construct and Predictive Validity," *Academy of Management Journal,* 41 (February 1998): 108–119.

12. See, for example, Jo Ellen Moore, "Are You Burning Out Valuable Resources?" *HRMagazine,* 44 (January 1999): 93–97. Also see Blake E. Ashforth, Glen E. Kreiner, and Mel Fugate, "All in a Day's Work: Boundaries and Micro Role Transitions," *Academy of Management Review,* 25 (July 2000): 472–491; and Peter W. Hom and Angelo J. Kinicki, "Toward a Greater Understanding of How Dissatisfaction Drives Employee Turnover," *Academy of Management Journal,* 44 (October 2001): 975–987.

13. Harrison, *Individuals and Groups,* p. 401.

14. For example, see Gary Blau, "Influence of Group Lateness on Individual Lateness: A Cross-Level Examination," *Academy of Management Journal,* 38 (October 1995): 1483–1496; Jeffrey A. LePine and Linn Van Dyne, "Peer Responses to Low Performers: An Attributional Model of Helping in the Context of Groups," *Academy of Management Review,* 26 (January 2001): 67–84; and Jennifer A. Chatman and Francis J. Flynn, "The Influence of Demographic Heterogeneity on the Emergence and Consequences of Cooperative Norms in Work Teams," *Academy of Management Journal,* 44 (October 2001): 956–974.

15. Adapted from Daniel C. Feldman, "The Development and Enforcement of Group Norms," *Academy of Management Review,* 9 (January 1984): 47–53. Also see Jose M. Marques, Dominic Abrams, Dario Paez, and Cristina Martinez-Taboada, "The Role of Categorization and In-Group Norms in Judgments of Groups and Their Members," *Journal of Personality and Social Psychology,* 75 (October 1998): 976–988.

16. See Kenneth J. Bettenhausen and Keith J. Murnigham, "The Development of an Intragroup Norm and the Effects of Interpersonal and Structural Challenges," *Administrative Science Quarterly,* 36 (March 1991): 20–35.

17. Gwendolyn Kelly, "Why This Med Student Is Sticking with Primary Care," *Business Week* (November 2, 1992): 125.

18. For related research, see Linda Klebe Trevino and Bart Victor, "Peer Reporting of Unethical Behavior: A Social Context Per-spective," *Academy of Management Journal,* 35 (March 1992): 38–64.

19. From *Group Effectiveness in Organizations* by L. N. Jewell and H. J. Reitz (Scott, Foresman, 1981). Reprinted by permission of the authors. Also see Jean Lipman-Blumen and Harold J. Leavitt, "Hot Groups 'with Attitude': A New Organizational State of Mind," *Organizational Dynamics,* 27 (Spring 1999): 63–73; and Lynn R. Offermann and Rebecca K. Spiros, "The Science and Practice of Team Development: Improving the Link," *Academy of Management Journal,* 44 (April 2001): 376–392.

20. Susan A. Wheelan and Felice Tilin, "The Relationship Between Faculty Group Development and School Productivity," *Small Group Research,* 30 (February 1999): 59.

21. For more, see Chao C. Chen, Xiao-Ping Chen, and James R. Meindl, "How Can Cooperation Be Fostered? The Cultural Effects of Individualism-Collectivism," *Academy of Management Review,* 23 (April 1998): 285–304.

22. See Vanessa Urch Druskat and Steven B. Wolff, "Building the Emotional Intelligence of Groups," *Harvard Business Review,* 79 (March 2001): 81–90.

23. The following discussion of the six stages of group development is adapted from *Group Effectiveness in Organizations* by Linda N. Jewell and H. Joseph Reitz. Copyright 1981, Scott, Foresman and Company, pp. 15–20. Reprinted by permission. For ground-breaking research in this area, see Warren G. Bennis and Herbert A. Shepard, "A Theory of Group Development," *Human Relations,* 9 (1956); 415–437; Bruce W. Tuckman and Mary Ann C. Jensen, "Stages of Small-Group Development Revisited," *Group & Organization Studies,* 2 (December 1977): 419–427; and John F. McGrew, John G. Bilotta, and Janet M. Deeney, "Software Team Formation and Decay: Extending the Standard Model for Small Groups," *Small Group Research,* 30 (April 1999): 209–234.

24. For a cross-cultural perspective, see Cristina B. Gibson, "Do They Do What They Believe They Can? Group Efficacy and Group Effectiveness Across Tasks and Cultures," *Academy of Management Journal,* 42 (April 1999): 138–152.

25. For example, see Mark C. Bolino, "Citizenship and Impression Management: Good Soldiers or Good Actors?" *Academy of Management Review,* 24 (January 1999): 82–98; Marjorie L. Randall, Russell Cropanzano, Carol A. Bormann, and Andrej Birjulin, "Organizational Politics and Organizational Support as Predictors of Work Attitudes, Job Performance, and Organizational Citizenship Behavior," *Journal of Organizational Behavior,* 20 (March 1999): 159–174; and Barry R. Schlenker and Thomas W. Britt, "Beneficial Impression Management: Strategically Controlling Information to Help Friends," *Journal of Personality and Social Psychology,* 76 (April 1999): 559–573.

26. As quoted in Anne Fisher, "Putting Your Mouth Where the Money Is," *Fortune* (September 3, 2001): 238.

27. Marcia Stepanek, "How Fast Is Net Fast?" *Business Week e.biz* (November 1, 1999): EB 54.

28. Data from "9-to-5 Not for Everyone," *USA Today* (October 13, 1999): 1B.

29. See Gerald R. Ferris, Pamela L. Perrewé, William P. Anthony, and David C. Gilmore, "Political Skill at Work," *Organizational Dynamics,* 28 (Spring 2000): 25–37; and Suzanne Koudsi, "You're Stuck," *Fortune* (December 10, 2001): 271–274.

30. Ethical implications are discussed in Erik W. Larson and Jonathan B. King, "The Systematic Distortion of Information: An Ongoing Challenge to Management," *Organizational Dynamics,* 24 (Winter 1996): 49–61; and Peter Troiano, "Nice Guys Finish First," *Management Review,* 87 (December 1998): 8.

31. Victor Murray and Jeffrey Gandz, "Games Executives Play: Politics at Work," *Business Horizons,* 23 (December 1980): 16.

32. Andrew J. DuBrin, *Fundamentals of Organizational Behavior: An Applied Perspective,* 2nd ed. (Elmsford, N.Y.: Pergamon Press, 1978): p. 154.

33. Dan Farrell and James C. Petersen, "Patterns of Political Behavior in Organizations," *Academy of Management Review,* 7 (July 1982): 407. Also see Andrea Nierenberg, "Masterful Networking," *Training & Development,* 53 (February 1999): 51–53; Jeff Barbian, "It's Who You Know," *Training,* 38 (December 2001): 22; and Stanley Bing, "Throwing the Elephant: Zen and the Art of Managing Up," *Fortune* (March 18, 2002): 115–116.

34. James R. Healey, "Covert Activity Saved Sports Car," *USA Today* (March 19, 1997): 1B. Also see Denis Collins, "Case Study: 15 Lessons Learned from the Death of a Gainsharing Plan," *Compensation & Benefits Review,* 28 (March–April 1996): 31–40.

35. Adapted from Dan L. Madison, Robert W. Allen, Lyman W. Porter, Patricia A. Renwick, and Bronston T. Mayes, "Organizational Politics: An Exploration of Managers' Perceptions," *Human Relations,* 33 (February 1980): 79–100. Also see Andrew J. DuBrin, "Career Maturity, Organizational Rank, and Political Behavioral Tendencies: A Correlational Analysis of Organizational Politics and Career Experience," *Psychological Reports,* 63 (October 1988): 531–537.

36. Madison et al., "Organizational Politics," p. 97.

37. These six political tactics have been adapted from a more extensive list found in DuBrin, *Fundamentals of Organizational Behavior,* pp. 158–170. Also see Roos Vonk, "The Slime Effect: Suspicion and Dislike of Likeable Behavior Toward Superiors," *Journal of Personality and Social Psychology,* 74 (April 1998): 849–864; Carol Memmott, "How to Play Cutthroat Office Politics and Win," *USA Today* (July 13, 1998): 2B; and David G. Baldwin, "How to Win the Blame Game," *Harvard Business Review,* 79 (July–August 2001): 55–62.

38. For more, see L. A. Witt, "Enhancing Organizational Goal Congruence: A Solution to Organizational Politics," *Journal of Applied Psychology,* 83 (August 1998): 666–674.

39. Adapted from DuBrin, *Fundamentals of Organizational Behavior,* pp. 179–182.

40. Blind conformity at Enron is discussed in Greg Farrell and Jayne O'Donnell, "Watkins Testifies Skilling, Fastow Duped Lay, Board," *USA Today* (February 15, 2002): 1B–2B.

41. See Solomon E. Asch, *Social Psychology* (Englewood Cliffs, N.J.: Prentice-Hall, 1952), ch. 16.

42. For details, see Taha Amir, "The Asch Conformity Effect: A Study in Kuwait," *Social Behavior and Personality,* 12, no. 2 (1984): 187–190; Timothy P. Williams and Shunya Sogon, "Group Composition and Conforming Behavior in Japanese Students," *Japanese Psychological Research,* 26, no. 4 (1984): 231–234.

43. Data from Rod Bond and Peter B. Smith, "Culture and Conformity: A Meta-Analysis of Studies Using Asch's (1952b, 1956) Line Judgment Task," *Psychological Bulletin,* 119 (January 1996): 111–137. Also see Sandra L. Robinson and Anne M. O'Leary-Kelly, "Monkey See, Monkey Do: The Influence of Work Groups on the Antisocial Behavior of Employees," *Academy of Management Journal,* 41 (December 1998): 658–672.

44. Irving L. Janis, *Groupthink,* 2nd ed. (Boston: Houghton Mifflin, 1982), p. 9. See also A. Amin Mohamed and Frank A. Wiebe, "Toward a Process Theory of Groupthink," *Small Group Research,* 27 (August 1996): 416–430; Kjell Granstrom and Dan Stiwne, "A Bipolar Model of Groupthink: An Expansion of Janis's Concept," *Small Group Research,* 29 (February 1998): 32–56; the entire February–March 1998 issue of *Organizational Behavior and Human Decision Processes;* Annette R. Flippen, "Understanding Groupthink from a Self-Regulatory Perspective," *Small Group Research,* 30 (April 1999): 139–165; Jin Nam Choi and Myung Un Kim, "The Organizational Application of Groupthink and Its Limitations in Organizations," *Journal of Applied Psychology,* 84 (April 1999): 297–306; and Walter Shapiro, "Groupthink a Danger for White House War Planners," *USA Today* (October 3, 2001): 7A.

45. Adapted from a list in Janis, *Groupthink,* pp. 174–175.

46. Ibid., p. 275.

47. See Rob Norton, "New Thinking on the Causes—and Costs—of Yes Men (and Women)," *Fortune* (November 28, 1994): 31.

48. For excellent discussions of the devil's advocate role, see Charles R. Schwenk, "Devil's Advocacy in Managerial Decision Making," *Journal of Management Studies,* 21 (April 1984): 153–168; and Richard A. Cosier and Charles R. Schwenk, "Agreement and Thinking Alike: Ingredients for Poor Decisions," *Academy of Management Executive,* 4 (February 1990): 69–74.

49. Adapted from a list in Janis, *Groupthink,* pp. 262–271.

50. Geoffrey Colvin, "America's Worst Boards," *Fortune* (April 17, 2000): 242. Also see Louis Lavelle, "The Best and Worst Boards," *Business Week* (October 7, 2002): 104–114.

51. An alternative form of groupthink is discussed in Paul F. Levy, "The Nut Island Effect: When Good Teams Go Wrong," *Harvard Business Review,* 79 (March 2001): 51–59.

52. As quoted in Sheila M. Puffer, "Continental Airlines' CEO Gordon Bethune on Teams and New Product Development," *Academy of Management Executive,* 13 (August 1999): 28.

53. See Lynda McDermott, Bill Waite, and Nolan Brawley, "Putting Together a World-Class Team," *Training & Development,* 53 (January 1999): 47–51; Donald Gerwin, "Team Empowerment in New Product Development," *Business Horizons,* 42 (July–August 1999): 29–36; Cheryl Dahle, "Xtreme Teams," *Fast Company,* no. 29 (November 1999): 310–326; Leigh L. Thompson, *Making the Team: A Guide for Managers*

(Upper Saddle River, N.J.: Prentice-Hall, 2000); and Hollis Heimbouch, "Should This Team Be Saved?" *Harvard Business Review,* 79 (July–August 2001): 31–40.

54. An instructive distinction between work groups and teams is presented in Jon R. Katzenbach and Douglas K. Smith, "The Discipline of Teams," *Harvard Business Review,* 71 (March–April 1993): 111–120. Also see Jon R. Katzenbach and Douglas K. Smith, *The Wisdom of Teams: Creating the High-Performance Organization* (New York: HarperCollins, 1999); Michelle A. Marks, John E. Mathieu, and Stephen J. Zaccaro, "A Temporally Based Framework and Taxonomy of Team Processes," *Academy of Management Review,* 26 (July 2001): 356–376; and Bradley L. Kirkman, Cristina B. Gibson, and Debra L. Shapiro, "'Exporting' Teams: Enhancing the Implementation and Effectiveness of Work Teams in Global Affiliates," *Organizational Dynamics,* 30 (Summer 2001): 12–29.

55. See Mary Uhl-Bien and George B. Graen, "Individual Self-Management: Analysis of Professionals' Self-Managing Activities in Functional and Cross-Functional Work Teams," *Academy of Management Journal,* 41 (June 1998): 340–350; Avan R. Jassawalla and Hemant C. Sashittal, "Building Collaborative Cross-Functional New Product Teams," *Academy of Management Executive,* 13 (August 1999): 50–63; Robert T. Keller, "Cross-Functional Project Groups in Research and New Product Development: Diversity, Communications, Job Stress, and Outcomes," *Academy of Management Journal,* 44 (June 2001): 547–555; and Kay Lovelace, Debra L. Shapiro, and Laurie R. Weingart, "Maximizing Cross-Functional New Product Teams' Innovativeness and Constraint Adherence: A Conflict Communications Perspective," *Academy of Management Journal,* 44 (August 2001): 779–793.

56. Dori Jones Yang, "Grace Robertson: Piloting a Superfast Rollout at Boeing," *Business Week* (August 30, 1993): 77.

57. See Nancy B. Kurland and Diane E. Bailey, "Telework: The Advantages and Challenges of Working Here, There, Anywhere, and Anytime," *Organizational Dynamics,* 28 (Autumn 1999): 53–68.

58. For a virtual team manager in action, see Riza Cruz, "At the Desk of Herman Miller's Greg Parsons," *Business 2.0,* 3 (April 2002): 114–115. Also see Faith Keenan and Spencer E. Ante, "The New Teamwork," *Business Week e.biz* (February 18, 2002): EB 12–EB 16.

59. See Kim Kiser, "Working on World Time," *Training,* 36 (March 1999): 28–34.

60. See Elizabeth Kelley, "Keys to Effective Virtual Global Teams," *Academy of Management Executive,* 15 (May 2001): 132–133; and Mitzi M. Montoya-Weiss, Anne P. Massey, and Michael Song, "Getting It Together: Temporal Coordination and Conflict Management in Global Virtual Teams," *Academy of Management Journal,* 44 (December 2001): 1251–1262.

61. See Suzanne G. Scott and Walter O. Einstein, "Strategic Performance Appraisal in Team-Based Organizations: One Size Does Not Fit All," *Academy of Management Executive,* 15 (May 2001): 107–116; Rudy M. Yandrick, "A Team Effort," *HRMagazine,* 46 (June 2001): 136–141; and Amy Edmondson, Richard Bohmer, and Gary Pisano, "Speeding Up Team Learning," *Harvard Business Review,* 79 (October 2001): 125–132.

62. See Hans J. Thamhain, "Managing Technologically Innovative Team Efforts Toward New Product Success," *Journal of Product Innovation Management,* 7 (March 1990): 5–18. Also see the following study of team effectiveness: Richard J. Magjuka and Timothy T. Baldwin, "Team-Based Employee Involvement Programs: Effects of Design and Administration," *Personnel Psychology,* 44 (Winter 1991): 793–812.

63. See Nancy Katz, "Sports Teams as a Model for Workplace Teams: Lessons and Liabilities," *Academy of Management Executive,* 15 (August 2001): 56–67; and Geoffrey Colvin, "Think You Can Bobsled? Ha!" *Fortune* (March 18, 2002): 50.

64. See Mark E. Haskins, Jeanne Liedtka, and John Rosenblum, "Beyond Teams: Toward an Ethic of Collaboration," *Organizational Dynamics,* 26 (Spring 1998): 34–50; Allan B. Drexler and Russ Forrester, "Interdependence: The Crux of Teamwork," *HRMagazine,* 43 (September 1998): 52–62; and Don Knight, Cathy C. Durham, and Edwin A. Locke, "The Relationship of Team Goals, Incentives, and Efficacy to Strategic Risk, Tactical Implementation, and Performance," *Academy of Management Journal,* 44 (April 2001): 326–338.

65. Three kinds of trust are discussed in Douglas A. Houston, "Trust in the Networked Economy: Doing Business on Web Time," *Business Horizons,* 44 (March–April 2001): 38–44.

66. See Gerald Andrews, "Mistrust, the Hidden Obstacle to Empowerment," *HRMagazine,* 39 (September 1994): 66–70; and Gretchen M. Spreitzer and Aneil K. Mishra, "Giving Up Control Without Losing Control," *Group & Organization Management,* 24 (June 1999): 155–187.

67. Stephanie Armour, "Employees' New Motto: Trust No One," *USA Today* (February 5, 2002): 2B.

68. Prusak and Cohen, "How To Invest in Social Capital," p. 90.

69. See Dale E. Zand, "Trust and Managerial Problem Solving," *Administrative Science Quarterly,* 17 (June 1972): 229–239.

70. Trustworthiness is discussed in Thomas A. Stewart, "Whom Can You Trust? It's Not So Easy to Tell," *Fortune* (June 12, 2000): 331–334. Also see the entire July 1998 issue of *Academy of Management Review;* John A. Byrne, "Restoring Trust in Corporate America," *Business Week* (June 24, 2002): 30–35; and Bruce Nussbaum, "Can Trust Be Rebuilt?" *Business Week* (July 8, 2002): 32–34.

71. Adapted from Fernando Bartolomé, "Nobody Trusts the Boss Completely—Now What?" *Harvard Business Review,* 67 (March–April 1989): 137–139. Also see Ron Zemke, "Can You Manage Trust?" *Training,* 37 (February 2000): 76–83; James Lardner, "Why Should Anyone Believe You?" *Business 2.0,* 3 (March 2002): 40–48; and Ron Zemke, "Honesty: Best Antidote," *Training,* 39 (October 2002): 14.

72. See Kimberly D. Elsbach and Greg Elofson, "How the Packaging of Decision Explanations Affects Perceptions of Trustworthiness," *Academy of Management Journal,* 43 (February 2000): 80–89; and Michele Williams, "In Whom We Trust: Group Membership as an Affective Context for Trust Development," *Academy of Management Review,* 26 (July 2001): 377–396.

# Chapter 15

**Opening Quotation**  As quoted in Thomas A. Stewart, "What's So New About the 'New Economy'? Glad You Asked . . . ," *Business 2.0*, 2 (August–September 2001): 78. As quoted in John A. Byrne and Heather Timmons, "Tough Times for a New CEO," *Business Week* (October 29, 2001): 70.

**Opening Case**  Stephanie N. Mehta, "Why Mentoring Works," *Fortune* (July 9, 2001): 119. Copyright © 2001, Time Inc. Reprinted by permission.

**Closing Case**  Excerpted from Eryn Brown, "A Smokeless Herb," *Fortune* (May 28, 2001): 78–79. Copyright © 2001, Time Inc. Reprinted by permission.

1. See Karen S. Peterson, "In Charge . . . and Out of Control," *USA Today* (July 31, 2000): 6D; and Robert B. Cialdini, "Harnessing the Science of Persuasion," *Harvard Business Review*, 79 (October 2001): 72–79.

2. See Gary Yukl and Cecilia M. Falbe, "Influence Tactics and Objectives in Upward, Downward, and Lateral Influence Attempts," *Journal of Applied Psychology*, 75 (April 1990); 132–140. Also see David Kipnis, Stuart M. Schmidt, and Ian Wilkinson, "Intraorganizational Influence Tactics: Explorations in Getting One's Way," *Journal of Applied Psychology*, 64 (August 1980): 440–452; and Chester A. Schriesheim and Timothy R. Hinkin, "Influence Tactics Used by Subordinates: A Theoretical and Empirical Analysis of the Kipnis, Schmidt, and Wilkinson Subscales," *Journal of Applied Psychology*, 75 (June 1990): 246–257.

3. Adapted from Yukl and Falbe, "Influence Tactics and Objectives in Upward, Downward, and Lateral Influence Attempts." Also see Gary Yukl, Cecilia M. Falbe, and Joo Young Youn, "Patterns of Influence Behavior for Managers," *Group & Organization Management*, 18 (March 1993): 5–28; Randall A. Gordon, "Impact of Ingratiation on Judgments and Evaluations: A Meta-Analytic Investigation," *Journal of Personality and Social Psychology*, 71 (July 1996): 54–70; Bennett J. Tepper, Regina J. Eisenbach, Susan L. Kirby, and Paula W. Potter, "Test of a Justice-Based Model of Subordinates' Resistance to Downward Influence Attempts," *Group & Organization Management*, 23 (June 1998): 144–160; William D. Crano and Xin Chen, "The Leniency Contract and Persistence of Majority and Minority Influence," *Journal of Personality and Social Psychology*, 74 (June 1998): 1437–1450; and Barbara Price Davis and Eric S. Knowles, "A Disrupt-Then-Reframe Technique of Social Influence," *Journal of Personality and Social Psychology*, 76 (February 1999): 192–199.

4. See George F. Dreher, Thomas W. Dougherty, and William Whitely, "Influence Tactics and Salary Attainment: A Gender-Specific Analysis," *Sex Roles*, 20 (May 1989): 535–550; and Herman Aguinis and Susan K. R. Adams, "Social-Role Versus Structural Models of Gender and Influence Use in Organizations," *Group & Organization Studies*, 23 (December 1998): 414–446.

5. See Mahfooz A. Ansari and Alka Kapoor, "Organizational Context and Upward Influence Tactics," *Organizational Behavior and Human Decision Processes*, 40 (August 1987): 39–49.

6. Dean Tjosvold, "The Dynamics of Positive Power," *Training and Development Journal*, 38 (June 1984): 72.

7. See Toddi Gutner, "A 12-Step Program to Gaining Power," *Business Week* (December 24, 2001): 88.

8. Morgan McCall Jr., "Power, Influence, and Authority: The Hazards of Carrying a Sword," *Technical Report*, 10 (Greensboro, N.C.: Center for Creative Leadership, 1978), p. 5.

9. For more on these three effects of power, see Anthony T. Cobb, "An Episodic Model of Power: Toward an Integration of Theory and Research," *Academy of Management Review*, 9 (July 1984): 482–493. Also see C. Marlene Fiol, Edward J. O'Connor, and Herman Aguinis, "All for One and One for All? The Development and Transfer of Power Across Organizational Levels," *Academy of Management Review*, 26 (April 2001): 224–242.

10. Based on Edwin P. Hollander and Lynn R. Offermann, "Power and Leadership in Organizations: Relationships in Transition," *American Psychologist*, 45 (February 1990): 179–189.

11. See William A. Kahn and Kathy E. Kram, "Authority at Work: Internal Models and Their Organizational Consequences," *Academy of Management Review*, 19 (January 1994): 17–50.

12. "There Is No State Here Anymore," *Newsweek* (February 24, 1997): 42.

13. For related discussion, see Allan R. Cohen and David L. Bradford, "Influence Without Authority: The Use of Alliances, Reciprocity, and Exchange to Accomplish Work," *Organizational Dynamics*, 17 (Winter 1989): 4–17; and Allan R. Cohen and David L. Bradford, *Influence Without Authority* (New York: Wiley, 1990).

14. See John R. P. French Jr. and Bertram Raven, "The Bases of Social Power," *Studies in Social Power*, ed. Dorwin Cartwright (Ann Arbor: University of Michigan Press, 1959), pp. 150–167. Eight different sources of power are discussed in Hugh R. Taylor, "Power at Work," *Personnel Journal*, 65 (April 1986): 42–49. Also see H. Eugene Baker III, "'Wax On—Wax Off': French and Raven at the Movies," *Journal of Management Education*, 17 (November 1993): 517–519.

15. John P. Kotter, "Power, Dependence, and Effective Management," *Harvard Business Review*, 55 (July–August 1977): 128. For related research, see Sydney Finkelstein, "Power in Top Management Teams: Dimensions, Measurement, and Validation," *Academy of Management Journal*, 35 (August 1992): 505–538; and Herminia Ibarra, "Network Centrality, Power, and Innovation Involvement: Determinants of Technical and Administrative Roles," *Academy of Management Journal*, 36 (June 1993): 471–501.

16. For a revealing case study, see John A. Byrne, "Chainsaw," *Business Week* (October 18, 1999): 128–147. Also see Jonathan Alter, "Citizen Clinton Up Close," *Newsweek* (April 8, 2002): 34–42.

17. Patricia Sellers, "What Exactly Is Charisma?" *Fortune* (January 15, 1996): 68. Also see Daniel Sankowsky, "The Charismatic Leader as Narcissist: Understanding the Abuse of Power," *Organizational Dynamics*, 23 (Spring 1995): 57–71.

18. See Mark R. Story, "The Secrets of Successful Empowerment," *National Productivity Review*, 14 (Summer 1995): 81–90;

Gretchen M. Spreitzer, "Psychological Empowerment in the Workplace: Dimensions, Measurement, and Validation," *Academy of Management Journal,* 38 (October 1995): 1442–1465; Mark G. Becker, "Lessons in Empowerment," *Training,* 33 (September 1996): 35–42; Robert E. Quinn and Gretchen M. Spreitzer, "The Road to Empowerment: Seven Questions Every Leader Should Consider," *Organizational Dynamics,* 26 (Autumn 1997): 37–49; Bradley L. Kirkman and Benson Rosen, "Beyond Self-Management: Antecedents and Consequences of Team Empowerment," *Academy of Management Journal,* 42 (February 1999): 58–74; and Christine S. Koberg, R. Wayne Boss, Jason C. Senjem, and Eric A. Goodman, "Antecedents and Outcomes of Empowerment: Empirical Evidence from the Health Care Industry," *Group & Organization Management,* 24 (March 1999): 71–91.

19. As quoted in Laurel Shaper Walters, "A Leader Redefines Management," *The Christian Science Monitor* (September 22, 1992): 14. For Frances Hesselbein's ideas about leadership, see Roundtable Discussion, "All in a Day's Work," *Harvard Business Review* (Special Issue: Breakthrough Leadership), 79 (December 2001): 54–66.

20. Based on discussion in Stephen R. Covey, *Principle-Centered Leadership* (New York: Simon & Schuster, 1991), pp. 214–216. Also see W. Alan Randolph, "Navigating the Journey to Empowerment," *Organizational Dynamics,* 23 (Spring 1995): 19–32; and Alan J. H. Thorlakson and Robert P. Murray, "An Empirical Study of Empowerment in the Workplace," *Group & Organization Management,* 21 (March 1996): 67–83; Kyle Dover, "Avoiding Empowerment Traps," *Management Review,* 88 (January 1999): 51–55; and W. Alan Randolph, "Re-Thinking Empowerment: Why Is It So Hard to Achieve?" *Organizational Dynamics,* 29 (Fall 2000): 94–107.

21. John A. Byrne, "The Environment Was Ripe for Abuse," *Business Week* (February 25, 2002): 119.

22. For a recent sampling, see Michael Useem, "The Leadership Lessons of Mount Everest," *Harvard Business Review,* 79 (October 2001): 51–58; Katharina Balazs, "Some Like it Haute: Leadership Lessons From France's Great Chefs," *Organizational Dynamics,* 30 (Fall 2001): 134–148; and Jane E. Dutton, Peter J. Frost, Monica C. Worline, Jacoba M. Lilius, and Jason M. Kanov, "Leading in Times of Trauma," *Harvard Business Review,* 80 (January 2002): 54–61.

23. See Jonathan E. Smith, Kenneth P. Carson, and Ralph A. Alexander, "Leadership: It Can Make a Difference," *Academy of Management Journal,* 27 (December 1984): 765–776; Janet M. Dukerich, Mary Lippitt Nichols, Dawn R. Elm, and David A. Vollrath, "Moral Reasoning in Groups: Leaders Make a Difference," *Human Relations,* 43 (May 1990): 473–493; Larry Bossidy, "The Job No CEO Should Delegate," *Harvard Business Review,* 79 (March 2001): 46–49; Melvin Sorcher and James Brant, "Are You Picking the Right Leaders?" *Harvard Business Review,* 80 (February 2002): 78–85; and Charles Fishman, "Isolating the Leadership Gene," *Fast Company,* no. 56 (March 2002): 82–90.

24. Inspired by the definition in Andrew J. DuBrin, *Leadership: Research Findings, Practice and Skills,* 2nd ed. (Boston: Houghton Mifflin, 1998), p. 2. Also see Francis J. Yammarino, Fred Dansereau, and Christina J. Kennedy, "A Multiple-Level Multidimensional Approach to Leadership: Viewing Leadership Through an Elephant's Eye," *Organizational Dynamics,* 29 (Winter 2001): 149–163.

25. As quoted in Oren Harari, *The Leadership Secrets of Colin Powell* (New York: McGraw-Hill, 2002): p. 13.

26. See Gary Yukl, "Managerial Leadership: A Review of Theory and Research," *Journal of Management,* 15 (June 1989): 251–289; Gary A. Yukl, *Leadership in Organizations,* 2nd ed. (Englewood Cliffs, N.J.: Prentice-Hall, 1989); and Karl O. Magnusen, "The Legacy of Leadership Revisited," *Business Horizons,* 38 (November–December 1995): 3–7.

27. See David L. Cawthon, "Leadership: The Great Man Theory Revisited," *Business Horizons,* 39 (May–June 1996): 1–4; Nathan A. Forney, "Rommel in the Boardroom," *Business Horizons,* 42 (July–August 1999): 37–42; Thomas A. Stewart, Alex Taylor III, Peter Petre, and Brent Schlender, "Henry Ford, Alfred P. Sloan, Tom Watson Jr., Bill Gates: The Businessman of the Century," *Fortune* (November 22, 1999): 109–128; and Richard S. Tedlow, "What Titans Can Teach Us," *Harvard Business Review* (Special Issue: Breakthrough Leadership), 79 (December 2001): 70–79.

28. Fred Luthans, *Organizational Behavior,* 3rd ed. (New York: McGraw-Hill, 1981), p. 419. Also see Gail Dutton, "Leadership in a Post-Heroic Age," *Management Review,* 85 (October 1996): 7.

29. Ralph M. Stogdill, "Personal Factors Associated with Leadership: A Survey of the Literature," *Journal of Psychology,* 25 (1948): 63.

30. See Daniel Goleman, *Emotional Intelligence* (New York: Bantam Books, 1995); Michaela Davies, Lazar Stankov, and Richard D. Roberts, "Emotional Intelligence: In Search of an Elusive Construct," *Journal of Personality and Social Psychology,* 75 (October 1998): 989–1015; and Quy Nguyen Huy, "Emotional Capability, Emotional Intelligence, and Radical Change," *Academy of Management Review,* 24 (April 1999): 325–345.

31. Michelle Neely Martinez, "The Smarts That Count," *HRMagazine,* 42 (November 1997): 72.

32. Based on and adapted from Daniel Goleman, Richard Boyatzis and Annie McKee, "Primal Leadership," *Harvard Business Review* (Special Issue: Breakthrough Leadership), 79 (December 2001): 49. Also see Daniel Goleman, Richard Boyatzis, and Annie McKee, *Primal Leadership: Realizing the Power of Emotional Intelligence* (Boston: Harvard Business School Press, 2002); and Bruce Rosenstein, "Experts: Leaders Can Motivate if They Exude the Right Vibes," USA Today (March 25, 2002): 9B.

33. Data from Judy B. Rosener, "Ways Women Lead," *Harvard Business Review,* 68 (November–December 1990): 119–125. Also see Chris Lee, "The Feminization of Management," *Training,* 31 (November 1994): 25–31; Rochelle Sharpe, "As Leaders, Women Rule," *Business Week* (November 20, 2000): 74–84; and Del Jones, "Many Successful Women Also Athletic," *USA Today* (March 26, 2002): 1B–2B.

34. See "Ways Women and Men Lead," *Harvard Business Review,* 69 (January–February 1991): 150–160.

35. Data from Alice H. Eagly and Blair T. Johnson, "Gender and Leadership Style: A Meta-Analysis," *Psychological Bulletin,* 108 (September 1990): 233–256. Also see Judith A. Kolb, "Are We Still Stereotyping Leadership? A Look at Gender and Other Predictors of Leader Emergence," *Small Group Research,* 28 (August 1997): 370–393; Virginia W. Cooper, "Homophily or the Queen Bee Syndrome: Female Evaluation of Female Leadership," *Small Group Research,* 28 (November 1997): 483–499; and Robert K. Shelly and Paul T. Munroe, "Do Women Engage in Less Task Behavior Than Men?" *Sociological Perspectives,* 42 (Spring 1999): 49–67.

36. Kurt Lewin, Ronald Lippitt, and Ralph K. White, "Patterns of Aggressive Behavior in Experimentally Created 'Social Climates,'" *Journal of Social Psychology,* 10 (May 1939): 271–299.

37. The risks of shifting styles are discussed in Thomas L. Brown, "Managerial Waffling: In Politics—or in Business—Waffling Suggests Bad Leadership," *Industry Week* (January 18, 1993): 34. Also see Oren Harari, "Leadership vs. Autocracy: They Just Don't Get It!" *Management Review,* 85 (August 1996): 42–45.

38. For an informative summary of this research, see Edwin A. Fleishman, "Twenty Years of Consideration and Structure," in *Current Developments in the Study of Leadership,* ed. Edwin A. Fleishman and James G. Hunt (Carbondale, Ill.: Southern Illinois University Press, 1973), pp. 1–40. Also see Vishwanath V. Baba and Merle E. Ace, "Serendipity in Leadership: Initiating Structure and Consideration in the Classroom," *Human Relations,* 42 (June 1989): 509–525.

39. Three popular extensions of the Ohio State leadership studies may be found in Robert R. Blake and Anne McCanse, *Leadership Dilemmas—Grid Solutions* (Houston: Gulf Publishing, 1990); William J. Reddin, *Managerial Effectiveness* (New York: McGraw-Hill, 1970); and Paul Hersey and Kenneth H. Blanchard, *Management of Organizational Behavior: Utilizing Human Resources,* 5th ed. (Englewood Cliffs, N.J.: Prentice-Hall, 1988), p. 171. Empirical lack of support for Hersey and Blanchard's situational leadership theory is reported in Jane R. Goodson, Gail W. McGee, and James F. Cashman, "Situational Leadership Theory: A Test of Leadership Prescriptions," *Group & Organization Studies,* 14 (December 1989): 446–461.

40. See Abraham K. Korman, "Consideration, 'Initiating Structure,' and Organizational Criteria—A Review," *Personnel Psychology,* 19 (Winter 1966): 349–361.

41. See Blake and McCanse, *Leadership Dilemmas—Grid Solutions.*

42. See Tom Lester, "Taking Guard on the Grid," *Management Today* (March 1991): 93–94.

43. For details of this study, see Robert R. Blake and Jane Srygley Mouton, "Management by Grid® Principles or Situationalism: Which?" *Group & Organization Studies,* 6 (December 1981): 439–455. Also see Robert R. Blake and Jane Srygley Mouton, "A Comparative Analysis of Situationalism and 9,9 Management by Principle," *Organizational Dynamics,* 10 (Spring 1982): 20–43. For another view of leader behavior, see Susan A. Tynan, "Best Behaviors," *Management Review,* 88 (November 1999): 58–61.

44. Fred E. Fiedler, "Job Engineering for Effective Leadership: A New Approach," *Management Review,* 66 (September 1977): 29.

45. For an excellent comprehensive validation study, see Michael J. Strube and Joseph E. Garcia, "A Meta-Analytic Investigation of Fiedler's Contingency Model of Leadership Effectiveness," *Psychological Bulletin,* 90 (September 1981): 307–321.

46. Fred E. Fiedler and Martin M. Chemers, *Leadership and Effective Management* (Glenview, Ill.: Scott, Foresman, 1974), p. 91.

47. Robert J. House and Terence R. Mitchell, "Path-Goal Theory of Leadership," *Journal of Contemporary Business,* 3 (Autumn 1974): 85. The entire Autumn 1974 issue is devoted to an instructive review of contrasting theories of leadership.

48. See Jan P. Muczyk and Bernard C. Reimann, "The Case for Directive Leadership," *Academy of Management Executive,* 1 (November 1987): 301–311.

49. Adapted from House and Mitchell, "Path-Goal Theory of Leadership," p. 83.

50. For path-goal research, see Abduhl-Rahim A. Al-Gattan, "Test of the Path-Goal Theory of Leadership in the Multinational Domain," *Group & Organization Studies,* 10 (December 1985): 429–445; Robert T. Keller, "A Test of the Path-Goal Theory of Leadership with Need for Clarity as a Moderator in Research and Development Organizations," *Journal of Applied Psychology,* 74 (April 1989): 208–212; John E. Mathieu, "A Test of Subordinates' Achievement and Affiliation Needs as Moderators of Leader Path-Goal Relationships," *Basic and Applied Social Psychology,* 11 (June 1990): 179–189; and Retha A. Price, "An Investigation of Path-Goal Leadership Theory in Marketing Channels," *Journal of Retailing,* 67 (Fall 1991): 339–361.

51. See J. McGregor Burns, *Leadership* (New York: HarperCollins, 1978). Also see Frederick F. Reichheld, "Lead for Loyalty," *Harvard Business Review,* 79 (July–August 2001): 76–84.

52. See David A. Nadler and Michael L. Tushman, "Beyond the Charismatic Leader: Leadership and Organizational Change," *California Management Review,* 32 (Winter 1990): 77–97; and Noel Tichy, "Simultaneous Transformation and CEO Succession: Key to Global Competitiveness," *Organizational Dynamics,* 25 (Spring 1996): 45–59. For more on "vision," see Laurie Larwood, Cecilia M. Falbe, Mark P. Kriger, and Paul Miesing, "Structure and Meaning of Organizational Vision," *Academy of Management Journal,* 38 (June 1995): 740–769; Maria L. Nathan, "What Is Organizational Vision? Ask Chief Executives," *Academy of Management Executive,* 10 (February 1996): 82–83; and Burt Nanus, "Leading the Vision Team," *The Futurist,* 30 (May–June 1996): 21–23.

53. A critique of charismatic leadership can be found in Joshua Macht, "Jim Collins to CEOs: Lose the Charisma," *Business 2.0,* 2 (October 2001): 121–122. Also see Jack Welch, *Jack: Straight From the Gut* (New York: Warner Business Books, 2001); and Bruce Horovitz and Theresa Howard, "Wendy's Loses Its Legend," *USA Today* (January 9, 2002): 1B–2B.

54. See Joseph Seltzer and Bernard M. Bass, "Transformational Leadership: Beyond Initiation and Consideration," *Journal of Management,* 16 (December 1990): 693–703.

55. For research support, see David A. Waldman, Gabriel G. Ramírez, Robert J. House, and Phanish Puranam, "Does Leadership Matter? CEO Leadership Attributes and Profitability Under Conditions of Perceived Environmental Uncertainty," *Academy of Management Journal,* 44 (February 2001): 134–143.

56. For example, see Jane M. Howell and Peter J. Frost, "A Laboratory Study of Charismatic Leadership," *Organizational Behavior and Human Decision Processes,* 43 (April 1989): 243–269; Bernard M. Bass, "From Transactional to Transformational Leadership: Learning to Share the Vision," *Organizational Dynamics,* 18 (Winter 1990): 19–31; Ronald J. Deluga, "The Effects of Transformational, Transactional, and Laissez-Faire Leadership Characteristics on Subordinate-Influencing Behavior," *Basic and Applied Social Psychology,* 11 (June 1990): 191–203; Robert T. Keller, "Transformational Leadership and the Performance of Research and Development Project Groups," *Journal of Management,* 18 (September 1992): 489–501; Philip M. Podsakoff, Scott B. MacKenzie, and William H. Bommer, "Transformational Leader Behaviors and Substitutes for Leadership as Determinants of Employee Satisfaction, Commitment, Trust, and Organizational Citizenship Behaviors," *Journal of Management,* 22, no. 2 (1996): 259–298; J. Bruce Tracey and Timothy R. Hinkin, "Transformational Leadership or Effective Managerial Practices?" *Group & Organization Management,* 23 (September 1998): 220–236; David A. Waldman and Francis J. Yammarino, "CEO Charismatic Leadership: Levels-of-Management and Levels-of-Analysis Effects," *Academy of Management Review,* 24 (April 1999): 266–285; and Warren Bennis, "The End of Leadership: Exemplary Leadership Is Impossible Without Full Inclusion, Initiatives, and Cooperation of Followers," *Organizational Dynamics,* 28 (Summer 1999): 71–80.

57. For more on the servant leader philosophy, see Robert K. Greenleaf, *Servant Leadership: A Journey into the Nature of Legitimate Power and Greatness* (New York: Paulist Press, 1977); and Walter Kiechel III, "The Leader as Servant," *Fortune* (May 4, 1992): 121–122.

58. David Leon Moore, "Wooden's Wizardry Wears Well," *USA Today* (March 29, 1995): 1C–2C. Also see "The 'Wizard' Turns 90," *USA Today* (October 11, 2000): 10C; Jerry Useem, "A Manager for All Seasons," *Fortune* (April 30, 2001): 66–72; and Chuck Salter, "Attention, Class!!!" *Fast Company,* no. 53 (December 2001): 114–126.

59. For good ideas about developing tomorrow's leaders, see Leigh Buchanan and Mike Hofman, "Everything I Know About Leadership, I Learned from the Movies," *Inc.,* 22 (March 2000): 58–70; Randy Hopper, "U.S. Military Academy: 'You Can't Lead Without Making Sacrifices,'" *Fast Company,* 47 (June 2001): 106–116; and James R. Fisher Jr., "Obstacles—and Overcoming Them—to Leadership Among Professional Workers," *Journal of Organizational Excellence,* 20 (Summer 2001): 27–34.

60. For more, see Andrea C. Poe, "Establishing Positive Mentor Relationships," *HRMagazine,* 47 (February 2002): 62–69; Harriet Rubin, "The Trouble with Mentors," *Fast Company,* no. 56 (March 2002): 44–46; Steve Bates, "Mentors Help Meld Cultures in Mergers," *HRMagazine,* 47 (March 2002): 10, 12; and Fara Warner, "Inside Intel's Mentoring Movement," *Fast Company,* no. 57 (April 2002): 116–120.

61. Abraham Zaleznik, "Managers and Leaders: Are They Different?" *Harvard Business Review,* 55 (May–June 1977): 76.

62. For details, see Ellen A. Fagenson, "The Mentor Advantage: Perceived Career/Job Experiences of Protégés Versus Non-Protégés," *Journal of Organizational Behavior,* 10 (October 1989): 309–320. More mentoring research findings are reported in Belle Rose Ragins and Terri A. Scandura, "Gender Differences in Expected Outcomes of Mentoring Relationships," *Academy of Management Journal,* 37 (August 1994): 957–971; Bennett J. Tepper, "Upward Maintenance Tactics in Supervisory Mentoring and Nonmentoring Relationships," *Academy of Management Journal,* 38 (August 1995): 1191–1205; Samuel Aryee, Yue Wah Chay, and Juniper Chew, "The Motivation to Mentor Among Managerial Employees: An Interactionist Approach," *Group & Organization Management,* 21 (September 1996): 261–277; and Belle Rose Ragins, John L. Cotton, and Janice S. Miller, "Marginal Mentoring: The Effects of Type of Mentor, Quality of Relationship, and Program Design on Work and Career Attitudes," *Academy of Management Journal,* 43 (December 2000): 1177–1194.

63. See Erik Gunn, "Mentoring: The Democratic Version," *Training,* 32 (August 1995): 64–67; and Ian Cunningham and Linda Honold, "Everyone Can Be a Coach," *HRMagazine,* 43 (June 1998): 63–66.

64. Jeremy Kahn, "The World's Most Admired Companies," *Fortune* (October 11, 1999): 275. Also see Frank Jossi, "Mentoring in Changing Times," *Training,* 34 (August 1997): 50–54.

65. For more, see Kathy E. Kram, "Phases of the Mentor Relationship," *Academy of Management Journal,* 26 (December 1983): 608–625.

66. Good discussions of women and mentoring can be found in R. J. Burke and C. A. McKeen, "Mentoring in Organizations: Implications for Women," *Journal of Business Ethics,* 9 (April–May 1990): 317–332; Belle Rose Ragins and John L. Cotton, "Easier Said Than Done: Gender Differences in Perceived Barriers to Gaining a Mentor," *Academy of Management Journal,* 34 (December 1991): 939–951; and Victoria A. Parker and Kathy E. Kram, "Women Mentoring Women: Creating Conditions for Connection," *Business Horizons,* 36 (March–April 1993): 42–51; and Susan J. Wells, "Smoothing the Way," *HRMagazine,* 46 (June 2001): 52–58.

67. For more, see George F. Dreher and Josephine A. Chargois, "Gender, Mentoring Experiences, and Salary Attainment Among Graduates of an Historically Black University," *Journal of Vocational Behavior,* 53 (December 1998): 401–416; David A. Thomas, "The Truth About Mentoring Minorities: Race Matters," *Harvard Business Review,* 79 (April 2001): 99–107; Robert J. Grossman, "Mentors in Demand," *HRMagazine,* 45 (March 2000): 42–43; and Jonathan A. Segal, "Mirror-Image Mentoring," *HRMagazine,* 45 (March 2000): 157–166.

68. For a contemporary perspective of behaviorism, see Richard J. DeGrandpre, "A Science of Meaning: Can Behaviorism Bring

Meaning to Psychological Science?" *American Psychologist,* 55 (July 2000): 721–738.

69. See Edward L. Thorndike, *Educational Psychology: The Psychology of Learning* (New York: Columbia University Press, 1913), II, 4.

70. For an instructive account of operant conditioning applied to human behavior, see B. F. Skinner, *Science and Human Behavior* (New York: Free Press, 1953), pp. 62–66. A good update is B. F. Skinner, "What Is Wrong with Daily Life in the Western World," *American Psychologist,* 41 (May 1986): 568–574. Also see Marilyn B. Gilbert and Thomas F. Gilbert, "What Skinner Gave Us," *Training,* 28 (September 1991): 42–48.

71. For example, see Tom Kramlinger and Tom Huberty, "Behaviorism Versus Humanism," *Training & Development Journal,* 44 (December 1990): 41–45; and Alfie Kohn, "Challenging Behaviorist Dogma: Myths About Money and Motivation," *Compensation & Benefits Review,* 30 (March–April 1998): 27, 33–37.

72. For example, see Bob Filipczak, "Why No One Likes Your Incentive Program," *Training,* 30 (August 1993): 19–25; and Alfie Kohn, "Why Incentive Plans Cannot Work," *Harvard Business Review,* 71 (September–October 1993): 54–63.

73. For positive evidence and background, see Alexander D. Stajkovic and Fred Luthans, "A Meta-Analysis of the Effects of Organizational Behavior Modification on Task Performance, 1975–95," *Academy of Management Journal,* 40 (October 1997): 1122–1149; Fred Luthans and Alexander D. Stajkovic, "Reinforce for Performance: The Need to Go Beyond Pay and Even Rewards," *Academy of Management Executive,* 13 (May 1999): 49–57; Cheryl Comeau-Kirschner, "Improving Productivity Doesn't Cost a Dime," *Management Review,* 88 (January 1999): 7; and Alexander D. Stajkovic and Fred Luthans, "Differential Effects of Incentive Motivators on Work Performance," *Academy of Management Journal,* 44 (June 2001): 580–590.

74. Dale Feuer, "Training for Fast Times," *Training,* 24 (July 1987): 28.

75. See Robert Kegan and Lisa Laskow Lahey, "More Powerful Communication: From the Language of Prizes and Praising to the Language of Ongoing Regard," *Journal of Organizational Excellence,* 20 (Summer 2001): 11–17; and Leigh Buchanan, "Managing One-to-One," *Inc.,* 23 (October 2001): 82–88.

76. Alan Farnham, "The Trust Gap," *Fortune* (December 4, 1989): 74.

77. Kenneth Blanchard and Spencer Johnson, *The One Minute Manager* (New York: Berkley, 1982), p. 45 (emphasis added). Also see Kenneth Blanchard and Robert Lorber, *Putting the One Minute Manager to Work* (New York: Berkley, 1984).

78. For detailed treatment of B. Mod. in the workplace, see Fred Luthans and Robert Kreitner, *Organizational Behavior Modification and Beyond: An Operant and Social Learning Approach* (Glenview, Ill.: Scott, Foresman, 1985); and Gerald A. Merwin Jr., John A. Thomason, and Eleanor E. Sanford, "A Methodology and Content Review of Organizational Behavior Management in the Private Sector: 1978–1986," *Journal of Organizational Behavior Management,* 10, no. 1 (1989): 39–57.

Also see Mark A. Friend and James P. Kohn, "A Behavioral Approach to Accident Prevention," *Occupational Hazards,* 54 (October 1992): 112–115; Thomas K. Connellan and Ron Zemke, *Sustaining Knock Your Socks Off Service* (New York: Amacom, 1993), ch. 13; Mark E. Furman, "Reverse the 80–20 Rule," *Management Review,* 86 (January 1997): 18–21; and Ahmad Diba, "If Pat Sajak Were Your CEO . . . ," *Fortune* (December 18, 2000): 330.

79. Ten items excerpted from a 25-item survey in Anne Fisher, "Success Secret: A High Emotional IQ," *Fortune* (October 26, 1998): 293–298.

## Chapter 16

**Opening Quotation** Dean Tjosvold, *Learning to Manage Conflict: Getting People to Work Together Productively* (New York: Lexington, 1993), p. xi.

**Opening Case** Reprinted by permission of *Harvard Business Review.* Excerpt from "The Business Case Against Revolution: An Interview with Nestlé's Peter Brabeck," by Suzy Wetlaufer. February 2001: 112–119. Copyright © 2001 by the Harvard Business School Publishing Corporation; all rights reserved.

**Closing Case** From "Bob Schmonsees Has a Tool for Better Sales, and It Ignores Excuses," by Thomas Petzinger, Jr., *The Wall Street Journal* (March 26, 1999). Copyright 1999 by Dow Jones & Co., Inc. Reproduced with permission of Dow Jones & Co., Inc. in the format textbook via Copyright Clearance Center.

1. See Pierre Mornell, "Nothing Endures but Change," *Inc.,* 22 (July 2000): 131–132; and Gary Hamel, "Revolution vs. Evolution: You Need Both," *Harvard Business Review,* 79 (May 2001): 150–154.

2. See Carrie R. Leana and Bruce Barry, "Stability and Change as Simultaneous Experiences in Organizational Life," *Academy of Management Review,* 25 (October 2000): 753–759.

3. Adapted from discussion in David A. Nadler and Michael L. Tushman, "Organizational Frame Bending: Principles for Managing Reorientation," *Academy of Management Executive,* 3 (August 1989): 194–204. Also see Loizos Heracleous and Michael Barrett, "Organizational Change as Discourse: Communicative Actions and Deep Structures in the Context of Information Technology Implementation," *Academy of Management Journal,* 44 (August 2001): 755–778; and Peter D. Sherer and Kyungmook Lee, "Institutional Change in Large Law Firms: A Resource Dependency and Institutional Perspective," *Academy of Management Journal,* 45 (February 2002): 102–119.

4. See Brian Dumaine, "Creating a New Company Culture," *Fortune* (January 15, 1990): 127–131.

5. See Tom Duening, "Our Turbulent Times? The Case for Evolutionary Organizational Change," *Business Horizons,* 40 (January–February 1997): 2–8.

6. Fred Vogelstein, "Can Schwab Get Its Mojo Back?" *Fortune* (September 17, 2001): 96. Also see Julia Kirby, "Reinvention with Respect: An Interview with Jim Kelly of UPS," *Harvard Business Review,* 79 (November 2001): 116–123; and Fara Warner, "Change Agent: John Dooner," *Fast Company,* no. 52 (November 2001): 116–120.

7. Kathy Rebello, "Inside Microsoft," *Business Week* (July 15, 1996): 57. For an update, see Jim Frederick, "Microsoft's $40 Billion Bet," *Money,* 31 (May 2002): 66–80. Also see Richard Leifer, Gina Colarelli O'Connor, and Mark Rice, "Implementing Radical Innovation in Mature Firms: The Role of Hubs," *Academy of Management Executive,* 15 (August 2001): 102–113; and Jim Collins, "Good to Great," *Fast Company,* no. 51 (October 2001): 90–104.

8. See Russ Vince and Michael Broussine, "Paradox, Defense and Attachment: Accessing and Working with Emotions and Relations Underlying Organizational Change," *Organization Studies,* 17, no. 1 (1996): 1–21.

9. See Robert H. Miles, "Beyond the Age of Dilbert: Accelerating Corporate Transformations by Rapidly Engaging All Employees," *Organizational Dynamics,* 29 (Spring 2001): 313–321.

10. See Timothy A. Judge, Carl J. Thoresen, Vladimir Pucik, and Theresa M. Welbourne, "Managerial Coping with Organizational Change: A Dispositional Perspective," *Journal of Applied Psychology,* 84 (February 1999): 107–122; Quy Nguyen Huy, "Emotional Capability, Emotional Intelligence, and Radical Change," *Academy of Management Review,* 24 (April 1999): 325–345; and Cheryl Dahle, "Big Learning, Fast Futures," *Fast Company,* no. 25 (June 1999): 46, 48.

11. For example, see Roundtable Discussion, "Fast Talk: The Old Economy Meets the New Economy," *Fast Company,* no. 51 (October 2001): 70–80.

12. Ichak Adizes, *Mastering Change: The Power of Mutual Trust and Respect in Personal Life, Family Life, Business and Society* (Santa Monica, Calif.: Adizes Institute, 1991), p. 6.

13. See Cynthia M. Hernandez and Donald R. Leslie, "When Change Hits the Fan," *Nonprofit Management & Leadership,* 10 (Summer 2000): 451–455; Sandy Kristin Piderit, "Rethinking Resistance and Recognizing Ambivalence: A Multidimensional View of Attitudes Toward an Organizational Change," *Academy of Management Review,* 25 (October 2000): 783–794; and Peter de Jager, "Resistance to Change: A New View of an Old Problem," *The Futurist,* 35 (May–June 2001): 24–27.

14. J. Alan Ofner, "Managing Change," *Personnel Administrator,* 29 (September 1984): 20.

15. Peter Coy, "The Perils of Picking the Wrong Standard," *Business Week* (October 8, 1990): 145. Also see Louis Woo, "Speech Technology Can Shrink World," *USA Today* (June 22, 1999): 6E.

16. This list is based in part on John P. Kotter and Leonard A. Schlesinger, "Choosing Strategies for Change," *Harvard Business Review,* 57 (March–April 1979): 106–114; and Joseph Stanislao and Bettie C. Stanislao, "Dealing with Resistance to Change," *Business Horizons,* 26 (July–August 1983): 74–78.

17. Robert Kegan and Lisa Laskow Lahey, "The Real Reason People Won't Change," *Harvard Business Review,* 79 (November 2001): 86.

18. For example, see Arnon E. Reichers, John P. Wanous, and James T. Austin, "Understanding and Managing Cynicism About Organizational Change," *Academy of Management Executive,* 11 (February 1997): 48–59; Jack Gordon, "Change Resistance," *Training,* 35 (June 1998): 8, 10; Kenneth E. Hultman, "Let's Stop the Change Game," *Training,* 35 (November 1998): 120; Oren Harari, "Why Do Leaders Avoid Change?" *Management Review,* 88 (March 1999): 35–38; and "Resistance Fighter," *Fast Company,* no. 30 (December 1999): 390–396.

19. As quoted in Del Jones, "Product Development Can Fill Prescription for Success," *USA Today* (May 30, 2000): 7B.

20. See Allison Rossett, "Training & Organization Development: Separated at Birth?" *Training,* 33 (April 1996): 53–59; Joseph A. Raelin, "Action Learning and Action Science: Are They Different?" *Organizational Dynamics,* 26 (Summer 1997): 21–34; and Robert N. Llewellyn, "When to Call the Organization Doctor," *HRMagazine,* 47 (March 2002): 79–83.

21. Philip G. Hanson and Bernard Lubin, "Answers to Questions Frequently Asked About Organization Development," in *The Emerging Practice of Organization Development,* ed. Walter Sikes, Allan Drexler, and Jack Grant (Alexandria, Va.: NTL Institute, 1989), p. 16 (emphasis added). For good background information of current OD practices, see W. Warner Burke, "The New Agenda for Organization Development," *Organizational Dynamics,* 26 (Summer 1997): 7–20; Chuck McVinney, "Dream Weaver," *Training & Development* 53 (April 1999): 39–42; and Ron Zemke, "Don't Fix That Company!" *Training,* 36 (June 1999): 26–33.

22. W. Warner Burke, *Organization Development: A Normative View* (Reading, Mass.: Addison-Wesley, 1987), p. 9. Also see Benjamin Schneider, Arthur P. Brief, and Richard A. Guzzo, "Creating a Climate and Culture for Sustainable Organizational Change," *Organizational Dynamics,* 24 (Spring 1996): 7–19.

23. See Robert H. Schaffer, "Overcome the Fatal Flaws of Consulting: Close the Results Gap," *Business Horizons,* 41 (September–October 1998): 53–60; Cheryl Dahle, "Change Course: That's His Message to the Navy," *Fast Company,* no. 34 (May 2000): 68, 70; and Julia Boorstin, "The Making of a Model Consultant," *Fortune* (January 22, 2001): 158, 160.

24. For example, see Joel Schettler, "Bruce Kestelman," *Training,* 38 (November 2001): 36–39.

25. This list is based on Wendell French, "Organization Development Objectives, Assumptions, and Strategies," *California Management Review,* 12 (Winter 1969): 23–34; and Charles Kiefer and Peter Stroh, "A New Paradigm for Organization Development," *Training and Development Journal,* 37 (April 1983): 26–35.

26. See Robert J. Marshak, "Managing the Metaphors of Change," *Organizational Dynamics,* 22 (Summer 1993): 44–56; Craig L. Pearce and Charles P. Osmond, "Metaphors for Change: The ALPs Model of Change Management," *Organizational Dynamics,* 24 (Winter 1996): 23–35; and Ian Palmer and Richard Dunford, "Conflicting Uses of Metaphors: Reconceptualizing Their Use in the Field of Organizational Change," *Academy of Management Review,* 21 (July 1996): 691–717.

27. A successful application of Lewin's model at British Airways is discussed in Leonard D. Goodstein and W. Warner Burke, "Creating Successful Organization Change," *Organizational Dynamics,* 19 (Spring 1991): 4–17. Also see Gib Akin and Ian Palmer, "Putting Metaphors to Work for Change in

Organizations," *Organizational Dynamics,* 28 (Winter 2000): 67–79; Richard S. Allen and Kendyl A. Montgomery, "Applying an Organizational Development Approach to Creating Diversity," *Organizational Dynamics,* 30 (Fall 2001): 149–161; and Mark Herron, "Training Alone Is Not Enough," *Training,* 39 (February 2002): 72.

28. For details on how poor "unfreezing" threatened the Hewlett-Packard/Compaq Computer merger plan, see Peter Burrows, "Carly's Last Stand?" *Business Week* (December 24, 2001): 62–70.

29. For example, see Anita Lienart, "Drawing on the Pioneer Spirit," *Management Review,* 87 (December 1998): 19.

30. Bill Breen and Cheryl Dahl, "Field Guide for Change," *Fast Company,* no. 30 (December 1999): 384. Also see Oren Harari, "Leading Change from the Middle," *Management Review,* 88 (February 1999): 29–32; and David Butcher and Sally Atkinson, "The Bottom-Up Principle," *Management Review,* 89 (January 2000): 48–53.

31. Debra E. Meyerson, *Tempered Radicals: How People Use Difference to Inspire Change at Work* (Boston: Harvard Business School Press, 2001), p. xi. Also see Debra E. Meyerson, "Radical Change, the Quiet Way," *Harvard Business Review,* 79 (October 2001): 92–100.

32. Adapted from "Tips for Tempered Radicals" in Keith H. Hammonds, "Practical Radicals," *Fast Company,* no. 38 (September 2000): 162–174.

33. For practical insights on organizational change, see Scott Kirsner, "How to Stay On the Move . . . When the World Is Slowing Down," *Fast Company,* no. 48 (July 2001): 113–121; Shaul Fox and Yair Amichai-Hamburger, "The Power of Emotional Appeals in Promoting Organizational Change Programs," *Academy of Management Executive,* 15 (November 2001): 94; and Robert A. F. Reisner, "When a Turnaround Stalls," *Harvard Business Review,* 80 (February 2002): 45–51.

34. Abraham Zaleznik, "Real Work," *Harvard Business Review,* 67 (January–February 1989): 59–60.

35. For example, see Karen A. Jehn and Elizabeth A. Mannix, "The Dynamic Nature of Conflict: A Longitudinal Study of Intragroup Conflict and Group Performance," *Academy of Management Journal,* 44 (April 2001): 238–251; and Margaret Boitano, "You Got a Problem with That?" *Fortune* (June 11, 2001): 196[B]–196[F].

36. Dean Tjosvold, *Learning to Manage Conflict: Getting People to Work Together Productively* (New York: Lexington, 1993), p. 8.

37. Ibid. Also see Allen C. Amason, "Distinguishing the Effects of Functional and Dysfunctional Conflict on Strategic Decision Making: Resolving a Paradox for Top Management Teams," *Academy of Management Journal,* 39 (February 1996): 123–148; and Samuel S. Corl, "Agreeing to Disagree," *Purchasing Today,* 7 (February 1996): 10–11.

38. For case studies of problems associated with competitive conflict, see Ben Elgin, "Inside Yahoo!" *Business Week* (May 21, 2001): 114–123; Stanley Holmes, "Pulp Friction at Weyerhaeuser," *Business Week* (March 11, 2002): 66, 68; and Peter Burrows, "What Price Victory at Hewlett-Packard?" *Business Week* (April 1, 2002): 36–37.

39. Walter Kiechel III, "How to Escape the Echo Chamber," *Fortune* (June 18, 1990): 130. For other good material on constructive conflict, see Dean Tjosvold, Chun Hui, and Kenneth S. Law, "Constructive Conflict in China: Cooperative Conflict as a Bridge Between East and West," *Journal of World Business,* 36 (Summer 2001): 166–183.

40. For a good overview of managing conflict, see Kenneth Cloke and Joan Goldsmith, *Resolving Conflicts at Work: A Complete Guide for Everyone on the Job* (San Francisco: Jossey-Bass, 2000).

41. See "Aggressive Behavior Bullies into Workplace," *HRMagazine,* 44 (February 1999): 30; Rudy M. Yandrick, "Lurking in the Shadows," *HRMagazine,* 44 (October 1999): 61–68; and Kevin Dobbs, "The Lucrative Menace of Workplace Violence," *Training,* 37 (March 2000): 54–62.

42. See Dean Tjosvold and Margaret Poon, "Dealing with Scarce Resources," *Group & Organization Management,* 23 (September 1998): 237–255.

43. For related research, see Steven M. Farmer and Jonelle Roth, "Conflict-Handling Behavior in Work Groups: Effects of Group Structure, Decision Processes, and Time," *Small Group Research,* 29 (December 1998): 669–713; and Russell Cropanzano, Herman Aguinis, Marshall Schminke, and Dina L. Denham, "Disputant Reactions to Managerial Conflict Resolution Tactics: A Comparison Among Argentina, the Dominican Republic, Mexico, and the United States," *Group & Organization Management,* 24 (June 1999): 124–154.

44. Stephen P. Robbins, *Managing Organizational Conflict: A Nontraditional Approach* (Englewood Cliffs, N.J.: Prentice-Hall, 1974), p. 62.

45. See William H. Ross and Donald E. Conlon, "Hybrid Forms of Third-Party Dispute Resolution: Theoretical Implications of Combining Mediation and Arbitration," *Academy of Management Review,* 25 (April 2000): 416–427; and Stephanie Armour, "Arbitration's Rise Raises Fairness Issue," *USA Today* (June 12, 2001): 1B–2B.

46. See M. Afzalur Rahim, "A Measure of Styles of Handling Conflict," *Academy of Management Journal,* 26 (June 1983): 368–376; Erich Brockmann, "Removing the Paradox of Conflict from Group Decisions," *Academy of Management Executive,* 10 (May 1996): 61–62; and Donald E. Conlon and Daniel P. Sullivan, "Examining the Actions of Organizations in Conflict: Evidence from the Delaware Court of Chancery," *Academy of Management Journal,* 42 (June 1999): 319–329.

47. See Lyle Sussman, "How to Frame a Message: The Art of Persuasion and Negotiation," *Business Horizons,* 42 (July–August 1999): 2–6; G. Richard Shell, "Negotiator, Know Thyself," *Inc.,* 21 (May 1999): 106–107; and James K. Sebenius, "Six Habits of Merely Effective Negotiators," *Harvard Business Review,* 79 (April 2001): 87–95.

48. Data from Laurie R. Weingart, Elaine B. Hyder, and Michael J. Prietula, "Knowledge Matters: The Effects of Tactical Descriptions on Negotiation Behavior and Outcome," *Journal of Personality and Social Psychology,* 70 (June 1996): 1205–1217. Also see Kimberly A. Wade-Benzoni, Andrew J. Hoffman, Leigh L. Thompson, Don A. Moore, James J. Gillespie, and

Max H. Bazerman, "Barriers to Resolution in Ideologically Based Negotiations: The Role of Values and Institutions," *Academy of Management Review,* 27 (January 2002): 41–57.

49. Margaret A. Neale and Max H. Bazerman, "Negotiating Rationally: The Power and Impact of the Negotiator's Frame," *Academy of Management Executive,* 6 (August 1992): 42–51.

50. See "Powers of Persuasion," *Fortune* (October 12, 1998): 160–164; and Paul Kaihla, "Dicker the Other Guy Senseless," **www.ecompany.com,** 2 (July 2001): 51–52.

51. See Maurice E. Schweitzer and Jeffrey L. Kerr, "Bargaining Under the Influence: The Role of Alcohol in Negotiations," *Academy of Management Executive,* 14 (May 2000): 47–57; and Anne M. Burr, "Ethics in Negotiation: Does Getting to Yes Require Candor?" *Dispute Resolution Journal,* 56 (May–July 2001): 8–15.

52. Cross-cultural negotiation is discussed in Élise Campbell and Jeffrey J. Reuer, "International Alliance Negotiations: Legal Issues for General Managers," *Business Horizons,* 44 (January–February 2001): 19–26; Pervez Ghauri and Tony Fang, "Negotiating with the Chinese: A Socio-Cultural Analysis," *Journal of World Business,* 36 (Fall 2001): 303–325; and James K. Sebenius, "The Hidden Challenge of Cross-Border Negotiations," *Harvard Business Review,* 80 (March 2002): 76–85.

53. Stephen R. Covey, *The Seven Habits of Highly Effective People* (New York: Simon & Schuster, 1989), p. 207. Also see H. Joseph Reitz, James A. Wall Jr., and Mary Sue Love, "Ethics in Negotiation: Oil and Water or Good Lubrication?" *Business Horizons,* 41 (May–June 1998): 5–14.

54. A good resource book is Roger Fisher and Danny Ertel, *Getting Ready to Negotiate: The Getting to Yes Workbook* (New York: Penguin, 1995). Also see Deborah M. Kolb and Judith Williams, "Breakthrough Bargaining," *Harvard Business Review,* 79 (February 2001): 88–97.

55. Roger Fisher and William Ury, *Getting to Yes: Negotiating Agreement Without Giving In* (Boston: Houghton Mifflin, 1981), p. 104.

56. See Chapter 9 in Max H. Bazerman and Margaret A. Neale, *Negotiating Rationally* (New York: The Free Press, 1992), pp. 67–76. Also see Joan F. Brett, Gregory B. Northcraft, and Robin L. Pinkley, "Stairways to Heaven: An Interlocking Self-Regulation Model of Negotiation," *Academy of Management Review,* 24 (July 1999): 435–451.

57. An informative and entertaining introduction to a four-step win-win model can be found in Ross R. Reck and Brian G. Long, *The Win-Win Negotiator: How to Negotiate Favorable Agreements That Last* (New York: Pocket Books, 1987).

58. Based on discussion in Karl Albrecht and Steve Albrecht, "Added Value Negotiating," *Training,* 30 (April 1993): 26–29.

59. Ibid., p. 29.

60. Excerpted from Cloke and Goldsmith, *Resolving Conflicts at Work,* pp. 114–116.

## Chapter 17

**Opening Quotation** As quoted in Regina Fazio Maruca, ed., "Masters of Disaster," *Fast Company,* no. 45 (April 2001): 88.

**Opening Case** Eric Hellweg, "Supply-Chain Hero," *Business 2.0,* 3 (January 2002): 74–75. Reprinted by permission.

**Closing Case** Excerpted from Charles Fishman, "But Wait, You Promised . . . ," *Fast Company,* no. 45 (April 2001): 110–128. Copyright 2001 by Bus. Innovator Group Resources/Inc. Reproduced with permission of Bus. Innovator Group Resources/Inc. in the format textbook via Copyright Clearance Center.

1. For example, see Carol Hymowitz, "How CEOs Can Keep Informed Even as Work Stretches Across Globe," *The Wall Street Journal* (March 12, 2002): B1.

2. For example, see Harold Koontz and Robert W. Bradspies, "Managing Through Feedforward Control," *Business Horizons,* 15 (June 1972): 27.

3. James Cox, "More Firms Hire Sleuths to Avoid Nasty Surprises," *USA Today* (June 26, 2001): 1B. Also see Erika Germer, "Job Titles of the Future: Director, Ethical Hacking," *Fast Company,* no. 52 (November 2001): 64.

4. For discussion of a small business that got out of control, see D. M. Osborne, "Fast-Paced Rivals Silence Talking-Beeper Service," *Inc.,* 21 (December 1999): 40. Also see Anne Stuart, "The Pita Principle," *Inc.,* 23 (August 2001): 58–64.

5. See Richard L. Daft and Norman B. Macintosh, "The Nature and Use of Formal Control Systems for Management Control and Strategy Implementation," *Journal of Management,* 10 (Spring 1984): 43–66.

6. See Harrison M. Trice and Janice M. Beyer, *The Cultures of Work Organizations* (Englewood Cliffs, N.J.: Prentice-Hall, 1993).

7. Based on Eric Flamholtz, "Organizational Control Systems as a Managerial Tool," *California Management Review,* 22 (Winter 1979): 50–59.

8. Data from "Volvo Names North American Chief as CEO," *USA Today* (June 7, 2000): 1B.

9. See Stanley F. Slater, Eric M. Olson, and Venkateshwar K. Reddy, "Strategy-Based Performance Measurement," *Business Horizons,* 40 (July–August 1997): 37–44.

10. For more, see "Benchmarking for the Future," *Purchasing Today,* 12 (January 2001): 40–49; Ilan Mochari, "Steal This Strategy," *Inc.,* 23 (July 2001): 62–68; and Gabriel Szulanski and Sidney Winter, "Getting It Right the Second Time," *Harvard Business Review,* 80 (January 2002): 62–69.

11. Chris Woodyard, "United Polishes Its First-Class Act," *USA Today* (March 2, 1999): 10B. Also see Faith Keenan, "The Marines Learn New Tactics—From Wal-Mart," *Business Week* (December 24, 2001): 74.

12. For more on strategic control, see John H. Lingle and William A. Schiemann, "From Balanced Scorecard to Strategic Gauges: Is Measurement Worth It?" *Management Review,* 85 (March 1996): 56–61; and Joseph C. Picken and Gregory G. Dess, "Out of (Strategic) Control," *Organizational Dynamics,* 26 (Summer 1997): 35–48.

13. For a brief case study of financial control problems in the Catholic Church, see William C. Symonds, "The Economic Strain on the Church," *Business Week* (April 15, 2002): 34–40.

14. Ian Wylie "Down the Up Staircase," *Fast Company,* no. 56 (March 2002): 34.

15. See Nanette Byrnes, "Accounting in Crisis," *Business Week* (January 28, 2002): 44–48; and Allan Sloan and Mark

Hosenball, "No Accounting for It," *Newsweek* (February 25, 2002): 34–35.

16. Data from Justin Fox, "What's So Great About GE?" *Fortune* (March 4, 2002): 64–67.

17. Lawrence B. Sawyer, "Internal Auditing: Yesterday, Today, and Tomorrow," *The Internal Auditor,* 36 (December 1979): 26 (emphasis added). Also see Joseph F. Berardino and Gregory J. Jonas, "Power to the Audit Committee People," *Financial Executive,* 15 (November–December 1999): 36–38.

18. See Scott Herhold, "The Blunt Bean Counter," *Business 2.0,* 3 (April 2002): 91–92; and Thomas Mucha, "The Fraud Cop," *Business 2.0,* 3 (April 2002): 90–91.

19. This list is based in part on Donald W. Murr, Harry B. Bracey Jr., and William K. Hill, "How to Improve Your Organization's Management Controls," *Management Review,* 69 (October 1980): 56–63.

20. Data from Anna Bernasek, "The Friction Economy," *Fortune* (February 18, 2002): 104–112. Also see Gary Strauss, "Catastrophe Suspends Business as Usual in USA," *USA Today* (September 12, 2001): 1B–2B; Bill Powell, "Battered but Unbroken," *Fortune* (October 1, 2001): 68–80; and Michelle Conlin, "When the Office Is the War Zone," *Business Week* (November 19, 2001): 38.

21. See James Lardner, "Be Prepared," *Business 2.0,* 3 (January 2002): 41–52; Susanne M. Bruyère and William G. Stothers, "Enabling Safe Evacuations," *HRMagazine,* 47 (January 2002): 65–67; and Jonathan Rosenoer, "Safeguarding Your Critical Business Information," *Harvard Business Review,* 80 (February 2002): 20–22.

22. Christine M. Pearson and Judith A. Clair, "Reframing Crisis Management," *Academy of Management Review,* 23 (January 1998): 60. Also see Karlene H. Roberts and Robert G. Bea, "When Systems Fail," *Organizational Dynamics,* 29 (Winter 2001): 179–191.

23. See Christine M. Pearson, Judith A. Clair, Sarah Kovoor-Misra, and Ian I. Mitroff, "Managing the Unthinkable," *Organizational Dynamics,* 26 (Autumn 1997): 51–64; Del Jones, "Paranoia Pays: Managing Risk Has Its Rewards," *USA Today* (May 5, 2000): 1B; and Joshua Piven and David Borgenicht, "How to Survive a Kidnapping," *Business 2.0,* 3 (April 2002): 115.

24. See Christine M. Pearson and Dennis A. Rondinelli, "Crisis Management in Central European Firms," *Business Horizons,* 41 (May–June 1998): 50–60; Milton Bordwin, "Plan B . . . or Is It Plan C for Crisis?" *Management Review* 88, (July–August 1999): 53–55; Alex S. L. Tsang, "Military Doctrine in Crisis Management: Three Beverage Contamination Cases," *Business Horizons,* 43 (September–October 2000): 65–73; Karlene H. Roberts and Robert Bea, "Must Accidents Happen? Lessons from High Reliability Organizations," *Academy of Management Executive,* 15 (August 2001): 70–78; and Emily Barker, "The 24-Hour Recovery Plan," *Inc.,* 23 (December 2001): 112–113.

25. See Marilyn Adams, "Southwest Manages a Crisis," *USA Today* (March 20, 2000): 6B.

26. See Dale D. McConkey, "Planning for Uncertainty," *Business Horizons,* 30 (January–February 1987): 40–45; and Brahim

Herbane, Dominic Elliot, and Ethne Swartz, "Contingency and Continua: Achieving Excellence Through Business Continuity Planning," *Business Horizons,* 40 (November–December 1997): 19–25.

27. Barbara Rudolph, "Coping with Catastrophe," *Time* (February 24, 1986): 53.

28. William C. Symonds, "How Companies Are Learning to Prepare for the Worst," *Business Week* (December 23, 1985): 76.

29. "Ford Ends Tire-Replacement Program," *USA Today* (April 1, 2002): 2B. Also see David Kiley and James R. Healey, "Ford CEO Takes Recall Reins as More Questions Arise," *USA Today* (August 17, 2000): 1B–2B.

30. See Paul Davidson, "Andersen Receives Mixed Grades for Crisis Management," *USA Today* (January 22, 2002): 3B; and Theresa Howard, "Experts: Admission Could Have Aided Andersen," *USA Today* (March 29, 2002): 1B.

31. See Woodruff Imberman, "The American Quest for Quality," *Business Horizons,* 42 (September–October 1999): 11–16.

32. See David A. Garvin, "How the Baldrige Award Really Works," *Harvard Business Review,* 69 (November–December 1991): 80–93; Robert Bell and Bernard Keys, "A Conversation with Curt W. Reimann on the Background and Future of the Baldrige Award," *Organizational Dynamics,* 26 (Spring 1998): 51–61; and John R. Dew, "Learning from Baldrige Winners at the University of Alabama," *Journal of Organizational Excellence,* 20 (Spring 2001): 49–56.

33. Chris Woodyard, Bruce Horovitz, Gary Strauss, and Anne Willette, "Quality Guru Now Plugs Innovation," *USA Today* (February 27, 1998): 8B.

34. Philip B. Crosby, *Quality Without Tears: The Art of Hassle-Free Management* (New York: Plume, 1984), p. 64. Also see Philip B. Crosby, *Completeness: Quality for the 21st Century* (New York: Dutton, 1992), p. 116.

35. Adapted in part from Ron Zemke, "A Bluffer's Guide to TQM," *Training,* 30 (April 1993): 48–55.

36. For subscription information, see **www.consumerreports. org.**

37. Stratford Sherman, "How to Prosper in the Value Decade," *Fortune* (November 30, 1992): 91. Also see Gerald E. Smith and Thomas T. Nagle, "Frames of Reference and Buyers' Perception of Price and Value," *California Management Review,* 38 (Fall 1995): 98–116.

38. Data from "5 Hundred Largest U.S. Corporations," *Fortune* (April 15, 2002): F1, F52.

39. See Roundtable Discussion, "Fast Talk: The State of the Customer Economy," *Fast Company,* no. 50 (September 2001): 80–90; Emily Barker, "You Just Don't Get It," *Inc.,* 23 (November 20, 2001): 120; and Lior Arussy, "Don't Take Calls, Make Contact," *Harvard Business Review,* 80 (January 2002): 16–17.

40. Data from Patricia Sellers, "Getting Customers to Love You," *Fortune* (March 13, 1989): 38–49.

41. Data from Patricia Sellers, "What Customers Really Want," *Fortune* (June 4, 1990): 58–68.

42. Based on discussions in M. Jill Austin, "Planning in Service Organizations," *SAM Advanced Management Journal,* 55 (Summer 1990): 7–12; Everett E. Adam Jr. and Paul M.

Swamidass, "Assessing Operations Management from a Strategic Perspective," *Journal of Management,* 15 (June 1989): 181–203; and Ron Zemke, "The Emerging Art of Service Management," *Training,* 29 (January 1992): 37–42.

43. See, for example, Ron Zemke, "Customer Service as a Performing Art," *Training,* 30 (March 1993): 40–44; Blake E. Ashforth and Ronald H. Humphrey, "Emotional Labor in Service Roles: The Influence of Identity," *Academy of Management Review,* 18 (January 1993): 88–115; and Richard B. Chase and Sriram Dasu, "Want to Perfect Your Company's Service? Use Behavioral Science," *Harvard Business Review,* 79 (June 2001): 79–84.

44. Data from Andrew Erdman, "Staying Ahead of 800 Competitors," *Fortune* (June 1, 1992): 111–112.

45. Ron Zemke and Dick Schaaf, *The Service Edge: 101 Companies That Profit from Customer Care* (New York: New American Library, 1989), p. 14. Also see Mohanbir Sawhney, "Don't Homogenize, Synchronize," *Harvard Business Review,* 79 (July–August 2001): 101–108; and Chun Hui, Simon S. K. Lam, and John Schaubroeck, "Can Good Citizens Lead the Way in Providing Quality Service? A Field Quasi Experiment," *Academy of Management Journal,* 44 (October 2001): 988–995.

46. See Leonard L. Berry, A. Parasuraman, and Valarie A. Zeithaml, "The Service-Quality Puzzle," *Business Horizons,* 31 (September–October 1988): 35–43; Leonard L. Berry, A. Parasuraman, and Valarie A. Zeithaml, "Improving Service Quality in America: Lessons Learned," *Academy of Management Executive,* 8 (May 1994): 32–45; Leonard L. Berry, Kathleen Seiders, and Larry G. Gresham, "For Love and Money: The Common Traits of Successful Retailers," *Organizational Dynamics,* 26 (Autumn 1997): 7–23; and Kathleen Seiders and Leonard L. Berry, "Service Fairness: What It Is and Why It Matters," *Academy of Management Executive,* 12 (May 1998): 8–20.

47. Based on Paul Hellman, "Rating Your Dentist," *Management Review,* 87 (July–August 1998): 64.

48. See Christopher Meyer, "While Customers Wait, Add Value," *Harvard Business Review,* 79 (July–August 2001): 24–26.

49. For example, see Steven N. Silverman and Lori L. Silverman, "TOM: The Story of How the Q Lost Its Tail," *Nonprofit World,* 18 (November–December 2000): 25–26; Thomas J. Douglas and William Q. Judge Jr., "Total Quality Management Implementation and Competitive Advantage: The Role of Structural Control and Exploration," *Academy of Management Journal,* 44 (February 2001): 158–169; William Roth and Terry Capuano, "Systemic Versus Nonsystemic Approaches to Quality Improvement," *Journal of Organizational Excellence,* 20 (Spring 2001): 57–64; and Richard S. Allen and Ralph H. Kilmann, "Aligning Reward Practices in Support of Total Quality Management," *Business Horizons,* 44 (May–June 2001): 77–84.

50. Inspired by a more lengthy definition in Marshall Sashkin and Kenneth J. Kiser, *Total Quality Management* (Seabrook, Md.: Ducochon Press, 1991), p. 25. Another good introduction to TQM is Arthur R. Tenner and Irving J. DeToro, *Total Quality Management: Three Steps to Continuous Improvement* (Reading, Mass.: Addison-Wesley, 1992). Also see the entire July 1994 issue of *Academy of Management Review.*

51. Richard J. Schonberger, "Total Quality Management Cuts a Broad Swath—Through Manufacturing and Beyond," *Organizational Dynamics,* 20 (Spring 1992): 18.

52. "Aiming for the Stars at Philips," Special Advertising Section, Quality '92: Leading the World-Class Company, *Time* (September 21, 1992): 26.

53. See John Shea and David Gobeli, "TQM: The Experiences of Ten Small Businesses," *Business Horizons,* 38 (January–February 1995): 71–77; Loyd Eskildson, "TQM's Role in Corporate Success: Analyzing the Evidence," *National Productivity Review,* 14 (Autumn 1995): 25–38; Richard Reed, David J. Lemak, and Joseph C. Montgomery, "Beyond Process: TQM Content and Firm Performance," *Academy of Management Review,* 21 (January 1996): 173–202; and William A. Hubiak and Susan Jones O'Donnell, "Do Americans Have Their Minds Set Against TQM?" *National Productivity Review,* 15 (Summer 1996): 19–32.

54. Adapted and condensed from David E. Bowen and Edward E. Lawler III, "Total Quality-Oriented Human Resources Management," *Organizational Dynamics,* 20 (Spring 1992): Exhibit 1, 29–41.

55. "Judge Orders Ford to Replace Faulty Device," *USA Today* (April 16, 2001): 1B.

56. Richard J. Schonberger, *Japanese Manufacturing Techniques: Nine Hidden Lessons in Simplicity* (New York: Free Press, 1982), p. 35. Also see Barry Berman, "Planning for the Inevitable Product Recall," *Business Horizons,* 42 (March–April 1999): 69–78.

57. For contrasting views, see Christopher W. L. Hart, "The Power of Internal Guarantees," *Harvard Business Review,* 73 (January–February 1995): 64–73; and Thomas A. Stewart, "Another Fad Worth Killing," *Fortune* (February 3, 1997): 119–120.

58. Andrew H. Szpekman, "Quality Service Sets You Apart," *HRMagazine,* 37 (September 1992): 74.

59. Richard S. Teitelbaum, "Where Service Flies Right," *Fortune* (August 24, 1992): 115. For another example, see Cathy Olofson, "Rough Seas, Tough Customers," *Fast Company,* no. 25 (June 1999): 56.

60. See Roger Brown, "How We Built a Strong Company in a Weak Industry," *Harvard Business Review,* 79 (February 2001): 51–57; Patricia B. Seybold, "Get Inside The Lives of Your Customers," *Harvard Business Review,* 79 (May 2001): 81–89; Anthony W. Ulwick "Turn Customer Input into Innovation," *Harvard Business Review,* 80 (January 2002): 91–97; and Darrell K. Rigby, Frederick F. Reichheld and Phil Schefter, "Avoid the Four Perils of CRM," *Harvard Business Review,* 80 (February 2002): 101–109.

61. Andy Reinhardt, "Meet Mr. Internet," *Business Week* (September 13, 1999): 136. Another customer-centered manager is profiled in David DuPree, "First-Class Operation," *USA Today* (December 21, 2001): 1C–2C.

62. Based on discussion in Richard J. Schonberger, "Is Strategy Strategic? Impact of Total Quality Management on Strategy," *Academy of Management Executive,* 6 (August 1992): 80–87.

63. See D. Keith Denton, "Creating a System for Continuous Improvement," *Business Horizons,* 38 (January–February

1995): 16–21; and Thomas Y. Choi, Manus Rungtusanatham, and Ji-Sung Kim, "Continuous Improvement on the Shop Floor: Lessons from Small to Midsize Firms," *Business Horizons,* 40 (November–December 1997): 45–50.

64. Edward E. Lawler III, "Total Quality Management and Employee Involvement: Are They Compatible?" *Academy of Management Executive,* 8 (February 1994): 68–76.

65. "Reinventing Chrysler," Special Advertising Section, Quality '92: Leading the World-Class Company, *Time* (September 21, 1992): 20.

66. Sashkin and Kiser, *Total Quality Management,* p. 42. Six Sigma, another set of quality improvement tools, is discussed in Lee Clifford, "Why You Can Safely Ignore Six Sigma," *Fortune* (January 22, 2001): 140; Kristine Ellis, "Mastering Six Sigma," *Training,* 38 (December 2001): 30–35; and Michael Hammer, "Process Management and the Future of Six Sigma," *MIT Sloan Management Review,* 43 (Winter 2002): 26–32.

67. Based on discussion in Mary Walton, *Deming Management at Work* (New York: Perigee, 1990), p. 16.

68. See Marta Mooney, "Deming's Real Legacy: An Easier Way to Manage Knowledge," *National Productivity Review,* 15 (Summer 1996): 1–8; and Pamela J. Kidder and Bobbie Ryan, "How the Deming Philosophy Transformed the Department of the Navy," *National Productivity Review,* 15 (Summer 1996): 55–63.

69. W. Edwards Deming, *Out of the Crisis* (Cambridge, Mass.: MIT Press, 1986): p. 5. Also see Oren Harari, "Beyond Zero Defects," *Management Review,* 88 (October 1999): 34–36.

70. Ken Western, "No Matter What It Takes, I'll Do It," *The Arizona Republic* (August 1, 1993): F1.

71. See Figure 5 in Deming, *Out of the Crisis,* p. 88.

72. Daniel Roth, "Craig Barrett Inside," *Fortune* (December 18, 2000): 260.

73. Adapted from discussion in Deming, *Out of the Crisis,* pp. 23–96; and Howard S. Gitlow and Shelly J. Gitlow, *The Deming Guide to Quality and Competitive Position* (Englewood Cliffs, N.J.: Prentice-Hall, 1987). Also see M. R. Yilmaz and Sangit Chatterjee, "Deming and the Quality of Software Development," *Business Horizons,* 40 (November–December 1997): 51–58.

74. Deming, *Out of the Crisis,* p. 59.

75. The debate is framed in Paula Phillips Carson and Kerry D. Carson, "Deming Versus Traditional Management Theorists on Goal Setting: Can Both Be Right?" *Business Horizons,* 36 (September–October 1993): 79–84.

76. Deming, *Out of the Crisis,* p. 24.

# Glossary

**Acceptance theory of authority**  Barnard's theory that authority is determined by subordinates' willingness to comply (Ch. 9)

**Accommodative social responsibility strategy**  assuming additional responsibilities in response to pressure (Ch. 5)

**Added value negotiating**  five-step process involving development of multiple deals (Ch. 16)

**Advocacy advertising**  promoting a point of view along with a product or service (Ch. 3)

**Affirmative action program (AAP)**  making up for past discrimination by actively seeking and employing minorities (Ch. 11)

**Alcoholism**  a disease in which alcohol abuse disrupts one's normal life (Ch. 11)

**Alternative dispute resolution**  avoiding courtroom battles by settling disputes with less costly methods, including arbitration and mediation (Ch. 3)

**Altruism**  unselfish devotion to the interests of others (Ch. 5)

**Amoral managers**  managers who are neither moral nor immoral, but ethically lazy (Ch. 5)

**Antecedent**  an environmental cue for a specific behavior (Ch. 15)

**Anticipatory changes**  planned changes based on expected situations (Ch. 16)

**Authority**  right to direct the actions of others (Ch. 9)

**Bargaining zone**  the gap between two parties' BATNAs (Ch. 16)

**Behavior-based interview**  detailed questions about specific behaviors in past job-related situations (Ch. 11)

**Behavior modification**  systematic management of the antecedents and consequences of behavior (Ch. 15)

**Behaviorally anchored rating scales (BARS)**  performance appraisal scales with notations about observable behavior (Ch. 11)

**Behaviorism**  belief that observable behavior is more important than inner states (Ch. 15)

**Benchmarking**  identifying, studying, and building upon the best practices of organizational role models (Ch. 17)

**Body language**  nonverbal communication based on facial expressions, posture, and appearance (Ch. 12)

**Break-even point**  level of sales at which there is no loss or profit (Ch. 6)

**Bureaucracy**  Weber's model of a rationally efficient organization (Ch. 9)

**Business cycle**  the up-and-down movement of an economy's ability to generate wealth (Ch. 3)

**Business ecosystem**  economic community of organizations and all their stakeholders (Ch. 7)

**Cafeteria compensation**  plan that allows employees to select their own mix of benefits (Ch. 13)

**Capability profile**  identifying the organization's strengths and weaknesses (Ch. 7)

**Causes**  variables responsible for the difference between actual and desired conditions (Ch. 8)

**Centralization**  the retention of decision-making authority by top management (Ch. 10)

**Closed system**  a self-sufficient entity (Ch. 2)

**Cluster organization**  collaborative structure in which teams are the primary unit (Ch. 10)

**Coercive power**  gaining compliance through threats or punishment (Ch. 15)

**Cohesiveness**  tendency of group to stick together (Ch. 14)

**Collaborative computing**  teaming up to make decisions via a computer network programmed with groupware (Ch. 8)

**Collectivist cultures**  cultures that emphasize duty and loyalty to collective goals and achievements (Ch. 4)

**Commonweal organization**  nonprofit organization serving all members of a given population (Ch. 9)

**Communication**  interpersonal transfer of information and understanding (Ch. 12)

**Comparative management**  study of how organizational behavior and management practices differ across cultures (Ch. 4)

**Concurrent control**  monitoring and adjusting ongoing activities and processes (Ch. 17)

**Concurrent engineering**  team approach to product design involving specialists from all functional areas including research, production, and marketing (Ch. 3)

**Condition of certainty**  solid factual basis allows accurate prediction of decision's outcome (Ch. 8)

**Condition of risk**  decision made on basis of incomplete but reliable information (Ch. 8)

**Condition of uncertainty**  no reliable factual information available (Ch. 8)

**Conflict**  incompatible behaviors that make another person less effective (Ch. 16)

**Conflict trigger**  any factor that increases the chances of conflict (Ch. 16)

**Conformity**  complying with prevailing role expectations and norms (Ch. 14)

**Contingency approach**  research effort to determine which managerial practices and techniques are appropriate in specific situations (Ch. 2)

**Contingency design**  fitting the organization to its environment (Ch. 10)

**Contingency plan**  a backup plan for emergencies (Ch. 17)

**Contingent time off**  rewarding people with early time off when they get the job done (Ch. 13)

**Contingent workers**  part-timers and other employees who do not have a long-term implicit contract with their ultimate employers (Ch. 3)

**Continuous reinforcement**  every instance of a behavior is rewarded (Ch. 15)

**Contribution margin**  selling price per unit minus variable costs per unit (Ch. 6)

**Control**   taking preventive or corrective actions to keep things on track (Ch. 17)

**Control chart**   visual aid showing acceptable and unacceptable variations from the norm for repetitive operations (Ch. 17)

**Corporate philanthropy**   charitable donation of company resources (Ch. 5)

**Corporate social responsibility**   idea that business has social obligations above and beyond making a profit (Ch. 5)

**Creativity**   the reorganization of experience into new configurations (Ch. 8)

**Crisis management**   anticipating and preparing for events that could damage the organization (Ch. 17)

**Critical path**   most time-consuming route through a PERT network (Ch. 6)

**Cross-cultural training**   guided experience that helps people live and work in foreign cultures (Ch. 4)

**Cross-functional team**   task group staffed with a mix of specialists pursuing a common objective (Ch. 14)

**Cross-sectional scenarios**   describing future situations at a given point in time (Ch. 7)

**Culture**   a population's taken-for-granted assumptions, values, beliefs, and symbols that foster patterned behavior (Ch. 4)

**Customer-centered**   satisfying the customer's needs by anticipating, listening, and responding (Ch. 17)

**Decentralization**   management shares decision-making authority with lower-level employees (Ch. 10)

**Decision making**   identifying and choosing alternative courses of action (Ch. 8)

**Decision rule**   tells when and how programmed decisions should be made (Ch. 8)

**Defensive social responsibility strategy**   resisting additional responsibilities with legal and public relations tactics (Ch. 5)

**360-degree review**   pooled, anonymous evaluation by one's boss, peers, and subordinates (Ch. 11)

**Delegation**   assigning various degrees of decision-making authority to lower-level employees (Ch. 10)

**Deming management**   application of W. Edwards Deming's ideas for more responsive, more democratic, and less wasteful organizations (Ch. 17)

**Demographics**   statistical profiles of population changes (Ch. 3)

**Departmentalization**   grouping related jobs or processes into major organizational subunits (Ch. 10)

**Differentiation (organizational)**   tendency of specialists to think and act in restricted ways (Ch. 10)

**Differentiation (strategic)**   buyer perceives unique and superior value in a product (Ch. 7)

**Downsizing**   planned elimination of positions or jobs (Ch. 9)

**Dynamic equilibrium**   process whereby an open system maintains its own internal balances with help from its environment (Ch. 9)

**E-business**   a business using the Internet for greater efficiency in every aspect of its operations (Ch. 1)

**Effect uncertainty**   impacts of environmental changes are unpredictable (Ch. 6)

**Effectiveness**   a central element in the process of management that entails achieving a stated organizational objective (Ch. 1)

**Efficiency**   a central element in the process of management that balances the amount of resources used to achieve an objective against what was actually accomplished (Ch. 1)

**Emotional intelligence**   the ability to monitor and control one's emotions and behavior in complex social settings (Ch. 15)

**Employment selection test**   any procedure used in the employment decision process (Ch. 11)

**Empowerment**   making employees *full* partners in the decision-making process and giving them the necessary tools and rewards (Ch. 15)

**Enlightened self-interest**   a business ultimately helping itself by helping to solve societal problems (Ch. 5)

**Entrepreneurship**   process of pursuing opportunities without regard to resources currently under one's control (Ch. 1)

**Equifinality**   open systems can achieve similar ends through different means (Ch. 9)

**Escalation of commitment**   people get locked into losing courses of action to avoid the embarrassment of quitting or admitting error (Ch. 8)

**Ethical advocate**   ethics specialist who plays a role in top-management decision making (Ch. 5)

**Ethics**   study of moral obligation involving right versus wrong (Ch. 5)

**Ethnocentric attitude**   view that assumes the home country's personnel and ways of doing things are best (Ch. 4)

**Event outcome forecasts**   predictions of the outcome of highly probable future events (Ch. 7)

**Event timing forecasts**   predictions of when a given event will occur (Ch. 7)

**Executive reality check**   top managers periodically working at lower-level jobs to become more aware of operations (Ch. 17)

**Exit interview**   brief structured interview with a departing employee (Ch. 12)

**Expectancy**   one's belief or expectation that one thing will lead to another (Ch. 13)

**Expectancy theory**   model that assumes motivational strength is determined by perceived probabilities of success (Ch. 13)

**Expert power**   compliance based on ability to dispense valued information (Ch. 15)

**Explicit knowledge**   documented and sharable information (Ch. 8)

**Extrinsic rewards**   payoffs, such as money, that are granted by others (Ch. 13)

**Feedback control**   checking a completed activity and learning from mistakes (Ch. 17)

**Feedforward control**   active anticipation and prevention of problems, rather than passive reaction (Ch. 17)

**Fishbone diagram**   a cause-and-effect diagram (Ch. 17)

**Fixed costs**   contractual costs that must be paid regardless of output or sales (Ch. 6)

**Flextime**   allows employees to choose their own arrival and departure times within specified limits (Ch. 13)

**Flow chart**   graphic display of a sequence of activities and decisions (Ch. 17)

**Forecasts**   predictions, projections, or estimates of future situations (Ch. 7)

**Formal group**   collection of people created to do something productive (Ch. 14)

**Formal leadership**   the process of influencing others to pursue official objectives (Ch. 15)

**Framing error**   how information is presented influences one's interpretation of it (Ch. 8)

**Functional authority**   gives staff temporary and limited authority for specified tasks (Ch. 10)

**Gantt chart**   graphic scheduling technique (Ch. 6)

**General systems theory**   an area of study based on the assumption that everything is part of a larger, interdependent arrangement (Ch. 2)

**Geocentric attitude**   world-oriented view that draws on the best talent from around the globe (Ch. 4)

**Glass ceiling**   the transparent but strong barrier keeping women and minorities from moving up the management ladder (Ch. 3)

**Global company**   a multinational venture centrally managed from a specific country (Ch. 4)

**Goal setting**   process of improving performance with objectives, deadlines, or quality standards (Ch. 13)

**Grand strategy**   how the organization's mission will be accomplished (Ch. 7)

**Grapevine**   unofficial and informal communication system (Ch. 12)

**Group**   two or more freely interacting individuals with a common identity and purpose (Ch. 14)

**Groupthink**   Janis's term for blind conformity in cohesive ingroups (Ch. 14)

**High-context cultures**   cultures in which nonverbal and situational messages convey primary meaning (Ch. 4)

**Histogram**   bar chart indicating deviations from a standard bell-shaped curve (Ch. 17)

**Hourglass organization**   a three-layer structure with a constricted middle layer (Ch. 10)

**Human capital**   all present and future employees, who need to develop to their fullest potential (Ch. 11)

**Human relations movement**   an effort to make managers more sensitive to their employees' needs (Ch. 2)

**Human resource management**   acquisition, retention, and development of human resources (Ch. 11)

**Human resource planning**   meeting future human resource needs with a comprehensive staffing strategy (Ch. 11)

**Idealize**   to change the nature of a problem's situation (Ch. 8)

**Incremental changes**   subsystem adjustments required to keep the organization on course (Ch. 16)

**Individualistic cultures**   cultures that emphasize individual rights, roles, and achievements (Ch. 4)

**Influence**   any attempt to change another's behavior (Ch. 15)

**Informal group**   collection of people seeking friendship (Ch. 14)

**Informal leadership**   the process of influencing others to pursue unofficial objectives (Ch. 15)

**Innovation lag**   time it takes for a new idea to be translated into satisfied demand (Ch. 3)

**Innovation process**   the systematic development and practical application of a new idea (Ch. 3)

**Instrumental value**   enduring belief in a certain way of behaving (Ch. 5)

**Integration**   collaboration needed to achieve a common purpose (Ch. 10)

**Intermediate planning**   determining subunits' contributions with allocated resources (Ch. 6)

**Intermittent reinforcement**   rewarding some, but not all, instances of a behavior (Ch. 15)

**Internal auditing**   independent appraisal of organizational operations and systems to assess effectiveness and efficiency (Ch. 17)

**Internal customer**   anyone in your organization who cannot do a good job unless you do a good job (Ch. 17)

**International management**   pursuing organizational objectives in international and cross-cultural settings (Ch. 4)

**Internet**   global network of servers and personal and organizational computers (Ch. 1)

**Intrapreneur**   an employee who takes personal responsibility for pushing an innovative idea through a large organization (Ch. 3)

**Intrinsic rewards**   self-granted and internally experienced payoffs, such as a feeling of accomplishment (Ch. 13)

**Iron law of responsibility**   those who do not use power in a socially responsible way will eventually lose it (Ch. 5)

**Issues management**   ongoing process of identifying, evaluating, and responding to important social and political issues (Ch. 3)

**Job analysis**   identifying task and skill requirements for specific jobs by studying superior performers (Ch. 11)

**Job description**   document outlining role expectations and skill requirements for a specific job (Ch. 11)

**Job design**   creating task responsibilities based upon strategy, technology, and structure (Ch. 13)

**Job enlargement**   combining two or more specialized tasks to increase motivation (Ch. 13)

**Job enrichment**   redesigning jobs to increase their motivational potential (Ch. 13)

**Job rotation**   moving people from one specialized job to another (Ch. 13)

*Kaizen*   a Japanese word meaning "continuous improvement" (Ch. 17)

**Knowledge management**   developing a system to improve the creation and sharing of knowledge critical for decision making (Ch. 8)

**Law of unintended consequences**   results of purposeful actions are often difficult to predict (Ch. 8)

**Leadership**　social influence process of inspiring and guiding others in a common effort (Ch. 15)

**Learning organization**　one that turns new ideas into improved performance (Ch. 9)

**Legal audit**　review of all operations to pinpoint possible legal liabilities or problems (Ch. 3)

**Legitimate power**　compliance based on one's formal position (Ch. 15)

**Line and staff organization**　organization in which line managers make decisions and staff personnel provide advice and support (Ch. 10)

**Longitudinal scenarios**　describing how the future will evolve from the present (Ch. 7)

**Low-context cultures**　cultures in which words convey primary meaning (Ch. 4)

**Management**　the process of working with and through others to achieve organizational objectives in a changing environment (Ch. 1)

**Management by objectives (MBO)**　comprehensive management system based on measurable and participatively set objectives (Ch. 6)

**Managerial ability**　the demonstrated capacity to achieve organizational objectives with specific skills and competencies (Ch. 1)

**Managerial functions**　general administrative duties that need to be carried out in virtually all productive organizations to achieve desired outcomes (Ch. 1)

**Managerial roles**　specific categories of managerial behavior (Ch. 1)

**Managing diversity**　process of helping all employees, including women and minorities, reach their full potential (Ch. 3)

**Matrix organization**　a structure with both vertical and horizontal lines of authority (Ch. 10)

**Mechanistic organizations**　rigid bureaucracies (Ch. 10)

**Media richness**　a medium's capacity to convey information and promote learning (Ch. 12)

**Mentor**　someone who develops another person through tutoring, coaching, and guidance (Ch. 15)

**Monochronic time**　a perception of time as a straight line broken into standard units (Ch. 4)

**Motivation**　psychological process giving behavior purpose and direction (Ch. 13)

**Motivation to manage**　desire to succeed in performing managerial functions and roles; one of the three elements of the basic formula for managerial success (Ch. 1)

**Multivariate analysis**　research technique used to determine how a combination of variables interact to cause a particular outcome (Ch. 2)

**Negotiation**　decision-making process among interdependent parties with different preferences (Ch. 16)

**New social contract**　assumption that employer-employee relationship will be a shorter-term one based on convenience and mutual benefit, rather than for life (Ch. 3)

**Noise**　any interference with the normal flow of communication (Ch. 12)

**Nonprogrammed decisions**　decisions made in complex and nonroutine situations (Ch. 8)

**Norms**　general standards of conduct for various social settings (Ch. 14)

**Objective**　commitment to achieve a measurable result within a specified period (Ch. 6)

**Objective probabilities**　odds derived mathematically from reliable data (Ch. 8)

**Open-book management**　sharing key financial data and profits with employees who are trained and empowered (Ch. 13)

**Open system**　something that depends on its surrounding environment for survival (Ch. 2)

**Operational approach**　production-oriented field of management dedicated to improving efficiency and cutting waste (Ch. 2)

**Operational planning**　determining how to accomplish specific tasks with available resources (Ch. 6)

**Operations management**　the process of transforming material and human resources into useful goods and services (Ch. 2)

**Optimize**　to systematically identify the solution with the best combination of benefits (Ch. 8)

**Organic organizations**　flexible, adaptive organization structures (Ch. 10)

**Organization**　cooperative and coordinated social system of two or more people with a common purpose (Ch. 9)

**Organization chart**　visual display of organization's positions and lines of authority (Ch. 9)

**Organization development (OD)**　planned change programs intended to help people and organizations function more effectively (Ch. 16)

**Organizational behavior**　a modern approach seeking to discover the causes of work behavior and develop better management techniques (Ch. 2)

**Organizational culture**　shared values, beliefs, and language that create a common identity and sense of community (Ch. 9)

**Organizational decline**　organization is weakened by resource or demand restrictions and/or mismanagement (Ch. 9)

**Organizational effectiveness**　being effective, efficient, satisfying, adaptive and developing, and ultimately surviving (Ch. 9)

**Organizational politics**　the pursuit of self-interest in response to real or imagined opposition (Ch. 14)

**Organizational socialization**　process of transforming outsiders into accepted insiders (Ch. 9)

**Organizational values**　shared beliefs about what the organization stands for (Ch. 9)

**Organizing**　creating a coordinated authority and task structure (Ch. 10)

**Ostracism**　rejection from a group (Ch. 14)

**Outplacement**　the ethical practice of helping displaced employees find new jobs (Ch. 9)

**Pareto analysis**　bar chart indicating which problem needs the most attention (Ch. 17)

**Participative management**　empowering employees to assume greater control of the workplace (Ch. 13)

**PDCA cycle**   Deming's plan-do-check-act cycle that relies on observed data for continuous improvement of operations (Ch. 17)

**Performance appraisal**   evaluating job performance as a basis for personnel decisions (Ch. 11)

**PERT (Program Evaluation and Review Technique)**   graphic sequencing and scheduling tool for complex projects (Ch. 6)

**PERT activity**   work in process (Ch. 6)

**PERT event**   performance milestone; start or finish of an activity (Ch. 6)

**PERT times**   weighted time estimates for completion of PERT activities (Ch. 6)

**Plan**   an objective plus an action statement (Ch. 6)

**Planning**   coping with uncertainty by formulating courses of action to achieve specified results (Ch. 6)

**Planning horizon**   elapsed time between planning and execution (Ch. 6)

**Polycentric attitude**   view that assumes local managers in host countries know best how to run their own operations (Ch. 4)

**Polychronic time**   a perception of time as flexible, elastic, and multidimensional (Ch. 4)

**Positive reinforcement**   encouraging a behavior with a pleasing consequence (Ch. 15)

**Power**   ability to marshal resources to get something done (Ch. 15)

**80/20 principle**   a minority of causes, inputs, or efforts tend to produce a majority of results, outputs, or rewards (Ch. 6)

**Priorities**   ranking of goals, objectives, or activities in order of importance (Ch. 6)

**Proactive social responsibility strategy**   taking the initiative with new programs that serve as models for the industry (Ch. 5)

**Problem**   the difference between actual and desired states of affairs (Ch. 8)

**Problem solving**   conscious process of closing the gap between actual and desired situations (Ch. 8)

**Product technology**   second stage of innovation process involving the creation of a working prototype (Ch. 3)

**Production technology**   third stage of innovation process involving the development of a profitable production process (Ch. 3)

**Programmed decisions**   repetitive and routine decisions (Ch. 8)

**Project**   a temporary endeavor undertaken to achieve a particular aim (Ch. 6)

**Quality**   conformance to requirements (Ch. 17)

**Quality control circles**   voluntary problem-solving groups committed to improving quality and reducing costs (Ch. 13)

**Reactive changes**   changes made in response to unexpected situations (Ch. 16)

**Reactive social responsibility strategy**   denying responsibility and resisting change (Ch. 5)

**Realistic job previews**   honest explanations of what a job actually entails (Ch. 13)

**Reengineering**   radically redesigning the entire business cycle for greater strategic speed (Ch. 7)

**Referent power**   compliance based on charisma or personal identification (Ch. 15)

**Refreezing**   systematically following up a change program for lasting results (Ch. 16)

**Response uncertainty**   consequences of decisions are unpredictable (Ch. 6)

**Reward power**   gaining compliance through rewards (Ch. 15)

**Rewards**   material and psychological payoffs for working (Ch. 13)

**Role**   socially determined way of behaving in a specific position (Ch. 14)

**Run chart**   a trend chart for tracking a variable over time (Ch. 17)

**Satisfice**   to settle for a solution that is good enough (Ch. 8)

**Scatter diagram**   diagram that plots relationships between two variables (Ch. 17)

**Scenario analysis**   preparing written descriptions of equally likely future situations (Ch. 7)

**Scientific management**   developing performance standards on the basis of systematic observation and experimentation (Ch. 2)

**Self-managed teams**   high-performance teams that assume traditional managerial duties such as staffing and planning (Ch. 13)

**Semantics**   study of the meaning of words (Ch. 12)

**Sexual harassment**   unwanted sexual attention that creates an offensive or intimidating work environment (Ch. 11)

**Situational analysis**   finding the organization's niche by performing a SWOT analysis (Ch. 7)

**Small business**   an independently owned and managed profit-seeking enterprise with fewer than 100 employees (Ch. 1)

**Span of control**   number of people who report directly to a given manager (Ch. 10)

**Stakeholder audit**   identifying all parties possibly impacted by the organization (Ch. 5)

**State uncertainty**   unpredictable environment (Ch. 6)

**Strategic business unit**   organizational subunit that acts like an independent business (Ch. 10)

**Strategic changes**   altering the overall shape or direction of the organization (Ch. 16)

**Strategic management**   seeking a competitively superior organization-environment fit (Ch. 7)

**Strategic planning**   determining how to pursue long-term goals with available resources (Ch. 6)

**Strategy**   integrated, externally oriented perception of how to achieve the organization's mission (Ch. 7)

**Structured interview**   a set of job-related questions with standardized answers (Ch. 11)

**Subjective probabilities**   odds based on judgment (Ch. 8)

**Synergy**   the concept that the whole is greater than the sum of its parts (Ch. 7)

**System**   a collection of parts that operate interdependently to achieve a common purpose (Ch. 2)

**Tacit knowledge**   personal, intuitive, and undocumented information (Ch. 8)

**Technology**   all the tools and ideas available for extending the natural physical and mental reach of humankind (Ch. 3)

**Telecommuting**   sending work to and from one's office via computer modem while working at home (Ch. 12)

**Tempered radicals**   people who quietly try to change the dominant organizational culture in line with their convictions (Ch. 16)

**Terminal value**   enduring belief in the attainment of a certain end-state (Ch. 5)

**Theory Y**   McGregor's optimistic assumptions about working people (Ch. 2)

**Time series forecasts**   estimates of future values in a statistical sequence (Ch. 7)

**Total quality management (TQM)**   creating an organizational culture committed to continuous improvement in every regard (Ch. 17)

**Training**   using guided experience to change employee behavior/attitudes (Ch. 11)

**Transformational leaders**   visionaries who challenge people to do exceptional things (Ch. 15)

**Transnational company**   a futuristic model of a global, decentralized network with no distinct national identity (Ch. 4)

**Trend analysis**   hypothetical extension of a past series of events into the future (Ch. 7)

**Trust**   belief in the integrity, character, or ability of others (Ch. 14)

**Unfreezing**   neutralizing resistance by preparing people for change (Ch. 16)

**Universal process approach**   assumes all organizations require the same rational management process (Ch. 2)

**Upward communication**   encouraging employees to share their feelings and ideas with management (Ch. 12)

**Values**   abstract ideals that shape one's thinking and behavior (Ch. 5)

**Variable costs**   costs that vary directly with production and sales (Ch. 6)

**Videoconference**   live television or broadband Internet video exchange between people in different locations (Ch. 12)

**Virtual organizations**   Internet-linked networks of value-adding subcontractors (Ch. 10)

**Virtual team**   task group members from dispersed locations who are electronically linked (Ch. 14)

**Whistle-blowing**   reporting perceived unethical organizational practices to outside authorities (Ch. 5)

# Photo Credits

# Name Index

Abbott, Ann S., R23
Abernathy, Donna J., R16, R33, R37
Abrams, Dominic, R43
Abrashoff, D. Michael, R5
Aburdene, Patricia, 93–94, R8
Ace, Merle E., R48
Ackoff, Russell L., 271, R5, R24
Acohido, Byron, 222
Adam, Everett E., Jr., R41, R54
Adams, J. Stacy, R40
Adams, James L., 275, R23, R24
Adams, Marc, 302, R7, R26
Adams, Marilyn, R15, R54
Adams, Scott, 19, 184, 357, R2, R16, R31
Adams, Susan K. R., R46
Adamson, Jim, R32
Adizes, Ichak, 535, R51
Adler, Jerry, R7
Adler, Nancy J., 111, R9, R11
Adler, Paul S., R42
Aggarwal, Raj, 446, R25, R41
Agle, Bradley R., R14
Agor, Weston H., 253, R21
Aguinis, Herman, R46, R52
Ahlstrom, David, R12
Aiello, Robert J., R36
Akers, George, 155
Al-Gattan, Abduhl-Rahim A., R48
Alba, Joseph W., 255
Albrecht, Karl, 551, R11, R35, R53
Albrecht, Steve, 551, R53
Aldrich, Howard E., R19
Alessi, Alberto, 260
Alexander, Larry D., 146
Alexander, Ralph A., R47
Alexander the Great, 503
Alexrod, Beth, R2
Aley, James, R3
Alford, Randall J., R30
Allen, James Sloan, R1
Allen, Lisa, 314
Allen, Louis A., R29
Allen, Richard S., R52, R55
Allen, Robert W., R44
Allen, Tammy D., R27
Allerton, Haidee E., R27
Allinson, Robert Elliott, R14
Allison, John R., R8
Alter, Jonathan, R32, R46
Alvarado, Elliott, R24
Alvarez, Jorge, 277
Amason, Allen C., R52
Amburgey, Terry L., R27
Amichai-Hamburger, Yair, R52

Amir, Taha, R44
Amparano, Julie, R2
Andelman, David A., R8, R10
Anders, George, R23, R31
Anderson, Barbara A., R12
Anderson, Douglas, R29
Anderson, Philip, R30
Anderson, Richard E., R29
Anderson, Robert O., 247
Andresky, Jill, R17
Andrews, Gerald, R45
Ansari, Mahfooz A., R46
Ante, Spencer E., R19, R45
Anthony, William P., R22, R24, R41, R44
Antonioni, David, R33
Anundsen, Kristin, 469
Appleby, Julie, R15
Arakawa, Minoru, 236
Archer, Earnest R., R2
Argyris, Chris, R25
Armacost, Robert L., R17
Armenakis, Achilles A., R26
Armendariz, Yvette, R3
Armour, Stephanie, 106, 304, 410, 413,
    538, R3, R6, R7, R8, R26, R31–R34,
    R36, R37, R42, R45, R52
Arndt, Michael, R9, R11, R26
Arnst, Catherine, R28
Arthur, Jeffrey B., R30
Arthur, Michael B., R31
Arussy, Lior, R54
Aryee, Samuel, R49
Asch, Solomon E., 479–480, R44
Ashe, Donna K., R33
Ashford, Susan J., R38
Ashforth, Blake E., R39, R43, R55
Assunto, Richard, 438
Atamer, Tugrul, R9
Atkinson, Sally, R52
Atkinson, William, R32, R42
Atwater, Leanne E., R33
Aubrey, Robert, R5, R6
Austin, James T., R51
Austin, M. Jill, R54
Austin, Nancy K., 349, R27
Auth, Rich, 41
Autzen, Richard, 106
Avolio, Bruce J., R12, R24

Baba, Vishwanath V., R48
Babcock, George D., R4
Babcock, Richard, R17
Bae, Johngseok, R30
Bagby, D. Ray, R9

Bahls, Jane Easter, R34
Bahner, Craig, 471
Baig, Edward C., R16
Bailey, Diane E., R45
Bain, Alexander, 98
Baker, Douglas D., R34
Baker, H. Eugene, III, R46
Baker, Stephen, R16, R25
Baker, Wayne E., R10
Bakken, Earl, 425
Balazs, Katharina, R47
Baldock, Robert, R21
Baldridge, David C., R32
Baldwin, David G., R44
Baldwin, Timothy T., R5, R45
Ball, Ben C., Jr., R20
Ball-Rokeach, Sandra J., R14
Ballon, Marc, 27
Balu, Rekha, 22
Bansal, Pratima, R1
Barada, Paul W., R36
Barber, Alison E., R40
Barber, Denise, 376
Barbian, Jeff, 510, R12, R27, R44
Barbour, Mary, 107
Barger, Dave, 524
Barkdull, C. W., R28
Barker, Emily, 38, R1, R17, R54
Barker, Paul, 246
Barker, Vincent L., III, R25, R26
Barley, Stephen R., 96
Barnard, Chester I., 56, 257, 292, R5,
    R22, R25
Barnard, Janet, R22
Barner, Robert, R6
Barnes-Farrell, Janet L., R23
Barnett, Rosalind Chait, R42
Barney, Jay B., R20
Baron, Robert A., R42
Barram, Dave, 404
Barrett, Colleen, 220
Barrett, Craig R., 14, 80, 587
Barrett, Gerald V., R33
Barrett, Michael, R50
Barrier, Michael, R31
Barry, Bruce, R50
Barry, Bryan W., R18
Bart, Christopher K., R16
Bartlett, Christopher A., R29, R41
Bartmess, Andrew, R20
Bartolomé, Fernando, 487, R45
Bass, Bernard M., 511, 512, R48, R49
Bassi, Pete, 110
Bateman, Thomas S., R13

I-1

Hofstede, Geert, 125, 126, 129, R11
Holland, Dutch, R28
Holland, Kelley, R14
Hollander, Edwin P., R46
Hollenbock, John R., R23
Holley, William H., R33
Holmes, Nigel, R37
Holmes, Stanley, R52
Holt, Jim, R30
Holtsberg, Warren, 229
Hom, Peter W., R38, R39, R43
Honold, Linda, R49
Hood, Neil, R10
Hopkins, Frank Snowden, R35
Hopkins, H. Donald, R21
Hopkins, Jim, 76, 518, R2, R6, R13, R17, R31
Hopkins, Michael, R24
Hopper, Randy, R49
Horovitz, Bruce, R13, R18, R21, R48, R54
Horton, Thomas R., 158, R14
Hosenball, Mark, R53, R54
Hosmer, LaRue Tone, R14, R15
House, Robert J., 510, R12, R38, R48, R49
Houston, Douglas A., R45
Hovanesian, Mara Der, 357
Hoversten, Paul, R13, R21
Howard, Theresa, R9, R13, R18, R31, R48, R54
Howell, Andre, 230
Howell, Jane M., R49
Howell, M. A., R39
Hsee, Christopher K., R21
Hsu, Jeffrey, R23
Hubbard, Nate, 293
Huber, George P., R20, R23, R27, R28
Huberty, Tom, R50
Hubiak, William A., R55
Hudson, Katherine M., R25
Huey, John, R6, R31, R39
Hufbauer, Gary, 95
Huffcutt, Allen I., R33
Hultman, Kenneth E., R51
Hummel, Ralph P., R24
Humphrey, Ronald H., R55
Hunt, Courtney Shelton, R19
Hunt, David M., R11
Hunt, James G., R48
Hunter, John E., R16, R17
Hurwitz, Alan, R30
Huselid, Mark A., R31
Hutchinson, J. Wesley, 255
Hyatt, Joshua, R21
Hyder, Elaine B., R52
Hymowitz, Carol, R10, R36, R53

Iacocca, Lee A., 300, 337, 338, 583
Iansiti, Marco, R28
Ibarra, Herminia, R46
Iem, Michael, 269

Ilgen, Daniel R., R23
Ilinitch, Anne Y., R28
Imberman, Woodruff, R38, R54
Immelt, Jeffrey R., 151, 305
Imperato, Gina, R24, R27
Imperiale, John, 495
Inglehart, Ronald, R10
Ireland, R. Duane, 64, 66, R5, R16, R18
Ishikawa, Kaoru, 11, 50
Isikoff, Michael, R8
Israel, David, R15
Itoh, Ryoji, R11
Ivancevich, John M., 298
Ivey, Mark, R18
Iyengar, Sheena S., R40

Jackson, Donald W., Jr., R38
Jacob, Rahul, R10, R28
Jacobsen, Patricia R., R40
Jacobson, Betsy, R27
James, David N., R25
James, Reggie, 87
Janis, Irving L., 480–481, R44
Janove, Nathan W., R34
Janson, Peter, 450
Jaques, Elliot, R24
Jardim, Ann, R24
Jarillo, J. Carlos, R3
Jarin, Kenneth M., R34
Jarley, Paul, R24
Jarvis, Lance P., R29
Jassawalla, Avan R., R45
Jauernig, Rohne L., R17
Javidan, Mansour, R12
Jawahar, I. A., R13
Jazwinski, Christine H., R36
Jeffries, Vincent, R13
Jehn, Karen A., R52
Jen-Hsun Huang, 25
Jenkins, Jennifer E., R17
Jenkins, Mary, R33
Jennings, Marianne M., R8
Jensen, Mary Ann C., R43
Jewell, Linda N., 473, R43
Ji-Sung Kim, R56
Jia Lin Xie, R39
Jick, Todd, 310
Jiménez, Maria Gabriela Gúzman, 11
Johannessen, Odd Jay, R41
Johns, Gary, R39
Johnson, Blair T., R48
Johnson, Heather, R30, R41
Johnson, Homer H., R13
Johnson, James P., R9, R11
Johnson, Jean L., R9
Johnson, Jonathan L., R3
Johnson, Kevin, R32
Johnson, Mike, R11
Johnson, Roy S., R7
Johnson, Spencer, R50
Johnston, Mark W., R43

Joinson, Carla, 369, R30, R31, R33, R41, R42
Jonas, Gregory J., R54
Jones, Bodil, R11
Jones, Carmen, 362
Jones, David, R16
Jones, Del, 93, 119, 149, 370, 402, R1, R4, R6, R8, R14, R24, R26, R33, R34, R36, R42, R47, R51, R54
Jones, Oswald, R4
Jones, Stephen R. G., R5
Jones, Steven D., R16
Jones, Thomas M., R13
Joni, Saj-Nicole A., R9
Joo Young Youn, R46
Jordon, Jean-Anne, R35
Jossi, Frank, R13, R31, R49
Joyce, William F., R29
Judge, Paul C., 567, R1, R8, R15, R35
Judge, Timothy A., R51
Judge, William Q., Jr., R1, R55
Julian, Scott D., R25
Julius, Mara, R23
Jung, Andrea, 3–4
Jung, Dong I., R12
Juran, Joseph M., 51, 584, R4

Kaestle, Paul, R28
Kahai, Surinder S., R24
Kahn, Herman, 236
Kahn, Jeremy, R13, R32, R49
Kahn, William A., R14, R46
Kaihla, Paul, R20, R53
Kakabadse, Andrew, 456
Kamuda, Alan R., R24
Kanigel, Robert, R4
Kanov, Jason M., 472, R47
Kanter, Rosabeth Moss, R18, R25
Kantrow, Alan M., R3
Kaplan, David A., R26
Kaplan, Robert D., R28
Kaplan, Robert E., R21
Kapoor, Alka, R46
Karren, Ronald J., R38
Kashy, Deborah A., R35
Kasoff, Mark, R9
Kast, Fremont E., 294, R25
Katz, Nancy, R45
Katzenbach, Jon R., R38, R45
Kaufman, Carol Felker, R11
Kaufman, Jonathan, R32
Kaul, James D., R5
Kavanagh, Jodie, 403
Kaye, Alan, 74
Kaye, Beverly, R27
Kaye, Steve, R2
Keats, Barbara W., R18
Keegan, Paul, R36
Keenan, A., R35
Keenan, Faith, R45, R53
Kegan, Robert, R35, R50, R51
Keidel, Robert W., R27, R28

# Company Index

# Subject Index